THE
NAZARENE GOSPEL
RESTORED

THE
NAZARENE GOSPEL
RESTORED

by

ROBERT GRAVES

and

JOSHUA PODRO

Garden City, New York

DOUBLEDAY & COMPANY, INC.

1954

Library of Congress Catalog Card Number 54-7314

First published, 1954, in the United States

COPYRIGHT, 1953, BY ROBERT GRAVES AND JOSHUA PODRO
ALL RIGHTS RESERVED
PRINTED IN THE UNITED STATES
AT
THE COUNTRY LIFE PRESS, GARDEN CITY, N. Y.
FIRST EDITION

FOREWORD

(*a*) The attitude of the Roman Church towards the New Testament is that the Canon has long been fixed: it is complete, consistent, and historical, and the interpretation of every text has been laid down in such irrefutable detail by a long line of Popes that devout Catholics need only read what they are told to read, interpret as they are told to interpret, make a personal effort of faith and repentance, and they will then be assured of salvation —because the keys of Heaven (*Matthew* xvi. 19—*see* LXXVII.*d*) are held by the Pope as St. Peter's lineal successor. The Protestant attitude is that Jesus's acts and sayings, in so far as they can be established historically, are of greater importance than any theological commentary on them, since Jesus speaks directly to the individual conscience. This 'in so far' is a concession to the large body of historically-minded Protestants who, not being forbidden to search the Scriptures for themselves and interpret what they find as best they may, have come to realize that the text of the New Testament is sadly inconsistent and strewn with anachronisms.

(*b*) Gospels written by members of the various Gentile Churches, after the Destruction of the Temple in 70 A.D., to support local doctrine, were piously attributed to the Apostles Matthew, John, James the Less, Peter, Thomas, Bartholomew, Andrew, and 'The Twelve'. Of these, the first two alone, with the addition of *Luke* and *Mark,* have become canonical, and then only after continuous drastic revision. Of the rest, some survive whole, some in part, some have been suppressed as heretical; and fragments of several other named and unnamed Gospels are extant. But none of these, whether canonical or uncanonical, can have been written by the author to whom it is ascribed. The introduction to *Luke* and the accounts quoted by Eusebius from the early second-century writer Papias (*see Introduction* IV.*g*) show that all the Gospels, except the patently fictitious ones, were based on notes taken by Greek-speaking converts from the Aramaic Gospel orally current among the Nazarenes; and that each evangelist, as Papias reports: 'interpreted them as best he could'—that is to say, uncritically and, in general, with studied ignorance of their historical background.

(*c*) After much patient research and experimentation, the Dean of York and Mr. O. Lazenby, a foreman glazier, have at last successfully restored the fourteenth-century 'Jesse' window in the nave of York Minster. This originally showed a vine with curved branches and twisted tendrils, Jesse lying at the foot, kings and queens standing within the trunk, prophets posted in the whorls, and a majestic crowned Virgin dominating the scene. In 1789, one William Peckitt, who was commissioned to repair the window, replaced Jesse with an erect king of his own creation, giving him a grotesque eight-

eenth-century head and a dress made from a fifteenth-century canopy enclosed in the frame of David's harp. He also removed the labels from the
twelve prophets, distributed their shoes and fragments of the Virgin's crown
in odd corners of the window, set a queen's head on Daniel's shoulders,
jumbled the vine's branches, and placed the Virgin's hand, with half the book
she was holding, on the ground at Samuel's feet. The window is now once
more in something like its original condition, though several heads, broken
or lost in Commonwealth days, have had to be replaced by later ones.

(d) We have undertaken much the same task here. Once the distortive technique of Gospel editing has been deduced: from contradictions and historical
discrepancies in the surviving documents; from a close study of Jewish life,
literature and religious beliefs in Jesus's time; and from early Christian ecclesiastical history, the original Nazarene tradition can be restored with a fair
degree of confidence. Only a few broken fragments of the story seem to be
lacking, though many are misplaced and have had their edges trimmed to
make them fit into a Peckitt's pattern.*

(e) Briefly, this restoration proves that Jesus was a devout Jew, belonging to a
small apocalyptic sect known as *Zophim,* or 'Watchers for the Kingdom', and
organized on Free Essene lines. He took the contemporary Pharisaic attitude
towards the Mosaic Law, making only minor reservations (*see* XLVIII.*d,*
LXXX.*e and* CVI.*f*), never equated himself with God and, though he performed
certain faith cures in God's name, neither did nor suffered anything that lay
outside the sphere of natural human experience. Granted, he was set apart
from his fellow-Israelites, because John the Baptist had chosen him as the
person to whom the whole corpus of Messianic prophecies referred, and secretly anointed him King of Israel; yet his deference to the Great Sanhedrin's
religious authority (*see* XIII.*a, and* XLVIII.*d-f*) continued to be no less sincere
than the devout Catholic's is to the Holy See to-day.

(f) Jesus was a man of unusual learning, wit and piety; his chief sponsors
were members of the religious aristocracy of Jerusalem (*see* VIII.*v*); and
under the synagogue system then in force the general educational level of the
Jewish artisan class, from which most of the disciples seem to have been
drawn, was higher than that of any other in the world, the Greek included.
All available evidence goes to show that the original Nazarene Gospel was
terse, factually accurate and intellectually satisfying to those chosen students

---

* In 1946, I published a historical novel, *King Jesus,* written from the standpoint of Agabus,
an Alexandrian scholar, in the year 98 A.D. Agabus made no claim to be an authority on Pharisaic law, believed in the supernatural and relied in part on already falsified texts; so that his
view does not correspond with ours on many points, particularly on the question of the Nativity.

I used the fictional device of letting the story be told by a Greek subject of the Emperor
Domitian, in order to emphasize the paradox of Christianity: namely, that the ancient Cyprian
Goddess on whom Jesus declared war in the name of Israelite Jehovah (*see* XXI.*n*) met his challenge and gained a partial victory. Jesus was hanged on a tree, as her sacred king had been
hanged in ancient times (*see* CXIII.*c*); and Christianity became a strange compound of laughter-
loving Mediterranean Goddess-worship, Gothic sword-worship, Greek speculative philosophy
and ascetic Jewish monotheism. R. G.

of the Law and the prophets for whom it was primarily intended. But Gentile heretics pirated it, mistranslated it into pedestrian Greek, recast it, and then subjected it to a century-long process of emendation and manipulation. The glamour of the early Jacobean prose in which the Gospels are now clothed, and their judicial authority, are most deceptive. Judged by Greek literary standards, they are poor; by historical standards, unreliable; and their doctrine is confused and contradictory. The late-Victorian atheist (was it Bradlaugh?) may be excused for remarking that they read as though 'concocted by illiterate, half-starved visionaries in some dark corner of a Graeco-Syrian slum.'

(g) A number of processes are distinguishable by which the original tradition became so sadly distorted. Some of these reflect editorial carelessness; some, doctrinal piety or perversity; others, polemical shrewdness. At times these categories overlap.

Editorial carelessness covers such cases as the following:

(1) Miscopying; with accidental omissions or duplications.

(2) Misunderstanding of the Aramaic original.

(3) Infiltration of marginal glosses into the text.

(4) Misreading of the Nazarene subject-arrangement for a chronological one.

(5) Choice of inappropriate contexts for sayings which bore no indication of context.

(6) Running together of such sayings into a single confused argument.

(7) Inclusion of anecdotes based on a misinterpretation of sacred pictures.

(8) Ill-considered stylistic improvements.

(9) Clumsy attempts to correct obvious absurdities or contradictions.

(10) Mistaking of figurative or ironical sayings for straightforward ones— and *vice versa*.

(h) Doctrinal piety or perversity covers such cases as the following:

(1) Identification of Jesus with the Second Person of the Gnostic Trinity: a process which involved the substitution of 'I' for 'God' in many of his sayings, and the omission of his prayers to God whenever he performed works of healing.

(2) Conversion of his symbolic acts into miracles; and attempts to make him rival or surpass the recorded feats of Moses, Elijah, Elisha and Apollonius of Tyana.

(3) Disguise of the motives which guided him during Passion Week.

(4) Removal of references to his humanity.

(5) Invention of miracles wherever he might have been expected to perform them.

(6) Borrowings from the Pauline *Epistles,* or from Church liturgy, in order to identify his message with Paulinism.

(7) Invention of sayings and incidents which would authorize second-century Church practice.

(8) Attempts to prove that he preferred the poor, sick, and outcast to the rich, healthy, and established.

(9) Disguise of his asceticism, but particularly of his insistence on complete sexual chastity.

(*i*) Polemical shrewdness covers such cases as the following:

    (1) Attempts to dissociate Jesus from Judaism by omitting nearly all his quotations from the Law and prophets.

    (2) Suppression or manipulation of any act or saying likely to offend the Roman authorities.

    (3) Attempts to prove that he deliberately flouted the Mosaic Law.

    (4) Attempts to prove that he rejected the Oral Law as an impossible burden.

    (5) Attempts to fasten the blame for his death on the Jews.

    (6) Attempts to prove that he debarred the Jews from the Kingdom of God in favour of the Gentiles.

    (7) Pro-Samaritan, pro-Grecian or pro-Phoenician tamperings with the text.

    (8) Deliberate misdirection against the Pharisees of denunciations originally intended for the Herodians and Sadducees.

    (9) Misdirection against the Pharisees of denunciations intended for the 'feigned Pharisees'.

These lists are by no means comprehensive.

(*j*) If all the corruptions in the Gospels had been due merely to carelessness or obtuseness, our task would have been comparatively easy. Yet even so, a restoration of the original text from internal and external evidence would doubtless have met with invincible opposition from the Protestant as well as the Roman Churches. Witness the Caliphate's refusal to permit the slightest textual recension of the Koran, once its various parts had been collected and placed in decreasing order of length, regardless of the contents, by Zaid ibn Thabit. This eccentric arrangement, which made havoc of the sense, seems to have been adopted because Mohammed referred to the separate passages of his revelation as *surahs*—that is to say, courses of brick or masonry —and it seemed architecturally appropriate to lay the largest course first. Thus Mohammed, who wrote in the rhythmic prose of contemporary Arab soothsayers, has won undeserved fame for ecstatic disorientation; and though many of the *surahs* are headed by such unexplained letters as *ALM, ALR, TH*—apparently the alphabetical labels of the baskets in which the various parts of his revelation were filed—no Arabic scholar has since dared to rearrange them in a logical sequence.

(*k*) Our suggestion (*see* (*g*) *above*) that many fictitious events, derived in good faith from a misreading of sacred pictures, have been incorporated into the Canonical Gospels—we call this process 'iconotropy'—has not, so far as we know, been made before. But New Testament scholars have been slow to realize that the Christian art of the Catacombs is not entirely of Gentile origin: that while the Gospels were being compiled, Jewish synagogues were decorated not only with mosaics, as in the Palestinian synagogues of Beth

Alpha and the North African synagogue of Hamman-Lif, but also with frescoes in Pompeian style similarly illustrative of Scriptural texts. Examples of the latter have survived, by an extraordinary accident, in the Great Synagogue of Doura-Europos,* on the Euphrates; though mid-third-century in date, they seem to have been copied from those of a second-century synagogue on the same site. Among the Doura frescoes† are several Old Testament scenes which vividly suggest Christian themes. The painting of Ahasuerus, Vashti, and Esther could serve as an illustration for the story of Antipas, Herodias, and Salome; that of the death of Joab, for the decapitation of John the Baptist; that of Elijah's reception by the widow of Sarepta, for the Syro-Phoenician woman's visit to Jesus; that of Elijah's raising of the widow's son at Sarepta, for Jesus's raising of the widow's son at Nain; that of Ezekiel's vision of the dry bones, for Jesus's harrowing of Hell. It is a wide-spread fallacy that the Jews, like the Moslems, were forbidden all representational art; the ban applied only to the making of images for worship. (*l*) No illustrated Christian manuscript survives of a date earlier than the fourth century A.D., but the tradition of sacred illustration, in the *Book of the Dead* style, had been firmly established among Greek Jews from pre-Christian times; and first-century copies of *Logia* (Jesus's oracular sayings), particularly the collection attributed to the Apostle Matthew, are likely to have been treated in the same way. Not only may such close parallels between Old and New Testament anecdotes as the rousing of Jonah from sleep during a storm at sea and the similar rousing of Jesus (*see* LXXV.*b*) be due to iconotropy, but so may patently unhistorical anecdotes such as the calling of Zacchaeus (*see* XIX.*g*); and mysterious or supernatural events such as *Mark's* accounts of the Temptation (*see* LXXVIII.*b*) and the Transfiguration (*see* LXXIX.*g*), with all others similarly distinguished by the appearance of angels or the sounding of God's voice from the sky. Additions to the Gospels were, it seems, made by Greek-speaking 'God-fearers': converts to Paulinism, who could not translate the Hebrew legends attached to the synagogue frescoes of Syria or Greater Greece, and had little Scriptural learning. One obvious cause of misunderstanding was the art-convention which permitted the same character to appear several times in a single painting. Thus the boy in the Doura-Europos 'Raising of the Widow's Son' is first shown dead in his mother's arms, next being healed by Elijah, lastly restored to his mother. Anyone unfamiliar with 2 *Kings* iv. 18–37 would suppose that Elijah healed three different boys (*see* XXXVI.*c*).

It may be charged that we have far too frequently sheltered behind the theory of iconotropy when confronted by supernatural incidents in the Gospels; but early literary sources are inadequate to account for all of these. To judge from Talmudic analogues dating back to the first century A.D., the

---

* When the city was besieged, this synagogue was incorporated into a hastily constructed rampart, and its whereabouts were forgotten after the massacre of the inhabitants.

† Comte du Mesnil du Buisson: *Les Peintures de la Synagogue de Doura-Europos* (Rome, Pontificio Istituto Biblico, 1939).

Nazarenes, though they credited Jesus with having cured many sick people by the 'finger of God', and with having himself defeated death on the Cross, soberly refrained from supernatural fantasy. And it would be unjust to suggest that the early Gentile Fathers deliberately concocted miracles. Granted, they were not above revising or lavishly embellishing the Nazarene tradition; their excuse was that the Jews had rejected Jesus and had therefore jealously minimized his divine feats. But they must have demanded an honest assurance, from local Church leaders anxious to add new miracles to the Canon, that these were backed by some traditional authority at least, even if this were a mere textual gloss (*see* xxxviii.*b and* lxiii.*c*); and pictorial evidence will have been acceptable enough.

(*m*) When all first-and-second-century changes and interpolations are removed from the Canon, what is left amounts to no more than an exceptionally dramatic incident in Jewish sectarian history. The Nazarenes and the Ebionites (*Ebionim,* 'poor men'—Nazarenes dedicated to a life of poverty) differed from the Pharisees only in their belief that the promised King-Messiah had appeared in the person of Jesus and that the Kingdom of God was hourly imminent. Later, their doctrine was transformed by Paul, who held that the coming of this Messiah marked a new epoch of emancipation from the Law. His view was adopted by Gentile 'God-fearers' of Syria, Asia Minor, Greece, and Italy who had found the Jewish ceremonial law a hardship and a handicap; and also by the 'Grecians' of Alexandria, who resented their dependence on Jerusalem for true doctrine. These, with a small but influential body of Samaritan converts, shaped the Nazarene tradition to their own convenience; and the Gentiles, recalling the violent diatribes which the prophets had pronounced on their fellow-Israelites, felt spiritually superior to a 'stiff-necked and adulterous nation'.

(*n*) The Gospels in circulation among the early Christian communities of the Dispersal will have been condemned as heretical by the Nazarene Council of Jerusalem, which claimed that the chosen companions of Jesus could alone speak from personal knowledge of his sayings and beliefs. Jesus's 'Oracles', as preserved by the Nazarenes, will have consisted partly of scattered epigrams, moral judgements, and denunciations of all who rejected Pharisaic authority or compounded with the 'Wicked Kingdom of Rome'; partly of *midrashim,* or comments, on Scriptural texts; partly of religious discussions with friends or opponents. They will have been supplemented by eye-witness accounts of his coronation, of his symbolic actions, of cures he performed, of his travels through the Kingdom of Israel and, finally, of his crucifixion, burial, resurrection, and farewell.

(*o*) Our findings are consistent with, and not greatly in advance of, contemporary Biblical criticism; but we appear to be the first to cross a wide stream at which even the most liberal scholars have long baulked. If these findings are to be accepted, historically-minded Protestants will conclude that only one honest course is left to them: namely, to revive Jesus's own form of Judaism and subject themselves to circumcision and the laws of ritual cleanliness in token of their sincerity. Yet if they decide to do so—as some of the Independents came close to doing under Cromwell*—they will be faced with a further moral problem. Jesus himself believed in the Old Testament as a trustworthy record of events, and divine orders, and Josephus, in several passages of his *Antiquities,* voiced the national belief that nothing had ever been added to or removed from it since the time of Moses, who lived two thousand years before him; whereas it had, in fact, been edited and re-edited many times since its first redaction, and wholly misrepresented primitive religious theory and practice in Israel. None of the books ascribed to Moses, David, and Solomon was—as Biblical scholars now generally agree—written by these; the prophecies of Isaiah and his successors were defaced by additions and interpolations; the national chronicles had been tampered with, and contained numerous anachronisms; miracles were recorded even less credible than those in the New Testament. Thus Protestants who, on historical grounds, may decide to Judaize, will either have to smile reproof at Jesus for taking the Old Testament literally, or else do so themselves. But if they can swallow the Old Testament with its miracles, why should the New stick in their throat? Why should the evangelists be blamed for ascribing fictitious sayings to Jesus, while the authors of the Old Testament are pardoned for ascribing fictitious sayings to Moses or David?

(*p*) It would be foolish, of course, to despise Jesus for knowing less about Old Testament origins than we do now. The Canon of the greater part of the Scriptures had been fixed and edited with care some two centuries before; only minor contradictions were discernible in its text, and these had been resolved by ingenious glosses. Nobody ever doubted that the Pentateuch was Moses's own original composition. Moreover Jesus, as a devout Jew, could follow a prescribed rule of moral conduct without distinguishing between civil and religious law. It is far more difficult for an intelligent modern Churchman to keep to the orthodox path, since the Canonical Gospels contradict one another freely and the *Epistles* enjoin obedience to the temporal power as distinct from the authority of the Church. Thus Christian morality, even under severe ecclesiastical discipline, has become proportionately more elastic; and the Pauline doctrine that faith takes precedence of works, and that all Christians are sinners, whether they keep the Law or not, has led the Church to reject most of the religious obligations on which Jesus insisted. For Jesus, though demanding from his people an earlier, more child-like, belief in the power and mercy of God, untroubled by legalistic obsesssions, had nevertheless bound them to a scrupulous regard for the unalterable Law.

(*q*) Paul considered this a cruel hardship: laws need lawyers to interpret them, and the more conscientious a lawyer, the finer will be the points he raises. Pharisee lawyers of the first century, holding that the personal salva-

---

* John Bunyan at one time even despaired of salvation because he was not of Jewish blood (*Grace Abounding to the Chief of Sinners*).

tion of each individual depended on his strict observance of the Law, made it their duty to anticipate and provide for every moral contingency, however trivial, that might arise in the course of daily life under Roman rule. Paul was convinced that the Law had already become a greater burden than many Jews themselves could bear, and that the Gentiles should not be forced to shoulder it. He decided that a clean start must be made, outside the synagogue system, and held that the Crucifixion had now abrogated the Law (*Galatians* iii. 13). It is not for us to judge whether this decision was right or wrong; but we may at least deplore his dishonesty in implementing it and the looseness of his terms, since the Ten Commandments, which continued to be read in Christian churches as they had been in synagogues,* were the essence of the Law. Paul's conduct fell short not only of Jewish but of Graeco-Roman moral standards, and it is the greatest of pities that a mitigation of the Law's demands was preached by him and not by some saint of irreproachable antecedents and unchallengeable integrity.

(*r*) Practically-minded Protestants, realizing the difficulty of literal obedience to Nazarene doctrine—if only because it presupposes the existence of the Temple-cult at Jerusalem—will continue to condone Paul's evasions and distortions and thus still regard Jesus as a rebel against Judaism. They will first dwell on the general plausibility of the Gospels as they have survived; then, though ready to admit the grave inherent contradictions in particular passages, will stress the hopelessness of trying to restore the original text; and, finally, if asked how their critical consciences allow them to accept a view that is not only unhistorical but defies scholarly scrutiny, will retreat in good order to their last, impregnable, third-century line of defence: 'No one who lacks faith can understand or criticize the Word of God.'

(*s*) 'Faith' in this sense is a very different concept from the faith which these same Protestants are content to rest in a mathematical or physiological principle; it is an assumption, made with a great dissociative effort of will, that at a certain period in history the Prime Cause suddenly intervened in human affairs, and that subsequent events transcended so many natural laws that no annalist of the time was able to give a coherent account of them. Such faith is prized today for its imaginative denial of the crudely mechanical views of existence. It preserves the sense of the unexpected and wonderful—if miracles have happened once, why not again? Life is not considered worth living in the West if completely controlled and behaviouristic; and the Gospel message combines evidence of miracles with an insistence on the individual's right to be master of his own spiritual fate. It is said: 'Look what has happened to personal liberty in Godless Russia! Destroy belief in the authenticity of the Gospels and you destroy belief in a man's right to think or act for himself.' This is not, of course, so: the most important contributions to modern imaginative literature and scientific discovery have been made by agnostics or

---

* Oddly enough, it was the synagogues which discontinued this practice, in the mid-second century A.D., to lessen the similiarity between the rival services.

atheists, and the chief difficulty with which the Western nations have to contend is not that the Russians are Godless or controlled by the Communist Party, but that, for better or worse, they are Russians.

(*t*) Reputable Christian apologists, finding our main theses hard to refute—except by a rallying call to orthodoxy—will either leave them unanswered or else evade the issue by disputing minor points. After all, when there is disagreement between the four Gospels even on essential facts—for instance, on Jesus's ancestry (*see* ii.*a*) or the circumstances of his betrayal by Judas (*see* cv.*a*) or his Resurrection (*see* cxv.*a*)—they will find it easy enough to demolish our reconstruction of the original tradition, merely by upholding as Gospel truth one of the texts which we have thought fit to reject; since it has never been an article of ecclesiastical logic that only a single set of harmonious facts can fit a given incident. And when one of Jesus's sayings is quoted by the evangelists in a wide range of different contexts (*see* xxv.*b*), they will say that he did indeed repeat himself, why not?, and that we have no right to place the saying in only one of these. As for the miracles, they will point out that scientists are still unable to account for a great number of common psychical and physical phenomena and that it would therefore be unscientific to reject any of the supernatural occurrences in the Gospels, even where the evangelists' accounts appear to be contradictory. Further, that belief in Jesus as the God and Saviour of mankind has led to a succession of latter-day miracles, many of them attested by persons of the highest veracity, which are sufficient to prove the Christian thesis. And further—a contention which we would be the last to dispute—that orthodox Christianity has been the sole inspiration and support of countless noble lives.

Protestantism, except in intellectually backward areas of Europe and the United States, has come to be a strategic position rather than a faith; a defence against Catholicism on one flank and Communism on the other. If the management of all Protestant Churches were entrusted to unpaid laymen, with an endowed priesthood engaged only in ritual observances, as among the Jews in Jesus's time (*see* xiii.*j*), the case might be different: there would not be the same unwillingness to keep religion abreast of contemporary thought and feeling, or the same insistence on the authenticity of the more fantastic miracles. It is remarkable that Hillel—a Jewish lay-teacher of the first century b.c., who became President of the Great Sanhedrin and to whom, paradoxically, the Christian ethic owes more even than to Jesus—always displayed a negative and incurious attitude towards the supernatural, though he was wholly dedicated to God. He regarded the Godhead as a mystery, notoriously beyond definition, which it was most improper for theologians to discuss in public. While conceding the need for strict ceremoniousness in obedience to the Law, he insisted that love for one's neighbour was the sole beginning and end of religion (*see* lxxxii.*l*); and used the Law and the prophets as his text-books, simply because they were traditionally invested with divine authority. Hillel avoided all discussion of miracles or other transcendental phenomena and made no attempt to justify Scriptural contradictions or anachronisms, which did not interest him even if he became aware of them. He was not bound by a formal creed—the creed was invented by the Catholics as a means of ecclesiastical discipline: his concern was with practical humanity in a universal sense, and he never taught mystical nonsense.

(*u*) This book is published not in challenge to the Catholic priesthood and their devoted congregations, but to reassure the lay public, which has lost its child-like faith in ecclesiastical dogma, that the original Gospel stood four-square—that, indeed, granted the introductory premiss 'I believe in God the Father Almighty, Maker of Heaven and earth,' the Apostles' Creed is historically acceptable, at least as far as 'On the third day he rose again from the dead'; and that Jesus the devout Jew, though an apocalyptic extremist, deserves far greater respect for his religious integrity than the Jesus of the Gospels. The ethical system of the West depends on his example; and whether or not he showed absolute devotion to principle—however ingenuous his beliefs—is therefore a matter of the highest importance. A common Protestant contention that Jesus, being God, might behave as irresponsibly as he pleased, is intellectual defeatism, which is liable to end either in an abandonment of traditional morality or in a transference of one's personal conscience to the perhaps conscienceless charge of a confessor. Once it is realized that Jesus, although he had won the honorific title 'Son of God' at his coronation (*see* 1.*b*), was humanly aware of his own frailties, and that his sayings made straightforward sense in the context of the Law and the prophets, then the Western ethical system can be strengthened by his example and the mystical concept of Godhead can remain—for those who care to embrace it—untarnished by human error. Even Jews may learn to forgive Jesus for the centuries of persecution and shame which they have suffered on his behalf.

(*v*) It remains for anthropologists to decide whether—always assuming the continued need for religion and the impracticability of reviving any of Christianity's defeated rivals—the Old Testament, as interpreted by Hillel and his successor Jesus, or the New Testament, as interpreted by the more enlightened Christian Churches, provides the better ethical education. Jesus's Judaism demands utter devotion to Jehovah as the national God of Israel, and a tradition of patient watching for the day of deliverance: when persecutions shall cease and the twelve tribes, purged and pardoned, shall be reassembled at Jerusalem, where their leaders will instruct the Gentiles in moral perfection. 'Salvation,' as he himself told the woman of Sychar, 'is from the Jews,' (*see* lxx.*c*) and from the Gentiles he expected nothing but grateful attention to the Law and prophets as expounded by his fellow-Pharisees. Christianity is patently a religion of compromise: not morally strict enough for the ethically inclined; too ecclesiastical for the mystically inclined; and for the historians deserving of *de facto* recognition only.

(*w*) Ought there, then, to be a division of Christianity into two separate religions: the religion of poetry and the religion of prose? Should the mystically and emotionally inclined worship Christ as an Osiris done to death by the tyrannical Set, mourned by Isis, and annually renewed as the Child Horus? But would this not imply a return to some form of orgiastic extravagance? Should the historically and ethically inclined worship Jesus the apocalyptic Pharisee, as a leading moral exemplar among other Jewish and non-Jewish saints, yet be guided in their daily life by Hillel's less ascetic rule and by his less literal faith in the supernatural and in the fulfilment of eschatological prophecy? But would this not imply some degree at least of Judaization and a renewed belief, among other things, in the now discredited doctrine of Hell-fire? These are questions which will eventually have to be answered by the heads of the Protestant Churches; though not, perhaps, in the lifetime of any parish priest or bishop contemporary with ourselves.* And would the Synagogue authorities give the Judaizer a wholehearted welcome? They have learned by bitter experience to discourage proselytes by every means short of downright rejection, and to suspect them of ineradicable *minuth.* (*x*) The logic of most Protestant apologists is so faulty, and they present so mean-spirited and vapid a picture of Jesus, that their readers are tempted to subject themselves once more to Catholic discipline; Catholicism may be unhistorical, and even anti-historical, but at least it is consistent.

Why, although the factual discrepancies and doctrinal differences between the Gospels are a matter of common knowledge among professional theologians, do these shrink from making a concerted attempt to investigate the processes by which the authentic tradition became distorted? And when lead-

---

* Meanwhile, Sir Henry Self, President of the Modern Churchmen's Union, speaking at their Cambridge Conference on August 14, 1950, is reported by *The Times* to have emphasized the disagreement between modern scientific views of the Universe and the 'outdated, outmoded fundamentalist dogmas of the Church,' and to have continued:

'It is essential for the Church, which has increasingly contributed by its ineptitude and dogmatism to the number of "humanists", now to re-proclaim its Gospel in terms which meet with modern understanding.'

Sir Henry was alluding to the Protestant Church; and the well-known preacher, Dr. W. R. Inge who, in his sermon at the opening service had, negatively at least, envisaged the sort of Gospel which would please these Modern Churchmen, said:

'Do you agree with me that our services are terribly clogged with Judaism? If you are clergymen, do you not hate having to read many of the Old Testament lessons? Some of them are frankly unedifying, others are unintelligible. . . . Of one thing we may be thankful, that the hideous hell-fire theology is heard no longer in our Churches.'

The same issue of *The Times* carried the following news item, which shows the bland rejection by the Roman Church of all modern scientific views and their wholehearted endorsement of the Immaculate Conception dogma proclaimed by Pope Pius IX in 1854:

'The *Osservatore Romano,* organ of the Vatican, announced today that the Pope is to hold a consistory on October 30, at which he will announce his intention of proclaiming a new dogma of the Roman Catholic Church, that of the Assumption of the Blessed Virgin Mary into Heaven—that she is in heaven not only in soul but also in body. . . . (*see* cxviii.*w*).

'While discussion of the possibility of proclaiming the dogma has been proceeding inside the Church since 1869, it was the present Pope who, during the past four years, made a world-wide survey among bishops of the Roman Catholic Church to determine whether it was considered "wise, prudent, and desirable" to proclaim the dogma. . . . According to a reliable Vatican source, 97 per cent. of the declarations made by cardinals, bishops, and others since the discussions opened have been in favour of proclaiming the dogma.'

The Assumption duly became dogmatic.

ing scholars admit to a despair of recovering the original truth, is their despair unqualified by the practical consideration: 'Perhaps such a recovery would not be altogether in the public interest'? Have they turned a blind eye to elements of the problem which are obvious to less interested students—particularly to the Gospel editors' skilful use of a technique described by Irenaeus in the context of the Gnostic forgeries (*see Introduction* iii.*u*) and now known in the film industry as *montage*?*

One device of *montage,* to which the Russian film director Eisenstein first called attention in the 1920's, is the insertion of unrehearsed shots into studio scenes as a means of heightening dramatic conviction. In a historical film, he said, the excited, unselfconscious faces of extras watching a Punch-and-Judy show will produce a far greater emotional impact than if taken while watching an imaginary Czarist massacre. Thus, while the commentators may be intellectually convinced, for instance, that Lazarus did not stumble out of his tomb, wrapped in cere-cloths, and that Pilate did not call for water and wash from his hands the guilt of Jesus's crucifixion, they nevertheless allow themselves to be emotionally deceived by these vivid circumstantial details. It seems to have occurred to none of them that such details, though genuine, may have been borrowed from another Gospel sequence, where they were politically or doctrinally dangerous, and transferred to an altogether different one (*see* lxxxvii.*e, Introduction* iv.*e and* cx.*g*).

(*y*) They do not fear the truth, but owe a duty of caution alike to their employers and to their dependants, and are particularly anxious not to offend any of the 'little ones': if only because these are quick to take offence and half-a-dozen strongly-worded protests to the Church or University authorities may cause a deal of trouble.

It happens that neither of us has a chair, post, or pulpit to lose. Working when and how we please and consulting our own libraries, we acknowledge no spiritual authority, except the still, small, nagging voice of conscience—a survival from our early Scriptural education—which urges us to tell the truth as we know it.

One of us grew up as a devout Eastern European Jew and passed his childhood in terror of Christian pogroms; the other an Irish bishop's grandson, born in the same year, grew up as a devout Anglican and soon learned to abhor the Jews 'who crucified Jesus'. It is less remarkable than may appear that we arrived eventually at a common point of view: both developed a historical conscience and ceased to hold orthodox beliefs long before we came to know each other in England during the recent war. We knew that an enormous intellectual effort was needed to wipe out the traditional misrepresentations of Jesus acquired in childhood. Comparing notes, we realized how much each could learn from the other; one of us had a special knowledge of the Graeco-Roman world, and of the early Church, which complemented

---

* *Montage* in the Gospels must be distinguished from mere *collage,* which is the less exacting art of, for example, filling any gap in a discourse of Jesus's with devotional excerpts from other contexts (*see* lxxxi.*b*).

the other's researches in Jewish history and literature. Once the relevant facts were established, no disagreement could be possible, though the Jew would remain temperamentally 'of the circumcision' and the Anglican 'of the uncircumcision'.

(z) One disadvantage of the method we have adopted—which is to arrange episodes or groups of sayings in roughly chronological sequence and devote a separate chapter to each—is that we must constantly assume the reader's acceptance of certain general principles previously submitted. If we write, for instance:

> '*Luke* — — is a *midrash* on *Isaiah* — —; it makes no sense in its present context and must have originally formed part of the dispute recorded in *Matthew* — —.'

this may seem an arbitrary pronouncement to anyone who dips into this book without following the argument. For the convenience of 'dippers', our general principles are summarized at the beginning of *Part* III.

We quote our authority for every historical statement not a matter of common knowledge; but have refrained from loading this already long book with even a select bibliography of the sixty or seventy thousand scholarly works on Christian origins.

Grateful acknowledgements are due to Kenneth Gay, who has helped us with the preparation of the manuscript; and to Beryl Graves, who has checked the references.

R. G. J. P.

CONTENTS

PART THREE

Summary of Critical Principles

Part One

CURIOSITIES OF NEW TESTAMENT CRITICISM

(*a*) Since even nominal Christians are required by Law to take a Court oath on the Bible, as the final repository of truth, and since the Protestant Churches agree with the Catholic and Orthodox on the desirability of belief in its literal accuracy, nearly a century of street-corner atheism has been needed to make the Protestant masses admit, for instance, on zoological grounds, that the whale's swallowing of Jonah may have been no more than an allegory. They are still, however, disinclined to abandon their faith in 'Gospel truth', even when they see plainly that the evangelists have contradicted one another or that Jesus is behaving inconsistently. Religious education in the schools has changed little during the past hundred years, and the artificial distinction between sacred and profane history has been jealously maintained at the Universities. Despite the remarkable development of Biblical criticism in the same period, a great part of the people and of the provincial clergy, though scientifically-minded in other respects, remain, outwardly at least, determined fundamentalists.

(*b*) Early prejudices stick. Ernest Renan who, in 1845, broke short his studies for the Roman priesthood after reading the rationalistic works of advanced German critics, would not apply his knowledge of Hebrew to dispersing the prejudices with which he had been imbued at the seminary of St. Nicholas du Chardonnet. In his *Vie de Jésus,* he insisted that Jesus fell a victim to the 'ferocious Mosaic Law', and that the Romans had no part in his judicial murder—which must therefore be laid at the door of the Jews as a nation (*see* cx.*b*). Even today educated Christian laymen cannot bring themselves to read the Gospel narrative as an exclusively Jewish one of the first century A.D.; they detach it from the contemporary background and it becomes an unaccountable enclave in historical time. The grateful love which they have been taught to feel for their Redeemer combines with the Old Master tradition in art to make them picture Jesus as a gentle, long-haired, blond-bearded Greek, in an Italianate setting, savagely beset by an alien horde of turbaned Jews. And whatever their mental reservations about certain of the miracles, they will at least agree with David Friedrich Strauss—whose *Leben Jesu* (1835) was the first scholarly attempt to free the Gospels of their supernatural element—that Jesus is 'beyond criticism as the creator of the religion of humanity'. For Strauss, though sponsoring the modern disbelief in miracles among the educated classes, also taught them to insist on the originality of Jesus's teaching.

(c) Advanced theologians of the succeeding generation, feeling it their duty to depreciate the religious and ethical ideas current in Judaea before Jesus's ministry, suggested that religious faith had been submerged in a dead sea of legalism. Later, when some of them entered the field of Jewish studies to substantiate their theory, and found that the *Mishnah,* the *Midrash* and the two Talmuds contained ethical teachings of a universalistic trend, they airily dismissed these as dating only from the second century. Thus Emil Schürer (*History of the Jewish People in the Time of Jesus Christ,* ii.1. 190), treating of the humanitarian laws in the *Mishnah* and their bearing on the Sanhedrin trials for capital offences, argued that they were 'purely theoretical in character' and added: 'We know from what took place in the case of Jesus that these laws were by no means strictly adhered to.'* An equally precarious theory, expressed by Professor Charles Guignebert in his recent *Jesus* (*p.* 401), is that the rabbis quoted in the *Mishnah* borrowed their ethical teachings from the Gospels.

(d) Some theologians, however, while conscientiously admitting that Jesus had preached little or nothing that was not implicit in the Pentateuch and the Pharisaic Oral Law, the *Torah she baal peh,* decided that though his teaching may not have been original in content, it was so in the manner of its delivery at least. Theodosius Harnack, in his *What is Christianity?* (*p.* 44), wrote of Julius Wellhausen's theories:

> 'I answer with Wellhausen: "It is quite true that what Jesus proclaimed, and what John the Baptist expressed before him in exhortations to repentance, was also to be found in the prophets and even in the Jewish tradition of their time; the rabbis said the same, but they were weak and did not carry it out." '

Harnack's meaning seems to be that the rabbis did not go on missionary journeys; and this is true enough, but they can hardly be accused of weakness on that account. Nor can it be contended that Jesus was more open-hearted than they; the doctrine of universality, which subsequently distinguished Christianity from the state religions of the Greek world, was borrowed from pre-Christian Pharisaic teaching. Jehovah had, indeed, ceased to be an exclusively national God ever since the prophets proclaimed him the Lord of Creation who watched with personal interest over everything that drew breath. The roots of Christianity are to be found in the prophecies of

---

* But Schürer's Jewish contemporary Isaac Hirsch Weiss, still the greatest authority on the subject, wrote:

'If we scrutinize the large literature of the oral law, namely the *Mishnah,* the *Baraitoth* and the Talmuds, we find that these laws attained their greatest perfection in the last days of the Temple, especially those administered in Palestine itself and connected with sacrifices, cleanliness, and capital punishment.' (*Dor Dor Ve'dorshov* i. 187; *2nd ed. Wilna,* 1893).

Jeremiah, who not only attacked blood-sacrifices and preached non-resistance to Babylon, but was the first prophet who addressed the individual heart.

(e) M. Goguel, in his *Jésus de Nazareth* (*Paris,* 1925), explains Jesus's supposed religious innovations as follows:

> 'In his eyes the value of rites was entirely secondary. . . . The Law expressed the Divine Will in a certain number of formulas, both positive and negative. It defined certain actions which a man ought to perform, and others from which he should refrain. But it left outside the moral sphere all that had not been foreseen and defined.'

Goguel here reveals a studied ignorance of the Oral Law, since Pharisaic teaching was primarily a guide to moral conduct in matters for which the Law did not explicitly provide. He continues:

> 'In Judaism, God is not known apart from the revelation of Himself in the Law. This revelation is insufficient, if the ideal which Jesus held up to his disciples in the words: "Be ye perfect, even as your Father in Heaven is perfect" (*Matthew* v. 48), be the true one.'

But this personal perfection had already been enjoined by the Law (*Leviticus* xi. 44): 'Ye shall be holy, for I am holy!' The Pharisees tried to imitate God's holiness and perfection, yet were aware that a full realization of this ideal was not humanly possible, and ruled that no greater demands should be placed on a community than it could bear.

(f) Wellhausen, in his *Israelitische und Jüdische Geschichte* (1907), suggested a novel compromise: namely, that Jesus's teaching, though anticipated by Hillel, a President of the Great Sanhedrin, and the Pharisees in general, was nevertheless original since he omitted some element from the doctrine he borrowed of them—it was his selective genius that distinguished him. Neither Wellhausen nor Guignebert holds that Jesus explicitly rejected any part of Pharisaism, but both maintain the compromise by stressing those elements of which he approved, and thus imply that he rejected the residue as burdensomely legalistic. Their view, however, is contradicted by Jesus's injunction, in *Matthew* xxiii. 23, not to omit the scrupulous tithing of mint, anise, and cummin (*see* XIII.*q*).

(g) Johannes Weiss, in his *Jesus von Nazareth: Mythus oder Geschichte?* (1911), also tries to uphold the originality of Jesus's message by advancing the theory that his contribution to contemporary thought was a 'new poetic creation'. He writes:

> 'Are Shakespeare's dramas of any smaller value because their sources can be traced even in minute particulars? What Jesus said can be found in *Job* and *Ecclesiasticus,* but he said it with greater warmth and with greater enthusiasm.'

As Weiss should have known, both Isaiah and Jeremiah wrote with striking enthusiasm and warmth of feeling, and their prophecies were, moreover,

original in content as well as in presentation. That the Almighty stood in no
need of blood-sacrifices was a revolutionary thesis which seemed to contradict
Genesis iv. 3–5, the story of Cain and Abel; and what earlier religious book
of any nation had refined the concepts of justice, love and truth so carefully
as Isaiah? Was Jesus's delivery of old truths, then, more poetical than Isaiah's
and Jeremiah's had been of new? Weiss, however, approves of the prophets
and holds that Jesus, finding their spirit suffocated by the legalistic narrow-
ness of his contemporaries—who granted no greater importance to notions
of justice and love than to petty ceremonial observances—courageously
recreated it.

If Weiss and his fellow-theologians discover, for instance, that Jesus, according to the Talmud, could not have been tried by a Pharisaic Sanhedrin
on the eve of a Sabbath, as the Synoptics report (*see* cix.*d*), they either ask:
'How do we know that these laws, redacted only at the close of the second
century, were framed during Jesus's lifetime?' Or else they declare with
Schürer (*see* (*c*) *above*): 'We know from the Gospels that they were not
adhered to.' Similarly, while convinced that the first-century synagogues were
ruled by the 'suffocating spirit' of the Talmud, they regard as second-century
borrowings from the Gospels all 'Christian' ideas found in it.

(*h*) Yet Weiss identifies as positively new only one of Jesus's doctrines:
Matthew v. 44, the command to love one's enemy. 'It is possible,' he writes,
'that this may have been preached by individual noble Jews—but what authoritative Jewish document or what Jewish community has ever made the
love of one's enemy a fundamental principle of action?' No community, of
course, whether Jewish or Christian, has ever done so; though *Proverbs* xxiv.
17 advises: 'Rejoice not when thine enemy falleth,' and *Proverbs* xxv. 21–22,
more positively: 'If thine enemy be hungry, give him bread to eat; and if he
be thirsty, give him water to drink: for thou shalt heap coals of fire upon his
head, and the Lord shall reward thee.' Jesus was here commenting on several
Scriptural texts in the spirit of the *Testaments of the Twelve Patriarchs* (*Gad*
vi. 3–4 and *Joseph* xviii. 2), a book written during the latter half of the second
century B.C. (*see* xxviii.*e*).

The author of the *Testaments* was aware that an enemy acts usually in
revenge of a real or fancied wrong done him; and that an amicable talk may
bring this wrong to light and thus allow it to be rectified. Jesus, therefore,
insisted on the need for gratitude to one's enemies when their hostility
pointed to faults in oneself which, if left unchecked, might lead to damnation. He said so most forcibly in *Matthew* v. 25: 'Agree with thine adversary
quickly . . . lest . . . the Adversary [of man] deliver thee to the Judge, and
the Judge cast thee into prison' (*see* xxii.*e*). But that was no more than an
elaboration of *Proverbs* xxv. 8–9: 'Go not forth hastily to sue . . . but debate
thy cause with thy neighbour himself.' Similarly, the Talmudic maxims: 'Let
the property of another be as dear unto thee as thine own,' and 'Let the
honour of another be as dear unto thee as thine own,' and 'Pray for the

wicked,' are elaborations of *Leviticus* xix. 18: 'Thou shalt love thy neighbour as thyself,' and of *Exodus* xxiii. 4, which orders a man to assist his personal enemy when he is in trouble.

(*i*) All these sayings present an ethical ideal that makes no concession to human frailty. Jewish religious teachers of the second and first centuries B.C., their eyes fixed on the Heavenly Kingdom, sought to create a perfect moral society. The rigorous humanitarian teachings of the Talmud are earlier even than the time of Hillel, and in their light the 'Sermon on the Mount' has a familiar look (*see* xxviii. *a and b*). Thus in *Matthew* v. 38–48 the ideal of human goodness is carried to a point where all personal pride must be surrendered: 'If your enemy sues you for your shirt, let him have your coat as well rather than prolong a quarrel in which you are as likely to be wrong as he is. Never resist a personal attack: if your enemy strikes you on the right cheek, show your peaceful intentions by also turning the left. But on God's behalf, or in defence of an ill-treated innocent, be unexceptionally firm and bold.'

(*j*) In *Matthew* v. 20, Jesus's counsels of perfection have been misrepresented as an order to outdo the Pharisees in virtue: 'Unless your righteousness exceed that of the scribes and Pharisees. . . .' He must really have said 'Sadducees' (*see* xxi.*j*), and a Gospel editor has mischievously introduced the refrain: 'Ye have heard it said. . . . But I say unto you . . .', though Jesus's teaching in *Matthew* v. 21 ff. is a typically Pharisaic strengthening of the Ten Commandments, meant for devotees who lived in hourly expectation of the Kingdom and thought only how best to save their souls.

The greater part of Jesus's teaching seems, originally, to have been delivered in the form of *midrashim,* or commentaries: he quoted a Scriptural text and applied it to a contemporary occasion—as in *Luke* xiv. 8–10 (*see* xlvi.*e*), where he told a parable based on *Proverbs* xxv. 6–7, or in *Matthew* v. 25, where he expanded *Proverbs* xxv. 8–9 (*see* xxii.*e*). Yet nearly always the introductory quotation has been omitted by a Greek editor who wished to emphasize Jesus's originality. This process of excision accounts for the many cases, especially in *Matthew,* where a text is introduced by an illogical *gar,* 'for'.

(*k*) At one point, Weiss asks an ingenuous question: 'If the words of Jesus are no more than a new edition of established Jewish ethics, how is it that so many of them are an attack on Judaism. . . ?' But Jesus no more attacked Judaism than did Isaiah who, though admonishing 'this sinful nation, a people laden with iniquity, a seed of evildoers, children that deal corruptly', yet found words of comfort for them. Time and again the prophets had reminded the Israelites of their unworthiness for the task to which they were appointed by God. No other nation regarded itself as 'chosen' in the religious sense or had such fierce internal critics. In the Graeco-Roman world it was a crime to disparage one's own tribe or city; satires were written only against individuals, and with the object of shaming rather than reforming them. The ideal historian was one who, like Livy, limited himself to recording the triumphs and virtues of his people. But the Jews meekly accepted all rebukes offered them in God's name, and humbly incorporated in their Scriptures even the most immoderate of these. Thus, when the Septuagint, the first Greek translation, was published in Ptolemaic Egypt, 'God's chosen people' suddenly stood self-condemned before a heathen world which marvelled at their long record of iniquity (*see* LXXXI.*e*).

(*l*) The Jews had contributed almost nothing towards research on Christian origins until the nineteenth century; and the Talmud and the *Midrash* add little to our knowledge of Jesus (*see* LIII *and* LXXX), though clearly revealing the Pharisees' attitude towards Pauline and allied forms of 'Grecian' Christianity during the late second century. The Nazarene Oracles have perished and no other independent Jewish records remain except a hostile biography, entitled the *Toldoth Yeshu,* the original text of which has been no less grossly overlaid with invention than the Apocryphal Gospels, though in an opposite sense.

When the Jews, under Bar-Cochba, had made their last stand against Rome in 132 A.D., the Pharisees, who assumed spiritual charge of the survivors, found themselves violently assailed by a former sect of their own persuasion; it had expanded and changed beyond recognition and was now composed almost exclusively of Jewish renegades and Gentile foes. Christianity was unmistakably a 'daughter' religion—but what daughter would side with her mother's alien oppressors, jeer at her calamities and declare herself the sole inheritrex of the family title and culture? The *Toldoth Yeshu,* which exists only in mediaeval versions, is a record of contemporary Jewish recriminations.

(*m*) The Pharisees had decided, even before Bar-Cochba's revolt, that, to survive at all, they must live in spiritual isolation. A decree, passed by the Great Sanhedrin as early as 116 A.D., which forbad the Jews to learn Greek, was one of a number of measures intended to cut cultural connexions with the outside world. Above all else, they feared assimilation and refused to interest themselves any longer in non-Jewish studies; still to possess the Law sufficed them. Thenceforth, for nearly fifteen hundred years, they ignored whatever might be written about them in Greek or Latin, and avoided all discussions of Christianity. Josephus was the last Jew for many centuries who replied to the libels of a Gentile (*Against Apion*), and even he had been not much better than a renegade. During the Middle Ages, Jews defended themselves in disputations with Christians only when compelled by force to do so. Every Christian was taught that the Jews had rejected and murdered their God but remained unrepentant, and since it was an axiom that the Christian, having the truth on his side, must always vanquish his opponent, the greater the eloquence shown by a Jewish apologist, the more likely were his co-religionists to suffer for it. Not until the end of the Middle Ages were theological works published to defend Judaism against attacks by Jewish con-

verts to Christianity; they were not, however, offered as historical contributions to the problem of Christian origins, since practically all the information
about Jesus then available came from Christian sources which it was dangerous to contradict.

(*n*) In the nineteenth century, Jewish historians begin to interest themselves
in New Testament research. The results were published piecemeal in their
own periodicals, but no scholarly Life of Jesus by a Jew had appeared before
Joseph Klausner's *Jesus of Nazareth* (1928). This book has been highly
regarded, even by Christians, for the past two decades, largely because
Klausner, a professor at the University of Jerusalem, is reluctant to distinguish
pre-Christian Pharisaic tradition in the Gospels from accretions of the first
and early second centuries, which makes his work read at times like that of
a Lutheran theologian who has acquired an exceptional knowledge of the
Talmud and the *Midrash*. Carefully following the path worn for him by a
generation of advanced Christian historians, who allow him to state that Jesus
was a pious and observing Jew, Klausner asks: 'Why, if Christianity was
born within Israel, did Israel as a nation reject it utterly?' And on the principle 'as the tree is, so also is the fruit', he assumes that if Jesus's teaching had
not contained some element that contradicted the religious views of Israel, a
new faith so irreconcilable with them could never have arisen from it. *Ex
nihilo nihil fit.*

(*o*) This goes to show how strong an influence Christian theology can exert
even on a Talmudist. Not only were the religious views of Israel in Jesus's
day extremely mixed—varying from Herodian-Sadducaic 'worldliness' to
Essene 'other-worldliness'—but Jesus's own views were widely held, especially by the apocalyptic extremists. Klausner would be justified in asking
why Israel rejected Jesus's message, which was a sincere and literal para-
phrase of Scriptural teaching, if any other nation had since accepted and followed it literally. And he should know that the Church of Jerusalem, headed
by James the Just, Simeon Cleophas and the other first-century Nazarenes,
continued to flourish even when Roman misrule in Palestine had forced most
Jews to abandon other-worldly quietism and break into open revolt; after
which it was gradually discredited by Gentile Christian libels against the
Jews in general and the Pharisees in particular.

Klausner then comes out with the surprising statement that Paul could
never have set aside the ceremonial laws and thus broken through the bar-
riers of national Judaism, if he had not found support for this reform in
Jesus's teaching. It is clear, from *Matthew* v. 18 (*see* xxi.i), that Jesus con-
sidered the Law so sacred and immutable that none who transgressed the
least of its ordinances might hope to partake of God's Kingdom. Also, that
Paul makes only scanty reference in his *Epistles* to the life and teaching of
Jesus; that he came into sharp conflict with the Twelve, whose view of the
Law was diametrically opposed to his; and that the texts of all the Canonical
Gospels have been manipulated in favour of the Pauline view.

(*p*) The article on the *Gospels* in the learned and liberal *Encyclopaedia Biblica* is characteristically wrong-minded: after dwelling at length on textual inconsistencies and anachronisms, its author, Dr. Paul Schmiedel, Professor of New Testament Exegesis at Zürich, comes to the conclusion that:

> '. . . the passage in *Matthew* xxiii. 2–3*a*, so friendly to the Pharisees, and all the Jewish particularistic passages listed above—*Matthew* xv. 24, "lost sheep of Israel"; x. 5*ff.*, "go not into the way of the Gentiles"; v. 17–20, "I come not to destroy the Law but to fulfil it"; xxiv. 20, "pray ye that the flight be not on a Sabbath"—which it is impossible to ascribe to Jesus . . . are attributable to a Judaistic redaction which the *Logia* underwent before they were made use of and altered to an opposite sense by Matthew. . . .
>
> 'The character of the original *Logia* becomes in this way more uniform and more in accordance with the free attitude of Jesus towards the Law.'

THE PAULINE HERESY

(*a*) The attempt to reconstruct lost or damaged parts of any ancient narrative calls for a sharp intuition as to what is true or false in the surviving documents. Almost every historian has his personal bias, which is usually betrayed by slight departures from abiding fact; once this has been identified, more serious inaccuracies may come to light. The task of discovering what Jesus really did and said is complicated by the many layers of misrepresentative editing from which the canonical and apocryphal Gospels suffer; yet every contradiction or anachronism is a useful indication of bias. If it is permissible to assume, as we do, that Jesus was single-minded in his pursuit of truth, that he impressed the necessity of truth on the disciples, and that they did not deliberately falsify their accounts, considerable progress can be made.

Motives for the extensive distortion of facts by Gospel editors must be looked for in early Church politics, particularly in the bitter quarrels that, less than thirty years after the Crucifixion, divorced the Gentile Churches of Greece, Asia Minor, and Italy, largely controlled by Paul—and also the 'Grecian' churches of Egypt and Libya, largely controlled by the Gnostics—from the Nazarene Church, headed by James the Just and Jesus's other disciples, which continued to obey the authority of the Pharisaic Sanhedrin, the fountain-head of orthodox Jewish doctrine. That the word *Pharisee*, which originally meant 'separated'—one who dedicated himself to a life of religious purity—has now acquired the meaning of 'pompous hypocrite', and that the scribes and Pharisees are presented in the Gospels as Jesus's chief opponents, makes it difficult for even the shrewdest reader to realize how deep a deception has been practised upon him.

(*b*) Consider, for instance, *John* viii. 1–11, where the Jerusalem Pharisees tempt Jesus in the matter of the adulterous woman (*see* LXX.*h*). Though the story rings true, its setting is historically impossible. The adulteress would have been in no danger of stoning: all Judaean and Galilean cases of this kind were tried by Pharisaic law and the Great Sanhedrin long before this date had abolished the death penalty for adultery (*Sanhedrin* 41*a*). A convicted adulteress, at the worst would lose her property rights under the marriage contract (Maimonides: *Yad Ha'hazakah, Ishuth* xxiv. 6); but the Court's insistence on witnesses, and on proof that the accused understood every article of the Law relating to her crime, made execution impossible in practice.

(c) A single exception, in which a priest's daughter is said to have been condemned to death for adultery shortly before the destruction of the Temple, has often been adduced in support of the Gospel account. However, this woman, being a priest's daughter, was burned (*Leviticus* xxi. 9), not stoned, and the Talmud mentions her case only to question its authenticity. The facts are these. According to a *Baraita* (*Sanhedrin* 52a), Rabbi Eliezer ben Zadok related, about 120 A.D., that when carried on his father's shoulders as a child, he once saw a priest's daughter being burned alive between stacked faggots. Eliezer's colleagues questioned his statement, which was incredible in several respects. First, no one but Eliezer had heard of this extraordinary case; next, the Court could not have burned the woman's body and thus denied her resurrection—it had been customary in earlier times to thrust a firebrand down an adulteress's throat; lastly, a priest would not have taken his child to witness such a spectacle before he was old enough to understand the meaning of adultery. Eliezer's critics were, however, content to say politely: 'A child's evidence is not acceptable.' The story of the priest's daughter occurs also in the *Mishnah* (*Sanhedrin* vii. 2), without reference to Eliezer, and the rabbis decide there that the woman's judges must have been ignorant of the correct procedure in capital cases. Thus, the court in question will have been a Sadducaic one, convened before the days of Shemaiah and Abtalion (mid-first century B.C.) when all judges were appointed by the Pharisees and bound to keep their judicial rules. And the explanation of Eliezer's testimony may be that he associated an early recollection of having seen a female leper's garments ritually burned, with a story he heard from his father: how a priest's daughter had been burned for adultery more than a hundred years previously.

(d) The one place, in fact, where Jesus could have been tempted with the question: 'Moses in the Law commanded us that such be stoned, but what sayest thou?' was Samaria, which was not subject to Pharisaic jurisdiction and in which the Law of Moses was still enforced with primitive rigour. Therefore it will have been the Samaritans who accused Jesus, as an over-indulgent Pharisee, of weakening the Law. And Jesus's 'He that is without sin among you, let him cast the first stone', so far from being a bold anti-Pharisaic pronouncement, was a vindication of the humane Pharisaic point of view as laid down by Hillel (*Aboth* ii. 5): 'Judge not thy neighbour till thou be in his place' (*see* LXX.i).

(e) This mischievous shift of scene and emphasis might be excused as accidental, if the same anti-Pharisaic prejudice did not appear elsewhere; particularly in *Matthew* xxii. 15–22, the tribute-penny narrative (*see* XCIII.c). It cannot have been the Pharisees who confronted Jesus with the dilemma reported in *Matthew,* since they were forbidden to bring unclean coin into the Temple—the inscription celebrated the Emperor Tiberius as son of the God

Augustus—and would not have dared to produce it at his challenge even if they had disregarded this prohibition. Similarly, they could not have made common cause with the Herodians, who were Hellenizers and collaborated with the Romans. *Luke* xx. 15-26, a more plausible version, mentions the Sadducaic Chief Priests, who were pro-Roman, as Jesus's main opponents; if so, they will have prompted one of the Herodians to ask the question and produce the coin.

(*f*) These two libels on the Pharisees point to a more serious instance of editorial guile: *Luke* x. 33-37, the parable of the so-called Good Samaritan (*see* LXXXII.*m-o*). The original account—it has been doubled and confused in the Gospels (*Matthew* xix. 16 *and* xxii. 35)—will have opened with Jesus's answer to a lawyer, namely that Hillel, when asked much the same question by a Gentile scoffer (*Shabbath* 31*a*), had replied: 'Do not unto thy neighbour what is hateful unto thee', a reference to *Leviticus* xix. 18, the 'love thy neighbour' text. Jesus's acknowledgement to Hillel, who continued: 'This is the essence of the Law; the rest is commentary', has been suppressed by all the evangelists (*see* LXXXII.1). The lawyer then asks for a definition of 'neighbour'. Jesus seems to have answered by telling a moral story in conventional Pharisaic style, about a Priest, a Levite and a Son of Israel: the first two, being unregenerate Sadducees, obey the letter of the Law, whereas the Son of Israel, being an enlightened Pharisee, obeys its spirit—and is, therefore, held up as a model of virtue. The Priest, the Levite, and the Son of Israel find a *Samaritan* lying naked and wounded by the roadside; Priest and Levite pass by in contempt, but the Son of Israel shows him mercy as a fellow-worshipper of Jehovah. 'Who was the neighbour in this case?' And the Lawyer, though aware that the Samaritans have recently defiled the Temple by throwing dead men's bones in at the gates (*see* LXXXII.*n*), is forced to reply: 'The man to whom he shewed mercy.'

(*g*) The evangelists' version is illogical: Jesus is made to vary the traditional formula pointlessly and to deny the earnest young man his definition. Their anti-Pharisaic obsession, which has falsified these and other original texts, conceals Jesus's wholehearted acceptance of the enlightened Pharisaic principle known as *tikkun ha'olam,* or 'improvement of social order', which mitigated the literal severity of the Mosaic code. This principle implied, among other things, the supersession of *Exodus* xxi. 24, the eye-for-an-eye law, by a scale of monetary compensation (*Baba Kamma* viii. 1); and of *Deuteronomy* xv. 1-3, which cancelled all debts at the end of every seventh year, by a legal fiction that would encourage people to lend to their needy neighbours, as enjoined by *Deuteronomy* xv. 8, even during the seventh year (*Shebiith* x. 3 *and Gittim* iv. 3). Jesus's castigation of a few narrow-minded provincial Pharisees who despised the Galilean peasantry because they were not of pure Israelite descent, and because their work often prevented them from observing the oral tradition in the matter of ceremonial washings, has here been twisted into an annulment of the entire written Law.

(*h*) Another example of falsification in this sense is the excision of the word 'only' from *Mark* vii. 15: 'It is not *only* the thing from without which goeth into a man that can defile him . . .' (*see* xx.*i*). Jesus is speaking of religious bigots who, even when they eat the undefiled honey of the Law (*Ezekiel* iii. 1–3), or the bread of Wisdom (*Ecclesiasticus* xxiv. 21–23), contrive to void it in uncharitableness. He takes his stand on the 'love thy neighbour' text, and declares that the *tikkun ha'olam* principle as expounded by Hillel: 'Be of the disciples of Aaron, lovers of peace and of God's creatures, and bring them nigh unto the Law' (*Aboth* i. 12), must be applied to the case of these peasants. Insistence on impossible standards of ritual cleanliness would debar them from the synagogues and thus prevent their instruction in the Law; and whatever their ancestry, they were full members of the congregation. Jesus never called the Pharisees hypocritical as a body; he accused certain Pharisees of being unworthy to bear the name (*Matthew* xxiii. 27), and upheld the religious authority of the Great Sanhedrin (*Matthew* xxiii. 2): 'The scribes and Pharisees sit in Moses's seat. All therefore they bid you observe, that observe and do' (*see* xiii.*a*). He was by no means the only Pharisee to condemn certain of his fellows for falling short of their austere ideals; mutual exhortations to practise what was preached had long been a commonplace of Pharisaic religious life (*see* xiii.*k*).

(*i*) Whether Christianity is to be regarded as a great spiritual advance on Judaism, or as a serious falling-off, need not concern us here; what matters is that the later faith derives from the earlier. This, according to Tacitus (*Sulpicius Severus Fragm. Hist. Chron.* ii. xxx. 6), was recognized by Titus in 70 A.D.

> 'It is said that Titus before committing himself to the destruction of such a mighty Temple called a council to advise him on the matter. Some members agreed that he should spare what was after all the most glorious shrine in the world, because to do so would testify to the clemency of Rome, whereas its destruction would be a perpetual mark of her cruelty. Others, including Titus himself, took the opposite view, holding that it was more important to destroy the Temple, in order to eradicate the more completely both the Jewish and the Christian faiths; they argued that, though mutually hostile, these faiths had flowered from the same root—the Christian had derived from the Jewish—and that if this root were destroyed the stem would easily perish.'

A close scrutiny of the Gospels reveals the astonishing paradox that Jesus, an apocalyptic Pharisee whose message was neither unorthodox nor original, came by a series of accidents and misunderstandings to be posthumously worshipped as a heathen God—to use 'heathen' in its strict Old Testament sense—and was only then rejected by his own nation.

(*j*) The acceptance of his missionary teaching, not long after the Crucifixion, by very large numbers of devout Jews, further sharpens the paradox. These included many members of the Sadducaic priesthood;* and there were as yet no Gentile converts. Jesus's message was simple: that the Day of Judgement described in great detail by the prophets Zechariah, Zephaniah, Malachi† and others, was at hand, and that all must repent and prepare for the coming trials (*see* ci.*c*).

(*k*) They accepted this message because, though Jesus could not have been the Warrior Messiah—since he had fought no battles in the expected sense—they confidently identified him with the anointed prophet foretold in *Zechariah,* who would take upon himself Israel's sins and whose death was to inaugurate the Messianic Kingdom (*see* cii.*e*); and also with the prophet foretold in *Deuteronomy* xviii. 15, a text of even greater authority because part of the immutable Law (*see* lxxvii.*b*). It was further held that Jesus, by becoming Israel's royal scapegoat, as an anointed Son of David, had equated himself with the 'Suffering Servant' of *Isaiah* liii, a figure representing the whole nation of Israel, not (as is usually thought) a particular Messiah. This Suffering Servant—a marred, uncomely, despised man, reckoned a sinner, sentenced to dishonourable death, dumb before his accusers and hurried by them to the grave—was nevertheless to be rewarded with the spoils of victory after his death.

(*l*) The Son of David was the most popular Messianic concept. This Messiah would be a monarch in the ordinary temporal sense, ruling the same territory over which David had once ruled. He was the pastoral king foretold by Ezekiel, by the author of *Psalms* xvii and xviii, by Zechariah and Malachi, by the author of the second part of *Isaiah,* by the Sibyl of the *Oracles,* by the author of the *Psalter of Solomon,* by Esdras and by many others. He would be born of a young mother in Judaean Bethlehem—Bethlehem of Ephratah —after a period crowded with wars, famines, and natural calamities, the so-called Pangs of the Messiah, when the Jews were floundering in a slough of misery. He would be summoned from an obscure home and anointed King by the ever-young prophet Elijah, of whom the Preacher had written:

'You who are ready for the Time, as it is prophesied, to still men's anger before the fierce anger of the Lord, to turn the hearts of the fathers to the children and restore the tribes of Israel.'

Elijah was to prepare the way for the Messiah, who would thereupon enter Jerusalem riding in triumph on a young ass. This would be the signal for a bloody war against Jerusalem by the oppressors of Israel, in the course of which the city would be taken and two-thirds of the inhabitants massacred.

---

* *Clementine Recognitions* i. 43.

'We who had been very few became in the course of a few days, by God's help, far more numerous than they; so that the priests were afraid at one time that the whole of the people might come over to our faith.'

And *Acts* vi. 7:

'And the number of disciples multiplied in Jerusalem greatly; and a great company of the priests were obedient to the faith.'

† Daniel, Enoch, and similar hagiographers did not officially rank as 'prophets'.

The Messiah, however, encouraged by divine portents, would rally the faithful survivors on the Mount of Olives and lead them to final victory. He would then re-unite the scattered tribes and reign peacefully for four hundred years or, some said, a thousand years, with the rulers of Egypt and Assyria and all the rest of the world paying homage to his throne in the newly sanctified city of Jerusalem. This Kingdom of Heaven would be an era of unexampled prosperity, a new Golden Age.

(*m*) The Son of Joseph, or the Son of Ephraim, was another warlike Messiah, whose reign was similarly to be crowned with universal peace. His birthplace, too, would be Judaean Bethlehem, the seat of his ancestress Rachel; but he was to reign principally over the ten tribes of the North which had seceded from Rehoboam, the last King of all Israel. Since Shechem had been defiled by the Samaritans, it was expected by some that he would reveal himself on Mount Tabor, the holy mountain of Galilee; others, however, expected that he would return to Shechem and cleanse it. The Son of Joseph was, in fact, a rival concept to the Son of David, whose cult was centred on Jerusalem: the Northerners held that the blessing conferred by Jacob on his sons, according to *Genesis* xlix. 10, did not justify Judah's claim to the perpetual leadership of Israel. This prophecy ran, somewhat ambiguously, as follows:

> 'The sceptre shall not depart from Judah, nor the commander's baton from between his feet, until he approaches the man to whom they belong—him for whom the people wait.'

When this happened, the Northerners held, the royal sceptre and the commander's baton would be made over by Judah to the Messiah—who must necessarily be a Josephite, since Jacob had prophesied that from Joseph would spring the Shepherd, the Rock of Israel, and that blessings were in store for him 'to the utmost bounds of the everlasting hills'. This warrior Son of Joseph was associated with a preacher of repentance, who might be Elijah.

(*n*) But what did 'Joseph' signify? Did it not perhaps mean the whole holy nation of Israel which had been led out of Egypt by Moses, rather than the two tribes of Ephraim and Manasseh with whom the name later became identified, and all but the poor remnants of whom had been carried away into Assyrian captivity seven hundred years previously, never to return? In that case, the Son of David might also be the Son of Joseph, and the meaning of Judah's blessing might be that he should keep his tribal sovereignty until the time came to extend it to Israel.

(*o*) A puzzling particular about the Warrior Messiah—whether the Son of David or the Son of Joseph had been intended could not be agreed—was that, according to Isaiah, he would come marching out of Edom which, in Isaiah's day, lay outside Israelite territory, in dyed garments from Bozrah. If Bozrah were given its obvious connotation, namely the Edomite capital city, this would make him an Edomite prince. But, perhaps, critics suggested, the other Bozrah on the Persian Gulf was meant, where a purple-dyeing industry had been established for centuries.

(*p*) The third Messiah was the Son of Man, but his Messiahship was a doubtful tradition deduced from *Daniel* vii, where a certain Son of Man is given everlasting dominion by the Ancient of Days over all nations and tongues. The Son of Man was no human king, and would enter Jerusalem, so Daniel said, riding not an ass but a storm-cloud. He might, however, be regarded as the spirit or emanation of either the Son of David or the Son of Joseph, performing in the Heavens what was simultaneously being performed on earth.

(*q*) The fourth Messiah was to be a priest-king, supported by a Judaean general. The best text for studying his claims was the eloquent, if uncanonical, *Testament of Levi*. As a priest, this Messiah must necessarily come from the tribe of Levi. He would sanctify the conquests of his general, institute universal peace, reform the calendar, revise the Scriptural Canon, and cleanse the people from their sins.*

(*r*) Jesus had survived the Crucifixion and, after a decisive farewell, walked up the Mount of Olives, towards Bethany, until he disappeared into cloud (*Acts* i. 9–12—*see* cxvii.*n*)—an event which in *Mark* and *Luke* has been transformed into an aerial ascension, his body losing weight and rising miraculously into the air. He never came back again and, as in the case of Moses, who was also last seen on a mountain top: 'No man knoweth his sepulchre to this day' (*Deuteronomy* xxxiv. 1–6). But he was generally thought to be still alive in the flesh, and when he did not re-appear, the prophecy in *Psalm* cx: 'The Lord said unto my Lord: "Sit thou on the right hand of God until I make thine enemies thy footstool . . . thou art a priest for ever after the order of Melchizedek" ', was applied to him by literal-minded Grecian devotees (*Acts* ii. 29–35—*see* cxviii.*g*). It was believed, in fact, that he had been granted the same dispensation as Enoch and Elijah, who had been drawn up to Heaven without first suffering death (*Book of Jubilees* iv *and* 2 *Kings* ii), and was waiting there for the disciples to complete his work—when he would return as the Warrior Messiah. On one occasion, he had assured them that the Kingdom of God would come in the lifetime of many (*Matthew* xvi. 28 and xxiv. 34—*see* ci.*b*), and his qualifications of this assurance (*Acts* i. 7 *and John* xxi. 18), made after the Crucifixion (*see* cxvii.*m*), were now conveniently overlooked. In *Acts* iii. 19–26, Peter and John are said to have preached this eschatological doctrine in the Temple—the anti-Jewish passages of *Acts* ii. 23 and iii. 12–18, which exculpate the Romans from all blame for the Crucifixion, must be discounted as an interpolation—and to have made three thousand (thirty?) converts in a single day (*Acts* ii. 41).

(*s*) Among the Nazarenes' opponents was Saul, or perhaps Solon (*see* cxviii.*e–f*), later Paul, a Greek-speaking adventurer from Tarsus in Cilicia

* Paragraphs (*l–q*) are quoted from *King Jesus* (Robert Graves, 1946).

who, as a pretended Pharisee in the pay of the Sadducees, assisted in the murder of the deacon Stephen, persecuted the Nazarenes (*Acts* viii. 1–3), and is alleged to have thrown James the Just down the fifteen steps of the Nicanor Gate in the Temple (*Clementine Recognitions* i. lv–lxxi). Saul presently became a convert to the Nazarene faith, after a vision of, or meeting with, Jesus (*Acts* ix. 1–20—*see* cxviii.*j–n*), and offered his services to James, Peter, and John as the leaders of the Church (*Acts* ix. 27). Then he announced his intention of converting the Gentiles to the 'Way', in accordance with Jesus's alleged instructions on the road to Damascus, and they gave him their right hands in friendship (*Galatians* ii. 9); relieved, perhaps, to be so easily rid of this embarrassing guest (see cxviii.*o*). That his mission was to the 'uncircumcised' made it unlikely that their ways would ever cross again. He might have been going to a leper colony, since daily contact with ritually unclean Gentiles would make continued social relations with his co-religionists impossible. James therefore asked no more of him (*Galatians* ii. 10) than that his converts should contribute towards the maintenance of 'the poor', namely the Ebionites; and this he did (*Acts* xi. 30).

(*t*) Saul's prospective converts were already so-called 'God-fearers'—mainly Syrians, Greeks, and Cypriots—who accepted the ethical principles of the Mosaic Law as contained in the Ten Commandments, but did not feel bound to undergo circumcision, which was not mentioned in the Decalogue and was disparaged by the Romans as a mutilation. Many of them were genuinely attracted by the moral rectitude of the Jews; others seem to have become God-fearers for commercial reasons—it was advantageous to be on good terms with the Jews who controlled much of the trade in the Mediterranean. Saul's task, it will have been understood in Jerusalem, was to convince these God-fearers that they must now shoulder the whole burden of the Law, of which, as Jesus had said, not a jot nor tittle should pass away before Heaven and earth also passed away (*Matthew* v. 18—*see* xxi.*i*). Saul seems himself to have begun his religious career as a God-fearer (*see* cxviii.*e*).

(*u*) The Kingdom of God, which Jesus preached, was to lie about a re-sanctified Jerusalem peopled, at first, with the faithful of Israel who had survived the horrors of the Last Days (*Zechariah* xiv. 9–11—*see* lxxxviii.*h*); later, the scattered remnants of other nations might apply for admission and be accepted as honorary Sons of Abraham, in proof of Jehovah's universality. But they must also accept the Law and be circumcised; and any who failed to come up yearly for the Feast of Tabernacles would be punished with drought or plague (*Zechariah* xiv. 16–19). However, in epistles addressed to his new converts in Thessalonica and Galatia between 48 and 50 A.D., Paul foretold Jesus's return to inaugurate the Kingdom, while declaring that the Law was no longer binding on them. He called them foolish for having scruples about ritual cleanliness: if they had led a life of love and rectitude, they could enjoy the lavish delights of the Kingdom merely by calling on Jesus's name. This argument (*Galatians* iii. 13) Paul based on *Deuteronomy*

xxi. 23: 'He that is hanged upon a tree is accursed of the Lord', suggesting that since Jesus had been hanged on a tree and, far from being accursed, had actually been taken up to Heaven, the Law was clearly superseded in this respect (*Galatians* iii. 25). But, if in one respect, why not in others? He assured them that the 'curse of the Law' (*Deuteronomy* xxvii. 26—*see* cxiii.*a*), which made ritual cleanliness a prerequisite of salvation, was now annulled for all but Jews (*Galatians* iii. 10). Later, in his *Epistle to the Romans* iii, he debates the advantages of being a Jew and can find none except that descent from ancestors to whom God committed His oracles would be a proud boast, if boasting were allowed—which it was not—or if the Jews had not sinned equally with the Gentiles, or if Jehovah were not a universal God. 'We conclude that a man is justified by faith [in Jesus] without observance of the Law.' Paul, despite his claims, cannot have been of Jewish birth (*see* cxviii.*f*); had he been so, he could not have argued as he did, since he neglected the ritual cleanliness still incumbent upon him.

(*v*) In *Galatians* ii. 11–21, Paul describes a stormy meeting with Peter, who had been reproved by emissaries from James the Just, his superior, for eating with Gentiles at Antioch. Peter, being a Galilean fisherman, may not have been so strict as the Jerusalem Pharisees whose oral tradition forbad them many things not specifically mentioned in the Scriptures; he may also have remembered Jesus's missionary work among the outcasts of Israel, and his strictures on those who carried ritual cleanliness to the point of absurdity. He apparently thought that a case could be made out for eating with God-fearers, so long as their food and cooking utensils were ritually clean (*see* lxx.*e*). Moreover, impressed by Paul's success in the mission field, he may have decided that God was with him (*Galatians* ii. 7–9). Nevertheless, he accepted James's reprimand as deservedly given and withdrew from the Gentile table. When Paul protested and called him doublefaced, Barnabas came forward on Peter's side (*Galatians* ii. 13). There is no reliable evidence that Peter and Paul ever met or corresponded again as friends. However, the principle of apostolic harmony had to be preserved, and Clement of Alexandria in his *Fifth Book of the Hypotyposeis,* quoted by Eusebius (*Ecc. Hist.* 1. xii. 2), tried to make it appear that the Cephas with whom Paul quarrelled was not Peter, but an unknown namesake.*

(*w*) This scandal is also slurred over in the *Acts,* a book which attained something like its present shape at the close of the first century, as a reconciliation between the doctrines then held by Peter's followers and those held by Paul's; its editors try to show that Paul was always on good terms with the original disciples and that he and Peter brought James the Just round to their view. *Acts* xv. 22–35, the account of the dispute at Antioch, flatly contradicts Paul's statement in *Galatians* ii. 11–21. Verses 23–29, a pastoral letter said to have been sent from Jerusalem by James and his fellow-elders to the

---

* It is recorded in the same work (*Ecc. Hist.* 2. i. 3) that James the Just was elected Bishop of Jerusalem by Peter, James and John 'who did not themselves contend for the honour'.

Gentiles at Antioch, commending Paul and freeing them from the obligations of the Law, is clearly forged; so is Peter's speech, said to have convinced James and the other apostles that neither they nor their fathers had been able to bear the yoke of the Mosaic Law (*see* xv.*c*), and that faith in Jesus was sufficient for Salvation (*Acts* xv. 6–11). James will have held that though Paul's Gentile converts were free to continue in their minimum observance of the Law, no mere God-fearer could be admitted to the Messianic Kingdom—which was reserved for the circumcised who had joyfully borne its burden. Moreover, in *Acts* xv. 1–35, Barnabas is represented as taking Paul's side, and their quarrel has been altered to a personal, rather than a doctrinal, disagreement (*Acts* xv. 39). *Galatians* vi. 12 makes it clear that James's emissaries continued to invade Paul's territory and preach the necessity of circumcision.*

(*x*) Similarly, *Acts* xvi. 1–3:

> 'Then came Paul to Derbe and Lystra: and, behold, a certain disciple was there, named Timothy, the son of a certain woman, which was a Jewess and believed; but his father was a Greek. . . . Him would Paul have to go forth with him; and took and circumcised him because of the Jews which were in those quarters: for they knew all that his father was a Greek.'

discredits the sincerity of Paul's pronouncement in *Galatians* v. 2–4:

> 'Behold, I Paul say unto you, that if ye be circumcised, Christ shall profit nothing. For I testify again to every man that is circumcised, that he is a debtor to do the whole Law. Christ is become of no effect unto you, whosoever of you are justified by the Law; ye are fallen from grace.'

(*y*) Afterwards, on a visit to Jerusalem, probably in 58 A.D., James the Just questioned Paul about his activities and charged him with having dissuaded Jews from circumcising their sons (*Acts* xxi. 17–21). James, evidently finding his defence unsatisfactory, prevailed on him (*Acts* xxi. 23–24) to undergo a seven days' ceremony of purification and offer a sacrifice in atonement for his breaches of the Law. But Paul then committed the crime of polluting the Temple, and the people of Jerusalem were so strongly incensed (*Acts* xxi. 27–31) that he escaped death only by revealing his Roman citizenship—seemingly acquired during a visit to Cyprus in 47 A.D., when it was under the Governorship of Sergius Paulus†, and appealing to the Emperor (*Acts* xxi.

---

* This doctrinal war seems to have been fought bitterly on both sides. Thus, in the *Clementine Recognitions* iv. 35, an anti-Pauline document, Peter writes to the Church of Tripolis:

> 'Be careful to believe no teacher who does not bring a testimonial from James the brother of Our Lord at Jerusalem. For none who has not gone thither and been approved as a fit and faithful preacher of the words of the Anointed One—and has not, as I say, brought his testimonial thence—is by any means to be received.'

† Paul's 'But I was free born' (*Acts* xxii. 28) is disingenuous. Though he would hardly have dared to claim Roman citizenship if he were not entitled to it, he certainly had been known as 'Saul' before his Cyprian visit (*Acts* xiii. 1–13); the name 'Paul' was doubtless taken by permission, and in honour, of the Governor from whom he bought his citizenship. Had he been a Roman by birth, he could not have been flogged eight times (2 *Corinthians* xi. 24–25); and

28). This evasion of his duty towards God, followed by his dishonest plea before the Council of Priestly Elders (*Acts* xxiii. 6—*see* cviii.*f and m*), caused the final breach between Paul and the Nazarene Church. He now gloried in playing the Jew among Jews, the Gentile among Gentiles, and being 'all things to all men' in order to gain converts (1 *Corinthians* ix. 20–22— *see* cviii.*f, footnote and* cxix, *passim*) for his religion.

(*z*) The 'Party of Peter' (1 *Corinthians* i. 12) remained undecided between the 'Party of Paul' and the 'Party of the Messiah', that is to say, the Nazarenes, until persuaded to join forces with the former—when Peter was at last awarded a common Saint's Day with Paul and, unhistorically, associated with him in the foundation of the Roman Catholic Church.*

---

there is no mention in the *Acts,* except for the patently unhistorical incident at Philippi in xvi. 14–40, of his having been flogged at all after his visit to Cyprus.

So it seems that he was here casuistically recording his citizenship of Tarsus, which Mark Antony (Appianus: *Civil War* v. 7) had created a *civitas libera et immunis* for its attachment to Caesar's cause during the Civil War. While he remained at home, he enjoyed its freedom from Roman taxes and interference with internal revenue; but this, of course, was not the same as being a Roman citizen. Perhaps he knew that Claudius Lycias, the 'Chief Captain' (*see* cxix.*e*), who had bought his Roman citizenship so dearly, was born in a less favoured city than Tarsus.

The interesting question remains: how did Paul find the money necessary for buying his citizenship at Paphos? It will at once have occurred to James the Just and Peter that this sum had been taken from the alms collected for the Ebionites, and that he had charged it to his expenses under the heading: 'Provision for honest things in the sight of men out of this abundance, which is administered by me' (2 *Corinthians* viii. 20).

Was Paul to be trusted when he said, in *Acts* xxi. 3, that his ship from Patara had left Cyprus to the larboard without touching Paphos? He certainly had arrived in Jerusalem, accompanied by a Cypriot Jew (*Acts* xxi. 16).

* The first suggestion that Peter went to Rome is made by Irenaeus in 170 A.D. Earlier writers, who would have mentioned the visit if it had taken place, are silent. It seems that he remained at Antioch until he died.

THE HAND OF SIMON MAGUS

(*a*) Eusebius's account (*Ecc. Hist.* 2. xxiii) of James the Just's martyrdom proves that the Nazarenes continued for many years to sacrifice in the Temple and to keep the Law of Moses in accordance with Pharisaic usage. The impartial attitude of Gamaliel I, President of the Great Sanhedrin, towards the Church in Jerusalem is recorded in *Acts* v. 34-40 (*see* cxviii.*c*); and his successor, Rabbi Johanan ben Zakkai, whose many doctrinal disputes from 40 A.D. to 80 A.D. are reported in the *Mishnah* and *Gemara*—with the Sadducees in *Yadaim* iv. 6 and *Baba Bathra* 115*b*; with the Boethians in *Menahoth* 65*a*; with the Gentiles in *Hullin* 27*b*, *Bekoroth* 5*b*, *Numbers Rabbah* xix.4—is nowhere stated to have denounced it. Yet if any conflict had arisen between Nazarene and Pharisaic doctrine, the Great Sanhedrin would have been called upon to settle it; and would have been quick to detect and condemn the least sign of heresy.

(*b*) Eusebius records (*Ecc. Hist.* 3. v. 3) that in 66 A.D. the Nazarenes refused to join the forces of insurrection against Rome, believing that the heathen should be left to God's vengeance rather than opposed by force, and 'at the command of an oracle' moved in a body to Pella in Decapolis. They regarded the subsequent fall of Jerusalem as a partial fulfilment of Jesus's prophecy (*Mark* xiii. 2—*see* xcvii.*a-c*) and a justification of their secession. Later, in 132 A.D., they refused to join Bar-Cochba who, according to Justin Martyr (*First Apology* xxxi), tried to extract from them by cruel means an acknowledgement of his Messiahship (*see* xiii.*w*). Bar-Cochba failed to liberate Israel and Jesus's prophecy was now wholly fulfilled: the Temple ruins were razed to make way for a shrine dedicated to Aelian Jupiter. Judaism was placed under the Imperial ban and the Nazarenes suffered equally with the rebels. According to Eusebius (*Ecc. Hist.* 4. v. 4), the Bishopric of Jerusalem was abolished at this time; but presently, when the city was colonized by foreigners and renamed Aelia, the Gentile Christians founded a church of their own there, headed by an uncircumcised bishop named Marcus (*Ecc. Hist.* 4. vi. 4).

(*c*) The Pharisees of Hillel's school had similarly provoked the scorn of the Zealots during the first Revolt, to which, being quietists, they were bitterly opposed. When Jerusalem was besieged, Johanan ben Zakkai persuaded the Emperor Vespasian to let him and his disciples return to the township of Jamnia in Southern Palestine and re-establish his academy there. Afterwards, when these disciples stood aghast at the sight of the burning Temple, Johanan consoled them by saying that the study of the Law would compensate for its loss.

Now that the Temple was desecrated and its religious services suppressed, the priesthood became unemployed and the Sadducees ceased to exist as a sect; but much of the opprobrium attached to them in the early Nazarene 'Oracles' was maliciously transferred by Gentile evangelists to the Pharisees, now the acknowledged leaders of Israel and still at peace with the Nazarene Church.

(d) It was not until the reign of Trajan, in the early second century, that the Pharisees came to distrust the Nazarenes (see LIII.b) for their belief in Jesus's Messiahship—a doctrine also held by the Paulines, whose heresy was threatening the very existence of the synagogue system. But though the then leader of the Pharisees, Gamaliel II, required devout Jews to keep their distance from all Nazarenes, lest their heterodoxy might be tainted by Paulinism or Gnosticism, these were not regarded as utterly damned or even debarred from the synagogues. Indeed, in the first half of the third century, Rabbi Joshua ben Levi refused to exclude from the office of synagogue-reader (see XXXVII.f) even Nazarenes suspected of being *minim,* or heretics, and quoted as his authority the verses from *Psalm* cxlv. 9–15 (*Berakoth 7a*):

'The Lord is good to all, and His tender mercies are over all His works.
'All Thy works shall praise Thee, O Lord, and Thy saints shall bless Thee.
'For Thou satisfiest the desire of every living thing.'

(e) Thus the Nazarenes, who were far more heretical in the eyes of the Gentile Christians than in those of the Pharisees, contrived to keep their identity as a sect until the fifth century, when some returned to orthodox Judaism and others were absorbed into the Gentile Church (Krauss: *Jewish Encyclopaedia* ix. 194). Their equivocal position towards the close of the first century explains the early Talmudic use of the synonym 'Balaam' for Jesus, first pointed out by Geiger (*Jüdische Zeitschrift für Wissenschaft und Leben* vi. 31–37). Balaam (*Numbers* xxii, xxiii *and* xxiv) was the Scriptural prototype of all false prophets who set themselves to oppose Israel for the sake of personal gain. Geiger quotes the passage in *Sandhedrin* 106b, which reads:

'A heretic once asked Rabbi Haninah: "Hast thou perchance ascertained the age of Balaam?"'
'He answered: "Nothing is recorded concerning his age; but since it is written: 'Bloody and deceitful men shall not live out half their days.' [*Psalm* lv. 23] he will have been thirty-three or thirty-four years old."'
'The heretic said: "Thou speakest well; for I myself have seen a chronicle

of Balaam in which it is written: 'Thirty-three years old was Balaam the Lame when the robber Phinias [? *i.e. Pintias, i.e. Pontius Pilate*] slew him.'" '

and another from *Aboth* v. 19:

'. . . The disciples of the wicked Balaam shall inherit Gehenna and go down to the pit of destruction. As it is written: "Bloody and deceitful men shall not live out half their days." '

The reference here is to Israelites who have no share in the world to come, and Geiger argues that, since the original Balaam was no Israelite, but a Mesopotamian in Moabite pay, 'Balaam' must be the pseudonym for a Jewish renegade. This view has been accepted by Laible, Herford and their successors.

(*f*) Klausner dissents (*Jesus of Nazareth p.* 32). He disregards *Sanhedrin* 106*a*, a clear reference to *Luke* i. 27 and *Matthew* xiii. 55:

'They say that his [*Balaam's*] mother was descended from princes and rulers but consorted with carpenters. . . .'

and questions Jesus's identification with Balaam, by citing *Gittin* 56*b*–57*a*:

'It is told of Onkelos son of Kalonymos, who was a son of the Emperor Titus's sister, that he wished to become a proselyte. Therefore, by means of spells, he first evoked Titus, who advised him not to become a proselyte, since he would then have to observe many hard commandments, but rather to oppose Israel.

'Onkelos next evoked Balaam, who raged against Israel, saying: "Seek neither their peace nor their good." [*Deuteronomy* xxiii. 6, *quoted from a passage aimed at the Moabites who had hired Balaam.*]

'Not until then did Onkelos evoke Jesus, whom he asked: "What is the most important thing in the world?" Jesus answered: "Israel."

'Onkelos asked again: "How would it go with me if I joined myself to this people?" Jesus replied: "Seek not their harm, but their good. For whosoever shall touch them, it is as though he touched the apple of God's eye." [*A quotation from Zechariah* ii. 7–8, *beginning:* 'Deliver thyself, O Zion, thou that dwellest with the daughter of Babylon. . . .']

'Onkelos asked again: "What is the fate of that man [*Balaam*]?" Jesus answered: "Boiling filth."

'It is said in a *Baraita*: "Whosoever scoffeth against the words of the wise, the same shall be condemned to boiling filth." Come and see what there is between the transgressors in Israel and the prophets of the nations of the world!'

(*g*) Klausner points out that Flavius Clemens—corrupted to 'Kalonymos' and 'Kalonikos'—Titus's nephew, was executed as an atheist, i.e. a convert to Judaism, about 96 A.D.; and that the tradition preserved in *Gittin* is therefore an early one. He claims, however, that 'Balaam' cannot be Jesus, since Jesus is there distinguished from the Balaam who was the hero of the story. But Klausner has missed its point: namely, the Pharisees' rejection of Jesus's false *imago,* which the Gentile Christians had evoked to denounce Israel, as Balaam had formerly been hired to do by Balak, King of Moab. The Pharisees agreed with the Nazarenes that the historical Jesus held Israel to be 'the most important thing in the world' (*John* iv. 22—*see* LXX.*c*) and would have condemned the fictitious Balaam-Jesus to boiling filth; they have even made him quote Zechariah as his authority for defying, instead of courting, the oppressors of Israel—'daughter of Babylon' being a common Talmudic synonym for Rome.

(*h*) Both Herford and Laible, on the other hand, plausibly suggest that Balaam, Doeg, Ahithophel and Gehazi who, in *Sanhedrin* x. 2, are stated to 'have no share in the world to come', represent Jesus and three of his disciples, though they disagree in identifying these. Judas, from the Nazarene point of view, fits Ahithophel (2 *Samuel* xvii. 1–23—*see* CXII.*c*), since he betrayed his master and afterwards hanged himself. Paul fits Doeg the Edomite—'Edom' was another Talmudic synonym for Rome, of which Paul was a citizen—who treacherously murdered the priests of Nob and their families (1 *Samuel* xxii. 17–18 *and Acts* viii. 1–3). Gehazi (2 *Kings* v. 22–27) who, for private gain, lied to his master Elisha and was summarily punished, fits Ananias (*Acts* v. 1–5). Nevertheless, all three are perhaps better regarded as types of infidelity than as particular persons.

(*i*) In *Sanhedrin* 105*a*, the fictitious Balaam-Jesus is said to be not only lame but blind in one eye—possibly a glancing reference to *Matthew* xviii. 9 (*see* XXI.*g*)*—and his disciples are described as having 'an evil eye, a haughty bearing and an avaricious spirit,' none of which were traits of the Nazarenes, though all could be attributed to the Paulines by their foes. This Pharisaic text has, confusingly, been borrowed by the Pauline editor of 2 *Peter*—a late second-century epistle, not mentioned in the *Muratorian Fragment,* which according to Eusebius (*Ecc. Hist.* 3. iii. 1) was rejected from the Canon—as a denunciation of certain anti-Pauline 'false teachers who privily bring in damnable heresies' (2 *Peter* ii. 14–18):

> 'Having eyes full of adultery and that cannot cease from sin, beguiling unstable souls, an heart they have exercised with covetous practices, cursed children,
> 'Which have forsaken the right way and have gone astray following the way of Balaam of Bosor who loved the wages of unrighteousness,
> 'But was rebuked for his iniquity, the dumb ass speaking with a man's voice forbad the madness of the prophet . . . .
> 'For when they speak swelling words of vanity they allure through the lust of the flesh. . . .'

This passage seems originally to have formed part of a Nazarene document criticizing Paul himself (*see* CXVIII.*s*).

---

* The original Balaam 'walked haltingly' (*Numbers* xxiii. 3); this is mistranslated in the Authorised Version as 'went to an high place'. He kept his eyes shut (*Numbers* xxiv. 3) the Hebrew is *shetum ha'ain,* rendered by the Talmud as 'with a shut eye' (*Sanhedrin* 105*a*).

(*j*) The confusion increases in later Pharisaic tradition when the Scriptural Balaam who blessed the Israelites, albeit against his will, is judged to have been a far worthier person than the fictitious Balaam-Jesus who cursed and persecuted them; he is even invoked to denounce his namesake as one who showed no respect for God. Thus, in the second century, Rabbi Eliezer Ha'Kappar is reported as saying (*Yalkut Shimeoni* 1.766):

> 'God gave strength unto Balaam's voice so that it went from one end of the world to the other, because he looked forth and beheld the nations that bowed down to the sun and moon and stars and to wood and stone, and he looked forth and saw that a man born of a woman should rise up and seek to make himself God and cause the whole world to go astray.
>
> 'God therefore gave power unto the voice of Balaam, that all the prophets of the world might hear, and thus he spake in His name: "Give heed, that ye go not astray after that man, for it is written: 'God is not a man that he should lie.' [*Numbers* xxiii. 19, *quoting Balaam's reproof to Balak, King of Moab.*] And if he says that he is God, he lieth; and he will deceive and saith that he will depart now and come again at the End. . . ." '

(*k*) Very early in their history the Gentile Christians had fallen under suspicion as crypto-Jews. Suetonius records (*Twelve Caesars: Claudius* 25), that tumults arose in Rome, *impulsore Chresto,* 'with Christ as the instigator', during Claudius's reign (*see* cxviii.*q*), which caused the entire Jewish colony to be expelled (*c.f. Acts* xvii. 2); and Tacitus reports (*Annals* xv. 45) that in 64 A.D. Christians—presumably the followers of Paul—were accused by Nero of having set fire to the City. Since, in 132 A.D., their Messianic beliefs could easily be mistaken for Bar-Cochba's, they were anxious to convince the Romans that Jesus was a universalist and a pacifist, and that they themselves opposed militant Jewish nationalism. Paul had identified Jesus with the Son of Man, or the Second Adam (1 *Corinthians* xv. 45), a supernatural Saviour of the World, rather than with the Son of David, the Warrior Messiah, to whom the Galilean Zealots looked for deliverance from Rome; and at the collapse of Bar-Cochba's revolt this mystical identification seemed justified by events. Paul's successors were ignorant of the true facts of Jesus's life and convinced that he was a rebel against the Mosaic Law. Eusebius records (*Ecc. Hist.* 4. iii) that two of them, named Quadratus and Aristides, sent the Emperor Hadrian letters of apology; as though to reassure him that Christianity had no connexion with Judaism.

(*l*) After discarding all Jewish ritual observances, even the ban on food that had been offered to idols (1 *Corinthians* x; *but see Acts* xv. 20), the Gentile Christians equated Jesus with one aspect of God—this was regarded by the Nazarenes as gross blasphemy—namely His Word, or the expression of His Mind, and transformed Jesus's teaching into a Greek mystery-cult. Many Christians, as Justin Martyr wrote about 148 A.D. (*Dialogue* 80. 306*b*), no longer looked forward to the millennium in a restored and beautified Jerusalem; instead, they expected the promised Kingdom to be a heavenly, not an earthly, one. Their bishops persuaded the Roman authorities that the connexion between Christianity and Judaism was tenuous; that the Jewish nation had rejected and crucified Jesus, despite Pilate's intervention; and that they themselves were loyal subjects of the Emperor. They could produce Paul's *Epistle to the Romans* xiii. 1–7 as a direct order to obey the Imperial power under pain of damnation. By the end of the first century Ignatius, the second Bishop of Antioch, could write in his *Epistle to the Magnesians* x, that it was 'monstrous to speak of Jesus Christ yet practise Judaism' and, by the third century, according to Eusebius (*Ecc. Hist.* 3. xxxix, 12), the doctrine of the earthly millennium was considered heretical.

(*m*) This pro-Roman view is reflected in the editing of the Gospels and the *Acts*. Close scrutiny reveals that the tribute-penny narrative has been doubly falsified. The Pharisees could not have produced the unclean coin (*see* xciii.*c*), neither could Jesus have advised them to 'render unto Caesar that which is Caesar's': this would have been a breach of the First Commandment (*see Introduction* 11.*e*). His actual words will have been: '*Render not unto Caesar that which is God's, nor unto God that which is Caesar's.*' It is equally difficult to accept the three pious centurions mentioned in the Gospels (*Matthew* viii. 5 *and* xxvii. 54) and in *Acts* x. 1 (*see* xxxiii.*a and* cxiii.*p*); two of them, at least, seem to have been introduced in order to propitiate the Roman Army.

In retaliation for these and other forgeries, the Jews began to invent hostile and even obscene libels about Jesus, some of which survive in the Talmud (*Sanhedrin* 43*a*, 51*a*, 107*b*; *Sotah* 47*b* and *Tractate Kallah p.* 146 ed. Higger) and in the *Toldoth Yeshu*. Like the Paulines, they had forgotten the true facts and now confused Jesus with the fictitious Balaam-Jesus, soon to become the tutelary God of the Roman Empire. Thus Rabbi Abbahu taught (*Jer. Ta'anith* ii.1):

> 'If a man saith unto thee: "I am God," he lieth; if he saith: "I am the Son of Man," he will live to rue his words; and if he saith: "I ascend to Heaven," he will not bring to pass that which he saith.'

And Rabbi Hisda commented on *Psalm* xci. 10 (*Sanhedrin* 103*a*):

> 'The words "There shall no evil befall thee," signify: "No evil dreams nor inclinations shall trouble thee." The words "Neither shall any plague come near thy dwelling," signify: "Thou shalt have neither a son nor a disciple who will publicly let his food burn as, for example, did Jesus the Nazarene." '

By this he seems to have meant: 'who will forfeit his salvation by making a public display of sin' (*see* cii.–cvi. *passim*).

(*n*) Origen reports that Josephus acknowledged the righteousness of James the Just, regarding the Fall of Jerusalem as a punishment for his judicial murder (*see* liii*a*); but that he rejected Jesus's claim to the Messiahship (*On Matthew* x. 17 and *Against Celsus* i. 47). The omission of both these statements from existing texts of the *Antiquities* suggests that the Gentile Christian editors were as hostile to James the Just's uncompromising Judaism as they were sensitive to Josephus's repudiation of Jesus's divinity. In the Slavonic *Wars of the Jews,* apparently a genuine and undoctored translation of an early version—it contains first-hand military details which Josephus afterwards omitted—Jesus is described as a wonder-worker who performed many acts of healing and, though he broke the Law and violated the Sabbath (here Josephus seems to have been misled by Pauline propaganda) 'performed nothing shameful'. Josephus goes on to say that many Jews, led to fix their eyes on Jesus as the leader who would free them from Roman domination, invited him to head an armed revolt. . . . '*This he did not disdain to do,*' or (according to another, equally good reading): '*But to this he gave no heed,*' (*Codex Moscow Acad.* 651. 47. v.; *Codex Synod* 770 *and* 991). When the High Priests warned Pilate about the growing danger of the movement, he condemned Jesus to death as a pretender to the Jewish throne. Again, in the reign of Claudius, the followers of the same wonder-worker excited the poor of Jerusalem by declaring that he was still alive and would free them from bondage (*see* cxviii.*m*.) This new movement was similarly crushed.

Josephus's experiences as an officer in the Jewish War had soured him against militant Messianism. He records that the Jews were led to their fatal uprising by 'an ambiguous oracle: how, about this time, a man of their own country would become ruler of the world'—by which, he says, Vespasian must have been meant, since the legions acclaimed him Emperor while still in Palestine (*Wars* vi. 5. 4). But he knew that James was a saintly quietist, and deplored his irregular trial and execution, as the Romans also did; and this account of Jesus's mission is moderately phrased. In the *Antiquities,* his scorn seems to have been reserved for the credulous Gentile Christians only.

(*o*) The persistent bias of the Gospels in favour of Samaria—shown in the accounts of the so-called Good Samaritan (*Luke* x. 33—*see* lxxxii.*m*), of the woman taken in adultery (*John* viii. 1-11—*see* lxx.*h*), and of the ten lepers healed, of whom the only grateful one was a Samaritan (*Luke* xvii. 16—*see* xxxii.*c*)—suggests that the most cynical of the early tamperers with the Nazarene tradition came from that region. It is even possible to make a plausible guess at his identity and do this without incriminating any reputable Church Father.

(*p*) Celsus, a second-century critic of Christianity, was justified in his charge (Origen: *Against Celsus* ii. 18) that:

> 'Certain Christians, like men who are overcome by the fumes of wine and care not in the least what they say, alter the original text of the Gospels so that they admit of various and almost indefinite readings. And this, I suppose, they have done out of worldly policy, so that when we press an argument home, they might have the more scope for their pitiful evasions.'

Origen rejoined that he knew of no tampering with Gospel texts, except
by two or three notorious heretics, such as Marcion, Lucian and Valen-
tinus, whose writings were disowned by the Catholic Church (*ibid.*). He
was relying on Irenaeus who—in his *Against Heresies* (about 180 A.D.), an
expansion of a lost work of Justin Martyr's—had proclaimed the four
Canonical Gospels to be genuine and unfalsified accounts of Jesus's life,
and denounced the Gnostic variants only. Yet even Origen seems to have
had his suspicions, because he adds:

> 'Besides, it is not at all fair to bring this charge against the Christian re-
> ligion as a crime unworthy of its pretended purity; only those persons who
> were concerned in the fraud should, in equity, be held answerable for it.'

Irenaeus had written (*Against Heresies* i. 22):

> 'Since therefore the detection and conviction of all heretics is a complicated
> business, and my aim here is to refute them individually, I have decided that
> I should first state from whom they all first sprang; so that, when you learn
> the name of their most sublime "Abyss", you may know from what sort of
> tree fruits like these were gathered.'

He then reveals this arch-heretic to be one Simon Magus, mentioned in
Acts viii. as a sorcerer who had long bewitched the people of Samaria
but was converted by the Apostle Philip; later, Simon was rebuffed by
Peter, allegedly for trying to buy the gift of the Holy Spirit. But Jesus
had never awarded the Twelve the sole prerogative of dispensing the Holy
Spirit, and Simon's real misdemeanour must have been Paulinism, the
denial that submission to the Law was necessary; because in the polemic
pseudo-Clementine *Homilies* xvii. 19 and *Recognitions* x. 61 a recognizable
caricature of Paul's, who behaves like him and uses his peculiar Greek
idioms, is named 'Simon Magus.' Since the *Acts* is known to embody
passages of anti-Pauline invective from a Nazarene source—carefully disguised by the Pauline editor—it has been plausibly suggested that Peter's
reproof of Simon for trying to buy the gifts of the Holy Spirit was originally aimed at Paul. Paul had been denied equal rank with the Twelve
(1 *Corinthians* ix. 1), and seems to have been accused of 'simony' when he
arrived at Jerusalem with the alms collected for the Ebionites (1 *Corinthians* xvi. 1-4, 2 *Corinthians* viii, 1-22 and *Romans* xv. 25-28), though he
imagined himself particularly favoured by God on this account (*Galatians* ii. 9). His disparaging comments on James the Just, Peter, and John,
suggest that these refused to accept him at his own high valuation.

(*q*) Simon Magus is described in *Acts* viii. 10 as a religious megalomaniac
even before his conversion; but this is probably a mistake, and so is the
statement in the pseudo-Clementine *Homilies* ii. 23, that he had been a
leading disciple of John the Baptist's. Later, he seems to have borrowed
theological concepts partly from the mystical Pharisaic speculations on

the Trinity—which, at the time, existed in a secret oral tradition only and were not committed to writing* for another thirteen hundred years—but partly from pagan Gnosticism, according to which 'Thrice Great Hermes son of the All Highest, dwelling in the eightfold city of light'† illuminated the mind of man. Simon may have identified Jesus with the Son—a counterpart of the Gnostic Hermes—in what might be called the proto-Zoharic Trinity: '*Father* as knowledge; *Mother* as knower; and *Son* as that which is known.'‡

(*r*) This Trinity was foreshadowed in *Numbers* vi. 22–26, the Blessing of Aaron, which only priests were authorized to utter:

> 'The Lord bless you and keep you,
> 'The Lord make His face shine upon you and be gracious unto you.
> 'The Lord lift up the light of His countenance upon you,
> 'And give you peace!'

The Father here was the merciful Lord; the Mother was 'the light of His countenance'—namely, as Rabbi Nathan pointed out in *Sifre* (*Naso*) the *shekinah,* or Glory—the ineffable female emanation of God, who did not exist apart from Him, and whom the Pharisaic mystics identified with Wisdom; the son was 'Peace', and the distinguishing title of the Anointed King in *Isaiah* ix. 6 was 'Prince of Peace'. *Pesikta Rabbati* 33 (Ed. Friedmann) records that: 'At the beginning of creation was born the Anointed King'—the transcendental 'Son of Man' of *Daniel* vii.—'who mounted into God's thoughts before the world was made.' In *Numbers* vi. 27, which follows the Blessing, the co-identity of these three divine concepts—Light, Wisdom, and Peace—is proved by an injunction to Aaron and his sons: 'And they shall put My name upon the children of Israel; and I will bless them.'

The formula conjoining Father, Holy Spirit, and Son in a mystical Trinity is the one which, according to Epiphanius (*Heresies* lxii. 2), Jesus was said to have revealed to his disciples (*see* LXXXIV.*e–f*), though without claiming to be the Son himself. Moreover, in the *Gospel according to the Hebrews,* he refers to 'My Mother, the Holy Spirit' who rapt him by the hair to the summit of Mount Tabor; and identifies this 'Mother' with the Spirit of Divine Wisdom (Origen: *On John* ii. 12 *and On Isaiah* xi. 9—*see* LXXVIII.*g*). In *Matthew* vii. 7, he is clearly referring to the Trinity, when he says: 'Ask [*for peace*] and it shall be given you; seek, and ye shall find [*wisdom*]; knock, and it [*the gate of mercy*] shall be opened unto you,' though the Scriptural quotations on which he based his promises have been suppressed by the Greek editors (*see* XXVII.*i*).

---

* With the publication of Zohar.

† This probably referred to God's eight-letter name.

‡ Augustine's famous definition of the Trinity is an emotional variant of the same concept, but the roles of the Mother and Father have been interchanged: 'The Father is the Lover, the Son is the Beloved, the Holy Spirit is the Love that subsists between them.'

(*s*) If Simon Magus had contented himself with these theosophic speculations, he would now be considered wholly orthodox, since the co-identity
of the Trinity—though regarded as a Sabellian heresy by Epiphanius—
later became good Catholic doctrine. Thus the *Gospel according to St. John,*
as we have it, begins with a Christian Gnostic formula: 'In the beginning
was the Word . . . and the Word was made flesh and dwelt among us';
and the Nicene Creed presents Jesus as 'begotten by the Father before all
the world.' But, according to Irenaeus (*Against Heresies* i. 23), Simon came
to identify himself personally with his more grandiose concepts and claimed
to be the 'Established One', a re-incarnation of:

> '. . . him who appeared among the Jews as the Son (*Matthew* iii. 17); who
> had descended as the Father in Samaria (*Genesis* xii. 7); and who visited the
> Gentiles as the Holy Spirit (*Acts* ii. 1–8).'

According to Justin Martyr's *Apology,* quoted by Eusebius, Simon Magus
'was worshipped by almost all the Samaritans and a few people elsewhere
as the God above all authority, rule, and power.' He also preached (*Ecc.
Hist.* 2. xiii. 4) that Helena, an ex-prostitute who lived with him, was:

> '. . . . the first Idea of his mind, the mother of all living, through whom,
> in the beginning, he mentally begot angels and archangels.'

This act of creation he had performed while still the 'Sublime Abyss', as
Irenaeus ironically calls him (*see* (*o*) *above*).

(*t*) The early Fathers' intense preoccupation with Simon Magus suggests
that, before his megalomanic derangement, he had assisted greatly in the
formation of Church doctrine. According to Eusebius (*Ecc. Hist.* 4. vii.
1–6), he had founded the Christian Gnostic school some time before the
close of the first century: for Menander, his Samaritan disciple, taught the
Alexandrian Gnostic Basilides who lived in the reign of Hadrian.

It has long puzzled Biblical scholars that Paul and Simon Magus should
have become so closely associated in the polemics of Peter's party, but this
is simply explained: both were regarded as doubly or trebly turncoats. At
first, Simon Magus had been a Samaritan mystic connected with the local
cult of the Dove-goddess Astarte—as may be deduced from a reference
to his love-charms in *Ecc. Hist.* 4. vii. 9; next, he became a convert to the
Nazarene faith; and then a Pauline, with Gnostic leanings. Paul probably
began as a Grecian 'God-fearer' (*see Introduction* 11.*t and* cxviii.*f*); next,
he became a pretended Pharisee in Sadducaic pay; and then a convert to the
Nazarene faith. Each ended by founding a new religion and advancing
extravagant claims for himself. Thus, in the pre-Catholic *Acts of Peter,*
Simon Magus is caricatured as Paul by being made to boast that he will
fly straight to Heaven—Paul had claimed in 2 *Corinthians* xii. 2 that he was
bodily caught up into the third of *Enoch's* seven heavens, and there heard

'words which it is unlawful to utter'—a boast which clearly outraged the Twelve (2 *Corinthians* XII. 11).

Another link between them is Simon's use of the divine title 'the Abiding One', which is taken from the third line of a panegyric on Zeus, attributed to King Minos, and preserved in the Nestorian commentary *Gannat Busamé* ('The Garden of Delights'):

> 'The Cretans have fashioned a tomb for Thee, O Holy and Most High—
> Liars, evil beasts, idle bellies!
> For Thou diest not, but ever Thou livest and abidest.
> For in Thee we live and move and have our being.'

This verse was much in Paul's mind. He quoted the second line in *Titus* i. 12, and the fourth in *Acts* xvii. 28. The probability is that later editors have suppressed his quotation of the intervening line which is implied in each case, because it served as a reminder that he and Simon were for a short time religious associates. Epimenides (early sixth century B.C.) was the actual author of the panegyric. A shorter version occurs in Callimachus (*Hymn to Zeus* 8–10).

The similarity of the two cases has been obscured by the very different fates of Paul's and Simon's doctrines: Paul's Christianity developed into Catholicism, whereas already by Origen's time (*Against Celsus* i. 46), the Simonians had dwindled to 'barely thirty persons'. Nevertheless, except for Jesus himself, Simon Magus was the earliest teacher to be historically associated with the all-important Christian doctrine of the co-identity of the Trinity—and that he subsequently misused it to further his own glorification does not affect his theological distinction. In Canonical literature, this doctrine first appears in 1 *John* v. 7, an Alexandrian tract written at the beginning of the second century and, less clearly, in the *Gospel according to St. John* x. 30, which is a text of about the same date (*see* LXXXIV.*d*). Thus Harnack, in his *Lehrbuch,* credits Simon Magus with a 'new universal religion of the Supreme God,' and Kreyenbühl, in his *Evangelium der Wahrheit,* with 'having first formulated the fundamental principle of all Christian philosophy . . . namely an absolute and universal theanthropologism.'

(*u*) Boldly disavowing the strong Gnostic element in *John* i. 1–8, Irenaeus wrote (*Against Heresies* i. 9) that the Gnostics:

> '. . . confuse the minds of simpletons by their wanton mishandling of the Sayings of Our Lord, and become evil interpreters of the very things they praise.'

And again (*ibid.*):

> 'You observe, beloved, their method of deceiving themselves and abusing the Scriptures, by forgeries intended to commend their fictions; I quote their

statements in evidence of this wanton deceit. . . . They collect scattered words and phrases and transfer them, as I have said, from a proper to an improper context; as one might invent some new-fangled theory or other and try to support it by quotation from Homer—so that a simpleton would think that Homer had written his poems to support that particular theory.'

(*v*) Irenaeus, the first writer to name the four Canonical Gospels (*see* (*o*) *above*), was treading on dangerous ground. No Samaritan forgeries are found in the 'Triple Tradition'—the common source of the 'Synoptics', *Matthew, Mark,* and *Luke*—yet it is possible, if Simon Magus was indeed converted by Philip, that he took an ingenious vengeance on Peter, who had rebuffed him: by the deliberate misediting for Gentile use of one particular collection of Nazarene 'Oracles', on which the Greek-speaking author of *Luke* trustingly relied.* Furthermore, the Samaritan interpolations in *John* suggest that Simon, after embracing Gnosticism, tampered with another collection of 'Oracles'—said to have been compiled by John the Apostle, but more likely the work of 'John the Elder', or 'John son of Annas' (*see* LXXXII.*a–b*)—which ultimately became the Fourth Gospel. This suspicion is greatly strengthened when passages in Simon Magus's *Great Announcement*—a seemingly genuine first-century document, quoted in the anonymous *Philosophoumena*—are compared with similar passages in *John:* for instance, 'if a tree abide alone' and 'remain alone in potentiality' (*John* xii. 24—*see* LXXXI.*b*); and when Simon's trinitarian reference to the 'Three Abiding Ones' is carefully examined.

(*w*) Irenaeus's condemnation of Gospel forgeries traced to early second-century Gnostics was also deserved by many first-century texts which he regarded as authentic; and he shows that Simon Magus was obsessed by the superiority of his own nation over the Jews—he insisted, for instance (*see* (*s*) *above*), that God the Father honoured Samaria with a visit before He ever went to Jerusalem. Thus, if it was not Simon Magus who, during the middle period of his career, made the pro-Samaritan changes in the 'Oracles' which were later incorporated in *Luke* and *John,* it must have been another Pauline Christian of the same generation, the same race, and the same obsessive spite. The Samaritan touch is similarly noticeable in *Acts* i. 8 where, shortly before his Ascension, Jesus finds a special word to say for Samaria; but is absent from *Mark;* and in *Matthew* appears in xxi. 42-44 only, interrupting the Parable of the Corner-stone (*see* c.*b*). The Corner-stone of *Psalm* cxviii. 22, which Jesus quotes, is Israel; and in *Zechariah* xii. 3, and *Daniel* ii. 34-35, which he also quotes, it has the same metaphorical meaning. Yet in the interpolated *Matthew* xxi. 43, Jesus promises the Kingdom of God, the rightful inheritance of Israel prophesied in *Zechariah* and *Daniel,* to 'another nation'. Not to all nations equally, but

* This was not the collection now known as 'Q' which Papias, writing about 140 A.D., records as having been compiled by the Apostle Matthew, and on which the authors of *Matthew* and *Luke* both drew, but the source known as 'L'.

presumably to Samaria; where, according to *Acts* viii. 14 and ix. 31, the Nazarene faith had flourished before the time of Paul's conversion.

(*x*) The deceitful hand of 'Simon Magus' alienated Christian and Jew even more than the schismatic preachings of Paul. 'Good Samaritan'* implies 'Evil Jew'; and by 148 A.D. Justin Martyr could marvel in his *Apology* (xxx–xlii) at the bitter hatred felt by the Jews for Christians—had Jesus not been prophesied in their own Scriptures?—and, a few years later, in his *Dialogue with Trypho,* could complain of their remorseless slanders. Justin also happened to be a Samaritan, but dissociated himself from Simon Magus's view by admitting that the Samaritans had 'rejected Christ equally with the Jews'.† His own contribution to the vexed question, 'should the Law be observed?' was that its temporal provisions were allegories of eternal truths; and that, being allegorical, they had lost their literal force at the advent of Jesus.

> (*y*) 'Perhaps the greatest hindrance to a reasonable view of Jesus is not that a large part of his secret history has been lost, but that the influence of the late and propagandist *Gospel according to St. John* remains so strong. Though this embodies fragments of a genuine tradition not found in the Synoptic Gospels, serious critical reservations are demanded by the metaphysical prologue, which makes no sense whatever in the original context; by the author's wilful ignorance of Jewish affairs; and by the Alexandrian Greek rhetoric unfairly ascribed to a sage who never wasted a word.'‡

Moreover, a malicious Samaritan editor had tampered with it before its Alexandrian recension towards the close of the first century.

(*z*) Celsus's account of Christian forgeries in general (*see* (*o*) *above*) so closely resembles Irenaeus's account of Gnostic forgeries (*see* (*u*) *above*) that both may have been quoting from Justin Martyr's lost treatise on the latter; and it must be remembered that, for Justin, the *Gospel according to St. John* was still uncanonical§ and therefore no more reliable than any other Gnostic work (*see* LXXXI.*h*).

---

* The Pauline Christians had no quarrel with the Samaritans as a nation and could flatter them without offence to Rome. Though obeying the Mosaic Law, they took no part in the insurrection of 70 A.D., and their temple on Mount Gerizim, destroyed by the Hasmonean John Hyrcanus in 128 B.C., was re-built by the Romans as a reward for their help in suppressing Bar-Cochba's Revolt.

† Justin makes one wild mistake in reporting (*Dialogues* 120) that, when Simon went to practise his demonic arts at Rome during the reign of Claudius, he was honoured by the Senate and people with a statue on an island in the Tiber, bearing the inscription *Simoni Deo Sancto*—'to the Holy God Simon'. The base of this statue has since been found on the island, and the inscription shows it to have been dedicated in late Republican times by Sextus Pompeius to the God Semo Sancus, of the Sabines—*Semoni Sanco Deo* (Ovid: *Fasti* vi. 213–218).

‡ Introduction to *King Jesus.*

§ The *Muratorian Fragment* (about 170 A.D.), gives *John* its official *testamur*, by recording that John the Disciple wrote it at the express desire of his fellow-disciples and bishops: after a three days' fast, at Ephesus, it was revealed to Andrew that John should write it in his own name, though all should revise it. The author of the *Fragment* insists that one Catholic spirit pervades all four Gospels, though different Catholic truths are taught in each of them.

THE PROCESS OF GOSPEL-MAKING

(*a*) In *Matthew* xxiii. 2–3, Jesus enjoins his followers to obey the religious authority of the Pharisees (*see Introduction* i.*p* and xiii.*a*). This had been absolute for nearly a century: when raised to power under Queen Alexandra and her brother Shimeon ben Shetah, they had annulled the Sadducaic Book of Edicts (*Sefer Gezerta*) and proclaimed the day of annulment a half-holiday (*Migilat Ta'anith and Dor Dor Ve'dorshov* i. 128).

(*b*) Pharisaic tradition was wholly oral. The author of the *Book of Enoch* had bewailed the invention of writing by an angel named Peneme, who subsequently fell from grace and turned Satanic (*Enoch* lxix. 8–11); Peneme may be identified with the evil Cosmocrator who, as Nabu, Thoth, or Hermes, had made the same invention (*see* LXX.*f* and CI.*e*):

> 'He taught the children of men the bitter and the sweet, and he taught them all the secrets of their wisdom. And he instructed mankind in writing with ink on paper, and thereby many sinned from eternity to eternity, and until this day.
>
> 'For men were not created for such purposes, to give confirmation to their good faith with pen and ink . . . through their learning they are perishing.'

Here he had the support of *Jeremiah* viii. 8:

> 'How say ye: "We are wise, the Law of the Lord is with us"? Certainly He made it in vain, when the false pen of the scribe worketh for falsehood.'

Jeremiah meant that the Law had been delivered orally to Moses, and by him to the people, except such parts of it as were engraved on stone; and that the priesthood were foisting written laws upon the people, at variance with the oral tradition. This view impressed the Pharisees who, when they assumed the responsible task of keeping the Law and the prophets free from error, decided to trust their memories rather than written records, though not abandoning pen and ink altogether: a perfect text of the Scriptures was kept in the Temple, and the synagogue copies were faithful transcriptions of it. Thenceforth, neither additions nor amendments might be recorded in writing, not even those of the highest authority, such as juridical pronouncements by the Sages. Teachers were also required to quote their authority for every oral tradition (a method afterwards adopted in Islam): 'He that telleth a thing in the name of him that said it, the same bringeth deliverance to the world; for it is written: "And Esther told the King thereof in Mordecai's name," ' (*Megillah* 15a, referring to Esther ii. 22).

(*c*) Towards the close of the first century, Rabbi Johanan ben Zakkai (*see* LXXXIII.*f*) praised his disciple Eliezer ben Horkynas (*see* LIII.*b and* LXV.*e*) as 'a cistern which loses not a drop' (*Aboth* ii. 11); and in his old age, Eliezer prided himself on having never uttered an original word (*Sukkah* 27b–28a, *Yoma* 66b *and Berakoth* 27b)—since it was then regarded as a virtue to teach only what one learned and not to volunteer a new opinion. Such conscientiousness had been unknown in pre-Pharisaic times: earlier editors of the Scriptures had carelessly ascribed anonymous sayings, and self-effacingly ascribed their own sayings, to Moses, David, and Solomon. The Canon was now at last established, and the recent discovery of the Dead Sea Scrolls, containing Scriptural manuscripts more than a thousand years older than any that had hitherto survived, proved the extreme accuracy of Pharisaic transmission: hardly a word was found to differ from the Massoretic text.

(*d*) Thus the Gospel, or 'Good Tidings', of Jesus's acts and sayings, the authentic and harmonious Apostolic tradition, will have been faithfully taught by rote to catechumens; but not set down in writing until, thirty years or so after the Crucifixion, a body of proselytes seceded and displayed their independence by translating it into Greek. Presently, the Greek-speaking Paulines, Gnostics, and others seized their pens and revived the old, unhistorical method of compilation. They considered themselves justified in emending the Apostolic tradition to Jesus's advantage, or that of the Church. In Cardinal Newman's words: 'They thought that, when there was a *causa justa,* an untruth need not be a lie.' The pirated Gospel multiplied into 'Gospels', strewn with contradictions about even the most striking events of Jesus's life, such as the Nativity, the Miracles, the Crucifixion, the Resurrection, and the Ascension.

(*e*) The Pharisees had stressed the importance of carefully cross-examining witnesses before a verdict was reached (*Sanhedrin* 41a):

> 'Rabbi Johanan ben Zakkai once cross-examined witnesses who had testified before him in the case of a murder committed underneath a fig-tree.
>
> 'He asked them: "As to the fig-tree, were its branches slender or thick, and were its figs blue or green?" [*Their testimony did not agree.*] The man who cross-examines witnesses with care is deserving of praise.'

The story of Susanna and the Elders, a moral anecdote invented by a Pharisaic teacher to illustrate this point, is particularly interesting because in *Susanna* v. 46, Daniel anticipates *Matthew* xxvii. 24: 'I am innocent of the blood of this just person' (*see* cx.*g*).

> 'Then said Daniel unto the elders: "Put these two witnesses aside, one far from another, and I will examine them. . . .

'And he called one of them, and said: "Under what tree sawest thou them [*Susanna and the young man*] companying together?" Who answered: "Under a mastic-tree. . . ."

'And Daniel commanded to bring the other . . . who answered: "Under an holm-tree. . . ."

'With that all the assembly cried out with a loud voice and praised God who saveth them that trust in Him.

'And they arose against the two elders, for Daniel had convicted them of false witness by their own mouth . . . and put them to death. Thus the innocent blood was saved the same day.'

Whenever (so to speak) *Matthew* and *Mark* have 'holm-oak', but *Luke* has 'mastic' and *John* 'terebinth', at least two of the four must be giving false witness. The task of restoring the primitive Apostolic tradition is complex, because an adequate historical or textual reason should be suggested for each evangelist's divergence from it; and since every Gospel text is suspect—as are all relevant Greek, Latin, Hebrew, and Aramaic sources—no restoration can be made that is not challengeable on a score of technical points.

(*f*) The evangelists' readiness to recast the Nazarene tradition becomes most striking when the Synoptics are compared with *John*—according to *John,* for instance, Jesus overturns the tables of the money-changers, foretells his own death, and makes a priestly convert before he has even attended the marriage at Cana (*see* xc.*f and* LXXXIII.*a*). But neither are the Synoptics consistent in their rearrangement of Jesus's sayings and deeds (*see* VIII.*h,* LXXXIV.*a,* LXXXVII.*b and* CIV.*a*).

Thus, since no Aramaic Gospel or collection of Oracles survives, or could indeed have been committed to writing by a first-century Nazarene, all that can be done is to apply one's analeptic intelligence to the existing records; and these are so Greek in form and tendency that most, if not all, of their Scriptural quotations were copied not from the Hebrew original but from the Septuagint translation.

(*g*) The Gospel-making procedure is helpfully explained by Eusebius (*Ecc. Hist.* 3. XXXIX. 12–16):

'. . . Papias [*an early second-century bishop of Phrygian Hierapolis*] adduces strange parables and teachings of the Saviour, and other more mystical things. Among them he says that there will be a millennium after the resurrection of the dead, when the Kingdom of the Messiah will be set up in material form on this earth. I suppose that he acquired these notions from a perverse reading of the apostolic accounts, not realizing that they had spoken only figuratively, for he was a man of very little intelligence. . . . But many subsequent Christian writers have followed him in this: Irenaeus, for example, relying on his antiquity. . . .

'Papias says that he heard . . . from the mouth of the elder John . . . that Mark became Peter's interpreter and wrote accurately all that Peter remembered, not indeed in order, of the sayings and acts of our Lord. . . . Peter used to teach as necessity commanded, but made no formal arrangement of Our Lord's Oracles, so that Mark was quite right to set down single points as he recalled them. To one thing only he gave attention: to leave out nothing of what he had heard, and not to misreport.

'About Matthew, Papias said: "He collected the Oracles in Hebrew, and everyone has since interpreted them as best he could."'

It should be noted that Matthew is here said to have collected Jesus's 'Oracles' in Hebrew, which probably means Aramaic—and 'collected' suggests that he arranged them under subject headings—but not to have written them down, still less to have made them into what is now called a 'gospel', namely a brief biography.* Mark is said merely to have translated and recorded Peter's memoirs of Jesus, without troubling to arrange them in chronological order. Thus the *Gospel according to Matthew* and the *Gospel according to Mark* are later compilations, based on these and similar records which continued for awhile in devotional use. Luke mentions the title of one of these 'Oracles', *The Divine Wisdom* (*Luke* xi. 49—see XIII.*u*), which may have been the source now known as 'L' (*see Introduction* III.*v*, footnote). Fragments of another collection, the *Oxyrhynchus Papyri* 1 *and* 654, survive in Greek (*see* LXV.*b and* LXXI.*h*). The Early Fathers also refer to a collection called *The Tradition of Matthias* (*see* XXI.*q and r.*); and to another called *The Teaching of Peter* (*see* XIX.*k and* LXVII.*a*), which may have been the source on which *Mark* drew.

(*h*) According to Eusebius (*Ecc. Hist.* 3. xxxix. 1), Papias wrote five Commentaries on the 'Oracles', but these have perished; and the compiler of *Luke* explains in his introduction (*Luke* i. 1–4) that, before him, several other evangelists had tried their hands at composing a chronological sequence which should most nearly satisfy the doctrinal needs of their readers, and had reduced to writing what had hitherto been orally handed down by eye-witnesses:

> 'Forasmuch as many have taken in hand to set forth in order a declaration of those things which are most surely believed among us, even as they delivered them unto us, which from the beginning were eyewitnesses, and ministers of the word; it seemed good to me also, having had perfect understanding of all things from the very first, to write unto thee in order, most excellent Theophilus,† that thou mightest know the certainty of those things, wherein thou hast been instructed.'

---

* The Pharisees also used subject-headings in the arrangement of the *Halakah*, or 'records for legal guidance', and though this aided the memory, it interfered with their chronological sequence. The Mishnaic material contained not only juridical discussions, but a wealth of miscellaneous tradition, ranging from legend to personal memoirs. Thus, in the later *Mishnah*, compiled towards the end of the second century A.D. by Rabbi Judah the Primate, important historical facts are often introduced into a legal dispute to which they bear only a vague relevance.

† Eisler suggests that Theophilus was one of the sons of Annas the High Priest, who is known to have borne that name; if so, he will have been a very old man when this Gospel was composed.

(*i*) Many of the discrepancies in the written Gospels occurred because the 'Oracles' were, it seems, arranged not chronologically, but under subject-headings, such as 'Light' (*see* xxiv.*a*), 'Why Wail Ye?' (*see* xxvi.*a*), 'Fruit-ful Trees' (*see* xlv.*d*), 'Importunity' (*see* lxiv.*a*) and 'Master, Master!' (*see* lxix.*a*); and because there was no break between the items. Thus Luke has combined into a single inconsistent parable as many as five separate ones (*see* xxx.*a and d*), all on the subject of watching, four of which appear in *Matthew*. Similarly, the historical difficulties about the disciples' corn-plucking on the Sabbath, an incident which the Synoptics place im-mediately before the healing of the withered arm, can be resolved by pre-suming that these two incidents were found under the same subject-heading, namely 'Conflict with Authority', and that in the first Jesus answered a charge of sacrilege, but in the second a charge of Sabbath-breaking. Their juxtaposition led the author of the 'Triple Tradition' to suppose that both took place on a Sabbath, though the corn could have been plucked and husked on a week-day only (*see* lxxi.*a and* lxxiv.*b*). Similarly also, the editor of *John* made Jesus cast out the money-changers early in his ministry, rather than just before his Crucifixion (*see* xc.*f*), because he found the incident under the subject-heading 'Our Master in the Temple', and decided that Jesus could not have turned a blind eye to their dishonest practices for three years, but must have expelled them during his first visit there.

(*j*) Irresponsible additions to the Gospel narrative—apart from the Chris-tological discourses in *John, Luke's* nativity fable of the Shepherds (*see* i.*s*), and his story of Zacchaeus (*see* xix.*g*)—seem to be on a small scale; they consist mostly of an occasional word or phrase. When anecdotes are in-vented, these are usually pious variants of others in the same Gospel—such as the story of the crooked woman and dropsical man in *Luke* xiii. 11–17 and xiv. 1–6 (*see* lxxiv.*f*); or are intended either to make good a prophecy, such as the account of the gall offered to Jesus on the Cross (*Matthew* xxvii. 34—*see* cxiii.*q*); or to underline a Scriptural parallel, such as the raising of the Widow's son at Nain (*Luke* vii. 11–18—*see* xxxviii.*b*).

(*k*) The omissions are as illuminating as the interpolations. Papias's credible account of Jesus's belief in the Messianic Kingdom on earth, which would last a thousand years, and of his 'strange parables' that did not suit the Gentile faith (*see* (*g*) *above*), was suppressed as 'perverse'. Neither *Matthew* nor *Luke* mentions *Mark's* reports that Jesus was unable to perform any mighty work at Nazareth (*Mark* vi.5—*see* xxxvii.*g*) and that his family thought him temporarily insane (*Mark* iii. 20–21—*see* civ.*c*). The author of *John,* though alone in supporting the quotation from *Zechariah* ix. 9 in *Matthew* xxi. 5: 'Behold thy King cometh!', omits the word 'meek' on which the Pharisees laid particular emphasis (*see* lxxxix.*q*); being anxious to divert attention from the Messiah of *Zechariah's* prophecy, since the Gnostic Christ was far from meek.

The four Canonical Gospels developed by accretion until about 130 A.D.;

and their text was not established even then, as is proved by important variants found in the fourth-century *Codex Vaticanus* and *Codex Sinaiticus* (*see* II.*g*).

(*l*) If the setting of the Gospels were some legendary island, unmarked on any map, they could be read as an allegory; but since it is first-century Palestine, no supernatural element, unless presented as the religious belief or visionary experience of one of the characters concerned, can make acceptable sense. In allegory, Jesus may be God; in history he must be man. *Mark* x. 18 and *Luke* xviii. 19 show that he carefully distinguished himself from God: 'Why callest thou me "good"? None is good save one, that is God!' (*see* LXXXII.*c*); and his alleged saying in *John* x. 30: 'I and the Father are one', is a breach of the First Commandment which he could never have committed (*see* LXXXIV.*d*). Jesus was not a vulgar miracle-monger; according to *Mark* viii. 12, he refused to give a sign in proof of his prophetic authority (*see* XCI.*a and f*). *John* ii. 1-11, the miracle of the water turned to wine (*see* x.*b*), and *Matthew* xiv. 15-21, the miracle of the loaves and fishes (*see* LXXII.*a*), must thus be read as symbolic acts, rather than as reversals of nature. The water was turned into wine allegorically, the people fed spiritually; and the importance of the acts lay only in the message conveyed by their performance. Those who witnessed them evidently understood; but the Gentile Church has preferred not to understand.

(*m*) Jesus's symbolic acts became misrepresented as miracles, at a time when Gentile Christianity had met with a strong rival in the 'gymnosophism' of Apollonius of Tyana, an ascetic philosopher who flourished under Nero. Apollonius was believed to have cast out devils, raised the dead, accurately prophesied several public disasters, appeared in two far distant towns on the same day, vanished into thin air from the Imperial Judgement Hall at Rome, and at last ascended into Heaven—whence he occasionally revealed himself to those who disbelieved in his apotheosis. The Gentile Christians were anxious to prove that Jesus had done equally wonderful things, forgetting his stern refusal to gratify the multitude by idle display or to let his disciples use magical incantations (*Matthew* vi. 7—*see* XXXI.*b* and XXVII.*e*). He had even declined all credit for his feats of healing (*Mark* v. 19—*see* LXIII.*f*).

(*n*) There are striking literary resemblances between the Canonical Gospels and Flavius Philostratus's *Life of Apollonius,* written about 217 A.D. *Book* 4. xliv reads (*see* XXXVI *and* XXXVIII):

> 'And in these days Apollonius wrought another miracle. A certain maiden had died in the very hour of her marriage and the bridegroom followed the bier, mourning, as was natural, that his marriage was unfilfilled. And the whole city mourned with him, for the maiden was a nobleman's daughter. Then Apollonius, seeing their grief, said: "Let them that bear the bier lay it down, for behold I will stay the tears that are shed for this maiden." And he asked: "What is her name?" [And they told him "Such-and-such."] Thereupon the multitude looked that he should deliver an oration unto them, this

being the custom at Rome, as much to honour the funeral as to provoke lamentation. Nevertheless he did not so, but touched her and whispered some words in secret, so that at once she awakened from what had seemed to be death, and returned to her father's house.'

And *Book* 3. xxxviii reads (*see* LXXIX):

'And a messenger brought unto Apollonius a poor woman who interceded with him for her child, a boy of sixteen years of age, who had been for two years possessed of a devil. Now this devil was amorous of him . . . and would not let him either go to school or stay at home . . . but drove him out into desert places. And Apollonius asked: "Is he at hand?" She answered: "No, lord, for when I sought to bring him to you the devil threatened to slay him. . . ." Then said Apollonius: "Take courage, for he will not slay the lad when he hath read this." And with that he drew a letter from his bosom and gave it to her. Now the letter was addressed to the devil and threatened him greatly if he did the boy further injury. . . .'

Apollonius also cured a blind man, and a man with a withered hand (*see* XL *and* LXXIV).

(*o*) Philostratus, who writes that 'his words had a ring about them as of judgements delivered by a sceptred King', may well have been influenced by the Gospels when he recorded Apollonius's discourses, miracles, and travels. He did this at the order of the Dowager-Empress Julia Domna, then living with the Emperor Alexander Severus, her great-nephew who, according to his biographer Lampridius, set up statues of Apollonius and Jesus in his private shrine side by side with those of Alexander the Great, Orpheus, and Abraham. Julia Domna provided Philostratus with the historical materials, particularly the contemporary memoirs of Apollonius's disciple, Damis of Nineveh.

The Gospels, however, before their text was finally established, may also have been influenced by miracles recorded in early lives of Apollonius. A hundred years after the publication of Philostratus's *Life,* Eusebius felt obliged to attack it in a treatise 'occasioned by the parallel drawn between Apollonius and Christ by Hierocles.' Hierocles, one of Diocletian's provincial governors, had remarked that 'whereas the tales of Jesus have been concocted by Peter and Paul and a few others like them (liars, uneducated, and wizards), the history of Apollonius was written by Maximus of Aegae, and his constant companion Damis the philosopher, and Philostratus the Athenian, all men of the highest education, lovers of truth and of mankind'; and that Apollonius was greater than Jesus.

(*p*) Eusebius was hampered in his controversy by the close parallels between these two: each was credited with a fabulous nativity, prophecies, miracles, an ascension to Heaven and posthumous appearances. If he ridiculed Apollonius, he would weaken Jesus's case, since Apollonius also was reputedly abstemious, wise, and noble and, unlike Jesus, had been worshipped as a God even during his lifetime. He therefore refused to be drawn into a comparative discussion of their rival histories, contenting himsel᷏ with a *tu quoque:* the discrepancies in Apollonius's *Lives* convicted theiɪ authors of being liars, uneducated, and charlatans, and Apollonius himself of wizardry.

Eusebius's position in the Church debarred him from constructive historical criticism. It would have been most interesting to know whether Apollonius was a worthy successor of Pythagoras and Empedocles who, as elected grand-masters of an originally Thraco-Libyan mystery-cult, were granted semi-divine honours by the initiates; or just another market-place adventurer exploiting the credulity of first-century provincials; and whether Damis's biography was published earlier or later than the Gospel passages with which it has so much in common.

Part Two

Part Two

I

THE NATIVITY

Matthew i. 18–25

[18]Now the birth of JESUS CHRIST was on this wise:

When as His mother Mary was espoused to Joseph, before they came together, she was found with child of the Holy Ghost. [19]Then Joseph her husband, being a just man, and not willing to make her a public example, was minded to put her away privily. [20]But while he thought on these things, behold, the angel of the Lord appeared unto him in a dream, saying: 'Joseph, thou son of David, fear not to take unto thee Mary thy wife: for that which is conceived in her is of the Holy Ghost. [21]And she shall bring forth a son, and thou shalt call His name JESUS: for He shall save His people from their sins.' [22]Now all this was done, that it might be fulfilled which was spoken of the Lord by the prophet, saying:

[23]*Behold, a virgin shall be with child,*
And shall bring forth a son,
And they shall call His name Emmanuel,
Which being interpreted is, God with us.

[24]Then Joseph being raised from sleep did as the angel of the Lord had bidden him, and took unto him his wife: [25]and knew her not till she had brought forth her firstborn son: and he called His name JESUS.

Matthew ii. 1–23

[1]Now when Jesus was born in Bethlehem of Judaea in the days of Herod the king, behold, there came wise men from the east to Jerusalem, [2]saying: 'Where is He that is born King of the Jews? for we have seen His star in the east, and are come to worship Him.' [3]When Herod the king had heard these things, he was troubled, and all Jerusalem with him. [4]And when he had gathered all the chief priests and scribes of the people together, he demanded of them where Christ should be born. [5]And they said unto him: 'In Bethlehem of Judaea: for thus it is written by the prophet,

[6]*And thou Bethlehem, in the land of Judah,*
Art not the least among the princes of Judah:
For out of thee shall come a Governor,
That shall rule my people Israel.'

[7]Then Herod, when he had privily called the wise men, inquired of them diligently what time the star appeared. [8]And he sent them to Bethlehem, and

Matthew ii. 1–23 (contd.)

said: 'Go and search diligently for the young Child; and when ye have found Him, bring me word again, that I may come and worship Him also.'
⁹When they had heard the king, they departed; and, lo, the star, which they saw in the east, went before them, till it came and stood over where the young Child was. ¹⁰When they saw the star, they rejoiced with exceeding great joy. ¹¹And when they were come into the house, they saw the young Child with Mary His mother, and fell down, and worshipped Him: and when they had opened their treasures, they presented unto Him gifts; gold, and frankincense, and myrrh. ¹²And being warned of God in a dream that they should not return to Herod, they departed into their own country another way.

¹³And when they were departed, behold, the angel of the Lord appeareth to Joseph in a dream, saying: 'Arise, and take the young Child and His mother, and flee into Egypt, and be thou there until I bring thee word: for Herod will seek the young Child to destroy Him.' ¹⁴When he arose, he took the young Child and His mother by night, and departed into Egypt: ¹⁵and was there until the death of Herod: that it might be fulfilled which was spoken of the Lord by the prophet, saying:

Out of Egypt have I called My Son.

¹⁶Then Herod, when he saw that he was mocked of the wise men, was exceeding wroth, and sent forth, and slew all the children that were in Bethlehem, and in all the coasts thereof, from two years old and under, according to the time which he had diligently inquired of the wise men. ¹⁷Then was fulfilled that which was spoken by Jeremiah the prophet, saying:

¹⁸*In Ramah was there a voice heard, lamentation,*
And weeping, and great mourning,
Rachel weeping for her children,
And would not be comforted, because they are not.

¹⁹But when Herod was dead, behold, an angel of the Lord appeareth in a dream to Joseph in Egypt, ²⁰saying: "Arise, and take the young Child and His mother, and go into the land of Israel: for they are dead which sought the young Child's life." ²¹And he arose, and took the young Child and His mother, and came into the land of Israel. ²²But when he heard that Archelaus did reign in Judaea in the room of his father Herod, he was afraid to go thither: notwithstanding, being warned of God in a dream, he turned aside into the parts of Galilee: ²³and he came and dwelt in a city called Nazareth: that it might be fulfilled which was spoken by the prophets:

He shall be called a Nazarene.

Luke ii. 1–20

¹And it came to pass in those days, that there went out a decree from Caesar Augustus, that all the world should be taxed. ²This taxing was first made when Cyrenius was governor of Syria. ³And all went to be taxed, every one into his own city. ⁴And Joseph also went up from Galilee, out of the city of Nazareth, into Judaea, unto the city of David, which is called Bethlehem, (because he was of the house and lineage of David) ⁵to be taxed with Mary his espoused wife, being great with child. ⁶And so it was, that, while they

Luke ii. 1–20 (*contd.*)

were there, the days were accomplished that she should be delivered. [7]And she brought forth her first-born son, and wrapped Him in swaddling clothes, and laid Him in a manger; because there was no room for them in the inn.

[8]And there were in the same country shepherds abiding in the field, keeping watch over their flock by night. [9]And, lo, the angel of the Lord came upon them, and the glory of the Lord shone round about them: and they were sore afraid. [10]And the angel said unto them:

Fear not:
For, behold, I bring you good tidings of great joy,
Which shall be to all people.
[11]*For unto you is born this day in the city of David a Saviour,*
Which is Christ the Lord.
[12]*And this shall be a sign unto you; Ye shall find the Babe wrapped in*
swaddling clothes, lying in a manger.

[13]And suddenly there was with the angel a multitude of the heavenly host praising God, and saying:

[14]*Glory to God in the Highest,*
And on earth peace, good will toward men.

[15]And it came to pass, as the angels were gone away from them into heaven, the shepherds said one to another, Let us now go even unto Bethlehem, and see this thing which is come to pass, which the Lord hath made known unto us. [16]And they came with haste, and found Mary, and Joseph, and the Babe lying in a manger. [17]And when they had seen it, they made known abroad the saying which was told them concerning this Child. [18]And all they that heard it wondered at those things which were told them by the shepherds. [19]But Mary kept all these things, and pondered them in her heart. [20]And the shepherds returned, glorifying and praising God for all the things that they had heard and seen, as it was told unto them.

Protoevangelium 17–18

[17]And there came an order from Augustus the King, that all in Bethlehem of Judaea should be enrolled. And Joseph said: 'I shall enrol my sons, but what shall I do with this maiden? How shall I enrol her? As my wife? I am ashamed. As my daughter then? But all the sons of Israel know that she is not my daughter. The day of the Lord shall itself bring it to pass as the Lord will.' And he saddled the ass and set her upon it; and his son led it, and Joseph followed. And when they had come within three miles, Joseph turned and saw her sorrowful; and he said to himself: 'Likely that which is in her distresses her.' And again Joseph turned and saw her laughing. And he said to her: 'Mary, how is it that I see in thy face at one time laughter, at another sorrow?' And Mary said to Joseph: 'Because I see two peoples with my eyes; the one weeping and lamenting, and the other rejoicing and exulting.' And they came into the middle of the road, and Mary said to him: 'Take me down from off the ass, for that which is in me presses to come forth.' And he took her down from off the ass, and said to her: 'Whither shall I lead thee, and cover thy disgrace? for the place is desert.'

Protoevangelium 17–18 (contd.)

¹⁸And he found a cave there, and led her into it; and leaving his two sons beside her, he went out to seek a midwife in the district of Bethlehem.

* * * * *

(a) The Nazarenes, like the Gentile Christians, feared to be suspected of militant nationalism, and therefore disguised the tradition of Jesus's having been crowned King of Israel without Roman assent or knowledge and having thus become the titular Son of God. They taught that his kingdom had not been an earthly one—which was true in fact, because when at last he had publicly claimed his kingdom he had so signally failed to win popular support that the Romans were able to crucify him without hindrance. The political value of this doctrine was proved at the close of the first century by the acquittal of Jesus's Nazarene grand-nephews 'according to the flesh,' when they were brought before the Emperor Domitian on a capital charge of treason (Eusebius: *Ecc. Hist.* 3. xix–xx).

(b) The Gentile Christians had already come to hold an independent view: they first tolerated, then encouraged, and finally came to accept the Hellenistic notion that Jesus had been spiritually begotten by God on a virgin and, in due course, physically born from her womb. It seems that this view originated in an extravagant metaphor used by Philo, the 'Grecian' (i.e. the Alexandrian Jewish) philosopher who, in the first half of the first century A.D., allegorized the Old Testament for the instruction of the Greek world in an attempt to reconcile it with the Platonic system (*see* LXXXI.*c*). Philo uses this metaphor when speaking of the birth of several distinguished Pentateuchal characters. Thus Leah (*Genesis* xxix. 31) is impregnated by 'the quiet one' before she bears the patriarchs Judah and Levi, though Jacob is her husband (Philo: i. 147). Also, Samuel is 'born of a human mother who became pregnant after receiving divine seed' (i. 148), though Philo is aware that in 1 *Samuel* i. 19: 'Elkanah knew Hannah' before she conceived. And of Isaac (*Genesis* xxi. 1–3) he writes (i. 215): 'It is most fitting that God should converse in an other than human manner with a creature of so marvellous, unpolluted, and pure a nature.' As Grecian influence strengthened in the early Gentile Church—and Jesus is credited by *Luke* and *Matthew* with a parable borrowed directly from Philo (*see* XLIV.*a*)—the Philonian view of Mary's divine impregnation became orthodox, but its metaphorical origin was forgotten. Jesus was now thought to have been born from Mary, the carpenter's betrothed, very much as Perseus had been born from Danaë: after the Father of Heaven had visited her in a shower of glory.

(c) Though this doctrine could be reconciled neither with *Romans* i. 3 and *Hebrews* vii. 14, nor with *Galatians* iv. 4—documents which are earlier in date than any of the Canonical Gospels (*see* II.*g*)—its polemical value in proving the divinity of Jesus and glorifying him equally with heathen gods was remarked upon by Justin Martyr in his philosophical *Apology for the Christians* in 139 A.D. It was defended by Origen, Lactantius, and other early Christian apologists on the zoological ground that even vultures and Spanish mares were capable of parthenogenous birth; but it excited the horror of Palestinian Jews and the ridicule of Romans and Greeks, who naturally concluded that Jesus was a bastard. Celsus, for instance (Origen: *Against Celsus* i. 19. 1), writing about the year 175 A.D., describes him as the fruit of his mother's seduction by a Roman soldier named Pantherus; and it is recorded in the Talmud (*Sanhedrin* 43a) that he was 'related to the Government (or "Royalty")'. Though the Talmudic authority for this, Ulla, a fourth-century scholar, has here confused Jesus with a Messianic pretender from Lydda, who appeared in the time of Hadrian, and states that forty days elapsed between his apprehension and his death, a more plausible version of the libel appears in a third-century Talmudic record (*Shabbath* 104a—*see* vii.h). Moreover, the Jews could disprove the legitimacy of Jesus's birth merely from the account given in *Matthew* i. 18 and the *Protoevangelium* 17. Their God did not father sons on mortal maidens in the style of Zeus, and if Mary had already been contracted in marriage to Joseph before he found her pregnant, this would in Jewish law (*Deuteronomy* xxii. 13–21) have bastardized her child even if the marriage had not been consummated and she had in the interval married some other man.

(*d*) Though nothing is related of this Mary in the Canonical Gospels except that she was cousin to the priest Zacharias's wife Elisabeth, a daughter of Aaron (*Luke* i. 5), the tradition embodied in the second-century *Protoevangelium* makes her the only daughter of one Joachim and his wife Hannah (St. Ann); and it is not historically impossible that she was pledged by her parents to the service of the Temple, as Samuel had been (1 *Samuel* i. 28), in accordance with the provisions of *Leviticus* xxvii. 6.* But it is most unlikely that a daughter of a priestly house at Jerusalem would have married a Galilean carpenter, even a scion of the House of David. Priests' daughters were notoriously proud of their descent from Aaron, and though the Mosaic ban on inter-tribal marriages (*Numbers* xxxvi. 8–9), designed to keep landed property under the same local authority, had now been repealed by the Pharisees (*Ta'anith* 30b), it seems to have still kept a certain superstitious force. We know, certainly, that Mariamne the Hasmonean detested her forced marriage to Herod (Josephus: *Wars* i. 22. 2), and though the Talmud lists the kinds of families worthy of supplying wives to the priesthood (*Kiddushin* iv. 1), the priests seem to have shrunk from giving their daughters in marriage to non-Levites. 'Scripture advised these daughters to marry only such as were worthy of them' (*Baba Bathra* 120a).

* The first eight verses of this chapter are usually read as laying down the varying amounts due to the Sanctuary in fulfilment of specific vows; but the remainder, which concern the dedication of beasts, houses, and land to the Temple, make it clear that the first eight concern the *hierodouloi*, or slaves of God, who either sold themselves, or were sold by their parents, to the Temple service.

(*e*) Nevertheless, Nazarene tradition has taken pains to preserve this mysterious paradox about Jesus's birth: that though physically born of the non-priestly House of David he was, however, legally entitled to wear a priestly garment (*see* cxiii.*t*), and had Levite kinsfolk, including his brother James (*Galatians* i. 19) who served in the Temple as a priest (*see* viii.*t–v*). It may be postulated, therefore, that two Marys were concerned in Jesus's nativity: his physical mother Mary, Joseph's wife, a Galilean woman; and Mary, a kinswoman of John the Baptist's mother Elisabeth, who became his adoptive mother when he was formally engrafted into the tribe of Levi. This ceremony was needed to fulfil the expectation of the Apocalyptics, of whom John was one, that the Messiah would be 'of Judah and of Levi', namely a Priest-king of the tribe of Levi, yet born of the seed of David.

(*f*) The authority for the coming of such a Priest-king was found in the *Testament of Levi* ii. 10–11: 'Thou, Levi, shalt proclaim concerning him that shall redeem Israel, and by thee and Judah shall the Lord appear among men.' And again in xviii. 2–14, a passage of frequent allusion in the Gospels:

'Then shall the Lord raise up a new priest.
And to him all the words of the Lord shall be revealed;
And he shall execute a righteous judgement upon the earth for a multitude
    of days.
And his star shall arise in heaven as of a king,
Lighting up the light of knowledge as the sun the day,
And he shall be magnified in the world.
He shall shine forth as the sun on the earth,
And shall remove all darkness from under heaven,
And there shall be peace in all the earth.
The heavens shall exult in his days,
And the earth shall be glad,
And the clouds shall rejoice,
And the angels of the glory of the presence of the Lord shall be glad in him.
The heavens shall be opened.
And from the temple of glory shall come upon him sanctification,
With the Father's voice as from Abraham to Isaac.
And the glory of the Most High shall be uttered over him,
And the spirit of understanding and sanctification shall rest upon him.
For he shall give the majesty of the Lord to His sons in truth for evermore;
And there shall none succeed him for all generations for ever.
And in his priesthood the Gentiles shall be multiplied in knowledge upon the
    earth.
And enlightened through the grace of the Lord:
And in his priesthood shall sin come to an end,
And the lawless shall cease to do evil.
And he shall open the gates of paradise,
And shall remove the threatening sword against Adam.
And he shall give to the saints to eat from the tree of life,
And the spirit of holiness shall be on them.

And Beliar ['Belial'] shall be bound by him.
And he shall give power to His children to tread upon the evil spirits.
And the Lord shall rejoice in His children,
And be well pleased in His beloved ones for ever.
Then shall Abraham and Isaac and Jacob exult,
And I [Levi] will be glad,
And all the saints shall clothe themselves with joy.'

It was also prophesied in the *Testament of Levi* viii. 11-15:

'Levi, thy seed shall be divided into three offices, for a sign of the glory of the
Lord that is to come. And the first portion shall be great; yea, greater than it
none shall be. The second shall be in the priesthood. And the third shall be
called by a new name, because a king shall arise in Judah and shall establish
a new priesthood, after the fashion of the Gentiles. And his presence is beloved, as a prophet of the Most High, of the seed of Abraham our father.'

That this referred to John Hyrcanus, the Hasmonean King, as possessing
'the government of the nation, the dignity of the high priesthood, and
prophecy' (Josephus: *Antiquities* xiii. 10. 7), had been forgotten by the time
of John the Baptist, because the later Hasmoneans fell away from John
Hyrcanus's idealistic example and Levi's words were relegated to the mount-
ing store of unfulfilled Messianic prophecy.

(g) Again, in the *Testament of Judah* xxi. 1-4, the patriarch Judah says:

'And now, my children, love Levi that ye may abide, and exalt not yourselves
against him, lest ye be utterly destroyed. For to me the Lord gave the kingdom, and to him the priesthood, and He set the kingdom beneath the priesthood. To me He gave earthly things; to him the heavenly things. As the
heaven is higher than the earth, so is the priesthood of God higher than the
earthly kingdom, unless it falleth away through sin from the Lord and is
dominated by the earthly kingdom.'

Judah further prophesies (*Testament of Judah* xxiv. 1-6 and xxv. 3-5, [*omitting Christian interpolations*]):

'And a man shall arise, like the sun of righteousness,
Walking with the sons of men in meekness and righteousness;
And no sin shall be found in him.
And the heavens shall be opened unto him,
To pour out the spirit, the blessing of the Holy Father;
And he shall pour out the spirit of grace upon you;
And ye shall be unto Him sons in truth,
And ye shall walk in His commandments first and last.
Then shall the sceptre of my kingdom shine forth;
And from your root shall arise a stem;
And from it shall grow a rod of righteousness to the Gentiles,
To judge and to save all that call upon the Lord.

*   *   *   *   *

And ye shall be the people of the Lord, and have one tongue;
And there shall be there no spirit of deceit of Beliar,
For he shall be cast into the fire for ever.
And they who have died in grief shall arise in joy,
And they who were poor for the Lord's sake shall be made rich,
And they who are put to death for the Lord's sake shall awake to life.
And the hearts of Jacob shall run in joyfulness,
And the eagles of Israel shall fly in gladness;
And all the peoples shall glorify the Lord for ever.'

Thus Jesus had to be born according to the flesh from the line of David, in agreement with the prophecies of *Isaiah* ix. 6–7, *Jeremiah* xxiii. 5; *Amos* ix. 11; *Ezekiel* xxxiv. 23, etc., but according to the spirit from the line of Aaron. (*h*) St. Ephraim the Syrian in his *Gospel Commentaries* (373 A.D.) insists that Jesus was physically sprung from Judah through both his parents:

'If because the Scripture saith: "Elisabeth thy sister", ye suppose that this is said that it might be made manifest that Mary was of the tribe of Levi, [ye err since] in another part the same Scripture saith that both Joseph and Mary were of the House of David.'

Yet St. Ephraim, though he failed to distinguish between the first Mary, a daughter of Judah, Jesus's mother according to the flesh, and Mary the Levite, his mother according to the Spirit, seems to have known that Jesus had been adopted into the tribe of Levi. He may have relied principally on a text in *Matthew* xvii, later suppressed (*see* XLVIII.*d*); but this was supported by a statement of Paul's—if Paul was indeed the author of *The Epistle to the Hebrews*. There addressing the submerged Israelite population of Samaria (*see* LXX.*c*) who are known to have been daily expecting 'that prophet' promised in *Deuteronomy* xviii. 15–19 (*see* LXXVII.*b*), yet careful not to fall foul of the Romans, Paul slurs over Jesus's title as King of the Jews and stresses his High Priesthood (*Hebrews* v. 5–6):

'So also Christ glorified not himself to be made an High Priest. But He did so which said unto him: "Thou art my Son, this day have I forgotten thee." As He saith also in another place: "Thou art a priest for ever after the order of Melchizedek." '

(*i*) This promise, in *Psalm* cx. 4, had been made on behalf of God by an unknown prophet apparently in honour of Simon Maccabaeus (142–135 B.C.) the Levite King who assumed the title 'Priest of the Most High God', previously borne by Melchizedek King of Salem (*Genesis* xiv. 18); but it was now accepted as still another Messianic prophecy. True, Paul continues tortuously (*Hebrews* vii. 4–16):

'Now consider how great this man was, unto whom even the patriarch Abraham gave the tenth of the spoils. . . . And, as I may so say, Levi also who receiveth tithes, paid tithes in Abraham. . . . For he was yet in the loins of his father when Melchizedek met him. . . . If therefore perfection were by the Levitical priesthood, for under it the people received the Law, what further need was there that another priest should rise after the order of Melchizedek, and not to be called after the order of Aaron? For the priesthood being changed, there is made of necessity a change also in the Law. For he of whom these things are spoken pertaineth to another tribe, of which no man gave attendance at the altar. For it is evident that our Lord sprang out of Judah, of which tribe Moses spake nothing concerning priesthood. And it is yet far more evident: for that after the similitude of Melchizedek there ariseth another priest who is made, not after the Law of carnal commandment, but after the power of an endless life.'

Nevertheless, he has stated that Jesus was born legitimately (*Galatians* iv. 4–5), and here testifies that he came of the tribe of Judah; and furthermore makes him a High Priest, connecting this appointment with the Baptism which, as we shall show, was a Coronation rite. The Melchizedek argument seems only to confuse the issue, yet Paul, though he disguises the political aspects of his doctrine, is making a correct analogy between Jesus the Messiah and the ancient priest-king of Jerusalem who was, in religious theory, 'without father or mother' because 'made as it were the Son of God' (*Hebrews* vii. 1–3). Again in *Romans* i. 3, Paul insists that 'God's son, Jesus Christ Our Lord, which sprang from the seed of David according to the flesh' (in *Romans* viii. 3, he characterizes this flesh as 'sinful') had been 'declared to be the Son of God with power': namely as his re-birth, or Epiphany, a prelude to the Coronation (*see* viii.*a*). This doctrine Paul may well have learned from the New Covenanters at Damascus (*see* cxviii. *end*). It is known that the Early Church before stabilizing the date of Jesus's birth as December 25th (in order to benefit from a pagan public holiday, 'The Nativity of the Unconquered Sun'), celebrated the birth and Epiphany as a single feast. The Armenian Church still preserves this tradition.

(*j*) If, then, the second Mary who adopted Jesus into the tribe of Levi was a virgin at the time of his ritual re-birth, the Virgin Birth doctrine must be read not as a Gentile fiction, but as an authentic Nazarene tradition. That the view of Jesus's literal parthenogenesis was current in the Gentile Churches as early as the reign of Domitian is suggested by the Christian interpolation in Josephus (*Antiquities* xviii. 3. 3—*see* cx.i):

> 'Now there was about this time Jesus a wise man, if it be lawful to call him a man, for he was a doer of wonderful works—a teacher of such men as receive the truth with pleasure. He drew over to him both many of the Jews and many of the Gentiles. He was the Christ; and when Pilate, at the suggestion of the principal men among us, had condemned him to the cross, those that loved him at the first did not forsake him, for he appeared to them alive again the third day, as the divine prophets had foretold these and ten thousand other wonderful things concerning him; and the tribe of Christians, so named after him, are not extinct to this day.'

(*k*) This passage has evidently been substituted for another far less flattering one, a fragment of which remains in the illogical: 'those that loved him at

the first did not forsake him, for he appeared. . . .' Josephus is more likely
to have written: 'for they claimed that he appeared . . .', and his 'ten thousand other wonderful things' conveys scorn, not admiration. Had the Christian editor been a more skilful forger he would have made Josephus particularize one or two of the more sensational miracles. The account follows
the story of a riot provoked by Pilate's attempt to build an aqueduct for
Jerusalem with Temple funds (*see* LI.*a*), and is itself followed by:

> 'About this same time also another sad calamity put the Jews into disorder
> and certain shameful practices happened about the temple of Isis, at Rome.'

The 'shameful practices' are given first. They have nothing to do with Jewish
history and concern one Mundus who, by impersonating the God Anubis,
tricked Paulina, a Roman matron, into letting him seduce her in the Temple
of Isis. Tiberius, who examined the case, found that the priests had been
bribed and ordered them to be crucified. The 'sad calamity' refers to the trick
played on a Roman woman named Fulvia, a proselyte to the Jewish religion,
by four Jews who had persuaded her to send treasure to the Temple at Jerusalem and then kept it for themselves; Tiberius, after trying the case, banished the embezzlers from Rome. It seems, then, that Josephus who was a
clear and careful, though often dishonest, writer, found a close connexion
between the story of Jesus, the story of Paulina, and the story of Fulvia; it
must not be forgotten that he enjoyed the patronage of Domitian's wife and
wrote at a time when the Christians were under the Imperial ban.

(*l*) The original may well have run as follows:

> 'There was another sedition made at this time by the followers of one Jesus,
> a wonder-worker and preacher of the Kingdom of God, whom certain Zealots
> rashly acclaimed as the Messiah. When blood was shed by them on the Eve
> of the Feast of Unleavened Bread, Pilate after consultation with the Chief
> Rulers, condemned him to be crucified. But those who had loved him at first
> did not forsake him, and claimed that he appeared to them alive again after
> the third day in fulfilment of a prophecy. The tale drew both many of the
> Jews to belief in him and also many Gentiles, who invented ten thousand other
> wonderful things about him: these even said that it was not lawful to call him
> a man since he had been begotten by God, and that his mother Mary was at
> that time a virgin betrothed to a Galilean carpenter. He is still worshipped as
> a God by a few stubborn "Christians", as they call themselves, though the cult
> is under an Imperial ban.
>
> 'I do not know who his true father was, but some say that his mother was
> grossly deceived, as happened at Rome to one Paulina.'

Clearly, Josephus must have known in what sense Jesus was a Son of God;
but it amused him to feign ignorance in order to present the Gentile Christians as fools or rogues. The Mundus-Paulina parallel was made the closer
by an Alexandrian identification of Anubis with the Angel Gabriel*; which

---

* There is a description in de Haas's *Bilderatlas* of an Egyptian gem showing Anubis with
palm and pouch on the obverse, and on the reverse an archangel described as GABRIER SABAO,
meaning Gabriel Sabaoth; the Egyptians having, as usual, converted the *l* into an *r*.

in the light of *Luke* i. 26–28 (*see* vii.*a and e*) may have given rise to the libel against Mary the Virgin, found in the *Toldoth Yeshu,* and also in the Talmud (*Kallah* p. 148, ed. Higger), that she was seduced by her husband's paranymph, i.e. 'best man', before her wedding. *Luke* i. 28, 'The angel came in unto her', is an unfortunate reminiscence of *Genesis* xix. 31, where 'come in unto' has a sexual connotation.

(*m*) The question of Jesus's identity has been confused by yet another view, apparently held by a section of first-century Gentile Christians, which has left strong traces on the Nativity story in *Luke* and *Matthew*. It was based on the romantic notion that the Messiah was necessarily a lost royal heir, brought up in poverty until he made a sudden radiant appearance in his ancestral city—such another as King Cyrus who, in *Isaiah* xl–xlviii, was acclaimed as a Messiah, God's chosen instrument for vengeance on Babylon and rescue of the captive Jews; he would be acclaimed and anointed by the ever-young prophet Elijah. This view is also implied in *John's* account of Pilate's question to Jesus, and the answers he received (*see* cx.*d*). Pilate is said to have asked him: 'Art thou the King of the Jews?' (*John* xviii. 33), knowing that Jesus had been hailed as King by the pilgrim crowd and had not discouraged them; and what this would have meant to *John's* Greek readers was: 'Have you a right under Roman Law to claim the title?' Jesus is said to have replied by asking the source of the information on which Pilate's question was based (*John* xviii. 34), but then admitted that he was indeed King of the Jews, though waiving his claim to the temporal power that the title carried with it (*John* xviii. 36–37). Pilate, *John* records, did not contradict Jesus and found no fault in him. But the Hasmonean dynasty was extinct and to be 'King of the Jews' could have meant only one thing in Roman Law, namely to be the lost heir-at-law to the only Jewish throne recognized at Rome—the Herodian. It follows, therefore, unless they were talking at cross-purposes, that Jesus admitted Pilate's information to be correct: he had been legitimately fathered on Mary by King Antipater, the eldest son of King Herod and a Roman army officer.

(*n*) It is at first reading a plausible view. Antipater shared the throne with his father (*Antiquities* xvii. 1. 1), who had him murdered five days before his own death (*Antiquities* xvii. 8. 1).* Herod, who was an Edomite, had made his Will in Antipater's favour; the Emperor Augustus had duly re-

* It is clear from the account of his rigged trial that Antipater was innocent of the formal charges brought against him—the Roman Governor of Syria showed his dissatisfaction by leaving the Court before proceedings were over (*Antiquities* xvii. 5. 7)—and the reason of Herod's desire to kill him was not necessarily that he had committed a crime. It is possible that, suffering from a horrible and incurable complaint (*Antiquities* xvii. 6. 5), he wished to offer him up as a human sacrifice in propitiation of Jehovah; Herod was a religious maniac and only the approach of death prevented his wanton massacre of twenty thousand Jewish notables (*Antiquities* xvii. 6. 5 and 8. 2) in the hippodrome at Jericho. Royal sacrifice of an eldest son in times of crisis was a well-attested practice. Abraham was about to sacrifice Isaac (*Genesis* xxii. 2) when prevented; Saul tried to kill Jonathan by a trick but was given another life in ransom (1 *Samuel* xiv. 39–45); the King of Moab offered his eldest son and heir as a burned offering (2 *Kings* iii. 27).

ceived and approved it and must have laid it up in the temple of Vesta
(Herod being a Roman citizen of consular rank), where it was inviolable
(*Antiquities* xvii. 3. 2). No other son of Herod afterwards became king or
could transmit to his heirs a claim to the throne, and Antipater's son by a
former union with a Hasmonean princess (*Antiquities* xvii. 4. 1 and xvii. 5.
2) does not appear to have survived him and was probably murdered at
Herod's orders. Jesus would thus have become Herod's heir, though his
existence might not have been known to Augustus when he divided the
kingdom into unroyal 'tetrarchies' among three of Herod's four surviving
sons, namely Archelaus, Antipas, and Philip (*Antiquities* xvii. 11. 4); the
fourth, Herod Philip, originally next in succession according to the Will, had
been 'blotted out' in a codicil before Antipater's death (*Wars* i. 30. 7).

(*o*) In this view, the news of Antipater's arrest and trial would account for
Mary's hurried flight to Elisabeth (*Luke* i. 39–40) and for the unusual circumstances of her subsequent marriage (*Matthew* i. 18–19) which suggest a
subterfuge to conceal her from Herod's agents: while pregnant of Antipater's
child she could expect no mercy. Herod's Massacre of the Innocents at
Bethlehem (*Matthew* ii. 16) also makes sense if he had heard rumours that
a surviving grandson by Antipater, not more than two years old, had been
adopted into the House of David. The editor of *Luke* ii. 1 unhistorically gives
the occasion as a general census; but the *Protoevangelium* points to a particular registration of the House of David, under orders from 'the King':
presumably Herod, though a stupid gloss 'Augustus' has crept into the text
—Augustus was not a king (*Protoevangelium* 17. 1). Herod had previously
desecrated David's tomb (*Antiquities* xvi. 7. 1), and was so jealous of the
House of David that he destroyed* its family records, as Eusebius states on
the authority of Africanus (*Ecc. Hist.* i. vii. 13), though Jesus's relations had

---

* Eusebius suggests that Herod destroyed all the genealogies of prominent Jews, and the
Talmud says: 'Since the day that the *Book of Genealogies* was removed from sight, the strength
of the sages has been impaired and their eyesight dimmed' (*Pesahim* 62*b*). According to Rashi,
this book contained the reasons, since forgotten, for many Scriptural Laws; but the destruction or confiscation is not mentioned as Herod's deed, and the book seems to have contained
only royal genealogies; for Josephus (*Life* i.) found his own in the yet unburned Temple
archives. The Pharisees were not interested in the genealogies so much as in the legal commentaries; they held that 'a learned bastard takes precedence over an ignorant High Priest'
(*Horayoth* iii. 8).

Herod's own ancestry is disputed. According to Africanus, a careful writer quoted by
Eusebius (*Ecc. Hist.* i. vi. 2) and supported by inscriptional evidence, his grandfather Antipater was a 'Slave of the God' in the Temple of Hercules at Ascalon, whom the Edomites
captured in a raid and who became one of their noblemen. When the Edomites were conquered by the Hasmonean King Alexander Jannaeus and forced to accept the Law of Moses,
Herod's father, also called Antipater, was brought up at Alexander's court, and made commander-in-chief of the Edomite army (*Antiquities* xiv. 1. 3). Nicolaus of Damascus, quoted by
Josephus in the same context, claimed on the contrary that Herod's family was 'of the stock
of the principal Jews who came out of Babylon into Judaea'. The two views can, however, be
reconciled: if the family was a princely Jewish one, it may well have been among those who
adopted the cult of Hercules in the time of the Seleucid Kings (2 *Maccabees* iv. 9–20), and
who were expelled by the Hasmoneans (1 *Maccabees* iv. 34–43). To be a 'Slave of the God' at
Ascalon would have meant being a foreign devotee of Hercules, who had taken refuge there.
The family name was Antipater, the Hebrew equivalent of which is Abiathar; 'Herod' was the
Greek cognomen and means 'heron', a sacred bird much studied by augurs and tabooed in
Leviticus xi.

memorized their genealogy. That Herod himself had Messianic pretensions is shown by the star which appeared on some of his copper coins; others bear an X within a wreath, the X being the Messiah's Greek initial and also the manner of his anointing.

(*p*) However, this engaging view, though given verisimilitude by a partial concealment under the Hellenistic doctrine of the Virgin Birth, and by Origen's hints at 'state secrets' of the Christian faith (*Against Celsus* i. 8), cannot stand careful historical scrutiny. It is based on *John's* account of the interview with Pilate, which has clearly been re-written to propitiate the Romans and to lay the blame for Jesus's judicial murder on the Jews; and Jesus's 'Thou sayest that I am King', which in Greek means 'yes', has an altogether different meaning in Aramaic (*see* cix.*k*). Besides, it is impossible that John the Baptist would have acclaimed and anointed a Roman citizen, a scion of the usurping and pagan House of Herod, whose death was proclaimed a festival in the Jewish calendar; nor is the Massacre of Bethlehem recorded in any other document, either non-Jewish or Jewish.

(*q*) The early Christians, though not above modifying a story for political ends, were truthful in intention and the picturesque Nativity story in *Matthew* and *Luke* hints at Jesus's royal birth; it has obviously, however, been influenced by the Pharaonic myth, which underlies the Mosaic legend, of the attempted slaying by the God Set of his nephew, Horus, the infant Sun-god. A late variant, current at the time that the Gospels were composed, is recorded by Suetonius (*Twelve Caesars: Octavius* 94), the part of Horus being taken by the infant Augustus, who was destined to succeed the Pharaohs.

> 'Julius Marathus . . . the freedman of Augustus writeth in the history of Augustus's life . . . that some six months before Augustus's nativity there happened at Rome a prodigy publicly known, whereby foreshown and denounced it was that Nature was about to bring forth a King over the people of Rome; at which the Senate being affrighted made an Act that no man-child born should be reared and brought up. But they whose wives were great-bellied (for every one was ready to draw the hope unto himself) took order that the said Act of the Senate should not be brought into the City Chamber and there enrolled.'

The confused Gospel account of Jesus's nativity, in fact, is composed of several unrelated elements: the secret tradition of his ritual re-birth at the Coronation, the Cyrus legend, the Horus legend, the Philonian metaphor of divine seed, the tradition that he was born at Bethlehem on the occasion of the Davidic registration, and the tradition that Herod destroyed the genealogical records as ruthlessly as he had destroyed three of his own children, who were innocent of any crime.

(*r*) It seems, further, that the confusion was prompted by a misreading of Jewish synagogue murals. *Matthew* ii. 1–8 and 13–18 could be derived from a

picture of Pharaoh ordering all Israelite children to be drowned as soon as
born (*Exodus* i. 22). The scene may be postulated as follows: Jewish mothers
are shown in full flight, with Egyptian soldiers in pursuit, but Amram and
Jochebed, concealed behind a bush, bend over a harvest basket daubed with
pitch in which they have laid the infant Moses; Israelite shepherds are at
hand, the Nile flows by, and the pyramids appear in the background. The
rescue of Moses was a favourite subject in Jewish and early Christian art;
four scenes are devoted to it in the Doura-Europos frescoes (*see Foreword k*).

Matthew ii. 9–11 suggests a second picture illustrating the Messianic prophecies of *Isaiah* lx. 3:

> 'The Gentiles shall come to thy light and Kings to the brightness of thy
> rising.'

and of *Psalm* lxxii. 11–17:

> 'All kings shall fall down before him, all creatures shall serve him. . . . And
> he shall live and unto him shall be given the gold of Sheba, and daily shall
> he be praised. His name shall endure for ever.'

But it may have an historical basis in a visit from Damascus of three Zado-
kites of the New Covenant (*see* VIII.*l*). *Matthew* ii. 18 suggests a third picture: Rachel weeping for the Children of Israel taken off into Captivity
(*Jeremiah* xxxi. 15). The editor of *Matthew* forgets that these children were
not killed and that Jeremiah, in his next two verses, promised their safe return.*

(*s*) The cave of the Nativity is mentioned in the *Protoevangelium,* and
Jerome wrote to Paulinus:

> 'Bethlehem used to be overshadowed by a grove of Adonis, and in the cave
> where Christ formerly wailed as an infant, they used to wail for the beloved
> of Venus.'

But the stable with its ox and its ass is an uncanonical fiction perhaps suggested by the manger and by the tradition that the Ox was the symbol of the
Messiah son of Joseph and the Ass that of the Messiah son of David. 'The
feet of the ox and the ass' (*Isaiah* xxxiii. 20) is so interpreted by the Rabbis
(*see* LXXVIII.*d*).

Jesus, as the Messiah, was necessarily connected with Bethlehem because
of the prophecy in *Micah* v. 2, and we have no reason to reject the Nazarene

---

* Hugh Schonfield in his *The Lost Book of the Nativity of John* (1929) suggests that the
Nativity legends of Jesus were originally applied to John the Baptist; he shows that traditions,
possibly earlier than the *Protoevangelium,* centred around the escape of the infant John from
the Bethlehem massacre, and that he was regarded by his Mandaean followers as the true
Messiah, in rivalry with Jesus. This may well be so; but the substitution of Jesus's name for
John's does not affect our argument that these legends had an iconotropic origin; indeed, Mr.
Schonfield underlines the close parallel between the Nativity legend of John as embodied in the
Mandaean *Sidrā d' Yahyā* (Book of John), a document based on first or second century tradi-
tions, and that of Moses.

belief that he was born there when Joseph went to record his pedigree. *Luke's* story of the adoration by the shepherds (*Luke* ii. 1–20) seems to be based on a tradition that shepherds tended Mary when she was overtaken by her birthpangs at night and without shelter. But *Luke* has perhaps also studied a mural, or an illustration to a Messianic book, showing a number of prophets in pastoral dress gazing up to Heaven where a large star appears among many lesser ones with open-mouthed angel faces. The prophets are addressed by a figure in resplendent dress who points to the large star—Moses, prophesying the star of the Messiah in *Numbers* xxiv. 17. Such a picture would also have referred to *Job* xxxviii. 7:

'The morning stars sang together and all the sons of God shouted for joy.'

(*t*) The taxing of 'Cyrenius' (*Luke* ii. 2)—Publius Sulpicius Quirinius—took place not during Herod's reign but in 6 A.D., after Archelaus's deposition (*Antiquities* xvii. 13. 5 and xviii. 1. 1) when, as Legate of the Imperial Governor of Syria, Quirinius ruled Judaea as a Roman protectorate; moreover, during an Imperial census everyone was required to stay in the town or village of his domicile. The historical facts, therefore, seem to be that Jesus was registered as a Galilean in the census of the year 6 A.D., but that Joseph had visited the Judaean Bethlehem in 4 or 5 B.C., when Herod ordered the House of David to give documentary proof of their pedigrees—which he then destroyed—and that Jesus had been born on this occasion.

(*u*) The author of *Matthew* ii. 23 is plainly uneducated: he quotes *Judges* xiii. 5 as though it were the prophets, and tries to connect 'Nazareth' with the Nazirite vow imposed on Samson before his birth—'Nazir' meaning a dedicated person. There is no record in either the Old Testament, the works of Josephus, or the Talmud, that such a place as Nazareth existed in Jesus's time; the word seems to have been an adjective *nōseriyyah,* meaning 'Galilean', applied to a village of another name—probably 'Bethlehem in Galilee', thus distinguishing it from 'Bethlehem in Judaea'. The name 'Bethlehem Nōseriyyah', which appears in the Jerusalem Talmud (*Megillah* i. 1) as 'Bethlehem 'Tsarayah' may have also been shortened to 'Nazara'; Eusebius mentions (*Ecc. Hist.* i. vii. 14) that relatives of Jesus were living at 'Nazaron' in later times. This northern Bethlehem lies in the vale of Esdraelon, a two-hours' journey from the modern Nazareth.

(*v*) That Jesus abstained from wine like John the Baptist and his disciples (*see* xxxix.*e and g*) and his 'brother' James the Just (*see* viii.*v*), seems certain, but he was not himself a Nazirite (*see* x.*d*). The word 'Nazarene' seems to have become attached to Jesus's followers from a punning combination of the unrelated words *Nazara, Nazirite,* and *Netzer* ('Branch'). (*Isaiah* xi. 1–11, *Jeremiah* xxiii. 5, *Isaiah* iv. 2–3—*see* lvi.*h*—and *Zechariah* iii. 8, and *The Testament of Levi* viii. 8—*see* viii.*n*). The variant 'Nazoraeans' may be a Greek form of *Nozrim,* the guardians, because they preserved the oral tradition of Jesus's acts and sayings. Further: we have every reason to suppose that Jesus worked at his father's trade of carpentry (*Matthew* xiii. 46 and *Mark* vi. 3—see xxxvii.*b*) until his thirtieth year; this was not incompatible with coming to Jerusalem and there studying under an able and distinguished Pharisaic teacher, as the *Toldoth Yeshu* records. Students were expected to work at a trade, as even the Heads of Academies prided themselves on doing (*see* xiii.*j*), and Justin Martyr notes (*Dialogue with Trypho,* 80) that in his time yokes and ploughs made by Jesus were still in existence. 'Jesus the Nazarene' may therefore have been a distinguishing nickname based on the Aramaic *n'sar,* a saw; as Judas Maccabaeus took his name from the hammer he wielded.

(*w*) 'Out of Egypt have I called my Son', quoted in *Matthew* ii. 11, comes from *Hosea* xi. 1; it is not a Messianic prophecy but concerns the Egyptian captivity of Israel.

The comment on Joseph's dream in *Matthew* i. 22–23 refers to the prophecy in *Isaiah* vii. 14–16, which is important as fixing the date of Jesus's birth: namely that while 'Emmanuel' was an infant both the ruling kings should die. This happened in 4 B.C., when Herod the Great executed his co-king Antipater and died himself five days later (Josephus: *Antiquities* xvii. 5.7 and 8.1); 'the land which Thou abhorrest' is not, however, to be read as 'Israel' in this context, but as 'the Wicked Kingdom of Edom', of which Herod had been a native. The quotation from *Isaiah* seems to have been curtailed by an editor who held that Jesus had known the difference between good and evil since birth. Joseph's dream (*Matthew* i. 19) and its result (*Matthew* i. 24–25) belong to an altogether different context (*see* viii.*q*). The introductory exclamation, which also greeted Jesus during his royal entry into Jerusalem (*see* lxxxix.*c*), is from *Psalm* cxlviii. 1.

We may restore the Nazarene oral tradition as follows:—

(1) *Glory to God in the highest; on earth peace; good will towards men!*

The birth of Jesus which became our Master, the Anointed One, was on this wise:

There went out a decree of Herod the Wicked, King of the Jews, that all they of the House of David should be gathered together at the city of David, which is called Bethlehem Ephratah, and there prove their lineage.

And one Joseph, son of Eli, which dwelt in that other Bethlehem called Nazara, a just man, took the roll of his lineage and went thither with his wife Mary, being great with child.

But when they entered into the city they found no room at the inn, for a great concourse of the Sons of David lodged there.

Then were the days accomplished that Mary should be delivered. And as they sought a house or a stable where they might find rest until morning, behold the pangs of travail came upon her and she cried out.

Now, there were shepherds abiding in the field, keeping watch over their flocks by night,

Which, when they heard her cries, came running to her and cared for her.

And she brought forth her first-born son in a cave that was nigh at hand,

and wrapped him in swaddling clothes and laid him in a harvest basket which the shepherds set before her.

And she called his name Jehoshua (which is Jesus); the same signifieth 'He shall save'.

For behold, an angel of the Lord had appeared unto her husband Joseph in a dream, saying: 'That which is conceived in thy wife Mary is full of the Holy Spirit.

'And she shall bring forth a son, and thou shalt call his name Jesus, for he shall save Israel from their sins.'

Now, certain of the Sons of David, when they heard the tidings of Jesus's birth which were given to them by the shepherds, came to salute Joseph and Mary and found them in the cave, and the babe lying in a basket.

And when they heard of the dream that Joseph had dreamed, they wondered and made known abroad the saying which was told them concerning the child, and returned to their own cities, glorifying and praising God.

* * * * *

(2) This Jesus was the prophet which should redeem Israel from the hands of Belial. Therefore he tasted no wine, like unto Samson the Nazirite which redeemed Israel from the hands of the Philistines.

Yea, more, he was that Branch whereof Isaiah prophesied: 'A branch' shall grow out of the roots of Jesse, and the Spirit of the Lord shall rest upon him, the Spirit of wisdom and understanding, the Spirit of counsel and might, the Spirit of knowledge and of the fear of the Lord.

'And shall make him of quick understanding in the fear of the Lord, and righteousness shall be the girdle of his loins.

'And it shall come to pass in that day that the Lord shall set His hand again the second time to recover the remnant of His people.

'In that day the Branch of the Lord shall be beautiful and glorious and the fruit of the earth excellent for them that are escaped of Israel.

'And he that is left in Zion shall be called holy, even every one that is written among the living of Jerusalem.'

Jeremiah also spake of him, saying: 'I will raise unto David a righteous Branch, and a King shall reign and prosper.'

That day was the prophecy of Micah fulfilled: 'But thou, Bethlehem Ephratah, though thou be little among the thousands of Judah, yet out of thee shall come forth unto Me that is to be ruler in Israel!'

* * * * *

(3) Then Herod the King, when they of the House of David brought their records unto him, destroyed them; for he was envious. Yet Mary kept the lineage of Jesus in her heart.

And it came to pass that while Jesus was yet a suckling, this same Herod having slain other children of his own, princes innocent of the charges he laid against them, went further and slew Antipater, his eldest son, which reigned beside him in Edom.

After these things Herod also died himself; nor did the Romans grant the title of King to Archelaus when he came to reign in Judaea in the room of his father Herod, nor unto any other man.

Thus was the prophecy fulfilled which Isaiah spake, saying: 'Behold, a damsel shall conceive and bear a son and shall call his name "Emmanuel", which is "God with us".

'Milk and honey shall he eat, that he may know to refuse the evil and choose the good.

'But before the child shall know to refuse the evil and choose the good, the land which Thou abhorrest shall be forsaken of both her Kings.'

* * * * *

(*x*) If, in the original Nazarene tradition, Isaiah's prophecy had been explained as thus referring to Herod and Antipater, that would account for the Alexandrian view, later suppressed, that Jesus was Antipater's son by a secret marriage to Mary.

(*y*) The first-century Nativity doctrine has been strongly influenced by the Eleusinian Mysteries. Catacomb paintings show that the Roman Christians made frequent use of Greek myth for devotional purposes: Ulysses and the Sirens symbolized the Christians' rejection of pagan lusts; Orpheus with his lute symbolized Jesus's sweet domination of mankind. In the Mysteries, the child Dionysus was displayed in a harvest basket by torchbearers in shepherds' dress:

> 'And the Hierophant himself cries in a loud voice: "Holy Brimo has borne a child! Holy is the generation that is spiritual, that is heavenly, that is from above, and mighty is he so engendered!" ' (*Philosophoumena:* Cruise's text, Paris 1860, *p.* 17).

The Goddess Brimo was a virgin and her child was a newly-reaped sheaf of corn, apparently made up into the semblance of a child, like the harvest 'corn dollies' of Essex; and that Jesus was born at Bethlehem, 'The House of Bread', and believed to have offered his flesh to be eaten as bread, made the parallel irresistibly close. Later, the Christian Fathers, in revenge for the calumnies of Celsus, depreciated the Eleusinian Mysteries as incestuous, saying that Zeus had begotten a bastard on his daughter; and eventually succeeded in suppressing them.

(*z*) This is not to suggest that the Gentile Christian equation of Jesus with bread was wholly Greek; it may well have been influenced by Egyptian, or Libyan, or Syrian, religious theory. In Haran, Abraham's former home in Syria, the women were still weeping for the Corn-Tammuz in the tenth century A.D. In Egypt and Libya the annually slain god Osiris was said to have announced: 'I am the barley!' and, according to a Coptic legend, God took a part of his own body and gave it to Jesus in the form of a grain of wheat with instructions to hand it to Michael, who in turn must hand it to Adam and teach him to sow and reap. Also in the Ugarit texts from Ras Shamra in the Sinai peninsula, both Alain (Baal) and his divine brother Mot (Tammuz) are referred to as foods: the goddess Anatha—who once had a temple at Jerusalem and gave her name to the village of Bethany—took Mot, cleft him with her sword, winnowed him in her harvest-basket, parched him at the fire, ground him in the mill and sowed him in the field; which recalls the ancient Scottish ballad of Sir John Barleycorn, borrowed by Burns. Finally Mot, like Sir John Barleycorn, sprouted as grain from the soil, and was eaten at the Feast of Unleavened Bread. The Jews of Jesus's day had, of course, no regard for pagan divinities such as Tammuz, Osiris, Maneros, or Mot, but outside Jewry the theory of the slain god's body being eaten as bread was a commonplace; and the Christian Manichees held that Jesus lived on in the vegetable kingdom, the whole of which they named *Jesus patibilis* —'Jesus perceptible'.

II

THE GENEALOGY

Matthew i. 1–17

[1]The book of the generation of Jesus Christ, the son of David, the son of Abraham.

[2]Abraham begat Isaac; And Isaac begat Jacob; And Jacob begat Judah and his brethren; [3]And Judah begat Phares and Zara of Thamar; And Phares begat Esrom; And Esrom begat Aram; [4]And Aram begat Aminadab; And Aminadab begat Naasson; And Naasson begat Salmon; [5]And Salmon begat Boaz of Rahab; And Boaz begat Obed of Ruth; And Obed begat Jesse; [6]And Jesse begat David the king.

And David the king begat Solomon of her that had been the wife of Uriah; [7]And Solomon begat Rehoboam; And Rehoboam begat Abijah; And Abijah begat Asa; [8]And Asa begat Jehosaphat; And Jehosaphat begat Joram; And Joram begat Uzziah; [9]And Uzziah begat Jotham; And Jotham begat Ahaz; [10]And Ahaz begat Hezekiah; And Hezekiah begat Manasseh; And Manasseh begat Amon; And Amon begat Josiah; [11]And Josiah begat Jechoniah and his brethren, about the time they were carried away to Babylon.

[12]And after they were brought to Babylon, Jechoniah begat Salathiel; And Salathiel begat Zerubbabel; [13]And Zerubbabel begat Abiud; And Abiud begat Eliakim; And Eliakim begat Azor; [14]And Azor begat Sadok; And Sadok begat Achim; And Achim begat Eliud; [15]And Eliud begat Eleazar; And Eleazar begat Matthan; And Matthan begat Jacob; [16]And Jacob begat Joseph the husband of Mary, of whom was born Jesus, Who is called Christ.

[17]So all the generations from Abraham to David are fourteen generations; and from David until the carrying away into Babylon are fourteen generations; and from the carrying away into Babylon unto Christ are fourteen generations.

Luke iii. 23–38

[23]And Jesus Himself began to be about thirty years of age, being (as was supposed) the son of Joseph, which was the son of Heli,

[24]Which was the son of Matthat, Which was the son of Levi, Which was the son of Melchi, Which was the son of Janna, Which was the son of Joseph, [25]Which was the son of Mattathias, Which was the son of Amos, Which was the son of Nahum, Which was the son of Esli, Which was the son of Nagge, [26]Which was the son of Maath, Which was the son of Mattathias, Which was the son of Semei, Which was the son of Joseph, Which was the son of Juda,

Luke iii. 23–38 (*contd.*)

²⁷Which was the son of Joanna, Which was the son of Rhesa, Which was the son of Zerubbabel, Which was the son of Salathiel,

Which was the son of Neri, ²⁸Which was the son of Melchi, Which was the son of Addi, Which was the son of Cosam, Which was the son of Elmodam, Which was the son of Er, ²⁹Which was the son of Jose, Which was the son of Eliezer, Which was the son of Jorim, Which was the son of Matthat, Which was the son of Levi, ³⁰Which was the son of Simeon, Which was the son of Juda, Which was the son of Joseph, Which was the son of Jonan, Which was the son of Eliakim, ³¹Which was the son of Melea, Which was the son of Menan, Which was the son of Mattatha, Which was the son of Nathan, Which was the son of David,

³²Which was the son of Jesse, Which was the son of Obed, Which was the son of Booz, Which was the son of Salmon, Which was the son of Naasson, ³³Which was the son of Aminadab, Which was the son of Aram, Which was the son of Esrom, Which was the son of Phares, Which was the son of Judah, ³⁴Which was the son of Jacob, Which was the son of Isaac, Which was the son of Abraham,

Which was the son of Terah, Which was the son of Nahor, ³⁵Which was the son of Saruch, Which was the son of Ragau, Which was the son of Peleg, Which was the son of Heber, Which was the son of Sala, ³⁶Which was the son of Cainan, Which was the son of Arphaxad, Which was the son of Shem, Which was the son of Noah, Which was the son of Lamech, ³⁷Which was the son of Methuselah, Which was the son of Enoch, Which was the son of Jared, Which was the son of Mahalaleel, Which was the son of Cainan, ³⁸Which was the son of Enos, Which was the son of Seth, Which was the son of Adam, Which was the son of God.

(*a*) These two genealogies cannot be reconciled with each other, even if one takes into consideration, as Eusebius did (*Ecc. Hist.* i. vii. 16), the Levirate Law which made it possible for a man 'to raise up seed unto his brother' (*Deuteronomy* xxv. 5). *Matthew's,* the shorter genealogy, is the more distinguished because it follows the royal line of Solomon down to Josiah, the last independent King of Judah before the Captivity; but *Luke's* is the more credible because it runs modestly through Nathan, a son of David who never came to the throne. By the forms of the Old Testament names they contain, both genealogies are shown to have been checked against the Greek translation of the Hebrew Scriptures. The traditional view is that *Matthew's* genealogy is really Mary's; yet like *Luke's,* it is made to end in Joseph the Carpenter. Joseph's Davidic descent seems to be established by the testimony of Hegesippus (Eusebius: *Ecc. Hist.* 3. xx. 1–2), that the grandsons of Jude, Jesus's brother according to the flesh, Galilean small-holders, admitted before the Emperor Domitian that they came of the House of David. They were by no means the only poor Jews of the first century who could trace their ancestry in a direct male line to David; the famous Hillel, another of them, had arrived at Jerusalem from Babylonia in a destitute condition. If our argument is sound, Hillel will have been in Bethlehem on the occasion of the Nativity.

(*b*) *Matthew* follows the linguistic form of *Genesis* iv. 18, *Ruth* iv. 18–22 and 1 *Chronicles* ii. 1–14, and takes his title 'The Book of the Generation' from *Genesis* v. 1. The table contains three sets of fourteen names each: from Abraham to David, from David to Jechoniah, from Jechoniah to Jesus. But there is a mistake in the reckoning: the first series needs both Abraham and David, and the third both Jechoniah and Jesus, to make up the canonical number.* Also, if the second series is compared with 1 *Chronicles* iii. 11, four Kings, namely Joash, Amaziah, Azariah, and Jehoiakim are found to have been omitted. The third series is seven generations shorter than the corresponding one in *Luke*. Of the three women in the genealogy, Tamar is mentioned apparently because she played the harlot with Judah; Rahab, because she was both a harlot and a heathen; Ruth, because she was a Moabitess— the Israelites were warned against having any dealing with Moab (*Deuteronomy* xxiii. 3–6) and children of a Moabite marriage were debarred from full citizenship for ten generations. Here the Christian editor emphasizes Jesus's humility in not abhorring such a line of sinful wombs, and his approval of mixed marriages. But that Rahab was the mother of Boaz is against Old Testament tradition and chronology. *Matthew's* genealogy, as we shall suggest, consists of two unrelated lines tacked together: the first Davidic, the second Aaronic (*see* VIII.*t and u*).

(*c*) *Luke* follows the lists of 1 *Chronicles* ii. 1–14, 24–27 and *Ruth* iv. 18–22 in the series from David to Adam. In the series from Abraham to Adam, however, *Cainan* occurs twice; and in the series from David to Abraham, *Admin* and *Arni* appear in place of the single name *Aram*. This has been done, it seems, to make the genealogy run in eleven sets of seven names each, with pauses at the more illustrious names. It is remarkable that no genealogy corresponding with *Luke's* record from Nathan to Jesus can be found anywhere in Hebrew literature; it has in common with *Matthew's* only the distinguished names *Salathiel* and *Zerubbabel* and that of Joseph's grandfather *Matthan,* if this is the same as *Matthat*. A confusion occurs in the part concerning Zerubbabel's parentage and posterity: *Luke* gives his grandfather as Neri, but this is probably a mistake for 'Assir'. Salathiel, Zerubbabel's father, was Jechoniah's son (1 *Chronicles* iii. 17) and the Talmud has Assir, 'prisoner' (*see Matthew* i. 11) either as Jechoniah's nickname or, in some texts, as the name of a second son, Salathiel's brother (*Vayikra Rabbah* x.). 'Judah, son of Johanan' is preferable to *Luke's* 'Joanna son of Rhesa'—'Rhesa' being probably Resha, 'the chief', a title of Zerubbabel's who was Governor of Judaea. Too many characteristically Levite names intrude into *Luke's* list for us to accept more than a small part of it, though he gives a probable number of generations for the period covered. After allowance has been made for

---

* Hugh Schonfield has restored a missing name in the third series from an old Hebrew text of *Matthew;* it is Abner, and has dropped out between Abiud and Eliakim. (Schonfield: *An Old Hebrew Text of Matthew's Gospel,* pp. 21–23).

the miscopying of Hebrew names by Greek scribes, it may be unconfidently
restored as follows:

(4) *Now this is the genealogy, according to the flesh, of Jesus which afterwards was called The Branch:*

He was the son of Joseph,
The son of Eli,
The son of Matthan,
The son of Levi,
The son of Johanan,
The son of Joseph,
The son of Mattathias,
The son of Amos,
The son of Nahum,
The son of Esli,
The son of Naggai,
The son of Maaz,
The son of Mattathias,
The son of Shimei,
The son of Joseph,
The son of Judah,
The son of Johanan,
The son of Zerubbabel the Governor,
The son of Salathiel,
The son of Jechoniah the captive,
The son of Melcheiram,
The son of Addi,
The son of Osamoth,
The son of Elmodam,
The son of Er,
The son of Joseph,
The son of Eliezer,
The son of Joram,
The son of Matthan,
The son of Levi,
The son of Simeon,
The son of Judah,
The son of Joseph,
The son of Johanan,
The son of Eliakim,
The son of Malchiah,
The son of Menahem,
The son of Mattathias,
The son of Nathan,
The son of David.

* * * *

(d) This younger Davidic line through Nathan had the advantage of escap-
ing both the curse of *Jeremiah* xxii. 28–30 and xxxvi. 30 on the elder line

fathered by the other Jechoniah (*Matthew* i. 11-12), and the censure of Ecclesiasticus (*Ecclesiasticus* xlix. 4) who announces that the royal line of David has proved itself unworthy of divine favour, only three kings having kept faith with God, and that their power has therefore been bestowed elsewhere.

(*e*) The Gnostics' identification of Jesus with 'The Word', the Second Person of an already formulated mystical Trinity (*see Introduction* III. *p-q*), could be reconciled with the tradition that, though incarnate in flesh, he had not been carnally begotten—'just as Hermes was the Word of Zeus', they said. The notion of his parthenogenous birth, in the literal and physical sense, was supported, for Greek readers of the Scriptures, by the Messianic prophecy in *Isaiah* vii. 14: 'Behold, a virgin shall conceive'; though 'virgin', as Celsus's Jewish mentor first pointed out (Origen: *Against Celsus* i. 30), is a Septuagint mistranslation* for 'young woman'. Yet the true tradition survived in *Luke* iii. 23, namely that 'Jesus himself began to be when about thirty years of age': then he was ceremonially re-born as the Son of God from an adoptive virgin mother—after which his original nativity ceased to be of importance, except to refute the charges of bastardy that were early brought against him.

(*f*) It is clear from several passages in the Gospels that Jesus was generally regarded as the son, by physical parenthood, of Joseph the Carpenter and his wife Mary. 'Is not this the son of Joseph?' (*Luke* iv. 22) and 'Is not this Jesus the son of Joseph whose father and mother we know?' (*John* vi. 42—*see* XXXVII.*b*). 'Joseph the husband of Mary, of whom was born Jesus, the Christ' (*Matthew* i. 16—*see* I.*c*). 'Son, thy father and I have sought thee sorrowing' (*Luke* ii. 48—*see* III.*b*).

(*g*) The earliest New Testament book mentioning the Nativity is the *Epistle to the Galatians*. There Paul writes: 'God sent forth His Son, made of women, made under the Law'—that is, legitimately—'that he might redeem those that were under the Law' (*Galatians* iv. 4-5). This is further supported by *Romans* i. 3 and *Hebrews* vii. 14, documents earlier than any of the Gospels; by the original text of *Matthew* i. 16, quoted in the *Dialogue of Timothy and Aquila,* and confirmed by the Sinaitic Syriac text, according to which 'Joseph to whom was espoused the Virgin Mary, begat Jesus who is called the Christ'; by almost precisely the same reading in the Vatican *Diatessaron;* by Peter's testimony (*Acts* ii. 30), that Jesus was 'of the fruit of David's loins according to the flesh'; finally by Irenaeus's statement (*Heresies* 3. xxi. 1), that the Ebionites (i.e. poor Nazarenes) considered Jesus to have been the son of Joseph—'thus adopting the view that the word "virgin" used by Isaiah means "young woman".'

(*h*) There can be little doubt that the original tradition made Jesus physically

---

* Isaiah's word is *almah* ('wench'), not *betulah* ('virgin'). Almah occurs in the plural *alumoth* in *Canticles* vi. 8: 'Sixty queens had Solomon, eighty concubines, *alumoth* without number'—where the word certainly does not mean 'virgins', but young women of a less exalted rank than the concubines—presumably they were expected to work in the Palace as well as to be ready for a summons to Solomon's couch.

the son of Joseph, the Galilean carpenter who claimed Davidic descent, and of his wife Mary. That he was not a senior member of the senior branch of the House of David may be taken for granted. Recognition by a divinely inspired prophet enroyalled Saul, David, and Jehu, none of whom had been born of royal stock; David was even a youngest son. If John the Baptist anointed Jesus King, and if the pilgrims and people of Jerusalem later so acclaimed him, then he was indeed King according to Jewish law, unless a rival came forward to dislodge him—as when Solomon brushed aside Adonijah's claims (1 *Kings* i. 39–53), or David re-asserted his kingship against Absalom (2 *Samuel* xviii. 1–4).

Jesus himself later raised in the Temple the only other question relevant to his acceptance as King (*Mark* xi. 30 and *Matthew* xxi. 25—*see* xciv.*a*), namely whether John was, or was not, a divinely inspired prophet. The Pharisees, in order to discourage sectarianism, had ruled that the age of prophecy terminated when the Law had been handed over by the minor prophets to the Men of the Great Assembly, afterwards to be known as the Great Sanhedrin (*Aboth* i. 1). It was recognized, however, that Elijah would return just before the Last Days (*Malachi* iv. 5–6), which explains why the membership of the Sanhedrin had been kept down to the uncanonical seventy-one—seventy-two being the number of letters in JHWH's full name— with one seat left vacant for Elijah. Until he arrived to claim it, the Sanhedrin exercised all the functions previously enjoyed by the prophets except that of adding to the canon of Scripture. Jesus himself regarded John the Baptist as Elijah (*Mark* ix. 13 and *Matthew* xvii. 12–13—*see* lxxix.*h*), and John seems to have quoted *Malachi* iii. 1–3 in the same sense (*see* v.*d*). *John* i. 21, where he denies that he is Elijah, must be a forgery, because it destroys Jesus's claim to royal Messiahship (*ibid.*).

(*i*) But if John were not a divinely inspired prophet, which meant Elijah and no other, then the coronation had to be regarded as a sectarian act until everyone understood by the fulfilment of prophecies that Jesus was the true Messiah (*see* xxxix.*f*). The Sanhedrin would not officially endorse his claims, and thereby risk an open revolt against Rome, until they were quite certain that he was no impostor; but neither would they oppose him, 'lest haply ye be found even to fight against God,' as Gamaliel I, their President, ruled shortly after the Crucifixion (*Acts* v. 34–40—*see* cxviii.*c*). What could not be disregarded was that John had died without having entered the Sanhedrin to claim Elijah's seat and deal with all the cases whose settlement had been postponed until his coming (*see* cxiii.*m*).

III

THE INFANCY

Luke ii. 21–52

²¹And when eight days were accomplished for the circumcising of the Child, His name was called JESUS, which was so named of the angel before He was conceived in the womb.

²²And when the days of her purification according to the law of Moses were accomplished, they brought Him to Jerusalem, to present Him to the Lord; ²³it is written in the law of the Lord,

Every male that openeth the womb shall be called holy to the Lord;

²⁴and to offer a sacrifice according to that which is said in the law of the Lord—*a pair of turtledoves, or two young pigeons.*

²⁵And, behold, there was a man in Jerusalem, whose name was Simeon; and the same man was just and devout, waiting for the consolation of Israel: and the Holy Ghost was upon him. ²⁶And it was revealed unto him by the Holy Ghost, that he should not see death, before he had seen the Lord's Christ. ²⁷And he came by the Spirit into the temple: and when the parents brought in the Child Jesus, to do for Him after the custom of the law, ²⁸then took he Him up in his arms, and blessed God, and said:

²⁹'Lord, now lettest Thou Thy servant depart
    According to Thy word, in peace:
³⁰For mine eyes have seen Thy salvation,
³¹Which Thou hast prepared before the face of all people;
³²A light to lighten the Gentiles,
    And the glory of Thy people Israel.'

³³And Joseph and His mother marvelled at those things which were spoken of Him. ³⁴And Simeon blessed them, and said unto Mary His mother:

'Behold, this Child is set for the fall and rising again of many in Israel;
    And for a sign which shall be spoken against;
³⁵(Yea, a sword shall pierce through thy own soul also,)
    That the thoughts of many hearts may be revealed.'

³⁶And there was one Anna, a prophetess, the daughter of Phanuel, of the tribe of Aser: she was of a great age, and had lived with an husband for seven years from her virginity: ³⁷and she was a widow of about fourscore and four years, which departed not from the temple, but served God with fastings and prayers night and day. ³⁸And she coming in that instant gave thanks likewise unto the Lord, and spake of Him to all them that looked for redemption in Jerusalem.

Luke ii. 21–52 (*contd.*)

³⁹And when they had performed all things according to the law of the Lord, they returned into Galilee, to their own city Nazareth.

⁴⁰And the Child grew, and waxed strong in spirit, filled with wisdom: and the grace of God was upon Him.

⁴¹Now his parents went to Jerusalem every year at the feast of the passover. ⁴²And when He was twelve years old, they went up to Jerusalem after the custom of the feast. ⁴³And when they had fulfilled the days, as they returned, the Child Jesus tarried behind in Jerusalem; and Joseph and His mother knew not of it. ⁴⁴But they, supposing Him to have been in the company, went a day's journey; and they sought Him among their kinsfolk and acquaintance. ⁴⁵And when they found Him not, they turned back again to Jerusalem, seeking Him. ⁴⁶And it came to pass, that after three days they found Him in the temple, sitting in the midst of the doctors, both hearing them, and asking them questions. ⁴⁷And all that heard Him were astonished at His understanding and answers. ⁴⁸And when they saw Him, they were amazed: and His mother said unto Him: 'Son, why hast Thou thus dealt with us? behold, Thy father and I have sought Thee sorrowing.' ⁴⁹And he said unto them:

'How is it that ye sought Me? wist ye not that I must be about My Father's business?'

⁵⁰And they understood not the sayings which He spake unto them. ⁵¹And He went down with them, and came to Nazareth, and was subject unto them: but His mother kept all these sayings in her heart.

⁵²And Jesus increased in wisdom and stature, and in favour with God and man.

(*a*) The many miraculous stories of Jesus's childhood in the *Protoevangelium,* the *Pseudo-Matthew* and the *Gospel of Thomas* are not worth examining or even recording here.

It is usually taken for granted that Jesus was publicly circumcised in the Temple, but the rite in his day remained a private one performed in the home by a *mohel,* or qualified surgeon (*Antiquities* xx. 2. 4); not until the Middle Ages did the custom arise of circumcising in the synagogue. Mary's purification ceremony will have taken place thirty-two days later (*Leviticus* xii. 4). The prescribed sacrifice was a lamb for a burned offering, and a turtle-dove or pigeon for a sin-offering (*Leviticus* xii. 6), but since Jesus was later supposed to have been begotten without sin, the editor of *Luke* does not mention that it was a sin-offering (*Luke* ii. 24). That old Anna, or Hannah, prophesied his future is credible; but since Jesus the infant was not yet the Anointed One of *Luke* ii. 26, Simeon's prophecy must belong to a later context (*see* viii.*w*), and his song, the *Nunc Dimittis,* to a still later one (*see* cxvi.*f*). For Simeon's identity *see* viii.*q, u and v.*

(*b*) It need not be doubted that Jesus was lost by his parents during the Passover, and found in the Temple, though it has been suggested by J. M. Robertson that the story is borrowed from pagan myth. According to Jewish folklore, twelve years was the age when both Moses and Samuel began to prophesy, and Jesus may have felt that he had now reached a turning-point in his religious life. But a twelve-year-old child, however brilliant, would hardly have been allowed to intervene in a doctorial dispute. Neither, if he was so well versed in the Law, would he have dishonoured his parents by the rude rejoinder, quoted in *Luke* ii. 49; this detail seems rather to reflect the manners of the Gentile Christian period, when the family peace was often broken by the conversion of a son or daughter. Some explanation of his failure to notify Joseph that he wished to stay behind must have dropped out, and also an antecedent remark which would explain 'My Father's business'.

(5) *And when the eight days were accomplished, the child was circumcised, and when the forty days were accomplished for the purification of Mary his mother, Joseph brought these twain from Bethlehem to the Temple at Jerusalem.*

There he offered the sacrifice ordained by the law, namely a lamb for a burned offering, and a turtledove for a sin-offering, and he presented the child Jesus to the Lord.

Now, there was one Hannah a prophetess, the daughter of Phanuel of the tribe of Assher. She was of a great age and had lived with an husband seven years from her virginity.

And she was now a widow of about four-score and four years, which departed not from the women's court of the Temple, but served God with fastings and prayers night and day.

She coming in that instant when the child was presented, gave thanks unto the Lord, and prophesied of him to all the saints of her acquaintance, saying: 'He will be a great one and a present help in the redemption of Israel.'

But when his parents had performed all things according to the Law they returned into Galilee, to their own city Nazara.

And the Child grew and waxed strong in spirit, filled with wisdom, and the grace of the Lord was upon him.

* * * * *

(6) *When the child Jesus was twelve years old, his parents went to Jerusalem to keep the feast of Passover, as their custom was.*

And after that they had fulfilled the days, as they returned, the child tarried behind in Jerusalem.

But his mother and father supposing him to have been in the company of their kinsfolk and acquaintance, went a day's journey.

And when they found him not that night, on the morrow they turned back again to Jerusalem, seeking him. And it came to pass that on the third day they found him in a porch of the Temple, where the doctors expounded the Law, sitting in the midst of their disciples.

Now, the doctors were astonished to find such love of learning in so young a child; for he had asked them many questions as they entered into the porch where they taught.

But Mary said unto him: 'Son, why hast thou thus dealt with us? Behold, thy father and I have sought thee suffering.'

And Jesus fell at their feet and desired their forgiveness, but he asked them: 'How is it that ye sought me?'

For one of his kinsfolk, having business to perform in Jerusalem, had undertaken to plead with Joseph and Mary that Jesus might tarry with him there for certain days, and afterwards return to Galilee in his company.

And when they asked further: 'But wherefore didst thou desire to tarry here, not being also a merchant?' he answered: 'Wist ye not that I must be about the Father's business?'

Then he went down with them and came again to Nazara, and was subject unto them until Joseph his father died.

And he increased in wisdom and stature, and in the favour of God and man.

*   *   *   *   *

IV

JOHN'S BIRTH

Luke i. 5–25

5There was in the days of Herod, king of Judaea, a certain priest named Zacharias, of the course of Abia: and his wife was of the daughters of Aaron, and her name was Elisabeth. 6And they were both righteous before God, walking in all the commandments and ordinances of the Lord blameless. 7And they had no child, because that Elisabeth was barren, and they both were now well stricken in years.

8And it came to pass, that while he executed the priest's office before God in the order of his course, 9according to the custom of the priest's office, his lot was to burn incense when he went into the temple of the Lord. 10And the whole multitude of the people were praying without at the time of incense. 11And there appeared unto him an angel of the Lord standing on the right side of the altar of incense. 12And when Zacharias saw him, he was troubled, and fear fell upon him. 13But the angel said unto him:

'Fear not, Zacharias: for thy prayer is heard; and thy wife Elisabeth shall bear thee a son, and thou shalt call his name John. 14And thou shalt have joy and gladness; and many shall rejoice at his birth. 15For he shall be great in the sight of the Lord, and shall drink neither wine nor strong drink; and he shall be filled with the Holy Ghost, even from his mother's womb. 16And many of the children of Israel shall he turn to the Lord their God. 17And he shall go before Him in the spirit and power of Elijah, to turn the hearts of the fathers to the children, and the disobedient to the wisdom of the just; to make ready a people prepared for the Lord.'

And Zacharias said unto the angel: 'Whereby shall I know this? for I am an old man, and my wife well stricken in years.' 19And the angel answering said unto him:

'I am Gabriel, that stand in the presence of God; and am sent to speak unto thee, and to shew thee these glad tidings. 20And, behold, thou shalt be dumb, and not able to speak, until the day that these things shall be performed, because thou believest not my words, which shall be fulfilled in their season.'

21And the people waited for Zacharias, and marvelled that he tarried so long in the temple. 22And when he came out, he could not speak unto them: and they perceived that he had seen a vision in the temple: for he beckoned unto them, and remained speechless. 23And it came to pass, that, as soon as the days of his ministration were accomplished, he departed to his own house.

24And after those days his wife Elisabeth conceived, and hid herself five months, saying, 25Thus hath the Lord dealt with me in the days wherein He looked on me, to take away my reproach among men.

Luke i. 39–80

[39]And Mary arose in those days, and went into the hill country with haste, into a city of Judah; [40]and entered into the house of Zacharias, and saluted Elisabeth. [41]And it came to pass, that, when Elisabeth heard the salutation of Mary, the babe leaped in her womb; and Elisabeth was filled with the Holy Ghost: [42]and she spake out with a loud voice, and said: 'Blessed art thou among women, and blessed is the fruit of thy womb. [43]And whence is this to me, that the mother of my Lord should come to me? [44]For, lo, as soon as the voice of thy salutation sounded in mine ears, the babe leaped in my womb for joy. [45]And blessed is she that believed: for there shall be a performance of those things which were told her from the Lord.' [46]And Mary said:

'My soul doth magnify the Lord,
[47]And my spirit hath rejoiced in God my Saviour.
[48]For he hath regarded the low estate of His handmaiden:
For, behold, from henceforth all generations shall call me blessed.
[49]For He that is mighty hath done to me great things;
And holy is His name.
[50]And His mercy is from generation to generation,
On them that fear Him.
[51]He hath shewed strength with His arm;
He hath scattered the proud in the imagination of their hearts.
[52]He hath put down the mighty from their seats,
And exalted them of low degree.
[53]He hath filled the hungry with good things;
And the rich He hath sent empty away.
[54]He hath holpen His servant Israel,
In remembrance of His mercy;
[55]As He spake to our fathers,
To Abraham, and to his seed for ever.'

[56]And Mary abode with her about three months, and returned to her own house.

[57]Now Elisabeth's full time came that she should be delivered; and she brought forth a son. [58]And her neighbours and her cousins heard how the Lord had shewed great mercy upon her; and they rejoiced with her. [59]And it came to pass, that on the eighth day they came to circumcise the child; and they called him Zacharias, after the name of his father. [60]And his mother answered and said: 'Not so; but he shall be called John.' [61]And they said unto her: 'There is none of thy kindred that is called by this name.' [62]And they made signs to his father, how he would have him called. [63]And he asked for a writing table, and wrote, saying: 'His name is John.' And they marvelled all. [64]And his mouth was opened immediately, and his tongue loosed, and he spake, and praised God. [65]And fear came on all that dwelt round about them: and all these sayings were noised abroad throughout all the hill country of Judaea. [66]And all they that heard them laid them up in their hearts, saying, 'What manner of child shall this be?' And the hand of the Lord was with him.

Luke i. 39–80 (*contd.*)

⁶⁷And his father Zacharias was filled with the Holy Ghost, and prophesied, saying:
⁶⁸'Blessed be the Lord God of Israel;
  For he hath visited and redeemed His people,
⁶⁹And hath raised up an horn of salvation for us
  In the house of His servant David;
⁷⁰As He spake by the mouth of His holy prophets,
  Which have been since the world began:
⁷¹That we should be saved from our enemies,
  And from the hand of all that hate us;
⁷²To perform the mercy promised to our fathers,
  And to remember His holy covenant;
⁷³The oath which He sware to our father Abraham,
⁷⁴That He would grant unto us, that we being delivered out of the hand
    of our enemies
    Might serve Him without fear,
⁷⁵In holiness and righteousness before Him,
  All the days of our life.
⁷⁶And thou, child, shalt be called the prophet of the Highest:
  For thou shalt go before the face of the Lord to prepare His ways;
⁷⁷To give knowledge of salvation unto His people
  By the remission of their sins,
⁷⁸Through the tender mercy of our God;
  Whereby the dayspring from on high hath visited us,
⁷⁹To give light to them that sit in darkness and in the shadow of death,
  To guide our feet into the way of peace.'
⁸⁰And the child grew, and waxed strong in spirit, and was in the deserts
  till the day of his shewing unto Israel.

(*a*) Another account of Zacharias's dumbness, quoted by Epiphanius from the lost Gnostic Gospel *The Descent of Mary* (*Against Heresies* xxvi. 12), is that an Ass-god appeared in the Sanctuary to Zacharias, which frightened him out of his wits, and that he was stoned to death for blasphemy when he reported the matter to the High Priest: the implication here is that the mysterious 'Blood of Zacharias son of Barachias' mentioned by Jesus shortly before the Crucifixion (*Matthew* xxiii. 35—*see* XIII.*u and v*), was shed on this occasion.*

(*b*) *Luke's* account, if less strange, is no more credible. We may believe that the prophet Isaiah had a vision of a seraph, or winged serpent, which fetched him a coal of fire from this very altar in token of his prophetic mission (*Isaiah* vi. 6); but the need for a premature domestic announcement to Zacharias, in interruption of a sacred rite, is not apparent. A similar announcement to Joseph the Carpenter about the far more important birth of Jesus was, according to *Matthew* i. 20, made merely in a dream.

---

* The historical possibilities of this incident, and of Jesus's alleged Herodian descent, are worked out in *King Jesus.*

(*c*) That John was the son of Zacharias—the Greek form of 'Zechariah'—a priest of the course of 'Abia', or Abijah, mentioned in 1 *Chronicles* xxiv. 10, may be accepted as historical; and it is possible that *Luke's* story has been deduced in good faith from a sacred picture of Isaiah having the coal placed on his mouth—the coal being mistaken for a gag—and that the legend ran: 'Hear ye indeed but understand not, and see ye indeed, but perceive not.' This was the message which Isaiah had been told by the angel to give, and which Jesus quoted at the Last Supper. If a companion picture showed Isaiah prophesying: 'Unto us a child is born' (*Isaiah* ix. 6), and if a third showed the prophet Zechariah in his rough garment enjoying a vision of the Son of Man as he stood upon the Mount of Olives, with the legend: 'The prophecy of Zechariah concerning the Messiah' (*Zechariah* xiv. 4)—then the story in *Luke* will have been deduced from these three loosely related pictures read in sequence. The first picture was interpreted as Zacharias the priest being struck dumb; the second as the birth of his son John; and the third as his prophecy that John would herald the Messiah. However, *Luke* i. 15–17, if transposed from the future to the historic tense, seems to be part of the genuine tradition. It contains a quotation from *Malachi* iv. 5–6.

(*d*) The praise of Zacharias and Elisabeth as blameless in their observance of the Law shows them to have been Pharisees; had they been Sadducees, they would have been condemned by the Nazarenes as lost souls. The word 'blameless' was later interpreted as 'sexually chaste' and gave rise to the story that John was also parthenogenously born. The legend of Elisabeth's bearing a child in her old age seems to be derived from that of Sarah (*Genesis* xxi. 2); an announcement of Isaac's birth had been made to Abraham by an angel under the oaks of Mamre (*Genesis* xvii. 9), and Sarah had laughed incredulously. *Luke* i. 25 similarly echoes Rachel's story, who had also been childless (*Genesis* xxx. 23); and in the *Protoevangelium* 17, just before the Nativity, Joseph turned to Mary as they went to register their pedigree at Bethlehem and saw her laughing (*see* 1.0).

(*e*) 'The Song of Zacharias' is clearly Nazarene in origin but seems to have been adapted to serve as a dramatic monologue in Gentile Christian churches. Over-familiarity with its phrases prevents most Christians from realizing that the verses, syntax, and argument are hopelessly confused. Verse 76, for instance, is clearly an interpolation; in verse 70 the prophets, not God, are absurdly made coeval with the world; and in verse 77 John is credited with the Messiah's task. The song is strongly reminiscent of a victory hymn in the recently discovered Hebrew scroll, apparently of the second century B.C., called 'The War Between the Sons of Light and the Sons of Darkness':

> And there all of them shall bless the God of Israel and together exalt his name with joy. Then they shall lift up their voices and say:
> 'Blessed be the God of Israel who layeth up kindness for the [people] of his covenant

'And [storeth up] the testimonies of his salvation to the people whom he hath redeemed . . .

'And we, thy holy people, will praise thy name by showing forth thy faithful acts

'And exalt thee by relating thy mighty deeds.

'Arise, arise, O most mighty God, and be lifted up in thy strength!'

(*f*) This Song is composed of quotations from the Law and the Prophets and seems to have been found prefacing a copy of the *Acts and Sayings*. Parts of it have been inappropriately added to Mary's *Magnificat* speech, in answer to Elisabeth, with verses 54 and 55 duplicating verses 68, 72 and 73 (*see* vii.*k*). It may originally have run as follows, the quotations at the end being from *Malachi* iii. 12 and *Psalms* lxxi. 19 and cxi. 9, traces of which appear in *Luke* i. 48–49. The 'dayspring from on high' is Jesus regarded as the Sun of Righteousness (*Malachi* iv. 2).

HYMN

Blessed be the Lord God of Israel, which hath visited and redeemed His people,

To perform the mercy promised to our fathers, and to remember His holy covenant, the oath which He sware to our father Abraham and his seed for ever:

That He would grant us delivery from our enemies and from the hands of all that hate us,

To serve Him with fear, in holiness and righteousness before Him, all the days of our life.

For He hath raised up an horn of salvation for us in the house of His servant David,

To give knowledge of salvation unto His people for the remission of their sins and to guide our feet into the way of peace.

Come, let us exalt the tender mercy of our God, which hath been since the world began and which shall continue on them that fear Him from generation to generation!

For thereby the dayspring from on high hath visited us, with healing in his wings: to give light to them that sit in darkness and in the shadow of death.

As God spake by the mouth of His holy prophets, saying:

'O Israel, all nations shall call you blessed, for ye shall be a delightful land.

'Thy righteousness, O God, is very high, which hast done great things. O who is like unto God?

'For He hath sent redemption unto His people; He hath commanded His covenant for ever; holy and reverend is His name!'

* * * * *

(7) *There was also in the days of Herod the Wicked, King of the Jews, a certain priest named Zechariah of the course of Abijah, and his wife was of the daughters of Aaron and her name was Elisabeth.*

*And they were both righteous before God, walking in all the command-
ments and ordinances of the Lord after the manner of the Pharisees, blameless.*

*And a son was born unto them which was called John, and he waxed
strong in spirit.*

*Now, John was great in the sight of the Lord and drank neither wine nor
strong drink, and was filled with the Holy Spirit even from his mother's
womb.*

*Many were the children of Israel which afterwards he turned to the Lord
their God,*

For he would not minister in the Temple as his father did,

But was seized by the spirit of prophecy, and driven out into the wilderness.

*And there he went before God in the spirit and power of Elijah, to turn
the hearts of the fathers unto the children (even as Malachi prophesied) and
the disobedient unto the wisdom of the just, to make ready a people prepared for the Lord.*

* * * * *

JOHN'S PREACHING

Mark i. 1–8

[1]The beginning of the Gospel of Jesus Christ, the Son of God. [2]As it is written in the prophets:

> *Behold I send my messenger before Thy face,*
> *Which shall prepare Thy way before Thee,*
> [3]*The voice of one crying in the wilderness,*
> *Prepare ye the way of the Lord,*
> *Make His paths straight.*

[4]John did baptize in the wilderness, and preach the baptism of repentance for the remission of sins. [5]And there went out unto him all the land of Judaea, and they of Jerusalem, and were all baptized of him in the river of Jordan, confessing their sins. [6]And John was clothed with camel's hair, and with a girdle of a skin about his loins; and he did eat locusts and wild honey; [7]and preached, saying:

> 'There cometh One mightier than I after me, the latchet of Whose shoes I am not worthy to stoop down and unloose. [8]I indeed have baptized you with water: but He shall baptize you with the Holy Ghost.'

Matthew iii. 1–12

[1]In those days came John the Baptist, preaching in the wilderness of Judaea, [2]and saying: 'Repent ye: for the kingdom of heaven is at hand. [3]For this is he that was spoken of by the prophet Isaiah, saying:

> *The voice of one crying in the wilderness,*
> *Prepare ye the way of the Lord,*
> *Make His paths straight.'*

[4]And the same John had his raiment of camel's hair, and a leathern girdle about his loins; and his meat was locusts and wild honey. [5]Then went out to him Jerusalem, and all Judaea, and all the region round about Jordan, [6]and were baptized of him in Jordan, confessing their sins. [7]But when he saw many of the Pharisees and Sadducees come to his baptism, he said unto them: 'O generation of vipers, who hath warned you to flee from the wrath to come? [8]Bring forth therefore fruits meet for repentance: [9]and think not to say within yourselves, We have Abraham to our father: for I say unto you, that God is able of these stones to raise up children unto Abraham. [10]And now also the axe is laid unto the root of the trees: therefore every tree which bringeth not forth good fruit is hewn down, and cast into the

Matthew iii. 1–12 (*contd.*)

fire. [11]I indeed baptize you with water unto repentance: but He that cometh after me is mightier than I, Whose shoes I am not worthy to bear: He shall baptize you with the Holy Ghost, and with fire. [12]Whose fan is in His hand, and He will thoroughly purge His floor, and gather His wheat into the garner: but He will burn up the chaff with unquenchable fire.'

Luke iii. 1–18

[1]Now in the fifteenth year of the reign of Tiberius Caesar, Pontius Pilate being governor of Judaea, and Herod being tetrarch of Galilee, and his brother Philip tetrarch of Ituraea and of the region of Trachonitis, and Lysanias the tetrarch of Abilene, [2]Annas and Caiaphas being the high priests, the word of God came unto John the son of Zacharias in the wilderness. [3]And he came into all the country about Jordan, preaching the baptism of repentance for the remission of sins; [4]as it is written in the book of the words of Isaiah the prophet, saying:

> *The voice of one crying in the wilderness,*
> *Prepare ye the way of the Lord,*
> *Make his paths straight*
> [5]*Every valley shall be filled, and every mountain and hill*
>   *shall be brought low;*
> *And the crooked shall be made straight,*
> *And the rough ways shall be made smooth;*
> [6]*And all flesh shall see the salvation of God.*

[7]Then said he to the multitude that came forth to be baptized of him: 'O generation of vipers, who hath warned you to flee from the wrath to come? [8]Bring forth therefore fruits worthy of repentance, and begin not to say within yourselves, We have Abraham to our father: for I say unto you, that God is able of these stones to raise up children unto Abraham. [9]And now also the axe is laid unto the root of the trees: every tree therefore which bringeth not forth good fruit is hewn down, and cast into the fire.' [10]And the people asked him, saying: 'What shall we do then?' [11]He answereth and saith unto them: 'He that hath two coats, let him impart to him that hath none; and he that hath meat, let him do likewise.' [12]Then came also publicans to be baptized, and said unto him: 'Master, what shall we do?' [13]And he said unto them: 'Exact no more than that which is appointed you.' [14]And the soldiers likewise demanded of him, saying: 'And what shall we do?' And he said unto them: 'Do violence to no man, neither accuse any falsely; and be content with your wages.'

[15]And as the people were in expectation, and all men mused in their hearts of John, whether he were the Christ, or not; [16]John answered, saying unto them all:

'I indeed baptize you with water; but One mightier than I cometh, the latchet of Whose shoes I am not worthy to unloose: He shall baptize you with the Holy Ghost and with fire; [17]Whose fan is in His hand, and He will thoroughly purge His floor, and will gather the wheat into His garner; but the chaff He will burn with fire unquenchable.'

[18]And many other things in his exhortation preached he unto the people.

John i. 1–38

¹In the beginning was the Word, and the Word was with God, and the Word was God. ²The same was in the beginning with God. ³All things were made by Him; and without Him was not any thing made that was made. ⁴In Him was life; and the life was the light of men. ⁵And the light shineth in darkness; and the darkness comprehended it not.

⁶There was a man sent from God, whose name was John. ⁷The same came for a witness, to bear witness of the Light, that all men through him might believe. ⁸He was not that Light, but was sent to bear witness of that Light. ⁹That was the true Light, which lighteth every man that cometh into the world. ¹⁰He was in the world, and the world was made by Him, and the world knew Him not. ¹¹He came unto His own, and His own received Him not. ¹²But as many as received Him, to them gave He power to become the sons of God, even to them that believe on His name: ¹³which were born, not of blood, nor of the will of the flesh, nor of the will of man, but of God.

¹⁴And the Word was made flesh, and dwelt among us, (and we beheld His glory, the glory as of the only begotten of the Father) full of grace and truth. ¹⁵John bare witness of Him, and cried, saying:

'This was He of whom I spake, He that cometh after me is preferred before me: for He was before me. ¹⁶And of His fulness have all we received, and grace for grace. ¹⁷For the law was given by Moses, but grace and truth came by Jesus Christ. ¹⁸No man hath seen God at any time; the only begotten Son, which is in the bosom of the Father, He hath declared Him.'

¹⁹And this is the record of John, when the Jews sent priests and Levites from Jerusalem to ask him: 'Who art thou?' ²⁰And he confessed, and denied not: but confessed: 'I am not the Christ.' ²¹And they asked him: 'What then? Art thou Elijah?' And he saith: 'I am not.' 'Art thou that prophet?' And he answered: 'No.' ²²Then said they unto him: 'Who art thou? that we may give an answer to them that hath sent us. What sayest thou of thyself?' ²³He said: 'I am

The voice of one crying in the wilderness,
Make straight the way of the Lord,

as said the prophet Isaiah.' ²⁴And they which were sent were of the Pharisees. ²⁵And they asked him, and said unto him: 'Why baptizest thou then, if thou be not that Christ, nor Elijah, neither that prophet?' ²⁶John answered them, saying: 'I baptize with water: but there standeth One among you, Whom ye know not. ²⁷He it is, Who coming after me is preferred before me, Whose shoe's latchet I am not worthy to unloose.' ²⁸These things were done in Bethabara beyond Jordan, where John was baptizing.

²⁹The next day John seeth Jesus coming unto him, and saith: 'Behold the Lamb of God, Who taketh away the sin of the world. ³⁰This is He of Whom I said, After me cometh a man Who is preferred before me: for He was before me. ³¹And I knew Him not: but that He should be made manifest to Israel, therefore am I come baptizing with water.' ³²And John bare record, saying:

John i. 1–38 (*contd.*)

'I saw the Spirit descending from heaven like a dove, and it abode upon Him. [33]*And I knew Him not: but He that sent me to baptize with water, the same said unto me: Upon Whom thou shalt see the Spirit descending, and remaining on Him, the same is He Who baptizeth with the Holy Ghost.* [34]*And I saw, and bare record, that this is the Son of God.'*

[35]Again the next day after John stood, and two of his disciples; [36]and looking upon Jesus as He walked, he saith: 'Behold the Lamb of God.' [37]And the two disciples heard him speak, and they followed Jesus. [38]Then Jesus turned, and saw them following, and saith unto them:

'What seek ye?'

They said unto Him: 'Rabbi, (which is to say, being interpreted, Master,) where dwellest Thou?'

(*a*) John the Baptist, who anticipated Jesus's view that the end of the world was imminent, followed in the footsteps of the ancient Hebrew prophets and wore the pastoral 'rough garment', mentioned in *Zechariah* xiii. 4, as a sign of his calling. Like Elijah he was girded in leather (2 *Kings* i. 8), and hid himself in the wilderness (1 *Kings* xvii. 3–5 *and* xix. 4–18).

(*b*) Baptism, one of the three ritual acts by which a Gentile became an adoptive Son of Abraham, is said to have attained greater importance in the first century A.D. than the other two, namely circumcision and Temple sacrifice. Indeed, Rabbi Joshua ben Hananyah (late first and early second centuries) held that baptism alone was sufficient initiation ceremony for a proselyte (*Yebamoth* 46a *and* b). The proselyte entered the water where 'two learned men, standing over him, taught him a few light and a few grave Commandments, and when he had dipped and emerged, he was like an Israelite in every respect.' He then uttered a benediction: 'Blessed art Thou, O Lord, who hast sanctified us by Thy Commandments and commandest us concerning baptism.' Proselytes were 'as children newly born' (*Yebamoth* 22a).

(*c*) Did John then intend to convey, by his baptism of certain Jews, that Israel as a whole was doomed, and that every man must look to his own salvation? This seems to be the meaning of *Matthew* iii. 10; his call is a traditional combination of threats with promises. If so, he will have used the cross symbol drawn in water on the brow, as a sign that the penitent was to be spared when the six angels of the Lord came to slay the faithless (*Ezekiel* ix. 4–6). Despite *Luke* iii. 1, Eisler maintains (on the strength of a passage in the Slavonic translation of Josephus's *Jewish Wars* (*see* XLI.*b*)), that John began his missionary work under the Ethnarch Archelaus in the year 5 A.D., which was some twenty-three years before he baptized Jesus in the 'fifteenth year of the reign of Tiberius'. The Gospels themselves suggest that John had worked for a long time previously, since he had a large following when Jesus first came to him (*Mark* i. 5).

(*d*) John clearly regarded himself as the 'voice crying in the wilderness' of

Isaiah xl. 3, the forerunner of the Lord (*Malachi* iii. 1–3) who turns out to be Elijah and reconciles the sons to the fathers (*Malachi* iv. 5–6). He intended to select and crown the Messiah who would redeem the remnant of Israel, as Samuel had selected and crowned the national saviours Saul and David. *Mark* i. 8 and *Matthew* iii. 11 are influenced by *Acts* ii. 4, where the flames of the Holy Spirit are said to have lighted upon the heads of the disciples after the Crucifixion. But it is not clear whether John's: 'He shall baptize you with fire,' referred only to the universal purifying blaze through which the remnant would have to pass before their regeneration in the Kingdom of Heaven (*Isaiah* iv. 4 and *Malachi* iv. 1)—this is explained in *Matthew* iii. 12—or whether he was also referring to the fire-kindling ceremony with which every King of Israel began his reign (*see* viii.*c and y*).

(*e*) What the 'locusts' in *Mark* i. 6 and *Matthew* iii. 4 were has been disputed. Some say 'locust beans', that is to say carobs, the 'food of repentance' (*see* xviii.*a*). Others, that they were winged locusts, some varieties of which are 'clean' according to *Leviticus* xi. 22; these could be gathered in large quantities when they rested in their flight across Palestine from Central Africa and, after the removal of their wings, pounded into a paste. But locust invasions were infrequent, and the paste would not remain edible for any great length of time. 'Carobs' is by far the better reading because John's 'bring forth the fruits of repentance' seems to refer to the repentant palm-tree that promised carobs (*Ahikar* viii. 35—*see* xvi.*b*). According to Epiphanius (*Against Heresies* xxx.), the early *Gospel of Matthew* in the possession of the Ebionites, contained the following:

> 'John's meat was wild honey, whereof the taste is of manna, and a cake dipped in oil.'

Epiphanius adds:

> '. . . that, forsooth, they may pervert the word of truth into a lie and for locust, *akris,* put a cake, *enkris.'*

But, by their mention of oil, the Ebionites point to the text quoted by John, namely *Deuteronomy* xxxii. 13–15, which concerns wild honey and oil. Josephus mentions a similar prophet, Banus the Nazirite, who lived in the wilderness, dressed in the leaves of a tree (presumably the tough leaves of the carob), ate only wild fruit and bathed night and day many times in cold water for purity's sake (*Life,* 2).

(*f*) *Matthew* iii. 11 preserves another version of the 'shoes' saying: 'Whose shoes I am not worthy to bear'. The literal Aramaic will have been: 'Whose shoes I am too small to bear' (*Erubin* 27*b*). In the Egyptian coronation ritual the King put on a pair of papyrus shoes, and Hocart shows in his *Kingship* that this is paralleled in many similar rituals, including the English until the reign of George II. The shoes were an emblem of the fertile land that would now become the King's domain. Even in common land-contracts an Israelite would draw off his shoe and hand it to the purchaser in token of seisin (*Ruth* iv. 7–12), and 'over Edom will I cast my shoe' (*Psalm* lx. 8), means 'I will take possession of Edom'. John here modestly expresses his own unworthiness as officiating priest to give seisin of the realm to the new King. (*g*) The 'Pharisees and Sadducees' of *Matthew* iii. 7 are greeted with words which either belong to a different context (*Matthew* xxiii. 33—*see* XIII.*w*), or are quoted, as there, from *Isaiah* lix. 5. John is calling his opponents vipers that have been hatched by the enemies of God; but he can hardly have meant to include the Pharisees in his denunciation of the Sadducees, since they had never collaborated with the Romans. In *Matthew* iii. 9 John reminds the Sadducees that, under Pharisaic Law, any wandering Arabian may become an honorary Son of Abraham. 'Stones' is a play on words: in Hebrew *abanim* means 'stones' and *banim* means 'sons'.* He is referring to Abraham as the Rock from which the people of Israel were hewn (*Isaiah* li. 1–2), and of which, according to *Deuteronomy* xxxii. 15, they were criminally unmindful. There are several midrashic passages in which the Children of Abraham are symbolized by stones. For instance: 'And Jacob took twelve stones from the altar whereupon his father Isaac had been bound and laid them under his head in that place for a sign that twelve tribes should spring from him in the fullness of time' (*Pirke di Rabbi Eliezer,* 35). For Jesus's quotation in *Matthew* iii. 8 and 10—*see* XLVII.*b*.

(*h*) The additions to John's preaching in *Luke* iii. 11–14 must be rejected. If the publicans had consulted him he would have warned them to collect no more taxes for the Romans; and he would have ordered the Israelite soldiers—also in Roman pay—to lay down their weapons. It may be that these interpolations, made by the same Gentile editor who improved on the story of the Centurion (*see* XXXIII.*a*), were at first attributed to Jesus, but later rejected as uncanonical and finally, as a compromise, attributed to John. The suggestion, in *Luke* iii. 15, that the people wondered whether John were the Messiah seems gratuitous.

(*i*) The Gnostic introduction to *John* (verses 1–19) is a clear warning that a great deal of the Gospel must be discounted as tendentious. This warning is made good at once by John's downright denial in verse 21 that he is Elijah, which contradicts *Matthew* xvii. 13 (*see* LXXIX.*h*) and has been patched in from a similar question addressed to Jesus in *Mark* vi. 15 (*see* LXXVII.*b*); the editor who thus destroyed Jesus's Messianic credentials (*see* II.*h*, XIII.*a and* XXXIX.*h*) must have realized that the Last Days which Elijah was expected to herald had not, in fact, come. But though it seems incredible at first sight that the priestly deputation sent from Jerusalem (*John* i. 24) were Pharisees, most of the priesthood being Sadducees, this is not to be dismissed as an invention; it is evident that Jesus was associated with a family of priestly Pharisees which provided leaders for the Nazarene Church after his departure (*see* VIII.*v*; CXVI.*b and* CXVIII.*w and x*).

---

* A curious parallel occurs in the Greek myth of Deucalion and Pyrrha, who, after the Universal Deluge, threw stones over their shoulders and found them magically converted into men and women: 'Hence, in Greek, *laos* means both a stone and a people.'

(*j*) *Beth-abara,* the 'House of Food', may be a misreading of *Beth-arabah,* 'the House in Arabah' (*Joshua* xv. 6), one of the six cities of the Negeb. Or it may be another place, the now traditional baptismal site near the mouth of the *Wadi el-Kelt,* where pilgrims bathe, at the north-west corner of the Dead Sea—for Origen could find no 'Beth-abara' or 'Beth-arabah' beyond Jordan. But some MSS read 'Bethany', not 'Bethabara', and Sir George Grove has suggested that the original text was *Bethanabra,* which is a Septuagint spelling of *Beth-nimrah* (*Joshua* xiii. 27), 'place of pure water', an oasis some thirteen miles east of Jordan, nearly opposite Jericho.

(*k*) Josephus records of John (*Antiquities* xviii. 5. 2) that 'he was a good man and commanded the Jews to exercise virtue and righteousness towards each other and piety towards God and so come to baptism'. He does not mention John's Messianic preaching as such, but says that Herod Antipas who 'feared that John's great influence over the people might put it into his power and intention to raise a rebellion, had him sent a prisoner to the castle of Machaerus [on the west coast of the Dead Sea] and there put to death.' Antipas's arrest of John shows that he was preaching within the tetrarchy, which included the part of Peraea (Transjordan) in which Beth-Nimrah lay (*see* XLI.*a and* LXXVI.*a*).

Mark begins by quoting *Malachi* iii. 1–3 and *Isaiah* xl. 3. John's saying about the axe being laid to the root of the tree is drawn from *Isaiah* v. 1–7. 'His fan is in his hands' is quoted from *Jeremiah* xv. 7.

PROEM

(ii) THE BEGINNING OF THE GOSPEL CONCERNING JESUS, THE ANOINTED SON OF GOD.

*   *   *   *   *

(8) *John baptized in the wilderness of Beth-Nimrah and preached the baptism of repentance, for the remission of sins.*

And there went over unto him multitudes from Jerusalem and from all the land of Judaea, and confessed their sins, and were baptized.

*   *   *   *   *

(9) *And when there came out unto him certain priests of his kinsfolk, which were Pharisees, to enquire what he did, he answered:* 'It is written in the book of the prophet Malachi:

' "*Behold, I will send my messenger and he shall prepare the way before me, and the Lord whom ye seek shall suddenly come to His Temple.*

' "*But who may abide the day of His coming? For He is like a refiner's fire. And I will come near to you in judgement."*

'*Also it is written in the book of the prophet Isaiah:* "*The voice of one crying in the wilderness: Prepare ye the way of the Lord, make straight in the desert a highway to our God.*

' "*For the glory of the Lord shall be revealed and all flesh shall see it together." '*

*   *   *   *   *

(10) *And John was clothed with a rough garment of camel's hair and with breeches of skin about his loins, and his meat was carobs of repentance.*

He ate wild honey also from the rock. For he said: 'Moses testified: "The Lord found Israel in this desert land, in the waste wilderness, and made him to suck honey out of the rock and oil out of the flinty rock.

' "But when Israel went into Canaan and ate butter of kine and milk of sheep and fat of lambs and wheat and drank the pure blood of the grape, then he waxed fat and kicked and forsook God and lightly esteemed the rock of his salvation." Therefore am I returned hither to the desert.'

And John preached: 'Now is the axe laid unto the root of trees in the vineyard; as Isaiah prophesied that every vine bearing wild grapes shall be hewn down and cast into the fire. Bring forth therefore the fruits of repentance.

'For there cometh one mightier than I, whose shoes I am not worthy to bear, nor stooping down to set them upon his feet.

'I indeed have baptized you with water, but he shall baptize you with consuming fire.

'Of him Malachi prophesied: "Behold, the day cometh that all the proud, and they that do wickedly, shall be burned up as stubble; but unto them that fear God shall the Sun of Righteousness arise with healing in his wings."

'And Jeremiah spake in the name of the Lord: "I will fan them with a winnowing fan and bereave them of children."

'Behold, now, God's fan is in His hand, and He will thoroughly cleanse His threshing floor and gather the wheat into the garner, but He will burn the chaff with unquenchable fire.

'For the anointed King is at hand, the Son of God.'

* * * *

(11) *And when certain men also of the Sadducees came to John to enquire what he did, he cried unto them: 'O ye that are hatched from the eggs of vipers, as the prophet Isaiah testified, who hath warned you to flee from the wrath to come?*

'Say not within yourselves: "We are children of Abraham, which is called the Rock." For in like manner as God once made the twelve stones that our forefather Jacob gathered to be his sons, and tribes in Israel, so He is able of these abanim, *which is stones, to raise up new* banim, *which is children, unto Abraham!'*

* * * *

(*l*) John's ascetic fare did not make for gentleness. A prolonged diet of carobs plays havoc with the intestines (*see* XVIII.*a*), and honey is notoriously bilious in effect.

* * * *

(*m*) [Here follows the Pharisees' decision not to accept John as a reincarnation of Elijah until they were certain that the prophecy of *Malachi* iv. 5–6 referred to him (*see* XXXIX.*h*).]

VI

THE ACCLAMATION

Jerome: Dialogue against Pelagius iii. 2

In the *Gospel according to the Hebrews* which is indeed in the Chaldaean and Syrian speech but is written in Hebrew letters, which the Nazarenes use to this day, called 'according to the apostles', or, as most term it, 'according to Matthew', which also is to be seen in the library of Caesarea, the story tells: 'Behold the mother of the Lord and his brethren said unto him: John Baptist baptizeth unto the remission of sins; let us go and be baptized of him. But he said unto them: Wherein have I sinned, that I should go and be baptized of him? unless peradventure this very thing that I have said is *a sin of* ignorance.'

Matthew iii. 13–15

[13]Then cometh Jesus from Galilee to Jordan unto John, to be baptized of him. [14]But John forbad Him, saying: 'I have need to be baptized of Thee, and comest Thou to me?' [15]And Jesus answering said unto him:

'Suffer it to be so now: for thus it becometh us to fulfil all righteousness.'

Then he suffered Him.

John i. 29–36

[29]The next day John seeth Jesus coming unto him, and saith: 'Behold the Lamb of God, Who taketh away the sin of the world. [30]This is He of Whom I said, After me cometh a man Who is preferred before me: for He was before me. [31]And I knew him not: but that He should be made manifest to Israel, therefore am I come baptizing with water.' [32]And John bare record, saying:

'*I saw the Spirit descending from heaven like a dove, and it abode upon Him.* [33]*And I knew Him not: but He that sent me to baptize with water, the same said unto me: Upon Whom thou shalt see the Spirit descending, and remaining on Him, the same is He Who baptizeth with the Holy Ghost.* [34]*And I saw, and bare record, that this is the Son of God.*'

[35]Again the next day after John stood, and two of his disciples; [36]and looking upon Jesus as He walked, he saith: 'Behold the Lamb of God.'

John i. 47–51

[47]Jesus saw Nathanael coming to Him, and saith of him:

'Behold an Israelite indeed, in whom is no guile.'

John i. 47–51 (*contd.*)

⁴⁸Nathanael saith unto Him: 'Whence knowest thou me?' Jesus answered and said unto him:

'Before that Philip called thee, when thou wast under the fig tree, I saw thee.'

⁴⁹Nathanael answered and saith unto Him: 'Rabbi, Thou art the Son of God; Thou art the King of Israel.' ⁵⁰Jesus answered and said unto him:

'Because I said unto thee, I saw thee under the fig tree, believest thou? thou shalt see greater things than these.'

⁵¹And He saith unto him:

'Verily, verily, I say unto you, hereafter ye shall see heaven open, and the angels of God ascending and descending upon the Son of Man.'

(*a*) The 'sin of ignorance' mentioned in *The Gospel according to the Hebrews* is a reference to *Psalm* xix. 12; Jesus is suggesting that John's baptism calls for an entire change of heart (*see* v.*c*), and should properly be reserved for gross sinners only. But he fears to be presumptuous, and therefore goes.

(*b*) John's recognition of Jesus has been characteristically altered in *John* i. 29–36, but his sudden choice of the destined King from among the brothers has a genuine ring: it recalls Samuel's choice of David in 1 *Samuel* xvi. 5–13 (*see* LXVIII.*e*). When he hails Jesus as the 'Lamb of God that taketh away the sins of the world' he is referring both to *The Testament of Levi* xviii. 6 (*see* i.*f*) and to *Enoch* xc.38 (*see* LXXXVIII.*h*). 'With the Father's voice as from Abraham to Isaac' is a reference to *Genesis* xxii. 8: 'Abraham said: "My son, God will provide Himself a lamb for a burned offering."' Abraham had received a divine command to offer up Isaac as a sin-offering instead of the usual lamb, and Isaac uncomplainingly followed him to Mount Zion. The Messiah was thus commanded to hold himself in readiness as the nation's sin-offering—according to the prophecy of *Zechariah* (*see* CII.*e*). Like the victim of *Isaiah* liii. 7: 'He was led like a lamb to the slaughter'—but trusted that, like Isaac, he would not be allowed to perish.

(*c*) John's choice was apparently made at first sight of Jesus, though he may have already heard rumours of his wisdom and his asceticism, and been aware of his Davidic genealogy. Jesus's looks recommended him perhaps: according to the earliest Christian art-tradition, he was red-haired like David. Also, St. Ephraim the Syrian records in his *Gospel Commentaries*: 'God took human form and appeared in a form of three human ells; he came down to us in small stature.' So John, seeing Jesus with his brothers, will have remembered Samuel's rejection of David's tall brother Eliab (1 *Samuel* xvi. 7—*see* LXVIII.*e*), in favour of little David. Jesus apparently refers to the missing ell of his own stature in *Matthew* vi. 27 (*see* LXV.*a*). Tertullian mentions Jesus's *corpusculum,* his 'insignificant little body' (*Against Marcion* iii. 17), and the best that Jerome can say of him is that 'if he did not have a heavenly look in

his face and eyes, the apostles would never have hastened to follow him'
(*Epistle* 65).

(*d*) The story of the Temptation suggests an interval between the Acclamation and the Coronation, paralleled in 1 *Samuel* x. 8, during which Jesus
fasted (*see* LXXVIII.*e*) while John visited Jerusalem to summon Mary the
Braider (*see* VII.*a*), and Bethany to summon Simeon the Chaste and his
daughter Mary (*see* VIII.*s*).

> (13) *Now it came to pass after that Joseph the son of Eli was dead in Nazara,
> that the brethren of Jesus called him from where he sat under a fig-tree; and
> his mother said unto him before them all:*
>
> *'John the Baptist baptizeth beyond Jordan unto the remission of sins. Let
> us go, thou and I and thy brethren, to be baptized of him.'*
>
> *Jesus answered and said unto her: 'Have we so greatly offended against
> God or against our neighbours that thou shouldest say this thing?*
>
> *'Nevertheless, our father David prayed: "O cleanse Thou me of my secret
> faults. Keep me from the sin of presumption." Therefore will I go with
> thee and with my brethren, according to thy word.'*

*   *   *   *   *

(*e*) The passage in *John* i. 47–51 is corrupt. According to the Nazarene
tradition, the only Israelite in whom there was no guile—that is to say deliberate, as opposed to unwitting, sin—was Jesus (1 *Peter* ii. 22); Nathanael
(Bartholomew) certainly showed guile when he fled and forsook his master
on the Mount of Olives. Perhaps the editor of *John* found the word 'Emmanuel', John's title for Jesus, copied in the *Acts and Sayings* as 'Nathanael'.
The opening of the heavens took place only at the Coronation, when
Nathanael, so far as is known, was not present.

(*f*) In *Matthew* iii. 14–15 John seems to be referring to the fire-baptism; but
Jesus's somewhat awkward answer fits another context far better (*see* VIII.*q*).

(*g*) *John* i. 30 is Gnostic doctrine: Jesus is identified with The Word, 'begotten before all the worlds'.

> (14) *And forthwith they left their dwellings and went to Beth-Nimrah across
> Jordan.*
>
> *John, seeing Jesus coming unto him in the midst of his brethren, stood amid
> two of his disciples,*
>
> *And looking upon Jesus as he walked, he said unto them: 'Behold Emman-
> uel, an Israelite indeed in whom there is no guile! Here cometh the Lamb
> of God which shall take away the sins of the world.*
>
> *'For He that sent me to baptize with water, the same said unto me:
> "In whom thou shalt see the Spirit of the Lord dwelling, the same is he
> which shall be called the Son of God." '*
>
> *John therefore baptized the mother of Jesus and his brethren, but when
> Jesus came to be baptized John forbade him, saying privily: 'Nay, for thou
> art set aside from all thy brethren, as was my father Levi.'*
>
> *Jesus saith unto him: 'Whence knowest thou me?'*

He answered him, saying: 'Wert thou not called hither from under thy fig-tree?'

Jesus said: 'I perceive that thou art indeed a prophet.'

John spake and said: 'I prophesy greater things than these. Thou shalt become the Son of God, thou shalt become the King of Israel! Hereafter thou shalt see Heaven open and the Spirit of God poured in a fountain upon thee! Then shall I have need to be baptized of thee.

'Now, behold, as the prophet Samuel spake to Saul, so speak I to thee: "Seven days shalt thou tarry till I come unto thee and shew thee what thou shalt do."'

Jesus therefore went apart into a mountain to pray, but his mother and his brethren turned back into Galilee.

* * * *

(*h*) Jesus's apparent unwillingness to be crowned conforms with ancient coronation etiquette. An early cylinder-seal from South Palestine, reproduced in *King Jesus,* shows the king modestly resisting the priest who comes to anoint and lead him up to the hill of coronation. So Saul, also, in modesty 'hid himself among his stuff' (1 *Samuel* x. 21–23).

(*i*) The fig-tree reference is to *Zechariah* iii. 10 (*see* VIII.*e*).

VII

THE ANNUNCIATION

Luke i. 26–56

[26]And in the sixth month the angel Gabriel was sent from God unto a city of Galilee, named Nazareth, [27]to a virgin espoused to a man whose name was Joseph, of the house of David; and the virgin's name was Mary. [28]And the angel came in unto her, and said:

'Hail, thou that art highly favoured, the Lord is with thee: blessed art thou among women.'

[29]And when she saw him, she was troubled at his saying, and cast in her mind what manner of salutation this should be. [30]And the angel said unto her:

'Fear not, Mary: for thou hast found favour with God. [31]And, behold, thou shalt conceive in thy womb, and bring forth a son, and shalt call His name JESUS. [32]He shall be great, and shall be called the Son of the Highest: and the Lord God shall give unto Him the throne of His father David: [33]and He shall reign over the house of Jacob for ever; and of His kingdom there shall be no end.'

[34]Then said Mary unto the angel: 'How shall this be, seeing I know not a man?' [35]And the angel answered and said unto her:

'The Holy Ghost shall come upon thee, and the power of the Highest shall overshadow thee: therefore also that holy thing which shall be born of thee shall be called the Son of God. [36]And, behold, thy cousin Elisabeth, she hath also conceived a son in her old age: and this is the sixth month with her, who was called barren. [37]For with God nothing shall be impossible.'

[38]And Mary said: 'Behold the handmaid of the Lord; be it unto me according to thy word.' And the angel departed from her.

[39]And Mary arose in those days, and went into the hill country with haste, into a city of Judah; [40]and entered into the house of Zacharias, and saluted Elisabeth. [41]And it came to pass, that, when Elisabeth heard the salutation of Mary, the babe leaped in her womb; and Elisabeth was filled with the Holy Ghost: [42]and she spake out with a loud voice, and said: 'Blessed art thou among women, and blessed is the fruit of thy womb. [43]And whence is this to me, that the mother of my Lord should come to me? [44]For, lo, as soon as the voice of thy salutation sounded in mine ears, the babe leaped in my womb for joy. [45]And blessed is she that believed: for there shall be a performance of those things which were told her from the Lord.' [46]And Mary said:

Luke i. 26–56 (*contd.*)

'My soul doth magnify the Lord,

[47]And my spirit hath rejoiced in God my Saviour.

[48]For He hath regarded the low estate of His handmaiden:

For, behold, from henceforth all generations shall call me blessed.

[49]For He that is mighty hath done to me great things;

And holy is his name.

[50]And His mercy is from generation to generation,

On them that fear Him.

[51]He hath shewed strength with His arm;

He hath scattered the proud in the imagination of their hearts.

[52]He hath put down the mighty from their seats,

And exalted them of low degree.

[53]He hath filled the hungry with good things;

And the rich He hath sent empty away.

[54]He hath holpen His servant Israel,

In remembrance of His mercy;

[55]As He spake to our fathers,

To Abraham, and to his seed for ever.'

[56]And Mary abode with her about three months, and returned to her own house.

Protoevangelium 10–11

[10]And there was a council of the priests, saying: 'Let us make a veil for the temple of the Lord.' And the priest said: 'Call to me undefiled virgins of the family of David.' And the officers went away, and sought, and found seven virgins. And the priest remembered the child Mary, that she was of the family of David, and undefiled before God. And the officers went away and brought her. And they brought them into the temple of the Lord. And the priest said: 'Choose for me by lot who shall spin the gold, and the white, and the fine linen, and the silk, and the blue, and the scarlet, and the true purple.' And the true purple and the scarlet fell to the lot of Mary, and she took them, and went away to her house. And at that time Zacharias was dumb, and Samuel was in his place until the time that Zacharias spake. And Mary took the scarlet, and span it.

[11]And she took the pitcher, and went out to fill it with water. And behold, a voice saying: 'Hail, thou who hast received grace; the Lord is with thee; blessed art thou among women!' And she looked round, on the right hand and on the left, to see whence this voice came. And she went away trembling, to her house, and put down the pitcher; and taking the purple, she sat down on her seat, and drew it out. And, behold, an angel of the Lord stood before her, saying: 'Fear not, Mary; for thou hast found grace before the Lord of all, and thou shalt conceive, according to His word.' And she hearing, reasoned with herself, saying: 'Shall I conceive by the Lord, the living God? and shall I bring forth as every woman brings forth?' And the angel of the Lord said: 'Not so, Mary; for the power of the Lord shall overshadow thee: wherefore also that holy thing which shall be born of thee shall be called the Son of the Most High. And thou shalt call His name Jesus, for He shall save His people

Protoevangelium 10–11 (*contd.*)

> from their sins.' And Mary said: 'Behold, the servant of the Lord before His face: let it be unto me according to thy word.'

(*a*) If the word 'angel', which in Greek and Hebrew means no more than 'messenger', is taken literally, there is no reason to doubt the historic truth of this strange announcement. 'Gabriel' can only have been John the Baptist. Jesus, in order to be engrafted into the tribe of Levi, and thus qualify as the Priest-king of the *Testament of Levi* (*see* VIII.*i and f*), needed an adoptive mother. John was aware that every Hebrew coronation ceremony implied ritual death and re-birth; in the *Protoevangelium* (x. 1–2) he emphasizes that the birth will not be a physical one. Samuel had told Saul at his anointing: 'The Spirit of the Lord shall come upon thee, and thou shalt be turned into another man' (1 *Samuel* x. 6). To ensure the pure perfection of Jesus's kingship, John seems therefore to have chosen a virgin, a relative of his mother's who, according to the *Protoevangelium* 7–12, had been dedicated to the Temple service at birth, in conformity with *Leviticus* xxvii. 6, and was employed on the work of making the 'veil of the Temple' (*Exodus* xxvi. 31), a very heavy carpet covering the entrance to the Holy of Holies. We must, of course, discount as nonsensical the story in the *Protoevangelium* of how the veil came to be made, though the author of it has got the main colours right. These were: the colour of Palestinean linen (a pale yellow) to represent the earth, purple for water, scarlet for fire, and blue for air (Josephus: *Wars* v. 5. 4). Six threads of each of these colours were contained in every 'lace', seventy-two laces forming the thickness of the veil (*Shekalim* viii. 5). The decision 'Let us make a veil for the Temple of the Lord,' reached by a Council of Priests, is charmingly naïve. Thirteen veils (curtains) hung at various doors and gates; a Temple official was responsible for their maintenance and renewal at regular intervals (*Kethuboth* 106*a* and *Shekalim* v. 1).

(*b*) Dr. Raphael Patai, Director of the Israeli Institute of Folklore and Ethnology, in his *Hebrew Installation Rites* (*Cincinnati,* 1947), emphasizes the importance of re-birth in Old Testament coronation references.

> It has already been noted by Hocart that the entering of the spirit of God into the newly anointed king (*Saul:* 1 *Samuel* x. 6 *and* 9; *David:* 1 *Samuel* xvi. 13), in consequence of which he 'turns into another man' (*Saul:* 1 *Samuel* x. 6, *cf.* v. 9), closely corresponds to other peoples' ceremonies which symbolize the death and re-birth of the king (Hocart: *Kingship p.* 86). According to Hocart, the general theory of the installation ritual is that 'the king (1) dies; (2) is re-born, (3) as a god' (*Op. cit. p.* 70). Traces of the existence of this theory in the Hebrew installation ritual can be found in *Psalm* ii, which puts the following words in the mouth of God: 'I have set up my King upon Zion, my sacred mountain.' This statement is answered by the king: 'I will declare the statute; the Lord hath said unto me, Thou art my son, this day have I borne thee . . .' (*Psalm* ii. 6–7—*in Hebrew*

'begotten, fathered', but lit. 'borne'). To quote only one African example in which the re-birth of the king on the day of his enthronement, referred to in this Psalm, is most strikingly enacted, let us mention the following detail from the coronation ceremonies of the Atah (the king) of Idah, a state lying in the angle formed by the Niger and the Benue. 'Two officers, the Onobe Ogbo, "the oldest man in the world", and the Oneda, the "birth giver", sport together as man and wife, then the Oneda mimics child-birth, and after a diviner has prophesied the child will be "a boy . . . lord of the earth", the Atah appears from beneath the skirts of the Oneda . . .' (Seligman: *Egypt and Negro Africa, p.* 44). While noting the parallelism between the African enactment and the Hebrew reference, one must not lose sight of the difference between the African King's ritual re-birth by a court-official, and the Hebrew king's re-birth by God. Though, also in the African installation rite, the theory seems to be that the king is 'reborn as a son of the gods' (Meek: *Sudanese Kingdom, p.* 137).

As to the ancient Hebrew concept that the Davidic king is the Son of God, there is ample evidence to this effect also, in addition to *Psalm* ii, in the Psalter and in other biblical writings (*e.g.* 2 *Samuel* vii. 14; 1 *Chronicles* xvii. 13; *Psalm* lxxxix. 27–28). According to later Jewish tradition, the king becomes on the day of his coronation 'like a one year old babe who has not known the taste of sin' (*Midrash Samuel* 17; *cf. Yoma* 22*b; Jer. Bikkurim* iii. 2), while the concept that the spirit of God enters into the anointed one so that he becomes the Son of God, re-appears in the Gospels in the baptism-story of Jesus (*John* i. 32–34; *Matthew* iii. 16–17; *Mark* i. 10–11; *Luke* iii. 21–22).

(*c*) Dr. Patai does not mention the importance attached to the King's mother in the royal chronicles of Israel and Judah, nor the fact that Solomon, first called Jedidiah, evidently had two mothers: a physical one, probably Abigail the Carmelitess, through whom (despite 2 *Samuel* xii. 24) it seems that he had a better right to the throne by primogeniture than his rival Adonijah (1 *Kings* i. 11); and his adoptive mother Bathsheba, who gave him his ritual name 'Solomon'*. The power of the Queen-mother was so great that Solomon abased himself before her and stationed her on his right hand (1 *Kings* ii. 19 and *Psalm* xlv. 9). It was her particular task to crown the new King (*Canticles* iii. 11):

'Go forth, O ye daughters of Zion, and behold King Solomon with the crown wherewith his mother crowned him in the day of his espousals.'

A coronation was, at the same time, an espousal (*see* viii.o).

(*d*) The ancient Hebrew ceremony of adoption must have been a mimic re-birth under the adoptive mother's skirts, as it was in ancient Greece,† and as it still is in Idah (*see* (*b*) *above*); since the expression 'I spread my skirt

---

* Adonijah's claim may have rested on his having been the first son born after David's accession to the throne of all Israel.

† Diodorus Siculus (iv. 39) relates that Zeus persuaded Hera to adopt Heracles as her son, when he became a god, by pretending to be in labour and then producing him from under her skirts—'the adoption ritual still in use among many barbarian tribes'.

over thee and covered thy nakedness,' is used in *Ezekiel* xvi. 8 to describe God's adoption of Israel, a bastard child abandoned in a field. In patriarchal times it became the custom for the father, not the mother, to spread his skirt over an adopted son or daughter, as Ruth asked Boaz to do (*Ruth* iii. 9). She was therefore 'borne' by Boaz, rather than 'begotten'. At a coronation re-birth, the purple mantle placed over the King represented the womb, and in royal Hindu ritual it is still so called. In *Zechariah* iii. 5–8 the angel of the Lord addresses the High Priest Joshua when thus invested and calls all the other priests to witness his re-birth as 'The Branch'. That Moses, though born of Jochebed, is called the 'adopted son of Bithiah, the daughter of Pharaoh' in the Talmud (*Megillah* 13a), suggests the tradition of a coronation ritual, at which a priestess representing the 'Daughter of Pharaoh', the Goddess to whom Solomon dedicated a shrine on Temple Hill (1 *Kings* vii. 8), acted as his virgin mother. Sir Flinders Petrie has suggested that Moses is an Egyptian word meaning: 'Unfathered son of a princess'—in other words: 'Royal son of a virgin'.

(e) J. M. Robertson (*Christianity and Mythology, pp.* 305ff) has found an Egyptian parallel to the Annunciation in the Luxor temple sculptures reproduced by Sharpe. The Virgin-queen Mautmes is approached by ibis-headed Thoth, the Egyptian Hermes, and told that she will bear a son. In the next scene, Nechbet the Goddess of Childbirth, and Hathor, Goddess of Love, take the Queen's hand and hold the *crux ansata,* symbol of life, to her mouth. Lastly, Pharaoh is born as an infant and adored by the deities and priests assisting at the Coronation. Mautmes was, in theory, impregnated by the Sun-god Amen-Ra, who in an inscription in honour of Rameses II and III says to the Pharaoh: 'I am thy father. I have begotten thee upon thy revered mother.' This, like *Psalm* ii. 7, 'Thou art my beloved Son, this day have I begotten thee', referred to a coronation re-birth, not to a physical birth. The parallel would be still closer if dog-headed Anubis, Gabriel's counterpart in Egypto-Jewish mythology, not Thoth, whose counterpart was the archangel Michael, had made the Annunciation; but that it was Gabriel who came emphasizes the authenticity of the story—Gabriel being, like John, the herald of the Last Days.

(f) The identity of this Mary to whom the Annunciation was made may be deduced from the account of the three women who went to the Tomb to anoint and take away Jesus's body (*see* cxv.b). No women except those of his immediate family would have had both the right and the obligation to do so. The three at the Tomb, according to *Mark,* were Mary ('of Cleophas') 'the mother of James the Less and of Joses'; Mary Magdalene; and Salome (*Mark* xv. 40, 47 and xvi. 1). Salome, the last mentioned, is identified by *Matthew* with the mother of Zebedee's children (*Matthew* xxvii. 56), two of Jesus's leading disciples; but this is probably a mistake. An early editor of *Matthew,* finding 'Salome' mentioned without a hint at her identity, held her to be the proud mother of James and John in *Matthew* xx. 20 (*see*

LXII.*c*). She is likely, rather, to have been the elderly virgin, a relative of the two Marys, whose conversation with Jesus, suppressed by the Synoptics, has been preserved by Clement of Alexandria (*see* XXI.*n*). The *Protoevangelium* 19 and 20 makes her assist at Jesus's birth; which may preserve the tradition that she played the ritual part of midwife in the re-birth ceremony at the Coronation (*see* VIII.*i*). Of the two Marys at the Tomb only Mary Magdalene is not known to have been married and thus to have forfeited the title of Virgin; and the Talmud states that Jesus's mother was 'Miriam *M'gadd'la'*, meaning 'Mary the Braider', which appears to be the original form of 'Magdalene'.

(*g*) The Talmudic account (*Shabbath* 104*b* and *Sanhedrin* 67*a*) is given in so elliptical a form that it is hardly intelligible*:

' "The son of Stada was he not [also called] the son of Pandera?"
'Rabbi Hisda replied: "[Are you suggesting] that his mother's husband was Stada and that Pandera was her paramour? And that the husband was like Pappus ben Yehuda? But [perhaps] his mother was [herself known as] Stada. Was not her real name Miriam M'gadd'la N'shaya? For as they say in Pumpeditha: '*S'tath da'*, which means, 'she went astray from her husband'." '

This is a third-century Babylonian pronouncement on Jesus's identity. Celsus's Jewish mentor had told him, a hundred years previously, that Jesus was Mary's illegitimate son by a soldier called Panthéros (Origen: *Against Celsus* i. 9. 1, 32, 33—*see* I.*c*). The story, which is reflected in *John* viii. 41 (*see* XCV.*c*), seems to have originated from the title given Jesus by the Gnostic Grecians: 'Jesus, son of the Virgin' (*Parthenos*). The *n* and the *r* of 'Parthenos' were purposely transliterated by orthodox Jews who regarded the Gnostic doctrine as blasphemous, to make it suggest the panther, a legendary wild animal emblematic of Bacchus.† A similar transliteration is Nabal ('fool') for Laban ('white') in 1 *Samuel* xxv. 5.

(*h*) Jesus, then, as the supposed founder of Gentile Christianity, which became violently anti-Pharisaic, had been posthumously given two nicknames by its opponents: 'The son of Pantheras (or Pandera)' and 'The son of Stada'. 'Son of Stada' (or, more properly 'Satda'), was really the name of an Egyptian prophet mentioned in *Antiquities* xx. 8. 6; *Acts* xxi. 38; *Shabbath* 104*b* and *Sanhedrin* 67*a*, who early in the reign of the Emperor Nero brought

---

* This passage, owing to mediaeval censorship, is not to be found in most editions of the Babylonian Talmud.

† Dr. Raphael Patai writes to us: 'I have a tentative hypothesis of my own as to the origin of the name "ben Pandera". Jesus was baptized, as you point out (*see* v.*j*), at Beth-Nimrah. Baptism was equivalent to re-birth. The name Beth-Nimrah, though meaning "the place of pure water", may have been popularly taken as meaning "house of the leopardess"; Jesus was therefore referred to as "He who was re-born at the house of the leopardess" or, in brief, "Son of the Leopardess". Nimrah, however, being a Hebrew word, was supplanted by its colloquial Aramaic equivalent, Panthera, from the Greek *panther*, leopard. When the origin of this name was forgotten, as it soon must have been, the spelling was changed and became unsteady.'

spells from Egypt 'hidden in a cut in his flesh', and beguiled the people—as Jesus himself was thought to have done. In the hostile account of Jesus's life, the *Toldoth Yeshu,* this same incident of the secret spells is mentioned, though Jesus is referred to only as 'ben Pandera', not as 'ben Stada'. Rabbi Hisda (217–309 A.D.) therefore pronounces, punning on the name *Stada:*

> 'As to whether the son of Stada is the same person as the son of Pandera: it may be that *Stada* was not the name of Mary's husband as some say. Perhaps it was what she herself was subsequently called, because as they say in Pumpeditha: *"S'tath da"* ('she went astray from her husband'). Her real name was Mary, the Braider of the Women. The paramour is said to have been Pantheras. Was her husband perhaps like Pappus son of Judah?'

The last reference is to an early second-century colleague of Rabbi Akiba's, of whom it is related in *Gittin* 90a and *Tosephta Sotah* v. 9:

> 'There are some who if a fly fall into their cup will pour it away and not drink it. Such was the nature of Pappus ben Yehuda who used to lock up his wife whenever he left his house [i.e. he was so sensitive about ocular adultery (*see* xxi.*f and g*) that he would not have slept with her, once she had been subjected to the lustful looks of neighbours].'

Rabbi Hisda's suggestion is that Mary took revenge on her husband by admitting a Roman lover into the house.

(*i*) The 'braider of the women' is usually taken to mean 'women's hairdresser', since the notice is a hostile one and hairdressing for women was a despised and unclean profession; this was a period of elaborate coiffures and the chief purveyors of hair for wigs were professional grave-robbers, who also supplied witches with corpse-flesh. A women's hairdresser will have been suspected of dealing in charms and philtres. But 'braider of the women' may refer, rather, to Mary's particular task among those who made the veil of the Sanctuary (*Protoevangelium* 10. 1)—namely, braiding the ends of the threads. That women weavers were employed on this work and paid out of the Sanctuary Tax is recorded in *Tosephta Shekalim* ii. 6. *Gedilim,* the word from which *M'gadd'la* is formed, are 'fringes', and cap-weavers are called *godle misnefeth* in the Talmud (*Kelim* xvi. 7). It seems that the Gospel editors, to scotch this hairdressing libel, turned *M'gadd'la* into 'Magdalene' (i.e. 'of Magdala' on the Lake of Galilee) and thus found themselves obliged to distinguish Mary of Magdala the Galilean from Mary the Virgin, who was a Judaean Levite. The original tradition survives in Greek only in the *Gospel of Bartholomew* ii. 22, where Jesus after his resurrection appears to Mary the Virgin, rather than to Mary Magdalene; but this is the wildest and most extravagant of all the Apocryphal Gospels.

(*j*) The Marys proved confusing to Grecian Christians who were not in the Nazarene secret. 'Mary the wife of Joseph the Carpenter' was the physical mother of Jesus; Mary his adoptive mother was called 'Mary the Braider'; and since Mary of Cleophas's son James was also called 'The Brother of our

Lord', this might be taken to mean that he was a blood-brother, and that Mary of Cleophas was Jesus's mother. The Copts solved the problem to their own satisfaction by making a single character of all three Marys (Budge: *Misc. Coptic Texts, p.* 626). For the pedigree of Jesus's adoptive family *see* VIII.*r.*

(*k*) The *Magnificat* was really Mary the Braider's quotation from Hannah's song of triumph after Samuel's unexpected birth; and this was remarkably apt if, as we suggest (*see* cxiv.*b*), Mary belonged to Samuel's own clan, coming from Ramathaim-Zophim, his birth-place. But the quotation has been tampered with by a Gentile editor who did not recognize its origin and added to it verses from the *Song of Zacharias* (*see* iv.*f*). *Luke* i. 56 may represent an original account of Mary's three-days' stay in Elisabeth's house before attending the ceremony at Beth-Nimrah.

(*l*) *Luke* i. 48 is a quotation from 1 *Samuel* i. 18 and will have been spoken by Mary to John the Baptist before she sang the song.

> (15) *And John, the messenger of the Lord, in likeness of the Angel Gabriel which leadeth in the Last Days, came filled with the Holy Spirit to Jerusalem unto a virgin named Mary, a duaghter of Aaron.*
>
> *The same had been given by her father and mother to the service of the Temple, in accordance with the Law.*
>
> *She it is that was called Mary Magaddla (which is Mary the Braider) because she was of the women that wove the veil of the Sanctuary and braided the fringes thereof.*

*   *   *   *   *

> (16) *Now it came to pass, when the virgins which braided the veil were athirst, that Mary took a pitcher and went out to fill it with water.*
>
> *And John, standing by the well, saluted her, saying: 'Hail, Mary, thou art highly favoured, the Lord is with thee: blessed art thou among women!'*
>
> *But Mary, when she heard his words, was troubled, and cast in her mind what manner of salutation this should be, and she set down the pitcher.*
>
> *And John said unto her: 'Fear not, Mary, for thou hast found favour with God.*
>
> *'Behold, not many days shall pass and thou shalt bring forth a son and shalt call his name The Branch.*
>
> *'He shall be great, and shall be called the Son of the Most High, and the Lord God shall give unto him the throne of his father David,*
>
> *'And he shall reign over the House of Jacob until this world hath ended.'*
>
> *Then said Mary unto John: 'How may this be, seeing that I have known no man, to lie with him carnally? Shall I in truth bring forth, as every woman bringeth forth?'*
>
> *John answered and said: 'Not so, Mary, for the Holy Spirit shall come upon thee, and the power of the Highest shall overshadow thee.*
>
> *'Therefore also that holy one which shall be born of thee shall be called the Son of God; and his name is now Jesus, for he shall save the people from their sins.'*

And Mary said: 'Let thine handmaid find grace in thy sight. If that thou sayest is true, be it unto me according to thy word.'

John answered: 'Go to the house of my mother Elisabeth, which is thy kinswoman, and hasten with her to the place that I have appointed.'

And he departed from her, and when she had filled the pitcher she went away trembling and sat down in her seat, saying naught to her companions.

* * * * *

(17) Mary arose in those days and went with haste into the hill country and entered into the house of Zechariah and saluted Elisabeth, her kinswoman.

And Elisabeth said: 'Blessed art thou among women! And whence is this that the mother of my Lord should come to me?'

When therefore Mary knew that the messenger spake no deceit, she said: 'Let me rejoice as our mother Hannah rejoiced in the birth of her son Samuel, saying:

' "My heart rejoiceth in the Lord, mine horn is exalted in Thee, O Lord, because I rejoice in Thy salvation!

' "The Lord maketh poor, and maketh rich; He bringeth low, He lifteth up.

' "He raiseth up the poor from the dust and the beggar from the dung hill to set them among princes and to make them inherit the throne of glory.

' "He will keep the feet of the saints, and the wicked shall be silent in darkness, for by strength shall no man prevail over God.

' "The adversaries of the Lord shall be broken into pieces, out of heaven shall He thunder upon them. The Lord shall judge the ends of the earth, He shall give strength unto His king and exalt the horn of His Messiah." '

And Mary abode with Elisabeth about three days and forthwith went with her to Beth-Nimrah across Jordan, even as John had appointed.

* * * * *

VIII

THE CORONATION

Mark i. 9–11

[9]And it came to pass in those days, that Jesus came from Nazareth of Galilee, and was baptized of John in Jordan. [10]And straightway coming up out of the water, He saw the heavens opened, and the Spirit like a dove descending upon Him. [11]And there came a voice from heaven, saying:

Thou art my beloved Son, in Whom I am well pleased.

Matthew iii. 13–17

[13]Then cometh Jesus from Galilee to Jordan unto John, to be baptized of him. [14]But John forbad Him, saying: 'I have need to be baptized of Thee, and comest Thou to me?' [15]And Jesus answering said unto him: 'Suffer it to be so now: for thus it becometh us to fulfil all righteousness.' Then he suffered Him. [16]And Jesus, when He was baptized, went up straightway out of the water: and, lo, the heavens were opened unto Him, and He saw the Spirit of God descending like a dove, and lighting upon Him. [17]And lo a voice from heaven, saying:

This is My beloved Son,
In Whom I am well pleased.

Luke iii. 21–23

[21]Now when all the people were baptized, it came to pass, that Jesus also being baptized, and praying, the heaven was opened, [22]and the Holy Ghost descended in a bodily shape like a dove upon Him, and a voice came from heaven, which said:

Thou art My beloved Son;
In Thee I am well pleased.

[23]And Jesus Himself began to be about thirty years of age, being (as was supposed) the son of Joseph, which was the son of Heli . . .

Jerome: On Isaiah xi. 2

(The Spirit of the Lord shall rest upon him) not partially as in the case of other holy men: but, according to the Gospel written in the Hebrew speech, which the Nazarenes read, 'There shall descend upon him the whole fount of the Holy Spirit' . . . In the Gospel I mentioned above, I find this written: 'And it came to pass when the Lord was come up out of the water, the whole fount of the Holy Spirit descended and rested upon him, and said

Jerome: On Isaiah xi. 2 (*contd.*)

unto him: My son, in all the prophets was I waiting for thee that thou shouldst come, and I might rest in thee. For thou art my peace, thou art my first begotten son, that reignest for ever.'

Epiphanius: Against Heresies xxx.

And after a good deal more it [*The Gospel of the Ebionites*] continues:

After the people were baptized, Jesus also came and was baptized by John; and as he came up from the water, the heavens were opened, and he saw the Holy Ghost in the likeness of a dove that descended and entered into him: and a voice from heaven saying: Thou art my beloved Son, in thee I am well pleased: and again: This day have I begotten thee. And straightway there shone about the place a great light. Which when John saw (it saith) he saith unto him: Who art thou, Lord? and again *there was* a voice from heaven saying unto him: This is my beloved Son in whom I am well pleased. And then (it saith) John fell down before him and said: 'I beseech thee, Lord, baptize thou me. But he prevented him saying: Suffer it (*or* let it go): for thus it behoveth that all things should be fulfilled'.

*   *   *   *   *

Mark ii. 18–20

18 And the disciples of John and of the Pharisees used to fast: and they come and say unto Him: 'Why do the disciples of John and of the Pharisees fast, but Thy disciples fast not?' 19 And Jesus said unto them: 'Can the children of the bride-chamber fast, while the bridegroom is with them? as long as they have the bridegroom with them, they cannot fast. 20 But the days will come when the bridegroom shall be taken away from them, and then shall they fast in those days.'

Mark xiv. 65

65 And some began to spit on Him, and to cover His face, and to buffet Him, and to say unto Him, Prophesy: and the servants did strike Him with the palms of their hands.

Mark xv. 17–20

17 And they clothed Him with purple, and platted a crown of thorns, and put it about His head, 18 and began to salute Him: 'Hail, King of the Jews!' 19 And they smote Him on the head with a reed, and did spit upon Him, and bowing their knees worshipped Him. 20 And when they had mocked Him, they took off the purple from Him, and put His own clothes on Him.

Matthew ix. 14–15

14 Then came to Him the disciples of John, saying: 'Why do we and the Pharisees fast oft, but Thy disciples fast not?' 15 And Jesus said unto them: 'Can the children of the bridechamber mourn, as long as the bridegroom is with them? but the days will come, when the bridegroom shall be taken from them, and then shall they fast.'

Matthew xxvi. 67–68

⁶⁷Then did they spit in His face, and buffeted Him; and others smote Him with the palms of their hands, ⁶⁸saying, 'Prophesy unto us, Thou Christ, Who is he that smote Thee?'

Matthew xxvii. 28–31

²⁸And they stripped Him, and put on Him a scarlet robe. ²⁹And when they had platted a crown of thorns, they put it upon His head, and a reed in His right hand: and they bowed the knee before Him, and mocked Him, saying: 'Hail, King of the Jews!' ³⁰And they spit upon Him, and took the reed, and smote Him on the head. ³¹And after that they had mocked Him, they took the robe off from Him, and put His own raiment on Him, and led Him away to crucify Him.

Luke v. 33–35

³³And they said unto Him: 'Why do the disciples of John fast often, and make prayers, and likewise the disciples of the Pharisees; but Thine eat and drink?' ³⁴And He said unto them: 'Can ye make the children of the bride-chamber fast, while the bridegroom is with them? ³⁵But the days will come, when the bridegroom shall be taken away from them, and then shall they fast in those days.'

Luke xxii. 63–65

⁶³And the men that held Jesus mocked Him, and smote Him. ⁶⁴And when they had blindfolded Him, they struck Him on the face, and asked Him, saying: 'Prophesy, who is it that smote Thee?' ⁶⁵And many other things blasphemously spake they against Him.

Luke xxiii. 11

¹¹And Herod with his men of war set Him at nought, and mocked Him, and arrayed Him in a gorgeous robe, and sent Him again to Pilate.

John xix. 1–5

¹Then Pilate therefore took Jesus, and scourged Him. ²And the soldiers platted a crown of thorns, and put it on His head, and they put on Him a purple robe, ³and said: 'Hail, King of the Jews!' and they smote Him with their hands. ⁴Pilate therefore went forth again, and saith unto them: 'Behold, I bring Him forth to you, that ye may know that I find no fault in Him.' ⁵Then came Jesus forth, wearing the crown of thorns, and the purple robe. And [Pilate] saith unto them: 'Behold the man!'

John iii. 23–36—John iv. 1–3

²³And John also was baptizing in Aenon near to Salim, because there was much water there: and they came and were baptized. ²⁴For John was not yet cast into prison.

John iii. 23–36—John iv. 1–3 (*contd.*)

25Then there arose a question between some of John's disciples and the Jews about purifying. 26And they came unto John, and said unto him: 'Rabbi, He that was with thee beyond Jordan, to Whom thou barest witness, behold, the same baptizeth, and all men come to Him.' 27John answered and said: 'A man can receive nothing, except it be given him from heaven. 28Ye yourselves bear me witness, that I said, I am not the Christ, but that I am sent before Him. 29He that hath the bride is the bridegroom: but the friend of the bridegroom, which standeth and heareth him, rejoiceth greatly because of the bridegroom's voice: this my joy therefore is fulfilled. 30He must increase, but I must decrease.

31'He that cometh from above is above all: he that is of the earth is earthly, and speaketh of the earth: He that cometh from heaven is above all. 32And what He hath seen and heard, that He testifieth; and no man receiveth His testimony. 33He that hath received His testimony hath set to his seal that God is true. 34For He Whom God hath sent speaketh the words of God: for God giveth not the Spirit by measure unto Him. 35The Father loveth the Son, and hath given all things into His hand. 36He that believeth on the Son hath everlasting life: and he that believeth not the Son shall not see life; but the wrath of God abideth on him.'

1When therefore the Lord knew how the Pharisees had heard that Jesus made and baptized more disciples than John, 2(though Jesus himself baptized not, but His disciples) 3He left Judaea, and departed again into Galilee.

John xix. 25–27

25Now there stood by the cross of Jesus His mother, and His mother's sister, Mary the wife of Cleophas, and Mary Magdalene. 26When Jesus therefore saw His mother, and the disciple standing by, whom He loved, He saith unto His mother:

'Woman, behold thy son!'

27Then saith He to the disciple:

'Behold thy mother!'

And from that hour that disciple took her unto his own home.

Revelation xix. 6–9

6And I heard as it were the voice of a great multitude, and as the voice of many waters, and as the voice of mighty thunderings, saying:

'Alleluia:
For the Lord God omnipotent reigneth.
7Let us be glad and rejoice and give honour to Him:
For the marriage of the Lamb is come,
And His wife hath made herself ready.'

8And to her was granted that she should be arrayed in fine linen, clean and white: for the fine linen is the righteousness of saints.

9And he saith unto me: 'Write, Blessed are they which are called unto the marriage supper of the Lamb.' And he saith unto me: 'These are the true sayings of God.'

Luke ii. 25–35

²⁵And, behold, there was a man in Jerusalem, whose name was Simeon; and the same man was just and devout, waiting for the consolation of Israel: and the Holy Ghost was upon him. ²⁶And it was revealed unto him by the Holy Ghost, that he should not see death, before he had seen the Lord's Christ. ²⁷And he came by the Spirit into the temple: and when the parents brought in the Child Jesus, to do for Him after the custom of the law, ²⁸then took he Him up in his arms, and blessed God, and said:

²⁹'Lord, now lettest Thou Thy servant depart
According to Thy word, in peace:
³⁰For mine eyes have seen Thy salvation,
³¹Which Thou hast prepared before the face of all people;
³²A light to lighten the Gentiles,
And the glory of Thy people Israel.'

³³And Joseph and His mother marvelled at those things which were spoken of him. ³⁴And Simeon blessed them, and said unto Mary His mother:

'Behold, this Child is set for the fall and rising again of many in Israel;
And for a sign which shall be spoken against;
³⁵(Yea, a sword shall pierce through thy own soul also,)
That the thoughts of many hearts may be revealed.'

(*a*) There need be no doubt that Jesus was anointed and crowned King of Israel; but the Gospel editors have done their best to conceal this, for political reasons, even while referring to him as 'Christ' ('The Messiah' or 'The Anointed One') and 'The Chosen One' (*Luke* xxiii. 35), one of the titles of the royal Messiah in *Enoch* (xlv. 3), and prophesying for him the everlasting throne of his father David (*Luke* i. 32–33).

That the Baptism was a royal lustration is clear from the account in the Synoptic Gospels (*Luke* iii. 22, *Matthew* iii. 17 and *Mark* i. 11). A verse from the Coronation psalm is quoted: 'My beloved son thou art; this day have I begotten thee' (*Psalm* ii. 7), though in each case the second part of the sentence, preserved in *Acts* xiii. 33, *Hebrews* i. 5 and in the *Gospel according to the Hebrews* (Jerome: *On Isaiah* xi. 2), and hinted at in *John* i. 34, has for doctrinal reasons been changed to 'in whom I am well pleased' (from the *Testament of Levi* xvii. 2–14—see 1.*f*). This account is supplemented in *Luke* iii. 21–22 by the descent of the dove from heaven. The dove was an emblem of peace (*Genesis* viii. 11), and of love (*Canticles* i. 14 and v. 2); whereas at the coronation of a Pharaoh his *ka*, or double, descended upon him in the form of a hawk, an emblem of warfare. The species of the bird that descends on the King's loins at his Coronation, according to the Southern Palestinian cylinder-seal (*see* vi.*h*), is not easily determined, but it seems to be a hawk. The King is wearing a pair of wings, which are clearly hawk's wings and show his solar power.

(*b*) The account by Epiphanius from the lost *Gospel of the Ebionites* (*Heresies* xxx.) is even more explicit:

'. . . It saith that . . . as Jesus came up from the water, the heavens were opened, and he saw the Holy Ghost descending and entering into him in the likeness of a dove; and a voice from heaven saying: "Thou art my Beloved Son, in thee I am well pleased," and again: "This day I have begotten thee." And that straightway there shone about the place a great light . . . On this account they say that Jesus was begotten of the seed of a man and was chosen; and so by the choice [of God] he was called the Son of God from the Anointed One that entered into him from above in the likeness of a dove.'

Thus, according to the Nazarene tradition, John the Baptist was reviving the Jewish monarchy which had been in demise since the death of the Edomite usurper Herod. The Hasmonean kings had been acclaimed 'Sons of God'*, a title promised to all successors of David (2 *Samuel* vii. 14) for ever, in the special sense that is here applied to Jesus. He must have been anointed on this occasion with sacred oil from the Mount of Olives, and thereby become the 'Messiah' or 'Christ'; lay kings were anointed with a circlet of oil around the poll, priests with the Greek letter X marked on the brow (*Horayoth* 12a; *Kerithoth* 5b).

(c) Dr. Raphael Patai, in his carefully documented *Hebrew Installation Rites* (*see* VII.b) shows that of the twenty-seven rites connected with coronation in the African systems studied by Tor Irstam (*The King of Ganda: Studies in the Institution of Sacred Kingship in Africa; Stockholm,* 1944) no less than twenty-one are recorded in, or can be deduced from, different Old Testament accounts of how the Kings of Israel or Judah were crowned; and holds that the modern African ritual is ultimately derived from a Near Eastern prototype.

He gives the twenty-one rites as follows, with numbers borrowed from Irstam's list:

(1) The Hebrew king was conceived of as being re-born at the time of his installation as the son of God.

(2) He was dressed in purple royal robes.

(4) The prophet, or the person functioning as his anointer, addressed him. The King answered. He was proclaimed as King.

(5) A real fight preceded the king's final installation. The king's (ritual) victory over his enemies is often alluded to.

(6) After the initial stage, the installation ritual was interrupted for the duration of a week.

(7) The king received communion by partaking of a sacrificial meal.

(8) He was baptized.

(9) He mounted a hill, the Bamah, or the 'pillar'.

(10) The king set up for himself a memorial pillar.

(11) He was admonished by the prophet, and promised to follow the divine instructions.

(12) The king was anointed with oil.

---

* 'Son of God' had two senses: it applied particularly to a king or ruler, but generally to the whole of God's chosen people, as in *Psalm* lxxxii. 6 or *Exodus* iv. 22.

(14) The king received as his regalia a spear, a shield, etc.

(15) The king sat on the throne.

(16) The king was crowned.

(17) A fire rite took place.

(18) The king distributed baker's ware among the people.

(20) He made the round of his dominion.

(21) Festivities were held.

(22) The king was made the butt of the people.

(24) Human sacrifices.

(26) Substitute king.

(*d*) Dr. Patai overlooks Irstam's No. 3: 'The king received a new name',: Hoshea becomes Jehoshua (*Numbers* xiii. 16), though the occasion has been disguised; Jedidiah becomes Solomon (2 *Samuel* xii. 25); Eliakim becomes Jehoiakim (2 *Kings* xxiii. 34), and Mattaniah becomes Zedekiah (2 *Kings* xxiv. 17).* He perhaps also overlooks Irstam's No. 13: 'The king drew on his shoes' (*Psalm* lx. 8). He continues to list other distinctive features of the Hebrew coronation and suggests (*see* vii.*b*) that the tradition lasted until the time of Jesus's reported installation by John the Baptist:

(1) The king is chosen by both electors and oracle.

(2) A high official (priest, prophet) functions at the election as well as at the installation.

(3) Animosity or incompatibility exists between this official and the king.

(4) The king must be of unblemished body, healthy, strong, and beautiful.

(5) The king must not defile himself with a dead body.

(6) Ceremonial marriage in a special hut.

(7) The king marries the widow of his predecessor.

(8) The king rides on a mount.

(9) The king hides, is sought and found.

(10) The 'shooting of the nations'.

(11) Ritual combat; omitted if real fighting happens to break out.

(12) Installation ritual very protracted.

(13) Periodical (annual, on New Year's day) repetition of installation rites.

(14) Monthly new moon festivals.

(15) The king is the chief priest of his people.

(*e*) The ceremonies of crowning a king and crowning a High Priest were, Dr. Patai shows, originally identical; so the vision in *Zechariah* iii. 1–10, where Joshua (Greek: Jesus) is to be crowned Priest-king in order to inaugurate the Kingdom of Heaven is of great importance to the story, and supplies much that is missing in the Gospel account of the ritual.

(1) And he shewed me Joshua the high priest standing before the angel of the Lord, and Satan standing at his right hand to resist him.

* In the two latter cases the change of name is made, apparently, by order of an over-lord —the King of Egypt or the King of Babylon; but this is a mistake. The subject of the verb 'changed' is the new King of Judah himself, as the significance of the chosen names proves.

(2) And the Lord saith unto Satan, The Lord rebuke thee, O Satan; even the Lord that hath chosen Jerusalem rebuke thee: is not this a brand plucked out of the fire?

(3) Now Joshua was clothed with filthy garments, and stood before the angel.

(4) And he answered and spake unto those that stood before him, saying: 'Take away the filthy garments from him.' And unto him he said: 'Behold, I have caused thine iniquity to pass from thee, and I will clothe thee with change of raiment.'

(5) And I said: 'Let them set a fair mitre upon his head.' So they set a fair mitre upon his head, and clothed him with garments. And the angel of the Lord stood by.

(6) And the angel of the Lord protested unto Joshua, saying:

(7) 'Thus saith the Lord of Hosts; If thou wilt walk in my ways, and if thou wilt keep my charge, then thou shalt also judge my house, and shalt also keep my courts, and I will give thee places to walk among these that stand by.

(8) 'Hear now, O Joshua, the high priest, thou, and thy fellows that sit before thee: for they are men of a sign: for, behold, I will bring forth my servant the BRANCH.

(9) 'For behold the stone that I have laid before Joshua; upon one stone shall be seven eyes: behold, I will engrave the graving thereof, saith the Lord of Hosts, and I will remove the iniquity of that land in one day.

(10) 'In that day, saith the Lord of Hosts, shall ye call every man his neighbour under the vine and under the fig-tree.'

* * * *

(f) God's promise: 'I will remove the iniquity of that land *in one day'*, is relevant to the story of the Passion, where Jesus was attempting to fulfil a later prophecy of Zechariah. Also, when Jesus told Peter on the occasion of the Disclosure, that he had been tempted by Satan (*see* LXXVIII.*e*), he must have had this passage from *Zechariah* in mind; it is again plainly referred to in the story of Nathanael (*see* VI.*e*); and accounts for his 'keeping the courts' of the Temple (*see* XC.*a*). As Dr. Patai points out, only kings who founded new dynasties were anointed by prophets, unless a rival claimant appeared (*Horayoth* iii. 2, *Sotah* viii. 3); but Jesus's was a new dynasty.

It is likely that the baptism and subsequent anointing took place not in the Jordan but at Beth-Nimrah, or perhaps 'Aenon' (*John* iii. 23), because of the tradition that a king should be anointed at a spring so that his reign might be pure and long drawn out like its waters (*Tosephta Sanhedrin* iv. 10). Thus Solomon was anointed at the spring of Gihom (1 *Kings* i. 45) and his rival Adonijah at the spring of Rogel (1 *Kings* i. 9).

(g) The scorn with which Jesus was greeted on his return to Nazara (*see* XXXVII.*d*) suggests that he received some visible and permanent injury during his coronation; this would be in keeping with *Isaiah* lii. 14. He may have been lamed (*see* CXIII.*j*).

At this point we reach debatable ground, but as the authentic text of

Jesus's sayings may be recovered with a fair degree of certainty by restoring the Old Testament quotations on which they are *midrashim,* so here with his actions. That the Hebrew text of the Old Testament which we now possess has changed hardly at all since the time of Jesus is proved by the pre-Christian scrolls recently discovered in a cave near the Dead Sea; and if it may be assumed that Jesus quoted accurately from the Law and the Prophets, these and such later apocalyptic books as *Enoch* and *The Testaments of the Twelve Patriarchs (see* LXXXVIII.*h)* provide a critical control to the Gospels. Similarly, if the installation ceremony was not modified by John the Baptist, Dr. Patai's list of Old Testament rites should be a trustworthy guide to what happened in Jesus's case.

(*h*) At first sight, the account of all the rites except the lustration seems lost beyond recovery; but if we find incidents precisely corresponding to them inserted in later chapters of the Gospels and demonstrably out of place there, we may postulate that early editors, not wishing the Romans to realize that Jesus had been crowned King of Israel without the Emperor's sanction, yet loth to destroy the records, broke up a consecutive account of the Coronation and distributed the pieces elsewhere. This would imply a secret oral tradition among Nazarene initiates, to which the Gentile Christian camp-followers had no access and which was eventually suppressed and lost.

(*i*) The promise to Mary the Braider at the Annunciation that the power of the Most High would overshadow her is seen to have been made good, if the command 'Mother, behold thy son; Son, behold thy mother' is excised from the Crucifixion context (*John* xix. 26–27) where it does not make sense, and placed here, where it does. Jesus could not have handed over his physical mother, Mary the wife of Joseph the Carpenter, to the care of his disciple John. That would have been to accuse his three brothers (*Mark* vi. 3) of re-fusing to support her and therefore of being 'murderers' in Pharisaic Law; besides, at the Crucifixion the women were standing afar off (*Mark* xv. 40) and could hardly have heard his words even if he had spoken to them (*see* CXIII.*v*). The account in *John* xix. 25–27 seems to be based on a complete mis-reading of a passage found in the *Acts and Sayings:*

> 'John [the Baptist] bore record that he [John the Baptist] looking upon Mary [the Braider] said: "Woman, behold thy son; Son, behold thy mother." And thereafter he [Jesus] took her unto him as his own mother.'

which the editor read as:

> 'John, the disciple whom Jesus loved, bears record that Jesus seeing Mary his mother [at the Cross] said unto her: "Woman, behold thy son," and unto him: "Son, behold thy mother." And from that hour he took her into his own house.'

Mary will have spread her skirt over Jesus and thus borne him; with Salome, a kinswoman, acting as midwife and testifying to her virginity (*see* VII.*f*).

(*j*) There remain the less easily disguised coronation rites, namely the award of the sceptre, the investment with a purple mantle, the crowning, and the ritual mocking—the Biblical parallel for this is 1 *Samuel* x. 27, where Saul is mocked at Mizpah by the 'sons of Belial'* yet holds his peace. Is it not likely that these have been ingeniously transferred in *Luke* to the scene of Jesus's appearance before Herod Antipas, and in *Mark* and *Matthew* and *John* to that of his appearance before Pilate, and again in *Mark, Matthew,* and *Luke* to the previous trial-scene where the Sanhedrin play 'Blind Man's Buffet' with him?

The compilers of the four canonical Gospels, and their editorial successors, seem on the whole to have abstained from wanton invention, and to have used genuine material with which to build even their most extravagant stories. Since it is incredible that the High Priest and his family would have mishandled their prisoner in so vulgar a style, and unlikely that Pilate's body-guard would have conveniently found a spray of desert thorn for his crown, or even a green reed for his sceptre, in the hill-top palace where they were quartered at Jerusalem, or that they would have been able to borrow a costly purple robe for their horse-play, it is reasonable to presume that these incidents really belong to the Coronation sequence. 'Prophesy who buffeted thee, Anointed One!' (*Matthew* xxvi. 68) refers plainly to the spirit of prophecy which seized the newly acclaimed King (1 *Samuel* x. 11). It may be that the mockery was not 'Prophesy: who smote thee?' but the formula quoted in 2 *Chronicles* xviii. 23 and 1 *Kings* xxii. 24:

> Then Zedekiah the son of Chenaanah came near and smote Micaiah upon the cheek and said: 'Which way went the spirit of the Lord from me to speak unto thee?'

(*k*) Purple was worn by the kings of Midian (*Judges* viii. 26) and by the Hasmonean kings (1 *Maccabees* viii. 14 *and* x. 20, 62, 64), and the Messiah was hailed in *Isaiah* as coming in garments dyed with Bozra purple (*Isaiah* lxiii. 1). The garments with which the High Priest Joshua was clothed (*Zechariah* iii. 5) were a tunic, linen breeches, and vestment, a girdle, and a purple robe† decorated with bells and pomegranates. A purple robe was also worn by the High Priest at Hierapolis (Lucian: *De Dea Syria,* 42) where the religious rites were indistinguishable from those originally performed in Solomon's Temple. John would have been able to obtain these garments from his relatives at Jerusalem—even a purple robe, which was used by others than High Priests (*Luke* xvi. 19—*see* LXXXII.*j*). The priestly vestment (*Exodus* xxiv. 5 *and* 8) was remarkable for being woven on a special loom without seam (Josephus: *Antiquities* iii. 7. 4; and *Yoma* 72b), and if *John*

* *Belial* is a Hebrew cacophemism, *B'li Yaal* ('without use or avail', i.e. 'good for nothing') used as a disguise for *Belili,* a title of the Love-goddess Ishtar. So here the 'sons of Belili' are merely 'the children of the bride chamber', not 'Sons of Destruction'.

† *See* van Hoonaker: *Le Sacerdoce Lévitique,* p. 341ff.

is right in recording that Jesus wore one at the Crucifixion (*John* xix. 23—
see cxiii.*q*), then he was certainly regarded as a Priest-king.

(*l*) According to Josephus (*Wars* i. 33. 9), King Herod had a 'wreath' for his
crown as well as a heavy gold 'diadem'. (The King of Rabbah's diadem
(2 *Samuel* xii. 30), which David took for his own use, weighed a talent.)
John would not have easily procured such a costly gaud from his own re-
sources, but if the wise men of *Matthew* ii. 1–2 were 'New-Covenanters', i.e.
Zadokite apocalyptics from Damascus, on a visit to their co-religionists at
Bethany or Ramathaim (*see* cxiv.*b*) and had brought presents of gold,
myrrh, and frankincense for the King whom they were expecting, this gold
may well have been worked into a diadem. It would have been raised by the
monthly subscription for communal expenses to which we know the New-
Covenanters were bound. The frankincense and myrrh also were costly items
needed for the coronation ceremony. This numerous sect dated from perhaps
the third century B.C.; the 'New Covenant' referred to God's promise in
Jeremiah xxxi. 31–34. They named the Messiah 'The Star' or 'The Coming
One' and were ruled by a tribunal of ten (*see* cxviii.*p*). Justin (*Dialogues*
78) records a tradition that the wise men came from Arabia; he probably
means Damascus, which a few years later was ceded to Aretas IV, 'King of
Arabia' (2 *Corinthians* xi. 32).

(*m*) Was it perhaps the arrival of the wise men that prompted John the
Baptist's acclamation of Jesus? Among the Dead Sea Scrolls is a commentary
on Habbakuk, which Professor André Dupont-Sommer dates from 42 B.C.
The New-Covenanters' leader, styled 'The Master of Justice and the Elect
of God', had been put to death by the Hasmonean Aristobulus II (66–63 B.C.),
but avenged in 63 B.C. by Pompey's capture of Jerusalem. Professor Dupont-
Sommer shows that the New-Covenanters' oath was identical with the
Essene oath, and that, already two generations before the Crucifixion, the
End of the World was thought to be imminent. The martyred Master of
Justice was expected to appear again just before this occurred; and it seems
therefore that John chose Jesus to fill the part. This character, to whom the
New-Covenanters also referred as 'The Coming One'—cf. 'Art thou he that
should come?' (*see* xxxixa)—was, in fact, the Messiah, and they insisted on
the authority of *The Testaments of the Twelve Patriarchs,* that he would be
a 'priest of the race of Aaron'; and yet, on that of the *Book of Jubilees* (which
they regarded as equally inspired), that he would be begotten of the House
of David. Though the theory of the Messiah's claim to belong both to Judah
and Levi is expressed in the *Twelve Patriarchs* (*see* 1.*g*–*h*), the impulse for
Jesus's adoption ceremony may well have come from the New-Covenanters.
One of the last Gentile Christian records of his double birth is found in a
fragment of Irenaeus taken from a *catena* on *Deuteronomy*: 'From Levi, and
also from Judah according to the flesh, he became both king and priest,'
(quoted by Guignebert: *The Jewish World in the Time of Jesus, p.* 144).
But it is implicit in the Christian interpolations in the *Twelve Patriarchs*

(e.g. *Simeon* vii. 2) : 'For the Lord shall raise up from Levi as it were a High Priest and from Judah as it were a king [*God and man*]. He shall save all [*the Gentiles and*] the race of Israel.' (*See also* XLVIII.*d*).

> (21) *For certain wise men had journeyed from Damascus to Jerusalem, being Zadokite priests of the New Covenant,*
>
> *Which came unto the Watchers of Bethany (the same is nigh to Jerusalem) and said unto them: 'Where is he that shall be re-born King of Israel? Behold the Star, the Coming One, is foretold in the heavens; and we are journeyed hither to worship him.'*
>
> *Then the Watchers enquired diligently of them at what time this birth should come to pass, and they answered 'on such a day'.*
>
> *These wise men therefore were abiding in Jerusalem until the time that John chose Jesus to be King.*
>
> *And when they heard that Jesus was chosen, they rejoiced with exceeding great joy and went out with the Watchers unto Beth-Nimrah,*
>
> *Where seeing Mary and her new-born son, they fell down and worshipped him.*
>
> *And when they had opened their treasures, they presented unto him gifts: a golden diadem and precious ointment and frankincense.*

* * * *

(*n*) The 'burning bush' in which God appeared to Moses (*Exodus* iii. 2) was traditionally a thorned acacia and would have provided the most suitable wreath for a priestly coronation. According to Philo (*Legation to Gaius,* 13), it was the ancient nimbus of the Sun-god, and Bühr (*Symbolik* i. *p.*363) enlarges on its sacral use in Egypt.

As an emblem of his pacific mission Jesus was given a canna-reed instead of the spear which Saul carried (1 *Samuel* xiii. 22, 2 *Samuel* i. 6, etc.). The reed (2 *Kings* xviii. 21) was emblematic of royalty in Egypt where it alluded to the fertilizing flow of the Nile; and reeds, used for a variety of domestic and agricultural needs, will have been cultivated at Beth-Nimrah. The close parallels between the Hebrew and the Egyptian coronation rituals are not surprising; Palestine was for centuries under Egyptian protection.

It is likely that an olive-branch as well as a reed was presented to Jesus, which would account for his new name 'The Branch' (*see* I.*v and* LVI.*g*). This, at least, was in accordance with the coronation ritual of Levi the High Priest (*Testament of Levi* viii. 4–10);

> (4) And the first of the seven [men in white raiment] anointed me with holy oil and gave to me the staff of judgement.
>
> (5) The second washed me with pure water and fed me with bread and wine, the most holy things, and clad me with a holy and glorious robe.
>
> (6) The third clothed me with a linen vestment like an ephod.
>
> (7) The fourth tied about me a girdle like unto purple.
>
> (8) The fifth gave me a branch of rich olive.

(9) The sixth placed a crown on my head.

(10) The seventh placed on my head a diadem of priesthood and filled my hands with incense, that I might serve as priest to the Lord God.

(o) However, to judge from *Canticles* iii. 11,* the wreath-crown will have been placed on Jesus's head not by one of the seven priests (who seem to be the seven 'eyes', or eyewitnesses, of Joshua's coronation) but by his mother; and if it was she who braided, or plaited it, this may be an allusion to her name, Mary the Braider. The occasion in *Canticles* is given as 'the king's espousals', and indeed when a king was crowned in the ancient style (as Hocart, Irstam, and Patai all show) he also married.

It had always been so in Israel: the feast of Saul after his acclamation (1 *Samuel* ix. 22) was a wedding feast with Samuel acting as paranymph, or 'best man', like the one recorded in *Judges* xiv. 10–11, when Samson feasted with thirty 'sons of the bride chamber'. *Psalm* xlv. is the royal marriage-song, and refers to several of the coronation rites that precede the nuptials. It is noteworthy that Jesus refers to his followers as 'sons of the bride chamber' in *Mark* ii. 19 and *Matthew* ix. 15, as though he had taken a bride. If he was speaking metaphorically, the reference must be explained; it is too easy to say, *a posteriori*: 'Christ was referring to his love of the Church.' Moreover, John the Baptist speaks of himself as Jesus's paranymph (*John* iii. 29—see 1.*l*). Has the story of the marriage also been disguised, lest the Romans might conclude that Jesus had left an heir to the Kingdom? If so, the original of *Mark* ii. 19 and *Matthew* ix. 15, may have run:

(30) *When presently these twain came out of the bride chamber they found a feast prepared for them.*

But Jesus, perceiving that the disciples of John fasted and were of a sorrowful countenance, said unto them:

'Shall the sons of the bride chamber mourn and fast while the bridegroom is with them?' (For the espousals of a king absolve men of their vows of fasting). 'But when the bridegroom is gone from you, then may ye fast again.'

Therefore did they also eat with him, and were merry.

* * * * *

(p) The original of *John* iii. 23–36, *John* iv. 1–3, a passage which seems to have been altered to suit a later dispute between the disciples of John and the Nazarenes, may be restored as follows:

(31) *And the disciples of John the Baptist, seeing him of good cheer which before was sorrowful, and full of laughter and blessings which before was full of lamentations and curses, were amazed, because it was as though he were himself the bridegroom.*

---

* There is no need to question the authority of the *Canticles* in this matter, dismissing them as a 'collection of popular love songs'; their symbolism everywhere reflects a very early religious tradition—*Canticles* iii. 4 even implies an exogamic and therefore matrilineal system, as in the legend of Samson and Delilah and in the order (*Genesis* ii. 24) that a man shall quit his own tribe when he marries. The Pharisees did not dare to exclude them from the Canon.

> *But he answered and said unto them: 'The friend of the bridegroom which standeth and heareth him, rejoiceth greatly in his voice. This my joy therefore is fulfilled, that the Father loveth His son and hath given all things into his hand.*
>
> *'He must increase, but I must decrease.'*

* * * * *

And here is the conclusion of the Coronation sequence:

> (38) *When therefore all things were accomplished, Jesus returned into Galilee, and John was baptizing in Karim, nigh unto Jerusalem, because there was much water there.*

* * * * *

(*q*) The royal marriage cannot have been consummated. John was an ascetic and Jesus held that the imminence of the end of the world made it necessary to abstain from the sexual act (*see* xxi.*k and l and* xcviii.*i*) which detracted from full holiness (*Exodus* xix. 15). Thus in *Revelation* xiv. 4, originally a Nazarene document, the 'elect' who stand with the Lamb on Mount Zion are 'virgins that have never defiled themselves with women'. Yet the espousal was an integral part of the ceremony. Jesus's dilemma recalls *Matthew* i. 19–25, which runs:

> Then Joseph, being a just man, and not willing to make her a public example, was minded to put her away privily. But while he thought on these things the messenger of the Lord . . . saith unto him: 'Fear not, thou son of David, to take unto thee Mary thy wife.
>
> 'For . . .'
>
> Then he did as the messenger of the Lord had bidden him and took unto him his wife, but he knew her not.

Since, as has been shown, the story of Joseph the Carpenter's discovery of his wife's parthenogenous conception makes no historical sense (*see* 1.*c*), it looks as if this is yet another part of the Coronation story, with 'Jesus' substituted for 'Joseph'; and perhaps followed by Jesus's saying, in *Matthew* iii. 15: 'Suffer it to be so now, for thus it becometh us to fulfil all righteousness' (*see* vi.*f*). This raises the difficult question of Jesus's Queen. Was she still another Mary? The only two women for whom he is particularly recorded to have felt love were Mary and Martha the sisters of Lazarus, with whom he lodged at Bethany (*John* xi. 5—*see* xi.*f and* lxxxvii.*a*). The wording of the passage, 'Now Jesus loved Martha and her sister and Lazarus,' suggests that attention is being detracted from Mary, the more important character in the story. She is said to have wiped Jesus's feet with her hair (*John* xii. 3), an act which, if Jesus indeed avoided all intimate contact with women, could have been pardoned only in a wife. The incident seems to be the same as the one recorded in *Mark* xiv. 3, where the owner of the house is described as 'Simon the Leper' (*see* xi.*a–c*); if so, Simon (Simeon) will have been the father of Eliezer (Lazarus), Mary, and Martha. He may also be identified with 'Simeon son of Cleophas, or Clopas, or Kalpus', first cousin of 'James the brother of our Lord', *alias* James of Alphaeus, *alias* James the Less, *alias* James the Just.

(*r*) 'James the brother of our Lord' was one of the heads of the Nazarene Church when Paul visited Jerusalem (*Galatians* i. 19)—and, indeed, supreme head, as appears in *Acts* xxi. 8, Eusebius (*Ecc. Hist.* 2. i. 3) and *Galatians* ii. 12—because Paul mentions him there as 'one of the Apostles' and only two Jameses appear in the list, the other being James the son of Zebedee (*see* LVI.*b and c*). Of the patristic writers, Chrysostom, Jerome (*see* CXVI.*c*) and Theodoret support this identification and make James a kinsman of Jesus, but Hegesippus (as quoted by Eusebius), the Pseudo-Clementine, and the author of the *Apostolic Constitutions,* oppose it: they suggest that James, surnamed the Just, was Jesus's physical half-brother, a younger son of Joseph the Carpenter and his wife Mary, mentioned in *Mark* vi. 3 and, though originally not a believer, converted after the Resurrection (1 *Corinthians* xv. 7) when he took precedence over the other disciples. This second view is contradicted by Hegesippus's own detailed account of James the Just's martyrdom in the Temple, which Epiphanius confirms: James wore linen and served in the Sanctuary (Eusebius: *Ecc. Hist.* 2. xxiii. 6)—in other words, he was a Levite priest. No son of Joseph the Carpenter, who was of the House of David, could have become a priest, except by virtue of the rare ceremony of adoption into the tribe of Levi with which Jesus was honoured. The solution to this problem seems to be that James the Just was 'the son of Alphaeus' and, also, 'the brother of our Lord' as the result of Jesus's ritual re-birth from Mary the Braider, the ward of James's father 'Alphaeus.'

(*s*) We suggest (*see* (*q*) *above*) that Jesus's Queen was Mary, sister of 'Lazarus' (Eliezer) and Martha, and that these three lived together at Bethany and were children of one Simeon Cleophas the Chaste, whom *Matthew* and *Mark* mistakenly call 'Simon the Leper' (*Mark* xiv. 3 and *Matthew* xxvi. 6), but who is called by *Luke* 'a Pharisee' (*Luke* vii. 36). The mistake of 'Leper'—Jesus could not have eaten with a leper, nor did lepers live in houses—provides a clue to James's identity. Though *Alphaios* is usually taken to mean 'of the town of Heleph' (*Joshua* xix. 33), *alphos* in Greek means *vitiligo,* a skin disease suggesting leprosy (*see* XXXII.*a*)—and *alpheios* is used by Curtius, the late first-century historian, as an adjective formed from it. If 'Alpheios' then means 'the vitiliginous', a nickname also given to Matthew the publican's father (*see* XIX.*g*)—but we suggest that 'the vitiliginous' (*garba* in Aramaic) is, in the first case, a mistranslation of *garosh,* 'the chaste' (*see* XI.*c*)—the real name of James's father is still to be found.

(*t*) Now, Mary of Cleophas is mentioned in *John* xix. 25 (*see* CXIII.*v*) as having been at the Crucifixion, and must therefore be 'the mother of James and Joses', mentioned in the corresponding texts of *Matthew* xxvii. 56 and *Mark* xvi. 1, where James is called 'the Less' to distinguish him from James the son of Zebedee; and according to *Mark,* she is 'of Joseph', i.e. married to Joseph. Therefore James was the son of Mary daughter of Cleophas (perhaps a

Hebrew form of the Greek *Cleopatros,* spelt 'Kalpus' in the *Toldoth Yeshu*),
by her marriage to a certain Joseph. But this same Mary is described as a
sister of Jesus's mother (*John* xix. 25), and must in effect have been a sister-
in-law, not a sister, because two sisters never bore the same name unless they
were princesses by birth. And since James was a Levite, his mother must have
been sister-in-law not of Jesus's physical mother (namely the wife of Joseph
the Carpenter) who is said in the *Codex Sinaiticus* to have been 'also of the
seed of David', but of his adoptive mother Mary the Braider, who was a
Levite. Further, Hegesippus, quoted by Eusebius (*Ecc. Hist.* 3. xi. 1), describes Cleophas as 'the brother of Joseph who was called the father of Jesus',
and since this Joseph cannot have been the Galilean carpenter, because
Cleophas also was a Levite, it follows that he was a brother of Joseph, Mary
the Braider's brother, who legally ranked as Jesus's father, Mary having had
no husband.

(*u*) These relationships oblige us to reconsider the genealogy found in *Matthew* i. 17, which cannot be that of Joseph the Carpenter (*see* 11.*a and b.*).
Since the latter part, from the Judaean prince Zerubbabel downwards, contains certain characteristically Levite names—Matthan (2 *Kings* xi. 18),
Eleazar (*Exodus* xxviii. 1), Eliud=Elihu (1 *Samuel* i. 1), Achim=Jachin
(1 *Chronicles* xxiv. 17), Zadok (2 *Samuel* viii. 17), Azur (*Jeremiah* xxviii. 1),
Eliakim (*Nehemiah* xii. 4) and Abiud=Abihu (*Exodus* xxiv. 1)—it is possible that this belongs to the pedigree of Joseph the brother and guardian of
Mary the Braider, and that it was originally traced back to Aaron. If so, the
earlier part has been suppressed, for doctrinal reasons, and the last few generations have been tacked on to the royal genealogy that ended with Zerubbabel. In this case, the father of Mary the Braider will have been Jacob son
of Matthan, not Joachim; and the Church tradition that the *Matthew* genealogy was that of Mary the Virgin will be confirmed. Another tradition, that
Joseph who was called the father of Jesus married his niece Mary, is also
confirmed if it refers to Joseph of Arimathea (Ramathaim-Zophim) and
Mary of Cleophas.

(39) *Now, this was the generation of Joseph of Ramathaim, which was called
the father of Jesus, seeing that Mary the Braider, his sister of whom Jesus was
born by the spirit, was an unwedded virgin:*

Joseph was the son of Jacob,
Which was the son of Matthan,
Which was the son of Eleazar,
Which was the son of Elihu,
Which was the son of Jachin,
Which was the son of Zadok,
Which was the son of Azur,
Which was the son of Eliakim,
Which was the son of Abner,
Which was the son of Abihu,

Which was of the line of Zadok son of Ahitub, which was of the line of Eleazar son of Aaron, whom the Lord God (blessed be He!) chose to be High Priest of Israel.

* * * * *

It is likely that the Levite names which intrude into Jesus's Davidic genealogy have been borrowed from this passage (*see* 11.*c*).

(*v*) Hegesippus further reports that Simeon the son of Cleophas was James the Just's cousin (Eusebius: *Ecc. Hist.* 4. xxii. 4) and after James's martyrdom became his successor as head of the Nazarene Church; he lived to a remarkable old age. In the *Codex Wagenseil* of the *Toldoth Yeshu* he is mentioned as 'a certain aged man from among the elders who frequented the Holy of Holies' and led the exodus of the Nazarenes from Jerusalem. In the *Codex Huldreich* he is described as 'Simeon son of Kalpus the uncle of Jesus.' According to Epiphanius (*Heresies* lxxviii. 14), who says that he was a Rechabite, Simeon had tried in vain to save James from his assailants. This is why we now identify him with Simeon the Chaste, who has the same appellative ('*Ha-Zenuna*') in the *Tosephta* (*see* cix.*k*). That Joseph the father of James was 'Joseph of Arimathea' is indicated by his claiming of Jesus's body from Pilate, after the Crucifixion, presumably as his male next-of-kin (*see* cxiv.*a*). Doubt has been cast on the possible existence of a Rechabite priest, but according to *Yalkut Shimeoni* ii. 323, the Rechabites married their daughters to priests and had grandchildren among the priesthood, of whom Jeremiah was one (*Megillah* 14*b*), and the celebrated Rabbi Jose ben Halafta another (*Genesis Rabbah* xcviii. 13). Priests of Rechabite blood had a specially appointed time for Temple service, namely the seventh of Ab (*Ta'anith* iv. 5) and the rabbis held that God's covenant with them (*Jeremiah* xxxv. 19) was superior to his covenant with David (*Psalm* cxxxii. 12) since theirs was unconditional (*Mechilta* ii. 157, *ed. Lauterbach*). If Simeon was a Rechabite, so was his first cousin James the Just; and this is in part confirmed by Eusebius who records (*Ecc. Hist.* 2. xxiii. 5) that James touched neither wine nor strong drink.

(26) *Then John brought unto Jesus the other Mary, daughter of Simeon the Chaste, of Bethany, arrayed in white linen and espoused her unto him.*

* * * * *

(28) *Now Jesus, after the manner of the saints, had kept himself from women all the days of his life lest the Day of Judgement might find him defiled. As Moses said on Sinai: 'Be ready against the third day' (which is the Day of Resurrection); 'come not at your wives!'*

* * * * *

(29) *Then he, being a just man, was minded to put her away privily, not wishing to shame her before the guests.*
But while he thought on these things John counselled him, saying: 'Fear not, thou son of David, to take unto thee Mary, thy espoused wife,

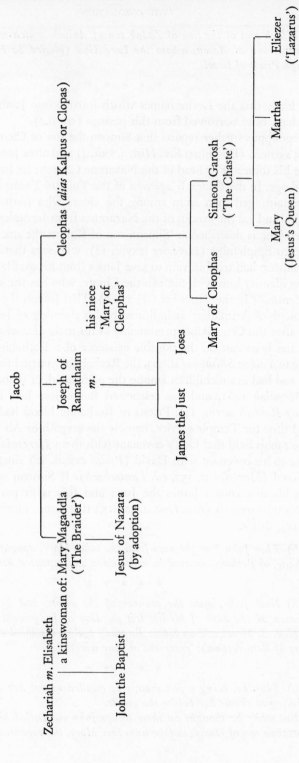

THE LEVITE KINSFOLK OF JESUS

'For she shall be unto thee as Abishag the Shunemite was, that ministered unto thy father David; though she was very fair, yet David knew her not and he named her his sister, though she was his spouse.'

And Jesus said unto Mary his wife: 'Suffer it to be so, for thus it becometh us to fulfil all righteousness.'

Therefore he took unto him his wife as John bade, but he knew her not. Yet he entered with her into the bride chamber which the disciples had builded for him, and tarried there awhile with her.

*   *   *   *   *

(*w*) Sister-wives seem to have been the rule in the early Church, (1 *Corinthians* ix. 5) : 'Have we not power to lead about a sister wife?'; and sexless cohabitation between clerics and nuns was practised in the medieval Irish Church until scandals caused its prohibition.*

The passage seems to be introduced by another which has been hidden in *Revelation* xix. 6–8, where it is certified as authentic Scripture (verse 9). Only very slight modifications need be made here:

(25) *And John spake from beside the throne, saying in a voice of mighty thunderings: 'Praise our God, all ye His servants, and ye that fear Him, both great and small!'*

And they that stood by answered in a voice of many waters: 'Halleluiah! For the Lord God Omnipotent reigneth!'

Then said John: 'Let us be glad and rejoice and give honour to our King. For the marriage of the Lamb is come, and his wife hath made herself ready.

'And to her is granted that she should be arrayed in fine linen, clean and white; for fine linen is the righteousness of saints.

'Blessed are they that are called to the marriage supper of the Lamb.'

*   *   *   *   *

White linen (a symbol of chastity) was the dress of the Essenes, and of the priests.

This seems to be the point at which Simeon blessed the couple (*see* III.*a*), but his *Nunc Dimittis* belongs to a much later context (*see* cxvi.*f*). His remark to Mary the mother of Jesus (*Luke* ii. 35): 'Yea, a sword shall pierce thy soul also', reads like an interpolation, a prophecy made after the event; or did Simeon really foresee that Jesus would identify himself with *Zechariah's* shepherd (*see* cii.*e*) who was fated to be run through by the sword? But the 'also' is important as suggesting that in the original Apostolic tradition, preserved by the Copts, Jesus was pierced on the Cross, by a sword, not a spear (*see* cxiii.*y*). The Joseph who is said to have marvelled, together with the mother of Jesus, at Simeon's prophecy, will have been Joseph of Ramathaim, the brother of Mary the Braider. His son James the Just is likely to have been present.

(27) *And Simon the Chaste, a just and devout man, of those Watchers which awaited the consolation of Israel, was filled with the Holy Spirit.*

* J. Loth: *Révue Celtique,* 15; L. Gougaud: *Eriu* ix.

He blessed the bridegroom and the bride and said unto Mary the Braider, the mother of Jesus:

'This thy son is set for the fall and rising again of many in Israel, and for a sign that shall be spoken against, that the thoughts of many hearts may be revealed.'

Yes, a sword shall pierce thy soul also.

And the mother of Jesus and Joseph of Ramathaim, her brother, marvelled at these things which were spoken of him.

*   *   *   *

(*x*) The only known occasion on which Jesus 'went up into' a hill and formally seated himself, was when he preached the so-called 'Sermon on the Mount', the longest and most carefully composed of all his utterances; and *Matthew* places it at the beginning of the ministry. The account of the Coronation would have been of little interest to the Nazarenes if Jesus had not improved the hour by a solemn statement of religious policy (*see* IX.*a*).

(*y*) The order of ritual events may now be postulated as follows:

(*a*) John the Baptist acclaims Jesus the future king (see VI.*b*).

(*b*) John goes to Jerusalem to summon Mary the Braider, his maternal kinswoman (*see* VII.*a*), and thence to Bethany to summon Mary daughter of Simeon the Chaste.

(*c*) In the interval Jesus fasts, and has a vision of his good and evil angels (*see* LXXVIII.*e*).

(*d*) Mary the Braider arrives and Jesus is lustrated in the spring.

(*e*) He is given a new name and proclaimed the Son of God.

(*f*) Mary the Braider becomes his new mother.

(*g*) He is duly anointed and shod.

(*h*) He is clad in a purple robe, sceptred and crowned.

(*i*) He mounts a hill.

(*j*) He delivers his address from the throne.

(*k*) He is espoused to the other Mary and admonished by John.

(*l*) He retires for awhile to the bride chamber with his Queen.

(*m*) The feast is celebrated; Jesus is perfumed.

(*n*) He lights a new fire.

(*o*) He is mocked and assaulted.

(*p*) He returns to Galilee.

(*q*) He distributes bread (*see* LXXII.*d*).

(*r*) He symbolically sets up his memorial pillar (*see* LVI.*f*).

(*s*) He makes the round of his Kingdom (*see* LXXIX.*a*).

(*t*) He finally rides into Jerusalem on ass-back amid plaudits (*see* LXXXIX.*a*).

*   *   *   *

The sequence begins here:

(18) *When therefore Mary came with Elisabeth unto Beth-Nimrah, and Jesus which should be made king was also returned thither from the mountain where he fasted,*

He, being clad in filthy garments, stood before John the messenger of the Lord, even as Zechariah prophesied.

And John said to the seven priests which stood by: 'Take away these filthy garments!' And unto Jesus he said: 'Behold, I have caused thine iniquity to pass from thee, and I will clothe thee with change of raiment.'

* * * * *

(19) Then John protested unto Jesus according to the prophecy of Zechariah, saying:

'Thus saith the Lord of Hosts: "If thou wilt walk in My ways and if thou wilt keep My charge, then thou shalt also judge My house and keep My courts, and I will give thee walks to walk in among them that stand by.

' "Hear now, Jesus, thou and thy fellows that sit before thee, for they are men of a sign; behold, I will bring forth my servant The Branch!" '

Then it came to pass that Jesus went into the water of his cleansing and when he came out a great light shone upon him.

John bare record, saying: 'Behold, I saw the heavens opened, as my father Levi prophesied, and the Spirit of God that descended and lighted upon thee in the form of a dove. And the voice of the Lord uttered glory upon thee.'

And John, casting his eye upon Mary the Braider, said unto her: 'Woman, behold thy son!' and to Jesus he said: 'Son, behold thy mother!'

Then Mary spread her skirt over Jesus to cover his nakedness, and he was born again of her and was received into the tribe of Levi.

And Salome, her kinswoman, who ministered unto her as a midwife, testified saying: 'This child is born of a virgin which hath known no man.'

Thereafter Jesus took Mary unto him as his own mother, and she called his name The Branch.

* * * * *

(20) John took a cruse of sacred oil and anointed the brow of Jesus.

Then went Jesus into the tiring chamber and there his mother set upon his brow a wreath of thorn which she had plaited for his espousals.

As it is written: 'Go forth, ye daughters of Zion, and behold the King with the wreath wherewith his mother crowned him in the day of his espousals and in the gladness of his heart.'

Then of the seven priests which stood by, the first fastened shoes upon his feet.

And the second clad him in a tunic of fine linen without seam, and the third put a purple mantle upon him.

And the fourth set a green reed in his right hand, and the fifth, a branch of fruitful olive.

And the sixth filled his left hand with frankincense, and the seventh crowned him with a diadem of gold.

* * * * *

[This section is followed by the explanatory story (*see (m) above*) of the wise men who brought the diadem and the frankincense.]

(22) *When he therefore came forth from the tiring chamber, wearing the diadem and the crown of thorn and the purple mantle, John saith: 'Behold, the man!'*

Then Jesus, seeing the solemn assembly, went up into a mount, as David his father had prophesied, saying: 'Yet have I set my King upon my holy hill,

'I will declare the statute: the Lord hath said unto me: "Thou art my Son, this day art thou born to me." '

And when Jesus was set, the disciples came unto him and they began to salute him saying: 'Hail, King of the Jews!' and bowed the knee before him and worshipped him.

* * * * *

[Here follows, first, his speech from the throne (*see* ix.*c*), next his marriage and marriage feast (*see* (*o–w*) *above*), then the incident of the precious ointment (*see* xi.*i*), finally his resolve to abstain from wine (*see* x.*e*).]

(35) *Afterward, according to the word that John had spoken, Jesus kindled a great fire of thorns, and burned incense therein, wherewith the disciples were baptized, and John, and all the company.*

* * * * *

(36) *But certain of the sons of the bride chamber took the reed from Jesus and smote him on the head withal, and did spit on his face.*

And others blindfolded him and smote him with the palms of their hands, saying: 'Prophesy unto us, thou Anointed One: which is he that smote thee?'

And they heaped many curses upon him and buffeted him.

That it might be fulfilled which was spoken of Isaiah the prophet:

'Behold, my servant shall be exalted and extolled and be very high. And many were astonished: his visage was so marred more than any man's, and his form more than the sons of man.'

* * * * *

(37) *And when they had done mocking him, they took the purple off him and put his own raiment on him, and led him away, for his visage was bruised so that for awhile he had no sight, and his body was maimed.*

Thus Jesus himself began to be, about thirty years of age.*

(*z*) Dr. Patai observes that the King after his coronation had no further friendly contact with the prophet who performed the ceremony (1 *Samuel* xv. 35 *and* xvi. 13; 2 *Kings* ix. 3–10)—which may explain why John the Baptist thereafter communicated with Jesus only through his disciples (*Matthew* ix. 14 *and* xi. 2–3—*see* xxxix.*a*).

* * * * *

---

* As late as the third century Paul of Samosata and Archelaus of Armenia denied that Jesus was divine before the spirit descended upon him at his lustration.

IX

THE ADDRESS

Matthew v. 1–12

¹And seeing the multitudes, He went up into a mountain: and when He was set, His disciples came unto Him: ²and He opened His mouth, and taught them, saying:

³'Blessed are the poor in spirit:
For theirs is the kingdom of heaven.

⁴Blessed are they that mourn:
For they shall be comforted.

⁵Blessed are the meek:
For they shall inherit the earth.

⁶Blessed are they which do hunger and thirst after righteousness:
For they shall be filled.

⁷Blessed are the merciful:
For they shall obtain mercy.

⁸Blessed are the pure in heart:
For they shall see God.

⁹Blessed are the peacemakers:
For they shall be called the children of God.

¹⁰Blessed are they which are persecuted for righteousness' sake:
For theirs is the kingdom of heaven.

¹¹Blessed are ye, when men shall revile you, and persecute you,
And shall say all manner of evil against you falsely, for My sake.

¹²Rejoice, and be exceeding glad:
For great is your reward in heaven:
For so persecuted they the prophets which were before you.

Luke vi. 20–26

²⁰And He lifted up His eyes on His disciples, and said:
'Blessed be ye poor: for yours is the kingdom of God.

²¹Blessed are ye that hunger now: for ye shall be filled.
Blessed are ye that weep now: for ye shall laugh.

²²Blessed are ye, when men shall hate you, and when they shall separate you from their company,
And shall reproach you, and cast out your name as evil, for the Son of Man's sake.

²³Rejoice ye in that day, and leap for joy:
For, behold, your reward is great in heaven:
For in the like manner did their fathers unto the prophets.

Luke vi. 20–26 (*contd.*)

²⁴But woe unto you that are rich! for ye have received your consolation.
²⁵Woe unto you that are full! for ye shall hunger.
   Woe unto you that laugh now! for ye shall mourn and weep.
²⁶Woe unto you, when all men shall speak well of you! for so did their
   fathers to the false prophets.

(*a*) Jesus's 'Beatitudes' are a series of ten *midrashim* on the theme of other-
worldly consolation for present suffering. This carefully composed sermon
was preached to a chosen gathering, rather than to 'a multitude'; and both
the formality of the introduction and its early place in *Matthew* suggest that
it was a statement of religious policy, a speech from the Throne. The evangelists have omitted all quotations from the Prophets; if Jesus had been presented as uttering no truth unsubstantiated by the Hebrew Scriptures, the
Gentile Christians could hardly have been expected to revere him as 'speaking with authority, not as the Scribes' (*Matthew* vii. 29—*see* XLII.*f*).
   The parallels are as follows:

> *Matthew* v. 3=*Isaiah* lvii. 15
> *Matthew* v. 4=*Isaiah* lx. 20
> *Matthew* v. 5=*Psalm* xxxvii. 11
> *Matthew* v. 6=*Proverbs* xxi. 17 and 21
> *Matthew* v. 7=*Psalm* xli. 1
> *Matthew* v. 8=*Psalm* xxiv. 3–4 and xi. 7
> *Matthew* v. 9=*Psalm* xxxiv. 11–14
> *Matthew* v. 10=*Isaiah* l. 6–7
> *Matthew* v. 11=*Isaiah* lx. 15

If these quotations are restored to the text, amendments will be needed in
Matthew v. 10 (the second part of which clearly should not repeat *Matthew*
v. 3), and in the Christological *Matthew* v. 11. In *Luke* v. 20–26, where the
scene of the address is a plain, not a mountain, all the beatitudes are over-
simplified except that in *Luke* vi. 22, which fortunately confirms our
amended text of *Matthew* v. 11.
(*b*) Ten was the number of completeness* in Pharisaic mystical theory.
Moses delivered ten Commandments, and ten men constituted a congregation; it is thus unlikely that any beatitudes are missing; but there must have
been ten complementary woes. Of these *Luke,* perhaps not wishing to weary
his readers, has preserved only four, as he has preserved only four beatitudes.
Two woes survive vestigially in *Matthew* v. 12, which corresponds with the
second part of *Luke* vi. 25 and with *Luke* vi. 26. The quotations omitted
from *Luke's* woes are as follows:

> *Luke* vi. 24=*Amos* vi. 1–9
> *Luke* vi. 25=*Isaiah* lxv. 13, and also 14
> *Luke* vi. 26=2 *Chronicles* xxxvi. 16.

* The Pythagoreans concurred.

(*c*) The six missing woes will probably have been uttered against the proud, the deceitful, the foolish, the hard-hearted, the avaricious, and the bloody-minded. The relevant texts may be found in:

> *Proverbs* xv. 25
> *Psalm* v. 6
> *Proverbs* xix. 29
> *Proverbs* xxviii. 14
> *Isaiah* v. 8
> *Psalm* lv. 23.

The woes uttered against the Feigned Pharisees in *Matthew* xxiii. 13 belong to a different series (*see* xiii.*c–x*).

'The disciples' will have been John the Baptist's, Jesus having not yet chosen the Twelve.

[And seeing the solemn assembly, he went up into a mount. And when he was set, the disciples came unto him . . . *see* viii.*y*]

*   *   *   *   *

(23) *And he opened his mouth and uttered ten blessings upon those that forsook all for the Kingdom's sake, saying:*

'*Blessed are the poor in spirit; theirs is the Kingdom of Heaven! For Isaiah prophesied in God's name, saying: "I dwell in the high and holy place with him also that is of a contrite and humble spirit."*

'*Blessed are they that mourn; they shall be comforted! For Isaiah also prophesied, saying: "The Lord shall be thine everlasting light and the days of thy mourning shall be ended."*

'*Blessed are the meek; they shall inherit the earth! For David prophesied: "The meek shall inherit the earth, and shall delight themselves in the abundance of peace."*

'*Blessed are they that hunger and thirst after righteousness and mercy; they shall be filled! For Solomon prophesied: "He that loveth wine and oil shall not be rich, but he that seeketh after righteousness and mercy findeth life and righteousness and honour."*

'*Blessed are the merciful; they shall receive mercy! For David prophesied: "He that hath mercy upon the poor, the Lord will deliver him in time of trouble."*

'*Blessed are the pure in heart; they shall see God! For David prophesied: "He that hath clean hands and a pure heart, he shall receive the blessing of the Lord." And David also declared this blessing, what it was, saying: "I will behold Thy face in righteousness, when I awaken."*

'*Blessed are the peacemakers; they shall be called the Children of God! For David prophesied, saying: "Come, ye children, hearken unto me and I will teach you the fear of the Lord: which is to depart from evil and to do good, to seek peace and to ensue it."*

'*Blessed are they that are reproached for righteousness' sake; they shall not be confounded! For Isaiah prophesied: "I hid not my face from shame and*

*spitting. But the Lord God will help me; therefore shall I not be confounded
and I have set my face like a flint."*

*'Blessed are they that men hate and forsake; many generations shall love
them! For Isaiah prophesied: "Whereas thou hast been forsaken and hated,
I will make thee an eternal excellence, a joy of many generations." '*

* * * *

(24) *And he uttered also ten woes upon those that repented not, saying:*

*'Woe unto them that take delight in riches and put far off the evil day; they
shall perish in the destruction of their palaces! For Amos prophesied of them:
"Woe unto them that are at ease in Zion and lie upon beds of ivory and chant
to the sound of viols; if there remain ten men in one house, they shall all die."*

*'Woe unto them that are filled; they shall hunger! For Isaiah prophesied
against them in the name of the Lord: "Behold, my servants shall eat, but ye
shall be hungry."*

*'Woe unto them that laugh now; they shall weep! . . . For Isaiah proph-
esied against them also: "Behold, my servants shall sing for joy, but ye shall
weep for sorrow of heart and cry from vexation of spirit."*

*'Woe unto the proud; they shall be left without shelter! For Solomon
prophesied: "The Lord will break down the house of the proud."*

*'Woe unto the deceitful; they shall be destroyed! For David prophesied:
"Thou shalt destroy them that speak leasing."*

*'Woe unto the fools that despise righteousness; they shall receive many
stripes! For Solomon prophesied: "Judgements are prepared for scorners and
stripes for the backs of fools."*

*'Woe unto the hard-hearted; they shall find no mercy! For Solomon
prophesied: "He that hardeneth his heart shall fall into mischief."*

*'Woe unto them that are greedy of gain; they shall want! For Isaiah
prophesied: "Woe unto them that join house to house, that lay field to field!
Of a truth many great and fair houses shall be desolate, and the seed of an
homer shall yield but an ephah."*

*'Woe unto the blood-thirsty; they shall be cut off! For David prophesied:
"Bloody and deceitful men shall not live out half their days."*

*'Woe unto them that speak well of false prophets, but despise the mes-
sengers of God; they shall perish utterly! As it is written in the Chronicles of
the Kings of Judah: "But they mocked the messengers of God and despised
His prophets, until the wrath of the Lord arose against His people and He
sent him against them which slew their young men with the sword in the
house of their sanctuary, and had no compassion upon young man or maiden,
or him that stooped for age." '*

(d) Jesus is keeping faithfully to the ethical teaching found in *The Testaments of the Twelve Patriarchs (Issachar* iv. 2–6):

'The single-minded man coveteth not gold,
He over-reacheth not his neighbour,
He longeth not after manifold dainties,
He delighteth not in varied apparel,
He doth not desire to live a long life

But only waiteth for the will of God.
And the spirits of deceit have no power against him,
For he hath looked not on the beauty of women,
Lest he should pollute and corrupt his mind.
There is no envy in his thoughts,
Nor any troubling of insatiable desire in his mind,
For he hath walked in singleness of soul
And beholdeth all things in uprightness of heart
Shunning the eyes that are made evil through the error of the will.
Lest he should see the perversion of any Commandment of the Lord.

* * * * *

X

THE WATER POTS

John ii. 1–11

¹And the third day there was a marriage in Cana of Galilee; and the mother of Jesus was there: ²and both Jesus was called, and His disciples, to the marriage. ³And when they wanted wine, the mother of Jesus saith unto Him: 'They have no wine.' Jesus saith unto her: 'Woman, what have I to do with thee? Mine hour is not yet come.' ⁵His mother saith unto the servants: 'Whatsoever He saith unto you do it.' ⁶And there were set there six waterpots of stone, after the manner of the purifying of the Jews, containing two or three firkins apiece. ⁷Jesus saith unto them: 'Fill the waterpots with water.' And they filled them up to the brim. ⁸And He saith unto them: 'Draw out now, and bear unto the governor of the feast.' And they bare it. ⁹When the ruler tasted the water that was made wine, and knew not whence it was, (but the servants which drew the water knew) the governor of the feast called the bridegroom, ¹⁰and saith unto him: 'Every man at the beginning doth set forth good wine; and when men have well drunk, then that which is worse: but thou hast kept the good wine until now.' ¹¹This beginning of miracles did Jesus in Cana of Galilee, and manifested forth His glory; and His disciples believed on Him.

Mark xiv. 23

²³And He took the cup, and when He had given thanks, He gave it to them: and they all drank of it.

Mark xiv. 25

²⁵Verily I say unto you, I will drink no more of the fruit of the vine, until that day that I drink it new in the kingdom of God.

Matthew xxvi. 27

²⁷And He took the cup, and gave thanks, and gave it to them, saying:
'Drink ye all of it.'

Matthew xxvi. 29

²⁹But I say unto you, I will not drink henceforth of this fruit of the vine, until that day when I drink it new with you in My Father's kingdom.

Luke xxii. 17–18

¹⁷And He took the cup, and gave thanks, and said: 'Take this, and divide it among yourselves: ¹⁸for I say unto you, I will not drink of the fruit of the vine, until the kingdom of God shall come.'

(*a*) Jesus performed the symbolic act of presenting lustral water to guests at a wedding as though it were wine, after his return to Galilee. The account was omitted from the synoptic Gospels, perhaps because its original ascetic meaning did not suit Gentile Christian doctrine; but an editor of *John* had the notion of transforming it into an impressive, if pointless, conjuring trick of the sort ascribed to Apollonius of Tyana (*see Introduction* IV.*m*).

'Woman, what have I to do with thee?' cannot have been spoken by Jesus to his mother; that would have been a breach of the Third Commandment. He must have been rejecting some other woman's invitation to go against his conscience. The same formula was used by David in 2 *Samuel* xix. 22, when called upon by the sons of Zeruiah to punish Shemei though he had acted under orders from God. The clue to the situation is found in 'My time is not yet come', a saying paralleled by *John* vii. 6 (*see* XLIX.*b*): Jesus means that he has resolved to drink no wine until a certain day which has not yet arrived. A simple substitution of 'Thou hast no wine' for 'They have no wine', and of 'Mary' for 'his mother' at once makes sense of the story; the Mary in question is his Queen, the daughter of Simeon the Chaste. In contemporary theory (*Baba Mezi'a* 59*a*), the man who listened to his wife's advice was in constant danger of hell fire.

(*b*) It seems that Jesus assisted at the marriage of a Galilean kinsman—perhaps his brother Judah, whose grandchildren became Nazarenes (*see* I.*a*)—that the guests drank deep and that Mary begged him to do the same, since the wedding gave him dispensation. He refused, probably quoting from the *Testament of Judah* xiv. 1, *Isaiah* v. 11–12 and *Zechariah* xiv. 21. Instead, he made the servants fill the pots from which water was drawn before and after meals for ritual washing, and replenish the wine-cups from them. This signified that, since the Kingdom of God was imminent, water of purification was better than wine, the inflamer of carnal desire, even at a wedding; that, in fact, love between the sexes should not be physically consummated. Jesus later enlarged on the theme in *Matthew* xxiv. 38 and in the *Gospel according to the Egyptians* (*see* XXI.*k and n*). The master of ceremonies understood his meaning and conveyed it to the bridegroom, for whom it was intended.

(*c*) Since the introduction of idle detail into a narrative is not characteristic of the Gospels, we conclude that the number of the water-pots, namely six, had some special significance in the context either for Jesus himself or for the Grecian editor of *John*. If for Jesus, it recalled the prophecy in *Zechariah* xiv. 21 about the pots being 'holiness to the Lord': he will have been insisting that the six labouring days of the week should be kept holy as the Sabbath during which sexual dalliance was forbidden (*see* XXI.*l*) and the pious kept their thoughts fixed on the Law. For the editor of *John*, however, *six* will have been a mathematic metaphor borrowed from Philo (*Allegories of the Law* ii. 281): 'What the number 6 generated, that the number 7 exhibited in full perfection.' 'Two or three firkins' is probably a Grecian addition, the number 2 being female and 3 being male in Philonian philosophy (*ibid.*); but it is just possible that they had the same significance in secret Pharisaic doctrine, and that Jesus meant to deliver the message equally for men and women.

> (66) *There was a marriage in Cana of Galilee, and Jesus was called thither, for the bridegroom was his kinsman according to the flesh.*
>
> *And coming with his disciples on the third day he found the guests merry with music and laughter, but he would drink no wine with them.*
>
> *Then Mary his wife said unto him: 'Lord, thou hast no wine. Let me command the servants to fill thy cup.'*
>
> *He answered and said unto her: 'Woman, what have I to do with thee? The time of my drinking is not yet come.'*
>
> *But his mother, which was of the House of David, said unto him: 'Yet this day looseth all vows.'*
>
> *He answered her: 'Our forefather Judah commanded us: "My children, be not drunk with wine, which turneth the mind away from the truth, leadeth in lust, and guideth the eyes into error."*
>
> *'And Isaiah prophesied against the drunken, saying: "The tabret and pipe are in their feasts but they regard not the work of the Lord."*
>
> *'Therefore will I drink no wine until the Kingdom of God cometh. I pray thee, let me now command the servants as it seemeth good unto me. For behold, that time is at hand when, as Zechariah prophesied, every pot shall be holiness unto the Lord of Hosts.'*
>
> *His mother commanded the servants, saying: 'Whatsoever he may bid you do, do it!'*
>
> *And he bade them fill up six stone water-pots being of two or three firkins apiece. They filled them with water to the brim.*
>
> *Then he said: 'Bear out now unto the ruler of the feast!' And they bare them.*
>
> *And when that the ruler of the feast had tasted of the water that was poured out as wine, he understood, and said unto the bridegroom: 'The better drink is used to be set out first, and then, when men have well drunk, that which is worse. But thou hast kept the better until now.'*
>
> *Jesus answered and said unto him: 'These six pots shall be as the six days of the week wherein we labour: each shall be holiness unto the Lord, both for the male and for the female, even as the Sabbath is holy.'*
>
> *This was the first notable act which Jesus performed in Galilee after that he turned back thither from his anointing.*

* * * * *

(*d*) The occasion of this resolve to abstain from wine has been disguised by the author of *Mark*. He places it at the end of the Last Supper, as a prophecy of Jesus's coming death (*see* cvi.*k–p*). Probably the resolve was announced during the Coronation banquet, as a token of his complete self-dedication to God. Jesus refrained from using the word *corban* (*see* xx.*b* and xxiii.*c*): though no less binding than a formal vow his words, should he fail to keep them, would not involve him in a breach of the Third Commandment (*see* xx.*e*). Prophets drank no wine (*Amos* ii. 12)—neither did priests while employed in divine service (*Leviticus* x. 9)—and Jesus may have privately reminded his Queen that as a King he was forbidden all carnal indulgence (*Proverbs* xxxi. 3–5):

'Give not thy strength unto women, nor thy ways to that which destroyeth kings.

It is not for kings, O Lemuel, it is not for kings to drink wine, nor for princes to drink strong drink,

Lest they drink and forget the Law and pervert the judgement of any of the afflicted.'

From *Ezekiel* xliv. 20 it would appear that he was a Nazirite only in so far as he abstained from wine; being a Levite by adoption he was not allowed to let his hair grow long.

(*e*) The particular wine to which he refers in *Mark* xiv. 25 and *Matthew* xxvi. 29 is the *Yayin ha-Meshummar,* said to have been prepared by God during the six days of creation and to be still existent in its original grapes, ready for serving new at the banquet given to the just in the Kingdom of Heaven (*Sanhedrin* 99*a* and *Berakoth* 34*b*).

(34) *Then Jesus took a cup of wine that was prepared for him, and blessed it and gave thanks. And unto the sons of the bride chamber he said: 'Take this and drink ye all of it. But I will not drink henceforth of the fruit of the vine until I may drink it new in the Kingdom of my Father.*

'That wine shall be pressed from grapes which have been since the world began.'

*   *   *   *   *

XI

THE PRECIOUS OINTMENT

Mark xiv. 3–9

[3]And being in Bethany in the house of Simon the leper, as He sat at meat, there came a woman having an alabaster box of ointment of spikenard very precious; and she brake the box, and poured it on His head. [4]And there were some that had indignation within themselves, and said: 'Why was this waste of the ointment made? [5]For it might have been sold for more than three hundred pence, and have been given to the poor.' And they murmured against her. [6]And Jesus said: 'Let her alone; why trouble ye her? she hath wrought a good work on Me. [7]For ye have the poor with you always, and whensoever ye will ye may do them good: but Me ye have not always. [8]She hath done what she could: she is come aforehand to anoint My body to the burying. [9]Verily I say unto you, wheresoever this Gospel shall be preached throughout the whole world, this also that she hath done shall be spoken of for a memorial of her.'

Matthew xxvi. 6–13

[6]Now when Jesus was in Bethany, in the house of Simon the leper, [7]there came unto Him a woman having an alabaster box of very precious ointment, and poured it on His head, as He sat at meat. [8]But when His disciples saw it, they had indignation, saying: 'To what purpose is this waste? [9]For this ointment might have been sold for much, and given to the poor.' [10]When Jesus understood it, He said unto them: 'Why trouble ye the woman? for she hath wrought a good work upon Me. [11]For ye have the poor always with you; but Me ye have not always. [12]For in that she hath poured this ointment on My body, she did it for my burial. [13]Verily I say unto you, wheresoever this Gospel shall be preached in the whole world, there shall also this, that this woman hath done, be told for a memorial of her.'

Luke vii. 36–50

[36]And one of the Pharisees desired Him that He would eat with him. And He went into the Pharisee's house, and sat down to meat. [37]And, behold, a woman in the city, which was a sinner, when she knew that Jesus sat at meat in the Pharisee's house, brought an alabaster box of ointment, [38]and stood at His feet behind Him weeping, and began to wash His feet with tears, and did wipe them with the hairs of her head, and kissed His feet, and anointed them with the ointment. [39]Now when the Pharisee which had bidden Him saw it, he spake within himself, saying, This man, if He were a prophet, would have known who and what manner of woman this is that toucheth

Luke vii. 36–50 (*contd.*)

Him: for she is a sinner. [40]And Jesus answering said unto him: 'Simon, I have somewhat to say unto thee.' And he saith: 'Master, say on.' [41]'There was a certain creditor which had two debtors: the one owed five hundred pence, and the other fifty. [42]And when they had nothing to pay, he frankly forgave them both. Tell me therefore, which of them will love him most?' [43]Simon answered and said: 'I suppose that he, to whom he forgave most.' And He said unto him: 'Thou hast rightly judged.' [44]And he turned to the woman, and said unto Simon: 'Seest thou this woman? I entered into thine house, thou gavest Me no water for My feet: but she hath washed My feet with tears, and wiped them with the hairs of her head. [45]Thou gavest Me no kiss: but this woman since the time I came in hath not ceased to kiss My feet. [46]My head with oil thou didst not anoint: but this woman hath anointed My feet with ointment. [47]Wherefore I say unto thee, Her sins, which are many, are forgiven; for she loved much: but to whom little is forgiven, the same loveth little.' [48]And He said unto her: 'Thy sins are forgiven.' [49]And they that sat at meat with Him began to say within themselves, 'Who is this that forgiveth sins also?' [50]And He said to the woman: 'Thy faith hath saved thee; go in peace.'

John xi. 1–2

[1]Now a certain man was sick, named Lazarus, of Bethany, the town of Mary and her sister Martha. [2]It was that Mary which anointed the Lord with ointment, and wiped His feet with her hair, whose brother Lazarus was sick.

John xii. 1–8

[1]Then Jesus six days before the passover came to Bethany, where Lazarus was which had been dead, whom He raised from the dead. [2]There they made Him a supper; and Martha served: but Lazarus was one of them that sat at the table with Him. [3]Then took Mary a pound of ointment of spikenard, very costly, and anointed the feet of Jesus, and wiped His feet with her hair: and the house was filled with the odour of the ointment. [4]Then saith one of His disciples, Judas Iscariot, Simon's son, which should betray Him: [5]'Why was not this ointment sold for three hundred pence and given to the poor?' [6]This he said, not that he cared for the poor; but because he was a thief, and had the bag, and bare what was put therein. [7]Then said Jesus: 'Let her alone: against the day of My burying hath she kept this. [8]For the poor always ye have with you; but Me ye have not always.'

(*a*) 'Simon the Leper' (*Mark* xiv. 3 and *Matthew* xxvi. 6) is now generally admitted to be a fantastic mistranslation. Under the Mosaic Law, a leper was evicted from his home and forced to live outside the town or settlement (*Leviticus* xiii. 46—see xxxii.*a*). The suggestion that Jesus of his infinite charity consorted with lepers does not bear a moment's scrutiny.* Of what

* This misunderstanding was largely responsible for the frightful spread of leprosy in the Dark Ages, when Graeco-Roman hygienic principles had been undermined: pious Christians identified bathing with debauchery, hand-washing with hypocrisy, and quarantine with sheer uncharitableness. A man who laid a leper in his own bed was regarded as a saint, not as an anti-social pervert.

Aramaic word, then, is 'leper' a mistranslation? *Mezora* is the correct equivalent of 'leper' in Hebrew, and *segira* in Aramaic; but it may be assumed
with confidence that the word which the translator found was *garba;* because the Syriac text of *Matthew* xxvi. 6, which is of great antiquity, reads:

> *Vekad hava Jeshua bebet-ania bebetah de'Shimeon* garba.

(*b*) *Garba* means 'sufferer from a non-contagious skin-disease', (*garab* in
Hebrew) and according to *Leviticus* xxi. 20, such a man, though not 'cast
out from the camp', was disqualified from serving as a priest. *Garba* included those with scrofula or 'false leprosy' (*vitiligo*) for which the Greek is
alphos; so *garba, garab,* or *garban* (this last is the Aramaic form occurring in
the *Targum to Leviticus* xxi. 20) would be more properly translated *alpheios*
—thus recalling the name given to the fathers of 'James the brother of our
Lord' and of Matthew the Levite (*see* VIII.*s* and XIX.*g*). If, *alphaeus,* which
has no meaning in Greek, stands for *alpheios,* 'vitiliginous', then 'this is a
sort of leprosy', an early gloss for the benefit of ignorant readers, may well
have crept into the Greek text: *Simōnos tou Leprou* replacing *Simōnos tou
Alpheiou.* But since Simon Alpheios—whom we identify with 'Simon Cleophas' and 'Simon the Chaste' of the Talmud (*see* VIII.*v,* CIX.*k,* and CXVI.*b*)
was a Levite priest who served in the Sanctuary (Epiphanius: *Heresies*
lxxviii. 14; *Tosephta Kelim* 1-6), he could not have been *garba,* 'vitiliginous',
any more than he could have been *segira,* 'a leper', owing to the provisions
in *Leviticus* xxi. 20 mentioned above. Therefore *garba* must be a misreading
of an Aramaic word of which the Greek is a translation.

(*c*) Textual corruption is generally admitted, and various scholarly guesses
have been made at the original word. Since Simon is called 'a Pharisee' in
Luke vii. 36, some read *zenua,* 'the pious' or *zadika,* 'the innocent', or *kana,*
'the just'—all words which, when written in Hebrew characters of the
period, carry a vague resemblance to *garba.* But the missing word is likely
to have resembled *garba* far more closely than any of these three, and to have
been unfamiliar enough to puzzle the Greek translator (probably a Graeco-
Syrian convert). Our own suggestion is *garosh,* which means: 'one who
separates himself from his wife'. It is known that the organization of Jesus's
disciples closely resembled that of the Essenes described by Josephus (*see*
LVI.*i*); and also that the Free Essenes—the Strict Essenes were monastic
celibates—'came at their wives' only when deliberately attempting procreation: 'to demonstrate that they do not marry for lust but for the sake of
posterity', as Josephus explains (*Wars* ii. 8. 13). It is difficult, however, to
decide whether *'the of Alphaeos'* (=*alpheios*=*garba*=*garosh*) means that
James's father separated himself from his wife or that James did so himself;
and whether, in the latter case, *garosh* meant one who practised complete
marital chastity (*see* XXI.*n*) or one who occasionally took grudging thought
for posterity. In any case, 'Simon the Leper' may be plausibly re-translated
'Simeon the Chaste'.

(*d*) Our reading would account for 'the Pharisee' in *Luke* vii. 36; the translator here has also been baffled by *garosh* and guessed *parusha* ('Pharisee'). The author of *Luke,* who could never refrain from knitting together sayings and acts of Jesus's which should have been left separate, has been particularly mischievous in his presentation of the story. Its earliest form appears in *Mark* xiv. 3-9, and from *John* xii. 1-2 we are able to identify the woman as Mary, daughter of Simeon the Chaste who, we suggest, was Jesus's Queen (*see* VIII.*s*). But *Luke,* who dates the incident much earlier than either *Mark* or *Matthew,* combines the anointing of Jesus's head with the weeping over his feet, a new detail which he is unlikely to have invented (*Luke* vii. 36-50). Let us see what remains of the story after *Luke's* special contribution is disentangled from the ointment context and from the impossible incident of a prostitute's familiar entry into a Pharisaic household.

(*e*) But the other omissions and accretions must first be repaired. Half a verse has dropped out from *Luke* vii. 37, since 'stood at his feet, behind him' makes no sense: Jesus was not grazing like a sheep. Also, Simeon would have been scrupulous to offer his guest a foot bath (*Luke* vii. 44), if he had come from another town, though not himself a ceremonialist about ritual washing (*see* CIX.*k*). The last two verses have been patched in from *Matthew* ix. 3, ix. 22, and *Luke* viii. 48. Jesus had no right to forgive sins against other men, or against God; he could forgive only wrongs done to himself (*see* XXXV.*b*). How Mary had wronged him does not appear; however, 'she loved much' suggests not that she was sexually faithless to him, but that she opposed certain of his actions from wifely solicitude. The meaning now attached to the words by Protestant sentimentalists, namely that she kept falling in love with different men and allowing herself to be seduced by them from mere goodness of heart, is utterly alien to Jewish thought.

(*f*) Jesus is telling a 'Thou art the Man!' fable, like the one told by the prophet Nathan to David (2 *Samuel* xii. 1-6); and Simeon, as the lesser debtor, must therefore have been implicated in the wrong. The nature of the quarrel can be recovered by a critical examination of the story of Lazarus (*see* LXXXVII.*e*). It seems that Mary tried to make Jesus drink wine at a wedding (*see* X.*a*), but her other sins are not known; perhaps she chafed at the nonconsummation of her marriage. If so, the story will have been that shortly before the Crucifixion, Jesus stopped at Bethany on his way to Jerusalem, but reproached neither Simeon nor Mary, and that after a while she fell at his feet in a fit of repentance. The second part of *John* xii. 2 is misplaced; Lazarus cannot have been present (*see* LXXXIV.*d*).

(*g*) The woman's long hair has been quoted as evidence that she was a prostitute because, in later times, Jewish women shaved their heads after marriage. But this is unhistorical. *Canticles* vii. 5, which continued to reflect popular customs in Jesus's day, praises the Queen's glossy black hair; and though women's hair was held to cause sexual excitement (*Berakoth* 24*a*) and married women therefore covered their heads in the synagogue as a precaution against *Yezer Hara* ('the wicked councillor')—this is mentioned in 1 *Corinthians* xi. 10—the occasion here was family gathering. Tresses were cut off only as a sign of mourning (*Jeremiah* vii. 29) or degradation (*Deuteronomy* xxi. 12).*

> (313) *And he came unto Bethany and entered into the home of Simeon the Chaste. He said: 'Peace be to this house!' and offered no reproaches either unto his kinsmen or unto Mary his wife.*
>
> *As he sat at meat with Simeon and his other kinsmen, Mary stood behind him and ministered unto him, weeping.*
>
> *On a sudden she cried out and came and fell at his feet and began to wet them with tears and wipe them with the hairs of her head, and kissed them.*
>
> *And Simeon spake within himself, saying: 'If this man were indeed a prophet he would know how greatly she has trespassed against him.'*
>
> *Then Jesus said unto Simeon: 'I have somewhat to say unto thee.' And Simeon answered: 'Say on!'*
>
> *He said again: 'There was a certain creditor which had two debtors: the one owing five hundred pence and the other fifty.*
>
> *'And when they had nothing to pay, he frankly forgave them both. Tell me therefore which of them will love him the most?'*
>
> *Simeon answered and said: 'I suppose, he to whom he forgave most.'*
>
> *And Jesus said: 'Thou hast rightly judged. Thou gavest me no kiss when I entered, nor weepedst upon my neck; but Mary hath both kissed my feet and washed them with her tears since the time I came in.*
>
> *'Wherefore I say: Her trespasses against me which are many, are forgiven, for she loved me much. Thy trespasses, which are few, are likewise forgiven, but I see that thou lovest me less.'*

* * * * *

(h) *John's* account of Mary's actions has been influenced by *Luke* and makes no sense. Mary, dry-eyed, applies a whole pound of precious ointment to Jesus's feet, leaving his head unanointed, and then transfers it to her own hair. There is also an unwarranted suggestion that Judas stole from the alms-bag, and that Lazarus was present at the meal. Martha's service at table seems to be part of the genuine tradition, since the story of Martha and Mary (*Luke* x. 38–42) clearly belongs to that of Mary's forgiveness. The substance of *Mark* xvi. 9: 'Mary Magdalene, out of whom he had cast seven devils,' echoed in *Luke* viii. 2, probably belongs here. (For a confusion of the three Marys *see* VII.*i*.)

> (314) *Now, Martha the sister of Mary also ministered unto the company.*
>
> *And when she saw that Mary sat at Jesus's feet and heard his words and did nought, she came unto him, saying:*

---

* An exceptionally pious woman, such as the mother of the High Priest Ishmael ben Kimhit, might keep her hair perpetually covered: 'Throughout the days of my life the beams of my house have not seen the plaits of my hair.' But the rabbis replied with dry politeness to her boasts: 'Many other women have covered their heads, but have not enjoyed the honour of having their sons appointed High Priests' (*Yoma* 47*a*). In other words: 'such puritanical scrupulousness is not necessarily a sign of virtue.'

'Behold, I am cumbered with much serving. Dost thou not care, Master, that my sister hath left me to serve alone? Bid her therefore that she help me.'

Jesus answered and said: 'Martha, Martha, thou art careful and troubled about many things. But one thing is needful, which is repentance.

'Mary hath chosen that good part which shall not be taken away from her. For seven devils entered into her, but now are they come forth.'

* * * * *

(*i*) There remains the simple story of the ointment:

(32) *As Jesus sat at meat, Mary took an alabaster box of ointment of nard, mixed with myrrh, very precious, and breaking the box, poured it upon his head. And the house was filled with the savour.*

And the disciples were offended and one said: 'Why was this waste of ointment made? It might have been sold for three hundred pence and given to the poor?' And they murmured against her.

Jesus said: 'Let her alone, why trouble ye her?

'For it is written: "The poor shall never cease out of the land," and whensoever ye will, ye may open your hand wide unto them. But me ye have not always with you.

'My sister hath wrought a good work: she hath done this as a memorial unto me, anointing my body aforehand for the grave, that my soul may live for ever more.'

* * * * *

'Me ye have not always with you' recalls the saying about the sons of the bridechamber (*Luke* v. 33-35); both belong to the Coronation context (*see* VIII.*o*). The disciples mentioned were evidently those of John the Baptist who, as ascetics, objected to the use of ointments even at a marriage feast. Jesus defends Mary's action: it was part of the marriage ritual that the King's garments should smell of perfumes (*Psalm* xlv. 8), and he quotes *Deuteronomy* xv. 11 to show that the poor would always be in need of assistance. The same point is made in the Talmud (*Berakoth* 34*b*):

'Samuel declared: there shall be no difference between this world and the days of the Messiah save that then there shall be no bondage of foreign powers; for it is written: "The poor shall never cease out of the land".'

Jesus adds that he regards the ointment as symbolizing not erotic stimulation but the required burial of his bodily lusts.

(*j*) The value of the box and its contents has probably not been overestimated. The Talmud states (*Kethuboth* 66*b*) that Nicodemon ben Gorion's daughter spent as much as four hundred gold denarii on perfume in a single day; and 'three hundred pence' amounted to only twelve gold denarii. But the true nard imported from North-eastern India, being excessively dear, was usually mixed with other spices; and it was myrrh, not nard, which Nicodemon provided to anoint Jesus's body for burial (*John* xix. 39—*see* cxiv.*d*). So the box, if part of the New Covenanters' coronation gift from Damascus

—gold, myrrh, and frankincense (*see* viii.*l*)—is likely to have contained a compound of Arabian myrrh and Indian nard, both of which are mentioned in Solomon's marriage song (*Canticles* i. 12–13).

Alabaster was regarded as the best material for such boxes (Pliny: *Natural History* xiii. 3) and up to four hundred pence a pound had been paid for unguents (*ibid.* 4).

(*k*) 'Wheresover the Gospel shall be preached throughout the whole world this also that she hath done shall be spoken of for a memorial of her,' is a late Gentile Christian addition. It has its origin, perhaps, in the last words of *Psalm* cxxxiii, the psalm of the High Priest's consecration.

> (33) *And Jesus sang the psalm of David which saith:*
> *'Behold, how good and how pleasant it is for brethren to dwell in unity!*
> *'It is like the precious ointment upon the head that ran down upon the beard, even the beard of Aaron, that went down to the skirts of his garments,*
> *'As the dew that fell upon Hermon and upon the mountains of Zion: for there the Lord commanded the blessing, even life for ever more.'*

* * * * *

XII

THE MEN OF THE LAND

(a) While Josephus particularizes only four contemporary sects (*Antiquities* xviii. 1. 2–6), the Talmud records (*Jer. Sanhedrin* x. 5) that: 'Israel was not exiled until there appeared twenty-four sects of dissenters.' These twenty-four (a number glossed by Pene Mosheh as merely meaning 'very many') would not, of course, have included the sect of the Pharisees by whom the Talmud was itself compiled; yet they too were divided into the quietistic school of Hillel and the more nationalistic school of Shammai.

The Pharisees were the central party. On one flank stood the Sadducees; on the other the apocalyptic extremists, who are proved by their literature to have disagreed on important points of doctrine and policy. They included the Essenes, sub-divided into the Strict Essenes, who chose complete monastic seclusion; the Therapeutics, who preferred convents where the sexes were segregated except during communal worship; and the Free Essenes, who lived in towns, married, and even took part in politics.

The Sadducees, whose main strength lay in the priesthood, were similarly divided among themselves. The poorer priests were always at odds with the patricians, who were less scrupulous than they in the observance of Levitical purity. As for the unpriestly Levites who were also Sadducees but who, apart from musicians, official money-changers and the like, had been reduced to manual labour in the Temple, they bore a grudge against all priests.* Finally the Sadducaic Herodians, the most lax of all in their observance of the Law, quarrelled among themselves for the surviving perquisites of monarchy.

(b) Nevertheless, all sects, apart from the few renegades, were united in reverence for the Mosaic Law and treated the Roman rule as a sacrilegious usurpation; nothing in Judaea or Galilee should be regarded as Caesar's, and no tribute was legally due to him. The Land of Israel—perhaps the most heavily taxed of all Roman protectorates—was waiting for a Messiah who,

---

* Tithes provoked this quarrel. Originally the tithe was collected from the other tribes for the Levites as a whole, and a tithe of this tithe devoted to the priests and Temple servants (*Nehemiah* x. 38–39); but for a long time now the House of Boethus had collected the entire sum and shared it grudgingly with their fellow-tribesmen. Soon not even the poorer priests benefited. Josephus records (*Antiquities* xx. 8. 8):

'The Chief Priests had the hardness to send their servants to the threshing floors to take away those tithes that were due to the priests, insomuch as the poorer sort died for want.'

with God's fullest approval, would come to the rescue of His oppressed people. The announcement of his arrival would make thrones totter and fall and the light of his face would illumine the world. It was believed that the Romans would then either recognize the sovereignty of the True God, or else be utterly destroyed.

(*c*) Several claimants to the Messiahship had made their appearance since the death of Herod the Great. Josephus (*Antiquities* xvii. 10. 5–7) mentions three: Judas of Galilee, son of Hezekiah, an earlier rebel; Simon, an ex-slave; and Athronges, a shepherd. They were proved to be impostors only by their failure; anyone who could successfully defy the Romans and literally fulfil the ancient Messianic prophecies would be the Messiah. It was easy enough for these self-appointed saviours to gain a following among the Zealots, or militant nationalists; but, since they were not recognized by the other sects, none had hitherto become more than a notorious bandit-leader.

(*d*) Continuous repression at the hand of the Romans, and frequent punitive expeditions, which increased in severity as the Zealots took reprisals, turned many ordinary Jews into quietists. Disillusioned by the world, they joined the ranks of the Pharisees and devoted themselves to religious study. The physical body was for them a standing hindrance to the attainment of perfect bliss, and this world a slough of uncleanness, selfishness, falsity, and lust. Their chief ambition was to fit themselves for the next world by abstinence, prayer, and solitary meditation. They were direct successors of the second-century sect of Hasidim, who had offered armed resistance to Antiochus Epiphanes when he tried to Hellenize the Temple but, as soon as freedom of worship was finally won, had refused to assist the Hasmoneans in their further struggle for national sovereignty (1 *Maccabees* vii. 12–14). Those who wished to isolate themselves entirely became Essenes.

(*e*) Much teaching of an Essene character is to be found in the New Testament. Jesus will have first been connected with the sect through the Zophim of Bethany (*see* cxiv.*a and b*) or some other community of Free Essenes. These all aimed at 'seeing God': 'Blessed are the pure in heart, for they shall see God' (*Matthew* v. 8), which could be achieved only after a rooting out of all sensual desires, to the extent of punishing any bodily member that showed a tendency to sin (*Matthew* xviii. 8 and xix. 12). Paul paid lip-service to the same doctrine (*Romans* viii. 13): 'If ye live after the flesh ye shall die, but if ye through the spirit mortify the flesh, ye shall live'—though the Pauline rule, which granted indulgences for wine (1 *Timothy* v. 23), meat (*Romans* xiv. 20), marital lust (1 *Corinthians* vii. 9), and liberal traveling expenses (2 *Corinthians* viii. 21), was regarded by the Nazarene Church of Jerusalem, which remained true to Jesus's ascetic teaching, as gross libertinism.

(*f*) The orthodox Pharisees also reacted against Essene strictness, but only where it ran counter to the spirit of the Law. A Talmudic reference to the 'Saintly Fool' (*Hasid Shoteh*) can have been meant only for the Essenes (*Sotah* 21*b*):

'If the Saintly Fool saw a woman about to drown in a river, he would say: "It is improper for me to come to her rescue, since I could not then avoid looking at her more closely." '

It is folly, not saintliness, that is here being criticized. A second-century Pharisee, Phineas ben Yair, thus describes the wise saint's progress to Salvation (*Abodah Zarah* 20*b*) :

'Study leads to care, care to zeal, zeal to cleanliness, cleanliness to restraint, restraint to purity, purity to holiness, holiness to meekness, meekness to fear of sin, fear of sin to saintliness, saintliness to the holy spirit, and the holy spirit to Salvation.'

The Strict Essene's folly lay in a refusal to think of anyone's salvation but his own. Retirement to an all-male monastery, in the hope that the surrounding thorn hedge would keep out the Devil, seemed absurd to the Pharisees. Already, towards the close of the first century B.C., Hillel had published the admonition (*Aboth* ii. 5): 'Do not separate thyself from the congregation.' He saw clearly that asceticism would lead to monasticism, and monasticism to 'presumptuous sin' (*Psalm* xix. 13)—the placing of one's own spiritual needs above those of the community. Hillel himself led a frugal, not an ascetic, life. He felt a deep sense of responsibility for the welfare of the nation as a whole, and set himself to humanize the Law, not to annul it as Paul tried to do.

(*g*) In the Pharisaic view, all moral problems, whether great or small, must be related to the Law. An individual was of importance only as a member of the nation chosen by God to implement His divine will; cut off from them he was lost, as the nation was similarly lost if cut off from God. Yet, though Judaism was a national religion, the Jews might not keep it exclusively to themselves. The prophets had declared that the God of Israel ruled the Universe, and that all mankind was in His care. Therefore, since only the Jews knew exactly what conduct God demanded of His children, it was their duty to communicate this knowledge to other nations and invite them to become His worshippers in strict obedience to the Mosaic Law, sharing the hope of salvation on equal terms with the Sons of Abraham. In fact, Hillel turned away no would-be convert of any race, even if he were a Roman (*see.* LXXXII.*l*). But with this invitation went a warning of the difficulties and responsibilities that faced the honorary Jew: 'Let thy right hand ever repel, and thy left hand invite' (*Sanhedrin* 107*b* and *Sotah* 47*a*).

(*h*) Unlike the Greek mystery cults, which were reserved for the ruling classes, Judaism was a popular religion. The Pharisees discouraged excessive mourning, fasting, self-castigation, and philosophic speculations about 'what is above, below, in front, or behind', and promoted feasts and pageants. When some of the Canaanite customs adopted on Joshua's entry into the country proved difficult to eradicate, the pre-Pharisaic editors of the Law had given them a new meaning: thus the corn left uncut at harvest in propitiation of the Earth-goddess, and the olives and grapes left ungleaned, were devoted to the widow, the orphan, and the stranger (*Deuteronomy* xxiv. 19–21). The barbarous rites of the 'Pesach', a Spring festival in honour of Tyrian Hercules and his orgiastic mother, the Partridge-goddess, were also modified and made to commemorate incidents in the Exodus from Egypt. The Pharisees now pursued this principle of religious refinement by casting a cloak of allegory over any scandalous or anomalous event in Biblical history. And though they would never admit the individual's right of choice between obedience or disobedience to the Law, they expected him to use commonsense whenever two commandments happened to make irreconcilable demands on him: for instance, when a crisis arose on the Sabbath which obliged him to work for the greater glory of God (*see* LXXIV.*a*). In this way they tried to steer Judaism between the two extremes of Herodian worldliness and Strict Essene other-worldliness.

(*i*) The tighter the Roman hold, the more rapidly the apocalyptics drifted from the sense of physical reality to which the main body of the Pharisees clung: they no longer even felt the need for personal possessions. This present, illusory world, in which Satan had been granted a temporal freedom of action, was for them no more than a gloomy ante-room to the Palace, made still darker by anticipation of the stupendous sufferings that would herald the coming of the Messiah. No power on earth could precipitate or retard the Day of Judgement; yet those gifted with prophecy might preach the danger of imminent doom—as men who see that a dam is about to burst cry out a warning of the approaching flood (*see* XCVIII.*j and* CI.*c*).

(*j*) The apocalyptics were well versed in eschatology and knew what signs to expect (*Enoch* xci. 7):

'When sin and unrighteousness and blasphemy
And violence in all manner of deeds shall increase,
And apostasy and transgression and uncleanness shall also increase,
A great chastisement shall come from heaven upon all these
And the holy Lord will come forth with wrath and vengeance
To execute judgement on earth.'

This chastisement would not merely overtake certain sinful nations or individuals; but the entire world in its familiar form would cease to be. The chosen saints alone would survive the fire, flood, and sword (*see* XCVIII.*k and o*). Different apocalyptic communities had in mind different classes of people whom they hoped to see damned; but it was generally agreed that those who most deserved damnation were the heathen oppressors, their Israelite collaborators, and the boastful, hard-hearted rich—above all the Sadducees, since they refused to believe in the Resurrection. God would tumble the proud from their high seats and exalt the meek, and in the subsequent new Heaven upon earth, the true world (*Olam ha'Emeth*), justice and bliss would reign: the chosen would dwell in angelic harmony for four hundred (or some said a thousand) years until their final, non-corporeal union with God.

(*k*) Each sect or sub-sect in Israel, including the Sadducees, regarded itself as the only orthodox one, and looked with sorrow, anger, or compassion on its rivals. But there was a large group which could be termed neither a sect nor a party: the unorganized and inarticulate manual labourers known as *Ame ha'Aretz,* or 'Men of the Land'. This name implied ignorance of the Law or carelessness in its observance, but did not particularly refer to the peasantry; the alleys and by-streets of Jerusalem were also thronged with *Ame ha'Aretz.*

It can be deduced from both the *Mishnah* and the *Tosephta* that the Men of the Land were despised by the Sadducaic patricians for their poverty, and distrusted by the Pharisees for their violence and religious laxity: the word 'Pharisee' implied self-separation from all who failed to keep the Law—uncleanness was held to be infectious. The patricians had adopted the Graeco-Roman plutocrats' scorn of the lower orders.* The lot of a poor freeman anywhere in the Roman Empire might be far worse than that of the plutocrat's household slave, and spiritual equality was not restored even in the next world: only a citizen who could afford the initiation fee of a respectable mystery cult had any prospect of achieving immortality.

(*l*) Those of the *Ame ha'Aretz* who were peasants resented paying tithes on their produce in order to support the priesthood, especially when few of the Pharisees, being mainly artisans or city-dealers, were liable to this tax. It was the same with the question of Levitical purity: in the better quarters of a predominantly Jewish city like Jerusalem, strict observance of the Law was easier than in the slums, or in the countryside, where more occasions for contamination offered. The Men of the Land condemned the Pharisees' scrupulous piety as hypocritical, and needed little provocation to rail against them (*see* xix.*l*). Besides, though regarded by pious synagogue-goers as theoretically equal with themselves before God and as capable of achieving the Heavenly Kingdom, what chance had they of approaching an ideal of purity which was difficult even for a dedicated saint to maintain?

(*m*) Jesus, however, chose to work among the *Ame ha'Aretz*—not because he admired them or was one of them, but because, the Kingdom being imminent, he felt constrained to give them the opportunity of repentance which they had forfeited as outcasts from the synagogues. While not neglecting the ninety-and-nine sheep safe in the fold, he went in search of lost lambs and it was without the least irony that he pronounced the Pharisees and their followers to be in good spiritual health and thus in no need of a physician (*Matthew* ix. 12—*see* xix.*b*); he had preached in the synagogues and was satisfied with their reception of his message.

---

* Even Plato's views about the common people differed little from those of the ordinary unphilosophical patrician; he despised them as the prey of demagogues and held out no hope to them of everlasting bliss.

(*n*) The ragged, evil-smelling proletarians were flattered when Jesus contrasted them favourably with the Sadducees, the well-to-do guests who had excused themselves from attendance at the wedding feast (*Matthew* xxii. 3 and *Luke* xiv. 18—*see* xlvi.*b*); and he convinced himself that, by threats and promises, they could be brought to fill the vacant seats. But in identifying himself with their cause he forfeited the confidence of the well-to-do; and as a quietist he had trouble with his restive Galilean disciples, some of them ex-Zealots, who expected an immediate reward in kind for their self-denials (*Matthew* xix. 27—*see* ci.*f*).

(*o*) Jesus kept perfect faith in God and in the literal fulfilment of Messianic prophecy. Nothing could daunt him. He believed himself to be the destined prophet who, instead of 'reconciling fathers to sons and sons to fathers', as Malachi had foretold of Elijah in the last verse of his book (*see* iv.*d*), would bring 'not peace but a flaming fire' (*see* ci.*g*) and, as Micah had prophesied (*Micah* vii. 6—*see* ci.*d*), divide every family against itself.

(*p*) The Pharisees were assured that the Messiah would come in a generation which was altogether righteous or altogether wicked; that is to say, when every Israelite had made up his mind either to accept or reject the Law (*Sanhedrin* 98*a*). This ancient belief was voiced by Rabbi Johanan: 'When thou seest a generation overwhelmed by many troubles as by a river, then await the Messiah' (*ibid.*). Jesus concluded that this time had now come, and that by preaching himself and also sending out chosen missionaries throughout the land, he could give every Israelite the choice to accept or reject the Law. The action, predetermined by the Prophets, which he then intended to take, would shock the entire nation into repentance, inaugurate the 'Pangs of the Messiah' and so bring the world to a sudden cataclysmic end.

(*q*) It would be wrong to accuse Jesus of megalomania, as many critics have done. He had not planned his own fate, nor even cast himself for the part of national redeemer. John the Baptist had chosen him out of a crowd of pilgrims, anointed him King, given him general instructions in God's name, and left him to play the Messiah as best he might. But the part was implicit in the Law and Prophets, which Jesus had studied with loving care, and though on one occasion John sent an embassy questioning his interpretation of it, Jesus quoted chapter and verse in self-justification (*see* xxxix.*a and b*), not being himself the author of the drama.

* * * * *

XIII

FEIGNED PHARISEES

Luke iv. 14–15

[14]And Jesus returned in the power of the Spirit into Galilee: and there went out a fame of Him through all the region round about. [15]And He taught in their synagogues, being glorified of all.

Matthew xxiii. 1–36

[1]Then spake Jesus to the multitude, and to His disciples, [2]saying: 'The scribes and the Pharisees sit in Moses's seat: [3]all therefore whatsoever they bid you observe, that observe and do; but do not ye after their works: for they say, and do not. [4]For they bind heavy burdens and grievous to be borne, and lay them on men's shoulders; but they themselves will not move them with one of their fingers. [5]But all their works they do for to be seen of men: they make broad their phylacteries, and enlarge the borders of their garments, [6]and love the uppermost rooms at feasts, and the chief seats in the synagogues, [7]and greetings in the markets, and to be called of men, Rabbi, Rabbi. [8]But be not ye called Rabbi: for One is your Master, even Christ; and all ye are brethren. [9]And call no man your father upon the earth: for One is your Father, which is in heaven. [10]Neither be ye called masters: for One is your Master, even Christ. [11]But he that is greatest among you shall be your servant. [12]And whosoever shall exalt himself shall be abased; and he that shall humble himself shall be exalted.

[13]But woe unto you, scribes and Pharisees, hypocrites! for ye shut up the Kingdom of Heaven against men: for ye neither go in yourselves, neither suffer ye them that are entering to go in. [14]Woe unto you, scribes and Pharisees, hypocrites; for ye devour widows' houses, and for a pretence make long prayer: therefore ye shall receive the greater condemnation. [15]Woe unto you, scribes and Pharisees, hypocrites! for ye compass sea and land to make one proselyte, and when he is made, ye make him twofold more the child of hell than yourselves. [16]Woe unto you, ye blind guides, which say, Whosoever shall swear by the temple, it is nothing; but whosoever shall swear by the gold of the temple, he is a debtor! [17]Ye fools and blind: for whether is greater, the gold, or the temple that sanctifieth the gold? [18]And, Whosoever shall swear by the altar, it is nothing; but whosoever sweareth by the gift that is upon it, he is guilty. [19]Ye fools and blind: for whether is greater, the gift, or the altar that sanctifieth the gift? [20]Whoso therefore shall swear by the altar, sweareth by it, and by all things thereon. [21]And whoso shall swear by the temple, sweareth by it, and by Him that dwelleth therein. [22]And he that shall swear

Matthew xxiii. 1–36 (contd.)

by heaven, the same sweareth by the throne of God, and by Him that sitteth thereon. ²³Woe unto you, scribes and Pharisees, hypocrites! for ye pay tithe of mint and anise and cummin, and have omitted the weightier matters of the law, judgment, mercy, and faith: these ought ye to have done, and not to leave the other undone. ²⁴Ye blind guides, which strain at a gnat, and swallow a camel. ²⁵Woe unto you, scribes and Pharisees, hypocrites! for ye make clean the outside of the cup and of the platter, but within they are full of extortion and excess. ²⁶Thou blind Pharisee, cleanse first that which is within the cup and platter, that the outside of them may be clean also. ²⁷Woe unto you, scribes and Pharisees, hypocrites! for ye are like unto whited sepulchres, which indeed appear beautiful outward, but are within full of dead men's bones, and of all uncleanness. ²⁸Even so ye also outwardly appear righteous unto men, but within ye are full of hypocrisy and iniquity. ²⁹Woe unto you, scribes and Pharisees, hypocrites! because ye build the tombs of the prophets, and garnish the sepulchres of the righteous, ³⁰and say, If we had been in the days of our fathers, we would not have been partakers with them in the blood of the prophets. ³¹Wherefore ye be witnesses unto yourselves, that ye are the children of them which killed the prophets. ³²Fill ye up then the measure of your fathers. ³³Ye serpents, ye generation of vipers, how can ye escape the judgment of hell? ³⁴Wherefore, behold, I send unto you prophets, and wise men, and scribes: and some of them ye shall kill and crucify; and some of them shall ye scourge in your synagogues and persecute them from city to city: ³⁵that upon you may come all the righteous blood shed upon the earth, from the blood of righteous Abel unto the blood of Zacharias son of Barachias, whom ye slew between the temple and the altar. ³⁶Verily I say unto you, all these things shall come upon this generation.'

Luke xi. 37–54

³⁷And as He spake, a certain Pharisee besought Him to dine with him: and He went in, and sat down to meat. ³⁸And when the Pharisee saw it, he marvelled that He had not first washed before dinner. ³⁹And the Lord said unto him: 'Now do ye Pharisees make clean the outside of the cup and the platter; but your inward part is full of ravening and wickedness. ⁴⁰Ye fools, did not He that made that which is without make that which is within also? ⁴¹But rather give alms of such things as ye have; and, behold, all things are clean unto you. ⁴²But woe unto you, Pharisees! for ye pay tithe of mint and rue and all manner of herbs, and pass over judgment and the love of God: these ought ye to have done, and not to leave the other undone. ⁴³Woe unto you, Pharisees! for ye love the uppermost seats in the synagogues, and greetings in the markets. ⁴⁴Woe unto you, scribes and Pharisees, hypocrites! for ye are as graves which appear not, and the men that walk over them are not aware of them.' ⁴⁵Then answered one of the lawyers, and said unto Him: 'Master, thus saying Thou reproachest us also.' ⁴⁶And He said: 'Woe unto you also, ye lawyers! for ye lade men with burdens grievous to be borne, and ye yourselves touch not the burdens with one of your fingers. ⁴⁷Woe unto you! for ye build the sepulchres of the prophets, and your fathers killed them. ⁴⁸Truly ye bear witness that ye allow the deeds of your fathers: for they in-

Luke xi. 37–54 (contd.)

deed killed them, and ye build their sepulchres. [49]Therefore also said the wisdom of God, I will send them prophets and apostles, and some of them they shall slay and persecute: [50]that the blood of all the prophets, which was shed from the foundation of the world, may be required of this generation; [51]from the blood of Abel unto the blood of Zacharias, which perished between the altar and the temple: verily I say unto you, it shall be required of this generation. [52]Woe unto you, lawyers! for ye have taken away the key of knowledge: ye entered not in yourselves, and them that were entering in ye hindered.'

[53]And as He said these things unto them, the scribes and the Pharisees began to urge Him vehemently, and to provoke Him to speak of many things: [54]laying wait for Him, and seeking to catch something out of His mouth, that they might accuse Him.

Mark vii. 1–8

[1]Then came together unto Him the Pharisees, and certain of the scribes, which came from Jerusalem. [2]And when they saw some of His disciples eat bread with defiled, that is to say, with unwashen, hands, they found fault. [3]For the Pharisees, and all the Jews, except they wash their hands oft, eat not, holding the tradition of the elders. [4]And when they come from the market, except they wash, they eat not. And many other things there be, which they have received to hold, as the washing of cups, and pots, brasen vessels, and of tables. [5]Then the Pharisees and scribes asked Him: 'Why walk not Thy disciples according to the tradition of the elders, but eat bread with unwashen hands?' [6]He answered and said unto them: 'Well hath Isaiah prophesied of you hypocrites, as it is written,

> This people honoureth Me with their lips.
> But their heart is far from Me.
> [7]Howbeit in vain do they worship Me,
> Teaching for doctrine the commandments of men.

[8]For laying aside the commandments of God, ye hold the tradition of men, as the washing of pots and cups: and many other such like things ye do.'

Matthew xv. 1–2

[1]Then came to Jesus scribes and Pharisees, which were of Jerusalem, saying: [2]'Why do Thy disciples transgress the tradition of the elders? for they wash not their hands when they eat bread.'

Luke x. 19

[19]Behold, I give unto you power to tread on serpents and scorpions, and over all the power of the enemy: and nothing shall by any means hurt you.

Mark xvi. 18

[18]They shall take up serpents; and if they drink any deadly thing, it shall not hurt them; they shall lay hands on the sick, and they shall recover.

(a) The text of Matthew xxiii seems to have reached its present state of corruptness between the years 115 and 130 A.D. An unexpected feature is the retention of the first two verses and half of the third, in which Jesus, after declaring that he has come neither to augment nor to diminish the Law (*Matthew* v. 17—*see* xxi.*i and* lxxx.*b*) acknowledges that the Pharisees, as opposed to the Sadducaic priesthood, are the sole body with a right to interpret it. Here he follows the teaching of the *Mishnah* (*Aboth* i. 1), which opens with:

> 'Moses received the Law at Sinai and delivered it to Joshua, and Joshua to the elders, and the elders to the prophets, and the prophets to the men of the Great Assembly,'

and then gives a list of sages through whom the Law reached Hillel. Nor does he seem ever to have questioned Hillel's authority on any point of Law or morality.

For Jesus, the tradition that the prophets had delivered the Law to the men of the Great Assembly was of great importance. Like the Pharisees, he took it to mean that the great age of prophecy had ended: that the only prophet who could now appear was Elijah (*Malachi* iv. 5—*see* xxxix.*f*). Yet since none but a prophet could anoint a king, Jesus might not expect recognition by the Pharisees unless they acknowledged that John the Baptist had been Elijah. This they had hitherto been unwilling to do (*see* xxxix.*h*).

The rest of the chapter, with its seven woes and twenty-four invectives, repudiates this introduction. Jesus's principle, shared with the Pharisees, was: 'As the tree is, so is the fruit.' It would clearly have been spiritual suicide for his disciples to accept the guidance of such monsters of iniquity as he is here alleged to have portrayed.

(*b*) Josephus's testimonial to the Pharisees is relevant at this point: an unsolicited one, because when he wrote it he had long broken with them and gone over to the Romans (*Antiquities* xviii. 1. 3):

> 'They live simply and despise delicacies of diet, following the conduct of reason and observing its prescription since they think that they ought to strive earnestly to reconcile theory with practice. They also venerate their elders, never daring to reject any of their innovations. Though they regard destiny as ruling everything, they do not deny free will in men, their notion being that it has pleased God to make an arrangement by which His will is done but man is allowed to choose between virtue and vice. They also believe that souls have immortal vigour in them, and that in the underworld there will be punishments and rewards according to their deserts: the evil are to be detained in an everlasting prison, the righteous will be revived and live again. These doctrines give them a great hold over the people, who obey all their rules for divine worship, prayers and sacrifices. The cities have given them high praise for their entirely virtuous conduct and the correspondence between their deeds and words.'

'Correspondence between their deeds and words' is the key phrase, but according to the Talmud, King Alexander Jannaeus had left his widow, Queen Alexandra (75–61 B.C.), the following warning (*Sotah* 22*b*):

'Fear neither the Pharisees, nor those of the other party [i.e. the Sadducees], but fear the painted ones, the feigned Pharisees, whose works are like the work of Zimri, yet who seek the reward of Phineas.'

[Phineas the zealous priest transfixed Zimri and his Midianite wife Cozbi with a spear, for disobeying the law against mixed marriages, and was rewarded by God with the everlasting priesthood (*Numbers* xxv. 6-15).]

(c) Verses 6, 7, 8, and 14 of *Matthew* xxiii belong to a denunciation of the Sadducaic State scribes, or lawyers (*see* xxix.*b*). So does verse 35 (*see* (*z*) *below*). The rest of the chapter is built around Jesus's denunciation of the 'painted', or feigned, Pharisees* who lived on the credit of the true Pharisees; with the insertion, however, of much extraneous material.

(d) For instance, verse 4 seems to be borrowed from a Sadducaic source, in support of Paul's remark (*Galatians* vi. 13): 'For even they who are circumcised keep not the Law themselves, but desire to have you circumcised that they may glory in your flesh.' The Sadducees rejected the Oral Law of the Pharisees, regarding it as an unreasonable burden. But Jesus used the word 'burden' as the Pharisees did, in a good sense; indeed, Paul himself, in the same chapter of *Galatians* (vi. 2), urges his disciples to take upon themselves the burden of the Kingdom of Heaven—a phrase used by the Pharisees to mean the preparing of one's mind for prayer (*see* xv.*c*). It is clear that by an anticipation of the Simon of Cyrene incident (*Mark* xv. 21—*see* cxiii.*j and u*), 'cross' has been substituted for an original 'burden of the Kingdom of Heaven' in six passages (*Mark* viii. 34, *Matthew* x. 38 and xvi. 24, *Luke* ix. 23 and xiv. 27—*see* ci.*a and j*; and *Mark* x. 21—*see* lxxxii.*c*).

* * * * *

(e) The Oral Law fell under four general categories:†

(1) *Halaka* (plural: *halakot*)—usage or guiding custom. Some of these regulations, especially the ceremonial *halakot,* many of them pre-Pentateuchal, were based on tradition. Others were derived from the Pentateuch by interpretative rules; since the Mosaic Law proved inadequate to the more civilized requirements of their day, the Pharisees had set themselves the task of preserving its letter, while changing its spirit. *Numbers* xxxv. 19 and *Deuteronomy* xix. 6, for instance, allowed the 'avenger of the blood' (*goel ha'dam*) to be the sole judge and executioner of a homicide; the Pharisees decided that both the homicide and the deliberate murderer (*Deuteronomy* xix. 11-12) must be tried by a duly constituted court of no less than twenty-three qualified judges. The *Mishnah,* in which the Oral Law was finally codified by Rabbi Judah the Primate at the end of the second century, gives

---

* The word *hypocrite,* which in pre-Christian Greek merely meant a play-actor, but now means 'one who is well aware that he is acting a lie', has no Aramaic equivalent in either sense, because the Jews possessed no dramatic tradition; and is therefore a mistranslation. A 'painted' Pharisee was simply one who went through the motions of being a Pharisee, yet lacked all inner conviction.

† These categories are discussed by Professor Zeitlin in Jewish Quarterly Review, Vol. XXXIX, pp. 21-28.

the majority as well as the minority opinion in many questions concerning *halakot.*

(*f*) (2) *Gezera*—a particular enactment, independent both of the Pentateuch and of accepted *halakot.* When the occasion for the *gezera* disappeared, it became a dead letter (*Dor Dor ve'Dorsov* i. *p.* 136). During the Maccabean struggle, for instance, to counteract the influence of the rival Temple in Egypt built by the ejected High Priest Onias (*Antiquities* xiii. 3. 3), and to prevent Jews from emigrating, it was decreed that the lands of the heathen were in a state of Levitical uncleanness (*Shabbath* 14*b*). This *gezera* fell into desuetude when the Maccabeans had established themselves firmly, but was revived by the 'Rabbis of the Eighty Years', those who lived in the period between the building and the destruction of Herod's Temple—which included the lifetime of Jesus.

(*g*) (3) *Takkana*—an amendment to a Mosaic Law that adapted it to new circumstances. The *takkana* was always liberally intended. For instance: according to *Exodus* xxi. 7–10, a woman was considered the property first of her father, and then of her husband. But Simon ben Shetah and his fellow-sages of the second century B.C. introduced the *kethubah* (marriage contract —*see* LXXX.*c*) which insured widows and divorced women against destitution; a wife thus ceased in practice to belong to her husband, because she had acquired possessions in her own right. The *kethubah,* though not provided for by the Law, was instituted 'for the sake of the daughters of Israel' (*Kethuboth* 10*a*). Similarly, when Hillel found that at the approach of each Sabbatical Year, which cancelled all debt, people refrained from lending freely to one another and thereby transgressed *Deuteronomy* xv. 9, he ordained the *prozbul:* namely, a declaration made before a court of law that a particular loan was not subject to the sabbatical law of remission (*Shebiith* x. 3).

(*h*) (4) *Syag*—a 'fence' around the Law, to guard it against infringements. For instance: a man was forbidden to carry money or pick up a lamp on the Sabbath Day, lest he thoughtlessly either spent that money or lit the lamp (*see* cxviii.*p*). Paul's followers, who sought to demolish the garden of the Law, naturally denounced these fences. Yet Jesus himself set fences around the Commandments: for instance, by making ocular adultery a crime equal with phallic adultery (*see* xxi.*d*), and by recommending abstention from all oaths (*see* xxiii.*a*).

* * * * *

(*i*) *Matthew* xxiii. 5 refers to the praying garment, the *talith,* which Pharisees wore all the day, not merely when praying. Jesus must have been a member of the sect of Pharisees, if it is true that the fringes of his garment were touched by a woman whom he met in the street (*see* xxxvi.*e*). Like all Jews, he will also have worn a phylactery on his brow and on his left arm (*Exodus* xiii. 9 and *Canticles* viii. 6); they both contained the *shemā,* the

'Hear O Israel' passage (*see* xxvii.*a and* lxxxii.*l*). The feigned Pharisees are accused of displaying exaggeratedly long fringes and prominent phylacteries. This verse is in keeping with Hillel's warning (*Aboth* i. 13): 'Whosoever seeks to make a name for himself, the same shall lose his name; whosoever crowns himself with the tiara [i.e. uses the Law for self-glorification], the same shall perish.' It is laid down in the Talmud (*Sanhedrin* 103*a* and *Sotah* 42*a*): 'Four sorts of men will not be received in the Divine Presence: the scoffers, the liars, the self-glorifiers, and the tale-bearers.'

(*j*) The appearance of what was termed 'the plague of the Pharisees', namely the feigned Pharisees, proves the popular esteem in which the teachers, or 'doctors' of the sect were held. These numbered some six thousand and, by order of Rabban Gamaliel ii, aspirants to the doctorate were expected to be 'gold within and without—let no disciple who is not inwardly as he is outwardly enter the lecture hall' (*Barakoth* 28*a*). Their chief virtues were self-denial, simplicity, studiousness, and lack of worldly ambition; their love for children extended even to those of the *Ame ha'Aretz* (*see* lx.*c*); and their meticulous laws of cleanliness did not prevent them from becoming the most democratic party in Jewry. They successfully disputed the priesthood's claim to be the sole body qualified to intercede with God or enunciate His will, and established synagogues in which Jews of all classes were allowed to officiate.

What recommended the Pharisees to the common people was that, unlike the priests, they had no financial stake in endowed religion. They enjoyed neither sacrificial perquisites nor income from tithes, and admission to their lectures was free. Many prominent 'doctors' earned their livelihood by such humble trades as cobbling, carpentering, and job-gardening. (Abba Shaul was a grave-digger—*Niddah* 24*b*).

(*k*) It was expected that, in the Day of Judgement, God would deal severely with the feigned Pharisees. Rabbi Joshua ben Hananiah (a needle-maker by trade, who found it difficult to combine study and judicial duties with the task of supporting his family—*Berakoth* 28*a*) even prophesied: 'The plague of the Pharisees will bring about the destruction of the world' (*Sotah* 22*b*).

The Babylonian Talmud (*ibid.*) and the Jerusalem Talmud (*Sotah* v. 5) divide the feigned Pharisees into seven categories. The nicknames given in the two Talmuds differ somewhat and so do the explanations for them; but the best readings are these:

(1) The 'Shoulder Pharisee'—he who ostentatiously wears his good deeds on his shoulder. (*Jer. and Bab.*)

(2) The 'Anon Pharisee'—he who when asked to do an act of kindness, answers: 'Anon, but first I have a duty to perform.' (*Jer.*)

(3) The 'Calculating Pharisee'—he who says: 'May my bad actions, which are few, be set against my virtues, which are many.' (*Jer.*)

(4) The 'Pestle Pharisee'—he who walks with his head bowed in mock humility, like unto a pestle in a mortar. (*Bab.*)

(5) The 'Virtue-collecting Pharisee'—he who asks: 'Does any new virtue still remain which I have not yet acquired? If so, tell me, and I will seek it.' (*Jer. and Bab.*)

(6) The 'Reward-loving Pharisee'—he whose mind dwells on rewards only. (*Bab.*)

(7) The 'Doom-fearing Pharisee'—he who thinks only how to avoid the tortures of Gehenna. (*Bab.*)

Since it was legitimate to long for the rewards of Paradise and to fear the tortures of Hell, these last two categories were later thought over-severe and omitted from the Jerusalem Talmud; yet in Jerusalem as well as in Babylon it was understood that the true Pharisee served God for His own sake (*lishmah*), without any thought of self-interest. Jesus took the earlier view: he forbade his disciples to serve God either for fear of punishment (*Matthew* xxiii. 23—*see* (*q*) *below*) or for hope of reward (*Luke* xvii. 7-10— *see* xiv.*a* and xxvii.*f and g*).

(*l*) *Matthew* xxiii. 6-8 wrongly suggests that Pharisee teachers had been re-ferred to as 'rabbi' (master) in Jesus's time: the title was first officially bestowed on Gamaliel I. Nor, despite *Matthew* xxiii. 9, were they referred to as 'father'; this saying seems either to have strayed from the context 'Suffer me first to bury my father' (*see* lxxxv.*c*), or to have been earlier used by the Nazarenes against Paul who had written in 1 *Corinthians* iv. 15: 'It was I who in Christ Jesus became your father by means of the Gospel,' and who frequently addressed the Church he had founded as 'my children'.* Also, there were no 'chief seats' in the synagogue, apart from those allotted to the 'ruler' and the reader, which faced the congregation; for 'synagogue' read 'Council' (*see* xxix.*b*). The ruler's seat, called 'The Chair of Moses', is re-ferred to in verse 2; a massive example in basalt has been recovered from the ruins of the synagogue of Chorazin.

(*m*) Verses 11 and 12 are unconnected with the preceding attack on the priests and their employees, the State scribes. The first has been brought in from a saying about the Princes of the Gentiles (*Matthew* xx. 25—*see* lxii.*c* and *d*); the second really belongs to the wedding-feast story in *Matthew* xxii. 1-14), and is a combination of *Job* xxii. 29 with *Psalm* xviii. 27 (*see* xlvi.*e*).

(*n*) Verse 13 was misinterpreted early in the second century, when the Pharisees closed the synagogues to Gentile Christian missionaries. Originally, it had been a complaint against certain feigned Pharisees of Galilee, that their scorn kept the Men of the Land (*see* xii.*h and l*) away from the synagogues and thereby debarred them from instruction in the Law. It may have been joined with the charge in verse 15, that they were more interested in the con-version of rich foreigners than in the salvation of their own needy co-religionists. A great access of proselytes to Judaism is recorded in Jesus's

---

* That he does not so address the Romans in his *Epistle* is a strong reason for supposing that he had no part in the foundation of the Church of Rome (*see* cxviii.*s*).

time, including the famous Queen of Adiabene whose sarcophagus may be seen in the Louvre; Hillel had welcomed them, though never at the expense of the Men of the Land. The feigned Pharisees, however, did not work in the foreign mission-field: the Pauline resentment in verse 15 is against Nazarene preachers from Jerusalem who persuaded Gentile Christians that salvation could not be won without strict observance of the Law (*see Introduction* II.*w*).

The devourers of widows' houses in verse 14 are the State scribes again (*see* XXIX.6).

(*o*) Verses 16–22 are an interpolation by an editor who had evidently heard of a second-century Rabbinical discussion on vows and tried to join in it, but lacked sufficient legal knowledge.

There were two main kinds of vow: namely *nidre heḳdash,* promises to make a sacrifice or dedication; and *nidre isser,* promises of abstention, meant to combat such vices as gluttony or drunkenness (*see* xx.*b*). In general, the Pharisees discouraged vows (*Nedarim* 20*a*—*see* xx.*e*), and Jesus seems to have agreed with them (*see* XXIII.*a*); though promises of abstention helped the weak-willed to sobriety without committing them to an oath which might involve a breach of the Law: 'If a man vow unto the Lord, he shall not profane his word' (*Numbers* xxx. 2). Anyone who declared: 'May my staying in bed after the first hour be no less forbidden to me than the Levites' portion!' was under an obligation to rise punctually at the second hour. Thus the *Mishnah* (*Nedarim* i. 3) lays down:

> '[If he said, may it be to me] as the lamb [the daily whole-offering which was forbidden him], or as the [Temple] sheds, or as the wood [for burning on the Altar], or as the fire offerings, or as the Altar, or as Jerusalem, or if he vowed by any utensils of the Altar, although he did not utter [the word] *corban* ['an offering'], it was a vow as binding as if he had uttered the word *corban.*'

(*p*) The resolve, then, remained a solemn one whether he said 'I vow by the altar,' or 'I vow by the gift upon the altar'; and even if the problem of how the formula ought to be worded had arisen in Jesus's time, it would have been of insufficient importance to warrant his special curse upon the 'blind guides' who discussed it. The particular debate to which the editor here refers is recorded in *Nedarim* 14*b*, where a rabbi holds that 'if a vow is taken by the scroll of the Law, it is of no effect [for the speaker may have had in mind no more than the parchment on which the Law is written]; but if it is taken by what is contained in the scroll, then it is binding.'

(*q*) In verse 23, Jesus proclaims the three fundamental needs of humanity: justice, mercy, and faith. They are a *midrash* on *Isaiah* lix. 7–9. Those who tithed mint, dill, and cummin were 'Doom-fearing Pharisees'. No law compelled a farmer to tithe such self-sown herbs (*Menahoth* i.), but Jesus agreed that to do so for the love of God was good. The Doom-fearers treated it only as a safeguard against the tortures of Hell: they remembered the precept that those who tithed meticulously, even if otherwise sinful, might yet hope to escape punishment during their twelve months' passage through Gehenna (*Midrash Mishle* xxxi). This verse, with the ten succeeding ones, is an invective against the same feigned Pharisees, paralleled in *Luke* xi. 37–54. In *Luke* the occasion is a meal at a Pharisee's house; but Jesus would not have refused to wash his hands with the water set before him, nor, when they looked at him in surprise, would he have flown into a sudden fury and accused his host and fellow-guests of hypocrisy, malice, and greed.

(*r*) The editor of *Luke* xi. 40 has missed the point. A Pharisaic rule about the defilement of cups was that if the outside only were defiled, the inside might be considered clean, whereas if the inside were defiled, it became unclean both inside and out (*Berakoth* 52*a* and *b*.).

The Rabbis deduced the rules of washing from *Leviticus* xv. 11, which treats of persons suffering from an unclean issue. Anyone touching them or anything that they had touched must wash his hands. This necessitated washing before and after all meals, because in Mosaic times, as among the Bedouin today, the whole company helped themselves from the common dish, and someone might be unclean without realizing it. Washing of hands was also required after performing one's natural bodily functions, and before prayer. It is possible that the ritual of washing before and after meals became stricter once the Temple had been destroyed, because it preserved a memory of how the priests had washed before and after the Temple service—to make a separation (*lehavdil*) between the profane and the sacred state. The Gentile Christians scoffed at all this, holding that the laws of ritual cleanliness were unimportant compared with the giving of alms to the poor (*Galatians* ii. 9–13); and Jesus is therefore made to tell the Pharisees so in *Luke* xi. 41. But the theory that the disciples did not wash their hands before meals may have its origin in Rabbi Eliezer ben Horkinas's rebuke to Simeon the Chaste, for failing to make *lehavdil* before entering the Sanctuary (*see* cix.*k*).

(*s*) Sepulchres were whitewashed not only to make them show up in the dark, but also to protect from defilement people who accidentally touched them: the lime interposing a protective layer. The editor of *Matthew* xxiii. 27 seems, however, to have thought that whitewash was an adornment; and the English expression 'to whitewash' perpetuated this misconception. The editor of *Luke* xi. 44 was better informed: he omitted 'the whited sepulchres' in favour of 'graves that appear not'. Perhaps the original was 'graves that appear not, being unwhited' (*see* cviii.*h*).

(*t*) Many guesses have been made at the identity of the prophets whose tombs the scribes and Pharisees, according to *Matthew* xxiii. 29 (or the lawyers, according to *Luke* xi. 47) garnished so splendidly, saying: 'If we had lived in our fathers' days we should not have been partakers with them in the blood they shed.' Only one such prophet is mentioned by name, though with an incorrect patronymic, namely Zechariah the son of Jehoiada; but he had been killed more than eight hundred years before, in the reign of

Jehoash, much to the horror of the people of Jerusalem, who held that his blood and that of his successor Urijah had remained unexpiated until the destruction of Solomon's Temple in 586 B.C. These were indeed the only two Hebrew prophets recorded to have been killed (*see* xcvii.*b* *and* xcvi.*b*) until Herod Antipas beheaded John the Baptist; and this act was regarded with detestation by the Jews, who ascribed to it Herod's ill-success in his war against King Aretas of Nabataea or 'Arabia' (Josephus: *Antiquities* xviii. 5. 2—*see* lxxvi.*a*).

The explanation of the passage, however, is not far to seek: the 'prophets' who had been killed and whose sepulchres were being demonstratively garnished at some time during the second half of the first century, were the 'Grecian' martyrs, victims of Paul's persecution, including the deacon Stephen (*Acts* viii. 2). The garnishing will have been accompanied by exclamations of 'Woe unto the murderers!' Gentile Church leaders here hotly take up this Grecian provocation: 'You are Jews; it was your fathers, not ours, who murdered Stephen, as they also murdered Jesus.' They have even dared to put these words into Jesus's own mouth as a prophecy.

(*u*) The reference to the 'blood of Zechariah the son of Barachias' has long puzzled commentators. Those who reject both the reading 'Son of Jehoiada', quoted by Jerome from the *Gospel according to the Hebrews,* and the fantastic but strangely plausible story in the lost Gnostic Gospel, *The Descent of Mary,* quoted by Epiphanius*—hold that Jesus was prophetically pointing to one Zechariah son of Baruch, a pro-Roman priest, murdered a generation later by Zealots and Edomites in the heart of the Temple (*Wars* iv. 5. 4). But none of these three explanations fits the case. Nor is it enough to assume from *Luke's* detailed knowledge of the Siege of Jerusalem (*see* xcvii.*c*) that the passage was re-written after the destruction of the Temple, and that Josephus's 'Zacharias son of Barachias' was then substituted for 'Zechariah the son of Jehoiada'; because the reference to the 'son of Jehoiada' still remains enigmatic. All that we can be sure of is that the author of *Luke* found the saying in a collection of 'Oracles', presumably of Nazarene origin, called 'The Divine Wisdom' (*Luke* xi. 49).

(*v*) The only 'Zacharias son of Barachias' mentioned in the Bible or the Jewish apocrypha was the prophet Zechariah, who is not known to have met a violent death. But what if 'the blood of Zechariah' means 'the blood of which Zechariah prophesied in the concluding chapters of his work'? And if 'whom ye slew between the Temple and the altar' is not part of Jesus's original statement but a gloss that crept into the text of *Matthew* when it was decided that Jesus had been referring to the son of Jehoiada? Then there remains no doubt about the meaning of the passage, which is of the utmost importance as an indication of what Jesus already had in mind. It will be shown (*see* cii.*a–f*) that the Passion narrative cannot be properly understood

---

* The stoning of Zechariah the father of John the Baptist, as a result of the strange vision which he saw in the Temple (*see* iv.*a*).

except by a close critical analysis of this very prophecy—the work of the Deutero-Zechariah, living in the early second century B.C., which has been canonically fathered on the sixth-century Son of Barachias. Jesus identified himself with the ironically-named 'worthless shepherd' (*Zechariah* xi–xiv), whose assassination was to prelude the so-called 'Pangs of the Messiah' (*see* CII.*a–k*). His strange words and actions of the last few days before the Crucifixion, which Gentile Christians either did not understand or did not wish to understand, are explicable only in this sense.

The change from 'the blood of Zechariah son of Baruch' to 'the blood of Zechariah the son of Jehoiada whom ye slew between the Temple and the altar' (the reading preserved in the *Gospel according to the Hebrews*) may well have been a deliberate blind. Though scores of quotations from Zechariah's prophecies occur in the Gospels and *Acts,* this is the only direct mention of his name, whereas Isaiah's occurs thirteen times; and the crucial passage in *Zechariah* xi. 12 is wrongly attributed to Jeremiah (*Matthew* xxvii. 9). We suggest that the original reading 'Zechariah son of Baruch' had survived in 'The Divine Wisdom' and that, after the destruction of the Temple, an editor of *Matthew* (or it may have been *Luke*) collated it with Josephus's *Wars* iv. 5. 4 and decided that Jesus had been speaking prophetically. (For another reference to *Wars* iv. in the Gospels, *see* LXIII.*c*).

(*w*) *Luke* xi. 53–54 has been patched in from another context and refers to the State scribes and the Herodians, not the 'Scribes and Pharisees' (*see* LXXXIX.*i*).

Matthew xxiii. 33 is a *midrash* on *Isaiah* lix. 5. *Matthew* xxiii. 34, also found in *Luke* xi. 49, is an interpolation of not earlier than 132 A.D., when Bar-Cochba, who had the support of some of the Pharisees, including the influential Rabbi Akiba, dealt roughly with Pauline Christians who opposed his revolt (*see Introduction* III.*b*).

Another version of the platter-and-cup story, written for Gentile Christians who had long lost all contact with the Nazarenes, is connected in *Mark* vii. 1–13 with the muddled *corban* argument—which has quite a different context in *Matthew* xv. 1–20 (*see* xx.*a*). Here Jesus is not a guest of the Pharisees, but it is they who ill-mannerly interrupt his meal to criticize him. The only merit of this version is that *Mark* vii. 6–7 points to a *midrash* on *Isaiah* xxix. 13–15, which has dropped out in the other two versions; the quotation from *Isaiah* is also found in *Matthew* xv. 7–8 (*see* xx.*i*), but applied to a different argument.

Mark vii. 4 seems to be borrowed from a Sadducaic source.

An account of how Jesus's ministry began has been preserved in *Luke* iv. 14–15.

> (40) *When therefore Jesus returned in power of the spirit unto Galilee, there went out a fame of him in all the region round about. And he preached in the synagogues, being glorified of all.*

*   *   *   *   *

(41) *Thus he taught the people, saying:*

'The scribes and Pharisees sit in Moses's seat. For Moses received the Law upon Sinai, and delivered it to Joshua, and Joshua to the elders, and the elders to the prophets, and they to the men of the Great Council, the sages of whose line came Hillel—blessed be his memory!

'All therefore that they bid you observe, that observe and do.

'But take heed ye walk not in the way of the feigned Pharisees.

'For the feigned ones are they of whom Isaiah prophesied, saying: "This people draw near Me with their mouth, and with their lips do honour Me, but have removed their heart from Me, and their fear towards Me is taught by the precept of men."

'Behold, they worship not God for His own sake as do the true Pharisees:

'And hark ye how Isaiah beareth witness against their dissembling, saying: "Woe unto them that seek deep to hide their counsel from the Lord, and whose works are in the dark! They say: 'Who seeth us, and who knoweth us?'"

'Woe therefore unto those feigned Pharisees that serve not for love of God, but think only of rewards! For they make broad their phylacteries and enlarge the fringes of their garments of prayer, to be seen of men.'

* * * * *

(*x*) [Here follows a passage about the need of fasting from this world (*see* xxvii.*g*); and then a passage about serving for reward (*see* xiv.*b*).]

(45) *He said also:* 'Woe unto those feigned Pharisees that serve only for fear! For they tithe mint and dill and cummin, as indeed they ought to do, but hope thereby to abate a punishment; and omit the weightier matters of judgement, mercy and faith.

'Against them Isaiah witnesseth:

"They make haste to shed innocent blood; there is no judgement in their goings; they have made them crooked paths, whosoever goeth in them shall not know peace. They hatch vipers' eggs, and weave the spider's web."

'Woe therefore unto those feigned Pharisees! For they strain that which they drink lest they swallow a gnat, but (as men say) swallow a camel.

'Which wash well the outside of their dish, yet eat therefrom the meat of defilement.

'Which triumph in the rich proselyte coming from a land that lieth beyond the sea, yet despise the lost sheep of the House of Israel.

'By their scorn repelling them from the synagogue, and taking away the key of knowledge, whereby the Kingdom of Heaven is shut against them; for they know not that by so doing they shut themselves out also.

'Beware of such, for they are like sepulchres that appear not, being unwhited, against which ye may stumble and be defiled.

'Avoid their crooked paths, lest the vipers that lurk therein bite you and ye die.

'But keep faith with God, shew mercy, use judgement, and ye shall live!'

* * * * *

(y) The saying in *Luke* x. 19 is explained by the 'generation of vipers' text in *Matthew* xxiii. 33. It has been borrowed by the author of the concluding verses of *Mark* (xvi. 9–20)—Conybeare (*Exposition* 93*b*. 241–245) proves that he was the presbyter Aristion—and is a *midrash* on *Psalm* xci. 10–13. Aristion altered the saying either because he had misread a sacred picture illustrating *Exodus* vii. 10–11 (the story of Pharaoh and the magical serpents), or because he wanted to apply it to the case of Paul who at Malta had been bitten in the hand by an adder (*see* cxix.*k*) but took no harm (*Acts* xxviii. 5). Maltese adders, however, are not venomous,* though the writer of *Acts* seems to have been unaware of this; and Paul's miraculous escape was wrongly advanced as a proof that Jesus had chosen him to be a disciple.

(46) *'For David prophesied in a psalm, saying:*
' "If thou makest the Most High God thy refuge and dwelling, no evil shall befall thee: thou shalt trample upon the asp and viper." '

* * * * *

(z) The saying in *Matthew* xxiii. 35 belongs to a denunciation of the Sadducaic priesthood (*see* xciv.*m* and xcvii.*f*), uttered at a later stage.

(360) *'Woe unto these faithless priests, unbelievers! For on their head shall fall all the righteous blood shed upon the earth; from the blood of righteous Abel until that of which Zacharias the son of Barachias prophesied, which is yet to be shed.'*

* * * * *

---

* Paul is locally credited with having removed their stings for ever.

UNPROFITABLE SERVANTS

Luke xvii. 7–10

[7]'But which of you, having a servant plowing or feeding cattle, will say unto him straightway, when he is come from the field, Go and sit down to meat, [8]and will not rather say unto him, Make ready wherewith I may sup, and gird thyself, and serve me, till I have eaten and drunken; and afterward thou shalt eat and drink? [9]Doth he thank that servant because he did the things that were commanded him? I trow not. [10]So likewise ye, when ye shall have done all those things which are commanded you, say, We are unprofitable servants: we have done that which was our duty to do.'

(a) The saying in *Luke* xvii. 7-10 has probably not been tampered with, except for the removal of the quotations (*Leviticus* xxv. 55, *Deuteronomy* xxxii. 6 and *Job* xxxv. 7) on which it is a *midrash;* and of the definition of a servant's duty taken from *Ecclesiastes* xii. 13. It should follow on Jesus's denunciation of the 'Reward-loving Pharisees' (*see* xiii.*k and* xxvii.*f and g*). The servant here is a bondman, the property of his master, wageless and destitute of civil rights, though treated as a member of the family and protected by law from serious ill-usage.

(b) The *Midrash* (*Exodus Rabbah* xxiv.1) emphasizes the apparent contradiction in *Deuteronomy* xxxii. 6 between children and bondmen:

'It is written: "Do ye thus requite the Lord, O foolish people and unwise? Is He not thy father that hath bought thee?"'

'This is to teach you Israelites that if ye do God's will, He will show you mercy, as a father shows his children; but if ye do not, he will chastise you, as a master his bondman. And as a bondman must perforce minister unto his master, so will ye likewise be forced to minister unto God.'

(43) *And Jesus said:*
'*Moses spake in God's name, saying: "Unto Me the children of Israel are bondmen which I brought from Egypt."*
'*Now a bondman serveth not for reward, but because he is a bondman.*
'*Therefore Elihu the Jebusite asked of Job: "If thou be righteous, what givest thou unto God? Or what receiveth He of thine hand?"*
'*For which of you, having a bondman ploughing or feeding cattle, will say unto him, by and by, when he is come from the field: "Go and sit down to meat"?*

'But will not rather say unto him: "Make ready wherewith I may sup, and gird thyself and serve me, till I have eaten and drunken, and afterward thou shalt eat and drink"?

'Doth he praise that servant because he doeth the things that were commanded him? I trow not.

'So likewise ye, when ye shall have done all those things which are commanded you in the Law, shall say: "We are unprofitable bondmen: we have done no more than was our duty."

'As the Preacher saith: "Fear God and keep His commandments; for this is the whole duty of man." '

* * * *

THE YOKE OF THE LAW

Matthew xi. 28–30

²⁸Come unto Me, all ye that labour and are heavy laden,
And I will give you rest.
²⁹Take My yoke upon you, and learn of Me:
For I am meek and lowly in heart:
And ye shall find rest unto your souls.
³⁰For My yoke is easy,
And My burden is light.

John v. 39–47

³⁹Search the scriptures; for in them ye think ye have eternal life: and they are they which testify of Me. ⁴⁰And ye will not come to Me, that ye might have life. ⁴¹I receive not honour from men. ⁴²But I know you, that ye have not the love of God in you. ⁴³I am come in My Father's name, and ye receive Me not: if another shall come in his own name, him ye will receive. ⁴⁴How can ye believe, which receive honour one of another, and seek not the honour that cometh from God only? ⁴⁵Do not think that I will accuse you to the Father: there is one that accuseth you, even Moses, in whom ye trust. ⁴⁶For had ye believed Moses, ye would have believed Me: for he wrote of Me. ⁴⁷But if ye believe not his writings, how shall ye believe My words?

(*a*) The use of the word 'yoke' proves this to be one of the many cases where the word 'I' has been substituted for 'God' by editors who wished to suggest that Jesus identified himself with God. 'Yoke' is a technical term for the discipline of the Law (*see* XIII.*d*). Thus the *Apocalypse of Baruch* xxxi. 3 reads: 'For lo, I see many of Thy people that have removed from Thy Covenant and cast from them the yoke of Thy Law.' But the yoke of divine Wisdom was one that pious Jews delighted to wear (*Ecclesiasticus* vi. 30): 'An ornament of gold is her yoke, and her traces a riband of purple silk.' The same metaphor is found in *Ecclesiasticus* li. 26–27.

(*b*) 'For I am meek and lowly in heart' (*Matthew* xi. 29), is a late addition, a reference to *Zechariah* ix. 9, where the Messiah is applauded as he rides on ass-back into Jerusalem. Jesus, who protested at being called 'good' (*Mark* x. 17–18—*see* LXXXII.*c*) could not have glorified himself in this manner. He says in *John* v. 31 and *John* viii. 54: 'If I bear witness of myself, my witness is not true; if I honour myself, my honour is nothing' (*see* xcv.*e*), and that he is far from introducing a new dispensation appears in 'Ye shall find rest unto your souls', which shows that this passage is a *midrash* on *Jeremiah* vi. 16, where 'the old paths, the good way' are praised.

(*c*) The Pharisees insisted that the yoke, when willingly shouldered, was a delightful burden and quoted *Psalms* cxii. 1 and c. 2 in support:

> 'Blessed is the man that feareth the Lord, that delighteth greatly in His Commandments. . . . Serve the Lord with gladness and come before His presence with a song.'

Thus in *Tanna Debe Eliyahu* xvi. it is asked, in reference to *Isaiah* vi. 8: 'Here am I, send me!':

> 'What distinguished Isaiah the son of Amos from all other prophets who likewise prophesied good things and consolation unto Israel? Was it that he took upon himself [the yoke of] the Kingdom of Heaven with joy?'

and the comment follows:

> 'Moses spake unto God: "Lord of all things created, Thou layest two yokes upon Thy children: that of the Law and that of servitude to the governments of this world."
>
> 'God made answer: "All his elect are in thy hand [*Deuteronomy* xxxiii. 3]. And whosoever occupieth himself with the Law, the same shall be no slave unto the governments of this world." '

Rabbi Nehuniah ben Ha'Kanah, who was born not long after the Crucifixion, said (*Aboth* iii. 6):

> 'Whosoever taketh upon himself the yoke of the Law, from him shall the yoke of government and the yoke of earthly cares be removed.'

(*d*) God's Law was timeless, which allowed the Pharisees to attribute to Moses many sayings that were utterly irrelevant to desert life in the Wilderness, and also a respect for commandments delivered through David centuries later. Thus, according to *Sifre* (*Pinhas*) on *Numbers* xxvii. 22: 'Moses did as the Lord commanded him,' means that Moses fulfilled the Law with joy (*Psalm* c. 2); similarly, according to *Sifre* (*Tavo*): 'I have done according to all that Thou hast commanded me,' means 'I have rejoiced and caused others to rejoice,'—in other words: 'I have taken the yoke of the Law upon me with joy.' But the editor of *Matthew* is steeped in Paulinism (*see Introduction* 11.*w*): he prefers to think that Jesus simplified Judaism to the point where nothing that entered into a man defiled him (*Mark* vii. 18—*see* xx.*i*).

> (44) *But lest they should deceive themselves and suppose that such bondage was weariness, he said:*
>
> '*Come unto the Lord, all ye that labour and are heavily laden under burdens of this world, and He will give you rest.*
>
> '*Take upon you the easy yoke of the Law, and learn wisdom of God.*
>
> '*As Jeremiah prophesied:* "*Thus saith the Lord:* '*Ask ye for the old paths,*

where is the good way, and walk therein, and ye shall find rest for your souls.'"

'*And as the Preacher, the Son of Sirach, exhorted us: "Put your neck under the yoke and let your soul receive instruction, she is close at hand to find.*

'*"Behold with your eyes how I have had but little labour and have gotten unto me much rest."*

'*And the Preacher saith likewise of Wisdom: "An ornament of gold is her yoke, and her traces a ribband of purple silk."*'

* * * * *

(*e*) *John* v. 39–47 is a boastful second-century sermon impossibly attributed to Jesus; the reference in verse 43 may be to Andrew of Lycia, a revolutionary leader of 115 A.D.* But its nucleus is an authentic saying (verse 39) which Jesus probably addressed to the Sadducees who refused to listen to the prophets and contented themselves with Moses (*see* xci.g):

(330) '*Search the Scriptures therefore, for in them ye shall find the way of everlasting life.*'

* * * * *

The interpolated 'ye think' is most mischievous.

(*f*) Verse 46 may also be authentic in origin, if Jesus by a quotation from *Deuteronomy* xviii. 18–19 is strengthening his argument that Moses had authorized belief in the prophets. He is speaking of himself, though not so crudely as the editor of *John* suggests:

(348) '*And if ye believe Moses, which ye know and acknowledge, ye are accused by him that ye reject the prophets.*

'*For Moses spake in the name of the Lord: "I will raise them up a prophet from among their brethren, like unto thee and will put My words in his mouth; and he shall speak unto them all that I shall command him.*

'*"And it shall come to pass that whosoever will not hearken unto My words which he shall speak in My name, I will require it of him."*'

* * * * *

(*g*) These two verses seem to have been inserted in *Deuteronomy*, when it was written or 'discovered' during the reign of Josiah (637–608 B.C.—2 *Kings* xxii. 8–11), in order to invest it with Mosaic authority; the 'prophet' being its author, the High Priest Hilkiah. But this was forgotten long before the time of Jesus and the verses had now acquired a Messianic interpretation (*see* LXXVII.*f* and xciv.*c*).

* * * * *

* Eisler: *Enigma of the Fourth Gospel*, p. 166.

THE BARREN FIG TREE

Luke xiii. 6–9

[6]He spake also this parable: 'A certain man had a fig tree planted in his vineyard; and he came and sought fruit thereon, and found none. [7]Then said he unto the dresser of his vineyard, Behold, these three years I come seeking fruit on this fig tree, and find none; cut it down; why cumbereth it the ground? [8]And he answering said unto him, Lord, let it alone this year also, till I shall dig about it, and dung it: [9]and if it bear fruit, well: and if not, then after that thou shalt cut it down.'

(*a*) The parable of the Fig-tree needs no critical emendation, and has an important bearing on Jesus's actual destruction of a fig-tree, which seems at first sight to contradict it (*see* CIII.*a*).

There can be no doubt as to the meaning of the parable. The fig-tree, like the vine (*see* LIV.*c*), was a symbol of Israel. Joel used it in this sense (*Joel* i. 6–7—*see* XLVII.*b*):

'A nation is come upon my land like a lion: he hath laid my vine waste and barked my fig-tree: he hath made it clean bare and cast it away, the branches thereof are made white.'

Jesus here extols God's patience: Israel is always given new opportunities to repent and 'bring forth the fruits of righteousness'. Both the owner of the vineyard, as in *Matthew* xxi. 33 (*see* XCVI.*c and* XLVII.*b*), and the dresser, or husbandman, as in *John* xv. 1 (*see* LIV.*c*) are God, who, in the Old Testament, is often represented as thus alternating between exasperation and mercy. It would be wrong to read the parable as meaning that Jesus will intercede for Israel with God; this is a debate between God's sterner and milder selves.

(51) *And he taught them of the fig tree which is Israel: how God would yet once more shew mercy unto her and spare her; but if this time also she repented not, nor gave forth fruits of repentance, she should be hewn down.*

For he said: 'A certain man had a fig tree planted in his vineyard; and he came and sought fruit thereon, but found none.

'Then said he unto the dresser of the vineyard: "Behold, these three years I come seeking fruit on my fig-tree, and find none; cut it down; why cumbereth it the ground?"

'And he, answering, said unto him: "Lord, let it alone this year also, till I dig about it, and dung it: and if it bear fruit, well: and if not, then after that thou shalt cut it down."'

* * * * *

(*b*) There is a reminiscence here of the *Book of Ahikar*, the oldest of the surviving non-Canonical books of the Old Testament, dating from at least the fifth century B.C. (*Ahikar* viii. 35, *Syriac version*):

'My son, thou hast been to me like the palm-tree that stood by a river and cast its fruit [untimely] into the water. When its lord came to hew it down, the palm-tree said: "Let me be this year, and I will bring thee forth carobs."

'And its lord said unto it: "Since thou hast not laboured well in what is thine own, how wilt thou labour well in what is not thine own?"'

The palm-tree here promises carobs as the 'fruit of repentance' (*see* v.*e and* xviii.*a*), but the owner chooses to take it literally.

FISHERS OF MEN

Matthew xiii. 47–52

⁴⁷'Again, the Kingdom of Heaven is like unto a net, that was cast into the sea, and gathered of every kind: ⁴⁸which, when it was full, they drew to shore, and sat down, and gathered the good into vessels, but cast the bad away. ⁴⁹So shall it be at the end of the world: the angels shall come forth, and sever the wicked from among the just, ⁵⁰and shall cast them into the furnace of fire: there shall be wailing and gnashing of teeth.'

⁵¹Jesus saith unto them: 'Have ye understood all these things?' They say unto Him: 'Yea, Lord.' ⁵²Then said He unto them: 'Therefore every scribe which is instructed unto the Kingdom of Heaven is like unto a man that is an householder, which bringeth forth out of his treasure things new and old.'

Mark i. 16–20

¹⁶Now as He walked by the sea of Galilee, He saw Simon and Andrew his brother casting a net into the sea: for they were fishers. ¹⁷And Jesus said unto them: 'Come ye after Me, and I will make you to become fishers of men.' ¹⁸And straightway they forsook their nets, and followed Him. ¹⁹And when He had gone a little farther thence, He saw James, the son of Zebedee, and John his brother, who also were in the boat mending their nets. ²⁰And straightway He called them: and they left their father Zebedee in the boat with the hired servants, and went after Him.

Mark iii. 7–9

⁷But Jesus withdrew Himself with His disciples to the sea: and a great multitude from Galilee followed Him, and from Judaea, ⁸and from Jerusalem, and from Idumaea, and from beyond Jordan, and they about Tyre and Sidon, a great multitude, when they had heard what great things He did, came unto Him. ⁹And He spake to His disciples, that a small boat should wait on Him because of the multitude, lest they should throng Him.

Matthew iv. 18–22

¹⁸And Jesus, walking by the sea of Galilee, saw two brethren; Simon called Peter, and Andrew his brother, casting a net into the sea: for they were fishers. ¹⁹And He saith unto them: 'Follow Me, and I will make you fishers of men.' ²⁰And they straightway left their nets, and followed Him. ²¹And going on from thence, He saw other two brethren, James the son of Zebedee, and

Matthew iv. 18–22 (*contd.*)

John his brother, in a boat with Zebedee their father, mending their nets; and He called them. ²²And they immediately left the boat and their father, and followed Him.

Luke v. 1–11

¹And it came to pass, that, as the people pressed upon Him to hear the word of God, He stood by the lake of Gennesaret, ²and saw two boats standing by the lake: but the fishermen were gone out of them, and were washing their nets. ³And He entered into one of the boats, which was Simon's, and prayed him that he would thrust out a little from the land. And He sat down, and taught the people out of the boat. ⁴Now when He had left speaking, He said unto Simon: 'Launch out into the deep, and let down your nets for a draught.' ⁵And Simon answering said unto Him: 'Master, we have toiled all the night, and have taken nothing: nevertheless at Thy word I will let down the net.' ⁶And when they had this done, they inclosed a great multitude of fishes: and their net brake. ⁷And they beckoned unto their partners, which were in the other boat, that they should come and help them. And they came, and filled both the boats, so that they began to sink. ⁸When Simon Peter saw it, he fell down at Jesus' knees, saying: 'Depart from me; for I am a sinful man, O Lord.' ⁹For he was astonished, and all that were with him, at the draught of the fishes which they had taken: ¹⁰and so was also James, and John, the sons of Zebedee, which were partners with Simon. And Jesus said unto Simon: 'Fear not; from henceforth thou shalt catch men.' ¹¹And when they had brought their boats to land, they forsook all, and followed Him.

John i. 37–42

³⁷And the two disciples heard John speak, and they followed Jesus. ³⁸Then Jesus turned, and saw them following, and saith unto them: 'What seek ye?' They said unto Him: 'Rabbi, (which is to say, being interpreted, Master,) where dwellest Thou?' ³⁹He saith unto them: 'Come and see.' They came and saw where He dwelt, and abode with Him that day: for it was about the tenth hour. ⁴⁰One of the two which heard John speak, and followed him, was Andrew, Simon Peter's brother. ⁴¹He first findeth his own brother Simon, and saith unto him: 'We have found the Messiah,' which is, being interpreted, the Christ. ⁴²And he brought him to Jesus. And when Jesus beheld him, He said: 'Thou art Simon, the son of Jona: thou shalt be called Cephas,' which is, by interpretation, 'A stone.'

Matthew xiii. 1–2

¹The same day went Jesus out of the house, and sat by the sea side. ²And great multitudes were gathered together unto Him, so that He went into a boat, and sat; and the whole multitude stood on the shore.

John xxi. 1–14

¹After these things Jesus shewed Himself again to the disciples at the sea of Tiberius; and on this wise shewed He Himself. ²There were together Simon Peter, and Thomas called Didymus, and Nathanael of Cana in Galilee, and

John xxi. 1–14 (*contd.*)

the sons of Zebedee, and two other of His disciples. ³Simon Peter saith unto them: 'I go a fishing.' They say unto him: 'We also go with thee.' They went forth, and entered into a boat immediately; and that night they caught nothing. ⁴But when the morning was now come, Jesus stood on the shore: but the disciples knew not that it was Jesus. ⁵Then Jesus saith unto them: 'Children, have ye any meat?' They answered Him, No. ⁶And He said unto them: 'Cast the net on the right side of the boat, and ye shall find.' They cast therefore, and now they were not able to draw it for the multitude of fishes. ⁷Therefore that disciple whom Jesus loved saith unto Peter: 'It is the Lord.' Now when Simon Peter heard that it was the Lord, he girt his fisher's coat unto him, (for he was naked,) and did cast himself into the sea. ⁸And the other disciples came in a little boat; (for they were not far from land, but as it were two hundred cubits,) dragging the net with fishes. ⁹As soon then as they were come to land, they saw a fire of coals there, and fish laid thereon, and bread. ¹⁰Jesus saith unto them: 'Bring of the fish which ye have now caught.' ¹¹Simon Peter went up, and drew the net to land full of great fishes, an hundred and fifty and three: and for all there were so many, yet was not the net broken. ¹²Jesus saith unto them: 'Come and dine.' And none of the disciples durst ask Him: 'Who art Thou?' knowing that it was the Lord. ¹³Jesus then cometh, and taketh bread, and giveth them, and fish likewise. ¹⁴This is now the third time that Jesus shewed Himself to His disciples, after that He was risen from the dead.

Matthew xiii. 34

³⁴All these things spake Jesus unto the multitude in parables; and without a parable spake He not unto them.

John xvi. 17

¹⁷Then said some of his disciples among themselves: 'What is this that He saith unto us . . . . ?'

John xvi. 29

²⁹His disciples said unto Him: 'Lo, now speakest Thou plainly, and speakest no proverb.'

(*a*) In *Luke,* the 'miraculous draught of fishes' is associated with Jesus's summons to Peter, Andrew, James, and John to be his disciples; but in *John* with his third re-appearance after the Crucifixion. The origin of the story can be found in *Matthew* xiii. 47–49 and *Mark* i. 17 (paralleled in *Matthew* iv. 19). There is no mention of any miraculous draught in *Mark* i. 16–20 or in *Matthew* iv. 18–22—on the contrary, Peter and Andrew leave the net that they are casting and follow Jesus. The text of *Mark* iii. 7–9, from which *Luke* has borrowed the introduction to his account, is plainly corrupt since in verse 8 Jesus, followed by his Galilean disciples, is made to visit the Mediterranean, not the Lake of Galilee, there to be thronged by Phoenician admirers; but verses 7 and 9 seem genuine.

(*b*) Luke's account may be due to iconotropy (*see Foreword k*). Some sacred picture, perhaps a Nazarene synagogue-mural, showed the summons of Peter and Andrew while they were fishing. An editor of *Luke,* in all good faith, read Jesus's gesture to them not as an invitation to follow him but as an order to let down the net on the far side of the boat, and has combined *Matthew* xiii. 47 with *Matthew* iv. 18-22 and *Matthew* xiii. 2 (which introduces the parable of the Sower—*see* LXVI.*a*). Only *Luke* v. 8: 'Depart from me for I am a sinful man', seems genuine and should perhaps be inserted in the 'Walking on the Water' episode (*Matthew* xiv. 22-36) not found in *Luke* (see LXXIII.*d*). *Luke* may have seen this isolated text issuing from Peter's mouth in the same mural, a token of his humility.

(*c*) *John's* account (*John* xxi. 1-14) is still more confused, and can be explained only if the editor of *Luke* had written something of this sort in the margin: 'The authority for the following episode is what has been portrayed by the inspired illustrator of Saint Matthew's Gospel.' For it has apparently been deduced from a series of no less than four illustrations to *Matthew* read as a single story. On the left of the picture we postulate the summons of Peter, Andrew, James, and John (*Matthew* iv. 18-19); in the centre Jesus's re-appearance after Golgotha (*Matthew* xxviii. 16-18—*see* CXVII.*m*); on the right the 'Feeding of the Five Thousand' (*Matthew* xiv. 19-20—*see* LXXII.*a*), and its sequel the 'Walking on the Water' (*Matthew* xiv. 29-30—*see* LXXIII.*a*). The Summons appears in verses 2, 3, 4, 6, 8, and 10-11; the Re-appearance (which corresponds with *Matthew's* view that it took place in Galilee, not Jerusalem) in verses 1 and 14; the 'Walking on the Water' in verse 7; the 'Feeding of the Five Thousand' in verses 5, 9, 12, and 13.

(*d*) The one hundred and fifty-three great fishes* in *John* xxi. 11 are not hard to explain: this number was the contemporary Graeco-Roman estimate of the different nations of the world—the Jews remained true to the tradition that there were only seventy (*Genesis* x.—*see* LVII.*b*). Despite Jesus's warning against indiscriminate proselytizing in *Matthew* xxiii. 15 (*see* XIII.*n*), it is here stated that he ordered the disciples to 'compass sea and land' in an indefatigable chase of souls. *John* xxi. 14 has strayed from its context, which is *John* xx. 26 (*see* CXVII.*m*).

(*e*) In *Matthew* xiii. 47-52 the 'furnace of fire' seems inappropriate to the fish metaphor; and for 'good' and 'bad' we should read 'clean' and 'unclean', ascribing the change to a Pauline editor who did not admit the Levitical distinction between scaled and unscaled fish (*Leviticus* xi. 9). *Matthew* xiii.

---

* Augustine, with the help of Philonian numerology, explained that 153 means the Church as evolved from the Law and the Spirit. According to Philo, the fulfilment of any potentiality is the sum of the numbers which go to make it by arithmetical progression; thus the fulfilment of 5 is $1+2+3+4=10$. And the fulfilment of the Church, which is symbolized by 17 (10=the Law+7=the Spirit) is $1+2+3+4+5+6+7+8+9+10+11+12+13+14+15+16+17=$ 153. Other suggested examples of Philo's numerical symbolism in *John* are the 200 cubits swum by Peter, meaning 'Repentance' (*John* xxi. 8) and the 300 pence (*John* xii. 5) mentioned by Judas, meaning 'Harmony between God and Man'; but we do not take these seriously, if only because of the 200 pence in *John* vi. 7, which cannot be interpreted in the sense of Repentance.

49 is a *midrash* on *Enoch* lxii. 11–13. 'Weeping and gnashing of teeth' (*Matthew* xiii. 50), occurs six times in *Matthew* and may be omitted here. (*f*) The account given in *John* i. 37 of how Peter and Andrew became disciples of Jesus, on John's recommendation, contradicts the Synoptic version and was perhaps designed by a Gentile Christian editor to award Peter, as head of the Catholic Church, spiritual priority over Jesus's Levite kinsmen who had attended his coronation (*see* VIII.*q–v*), and especially over James the Just and his cousin Simeon the Chaste, the successive heads of the Nazarene Church. Much the same manipulation of texts is found in *Luke* xxiv. 34, where James and Simeon were really the first to see Jesus after the Resurrection (*see* CXVI.*b–c*).

The 'Come and see!' dialogue is modelled on that of Philip and Nathanael in *John* i. 43–46 (*see* LVI.*h*). Nevertheless, *John* i. 37–39 has a genuine ring and probably formed the close of the original account on which the Synoptics drew. Jesus's cautious 'What seek ye?' suggests that his call for fishers of men was made generally to the whole fishing fleet, not particularly to Peter and Andrew. For Jesus's address to Peter, *see* LVI.*f*.

> (50) *Jesus, walking by the Sea of Galilee, preached to the great multitude that followed him, and lest they should throng him he entered into a small boat.*
>
> *And he preached unto them, saying: 'The Day of Judgement is like a net that was cast into a sea and gathered of every kind of fish, clean and unclean, which when it was full the fishers drew to shore. Then gathered they the clean into baskets, but cast the unclean away.*
>
> *'So shall it be in the Last Days. The angels shall come forth and sever the wicked from the just.*
>
> *'For Enoch testifieth: "The Most High will deliver those evil ones to His angels for punishment because they have oppressed His children.*
>
> *'"But the righteous and elect shall be saved on that day and thenceforward shall never see the face of the sinners and unrighteous."'*
>
> *Now, in a boat near by were Simon, afterwards called Peter, and Andrew his brother; and in another boat were James and John the sons of Zebedee, mending their nets.*
>
> *Jesus said: 'Who will preach the way of repentance? Come with me, that will, and I will make you fishers of men!'*
>
> *Simon and Andrew, hearing those words, forsook their nets and, when Jesus departed, they followed him. Then Jesus turned and saw them following, and said unto them: 'What seek ye?'*
>
> *They asked him: 'Master, where dwellest thou?' He saith unto them: 'Come and see!'*
>
> *They came and saw where he dwelt, and abode with him that day, for it was about the tenth hour, and became his disciples.*

*   *   *   *   *

[Here follows Jesus's symbolic act in Cana of Galilee (*see* X. *a–c*).]

(*g*) Jesus's defence of his habitual use of simple parables (*Matthew* xiii. 51–52) seems to be a *midrash* on *Ezekiel* xx. 49 and *Leviticus* xxvi. 10–12,

and introduced by *Matthew* xiii. 34, with supporting texts in *John* xvi. 17
and 29. We place it at the conclusion of his series of parables about watching
and praying (*see* xxx.*f*), and distinguish it from a misleadingly similar saying in *Mark* iv. 10–11, *Matthew* xiii. 10–11 and *Luke* viii. 9–10; the parables
to which Jesus there refers are not simple ones—they have a concealed sense
as well as an overt one (*see* xxv.*d*).

> (162) *All these things spake Jesus in parables, and without a parable spake
> he not unto them.*
>
> *But some said among themselves: 'What are these new things he telleth?
> Sufficeth it not to deliver the Law plainly unto us as it is written in the roll
> thereof?'*
>
> *Jesus answered and said: 'The prophet Ezekiel cried unto God: "Ah, Lord,
> they say of me: 'Doth he not speak parables?'"*
>
> *'Yet he that is instructed in the imminent coming of the Kingdom of
> Heaven and expoundeth the Scriptures, the same shall be like an householder
> that bringeth forth from his storeroom meat which is old, and also meat
> which is new.*
>
> *'As Moses commanded: "Ye shall eat old store and bring forth the old
> because of the new. And I will set My tabernacle among you, and abhor
> you not. I will walk among you and will be your God, and ye shall be My
> people."'*

✳ ✳ ✳ ✳ ✳

(*h*) The above instructions are to be found in *Leviticus* xxv. 22, where the
Jews are promised, every sixth year, a miraculous harvest that will last them
until the ninth; they are not to sow or harvest in the seventh (the Jubilee,
or Sabbatical) year, but only in the eighth. For the ninth they will still have
a store of corn and other produce saved from the sixth year. Jesus is saying
that in dangerous times like the present new parables or symbolic acts should
enliven the old truths of Scripture, as did Ezekiel's parables of the tile
(*Ezekiel* iv. 1–8), of the razor (*v.* 1–4), and of the hole dug through the wall
(xii. 1–7) during an earlier religious crisis.

✳ ✳ ✳ ✳ ✳

XVIII

THE PRODIGAL SON

Luke xv. 11–32

[11]And He said: 'A certain man had two sons: [12]and the younger of them said to his father, Father, give me the portion of goods that falleth to me. And he divided unto them his living. [13]And not many days after the younger son gathered all together, and took his journey into a far country, and there wasted his substance in riotous living. [14]And when he had spent all, there arose a mighty famine in that land; and he began to be in want. [15]And he went and joined himself to a citizen of that country; and he sent him into his fields to feed swine. [16]And he would fain have filled his belly with the husks that the swine did eat: and no man gave unto him. [17]And when he came to himself, he said, How many hired servants of my father's have bread enough and to spare, and I perish with hunger! [18]I will arise and go to my father, and will say unto him, Father, I have sinned against heaven, and before thee, [19]and am no more worthy to be called thy son: make me as one of thy hired servants. [20]And he arose, and came to his father. But when he was yet a great way off, his father saw him, and had compassion, and ran, and fell on his neck, and kissed him. [21]And the son said unto him, Father, I have sinned against heaven, and in thy sight, and am no more worthy to be called thy son. [22]But the father said to his servants, Bring forth the best robe, and put it on him; and put a ring on his hand, and shoes on his feet: [23]and bring hither the fatted calf, and kill it; and let us eat, and be merry: [24]for this my son was dead, and is alive again; he was lost, and is found. And they began to be merry. [25]Now his elder son was in the field: and as he came and drew nigh to the house, he heard music and dancing. [27]And he called one of the servants, and asked what these things meant. And he said unto him, Thy brother is come; and thy father hath killed the fatted calf, because he hath received him safe and sound. [28]And he was angry, and would not go in: therefore came his father out, and intreated him. [29]And he answering said to his father, Lo, these many years do I serve thee, neither transgressed I at any time thy commandment: and yet thou never gavest me a kid, that I might make merry with my friends: [30]but as soon as this thy son was come, which hath devoured thy living with harlots, thou hast killed for him the fatted calf. [31]And he said unto him, Son, thou art ever with me, and all that I have is thine. [32]It was meet that we should make merry, and be glad: for this thy brother was dead, and is alive again; and was lost, and is found.'

(*a*) Apart from the probable loss of two quotations from *Isaiah* and the *Psalms,* the parable of the Prodigal Son, which occurs only in *Luke,* has escaped editorial amendment. It follows on the incident of Matthew's conversion (*see* XIX.*a–g*). The elder brother in the story is the Pharisee who, never having sinned, has earned no reward for repentance.

Luke xv. 16 is accurate: in times of famine alone would pigs be fed on carob-beans ('husks'), which make for lean bacon and are the staple of human beings only when starving or mortifying the flesh. Thus 2 *Kings* vi. 25, after the removal of scribal errors, runs: 'And behold, they besieged the city until an homer of lentils was sold for fifty shekels, and a quarter of a cor of carob-beans for five shekels.' And the warning in *Isaiah* i. 19–20: 'If ye be willing and obedient, the good of the land shall ye eat; but if ye rebel and resist, ye shall be devoured by the sword (*hereb*),' is glossed in the *Midrash* (*Leviticus Rabbah* xxxv. 7) with a play on words: 'If ye rebel and resist, carobs (*harub*) shall ye eat,' and with the quotation: 'Israel needs carob-beans to do repentance.' This *midrash,* reflected in Rabbi Aha's 'When a Jew is forced to eat carobs, he repents,' (*Leviticus Rabbah* xiii. 4) may be a tradition derived from Jesus's own preaching.

Between verses 19 and 20 a quotation from *Psalm* xxxii. 5–6 should be inserted.

(*b*) The swine stand for the Graeco-Romans with whom Matthew has been associating (*see* LXIII.*e*). Jesus has here borrowed from the *Book of Ahikar.* Ahikar's son Nadan, after treating him most unfilially, repents and says, in the Armenian version (*Ahikar, Arm.* 24*b*):

> 'My father Ahikar, men sin unto God, and He forgiveth them when they say: "I have sinned unto Thee." [Therefore] forgive thou me and I will be thy slave henceforth and for ever.'

The Syriac version, probably influenced by *Luke* (since no devout Jewish father would have kept pigs) runs (*Ahikar, Syr.* 34):

> 'Forgive me this my folly, and I will tend thy horses and feed the swine which are in thy house.'

(*see also* XVI.*b*).

(69) *Jesus said,*
'A certain man had two sons: and he divided unto them his living.
'And not many days after, the younger son gathered all together, and took his journey into a far country, and there wasted his substance in riotous living.
'Now, when he had spent all, there arose a mighty famine in that land; and he began to be in want.
'Therefore he went and joined himself to a citizen of that country; and he sent him into his fields to feed swine, where he would fain have filled his belly with the carobs that the swine did eat: and no man gave aught else unto him.
'As the prophet Isaiah said: "If ye be willing and obedient, the good of

the land shall ye eat; but if ye rebel and resist, hereb (*which is the sword*) *shall eat you."*

'*Let the rebellious ones therefore hasten to eat* harub (*which is carobs*), *for verily this is the food of repentance!*

'*And when the son came to himself, he said: "How many hired servants of my father's have bread enough and to spare, and I perish with hunger!*

'"*I will arise and go to my father, and will say unto him: 'Father, I have sinned against heaven, and before thee.'*"

'*For David spake in a psalm: "I acknowledged my sin unto Thee, and mine iniquity have I not hid. I said: 'I will confess my transgressions unto the Lord.' And Thou forgavest the iniquity of my sin."*

'*And the son arose and came to his father.*

'*But when he was yet a great way off, his father saw him, and had compassion, and ran, and fell on his neck, and kissed him.*

'*Then said the son unto him: "Father, I have sinned against heaven and before thee and am no more worthy to be called thy son. Forgive me this my folly and I will be thy bondman and will tend thy asses and feed thy cattle."*

'*But the father said to his servants: "Bring forth the best robe, and put it on him; and put a ring on his hand, and shoes on his feet: for this my son was dead, and is alive again; he was lost, and is found."*

'*And they began to be merry.*

'*Now, his elder son was in the field: and as he came and drew nigh to the house, he heard music and dancing.*

'*And he called one of the servants, and asked what these things meant. The servant said unto him: "Thy brother is come; and thy father hath killed the fatted calf, because he hath received him safe and sound."*

'*The elder son was angry thereat, and would not go in; therefore came his father out, and intreated him.*

'*And he answering said to his father: "Lo, these many years do I serve thee, neither transgressed I at any time thy commandment: and yet thou never gavest me a kid, that I might make merry with my friends:*

'"*But as soon as this thy son was come, which hath devoured thy living with harlots, thou hast killed for him the fatted calf."*

'*The father said unto him: "Son, thou art ever with me, and all that I have is thine.*

'"*It was meet that we should make merry, and be glad: for this thy brother was dead, and is alive again; and was lost, and is found."'*

*   *   *   *   *

PUBLICANS AND SINNERS

Mark ii. 14–17

¹⁴And as He passed by He saw Levi the son of Alphaeus sitting at receipt of custom, and said unto him: 'Follow me.' And he arose and followed Him.

¹⁵And it came to pass that, as Jesus sat at meat in his house, many publicans and sinners sat also together with Jesus and His disciples: for there were many, and they followed Him. ¹⁶And when the scribes and Pharisees saw Him eat with publicans and sinners, they said unto His disciples: 'How is it that He eateth and drinketh with publicans and sinners?' ¹⁷When Jesus heard it, He saith unto them: 'They that are whole have no need of the physician, but they that are sick: I came not to call the righteous, but sinners to repentance.'

Matthew ix. 9–13

⁹And as Jesus passed forth from thence, He saw a man, named Matthew, sitting at the receipt of custom: and He saith unto him 'Follow Me.' And he arose, and followed Him.

¹⁰And it came to pass, as Jesus sat at meat in the house, behold, many publicans and sinners came and sat down with Him and His disciples. ¹¹And when the Pharisees saw it, they said unto His disciples: 'Why eateth your Master with publicans and sinners?' ¹²But when Jesus heard that, He said unto them: 'They that be whole need not a physician, but they that are sick. ¹³But go ye and learn what that meaneth,

I will have mercy, and not sacrifice:

for I am not come to call the righteous, but sinners to repentance.'

Matthew xviii. 11–17

¹¹'For the Son of Man is come to save that which was lost. ¹²How think ye? if a man have an hundred sheep, and one of them be gone astray, doth he not leave the ninety and nine, and goeth into the mountains, and seeketh that which is gone astray? ¹³And if so be that he find it, verily I say unto you, he rejoiceth more of that sheep, than of the ninety and nine which went not astray. ¹⁴Even so it is not the will of your Father which is in heaven, that one of these little ones should perish.

¹⁵'Moreover if thy brother shall trespass against thee, go and tell him his fault between thee and him alone: if he shall hear thee, thou hast gained thy

Matthew xviii. 11–17 *(contd.)*

brother. [16]But if he will not hear thee, then take with thee one or two more, that in the mouth of two or three witnesses every word may be established. [17]And if he shall neglect to hear them, tell it unto the Church: but if he neglect to hear the Church, let him be unto thee as an heathen man and a publican.'

Matthew xviii. 21–22

[21]Then came Peter to Him, and said: 'Lord, how oft shall my brother sin against me, and I forgive him? till seven times?' [22]Jesus saith unto him: 'I say not unto thee, until seven times: but, until seventy times seven.'

Luke v. 27–32

[27]And after these things He went forth, and saw a publican, named Levi, sitting at the receipt of custom: and He said unto him: 'Follow Me.' [28]And he left all, rose up, and followed Him. [29]And Levi made Him a great feast in his own house: and there was a great company of publicans and of others that sat down with them. [30]But their scribes and Pharisees murmured against His disciples, saying: 'Why do ye eat and drink with publicans and sinners?' [31]And Jesus answering said unto them: 'They that are whole need not a physician; but they that are sick. [32]I came not to call the righteous, but sinners to repentance.'

Luke xv. 1–10

[1]Then drew near unto Him all the publicans and sinners for to hear Him. [2]And the Pharisees and scribes murmured saying: 'This man receiveth sinners, and eateth with them.' [3]And He spake this parable unto them, saying: [4]'What man of you, having an hundred sheep, if he lose one of them, doth not leave the ninety and nine in the wilderness, and go after that which is lost, until he find it? [5]And when he hath found it, he layeth it on his shoulders, rejoicing. [6]And when he cometh home, he calleth together his friends and neighbours, saying unto them, Rejoice with me; for I have found my sheep which was lost. [7]I say unto you, that likewise joy shall be in heaven over one sinner that repenteth, more than over ninety and nine just persons, which need no repentance. [8]Either what woman having ten pieces of silver, if she lose one piece, doth not light a candle, and sweep the house, and seek diligently till she find it? [9]And when she hath found it, she calleth her friends and her neighbours together, saying, Rejoice with me; for I have found the piece which I had lost. [10]Likewise, I say unto you, there is joy in the presence of the angels of God over one sinner that repenteth.'

Luke xvii. 3–4

[3]'Take heed to yourselves: If thy brother trespass against thee, rebuke him; and if he repent, forgive him. [4]And if he trespass against thee seven times in a day, and seven times in a day turn again to thee, saying, I repent; thou shalt forgive him.'

Luke xviii. 9–14

⁹And He spake this parable unto certain which trusted in themselves that they were righteous, and despised others: ¹⁰'Two men went up into the temple to pray; the one a Pharisee, and the other a publican. ¹¹The Pharisee stood and prayed thus with himself, God, I thank Thee, that I am not as other men are, extortioners, unjust, adulterers, or even as this publican. ¹²I fast twice in the week, I give tithes of all that I possess. ¹³And the publican, standing afar off, would not lift up so much as his eyes unto heaven, but smote upon his breast, saying, God be merciful to me a sinner. ¹⁴I tell you, this man went down to his house justified rather than the other: for every one that exalteth himself shall be abased; and he that humbleth himself shall be exalted.'

Luke xix. 1–10

¹And Jesus entered and passed through Jericho. ²And, behold, there was a man named Zacchaeus, which was the chief among the publicans, and he was rich. ³And he sought to see Jesus who He was; and could not for the press, because he was little of stature. ⁴And he ran before, and climbed up into a sycomore tree to see Him: for He was to pass that way. ⁵And when Jesus came to the place He looked up, and saw him, and said unto him: 'Zacchaeus, make haste, and come down; for today I must abide at thy house.' ⁶And he made haste, and came down, and received Him joyfully. ⁷And when they saw it, they all murmured, saying, that He was gone to be a guest with a man that is a sinner. ⁸And Zacchaeus stood, and said unto the Lord: 'Behold, Lord, the half of my goods I give to the poor; and if I have taken anything from any man by false accusation, I restore him fourfold.' ⁹And Jesus said unto him: 'This day is salvation come to this house, forasmuch as he also is a son of Abraham. ¹⁰For the Son of Man is come to seek and to save that which was lost.'

Clement of Alexandria: Stromateis iv. 6. 35

It is said that Zacchaeus (or as some say Matthias) the chief publican, when he heard that the Lord condescended to come to him, said: 'Behold, the half of my goods I give in alms, Lord; and if I have defrauded any man of aught, I restore it fivefold.' Whereupon also the Saviour said: 'The son of man is come today and hath found that which was lost.'

Gregory of Nazianzus: Epistle xvi. (quoting from *The Teaching of Peter*)

'A soul in trouble is near unto God,' saith Peter somewhere—a marvellous utterance.

Jerome: Dialogue against Pelagius iii. 2

In the *Gospel according to the Hebrews:* 'If thy brother,' (saith he) 'have sinned in aught and made thee amends, seven times in a day receive thou him.'

Jerome: Dialogue against Pelagius iii. 2 (contd.)

> Simon, his disciple, asked him: 'Seven times in a day?'
> The Lord answered and said unto him: 'Yea, and I say unto thee, seventy times seven times. For in the prophets also, after they were anointed by the Holy Spirit, something of sin was found.'

(a) In *Mark* ii. 14 the apostle Matthew is called 'Levi the son of Alphaeus'—evidently a mistake for 'a certain son of Levi (i.e. a Levite), the son of Alphaeus'. In *Luke* he is simply called 'Levi'. Matthew and Levi have therefore been distinguished in certain early Christian works. Heracleon, for example, quoted by Clement of Alexandria (*Stromateis* iv. 9. 71) says that 'Matthew, Philip, Thomas, and Levi' died natural deaths; but in Heracleon's original text 'Matthew' was probably 'Matthias'.

Jesus's frank opinion of publicans (i.e. tax-collectors), is preserved in *Matthew* xviii. 17, where the Jew who has turned publican in the service of the 'Wicked Kingdom' is reduced to the moral level of the Romans themselves. A publican's evidence, or that of his family, was not accepted in any Jewish court of Justice since it was assumed that he habitually defrauded the taxpayer (*Sanhedrin* 25*b* and *Shebu'oth* 39*a*). He was placed in the same category as the robber and the murderer (*Baba Kamma* 113*a*); any alms that he might offer to the Temple Treasury were refused.

(b) The evangelists have obscured the point of Jesus's encounter with the publicans. According to *Luke,* he attends a publicans' banquet given in Matthew's house after his conversion; but *Mark* reports that when Matthew was brought to Jesus's house, several of his publican friends followed out of curiosity and were fed there. The editors, who themselves cared nothing for ritual cleanliness, liked to think that Jesus must have willingly exposed himself to such contamination.

His reply to the Pharisees, however, suggests that it was not a real, but a figurative meal (*see* (*g*) *below*). Matthew would have had to be purified by baptism and a sin-offering before being accepted at Jesus's table. Jesus certainly could not have entered a publican's house and associated with his friends. What seems to have happened is that a party of Pharisees, coming to call on Jesus, were surprised and offended to find a group of publicans with him, and would not enter; and that they afterwards asked the disciples, some of whom had also been offended, why he did not reserve his preaching for the synagogue. Jesus then explained that he had no need to preach to the already converted; like the Men of the Land, these publicans were lost sheep of the House of Israel and estranged from the synagogues by the nature of their profession. If he could persuade them to abandon their evil ways, as Matthew had done, the Kingdom would be brought so much the nearer. The proper context of the quotation from *Hosea* vi. 6, found in *Matthew* ix. 13, is *Matthew* xii. 7 (*see* LXXI.*g*).

It may be that the story of Jesus's dinner with the publicans is derived from the saying: 'They that are full have no need of bread,' which balanced: 'They

that are whole need not a physician'; and from the subsequent parable of the
Prodigal Son and the slaying of the fatted calf. The controversy, whether a
Jew should eat with Gentiles (*see Introduction* ii.*v*), or with Jews who had
polluted themselves in the Roman service, was here unhistorically settled by
making Jesus himself do so.

(*c*) The parable of the Lost Sheep is a *midrash* on *Zechariah* xi. 4–9, a critical
text in the Passion narrative (*see* cxviii.*m*). Similarly *Matthew* xviii. 14:
'Even so it is not the will of your Father which is in heaven that one of these
little ones should perish,' paraphrases the second part of *Zechariah* xiii. 7, the
first part of which Jesus was to quote at the Last Supper (*see* cvi.*s*) : ' "I shall
smite the shepherd and the sheep shall be scattered", saith the Lord of Hosts,
"and I shall turn My hand upon the little ones" ' (*see* cii.*a and b*).

(*d*) *Luke* xvii. 3–4, the saying about the brother who trespasses, should be
attached to *Luke* xii. 13–14, where Jesus is asked to judge between two
brothers and refers the applicant to *Deuteronomy* xix. 15 (*see* xxvi.*c*).

Matthew xviii. 15 is a quotation from the *Testaments of the Twelve Patriarchs* (*Gad* vi. 3).

'Church' in *Matthew* xviii. 17 is a mistranslation of 'Council', namely the
local court of arbitration. Jesus will hardly have refrained here from quoting
Gad's exhortation to his sons: 'Leave to God the avenging!' (*Gad* vi. 7).
Jerome in his *Dialogue against Pelagius* has preserved the reason which Jesus
gave for this counsel of forgiveness: no man, even an anointed prophet, was
without sin and, as he hoped for forgiveness from God, so he should forgive
his neighbour (*see* xxvii.*b and* cxviii.*z*)

---

(108) *And Jesus taught them saying: 'Take heed to yourselves. If thy brother
trespass against thee, rebuke him gently; and if he repent, forgive him.*

*'Though he trespass against thee seven times in a day, and seven times
in a day turn again to thee, saying: "I repent," thou shalt forgive him.'*

Peter saith: 'Shall I indeed forgive him seven times?'

*Jesus answered: 'Yea, and unto seventy times seven! For even in the
prophets, after that they were anointed and the Spirit of the Lord had come
upon them, something of sin was yet found.*

*'Moreover, if thy brother shall have trespassed against thee and repented
not, the Law giveth thee redress.*

*'But first go and tell him his fault between him and thee alone, and if he
shall hear thee and acknowledge it, thou hast regained thy brother.*

*'For the patriarch Gad exhorted his sons in his Testament, saying: "My
children, love ye one another from the heart! And if a man sin against thee,
speak peaceably to him and in thy soul hold not guile; and if he repent and
confess, forgive him."*

*'But if thy brother will not hear thee, then take with thee another witness
or, if thou wilt, twain. For Moses said: "One witness shall not rise up against
a man for any sin that he sinneth; at the mouth of two witnesses or three
shall the matter be established." And if he shall hear them, well.*

'But if he shall neglect to hear them, tell it unto the council; and if he shall hear the council, well.

'But if he shall neglect to hear the council, let him be unto thee as a heathen and a publican, and thou hast lost thy brother.

'Nevertheless, forgive him from thy heart. For Gad saith again: "But if he be shameless and persist in his wrongdoing, even so forgive him from the heart, and leave to God the avenging."'

* * * * *

(e) The story of Zacchaeus appears only in *Luke* xix. 1–10, and makes little sense except in so far as the editor is trying both to justify the Pharisees' complaint: 'This man eateth with publicans and sinners,' and to absolve Jesus from the charge of opposing Roman sovereignty, by suggesting that he invited himself to dinner with the chief publican of Jericho.

There has been unnecessary argument as to which of the two was the smaller, Jesus or Zacchaeus; someone suggests that if the crowd obscured him from Zacchaeus's sight it may well have been Jesus, since Tertullian says that he looked insignificant (*see* vi.c) and the same tradition is recorded in the mid-second-century *Acts of John*, 89: 'A small man and uncomely.' Since we know that Jesus could not have used the words quoted in verse 5, we must find out why Zacchaeus had climbed a tree, and why it is particularized as a sycomore.

(f) We shall show that an ingenious early editor of *Matthew* turned the fig-tree which Jesus barked into a fig-mulberry (*see* xlv.e), in order to reconcile Jesus's action with the parable of the Barren Fig-tree (*see* xvi.a). The barking is not mentioned by *Luke,* but *Matthew* and *Mark* place it immediately after Jesus's Entry into Jerusalem and his overturning of the money-changers' tables. In *Luke,* the Entry occurs immediately after the Zacchaeus story, but the overturning of the tables is omitted. Clement of Alexandria notes (*Stromateis* iv. 6. 35) that some authorities attributed to Matthias the chief publican what others attributed to Zacchaeus. 'Matthias' in Greek is *Matthias* and 'Matthew' is *Matthaios*—only a slight difference in spelling; so, since Matthias was not a publican, Matthew must have been intended here (*see* (a) *above*).

(g) All this suggests that Zacchaeus is an iconotropic fiction deduced in good faith by the editor of *Luke* from an early mural or other illustration to *Matthew,* depicting the Entry in triptych. Jesus rides up to the Temple between cheering ranks, and the legend below reads: '*Zacch.* saw it'—meaning that this event was prophesied in *Zechariah* ix. Next, the money-changers are shown seated at their tables; one of these has been overturned and the mob are scrambling for fallen coins. The legend here reads: 'The poor are given the profits of extortion.' Next, Jesus curses the spirit of the barren sycomore-tree, represented as a manikin perched in its branches. The legend reads: 'I need food.' The whole triptych bears the abbreviated inscription: '*Kat. t. Math. t. telōn.*', meaning: 'According to Matthew the publican'. From this sequence *Luke* has concocted the story of little Zacchaeus who climbed into the sycomore, and who was a rich publican—translating '*t. Math. t. telōn.*' as 'the *disciple* (Greek: *matheta*) who was a publican'; and how he gave half his fortune to the poor and restored fourfold his wrongful gains; and how Jesus invited himself to dinner at Zacchaeus's magnificent house—the distant Temple.

But *Luke* must have found a basis for the story in a collection of 'Oracles': an account of Matthew the publican's conversion. 'Zacchaeus' here takes a vow to restore his ill-gotten gains according to the Law (*Exodus* xxii. 1) and to give half his fortune to the poor—leaving only enough for the needs of his household. Thereupon Jesus accepts him as a disciple. If 'Zacchaeus' was really Matthew the Levite, this may account for the strange 'Son of Abraham' in *Luke* xix. 9: a misreading for 'Son of Aaron'. And if 'the son of Alphaeus' means 'the son of the Chaste One' (*alpheios*)—(*see* viii.*s* and xi.*b*)—Matthew must have been a well-educated young Zadokite apocalyptic, one of the Zophim, who had associated with the Romans but was considering a return to the fold. The success of Jesus's sudden appeal now becomes credible; a Levite publican of orthodox Sadducaic upbringing would merely have stared at him and shrugged.

(68) *As Jesus passed by the receipt of custom, he saw Matthew the Levite, which had been a Watcher, sitting there and said unto him:*

'*Why sittest thou there, Matthew? Art thou not also a son of Aaron? Make haste and come down!*'

Matthew, being overcome with shame, asked him: 'Sir, what shall I do to be saved?'

Jesus answered, and said: 'Restore fourfold whatsoever thou hast taken by fraud, as the Law commandeth, and bestow upon thy household the remainder of thy substance, and come, follow me!'

Matthew said: 'Sir, I will do even as thou sayest.'

And he made haste and came down and followed him.

Now, it came to pass that many Hebrew publicans, which saw it, repented likewise and were drawn to follow after Matthew.

And they all entered into the house where Jesus lodged with his disciples, and sat down there.

Then did Jesus rejoice, saying: 'This day is salvation come to this house!' And he preached the word of God to them. But some of his disciples were offended that the publicans were come into the house.

* * * * *

(70) *But when certain Pharisees came to converse with Jesus and desired him to preach in their synagogue, they also were offended at that they saw and would not enter into his house.*

They said to the disciples privily: 'How is this? Why doth your master preach to publicans and sinners?'

When Jesus heard that the Pharisees were offended, he went out and said unto them: 'They that are whole have no need of the physician, but they that are sick. They that are well filled have no need of bread, but they that are hungry. I am come not to call the righteous, but sinners to repentance.'

*　*　*　*　*

(*h*) The parable of the Lost Sheep is carelessly told in *Luke* xv. 4–6: the shepherd leaves his flock in the *wilderness,* not the fold, while he goes to look for the stray—as though Jesus did not trouble about the fate of the righteous. For the Son of Man read 'this son of man', i.e. 'myself'.

(71) *And he spake this parable unto them, saying:*

'The words of the prophet Zechariah: "Thus saith the Lord my God, feed the flock of the slaughter. Therefore will I feed the flock of the slaughter, even you, the poor of the flock."

'What man of you having an hundred sheep, if he lose one of them doth not leave the ninety and nine in the fold, and go into the mountains and seek that which is gone astray?

'And if so be that he find it, verily I say unto you, he calleth to his friends and neighbours, saying unto them: "Rejoice with me, for I have found my sheep which was lost."

'Or what woman having ten pieces of silver, if she lose one doth not light a lamp and sweep the house, and seek diligently until she find it?

'And when she hath found it, she calleth her friends and neighbours together, saying unto them: "Rejoice with me, for I have found my piece which was lost."

'Likewise I say unto you, that there is joy in the presence of the angels of God over one sinner that repenteth.

'This son of man is sent to seek and save that which is lost, and today he hath found him.'

*　*　*　*　*

(*i*) The parable of the Pharisee and the Publican has been mischievously introduced into *Luke* xviii. 9. Jesus made use of it to illustrate the saying—a Talmudic commonplace—that 'the most righteous man alive is unworthy to stand in the place of a repentant sinner' (*Sanhedrin* 99a). The Pharisee here is a caricature. He could not have prayed as he is said to have done, but would merely have given thanks to God for keeping him from gross transgression. (*j*) Nor, if he were an ordinary Pharisee, as opposed to an apocalyptic extremist, would he have claimed to fast twice a week. In Jesus's time no more than one regular fast-day a year was prescribed, namely the Day of Atonement. Extraordinary fast-days were sometimes decreed, mainly during droughts. After the destruction of the Temple, however, fasting became more frequent and *Luke* xviii. 12 perhaps refers to a fast ordered for the Monday, the Thursday, and the second Monday after Tabernacles and Passover, to atone for 'the excessive merriment enjoyed during these feasts' (*Megilath Ta'anith, end*). Nor would the Pharisee have glorified himself for giving tithes; besides, tithes were levied on produce, not 'possessions'.

(*k*) This Pharisee was one of the ninety-and-nine safe in the fold; and to have accused himself of adultery, extortion, and the like would have been hypocritical. The sinner's repentance in the parable belongs to the story of Matthew's conversion; the lost sheep was found, it did not return to the fold of its own volition. 'A publican' should be read for 'this publican', since the one in question was standing far in the Pharisee's rear. *Sanhedrin* 99*a* (*see* (*i*) *above*), continues:

> 'For it is written: "Peace, peace to him that is far off, and to him that is near" (*Isaiah* lvii. 19). This signifies: peace is first given to him who stands far off, having strayed from God's presence, and then to him who is near, never having strayed from His presence.'

Thus the publican who stood far off from God's sanctuary, both literally and figuratively, would have earned God's peace the sooner; and Jesus is recorded in the *Teaching of Peter,* as quoted by Gregory of Nazianzus, to have said so.

> (72) *And Jesus also spake this parable:*
> '*Two men went up into the Temple to pray, the one a Pharisee which fasted when fasting was required of him and paid tithes of all his produce; the other a publican which had repented of his evil.*
> '*The Pharisee stood and prayed: "O Lord, I thank Thee that Thou hast heard my prayer, and kept me from adultery and theft and blasphemy and from all such greater offences. Were it not for Thy grace I might be even as a publican."*
> '*But the publican, standing far from the Sanctuary, would not lift up so much as his eyes unto heaven but smote upon his breast, saying: "God be merciful unto me, a sinner!"*
> '*I say unto you: that the Lord bestowed His peace first upon this publican, and then upon the Pharisee. For Isaiah prophesied: "Peace, peace to him that is far off, and to him that is nigh."*
> '*Behold, a soul which is in trouble standeth nigh unto God. And joy shall be in heaven over one such sinner that repenteth more than over nine-and-ninety just persons that need no repentance.'*

*   *   *   *   *

(*l*) 'Sinners' as distinct from 'publicans' are the Men of the Land (*see* xii.*k–n*), the peasants and city proletariat who paid as little attention to the Law as they dared. The Pharisees would not eat with them, suspecting them not only of ritual uncleanness, but of withholding part of the required tithes, which would have made their food unhallowed even if prepared according to the Law (*Hagigah* 22*b*). Rabbi Akiba (late first and early second century A.D.), who had been one of them, confessed:

> 'While I was yet an *Am ha'Aretz* I was often tempted to bite the disciples of the wise like a wild ass.'

Asked by his pupils: 'Why a wild ass rather than a dog?', he replied: 'Because a dog mauls only the flesh, but a wild ass crushes the bones' (*Pesahim* 49*b*).

His contemporary, Rabbi Hiya, said (*ibid.*):

'The hatred of the *Ame ha'Aretz* against the rabbis surpasses that of the heathen against the Jews.'

The Pharisees at times could not help reciprocating this hatred. Perhaps the most intemperate·remark in the entire Talmud is Rabbi Eliezer's (*ibid.*):

'It is legitimate to take up a knife and cut the throat of an *Am ha'Aretz* even on a Day of Atonement that falls on the Sabbath. . . . If they did not stand in need of our custom, they would have murdered us long ago.'

But the approved policy was to convert and guide them (*Baba Mezi'a* 85*a*):

'Whosoever teaches the Law to the son of an *Am ha'Aretz*, the Holy One (blessed be He!) will annul any judgement He made against that man.'

* * * * *

BLIND GUIDES

Mark vii. 9–23

⁹And He said unto them: 'Full well ye reject the commandment of God, that ye may keep your own tradition. ¹⁰For Moses said,

Honour thy father and thy mother;
and,
Whoso curseth father or mother, let him die the death:

¹¹but ye say, If a man shall say to his father or mother, It is Corban, that is to say, a gift, by whatsoever thou mightest be profited by me; he shall be free. ¹²And ye suffer him no more to do ought for his father or his mother; ¹³making the word of God of none effect through your tradition, which ye have delivered: and many such like things do ye.'

¹⁴And when He had called all the people unto Him, He said unto them: 'Hearken unto Me every one of you, and understand: ¹⁵there is nothing from without a man, that entering into him can defile him: but the things which come out of him, those are they that defile the man. ¹⁶If any man have ears to hear, let him hear.' ¹⁷And when He was entered into the house from the people, His disciples asked Him concerning the parable. ¹⁸And He saith unto them: 'Are ye so without understanding also? Do ye not perceive, that whatsoever thing from without entereth into the man, it cannot defile him; ¹⁹because it entereth not into his heart, but into the belly, and goeth out into the draught, purging all meats?' ²⁰And He said: 'That which cometh out of the man, that defileth the man. ²¹For from within, out of the heart of men, proceed evil thoughts, adulteries, fornications, murders, ²²thefts, covetousness, wickedness, deceit, lasciviousness, and evil eye, blasphemy, pride, foolishness: ²³all these evil things come from within, and defile the man.'

Matthew xv. 1–20

¹Then came to Jesus scribes and Pharisees, which were of Jerusalem, saying: ²'Why do Thy disciples transgress the tradition of the elders? for they wash not their hands when they eat bread.' ³But He answered and said unto them: 'Why do ye also transgress the commandment of God by your tradition? ⁴For God commanded, saying:

Honour thy father and mother:
and,
He that curseth father or mother, let him die the death.

Matthew xv. 1–20 (*contd.*)

[5]But ye say, Whosoever shall say to his father or his mother, it is a gift, by whatsoever thou mightest be profited by me; [6]and honour not his father or his mother, he shall be free. Thus have ye made the commandment of God of none effect by your tradition. [7]Ye hypocrites, well did Isaiah prophesy of you, saying:

[8]*This people draweth nigh unto Me with their mouth,*
And honoureth Me with their lips:
But their heart is far from Me.
[9]*But in vain they do worship Me,*
Teaching for doctrines the commandments of men.

[10]And He called the multitude, and said unto them: 'Hear and understand. [11]Not that which goeth into the mouth defileth a man; but that which cometh out of the mouth, this defileth a man.'

[12]Then came His disciples, and said unto Him: 'Knowest Thou that the Pharisees were offended, after they heard this saying?' [13]But He answered and said: 'Every plant, which My heavenly Father hath not planted, shall be rooted up. [14]Let them alone: they be blind leaders of the blind. And if the blind lead the blind, both shall fall into the ditch.'

[15]Then answered Peter and said unto Him: 'Declare unto us this parable.' [16]And Jesus said: 'Are ye also yet without understanding? [17]Do not ye yet understand that whatsoever entereth in at the mouth goeth into the belly, and is cast out into the draught? [18]But those things which proceed out of the mouth come forth from the heart; and they defile the man. [19]For out of the heart proceed evil thoughts, murders, adulteries, fornications, thefts, false witness, blasphemies: [20]these are the things which defile a man: but to eat with unwashen hands defileth not a man.'

Matthew xxiii. 24

[24]Ye blind guides, which strain at a gnat, and swallow a camel.

Luke vi. 39

[39]And He spake a parable unto them: 'Can the blind lead the blind? shall they not both fall into the ditch?'

John ix. 39–41

[39]And Jesus said: 'For judgement I am come into this world, that they which see not might see; and that they which see might be made blind.' [40]And some of the Pharisees which were with Him heard these words, and said unto Him: 'Are we blind also?' [41]Jesus said unto them: 'If ye were blind, ye should have no sin: but now ye say, We see; therefore your sin remaineth.'

1 Epistle of John iv. 6–21

[6]We are of God: he that knoweth God heareth us; he that is not of God heareth not us. Hereby know we the spirit of truth, and the spirit of error.

[7]Beloved, let us love one another: for love is of God; and every one that loveth is born of God, and knoweth God. [8]He that loveth not knoweth not

1 Epistle of John iv. 6–21 (*contd.*)

God; for God is love. [9]In this was manifested the love of God toward us, because that God sent His only begotten Son into the world, that we might live through Him. [10]Herein is love, not that we loved God, but that He loved us, and sent His Son to be the propitiation for our sins.

[11]Beloved, if God so loved us, we ought also to love one another. [12]No man hath seen God at any time. If we love one another, God dwelleth in us, and His love is perfected in us. [13]Hereby know we that we dwell in Him, and He in us, because He hath given us of His Spirit. [14]And we have seen and do testify that the Father sent the Son to be the Saviour of the world. [15]Whosoever shall confess that Jesus is the Son of God, God dwelleth in him, and he in God. [16]And we have known and believed the love that God hath to us.

God is love; and he that dwelleth in love dwelleth in God, and God in him. [17]Herein is our love made perfect, that we may have boldness in the day of judgement: because as He is, so are we in this world. [18]There is no fear in love: but perfect love casteth out fear: because fear hath torment. He that feareth is not made perfect in love. [19]We love Him because He first loved us. [20]If a man say, I love God, and hateth his brother, he is a liar: for he that loveth not his brother whom he hath seen, how can he love God Whom he hath not seen? [21]And this commandment have we from Him, that he who loveth God love his brother also.

(*a*) In *Mark* vii. 9–13 and *Matthew* xv. 3–14 the *corban* passages succeed the episode of the unwashed hands (*see* XIII.*q*), whereas the short parallel 'blind guides' passage in *Luke* vi. 39 is part of the Sermon of the Mount. Jesus is here made to indict the Pharisees in words that they themselves used two generations later against unscrupulous fellow-members of their society.

(*b*) Anciently it was common to dedicate part of one's possessions to the Temple Treasury by use of the word *corban* ('sacrifice'). Even before the destruction of the Temple, however, this had come simply to mean 'tabooed', and could introduce vows of abstention (*see* XIII.*o*) such as: 'May wine be no less tabooed to me than if it were dedicated to the Temple!' *Corban* was also used loosely to emphasize an asseveration. For instance (*Nedarim* iii. 2): '*Corban* [I vow] if I saw not a serpent as thick as the beam of an olive-press!'; and the same tractate refers to minced vows, the substitution of *conam* or *conah,* to avoid the serious consequences of *corban;* yet these euphemisms, the Pharisees decided, had equal force with true vows (*Nedarim* iii. 1—*see* XXIII.*a*). The *Mishnah* gives a typical example of the use of *conam*: 'Suppose a man said (for the purpose of bargaining) "*conam* if I take of thee less than a *Sela*", i.e. two shekalim, and the other said: "*Conam* if I give thee more than a shekel"; and suppose that subsequently both agreed on one shekel and a half; in this case, it is a vow of incitement and invalid.'

(*c*) There are two cases in the Talmud of *corban* being legitimately uttered in order to prevent someone from taking what was not his own. In both the more usual formula: 'May this be *corban* to you!' seems to have been found insufficient and the consecrated goods were in fact handed over to the Treasury (*Pesahim* 57*a*):

> 'Abba Shaul relates: "There was a store of sycomore trunks in Jericho and the men of violence [i.e. armed servants of the Chief Priests] seized them by force, whereupon their owners arose and consecrated them to heaven [i.e. the Temple]."
>
> 'Again: the skins of the sacrificial victims [perquisites of the priesthood] used to be placed in the chamber of *Beth ha'Parwah*. Every evening these were divided among the men of the paternal division [i.e. a subdivision of each weekly "ward" of the priesthood]. But the men of violence would seize them by force.
>
> 'It was then enacted that the skins should be divided on the Sabbath eve, and that all wards should gather to receive their share at this time. Yet the [servants of] the Chief Priests still seized the skins by force. Thereupon the owners [i.e. the ward-leaders] arose and consecrated them to heaven.'

The money realized by their sale then went into the Temple Treasury, not the private pockets of the High Priest's family (*see* xii.*a*, *footnote*). No more than one batch of skins was so consecrated; but the manœuvre could be repeated whenever the men of violence appeared.

(*d*) After the destruction of the Temple it was found that an undutiful son could defraud his parents by declaring *'corban'* a part of his possessions reserved for the support of their old age. Since the Treasury could no longer benefit, because both the Temple and its Treasurers had ceased to exist, the son's property remained in his hands. When instances of this unfilial behaviour came to the notice of Rabbi Eliezer ben Horkinas (*see* liii.*b*), he declared (*Nedarim* ix. 1) that any vow* against the interests of one's parents must be annulled at once. A rabbi should approach the son, explaining to him that the Fifth Commandment took precedence over his vow, and should seek to make him retract this. Rabbi Meir who taught some forty years later, recommended the same procedure in the case of all inhumane vows: the fraudulent person should be asked 'Did you know that you were breaking a Commandment when you made this vow?' If the answer were 'no!', he might be absolved from it; if 'yes!', he was to be left to God's vengeance. But in *Nedarim* 64*b* it is doubted whether an appeal to the son's conscience would be sufficient to make him reconsider his decision; once he had uttered such a wicked vow he would probably continue in his shamelessness and refuse to be absolved.

(*e*) Though vows could not be entirely forbidden, because they were permitted by the Law, the rabbis discouraged even those of abstention as unlikely, in the long run, to benefit the community. Thus in *Jer. Kiddushin* vi. 12 it is laid down:

---

* According to *Nedarim* iii.2 (*see* (*e*) *below*) such a vow would fall under the category of 'vows made in error'.

'On the Day of Judgement an account will be required from men of the good things which they might have enjoyed but refrained from enjoying.'

The Nazirite vow itself was regarded with suspicion: it was pointed out that the sacrifice due to the Treasury, when the period of the vow had expired, was a sin-offering (*Numbers* vi. 14); the only Nazirite of whom Simeon the Just approved was a shepherd who shore off his locks to avoid the sin of narcissism (*Nazir 4b*). And Rabbi Gamaliel I went even farther (*Nedarim 22a*) in a *midrash* on *Proverbs* xii. 18: 'Whoever opens his mouth to vow, deserves to be transfixed by a sword; but the tongue of the wise grants him absolution.'

(*f*) Rabbis Eliezer, Meir, and the rest had, as a matter of fact, been anticipated in a discussion which probably dates from before Jesus's ministry and is based on the principle that vows against the interest of parents are 'vows made in error' and invalid. *Nedarim* iii. 2 reads:

'If a man who has surprised a crowd of people in the act of eating his figs, tells them: "May they be *corban* to you!", and his father and brothers proved to be among the eaters, then the School of Shammai say: "The vow is not binding on his own family; though it is binding on the rest." But the School of Hillel say: "The vow is binding on neither part." [On the principle that a vow cannot be invalidated in part only.]

If, therefore, a son might not even withhold a few figs from his parents by means of a vow, how much less might he withhold the support of their old age? This disposes of the alleged Pharisaic transgression of the Fifth Commandment.

(*g*) Nevertheless, the *Mishnah* (*Hagigah* i. 8) confesses: 'The rules about absolution from vows hang in the air' [i.e. without support from Scripture], and Pharisee opinion was divided on the subject. The majority held that a vow contravening the laws that one must love one's neighbour and honour one's parents should be declared null and void; but the minority held that God would be dishonoured by such a declaration and pointed to the case of Jephthah (*Judges* xi. 1–40) who, as the result of a rash vow, was forced to sacrifice his daughter. Jesus is here probably defending the majority view, and *Mark* vii. 13: 'Making the word of God of no effect through your tradition which ye have delivered,' has been quoted from a minority spokesman's protest against it. If so, Jesus's answer may be recovered from the *First Epistle of John* (iv. 6–21), a rhetorical passage on the subject of Love which, like similar passages in the Gospel of the same alleged authorship and date (*see* xxvi.*d*; liv.*a*; lxxii.*i*; lxxx.*b and* cvii.*e*) seem to have been built around the nucleus of authentic and characteristic Oracles.

(*h*) *Mark* vii. 10 and *Matthew* xv. 4 are evidence of a *midrash* on the Fifth Commandment. In the Pharisaic view parents were God's representatives to their children, and the Oral Law was clear: sons were bound to provide for their parents' maintenance—'to take them out and bring them in and meet them ever with gladness' (*Kiddushin* 31*a*). 'Whosoever has possessions and feeds not his parents, he is before God like a murderer' (*Yalkut Shimeoni* i. 830).

> (90) *'It is written also: "Thou shalt honour thy father and thy mother!"*
>
> *'And know ye not that whosoever hath possessions and will neither feed nor clothe his father or mother, the same is before God like unto a murderer?*
>
> *'Therefore make no rash vow, by which they may haply be deprived of that thou owest unto them.*
>
> *'But if thou hast made such a vow, yet shalt thou be released from it, as one that spake in ignorance.'*
>
> *A certain lawyer therefore asked Jesus, saying: 'Master, how may a man be released from his vow because he spake rashly? Was Jephthah released from the vow which he made concerning the burned offering?*
>
> *'For he said unto his daughter: "Alas, daughter, I have opened my mouth unto the Lord, and I cannot go back." And she, lest the word of God might be dishonoured, agreed thereto, saying: "Let the thing be done unto me."*
>
> *'This, therefore, that thou preachest hangeth in the air without support from the Law. Dost thou indeed love God and wouldst thou make His word of none effect?'*
>
> *Jesus answered and said: 'Love is of God, and hereby we know the spirit of truth and the spirit of error.*
>
> *'For though men rightly fear to break a rash vow which they have made, yet perfect love casteth out fear; and he that saith "I love God," but doeth his neighbour an injury, or dishonoureth his parents, the same is a liar.*
>
> *'For he that loveth not his neighbour or his parents which he hath seen, how can he love God which he hath not seen?'*

* * * * *

(*i*) As for Jesus's unbelievable dictum about defilement (*Matthew* xv. 17–20), it seems originally to have been a *midrash* on *Ezekiel* iii. 1–3; but the key-word *only* has been omitted (*see Introduction* 11.*h*). The list of defilements correspond with the 'shalt not's' of the Decalogue (*see* LXX.*f*).

The saying about the blind leading the blind must belong to the indictment of the feigned Pharisees (*see* XIII.*c*), and so must the quotation from *Isaiah* xxix. 13–15 in *Matthew* xv. 7–8 (*see* XIII.*w*).

> (47) *And he spake again of the feigned Pharisees, saying:*
>
> *'It is not only that which goeth into a man that defileth a man, but also that which cometh out of him.*
>
> *'For though ye eat clean food it entereth into the belly and descendeth into the draught and is presently voided as dung that defileth.*
>
> *'The Lord gave Ezekiel a scroll of a book to eat, and it was in his mouth as honey for sweetness.*
>
> *'Yet some there are which, when the scroll of the Law is given them to feed upon in their hearts, void it wickedly in murders, adulteries, thefts, false witness and covetousness.'*

* * * * *

(48) *'Walk not in their company, open thine eyes to their deceit, and be not guided by them: for if the blind lead the blind, shall they not both fall into a ditch?'*

* * * * *

(*j*) *Matthew* xv. 13: 'Every plant which our heavenly Father hath not planted shall be rooted up,' probably belongs to a passage about the Kingdom of Heaven (*see* LV.*b*).

(*k*) *John* ix. 39–41 must be related to *Luke* vi. 39, but the first verse contradicts *John* xii. 47, where Jesus is made to declare that he has not come to judge the world (*see* XXVI.*c*), and is an unintelligent comment on *Matthew* xiii. 13–15 (*see* XXV.*b*).

The next two verses are influenced by the anti-Nazarene *Romans* ii. 19–29:

'Thou, Jew, art confident that thou art a guide of the blind, a light of them which are in darkness. . . . Wherefore teachest thou not myself? Thou, which preachest a man should not steal, dost thou steal? Thou, which preachest a man should not commit adultery, dost thou commit adultery?'

Yet there may be an authentic saying concealed here: a general statement as opposed to a personal indictment.

(49) *'To be blind is no sin, but to be blind and say: "We see, let us guide thee," the same is deceit and sin.'*

* * * * *

ON CHASTITY

Mark x. 1–12

¹And He arose from thence, and cometh into the coasts of Judaea by the farther side of Jordan: and the people resort unto Him again; and, as He was wont, He taught them again. ²And the Pharisees came to Him, and asked Him: 'Is it lawful for a man to put away his wife?' tempting Him.

³And He answered and said unto them: 'What did Moses command you?' ⁴And they said: 'Moses suffered to write a bill of divorcement, and to put her away.'

⁵And Jesus answered and said unto them: 'For the hardness of your heart he wrote you this precept. ⁶But from the beginning of the creation God made them male and female. ⁷For this cause shall a man leave his father and mother, and cleave to his wife: ⁸and they twain shall be one flesh; so then they are no more twain, but one flesh. ⁹What therefore God hath joined together, let not man put asunder.' ¹⁰And in the house His disciples asked Him again of the same matter. ¹¹And He saith unto them: 'Whosoever shall put away his wife, and marry another, committeth adultery against her. ¹²And if a woman shall put away her husband, and be married to another, she committeth adultery.'

Matthew xix. 1–12

¹And it came to pass, that when Jesus had finished these sayings, He departed from Galilee, and came into the coasts of Judaea beyond Jordan; ²and great multitudes followed Him; and He healed them there.

³The Pharisees also came unto Him, tempting Him, and saying unto Him: 'Is it lawful for a man to put away his wife for every cause?' ⁴And He answered and said unto them: 'Have ye not read, that He Who made them at the beginning made them male and female, ⁵and said:

> For this cause shall a man leave father and mother, and shall cleave to his wife: and they twain shall be one flesh?

⁶Wherefore they are no more twain, but one flesh. What therefore God hath joined together, let not man put asunder.' ⁷They say unto Him: 'Why did Moses then command to give a writing of divorcement, and to put her away?' ⁸He saith unto them: 'Moses because of the hardness of your hearts suffered you to put away your wives: but from the beginning it was not so. ⁹And I say unto you, whosoever shall put away his wife, except it be for

Matthew xix. 1–12 (*contd.*)

fornication, and shall marry another, committeth adultery; and whoso marrieth her which is put away doth commit adultery.' [10]His disciples say unto Him: 'If the case of the man be so with his wife, it is not good to marry.' [11]But He said unto them: 'All men cannot receive this saying, save they to whom it is given. [12]For there are some eunuchs, which were so born from their mother's womb; and there are some eunuchs, which were made eunuchs of men: and there be eunuchs, which have made themselves eunuchs for the Kingdom of Heaven's sake. He that is able to receive it, let him receive it.'

Matthew v. 17–20

[17]'Think not that I am come to destroy the law, or the prophets: I am not come to destroy, but to fulfil. [18]For verily I say unto you, till heaven and earth pass, one jot or one tittle shall in no wise pass from the law, till all be fulfilled. [19]Whosoever therefore shall break one of these least commandments, and shall teach men so, he shall be called the least in the kingdom of heaven: but whosoever shall do and teach them, the same shall be called great in the kingdom of heaven. [20]For I say unto you, that except your righteousness shall exceed the righteousness of the scribes and Pharisees, ye shall in no case enter into the kingdom of heaven.'

Matthew v. 27–32

[27]'Ye have heard that it was said by them of old time, Thou shalt not commit adultery: [28]but I say unto you, that whosoever looketh on a woman to lust after her hath committed adultery with her already in his heart. [29]And if thy right eye offend thee, pluck it out, and cast it from thee; for it is profitable for thee that one of thy members should perish, and not that thy whole body should be cast into hell. [30]And if thy right hand offend thee, cut it off, and cast it from thee: for it is profitable for thee that one of thy members should perish, and not that thy whole body should be cast into hell.

[31]'It hath been said, Whosoever shall put away his wife, let him give her a writing of divorcement: [32]but I say unto you, that whosoever shall put away his wife, saving for the cause of fornication, causeth her to commit adultery: and whosoever shall marry her that is divorced committeth adultery.'

Luke xvi. 17–18

[17]And it is easier for heaven and earth to pass, than one tittle of the law to fail. [18]Whosoever putteth away his wife, and marrieth another, committeth adultery; and whosoever marrieth her that is put away from her husband committeth adultery.

Mark ix. 42–48

[42]And whosoever shall offend one of these little ones that believe in Me, it is better for him that a millstone were hanged about his neck, and he were cast into the sea. [43]And if thy hand offend thee, cut it off: it is better for thee to enter into life maimed, than having two hands to go into hell,

Mark ix. 42–48 (*contd.*)

into the fire that never shall be quenched: [44]where their worm dieth not, and the fire is not quenched. [45]And if thy foot offend thee, cut it off: it is better for thee to enter halt into life, than having two feet to be cast into hell, into the fire that never shall be quenched: [46]where their worm dieth not, and the fire is not quenched. [47]And if thine eye offend thee, pluck it out: it is better for thee to enter into the kingdom of God with one eye, than having two eyes to be cast into hell fire: [48]where their worm dieth not, and the fire is not quenched.

Matthew xviii. 7–10

[7]Woe unto the world because of offences! for it must needs be that offences come; but woe to that man by whom the offence cometh!

[8]'Wherefore if thy hand or thy foot offend thee, cut them off, and cast them from thee: it is better for thee to enter into life halt or maimed, rathei than having two hands or two feet to be cast into everlasting fire. [9]And it thine eye offend thee, pluck it out, and cast it from thee: it is better for thee to enter into life with one eye, rather than having two eyes to be cast into hell fire.

[10]'Take heed that ye despise not one of these little ones; for I say unto you, that in heaven their angels do always behold the face of My Father which is in heaven.'

Mark xii. 18–27

[18]Then come unto Him the Sadducees, which say there is no resurrection; and they asked Him, saying: [19]'Master, Moses wrote unto us, if a man's brother die, and leave his wife behind him, and leave no children, that his brother should take his wife, and raise up seed unto his brother. [20]Now there were seven brethren: and the first took a wife, and dying left no seed. [21]And the second took her, and died, neither left he any seed: and the third likewise. [22]And the seven had her, and left no seed: last of all the woman died also. [23]In the resurrection therefore, when they shall rise, whose wife shall she be of them, for the seven had her to wife?' [24]And Jesus answering said unto them: 'Do ye not therefore err, because ye know not the scriptures, neither the power of God? [25]For when they shall rise from the dead, they neither marry, nor are given in marriage; but are as the angels which are in heaven. [26]And as touching the dead, that they rise: have ye not read in the book of Moses, how in the portion called "The Bush" God spake unto him, saying,

I am the God of Abraham, and the God of Isaac, and the God of Jacob?

[27]He is not the God of the dead, but the God of the living, ye therefore do greatly err.'

Mark xii. 35–37

[35]And Jesus answered and said, while He taught in the temple: 'How say the scribes that Christ is the Son of David? [36]For David himself said by the Holy Ghost,

Mark xii. 35–37 (contd.)

> The Lord said to my Lord,
> Sit Thou on My right hand, till I make Thine enemies Thy footstool.

[37]David therefore himself calleth Him Lord; and whence is He then his son?' And the common people heard Him gladly.

Matthew xxii. 23–33

[23]The same day came to Him the Sadducees, which say that there is no resurrection, and asked Him, [24]saying: 'Master, Moses said, If a man die, having no children, his brother shall marry his wife, and raise up seed unto his brother. [25]Now there were with us seven brethren: and the first, when he had married a wife, deceased, and, having no issue, left his wife unto his brother: [26]likewise the second also, and the third, unto the seventh. [27]And last of all the woman died also. [28]Therefore in the resurrection whose wife shall she be of the seven? for they all had her.' [29]Jesus answered and said unto them: 'Ye do err, not knowing the scriptures, nor the power of God. [30]For in the resurrection they neither marry, nor are given in marriage, but are as the angels of God in heaven. [31]But as touching the resurrection of the dead, have ye not read that which was spoken unto you by God, saying,

> [32]I am the God of Abraham, and the God of Isaac, and the God of Jacob?

God is not the God of the dead, but of the living.' [33]And when the multitude heard this, they were astonished at His teaching.

Matthew xxii. 41–46

[41]While the Pharisees were gathered together, Jesus asked them, [42]saying: 'What think ye of the Christ? whose Son is He?' They say unto Him, The Son of David. [43]He saith unto them: 'How then doth David in spirit call Him Lord, saying,

> [44]The Lord said unto my Lord,
> Sit Thou on My right hand,
> Till I make Thine enemies Thy footstool?

[45]If David then call Him Lord, how is He his son?' [46]And no man was able to answer Him a word, neither durst any man from that day forth ask Him any more questions.

Luke xx. 27–44

[27]Then came to Him certain of the Sadducees, which deny that there is any resurrection; and they asked Him, [28]saying: 'Master, Moses wrote unto us,

> If any man's brother die, having a wife, and he die without children,
> that his brother should take his wife, and raise up seed unto his brother.

[29]There were therefore seven brethren: and the first took a wife, and died without children. [30]And the second took her to wife, and he died childless. [31]And the third took her; and in like manner the seven also: and they left no children, and died. [32]Last of all the woman died also. [33]Therefore in the resurrection whose wife of them is she? for seven had her to wife.' [34]And

Luke xx. 27–44 (contd.)

Jesus answering said unto them: 'The children of this world marry, and are given in marriage: ³⁵but they which shall be accounted worthy to obtain that world, and the resurrection from the dead, neither marry, nor are given in marriage: ³⁶neither can they die any more: for they are equal unto the angels; and are the children of God, being the children of the resurrection. ³⁷Now that the dead are raised, even Moses shewed in "The Bush", when he calleth the Lord the God of Abraham, and the God of Isaac, and the God of Jacob. ³⁸For He is not a God of the dead, but of the living: for all live unto Him.' ³⁹Then certain of the scribes answering said, Master, Thou hast well said. ⁴⁰And after that they durst not ask Him any question at all.

⁴¹And He said unto them: 'How say they that Christ is David's son? ⁴²And David himself saith in the book of Psalms,

> The Lord said unto my Lord,
> Sit Thou on My right hand,
> ⁴³Till I make Thine enemies Thy footstool.

⁴⁴David therefore calleth Him Lord, how is He then his son?'

Acts of Philip xxxiv.

For the Lord said unto me: 'If ye make not that which is below in you to be above, and the left hand things to be right, ye shall not enter into my Kingdom.'

Acts of Peter xxxviii.

The Lord said in a mystery: 'If ye make not the things of the left hand as those of the right, and those of the right hand as those of the left, and the things above as the things below, and the things before as the things behind, ye shall not know the Kingdom of God.'

Clement of Alexandria: Stromateis

iii. 9. 64. Whence it is with reason that after the Word had told about the End, Salome saith: Until when shall men die? (Now the Scripture speaks of man in two senses, the one that is seen, and the soul: and again, of him that is in a state of salvation, and him that is not: and sin is called the death of the soul) and it is advisedly that the Lord makes answer: So long as women bear [children].

iii. 9. 66. And why do not they who walk by anything rather than the true rule of the Gospel quote the rest of that which was said to Salome: for when she had said, 'I have done well, then, in not bearing [children]?' (as if child-bearing were not the right thing to accept) the Lord answers and says: Every plant eat thou, but that which hath bitterness eat not.

iii. 13. 92. When Salome inquired when the things concerning which she asked should be known, the Lord said: When ye have trampled on the garment of shame, and when the two become one and the male with the female [is] neither male nor female. In the first place, then, we have not this saying in the four Gospels that have been delivered to us, but in that according to the Egyptians.

Clement of Alexandria: Stromateis (contd.)

(*The so-called Second Epistle of Clement has this, in a slightly different form, c. xii. 2.:*

For the Lord himself being asked by some one when his kingdom should come, said: When the two shall be one, and that which is without as that which is within, and the male with the female neither male nor female.)

iii. 6. 45. The Lord said to Salome when she inquired: How long shall death prevail? 'As long as ye women bear [children]', not because life is an ill, and the creation evil: but as showing the sequence of nature: for in all cases birth is followed by decay.

iii. 9. 63. But those persons who set themselves against God's creation because of continence, which has a fair-sounding name, quote also those words which were spoken to Salome, of which I made mention before. They are contained, I think [*or* I take it] in the Gospel according to the Egyptians. For they say that the Saviour himself said: 'I came to destroy the works of the female.' By *female* he means lust: by *works*, birth and decay.

vii. 13. 82. They say that in the *Traditions*, Matthias the Apostle said that on every occasion, if the neighbour of an elect one sin, the elect one hath also sinned; for had he behaved himself as the Word [of God] enjoins, his neighbour would have been ashamed of his way of life and not sinned.

iii. 4. 26. They say that Matthias also taught thus: that we should fight with the flesh and chasten it, not yielding to it at all for licentious pleasure, but making the soul grow by faith and knowledge.

Clement of Alexandria: Excerpts from Theodotus

2. As the Valentinians say . . . on this account the Saviour saith: 'Save thyself, and thy soul.'

67. And when the Saviour says to Salome that there shall be death as long as women bear [children], he did not say it as abusing birth, for that is necessary for the salvation of believers.

Tertullian: On Baptism 20

The disciples were tempted because they fell asleep, so that they forsook the Lord when he was taken . . . for the saying had gone before: 'No man that is not tempted shall obtain the Kingdom of Heaven.'

Didascalia ii. 8

The Scripture saith: 'A man that is not tried is not approved.'

(*a*) *Mark* x. 1, expanded in *Matthew* xix. 1, should probably conclude the account of Jesus's visit to Jerusalem for the Feast of Dedication (*see* LXXXIV.*f*). In order to go from Galilee to Peraea ('the coasts of Judaea by the farther side of Jordan') which was another part of Herod Antipas's domain (*Wars* ii. 6. 3), he would have had to pass through either Samaria or the tetrarchy of Philip, but this is not mentioned in *Mark* or *Matthew*.

(*b*) *Mark* x. 2 has an artificial ring; so have the next two verses. Neither the Pharisees nor Jesus would have put questions the answers to which were generally agreed upon. It is likely, however, that the corresponding question in *Matthew* xix. 3, on the meaning of *Deuteronomy* xxiv. 1, is genuine; this was an outstanding point of disagreement between the School of Hillel and that of Shammai. Shammai had held that only adultery justified divorce; whereas Hillel had declared that, legally speaking, a man might divorce his wife on the slightest grounds, even for bad cookery.* Hillel's patently ironical pronouncement, a *reductio ad absurdum* of the Law, has been misinterpreted by Christians as a licence to libertinism; he laid special emphasis on the word *might,* the implication being that a husband who wishes for salvation should forgive even adultery in a wife, as God figuratively does in *Jeremiah* iii. 1; thus his follower Rabbi Eliezer ben Pedat said that 'the very altar sheds tears for him that divorces his first wife' (*Gittin* 90*b*). Hillel, however, held that in rare instances, where invincible dislike had estranged the spouses, Mosaic divorce was the sole remedy.

(*c*) Jesus will have taken this view, which had now been officially adopted by the Great Sanhedrin; but the word *lightly* has been omitted by some ascetic editor from 'Let no man lightly put asunder' (*Matthew* xix. 6), so that he is made to annul the Mosaic Law by a refusal to permit divorce on any account. This is impossible in the light of *Luke* xvi. 17; so is his downright 'He that putteth away his wife and marrieth another, committeth adultery against her, and whosoever marrieth her that is put away, committeth adultery'—because Moses in *Deuteronomy* xxiv. 2 expressly sanctioned the subsequent re-marriage of a divorced woman. Here the words 'for slight cause' seem to have been omitted from the first part of the saying; and the true version of the second is to be supplied from *Matthew* v. 32: 'He that putteth away his wife [for slight cause] guideth her feet in the path of adultery.'

A later editor of *Matthew* evidently found these amended prohibitions too severe; and, with the object of permitting a wronged husband to marry again, changed *Matthew* v. 32 from 'for slight cause' to 'save for fornication'. Then, since the original text survived in *Matthew* xix. 9, 'save for fornication' was subsequently introduced here too, thus converting Jesus to Shammai's view; and the Pauline Church, though accepting adultery as an excuse for separation, chose to read: 'Whom God hath joined let no man put asunder,' as Jesus's annulment of the Mosaic sanction for the re-marriage of divorced spouses. This is still Canon Law; but many loopholes are found for its evasion.

The Pharisaic Oral Law, to which Jesus enjoined strict obedience (*Matthew* xxiii. 2—*see* XIII.*a*) confirmed *Deuteronomy* xxiv. 1, which permitted divorce at the husband's discretion; insisting, however, on certain delays of procedure in the hope of a reconciliation. It also permitted the wife to sue her husband for divorce on grounds of impotence, denial of conjugal rites, unrea-

---

* Rabbi Akiba, in the early second century, added: 'Or loss of beauty.'

sonable restrictions on her freedom, loathsome ailments, or odorous occupa-
tions—such as tanning (*Nedarim* xi. 12; *Kethuboth* v. 5; vii. 2–5 *and* 9).

(*d*) In *Matthew* v. 27–28, Jesus sets a fence around the Seventh Command-
met by forbidding ocular as well as phallic adultery. *Ecclesiasticus* (xxxi. 13)
had declared: 'Nothing is created more evil than the eye.' Jesus could not recommend castration, which was a crime in Jewish Law, and therefore spoke
figuratively in *Matthew* xix. 10–12. The orgiastic devotee of Cybele might
castrate himself; the apocalyptic Pharisee committed no self-injury but restrained his passions and emulated the eunuch. The man-made eunuch, *saris
adam,* was despised (*Ecclesiasticus* xx. 4 and xxx. 20) and liable to severe
punishment (*Shabbath* 111*a*) if he had undergone castration for the sake of
acquiring a position of trust in a royal harem*; such an act set aside God's
first command to man (*Genesis* i. 22): 'Increase and multiply!' Sympathy, on
the other hand, was felt for the 'Sun eunuch' (*saris hamma*), one on whom
the sun had never shone as a man (*Wisdom of Solomon* iii. 14):

> 'Happy is the eunuch that hath wrought no lawless deed,
> For there shall be given him for his faithfulness a peculiar grace
> And a portion of great delight in the sanctuary of the Lord.'

(*e*) The law that no man-made eunuch might enter the congregation of
Israel (*Deuteronomy* xxiii. 2), was interpreted by the Pharisees to mean that
he might not marry a Jewess, for *Ecclesiasticus* (*see* (*d*) *above*) had satirized
the lust of the eunuch to deflower a virgin, and his sighs during an ineffectual
embrace.† His condition did not, however, debar him from the synagogue,
because of *Isaiah* lvi. 4–5: 'Unto the eunuchs will I give a place in My house
and a name for everlasting.' Several early Gentile ascetics, including Origen
(Eusebius: *Ecc. Hist.* 6 viii. 2) read *Matthew* xix. 12 in conjunction with *Matthew* v. 29–30, and thereupon castrated themselves; this practice was condemned in 325 A.D. by the Council of Nicaea (*Canon* i).

(*f*) *Mark* ix. 42–48 and *Matthew* xviii. 7–10 both contain instructions to rid
oneself of an offending foot, hand, or eye, though not in the adultery context:
the hypothetical offence is against children of the Men of the Land (*see* LX.*c
and e*). But since the threat of hell-fire and the undying worm is over-severe
after the mention of the millstone and the sea, which reads authentically
enough, the editor of *Mark* appears to have combined two unrelated sayings
found in a collection of Oracles, under the subject-heading 'Offence': one
concerned with the 'little ones' and the other with being offended by an erring member. Probably, then, the editor of *Matthew* borrowed *Mark's* version,
which he revised for insertion in *Matthew* xviii. 7–10; while also using a text
(*Matthew* v. 30) from a different collection of Oracles, where the offence of
the erring member is correctly placed in the adultery context.

---

* Herod the Great relied largely on eunuchs as household officers (*Antiquities* xvi 8. 1. etc.).

† Juvenal similarly satirizes eunuch marriages at Rome (*Satires* i. 22): '*Cum tener uxorem
ducat spado. . . .*'

(g) Foot, hand, and eye seem too many particulars at once to fit Jesus's concise style. It is possible, therefore, that only eye and foot* belong to the adultery context, and that a separate saying about the removal of a lazy right hand and the plucking out of a dull eye was quoted by Jesus from the *Book of Ahikar* (*Syr.* viii. 20) in the context of 'Lift up your eyes and see the fields that are white with harvest' (*John* iv. 35—see LXX.*j*); and that this became confused (again because of the subject-arrangement used in the Oracles) with the removal of the lascivious 'foot' and the plucking out of the concupiscent eye.

(297) *'And see that ye labour abundantly. For it is written in the* Book of Ahikar: *"The hand that laboureth not shall be cut off at the shoulder, and the eye in which there is no vision, the raven shall pluck it out."'*

* * * * *

(h) *Mark* ix. 44–48, which concerns the undying worm and the unquenched fire, is a reminiscence of *Isaiah* lxvi. 24, and has been expanded into a litany; the bishop or elder intones the three warning verses and the congregation chants the same response to each: 'Where the worm dieth not, and the fire is not quenched.'

(73) *Jesus went across Jordan and a multitude followed him, and as he was wont he taught them.*

And a Pharisee asked Jesus: 'Master, holdest thou that a man may put away his wife for any cause, or for fornication only?'

Jesus answered and said: 'Hast thou not read how that He which made men at the beginning made them male and female.

'For which cause shall a man leave his father and mother and shall cleave to his wife, and they twain shall be one flesh?

'What therefore God hath joined, let no man lightly put asunder.'

The Pharisee asked him again: 'Why then did Moses suffer a man to give a bill of divorcement, and to put away his wife?'

Jesus answered: 'Moses, truly, because of the hardness of our fathers' hearts, suffered them to put away their wives, if matter of uncleanness were found in them.

'Yet have ye not read what the prophet Jeremiah spake in the name of the Lord?

'For he said: "It is written: 'If a man put away his wife and she go from him and become another man's shall he return unto her again? Shall not that land be greatly polluted?' But thou, Israel, hast played the harlot with many lovers and under every green tree.† Yet return again to Me, saith the Lord."

'Therefore, if God thus forgiveth Israel her manifold whoredoms, how much more should not a man forgive a matter of uncleanness in the wife of his bosom?

---

* The original euphemism for 'privy member' was 'feet', as in *Exodus* iv. 25: 'Zepporah cast the foreskin at Moses's feet'; a later variant was 'fore-arm' (*Kiddushin* 25a).

† Trees sacred to the Love-goddess, see CXIII.*s*.

'And I say unto you that if a man put away his wife for slight cause he guidedth her feet in the path of adultery; and if he then take another in her stead, he himself committeth adultery.'

* * * * *

(*i*) *Matthew* v. 17–19, which concerns the immutability of the Law, and which the editor of *Luke* xvi. 17 rightly connects with the passage above, has been separated from it in *Matthew* by a few verses. It is a citation of *Deuteronomy* iv. 2 *and* 40, and the correct version of Jesus's words is to be found in the Talmud (*see* LXXX.*b*). He declares that Moses has not said that one *must* divorce one's faithless wife, but only that one *may* and that (in the words of the *Mishnah—Aboth* ii. 1): 'Ye cannot know how great or how small the sin will be reckoned that proceedeth from the breach of any commandment; be ye wise therefore and obey all!'

'Scribes and Pharisees' in *Matthew* v. 20 should read 'Sadducees'—who did not recognize the prophets as having almost equal authority with the Law.

(74) *They said unto him: 'But what Moses permitted, is not that the Law?'*

He answered and said: 'Think not that I am come to subvert the Law. I am come neither to increase it nor to diminish it, but to fulfil the will of God, which hath interpreted the Law by the mouth of His holy prophets.

'For Moses commanded Israel: "Ye shall not add unto the word which I command you, neither shall ye diminish ought from it, but ye shall keep the commandments of the Lord for ever!"

'Verily, therefore, until heaven and earth pass away, not one jot or tittle shall in any wise pass from the Law, but all shall be fulfilled!

'And whosoever breaketh the least of the commandments that God committed unto His prophets and excuseth himself, saying: "It is permitted in the Law," the same shall be called the least in the Kingdom of Heaven.'

* * * * *

(*j*) 'Verily' in *Matthew* v. 18 stands for *amen*, a Hebrew word originally meaning 'He was firm', which later acquired adverbial force. '*Amen* implies an oath, an acceptance of words, a confirmation of words' (*Shebu'oth* 36a). Dalman (*The Words of Jesus, p.* 226) states that Jesus was unique in beginning, rather than ending, a pronouncement with *amen;* and it seems to be because of this idiosyncrasy that he is referred to as 'The Amen' in *Revelation* iii. 14. Apparently he used this formula, which in *John* becomes *verily, verily* (*John* v. 19, 24, 25; vi. 26, 32, 47, 53, etc.) when speaking as a prophet, instead of saying: 'Thus saith the Lord.' By beginning his pronouncement with an assent, he meant to indicate that God, not himself, was its author; but the evangelists often interpolated an *amen* to underline a doctrinal point of their own.

The word had a strong Messianic flavour. Rabbi Eliezer ben Horkinas said (*Erubin* 19a), that on the Last Day the souls in Gehenna would chant *amen* when the Holy Name was praised by the congregation of the just. The doors of Hell would yield and angels would robe the sinners in white linen and carry them off to Paradise. This, according to Rabbi Joshua ben Levi (*ibid.*), would be their reward for testifying to the justice of their punishment, and glorifying God even in their torments.

The following passage belongs to the discussion of Pharisaic interpretations of the Law (*see* xxviii.*a–e*).

> (104) *'Verily I say unto you, that except your righteousness shall exceed the righteousness of the Sadducees, which keep all the Laws but not that of mercy and loving-kindness, ye shall in no wise enter into the Kingdom of Heaven!'*

*   *   *   *   *

(*k*) Jesus, having made a statement on divorce, answers a question arising from it. The Sadducee here quoted the Levirate Law of *Deuteronomy* xxv. 5, originally framed to prevent widows from marrying out of the clan and conferring their property on strangers. *Luke's* version is remarkable in that it forbids marriage to any who wish to enter the Kingdom—the Strict Essene view, which would have closed the door against Peter who was already married when he became a disciple (*Matthew* viii. 14), and against Philip the Deacon (*Acts* xxi. 8–9). Jesus (*see* viii.*q and* x.*b*) took the Free Essene view: that marriage, though permitted, should be consummated only when children were desired, and that, otherwise, spouses should enjoy a wholly spiritual communion. He was, in fact, recommending either unconsummated marriage or no marriage at all, since it would be madness to beget children when the frightful cataclysm of Judgement was hourly expected: 'Woe unto them that are with child and unto them that give suck in those days!' (*Matthew* xxiv. 19—*see* xcix.*i*).

(*l*) In *Matthew* xxiv. 38, Jesus goes on to speak of those who ate, drank, and celebrated weddings until the very day before the Deluge, when Noah and his family entered the Ark. In Pharisee doctrine, resurrected souls were like angels and did not marry (*Berakoth* 17*a* and *Aboth di Rabbi Nathan* c. 1). This was because the Messianic Kingdom would be one long Sabbath Day, perpetually illuminated by God, and because, according to the severe *Book of Jubilees* (i. 8), to lie with one's wife during the daylight hours of the Sabbath was to break it.* It was, however, expected by some that the elect would

---

* The objection to intercourse on the Sabbath Day was expressed by Rabbi Hune: 'Israelites do not cohabit in the light of the sun.' He referred to the public orgies in Syrian temples and under sacred trees (*see* (*h*) *above*). 'It happened once that a man lay with his wife under a fig-tree. He was brought before the Sanhedrin and flogged, not because he broke the Law, but *because the times required it*' (*Sanhedrin* 46*a*).

According to *Niddah* 38*a*, 'the pious men of old performed their marital duty only on the evening before the third day, lest their wives should be led to desecration of the Sabbath.' This is glossed as meaning that the average period of 273 days between conception and birth made intercourse dangerous except in the middle of the week; if a child were born on the Sabbath, that would involve such prohibited labour as drawing water and lighting a fire.

Nevertheless, this explanation is probably wrong. The Talmudic term for sexual intercourse is 'to eat garlic'; not only because garlic was considered a legitimate aphrodisiac (*Jer. Megillah* iv. 1), but because, as raw garlic taints the breath for three days, so cohabitation kept

beget thousands of children (*Enoch* x. 17), when they entered alive into the Messianic Kingdom on earth. The Kingdom would endure for seventy generations before the ultimate disappearance of the material world and the subsequent return of all souls to God (*see* LXXXVIII.*n*). The Sadducees, however, did not believe in the Resurrection (*see* LXIX.*d*).

For *Mark* xii. 27—*see* XCV.*c*.

(75) *But a Sadducee said to Jesus: 'If then a man and his wife be one flesh, there can be no resurrection.'*

Jesus asked: 'How so?'

He answered and said: 'Moses wrote that if a man die and leave no children, his brother shall take the widow and raise up seed unto him that is dead.

'Now, there were seven brethren, the first of which died without issue.

'The second took the widow unto himself and married her, neither left he any issue.

'The third likewise, and the fourth, until all seven had her.

'Last of all the woman died also.

'If there be a resurrection, how can this woman be one flesh with seven men?'

Jesus answered and said: 'Thou errest. Those that arise from the dead shall neither marry nor be given in marriage, but shall be like the angels in heaven. None thereafter shall either be born or die.

'And ye Sadducees that reject the prophets, how do ye reject the resurrection of the dead, having read the Law and knowing the power of God?

'Did not God speak to Moses out of the bush, saying: "I am the God of Abraham, Isaac and Jacob"?

'He therefore is not the God of the dead, but of the living. They that are called dead according to the flesh live unto Him in the spirit and shall be raised again at the Last Judgement when the Anointed One, the Son of David, cometh to judge the world.'

* * * * *

The remainder of Jesus's argument can be supplied from the Talmud (*Sanhedrin* 90*b*), where *Exodus* vi. 4 is discussed in this eschatological sense:

(76) *'And the Kingdom of Heaven to which they are called shall be in this land where we now are. As it is written: "And I also kept My covenant with Abraham, Isaac and Jacob to give them the Land of Canaan."'*

* * * * *

---

one from perfect cleanliness for an equal length of time (*Exodus* xix. 15 and 1 *Samuel* xxi. 5). In order to be clean on the Friday it was necessary not to 'eat garlic' after Tuesday evening.

In the second century, the Pharisees were enjoined to have marital intercourse on the Sabbath Eve (*Kethuboth* 65*b*; *Nedarim* iii. 10 *and* viii. 6); perhaps because the population had been dangerously reduced by war and famine, and the contemporary view was that hard work or exercise on the day after coition prejudiced conception. The Karaite Jews (Singer: *The Karaite Jews* pp. 198–9, *note*) and the modern Samaritans (Eichorn: *Repertorium* xiii. pp. 257–82) still keep to the older law, from a literal interpretation of *Exodus* xxxiv. 21: 'On the Seventh Day shalt thou rest!'

Whether one should normally 'eat garlic' on this or that day of the week will have been of only academic interest to Jesus, who was now prescribing complete marital chastity '*because the times required it*'.

(*m*) The saying in *Mark* xii. 35-37, *Matthew* xxii. 41-46 and *Luke* xx. 39-44, which refers to *Psalm* cx. 1, has been wrongly reported. Jesus could not have quibbled in a sense so contrary to Pharisaic doctrine. The quibble must have been introduced by the Sadducaic lawyers with whom, according to *Mark* and *Luke,* the conversation took place; an obtuse editor of *Matthew* here copied from *Luke* xx and misread the 'they' in verse 41. Much the same point is discussed in *Yalkut Shimeoni* ii. 869, where Abraham's face is said to have darkened because, in *Psalm* cx. 1, the Messiah was placed on God's right hand and thus given greater honour than himself, although his own remote descendant.

> (77) *Then certain of the scribes answered:* 'Master, thou hast well said!'
> *But the same Sadducee asked again:* 'By what authority sayest thou that the Anointed One, the Son of David, will come to judge the world?'
> *He answered and said:* 'Though ye Sadducees reject the prophets, yet sing ye the psalm of David which saith: "The Lord said unto my Lord: 'Sit thou on My right hand till I make thine enemies thy footstool.'"'
> *But the Sadducee laughed him to scorn, saying:* 'If David calleth him Lord, how is he then his son? And if he is David's son, how shall he be given greater honour than David?'

* * * *

Jesus's reply, as in *Yalkut Shimeoni* (*ibid.*) will have been to refer the questioner to verse 5 of the same *Psalm:*

> (78) *Jesus answered and said:* 'It is written in the same psalm: "The Lord at thy right hand shall strike through kings in the day of His wrath."
> 'Therefore shall David sit on the left hand, for something of sin was found in him, but his son shall be perfected and shall sit on the right hand.'

* * * *

> (79) *Jesus also said:*
> 'It is written: "Thou shalt not commit adultery!"
> 'Yet whosoever looketh upon a woman to lust after her, the same committeth adultery with her in his heart.
> 'Therefore, if thine eye offend thee, pluck it out and cast it from thee; or if thy foot offend thee, cut it off.
> 'It is better to enter halt or blind into the Kingdom, than that thy whole body should be cast into hell. Save thyself and thy soul!
> 'For Isaiah the prophet saith: "In the carcases of those that transgress against Thee, O Lord, their worm dieth not and the fire is not quenched."'
> *His disciples say unto him:* 'Not all men can receive this saying.'
> *Jesus answered:* 'I speak not according to the flesh. Some are born eunuchs and earn no praise therefrom, neither condemnation; some are made eunuchs of men and earn condemnation; but some shall make themselves as *it were*

eunuchs for the Kingdom of God, and these shall earn praise from the Father. 'He that can receive this saying, let him receive it!'

* * * * *

(*n*) Other sayings of Jesus's on this subject appear in the *Gospel according to the Egyptians* which, according to Origen (*On Luke: Homilies* i), was one of those early attempts at composing a Gospel mentioned in the prologue to *Luke* (*see Introduction* iv.*h*); but it lacked the gift of Grace. In other words, it was written before the late first-century or early second-century *Luke,* and its author had access to a collection of Oracles from which he selected several that were afterwards suppressed as conflicting with Catholic doctrine.

The remarkable conversation between Jesus and Salome, referred to by Clement of Alexandria in six different passages, is taken from this Gospel. In *Stromateis* iii. 9. 64, the 'Word' is a synonym for Jesus; and Salome is the woman who, according to *Mark* xv. 40, stood at the Cross with Mary Magdalene and later came to the tomb to anoint Jesus's body (*Mark* xvi.1—*see* vii.*f*). Since no account of her identity is given in *Mark* and her name is omitted from *Matthew* and *Luke,* it may well be that, in the Triple Tradition, she was presented as taking part in this very conversation, afterwards suppressed for doctrinal reasons. In the miracle story of the *Protoevangelium* 19–20, Salome's relationship to Jesus is not indicated, but she bears witness that his mother's hymen had been unbroken until she conceived. Though this is a common enough phenomenon (as appeared in the celebrated British Court case of Russell *v.* Russell), it seems that the Nazarene tradition of her having acted as midwife at Jesus's ceremonial re-birth was seized upon by the Gentile Christians to prove their dogma of his physical parthenogenesis (*see* viii.*i*).

The Female on whom Jesus declared war was *Aggrath Bat Machlat* (*see* lxiii.*e*), otherwise known as the *Alukah,* or 'horse-leech' (*Proverbs* xxx. 15), whose two daughters, the Womb and the Grave, constantly cry 'Give, give!' She was, in fact, the lustful and destructive Love-and-Death-goddess Ishtar, whom Jehovah had superseded as chief deity in Palestine. Jesus reasoned that procreation implied death; hence 'no more procreation, no more death.' Only chastity could confer immortality (*see* (*s*) *below*).

(*o*) A more complex version of Jesus's pronouncement on the relation of the sexes is quoted in the apocryphal *Acts of Philip* and *Acts of Peter,* the latter giving the more dependable version. In Israel, the husband always took precedence of his wife: on all ceremonial occasions he was placed above or ahead of her, and she took the left, or north, side while he took the right, or south, the side of honour. But Jesus claimed that these distinctions disappeared when perfect spiritual love prevailed between man and wife; which may be one of the reasons why early Christianity gained such support among pious but spirited women.

Stromateis iii. 9. 66, which concerns the bitter plant, may refer to *Proverbs* xxvii. 7.

(82) *Salome (which was midwife when he was born again of Mary the Braider by the Spirit of God, and which testified to her virginity) asked Jesus: 'Lord, how long shall Death prevail?'*

He answered: 'So long as ye women bear children.'

She asked again: 'I have done well, then, in bearing none?'

He said unto her: 'It is written in the Proverbs of Solomon: "To the hungry soul, every bitter thing is sweet." Eat of every healthful plant, but of that which is bitter eat not; for the time will come wherein the childless shall account themselves blessed.'

She asked: 'Shall a man then marry a wife and know her not?'

He answered: 'It is written in the same book that the Alukah hath two daughters, which are the womb and the grave, and they cry "Give, give!" I am sent to destroy her works.'

She asked him again: 'Lord, when shall these things be accomplished?'

He said unto her: 'When ye women shall have trampled upon the garment of shame: and when the two shall have become one in spirit, the male with the female being neither male nor female.

'Verily, I say unto you all, both men and women: if ye make not that which was on the left hand to be neither on the right nor yet on the left; and that which was below to be neither above nor yet below; and that which was behind to be neither before nor yet behind, ye shall not know the Kingdom of God!'

* * * *

(*p*) The Moslem formula of refusing marital rites to a wife is to call her 'my sister' and so make all further congress incestuous. This may have been borrowed from Hebrew practice (*see* VIII.*w*).

(*q*) Jesus's ruling consideration seems to have been that no woman would commit adultery unless she had been treated inconsiderately by her husband; the same view was later expressed by Rabbi Akiba (*Sifre Naso* and *Sotah* 47*b*), when discussing the 'bitter water' ordeal of a woman's chastity laid down in *Numbers* v. 11–24: 'The bitter waters will be an unfailing test of a wife's guilt only if her husband is himself guiltless.' And as with a husband's responsibility for his wife's faithfulness, so with a man's responsibility for his neighbour's good behaviour. Jesus's saying on this head is preserved in the *Traditions of Matthias,* a Gospel mentioned by Origen (*On Luke: Homilies* i.), and quoted by Clement of Alexandria (*Stromateis* vii. 13. 82). It is likely to have been spoken in the context of 'Judge not!' (*see* XXVI.*a–g*):

'They say that in the tradition [of Jesus], Matthias the Apostle records: "On every occasion if the neighbour of an elect one sin, the elect one hath also sinned; for had he comported himself as the word [of God] enjoins, his neighbour would have been ashamed to sin." '

(110) *'Moreover, if the neighbour of a man that accounteth himself righteous should sin, then hath he also something of sin in him.*

'For had he kept the Law according to the spirit of righteousness, then his neighbour would have repented him of his own ways and not sinned.'

* * * * *

(*r*) Another quotation from the *Traditions of Matthias* (*Stromateis* iii. 4. 26) supports the saying (*Matthew* xix. 12) about making oneself a eunuch for God's sake. It may be restored as follows; with the addition of a saying quoted by Tertullian (*On Baptism* 20 supplemented by another in *Didascalia* ii. 8):

(80) *'And let him strive with the flesh and chasten it, not yielding unto its lusts, but making his soul to wax strong by faith and wisdom.*

'For no man that is not tried can be approved, and no man that is not approved shall enter into the Kingdom.'

* * * * *

To this we may add (*see* LVII.*f*):

(81) *The disciples say unto him: 'Master, we receive this saying.'*

And Jesus rejoiced, and said: 'Now, behold, I see Satan as lightning fallen from heaven.'

* * * * *

(*s*) Satan, here, is the Cosmocrator, the author of the False Creation (*see* LXX.*f and* CI.*e*). Jesus's argument comes out clearly in a text excised from the *Acts of John,* a document of the mid-second century, and preserved only in the *Epistle of Titus,* a Latin document of six hundred years later. There John, addressing a group of virgins at a wedding, which he 'attended only for the sake of chastity,' is said to have told them:

'Little children, while yet your flesh is pure and ye have your bodies yet untouched and undestroyed, undefiled by Satan, the great and shameless foe of chastity, learn from me more fully the mystery of the nuptial act. It is the trial of the serpent, the ignorance of doctrine, injury of the seed, the gift of death . . . the impediment which separateth from the Lord, the beginning of disobedience, the end of life, namely death.'

In other words, the fruit which the Cosmocrator gave Eve, and which she shared with Adam, was the death-dealing gift of sexual love.

The *Epistle of Titus* contains a further quotation from the *Acts of John,* 113, which has also survived in many other manuscripts. John, as he dies, exclaims:

'O thou, who hast kept me until this hour for thyself and untouched by union with a woman; who, when in my youth I first desired to marry, didst appear unto me and say: "John, I have need of thee"; who at the second time didst prepare for me bodily sickness; and who, when for the third time I desired to marry, didst forthwith prevent me, and then at the third hour of the day* didst say to me upon the sea: "John, hadst thou not been mine, I should have suffered thee to marry. . . ." '

* * * * *

Previously (*Acts of John,* 63), he had persuaded Andronicus the praetor of Ephesus and his beautiful wife Drusiana to live together as brother and sister; but the arguments he used, perhaps taken from the *Gospel according to the Egyptians,* have been suppressed in all manuscripts.

(*t*) At a lesser Council of Nicaea (787 A.D.), the *Acts of John* were rejected from the New Testament Canon; and physically consummated marriage which was first banned, next condoned (1 *Corinthians* vii. 9), next celebrated in the Church porch only, has finally been accepted and converted into a sacrament. The 144,000 saints who alone gained the Kingdom of Heaven by keeping themselves undefiled of women (*Revelation* xiv. 4) are forgotten. The rite is now performed on the altar steps and the priest reads the solemn injunction: 'Marriage is ordained for the procreation of children.' He also refers to Jesus's hallowing of the wedding at Cana as though he had not 'attended only for the sake of chastity' (*see* x.*b*).

* * * * *

* The 'Hour of Revelation' in Gnostic religious theory.

ON MURDER

Matthew v. 21–24

²¹'Ye have heard that it was said by them of old time, Thou shalt not kill; and whosoever shall kill shall be in danger of the judgement: ²²but I say unto you, that whosoever is angry with his brother without a cause shall be in danger of the judgement: and whosoever shall say to his brother, Raca, shall be in danger of the council: but whosoever shall say, Thou fool, shall be in danger of hell fire. ²³Therefore if thou bring thy gift to the altar, and there rememberest that thy brother hath ought against thee; ²⁴leave there thy gift before the altar, and go thy way; first be reconciled to thy brother, and then come and offer thy gift.'

Luke xii. 58–59

⁵⁸When thou goest with thine adversary to the magistrate, as thou art in the way, give diligence that thou mayest be delivered from him; lest he hale thee to the judge, and the judge deliver thee to the officer, and the officer cast thee into prison. ⁵⁹I tell thee, thou shalt not depart thence, till thou hast paid the very last mite.

Matthew xii. 34–37

³⁴O generation of vipers, how can ye, being evil, speak good things? for out of the abundance of the heart the mouth speaketh. ³⁵A good man out of the good treasure of the heart bringeth forth good things: and an evil man out of the evil treasure bringeth forth evil things. ³⁶But I say unto you, that every idle word that men shall speak, they shall give account thereof in the day of judgement. ³⁷For by thy words thou shalt be justified, and by thy words thou shalt be condemned.

Luke vi. 45

⁴⁵A good man out of the good treasure of his heart bringeth forth that which is good; and an evil man out of the evil treasure of his heart bringeth forth that which is evil: for of the abundance of the heart his mouth speaketh.

Jerome: On Ephesians v. 4

As we also read in the *Gospel according to the Hebrews:*
'And never,' saith he, 'be ye joyful, save when ye behold your brother with love.'

(*a*) *Matthew* v. 21–22 is a *midrash* on the Sixth Commandment and on the subsidiary text (*Deuteronomy* xix. 5–13) which differentiates between murder and homicide. This follows the *midrash* on the Seventh Commandment (*see* xxi.*d*), and is succeeded in verses 23 and 24 by a *midrash* on the Ninth; in verses 33–37 by one on the Third (*see* xxiii.*a*); in *Matthew* vi. 22–23 by one on the Tenth (*see* xxiv.*b*); in *Matthew* vi. 24 by one on the First (*see* lxviii.*a*); and in *Matthew* xv. 4 by one on the Fifth (*see* xx.*h*).

The remaining three *midrashim* of this series, those on the Second, Fourth, and Eighth Commandments, are missing. But 'Thou shalt not make to thyself any graven image!' is implicit in Jesus's warning to the apostles not to enter Greek territory where such images were on display (*see* lvii.*g*); and 'Thou shalt not steal!', in the order to bestow all one's goods on the poor (*see* lxxxii.*g*); and 'Thou shalt keep holy the Sabbath Day!', in the assumption that his hearers will not exceed a Sabbath Day's journey even when fleeing from a rain of fire (*see* xcviii.*k*).

The text of *Matthew* v. 21–22 is corrupt. The presumptuous 'But I say' has been introduced to suggest that this is not accepted Pharisaic doctrine but an original and daring innovation; yet the reference to *Leviticus* v. 1–10 in *Matthew* v. 22 at once disproves the notion that the Law is obsolescent. Moreover, the editor has not realized that in Aramaic *raca* means 'fool'.

(*b*) The Pharisees considered libel, slander, and disparagement as the equivalent of murder (*Baba Mezi'a* 58*b*):

'Whosoever shames his neighbour, or gives him an evil name, the same is destined for Gehenna: it is as though he had spilled his blood.'

and in *Jer. Pe'ah* 1–2:

'It is said of the slanderer: "He speaketh here and he killeth in Rome; he speaketh in Rome and killeth in Syria."'

The theory that God abhors the slanderer was proved by the case of Miriam who was stricken with leprosy for her defamation of Moses's wife (*Numbers* xii. 1), and by that of the spies who brought back a misleading report on the Promised Land and died of plague (*Numbers* xiv. 37). Moreover, in the *Testaments of the Twelve Patriarchs* (*Dan* ii. 2) there is a warning against the sin of anger:

'For anger is blindness which suffereth not a man to look upon his neighbour's face with the truth.'

This accounts for the saying attributed to Jesus in the *Gospel according to the Hebrews* (Jerome: *On Ephesians* v. 4). But Solomon had treated slander as mere folly (*Proverbs* x. 18), and a fool as deserving no worse than stripes (*Proverbs* xix. 29).

(111) *Again he taught them saying:*
  '*It is written: "Thou shalt do no murder!", and he that doth murder shall be in danger of the judgement.*

'*Also Solomon hath declared that he that slandereth his neighbour is a fool, and deserving of stripes.*

'*These are the punishments of this world; but verily, in the world to come he that hath been angry with his neighbour without cause, the same shall be in danger of God's judgement; and he that hath slandered his neighbour, or hath shamed him, the same shall be in danger of hell fire!*'

* * * * *

(*c*) *Matthew* xii. 34–37, abbreviated in *Luke* vi. 46, is probably a *midrash* on *Psalm* iv. 2–4. 'Generation of vipers' is used here, as again in *Matthew* xxiii. 33 (*see* XIII.y) to support an indictment of the Pharisees wrongly deduced from the psalm.

(112) '*But since from the abundance of the heart the mouth speaketh, good if it be good, evil if it be evil,*

'*Therefore, if thy heart be evil, hold thy peace; for of every vain word that thou shalt speak, thou shalt be called to account in the Day of Judgement.*

'*By thy words as much as by thy deeds thou shalt be justified, or shalt be condemned.*

'*As David prophesied in the name of the Lord: "O ye sons of men, how long will ye turn My glory into shame? How long will ye love vanity and seek after leasing?*

'*"Stand in awe of Me and sin not, commune with your own heart upon your bed and let your tongues be still!"*

'*As it is written in the Testament of the patriarch Dan: "Unless ye keep yourselves from the spirit of lying and anger ye shall perish. For anger is blindness and suffereth not a man to see the face of his neighbour with truth."*

'*Therefore, let your mouths never speak so freely as doth your heart save when ye behold your neighbour with joy and love.*'

* * * * *

(*d*) That *Matthew* v. 23–24 is a *midrash* on the Ninth Commandment can be deduced from *Leviticus* v. 1–10, where a case is quoted of the conceal-ment, by witnesses to a contract, of the oath sworn in ratification of it, and where the atonement due for this negative breach of the Commandment is laid down.

(87) *Jesus spake of others of the Ten Commandments, saying:* '*It is written: "Thou shalt bear no false witness!", and likewise: "If a man heareth the voice of swearing and is a witness to an oath, and afterwards concealeth his knowl-edge of it, then when he confesseth his sin he shall bring a trespass offering unto the Lord, according to his substance, and the priest shall sprinkle of its blood upon the altar."*

'*But if ever thou bringest such a trespass offering unto the Lord, first con-sider whether by any words lightly spoken thou hast offended thy neighbour, whose oath thou concealedst because he wronged thee.*

'*And if thou rememberest aught, leave there thine offering before the altar and go thy way. First, be reconciled to thy neighbour, and then come again and offer thy gift.'*

* * * * *

(e) *Luke* xii. 58–59 is a *midrash* on *Proverbs* xxv. 8–9, which arises from Jesus's advice to be reconciled with one's neighbour. The Talmudic parallel is *Yoma* viii. 9:

'The Day of Atonement brings forgiveness for trespass against God; but for trespass against a neighbour the Day of Atonement brings no forgiveness until a man shall be reconciled with him.'

(88) *'Moreover, Solomon counselleth thee: "Go not forth hastily to strive lest thou know not what to do in the end thereof, when thy neighbour hath put thee to shame.*

' *"Debate thy cause with thy neighbour himself, and discover it not to another, lest he that heareth thee put thee to shame."*

'*Therefore, agree with thy neighbour whilst thou art with him in this world, lest in a time to come the Adversary deliver thee to the Judge and the Judge to his officer, and the officer cast thee into prison,*

'*Whence thou shalt not depart until thou hast paid the uttermost farthing of the debt that thou owest unto thy neighbour.'*

* * * * *

XXIII

ON OATHS

Matthew v. 33–37

33Again, ye have heard that it hath been said by them of old time, Thou shalt not forswear thyself, but shalt perform unto the Lord thine oaths. 34But I say unto you, swear not at all; neither by heaven; for it is God's throne: 35nor by the earth; for it is His footstool: neither by Jerusalem; for it is the city of the great King. 36Neither shalt thou swear by the head, because thou canst not make one hair white or black. 37But let your communication be, Yea, yea; Nay, nay: for whatsoever is more than these cometh of evil.

James v. 12

12But above all things, my brethren, swear not, neither by heaven, neither by the earth, neither by any other oath; but let your yea be yea; and your nay, nay; lest ye fall into condemnation.

(a) This saying, which is a *midrash* on the Third Commandment, seems to have been misquoted. Since oaths were sanctioned by the Law, Jesus could not have forbidden them altogether: the Third Commandment (*Exodus* xx. 7) warns against oaths idly sworn in the name of God. But according to the *Mishnah* (*Shebu'oth* iv. 13), an oath by heaven, by earth, or by Jerusalem was invalid unless it referred specifically to God—in *Psalm* xlviii. 1–2 Jerusalem is called the 'City of the Great King', namely God. So here Jesus was condemning idle oaths only.

He was, furthermore, 'setting a fence about the Law' by warning his disciples against the use of any oaths whatever, lest they might forswear themselves (*see* xxi.*e*). In this he followed Pharisaic tradition (*see* xx.*e*): 'Beware of swearing even on a truth' (*Gittin* 35*a*); 'Let thy nay be an honest nay and thy yea an honest yea—and say not one thing with thy heart but another with thy mouth' (*Sifra Leviticus* xix. 36). Anyone about to swear an oath was warned (*Shebu'oth* 38*b*–39*a*): 'Knowest thou not that the whole world shook when the Holy One (blessed be He) pronounced on Sinai: "Thou shalt not take the name of thy God in vain"?'

(b) Nevertheless, the *Mishnah* makes certain exceptions: the faithful were allowed to dissemble when confronted by tax-gatherers, robbers, or murderers. The School of Shammai held (*Nedarim* iii. 4): 'They may declare that what they carry is an heave-offering, although it be not an heave-offering; or that it belongs to the king, although it belong not to the king.' The School of Hillel assented and added (*ibid.*) that a false declaration might even take the form of an oath. This generous stretching of the principle of *tikkun ha'olam* (*see Introduction* ii. *g*) was intended to protect honest men from victimization.

> (69) '*It is written also:* "*Thou shalt not take the Name of the Lord thy God in vain!*"
>
> '*Therefore do thou set a fence about this commandment, and swear not at all save under compulsion, lest haply thou forswear thyself.*
>
> '*Let thy yea be yea, and thy nay, nay; for what is more than this proceedeth from evil,*
>
> '*As who would seek to deceive with an oath sworn by heaven, or by earth, or by Jerusalem, seeming to swear by Him that sitteth enthroned in heaven and that maketh the earth His footstool and that hath chosen Jerusalem as the city whereof He is the Great King.'*

✳　✳　✳　✳

The oath sworn by one's own head was not Jewish, and does not apply to these injunctions which solely concern oaths sworn in the name of God; it was, however, a favourite Graeco-Roman oath and must have been added by a devout Gentile editor.

(*c*) Jesus may have quoted from the original Hebrew text, no longer extant, of the *Secrets of Enoch* xlix. 1:

> 'I will swear no single oath, either by heaven or by earth, or by any creature which God hath made. If there be no truth in men, let them swear by a word: yea, yea, or nay, nay.'

Or the Grecian translator of the *Secrets of Enoch* may have borrowed from Jesus; or both may have quoted from a common source—the oral tradition recorded in *Sifra Kedoshim* xix. 36 (*see* (*a*) *above*). The saying also occurs in *James* v. 12.

The Essenes held the same view as Jesus; Josephus records in *Wars* ii. 8. 6:

> 'Whatsoever they say also is firmer than an oath, but they avoid swearing and esteem it worse than perjury, for they say that he who cannot be believed without invocation of God is already condemned.'

This was the orthodox Pharisaic view too, as expressed in the *Mishnah* (*Nazir* i. 1), which dispenses with the formal oath sworn on making a vow: 'If a man said: "I will be a Nazirite," a Nazirite he became.'

✳　✳　✳　✳

XXIV

ON LIGHT

Mark iv. 21

[21]And he said unto them: 'Is a lamp brought to be put under a bushel, or under a bed? and not to be set on a lamp-stand?'

Matthew v. 14–16

[14]'Ye are the light of the world. A city that is set on an hill cannot be hid. [15]Neither do men light a lamp, and put it under a bushel, but on a lamp-stand; and it giveth light unto all that are in the house. [16]Let your light so shine before men, that they may see your good works, and glorify your Father which is in heaven.'

Matthew vi. 22–23

[22]'The light of the body is the eye: if therefore thine eye be single, thy whole body shall be full of light. But if thine eye be evil, thy whole body shall be full of darkness. If therefore the light that is in thee be darkness, how great is that darkness!'

Luke viii. 16

[16]'No man, when he hath lighted a lamp, covereth it with a vessel, or putteth it under a bed; but setteth it on a lamp-stand, that they which enter in may see the light.'

Luke xi. 33–36

[33]'No man, when he hath lighted a lamp, putteth it in a secret place, neither under a bushel, but on a lamp-stand, that they which come in may see the light. [34]The light of the body is the eye: therefore when thine eye is single, thy whole body is full of light; but when thine eye is evil, thy body also is full of darkness. [35]Take heed therefore that the light which is in thee be not darkness. [36]If thy whole body therefore be full of light, having no part dark, the whole shall be full of light, as when the bright shining of a lamp doth give thee light.'

Oxyrhynchus Papyrus I

Jesus saith: 'A city built upon the top of a high mountain and established can neither fall nor be hidden.'

John xi. 9–10

⁹Jesus answered: 'Are there not twelve hours in the day? If any man walk in the day, he stumbleth not, because he seeth the light of this world. ¹⁰But if a man walk in the night, he stumbleth, because there is no light in him.'

John xii. 35–36

³⁵Then Jesus said unto them: 'Yet a little while is the light with you. Walk while ye have the light, lest darkness come upon you; for he that walketh in darkness knoweth not whither he goeth. ³⁶While ye have light, believe in the light, that ye may be the children of light.'

John iii. 20–21

²⁰'For every one that doeth evil hateth the light, neither cometh to the light, lest his deed should be reproved. ²¹But he that doeth truth cometh to the light, that his deeds may be made manifest, that they are wrought in God.'

John viii. 12

¹²Then spake Jesus again unto them, saying: 'I am the light of the world: he that followeth Me shall not walk in darkness, but shall have the light of life.'

John ix. 4–5

⁴'I must work the works of Him that sent Me, while it is day: the night cometh, when no man can work. ⁵As long as I am in the world, I am the light of the world.'

John xii. 46

⁴⁶'I am come a light into the world, that whosoever believeth on Me should not abide in darkness.'

(*a*) The parable of the Lamp and the Lamp-stand, which the Synoptics have incorporated in the Sermon on the Mount, seems to be a *midrash* on *Proverbs* iv. 18–19. In *Mark* iv. 21 and *Luke* viii. 16 it has been attached to: 'Nothing is hid that shall not be manifested' (*see* xliv.*c*), and in *Matthew* v. 14–16 to: 'Ye are the salt of the earth.' So haphazard has been the treatment of Oracles by the compilers of the Gospels, that in *Luke* xi. 33 this same passage is found again in the Signs from Heaven context, attached to: 'The light of the body is the eye', which occurs separately in *Matthew* vi. 22—where it is supported by a quotation from *Isaiah* lx. 1–3 as a *midrash* on the Tenth Commandment. The author of *Luke* xi. 33–36 probably found both the Lamp parable and the saying about the light of the body under the subject-heading 'Light' in a collection of Oracles.

(*b*) In *Matthew* vi. 22–23 Jesus warns his disciples against the *ain ha'ra*, the 'evil eye' which blights and causes darkness. In Jewish folklore the evil eye might induce sickness in a healthy person, the premonitory symptoms being yawns and drowsiness: it was cast either by the envious who hated others to be more fortunate than themselves, or by those cursed at birth with the power to 'overlook' unintentionally. *Habakkuk* i. 13: 'Thou art of purer eyes, O God, than to behold evil,' enjoins the pious to emulate God and thus avoid a breach of the Tenth Commandment. The source of light in *Matthew* v. 16 is the Law seen as a lamp lighted within the heart (*see* LXXX.*b footnote*), and the disciples are told to explain publicly that they are living by the light of the Law, not by their own righteousness.

(*c*) In *John* xi. 9 and xii. 35, Jesus also quotes from the *Testaments of the Twelve Patriarchs* (*Judah* xviii. 6). The saying about the city set on a hill, evidently found by the editor of *Matthew* under the same subject-heading, 'Light', has been turned inside-out in *Matthew* v. 14. The city on the hill was the heavenly Jerusalem upon which, as the version in the *Oxyrhynchus Papyrus* shows, they were to fix their hearts; this is a *midrash* on *Isaiah* ii. 2–5, ending with: 'Let us walk in the light of the Lord.'

'I' has characerically been substituted for 'the Law of God' in *John* viii. 12, ix. 5 and xii. 46 (*see Foreword. h*).

(91) '*It is written also: "Thou shalt not covet thy neighbour's house, nor his wife, nor his servant, nor his maid, nor his ox, nor his ass, nor anything that is his!"*

'*Therefore take heed that ye cast not looks that do injury.*

'*For verily, the light of the body is the eye: if thine eye be good and covet not, thine whole body shall be full of light; but if evil, then thy body shall be full of darkness,*

'*As it is written in the Testament of the Patriarch Judah: "A blinded soul stumbleth by day as though it were night."*

'*Take heed then that thine inner eye be good and covet not, that thou mayest see God; for if it be evil, how gross shall thy darkness be!*

'*Strive to look upon all things even as doth the eye of our Heavenly Father: for the prophet Habakkuk saith: "Thou art of purer eyes, O God, than to behold evil."*'

* * * * *

(92) '*Know ye not the words of Solomon: "The way of the just is a shining light, that shineth more unto the perfect day; but the way of the wicked is darkness"?*

'*For the Law is a lamp lighted within the heart of them that love the Lord.*

'*Be ye therefore as a light to the world, shine ye openly! For he that lighteth a lamp hideth it not under a bushel nor under a bed, but setteth it on a lampstand, whence it giveth light to all the household.*

'*Let your light so shine before men that they may know whence your good works proceed and may glorify our Father which is in heaven.*'

* * * * *

(94) '*And have ye not heard what Isaiah said? "Arise, be enlightened; for thy light cometh and the glory of the Lord is risen upon thee.*

'*"For behold, a darkness shall cover the earth, and a gross darkness the people, but the Lord shall rise upon thee and His glory shall be seen upon thee.*

'"And the generations shall come to Thy light, and kings to the brightness of Thy rising."

'Truly, God is the light of the world: he that obeyeth His Law shall not walk in darkness, but shall have the light of life.

'And know ye not what Isaiah also prophesieth? "And it shall come to pass in the last days that the mountain of the Lord's house shall be established on the mountain top and shall be exalted above the hills; and all nations shall flow unto it. O House of Jacob, come ye and let us walk in the light of the Lord!"

'Therefore, fix ye your hearts upon this heavenly city; which is an easy thing. For a city that is set on the top of a high mountain and established of God can neither fall nor be hidden.'

* * * * *

(d) *John* iii. 20–21, which follows a late doctrinal assertion that those who refuse to believe in the saving power of Jesus's name are already damned, is the remains of an authentic *midrash* on *Job* xxiv. 13–17.

(93) 'Is it not written in the Book of Job: "They rebel against the light; they know not the ways thereof, nor abide in the paths thereof.

'"The thief worketh by night; the eye also of the adulterer waiteth for the twilight; and in the dark they dig through the walls of houses.

'"The morning is to them even as the shadow of death."

'But he that doeth truth, the same feareth not the light, for it is manifest that his deeds are wrought in the name of God.'

* * * * *

This follows the *midrash* (*see* (c) *above*) on *Proverbs* iv. 18–19, and strengthens the association there made of the wicked with darkness.

* * * * *

EARS TO HEAR

Mark iv. 10–12

¹⁰And when He was alone, they that were about Him with the Twelve asked of Him the parable. ¹¹And he said unto them: 'Unto you it is given to know the mystery of the kingdom of God: but unto them that are without all these things are done in parables: ¹²that

> *Seeing they may see, and not perceive;*
> *And hearing they may hear, and not understand;*
> *Lest at any time they should be converted,*
> *And their sins should be forgiven them.'*

Mark iv. 25

²⁵'For he that hath, to him shall be given: and he that hath not, from him shall be taken even that which he hath.'

Matthew xiii. 10–17

¹⁰And the disciples came, and said unto Him: 'Why speakest Thou unto them in parables?' ¹¹He answered and said unto them: 'Because it is given unto you to know the mysteries of the Kingdom of Heaven, but to them it is not given. ¹²For whosoever hath, to him shall be given, and he shall have more abundance: but whosoever hath not, from him shall be taken away even that he hath. ¹³Therefore speak I to them in parables: because they seeing see not; and hearing hear not, neither do they understand. ¹⁴And in them is fulfilled the prophecy of Isaiah, which saith,

> *By hearing ye shall hear, and shall not understand;*
> *And seeing ye shall see, and shall not perceive:*
> ¹⁵*For this people's heart is waxed gross,*
> *And their ears are dull of hearing,*
> *And their eyes they have closed;*
> *Lest at any time they should see with their eyes,*
> *And hear with their ears,*
> *And understand with their heart,*
> *And should be converted, and I should heal them.*

¹⁶But blessed are your eyes, for they see: and your ears, for they hear. ¹⁷For verily I say unto you, That many prophets and righteous men have desired to see those things which ye see, and have not seen them; and to hear those things which ye hear, and have not heard them.'

Matthew xxv. 29

[29]For unto every one that hath shall be given, and he shall have abundance: but from him that hath not shall be taken away even that which he hath.

Luke viii. 8–10

[8]And when He had said these things, He cried, 'He that hath ears to hear, let him hear.'

[9]And His disciples asked Him, saying, 'What might this parable be?' [10]And He said: 'Unto you it is given to know the mysteries of the kingdom of God: but to others in parables; that seeing they might not see, and hearing they might not understand.'

Luke viii. 18

[18]Take heed therefore how ye hear: for whosoever hath, to him shall be given; and whosoever hath not, from him shall be taken even that which he seemeth to have.

Luke x. 23–24

[23]And He turned Him unto His disciples, and said privately: 'Blessed are the eyes which see the things that ye see: [24]for I tell you, that many prophets and kings have desired to see those things which ye see, and have not seen them; and to hear those things which ye hear, and have not heard them.'

Luke xix. 26

[26]For I say unto you, that unto every one which hath shall be given; and from him that hath not, even that he hath shall be taken away from him.

(a) *Mark* iv. 25: 'To him that hath shall be given, and from him that hath not shall be taken even that he hath,' is not (as might be supposed) a wry comment on the injustice of this world, but a *midrash* on *Proverbs* ii. 1–11, *Isaiah* xxix. 14 and *Ezekiel* xii. 2, and refers to the acquisition of wisdom only.

(155) *Jesus preached in the streets and lanes of Jerusalem, saying: 'Solomon spake this proverb of them that hearkened to the Law:*

' "My son, incline thine ear unto wisdom. If thou seekest after her as silver, then shalt thou understand the fear of the Lord, and understanding shall deliver thee from the ways of darkness."

'And Ezekiel spake of them that hearkened not. For he said:

' "Man, thou dwellest in the midst of a rebellious house which have eyes to see, and see not, and ears to hear but hear not."

'And Isaiah likewise prophesied in God's name:

' "Inasmuch as this people have removed their heart from Me, the wisdom of their learned men shall perish."

'Therefore, he that hath ears to hear, let him hearken; for unto him that

hearkeneth shall be given wisdom. And from him that hearkeneth not shall be taken even that wisdom which he seemeth to have.'

* * * * *

(*b*) The saying recurs, most mischievously, in *Matthew* xxv. 29 and *Luke* xix. 26, at the close of the parable of the Talents (*see* LII.*g*), and again in *Luke* viii. 18, in the context of 'nothing is secret that shall not be manifest' (*see* XLIV.*c*). Here, in *Mark* iv. 25, it is joined to 'with what measure ye mete' (*see* XXVI.*h*); and, as in *Matthew* xiii. 12–15, wrongly precedes a quotation from *Isaiah* vi. 9–10—a shortened version of which also occurs separately in *Mark* iv. 12 (*see* LXVI.*i*) without acknowledgement of the source, and again in *John* xii. 40, which is its correct context (*see* CV.*e*).

(*c*) In *Luke* viii. 10 the *Isaiah* quotation is once more briefly used, as in *Mark*. An editor of *Matthew* has deliberately altered 'Shut thou their eyes' to 'their eyes have they shut'. He must have realized that the original does not fit the context; and, indeed, it makes sense only later when Jesus has despaired of converting the people of Jerusalem. The author of *Isaiah* vi. 9–10 continued in verse 11 to prophesy a desolation for Israel, but in verse 13 offered a hope to the remnant, a tenth part; and this was read in Jesus's day as an eschatological prophecy.

(*d*) *Mark* iv. 10–11, paralleled in *Matthew* xiii. 10–11 and *Luke* viii. 9–10 has no connection with the *Isaiah* quotation; the Gentile Christians' postulate, that Jesus spoke in enigmas to prevent his Jewish audience from understanding him and so being converted, is a preposterous one. It is likely that this passage refers to the calendar mystery which he concealed under the parable of the Loaves and Fishes (*see* LXXII.*f*), rather than to the simpler parable of the Sower (*see* LXVI.*a–c*) with which *Mark* and *Matthew* connect it.

> (230) *The disciples asked him:*
> '*Why speakest thou in parables?*'
> *He answered them, saying:* '*Unto you it is given to understand the mysteries of the Kingdom of Heaven, but to others it is not yet given.*'

* * * * *

Jesus, while making plain the primary meaning of his loaves and fishes exposition, had a political reason for concealing its secondary meaning from all but those endowed with spiritual understanding: he had yet to reveal himself as the Messiah who, alone, was empowered to teach this secret doctrine (*see* LXXII.*d*), and could not risk a premature acclamation.

For further mystical secrets, *see* LXXXIV.*g* and CI.*j*.

For his defence of simple parables, *see* XVII.*h*.

(*e*) The saying in *Matthew* xiii. 16–17, which follows The Sower (*see* LXVI.*c*) is paralleled in *Luke* x. 23–24, where it has been applied to the Return of the Seventy (*see* LIX.*d*). But Jesus could never have called anyone blessed because privileged to hear his words: the blessing will have referred, conditionally, to the Last Days.

(156) *'Blessed be your eyes if they see and your ears if they hear, that by wisdom ye may live and not die.*

'For verily, I say unto you that many prophets and kings and righteous men of old have desired to see and hear such things as shall soon be seen and heard among us, but have neither seen nor heard them.'

* * * * *

XXVI

JUDGE NOT!

Mark iv. 23–24

23'If any man have ears to hear let him hear.'

24And he said unto them: 'Take heed what ye hear: with what measure ye mete, it shall be measured to you: and unto you that hear shall more be given.'

Matthew vii. 1–5

1'Judge not, that ye be not judged. 2For with what judgement ye judge, ye shall be judged: and with what measure ye mete, it shall be measured to you again. 3And why beholdest thou the mote that is in thy brother's eye, but considerest not the beam that is in thine own eye? 4Or how wilt thou say to thy brother, Let me pull out the mote out of thine eye; and, behold, a beam is in thine own eye? 5Thou hypocrite, first cast out the beam out of thine own eye; and then shalt thou see clearly to cast out the mote out of thy brother's eye.'

Luke vi. 37–38

37'Judge not, and ye shall not be judged: condemn not, and ye shall not be condemned: forgive, and ye shall be forgiven: 38give, and it shall be given unto you; good measure, pressed down, and shaken together, and running over, shall men give into your bosom. For with the same measure that ye mete withal it shall be measured to you again.'

Luke vi. 41–42

41And why beholdest thou the mote that is in thy brother's eye, but perceivest not the beam that is in thine own eye? 42Either how canst thou say to thy brother, Brother, let me pull out the mote that is in thine eye, when thou thyself beholdest not the beam that is in thine own eye? Thou hypocrite, cast out first the beam out of thine own eye, and then shalt thou see clearly to pull out the mote that is in thy brother's eye.

Luke xii. 13–14

13And one of the company said unto Him: 'Master, speak to my brother, that he divide the inheritance with me.' 14And He said unto him: 'Man, who made me a judge or a divider over you?'

John iii. 16–19

16'For God so loved the world, that He gave His only begotten Son, that whosoever believeth in Him should not perish, but have everlasting life. 17For God

John iii. 16–19 (*contd.*)

sent not His Son into the world to condemn the world; but that the world through Him might be saved. [18]He that believeth on Him is not condemned: but he that believeth not is condemned already, because he hath not believed in the name of the only begotten Son of God. [19]And this is the condemnation, that light is come into the world, and men loved darkness rather than light, because their deeds were evil.'

John v. 19–38

[19]Then answered Jesus and said unto them:

'Verily, verily, I say unto you, the Son can do nothing of Himself, but what He seeth the Father do: for what things soever He doeth, these also doeth the Son likewise. [20]For the Father loveth the Son, and sheweth Him all things that Himself doeth: and He will shew Him greater works than these, that ye may marvel. [21]For as the Father raiseth up the dead, and quickeneth them; even so the Son quickeneth whom He will. [22]For the Father judgeth no man, but hath committed all judgement unto the Son: [23]that all men should honour the Son, even as they honour the Father. He that honoureth not the Son honoureth not the Father Who hath sent Him. [24]Verily, verily, I say unto you, he that heareth My word, and believeth on Him that sent Me, hath everlasting life, and shall not come into condemnation; but is passed from death into life. [25]Verily, verily, I say unto you, the hour is coming, and now is, when the dead shall hear the voice of the Son of God: and they that hear shall live. [26]For as the Father hath life in Himself; so hath He given to the Son to have life in Himself; [27]and hath given Him authority to execute judgement also, because He is the Son of Man. [28]Marvel not at this: for the hour is coming, in the which all that are in the graves shall hear His voice, [29]and shall come forth; they that have done good, unto the resurrection of life; and they that have done evil, unto the resurrection of condemnation. [30]I can of Mine own Self do nothing: as I hear, I judge: and My judgement is just; because I seek not Mine own will, but the will of the Father Who hath sent Me.

[31]'If I bear witness of Myself, My witness is not true. [32]There is Another that beareth witness of Me; and I know that the witness which He witnesseth of Me is true. [33]Ye sent unto John, and he bare witness unto the truth. [34]But I receive not testimony from man: but these things I say, that ye might be saved. [35]He was a burning and a shining light: and ye were willing for a season to rejoice in his light. [36]But I have greater witness than that of John: for the works which the Father hath given Me to finish, the same works that I do, bear witness of Me, that the Father hath sent Me. [37]And the Father Himself, Who hath sent Me, hath borne witness of Me. Ye have neither heard His voice at any time, nor seen His shape. [38]And ye have not His word abiding in you: for whom He hath sent, Him ye believe not.'

John viii. 15–18

[15]'Ye judge after the flesh; I judge no man. [16]And yet if I judge, My judgement is true: for I am not alone, but I and the Father that sent Me. [17]It is also written in your law, that the testimony of two men is true. [18]I am one that bear witness of Myself, and the Father that sent Me beareth witness of Me.'

John x. 34

[34]Jesus answered them:
'Is it not written in your law,

I said, Ye are gods?'

John xii. 47

[47]And if any man hear My words, and believe not, I judge him not: for I came not to judge the world, but to save the world.

Acts vii. 24–28

[24]And seeing one of them suffer wrong, he defended him, and avenged him that was oppressed, and smote the Egyptian; [25]for he supposed his brethren would have understood how that God by his hand would deliver them: but they understood not. [26]And the next day he shewed himself unto them as they strove, and would have set them at one again, saying, Sirs, ye are brethren; why do ye wrong one to another? [27]But he that did his neighbour wrong thrust him away, saying, Who made thee a ruler and a judge over us? [28]Wilt thou kill me, as thou diddest the Egyptian yesterday?

Acts vii. 35

[35]This Moses whom they refused, saying, Who made thee a ruler and a judge? the same did God send to be a ruler and a deliverer by the hand of the angel which appeared to him in the bush.

(*a*) *Matthew* vii. 1–5 and *Luke* vi. 37–38 and 41–42, form a *midrash* on 2 *Chronicles* xix. 6, itself an elaboration of *Deuteronomy* i. 17 and referring to *Exodus* ii. 11–14. It deprecates any judgement delivered by other than official judges, and is anticipated by *Hosea* iv. 4: 'Let no man strive nor reprove another.'

In *John* x. 34, Jesus, quoting *Psalm* lxxxii. 6, reminds his audience that the Hebrew for 'judges' is *elohim,* 'gods', and that when seated in the judge's chair to dispense the Law, an otherwise fallible man spoke with divine authority. Part of his argument, omitted here, seems to have been expanded and incorporated in Stephen's speech to the Great Sanhedrin (*Acts* vii. 24–28 and 35) where it has little relevance.

(*b*) Light is thrown on the parable of the Mote and the Beam (*Matthew* vii. 4–5 and *Luke* vi. 41–44) by the Talmud (*Baba Bathra* 15*b*):

'Rabbi Johanan was asked: "What is the explanation of the saying: 'And it came to pass in the days of the judging of the judges' (*Ruth* i. 1)?"
'[He answered:] "It was a generation that judged its judges. Woe to that generation! If the judge commanded a man: 'Remove the splinter from between thy teeth!' he would answer: 'First do thou remove the beam from between thine eyes!' And if the judge said: 'Thy silver is dross,' he would answer him again: 'Thy wine is mingled with water.' " '

'Maharsha' (Samuel Edeles), an enlightened mediaeval commentator on the Talmud, explains the origin of this saying as follows:

'A certain man stole a beam and built it into his house where it served him for a post. A neighbour who passed by cut a splinter therefrom, and of it made himself a toothpick. The first man cried: "Restore the stolen splinter that is between thy teeth!" But the other answered: "First restore the stolen beam that is between [i.e. directly in front of] thy eyes!"'

Ta'anith 16a contains a particular ruling on the stealing of beams:

'He that hath stolen a beam and hath built it into his house, the same shall pull down that house, even if it serve as a fort, and shall restore the beam unto its owner.'

The silver and wine argument is less complex: the wine-seller complains that his customer has paid with silver which falls short of the required standard, but is rebutted with the more serious counter-charge of watering his wine. Since, therefore, the grossly hyperbolic language of the Gospel version is not consonant with Jesus's habit of precise speech, we can now make a confident guess at what he really said, and why (*see (f) below*).

(*c*) In *John* xii. 47, his refusal to act as unofficial arbiter, as in *Luke* xii. 13–14, is converted into a Christological statement that Jesus has come not to judge the world, but to save it—the judgement will follow later. In *John* viii. 15–18, he is made to add that he could, of course, judge if he so wished, since he has his Father's authority. The passage must be rejected, if only because he speaks of 'your Law', not 'our Law', and of God as subject to the Law in the same way as man. In *John* v. 22, it is stated positively, though incredibly, that God has delegated all judgement to Jesus, and this is expanded in verse 27 with the statement that he is the Son of Man. *John* iii. 16–19 contains the very late doctrine that all who refuse to believe in the saving power of his name will be damned to Hell.

(*d*) Five genuine sayings are, however, embedded in the Christological discourse of *John* v. 19–38. For the first, verse 24, *see* xciv. *b–d*. The second, verses 25, 27, 28, and 29, is a *midrash* on *Isaiah* xxvi. 19–21, and an assertion that the Son of Man (*Daniel* vii. 14) will judge the world during the Millennium. It forms part of Jesus's dispute with the Captain of the Temple (*see* xciv.*d*).

(340) '*Marvel not when I say: The hour is at hand when the dead shall hear the voice of the Son of Man and come forth from their tombs; they that have done righteousness into the Kingdom of Heaven, they that have done evil into the torments of Hell.*

'*For Isaiah prophesied: "Thy dead shall live and arise with their dead bodies.*

'*"Come, my people, enter into thy chambers and shut the door behind thee, hide thyself until His indignation be overpast.*

' "For behold, the Lord cometh out of His place to punish the inhabitants of the earth for their iniquity."

'And He shall give the Son of Man authority to execute judgement in his name, even as Daniel saith.'

* * * * *

(e) The third saying, verse 30, lacks only a conditional clause to make it a confession of Jesus's inability to settle a private dispute without error: 'Were I appointed a judge, then would my judgement be just,' (*Psalm* lxxxii. 1–6, *Exodus* xxii. 28 and 2 *Chronicles* xix. 6—*see* LXXXIV.*e*), which is part of the 'Judge not!' argument (*see* (*f*) *below*).

(f) The fourth, verse 31, has been borrowed from Jesus's contention with the Sadducees in the Temple (*see* xcv.*e*). The fifth, verse 35, is a commendation of John the Baptist (*see* xxxix.*c*).

(107) *On another day, one of the company besought Jesus, saying: 'Speak to my brother that he divide the inheritance with me.'*

Jesus said unto him: 'Man, who made me a judge or divider over you? I can of mine own self do nothing; I judge only as I hear men speak.

'But were I appointed to be a judge and sit in Moses's seat, then would my judgement be just, because I should seek not mine own will but the will of the Father which appointed me; the same readeth every man's heart.

'It is written that Jehoshaphat the King of Judah said unto the judges: "Take heed what ye do, for ye judge not for man, but for the Lord which is with you in judgement."

'Moses also said: "I charged your judges not to be respecters of persons in judgement, seeing that the judgement is the Lord's."

'And Jehoshaphat the King spake also with the voice of David, saying: "I have called my judges 'gods'; all of you are sons of the Most High God."

'Yet even Moses, before that he was sent of God to judge Israel, by the hand of the angel which appeared to him in the bush, the same suffered a reproach from his fellows as having judged without authority.

'For seeing one of them suffer wrong, he avenged him and smote the Egyptian. And the next day he shewed himself unto two of them as they strove and would have set them at one again, saying: "Ye are brethren, why wrong ye one another?"

'But he that did his neighbour wrong thrust Moses away, saying: "Who made thee a ruler and a judge over us? Wilt thou kill me, as thou didst the Egyptian yesterday?"*

'Therefore, let no man of you which is not appointed by authority set himself up as a judge, lest judgement itself be judged.

'For if thou sayest: "Restore the splinter that is between thy teeth," he that is judged shall answer: "First do thou restore the beam that is in the wall before thy very eyes!"

---

* There is a reference in *Jude* 9, to Moses's murder of the Egyptian, which greatly troubled the Pharisees. The Devil disputed with the Archangel Michael, claiming that this murder made Moses's body his own; and Michael could reply only with a lame '*The Lord rebuke thee*,' from *Zechariah* iii, 2. *Jude* is quoting *The Assumption of Moses*, a late apocalyptic book; the dispute is recorded in Chapter xiv.

'Or if thou sayest: "Thy silver is mingled with dross," he shall answer: "The wine which I bought from thee therewith is mingled with water."'

*   *   *   *   *

(g) Hillel had said (*Aboth* ii. 4) : 'Judge not thy fellow until thou findest thyself in his place!'—which came to much the same thing as 'Judge not!', because no two people can be under precisely the same temptation to sin.

[Here follows the passage quoted in the *Traditions of Matthias* (*see* xxi.*q*) about a man's responsibility for his neighbour's sins, and the passage about the brother who trespasses (*see* xix.*d*).]

Two sayings about good measure, evidently found in the Oracles under this subject-heading, have been run together in *Luke* vi. 38. Both must have described God's meting out to man, not man's meting out to his neighbour. The word 'bosom' suggests that the first is a *midrash* on *Psalm* lxxix. 12, supported by a quotation from *Proverbs* xix. 17.

(280) *'Solomon spake a proverb: "He that hath pity upon the poor lendeth unto the Lord, and that which he hath given shall the Lord pay him again."*

'David also saith in a psalm: "He that reproacheth his neighbour shall have the reproach repaid by the Lord sevenfold into his bosom." Then shall not God of His mercy likewise repay a kindness?

'Verily, sevenfold shall He repay it: good measure, pressed down, shaken together and running over shall He give into thy bosom!'

*   *   *   *   *

(h) The second saying, which also occurs in *Mark* iv. 23–24 combined with a third (*see* xxv.*b*), seems to be a *midrash* on *Proverbs* xi. 1:

(100) *'Know ye not the proverb which Solomon spake: "A false balance is abomination to the Lord, but a just weight is His delight."*

'Therefore, according to the measure wherewith ye mete, so shall He measure unto you.'

*   *   *   *   *

XXVII

ON PRAYER AND FASTING

Mark xi. 24–26

[24]'Therefore I say unto you, what things soever ye desire, when ye pray, believe that ye receive them, and ye shall have them. [25]And when ye stand praying, forgive, if ye have ought against any: that your Father also which is in heaven may forgive you your trespasses. [26]But if ye do not forgive, neither will your Father which is in heaven forgive your trespasses.'

Matthew vi. 1–18

[1]'Take heed that ye do not your alms before men, to be seen of them: otherwise ye have no reward of your Father which is in heaven. [2]Therefore when thou doest thine alms, do not sound a trumpet before thee, as the hypocrites do in the synagogues and in the streets, that they may have glory of men. Verily I say unto you, they have their reward. [3]But when thou doest alms, let not thy left hand know what thy right hand doeth: [4]that thine alms may be in secret: and thy Father which seeth in secret Himself shall reward thee openly.

[5]'And when thou prayest, thou shalt not be as the hypocrites are: for they love to pray standing in the synagogues and in the corners of the streets, that they may be seen of men. Verily I say unto you, they have their reward. [6]But thou, when thou prayest, enter into thy closet, and when thou hast shut thy door, pray to thy Father which is in secret; and thy Father which seeth in secret shall reward thee openly. [7]But when ye pray, use not vain repetitions, as the heathen do: for they think that they shall be heard for their much speaking. [8]Be not ye therefore like unto them: for your Father knoweth what things ye have need of, before ye ask Him. [9]After this manner therefore pray ye:

Our Father Which art in heaven,
Hallowed be Thy name.
[10]Thy kingdom come.
Thy will be done in earth, as it is in heaven.
[11]Give us this day our daily bread.
[12]And forgive us our debts, as we forgive our debtors.
[13]And lead us not into temptation, but deliver us from evil:
For Thine is the kingdom, and the power, and the glory, for ever.
Amen.

[14]For if ye forgive men their trespasses, your heavenly Father will also forgive you: [15]but if ye forgive not men their trespasses, neither will your Father forgive your trespasses.

Matthew vi. 1–18 (*contd.*)

[16]'Moreover when ye fast, be not, as the hypocrites, of a sad countenance: for they disfigure their faces, that they may appear unto men to fast. Verily I say unto you, they have their reward. [17]But thou, when thou fastest, anoint thine head, and wash thy face; [18]that thou appear not unto men to fast, but unto thy Father which is in secret: and thy Father, which seeth in secret, shall reward thee openly.'

Luke xi. 1–4

[1]And it came to pass, that, as He was praying in a certain place, when He ceased, one of His disciples said unto Him: 'Lord, teach us to pray, as John also taught his disciples.' [2]And He said unto them: 'When ye pray, say:

Our Father which art in heaven,
Hallowed be Thy name.
Thy kingdom come.
Thy will be done, as in heaven, so in earth.
[3]Give us day by day our daily bread.
[4]And forgive us our sins; for we also forgive every one that is indebted to us.
And lead us not into temptation; but deliver us from evil.'

Matthew vii. 7–11

[7]Ask, and it shall be given you; seek, and ye shall find; knock, and it shall be opened unto you. [8]For every one that asketh receiveth; and he that seeketh findeth; and to him that knocketh it shall be opened. [9]Or what man is there of you, whom if his son ask bread, will he give him a stone? [10]Or if he ask a fish, will he give him a serpent? [11]If ye then, being evil, know how to give good gifts unto your children, how much more shall your Father which is in heaven give good things to them that ask Him?

Luke xi. 9–13

[9]And I say unto you, 'Ask, and it shall be given you; seek, and ye shall find; knock, and it shall be opened unto you.' [10]For every one that asketh receiveth; and he that seeketh findeth; and to him that knocketh it shall be opened. [11]If a son shall ask bread of any of you that is a father, will he give him a stone? or if he ask a fish, will he for a fish give him a serpent? [12]Or if he shall ask an egg, will he offer him a scorpion? [13]If ye then, being evil, know how to give good gifts unto your children: how much more shall your heavenly Father give the Holy Spirit to them that ask Him?

John xiv. 7–14

[7]If ye had known Me, ye should have known My Father also: and from henceforth ye know Him, and have seen Him.
[8]Philip saith unto Him: 'Lord, shew us the Father, and it sufficeth us.'
[9]Jesus saith unto him: 'Have I been so long time with you, and yet hast thou not known Me, Philip? he that hath seen Me hath seen the Father: and how sayest thou then, Shew us the Father? [10]Believest thou not that I am in the

John xiv. 7–14 (*contd.*)

Father, and the Father in Me? the words that I speak unto you I speak not of Myself: but the Father that dwelleth in Me, He doeth the works. [11]Believe Me that I am in the Father, and the Father in Me: or else believe Me for the very works' sake. [12]Verily, verily, I say unto you, he that believeth on Me, the works that I do shall he do also; and greater works than these shall he do; because I go unto My Father. [13]And whatsoever ye shall ask in My name, that will I do, that the Father may be glorified in the Son. [14]If ye shall ask anything in My name, I will do it.

John xvi. 23–24

[23]Verily, verily, I say unto you, whatsoever ye shall ask the Father in My Name, He will give it you. [24]Hitherto have ye asked nothing in My name: ask, and ye shall receive, that your joy may be full.

Jerome: On Psalm cxxxv.

In the Hebrew *Gospel according to Matthew* it is thus: 'Our bread of the morrow, give us this day,' that is, 'the bread which Thou wilt give us in the Kingdom, give us this day.'

Oxyrhynchus Papyrus I

Jesus saith: 'If ye fast not from the world ye shall not find the Kingdom of God, and if ye keep not the Sabbath for the whole week, ye shall not see the Father.'

Origen: On Prayer 2

'Ask ye for the greater things and the small shall be added unto you; and ask for the heavenly things and the earthly shall be added unto you.'

Clement of Alexandria: Stromateis ii. 24. 150

'Ask ye for the greater things and the small shall be added unto you.'

(*a*) Either the 'Lord's Prayer' in *Matthew* vi. 9–13 and *Luke* xi. 2–4 has been developed by the Nazarenes from *Mark* xi. 24–26, paralleled in *Matthew* vi. 14–15; or, more likely, Jesus himself combined extracts from the Synagogue liturgy into this single example of how they should pray.

The Pharisees held that prayers should be brief, citing Moses's five-word plea for his leprous sister Miriam: 'Heal her now, O God, I beseech Thee!' (*Numbers* xii. 13). The Nazarene service seems to have been modelled on that of the Synagogue, which consisted of the *Shemā** and the Decalogue, with readings from the Pentateuch and the prophets not only on the Sabbath but also, for the benefit of peasants from outlying farms, on market days (Monday and Thursday). During the Hadrianic persecutions, however,

* The *Shemā* was a linking together of *Deuteronomy* vi. 4–9, xi. 13–21 and *Numbers* xv. 37–41, beginning 'Hear O Israel!' This composite passage, the essence of Judaism, was also recited daily in the Temple, and enclosed in every phylactery (*see* XIII.*e*) and *mezuzah* (*see* CIX.*i*). It is quoted in *Matthew* xxii. 37 (*see* LXXXII.*l*).

when all Jews were forbidden to recite the *Shemā* in public worship, the Lord's Prayer became its substitute among the Nazarenes.

(*b*) The following are the elements from which it is composed:

'Our Father which art in Heaven.' (*One of the three general forms of the address in the Jewish liturgy.*)

'Hallowed be Thine exalted Name in the world which Thou didst create according to Thy will. May Thy Kingdom and Thy dominion come speedily; and may it be acknowledged by all the world that Thy Name shall be praised in all eternity.' (*Kaddish, Kedusha, and Amidah—after Ezekiel* xxxviii. 23.)

'May Thy will be done in Heaven and also on earth give tranquillity of spirit to those that fear Thee. Yet in all things do what seemeth good to Thee.' (*Tosephta Berakoth* iii. 7.)

'Feed us with the bread of our allowance.' (*Proverbs* xxx. 8.)

'Father, forgive us our trespasses.' (*Amidah.*)

'Also all who have trespassed against us.' (*Megillah 28a.*)

'Even as we also forgive all.' (*Megillah 28a.*)

'Give us this day and every day, grace, favour and mercy in Thine eyes; lead us not into the power of sin or of temptation.' (*The Morning Prayer.*)

'For Thine is the Kingdom and for ever wilt Thou reign in glory.' (1 *Chronicles* xxix. 11–13 *and the Evening Prayer.*)

*   *   *   *

(*c*) 'Our daily bread', or 'bread sufficient for the coming day', is an explanation of 'the bread of my allowance' in *Proverbs* xxx. 8—itself a reference to *Exodus* xvi. 17–19, where the Israelites harvested the manna, each according to his needs, but not more than sufficed for the coming day. 'He that gathered much had nothing over, he that gathered little had no lack, and when some of them left it until the morning it bred worms and stank.' This provision of manna, which lasted for forty years, is mentioned by Jesus in *John* vi. 31, 35, 49, and 51 (*see* LXXII.*i*). Here, however, his prayer is for spiritual bread and is, in fact, identical with the prayer for grace, favour, and mercy. At its fullest, this passage would read:

'Do Thou who for forty years didst rain down manna for Thy people in the wilderness, to each according to his needs for the ensuing day, allow us this day and every day our portion of the bread of heaven, which is grace, favour, and mercy in Thine eyes.'

We should reject as presumptuous the version quoted from the *Gospel according to the Hebrews* by Jerome: a request to be given today the spiritual bread due tomorrow.

(*d*) The Lord's Prayer, for the sake of completeness (*see* IX.*b*), consists of ten requests, with a formal beginning and ending. The ending: 'For Thine is the Kingdom', is a denial of Roman authority, like that of Rabbi Alexandri's prayer (*Berakoth* 17*a*):

'Sovereign of the Universe; Thou knowest full well that our will is to perform Thy will. And what preventeth us? The leaven in our thoughts [the evil impulse] and our subjection to the hand of strangers. May it be Thy will to deliver us therefrom, that we may return to perform the statutes of Thy will with a perfect heart.'

Matthew vi. 2 is corrupt: 'as the hypocrites (*see* XIII.*c footnote*) do in the synagogues' has evidently been brought up from verse 5, and 'as it were' has dropped out. Jesus is referring to the feigned Pharisees who gave alms *'as it were* with trumpets sounded before them'—like princes scattering largesse in the streets; and verse 3 is paralleled in the Talmud (*Baba Bathra* 10*b*):

'He that giveth, it were better that he knew not to whom he giveth; and he that receiveth, it were better that he knew not from whom he receiveth.'

The word 'privately' has dropped out in verse 5: in the public synagogue services all Jews were expected to pray standing, except when certain passages in the liturgy demanded that they should kneel. Jesus asks his disciples to pray like Hannah (1 *Samuel* i. 13): 'And Hannah spake of her heart, only her lips moved, and her voice was not heard.' This is paralleled in the Talmud (*Berakoth* 24*b*):

'He that prays so that his words can be heard by them that stand by, is of small faith; he that cries aloud in praying is of the false prophets [a reference to 1 *Kings* xviii. 28, where the false prophets of Baal cry aloud to their god].'

(*e*) *Matthew* vi. 7 contradicts Jesus's recommendation to pray with importunity. The second part is spoken against long-winded prayers (*see* (*h*) *below*); the first, which is a warning to the Twelve not to use magical incantations (*Isaiah* viii. 19—*see* XXXI.*b*) when healing the sick, suits the context of *Mark* vi. 17 (*see* LVII.g).

(191) *'When ye pray that God will heal a sick person, peep not; neither mutter as the heathen do, but before the laying on of hands say openly: "Believe in God: He shall save!"'*

*   *   *   *   *

(*f*) 'Anoint thine head' (*Matthew* vi. 17) is suspect. To do so would suggest that the fast had been a banquet and Jesus cannot have recommended the deception, even if he approved the general use of toilet preparations—which is unlikely (*see* XI.*i*). 'Anoint thy head', therefore, should read 'comb thy hair'. Moreover, *during* a fast it was forbidden to anoint the head, wash the face, or comb the hair, except for medical reasons (*Ta'anith* 13*a*). But Jesus asks that all squalid traces of the ordeal should be removed before appearing again in public. The passage is aimed at the 'Reward-loving Pharisees (*see* XIII.*k*) who make broad their phylacteries and enlarge the fringes of their garments of prayer to be seen of men' (*Matthew* xxiii. 5). Pietistic indulgence in fasting was considered sinful by the true Pharisees (*Ta'anith* 11*a*— *see* XX.*e*).

(*g*) A saying, quoted in part by Clement of Alexandria (*Stromateis* ii. 24. 150), and in full by Origen (*On Prayer*, 2) has dropped out from *Mark* xi. 24–26.

(42) '*Being feigned Pharisees, they give alms as it were with trumpets sounded before them. They have their reward: to be praised of men.*

'*But thou, when thou givest alms, let not thy left hand know what thy right hand doth, that thine alms may be in secret; then in the world to come shalt thou earn praises from thy Father which watcheth in secret.*

'*Being but feigned Pharisees, they love also to pray openly in the synagogue or at the street corner. They have their reward: to be praised of men.*

'*But thou, when thou prayest, enter into thy closet and pray in secret; then in the world to come shalt thou earn praise from thy Father which hearkeneth in secret.*

'*Being but feigned Pharisees, they disarray their hair when they come from fasting, and make foul their cheeks with ashes and shew a sorrowful countenance. They have their reward: to be praised of men.*

'*But thou, when thou comest from fasting, comb thy hair and wash thy cheeks and be of a merry countenance. Then, though thou appearest unto men not to have fasted, yet shalt thou earn praise in the world to come from thy Father which watcheth in secret.*'

* * * * *

(*h*) [Here follows the saying about fasting from this world: one of two, preserved in the *Oxyrhynchus Papyrus* 1, the concluding phrases of which seem to have become interchanged (*see* LXXI.*h*).]

(83) '*But if ye fast not from the fleshly deceits of this world, ye shall not see the Father in the world to come.*'

* * * * *

Jesus is explaining that abstention from food has less spiritual value than abstention from the evil ways of the world. This was the orthodox Pharisaic view (*Ta'anith* 16*a*):

'During the fast the elder among them utters this exhortation: "Brethren, it is neither sackcloth nor fasting which wins God's favour, but only repentance and good deeds. For thus we find that it was said of the people of Nineveh, not: 'And God saw their sackcloth and their fasting,' but: 'God saw their works, that they turned from their evil way (*Jonah* iii. 10).' "'

(180) *Jesus therefore taught them saying:* '*Little children, when ye stand in prayer, forgive them that have wronged you; for if ye forgive not, neither will the Father forgive you the wrongs ye have done Him.*

'*Ask ye for the greater things, and the lesser shall be added unto you; ask for the heavenly things and the earthly shall be added unto you.*

'*And pray only for a sufficiency, saying: "Feed me with the bread of my allowance." For your Father will know before ye ask Him what your needs may be.*

'But when ye pray to Him for aught, add thereto: "Yet not as I will, but as Thou wilt."

'And make not long your prayers, thinking to be better heard by much speaking.'

* * * * *

(181) *Then said the disciples: 'Master, teach us to pray as John also taught his disciples.'*

He answered, and said: 'Thus pray ye:

' "Our Father which are in heaven!

' "Hallowed be Thy exalted name.

' "Thy Kingdom come speedily and be acknowledged by all the world.

' "Thy will be done in heaven,

' "And on earth be peace of heart to them that fear Thee.

' "Feed us with the bread of our allowance, which is grace, favour and mercy in Thy sight.

' "Forgive us our trespasses, Father,

' "And forgive them that trespass against us, as we also forgive them.

' "And lead us not into the power of sin,

' "Nor into temptation that is too great for us to bear.

' "Yet in all things do what seemeth good unto Thee.

' "For Thine is the Kingdom and ever more wilt Thou reign in glory!" '

* * * * *

(*i*) The saying about the scorpion and the egg (*Luke* xi. 12), has dropped out after *Matthew* vii. 10; and 'good things' (*Matthew* vii. 11) becomes 'the Holy Spirit' in *Luke* xi. 13, which reads like a promise of the gift that the apostles were to receive after the Resurrection (*see* cxviii.*a*).

The nature of the 'good things' which God would bestow has been concealed by a suppression of the texts on which Jesus's three injunctions are *midrashim:* namely *Psalm* ii. 8, which promises peace, or freedom from heathen oppression; *Proverbs* viii. 17 which promises wisdom—wisdom being the Holy Spirit of God (*see Introduction* iii.*r and* xlvii.*e*); and *Esther* vi. 10, which is allegorized in the Talmud as a promise of divine mercy. There (*Megillah* 12*b*) the efficacy of humble prayer is proved by Mordecai's patient supplication of King Ahasuerus: 'Because the Son of Kish [Mordecai] knocked at the Gates of Mercy, they were opened to him.' The sequel to 'knock and it shall be opened' is given in *Luke* xiii. 25 (*see* lxix.*b*).

(206) *And he taught them saying: 'David spake in the name of the Lord: "Ask of Me and I will give unto thee the heathen for thine inheritance and the uttermost parts of the earth for thy possession."*

'And Solomon says likewise of Wisdom: "They that seek Me diligently shall find Me; with Me are riches and honour."

'And it is written likewise in the Book *of Esther: "Let nothing fail of all that thou hast spoken for him that sitteth at the King's gate."*

'Therefore, ask for peace (which is the humbling of the heathen), and it

shall be given you; seek wisdom (which is the Holy Spirit), and ye shall find it; knock at the Gate of Mercy, and it shall be opened to you, as it was opened to Mordecai the son of Kish.

'If a son ask his father for bread, will he give him a stone? Or a serpent, if he ask for a fish? Or a scorpion, if he ask for an egg?

'Since therefore men that are sinners give good things to their children, how much more shall our Heavenly Father give good things to them that pray to Him?'

*   *   *   *   *

Jesus then quotes *Psalm* ciii. 13:

(207) *'For David saith: "Like as a father pitieth his children, so the Lord pitieth them that fear him."'*

*   *   *   *   *

(*j*) Nothing resembling any of these passages occurs in *John* where, in accordance with Pauline doctrine, the emphasis is wholly on Jesus's power to save by intercession with God.

John xiv. 7–14 and xvi. 23–24 must be rejected as late interpolations; they contradict the Lord's Prayer in which the requests are made directly to God, not transmitted to Him by Jesus, nor spoken in Jesus's name. A similar passage occurs in *John* xv. 7 (*see* LIV.*a*).

John xiv. 8 may be a genuine sequel to the injunction about fasting from this world (*see* (*h*) *above*). Philip asks to be made one of the pure in heart who shall see God (*see* LX.*a*), and says that, if rewarded so, his fasting from this world will not distress him. Jesus's alleged answer, though certainly a fabrication, may be based on a genuine saying in *John* xiv. 9–10, where he modestly objects to being called wise, as he elsewhere objects to being called 'good' (*see* LXXXII.*c*), and further disclaims all spiritual originality (*see Introduction* IV.*c*).

(84) *Philip saith: 'Teach us to see our Father, and it is enough. For wisdom dwelleth in thee, and thou revealest unto us new things.'*

Jesus answered: 'Have I been so long with thee, Philip, and yet hast thou not known me?

'The words that I speak, I speak not of myself, but I deliver the word of God to thee as it is delivered unto me in the scriptures and in the tradition of the elders.'

*   *   *   *   *

XXVIII

ON LOVE AND LENDING

Matthew v. 38–48

[38]Ye have heard that it hath been said, An eye for an eye, and a tooth for a tooth: [39]but I say unto you, that ye resist not evil: but whosoever shall smite thee on thy right cheek, turn to him the other also. [40]And if any man will sue thee at the law, and take away thy coat, let him have thy cloak also. [41]And whosoever shall compel thee to go a mile, go with him twain. [42]Give to him that asketh thee, and from him that would borrow of thee turn not thou away.

[43]Ye have heard that it hath been said, Thou shalt love thy neighbour, and hate thine enemy. [44]But I say unto you, love your enemies, bless them that curse you, do good to them that hate you, and pray for them which despitefully use you, and persecute you; [45]that ye may be the children of your Father which is in heaven: for He maketh His sun to rise on the evil and on the good, and sendeth rain on the just and on the unjust. [46]For if ye love them which love you, what reward have ye? do not even the publicans the same? [47]And if ye salute your brethren only, what do ye more than others? do not even the publicans so? [48]Be ye therefore perfect, even as your Father which is in heaven is perfect.

Matthew vii. 12

[12]Therefore all things whatsoever ye would that men should do to you, do ye even so to them: for this is the law and the prophets.

Luke vi. 27–36

[27]But I say unto you which hear,
Love your enemies, do good to them which hate you,
[28]Bless them that curse you, and pray for them which despitefully use you.
[29]And unto him that smiteth thee on the one cheek offer also the other;
And him that taketh away thy cloak forbid not to take thy coat also.
[30]Give to every man that asketh of thee;
And of him that taketh away thy goods ask them not again.
[31]And as ye would that men should do to you, do ye also to them likewise.

[32]For if ye love them which love you, what thank have ye? for sinners also love those that love them. [33]And if ye do good to them which do good to you, what thank have ye? for sinners also do even the same. [34]And if ye lend to

Luke vi. 27–36 (contd.)

them of whom ye hope to receive, what thank have ye? for sinners also lend to sinners, to receive as much again. [35]But love ye your enemies, and do good, and lend, hoping for nothing again; and your reward shall be great, and ye shall be the children of the Highest: for He is kind unto the unthankful and to the evil. [36]Be ye therefore merciful, as your Father also is merciful.

(a) *Matthew* v. 38 is not a novel pronouncement, a summary abrogation of the *lex talionis* found in *Exodus* xxi. 24, *Leviticus* xxiv. 20 and *Deuteronomy* xix. 21. By Jesus's time it was a commonplace that the all-important principle of love for one's neighbour took precedence of minor regulations in the Law. Although a tradition survives that the Sadducaic House of Boethus advocated a literal enforcement of the 'eye-for-an-eye' rule (*Megilat Ta'anith* iv.), there is no evidence that they ever gained their point. The Pharisees, who were the law-givers, deduced from *Numbers* xxxv. 31: 'Ye shall accept no ransom for the life of a murderer which is guilty of death,' that the principle of monetary compensation should, in contrast, be applied to all cases of lesser injury. It was observed that to knock out an aggressor's eye or tooth did not restore the victim's loss, and also argued more legalistically (*Leviticus* xxiv. 22 and *Baba Kamma* 84a): 'If a blind man put out the eye of a man with sight, what can be done to the offender by way of retaliation? Yet the Law saith: "Ye shall have but one manner of Law!" '

(b) Jesus cannot have used the contemptuous expression: 'Ye have heard it said', of a text in the Mosaic Law. He will have accepted the Pharisees' liberal interpretation of the *lex talionis* and called attention to another Pentateuchal passage forbidding anyone to harbour vengeful feelings (*Deuteronomy* xxx. 35). From this followed a recommendation that the victim of an assault should not insist even on his minimum legal rights, lest he might be motivated by revenge.

(c) *Matthew* v. 39–42 is a *midrash* on Proverbs xx. 22 and xxiv. 29, supported by a quotation from *Lamentations* iii. 30. With it belongs: 'Do as thou wouldst be done by' (*Matthew* vii. 12)—which is paralleled in the *Letter of Aristeas,* an apocryphal work written about 100 B.C. but ascribed to an Alexandrian Greek Jew who had lived more than a century earlier (*Aristeas,* 207):

'When the King asked: "What is the teaching of Wisdom?", one of the seventy-two sages [the translators of the Septuagint] made answer: "As thou wouldest that no evil should befall thee but only good, so do both to those that obey thee and to those that offend against thee; and in all tenderness admonish them that are set on virtue; for the Lord draweth all men unto Him with gentleness." '

Hillel stated this negatively (*Shabbath* 31a): 'Do not to others as thou wouldst not have them do unto thee'; he was quoting from the Aramaic text of *Tobit* iv. 15 (*ed.* Neubauer, *Oxford,* 1878, *p.*8), a book dating from the first or second century B.C.

(98) Jesus said also: 'It is written: "An eye for an eye and a tooth for a tooth."

'Now, if the eye of him that put out his neighbour's eye be likewise put out, or the tooth of him that broke his neighbour's tooth be likewise broken, is the neighbour's loss restored?

'Therefore, he giveth his neighbour satisfaction in silver or works, according to his loss. For the law of mercy is not to be set aside that the law of vengeance may be kept.'

*   *   *   *   *

(99) 'Moreover Solomon counselled you: "Say not thou: 'I will recompense evil, I will so do to my neighbour as he hath done to me,' but wait on the Lord and He shall save thee."

'And it is written in the Book of Lamentations: *"The Lord is good unto him that waiteth for Him, and unto him that giveth his cheek to the smiter."*

'Therefore, resist not evil, and if a man will sue thee at the Law and take away thy coat, let him have thy cloak also, if so be that thou mayest be at peace with him.

'And if he smite thee on the right cheek, turn thou also the other to him.

'And if he compel thee to go a mile, go with him twain.'

*   *   *   *   *

(d) Matthew v. 42 is an incomplete *midrash* on *Deuteronomy* xv. 7–8; the same argument is resumed in *Matthew* v. 46–48. Its full meaning can be deduced from the corresponding passage in *Luke* vi. 30–36, and in further support of his theme Jesus quotes *Psalm* xxxvii. 26. The Talmudic parallel (*Aboth* v. 10) reads:

'. . . he that saith: "What is thine is thine, and what is mine is also thine." '

Luke vi. 36: 'God is kind unto the unthankful and unto the evil,' seems unscriptural; but the parallel text in *Matthew* v. 46 points to an ingenious *midrash* on *Job* xxv. 3–4 and xxxviii. 26–27, on the lines of 'Judge not, that ye be not judged!' (*see* xxvi.*g*). As Bildad remarks, God's sun shines equally for all men, none of whom is perfect. Moreover, God Himself reminds Job that His rain falls both on desert places and on cultivated fields.

Luke vi. 36 is a reference to David's psalm in 2 *Samuel* xxii: 'With the merciful wilt Thou shew Thyself merciful, and with the upright man wilt Thou shew Thyself upright.'

(102) And again Jesus taught them saying: 'Moses commanded: "Thou shalt open thine hand wide unto thy poor neighbour and lend him sufficient for his need and turn not away from him."

'But to him that asketh thee to lend, give and exact no pledge, whosoever he may be.

'For if thou takest a pledge, what love shewest thou? The publicans also lend to their fellows, to receive as much again.

'Be ye therefore merciful, as your Father also is merciful: lend looking for

no payment, and without respect for persons, whether they be just or unjust.

'*For it is written in the* Book of Job: "*Upon whom doth not the light of God arise? And how can any man that is born of woman be clean in His sight?*"

'*Therefore, as He maketh the sun to rise both on the just and the unjust, and sendeth rain (as it is written in the same book) both upon the field that is plowed and upon the desolate waste ground,*

'*So do ye likewise give freely and judge not of your neighbour whether he be just or no, and your reward shall be great: ye shall be called the Children of the Highest.*

'*For David saith in a psalm: "He that is ever merciful and lendeth, his seed is blessed."*

'*And he saith also: "With the merciful Thou wilt shew Thyself merciful, O God, and with the upright man wilt Thou shew Thyself upright."* '

* * * * *

(e) *Matthew* v. 43–45 is corrupt. The Law neither commands nor permits anyone to hate his enemy. On the contrary: *Exodus* xxiii. 4–5 requires that good be returned for evil 'to him that hateth thee'. The nearest equivalent in Hebrew literature to the alleged injunction is found in the *Book of Ahikar* (*Greek version*, xxvi. 3):

'Let it be thy prayer that poverty and sickness may be the lot of thine enemies, that they may not have it in their power to injure thee.'

Jesus perhaps had this in mind, which would account for 'Ye have heard it said'; but he comments particularly on *Leviticus* xix. 18 and *Proverbs* xix. 11. The concealed quotations are from the *Letter of Aristeas* (227) and from the *Testaments of the Twelve Patriarchs* (*Joseph* xviii. 2 and *Gad* vi. 3–4). A Talmudic parallel is *Berakoth* 10a: 'Pray for the enemy and for the wicked!'

(103) '*Heed not them that counsel thee: "Let it be thy prayer that poverty and sickness may be the lot of thine enemies."*

'*For Moses commanded: "Thou shalt love thy neighbour as thyself," and Solomon declared: "It is a man's glory to pass over a transgression."*

'*Therefore, return not evil for evil, but pray for thy neighbour if he be at enmity with thee, and forgive him if he curse thee, and do good to him if he hate thee and use thee despitefully.*

'*As Aristeas counselleth: "All men hold that we should return good to those that do good unto us; but should we not also open our hand with gifts to those that shew enmity, that thereby we may draw them to righteousness?"*

'*Likewise the patriarch Joseph commanded in his testament: "And if any man seek to do you evil, do ye well unto him, and pray for him, and the Lord shall redeem you from evil."*

'*Likewise the patriarch Gad in his testament: "Love ye one another from the heart. If a man sin against thee, speak peaceably unto him, and hold no guile in thy soul. And if he repent and confess, forgive him, lest catching the poison from thee he take to swearing and thou sin doubly."*

'Do all these things therefore, and ye shall be called the children of your Father which reigneth in glory.'

* * * * *

(*f*) [Here follows a general warning not to be content with the lower morality of the Sadducees (*see* xxi.*j*).]

(*g*) *Matthew* v. 47 is a rhetorical interpolation meant to show that Jesus greeted Gentiles as affably as he greeted Jews. In *Luke* vi. 32–35 this is developed to the point of absurdity: Jesus is made to counsel his disciples against doing good to their friends—only when they do good to their enemies will they be entirely guiltless of mercenary motives.

* * * * *

XXIX

ON DEBTORS

Matthew xviii. 23–35

[23]Therefore is the Kingdom of Heaven likened unto a certain king, which would take account of his servants. [24]And when he had begun to reckon, one was brought unto him, which owed him ten thousand talents. [25]But forasmuch as he had not to pay, his lord commanded him to be sold, and his wife, and children, and all that he had, and payment to be made. [26]The servant therefore fell down, and worshipped him, saying, Lord, have patience with me, and I will pay thee all. [27]Then the lord of that servant was moved with compassion, and loosed him, and forgave him the debt. [28]But the same servant went out, and found one of his fellowservants, which owed him an hundred pence: and he laid hands on him, and took him by the throat, saying, Pay me that thou owest. [29]And his fellowservant fell down at his feet, and besought him, saying, Have patience with me, and I will pay thee all. [30]And he would not: but went and cast him into prison, till he should pay the debt. [31]So when his fellowservants saw what was done, they were very sorry, and came and told unto their lord all that was done. [32]Then his lord, after that he had called him, said unto him, O thou wicked servant, I forgave thee all that debt, because thou desiredst me: [33]shouldest not thou also have had compassion on thy fellowservant, even as I had pity on thee? [34]And his lord was wroth, and delivered him to the tormentors, till he should pay all that was due unto him. [35]So likewise shall My heavenly Father do also unto you, if ye from your hearts forgive not every one his brother their trespasses.

Matthew xxiii. 6–10

The scribes and the Pharisees . . . [6]love the uppermost rooms at feasts, and the chief seats in the synagogues, [7]and greetings in the markets, and to be called of men, Rabbi, Rabbi. [8]But be not ye called Rabbi: for One is your Master, even Christ; and all ye are brethren. [9]And call no man your father upon the earth: for One is your Father, which is in heaven. [10]Neither be ye called masters: for One is your Master, even Christ.

Matthew xxiii. 14

[14]Woe unto you, scribes and Pharisees, hypocrites! for ye devour widows' houses, and for a pretence make long prayer: therefore ye shall receive the greater condemnation.

Mark xii. 38–40

[38]And He said unto them in His teaching: 'Beware of the scribes, which love to go in long clothing, and love salutations in the marketplaces, [39]and the chief seats in the synagogues, and the uppermost rooms at feasts: [40]which devour widows' houses, and for a pretence make long prayers: these shall receive greater condemnation.'

Luke xx. 45–47

[45]Then in the audience of all the people He said unto His disciples: [46]'Beware of the scribes, which desire to walk in long robes, and love greetings in the markets, and the highest seats in the synagogues, and the chief rooms at feasts; [47]which devour widows' houses, and for a shew make long prayers: the same shall receive greater condemnation.'

(*a*) The parable of the Debtors in *Matthew* xviii. 23–25 needs little amendment. 'Ten thousand talents' in verse 24—an impossibly large sum—should be 'ten thousand pounds'; and 'my Heavenly Father' in verse 35 should be 'our Heavenly Father'. It is a *midrash* on *Ezekiel* xviii. 5, 7, 9, 12 and 13.

> (95) '*Hearken unto the words which Ezekiel the prophet spake, saying: "If a man be just and hath not oppressed any, but hath restored the debtor his pledge, he shall live; but he that hath oppressed the poor and needy and hath not restored the pledge, the same shall surely die."* '

*   *   *   *   *

In the last verse of the parable, Jesus returns to a theme contained in the Lord's Prayer (*see* xxvii.*b*).

> (96) '*Therefore is the Kingdom of Heaven likened unto a certain king which would take account of his servants.*
>
> '*And when he had begun to reckon, one was brought unto him, which owed him ten thousand pounds.*
>
> '*But forasmuch as he had not to pay, his lord commanded him to be sold, and his wife, and his children, and all that he had, and payment to be made.*
>
> '*The servant therefore fell down, and besought him, saying: "Lord, have patience with me, and I will pay thee all!"*
>
> '*Then the king was moved with compassion, and loosed him and forgave him his debt.*
>
> '*But the same servant went out, and found one of his fellow-servants, which owed him an hundred pence: and he laid hands on him, and took him by the throat, saying: "Pay me that thou owest!"*
>
> '*And his fellow-servant fell down at his feet, and besought him, saying: "Have patience with me, and I will pay thee all!"*
>
> '*Yet he would not: but went and cast him into prison, till he should pay the debt. So when the other servants saw this thing, they were very sorry, and came and told unto the king all that was done.*
>
> '*Then the king, after that he had called him, said unto him: "O thou wicked servant, I forgave thee all thy debt, because thou desiredst me: should-*

est not thou also have had compassion on thy fellow-servant, even as I had pity on thee?"

'And the king was wroth, and delivered him to the tormentors, till he should pay all that was due unto him.

'So, likewise, shall our Heavenly Father do also unto you, if ye from your hearts forgive not every one his fellows their trespasses.'

* * * * *

(*b*) In *Mark* xii. 38–40 (paralleled in *Matthew* xxiii. 6–10 and 14 and *Luke* xx. 45–47), Jesus refers to certain rich Jews who obeyed the letter of the Law while ignoring its spirit. They cannot have been Pharisees, as *Matthew* suggests, or even feigned Pharisees, and for 'synagogues' we must read 'councils'. Probably they were the Sadducaic scribes, or State lawyers, in the employ of the Chief Rulers. *Matthew* has embedded this saying, which seems to be a *midrash* on *Exodus* xxii. 22 (supported by quotations from *Deuteronomy* xxiv. 17 and *Job* xxiv. 3), in a long invective supposedly uttered against the Pharisees (*see* XIII.*c*).

(97) *Jesus said also: 'It is written: "Ye shall not afflict any widow or child!"*

'Woe, then, to the lawyers which serve the Chief Rulers. For they love long clothing, and salutations in the market place,

'And the chief seats in council and the uppermost places at feasts, and for a show make long prayers,

'The same forbear to take a widow's raiment in pledge, yet will take her ox (as Job testifieth), yea, and her house and land, and if she cannot pay her debt, will drive her thence, and her orphans with her;

'And will ask: "Was the woman not my debtor?"

'Therefore Job saith: "They are of those that rebel against the light."'

* * * * *

(*c*) Much the same denunciation is made in the *Assumption of Moses* (vii. 3–7, *ed.* Charles), an apocalyptic book written not later than Jesus's ministry:

'And, in the time of these, destructive and impious men shall rule, saying that they are just. And they shall stir up the poison of their minds, being treacherous men, self-pleasers, dissemblers in all their own affairs and lovers of banquets at every hour of the day; gluttons, belly-servers, devourers of the goods of the poor, saying that they work for justice, though in truth they seek to destroy them; complainers, deceitful, concealing themselves lest they should be known; impious, full of lawlessness and iniquity from sunrise to sunset.'

* * * * *

Matthew xxiii. 8 *and* 10, influenced by *Matthew* vii. 22 (*see* LXIX.*a*) may be disregarded as a second-century interpolation aimed at the Nazarenes who accepted the authority of the rabbis (*see* XIII.*l*). Verse 9 should be attached to *Matthew* viii. 21–22 and *Luke* ix. 59–60, where a disciple asks: 'Suffer me first to bury my father', and is told that an apostate is not entitled to his son's devotion (*see* LXXXV.*c*).

* * * * *

XXX

THE WATCHERS

Mark xiii. 34–37

[34]'For the Son of Man is as a man taking a far journey, who left his house, and gave authority to his servants, and to every man his work, and commanded the porter to watch. [35]Watch ye therefore: for ye know not when the master of the house cometh, at even, or at midnight, or at the cock-crowing, or in the morning: [36]lest coming suddenly he find you sleeping. [37]And what I say unto you I say unto all, Watch.'

Luke xii. 35–48

[35]'Yet your loins be girded about, and your lights burning; [36]and ye yourselves like unto men that wait for their lord, when he will return from the wedding; that when he cometh and knocketh, they may open upon him immediately. [37]Blessed are those servants, whom the lord when he cometh shall find watching: verily I say unto you, that he shall gird himself, and make them to sit down to meat, and will come forth and serve them. [38]And if he shall come in the second watch, or come in the third watch, and find them so, blessed are those servants. [39]And this know, that if the goodman of the house had known what hour the thief would come, he would have watched, and not have suffered his house to be broken through. [40]Be ye therefore ready also: for the Son of Man cometh at an hour when ye think not.'

[41]Then Peter said unto Him: 'Lord, speakest Thou this parable unto us, or even to all?' [42]And the Lord said: 'Who then is that faithful and wise steward, whom his lord shall make ruler over his household, to give them their portion of meat in due season? [43]Blessed is that servant whom his lord when he cometh shall find so doing. [44]Of a truth I say unto you, that he will make him ruler over all that he hath. [45]But and if that servant say in his heart, My lord delayeth his coming; and shall begin to beat the menservants and maidens, and to eat and drink, and to be drunken; [46]the lord of that servant will come in a day when he looketh not for him, and at an hour when he was not aware, and will cut him in sunder, and will appoint him his portion with the unbelievers. [47]And that servant, which knew his lord's will, and prepared not himself, neither did according to his will, shall be beaten with many stripes. [48]But he that knew not, and did commit things worthy of stripes, shall be beaten with few stripes. For unto whomsoever much is given, of him shall be much required: and to whom men have committed much, of him they will ask the more.'

Matthew xxiv. 42–xxv. 13

[42]Watch therefore: for ye know not what hour your Lord doth come. [43]But know this, that if the goodman of the house had known in what watch the thief would come, he would have watched, and would not have suffered his house to be broken up. [44]Therefore be ye also ready: for in such an hour as ye think not the Son of Man cometh. [45]Who then is a faithful and wise servant, whom his lord hath made ruler over his household, to give them meat in due season? [46]Blessed is that servant, whom his lord when he cometh shall find so doing. [47]Verily I say unto you, that he shall make him ruler over all his goods. [48]But and if that evil servant shall say in his heart, My lord delayeth his coming; [49]and shall begin to smite his fellowservants, and to eat and drink with the drunken; [50]the lord of that servant shall come in a day when he looketh not for him, and in an hour that he is not aware of, [51]and shall cut him asunder, and appoint him his portion with the hypocrites: there shall be weeping and gnashing of teeth.

[1]'Then shall the Kingdom of Heaven be likened unto ten virgins, which took their lamps, and went forth to meet the bridegroom. [2]And five of them were wise, and the five were foolish. [3]They that were foolish took their lamps, and took no oil with them: [4]but the wise took oil in their vessels with their lamps. [5]While the bridegroom tarried, they all slumbered and slept. [6]And at midnight there was a cry made, Behold, the bridegroom cometh; go ye out to meet him. [7]Then all those virgins arose, and trimmed their lamps. [8]And the foolish said unto the wise, Give us of your oil; for our lamps are gone out. [9]But the wise answered, saying, Not so; lest there be not enough for us and you: but go ye rather to them that sell, and buy for yourselves. [10]And while they went to buy, the bridegroom came; and they that were ready went in with him to the marriage: and the door was shut. [11]Afterward came also the other virgins, saying, Lord, Lord, open to us. [12]But he answered and said, Verily I say unto you, I know you not. [13]Watch therefore, for ye know neither the day nor the hour wherein the Son of Man cometh.

Matthew vii. 21–23

[21]Not every one that saith unto Me, Lord, Lord, shall enter into the kingdom of heaven; but he that doeth the will of My Father which is in heaven. [22]Many will say to Me in that day, Lord, Lord, have we not prophesied in Thy name? and in Thy name have cast out devils? and in Thy name done many wonderful works? [23]And then will I profess unto them, I never knew you: depart from Me, ye that work iniquity.

Luke xiii. 25–28

[25]When once the master of the house is risen up, and hath shut to the door, and ye begin to stand without, and to knock at the door, saying, Lord, Lord, open unto us; and He shall answer and say unto you, I know you not whence ye are: [26]then shall ye begin to say, We have eaten and drunk in Thy presence, and Thou hast taught in our streets. [27]But He shall say, I tell you, I know you not whence ye are; depart from me, all ye workers of iniquity. [28]There shall be weeping and gnashing of teeth, when ye shall see Abraham,

Luke xiii. 25–28 (*contd.*)

and Isaac, and Jacob, and all the prophets, in the kingdom of God, and you yourselves thrust out.

Luke xxi. 34–36

[34]'And take heed to yourselves, lest at any time your hearts be overcharged with surfeiting, and drunkenness, and cares of this life, and so that day come upon you unawares. [35]For as a snare shall it come on all them that dwell on the face of the whole earth. [36]Watch ye therefore, and pray always, that ye may be accounted worthy to escape all these things that shall come to pass, and to stand before the Son of Man.'

(*a*) The Synoptics have confused five parables (*Mark* xiii. 34–37, *Matthew* xxiv. 42–xxv. 13 and *Luke* xii. 35–48), all apparently found in the Oracles under the subject-heading 'Watch and Pray!' It was this watching, praying, and keeping perpetually chaste in expectation of the world's imminent end, that distinguished the ascetic apocalyptics from the main body of the Pharisees. These ascetics included Jesus and his kinsmen, the Nazarene 'Watchers' or *Zophim* (*see* cxiv.*b*) who, however, accepted their social obligations and did not retire, like the Strict Essenes, behind a thorn-topped entrenchment.

(*b*) *Mark* xiii. 34–37 contains only one parable, and that in its shortest form: how a householder went on a long journey, leaving his home in charge of servants who did not know on what day he would return from his travels, but were told to watch for him continuously.

Matthew xxiv. 42–xxv. 13 contains three parables. The first tells of a thief who came in the night and found no one on guard. The second tells of a householder who went on a journey—as in *Mark*—and left a trustworthy servant in charge; whereas another, who also went away, left his house in charge of an untrustworthy one. The third parable tells of ten bridesmaids who waited for the bridegroom; some of whom were found ready and some not.

In *Luke* xii. 35–48, these bridesmaids become bridemen and an attempt is made to combine all three parables into one—with the further addition of 'Let your loins be girded' (*see* (*d*) *below*).

(*c*) *Mark's* parable of the Traveller has an authentic ring, but the text is deficient, and in *Mark* xiii. 34 'Son of Man' has been gratuitously inserted. The parables of the Thief and the Bridesmaids have, it seems, dropped out at this point, leaving us no sure means of checking *Matthew's* unsatisfactory versions. In The Thief (*Matthew* xxiv. 34), it should be the porter, not the householder, who fails to watch; in The Bridesmaids (*Matthew* xxv. 1–13), the wise ones (verse 5) are no more watchful than the foolish, and verses 11 and 12 have been borrowed from the parable of The Closed Door (*Matthew* vii. 21–23) which is found at greater length in *Luke* xiii. 25–28 (*see* LXIX.*a and b*).

(*d*) The Neglectful Servants (*Matthew* xxiv. 45–51) is deficient—in verse 48 'that evil servant' has no antecedent—and at the close it is confused with the parable of the Talents, as in *Luke* xii. 48. *Luke's* synthetic parable (xii. 35–48) makes very poor sense even if one omits the phrase 'from the wedding' in verse 36, and the housebreaker reference in verse 39—which reads as though an attempt were made to steal the wedding presents. Verse 37 is an incongruous anticipation of Jesus's symbolic act at the Last Supper (*John* xiii. 5—*see* cvi.*t*): no bridegroom in his senses would wait on his servants as a reward for finding them awake. But *Luke* xii. 45–48 has preserved what must be the original parable of the *three* Neglectful Servants (*Matthew* mentions only one—*see* lii.*j*), though Peter's question that provoked it has probably been misreported. In *Luke* xii. 35 is found a vestige of still another parable, which compares those who watch for the Last Days to those who keep the Passover (*Exodus* xii. 11).

(*e*) *Luke* xxi. 34–36 furthermore preserves the metaphor of the snare, thus pointing to the text on which the parable of the Neglectful Servants is a *midrash*: namely *Proverbs* vii. 6–27, where the adulterous woman tells a lover that her husband is gone on a long journey and will not be back until the next day; he goes to her as a bird to the snare, and the following morning is found in her arms by the goodman. An editor of *Luke* has omitted the love-story as too suggestive for young catechumens, and has been content to mention only the crimes of violence, drunkenness, and surfeiting, quoted by Jesus from *Isaiah* lvi. 10–12.

It may be assumed that the other parables were also linked to a scriptural text: The Thief to *Jeremiah* xlix. 9; The Bridesmaids to *Psalm* xlv. 14–15; The Traveller to *Proverbs* vi. 4 and 9–10, and xiii. 4.

(157) *And he spake this parable unto them:* 'The Kingdom of Heaven is as when a man, taking a far journey, leaveth his house, and giveth authority to his steward, and allotteth to each man his work, and commandeth the porter to watch.

'Watch ye therefore, for ye know not when the master of the house shall come from travelling—at even, or at midnight, or at cock-crow, or in the morning—lest coming suddenly he find you sleeping or having neglected your tasks.

'As Solomon saith to the sluggard: "Desirest thou a little sleep, a little slumber, a little folding of the hands?

'"So shall thy poverty come upon thee as a man that travelleth."

'Blessed is that servant which the Lord shall find ready to receive Him, for he shall be rewarded.

'And Solomon saith likewise: "The soul of the sluggard desireth, and hath nothing; but the soul of the diligent shall be made fat.

'"Therefore give not sleep to thine eyes, my son, nor slumber to thine eyelids."'

* * * * *

(158) *Peter asked him:* 'And what of the servant which shall be found unready?'

Jesus answered and said: 'If a servant, knowing his lord's will, neglect it, then when the lord cometh in a day and an hour of which he is unaware, that servant shall be beaten with many stripes.

'And if a servant, not well knowing his lord's will, neglect it, that servant shall be beaten with few stripes.

'But if a servant hearken to the wiles of an adulteress, like her of which Solomon testified that she said: "Come, I have perfumed my bed. Let us take our fill of love until the morning. For the goodman is not at home, he is gone a long journey. He hath taken a bag of money with him and will come home at the day appointed";

'And if he, likewise, go in unto her as a bird goeth to a snare, and be drunken with the kisses of her mouth;

'And if the lord when he returneth find them in a bed together, he shall strike him in the liver with a dart.

'Verily, I say unto you that he shall afterwards cut the adulterous servant in sunder and bury him with unbelievers.

'Therefore take heed to yourselves lest at any time your hearts be over-charged with surfeiting, and drunkenness, and wantonness, so that the day come upon you unawares.

'For as a snare shall the Last Day come on all them that dwell on the face of the whole earth.

'Watch therefore, and pray always, that ye may be accounted worthy to escape the slaughter of that day, and stand on the Mount of Olives with the Son of Man.

'That which I say unto you, I say unto all: Watch!

'For Isaiah testifieth against the foolish: "His watchmen are blind and ignorant, dumb dogs that cannot bark, sleeping, lying down, loving to slumber, looking every one to his own gain,

'"Which say: 'Come, I will fetch wine, we will fill ourselves with strong drink, and tomorrow shall be as this day, but much more abundant.'"'

* * * * *

(159) Then said Jesus: 'The Kingdom of Heaven is like unto ten bridesmaids which lighted their lamps and went forth to meet the bridegroom by the way.

'And five of them were wise, but five foolish.

'The wise took oil in their oil vessels, besides that which was in their lamps, but the foolish took none.

'While the bridegroom tarried, the wise bridesmaids beholding how their lamps burned low, presently replenished and trimmed them.

'The foolish said to the wise: "Give us of your oil, for our lamps also burn low."

'The wise answered: "There is not enough both for us and for you. Go quickly to them that sell oil, and buy more while there is yet time."

'But they answered: "We go anon"; and they slumbered and slept, while the others kept watch.

'And at midnight a cry was made: "Behold, the bridegroom cometh: go ye out to meet him!"

'*Then all the bridesmaids arose together, and those that were ready went forth to meet the bridegroom.*

'*And those that were not ready ran to buy oil for their lamps, but coming to the house of the seller of oil found the door shut.*

'*Thus of the ten bridesmaids, only five went in to the wedding; and these were well received.*

'*As it is written in the Psalm of David: "The virgins, the companions that follow the bride shall be brought unto Thee: with gladness and rejoicing they shall enter the King's palace."*

'*Watch, therefore, and be prepared, for ye know neither the day nor the hour wherein the Son of Man cometh!*'

* * * * *

(160) *He said also: 'The Kingdom of Heaven shall come like a thief in the night.*

'*As Jeremiah saith: "If thieves come by night they will destroy till they have enough of destruction."*

'*Let not the porter therefore excuse himself to his master, saying: "Lord, had I known in what watch the thief would come, I should not have slept."*

'*The porter's office is to watch from nightfall even unto cock-crow.*'

* * * * *

(161) *And he said: 'While ye wait for the Kingdom of God, be like them that keep the Passover, with their loins girded and with shoes on their feet and with staffs in their hands, as for a journey undertaken in haste; for so Moses commanded our fathers as an ordinance for ever.*'

* * * * *

(*f*) [Here follows Jesus's defence of his habitual use of simple parables (*see* XVII.*g*).]

In *Matthew* xxiv. 48–51 and *Luke* xii. 43–46, Jesus borrows from the *Book of Ahikar* (*Syr.* iii. 1–3):

'But I, Ahikar, supposed that my son Nadan took hold of everything which I had been teaching him, and that he stood in my stead in the King's gate [i.e. interceded for me with God (*see* XXVII.*i*)] . . . But he began to [ill-treat] my servants by beating them and destroying them; yea, he shewed no mercy unto my servants and my handmaidens though they were diligent and well-beloved and excellent; and my horses he slew and my good mules he hamstrung.'

* * * * *

XXXI

THE DEAF MAN

Mark vii. 31–37

[31]And again, departing from the coasts of Tyre and Sidon, He came unto the sea of Galilee, through the midst of the coast of Decapolis. [32]And they bring unto Him one that was deaf, and had an impediment in his speech; and they beseech Him to put His hand upon him. [33]And He took him aside from the multitude, and put His fingers into his ears, and he spit, and touched his tongue; [34]and looking up to heaven, He sighed, and said unto him, 'Ephphatha,' that is, Be opened. [35]And straightway his ears were opened, and the string of his tongue was loosed, and he spake plain. [36]And He charged them that they should tell no man: but the more He charged them, so much the more a great deal they published it: [37]and were beyond measure astonished, saying, He hath done all things well; He maketh both the deaf to hear, and the dumb to speak.

Matthew xv. 29–31

[29]And Jesus departed from thence, and came nigh unto the sea of Galilee; and went up into a mountain, and sat down there. [30]And great multitudes came unto Him, having with them those that were lame, blind, dumb, maimed, and many others, and cast them down at Jesus' feet; and He healed them, [31]insomuch that the multitude wondered, when they saw the dumb to speak, the maimed to be whole, the lame to walk, and the blind to see: and they glorified the God of Israel.

(a) This modest feat, the healing of a deaf man (*Mark* vii. 31–37), recalls the healing of the blind man in *Mark* viii. 23–24, where Jesus also used spittle (*see* XL.*a*). A nervous impediment in speech can be cured by faith; and so can deafness caused not by any functional disorder, but by a failure in concentration.

In Jesus's time, spittle was widely employed as a repellent in cases of diabolical possession—devils were held responsible for most diseases—but had to be that of an only or eldest son on the father's side (*Baba Bathra* 126*b*). Whether Jesus was, in fact, the eldest of Joseph's family we have no means of knowing; however, his re-birth at the Coronation made him the only begotten son of the Father. His sighing and looking up to Heaven in *Mark* vii. 34 show that he prayed God to heal the patient, as Moses prayed for Miriam, though keeping silence like Hannah when she stood praying at the shrine of Shiloh (1 *Samuel* i. 13). The Aramaic EPHPHATHA proves the authenticity of the original tradition.

(*b*) A curative method frequently discussed in the Talmud was to drive out evil spirits by means of *lehisha* (whispered passages from Scripture), contemptuous spitting on the patient's body, and silent prayer. These whisperings, whether or not they included God's name, were permitted only as an introduction to the cure and had to precede the spitting. Jesus recommended his disciples to dispense with them altogether (*see* xxvii.*e*). He refrained even from spitting directly on the affected part, lest this might be interpreted as contempt for the patient rather than the devil; instead, he spat on his own fingers and so conveyed the spittle to the ears and tongue of the possessed. Similarly (*John* ix. 6—*see* xl.*f*) he spat on a lump of clay, with which he then touched the eyes of the blind man of Bethesda. In both cases he followed established practice by leading the patient away from the crowd: to prevent the devil from taking possession of some other body when finally expelled— in theory, if a spectator came too close, the devil could leap across this human bridge and so find a new home.

(*c*) The editor of *Matthew* xv. 30–31 improves on the miracle lavishly. He regards *Mark* vii. 37 as a licence to attribute to Jesus cures of all kinds, on the assumption that if this had been an isolated one, the crowd would hardly have felt 'astonished beyond measure' after the many previous miracles reported in *Mark* vi. 56.

(113) *Jesus preached in the seaward parts of Galilee, even unto the coasts of Tyre and Sidon.*

And departing thence he came again unto the Lake of Galilee by way of Philip's tetrarchy.

Now, men bring unto him one that was deaf and had an impediment in his speech, and they beseech him to lay his hand upon him.

And Jesus took him aside, and spat upon his own fingers and put them into the man's ears, and also touched the man's tongue withal.

Then, looking up to heaven, he sighed and prayed to God in his heart, and said: 'May they be opened; may it be loosed!'

And straightway his ears were opened and he heard; and the string of his tongue was loosed, and he spake plain.

But Jesus charged them that stood by to tell no man; yet the more he charged them, so much the more they published it,

For they were beyond measure astonished and said: 'He hath performed his twofold task well:

'By his intercession he that was dumb and deaf both speaketh and heareth.'

* * * * *

(*d*) The long sequence of cures which this initiated, suggests that the Watchers were closely allied to the Essenes. 'Essene' is the Greek form of *Issiim* ('healers'—from the Aramaic *asa*), healing having been one of their most notable functions, as it was of the early Christians (*Acts* v. 12–16—*see* cxviii.*c*).

For further resemblances see xi.*c*, xxiii.*c* and lvii.*c* and *j–l*.

* * * * *

XXXII

THE TEN LEPERS

Mark i. 40–45

40And there came a leper to Him, beseeching Him, and kneeling down to Him, and saying unto Him: 'If thou wilt, Thou canst make me clean.' 41And Jesus, moved with compassion, put forth His hand, and touched him, and saith unto him: 'I will; be thou clean.' 42And as soon as He had spoken, immediately the leprosy departed from him, and he was cleansed. 43And He straitly charged him, and forthwith sent him away; 44and saith unto him: 'See thou say nothing to any man: but go thy way, shew thyself to the priest, and offer for thy cleansing those things which Moses commanded for a testimony unto them.'

45But he went out, and began to publish it much, and to blaze abroad the matter, insomuch that Jesus could no more openly enter into the city, but was without in desert places: and they came to Him from every quarter.

Matthew viii. 1–4

1When He was come down from the mountain, great multitudes followed Him. 2And, behold, there came a leper and worshipped Him, saying: 'Lord, if Thou wilt, Thou canst make me clean.' 3And Jesus put forth His hand, and touched him, saying: 'I will: be thou clean.' And immediately his leprosy was cleansed. 4And Jesus saith unto him: 'See thou tell no man; but go thy way, shew thyself to the priest, and offer the gift that Moses commanded, for a testimony unto them.'

Luke v. 12–16

12And it came to pass, when He was in a certain city, behold a man full of leprosy: who seeing Jesus fell on his face, and besought Him, saying: 'Lord, if Thou wilt, Thou canst make me clean.' 13And He put forth His hand, and touched him, saying: 'I will: be thou clean.' And immediately the leprosy departed from him. 14And He charged him to tell no man: but 'Go, and shew thyself to the priest, and offer for thy cleansing, according as Moses commanded, for a testimony unto them.' 15But so much the more went there a fame abroad of Him: and great multitudes came together to hear and to be healed by Him of their infirmities. 16And He withdrew Himself into the wilderness, and prayed.

Luke xvii. 11–19

11And it came to pass, as He went to Jerusalem, that He passed through the midst of Samaria and Galilee. 12And as He entered into a certain village,

Luke xvii. 11–19 (*contd.*)

there met Him ten men that were lepers, which stood afar off: [13]and they lifted up their voices, and said, 'Jesus, Master, have mercy on us.' [14]And when He saw them, He said unto them: 'Go shew yourselves unto the priests.' And it came to pass, that, as they went, they were cleansed. [15]And one of them, when he saw that he was healed, turned back, and with a loud voice glorified God, [16]and fell down on his face at His feet, giving Him thanks: and he was a Samaritan. [17]And Jesus answering said: 'Were there not ten cleansed? but where are the nine? [18]There are not found that returned to give glory to God, save this stranger.' [19]And he said unto him: 'Arise, go thy way: thy faith hath made thee whole.'

(*a*) *Leviticus* xiii and xiv give detailed regulations for the diagnosis and quarantine of leprosy, and for the ritual purification of any who might recover from the disease. The symptoms there described are, however, characteristic not of true leprosy but of various other skin diseases such as ring-worm, scald-head, and 'English leprosy' (*psoriasis*); no description of true leprosy —which reached Palestine from Syria only about the time of Herod the Great —occurs in the Old Testament.

The account of the cure given by the Synoptics—it is not mentioned in *John*—suggests that Jesus's patient was no leper even in the Levitical sense. The Law laid down that suspects should be confined for seven days until a priest had satisfied himself either that it was not leprosy, when they were released; or else that it was, when he banished them to the desert. They must, thereafter, avoid the company of their fellow-men, wearing a mouth-cover and shouting 'unclean, unclean!' A certified leper could not have been living 'in a certain city', nor could Jesus have touched him. Origen realized this (*Against Celsus* i. 40), and over-ingeniously suggested that it was a spiritual, not a corporeal, touching.

(*b*) It is equally difficult to believe that Jesus in answer to 'Lord, if thou wilt, thou canst make me clean,' replied: 'I will; be thou clean!', thus claiming that power to heal rested in himself rather than in the leper's faith that God would take compassion on him. He would certainly not have permitted the leper to worship him; that would have been a flagrant breach of the First Commandment.

(*c*) *Luke* xvii. 11–19 seems to be another version of the same miracle: since, if Jesus really had healed ten lepers at a time, *Mark* and *Matthew* would surely not have ignored this multiple cure in favour of the single one.

Luke's version is meant to demonstrate that all Jews are ungrateful by nature: since only the Samaritan (*see Introduction* iii.*n*) returned to give thanks. Jesus's detailed instructions to the lepers must have been omitted before the abrupt 'Go shew yourselves to the priests'; and 'Thy faith hath made thee whole,' should have been spoken to all ten of them, whether or not they afterwards showed gratitude.

(*d*) Nevertheless, *Luke's* account is more plausible in some respects than either *Mark* or *Matthew*: the lepers are made to stand afar off, and Jesus refrains from touching them. But even if Jesus's lost instructions are restored, some difficulties remain. His 'Go shew yourselves to the priests and offer the gift that Moses commanded', would hardly have been said to a Samaritan. The only priests empowered to diagnose leprosy were Sons of Aaron (*Leviticus* xiii. 2), but no 'Son of Aaron' might examine, or offer the necessary sacrifices for, a Samaritan leper (*see* LXXXII.*n*); and a ceremony performed by Samaritan priests, who were not of Aaronic descent, would have been invalid in Jesus's eyes. Moreover, it is stated in *Mark* vi. 5, and implied in *Mark* i. 34, that Jesus could cure certain ailments only. If a leper was indeed healed on this occasion, he is likely to have been suffering from a rash or tetter of nervous origin (wrongly diagnosed as Levitical leprosy), which responded to faith treatment. Naaman's leprosy seems to have been of this variety. It did not prevent him from mixing with his fellows, and was readily cured by dipping seven times in Jordan at Elisha's orders (2 *Kings* v. 10–14). This treatment is paralleled in Pausanias's second century *Description of Greece* v. 5. 3–6:

> 'Going from the Neda you reach a place in Elis, named Samicum, which extends to the sea. Above it, to the right, is the district of Triphylia, with a city Lepreus . . . founded, some say, by Leprea, daughter of Pyrgeus. Others say that the first settlers in the land were attacked by leprosy, and that the city was named after their misfortunes . . .
>
> 'In Samicum, near the river Anigrus, is the cave of the Anigrian nymphs. A leper, entering the cave, prays to the nymphs and promises them a sacrifice of one sort or another. Then he wipes the affected part of his body, swims through the river,* leaves his uncleanness behind and emerges whole and with his skin of one colour.'

(*e*) But, granted that faith in God (or in river-nymphs) could heal nervous rashes, is it likely that all ten lepers were suffering from the same rare and uncontagious disease? Jesus's: 'Were there not ten cleansed, but where are the nine?' rings true only if the word 'cleansed' is omitted. It seems, in fact, that of the ten lepers who cried for mercy no more than one was cleansed, his case having been wrongly diagnosed; and that, soon afterwards, the account was altered in two distinct ways—the first version making no mention of the nine who were not healed, and the second stating that all ten were healed. The compiler of *Luke* used both versions, in the belief that they referred to different miracles, and a verse from *Luke* v. 12: 'The power of the Lord was present to heal him (or them),' has been transferred to the next cure (*see* XXXV.*a*). Jesus must have preferred Elisha's indirect method of cleansing, which he mentions in *Luke* iv. 27; it is probable, therefore, that his touching of the leper has been gratuitously introduced into the first version to prove

---

* Curiously enough, Pausanias states (*ibid.*) that an ancient name for the Acidas, a healing tributary of this otherwise foul river, was the Jardanus (*Iliad* vii. 136), which seems to be the same word as Jordan; there was another stream of the same name in Crete (*Odyssey* iii. 292). It may be that 'Jordan' is pre-Semitic and that its waters had the same healing property as the Jardanus; the grotto at its source was dedicated to Pan and the Nymphs (*see* LXXVII.*a*).

either his greater compassion or his scorn for the Law. The Egerton Papyrus Fragment 2, which dates from about 150 A.D. makes a leper come to Jesus and say absurdly: 'Master Jesus, journeying with lepers and eating with them in the inns, I myself also became a leper. If therefore thou wilt, I am made clean.' And Jesus, of course, heals him. Thus it became a Christian virtue to expose oneself to infection, and saints even shared their beds with lepers.

(*f*) Neither version is trustworthy; but that Jesus ordered the leper to perform the voodoo-esque ceremony prescribed in *Leviticus* xiv. 7 (*see* L.*a*) is not the sort of detail that a Gentile editor would have invented. It seems, then, that one certified 'leper' was, in fact, healed; that he stood afar off with nine companions, as recorded in the second version; and that Jesus did not touch him.

(150) *Now the Passover drew nigh and Jesus went to Jerusalem by way of Galilee and the eastern coasts of Samaria, and came to a certain village that lay nigh unto the Jordan.*

And when he had passed through to the other side, he saw ten lepers standing afar off, which lifted up their voices, and cried: 'Master, have mercy on us. If thou wilt, thou canst save us!'

Jesus said: 'Go, wash seven times in Jordan. For so Elisha the prophet commanded Naaman the Syrian.'

Then went they off hastily and did as he commanded. And one of them when he saw that he was healed, returned to Jesus glorifying God.

Jesus asked him: 'Were there not ten lepers? But where are the nine? Arise now and go thy way, shew thyself to the priest and offer the sacrifice of purification that Moses commanded, namely two sparrows.

'For thy faith hath made thee whole, but thy fellows doubted, though power was present from the Lord to heal them also.'

And he charged him that had been a leper to tell no man by whose orders he had washed in Jordan.

But so much the more went there a fame abroad of him, and great multitudes came together to hear and to be healed. And he withdrew himself into the wilderness and prayed.

* * * * *

XXXIII

THE CENTURION'S SERVANT

Matthew viii. 5–13

⁵And when Jesus was entered into Capernaum, there came unto Him a centurion, beseeching Him, ⁶and saying, Lord, my servant lieth at home sick of the palsy, grievously tormented. ⁷And Jesus saith unto him, I will come and heal him. ⁸The centurion answered and saith, 'Lord, I am not worthy that thou shouldest come under my roof: but speak the word only, and my servant shall be healed. ⁹For I am a man under authority, having soldiers under me: and I say to this man, Go; and he goeth; and to another, Come, and he cometh; and to my servant, Do this, and he doeth it.' ¹⁰When Jesus heard it, He marvelled, and said to them that followed: 'Verily I say unto you, I have not found so great faith, no, not in Israel. ¹¹And I say unto you, that many shall come from the east and west, and shall sit down with Abraham, and Isaac, and Jacob, in the kingdom of heaven. ¹²But the children of the kingdom shall be cast out into outer darkness: there shall be weeping and gnashing of teeth.' ¹³And Jesus said unto the centurion: 'Go thy way; and as thou hast believed so be it done unto thee.' And his servant was healed in the selfsame hour.

Luke vii. 1–10

¹Now when He had ended all His sayings in the audience of the people, He entered into Capernaum. ²And a certain centurion's servant, who was dear unto him, was sick, and ready to die. ³And when he heard of Jesus, he sent unto Him the elders of the Jews, beseeching Him that He would come and heal his servant. ⁴And when they came to Jesus, they besought Him instantly, saying, that he was worthy for whom He should do this: ⁵for he loveth our nation, and he hath built us a synagogue. ⁶Then Jesus went with them. And when He was now not far from the house, the centurion sent friends to Him, saying unto Him: 'Lord, trouble not Thyself: for I am not worthy that Thou shouldest enter under my roof: ⁷wherefore neither thought I myself worthy to come unto Thee: but say in a word, and my servant shall be healed. ⁸For I also am a man set under authority, having under me soldiers, and I say unto one, Go, and he goeth; and unto another, Come, and he cometh; and to my servant, Do this, and he doeth it.' ⁹When Jesus heard these things, He marvelled at him, and turned Him about, and said unto the people that followed Him: 'I say unto you, I have not found so great faith, no, not in Israel.' ¹⁰And they that were sent, returning to the house, found the servant whole that had been sick.

(a) *Matthew* viii. 5-13 and *Luke* vii. 1-10 contradict each other and neither can be accepted as it stands. Jesus must have resented the centurion's view of him as a magician who could send familiar spirits flying on whatever missions he pleased. The lesson which the evangelists are preaching here, as in the case of the other centurion who glorified God at the Crucifixion (*see* cxiii.*p*), is that Roman army officers venerated Jesus, and with good reason. These discrepancies, and the illogical 'For' in *Matthew* viii. 9 and *Luke* vii. 8, suggest that the original story has been turned inside-out. Since in *Matthew* the centurion makes his request in person, but in *Luke* sends a deputation of Jewish elders to report politely that he is unworthy of doing so, it is probable that Jesus, being a quietist, obeyed a message which the evangelists did not think consonant with his dignity.

(b) *Luke* vii. 5 is incredible since a Roman centurion could neither have afforded, wanted, or been permitted, to build a synagogue. And his obsequiousness in both versions is out of keeping with his official status. It is safe, therefore, to assume that he sent a message to Jesus peremptorily ordering him to heal his favourite Jewish servant; and that Jesus, when he arrived, ironically praised the centurion's faith; and that, though he refused to compound with the Wicked Kingdom by entering the barracks, he offered up an effective prayer outside. The suppressed sequel will have been that the servant resigned his appointment, lest the illness should recur.

(c) The original of *Matthew* viii. 11-12—a *midrash* on *Malachi* i. 7-12, to the effect that *some* Gentiles who accept the law, and *not all* the true-born Levite priesthood, should enter the Kingdom of Heaven—has been mischievously edited. It will have been one of many spoken by Jesus against the Sadducees; but now excludes all Israelites who keep the Law in favour of all Gentiles who believe in Jesus's divinity.

(122) *Now, when Jesus entered into Capernaum, a centurion sent a messenger which should bring him unto the camp.*

Jesus went thither, but would not enter lest he defile himself.

Then came the centurion out to him and said: 'My servant which is a Jew lieth within, grievously tormented with the palsy and desireth to be healed.

'Know now, that I am a man of authority. I say to this man "Go!" and he goeth; and to another "Come!" and he cometh; and to another "Do this!" and he doeth it.

'Therefore say I unto thee: Come in, and heal my servant! For I have heard that thy God worketh wonders for thee.'

Jesus turned to them that stood by him, and said as one that mocketh: 'I have not seen such faith, no, not in Israel!'

The centurion asked Jesus: 'Why delayest thou? Thinkest thou thyself unworthy to enter?'

Jesus answered: 'I may not come in, lest I defile myself. Yet will I pray to God, and peradventure thy servant shall be healed.'

And he prayed to God, and the sick man that lay within heard the voice of

Jesus which called him to repentance; and was made whole, and consorted no more with the Wicked Kingdom.

* * * * *

(359) *Jesus said also:* 'Malachi prophesied against the priests of Israel, saying: "Ye that offer polluted bread upon Mine altar, will I regard your persons?

'"For from the east unto the west shall My name be great among the Gentiles; yet have ye said of the table of the Lord: 'Behold, what a weariness it is,' and ye have sniffed at it."

'Therefore I say unto you, that though strangers come from the east and west and accept the Law with joy, and sit down to eat bread with Abraham, Isaac and Jacob in the Kingdom of Heaven, yet of these Sons of Levi, the children of the Kingdom, many shall be cast into outer darkness where shall be weeping and gnashing of teeth!'

* * * * *

XXXIV

BEELZEBUB

Mark iii. 22–30

²²And the scribes which came down from Jerusalem said: 'He hath Beelzebub, and by the prince of the devils casteth He out devils.' ²³And He called them unto Him, and said unto them in parables: 'How can Satan cast out Satan? ²⁴And if a kingdom be divided against itself, that kingdom cannot stand. ²⁵And if a house be divided against itself, that house cannot stand. ²⁶And if Satan rise up against himself, and be divided, he cannot stand, but hath an end. ²⁷No man can enter into a strong man's house, and spoil his goods, except he will first bind the strong man; and then he will spoil his house. ²⁸Verily I say unto you, All sin shall be forgiven unto the sons of men, and blasphemies wherewith soever they shall blaspheme: ²⁹but he that shall blaspheme against the Holy Ghost hath never forgiveness, but is in danger of eternal condemnation.'

³⁰Because they said, He hath an unclean spirit.

Mark ix. 38–40

³⁸And John answered Him, saying: 'Master, we saw one casting out devils in Thy name, and he followeth not us: and we forbad him, because he followeth not us.' ³⁹But Jesus said: 'Forbid him not: for there is no man which shall do a miracle in My name, that can lightly speak evil of Me. ⁴⁰For he that is not against us is on our part.'

Luke xi. 14–23

¹⁴And He was casting out a devil, and it was dumb. And it came to pass, when the devil was gone out, the dumb spake; and the people wondered. ¹⁵But some of them said: 'He casteth out devils through Beelzebub the chief of the devils.' ¹⁶And others, tempting Him, sought of Him a sign from heaven. ¹⁷But He, knowing their thoughts, said unto them: 'Every kingdom divided against itself is brought to desolation; and a house divided against a house falleth. ¹⁸If Satan also be divided against himself, how shall his kingdom stand? because ye say that I cast out devils through Beelzebub. ¹⁹And if I by Beelzebub cast out devils, by whom do your sons cast them out? therefore shall they be your judges. ²⁰But if I with the finger of God cast out devils, no doubt the kingdom of God is come upon you. ²¹When a strong man armed keepeth his palace, his goods are in peace: ²²but when a stronger than he shall come upon him, and overcome him, he taketh from him all his armour wherein he trusted, and divideth his spoils. ²³He that is not with Me is against Me: and he that gathereth not with Me scattereth.'

Matthew ix. 32–35

[32]As they went out, behold, they brought to Him a dumb man possessed with a devil. [33]And when the devil was cast out, the dumb spake: and the multitudes marvelled, saying, It was never so seen in Israel. [34]But the Pharisees said, He casteth out devils through the prince of the devils.

[35]And Jesus went about all the cities and villages, teaching in their synagogues, and preaching the Gospel of the kingdom, and healing every sickness and every disease among the people.

Matthew x. 25

[25]. . . If they have called the master of the house Beelzebub, how much more shall they call them of his household?

Matthew xii. 22–32

[22]Then was brought unto Him one possessed with a devil, blind, and dumb: and He healed him, insomuch that the blind and dumb both spake and saw. [23]And all the people were amazed, and said: 'Is not this the son of David?' [24]But when the Pharisees heard it, they said: 'This fellow doth not cast out devils, but by Beelzebub the prince of the devils.' [25]And Jesus knew their thoughts, and said unto them: 'Every kingdom divided against itself is brought to desolation; and every city or house divided against itself shall not stand: [26]and if Satan cast out Satan, he is divided against himself; how shall then his kingdom stand? [27]And if I by Beelzebub cast out devils, by whom do your children cast them out? therefore they shall be your judges. [28]But if I cast out devils by the Spirit of God, then the kingdom of God is come unto you. [29]Or else how can one enter into a strong man's house, and spoil his goods, except he first bind the strong man? and then he will spoil his house. [30]He that is not with Me is against Me; and he that gathereth not with Me scattereth abroad. [31]Wherefore I say unto you, all manner of sin and blasphemy shall be forgiven unto men: but the blasphemy against the Holy Ghost shall not be forgiven unto men. [32]And whosoever speaketh a word against the Son of man, it shall be forgiven him: but whosoever speaketh against the Holy Ghost, it shall not be forgiven him, neither in this world, neither in the world to come.'

John x. 19–21

[19]There was a division therefore again among the Jews for these sayings. [20]And many of them said, 'He hath a devil, and is mad; why hear ye him?' [21]Others said, 'These are not the words of him that hath a devil. Can a devil open the eyes of the blind?'

Luke ix. 49–50

[49]And John answered and said: 'Master, we saw one casting out devils in Thy name; and we forbad him, because he followeth not with us.' [50]And Jesus said unto him: 'Forbid him not: for he that is not against us is for us.'

Luke xii. 8–10

[8]Also I say unto you, whosoever shall confess Me before men, him shall the Son of Man also confess before the angels of God: [9]but he that denieth Me before men shall be denied before the angels of God. [10]And whosoever shall speak a word against the Son of Man, it shall be forgiven him: but unto him that blasphemeth against the Holy Ghost it shall not be forgiven.

(a) Jesus was undoubtedly charged with healing in the name of Beelzebul, *alias* Beelzebub; but *Mark* iii. 22 specifies 'the scribes which came down from Jerusalem', and *Matthew* ix. 34 the Galilean Pharisees, as his accusers, while *Luke* xi. 15 does not identify them. This suggests that the original tradition ran: 'A certain man . . .'

Beelzebul, 'Lord of the House', was an alternative title of the god Baal-sephon, 'Lord of the [House of the] North', who was worshipped by the Philistines and inherited this name from his Goddess-mother Baaltis Sapuna, a Canaanite diety of Death and Inspiration. The Canaanite Otherworld, like that of the Western Celts and the 'Hyperboreans' mentioned by Pindar, lay 'at the back of the North Wind'. In *Matthew* x. 25, Jesus refers to Beelzebul's title: 'If they have called the master of the house Beelzebub, how much more those of his household?' And again in *Luke* xi. 17: 'A house divided against itself must fall.'

(b) In 2 *Kings* i. 2, Ahaziah sends to Beelzebul's oracle, at Ekron in Philistia, to ask whether he will survive his fall from a window. The form 'Beelzebub', found both there and in the Gospels, is one of several cacophemistic names coined by the Jews (*see* VIII.*j footnote* and XCVIII.*a*): it means 'Lord of Flies' and suggests *zebel,* 'dung', the home of flies. Cacophemisms were made necessary by *Exodus* xxiii. 13, which forbad the mention of any alien deity's name. It is not clear, however, whether Jesus's critics used 'Beelzebub' in a loose sense to mean the Adversary of God, or whether they intended a particular reference to Mount Tabor, Beelzebul's ancient seat, to which Jesus claimed that his 'Mother, the Holy Spirit' had carried him (*see* LXXVIII.*g*). The word 'Tabor' is a worn-down form of 'Atabyrius' (*Hosea* v. 1), another title of the same God of the Dead, also cultivated at Agrigentum and in the island of Rhodes (Polybius: *History* 9. xxvii. 7), and the mountain was for long a rival in holiness to Mount Zion. Since the tribe of Zebulon worshipped there, this must have been the mountain mentioned in *Deuteronomy* xxxiii. 19—the 'house' which gave the tribe its name.

(c) The occasion of the charge differs in all four Gospels. *Mark* makes Jesus exorcize unclean spirits; *Luke* particularizes a devil of dumbness. *John's* Pharisees present their charge on three different occasions (*John* vii. 20, viii. 48–52 and x. 20), only the third of which, that of the blind man of Bethesda (*see* XXXIV.*d–e*), is concerned with a cure. *Matthew* ix. 32–35, paralleled in *Luke* xi. 14–15, has been combined with *John's* account, and made into a new story, so that Jesus cures the dumb man of blindness as well (*Matthew* xii.

22–30). The later editors of *Matthew* are peculiarly interested in blindness: they took literally the announcement attributed to Jesus that he came into the world to give light (*John* xii. 46—*see* xxiv.*c*). *Matthew* x. 25 also links the Beelzebub saying with that of the servant's not being above his master (*see* LVII.*n*).

(*d*) The parable of the Strong Man and the Robber (*Mark* iii. 27, *Matthew* xii. 29 and *Luke* xi. 21) is not logically connected with the Beelzebub passage; neither is the saying about those who blaspheme against the Holy Spirit (*Mark* iii. 28–29, *Matthew* xii. 31–32 and *Luke* xii. 8–10). But the parable probably concerns Beelzebub's inability to steal a man's soul while he keeps watch (*see* xxx.*b*); and the saying about blasphemy concerns those that abuse Jehovah's name for Beelzebub's designs—a custom well attested in Egyptian magical papyri of the period. All three sayings must have been found in the Oracles under the subject-heading 'The Power of Beelzebub'.

(*e*) *Luke* xi. 16, where Jesus's enemies ask him for a sign from heaven (*see* xci.*b*), is misplaced; and verse 20 refers to *Exodus* viii. 19, where Aaron performs miracles with the aid of God's finger.

(*f*) *Matthew* xii. 27, an addition to the brief and, in the main, credible Synoptic version, is a vulgar *tu quoque,* an unwarranted suggestion that the Pharisees, not Jesus, cured the sick by demonic agency.

Mark iii. 29: 'He that blasphemeth against the Holy Spirit shall be in danger of eternal damnation,' is altered in *Matthew* xii. 32 to the presumptuous: 'He that speaketh against the Holy Spirit, it shall not be forgiven him, neither in this world nor the next'; and 'hath never forgiveness' is introduced into *Mark* iii. 29 as well. The corresponding Christological passage in *Luke* xii. 8–10 reads even more severely.

> (117) *In those days Jesus cast out a dumb devil from a man, and the man spake, so that the people wondered, saying: 'The like was never seen in Israel!'*
>
> *But one of them said: 'He casteth out devils through Beelzebub, the prince of the devils.'*

*   *   *   *   *

[Here follows *John* viii. 48—*see* LXX.*m*.]

> (119) *Jesus answered:*
> *'Believest thou in truth that I cast out devils through him they call the Lord of the House? What sayest thou then? If the kingdom and household of the Lord of the House are divided against him, how shall they stand?*
>
> *'And if by the finger of God I am granted to cast out devils, will not God's kingdom be brought so much the nearer to you all?'*

*   *   *   *   *

> (120) *And he said also: 'When a strong man guardeth his house, with arms in his hand, his goods are secure. But if an enemy find the strong man sleeping, then will he bind him and spoil his goods.*

'Watch therefore, that the Lord of the House become not also the lord of thine house, to carry thy soul with him to the abode of darkness.'

* * * * *

(121) *'Verily, I say unto you: all sins shall be forgiven the sons of men if they repent, yea, even the taking in vain of God's name.*

'But if any of you shall utter magical spells in God's name, like as He were Beelzebub, the same standeth in danger of eternal damnation.'

* * * * *

(g) In *Mark* ix. 40, *Matthew* xii. 30 and *Luke* xi. 23, 'He that is not with me is against me, and he that gathereth not with me scattereth,' the 'me' in each case should be 'God'. It is an exhortation to work for the coming of the King-dom of Heaven; but whether this should be regarded as the complete saying depends on how we are to reconcile it with *Luke* ix. 50: 'He that is not against us is for us.' Either we must dismiss *Luke's* version as a forgery, be-cause it purports to answer: 'Master, we saw one casting out devils in thy name and we forbad him because he followeth not with us,'—an impossible statement, since Jesus cast out devils in God's name, not his own, and could claim no monopoly of healing. Or else we must assume that a careless editor has broken in two a delicately balanced antithesis. We have chosen the second alternative.

(193) *'In that day he that is not with God shall be against Him; and he that is not against Him shall be with Him.*

'He that gathereth not shall be as one which scattereth; he that scattereth not shall be as one which gathereth.'

* * * * *

In other words, on the Day of Judgement, those who have neglected their ac-tive duty towards God shall be damned; and those who have performed their passive duty of showing no hostility to the Kingdom of Heaven—Chief Rulers, for instance, who have not actively assisted the Romans—shall be spared; and so shall even slaves and foreigners. The saying must have been provoked by a question:

(198) *And seeing that they were sent forth to the House of Israel alone, the disciples said unto him: 'Master, at the Great Day shall all men, save only the elect of Israel, truly be cast into the everlasting fire?'*

He answered: 'Not so; for God shall spare them that set not their faces against Him.

'The prophet Zechariah hath testified that even such as are left alive of the Gentiles shall come up yearly to Jerusalem and worship the Lord of Hosts.'

* * * * *

(h) The School of Shammai taught that, at the Last Judgement, humanity would be divided into three categories: the wholly pious, the wholly wicked, and the betwixt-and-betweens. The wholly pious would win eternal life at once, the wholly wicked would be consigned to eternal torments, and the remainder, after a short purgatorial period, would also enjoy eternal bliss (*Zechariah* xiii. 9). The School of Hillel maintained, however (*Rosh Hasha-nah* 16*b*–17*a*), that there were only two categories, not three, since God of his boundless mercy would judge in favour of all doubtful cases. The gnashing of teeth by the wholly wicked would be the louder when they realized by how little they had failed to qualify for eternal life.

This doctrine is consistent with the parable of the Net and the Angels (*Matthew* xiii. 47–50—*see* xvii.*e*), and with the saying about the sheep and goats (*Matthew* xxv. 31–34—*see* xcviii.*m*). Any fish not forbidden by *Leviticus* xi. 10 would be regarded as good meat; and any man who had not sided with the goats would be accepted as a sheep.

(*i*) *Mark* ix. 39 seems to be of later composition than its corresponding text in *Luke* ix. 50: 'No man can lightly speak evil of me', does not point to an original 'No man can lightly speak evil of God', but is a Christological accretion.

*   *   *   *   *

THE PALSIED MAN

Mark ii. 1–13

[1]And again He entered into Capernaum, after some days; and it was noised that He was in the house. [2]And straightway many were gathered together, insomuch that there was no room to receive them, no, not so much as about the door: and He preached the word unto them. [3]And they come unto Him, bringing one sick of the palsy, which was borne of four. [4]And when they could not come nigh unto Him for the press, they uncovered the roof where He was: and when they had broken it up, they let down the bed wherein the sick of the palsy lay. [5]When Jesus saw their faith, He said unto the sick of the palsy: 'Son, thy sins be forgiven thee.' [6]But there were certain of the scribes sitting there, and reasoning in their hearts, [7]why doth this man thus speak blasphemies? who can forgive sins but God only? [8]And immediately when Jesus perceived in His spirit that they so reasoned within themselves, He said unto them: 'Why reason ye these things in your hearts? [9]Whether is it easier to say to the sick of the palsy, Thy sins be forgiven thee; or to say, Arise, and take up thy bed, and walk? [10]But that ye may know that the Son of Man hath power on earth to forgive sins, (He saith to the sick of the palsy,) [11]I say unto thee, Arise, and take up thy bed, and go thy way into thine house.' [12]And immediately he arose, took up the bed, and went forth before them all; insomuch that they were all amazed, and glorified God, saying: 'We never saw it on this fashion.'

[13]And He went forth again by the sea side; and all the multitude resorted unto Him, and He taught them.

Matthew ix. 1–8

[1]And he entered into a boat, and passed over, and came into His own city. [2]And, behold, they brought to Him a man sick of the palsy, lying on a bed: and Jesus seeing their faith said unto the sick of the palsy: 'Son, be of good cheer; thy sins be forgiven thee.' [3]And, behold, certain of the scribes said within themselves, This man blasphemeth. [4]And Jesus knowing their thoughts said: 'Wherefore think ye evil in your hearts? [5]For whether is easier, to say, Thy sins be forgiven thee; or to say, Arise, and walk? [6]But that ye may know that the Son of Man hath power on earth to forgive sins, (then saith He to the sick of the palsy) Arise, take up thy bed, and go unto thine house.' [7]And he arose, and departed to his house. [8]But when the multitude saw it, they marvelled, and glorified God, which had given such power unto men.

Luke v. 17–26

[17]And it came to pass on a certain day, as He was teaching, that there were Pharisees and doctors of the law sitting by, which were come out of every town of Galilee, and Judaea, and Jerusalem: and the power of the Lord was present to heal them. [18]And, behold, men brought in a bed a man which was taken with a palsy: and they sought means to bring him in, and to lay him before Him. [19]And when they could not find by what way they might bring him in because of the multitude, they went upon the housetop, and let him down through the tiling with his couch into the midst before Jesus. [20]And when He saw their faith, He said unto him: 'Man, thy sins are forgiven thee.' [21]And the scribes and the Pharisees began to reason, saying, 'Who is this which speaketh blasphemies? Who can forgive sins, but God alone?' [22]But when Jesus perceived their thoughts, He answering said unto them: 'What reason ye in your hearts? [23]Whether is easier, to say, Thy sins be forgiven thee; or to say, Rise up and walk? [24]But that ye may know that the Son of Man hath power upon earth to forgive sins, (He said unto the sick of the palsy) I say unto thee, Arise, and take up thy couch, and go into thine house.' [25]And immediately he rose up before them, and took up that whereon he lay, and departed to his own house, glorifying God. [26]And they were all amazed, and they glorified God, and were filled with fear, saying, We have seen strange things to day.

(*a*) The Synoptics place the healing of the palsied man soon after that of the leper, or lepers, which is said to have caused such a stir that Jesus was forced, for a time, to leave Capernaum.

Luke v. 17–26 is corrupt: the crowds, which in *Mark* consist of ordinary people and a few scribes (*Mark* ii. 2–6—*see Matthew* ix. 9), are there called 'Pharisees and doctors of the Law', and it is extravagantly added that they came 'from every village in Galilee and Judaea, and from Jerusalem,' a phrase borrowed from *Mark* iii. 7 (*see* xvii.*a*).

The promise in *Luke* v. 17: 'And the power of the Lord was present to heal them,' is not made good in the sequel; and an alternative manuscript reading: 'to heal him', is equally unsatisfactory. The original probably ran: 'There was power of the Lord [i.e. God] to heal them,' and must have referred to the nine lepers in verse 17, whose faith proved less than that of the tenth (*see* xxxii.*e*).

The removal of the tiles is omitted from *Matthew's* version; in compensation, Jesus is made to accuse the scribes of harbouring evil thoughts, and tells the palsied man: 'Son, be of good cheer!'

(*b*) Since the scribes would not merely have 'reasoned in their hearts' but protested energetically if Jesus had taken upon himself to forgive any man's sins—which was God's sole prerogative (*Isaiah* xliii. 25)—we must conclude that he did not. Apparently, in the original tradition, the palsied man's friends were disappointed with Jesus's prayer for his spiritual, rather than his bodily, health; and he then quoted 2 *Chronicles* vii. 12–14 to prove that bodily health depended on God's forgiveness of sin.

A public declaration of his Messiahship at this early stage in incredible. In *Mark* viii. 30, six chapters later, he charges his disciples to keep it a close secret. The incident has, in fact, been re-written to assure Gentile doubters that Jesus plainly declared himself, and showed himself to be, God; and that the Pharisees knew well what they were doing when they subsequently rejected his claim.

(*c*) The thronging of Jesus's house is the more remarkable for having taken place on a week-day; had it been a Sabbath, he could not have ordered the removal of the bed, which counted as work.

(178) *And he entered into Capernaum and it was noised abroad that he was in the house where he dwelt at this time.*

And straightway many were gathered together, insomuch as there was no room to receive them, no, not so much as about the door: and he preached the word unto them.

And there come four men to the house, bearing between them on a litter one that lay sick of the palsy.

And when they could not come nigh unto him, for the press, they went upon the roof of the house, and took off a part of the tiling and let the bed down by cords into the midst before Jesus, and themselves leaped down after.

And when Jesus saw their faith he prayed aloud, saying: 'O God, in Thy mercy forgive this man his sins!'

But they that brought the sick man murmured within themselves.

Jesus, perceiving their downcast countenances, said unto them: 'Why murmur ye within yourselves because I prayed that God might forgive him his sins, rather than that He should suffer him to rise and walk?

'For the Lord spake to Solomon by night, saying: "If I send sickness among My people, and if they humble themselves and turn from their wicked ways, then will I hear their prayers from heaven. I will forgive their sins and heal them."'

And even as he said these things, the man stirred and stood upon his feet, and gave thanks to God.

And Jesus said unto him: 'Son, take this bed hence that others may have the more room.'

And when he took up the bed and went forth before them all, they were amazed.

And certain of the scribes that sat by, said: 'We never saw it on this fashion.'

* * * * *

XXXVI

JAIRUS'S DAUGHTER

Mark v. 22–43

²²And, behold, there cometh one of the rulers of the synagogue, Jairus by name; and when he saw Him, he fell at His feet, ²³and besought Him greatly, saying: 'My little daughter lieth at the point of death: come and lay Thy hands on her, that she may be healed; and she shall live.' ²⁴And Jesus went with him; and much people followed Him, and thronged Him.

²⁵And a certain woman, which had an issue of blood twelve years, ²⁶and had suffered many things of many physicians, and had spent all that she had, and was nothing bettered, but rather grew worse, ²⁷when she had heard of Jesus, came in the press behind, and touched His garment. ²⁸For she said, 'If I may touch but His clothes, I shall be whole.' ²⁹And straightway the fountain of her blood was dried up; and she felt in her body that she was healed of that plague. ³⁰And Jesus, immediately knowing in Himself that virtue had gone out of Him, turned Him about in the press, and said: 'Who touched My clothes?' ³¹And His disciples said unto Him: 'Thou seest the multitude thronging Thee, and sayest Thou, Who touched Me?' ³²And He looked round about to see her that had done this thing. ³³But the woman fearing and trembling, knowing what was done in her, came and fell down before Him, and told Him all the truth. ³⁴And He said unto her: 'Daughter, thy faith hath made thee whole: go in peace, and be whole of thy plague.'

³⁵While He yet spake, there came from the ruler of the synagogue's house certain which said: 'Thy daughter is dead; why troublest thou the Master any further?' ³⁶As soon as Jesus heard the word that was spoken, He saith unto the ruler of the synagogue: 'Be not afraid, only believe.' ³⁷And He suffered no man to follow Him, save Peter, and James, and John the brother of James. ³⁸And He cometh to the house of the ruler of the synagogue, and seeth the tumult, and them that wept and wailed greatly. ³⁹And when He was come in, He saith unto them: 'Why make ye this ado, and weep? the damsel is not dead, but sleepeth.' ⁴⁰And they laughed Him to scorn. But when He had put them all out, He taketh the father and the mother of the damsel, and them that were with Him, and entereth in where the damsel was lying, ⁴¹and He took the damsel by the hand, and said unto her, 'TALITHA CUMI'; which is, being interpreted: 'Damsel, I say unto thee, arise.' ⁴²And straightway the damsel arose, and walked; for she was of the age of twelve years. And they were astonished with a great astonishment. ⁴³And He charged them straitly that no man should know it; and commanded that something should be given her to eat.

Matthew ix. 18–26

[18]While He spake these things unto them, behold, there came a certain ruler, and worshipped Him, saying: 'My daughter is even now dead: but come and lay Thy hand upon her, and she shall live.' [19]And Jesus arose, and followed him, and so did His disciples. [20]And, behold a woman, which was diseased with an issue of blood twelve years, came behind Him, and touched the hem of His garment: [21]for she said within herself, If I may but touch His garment, I shall be whole. [22]But Jesus turned Him about, and when He saw her, He said: 'Daughter, be of good comfort; thy faith hath made thee whole.' And the woman was made whole from that hour. [23]And when Jesus came into the ruler's house, and saw the minstrels and the people making a noise, [24]He said unto them: 'Give place: for the maid is not dead, but sleepeth.' And they laughed Him to scorn. [25]But when the people were put forth, He went in, and took her by the hand, and the maid arose. [26]And the fame hereof went abroad into all that land.

Luke viii. 41–56

[41]And, behold, there came a man named Jairus, and he was a ruler of the synagogue: and he fell down at Jesus' feet, and besought Him that He would come into his house: [42]for he had one only daughter, about twelve years of age, and she lay a dying. But as He went the people thronged Him. [43]And a woman having an issue of blood twelve years, which had spent all her living upon physicians, neither could be healed of any, [44]came behind Him, and touched the border of His garment: and immediately her issue of blood stanched. [45]And Jesus said: 'Who touched Me?' When all denied, Peter and they that were with Him said: 'Master, the multitude throng Thee and press Thee, and sayest Thou, Who touched Me?' [46]And Jesus said: 'Somebody hath touched Me: for I perceive that virtue is gone out of Me.' [47]And when the woman saw that she was not hid, she came trembling, and falling down before Him, she declared unto Him before all the people for what cause she had touched Him, and how she was healed immediately. [48]And He said unto her: 'Daughter, be of good comfort: thy faith hath made thee whole; go in peace.' [49]While He yet spake, there cometh one from the ruler of the synagogue's house, saying to him: 'Thy daughter is dead; trouble not the master.' [50]But when Jesus heard it, He answered him, saying: 'Fear not: believe only, and she shall be made whole.' [51]And when He came into the house, He suffered no man to go in, save Peter, and James, and John, and the father and the mother of the maiden. [52]And all wept, and bewailed her: but He said: 'Weep not; she is not dead, but sleepeth.' [53]And they laughed Him to scorn, knowing that she was dead. [54]And He put them all out, and took her by the hand, and called, saying: 'Maid, arise!' [55]And her spirit came again, and she arose straightway: and He commanded to give her meat. [56]And her parents were astonished: but He charged them that they should tell no man what was done.

* * * * *

Mark vii. 24–30

[24]And from thence He arose, and went into the borders of Tyre and Sidon, and entered into an house, and would have no man know it: but he could not

Mark vii. 24–30 (contd.)

be hid. [25]For a certain woman, whose young daughter had an unclean spirit, heard of Him, and came and fell at His feet. [26]The woman was a Greek, a Syrophenician by nation; and she besought Him that He would cast forth the devil out of her daughter. [27]But Jesus said unto her: 'Let the children first be filled: for it is not meet to take the children's bread and to cast it unto the dogs.' [28]And she answered and said unto Him: 'Yes, Lord: yet the dogs under the table eat of the children's crumbs.' [29]And He said unto her: 'For this saying go thy way: the devil is gone out of thy daughter.' [30]And when she was come to her house, she found the devil gone out, and her daughter laid upon the bed.

Matthew xv. 21–28

[21]Then Jesus went thence, and departed into the coasts of Tyre and Sidon. [22]And, behold, a woman of Canaan came out of the same coasts, and cried unto Him, saying: 'Have mercy on me, O Lord, Son of David; my daughter is grievously vexed with a devil.' [23]But He answered her not a word. And His disciples came and besought Him, saying: 'Send her away; for she crieth after us.' [24]But He answered and said: 'I am not sent but unto the lost sheep of the house of Israel.' [25]Then came she and worshipped Him, saying: 'Lord, help me.' [26]But He answered and said: 'It is not meet to take the children's bread, and to cast it to dogs.' [27]And she said: 'Truth, Lord: yet the dogs eat of the crumbs which fall from their masters' table.' [28]Then Jesus answered and said unto her: 'O woman, great is thy faith: be it unto thee even as thou wilt.' And her daughter was made whole from that very hour.

(a) The miraculous raising of Jairus's daughter, as described by the Synoptics, has so much in common with the even more miraculous raising of Lazarus, which *John* alone records, that we are led to suspect the authenticity of the latter. Both miracles, however, contain details unlikely to have been invented: the Aramaic *Talitha cumi,* for instance, in *Mark's* account of Jairus's Daughter (*Mark* v. 41), and Jesus's weeping for Lazarus in *John* xi. 35 (*see* LXXXVII.c). It seems, therefore, that both formed part of the original tradition, but that the Oracles consulted by the compiler of *Mark* contained the following brief mention of the Raising of Lazarus: 'When Jesus was called to the house where the corpse lay, he asked: "Why make ye such ado over one that is not dead but only sleepeth?" ', and that he linked it to the Raising of Jairus's Daughter, which preceded it under the subject-heading 'Why wail ye?'

(b) The account of 'The Bloody Issue' which, in all three Synoptics, interrupts the Raising of Jairus's Daughter, cannot be accepted. No woman known to be so cursed would have been allowed to mix with a crowd; it was a popular superstition that, if a menstruous woman passed between two men, one of these would die within the year. And had the woman touched him while still unclean, Jesus would have been defiled until the evening (*Leviticus* xv. 19) and thus debarred from entering Jairus's house. It seems, then, that this story was invented by Gentile Christians, unfamiliar with the Mosaic

Law, who had read about the curative virtue of Elijah's mantle (2 *Kings* ii. 14) and Elisha's bones (2 *Kings* xiii. 21) and wished to prove that Jesus was no less holy than they.

(*c*) This invention may have been prompted by an early Nazarene triptych illustrating three miraculous cures. The first showed Jesus summoned to heal the Centurion's servant, the sick-bed appearing in the background (*Luke* vii. 3—*see* xxxiii.*a and b*); the second showed the Syro-Phoenician woman (*Mark* vii. 24–30) as she grasped the fringe of his praying-garment and begged him to cure her daughter, 'laid on a bed' close by; the third showed the raising of Jairus's daughter. The Synoptics misread the triptych as a sequence, taking the three patients to be only one (see Foreword. *l*). As a result, the Centurion's summons became Jairus's appeal to Jesus; the raising of Jairus's daughter was correctly interpreted; but for the incident of the Syro-Phoenician woman, which intervened between these scenes, a new story had to be invented, namely 'The Bloody Issue'—Jesus's instinctive recoil from the unclean touch of a foreigner being construed as annoyance that 'virtue had gone out of him'. 'Twelve years', the duration of the disorder, seems to have been borrowed from the age of Jairus's daughter.

(*d*) This is not, however, to suggest that the Bloody Issue was a complete fabrication. The original tradition may have run thus:

(116) *Jesus also laid his hands upon a woman which for many years had a bloody issue.*

For thus he suffered himself to be made unclean until the evening, if haply she might be delivered of her plague for the remainder of her life.

And it pleased God to hearken unto his prayers, and straightway the fountain of her blood was dried up, though she had spent all her living on physicians and none had been able to heal her.

* * * * *

Later, the Bloody Issue became a favourite subject for the Catacomb painters: rich women converts felt flattered that Jesus should have sympathized with their menstrual disorders.

(*e*) To touch the fringes of a holy man's praying garment was popularly believed to be a prophylactic against evil dreams and inclinations, though not a cure for disease. In the triptych, the Syro-Phoenician's action will have been expressive of her desire to become a proselyte.

(*f*) A contradiction in *Mark's* account of Jairus's Daughter proves the corruptness of the text: a great crowd throngs after Jesus to watch the miracle (*Mark* v. 24), yet at the close (*Mark* v. 43) he strictly charges the parents not to publish any news of it.

In *Mark* v. 35 and *Luke* viii. 49, Jairus's daughter dies while Jesus is on his way to the sick-bed, as Lazarus also does (*John* xi. 14—*see* LXXXVII.*e*); but an editor of *Matthew*, while omitting all mention of Peter, James, and John, has improved the story by letting Jairus—though his name is not given—

appeal to Jesus when his daughter is already dead and the minstrels are playing the dirges (*Matthew* ix. 18). *Mark* v. 43, paralleled in *Luke* viii. 55, suggests that the girl (whose illness is not specified in any of the accounts) had been starved by the physicians in order to drive out the demon by which she was supposedly possessed. The scene of the raising seems to be Capernaum, Jesus's 'own city' (*Matthew* ix. 1 and *Luke* viii. 40).

(144) *And when Jesus was passed over again by boat unto the other side of the Lake, much people gathered unto him; and he was nigh to the water.*

And behold, there cometh one of the rulers of the synagogue, Jairus by name, who fell at Jesus's feet and besought him greatly, saying: 'My little daughter lieth at the point of death: come, lay thy hands upon her and pray that she may be healed.'

And Jesus went with him and much people followed, and he cometh to the ruler's house and heareth the dirges which the minstrels played.

And the kinsfolk and servants of the ruler wept and wailed greatly about the bed whereon the damsel lay, and she was about twelve years of age.

And Jesus asked: 'Why wail ye, as if for one already dead? Pray ye rather that the damsel may be restored to health!'

When therefore Jesus had caused them all to be put out, he entereth into the room with Jairus and the damsel's mother, and with his disciples Peter and James and John.

And having prayed to God, he saith to the damsel: 'Talyetha cumi!' which is: 'Damsel, arise!'

And straightway she arose and walked, and they were greatly astonished and wist not what to do.

But Jesus commanded that something should be given her to eat.

* * * * *

(g) *Mark* vii. 24–30, the story of the Syro-Phoenician woman, rings true; though Jesus's prayer and her subsequent conversion to Judaism are not mentioned. These are also omitted in *Matthew* xv. 21–28, where the woman, incredibly, addresses him as 'Thou son of David' (*see* XL.*c*). However, *Matthew's* account of Jesus's refusal to answer her at once seems genuine, and his description of the woman as an Aramaic-speaking Canaanite is more plausible than *Mark's*, where she appears as a Greek-speaking Syro-Phoenician.

Mark vii. 24 suggests that Jesus had left Capernaum to avoid arrest by Herod Antipas who wanted to kill him (*Luke* xiii. 31—*see* XCVII.*h*). But here the parallel with 2 *Kings* xvii. 1–24 (*see Foreword. k–l*)—where Elijah escapes from King Ahab's wrath, visits Sidon, and there heals the widow's son—is so close that the Sidonian setting of Jesus's miracle must be suspected (*see* XXXVIII.*a*). Even if he could speak Greek (but this is uncertain) he would not have gone to Phoenicia, a non-Jewish region which was ritually unclean (*see* XIII.*f*), while able to take refuge across the Lake in Philip's mainly Jewish tetrarchy. He had done so in *Mark* vi. 29–32, and does so again in *Mark* vii. 31, immediately after this act of healing. In *Matthew* xi. 21 and *Luke* x. 13, Tyre and Sidon are appreciatively mentioned, at the expense of Galilee—'if the mighty works that have been done in Bethsaida had been done there, they would long ago have repented.' The editor who attributes this saying to Jesus was probably a Phoenician (*see* LIX.*b*) and may also have had a hand in the composition of *Matthew* xv. 21–28.

(*h*) It is likely, therefore, that Jesus, after the death of John the Baptist, went not to Phoenicia, but to Decapolis, in Philip's tetrarchy, where he met a Canaanite woman, a devotee of the Syrian Goddess. The Jews called such people 'dogs', because of their promiscuous orgies and the ritual sodomy which, anciently, had also been practised in the Temple at Jerusalem (2 *Kings* xxiii. 7). In *Deuteronomy* xxiii. 18 and *Revelation* xxii. 15, 'dog' is a euphemism for 'sodomite'; and, according to *Genesis Rabbah* xxxvi. 7, the dog was so shameless an animal that it was sexually incontinent even in Noah's ark. As is shown in *Matthew* vii. 6 (*see* XLVII.*d*), Jesus shared this Jewish aversion to the offal-eating, masterless, pariah dog (2 *Samuel* iii. 8; 2 *Kings* viii. 13; *Poverbs* xxvi. 11 and *Isaiah* lvi. 10–11). But, according to *Kethuboth* 61*b,* the keeping of small Cyprian lap-dogs was permitted, and though both *Mark* and *Matthew* make Jesus speak of 'little dogs', he may have simply said 'dogs', whereas the Canaanite woman spoke of the little dogs, pleading: 'Not all dogs are savage and untameable; some are even household pets.' Her argument had the support of the *Book of Tobit* (v. 16 and xi. 4); where Tobias's dog faithfully accompanied him on a dangerous journey from Nineveh to Rages and back.

(143) *Jesus departed thence and went across the Lake to Decapolis, and entered into the house of a Galilean and would have no man know it.*

But he could not be hid, and when he came out at eventide, behold, a Canaanite woman cried unto him: 'Have mercy on me, Jesus of Nazara! My daughter is grievously vexed with a devil.'

He answered her not and turned again to go into the house. But though his disciples would have prevented her, she fell at his feet and took hold on the fringe of his garment, crying: 'Master, help me!'

He answered and said: 'Woman, I am not sent but unto the lost sheep of the House of Israel. Let the children first be filled. It is not meet to take their bread and cast it to the dogs.'

Then said she: 'Yea, but the little dogs that are taught to walk discreetly, the same eat of the crumbs that fall from their master's table.

'Behold, I would be baptized into the congregation of Israel, and my daughter also.'

Jesus answered: 'Woman, great is thy faith. Be it unto thee as thou wilt. Bring thy daughter hither, but tell no man.'

And he commanded the devil to go out of the damsel, and she was healed and both the woman and her daughter believed and were baptized.

* * * * *

XXXVII

JESUS IN NAZARA

Mark vi. 1–6

[1]And He went out from thence, and came into His own country; and His disciples follow Him. [2]And when the sabbath day was come, He began to teach in the synagogue: and many hearing Him were astonished, saying: 'From whence hath this man these things? and what wisdom is this which is given unto Him, that even such mighty works are wrought by His hands? [3]Is not this the carpenter, the son of Mary, the brother of James, and Joses, and of Juda, and Simon? and are not His sisters here with us?' And they were offended at Him. [4]But Jesus said unto them: 'A prophet is not without honour, but in his own country, and among his own kin, and in his own house.' [5]And He could there do no mighty work, save that He laid His hands upon a few sick folk, and healed them. [6]And He marvelled because of their unbelief. And He went round about the villages, teaching.

Matthew xiii. 53–58

[53]And it came to pass, that when Jesus had finished these parables, He departed thence. [54]And when He was come into His own country, He taught them in their synagogue, insomuch that they were astonished, and said: 'Whence hath this man this wisdom, and these mighty works? [55]Is not this the carpenter's son? is not His mother called Mary? and His brethren, James, and Joses, and Simon, and Judas? [56]and His sisters, are they not all with us? Whence then hath this man all these things?' [57]And they were offended in Him. But Jesus said unto them: 'A prophet is not without honour, save in his own country, and in his own house.' [58]And He did not many mighty works there because of their unbelief.

Luke iv. 14–30

[14]And Jesus returned in the power of the Spirit into Galilee: and there went out a fame of Him through all the region round about. [15]And He taught in their synagogues, being glorified of all.

[16]And He came to Nazareth, where He had been brought up: and, as His custom was, He went into the synagogue on the sabbath day, and stood up for to read. [17]And there was delivered unto Him a book of the prophet Isaiah. And when He had opened the book, He found the place where it was written:

[18]*The Spirit of the Lord is upon Me,*
Because He hath anointed Me to preach the Gospel to the poor;

Luke iv. 14–30 (*contd.*)

> *He hath sent Me to heal the brokenhearted, to preach deliverance to the*
> *captives, and recovering of sight to the blind,*
> *To set at liberty them that are bruised,*
> ¹⁹*To preach the acceptable year of the Lord.*

²⁰And He closed the book, and He gave it again to the minister, and sat down. And the eyes of all them that were in the synagogue were fastened on Him. ²¹And He began to say unto them: 'This day is this scripture fulfilled in your ears.' ²²And all bare Him witness, and wondered at the gracious words which proceeded out of His mouth. And they said: 'Is not this Joseph's son?' ²³And He said unto them: 'Ye will surely say unto Me this proverb, Physician, heal Thyself: whatsoever we have heard done in Capernaum, do also here in Thy country.' ²⁴And He said: 'Verily I say unto you, No prophet is accepted in his own country. ²⁵But I tell you of a truth, many widows were in Israel in the days of Elijah, when the heaven was shut up three years and six months, when great famine was throughout all the land; ²⁶but unto none of them was Elijah sent, save unto Sarepta, a city of Sidon, unto a woman that was a widow. ²⁷And many lepers were in Israel in the time of Elisha the prophet; and none of them was cleansed, saving Naaman the Syrian.' ²⁸And all they in the synagogue, when they heard these things, were filled with wrath, ²⁹and rose up, and thrust Him out of the city, and led Him unto the brow of the hill whereon their city was built, that they might cast Him down headlong. ³⁰But He passing through the midst of them went His way.

John vi. 41–42

⁴¹The Jews then murmured at Him, because He said, I am the bread which came down from heaven. ⁴²And they said: 'Is not this Jesus, the son of Joseph, whose father and mother we know? how is it then that He saith, I came down from heaven?'

John iv. 43–54

⁴³Now after two days He departed thence, and went into Galilee. ⁴⁴For Jesus Himself testified, that a prophet hath no honour in his own country. ⁴⁵Then when He was come into Galilee, the Galilaeans received Him, having seen all the things that He did at Jerusalem at the feast: for they also went unto the feast.

⁴⁶So Jesus came again into Cana of Galilee, where He made the water wine. And there was a certain nobleman, whose son was sick at Capernaum. ⁴⁷When he heard that Jesus was come out of Judaea into Galilee, he went unto Him, and besought Him that He would come down, and heal his son: for he was at the point of death. ⁴⁸Then said Jesus unto him: 'Except ye see signs and wonders, ye will not believe.' ⁴⁹The nobleman saith unto Him, 'Sir, come down ere my child die.' ⁵⁰Jesus saith unto him: 'Go thy way; thy son liveth.' And the man believed the word that Jesus had spoken unto him, and he went his way. ⁵¹And as he was now going down, his servants met him, and told him, saying, Thy son liveth. ⁵²Then inquired he of them the hour when he began to amend. And they said unto him: 'Yesterday at the seventh hour

John iv. 43–54 (contd.)

the fever left him.' [53]So the father knew that it was at the same hour, in the which Jesus said unto him, Thy son liveth: and himself believed, and his whole house. [54]This is again the second miracle that Jesus did when He was come out of Judaea into Galilee.

Oxyrhynchus Papyrus I

Jesus saith: 'A prophet is not acceptable in his own country, nor doth a physician do cures upon them that know him.'

(a) Accounts of Jesus's return to 'Nazareth', *alias* Bethlehem Nozeriyyah, or 'Nazara' (*see* I.*u*) must have existed in more than one collection of Oracles. According to *Mark* vi. 1, Jesus comes to Nazara after a visit to the farther side of the Lake of Tiberias, pausing by the way only to raise Jairus's daughter (*see* xxxvi.*f*). According to *Matthew* xiii. 54, he also crosses the Lake, but goes on a long missionary tour in Galilee before reaching Nazara. According to *Luke* iv. 14, he comes to Nazara, after preaching in various Galilean synagogues, but from Jerusalem, where he is tempted by the Devil (*see* lxxviii.*e*). According to *John* iv. 43, he comes by way of Samaria, also from Jerusalem, where he turns out the money-changers (*see* xc.*f*). It is probable that he had been keeping the Passover of 29 A.D.

(b) *John* iv. 43–44: 'Jesus departed thence and went into Galilee *for* . . . a prophet has no power in his own country,' does not make sense, because the 'thence' refers to Samaria. It seems that a Samaritan editor (*see Introduction* III.*n*) was claiming Jesus as a compatriot; and in *John* viii. 48 the Jews do indeed call him a Samaritan (though this may merely mean 'fool'—*see* lxx.*d*), and accuse him of being possessed by a devil.

It is likely, however, that the Samaritan incident is an interpolation, and that the 'thence' originally referred to Judaea: that, in fact, the author of *John* took Jesus for a Judaean, not a Galilean. This is borne out by the honourable reception accorded to him on his arrival in Galilee (*John* iv. 45–54), and by *John* vii. 1: 'After these things Jesus walked in Galilee, for he could not walk in Jewry, because the Jews sought to kill him.' Jesus's description in *John* i. 45, as being 'of Nazareth', need mean no more than that he had acquired a Galilean domicile. In *John* 'the Jews' are constantly mentioned as his enemies, and 'Jews' seems to exclude native Galileans, but to include all Judaeans living in Galilee: those of Capernaum, for instance (*John* vi. 41).

The Synoptics, however, are agreed that Nazara was 'the country' where Jesus had no honour; and it is admitted in *John* vi. 42 that his parents were living in Galilee. 'The carpenter's son' (*Matthew* xiii. 55) may be just another way of saying 'the carpenter', as in *Mark* vi. 3; but the context makes it clear that Jesus had practised a trade there—at first, possibly, as his father's apprentice.

(c) Only *Luke* iv. 16–30 records Jesus's sermon to his fellow-townsmen in the synagogue and their subsequent attempt to kill him. Verse 29 may be built on a theory, borrowed from *John,* that many such attempts were made before his eventual arrest. And though the account is free from further improbabilities, there are several lacunae: no explanation is offered for *Luke* iv. 23, 'Physician, heal thyself!', or for Jesus's angry tauntings (verses 24–27) of a congregation which (verse 22) 'bare him witness and wondered at the gracious words which proceeded from his mouth.'

(*d*) To fill these lacunae, we suggest that Jesus was seen to be lame in one leg on his return to Nazara from the Coronation; and that 'Physician, heal thyself!' was a personal insult provoked by his quotation of an adage mentioned in *Mark* vi. 4, *Matthew* xiii. 57, *Luke* iv. 24 and *John* iv. 44, but given at full length only in *Oxyrhynchus Papyrus I*: 'A prophet is without honour in his own country, nor doth a physician do cures upon them that know him.' Tertullian records (*Against Marcion* iii. 7—*see* vi.*c*) that Jesus was of small stature, and adds: '*nec humanae honestatis corpus*'—'his body was not even of honest human shape', but does not describe his deformity. In several Talmudic passages (*see Introduction III. e–j*), Jesus appears under the pseudonym 'Balaam the Lame'; and the account in the *Toldoth Yeshu,* that he was lamed when trying to fly,* may refer, maliciously, either to the Temptation (*see* LXXVIII.*g*), or to Christian portrayals of him as the Messiah, 'the Son of Righteousness with healing in his wings' (*Malachi* iv. 2—*see Luke* i. 78–79).

The wrestling-match at Peniel which won Jacob the title 'Israel' (*Genesis* xxxii. 24–32) is relevant here; the connexion between the ritual injury he then suffered and the sacred kingship is made in verse 32, and *Malachi* iv. 2 refers to the pinions worn by kings at their coronation in honour of their father the Sun-god (*see* VIII.*a*). Jacob's lameness (according to the Arabic lexicographers), was an anterior dislocation of the hip, which makes one leg appear longer than the other and induces a rolling limp. The same disability might account for the relaxation in Jesus's favour of the rule that obliged a felon to carry his cross-piece to the place of crucifixion (*see* CXIII.*j*); since a heavy burden would have thrown him off his balance.

It is probable, therefore, that 'Physician, heal thyself!' refers to an injury visible to the whole congregation; and that he had acquired this since his Acclamation (*see* VI. *c*), because according to 2 *Samuel* xiv. 25 candidates for the kingship had to be of unblemished body.

(*e*) His sayings about Elijah's sojourn with the widow of Zarephath (1 *Kings* xvii. 1–24) and Elisha's healing of Naaman (2 *Kings* v. 1–14—*see* XXXII.*d*) appear to be genuine. In *Luke* iv. 25–26, however, references to the cause of

---

* The *Acts of Peter* (xxxii) tells how Simon Magus tried to fly up to God in the presence of all Rome, but was dropped by the angels who carried him, broke a leg, and died at Terracina; and this may be echoed disrespectfully in the *Toldoth Yeshu.* But the account in the *Acts of Peter* may, on the other hand, have been intended as a counterweight to an already existing version of the *Toldoth Yeshu,* in which Jesus was lamed during the Temptation. This would be consistent with the *Clementine Recognitions* ii. 9, where Simon Magus is presented as Jesus's rival, and boasts: 'If ye throw me headlong from a high mountain, yet will I be borne up and conveyed safely to the ground.'

the famine and to Elijah's healing of the widow's son (*see* xxxvi.*g*) have dropped out; so has a reference in *Luke* iv. 27 to Elisha's being mocked by the Israelite children (2 *Kings* ii. 23-24). Jesus did not mean that his mission was, thereafter, to the Gentiles only; neither Elijah nor Elisha had deserted Israel for good.

(*f*) *Isaiah* lxi. was the passage expounded by Jesus. In the liturgy of the synagogue, readings from the prophets were followed by readings from the Law, which was divided into fifty-two portions, one for each Sabbath of the year; or perhaps, still, into one hundred and fifty-six portions to cover a three-year period.

It is, at first sight, surprising that Jesus, by implication, calls himself a prophet, since the age of prophecy was held to have ended (*see* xiii.*a*), and he had not yet revealed himself as a prophesying king (*see* viii.*j*). However, if he was invited to preach an expository sermon, as opposed to reading the prescribed text—*see Acts* xiii. 15—he could impersonally resent the taunt as being directed against his office.

While it seems incredible that the men of Nazara tried to murder him, the mention of the brow of the hill in *Luke* iv. 29 is a circumstantial detail unlikely to have been invented. Perhaps, then, this sequel to the sermon has been substituted for the true one which was that he retired to the brow of the hill (a Sabbath Day's journey), in order to ask God for forgiveness. He was aware that he had stumbled and well-nigh fallen (*Psalm* lxxiii. 2): because he should have turned away wrath with a soft answer (*Proverbs* xv. 1).

(*g*) According to *Mark* vi. 5, Jesus *could not do any* mighty works in his own country because of the unbelief there; in *Matthew* xiii. 58, '*he did not many* mighty works there because of their unbelief,' which is a very different matter.

> (172) *And when the Feast was accomplished, Jesus returned to Galilee in the power of the Spirit.*

* * * *

> (133) *And he came to Bethlehem Nazara where he had been brought up, and his fame had gone thither before him.*
>
> *But it was not granted unto him to do any mighty works among the people there, because of their unbelief.*
>
> *And when the Sabbath was come he went into the synagogue and, after the Law had been expounded, the roll of the prophet Isaiah was delivered unto him.*
>
> *And standing up, he read:*
>
> *'The spirit of the Lord God is upon me, because the Lord hath appointed me to preach good tidings unto the meek; He hath sent me to bind up the brokenhearted, to proclaim liberty to the captives and the opening of the prison to them that are bound.*
>
> *'To proclaim the acceptable year of the Lord, and the day of vengeance of our God, to comfort all that mourn.'*

Then said he: 'This scripture is fulfilled today.' And he preached the Kingdom to them, as had been desired of him.

And they all hearkened unto the gracious words that proceeded out of his
mouth.

But many were offended when he likewise preached the vengeance of God
and called them unto repentance; and they said one to another:

'Is not this the carpenter, the son of Joseph and Mary, the brother of James
and Joses and Judah and Simon? And are not his sisters here with us? Who
hath given him authority to speak thus threateningly unto us?'

And Jesus answered, and said: 'A prophet is not acceptable in his own country, nor doth a physician do cures upon them that know him.

'It is written that, when Israel hearkened not to the warning of God's
vengeance which Elijah the Tishbite preached, he departed into Sidon.

'There he was well received by a widow of Zarephath; and by the Lord's
grace he replenished her cruse of oil and her barrel of meal and also healed
her son, though many sons of Israel perished in the famine which God sent
upon them.

'For they lacked faith in the Lord, as ye likewise now lack faith.'

Then, one that sat near by, beholding that Jesus now halted upon his thigh
(even as our father Israel halted), mocked him, and said: 'Physician, heal
thyself!'

Jesus answered: 'Because of his baldness the prophet Elisha was mocked by
certain little children of Israel, and forty-two of them were destroyed by two
she-bears.'

And he said also: 'When Naaman the Syrian came to Elisha from afar to
be healed of his leprosy, he was made whole by the finger of God, though
there were many lepers of Israel in that day.

'For they lacked faith to be made whole, as ye likewise now lack faith.'

And they in the synagogue, when they heard these things, were filled with
wrath.

But Jesus delivered the roll again into the hands of the minister and, passing through the midst of them, he went his way.

And he came to the brow of the hill whereon the city was built, and there
prayed for forgiveness, because that he had not answered the man with mildness. As it is written: 'A soft answer turneth away wrath.'

And he humbled himself before God, saying in the words of his father
David:

' "As for me, I was almost gone, my steps had well nigh slipped.

' "Verily, I have cleansed my heart in vain and washed my hands in innocency.

' "So foolish was I and ignorant, like as a beast before Thee.

' "Nevertheless, I am continually with Thee, Thou hast holden me by the
right hand." '

* * * * *

(h) John iv. 43–54, the healing of the ruler's son at Capernaum, is a debased
version of Jairus's Daughter (see xxxvi.f) and must be disregarded. No other
Gospel contains it.

* * * * *

XXXVIII

THE WIDOW OF NAIN

Luke vii. 11–17

[11]And it came to pass the day after, that He went into a city called Nain; and many of His disciples went with Him, and much people. [12]Now when He came nigh to the gate of the city, behold, there was a dead man carried out, the only son of his mother, and she was a widow: and much people of the city was with her. [13]And when the Lord saw her, He had compassion on her, and said unto her: 'Weep not.' [14]And He came and touched the bier: and they that bare him stood still. And He said: 'Young man, I say unto thee, Arise.' [15]And he that was dead sat up, and began to speak. And He delivered him to his mother. [16]And there came a fear on all: and they glorified God, saying, that a great prophet is risen up among us; and, that God hath visited His people. [17]And this rumour of Him went forth throughout all Judaea, and throughout all the region round about.

(*a*) Elijah's healing of the widow's son at Zarephath strongly influenced the account of Jesus and the Canaanite's, or Syro-Phoenician's, daughter (*Luke* iv. 25-27—*see* xxxvi.g). *Luke* vii. 11-17 parallels a miracle of Elisha's: his raising, at Shunem, of the rich woman's child who had died of sun-stroke (2 *Kings* iv. 18-37).

(*b*) 'Nain' (or 'Naim' as it is written in some manuscripts), is perhaps a worn-down form of '[The Sheepfolds] of Shu*nem*', since both Eusebius (*Onomastica Sacra* 285. 41) and Jerome (143. 22) place it within a few miles of Shunem. It seems that an editor of *Luke* finding, in the margin of his collection of Oracles, a brief allusion to Elisha's feat at the city of which Nain was an outlying hamlet, mistakenly attributed a new miracle to Jesus; taking for his model the Raising of Jairus's Daughter (*see* xxxvi.f)—but keeping in mind a similar miracle attributed to Apollonius of Tyana (*see Introduction* iv.n). Though the Shunemite was not a widow like the mother of the boy cured by Elijah at Zarephath, her husband was old and impotent, and Elisha had procured her this only son by a miracle.

(*c*) *Luke* vii. 18-30 concerns the visit to Jesus of John's disciples; and since Jesus identified John with Elijah (*see* xxxix.f), and since they at once raised the question of Jesus's own identity, the original may have run:

(123) *And Jesus departed thence and came to the village of Nain.*

But the rumour of his healing of the centurion's servant ran ahead of him: and men said: 'A great prophet is arisen among us, like unto Elisha!'

(For Nain lieth not far from the city of Shunem where he restored the rich woman's son to life.)

And there came to meet Jesus at Nain certain disciples of John the Baptist.

* * * *

XXXIX

JOHN SENDS TO JESUS

Matthew xi. 2–15

[2]Now when John had heard in the prison the works of Christ, he sent two of his disciples, [3]and said unto Him: 'Art Thou He that should come, or do we look for another?' [4]Jesus answered and said unto them: 'Go and shew John again those things which ye do hear and see: [5]the blind receive their sight, and the lame walk, the lepers are cleansed, and the deaf hear, the dead are raised up, and the poor have the Gospel preached to them. [6]And blessed is he, whosoever shall not be offended in Me.'

[7]And as they departed, Jesus began to say unto the multitudes concerning John: 'What went ye out into the wilderness to see? A reed shaken with the wind? [8]But what went ye out for to see? A man clothed in soft raiment? behold, they that wear soft clothing are in kings' houses. [9]But what went ye out for to see? A prophet? yea, I say unto you, and more than a prophet. [10]For this is he, of whom it is written,

Behold, I send My messenger before Thy face,
Which shall prepare Thy way before Thee,

[11]Verily I say unto you, among them that are born of women there hath not risen a greater than John the Baptist: notwithstanding he that is least in the Kingdom of Heaven is greater than he. [12]And from the days of John the Baptist until now the Kingdom of Heaven suffereth violence, and the violent take it by force. [13]For all the prophets and the law prophesied until John. [14]And if ye will receive it, this is Elijah, which was for to come. [15]He that hath ears to hear let him hear.'

Matthew xi. 16–19

[16]But whereunto shall I liken this generation? It is like unto children sitting in the markets, and calling unto their fellows, [17]and saying,

We have piped unto you, and ye have not danced;
We have mourned unto you, and ye have not lamented.

[18]For John came neither eating nor drinking, and they say, He hath a devil. [19]The Son of Man came eating and drinking, and they say, Behold a man gluttonous, and a winebibber, a friend of publicans and sinners. But wisdom is justified of her children.

Matthew xii. 14–21

[14]Then the Pharisees went out, and held a council against Him, how they might destroy Him.

Matthew xii. 14–21 (*contd.*)

[15]But when Jesus knew it, He withdrew Himself from thence: and great multitudes followed Him, and He healed them all: [16]and charged them that they should not make Him known: [17]that it might be fulfilled which was spoken by Isaiah the prophet, saying:

> [18]*Behold My Servant, Whom I have chosen;*
> *My Beloved, in Whom My soul is well pleased:*
> *I will put My Spirit upon Him,*
> *And He shall shew judgement to the nations.*
> [19]*He shall not strive, nor cry;*
> *Neither shall any man hear His voice in the streets.*
> [20]*A bruised reed shall He not break,*
> *And smoking flax shall He not quench,*
> *Till He send forth judgement unto victory.*
> [21]*And in His name shall the nations trust.*

Luke vii. 18–35

[18]And the disciples of John shewed him of all these things. [19]And John calling unto him two of his disciples sent them to Jesus, saying: 'Art Thou He that should come? or look we for another?' [20]When the men were come unto Him, they said: 'John Baptist hath sent us unto Thee, saying, Art Thou He that should come? or look we for another?' [21]And in that same hour He cured many of their infirmities and plagues, and of evil spirits; and unto many that were blind He gave sight. [22]Then Jesus answering said unto them: 'Go your way, and tell John what things ye have seen and heard; how that the blind see, the lame walk, the lepers are cleansed, the deaf hear, the dead are raised, to the poor the Gospel is preached. [23]And blessed is he, whosoever shall not be offended in Me.'

[24]And when the messengers of John were departed, He began to speak unto the people concerning John: 'What went ye out into the wilderness for to see? A reed shaken with the wind? [25]But what went ye out for to see? A man clothed in soft raiment? Behold, they which are gorgeously apparelled, and live delicately, are in kings' courts. [26]But what went ye out for to see? A prophet? Yea, I say unto you, and much more than a prophet. [27]This is he, of whom it is written,

> *Behold, I send My messenger before Thy face,*
> *Which shall prepare Thy way before Thee.*

[28]For I say unto you, among those that are born of women there is not a greater prophet than John the Baptist: but he that is least in the kingdom of God is greater than he.' [29]And all the people that heard him, and the publicans, justified God, being baptized with the baptism of John. [30]But the Pharisees and lawyers rejected the counsel of God against themselves, being not baptized of him.

[31]And the Lord said: 'Whereunto then shall I liken the men of this generation? and to what are they like? [32]They are like unto children sitting in the marketplace, and calling one to another, and saying,

Luke vii. 18–35 (contd.)

> We have piped unto you, and ye have not danced;
> We have mourned to you, and ye have not wept.

³³For John the Baptist came neither eating bread nor drinking wine; and ye say, He hath a devil. ³⁴The Son of Man is come eating and drinking; and ye say, Behold a gluttonous man, and a winebibber, a friend of publicans and sinners! ³⁵But wisdom is justified of all her children.'

Luke xvi. 16

¹⁶The law and the prophets were until John: since that time the kingdom of God is preached, and every man presseth into it.

John v. 32–35

³²There is Another that beareth witness of Me; and I know that the witness which He witnesseth of Me is true. ³³Ye sent unto John, and he bare witness unto the truth. ³⁴But I receive not testimony from man: but these things I say, that ye might be saved. ³⁵He was a burning and a shining light: and ye were willing for a season to rejoice in his light.

(a) Herod Antipas will have kept John closely confined and *incommunicado;* it is incredible that he could have sent any message from prison. In *Matthew* xi. 2, an editor has inserted the phrase 'in prison' to explain John's absence, being unaware that it went against custom for the officiating prophet to pay the King friendly visits after his installation* (*see* viii.z). Only if the King failed in his duties would the prophet return, as Samuel did in the case of Saul, to deprive him of his throne (1 *Samuel* xv. 26). Since Jesus had not ventured, so far, to proclaim his kingship to the nation, John sent two disciples with a threatening message: 'Art thou the Coming One, the Anointed King whom Israel awaits, or must I seek and crown another?'

(b) Jesus then reassures John that he is faithfully attending to his royal affairs, and quotes *Isaiah* xliii. 1–7—which in *Matthew* xii. 14–21 has been given a different and unlikely setting. The evangelists, dissatisfied with this modest declaration of Jesus's aims, make him boast of his feats of healing; which would have been a sin of presumption, since the glory was God's alone (*see* xxxii.b). In *Luke* vii. 21 he is even made to stage a thaumaturgic display.

(c) John's disciples may have heard of certain miraculous cures (*see* xxxviii.c) and reported these to him; but if so, 'the dead are raised' must mean 'the dead in spirit', as in the Talmud (*Berakoth* 18b): 'The righteous are called living even after death; the wicked are called dead even in their lifetime.'

---

* John stood to Jesus in much the same relation as a film-director to his leading actor. The director is aware that the public, ignorant of his all-important function, will give the credit for a film's success to whatever actor he casts for the lead and drills in his performance. And if the actor is then prompted by public adulation to take the view that it is he, not the director, who is the more important, and insists on having his own temperamental way, the director may threaten to drop him in favour of someone more amenable to discipline.

Jesus's praise of John will have been unqualified, as Saul both before and after his denunciation by Samuel displayed abject humility in his presence. Since, therefore, 'the greatest prophet ever born of woman' places John above Jesus himself, *Matthew* xi. 11: 'He that is least in the Kingdom of God is greater than John,' must be a subsequent interpolation, dating from a time when John's followers had quarrelled with the Pauline, and perhaps also with the Nazarene, Church.

(*d*) *Matthew* xi. 7, 'a reed shaken with the wind', refers to an ancient type of oracle. Jehovah might raise a propitious sound of marching in the tops of sacred acacia-trees ('mulberries' in the R.V.—2 *Samuel* v. 24), but a heathenish reed-oracle like the one which spread the news of Midas's ears (Ovid: *Metamorphoses* xi. 146), or which gave Psyche good advice (Apuleius: *Metamorphoses* vi. 12), was abhorred by devout Jews. *Matthew* xi. 10, borrowed from *Matthew* iii. 3, seems to have superseded the praise of the Baptist preserved in *John* v. 35 (*see* XXVI.*f*).

(*e*) *Matthew* xi. 18–19 and its variant in *Luke* vii. 33–34 probably refer to John's diet of carobs instead of bread (*see* XLI.*b*), and of water instead of sour milk. We know that Jesus ate bread and fish (*see* CXVI.*e*), and *Isaiah* vii. 15 prescribed 'butter' (i.e. clotted cream) for the Messiah. However, both Jesus and John must have abstained from wine, which was held to seduce from truth and stimulate sexual desire (*Testament of Judah* xiv. 1) and was forbidden alike to a prophet (*Amos* ii. 11–12) and a king (*Proverbs* xxxi. 3–5—*see* X.*d*). The saying is quoted out of context; it may have been found in the Oracles under the subject-heading 'Jesus bears witness to John'.

(*f*) *Matthew* xi. 12 is contradicted by *Luke* xvi. 16, which also contradicts the following verse: 'It is easier for heaven and earth to pass away than for one tittle of the Law to pass away.' Its original meaning seems to have been praise for John's success in preaching repentance. In *Matthew* xi. 13, Jesus declares that all prophecies culminate in John, who is Elijah. An early tradition preserved in the Talmud (*Berakoth* 34*b*) was that 'all prophecies concern the Days of the Messiah'—which were expected after a universal repentance in Israel had caused Elijah to re-appear on earth (*Malachi* iv. 5-6).

(*g*) The suggestion in *Matthew* xi. 19 and *Luke* vii. 34, that Jesus was a boon-companion of publicans and sinners, is an obvious interpolation; Jesus neither ate nor drank with these (*see* XIX.*b*). 'Wine-bibber' may reflect a taunt later levelled by John's ascetic followers against Pauline Christians who celebrated the Eucharist and grossly abused it (1 *Corinthians* xi. 20–22).

(124) *Now, John the Baptist expected to hear great things of Jesus which he had anointed; but Jesus had not revealed himself to the people as King.*

Therefore John sent two disciples to say unto him: 'What dost thou of the things that are prophesied? Wherefore liftest thou not up thy voice, that all may know thee who thou art? Art thou verily he that should come, or shall I seek another to anoint him?'

Jesus answered them, and said: 'Isaiah prophesied in the name of the Lord:

"*Behold My servant whom I uphold, Mine elect in whom My soul delighteth. I have put My Spirit upon him: he shall bring forth judgement to the Gentiles.*

'*"He shall not cry, nor lift up, nor cause his voice to be heard in the streets.*

'*"A bruised reed shall he not break and smoking flax shall he not quench, yet he shall bring forth judgement unto truth.*

'*"He shall not fail nor be discouraged till he have set judgement in the earth: I the Lord have called thee in righteousness, and will hold thine hand and will keep thee and give thee for a covenant of the people, for a light to the Gentiles,*

'*"To open the blind eyes, to bring out the prisoners from confinement, and them that sit in darkness of the prison house."*

'*Go now, and shew John these things that ye have heard and seen!*'

And they returned to John and delivered unto him the words of Jesus, and said:

'*The blind indeed see, and the prisoners are freed, for he preacheth the Kingdom to the Men of the Land that hitherto dwelt in darkness.*

'*Moreover, the sick are healed, the dumb speak, the crooked are made straight, and they that were dead in the spirit are quickened.*'

* * * * *

[For the last words of their report to John, *see* XL.*i*.]

* * * * *

(126) *And when the disciples of John had departed, Jesus began to preach unto the multitude concerning John:*

He said: '*What went ye out into the wilderness for to see? A murmuring reed shaken by the wind? Nay, but such a thing speaketh foolishness.*

'*But what went ye out to see? A prophet? Yea, I say unto you, and more than a prophet! He is a burning and a shining light, and happy are ye to have rejoiced in that light for a season.*

'*Verily, among them that are born of woman, there hath not risen a greater than John.*

'*He that hath ears to hear, let him hear: this is Elijah come again!*

'*As the prophet Malachi saith: "Behold, I will send you Elijah the prophet before the coming of the great and terrible Day of the Lord.*

'*"And he shall turn the hearts of the fathers to their children and the hearts of the children to their fathers, lest I come and smite the earth with a curse."*

'*Lo, with his coming all prophecy hasteneth to fulfilment; for he hath preached repentance, and all men press into the Kingdom of Heaven.*'

* * * * *

The following seems to have been spoken during Jesus's visit to Jerusalem for the Passover of 29 A.D.:

(171) *And a report came unto Jesus how that certain men reproached him, saying:* '*He preacheth that a man shall take no heed what he shall eat or what he shall drink, yet he dineth every day with the rich men of this city.*'

Jesus answered: '*Whereunto shall I liken the men of this generation?*

'They are like unto little children sitting in the market place that reproach their fellows, crying: "We have piped as for a wedding, but ye have not danced; and we have wept as for a burial, but ye have not lamented."

'Wherefore should I heed their reproaches?

'When they saw that John's meat was carobs and his drink water, they said: "He hath a devil that driveth him into the wilderness and mortifieth his flesh."

'And when they see that I dine with honourable men and that bread is my meat and milk my drink, they say: "Behold a glutton and a belly server!"

'But wisdom is proved in her fruits.'

*   *   *   *   *

(*h*) For the malicious comparison between Pharisees and Publicans in *Luke* vii. 29-30—*see* LVIII.*d*. The passage must, however, be amended (*see* v.*m.*):

(12) *Then all they that were baptized of John, glorified God, saying: 'Is not this Elijah, which is come to fulfil the prophecy spoken of Malachi?'*

But the chief men of the Pharisees would not accept John that he was Elijah, for they declared that the signs prophesied of the Last Days were not yet appeared in Israel.

*   *   *   *   *

THE BLIND AND LAME

Mark viii. 22–26

²²And He cometh to Bethsaida; and they bring a blind man unto Him, and besought Him to touch him. ²³And He took the blind man by the hand, and led him out of the town; and when He had spit on his eyes, and put His hands upon him, He asked him if he saw ought. ²⁴And he looked up and said, I see men as trees, walking. ²⁵After that He put His hands again upon his eyes, and made him look up: and he was restored, and saw every man clearly. ²⁶And He sent him away to his house, saying: 'Neither go into the town, nor tell it to any in the town.'

Matthew ix. 27–31

²⁷And when Jesus departed thence, two blind men followed Him, crying, and saying: 'Son of David, have mercy on us.' ²⁸And when He was come into the house, the blind men came to Him: and Jesus saith unto them: 'Believe ye that I am able to do this?' They said unto Him: 'Yea, Lord.' ²⁹Then touched He their eyes, saying: 'According to your faith be it unto you.' ³⁰And their eyes were opened; and Jesus straitly charged them, saying: 'See that no man know it.' ³¹But they, when they were departed, spread abroad His fame in all that country.

Mark x. 46–52

⁴⁶And they came to Jericho: and as He went out of Jericho with His disciples and a great number of people, blind Bartimaeus, the son of Timaeus, sat by the highway side begging. ⁴⁷And when he heard that it was Jesus of Nazareth, he began to cry out, and say: 'Jesus, Son of David, have mercy on me.' ⁴⁸And many charged him that he should hold his peace: but he cried the more a great deal: 'Son of David, have mercy on me.'

⁴⁹And Jesus stood still, and commanded him to be called. And they call the blind man, saying unto him: 'Be of good comfort, rise; He calleth thee.' ⁵⁰And he, casting away his garment, rose, and came to Jesus. ⁵¹And Jesus answered and said unto him: 'What wilt thou that I should do unto thee?' The blind man said unto Him: 'Lord, that I might receive my sight.'

⁵²And Jesus said unto him: 'Go thy way: thy faith hath made thee whole.' And immediately he received his sight, and followed Jesus in the way.

Matthew xx. 29–34

[29]And as they departed from Jericho, a great multitude followed Him. [30]And, behold, two blind men sitting by the way side, when they heard that Jesus passed by, cried out, saying: 'Have mercy on us, O Lord, Son of David.' [31]And the multitude rebuked them, because they should hold their peace: but they cried the more, saying: 'Have mercy on us, O Lord, Son of David.' [32]And Jesus stood still, and called them, and said: 'What will ye that I shall do unto you?' [33]They say unto Him: 'Lord, that our eyes may be opened.' [34]So Jesus had compassion on them, and touched their eyes: and immediately their eyes received sight, and they followed Him.

Luke xviii. 35–43

[35]And it came to pass, that as He was come nigh unto Jericho, a certain blind man sat by the way side begging: [36]and hearing the multitude pass by, he asked what it meant. [37]And they told him that Jesus of Nazareth passeth by. [38]And he cried, saying: 'Jesus, Son of David, have mercy on me.' [39]And they which went before rebuked him, that he should hold his peace: but he cried so much the more: 'Son of David, have mercy on me.' [40]And Jesus stood, and commanded him to be brought unto Him: and when he was come near, He asked him, [41]saying: 'What wilt thou that I shall do unto thee?' And he said, Lord, that I may receive my sight. [42]And Jesus said unto him: 'Receive thy sight: thy faith hath saved thee.' [43]And immediately he received his sight, and followed Him, glorifying God: and all the people, when they saw it, gave praise unto God.

Luke vii. 21

And in that same hour He cured many of their infirmities and plagues, and of evil spirits; and unto many that were blind He gave sight.

Matthew xxi. 14

And the blind and the lame came to Him in the temple; and He healed them.

John ix. 1–38

[1]And as Jesus passed by, He saw a man which was blind from his birth. [2]And His disciples asked Him, saying: 'Master, who did sin, this man, or his parents, that he was born blind?' [3]Jesus answered: 'Neither hath this man sinned, nor his parents: but that the works of God should be made manifest in him. [4]I must work the works of Him that sent Me, while it is day: the night cometh, when no man can work. [5]As long as I am in the world, I am the light of the world.' [6]When He had thus spoken, He spat on the ground, and made clay of the spittle, and He anointed the eyes of the blind man with the clay, [7]and said unto him: 'Go, wash in the pool of Siloam,' (which is by interpretation, Sent). He went his way therefore, and washed, and came seeing.

[8]The neighbours therefore, and they which before had seen him that he was blind, said: 'Is not this he that sat and begged?' [9]Some said: 'This is he;' others said: 'He is like him:' but he said: 'I am he.' [10]Therefore said they unto him: 'How were thine eyes opened?' [11]He answered and said: 'A man

John ix. 1–38 (*contd.*)

that is called Jesus made clay, and anointed mine eyes, and said unto me, Go to the pool of Siloam, and wash: and I went and washed, and I received sight.' [12]Then said they unto him: 'Where is He?' He said: 'I know not.'

[13]They brought to the Pharisees him that aforetime was blind. [14]And it was the sabbath day when Jesus made the clay, and opened his eyes. [15]Then again the Pharisees also asked him how he had received his sight. He said unto them: 'He put clay upon mine eyes, and I washed, and do see.' [16]Therefore said some of the Pharisees: 'This man is not of God, because He keepeth not the sabbath day.' Others said: 'How can a man that is a sinner do such miracles?' And there was a division among them. [17]They say unto the blind man again: 'What sayest thou of Him, that He hath opened thine eyes?' He said: 'He is a prophet.' [18]But the Jews did not believe concerning him that he had been blind, and received his sight, until they called the parents of him that had received his sight. [19]And they asked them saying: 'Is this your son, who ye say was born blind? how then doth he now see?' [20]His parents answered them and said: 'We know that this is our son, and that he was born blind: [21]but by what means he now seeth, we know not; or who hath opened his eyes, we know not: he is of age; ask him: he shall speak for himself.' [22]These words spake his parents, because they feared the Jews: for the Jews had agreed already, that if any man did confess that He was Christ, He should be put out of the synagogue. [23]Therefore said his parents: 'He is of age; ask him.' [24]Then again called they the man that was blind, and said unto him: 'Give God the praise: we know that this man is a sinner.' [25]He answered and said: 'Whether He be a sinner or no, I know not: one thing I know, that whereas I was blind, now I see.' [26]Then said they to him again: 'What did He to thee? how opened He thine eyes?' [27]He answered them: 'I have told you already, and ye did not hear: wherefore would ye hear it again? will ye also be His disciples?' [28]Then they reviled him, and said: 'Thou art His disciple; but we are Moses' disciples. [29]We know that God spake unto Moses: as for this fellow, we know not from whence He is.'

[30]The man answered and said unto them: 'Why, herein is a marvellous thing, that ye know not from whence He is, and yet He hath opened mine eyes. [31]Now we know that God heareth not sinners, but if any man be a worshipper of God, and doeth His will, him He heareth. [32]Since the world began was it not heard that any man opened the eyes of one that was born blind. [33]If this Man were not of God, He could do nothing.' [34]They answered and said unto him: 'Thou wast altogether born in sin, and dost thou teach us?' And they cast him out.

[35]Jesus heard that they had cast him out: and when He had found him, He said unto him: 'Dost thou believe on the Son of God?' [36]He answered and said: 'Who is He, Lord, that I might believe on Him?' [37]And Jesus said unto him: 'Thou hast both seen Him, and it is He that talketh with thee.' [38]And he said: 'Lord, I believe.' And he worshipped Him.

John v. 1–16

[1]After this there was a feast of the Jews; and Jesus went up to Jerusalem. [2]Now there is at Jerusalem by the sheep market a pool, which is called in the

John v. 1–16 (*contd.*)

Hebrew tongue Bethesda, having five porches. ³In these lay a great multitude of impotent folk, of blind, halt, withered, waiting for the moving of the water. ⁴For an angel went down at a certain season into the pool, and troubled the water: whosoever then first after the troubling of the water stepped in was made whole of whatsoever disease he had. ⁵And a certain man was there, which had an infirmity thirty and eight years. ⁶When Jesus saw him lie, and knew that he had been now a long time in that case, He saith unto him: 'Wilt thou be made whole?' ⁷The impotent man answered Him: 'Sir, I have no man, when the water is troubled, to put me into the pool: but while I am coming, another steppeth down before me.' ⁸Jesus saith unto him: 'Rise, take up thy bed, and walk.' ⁹And immediately the man was made whole, and took up his bed, and walked.

And on the same day was the sabbath. ¹⁰The Jews therefore said unto him that was cured: 'It is the sabbath day: it is not lawful for thee to carry thy bed.' ¹¹He answered them: 'He that made me whole, the same said unto me, Take up thy bed, and walk.' ¹²Then asked they him: 'What man is that which said unto thee, Take up thy bed, and walk?' ¹³And he that was healed wist not who it was: for Jesus had conveyed Himself away, a multitude being in that place. ¹⁴Afterwards Jesus findeth him in the temple, and said unto him: 'Behold, thou art made whole: sin no more, lest a worse thing come unto thee.' ¹⁵The man departed, and told the Jews that it was Jesus which had made him whole. ¹⁶And therefore did the Jews persecute Jesus, and sought to slay Him, because He had done these things on the sabbath day.

(*a*) *Mark* viii. 22–26 is the earliest and most reliable of the eight Gospel passages which concern Jesus's cures of the blind. *Matthew* ix. 27–31 evidently refers to the same incident, that of the blind man of Bethsaida, despite a great discrepancy between the two versions. In *Mark*, to prevent the demon of blindness from entering into anyone else, Jesus leads his patient out of the city (*see* xxxi.*b*), then spits on his eyes and lays his hands upon him; in *Matthew*, he performs the cure in his own house, there are two blind men, not one, and he is content merely to touch their eyes. There is a similar discrepancy between the three Synoptic accounts of Blind Bartimaeus's* cure at Jericho. In *Mark* x. 46–52 and *Luke* xviii. 35–43, Jesus restores his sight without touching him; in *Matthew* xx. 29–34, there are again two blind men, and Jesus heals them both by touching their eyes.

The curing of total blindness, next to raising the dead, is one of the most spectacular of all therapeutic feats. It will be prudent, therefore, to accept the lowest estimate of these cures, namely *Luke's* one as against *Mark's* two and *Matthew's* four.

(*b*) The problem now to be faced, namely why the incidents in *Mark* are given two different settings, with different circumstantial details of each case,

---

* The meaning of 'Bartimaeus' is uncertain. It may be a Greek patronymic: 'the Son of Timaeus', a name which occurs as the title to one of Plato's *Dialogues*. Or it may be an Aramaic nickname, 'the Son of Uncleanness' (i.e. one disgracefully born), a sense which finds support in *John* ix. 2 (*see* (*d*) *below*).

is satisfactorily solved only on the following six premisses. First: that the compiler of the primitive Gospel known as the Triple Tradition consulted a collection of Oracles in which both cures were entered under the subject-heading 'The Blind and the Lame'. Second: that, according to one of these entries, Jesus healed a blind man of Bethsaida, while according to the other, Blind Bartimaeus hailed him as the Messiah when he was leaving, or (as *Luke* has it) entering, Jericho. Third: that it then seemed anomalous to this editor that Jesus had not restored Bartimaeus's sight in reward for his faith and perspicacity. Fourth: that the editor, assuming that this happy ending had been omitted by an oversight, added one modelled on previous cures—and though he suppressed the Bethsaida incident because it contained certain details reflecting on Jesus's dignity, saved others for insertion in this revised account of the Bartimaeus incident. Fifth: that his version was adopted by all the Synoptics. Sixth: that the Bethsaida account, still current in the Oracles, proved too popular for suppression, and later was incorporated, though not at its original length, in *Mark* viii. 22–26.

(*c*) The remaining discrepancies may be explained by the same premisses. Both *Matthew* and *Luke* had now recorded the healing of only one blind man, named Bartimaeus, against *Mark's* two. This did not trouble editors of *Luke,* however, since in vii. 21 they had presumed the healing of a number of blind men to explain Jesus's message in the next verse (*see* xxxix.*b*): 'Go now and shew John [the Baptist] these things that ye have heard and seen,' and their subsequent report: 'The blind see . . . the sick are healed, the lame walk, the crooked are made straight. . . .' But an editor of *Matthew,* who had not adopted *Luke's* addition, seems to have been distressed when he found only one cure in his Gospel, and to have written in the margin of the Bartimaeus passage: 'Jesus healed two blind men, not one', and then cited *Mark's* Bethsaida miracle. This new miracle was therefore patched into *Matthew* ix. 27–31, gloss and all, though without mention of the spittle. Finally, the gloss, over-literally accepted by the faithful, worked up into the text of both miracles—so that two men were said to have been healed at Bethsaida and two more at Jericho. A still later editor of *Matthew,* similarly finding that *Luke* vii. 21 contained a number of unparticularized cures not mentioned in his own Gospel, inserted these in the Jerusalem setting (*Matthew* xxi. 14), so that *Matthew* was now richer in this kind of miracle than all the other Gospels. He may have been the obtuse editor who spoilt the effect of Bartimaeus's acclamation of Jesus by letting both the blind men of Bethsaida (*Matthew* ix. 27) and the Canaanite woman (*Matthew* xv. 22— *see* xxxvi.*g*) hail him as the Son of David.

(*d*) In *John* ix. 1–38, the Bethsaida cure takes place at Jerusalem and, though inflated in the Johannine style, the account seems to be based on an early tradition and throws further light on the others. Verses 1–3 evidently belong to the Bartimaeus incident; they resemble Jesus's pronouncements in *Luke* xiii. 1–5 (*see* li.*b*), when he was questioned about the fate of those killed by the fall of an aqueduct pier. He denies that the blind man's name, 'The Son of Uncleanness', bears any relation to his disability. In verse 3, he is not promising a cure, but contending that blindness is compensated by inward sight in proof of God's compassion. Verse 4 appears to be a genuine, though unrelated, saying and may, originally, have introduced the Feeding of the Five Thousand (*Mark* vi. 35—*see* LXXII.*d*). Verse 5, borrowed, it seems, from Paul's description of Jesus as 'a light to lighten the Gentiles'—itself a quotation from *Isaiah* xlii. 6—is too boastful to be genuine.

(*e*) *John* ix. 13–38 deserves no credence whatever. It reverts to the old story (*Mark* ii. 11, *Matthew* ix. 6 and *Luke* v. 24—*see* LXXIV.*a–c*) of Jesus's reproof by the Pharisees for a breach of the Sabbath—the kneading of clay counted as work—and further exacerbates the ill-feeling between the Gentile and Nazarene Church by suggesting that Jesus rejected the Mosaic Law (verses 28–29), and that the Pharisees excommunicated not only Jesus (verses 34–35), but everyone who believed in him (verse 22). Verse 34 is the interesting result of a long editorial process. Originally based on verse 2, a discussion of Bartimaeus's name, it seems at one stage to have been changed to a slander against Jesus, and put into the Pharisees' mouths as a reinforcement of verses 24–25. It was, in fact, either the story quoted by Celsus (*Against Celsus* i. 29 —*see* I.*c*), that Jesus had been 'begotten in adultery by a wicked soldier on the body of a lustful female', or the one quoted in the Talmud (*Kallah* p. 146 ed. Higger*), that he was a 'son of menstruation', begotten on his mother by her paranymph while she was still unclean according to the Mosaic Law (*Leviticus* xv. 24). Bartimaeus (though he is given no name in *John*), is then made to defend Jesus by acknowledging his divinity. But the editor of *John* ix. 34 thought the slander too dangerous even as a self-condemnation of the wicked Pharisees who had dared to circulate it, and therefore cut it out. It survives, however, in the *Acts of Pilate* ii. 3, a second-century work otherwise called the *Gospel of Nicodemus,* which has strong literary affinities with *John*: 'The elders of the Jews said to Jesus: "Thou wast born of fornication." ' So Bartimaeus once more became the person slandered; yet was still invited to acknowledge Jesus as the Son of God—and thus, by implication, to scotch the story of Jesus's bastardy. Almost the only remark in this passage that has a genuine ring is 'Give God the praise', (verse 24), and this has been taken from Jesus and given to the Pharisees, with the gratuitous addition: 'We know that this man is a sinner.' Jesus must have said, more modestly: 'Give God the praise, not this sinner,' meaning himself. The Jews had an axiom that no man was without fault (*Proverbs* xx. 9): 'Who can say: "I have made my heart clean, I am pure of sin?" ' The Gentile Church adopted this axiom (*First Epistle of John* i. 8): 'If we say that we have no sin we deceive ourselves and the truth is not in us'—but always excepted Jesus, who was thought incapable of sinning.

(*f*) It seems, then, that an editor of *John* had found in the collection of

---

* Neither Jesus nor Mary is, however, mentioned by name in any extant texts of *Kallah*.

Oracles also consulted by the compiler of the Triple Tradition, and under the same subject-heading, both Jesus's pronouncement on Bartimaeus's inward sight and the blind man's cure which is mentioned in *Mark* viii. 22–26; and that he combined them. The circumstantial detail of the clay mixed with spittle and of the washing in the Pool of Siloam proves the authenticity of his material. But it also casts doubt on Bethsaida ('The House of Fisheries') in Galilee as the setting of the original cure; the Pool of Bethesda ('The House of Mercy') in Jerusalem (*John* v. 2), where the cripple was healed, is a far more likely setting. The 'troubling' of the pool may have been caused by a sudden subaqueous inrush of water. The *five* porches mentioned symbolize, perhaps, God's mercy as shown in the five books of the Law; and to divert attention from his cure, Jesus seems to have ordered the blind man to wash in the Pool of Siloam, where no miracles were expected, rather than in the Pool of Bethesda.

(*g*) The close association of the lame with the blind in *Matthew* xi. 4, *Luke* xiv. 13, and elsewhere—influenced by *Job* xxix. 15: 'I was eyes to the blind, feet to the lame'—suggests that *a* blind man and *a* lame man, of the many who waited for the movement of the waters at Bethesda, were healed by Jesus on the same day. Since both, clearly, expected to be cured by miraculous means (*John* v. 4), it is likely that their disabilities were the result of nervous shock rather than of disease or physical injury. Cases of 'psychological amaurosis' are not uncommon. Two of the best-known instances are Adolf Hitler's, while serving as a stretcher-bearer in World War I, and Saul's on the road to Damascus* (*see* cxviii.*k*). Clinical records show that, in most cases, the return of sight is a gradual process; the amaurotic is first aware of a mist, or film, over his field of vision. Paul's 'scales' (*Acts* ix. 18) probably refer to the flakes of mica used in lanterns, through which the light shines cloudily (1 *Corinthians* xiii. 12). Thus, in *Mark* viii. 24, the first stage of the blind man's recovery was 'seeing men as trees walking'. In *John* ix. 18–20, the editor is at pains to prove that the man of Bethesda was born blind, by citing the evidence of his parents; but, had he been, he would not, of course, have known what trees look like.

(*h*) Psychological paralytics are regularly cured at Lourdes, Monte Allegre, Fatima and other Catholic shrines. But after thirty-eight years (*John* v. 5) the leg-muscles of the cripple would have been atrophied and could not have obeyed him at once; it has been sensibly suggested that the thirty-eight years are symbolic of the Israelites' enforced wait before they might cross the brook Zered (*Deuteronomy* ii. 14); if so, Jesus, not the cripple, will have quoted this text, which was most apposite to the occasion. 'Take up thy bed and walk!' is a borrowing from *Mark* ii. 11 (*see* xxxv.*c*), where it is more to the point. The original sequence may have run as follows:

(312) *As Jesus went out from Jericho with his disciples, being in the midst of a great throng that went towards Jerusalem, one Bartimaeus (which is*

---

* The account of the amaurosis inflicted on Elymas, the sorcerer, at Paphos is, as Hilgenfeld has suggested, perhaps no more than a caricature of Paul's (*Acts* xiii. 16).

the Son of Uncleanness) sat begging by the highway, and he was blind from birth.

The same, when he heard that Jesus of Nazara was passing by, began to cry out for alms, saying: 'Have mercy upon me, Jesus! Have mercy upon me, thou anointed Son of David!'

And Jesus, giving him alms, charged him to hold his peace. But he cried the more: 'Thou anointed Son of David, blessed be thou!'

The disciples ask Jesus of the same Bartimaeus: 'Master, which hath sinned, this man or his parents, that he should be blind?'

Jesus answered: 'Neither he nor his parents, but this is done that the works of God might be manifested in him.

'For God of His compassion hath given him inward sight.'

* * * * *

(290) There is at Jerusalem by the sheep-market a pool called Bethesda (which is the Pool of Mercy), having five porches.

(For this is a parable of God's mercy towards the sheep of his hand; it lieth as a pool of healing amid the five books of the Law.)

In this place were gathered together a great multitude of impotent folk, the blind, the lame, and the withered, awaiting a troubling of the water.

For at a certain season an angel went down into the pool and troubled it; then whosoever first entered the water trusted to be healed of his infirmity.

And Jesus finding there a man which was crippled of both his legs, asked: 'How long hast thou lain here?'

He answered: 'For a great while, Master. Behold, I have no fellow to put me into the pool when it is troubled, and while I drag myself thither, another forestalleth me.'

Jesus said: 'It is written that Israel came to the waters of Zered, but was not suffered to wet her feet therein until all that was evil in her had perished.

'Therefore our fathers waited patiently for eight-and-thirty years, until at the last they were freed of their former evil and passed through and entered into the kingdom of their desire.'

The man answered: 'So be it with me!'

And Jesus, when he heard these words, prayed to God and laid his hands upon the man, and healed him, so that he stood upon his feet and walked.

And Jesus said: 'Go now, and make a thank-offering in the Temple.'

But meeting him there after a little while, he said: 'Behold, thou art made whole; sin no more lest a worse thing come upon thee!'

* * * * *

(291) Also among them that waited in Bethesda was a blind man. And his fellows, which brought him there, came unto Jesus and besought him urgently, saying: 'Lord, pray that our fellow may be healed!'

He answered: 'According to your faith be it unto him.'

And they call the blind man, saying: 'Be of good comfort, rise; he calleth thee!'

Then the blind man cast away the garment in which he was wrapped, and arose and came unto Jesus.

And Jesus said: 'What wilt thou of me?'

He answered: 'That through thee I may receive my sight of God.'

Then Jesus took the blind man by the hand and led him out from the city, to a place apart where he spat upon the ground and made clay of the spittle.

And, having anointed the blind man's eyes therewith, he prayed to God in silence and afterwards asked him whether he saw aught.

And he looked up, and said: 'I see men as trees walking.'

Then Jesus said: 'Go, wash in the Pool of Siloam and say no word to any man as thou goest, but return to me again.'

He went his way therefore, and washed, and returned seeing clearly. And he praised Jesus for what he had done.

But Jesus said: 'Give God the praise, not me which am a sinner. If any man worship God and do His will, to him will He hearken.'

* * * * *

(*i*) The following should be added to the report of John the Baptist's disciples (*see* xxxix.*c*) :

(125) *And they said also: 'Was it not of him that Job spake saying: "I was eyes to the blind, and feet to the lame; I was a father to the poor. The blessing of him that was ready to perish came upon me, and I caused the widow's heart to sing with joy"?'*

* * * * *

The disciples' report that Jesus had 'caused the widow's heart to sing with joy' may have influenced the ascription to him of Elijah's miracle at Shunem (*see* xxxviii. *b*).

* * * * *

XLI

JOHN IS TAKEN

Mark vi. 17–20

[17]For Herod himself had sent forth and laid hold upon John and bound him in prison for Herodias' sake, his brother Philip's wife: for he had married her. [18]For John had said unto Herod, It is not lawful for thee to have thy brother's wife. [19]Therefore Herodias had a quarrel against him, and would have killed him; but she could not. [20]For Herod feared John, knowing that he was a just man and an holy, and observed him; and when he heard him, he did many things, and heard him gladly.

Matthew xiv. 1–5

[1]At that time Herod the tetrarch heard of the fame of Jesus, [2]and said unto his servants: 'This is John the Baptist; he is risen from the dead; and therefore mighty works do shew forth themselves in him.' [3]For Herod had laid hold on John, and bound him, and put him in prison for Herodias' sake, his brother Philip's wife. [4]For John said unto him: 'It is not lawful for thee to have her.' [5]And when he would have put him to death, he feared the multitude, because they counted him as a prophet.

Luke iii. 19–20

[19]But Herod the tetrarch, being reproved by him for Herodias his brother Philip's wife, and for all the evils which Herod had done, [20]added yet this above all, that he shut up John in prison.

John iii. 24

For John was not yet cast into prison.

(*a*) Herod Antipas, tetrarch of Galilee since the death of his father Herod the Great in 4 B.C., had divorced the daughter of King Aretas IV of Nabataea (*see* LXXVI.*a and* LXXXVI.*b*); he had then according to Josephus (*Antiquities* xviii. 5. 4), married Herodias, his sister-in-law and first cousin, before the death of her husband, his half-brother Herod Philip, in defiance of the Mosaic Law (*Leviticus* xviii. 16 and *Deuteronomy* xxv. 5). Josephus also writes (*Antiquities* xviii. 5. 2) that Antipas imprisoned John in the fortress of Machaerus on the eastern shore of the Dead Sea as a 'disturber of the people, who seemed ready to do anything he should advise'—even to rising in rebellion. But nowhere in the *Antiquities* are these two events connected, nor does the Greek version of the *Jewish Wars* mention either of them.

(b) According, however, to the Slavonic translation of the *Jewish Wars* (*Codex Mosc. Acad.* 651 and *Codex Synod. Mosc.* 770), Antipater's marriage to Herodias took place after Herod Philip's death, when she already had four children by him, so that Antipas could not have contracted a Levirate marriage under the terms of *Deuteronomy* xxv. 5 and 'raised up seed unto his brother'; the alliance was therefore incestuous. This version of *Josephus* makes John denounce the marriage in so forthright a manner that Antipas first had him beaten and ejected from his palace, and finally, when he persisted in his denunciations, executed. It also states that John never ate bread, not even the unleavened Passover bread—which he regarded as a special dispensation for the Exodus 'because of the troublesomeness of the journey', and not as an annual institution.

None of the Gospels mentions whether Antipas married Herodias before or after the death of her husband. But if, as is possible, a Christian editor has altered the text of *Antiquities* xviii. 5. 4 which, originally, must have corresponded with that of the Slavonic *Wars,* he will have converted Antipas's crime into one readily recognized as immoral even by non-Jewish readers. Under Roman law, no objection was raised to marriage with a brother's widow, however many children she might have, but it was incest to marry one's mother, daughter, sister, half-sister, niece*, step-daughter, aunt, mother-in-law, or the wife of a still living brother.

> (134) *At this time Herod Antipas sent forth and laid hold on John and bound him in the Castle of Machaerus for Herodias's sake, the widow of his brother Herod Philip, which he had married.*
>
> *For John had stirred up the people against Herod, testifying of the many evil things that he did, and saying: 'He hath uncovered the nakedness of his brother's wife, and this was done for carnal lust, not that he might raise up seed unto his brother, as the Law requireth. Already she hath issue of Philip, namely four children.*
>
> *'Shall this man continue to rule over us?'*
>
> *And he spake these things to Herod himself and would not be silent, though many stripes were laid upon him.*
>
> *Therefore Herod would have put him to death, but that he feared the multitude because they accounted him a prophet.*

* * * * *

(c) [Here follows *Mark* i. 14–15 and *Matthew* iv. 12–17: how Jesus went into Galilee to preach repentance (*see* XLII.*a–c*).]

For *Matthew* xiv. 1–2—*see* LXXVII.*f.*

* * * * *

---

* Until Claudius married his niece Agrippina. Uncle-niece marriage was, however, permitted among the Jews (*see* VIII.*u*), as was marriage with a paternal half-sister (*Genesis* xx. 12).

XLII

THE UNCLEAN SPIRIT

Mark i. 14–15

[14]Now after that John was put in prison, Jesus came into Galilee, preaching the Gospel of the kingdom of God, [15]and saying: 'The time is fulfilled, and the kingdom of God is at hand: repent ye, and believe the Gospel.'

Mark i. 21–39

[21]And they went into Capernaum; and straightway on the sabbath day He entered into the synagogue, and taught, [22]and they were astonished at His doctrine; for He taught them as one that had authority, and not as the scribes. [23]And there was in their synagogue a man with an unclean spirit; and he cried out, [24]saying: 'Let us alone; what have we to do with Thee, Thou Jesus of Nazareth? art Thou come to destroy us? I know Thee who Thou art, the Holy One of God.' [25]And Jesus rebuked him, saying: 'Hold thy peace, and come out of him.' [26]And when the unclean spirit had torn him, and cried with a loud voice, he came out of him. [27]And they were all amazed, insomuch that they questioned among themselves, saying: 'What thing is this? what new teaching is this? for with authority commandeth He even the unclean spirits, and they do obey Him.' [28]And immediately His fame spread abroad throughout all the region round about Galilee.

[29]And forthwith, when they were come out of the synagogue, they entered into the house of Simon, and Andrew, with James and John. [30]But Simon's wife's mother lay sick of a fever, and anon they tell Him of her. [31]And He came and took her by the hand, and lifted her up; and immediately the fever left her, and she ministered unto them.

[32]And at even, when the sun did set, they brought unto Him all that were diseased, and them that were possessed with devils. [33]And all the city was gathered together at the door. [34]And He healed many that were sick of divers diseases, and cast out many devils; and suffered not the devils to speak, because they knew Him.

[35]And in the morning, rising up a great while before day, He went out, and departed into a solitary place, and there prayed. [36]And Simon and they that were with Him followed after Him. [37]And when they had found Him, they said unto Him: 'All seek for Thee.'

[38]And He said unto them: 'Let us go into the next towns, that I may preach there also: for therefore came I forth.'

[39]And He preached in their synagogues throughout all Galilee, and cast out devils.

Mark iii. 7–8

[7]But Jesus withdrew Himself with His disciples to the sea: and a great multitude from Galilee followed Him, and from Judaea, [8]and from Jerusalem, and from Idumaea, and from beyond Jordan; and they about Tyre and Sidon, a great multitude, when they had heard what great things He did, came unto Him.

Matthew iv. 12–17

[12]Now when Jesus had heard that John was cast into prison, He departed into Galilee: [13]and leaving Nazareth, He came and dwelt in Capernaum, which is upon the sea coast, in the borders of Zebulun and Naphtali: [14]that it might be fulfilled which was spoken by Isaiah the prophet, saying:

[15]*The Land of Zebulun, and the land of Naphtali,*
By the way of the sea, beyond Jordan,
Galilee of the Gentiles;
[16]*The people which sat in darkness*
Saw great light;
And to them which sat in the region and shadow of death
Light is sprung up.

[17]From that time Jesus began to preach, and to say: 'Repent: for the kingdom of heaven is at hand.'

Matthew iv. 23–25

[23]And Jesus went about all Galilee, teaching in their synagogues, and preaching the Gospel of the Kingdom, and healing all manner of sickness and all manner of disease among the people. [24]And His fame went throughout all Syria: and they brought unto Him all sick people that were taken with divers diseases and torments, and those which were possessed with devils, and those which were lunatic, and those that had the palsy; and He healed them. [25]And there followed Him great multitudes of people from Galilee, and from Decapolis, and from Jerusalem, and from Judaea, and from beyond Jordan.

Matthew vii. 28–29

[28]And it came to pass, when Jesus had ended these sayings, the people were astonished at His teaching: [29]for He taught them as one having authority, and not as the scribes.

Matthew viii. 14–17

[14]And when Jesus was come into Peter's house, He saw his wife's mother laid, and sick of a fever. [15]And He touched her hand, and the fever left her: and she arose, and ministered unto them.

[16]When the even was come, they brought unto Him many that were possessed with devils: and He cast out the spirits with His word, and healed all that were sick: [17]that it might be fulfilled which was spoken by Isaiah the prophet, saying:

Himself took our infirmities, and bare our sicknesses.

Luke iv. 14–15

[14]And Jesus returned in the power of the Spirit into Galilee: and there went out a fame of Him through all the region round about. [15]And He taught in their synagogues, being glorified of all.

Luke iv. 31–44

[31]And He came down to Capernaum, a city of Galilee, and taught them on the sabbath days. [32]And they were astonished at His doctrine: for His word was with power. [33]And in the synagogue there was a man, which had a spirit of an unclean devil, and cried out with a loud voice, [34]saying: 'Let us alone; what have we to do with Thee, Thou Jesus of Nazareth? art Thou come to destroy us? I know Thee Who Thou art; the Holy One of God.' [35]And Jesus rebuked him, saying: 'Hold thy peace, and come out of him.' And when the devil had thrown him in the midst, he came out of him, and hurt him not. [36]And they were all amazed, and spake among themselves, saying: 'What a word is this! for with authority and power He commandeth the unclean spirits, and they come out.' [37]And the fame of Him went out into every place of the country round about.

[38]And He arose out of the synagogue, and entered into Simon's house. And Simon's wife's mother was taken with a great fever; and they besought Him for her. [39]And He stood over her, and rebuked the fever; and it left her: and immediately she arose and ministered unto them.

[40]Now when the sun was setting, all they that had any sick with divers diseases brought them unto Him; and He laid His hands on every one of them, and healed them. [41]And devils also came out of many, crying out, and saying, Thou art Christ the Son of God. And He rebuking them suffered them not to speak: for they knew that He was the Christ.

[42]And when it was day, He departed and went into a desert place: and the people sought Him, and came unto Him, and stayed Him, that He should not depart from them. [43]And He said unto them: 'I must preach the kingdom of God to other cities also: for therefore am I sent.' [44]And He preached in the synagogues of Galilee.

Luke vi. 17–18

[17]And He came down with them, and stood in the plain, and the company of His disciples, and a great multitude of people out of all Judaea and Jerusalem, and from the sea coast of Tyre and Sidon, which came to hear Him, and to be healed of their diseases, [18]and they that were vexed with unclean spirits: and they were healed.

(*a*) The imprisonment of John the Baptist (*see* xli.*a*) decided Jesus, who regarded him as Elijah, to emulate Elisha (2 *Kings* ii. 13–14) by taking up his fallen mantle. Hitherto he had preached salvation without any great sense of urgency; but now he must prophesy the imminent Pangs of the Messiah. (*b*) The point of the story (*Mark* i. 21–28 and *Luke* iv. 31–37) about the man with an unclean spirit is that he was the first to recognize Jesus as a king travelling incognito. The point of the story (*Mark* i. 29–31, *Matthew* viii. 14–15 and *Luke* iv. 38–39) about Peter's wife's mother, which *Matthew* places much later in Jesus's ministry, is precisely that it was Peter's wife's mother, and no one else, who had fever. Though *Luke* tells of a 'great fever', it may be assumed that she had none at all, and that this was her only means of expressing antagonism towards Jesus for having seduced Peter and Andrew from their trade and left the family in want; and that Jesus then broke down her antagonism and persuaded her to join the Sabbath meal. Perhaps he whispered in her ear *Psalm* xxxiv. 10: 'The young lions do lack and suffer hunger, but they that fear the Lord shall want no manner of thing that is good.'

(*c*) *Matthew* and *Luke* improve on *Mark's* account of how Jesus subsequently healed divers sick. *Mark* records that he healed *many* of all those brought to him, and that he did not allow the demons to speak; *Matthew* that they brought to him *all* those that were sick and that he healed them; *Luke,* that he laid his hands on *every one of them* and healed them, adding that many of the demons acknowledged him as the Messiah and had to be rebuked. *Isaiah* ix. 1–7, from which *Matthew* iv. 14–16 purports to be a quotation, is the prophet's consoling message to 'the people that walketh [not "sat"] in darkness,' that help is coming from the south—except Verse 1, which in the Hebrew text completes the prophecies of misfortune at the close of Chapter VIII, and which the Authorised Version, based on the Septuagint, mistranslates:

> Nevertheless the dimness shall not be such as was in her vexation, when at the first he lightly afflicted the land of Zebulun and the land of Naphtali and afterward did more grievously afflict her by way of the sea, beyond Jordan, in Galilee of the nations.

Glil ha' goyim, does not mean 'Galilee of the Gentiles', but 'the district of the nations', namely 'a district of mixed population' lying north-east of Galilee; and, with the help of the Hebrew scholars Rashi and Kimhi, the passage may be correctly translated as follows:

> For there is no faintness in him [the Assyrian King] who is vexing her [the land of Israel]; at first [the enemy, under Tiglath-Pileser], only lightly troubled the land of Zebulon and the land of Naphtali, but at a later time, [under Shalmaneser, the attacks] were more grievous. They came by way of the sea [of Gennesaret], beyond the Jordan in the district of the nations.

The only possible excuse for *Matthew's* free handling of this text is that, as C. H. Dodd has suggested, not every Gentile Christian Church could afford to buy the full Greek translation of the Old Testament, and Gospel editors therefore contented themselves with a popular *Anthology of Messianic Prophecies.* Here the anthologist, baffled by the obscurity of Isaiah's prophecy, may have amended it in a Christological sense and led *Matthew* astray.

(d) *Matthew* iv. 25 is more convincing than its preceding verse: 'the whole of Syria' is a gross exaggeration. Jerusalem, Decapolis, Peraea (Transjordania), and 'the coasts of Tyre and Sidon' were all within a hundred miles of Capernaum, but the province of Syria extended to the Orontes and Euphrates. *Mark* iii. 8, another version of this text, paralleled by *Luke* vi. 17, is credible only if 'the coasts of Tyre and Sidon' are interpreted as the Galilean-Phoenician frontier, rather than the sea-coast (*see* XVII.*a and* LVII.*a*).

(135) *Now, after that John was cast into prison, Jesus came into Galilee, preaching and proclaiming: 'The time is now fulfilled and the Kingdom of God is at hand.*

'Accept ye this gospel: that if ye repent, ye shall be saved by God's mercy.'

* * * * *

[Here follow various parables of warning, including that of the leafing fig, and of the man who built his house on sand (*see* XLVII.*b* and *c*).]

(142) *And Jesus came with his disciples to Capernaum, where presently he entered into the synagogue and preached repentance.*

But as he taught, a certain man that was possessed with an unclean spirit, cried out: 'Let us alone, Jesus of Nazara! What have we to do with thee?'

And when Jesus rebuked him, speaking as one with authority, the unclean spirit tore the man, and cried: 'Art thou come to destroy us? I know thee who thou art. Thou art the Holy One of Israel, the son of the Most High God!'

Jesus therefore spake to the evil spirit, saying: 'If the Father shew me favour, let Him suffer me to cast thee out of this man! Hold thy peace and be-gone!'

And the devil cried again with a loud voice and came forth.

Then were the people all amazed, and asked: 'What was this name by which the unclean spirit called him? And by what authority was he cast forth?'

* * * * *

(e) The following events seem to have taken place on another occasion:

(60) *It was a Sabbath, and when Jesus was come out of the synagogue, he entered into the house of Simon Peter and Andrew to eat bread, and James and John were with him.*

But Peter's wife's mother kept her bed and would do naught for them, no, not so much as arise to salute Jesus.

For since Peter and Andrew had left their nets and followed after him, she feared lest the household might lack and suffer hunger.

They tell Jesus: 'She hath a fever. It were well for thee to dine in the house of another.'

But Jesus went to where she lay on her bed, and took her by the hand and spake a word to her privily: how that they which fear the Lord shall want no manner of thing that is good.

And immediately she arose and ministered unto them.

* * * * *

(61) *And when the sun had set, the men of Capernaum brought unto Jesus many that were lunatic or possessed of evil spirits, and all the city was gathered together at his door.*

Then was it granted unto him to work cures upon them; but he suffered no man to name him Son of God, lest the matter should come to the ears of them that served the Wicked Kingdom.

And rising up a great while before day was come, he went out and departed unto a solitary place and there prayed.

But Peter and they that were with him followed after, and when they find him, they say: 'Master, all men seek for thee.'

He answered: 'Let us go into the next cities, that I may preach there also; for unto this end was I sent: to proclaim the acceptable year of the Lord, and the day of His vengeance.'

* * * * *

[Here follows Philip's request to be accepted as a disciple (*see* LVI.*h*).]

* * * * *

(63) *Jesus preached in the synagogues throughout Galilee, and his fame went forth even to the coasts of Tyre and Sidon. And it passed also through Decapolis and across Jordan and came unto Jerusalem.*

And great multitudes followed him.

* * * * *

(*f*) *Mark* i. 22 and *Matthew* vii. 29, 'For he taught as one that had authority, and not as the scribes,' is a mistranslation. 'And not as' could mean either that the scribes taught without authority, or that Jesus held different religious views from theirs; but both these implications must be rejected. It should, perhaps, read 'though not of': meaning that Jesus, although not a graduate of a law-school, was held to teach with undeniable authority. The explanation, according to the *Toldoth Yeshu,* was that he had studied privately under a tutor. Equal surprise at his masterly exposition of the Law is recorded in *John* vii. 15, where he is teaching in the Temple; but this must be a variant of the same text (*see* XCIV.*b*).

(64) *Which marvelled at his teaching, for he spake with authority, though not being of the scribes.*

* * * * *

XLIII

THE STRAIT GATE

Matthew vii. 13–14

[13]'Enter ye in at the strait gate: for wide is the gate, and broad the way, that leadeth to destruction, and many there be which go in thereat: [14]because strait is the gate, and narrow the way, which leadeth unto life, and few there be that find it.'

Luke xiii. 22–24

[22]And He went through the cities and villages, teaching, and journeying toward Jerusalem. [23]Then said one unto Him: 'Lord, are there few that be saved?' And He said unto them: [24]'Strive to enter in at the strait gate: for many, I say unto you, will seek to enter in, and shall not be able.'

Revelation iii. 20

Behold, I stand at the door, and knock: if any man hear My voice, and open the door, I will come in to him, and will sup with him, and he with Me.

(*a*) The *Midrash* on *Canticles* v. 2. 2. runs:

God said unto Israel: 'Open unto Me, make Me an opening for repentance, and though it be as strait as the needle's eye, yet will I open the door widely that wagons and chariots may enter and pass.'

This seems to be the very *midrash* misquoted in *Matthew* vii. 13–14 and *Luke* xiii. 24. The prophets used the word 'highway' to symbolize the way of repentance, not that of damnation: it is so used in *Jeremiah* xxxi. 21. One part of Jesus's allegory has been incorporated in *Revelation* iii. 20.

For the metaphor of the needle's eye—*see* LXXXII.*e* and LXXXIII.*g*.

(151) *And he went through the cities and villages teaching and journeying towards Jerusalem.*

And one of the disciples asked of him: 'Master, are there few that shall be saved?'

He answered and said: 'Knowest thou not the Song of Solomon, how that he cried to his beloved, saying: "Open unto me, my sister, my spouse," whereat she put her hand to the hole of the door, and opened it?

'Now, Solomon spake a parable of the Virgin of Israel which should open the door unto God.

'For God crieth: "Behold, I stand at the door and knock. Open unto Me,

make Me an opening for repentance, and though it be as strait as the needle's eye, yet will I open the door widely, that wagons and chariots may enter."

'*Yea, wide is the highway of repentance, of which the prophet Jeremiah spake, saying: "Set thine heart towards the highway, turn again, thou Virgin of Israel!"*'

* * * *

XLIV

THE LEAVEN

Matthew xiii. 33–35

[33]Another parable spake He unto them: 'The Kingdom of Heaven is like unto leaven, which a woman took, and hid in three measures of meal, till the whole was leavened.'

[34]All these things spake Jesus unto the multitude in parables; and without a parable spake He not unto them: [35]that it might be fulfilled which was spoken by the prophet, saying:

I will open my mouth in parables;
I will utter things which have been kept secret from the foundation of the world.

Luke xiii. 20–21

[20]And again He said: 'Whereunto shall I liken the kingdom of God? [21]It is like leaven, which a woman took and hid in three measures of meal, till the whole was leavened.'

Mark viii. 14–16

[14]Now the disciples had forgotten to take bread, neither had they in the boat with them more than one loaf. [15]And He charged them, saying: 'Take heed, beware of the leaven of the Pharisees, and of the leaven of Herod.' [16]And they reasoned among themselves, saying, 'It is because we have no bread.'

Matthew xvi. 6–8

[6]Then Jesus said unto them: 'Take heed and beware of the leaven of the Pharisees and of the Sadducees.' [7]And they reasoned among themselves, saying: 'It is because we have taken no bread.' [8]Which when Jesus perceived, He said unto them: 'O ye of little faith, why reason ye among yourselves, because ye have brought no bread?'

Luke xii. 1–3

[1]In the mean time, when there were gathered together an innumerable multitude of people, insomuch that they trod one upon another, He began to say unto His disciples first of all: 'Beware ye of the leaven of the Pharisees, which is hypocrisy. [2]For there is nothing covered, that shall not be revealed; neither hid, that shall not be known. [3]Therefore whatsoever ye have spoken in dark-

Luke xii. 1–3 (contd.)

ness shall be heard in the light; and that which ye have spoken in the ear in closets shall be proclaimed upon the housetops.'

1 Corinthians v. 1–8

[1]It is reported commonly that there is fornication among you, and such fornication as is not so much as named among the heathen, that one should have his father's wife. [2]And ye are puffed up, and have not rather mourned, that he that hath done this deed might be taken away from among you. [3]For I, absent in the body but present in spirit, have already (as though I were really present) judged him that hath so done this deed, [4]in the name of our Lord Jesus Christ, when ye are gathered together, and my spirit, with the power of our Lord Jesus Christ, [5]to deliver such an one unto Satan for the destruction of the flesh, that the spirit may be saved in the day of the Lord Jesus. [6]Your glorying is not good. Know ye not that a little leaven leaveneth the whole lump? [7]Purge out therefore the old leaven, that ye may be a new lump, as ye are unleavened. For our passover, even Christ, is sacrificed for us: [8]therefore let us keep the feast, not with old leaven, neither with the leaven of malice and wickedness; but with the unleavened bread of sincerity and truth.

Mark iv. 22

[22]For there is nothing hid, which shall not be manifested; neither was any thing kept secret, but that it should come abroad. If any man have ears to hear, let him hear.

Matthew x. 26–27

[26]Fear them not therefore: for there is nothing covered, that shall not be revealed; and hid, that shall not be known. [27]What I tell you in darkness, that speak ye in light: and what ye hear in the ear, that preach ye upon the housetops.

Luke viii. 17

[17]For nothing is secret, that shall not be made manifest; neither any thing hid, that shall not be known and come abroad.

(a) The Pharisees used leaven to symbolize evil impulses because of its association with the Feast of Unleavened Bread (see xxvii.d); or any process of degeneration, as when wine turns to vinegar; and, in 1 Corinthians v. 1–8, Paul followed their example. Matthew xiii. 33 is therefore likely to be a borrowing by a Grecian editor from Philo of Alexandria, who comments (Book i. 173) on the 'three measures of the soul that are kneaded like cakes wherein the sacred doctrine must be hidden.'

The warning against the leaven, that is to say, the animating spirit of evil in those hostile to the Kingdom, was probably addressed to the Twelve when they set out on their mission (see lvii.h). In Mark viii. 15, these enemies are called 'the Pharisees and Herod'; in Matthew xvi. 6, 'the Pharisees and Sadducees'; in Luke xii. 1, merely 'the Pharisees'. The original is likely to have been: 'the Sadducees and Herodians which ally themselves adulterously with the Wicked Kingdom [i.e. Rome].' 1 *Corinthians* v. 6 and 8 may be a quotation from this very saying, since in verse 4 Paul invokes Jesus's authority.

(*b*) We must here assume a *midrash* on *Hosea* vii. 4, where leaven and adultery are connected, and on *Amos* iv. 4–5, where the northern Israelites offer flesh-sacrifices together with leavened cakes, in breach of *Leviticus* vi. 14–16, thus adopting the idolatrous practices of Egypt and Ashdod.

> (169) *And because that these were the days of unleavened bread he taught them, saying:*
>
> '*Beware of the leaven of the Sadducees and Herodians, which watch not for the Kingdom of God, but adulterously ally themselves with the Wicked Kingdom, and sleep and are in danger of Gehenna.*
>
> '*For the prophet Amos saith: "Come to Bethel and transgress; at Gilgal multiply your transgression, and offer a burnt sacrifice of thanksgiving with leaven."*
>
> '*And likewise the prophet Hosea saith: "They are all adulterers, as the oven is heated by the baker, which kneadeth the dough until he hath leavened it and thereafter sleepeth all night, and in the morning it burneth like a flaming fire."*
>
> '*Know ye not that a little leaven leaveneth the whole lump? Therefore feed in your hearts upon the unleavened bread of righteousness.*'

* * * * *

(*c*) The arrangement of these Gospel texts is more than usually confused. A quotation from *Psalm* lxxviii. 2, in *Matthew* xiii. 35, represents part of another *midrash* connected with Jesus's order to keep God's secrets for the Israelites only (*see* LXXXIV.*f and g*). This may be deduced from the saying in *Luke* xii. 2 which, however, in *Mark* iv. 22, succeeds the parable of the Lamp (as also in *Luke* viii. 17—*see* XXIV.*a*), and in *Matthew* x. 26 succeeds the warning against Beelzebub. *Matthew* xiii. 34 refers to another incident altogether (*see* XVII.*g*): Jesus's defence of his habitual use of parables.

> (208) '*David saith also: "Give ear, O my people, to my Law, incline your ears to the words of my mouth.*
>
> '"*I will open my mouth in a parable, I will utter dark sayings of old which our fathers have told us.*
>
> '"*We will not hide them from our children, but shew to the generation to come the praises of the Lord and His strength and His wonderful works."*
>
> '*For now there is nothing covered that shall not be revealed, neither hid that shall not be known.*'

* * * * *

(*d*) The next verse, though clearly belonging to a different context, must have been found in the Oracles attached to the preceding one, under the subject-heading 'Dark Sayings'. It probably introduced the royal entry into Jerusalem (*see* LXXXIX.*h*).

(317) *Then he called the Twelve unto him and said: 'What I have told you in darkness, that speak ye now in light; what ye whispered in the ear, that shout ye now from the housetops!'*

* * * * *

(e) *Matthew* x. 27 is more acceptable than *Luke* xii. 3, where an editor has taken the 'dark sayings' to mean wicked secrets, and not the divine parables of *Psalm* lxxviii. The change from the psalmist's 'dark sayings of old' to 'things that have been kept secret from the foundation of the world' (*Matthew* xiii. 35), is Christological: Jesus is made to claim that he was 'begotten before all the world' and therefore knows all its arcana.

(f) *Mark* viii. 14, where the disciples forget to bring bread, paralleled in *Matthew* xvi. 5-8, should preface Jesus's walking on the water (*see* LXXIII.*a-e*).

* * * * *

THE MUSTARD SEED

Mark iv. 30–32

30And He said: 'Whereunto shall we liken the kingdom of God? or with what comparison shall we compare it? 31It is like a grain of mustard seed, which, when it is sown in the earth, is less than all the seeds that be in the earth: 32but when it is sown, it groweth up, and becometh greater than all herbs and shooteth out great branches; so that the fowls of the air may lodge under the shadow of it.'

Matthew xiii. 31–32

31Another parable put He forth unto them, saying: 'The Kingdom of Heaven is like to a grain of mustard seed, which a man took, and sowed in his field; 32which indeed is the least of all seeds: but when it is grown, it is the greatest among herbs, and becometh a tree, so that the birds of the air come and lodge in the branches thereof.'

Luke xiii. 18–19

18Then said He: 'Unto what is the kingdom of God like? and whereunto shall I resemble it? 19It is like a grain of mustard seed, which a man took, and cast into his garden; and it grew, and waxed a great tree; and the fowls of the air lodged in the branches of it.'

Mark xi. 22–24

22And Jesus answering saith unto them: 'Have faith in God. 23For verily I say unto you, that whosoever shall say unto this mountain, Be thou removed, and be thou cast into the sea; and shall not doubt in his heart, but shall believe that those things which he saith shall come to pass; he shall have whatsoever he saith. 24Therefore I say unto you, what things soever ye desire, when ye pray, believe that ye receive them, and ye shall have them.'

Matthew xvii. 20

20And Jesus said unto them: 'Because of your unbelief: for verily I say unto you, if ye have faith as a grain of mustard seed, ye shall say unto this mountain, remove hence to yonder place; and it shall remove; and nothing shall be impossible unto you.'

Matthew xxi. 21–22

21Jesus answered and said unto them: 'Verily I say unto you, if ye have faith, and doubt not, ye shall not only do this which is done to the fig tree, but also

Matthew xxi. 21–22 (contd.)

if ye shall say unto this mountain, be thou removed, and be thou cast into the sea; it shall be done. [22]And all things, whatsoever ye shall ask in prayer, believing, ye shall receive.'

Luke xvii. 5–6

[5]And the Apostles said unto the Lord: 'Increase our faith.' [6]And the Lord said: 'If ye had faith as a grain of mustard seed, ye might say unto this sycamine tree, Be thou plucked up by the root, and be thou planted in the sea; and it should obey you.'

(a) The intemperate promise with which Jesus is credited in *Luke* xvii. 6 can be traced back through most of its stages to a simple and devout original.

Mark iv. 30–32 is a parable—occurring among others also concerned with seed—about the surprising results of a single brief missionary message. In the Talmud (*Berakoth* 40a), 'a grain of mustard' is similarly used for 'a minute amount'; and it is a fact that the plant may rise to twice the height of a man and flocks of birds alight in its branches to eat the seeds. But the editor of *Matthew* xiii. 31–32 has tried to improve on *Mark* by having a farmer sow the mustard—unaware that the Palestinian variety (*brassica nigra*) was a weed, not a field crop.

(b) The parable of the Mustard Seed is a *midrash* on what was regarded as a Messianic prophecy in *Ezekiel* xvii. 22–23. In *Luke* xiii. 18–19 it has been separated from the seed-sowing context, though part of the *Ezekiel* quotation still clings to it; and 'greater than all herbs' (*Mark* iv. 32) has consequently been altered to 'a great tree'. This parable also accounts for the mustard seed mentioned in Matthew xvii. 20 and Luke xvii. 6, a pronouncement on the faith that removes mountains. The corresponding text in *Mark* xi. 22–24, which is a *midrash* on *Job* ix. 5–8, makes no mention of mustard seed; yet the parable and the pronouncement will have been originally connected thus:

(196) *And he strengthened their spirits saying: 'Ezekiel prophesied of the tender twig that the Lord shall plant: "In the mountain of the height of Israel will I plant it, and it shall bring forth boughs and bear fruit and it shall be a goodly cedar tree, and under it shall be gathered all birds of every wing."*

'And though the work that ye are sent to do be as a grain of mustard seed, which is among the least of seeds that the earth yields,

'Yet when the grain is sown it sprouteth and runneth up and becometh greater than all other herbs; it throweth forth branches like unto a tree, and to them likewise shall the birds of the air be gathered.

'Have faith therefore in God whose Kingdom ye preach. Of Him Job prophesieth, saying: "He removeth the mountains, He casteth the earth out of her place, He treadeth upon the waves of the sea."

'And He shall also hearken unto your prayers.'

* * * * *

(c) The prayers will have been for the speedy coming of the Kingdom (*see* xxvii.*b*), not for the thaumaturgic removal of mountains.

(*d*) Evidently the second part of the above *midrash* appeared in the Oracles consulted by the compiler of the Triple Tradition, under the subject-heading 'Sown Seed'. But the editor of *Mark* xi. 22–24 seems to have found the whole of it, though in abridged form, in another collection under the subject-heading 'Fruitful Trees'. This led him into an unfortunate error: he identified the great cedar-tree of the Kingdom of God with the fig-tree later barked by Jesus (*see* cIII.*d*), and made this act of summary vengeance illustrate what faith in God might accomplish. His mistake was adopted in *Matthew* xxi. 21–22; and though a later editor, fearing that something was amiss, transferred it to the more appropriate context of the lunatic child healed by faith (*Matthew* xvii. 20—*see* LXXIX.*c*), the earlier version has survived.

(*e*) *Luke* xvii. 6 is now easier to understand, if we assume an original borrowing from *Mark* xi. 22–24. An early editor decided that the fig-tree's summary destruction contradicted the parable (*Luke* xiii. 6–9—*see* xvi.*a*) of the barren fig-tree which was promised another chance to fruit. In order to resolve this contradiction, he wrote an ingenious gloss in the margin of his Gospel: *'No; it was a sycomore!'*—meaning a 'fig-mulberry' (*see* xx.*b*), a tree with leaves resembling the mulberry's and a fig-like fruit. Jesus's promise thus remained good: the fig-tree would have another chance, but the sycomore was entitled to no such indulgence (*see* xIx.*g*). A later, and more than usually obtuse, editor misunderstood the reference: he took the gloss to mean that the sycomore, not the mountain, should be cast into the sea as a punishment for its barrenness, and amended the text accordingly. A still later editor then expunged the whole incident of the barked tree and misread *sycomore*, 'fig-mulberry', as *sycamine*, 'mulberry'—a mistake hallowed by the Septuagint translation of several passages in the Old Testament (*see* cIII.*b*). By this time all reference to prayer had dropped out: and the disciples were sanctioned to perform promiscuous acts of destructive magic in Jesus's name.

* * * * *

XLVI

GUESTS

Matthew xxii. 1–14

[1]And Jesus answered and spake unto them again by parables, and said: [2]'The Kingdom of Heaven is like unto a certain king, which made a marriage for his son, [3]and sent forth his servants to call them that were bidden to the wedding: and they would not come. [4]Again, he sent forth other servants, saying, Tell them which are bidden, Behold, I have prepared my dinner: my oxen and my fatlings are killed, and all things are ready: come unto the marriage. [5]But they made light of it, and went their ways, one to his farm, another to his merchandise: [6]and the remnant took his servants, and entreated them spitefully, and slew them. [7]But when the king heard thereof, he was wroth: and he sent forth his armies, and destroyed those murderers, and burned up their city. [8]Then saith he to his servants, The wedding is ready, but they which were bidden were not worthy. [9]Go ye therefore into the highways, and as many as ye shall find, bid to the marriage. [10]So those servants went out into the highways, and gathered together all as many as they found, both bad and good: and the wedding was furnished with guests. [11]And when the king came in to see the guests he saw there a man which had not on a wedding garment: [12]and he saith unto him, Friend, how camest thou in hither not having a wedding garment? And he was speechless. [13]Then said the king to the servants, Bind him hand and foot, and take him away, and cast him into outer darkness; there shall be weeping and gnashing of teeth. [14]For many are called, but few are chosen.'

Luke xiv. 1

[1]And it came to pass, as He went into the house of one of the chief Pharisees to eat bread on the sabbath day, that they watched Him.

Luke xiv. 7–24

[7]And He put forth a parable to those which were bidden, when He marked how they chose out the chief rooms; saying unto them: [8]'When thou art bidden of any man to a wedding, sit not down in the highest room; lest a more honourable man than thou be bidden of him; [9]and he that bade thee and him come and say to thee, Give this man place; and thou begin with shame to take the lowest room. [10]But when thou art bidden, go and sit down in the lowest room; that when he that bade thee cometh, he may say unto thee, Friend, go up higher: then shalt thou have worship in the presence of them that sit at

Luke xiv. 7–24 (*contd.*)

meat with thee. ¹¹For whosoever exalteth himself shall be abased; and he that humbleth himself shall be exalted.'

¹²Then said He also to him that bade Him: 'When thou makest a dinner or a supper, call not thy friends, nor thy brethren, neither thy kinsmen, nor thy rich neighbours; lest they also bid thee again, and a recompense be made thee. ¹³But when thou makest a feast, call the poor, the maimed, the lame, the blind: ¹⁴and thou shalt be blessed; for they cannot recompense thee: for thou shalt be recompensed at the resurrection of the just.'

¹⁵And when one of them that sat at meat with Him heard these things, he said unto Him: 'Blessed is he that shall eat bread in the kingdom of God.' ¹⁶Then said He unto him: 'A certain man made a great supper, and bade many: ¹⁷and sent his servant at supper time to say to them that were bidden, Come; for all things are now ready. ¹⁸And they all with one consent began to make excuse. The first said unto him, I have bought a piece of ground, and I must needs go and see it: I pray thee have me excused. ¹⁹And another said, I have bought five yoke of oxen, and I go to prove them: I pray thee have me excused. ²⁰And another said, I have married a wife, and therefore I cannot come. ²¹So that servant came, and shewed his lord these things. Then the master of the house being angry said to his servant, Go out quickly into the streets and lanes of the city, and bring in hither the poor, and the maimed, and the halt, and the blind. ²²And the servant said, Lord, it is done as thou hast commanded, and yet there is room. ²³And the lord said unto the servant, Go out into the highways and hedges, and compel them to come in, that my house may be filled. ²⁴For I say unto you, that none of those men which were bidden shall taste of my supper.'

(*a*) The editor of *Matthew* xxii. 1–14 has run together two separate *midrashim;* and the editor of *Luke* xiv. 7–24, three, including one of *Matthew's.* All must have been originally found in a collection of Oracles under the subject-heading 'Guests at a Feast'.

(*b*) *Matthew* xxii. 1–5 and 9–10, a *midrash* on *Proverbs* ix. 2, is Jesus's justification of his missionary preaching in the alleys of Jerusalem, delivered when certain of the well-to-do would not listen to him. *Matthew* xxii. 7–8 (omitted in the corresponding passage of *Luke*), is a clumsy intrusion based on Jesus's parable of the King's Son (*Mark* xii. 1–9—*see* xcvi.*a–c*) and aimed at persecutors of the early Gentile Church. The excuses offered by the guests are incompatible with a summons to a royal wedding; no motive is suggested for the killing of the servants; and the king's despatch of armies to burn down the entire city would have been an act of madness. Though the occasion in *Luke* xiv. 16–24 is a simple supper, *Matthew's* version has been influenced by the Lamb's Wedding Feast in *Revelation* xix. 9, and by the Destruction of Jerusalem, which seemed a judgement on the Jews for severing all connection with the Gentile Church.

(*c*) *Matthew* xxii. 11–13, a separate parable and probably a *midrash* on *Ecclesiastes* ix. 8, further confuses the story—guests dragged in from the highways could not be expected to possess wedding garments. The editor was aware of this difficulty and, at least, toned down the 'highways and hedges' preserved in *Luke* xiv. 23. Moreover, to bridge the two parables, he has borrowed 'both good and bad' from *Matthew* xiii. 47–48, and inserted it into *Matthew* xxii. 10. But by doing so he contradicts the Ebionite moral of the first: namely, that the proud and rich shall be deprived of their places at the heavenly feast while the meek and poor shall be welcomed. The white wedding-garment denotes purity. *Matthew* xxii. 14: 'For many are called, but few are chosen,' which occurs out of context in *Matthew* xx. 16, at the close of the Vineyard parable (*see* LVIII.*a*), is equally inappropriate as a comment on this feast, which was well attended by the meek and poor. But it may easily be Jesus's answer to his fellow-guest's pious ejaculation in *Luke* xiv. 15, which referred to the other saying about guests at a feast.

(*d*) The setting in *Luke* xiv. 1 is a Sabbath Day dinner with a Pharisee. 'They watched him', in verse 1, unfairly suggests that the Pharisees had invited Jesus not from kindliness, but because they hoped that he would commit some overt breach of the Law; that, in fact, they had by no means forgiven the violent rebuke with which he is credited in *Luke* xi. 37–39 (*see* XIII.*q*).

For the otherwise unrecorded account of how a dropsical man was healed, *see* LXXIV.*f*.

(*e*) *Luke* xiv. 7–10 is a *midrash* on *Proverbs* xxv. 6–7; and verse 11 combines *Psalm* xviii. 27 with *Job* xxii. 29. The Talmudic equivalent is *Leviticus Rabbah* i. 5:

> 'Hillel said: "When I humble myself I am exalted; and contrariwise."
> 'Shimeon ben Azzai [one of Hillel's successors] commented: "Refrain from taking thy due seat; but sit one, two, or three seats lower. There wait until they call to thee: 'Come up higher!' Come not up above thy due seat, lest afterwards thou be told: 'Make place!' For it is better to hear 'Come up higher!' than 'Make place, make place!' " '

Luke xiv. 12–14 is a *midrash* on *Nehemiah* viii. 10–12.

(*f*) *Luke* xiv. 15–21 is a less confused version of *Matthew* xxii. 1–10; verses 22–24, as also verse 8 in *Matthew's* version, are a late interpolation, paralleled in *Matthew* xxi. 43–44, completely disinheriting the Jews from the Kingdom of God, and also threatening Gentiles with hell fire if they reject their invitation to the Wedding Feast of the Lamb. In *Matthew's* version, there is no mention of the 'halt, maimed, and blind', who have been gratuitously introduced into *Luke* xiv. 21 from *John* v. 3; the late editor of *Luke* who made this change was confident that Jesus would have extended the wedding invitation not only to the poor and hungry, but also to the deformed. He did not understand that 'poor' meant 'the poor in spirit' and that 'hungry' meant 'those hungry for righteousness' (*see* IX.*c*)—a context into which the blind and maimed are most awkwardly introduced.

The guests' excuses in *Luke* xiv. 18–20 are carelessly reported. No man in his senses would buy a plot of land without first viewing it, or five yoke of oxen without testing their strength. And the man who had married probably pleaded the dispensation of *Deuteronomy* xxiv. 5: 'When a man hath taken a new wife, he shall not go out to war, neither shall he be charged with any business; he shall be free at home one year, and shall cheer up his wife whom he hath taken.'

(163) *On a sabbath day, when Jesus dined with a rich man of Jerusalem, the same asked him:* 'Friend, why preachest thou in the streets and lanes of this city?'

Jesus answered and said: 'Solomon prophesied that the poor of Jerusalem shall inherit everlasting life if they do but hearken to the voice of Wisdom.

'For she crieth in these streets, saying: "Wisdom hath killed her fatlings, she hath mingled her wine and also furnished her table.

' "She hath sent forth her maidens, she crieth upon the highest places of the city: 'Whoso is simple, let him turn in hither!'

' "And to him that is poor of understanding, she saith: 'Come, eat of my bread and drink of the wine which I have mingled. Forsake the foolish and live, and go in the way of understanding.' "

'For the foolish are the rich that hearken not unto her voice, but are busied with the cares of this world.

'Therefore, the Kingdom of Heaven is like unto one that prepared a great supper and invited many, and sent a servant at supper time to say: "Come, for all is now ready!"

'But they began with one consent to make excuses. The first said: "A piece of ground is offered for sale and I must view it forthwith, lest I lose the occasion of purchase. I pray thee, have me excused."

'Another said: "I have bought five yoke of oxen on a pledge that, if they serve not my purpose, their price shall be restored to me tomorrow; therefore I must go to prove them. I pray thee, have me excused."

'A third said: "I have lately married a wife and am wearied with feasting. Moreover, the Law biddeth me to stay at home and cheer up my wife which I have taken. I pray thee, have me excused."

'When the servant came and told his master these words, the master, being angry, said unto him: "Go out quickly into the streets and lanes of the city, and bring hither whatsoever poor and hungry thou mayest find, until all the places be filled!"'

* * * * *

(164) *Jesus said again:* 'In the day when Ezra the scribe first read the Law to our fathers, after that they returned unto Jerusalem from captivity, Nehemiah and Ezra beheld how the people wept.

'Then said they: "This day is holy to the Lord, therefore weep not, but go your way, eat the fat and drink the sweet. Yet send portions of your feast unto him for whom nothing is prepared."

'Wherefore, when thou preparest a supper, call not thy brethren, nor thy kinsmen, nor thy rich neighbours, hoping that they will bid thee in return.

But rather call the poor unto thy table, and thou shalt be blessed; for though they cannot recompense thee, thou shalt be recompensed at the resurrection of the just.'

* * * *

(165) *The rich man which heard these things sighed, and said unto Jesus: 'Blessed is he that shall eat bread in the Kingdom of Heaven.' Jesus answered: 'Many are called, but few are chosen.'*

* * * *

(86) *Jesus said also: 'Hearken unto the words of the Preacher: "Go thy way, eat thy bread, drink thy wine with a merry heart, for God now accepteth thy works. Let thy garment be always white and let thy head lack no ointment."*

'For to obey the Law is to be clothed in purity as in a linen garment; and to hearken unto the prophets is to be anointed with God's mercy as with ointment. Thus doing shalt thou rejoice as a guest rejoiceth at a wedding feast.

'Take heed therefore: behold, the Kingdom of Heaven is like unto a King that went to view the guests at the wedding feast to which he had called them.

'Among whom was one that had not on a wedding garment.

'And he said unto him: "Friend, how camest thou in hither not wearing a wedding garment?" And he was speechless.

'Then said the King unto his servants: "Bind him hand and foot and take him away! Cast him into outer darkness; there shall he weep and gnash his teeth!"'

* * * *

(g) The following belongs to the Wedding of Cana (*see* x.c) :

(67)*And when Jesus marked how they which were bidden to the wedding chose out the chief seats, he taught them, saying: 'Solomon spake a proverb: "Put not forth thyself in the presence of the king, and stand not in the place of great men.*

'"For better it is that it be said unto thee: 'Come up hither,' than that thou shouldest be put lower in the presence of the prince whom thine eyes have seen."

'And Job declareth: "When men are cast down then shalt thou say: 'There is lifting up, and He shall save the humble person.'"

'Verily, I say unto you: as it is in the presence of the prince whom thine eyes have seen, so shall it also be in the presence of Him whom they have not seen!

'For whosoever exalteth himself shall be abased; and he that humbleth himself shall be exalted.

'As David saith: "For Thou wilt save the afflicted people and bring down high lords."'

* * * *

Jesus uses 'The prince whom thine eyes have seen' as a synonym for the bridegroom who, at the wedding feast, was treated as a king.

* * * *

XLVII

TREE, ROCK, AND PEARLS

Matthew vii. 6

[6]Give not that which is holy unto the dogs, neither cast ye your pearls before swine, lest they trample them under their feet, and turn again and rend you.

Matthew vii. 15–20

[15]'Beware of false prophets, which come to you in sheep's clothing, but inwardly they are ravening wolves. [16]Ye shall know them by their fruits. Do men gather grapes of thorns, or figs of thistles? [17]Even so every good tree bringeth forth good fruit; but a corrupt tree bringeth forth evil fruit. [18]A good tree cannot bring forth evil fruit, neither can a corrupt tree bring forth good fruit. [19]Every tree that bringeth not forth good fruit is hewn down, and cast into the fire. [20]Wherefore by their fruits ye shall know them.'

Matthew xii. 33–37

[33]'Either make the tree good, and its fruit good; or else make the tree corrupt, and its fruit corrupt: for the tree is known by its fruit. [34]O generation of vipers, how can ye, being evil, speak good things? for out of the abundance of the heart the mouth speaketh. [35]A good man out of the good treasure of the heart bringeth forth good things: and an evil man out of the evil treasure bringeth forth evil things. [36]But I say unto you, that every idle word that men shall speak, they shall give account thereof in the day of judgement. [37]For by thy words thou shalt be justified, and by thy words thou shalt be condemned.'

Matthew vii. 24–27

[24]'Therefore whosoever heareth these sayings of Mine, and doeth them, I will liken him unto a wise man, which built his house upon a rock: [25]and the rain descended, and the floods came, and the winds blew, and beat upon that house; and it fell not: for it was founded upon a rock. [26]And every one that heareth these sayings of Mine, and doeth them not, shall be likened unto a foolish man, which built his house upon the sand: [27]and the rain descended, and the floods came, and the winds blew, and beat upon that house; and it fell: and great was the fall of it.'

Matthew xiii. 44–46

[44]'Again, the Kingdom of Heaven is like unto treasure hid in a field; the which when a man hath found, he hideth, and for joy thereof goeth and selleth all that he hath, and buyeth that field.

Matthew xiii. 44–46 (*contd.*)

⁴⁵'Again, the Kingdom of Heaven is like unto a merchant man, seeking goodly pearls: ⁴⁶who, when he had found one pearl of great price, went and sold all that he had, and bought it.'

Luke vi. 43–49

⁴³'For a good tree bringeth not forth corrupt fruit; neither doth a corrupt tree bring forth good fruit. ⁴⁴For every tree is known by his own fruit. For of thorns men do not gather figs, nor of a bramble bush gather they grapes. ⁴⁵A good man out of the good treasure of his heart bringeth forth that which is good; and an evil man out of the evil treasure of his heart bringeth forth that which is evil: for of the abundance of the heart his mouth speaketh. ⁴⁶And why call ye Me, Lord, Lord, and do not the things which I say? ⁴⁷Whosoever cometh to Me, and heareth My sayings, and doeth them, I will shew you to whom he is like: ⁴⁸he is like a man which built an house, and digged deep, and laid the foundation on a rock: and when the flood arose, the stream beat vehemently upon that house, and could not shake it: for it was founded upon a rock. ⁴⁹But he that heareth, and doeth not, is like a man that without a foundation built an house upon the earth, against which the stream did beat vehemently, and immediately it fell; and the ruin of that house was great.'

(*a*) Since Jesus was never embarrassed by false prophets, the reference in *Matthew* vii. 15 to those that came as wolves in sheep's clothing seems to have been borrowed from Paul's speech in *Acts* xx. 29–30.

(*b*) The Good and the Corrupt Tree in *Matthew* vii. 17 is probably a *midrash* on *Isaiah* v. 1–7 (*see* ci.*f*), with an additional citation of *Joel* i. 7. *Luke* vi. 44 is the better text: by substituting 'briers' for 'thistles', its editor has preserved Isaiah's metaphor. The confusion caused in Jesus's sayings by the omission of relevant quotations is clearly seen here: briers and thorns are what spring up when God, the owner of the Vineyard, roots out the vine and kills the fig-tree by girdling it (*see* ciii.*a–f*)—they are not examples of trees that yield corrupt fruit. In *Matthew* vii. 19–20, Jesus quotes John the Baptist (*Matthew* iii. 8–10 —*see* v.*g*); this quotation has been clumsily repeated in *Matthew* xii. 33–34, the passage concerning blasphemy against the Holy Spirit (*see* xxxiv.*f*).

(138) *And he expounded the prophecy of Isaiah which saith:* 'My well-beloved hath a vineyard in a very fruitful place, and he gathered out the stones thereof, and planted it with the choicest vines, and built a tower in the midst of it. And he looked that it should bring forth grapes and it brought forth wild grapes.

'I will therefore lay it waste, it shall not be pruned nor digged and there shall come up briers and thorns. For the Lord looked for judgement, but behold a scab; for righteousness, but behold a cry.'

He told them: 'Now, Israel is the vine which is judged by her fruit, whether it be good or whether it be cankered.

'As Joel prophesied, saying: "He hath laid My vine waste and barked My fig tree, the branches thereof are made white."'

'*And ye have heard how John the Baptist testified: "The axe is now laid to the root of the trees, and everyone that bringeth not forth good fruit is hewn down and cast into the fire."*

'*Beware, therefore, that ye bring forth the fruit of repentance! For if this vineyard be laid waste, shall men gather grapes of the thorns that spring up thereafter, or figs of the briers?*'

* * * * *

(*c*) *Luke* vii. 48 is a *midrash* on one of several texts in the *Psalms,* probably *Psalm* lxxiii. 26.

Though in *Luke* vi. 49 the foolish man's house is built on earth and a fresh-water stream undermines it, it will have been built on sand, as in *Matthew* vii. 26, and overwhelmed by the sea—which was Tyre's metaphorical fate (*Ezekiel* xxvi. 3–14). The sea symbolized corruption (*Isaiah* li. 9–10); hence 'There was no more sea' in *Revelation* xxi. 1.

(141) *And he expounded unto them the words of David: 'God is the rock of my heart and my portion for ever,' saying:*

'*Whosoever heareth the word of God and keepeth it, the same is like unto a wise man which builded his house on a rock.*

'*For the rain descended and the floods came and the winds blew and beat upon the house, but it fell not.*

'*But whosoever heareth not the word of God, but trusteth in his own conceits, the same is like unto a foolish man which builded his house upon the sands of the seashore.*

'*For the winds arose and the waves of the sea beat vehemently against the house, and great was the fall thereof.*

'*As Ezekiel prophesied: "Its place shall be for the spreading of nets."*'

* * * * *

(*d*) The Gentile Christians have taken *Matthew* vii. 6 as a reference to *Acts* xiii. 45–46, where 'the Jews' are said to have railed against Paul and Barnabas but to have been met with the retort: 'Since ye put the word of God from you and judge yourselves unworthy of eternal life, lo, we turn to the Gentiles!' It explains, on the contrary, why the disciples might not enter into any city of the Samaritans (*Matthew* x. 5) or of the Gentiles, and why Jesus himself avoided Caesarea Philippi, the capital of Philip's tetrarchy (*see* LXXVII.*a*), and Tiberias, the capital of Galilee. 'Dogs' and 'swine' were popular synonyms for the Syro-Phoenicians and the Graeco-Romans respectively (*see* XXXVI.*h* and XVIII.*b*).

(187) '*For ye shall not give what is holy unto the dogs, neither shall ye cast your pearls before swine, lest they trample them under their feet and turn again to rend you.*'

* * * * *

(*e*) The two short parables in *Matthew* xiii. 44–46 are *midrashim* on *Proverbs* ii. 4–5 and *Job* xxviii. 17–18 and 28; they elaborate a theme found in *Matthew* vii. 7 (*see* xxvii.*i*).

(53) *He expounded also a proverb of Solomon: 'If thou seekest Wisdom as silver and searchest for her as for hid treasures, then shalt thou find the knowledge of God,' saying:*

'Hearken therefore unto this parable: The Kingdom of Heaven is like to a treasure of silver and gold and precious stones hid in a field, the which when a wise man hath found he hideth again, and for joy thereof goeth and selleth all that he hath and buyeth that field,

'Or it is like unto a merchant man, seeking goodly pearls, which when he hath found one pearl of great price goeth and selleth all that he hath and buyeth it.

'As Job also saith: "Behold the fear of the Lord, that is wisdom; and to depart from evil, that is understanding.

'"The gold and the sapphire shall not equal wisdom, nor shall it be exchanged for jewels of fine gold. No mention shall be made of corals or of pearls, for the price of wisdom is above rubies."'

*   *   *   *   *

For *Matthew* xii. 34–37, abbreviated in *Luke* vi. 46, *see* xxii.c.

*   *   *   *   *

XLVIII

THE HALF-SHEKEL

Matthew xvii. 24–27

[24]And when they were come to Capernaum, they that received tribute money came to Peter, and said: 'Doth not your master pay tribute?' [25]He saith, Yes. And when he was come into the house, Jesus anticipated him, saying: 'What thinkest thou, Simon? of whom do the kings of the earth take custom or tribute? of their own children, or of strangers?' [26]Peter saith unto Him: 'Of strangers.' Jesus saith unto him: 'Then are the children free. [27]Notwithstanding, lest we should offend them, go thou to the sea, and cast an hook, and take up the fish that first cometh up; and when thou hast opened his mouth, thou shalt find a piece of money: that take, and give unto them for Me and thee.'

Clement of Alexandria: Stromateis i. 28. 177

The Lord said: 'Be ye approved money-changers.'

1 Thessalonians v. 18–21

This is the will of God in Christ Jesus concerning you: 'Quench not the Spirit; despise not prophecy; prove all things; hold fast that which is good.'

Codex Algerinae Peckover addition to Matthew xvii. 27

[Latin: reading *retem* for *rete, te* for *se*]

'Go thou to the sea and there let down thy net. Since they have thought me a stranger, let the sea teach thee that I am not a priest only but even a king. Go thou therefore and give for thyself [and for me] also, as if a stranger.'

St Ephraim the Syrian: On Matthew xvii. 27

Gospel Commentaries (about 373 A.D.)

And when he [Peter] had drawn out the fish which had in its mouth a stater the symbol of dominion, those haughty ones were reproved and confounded, because they believed not that he [Jesus] was a Levite, to whom the sea and the fishes were witnesses that he is King and priest.

(*a*) In the days of the early monarchy it was thought that to take a census of Israel was to tempt Providence: no sooner had the number been computed, than God would vengefully reduce it by a plague, as happened in the reign of David (2 *Samuel* xxiv. 10). An editor of *Exodus* evidently realized that Moses, when he received a half-shekel from every adult male in the congregation, could have deduced from the final amount of shekels, merely by doubling it, how many had contributed. This poll-tax was therefore explained (*Exodus* xxx. 11–16) as Israel's tribute, or 'ransom'—apparently, though this is not directly stated, a sin-offering for having been previously numbered at the instigation of Jethro, Moses's Midianite father-in-law (*Exodus* xviii. 21–24); since (*Numbers* xxv. 18) the Midianites were now represented as wily seducers of Israel. 'No plague' in *Exodus* xxx. 12 indicates a suppressed sequel to the numbering on that occasion.

The poll-tax was exacted yearly, six weeks before the Passover: collectors called 'Apostles' (*Shelihim*)—Paul described himself so when he set out to collect alms for the Nazarene Church (1 *Corinthians* iv. 9)—were sent to all the synagogues of the Dispersal. This system had been introduced in 79 B.C., when the Pharisees, under Queen Alexandra the Hasmonean, assumed spiritual power in Judaea. None withheld his half-shekel but many broke the letter of the Law (*Exodus* xxx. 15) by contributing more than their due.

(*b*) According to *Matthew* xvii. 24, Jesus and Peter arrived penniless in Capernaum and the collectors demanded the tribute from them. Peter, on being asked whether his master were a Jew and therefore liable to pay, replied, yes. Jesus then took Peter aside, discussed with him the legitimacy of the tax, and came to the conclusion that tribute is what one exacts from foreigners, not from one's own people.

(*c*) The explanation of this improbable discussion seems to be as follows. After Titus's destruction of the Temple, the tribute continued to be collected —but by and for the benefit of the Romans, in token of conquest (*Wars* vii. 6. 6), under the name of *fiscus Judaicus;* and a late editor of *Matthew* must have thought that they had also organized the collection in Jesus's time. Since, therefore, he pictured Jesus as a rebel against the Law, he misinterpreted him as having said on this occasion: 'We are obedient children of the Roman Empire and should not be forced to pay the tribute as though we were rebellious Jews. Nevertheless, we will pay rather than offend the authorities.' The editor had in mind a passage in *Romans* xiii. 1–6, where Paul threatens with damnation all those who do not acknowledge Roman rule and pay their taxes cheerfully.

(*d*) Since, until the destruction of the Temple, every devout Jew rejoiced to pay his half-shekel in token of national solidarity, Jesus could never have complained of the tax—much as he disliked the Chief Priests who were responsible for its collection—but only questioned the legitimacy of its present incidence. His point seems to have been that the Levites, 'the children of the Temple', were clearly not liable to pay, since the tax was a 'ransom' for being numbered and they had never been included in any census (*Numbers* i. 49). He was, in fact, exempting himself from payment by virtue of his formal adoption into the tribe of Levi, whose privileges he claimed; this is brought out in a suppressed verse of *Matthew* preserved in the *Codex Algerinae Peckover* alone, but referred to by St Ephraim the Syrian.

However, Jesus must have decided not to press the matter, because the Pharisaic High Court had ruled (*Shekalim* i. 4) that even Levites were liable to pay—Peter had better provide a whole shekel on behalf of both. 'Not a priest only but even a King', must be a literary embellishment unless the incident occurred after Jesus had privately revealed his kingship to Peter (*see* LXXVIII.*d*), explaining that he had been adopted into a priestly Levite house on the day when he was made king; but this would raise chronological difficulties. The Mishna admits that the Pharisees were defeated by the priesthood's stubborn refusal to pay: 'the shekel tax was not enforced upon the priests, for the sake of peace' (*Shekalim* 1.3).

(*e*) Peter's simple jest about finding the coin in a fish's mouth has been taken seriously by the evangelists and turned into a miracle. According to the folklore of the Lake of Tiberias, a much-prized fish, now called a *mouski*, opens its mouth as a refuge for its fry when enemies approach and then blocks it with a stone scooped from the lake-bottom. It seems that Peter went to the Lake, made a quick catch, sold his *mouski* in the market and returned at once with the price; then, when asked by the collectors where he had procured the money, he answered: 'With this coin a *mouski* stopped her mouth against her enemies.'

(*f*) Only two occasions are recorded of Jesus disputing a point of Oral Law. On this occasion he bows to the Pharisees' authority, not wishing to range himself on the side of the Sadducees, who claimed many privileges to which they were not entitled; on the other, though approving their decision, he submits that the times require its amendment (*see* LXXX.*f*).

(145) *Jesus and Peter returned together unto Capernaum, and the other disciples followed behind.*

And an apostle of the High Priest, which gathered tribute for the Sanctuary, came to Peter and asked him: 'Doth not thy master pay tribute?'

He answered: 'Yea, but both he and I have a vow of poverty.'

The apostle said: 'Yet go ye and earn an half-shekel apiece. For every son of Israel must pay according to the Law, both rich and poor alike.'

When Peter was returned to the house where they lodged, Jesus said unto him:

'Thinkest thou, Simon, that I should pay that which is required of me? For this tribute is ordained of God as a ransom for every man's soul when the Children of Israel are numbered, lest a plague fall upon them. Every man shall bring an half-shekel to the Sanctuary.

'But to the intent that the number of the congregation shall not be known by a computation of the shekels gathered, and the sin thereby multiplied, God hath set a fence about the offering.

'For He commanded Moses: "Thou shalt not number the tribe of Levi!"

'How, therefore, should they that are not numbered offer a ransom for their numbering? And that the Levites paid nought unto Moses, the word of tribute proveth.

'For of whom do the rulers of this world take tribute? Of their own children or of strangers?'

Peter answered: 'Of strangers.'

Jesus said: 'Then are the children of the Temple free, and I with them, who am enrolled in the House of Levi.

'Notwithstanding: lest we offend the Council which hath ruled otherwise, go thou to the Lake and cast an hook, if peradventure God may grant thee to catch aught.'

Peter therefore went to the Lake and did even as Jesus bade him, and with an hook he caught a great musc-fish and sold it in the market for fourpence, which make one shekel.

And he told it unto Jesus, which said: 'Go thou and give both for thyself and for me also, as though I were a stranger.'

Peter took the piece of money unto the apostle, which asked him: 'Whence, son of idleness, came this shekel? Hast thou begged it in alms?'

He answered: 'With this coin did a great musc-fish stop her mouth against her enemies; let it likewise stop thy mouth against my master!'

*   *   *   *

(g) A saying attributed to Jesus by Clement of Alexandria, and freely rendered by Paul in 1 *Thessalonians* v. 18–21, may have been occasioned by the sight of the Levite money-changers setting up their booths in the provinces to assist the collection of the poll-tax. They were salaried Temple servants, who had to pronounce on the 'cleanness' and weight of all money passing through their hands into the Treasury (*see* xc.*c*); had they been private usurers, Jesus could not have held them up for admiration (*see* lii.*f*).

(146) *Then the money-changer proved the piece and found it good.*

*   *   *   *

(149) *Afterwards, when Jesus saw the money-changers, how they rejected unclean money brought unto them, and also money that was of light weight, he exhorted his disciples, saying:*

'Be ye like unto approved money-changers, working for God, not for private gain! Mark all things with care and weigh them in a just balance; reject that which is evil, hold fast that which is good!'

*   *   *   *

XLIX

THE TABERNACLES

John vii. 1–13

[1]After these things Jesus walked in Galilee: for He would not walk in Judaea, because the Jews sought to kill Him. [2]Now the Jews' feast of tabernacles was at hand. [3]His brethren therefore said unto Him, 'Depart hence, and go into Judaea, that Thy disciples also may see the works that Thou doest. [4]For there is no man that doeth any thing in secret, and he himself seeketh to be known openly. If Thou do these things, shew Thyself to the world.' [5]For neither did His brethren believe in Him. [6]Then Jesus said unto them: 'My time is not yet come: but your time is alway ready. [7]The world cannot hate you; but Me it hateth, because I testify of it, that the works thereof are evil. [8]Go ye up unto this feast: I go not up yet unto this feast; for My time is not yet full come.' [9]When He had said these words unto them, He abode still in Galilee.

[10]But when His brethren were gone up, then went He also up unto the feast, not openly, but as it were in secret. [11]Then the Jews sought Him at the feast, and said: 'Where is He?' [12]And there was much murmuring among the people concerning Him: for some said: 'He is a good man'; others said: 'Nay; but He deceiveth the people.' [13]Howbeit no man spake openly of Him for fear of the Jews.

John vii. 37–39

[37]In the last day, that great day of the feast, Jesus stood and cried, saying: 'If any man thirst, let him come unto Me, and drink. [38]He that believeth on Me, as the scripture hath said, out of his belly shall flow rivers of living water.' [39]But this spake He of the Spirit, which they that believe on Him should receive: for the Holy Ghost was not yet given; because that Jesus was not yet glorified.

(a) The Synoptics make no mention of Jesus's journey to the Feast of Tabernacles at Jerusalem; but all pious Jews were expected to attend it every autumn and he can hardly have stayed away. Tabernacles was the most important of the annual festivals, and Zechariah insists that, in the Messianic Kingdom, even the Gentiles must go up to keep it (*Zechariah* xiv. 16–19).

(b) *John* vii. 1–13 and 37–39, though embodying a genuine tradition, are untrustworthy. Verses 11 and 13 advance the strange theory that the Galileans were not Jews, and that the Jews alone, Pharisees and Sadducees alike, wished to kill Jesus. The dialogue in verses 2–8 has been rewritten in a covert attempt to depreciate James, Jesus's brother by adoption, who was hostile to Paulinism (*see* VIII. *r–v*). It recalls a genuine occasion in the *Gospel according to the Hebrews* (*see* VI.*a*), when Jesus's brothers according to the flesh persuaded him to visit the Baptist and be cleansed of his sins.

John vii. 8–16 presents Jesus in a poor light: he is either deceiving his brothers or else breaking his word. In the original account he will have behaved with both caution and characteristic honesty when his Levite kinsmen urged him to announce his Messiahship to the people. *John* vii. 5: 'For neither did his brethren believe in him,' belongs to a different context altogether (*see* LXXXVII.*e*).

(*c*) The remainder of this chapter, beginning from verse 12, is almost wholly concerned with the events of the following Passover (*see* XCIV. *a–d*). Verses 37–39 alone are relevant to the Tabernacles, where Jesus interrupted the ritual on the most solemn evening of the nine-day feast by loudly quoting the summons of *Isaiah* lv. 1, which concerns the Messiah's imminent appearance. If any Zealots in the crowd had taken up his quotation with revolutionary fervour, the Chief Priests would have been bound to arrest Jesus for a breach of the peace; because this must have been the very Tabernacles during which Pilate massacred a number of Galilean pilgrims (*Luke* xiii. 1–5—*see* LI.*a*). The Christological part of the speech attributed to Jesus: 'He that believeth in me, as the Scripture hath said, out of his belly shall flow rivers of living water,' cannot be accepted. It is apparently based on *Proverbs* xviii. 4: 'The words of a [wise] man's mouth are as deep waters, and the well-spring of wisdom as a flowing brook'; and his *midrash* on it has been linked to *John* iv. 14 (*see* LXX.*g*).

(*d*) This was the eve of the Day of Willows, so called because willow-boughs decorated the Altar of Sacrifice. Every evening of the preceding seven a festal procession had gone down to the Pool of Siloam, headed by a priest bearing a golden pitcher of the capacity of three logs. After he had filled this with water, it was carried up the hill by torchlight and to the sound of trumpets; then taken through the Water Gate of the Temple into the Court of the Gentiles, where an assembly of priests received it from him, while they intoned *Isaiah* xii. 3: 'Ye shall draw water with joy from the wells of salvation.' At this, the trumpets sounded again. The Levites, chanting psalms and waving thyrsi, filed once around the altar, while the water from Siloam was poured over it by a priest, simultaneously with a libation of the new wine. Water and wine drained into a silver basin and disappeared down a pipe. The authority quoted for this rite—originally a Canaanite one, in honour of the Goddess Anatha, but adopted by the Israelites on their arrival in Palestine—was the tradition (*Sukkah* iv. 9 and *Yoma* 26*b*): 'The Holy One, blessed be He, said: "Pour out water before Me at the Feast, that the rains of the year may be blessed to you."' On the Day of Willows, however—the willow, being a water-loving tree, was expected to attract rain—the Levites filed not once, but seven times around the altar to commemorate, it was said, the seven days' encompassing of Jericho (*Sukkah* iv. 5).

(e) Jesus will have deprecated the unrestrained merriment and lavish show of the first evening, as being no longer 'required by the times'. Four giant golden lamps, each containing one hundred and twenty logs of oil, with wicks braided from the shredded linen of priestly garments, were lighted in the Temple (*Shabbath* 21a and *Yoma* 23a). To discourage 'light-headedness', the women were restricted to specially-built galleries, but the men sang hymns and danced in the court below all night. According to *Tosephta Sukkah* iv. 4, these dances were led by Pharisee notables, some of whom amused the crowd with inspired feats of tumbling, while others juggled miraculously with torches. A Levite choir, ranged on the fifteen steps of the Nicanor Gate (*see Introduction* II.s), broke into the fifteen 'Songs of Degrees' (*Psalms* cxx–cxxxiv—*Sukkah* iv. 4). Like everyone else, Jesus will have carried a thyrsus, or *lulab,* in his left hand, made up of willow, myrtle, and palm, and in his right an *ethrog*—a thick-rinded Indian citron which, since the Exile, had replaced the erotic quince—and joined in the processional cry of 'Hosanna! (*Hosha'na!,* Help now!—*see* LXXXIX.c), which had become a synonym for 'willow':

> 'Hosanna! For Thy sake, our God!
> Hosanna! For Thy sake, our Creator!
> Hosanna! For Thy sake, our Redeemer!
> Hosanna! For Thy sake, our Seeker!'

The illuminations were said to have been so bright that wheat could be separated from chaff anywhere in the city; and 'whosoever hath not seen the Joy of the House of Water-drawing, the same hath never seen true joy in all his life' (*Sukkah* v. 1).

> (213) *Now, the Feast of Tabernacles was at hand, and James the brother of Jesus according to the spirit, said unto him: 'Comest thou not with us to the feast? Let those of Judaea likewise see such works as thou doest in Galilee. Shew thyself to the world, for no man which seeketh to be known openly worketh alway in secret.'*
>
> *Jesus answered and said: 'Go thither now with thy brethren, and I follow. But that I do must not be openly done, for mine hour is not yet come.'*
>
> *And when they had gone up, then went he up also.*

* * * * *

(f) [Here follow Jesus's comments on Pilate's massacre (*see* (c) *above,* LI.d *and* L.c) and on the fall of the Tower (*see* LI.e).]

> (219) *And on the seventh day of the feast, when the priest stooped to fill the pitcher at the Pool of Siloam, Jesus lifted up his voice, and cried in the words of the prophet Isaiah:*
>
> *'"Ho, everyone that thirsteth, come ye to the waters, and he that hath no money; come ye, buy and eat; yea, come, buy wine and milk without money and without price!*
>
> *'"Wherefore spend ye money on that which is not bread, and your labour*

on that which satisfieth not? Hearken diligently unto Me, and eat ye that which is good, and let your soul delight in fatness!" '

And many that stood by, knowing the Scriptures, continued to cry out the words of Isaiah, saying:

' "Incline your ear and come unto Me and your soul shall live, and I will make an everlasting covenant with you, even the sure mercies of David.

' "Behold, I have given him for a witness to the people, a leader and a commander to the people!" '

Then were the Chief Rulers wroth, and asked: 'Who is this man that breaketh the holy silence?'

And they sought him out, but found him not; for the multitude was great.

* * * * *

L

TWO SPARROWS

Matthew x. 28–31

[28]And fear not them which kill the body, but are not able to kill the soul: but rather fear Him Who is able to destroy both soul and body in hell. [29]Are not two sparrows sold for a farthing? and one of them shall not fall on the ground without your Father. [30]But the very hairs of your head are all numbered. [31]Fear ye not therefore, ye are of more value than many sparrows.

Luke xii. 4–7

[4]And I say unto you, My friends, be not afraid of them that kill the body, and after that have no more that they can do. [5]But I will forewarn you whom ye shall fear: fear Him, which after He hath killed hath power to cast into hell; yea, I say unto you, fear Him. [6]Are not five sparrows sold for two farthings, and not one of them is forgotten before God? [7]But even the very hairs of your head are all numbered. Fear not therefore: ye are of more value than many sparrows.

Luke xxi. 18

[18]But there shall not an hair of your head perish.

Second Clementine Epistle v. 2–4

For the Lord saith: 'Ye shall be like lambs in the midst of wolves.' Peter answered and said unto him: 'But what if the wolves tear the sheep?'

Jesus saith to Peter: 'Let the lambs have no fear of the wolves after that they are slain by them. And do ye also not fear those that slay you but can do naught [else] to you; but rather fear ye Him that hath the power over both your souls and bodies, after ye are dead, to cast them into the flames of Hell.'

(a) *Matthew* x. 29: 'Are not two sparrows sold for a farthing?', is the correct version of a saying also found in *Luke* xii. 6. It refers to the sacrifice which formed part of a leper's cleansing ritual (*Leviticus* xiv. 4) and which Jesus recommended in *Matthew* viii. 4 (*see* xxxii.*d and f*); one of these sparrows was killed, the other set free. Here his point is that even the cheapest of sacrifices made to God will not be forgotten by Him; how much less will He then forget the sacrifice of a man's incomparably more precious life?

(b) *Luke* xii. 6: 'Five sparrows for two farthings', is an editorial blunder. The original Greek translation of the Oracles was probably: *strouthia B as-*

sariou; meaning 'sparrows, two for a farthing': but the figure *B,* 'two', was misread by the compiler of *Luke* as governing *assariou,* in the sense of 'sparrows for two farthings'. A later editor asked himself how many sparrows could be bought for this sum and concluded that, according to *Matthew,* four was the right number. But because 'four for two farthings' sounds queer in any language, he wrote 'five' to emphasize their cheapness, arguing that for two farthings the dealer would throw in an extra bird.

(c) *Matthew* x. 30 and *Luke* xii. 7 refer to 1 *Samuel* xiv. 45, where the people intervene when Saul tries to kill Jonathan. This is a *midrash* on *Isaiah* viii. 12–13, a denunciation of the proposed Jewish confederacy with Syria. Jesus is similarly warning his disciples not to compound with the Wicked Kingdom of Rome or its vassal states, such as the tetrarchies of Herod Antipas and his brother Philip. He assures them that, even if destroyed by the Romans, their bodies will be restored whole and entire in the Last Days. For the Pharisees believed in a literal resurrection of the body and consequently gave separate burial to any amputated limb. The saying seems to have been provoked by Pilate's massacre of the Galilean pilgrims who protested against an act of sacrilege (*see* li.*a*). In the so-called *Second Epistle of Clement of Rome to the Corinthians* v. 2–4, paralleled in *Clementine Homilies* xvii. 4 and Justin's *Apologia* i. 19, it is introduced after 'I send you as sheep to the wolves' (*Matthew* x. 16—*see* lvii.*f*), but the massacre context is the more suitable of the two, because the pilgrims, like the sparrows, fell as sacrifices to God.

(215) *'Serve not the Wicked Kingdom, neither make to yourselves friends of the Herodians.*

'As Isaiah prophesied: "Say ye not: 'Let us make a confederacy,' and fear not the fear of such as say so, neither be afraid. But fear the Lord Himself, in holiness, and He shall be for a sanctuary."

'Fear not them that kill the body, and are not able to kill the soul; fear, rather, Him which, after He hath killed, is able to cast both soul and body into the flames of hell.

'Are not two sparrows sold for one farthing to the leper that cometh for purification? Yet I say unto you: that sparrow of the twain which falleth a sacrifice to God shall not be forgotten of Him.

'Therefore, fear not lest ye likewise fall a sacrifice. Ye are of more value than many sparrows.

'As the people spake unto Saul, saying: "Shall he die which hath wrought this great salvation in Israel?", and Saul answered: "God forbid that an hair of his head shall fall to the ground,"

'So it shall likewise be with you. At the resurrection ye shall be raised up whole. For even the very hairs of your head are all numbered, and not one of them shall perish.'

* * * * *

(d) [Here follows *John* xv. 13, *see* liv.*g*.]

* * * * *

LI

SILOAM

Luke xiii. 1–5

[1]There were present at that season some that told Him of the Galilaeans, whose blood Pilate had mingled with their sacrifices. [2]And Jesus answering said unto them: 'Suppose ye that these Galilaeans were sinners above all the Galilaeans, because they suffered such things? [3]I tell you, nay: but, except ye repent, ye shall all likewise perish. [4]Or those eighteen, upon whom the tower in Siloam fell, and slew them, think ye that they were sinners above all men that dwelt in Jerusalem? [5]I tell you, nay: but, except ye repent, ye shall all likewise perish.'

(a) The massacre of *Luke* xiii. 1–5 must be the one mentioned in *Antiquities* xviii. 3. 2, the chapter containing the Christian interpolation about Jesus's life and crucifixion (*see* 1.*k*). Pilate had exacted a loan from the Temple Treasury for the purpose of building an aqueduct from Bethlehem to Jerusalem. Work had begun, it seems, without rousing any strong protest from the people of Jerusalem; but one day several thousand pilgrims, mostly Galileans who did not directly benefit from the project, held an indignation meeting and demanded that work should stop at once. Nothing in either the written or the oral Law prevented Temple funds from being used for aqueduct-building, and though Josephus merely states that 'the Galileans were not pleased with what had been done in the matter of the water,' their objection was evidently to the sponsoring of the aqueduct by Pilate, rather than by the High Priest—which seemed a sacrilegious use of consecrated money. Thereupon Pilate sent a number of his troops, dressed in native costume, with swords concealed beneath their cloaks, to surround the pilgrims. When these did not at once obey his order to disperse, he gave a signal and the soldiers butchered the unarmed Galileans, 'both those that were rebellious and those that were not'. Josephus fails to mention either the year or the season, but 'whose blood Pilate mingled with their sacrifices' shows that it was a Feast of Tabernacles, when pilgrims brought harvest fruits to the Temple.

(b) Nothing is known from other sources about the collapse of 'the Tower in Siloam'. Despite *Luke's* account of the first of these incidents (*see* (a) *above*), Jesus must have regarded the Galileans as martyrs because they were treacherously hewn down while protesting against the heathen's sacrilege, and against the Sadducaic High Priest's collaboration with God's enemies.

The victims of the second incident, on the other hand, died by accident while engaged in some task which Jesus was expected to think discreditable.

Yet these two disasters seem to be historically linked.

(c) Eisler (*The Messiah Jesus and John the Baptist, p.* 506), misled by the account in *Luke* xiii. 1–5, suggests that a defence-tower, standing at the head of 'Hezekiah's' aqueduct in Jerusalem, was seized by eighteen Galileans and held against Pilate—who demolished it with battering rams. He connects this imaginary incident with the disturbances provoked by the Bethlehem aqueduct; but had such armed resistance taken place, Josephus would have recorded it, and had these Galileans been members of the crowd that protested against Pilate's enterprise, Jesus could not have regarded them as sinners. Moreover, *Luke* calls them 'men of Jerusalem', not Galileans.

(d) 'The Tower in Siloam' must be a mistranslation of the Aramaic tradition. *Siloam* means 'conduit' or 'aqueduct', and 'the Tower in Siloam', when re-translated into Aramaic, means merely 'the aqueduct pier'. Roman aqueducts followed the natural contours of the ground with only occasional syphoning; but if a valley had to be crossed the conduit was supported by a series of arches springing from massive piers, like a railway viaduct. Several such valleys separate Bethlehem from Jerusalem and, to bridge them, Pilate will have employed local labour. If one of the piers had collapsed on a party of masons, the question might well have arisen: 'Were these men thus punished for serving the Wicked Kingdom in a sacrilegious enterprise?' That the accident, which was not sufficiently important to appear in *Antiquities,* occurred outside Jerusalem is suggested by *Aboth d'Rabbi Nathan ch.* 35, which lists among the 'ten wondrous mercies granted to our fathers in the sacred city' that no building in Jerusalem itself had ever collapsed.

> (214) *And the disciples met Jesus and told him concerning the Galileans whose blood Pilate had mingled with the offerings which they brought to the Temple.*
>
> *(For they made a great outcry against him because that he had built a conduit and paid the labourers with money consecrated to God.)*
>
> *Jesus answered and said: 'Those were just men which fell as an acceptable sacrifice to God, for they stood up unarmed to make protest against the despoilers of His House, and would not be silenced.'*

*   *   *   *   *

(e) This inevitable reply has been suppressed by the editor of *Luke* as being dangerously anti-Roman. Its sequel, found in the Two Sparrows context (*see* l.c), makes a further connexion between the massacre and the fall of the pier: in both cases Jesus refers to God's power of casting a man's soul into hell after having taken his life.

The second question, and Jesus's reply, will have run as follows:

> (217) *Again, they asked Jesus, saying: 'Of those eighteen whereon the tower of the conduit fell and slew them, thinkest thou that they were sinners above all men in Jerusalem?'*

He answered: 'Nay, for the Chief Priests consented to the work. Yet it pleased the Lord to take these lives before the Last Days; and presently, if their rulers repent not, He will not only slay them, but condemn their souls to hell also.'

* * * * *

Jesus must have answered these questions when he arrived late for the Feast of Tabernacles, presumably that celebrated in 29 A.D., seven months before his Crucifixion (*John* vii. 10—*see* L.*e*).

* * * * *

LII

THE TALENTS

Matthew xxv. 14–30

[14]'For the Kingdom of Heaven is as a man travelling into a far country, who called his own servants, and delivered unto them his goods. [15]And unto one he gave five talents, to another two, and to another one; to every man according to his several ability; and straightway took his journey. [16]Then he that had received the five talents went and traded with the same, and made them other five talents. [17]And likewise he that had received two, he also gained other two. [18]But he that had received one went and digged in the earth, and hid his lord's money. [19]After a long time the lord of those servants cometh, and reckoneth with them. [20]And so he that had received five talents came and brought other five talents, saying, Lord, thou deliverest unto me five talents: behold I have gained beside them five talents more. [21]His lord said unto him, Well done, thou good and faithful servant: thou hast been faithful over a few things, I will make thee ruler over many things: enter thou into the joy of thy lord. [22]He also that had received two talents came and said, Lord, thou deliveredst unto me two talents: behold, I have gained two other talents beside them. [23]His lord said unto him, Well done, good and faithful servant; thou hast been faithful over a few things: I will make thee ruler over many things: enter thou into the joy of thy lord. [24]Then he which had received the one talent came and said, Lord, I knew thee that thou art an hard man, reaping where thou hast not sown, and gathering where thou hast not strawed: [25]and I was afraid, and went and hid thy talent in the earth: lo, there thou hast that is thine. [26]His lord answered and said unto him, Thou wicked and slothful servant, thou knewest that I reap where I sowed not, and gather where I have not strawed: [27]thou oughtest therefore to have put my money to the exchangers, and then at my coming I should have received mine own with usury. [28]Take therefore the talent from him, and give it unto him which hath ten talents. [29]For unto every one that hath shall be given, and he shall have abundance: but from him that hath not shall be taken away even that which he hath. [30]And cast ye the unprofitable servant into outer darkness: there shall be weeping and gnashing of teeth.'

Luke xix. 11–27

[11]And as they heard these things, He added and spake a parable, because He was nigh to Jerusalem, and because they thought that the Kingdom of God should immediately appear. [12]He said therefore: 'A certain nobleman went into a far country to receive for himself a kingdom, and to return. [13]And he

Luke xix. 11–27 (*contd.*)

called his ten servants, and delivered them ten pounds, and said unto them, Occupy till I come. [14]But his citizens hated him, and sent a message after him, saying, We will not have this man to reign over us. [15]And it came to pass, that when he was returned, having received the kingdom, then he commanded these servants to be called unto him, to whom he had given the money, that he might know how much every man had gained by trading. [16]Then came the first, saying, Lord, thy pound hath gained ten pounds. [17]And he said unto him, Well, thou good servant: because thou hast been faithful in a very little, have thou authority over ten cities. [18]And the second came, saying, Lord, thy pound hath gained five pounds. [19]And he said likewise to him, Be thou also over five cities. [20]And another came, saying, Lord, behold, here is thy pound, which I have kept laid up in a napkin, [21]for I feared thee, because thou art an austere man: thou takest up that thou layedst not down, and reapest that thou didst not sow. [22]And he saith unto him, Out of thine own mouth will I judge thee, wicked servant. Thou knewest that I was an austere man, taking up that I laid not down, and reaping that I did not sow: [23]wherefore then gavest not thou my money into the bank, that at my coming I might have required mine own with usury? [24]And he said unto them that stood by, Take from him the pound, and give it to him that hath ten pounds. [25]And they said unto him, Lord, he hath ten pounds. [26]For I say unto you, that unto every one which hath shall be given; and from him that hath not, even that he hath shall be taken away from him. [27]But those mine enemies, which would not that I should reign over them, bring hither, and slay them before me.'

(*a*) A talent was one thousand gold pieces. As a pious Jew dedicated to a life of poverty, Jesus cannot have told this parable, which has given 'talent' its present meaning of 'natural capacity', as it is recorded in *Matthew* xxv. 14–30. Even in *Luke* xix. 12–27, where more of the original setting has been retained, something has either been altered or omitted at the close. Briefly, the man who hid the thousand gold pieces (or the single gold piece, according to *Luke* xix. 20), in a cloth rather than use it to support his master's capitalistic ventures, must originally have been the hero, not the villain, of the story.

(*b*) This parable should not be regarded as a companion piece to The Unjust Steward (*Luke* xvi. 1–9—*see* LXVIII.*d*) or The Hundred Pence (*Matthew* xviii. 23–35—*see* XXIX.*a*), though all these are concerned with a master, a servant, and a settlement of accounts between them. In both The Unjust Steward and The Hundred Pence, the master represents God and behaves with noble restraint. The Unjust Steward, in fact, concerns the Sadducees who, unwilling to pay their just debt of love to God, relax the spiritual demands of the Law for the ignorant masses as well as for themselves and thus lead them into sin. The master's praise is heavily ironic, as are his comments: 'The children of darkness are in their generation wiser than the children of light,' and 'Make friends with the Mammon of unrighteousness!' The Hundred Pence similarly concerns those defaulters who, though expecting pardon from God for serious offences against the spirit of the Law, show no mercy to subordinates who offend slightly against its letter.

(c) In The Talents, however, the master of the servants is, according to both *Matthew* and *Luke,* a crabbed, harsh, pitiless nobleman whom his fellow-citizens have every cause to hate. *Luke's* version, which is the more dependable, makes him visit a far country, evidently Rome, there to petition for the title of King; but in *Luke* xix. 14, his fellow-citizens send an embassy after him, pleading against his appointment. The situation recalls Prince Archelaus's visit to Rome in 4 B.C.; according to Josephus (*Antiquities* xvii. 9. 3), Archelaus petitioned the Emperor Augustus to confirm Herod the Great's will, by which he was to inherit the Kingdom of Judaea. An embassy of fifty Jews followed him to Rome with a counter-plea for the abolition of the Herodian monarchy (*Antiquities* xvii. 11. 1). Augustus confirmed the will in all but one article: impressed by the Jewish delegates, he withheld the courtesy title of King until Archelaus should have earned it by 'virtuous government' (*Antiquities* xvii. 11. 4). But he ruled despotically and avariciously until deposed by Augustus, whereupon Judaea became a Roman protectorate (*Antiquities* xvii. 13. 2).

(d) In 37 A.D., Archelaus's half-brother, Prince Herod Antipas, the tetrarch of Galilee, finally yielding to the importunities of his wife Herodias, visited Rome and petitioned the Emperor Tiberius for the title of King. Josephus records (*Antiquities* xviii. 7. 2) that he went against his better judgement. It is likely that the parable was told some eight years before, when Herodias was already urging Antipas to make the petition on the ground that, though Augustus had rejected a previous plea in 4 B.C. (*Antiquities* xvii. 9. 4), Tiberius had always shown them great friendship. If so, Antipas's excuse for not going will have been that Tiberius was living in retirement on Capri and that Pontius Pilate, the Governor-General of Judaea, with whom he had recently quarrelled (*Luke* xxiii. 12—*see* cx.*i*), was a nominee of Sejanus's, now the real ruler of Rome. Jesus, one of whose principal backers was Joanna, wife of Chuza, Antipas's finance minister (*Luke* viii. 3—*see* LXVI.*d*), may well have heard rumours of the proposed journey to Rome, and also rumours of a Jewish counter-petition which would be framed as on the former occasion. In fact, when Antipas did go—after the death of Tiberius and the accession of Caligula—he was met with an accusation of disloyalty and banished to Gaul (*Antiquities* xviii. 7. 2). Had Jesus perhaps heard from Joanna that if Antipas were appointed King, Chuza might become Governor of 'ten cities,' namely Decapolis?

(e) Jesus's disapproval of Herod Antipas is well known. When warned that Antipas, after killing John the Baptist, sought his life also, he called him a fox, that is to say 'unclean and a thief' (*Luke* xiii. 32—*see* xcvii.*e and h*). He had told his disciples (*Mark* viii. 15—*see* XLIV.*a*) to beware the leaven, by which he meant the animating evil spirit, of Antipas who, though nominally a Jew, had dedicated altars to heathen deities, notably in the islands of Cos and Delos.*

(*f*) When Jesus therefore told his parable of the nobleman who wished to be king but, like Archelaus and Antipas, was hated by his fellow-citizens, he cannot have been speaking either of the Messiah or of God. That he considered the people's hatred to be well deserved is shown by the nobleman's reply to the servant who had hidden the talent (or the gold piece) in a napkin. After admitting that he was, in fact, a harsh, ruthless man who harvested what he had not sown—that is, abused his political power for purposes of extortion—he asked the servant why, if unable to trade with the money, he had not banked it and let the interest accrue? To modern Christian ears the question sounds innocent enough. But the Mosaic Law absolutely forbade 'usury', which meant interest even at a half-per-cent (*Exodus* xxii. 25–26). And the Pharisaic Supreme Court at Jerusalem admitted no relaxation of this commandment when Jew dealt with Jew. Therefore, the servant would have been an enemy to God had he banked the money.

(*g*) Towards the close of the parable in *Luke,* where it follows immediately after Zacchaeus's repentance of his extortions (*see* xix.*g*), a saying of Jesus's from an earlier chapter (*Luke* viii. 18—*see* xxv.*b*) is repeated out of context: 'Unto him that hath shall be given, and from him that hath not shall be taken even that which he seemeth to have.' In *Matthew* xxv. 30, the saying about outer darkness has been borrowed from *Matthew* xxii. 11–13, the parable of the Wedding Garment, to which it properly belongs (*see* xlvi.*c*); earthly kings cast unprofitable servants into prison, not into outer darkness.

(*h*) How then did this parable originally end? Was the scrupulous servant perhaps the only one to survive a massacre of the King's household by the citizens whom they had defrauded? An ending of this kind would have been suppressed by early Gospel editors for fear of offending the Romans. The original, which seems to be a *midrash* on *Exodus* xxii. 25–26, supported by a quotation from *Ezekiel* xviii. 12–13, may be restored as follows:

(101) '*It is written in the Law: "If thou lend money to any of God's people, thou shalt not be to him as an usurer, neither shalt thou lay any usury upon him."*

'*Now, a certain nobleman before that he went to the Wicked Kingdom to sue for the title of King in his own country, called his ten servants to which he entrusted money, giving unto each of them a talent.*

'*He said unto them: "Occupy yourselves until I return." Then straightway he took his journey.*

'*But his fellow-citizens hated the nobleman, for the violence that he did them, and sent an embassy after him to Caesar, saying: "We will not have this man to reign over us."*

'*And it came to pass that, when he had received the kingdom and returned, he sent for the ten servants that he might know how much each had gained by his trading.*

* *Bulletin of Hellenic Correspondence* iii. 365*f*.

'*Then came the first, saying: "O King, thy talent hath gained ten talents."*

'*And he said unto him: "Well done, thou good and faithful servant: thou hast been faithful over a few things; I will make thee ruler over much. Have thou authority over ten cities."*

'*Then came another, saying: "O King, thy talent hath gained five talents."*

'*He said unto him likewise: "Well done, thou good and faithful servant: have thou authority over five cities."*

'*Then came the other seven and likewise earned their master's praise.*

'*For these nine servants had oppressed the poor and needy and used usury and fraudulent wiles, whereby they had increased the money committed unto them.*

'*Last of all came the tenth servant, which was a just man, and said: "O King, I knew thee for a hard man which reapest from fields where others have sown, and gatherest where others have reaped; and I feared to do as thou wouldst have had me do, lest I might offend against the Law.*

'*"Wherefore I wrapped my talent in a napkin and digged a hole and hid it in the ground: lo, here thou hast that is thine!"*

'*The King answered and said unto him: "Thou slothful and unprofitable servant, since thou knewest me for an hard man which reaped from fields where others had sown, why didst thou not at the least entrust my money to the bankers, and then at my coming I should have received mine own again with usury?"*

'*But the just servant asked him, saying: "Did not Ezekiel prophesy: 'He that hath given his money upon usury and taken increase, and hath oppressed the poor and needy, and hath spoiled by violence, the same shall surely die'?"*

'*Whereat the King was wroth, and said: "Cast this servant into prison; there shall he be fed upon bread of affliction and water of affliction! And those mine enemies which would not that I should reign over them, bring them hither and slay them!"*

'*Howbeit, the servants of the King could not prevail against them that made complaint, for all the people hated him.*

'*Then made they insurrection, running by night with torches to set fire to the King's house, and with swords to slay the King and his nine wicked servants withal.*

'*But the just servant which had not defiled his hands with offences against the Law, him they set free and entreated him well, as Jeremiah was likewise set free, and appointed him to be their judge.*

'*He that hath ears to hear, let him hear!*'

* * * *

(*i*) *Luke* xix. 11 is a late interpolation, probably of the mid-second century, when the Gentile Christians had begun to despair about the immediate coming of the Kingdom (*see Introduction* III.*l*). The parable may have been intended to reach the ears of Chuza—as a particular warning not to exploit his position if Antipas should go to Rome. But it had, of course, a more general meaning: it warned all who wished to qualify for the Kingdom of God that they must forsake this evil world, and shun any commerce not sanctioned by the Law.

(*j*) The discrepancies between the three accounts of the neglectful servant's fate (*Matthew* xxv. 30, *Luke* xix. 24 and *Luke* xii. 48—*see* xxx.*d*) has long troubled theologians. Hegesippus in his *Theophany* iv. 12 writes:

'But since the *Gospel according to the Hebrews* which hath reached my hands turns the threat not against the man who hid [the talent], but against him who had lived riotously—for it tells of these servants, one who devoured his master's substance with harlots and flute-girls, another who multiplied it by trading, and another who hid the talent, and made the one to be accepted, another only rebuked and the third imprisoned—it occurs to me to ask whether in *Matthew*, after the conclusion of the speech against the man who did nothing, the threat which follows may refer, not to him but, by resumption of a former topic, to the servant who ate and drank with the drunken.'

The editor of the *Gospel according to the Hebrews* evidently rejected the canonical version of the parable as immoral, and re-wrote it in conformity with *Luke* xii. 47; arguing that the servants' multiplication of their master's money was worthy of praise if achieved by honest trade, and not by usury.

* * * * *

THE HIRE OF A HARLOT

Abodah Zarah 16b–17a; Tosephta Hullin ii. 24

Our teachers have taught: When Rabbi Eliezer [the Great] was arrested for *minuth* they brought him to the tribunal for judgement. The Procurator said to him: 'Why does an old man like you concern himself with such idle matters?' He answered: 'I acknowledge the authority of my judge.' Therefore the Procurator thought that he spoke of him, whereas he spoke of his heavenly Father. The Procurator then said to him: 'Since you acknowledge my authority you are *dismissus,* acquitted.'

He went home distressed; when his disciples came to console him, he would not accept their consolations. Rabbi Akiba said to him: 'Suffer me to tell you one thing of what you have taught me.' He answered: 'Say on.' He said: 'Perhaps some of the teaching of the *Minim* had been transmitted to you and pleased you and therefore you were arrested?' (*Tosephta* reads: 'Perhaps one of the *Minim* had said to thee a word of *minuth* and it pleased thee?') He answered: 'Akiba, you have reminded me! Once as I walked along the upper market (*Tosephta* reads 'street') of Sepphoris I met with one (of the disciples of Jesus the Nazarene*) and Jacob of Kefar Sekanya (*Tosephta* reads 'Sakkanin') was his name. He said to me: "It is written in your Law: 'Thou shalt not bring the hire of a harlot, etc.' What was to be done with it—a house of easement for the High Priest?" But I answered not a word. He said to me: "Thus (Jesus the Nazarene*) taught me (*Tosephta* reads 'Yeshu ben Pantere'): 'For of the hire of an harlot hath she gathered them, and unto the hire of an harlot shall they return; from the place of filth they come, and unto the place of filth they shall go.'" The saying pleased me, and because of this I was arrested for *minuth*. And I transgressed against what is written in the Law: "Keep thy way far from her"—that is *minuth;* "and come not nigh the door of her house"—that is civil government.'

(*a*) Only two authentic sayings, among several libellous inventions, are credited to Jesus in the Talmud. This is partly because the Gentile Christians had used his name for what seemed blasphemous ends, so that favourable references to him were suppressed; but mainly because he never taught in a Pharisee academy. For one of these sayings, *see* LXXX.*b*.

---

* Not in text but supplied by Dikduke Sof'rim, a collection of passages expunged from the printed editions of the Talmud and of *variorum* readings.

The authority for the other is Rabbi Eliezer the Great, who heard it from Jesus's disciple 'James of Kefar Sekanya', (the modern village of Sukneh in Central Galilee, not far from Sepphoris). Klausner in his *Jesus of Nazareth* (*p.* 41), identifies this disciple with James the Just, who lived until 62 A.D., when the High Priest Annas II wrongfully condemned him to death. Josephus mentions this judicial murder (*Antiquities* xx. 9. 1)—which occurred during an interregnum between the death of one governor-general (*procurator*) and the arrival of another—and the resulting deposition of Annas. Klausner may be right, though James the Just is not known to have visited Galilee in later life, or indeed ever to have stirred far from the Temple (*see* cix.*k*).

(*b*) It appears that during Trajan's persecution of the Gentile Church, Rabbi Eliezer, then in his sixties, was arrested on a charge of being a crypto-Christian, but acquitted. A pupil, Rabbi Akiba, suggested that his arrest was God's warning to him never again to keep company with the *minim* ('heretics') or to cherish any of their sayings; for by this time, the orthodox Nazarenes too were under suspicion as heretics. Rabbi Eliezer, while regretting his association with the Nazarenes which made his fellow-Pharisees distrust him, admitted that he had been pleased by Jesus's apt quotation from *Micah* i. 7. He added wryly: 'This, I suppose, was my undoing.' Nevertheless, he made no attempt to rebut the saying.

It may have been while living under an official ban that Rabbi Eliezer came into close contact with the Galilean Nazarenes; he was being disciplined for an obstinate refusal to accept certain views held by his brother-in-law, Rabban Gamaliel II—the President of the Great Sanhedrin who forbade the Pharisees to have any further dealings with the Nazarenes (*see Introduction* III.*d*).

For 'Yeshu ben Pantere', *see* vii.*g*. For another, unacknowledged, quotation from Jesus by Rabbi Eliezer, *see* lxv.*e*.

(*c*) The historical problems here involved are discussed at length by Klausner (*see (a) above*); but he misses the point of Jesus's quotation, as he has also missed the point of 'Pappus ben Yehuda' in Rabbi Hisda's statement about Jesus's birth (*see* vii.*h*).

The text forbidding the Treasurers to accept money immorally earned was *Deuteronomy* xxiii. 18.

(275) *It was told unto Jesus by James, his brother according to the spirit:*
'*There was brought unto the Treasury the hire of an harlot and with it the Chief Rulers have builded a chamber of easement for the High Priest, against the Day of Atonement when he abideth in the Temple.*'
Wherefore James asked him: '*Master, what sayest thou? Is it not written: "Thou shalt not bring the hire of an harlot into the House of the Lord"?*'
Jesus answered and said: '*Yea, and shall a High Priest which fasteth on the Day of Atonement have need of a chamber of easement? Verily, that which was gained in filth, is spent upon a work of filth.*'

'Therefore did Micah preach against the Temple which was in Samaria, saying of the golden adornment that hanged there, the hire of harlots: "She gathered it from the hire of harlots, and unto such it will return again."

'And he prophesied, saying: "This evil is incurable; it is also come unto Judah."'

* * * * *

THE VINE

John xv. 1–27

¹"I am the true vine, and My Father is the husbandman. ²Every branch in Me that beareth not fruit He taketh away: and every branch that beareth fruit, He purgeth it, that it may bring forth more fruit. ³Now ye are clean through the word which I have spoken unto you. ⁴Abide in Me, and I in you. As the branch cannot bear fruit of itself, except it abide in the vine; no more can ye, except ye abide in Me. ⁵I am the vine, ye are the branches: he that abideth in Me, and I in him, the same bringeth forth much fruit: for without Me ye can do nothing. ⁶If a man abide not in Me, he is cast forth as a branch, and is withered; and men gather them, and cast them in the fire, and they are burned. ⁷If ye abide in Me, and My words abide in you, ye shall ask what ye will, and it shall be done unto you. ⁸Herein is My Father glorified, that ye bear much fruit; so shall ye be My disciples. ⁹As the Father hath loved Me, so have I loved you: continue ye in My love. ¹⁰If ye keep My commandments, ye shall abide in My love; even as I have kept My Father's commandments, and abide in His love. ¹¹These things have I spoken unto you, that My joy might remain in you, and that your joy might be full. ¹²This is My commandment, that ye love one another, as I have loved you. ¹³Greater love hath no man than this, that a man lay down his life for his friends. ¹⁴Ye are My friends, if ye do whatsoever I command you. ¹⁵Henceforth I call you not servants; for the servant knoweth not what his lord doeth: but I have called you friends; for all things that I have heard of My Father I have made known unto you. ¹⁶Ye have not chosen Me, but I have chosen you, and ordained you, that ye should go and bring forth fruit, and that your fruit should remain: that whatsoever ye shall ask of the Father in My name, He may give it you.

¹⁷"These things I command you, that ye love one another. ¹⁸If the world hate you, ye know that it hated Me before it hated you. ¹⁹If ye were of the world, the world would love his own: but because ye are not of the world, but I have chosen you out of the world, therefore the world hateth you. ²⁰Remember the word that I said unto you, "The servant is not greater than his lord." If they have persecuted Me, they will also persecute you: if they have kept My saying, they will keep yours also. ²¹But all these things will they do unto you for My name's sake, because they know not Him that sent Me. ²²If I had not come and spoken unto them, they had not had sin: but now they have no cloak for their sin. ²³He that hateth Me hateth My Father also. ²⁴If I had not done among them the works which none other man did, they had not had sin: but now have they both seen and hated both Me and My Father.

John xv. 1–27 (*contd.*)

²⁵But this cometh to pass, that the word might be fulfilled that is written in their law,

They hated Me without a cause.

²⁶But when the Comforter is come Whom I will send unto you from the Father, even the Spirit of truth, Who proceedeth from the Father, He shall testify of Me: ²⁷and ye also shall bear witness, because ye have been with Me from the beginning.'

(*a*) The rambling discourse of *John* xv. 7–27, introduced by the parable of The Vine, is evidently built around several short genuine sayings of Jesus's, most of them altered for doctrinal reasons. Verses 18–25 propose the improbable thesis that the Jews hated, rejected and persecuted Jesus, though he clearly revealed his Godhead by signs and wonders, and that they are thus all destined to burn in hell, except for the few faithful disciples mentioned in verse 7.

(*b*) 'I am the true vine', is one of the seven 'I am's' which the author of *John* placed into Jesus's mouth, followed by a predicate. The other six are:

The Bread of Life (vi. 35—*see* LXXII.*i*)
The Light of the World (viii. 12—*see* XXIV.*c*)
The Door (x. 9—*see* LXXXI.*f*)
The Good Shepherd (x. 14—LXXXIV.*d and f*)
The Resurrection and the Life (xi. 25—*see* LXXXVII.*a*)
The Way, the Truth, and the Life (xiv. 6—*see* CVI.*s and w*)

'I am' was a divine name of Jehovah's (*Exodus* iii. 14), and in *John* Jesus uses it, even without a predicate, during his dispute with the Sadducees (*John* viii. 58—*see* XCV.*f*); whereupon 'the Jews' allegedly try to stone him. (*c*) 'True' as a qualification of 'vine' shows that the author of *John* had another, 'false', vine in mind: namely the people of Israel. The rabbis constantly used the vine as an emblem of Israel, borrowing it from *Psalm* lxxx. 8: 'Thou didst bring a vine from Egypt', and from *Jeremiah* ii. 21: 'Yet I had planted you a noble vine of right good stock'. The commentator of *Exodus Rabbah* xliv. 1 explains the 'good stock' as being Abraham, Isaac, and Jacob: 'As a vine thriveth when supported by a stake of dry wood, so also Israel when supported by the patriarchs.' The emblem was well established in religious art: an enormous golden vine, with clusters as tall as a man, hung above the gate leading to the Sanctuary (*Wars* v. 5. 4). God was held to be the owner of this vineyard, and also its husbandman. For Jesus's further use of the same metaphor, *see* XCVI.*a* and CI.*l*.

(*d*) Jesus, however, far from agreeing with the Johannine view that the Jews were damned and that he himself was God, believed that they would lead all other nations to God (*John* iv. 22—*see* LXX.*c*), and that he was a sinner (*see* VI.*a and* LXXXII.*c*). Thus the original text of this parable, which now propounds the doctrine that faith in Jesus is the only means of salvation, may be restored as follows:

(136) 'David said in a psalm: "Thou didst bring a vine out of Egypt," and Jeremiah prophesied in the name of the Lord: "Yet I had planted you a noble vine of right good stock."

'For Israel is the vine, our Father is the vine-dresser; without Him we are as nothing.

'The branches that bear no grapes, those He cutteth off and casteth away; they wither and are gathered up for burning.

'But the fruitful branches He pruneth that they may bear yet more abundantly.'

* * * * *

(e) The main emphasis here is on the pruning: if his disciples lead an ascetic life, they will secure the everlasting joys of the Kingdom of Heaven. The missing summary of the parable may be deduced from *John* xv. 8, and from the editor's deliberate perversion of the vine metaphor.

(137) 'Delight therefore in the pruner's hook; thus shall God be glorified with much fruit in a latter season.

'For David said: "Blessed is he whom Thou chastenest, O Lord, and teachest of Thy Law! For the Lord will not cast off His people, neither will He forsake His inheritance."'

* * * * *

(f) The genuine sayings of Jesus contained in this chapter seem to have been found in a collection of Oracles under the subject-heading 'Love'. 'This is my commandment that ye love one another, as I have loved you,' in verse 12, repeated in verse 17, cannot be accepted. As the author of 2 *John.* 5 knew, it was God's commandment (*Leviticus* xix. 18), not Jesus's; and had been restated in the *Testament of Gad* vi. 1:

'And now, my children, love ye each his brother, and put away hatred from your hearts; love one another in deed and in word and inclination of the soul.'

Jesus might have quoted it on almost any occasion, but perhaps it should be associated with *Amos* iii. 3: 'Can two walk together except they be agreed?', and assigned to the Mission of the Twelve (*see* LVII.g).

(185) And he said: 'I send you out two by two, for Amos saith: "Can two walk together except they be agreed?", and ye know that God commandeth you so to love one another as He hath loved you.'

* * * * *

(g) Verse 13 may be part of the Two Sparrows context (*see* L.d).

(216) 'And what though you perish in your labours, which ye perform that others may repent and be saved?

'Greater love hath no man than this, that he lay down his life for his friends.'

* * * * *

(*h*) Verses 14–16 probably record Jesus's commendation of the Twelve when they returned from their mission (*Mark* vi. 30—*see* LVII.*h and n*).

(201) *And Jesus received them joyfully, saying: 'I chose and ordained you to go and gather fruit, and ye were my servants, for ye obeyed me.*

'But henceforth I call you not my servants, for the servant knoweth not that which his master doeth. I call you my friends; for the work of love which God hath granted me to perform, that ye likewise now perform.'

* * * * *

(*i*) Verses 18, 19, and 25 are too diffuse and boastful to be genuine. They may be a reassurance to the Twelve that they need not be dejected by Chorazin's disregard of their message, if it was lovingly delivered (*see* LIX.*c*).

(197) *'But if this world hate you without a cause, rejoice; for it loveth but its own.'*

* * * * *

(*j*) Verse 20 conceals a quotation from *Ezekiel* iii. 7, which should be attached to *Mark* viii. 33 (*see* LXXVIII.*i*). It is part of Jesus's announcement that he intends to defy the Chief Rulers when he goes up to Jerusalem (*see* LXXVII.*h*).

(249) *'The Lord said unto Ezekiel the prophet: "The House of Israel will not hearken unto thee, for they will not hearken unto Me.*

' "Behold, I have made thy face strong against their faces, and thy forehead strong against their foreheads. Fear them not, neither be dismayed." '

* * * * *

(*k*) 'Ye have been with me from the beginning', in verse 27, is inaccurate. Jesus had chosen Peter and the Galilean disciples only when he returned from his Coronation (*see* XVII.*a and* LVI.*f*).

* * * * *

ON ABUNDANCE

Irenaeus: Against Heresies v. 33. 3

As the elders remember, which saw John the Lord's disciple, that they heard from him how the Lord taught concerning those times, and said: The days shall come wherein vines shall grow each having ten thousand branches, and on one branch ten thousand shoots, and on every shoot ten thousand clusters, and in every cluster ten thousand grapes, and every grape when it is pressed shall yield five and twenty measures of wine. And when any of the saints taketh hold of one of the clusters, another will cry out: I am a better cluster, take me, through me bless thou the Lord. Likewise also he said that a grain of wheat shall bring forth ten thousand ears, and every ear shall have ten thousand grains, and every grain shall yield five double pounds of white clean flour; and all other fruits and seeds and plants according to the agreement that followeth with them: and all animals using those foods which are got from the earth shall be peaceable and in concord one with another, subject unto men with all obedience. These things Papias also, a hearer of John, and an associate of Polycarp, an ancient man, testifieth in writing in the fourth of his books—for he wrote five. And he addeth, saying: But these things are credible unto believers. And he saith that when Judas the traitor believed not, and asked: How then shall these growths be accomplished by the Lord? the Lord said: They shall see who shall come thereto.

Hippolytus: On Daniel iv. 60

So when the Lord was telling the disciples about the future kingdom of the saints, how glorious and wonderful it should be, Judas was struck by his words, and said: Who then shall see these things? And the Lord said: These things shall they see who are worthy.

(*a*) The Nazarene and other apocalyptics believed that an earthly paradise, lasting for a thousand years (*see* LXXXVIII.*x*) would succeed the Pangs of the Messiah. But since this paradise was not, in fact, initiated by the Crucifixion, Jesus's statements about it were eventually suppressed (*see Introduction* III.*l*).

The saying quoted by Irenaeus and Hippolytus appears to be a genuine relic of the original tradition. It is a *midrash* on the *Apocalypse of Baruch* xxix. 5 and *Isaiah* xi. 6–9; and should be inserted at the close of The Sower (*see* LXVI.*j*).

(174) *Then Judas of Kerioth asked Jesus: 'Shall the earth verily bring forth fruit of herself in the Kingdom of Heaven?'*

Jesus answered and said: 'Baruch foretold these things: "Behold, the earth will yield fruit ten thousandfold, and one vine shall bear a thousand branches, and each branch a thousand clusters, and each cluster a thousand grapes, and from each grape shall be pressed a cor of wine."

'And I say unto you that when any one of the elect shall take hold on a cluster of such a vine, another will (as it were) cry out to him: "I am better, take thou me and through me bless the Lord!"

'Likewise shall it be with the wheat. One grain shall bring forth ten thousand ears, and each ear ten thousand grains, and from every grain shall be ground five double pounds of clean white flour.

'And so shall it be with all other fruits and grains and herbs according to the same measure.'

* * * * *

(*b*) Here follows *Matthew* xv. 13 (*see* xx.*j*).

(175) *'But every plant which our heavenly Father hath not planted shall be rooted out.'*

* * * * *

(176) *'Moreover, the beasts that eat of these fruits and grains and herbs shall be at peace one with another and subject unto men in all obedience.*

'For Isaiah likewise prophesied of those days: "The wolf shall dwell with the lamb and the leopard shall lie down with the kid, the calf and the young lion and the fatling together, and a little child shall lead them.

' "The lion shall eat straw like an ox; they shall not hurt nor destroy in all My holy mountain, saith the Lord; for the earth shall be full of the knowledge of the Lord." '

And Judas asked: 'But how shall all these things be accomplished?'

Jesus answered and said: 'They shall see that are worthy to come thereto.'

* * * * *

(*c*) Since Jesus himself quoted 'The poor shall never cease out of the land,' (*Matthew* xxvi. 11—*see* xi.*h*), it is doubtful whether he believed in the literal fulfilment of these prodigies. But in *Judges* ix. 13, the grape was a symbol of joy, 'which cheereth God and man', as bread was a symbol of God's spiritual bounty (*see* xxvii.*c*), and neither would ever fail the elect.

A similar, though more restrained, prophecy about alimentary abundance in the Messianic Kingdom is made in *Enoch* x. 18–19:

'Then shall the whole earth be tilled in righteousness and all shall be planted with trees and be filled with blessing.

'And all desirable trees shall be planted on it and they shall plant vines on it, and the vine which is planted shall yield wine in abundance, and as for all the seed which is sown thereon, each measure shall bear a thousand, and each measure of olives shall yield ten presses of oil.'

* * * * *

THE TWELVE

Mark iii. 10–19

¹⁰For He had healed many, insomuch that they pressed upon Him for to touch Him, as many as had plagues. ¹¹And unclean spirits, when they saw Him, fell down before Him, and cried saying: 'Thou art the Son of God.' ¹²And He straitly charged them that they should not make Him known.

¹³And He goeth up into a mountain, and calleth unto Him whom He would: and they came unto Him. ¹⁴And He ordained twelve, that they should be with Him, and that He might send them forth to preach, ¹⁵and to have power to heal sicknesses, and to cast out devils—¹⁶Simon (surnamed Peter), ¹⁷and James the Son of Zebedee, and John the brother of James (and He surnamed them Boanerges, which is the 'sons of thunder'), ¹⁸and Andrew, and Philip, and Bartholomew, and Matthew, and Thomas, and James the son of Alphaeus, and Thaddaeus, and Simon the Canaanite, ¹⁹and Judas Iscariot, which also betrayed Him. . . .

Matthew x. 1–4

¹And when He had called unto Him His twelve disciples, He gave them power against unclean spirits, to cast them out, and to heal all manner of sickness and all manner of disease.

²Now the names of the twelve apostles are these: The first, Simon, who is called Peter, and Andrew his brother; James the son of Zebedee, and John his brother; ³Philip, and Bartholomew; Thomas and Matthew the publican; James the son of Alphaeus, and Lebbaeus, whose surname was Thaddaeus; ⁴Simon the Canaanite, and Judas Iscariot, who also betrayed Him.

Luke vi. 13–19

¹³And when it was day, He called unto Him His disciples: and of them He chose twelve, whom also He named apostles; ¹⁴Simon, (whom He also named Peter,) and Andrew his brother, James and John, Philip and Bartholomew, ¹⁵Matthew and Thomas, James the son of Alphaeus, and Simon called Zelotes, ¹⁶and Judas the brother of James, and Judas Iscariot, which also was the traitor. ¹⁷And He came down with them, and stood in the plain and the company of His disciples, and a great multitude of people out of all Judaea and Jerusalem, and from the sea coast of Tyre and Sidon, which came to hear Him, and to be healed of their diseases; ¹⁸and they that were vexed with unclean spirits: and they were healed. ¹⁹And the whole multitude sought to touch Him: for there went virtue out of Him, and healed them all.

Acts i. 13

¹³And when they were come in, they went up into an upper room, where abode both Peter, and James, and John, and Andrew, Philip, and Thomas, Bartholomew, and Matthew, James the son of Alphaeus, and Simon Zelotes, and Judas the brother of James.

Acts i. 16–17

¹⁶Judas, which was guide to them that took Jesus. ¹⁷For he was numbered with us, and had obtained part of this ministry.

John i. 37–51

³⁷And the two disciples heard him speak, and they followed Jesus. ³⁸Then Jesus turned, and saw them following, and saith unto them: 'What seek ye?' They said unto him: 'Rabbi, (which is to say, being interpreted, Master), where dwellest thou?' ³⁹He saith unto them: 'Come and see.' They came and saw where He dwelt, and abode with Him that day: for it was about the tenth hour. ⁴⁰One of the two which heard John speak, and followed him, was Andrew, Simon Peter's brother. ⁴¹He first findeth his own brother Simon, and saith unto him: 'We have found the Messiah,' which is, being interpreted, the Christ. ⁴²And he brought him to Jesus. And when Jesus beheld him, He said: 'Thou art Simon the son of Jona: thou shalt be called Cephas,' which is by interpretation, 'A stone'.

⁴³The day following Jesus would go forth into Galilee, and findeth Philip, and saith unto him: 'Follow Me.' ⁴⁴Now Philip was of Bethsaida, the city of Andrew and Peter. ⁴⁵Philip findeth Nathanael, and saith unto him: 'We have found Him, of whom Moses in the law, and the prophets, did write, Jesus of Nazareth, the son of Joseph.' ⁴⁶And Nathanael said unto him: 'Can there any good thing come out of Nazareth?' Philip saith unto him: 'Come and see.' ⁴⁷Jesus saw Nathanael coming to him, and saith of him: 'Behold an Israelite indeed, in whom is no guile.' ⁴⁸Nathanael saith unto Him: 'Whence knowest thou me?' Jesus answered and said unto him: 'Before that Philip called thee, when thou wast under the fig tree, I saw thee.' ⁴⁹Nathanael answered and saith unto Him: 'Rabbi, Thou art the Son of God; Thou art the King of Israel.' ⁵⁰Jesus answered and said unto him: 'Because I said unto thee, I saw thee under the fig tree, believest thou? thou shalt see greater things than these.' ⁵¹And He saith unto him: 'Verily, verily, I say unto you, hereafter ye shall see heaven open, and the angels of God ascending and descending upon the Son of Man.'

The Gospel of the Ebionites
(quoted by Epiphanius: Heresies xxx.)

. . . In the Gospel they have called *According to Matthew* . . . but falsified and mutilated, it is contained that: 'There was a certain man named Jesus and he was about thirty years old, who chose us. And coming into Capernaum he entered into the house of Simon Peter and opened his mouth and said: "As I passed by the Lake of Tiberias, I chose John and James the sons of Zebedee and Simon and Andrew and [. . . . .], Thaddaeus and

The Gospel of the Ebionites (*contd.*)

> Simon the Zealot and Judas Iscariot; and thee Matthew, as thou satest at the receipt of custom I called and thou followedst me. You therefore I will to be twelve apostles for a testimony unto Israel." '

Sanhedrin 43a.

> Jesus had five disciples: Mattai, Naquai, Netzer, Buni and Todah.

(*a*) The names of the Twelve Apostles in the five early lists (*Mark* iii. 16–19, *Matthew* x. 2–4, *Luke* vi. 14–16, *Acts* i. 13 *and* 16–17 and the *Gospel of the Ebionites,* quoted by Epiphanius) are arranged in three groups of four, the first name of each group being constant, while the order of the rest varies. No list occurs in *John,* and the Ebionite one is incomplete.

(1) *Mark*	: *Peter*	*James*	*John*	*Andrew*
Matthew & Luke	: *Peter*	*Andrew*	*James*	*John*
Acts	: *Peter*	*John*	*James*	*Andrew*
Ebionites	: *John*	*James*	*Simon*	*Andrew*

* * * * *

(2) *Mark & Luke*	: *Philip*	*Bartholomew*	*Matthew*	*Thomas*
Matthew	: *Philip*	*Bartholomew*	*Thomas*	*Matthew*
Acts	: *Philip*	*Thomas*	*Bartholomew*	*Matthew*
Ebionites	: —	—	—	*Matthew*

* * * * *

(3) *Mark &* *Matthew*	:	{ *James of Alphaeus*	*Thaddaeus*	{ *Simon the Canaanite*	{ *Judas Iscariot*
Luke & Acts	:	{ *James of Alphaeus*	{ *Simon Zelotes*	{ *Judas of James*	{ *Judas Iscariot*
Ebionites	:	—	*Thaddaeus*	{ *Simon Zelotes*	{ *Judas Iscariot*

* * * * *

(*b*) The first to appear in *Mark's* list are Peter and the two sons of Zebedee, the three witnesses to the Raising of Jairus's Daughter (*Mark* v. 37 and *Luke* viii. 51—*see* xxxvi.*f*) and the Agony in the Garden (*Mark* ix. 2—*see* cvii.*f*). 'Thaddaeus', ('bosom'), is a nickname for Judas son of James—a reference, perhaps, to his matronly figure. In Western texts he is called by the more dignified name 'Lebbaeus' ('heart'). 'Simon the Canaanite' may stand for 'Simon of Cana'. But since he is also called 'Simon Zelotes', the original is likely to have been 'Simon Kanan', Kanaim being an Aramaic synonym for the Zealots, or militant nationalists; if so, he will have turned quietist when he became a disciple. For Peter's militancy, *see* lxxviii.*e*, cviii.*c* and cxvii.*m*.

(*c*) For 'James of Alphaeus', otherwise known as 'James the Less', 'James the Just', or 'James the brother of our Lord', see viii.*r–v*, xi.*b–c*, liii.*a,* and cxvi.*c*.

The Authorised Version of *Luke* vi. 16 and *Acts* i. 13 suggests that he was brother to Judas Thaddaeus; but the Greek merely calls Thaddaeus 'Judas of James', meaning 'Judas *son* of James'—which James is not specified. James of Alphaeus seems to have had only one brother worthy of record, namely Joses (*Mark* xvi. 1 and *Matthew* xxvii. 56—*see* VIII. *t and v*).

James the son of Zebedee was executed by Herod Agrippa in 44 A.D. (*Acts* xii. 1-2); despite Jesus's high regard for him, he remains an obscure figure, like his brother.

Whether the John described with Peter and James in *Galatians* ii. 9 as 'seemingly a pillar of the Church' was John the son of Zebedee, or whether he was 'the beloved disciple', identified by us with 'the rich young man' (*see* LXXXII.*a–b*), cannot be determined.

'Iscariot', the surname of Judas, means 'of Kerioth', a town close to the Dead Sea. Apart from the two Levites, James of Alphaeus and Matthew (*see* XIX.*a*), he was the only Judaean, as opposed to Galilean, among the Twelve.

Nathanael is generally identified with Bartholomew, 'Son of Tholomaeus', because he is placed by the Synoptics immediately after Philip, who discovered him (*John* i. 45). 'Tholomaeus' occurs as the name of a robber-chief in *Antiquities* xx. 1. 1. In *John* xxi. 2, Nathanael is described as being 'of Cana'; but this, too, may be an error for 'of the Kanaim' (*see* (*b*) *above*).

It is not known why Thomas was called Didymus, or 'The Twin'.

(*d*) Jesus cannot have invested the Twelve with any particular power over unclean spirits as stated in *Mark* iii. 14 and *Matthew* x. 1. Though he may have taught them a simple formula of expulsion, it is more probable that he instructed them merely to heal the sick (*see* XIX.*b*) and destroy the works of the Devil (*see* XXI.*r–s*).

An attempt is made in *Luke* vi. 17–19 to improve on *Mark* iii. 11 (*see also* XLII.*c*).

Since the statement that virtue went out of Jesus has evidently been borrowed from *Mark* v. 30, the story of the Bloody Issue, which can be disproved from internal evidence (*see* XXXVI.*b*), the suggestion in *Luke* vi. 19 that merely to touch Jesus cured every sufferer of whatever ailment, need not be accepted either. But many members of the crowd may have touched the fringes of his praying garment, hoping thereby to free themselves from evil dreams and inclinations (*see* XXXVI.*e*).

(*e*) The meaning of 'Boanerges' is disputed. It stands either for *Beni Ragas,* 'Sons of Tumult' or, as Jerome plausibly emends (*On Daniel* i. 7), for *Beni Rehem,* 'the Sons of the Reem'—or wild ox, translated 'unicorn' in the Authorised Version. When Jesus distinguished James and John from the remainder of the Twelve by calling them 'the Sons of the Wild Ox,' he was comparing them to Ephraim and Manasseh, the sons of Joseph the Wild Ox (*Deuteronomy* xxxiii. 16–17), who were separated by Jacob from their brethren and given his peculiar blessing. The wild ox was proverbially untameable (*Job* xxxix. 9–12); thus 'Sons of the Wild Ox' and 'Sons of Tumult' have a similar meaning, namely 'The Irresistible Ones', which is also found in *Deuteronomy* xxxiii. 17.

(*f*) Since there is no evidence whatever that Jesus tried to replace the synagogue system with one of his own, it is hard to believe that he said: 'Thou art Peter, on this rock will I build my Church.' The promise is omitted in *John* i. 42, though Peter is there awarded his new name. What Jesus may well have said was: 'Thou art Peter; on this stone will I raise my pillar to the Lord'—a reference to 1 *Samuel* xv. 12, where Saul erects a pillar at Carmel during his coronation ceremony. E. R. Goodenough in his *Kingship in Early Israel* (1929, *p.* 186), writes 'The twelve stones which Joshua had piled up at Gilgal* after his crossing of the Jordan (*Joshua* iv. 20) may have been in the form of a pillar, and here is another association of the King with a pillar' (*see* VIII.*c*). The saying is peculiarly apposite, since Jesus after his Coronation decided to enlist the help of twelve disciples, one for each tribe, of whom Peter was the first—'for a testimony unto Israel' (*The Gospel of the Ebionites,* quoted by Epiphanius: *Heresies* xxx). Paul refers to Simon as 'Cephas' on several occasions (1 *Corinthians* i. 12; iii. 22; ix. 5 and *Galatians* ii. 9). That he was the first of the apostles to be chosen did not subsequently give him precedence over James the brother of Jesus (*Eusebius: Ecc. Hist.* 2. i. 2–3), though Catholic doctrine insists that it did; Peter was the base of the pillar, not its summit.

(*g*) The corrupt list of Jesus's five disciples in the Talmud (*Sanhedrin* 43*a*) is followed by a late Amoraitic addition full of cruel puns explaining why they deserved execution. 'Mattai' may be either Matthew or Matthias; 'Naquai' may be Nathanael, 'an Israelite in whom there is no guile', because *naqui* means 'innocent'; 'Todah' may be Thaddaeus. 'Netzer' ('branch'), though generally taken to be Andrew's Hebrew name (Greek: *Andreios,* 'manly'), is almost certainly Jesus himself (*Matthew* ii. 23—*see* I.*v and* VIII.*n*); 'Buni' is 'Nicodemus', the secret disciple (*see* LXXXIII.*a*–*g*).

(65) *And there pressed upon him, to touch the fringe of his garment, as many as were plagued by evil dreams and evil inclinations.*

* * * * *

(182) *And Jesus took apart into a mountain twelve men of his disciples, which he chose that they might abide with him until he should send them forth to preach: to heal all them that were sick in spirit and to destroy the works of the devil.*

First he chose Simon, and called him Cephas (which is The Stone), for he said: 'On this stone will I raise my pillar to the Lord.'

And he chose also James and John the sons of Zebedee, and called them Beni Rehem (which is The Sons of the Wild Ox); and Andrew, Simon's brother.

---

* *Gilgal* means 'stone circle'; but it is likely that the circle there was already a Canaanite shrine when Joshua arrived, and that he merely raised a pillar of twelve stones in the centre of it.

And Philip, and Nathanael his brother, sons of Tholomaeus, and Matthew the Levite, and Thomas called The Twin.

And his own brother James; and Judas called Of the Bosom; and that Simon which had been a Zealot; and lastly Judas of Kerioth.

And he said unto them: 'Behold, I will you to be twelve apostles for a testimony unto Israel, one man for every tribe.'

And they went together into a house at Capernaum, and abode there.

*   *   *   *

[Here follows the substance of *Mark* viii. 34–38, paralleled in *Matthew* x. 32–39 and *Luke* ix. 23–26 (*see* CI.*j*).]

*   *   *   *

(*h*) John i. 37–51 belongs to John the Baptist's acclamation of Jesus (*see* VII.*e*); the remainder is acceptable in the present context, though Jesus will hardly have told Philip to follow him, unless he had first been importuned for the honour. Philip, it appears, told Nathanael that Jesus's home was the northern Bethlehem, 'Bethlehem Noseriyyah', or 'Nazara' (*see* I.*u*); to which he rightly objected (*John* i. 46): 'Surely, no good can come out of *that* Bethlehem? Bethlehem Ephratah is the one mentioned in the prophecies.' This passage contains a pun, omitted in *John* i. 46, but preserved in *John* vii. 52: 'Can a *nazir* [one dedicated to God] come from Nazara?' Philip may have retorted: 'Come and see! He is more than *Nazir*, he is *Netzer*—The Branch.'

John i. 44, which mentions that Philip was a fellow-townsman of Peter and Andrew, belongs to another context (*see* LXXIII.*e*).

(62) *On the morrow therefore, Jesus would go forth into Galilee.*

And Philip besought him, saying: 'Master, suffer me to be thy disciple.'

Jesus answered and said: 'Follow me!'

Then Philip sought out Nathanael his brother, and said unto him: 'He hath been found, of whom Moses and the prophets did write! The same is Jesus, of Bethlehem Nazara, and he is dedicated unto God.'

But Nathanael asked: 'Is it not written that the Holy One shall proceed from Bethlehem Ephratah? And how can any man that proceedeth from Bethlehem Nazara be nazir *(which is Dedicated unto God)?'*

Philip said: 'Come and see! He is more than a man dedicated, he is Netzer *(which is The Branch), whereof Isaiah prophesied, saying: "And a branch from his roots shall blossom."'*

(Wherefore to this day we are called Nazarenes.)

And Nathanael likewise was chosen to be a disciple.

*   *   *   *

LVII

THE MISSION

John iv. 35

35Say not ye, There are yet four months and then cometh harvest? behold, I say unto you, Lift up your eyes, and look on the fields; for they are white already to harvest.

Mark vi. 7–13

7And He called unto Him the Twelve, and began to send them forth by two and two; and gave them power over unclean spirits; 8and commanded them that they should take nothing for their journey, save a staff only; no scrip, no bread, no money in their purse: 9but be shod with sandals; and not put on two coats. 10And He said unto them: 'In what place soever ye enter into an house, there abide till ye depart from that place. 11And whosoever shall not receive you, nor hear you, when ye depart thence, shake off the dust under your feet for a testimony against them. Verily I say unto you, It shall be more tolerable for Sodom and Gomorrha in the day of judgement, than for that city.' 12And they went out, and preached that men should repent. 13And they cast out many devils, and anointed with oil many that were sick, and healed them.

Mark xiii. 9–11

9But take heed to yourselves: for they shall deliver you up to councils; and in the synagogues ye shall be beaten: and ye shall be brought before rulers and kings for My sake, for a testimony against them. 10And the Gospel must first be published among all nations.

11But when they shall lead you, and deliver you up, take no thought beforehand what ye shall speak, neither do ye premeditate: but whatsoever shall be given you in that hour, that speak ye: for it is not ye that speak but the Holy Ghost.

Mark xvi. 15–18

15And He said unto them: 'Go ye into all the world, and preach the Gospel to every creature. 16He that believeth and is baptized shall be saved; but he that believeth not shall be condemned. 17And these signs shall follow them that believe: In My name shall they cast out devils; they shall speak with new tongues; 18they shall take up serpents; and if they drink any deadly thing, it shall not hurt them; they shall lay hands on the sick, and they shall recover.'

Matthew x. 5–25

⁵These twelve Jesus sent forth, and commanded them, saying: 'Go not into the way of the Gentiles, and into any city of the Samaritans enter ye not: ⁶but go rather to the lost sheep of the house of Israel. ⁷And as ye go, preach, saying:

The Kingdom of Heaven is at hand.

⁸Heal the sick, cleanse the lepers, raise the dead, cast out devils: freely ye have received, freely give. ⁹Provide neither gold, nor silver, nor brass in your purses, ¹⁰nor scrip for your journey, neither two coats, neither shoes, nor yet staves: for the workman is worthy of his meat. ¹¹And into whatsoever city or town ye shall enter, inquire who in it is worthy; and there abide till ye go thence. ¹²And when ye come into an house, salute it. ¹³And if the house be worthy, let your peace come upon it: but if it be not worthy, let your peace return to you. ¹⁴And whosoever shall not receive you, nor hear your words, when ye depart out of that house or city, shake off the dust of your feet. ¹⁵Verily I say unto you, it shall be more tolerable for the land of Sodom and Gomorrha in the day of judgement, than for that city.

¹⁶'Behold, I send you forth as sheep in the midst of wolves: be ye therefore wise as serpents, and harmless as doves. ¹⁷But beware of men: for they will deliver you up to the councils, and they will scourge you in their synagogues; ¹⁸and ye shall be brought before governors and kings for My sake, for a testimony against them and the Gentiles. ¹⁹But when they deliver you up, take no thought how or what ye shall speak: ²⁰for it shall be given you in that same hour what ye shall speak. For it is not ye that speak, but the Spirit of your Father which speaketh in you. ²¹And the brother shall deliver up the brother to death, and the father the child: and the children shall rise up against their parents, and cause them to be put to death. ²²And ye shall be hated of all men for My name's sake: but he that endureth to the end shall be saved. ²³But when they persecute you in this city, flee ye into another: for verily I say unto you, ye shall not have gone over the cities of Israel, till the Son of Man be come. ²⁴The disciple is not above his master, nor the servant above his lord. ²⁵It is enough for the disciple that he be as his master, and the servant as his lord.'

Luke vi. 40

⁴⁰The disciple is not above his master: but every one that is perfect shall be as his master.

Matthew x. 40–41

⁴⁰'He that receiveth you receiveth Me, and he that receiveth Me receiveth Him that sent Me. ⁴¹He that receiveth a prophet in the name of a prophet shall receive a prophet's reward; and he that receiveth a righteous man in the name of a righteous man shall receive a righteous man's reward.'

Matthew vi. 7

⁷But when ye pray, use not vain repetitions, as the heathen do: for they think that they shall be heard for their much speaking.

Matthew xxiv. 9–13

[9]Then shall they deliver you up to be afflicted, and shall kill you: and ye shall be hated of all nations for My name's sake. [10]And then shall many be offended, and shall betray one another, and shall hate one another. [11]And many false prophets shall rise, and shall deceive many. [12]And because iniquity shall abound, the love of many shall wax cold. [13]But he that shall endure unto the end, the same shall be saved.

Luke ix. 1–6

[1]Then He called His twelve disciples together, and gave them power and authority over all devils, and to cure diseases. [2]And He sent them to preach the kingdom of God, and to heal the sick. [3]And He said unto them: 'Take nothing for your journey, neither staves, nor scrip, neither bread, neither money; neither have two coats apiece. [4]And whatever house ye enter into, there abide, and thence depart. [5]And whosoever will not receive you, when ye go out of that city, shake off the very dust from your feet for a testimony against them.' [6]And they departed, and went through the towns, preaching the Gospel, and healing everywhere.

Luke x. 1–12

[1]After these things the Lord appointed other seventy also, and sent them two and two before His face into every city and place, whither He Himself would come. [2]Therefore said He unto them: 'The harvest truly is great, but the labourers are few: pray ye therefore the Lord of the harvest, that He would send forth labourers into His harvest. [3]Go your ways: behold, I send you forth as lambs among wolves. [4]Carry neither purse, nor scrip, nor shoes: and salute no man by the way. [5]And into whatsoever house ye enter, first say, "Peace be to this house." [6]And if the son of peace be there, your peace shall rest upon it: if not, it shall turn to you again. [7]And in the same house remain, eating and drinking such things as they give: for the labourer is worthy of his hire. Go not from house to house. [8]And into whatsoever city ye enter, and they receive you, eat such things as are set before you. [9]And heal the sick that are therein, and say unto them, The kingdom of God is come nigh unto you. [10]But into whatsoever city ye enter, and they receive you not, go your ways out into the streets of the same, and say, [11]"Even the very dust of your city, which cleaveth on us, we do wipe off against you": notwithstanding be ye sure of this, that the kingdom of God is come nigh unto you. [12]But I say unto you, that it shall be more tolerable in that day for Sodom, than for that city.'

Luke x. 16

[16]He that heareth you heareth Me; and he that despiseth you despiseth Me; and he that despiseth Me despiseth Him that sent Me.

Luke x. 19–20

[19]Behold, I give unto you power to tread on serpents, and scorpions, and over all the power of the enemy: and nothing shall by any means hurt you. [20]Notwithstanding in this rejoice not, that the spirits are subject unto you; but rather rejoice, because your names are written in heaven.

Luke xii. 11–12

¹¹And when they bring you unto the synagogues, and unto magistrates, and powers, take ye no thought how or what thing ye shall answer, or what ye shall say: ¹²for the Holy Ghost shall teach you in the same hour what ye ought to say.

Mark vi. 30

³⁰And the Apostles gathered themselves together unto Jesus, and told Him all things, both what they had done, and what they had taught.

Luke ix. 10

¹⁰And the Apostles, when they were returned, told Him all that they had done. . . .

Luke x. 17–18

¹⁷And the Seventy returned again with joy, saying: 'Lord, even the devils are subject unto us through Thy name.' ¹⁸And He said unto them: 'I beheld Satan as lightning fall from heaven.'

Luke xxi. 14–15

¹⁴Settle it therefore in your hearts, not to meditate before what ye shall answer. ¹⁵For I will give you a mouth and wisdom, which all your adversaries shall not be able to gainsay nor resist.

(a) The mission of the Twelve begins with *John* iv. 35 (*see* LXX.*j*). Time was running short, and Jesus, anxious to cover the whole of the home mission field, delegated part of his self-imposed task to the disciples, who were now to be regarded as his spokesmen. Their assignment was to convert the 'lost sheep of the House of Israel' (*Matthew* x. 6), that is to say, the Men of the Land (*see* XII.*k*). The Jews of the synagogue, safe in the Pharisaic fold, needed no conversion. Jesus himself would preach to the Jerusalem Sadducees; and the Greeks, Phoenicians, and city-dwelling Samaritans must wait until the Last Days (*see* LXX.*e*), when their remnants would become provincial subjects of the Messianic Kingdom (*see* LXXXVIII.*e*). 'Salvation is from the Jews', he had told the woman of Sychar (*see* LXX.*d*).

(b) An editor of *Luke* realized that Jesus was here discriminating against the Gentiles. He therefore invented a second mission, not recorded elsewhere, for seventy disciples (*Luke* x. 1)—seventy being the canonical number of all the nations in the world (*Genesis* x. 1–32). Though these are not restricted to the Jewish mission-field (*Luke* x. 8–10), neither are they ordered to 'go into all the world and preach the Gospel to every creature', as in the patently fictitious passage of *Mark* xvi. 9–20. *Luke's* seventy apostles were later confused with the Nazarene Council formed after Jesus's departure, which consisted, like the Great Sanhedrin, of seventy elders and two joint-presidents, called *zugim* ('pairs'), namely James and Peter (*Clementine*

Recognitions xl.). When the Pseudo-Dorotheus and the Pseudo-Hippolytus mention Agabus (*Acts* xi. 28 and xxi. 10) as one of the seventy, they may have meant that he was one of these elders.

Luke x. 8 is typically Pauline in its flaunting of the Law: it amounts to 'Do not enquire whether the meat set before you is clean or unclean.'

In *Luke* x. 16, Jesus is made to speak of himself, Christologically, as the second person of the Trinity.

(c) *Matthew* x. 8b: 'Freely ye have received, freely give', warns the apostles not to accept fees for their preaching or for any cures performed in God's name. The story of Gehazi (2 *Kings* v. 20–27) pointed a moral against the acceptance of payment for spiritual gifts; and *Hosea* xiv. 4 laid down the principle: 'I will love them freely.'

Matthew x. 8a: 'Cleanse the lepers, raise the dead', must be an interpolation; and *Matthew* x. 10: 'nor yet staves', meaning 'Do not carry a spare staff', is superfluous—the original may have been 'a spare shift'. A staff was, however, a necessity even for the youngest and sturdiest disciples: not only to help them negotiate flooded watercourses in the rainy season, or for fending off pariah dogs, but as an instrument of ritual cleanliness. Every Essene novice on taking his vows, was given a staff shaped like a paddle and taught how to dig a sanitary pit, whenever he needed to 'cover his feet' (*Wars* ii. 8. 9).

(d) The remainder of *Matthew* x. 10, paralleled in *Luke* x. 7: 'The labourer is worthy of his hire (or meat)', is suspect; it may be a borrowing from 1 *Timothy* v. 18, one of the very few texts common to both the Epistles and the Gospels. Paul's followers insisted that preaching should count as labour, which was neither the Pharisaic view (*see* cxviii.*h*), nor likely to have been Jesus's. The original of this saying seems to be preserved in the third-century *Didache* xii. 3: 'Let him work and therefore eat,' paralleled in 2 *Thessalonians* iii. 10: 'If any will not work, neither let him eat.' *Luke* x. 4: 'Salute no man by the way', means 'do not stay to gossip'.

(e) The anointing of the sick with oil is mentioned in *Mark* vi. 13 alone; both *Luke* and *Matthew* hold that the mere utterance of Jesus's name sufficed. Most of *Matthew* x. 16–23, paralleled in *Luke* xii. 11–12, dates from Domitian's persecutions of the Gentile Church. A late editor of *Mark*, who borrowed the passage, seems to have realized that it did not fit the context and has therefore presented it as Jesus's final instructions from the Mount of Olives (*Mark* xiii. 9–11). 'My name' in *Matthew* x. 22, cannot be accepted. The Twelve went out in God's name, not Jesus's, though in their laying-on of hands they may have used the formula 'Trust in God; *He shall save!*' and thus pronounced the word 'Jesus' (*see* (g) *below*). Neither did they meet any kings in the course of their mission, and all returned safely. Jesus may, however, have mentioned kings in his instructions, when he quoted *Psalm* cxix. 46. In *Matthew* x. 41 he cites *Genesis* xlvii. 10–20, 1 *Kings* xvii. 10 and 2 *Kings* ii. 8.

Matthew x. 40 is paralleled in *Luke* x. 16 (*see* LIX.*e*) and in *John* xii. 44 and xiii. 20 (*see* CV.*g*).

For Sodom and Gomorrah's fate (*Matthew* x. 15), see *Genesis* xix. 24.

(*f*) Jesus could not have told the apostles to be as subtle as serpents (*Matthew* x. 16), and thus to model themselves on Satan the Cosmocrator (*Genesis* iii. 1 and *Revelation* xii. 9). It was Paul who practised such subtlety (*see* CXIX.*l*), not Jesus, and elsewhere in the Gospels, apart from the peculiar case of *Numbers* xxi. 9 (*see* LXXXIII.*j*), the serpent always symbolizes evil which must be trodden in the dust. Moreover, this verse is too confusedly zoological for acceptance, until restored to its original balance: 'I send you as sheep to wolves, as doves to serpents'—serpents being popularly held to fascinate birds with their 'basilisk' eye.

Matthew xxiv. 13: 'He that shall endure to the end', is a quotation from *Daniel* xii. 13.

Matthew does not mention the disciples' return; *Mark* mentions it briefly, and without suggesting that they had been successful (*see* LIX.*a*). *Luke* here follows *Mark*, except that he records the spectacular success of the Seventy's mission (*Luke* x. 17–18). The joyful remark about Satan's fall from heaven recalls *Revelation* xii. 9, which is based on *Isaiah* xiv. 12; Jesus will have made it, if at all, when the disciples consented to become eunuchs for the sake of the Kingdom and so defeat the wiles of the Cosmocrator (*see* XXI.*r–s*).

Luke x. 20: 'Your names are written in heaven', refers to *Enoch* xliii. 1–4, where God is said to keep a record of the Elect in the firmament, spelt out in stars.

(184) *And when certain days had passed, Jesus called unto him the Twelve and began to send them forth two by two, and commanded them that they should take nought for their journey save a staff only.*

No scrip, no bread, no money in the fold of their garments; neither two pairs of shoes, nor two tunics, nor two shifts; nor salute any man by the way.

And if any of them would eat, let him undertake any labour that fell to him to perform.

* * * * *

(*g*) [Here follows Jesus's reason for sending them out two by two (*see* LIV.*f*).]

(186) *'But go not into any region of the Gentiles, nor into any city of the Samaritans.'*

* * * * *

[Here follows the injunction against casting pearls before swine (*see* XLVII.*d*).]

(188) *'Go only to the strayed sheep of the House of Israel.*

'And as ye go, preach, saying: "The Kingdom of Heaven is at Hand!"

'Into whatsoever city or village ye shall enter, enquire which house in it is worthy to receive you.

'*And when ye come to that house, salute it, and if it be worthy, let your peace come thereupon. But if not, let your peace return unto you.*

'*And when ye have found a house that is worthy, enter in and abide until ye depart thence.*

'*And know that whosoever receiveth a prophet, the same shall be rewarded by God in the prophet's name; as was the widow of Zarephath which received Elijah, and the great woman of Shunem which received Elisha.*

'*And whosoever receiveth a righteous man, the same shall be rewarded by God in that righteous man's name, as when Jacob blessed Pharaoh which received him into Egypt for Joseph's sake.*'

* * * * *

[Here follows the substance of *Matthew* x. 42 (*see* LX.*d*) and *Matthew* xxv. 34–46 (*see* LX.*e*).]

(190) '*And if there be any sick brought unto you, or any tormented by evil spirits, anoint them with oil and pray God to heal them.*

'*And as He spake by the mouth of the prophet Hosea, saying: "I will love you freely," so, having freely received, do ye freely give.*

'*Fall not into the sin of Gehazi which sought to exact payment for the healing that Elisha had wrought by the finger of God.*

'*Neither boast ye if evil spirits obey your voice and come forth; the glory is God's. But pray to Him that your names be inscribed among the stars of heaven.*

'*Even as Enoch testified, saying: "God called the stars by their names and they hearkened unto Him; and these are the names of the holy which dwell on earth and believe in the name of the Lord of Souls for ever and ever."*'

* * * * *

[Among his instructions were: 'Peep not and mutter not as the heathen do, but say openly: "Trust in God, He shall save!" ' (*See* XXVII.*e and* XXXI.*b*).]

(192) '*And if there be found no house in that city or village that is worthy, go your ways out from the streets of the same, and say:*

' *"The dust of your city which cleaveth to our shoes, we shake off as a testimony against you."*

'*And if they do not hearken to these words and so repent, I say unto you it shall be less tolerable in the Day of Judgement for that city than it was for Sodom and Gomorrah when God rained fire and brimstone upon them.*

'*For he that heareth you, heareth Him that sent you; and he that despiseth you, despiseth Him that sent you. Depart thence and go to another.*

'*Verily, when ye have visited all the cities of the land, the time shall be at hand that the Son of Man is revealed.*

'*Even as Daniel spake in the name of the Lord: "Go thou thy way until the end be; for thou shalt find rest and stand in thy allotted place at the end of the days."*'

* * * * *

[Here follows: 'In that day he that is not with God shall be against Him' (*see* xxxiv.*g*).]

(194) *'Behold, I send you forth as harmless sheep into the midst of ravening wolves, and as guileless doves into the midst of subtle serpents.*

'And if ye are taken before the rulers of synagogues, or before magistrates, or before the servants of Herod, take no thought beforehand what ye shall speak.

'But whatsoever shall be given you in that same hour, that speak ye; the Holy Spirit shall teach you what words ye may use.

'For David saith in a psalm: "I will speak of Thy testimonies even before kings, and will not be ashamed." '

* * * * *

(*h*) [Here follow Jesus's quotation from *Daniel* xii. 3 (*see* lxvi.*i*); his parable of the Mustard Seed (*see* xlv.*b*); his saying: 'If this world hate you without a cause . . .' (*see* liv.*i*); and his answer to a question about the fate of the Gentiles (*see* xxxiv.*g*).]

(199) *And the Twelve went forth as Jesus bade them and preached that men should repent.*

They also anointed with oil those that were sick or possessed of devils, and healed many.

* * * * *

(200) *And they gathered themselves together unto Jesus again, and told him all things, both that they had done and that they had taught.*

* * * * *

[Here follows Jesus's commendation (*see* liv. *f; and* (*n*) *below*).]

* * * * *

(*i*) His instructions to the apostles recall Josephus's *Wars* ii. 8. 4 which, in turn, recalls the communism of the Early Church as described in *Acts* ii. 44–46 (*see* cxviii.*a*):

'They have no certain city but many dwell in every city. And if any of their sect come from other places, what they have lies open for them, as if it were their own. And they go into such as they never knew before, as if they had been long acquainted with them. For which reason they carry nothing with them. . . . Accordingly there is, in every city where they live, one appointed particularly to take care of strangers and provide garments and other necessaries for them. . . . Nor do they allow the change of garments or of shoes till they be first entirely torn to pieces or worn out by time. Neither do they either buy or sell of another, but every one gives to him that needs aught . . . and although no requital be made they are fully permitted to take what they want of whomsoever they please.'

(*j*) Jesus does not appear to have accepted Strict Essene discipline. He did not share the Essene reluctance to take part in Temple worship; and, later, the Nazarenes even made the Temple their headquarters (*see* CXVIII.*a*). Again, according to Philo (*Quod Omnis Probus* 12), the Essenes were never molested by the successive rulers of Palestine; as happened to both John the Baptist's disciples and the Nazarenes. And it is impossible that Jesus, who dared preach to the Men of the Land (*see* XII.*m and* XIX.*e*), shared the Strict Essenes' morbid fear of defilement; a large part of their days was spent in ritual washing and, on the Sabbath, they even refrained from performing their bodily functions.

According to Pliny's *Natural History,* Josephus's *Antiquities* and *Wars,* Philo's *Quod Omnis Probus,* and Epiphanius's *Heresies,* the Essenes, unlike the Pharisees, seem to have reconciled the Scriptures with a cult of *Daniel's* 'Son of Man', a demi-god standing in much the same relation to Jehovah, the Ancient of Days, as the Orphic Dionysus stood to immortal Apollo-Helios; and were akin, philosophically, to the Pythagoreans and the devotees of Canopic Hercules. They lived ascetically, guarded certain mystical secrets connected with angelic powers and the progress of the Sun about the Zodiac, and were experts in medicine and agriculture.

(*k*) Philo and Josephus agree that there were about four thousand Essenes in all (*Quod Omnis Probus* 12 and *Antiquities* xviii. 1. 5); a number comprising both the Strict Essenes who were celibate and kept within their monastic cloisters near the Dead Sea, and the Free Essenes who married and kept guest-houses (*see* (*i*) *above*) in the Judaean towns and villages. The Hemero-Baptists, or 'washers-at-daybreak', were yet another branch, who appear in the Talmud (*Tosephta Yadaim* ii. 20) as *toble shahrith;* they seem to have been apocalyptic hermits like John the Baptist and 'Banus', Josephus's teacher (*see* v.*e*). The *Toble Shahrith* survived into the second century when, according to *Jer. Berakoth* iii. 4, Rabbi Haninah passing the gates of the baths (at Caesarea?) early one morning, found them at their ablutions and suggested that they would be better employed in studying the Law. He said on the same day: 'Whosoever has work to do let him go and do it.'

The word *Essenes* (Greek: *Essēnoi, Essaioi* or *Esaioi;* Latin: *Esseni*) may be derived from either the Hebrew *Hashaim,* 'the Silent Ones'—because, like Benedictine monks, they did not speak at meal-times—or from *Issiim,* 'Healers'; and was probably applicable to any communistic ascetic-quietistic order, among them the Zophim of Bethany and Arimathaea (*see* CXIV.*a and b*). Another Talmudic term for them is *Tsenuyim,* 'the Chaste Ones'.

(*l*) 'Banus' recalls *banaim,* still another Talmudic name for the Essenes (*Shabbath* 114*a* and *Mikwaoth* ix. 6). It means 'masons', though their masonry may have been metaphorical, like that of the Free Masons today,* and concerned with certain mystical pillars, or celestial arches, set up by their demi-god and watched over by angelic Powers. When Paul, in *Galatians* iv. 8–10 and *Colossians* ii. 8 *and* 20, inveighs against the astrological worship of

---

* The Talmud explains these builders as scholars: 'because they occupy themselves with building up the world'.

'weak and cringing elements' now vanquished by Jesus Christ, the sole mediator with the Father, he has these or similar Powers in mind.

(*m*) It is known that the heads of the Pharisee academies communicated certain divine secrets, such as 'The Work of the Chariot' (*Ezekiel* i.), 'The Work of the Creation' (*Genesis* i.), and 'The Sacred Name of God', to favourite pupils. Those arcana were never recorded in the Talmud lest they fell into wrong hands; and Paul's influence would have expunged any similar record from the Canonical Gospels. *The Gospel according to the Egyptians,* however, credits Jesus with a private mystical teaching (*see* LXXXIV.g), though this may not have been of an Essene character. It cannot therefore be decided whether the Hebrew mysteries taught to the Jews of Galatia, Corinth, and Colossi—and preached against by Paul who, in *Galatians* iv. 12, confesses to have himself once embraced them: 'Brethren, I beseech you, be as I am; for I [was] as ye [are]!'—were Nazarene ones of Essene origin.

(*n*) *Matthew* x. 21-23, paralleled in *Mark* xiii. 12-13 and repeated in *Matthew* xxiv. 9-13, belongs to Jesus's account of the Last Days (*see* XCVIII.d).

Matthew x. 24-25, paralleled and mistakenly expanded in *Luke* vi. 40, belongs to his confirmation of the Twelve as teachers in their own right, released from pupillage to him (*see* LIV.h *and* CVI.h).

> (202) *'Yet think not that the disciple is above his master or the servant above his lord; it is enough for the disciple that he be as his master, and the servant as his lord.'*

* * * * *

(*o*) The difference between Jesus's missionary zeal and that of Hillel lay in the degree of urgency felt by each. Hillel's mild dictum (*Tosephta Berakoth* vii. 24): 'Where men gather, do thou scatter; where they scatter, do thou gather,' is explained in *Gemarah* (*Berakoth* 63a):

> 'If thou seest a generation eagerly desiring knowledge of the Law, disseminate it; but if thou seest a generation having no such desire, withhold thy knowledge.'

In other words: 'Do not force enlightenment on your fellows, nor show anger if they fail to ask for it.' Jesus, living a generation later, had decided that the times required a change of religious policy: the Last Days were imminent (*see* CI.c), and everyone must now declare whether he stood on God's side, or on Satan's—that is, whether he accepted or rejected the call to repentance (*see* XXXIV.g *and* XLVI.c).

* * * * *

LVIII

THE VINEYARD

Matthew xx. 1–16

[1]'For the Kingdom of Heaven is like unto a man that is an householder, which went out early in the morning to hire labourers into his vineyard. [2]And when he had agreed with the labourers for a penny a day, he sent them into his vineyard. [3]And he went out about the third hour, and saw others standing idle in the marketplace, [4]and said unto them; Go ye also into the vineyard, and whatsoever is right I will give you. And they went their way. [5]Again he went out about the sixth and ninth hour, and did likewise. [6]And about the eleventh hour he went out, and found others standing idle, and saith unto them, Why stand ye here all the day idle? [7]They say unto him, Because no man hath hired us. He saith unto them, Go ye also into the vineyard; and whatsoever is right, that shall ye receive. [8]So when even was come, the lord of the vineyard saith unto his steward, Call the labourers, and give them their hire, beginning from the last unto the first. [9]And when they came that were hired about the eleventh hour, they received every man a penny. [10]But when the first came, they supposed that they should have received more; and they likewise received every man a penny. [11]And when they had received it, they murmured against the goodman of the house, [12]saying, These last have wrought but one hour, and thou hast made them equal unto us, which have borne the burden and heat of the day. [13]But he answered one of them, and said, Friend, I do thee no wrong: didst thou not agree with me for a penny? [14]Take that thine is, and go thy way: I will give unto this last, even as unto thee. [15]Is it not lawful for me to do what I will with mine own? Is thine eye evil, because I am good? [16]So the last shall be first, and the first last: for many be called, but few chosen.'

Matthew ix. 36–38

[36]But when He saw the multitudes, He was moved with compassion on them, because they fainted, and were scattered abroad, as sheep having no shepherd. Then saith He unto His disciples:

[37]'The harvest truly is plenteous, but the labourers are few; [38]pray ye therefore the Lord of the harvest, that He will send forth labourers into His harvest.'

Luke x. 2

[2]Therefore said He unto them: 'The harvest truly is great, but the labourers are few: pray ye therefore the Lord of the harvest, that he would send forth labourers into his harvest.'

Matthew xxi. 28–32

[28]But what think ye? A certain man had two sons; and he came to the first, and said, Son, go work today in my vineyard. [29]He answered and said, I will not: but afterwards he repented, and went. [30]And he came to the second, and said likewise. And he answered and said, I go, sir: and went not. [31]Whether of them twain did the will of his father?' They said unto Him, 'The first.' Jesus saith unto them: 'Verily I say unto you, that the publicans and the harlots go into the kingdom of God before you. [32]For John came unto you in the way of righteousness, and ye believed him not: but the publicans and the harlots believed him: and ye, when ye had seen it, repented not afterward, that ye might believe him.'

Luke vii. 29–30

[29]And all the people that heard him, and the publicans, justified God, being baptized with the baptism of John. [30]But the Pharisees and lawyers rejected the counsel of God against themselves, being not baptized of him.

(a) *Matthew* xx. 1–16, the parable of the Vineyard, has been inserted into Jesus's dispute with the Jerusalem Sadducees: probably because a Pauline editor understood it to mean that Gentiles who accept Christianity are not only the equal of Jews who have kept the Law all their lives, but superior to them. Hence the last verse, which does not fit the context and has been borrowed partly from *Mark* x. 31, *Luke* xiii. 30, or *Matthew* xix. 30 (*see* LXXXII.*d*), and partly from *Matthew* xxii. 14, itself quoted out of context (*see* XLVI.*c*). The parable's appropriate place is immediately after the Return of the Twelve (*see* LVII.*h*). Its true meaning recalls that of the Prodigal Son (*see* XVIII.*a*), but here the argument has been taken one stage further.

(b) The vineyard is Israel, the labourers are those who assist God as the Lord of the Vineyard (*see* LIV.*c*); presumably the steward is Enoch, or 'Metatron', who was regarded by the Jews very much as St Peter is now regarded by Catholics (*see* LX.*b*). Jesus declares that it will be a sin of jealousy (*see* XXIV.*b*) if veteran synagogue teachers resent the apostles' being placed on an equal footing with themselves.

In support of the parable's Pauline interpretation, the last-hired labourers are wrongly represented as coming to the pay-table first—which would have given the first-hired a just grievance. This change has made verse 14 illogical. Since the last-hired have already been paid (verses 8–9), 'I will give to this last' makes no sense. But 'this last' being singular, not plural, preserves a fragment of the original tradition. The structure of Jesus's parables is usually a cumulative sequence of first, next, and last; it is unlikely therefore that more labourers were hired between the sixth and the ninth hours.

(211) *Now, certain jealous men, feigning themselves to be Pharisees, heard that Jesus made much of the Twelve, and were offended, saying: 'Shall these verily be received with as much honour as they that have studied the Law and kept it from their youth up?*

'For some of these were sinners but yesterday, and today they continue in ignorance of the Law.'

Therefore Jesus spake a parable unto them, saying:

'The Kingdom of Heaven is like unto an householder, which went out early in the morning to hire labourers unto his vineyard.

'And when he had agreed with certain tried labourers of his acquaintance for a penny a day, he sent them into his vineyard.

'About the third hour he went out again and saw men standing idle in the market place, as sheep having no shepherd, and said unto them: "Go ye also into the vineyard and whatsoever is right I will give you. For the harvest truly is plenteous and the labourers are few." And they went their way.

'Now, it chanced as he passed through the market place at about the eleventh hour, that he saw a poor man, which had been waiting there since the third hour, and saith unto him: "Why standest thou here all the day idle?"

'He answered and said: "Because no man hath hired me; wherefore tomorrow we must go hungry, I and my children."

'Then he was filled with compassion, and said unto the man: "Go thou also into the vineyard and whatsoever is right, that thou shalt receive."

'When even was come, the householder saith unto his steward: "Call the labourers and give them their hire."

'And when the first came, they received every man a penny, but when they saw that those which were hired at the third hour likewise received a penny, they murmured among themselves and waited to see how much the last man should receive.

'But the householder said unto his steward: "Let this man likewise receive a penny."

'Then were those which were first hired filled with wrath, and said unto the householder: "This last hath laboured one hour only, and thou hast made him equal unto us which have borne the burden and heat of the day."

'But he answered one of them, and said: "Friend, I do thee no wrong. Didst thou not agree with me for a penny? Take that thine is, and go thy way. Wherefore shall I not give unto this last even as unto thee? Is it not lawful for me to do what I will with mine own?

'"Let not thine eye be evil because I do good unto this man which laboureth for me."'

And Jesus said unto them: 'Pray ye rather the Lord of the Vineyard, that he will send forth many more labourers into His harvest. For the harvest is great, but the labourers are few.'

* * * * *

(c) This should be followed by *Matthew* xxi. 28–32, the parable of the Two Sons. Jesus's opponents seem to have argued that the synagogue was the only legitimate centre of religious instruction to the faithful, and that enlightenment should not be forced on those unwilling to receive it (*see* LVII.o). Jesus replied that it was no longer enough to preach to the faithful alone; that the duty of all true Pharisees was to convert the Men of the Land; and that, since trained teachers had neglected this task, his recently baptized and still ignorant disciples must undertake it. He added that a repentant sinner stood higher in God's favour than the man who had never sinned (*Berakoth* 34*b*—see XIX.*k*).

(*d*) *Matthew* xxi. 31, 'publicans and harlots', should read: 'men who once served the Wicked Kingdom and partook of her harlotries but now have repented.'

The reference to the Baptist seems to have been altered in order to deny him credit for having baptized most of Jesus's disciples. There was never any question of John's converting the Pharisees, who were already saved; and 'publicans' has been mischievously inserted in *Luke* vii. 29–30, to emphasize the parable of the Pharisee and Publican (*see* XIX. *i*–*k*). The Pharisees' and lawyers' unwillingness to accept the popular identification of John with Elijah (*see* XXXIX.*h*), has been twisted into a downright rejection of his message.

(212) *They said again: 'Every Sabbath day the Law is expounded in the synagogue, whither all they that are faithful come to be taught.'*

But since they had rejected John's counsel which bade them preach to the men of the land, Jesus answered:

'It is not enough to teach the righteous only.'

He said unto them also: 'A certain householder had two sons. And he came to the first, and said: "Son, go work today in my vineyard!"

'He answered and said: "I will not," but afterwards he repented, and went.

'And the householder came to the second, and said likewise.

'And this son answered him dutifully, and said: "I go, sir," but went not.

'Did not the first of the twain honour his father rather than the second?

'Verily, I say unto you: these men which aforetime served the Wicked Kingdom and partook of her harlotries, but repented and were baptized of John, shall they be less honoured in the Kingdom of Heaven than ye?

'For John came and shewed unto you the way of righteousness, but ye which are skilled in the Law heeded him not, and went not forth to preach as he counselled you in God's name.

'But these, which are less skilled, hearkened to him and now they go forth to preach in your stead.'

*   *   *   *   *

LIX

WOE TO CHORAZIN!

Matthew xi. 20–27

20Then began He to upbraid the cities wherein most of His mighty works were done, because they repented not: 21'Woe unto thee, Chorazin! woe unto thee, Bethsaida! for if the mighty works, which were done in you, had been done in Tyre and Sidon, they would have repented long ago in sackcloth and ashes. 22But I say unto you, it shall be more tolerable for Tyre and Sidon at the day of judgment, than for you. 23And thou, Capernaum, which art exalted unto heaven, shalt be brought down to hell: for if the mighty works, which have been done in thee, had been done in Sodom, it would have remained until this day. 24But I say unto you, that it shall be more tolerable for the land of Sodom in the day of judgment, than for thee.'

25At that time Jesus answered and said: 'I thank Thee, O Father, Lord of Heaven and earth, because Thou hast hid these things from the wise and prudent, and hast revealed them unto babes. 26Even so, Father: for so it seemed good in Thy sight. 27All things are delivered unto Me of My Father; and no man knoweth the Son, but the Father; neither knoweth any man the Father, save the Son, and he to whomsoever the Son will reveal Him.'

Luke x. 13–16

13Woe unto thee, Chorazin! woe unto thee, Bethsaida! for if the mighty works had been done in Tyre and Sidon, which have been done in you, they had a great while ago repented, sitting in sackcloth and ashes. 14But it shall be more tolerable for Tyre and Sidon at the judgment, than for you. 15And thou, Capernaum, which art exalted to heaven, shalt be thrust down to hell. 16He that heareth you heareth Me; and he that despiseth you despiseth Me; and he that despiseth Me despiseth Him that sent Me.'

Luke x. 21–22

21In that hour Jesus rejoiced in spirit, and said: 'I thank Thee, O Father, Lord of heaven and earth, that Thou hast hid these things from the wise and prudent, and hast revealed them unto babes: even so, Father; for so it seemed good in Thy sight. 22All things are delivered to Me of My Father: and no man knoweth Who the Son is, but the Father; and Who the Father is, but the Son, and he to whom the Son will reveal Him.'

(a) Since it was strictly forbidden to glorify anyone but God (*Isaiah* xlii. 8 and *Acts* xii. 23), Jesus cannot have praised his own mighty works, as stated in *Matthew* xi. 21.

Luke x. 13-15, paralleled in *Matthew* xi. 21-24, follows on the Mission of the Seventy, and *Luke* x. 16 forms part of their instructions (*see* LVII.*b*); Jesus's commination is therefore likely to have been directed against those towns that rejected the Twelve.

(*b*) Bethsaida, according to *John* i. 44 and xii. 21, was the home of Peter, Andrew, and Philip; it lay a little east of where the Jordan enters the Lake of Galilee, and formed a Jewish suburb of Julias, a Greek city built by Philip the Tetrarch in honour of the Emperor Augustus's only daughter (*Antiquities* xviii. 2. 1). 'Chorazin', or Kerazeh, lay west of the river, two miles north of Capernaum, and not far from the highroad linking Egypt with Damascus. However, if the disciples obeyed Jesus's instructions, they would not have performed 'mighty works' in any town which did not welcome them. 'Mighty words' is the more likely reading.

'Tyre and Sidon' in *Matthew* xi. 22 and *Luke* x. 13, should be 'Sodom and Gomorrah', as in *Matthew* x. 15 (*see* LVII.*e*), since Tyre and Sidon could not repent of a breach of the Law by which they were not bound. This pro-Phoenician alteration recalls the improbable account of Phoenician converts in *Mark* iii. 8 (*see* XVII.*a*), which is omitted in the corresponding text, *Matthew* iv. 25, and seems to be borrowed from *Luke* vi. 17.

(*c*) 'Capernaum' cannot have been the original reading in *Matthew* xi. 23, paralleled in *Luke* x. 15: once this town had rejected the disciples and they had shaken its dust from their feet, they could not have revisited it, as Peter seems to have done in Jesus's own company (*Matthew* xvii. 24—*see* XLVIII.*b*). And 'exalted unto heaven', in the same verse, a phrase applied to Jerusalem in *Lamentations* ii. 1-7, does not suit a small, historically undistinguished market-town. This saying is unconnected with the woe against Chorazin and Bethsaida in the preceding verses, and will have been found in the same collection of Oracles under the subject heading 'Woe upon this City!' Its proper context is the 'O Jerusalem, Jerusalem!' lament in *Matthew* xxiii. 37 (*see* XCVII.*f*). Here it has been modified to suit *Matthew* xi. 20, where Jesus is said to have upbraided the cities that witnessed most of his mighty works. A later editor will have asked himself: 'Why no mention of Capernaum, Jesus's headquarters?', and made the change in all good faith.

If, in verse 22, 'Sodom and Gomorrah' is substituted for 'Tyre and Sidon', and the first half of *Matthew* xi. 23 is removed, then 'for' which introduces the second half of the saying, becomes logical again.

(362) *'Woe unto thee, Zion! As it is prophesied in the* Book of Lamentations:
'"How hath the Lord cast down from Heaven unto earth the beauty of Israel, and in the day of His anger remembered not His footstool!
'"He hath cast off His altar, He hath abhorred His sanctuary, He hath given up into the hand of the enemy the walls of her palaces.''

* * * * *

(203) *And when Jesus heard that they had shaken the dust off their feet as a testimony against Chorazin and against Bethsaida, he said:*

'Woe unto thee, Chorazin! Woe unto thee, Bethsaida! For if the mighty words spoken in your streets had been spoken in Sodom and Gomorrah, they would have repented in sack-cloth and ashes, and have remained standing until this day.'

* * * * *

(*d*) The strange praise supposedly given to God in *Matthew* xi. 25-27, for hiding the fate of these Galilean cities from the wise and revealing it to Jesus's disciples, occurs in a different context in *Luke* x. 21, where the Seventy have joyfully returned from their successful mission (*see* LVII.*f*). Jesus will have been pleased, not that the wise were debarred from knowing things revealed to babes, but rather that babes were admitted to knowledge formerly held only by the wise.

Luke x. 22, the saying about the Father and the Son, recalls several Christological passages, such as *John* iii. 35 (*see* VIII.*p*), *John* v. 20 (*see* XXVI.*d*) and *John* xiii. 3 (*see* CVI.*t*); it is followed by a text which, in *Matthew* xiii. 16-17, follows the parable of The Sower (*see* XXV.*e*).

(242) *And he lifted his eyes to heaven, and gave thanks to God, saying: 'I rejoice, Father, that Thou has not hid from simple men things that before were revealed to the wise and prudent alone.'*

* * * * *

LITTLE CHILDREN

Mark ix. 33–37

³³And He came to Capernaum: and being in the house He asked them: 'What was it that ye disputed among yourselves by the way?' ³⁴But they held their peace: for by the way they had disputed among themselves, who should be the greatest. ³⁵And He sat down, and called the Twelve, and saith unto them: 'If any man desire to be first, the same shall be last of all, and servant of all.' ³⁶And He took a child, and set him in the midst of them: and when He had taken him in His arms, He said unto them: ³⁷'Whosoever shall receive one of such children in My name, receiveth Me: and whosoever shall receive Me, receiveth not Me, but Him that sent Me.'

Mark ix. 41–42

⁴¹For whosoever shall give you a cup of water to drink in My name, because ye belong to Christ, verily I say unto you, he shall not lose his reward. ⁴²And whosoever shall offend one of these little ones that believe in Me, it is better for him that a millstone were hanged about his neck, and he were cast into the sea.

Mark x. 13–16

¹³And they brought young children to Him, that He should touch them: and His disciples rebuked those that brought them. ¹⁴But when Jesus saw it, He was much displeased, and said unto them: 'Suffer the little children to come unto Me, and forbid them not: for of such is the kingdom of God. ¹⁵Verily I say unto you, Whosoever shall not receive the kingdom of God as a little child, he shall not enter therein.' ¹⁶And He took them up in His arms, put His hands upon them, and blessed them.

Matthew x. 42

⁴²'And whosoever shall give to drink unto one of these little ones a cup of cold water only in the name of a disciple, verily I say unto you, he shall in no wise lose his reward.'

Matthew xviii. 1–6

¹At the same time came the disciples unto Jesus, saying: 'Who is the greatest in the Kingdom of Heaven?' ²And Jesus called a little child unto Him, and set him in the midst of them, ³and said: 'Verily I say unto you, except ye be

Matthew xviii. 1–6 (*contd.*)

converted, and become as little children, ye shall not enter into the Kingdom of Heaven. [4]Whosoever therefore shall humble himself as this little child, the same is greatest in the Kingdom of Heaven. [5]And whoso shall receive one such little child in My name receiveth Me. [6]But whoso shall offend one of these little ones which believe in Me, it were better for him that a millstone were hanged about his neck, and that he were drowned in the depth of the sea.'

Matthew xviii. 10

[10]'Take heed that ye despise not one of these little ones; for I say unto you, that in heaven their angels do always behold the face of My Father which is in heaven.'

Matthew xix. 13–15

[13]Then were there brought unto Him little children, that He should put His hands on them, and pray: and the disciples rebuked them. [14]But Jesus said: 'Suffer little children, and forbid them not, to come unto Me: for of such is the Kingdom of Heaven.' [15]And He laid His hands on them, and departed thence.

Luke ix. 46–48

[46]Then there arose a reasoning among them, which of them should be greatest. [47]And Jesus, perceiving the thought of their heart, took a child, and set him by Him, [48]and said unto them: 'Whosoever shall receive this child in My name receiveth Me: and whosoever shall receive Me receiveth Him that sent Me: for he that is least among you all, the same shall be great.'

Luke xvii. 1–2

[1]Then said He unto the disciples: 'It is impossible but that offences will come: but woe unto him, through whom they come! [2]It were better for him that a millstone were hanged about his neck, and he cast into the sea, than that he should offend one of these little ones.'

Luke xviii. 15–17

[15]And they brought unto Him also infants, that He would touch them: but when His disciples saw it, they rebuked them. [16]But Jesus called them unto Him, and said: 'Suffer little children to come unto Me, and forbid them not: for of such is the kingdom of God. [17]Verily I say unto you, whosoever shall not receive the kingdom of God as a little child shall in no wise enter therein.'

Matthew xxv. 34–46

[34]'Then shall the King say unto them on His right hand, Come, ye blessed of My Father, inherit the kingdom prepared for you from the foundation of the world: [35]for I was an hungred, and ye gave Me meat: I was thirsty, and ye gave Me drink: I was a stranger, and ye took Me in: [36]naked, and ye clothed Me: I was sick, and ye visited Me: I was in prison, and ye came unto Me.

Matthew xxv. 34–46 (contd.)

[37]Then shall the righteous answer Him, saying, Lord, when saw we Thee an hungred, and fed Thee? or thirsty, and gave Thee drink? [38]When saw we Thee a stranger, and took Thee in? or naked, and clothed Thee? [39]Or when saw we Thee sick, or in prison, and came unto Thee? [40]And the King shall answer and say unto them, Verily I say unto you, inasmuch as ye have done it unto one of the least of these My brethren, ye have done it unto Me. [41]Then shall He say also unto them on the left hand, Depart from Me, ye cursed, into everlasting fire, prepared for the devil and his angels: [42]for I was an hungred, and ye gave Me no meat: I was thirsty, and ye gave Me no drink: [43]I was a stranger, and ye took Me not in: naked, and ye clothed Me not: sick, and in prison, and ye visited Me not. [44]Then shall they also answer him, saying, Lord, when saw we Thee an hungred, or athirst, or a stranger, or naked, or sick, or in prison, and did not minister unto Thee? [45]Then shall He answer them, saying, Verily I say unto you, inasmuch as ye did it not to one of the least of these, ye did it not to Me. [46]And these shall go away into everlasting punishment: but the righteous into life eternal.'

(a) A somewhat forced *midrash* on *Lamentations* i. 5–6: 'Her children are gone into captivity, from Zion her splendour is departed,' runs (*Lamentations Rabbati* i. 32):

'See how beloved the little children are before God. When the Council [Sanhedrin] went into Captivity [i.e. under Nebuchadnezzar] the Glory [*shekinah*] went not with them, nor went it with . . . the priests. But when the little children went into Captivity, then went the Glory with them.'

In *Mark* x. 13–16, *Matthew* xviii. 2–3 and *Luke* xviii. 16–17, Jesus appears to be linking this *midrash* to one of his own on *Psalm* cxxxi. 1–2, where he extols the childish innocence of an adult, and this to a third *midrash* on Ezekiel's vision of the Chariot (*see* LVII.*m*): he warns his disciples 'not to enquire what is above, what is below, what is ahead or what is behind'. Because of their innocence, he declares, little children are permitted to see the Glory (a theory introduced into English poetry by Henry Vaughan and borrowed from him by Wordsworth in his *Intimations of Immortality*).

(b) In the original tradition, the disciples' dispute about precedence in the Kingdom (*Mark* ix. 33–35, *Matthew* xviii. 1 and *Luke* ix. 46), seems to have been unconnected with this saying; and unconnected, too, with the plea by the mother of James and John (*Matthew* xx. 20), or (less probably) by James and John themselves (*Mark* x. 35), that they should be seated on Jesus's left and right hand in the Kingdom (*see* LXII.*b*). The dispute was probably no more than a theological argument about the patriarchs' precedence in heaven. In the orthodox view, Abraham would have first place, Isaac and Jacob the second and third, and Moses the fourth; but the disciples may well have wondered about the precedence of Abraham's ancestor Enoch—Jehovah's Keeper of Records who, for the apocalyptics, ranked higher than any other Power in God's Court*—and perhaps also about Elijah's. Jesus settled the argument by quoting *Isaiah* xi. 6: 'A little child shall lead them'—held to be a prophecy about the Heavenly Kingdom. This saying and the one concerning school-children seem to have been found, together with a third and fourth, in a collection of Oracles, under the subject-heading 'Little Children.' (*c*) The third saying, *Mark* ix. 42, *Matthew* xviii. 6 and 10 and *Luke* xvii. 2: 'Take heed not to offend the little ones', will have been spoken by Jesus while fondling a child (*Mark* x. 13–16, *Matthew* xviii. 2 and *Luke* ix. 47–48). It is paralleled in the Talmud (*Sanhedrin* 96a): 'Care well for the children of the men of the land, for from them will the Law proceed', which is derived from a *midrash* on 1 *Chronicles* xvi. 22: 'Touch not Mine anointed and do My prophets no harm'. This runs:

> 'The anointed are children who learn the Law, and the prophets are their teachers.'

The millstone curse, a proverbial one, is fastened by Jesus on anyone who dares to offend school-children. The children's 'angels' in *Matthew* xviii. 10, should be 'angel': namely this same busy Enoch who, among his other duties, helped them to memorize the Law. (Individual guardian angels were deduced by Gentile Christians from this passage; in Hebrew tradition, only a king was entitled to one.†) Despite the attachment of the millstone saying to Jesus's praise of childish innocence in adults (*Mark* x. 13–16, *Matthew* xix. 13–15 *and Luke* xviii. 15–17), they do not seem to have been originally connected. Such innocence stood, above all things, for physical virginity: once a man had enjoyed sexual congress, he was delivered into the power of the Serpent, or Cosmocrator. Jesus held, therefore, that God valued the patriarchs Abraham and Enoch less highly than a child who had never known women (*see* xxi.*o–s*).

(*d*) The fourth saying, which concerns the cup of cold water, is found both in *Matthew* x. 42, where it has become detached from *Matthew* xviii. 5, and in *Mark* ix. 41, where it is confused with the millstone curse. *Luke* ix. 48 omits it altogether. It refers to the people's reception of the Twelve when they went out, in poverty and chastity, to preach the Kingdom of God (*see* lvii.*g*). A gloss to that effect must have been inserted in the margin of *Matthew* x. 42: 'This is said of a disciple'; but an obtuse editor (*see* lxiii.*a*), thinking that the gloss referred to *name,* not to *little one,* altered 'name of God' to 'name of a disciple'.

---

* The apocalyptics called him *Metatron,* a variant of the Greek word *metadromos,* 'He who courses about'. In the *Midrash,* he even instructs the Almighty in religious etiquette (*Lamentations Rabbati* xxiv):

'When God wept over the destruction of the Temple, Metatron said: "I will weep, but Thou must not."

'God answered: "If thou wilt not suffer me to weep, I will go where thou canst not follow and there will I weep and lament." '

† According to *Canticles Rabbah* viii. 14, 'no King suffers judgement unless his prince in heaven be first overthrown.'

(e) *Matthew* xxv. 34–46, a continuation of this saying, is a *midrash* on *Proverbs* xiv. 31 and xix. 17.

Verse 36 is a Pauline interpolation; the 'little children' who would benefit from the hospitality of the devout were neither naked, sick, nor imprisoned.

> (147) *And the other disciples also came to Capernaum, and when they were together in the house, Jesus asked them: 'What was it that ye disputed among yourselves by the way?'*
>
> *They answered: 'We disputed who should be counted most honourable in the Kingdom of God, whether our father Abraham which died and was buried, or whether his forefather the prophet Enoch, which was spared death as being a man without sin.'*
>
> *Jesus said: 'Neither the one nor the other. For Isaiah hath testified: "A little child shall lead them all."'*

*   *   *   *   *

> (148) *'Know ye not what David spake in a psalm? He said: "Lord, my heart is not haughty, neither do I exercise myself in great matters or things too high for me.*
>
> *'"Surely, I have behaved and quieted my soul as a weaned child."*
>
> *'Now, the things that are too high signify the Works of the Chariot, namely the vision of the Glory of God which Ezekiel saw, whereof we are warned by the Sages: "Enquire not what is above, nor what is below, nor what is ahead, nor what is behind."*
>
> *'Be ye therefore as the little children. For it is written in the* Book of Lamentations: *"Her children are gone into captivity, from Zion her glory is departed."*
>
> *'And the Sages have taught us: "See how beloved the little children are before God. When the Council went into captivity, the Glory of God went not with them; nor went it with the priests; but when the little children went into captivity, then went the Glory of God with them."*
>
> *'If therefore ye be not humble in heart and become as little children, ye shall neither see the Glory nor enter into the Kingdom.'*

*   *   *   *   *

> (179) *And when little children were brought unto Jesus that he should teach them the Law, his disciples drave them away, and rebuked those that brought them.*
>
> *But Jesus, being much displeased, took a little child in his arms and stood in their midst, and said: 'Suffer little children to come unto me and drive them not hence.*
>
> *'For David saith: "Touch not Mine anointed nor do My prophets any harm," and the Sages have taught us that the anointed signify the little children which learn the Law.*
>
> *'Therefore care ye well for the children of the Men of the Land; from them the Law shall proceed.*
>
> *'Verily, I say unto you: whosoever shall offend against one of these little ones, it were better for him that a millstone were hanged about his neck and that he were drowned in the depth of the sea.*

'*For Enoch, which is God's messenger unto such children as learn the Law, he ever beholds the face of our Father which is in heaven.*'

* * * * *

(189) '*And whosoever receiveth any of you little ones, and giveth him so much as a cup of cold water in God's name, the same shall receive his reward in the Day of Judgement.*

'*For Solomon prophesied: "He that hath pity upon the poor lendeth unto the Lord, and the Lord will repay him."*

'*In that day the King of Glory shall say unto certain righteous men that come before him: "Come, ye blessed of my Father, inherit the Kingdom of Heaven prepared for you from the foundation of the world.*

'*"For I was an-hungered, and ye gave me meat; I was a-thirst and ye gave me drink, I was a stranger and ye took me in."*

'*Then shall the righteous ask: "Lord, when did we so?"*

'*And the King of Glory shall answer and say unto them: "Insomuch as ye have done it unto the least of my children, ye have done it unto me."*

'*And it is written in the same book: "He that useth the poor ill, the same reproacheth his Maker."*

'*Therefore, in that day the King of Glory shall say unto certain others: "I was an-hungered and ye gave me no meat, I was a-thirst and ye gave me no drink, but ye reproached me and sent me away empty-handed."*

'*Then shall these unrighteous ones ask: "Lord, when did we so?"*

'*And the King of Glory shall answer and say unto them: "Insomuch as ye have done unto the least of my children, ye have done unto me to my reproach.*

'*"Depart from me, cursed ones, into the everlasting fire prepared for Belial and his angels!"*'

* * * * *

(*f*) For this judgement by the King of Glory, *alias* the Son of Man, *see* LXXXVIII.*g and h* and XCVIII.*m.*

* * * * *

LXI

ON SALT

Mark ix. 49–50

[49]'For every one shall be salted with fire, and every sacrifice shall be salted with salt. [50]Salt is good: but if the salt have lost its saltness, wherewith will ye season it? Have salt in yourselves, and have peace one with another.'

Matthew v. 13

[13]'Ye are the salt of the earth: but if the salt have lost its saltness, wherewith shall it be salted? it is thenceforth good for nothing, but to be cast out, and to be trodden under foot of men.'

Luke xiv. 34–35

[34]'Salt is good: but if the salt have lost its savour, wherewith shall it be seasoned? [35]It is neither fit for the land, nor yet for the dunghill; but men cast it out. He that hath ears to hear, let him hear.'

(a) The saying found in *Mark* ix. 49–50, *Matthew* v. 13 and *Luke* xiv. 34–35 is a *midrash* on *Leviticus* ii. 13 and *Numbers* xviii. 19, to which Jesus has added a topical comment on the general adulteration of salt—a result of the Imperial salt tax imposed on Judea and Galilee. It is aimed at the Sadducees who collaborated with the Romans. Salt, as an antidote to poison, is mentioned in 2 *Kings* ii. 19–22: a passage which explains the phrase 'salt of the earth' as implying not universal missionary activity, but the fertilization of a single barren region.

(170) *In these same days, when the disciples murmured, saying that the salt which they bought had no savour, Jesus said: 'The Chief Rulers, the sons of Aaron, love the princes of the Wicked Kingdom; wherefore the salt is corrupted.*

'For the Lord said unto Aaron: "With all thy sacrifices shalt thou offer salt and it shall be a covenant of salt for ever before the Lord unto thee and thy seed for ever."

'But these sons of Aaron have forsaken His covenant. And this salt, that hath lost its savour, wherewith shall it be salted?

'It is fit neither for the land, nor yet for the dung hill, but only to be cast upon the highway and trodden underfoot.

'Is it not written: "Every sacrifice that is burned upon the altar shall be seasoned with pure salt"?

'Therefore, keep ye faith, though they fail. Be ye as the salt which Elijah cast into the corrupt spring of Jericho, crying in the name of the Lord: "I have healed these waters. There shall not be from thence any more death or barren land." '

* * * * *

(*b*) In *Sopherim* xv. 6 (ed. Higger), the Law is compared to salt, because the world could not continue long without either, and in *Kethuboth* 66*b*, 'the salt of money' is used as a synonym for charity; and as 'salt' meant 'literary wit' in Athens, so it meant 'spiritual discernment' in Jerusalem.

(*c*) *Mark* ix. 50: 'Have peace with one another', is a separate saying and may be restored in its entirety from *Romans* xii. 18–21, where many of Jesus's sayings are briefly quoted (*see* xci.*e*).

(109) *'Yea, have peace with all men and take no vengeance, for it is written: "Vengeance is Mine, I will repay, saith the Lord."*

'And Solomon likewise saith: "If thine enemy be hungry, give him bread to eat, and if he be thirsty, give him water to drink. For thou shalt heap coals of fire upon his head, and the Lord shall reward thee."

'Wherefore, be not overcome of evil, but overcome evil with good.'

* * * * *

LXII

PRECEDENCE

Mark x. 35–45

³⁵And James and John, the sons of Zebedee, come unto Him saying: 'Master, we would that Thou shouldst do for us whatsoever we shall desire.'

³⁶And He said unto them: 'What would ye that I should do for you?'

³⁷They said unto Him: 'Grant unto us that we may sit, one on Thy right hand, and the other on Thy left hand, in Thy glory.'

³⁸But Jesus said unto them: 'Ye know not what ye ask: can ye drink of the cup that I drink of? and be baptized with the baptism that I am baptized with?'

³⁹And they said unto Him: 'We can.' And Jesus said unto them: 'Ye shall indeed drink of the cup that I drink of; and with the baptism that I am baptized withal shall ye be baptized; ⁴⁰but to sit on My right hand and on My left hand is not Mine to give; but it shall be given to them for whom it is prepared.' ⁴¹And when the ten heard it, they began to be much displeased with James and John. ⁴²But Jesus called them to Him, and saith unto them: 'Ye know that they which are accounted to rule over the Gentiles exercise lordship over them; and their great ones exercise authority upon them. ⁴³But so shall it not be among you: but whosoever will be great among you, shall be your minister: ⁴⁴and whosoever of you will be the chiefest, shall be servant of all. ⁴⁵For even the Son of Man came not to be ministered unto, but to minister, and to give His life a ransom for many.'

Matthew xix. 27–28

²⁷Then answered Peter and said unto Him: 'Behold, we have forsaken all, and followed Thee; what shall we have therefore?' ²⁸And Jesus said unto them: 'Verily I say unto you, that ye which have followed Me, in the regeneration when the Son of Man shall sit in the throne of His glory, ye also shall sit upon twelve thrones, judging the twelve tribes of Israel.'

Matthew xx. 20–28

²⁰Then came to Him the mother of Zebedee's children with her sons, worshipping Him, and desiring a certain thing of Him. ²¹And He said unto her: 'What wilt thou?' She saith unto Him: 'Grant that these my two sons may sit, the one on Thy right hand, and the other on the left, in Thy kingdom.' ²²But Jesus answered and said: 'Ye know not what ye ask. Are ye able to drink of the cup that I shall drink of, and to be baptized with the baptism that I am baptized with?' They say unto Him: 'We are able.' ²³And He saith unto

Matthew xx. 20–28 (*contd.*)

them: 'Ye shall drink indeed of My cup, and be baptized with the baptism that I am baptized with: but to sit on My right hand, and on My left, is not Mine to give, but it shall be given to them for whom it is prepared of My Father.' [24]And when the ten heard it, they were moved with indignation against the two brethren. [25]But Jesus called them unto Him, and said: 'Ye know that the princes of the Gentiles exercise dominion over them, and they that are great exercise authority upon them. [26]But it shall not be so among you: but whosoever will be great among you, let him be your minister; [27]and whoever will be chief among you, let him be your servant: [28]even as the Son of Man came not to be ministered unto, but to minister, and to give His life a ransom for many.'

Luke xxii. 24–30

[24]And there was also a strife among them, which of them should be accounted the greatest. [25]And He said unto them: 'The kings of the Gentiles exercise lordship over them; and they that exercise authority upon them are called benefactors. [26]But ye shall not be so: but he that is greatest among you, let him be as the younger: and he that is chief, as he that doth serve. [27]For whether is greater, he that sitteth at meat, or he that serveth? is not he that sitteth at meat? but I am among you as He that serveth. [28]Ye are they which have continued with Me in My temptations. [29]And I appoint unto you a kingdom, as My Father hath appointed unto Me; [30]that ye may eat and drink at My table in My kingdom, and sit on thrones judging the twelve tribes of Israel.'

(*a*) In *Mark* x. 35–45 and *Matthew* xx. 20–28, Jesus refuses to promise his disciples the right to sit on thrones in the Kingdom of Heaven; in *Matthew* xix. 27–28 and *Luke* xxii. 24–30, he does so. It seems that the editors of these two latter passages recalled *Revelation* iii. 21: 'To him that overcometh will I [Jesus] grant to sit with me in my throne . . .', and *Revelation* xx. 4: 'I saw thrones and they sat upon them and judgement was given unto them,' and were therefore convinced that Jesus's refusal to grant thrones had been misreported. A further reference to *Revelation* xix. 9 occurs in *Luke* xxii. 30.

(*b*) Though in *Revelation* iii. 21 Jesus arrogates to himself powers which in *Mark* x. 40 and *Matthew* xx. 23 he explicitly reserves for God, it may be assumed that he did mention the thrones of judgement in his *midrash* on *Isaiah* i. 26–28 and *Psalm* cxxii. 5 to which *Revelation* xx. 4 refers, but did not speculate on the identity of their occupants. The need for judges to scrutinize entrants into the Heavenly Jerusalem is emphasized in the Talmud (*Baba Bathra* 75*b*):

'Rabbi Jonanan said: "The Jerusalem of the world to come is not like unto the Jerusalem of this world. Into the Jerusalem of this world all may enter who will, but into the Jerusalem of the world to come they only may enter who are appointed thereto." '

According to *Hagigah* 12*b,* the Otherworldly Jerusalem existed already, complete with its Temple which was to replace the present one (*see* xc.*h*); and the Archangel Michael was the High Priest Designate.

(*c*) The mother of James and John probably made the request for precedence in the Kingdom without her sons' knowledge; she may have been let into the secret of Jesus's kingship (*see* LXXVII.*b*) before it was publicly announced. A Pauline editor of *Mark* x. 35–37 has seized this opportunity to discredit two leading disciples by suggesting that they made the request themselves and, moreover, that it provoked a quarrel among the rest. The editor of *Luke* stages the incident at the Last Supper, wishing further to emphasize their indecent ambition.

The quarrel, if there was one at all, will have been about precedence in this world, not the next: it may be hazarded that, on some previous occasion, Jesus had committed the other disciples to the charge of James, his adoptive brother, and Peter, who afterwards assumed the joint leadership of the Nazarene Church (*Galatians* ii. 9), and that this was resented.

The editor of *Luke* xxii. 25 overreaches himself when he makes Jesus warn his disciples not to earn the name of 'Benefactors'.

(260) *And as they went Jesus taught his disciples, saying: 'Isaiah prophesied unto Jerusalem in the name of the Lord: "I will restore thy judges as at the first and thou shalt be called the City of Righteousness."*

'And David also prophesied, saying: "Jerusalem is built as a city that is at unity with itself; and thither the tribes go up to give thanks unto the name of the Lord. For there are set thrones of judgement, the thrones of the household of David."

'Verily, I say unto you: in the Heavenly Jerusalem they that have continued faithful under temptation, the same shall be chosen to be judges and shall sit on thrones beside the Son of David to judge the tribes and to judge the Gentiles that come up thither to worship.'

* * * * *

(261) *Then came the mother of James and John unto Jesus, desiring a boon of him.*

And he asked her, saying: 'What wilt thou?'

She saith unto him: 'Grant that these my two sons may sit, the one on thy right hand and the other on thy left in the Kingdom, when thou deliverest judgement.'

Jesus was moved with indignation, and said: 'Thou knowest not what thou askest!'

And in the presence of James and John he said unto her: 'To drink of the bitter cup that I must drink of and to be baptized with the fiery baptism that I must be baptized with, that can I give thy sons, if they are able to receive it.

'But to sit on the right hand and on the left of the Son of David, is not mine to give. For the Father shall give it unto them for whom it is prepared.'

* * * * *

(183) *And it came to pass one day that Jesus departed from the house where he abode and went to pray upon a mountain alone. And he committed the ten disciples unto the charge of James his brother and of Simon Peter.*

Then were the ten filled with wrath and murmured, saying: 'Are these greater than we?'

Therefore Jesus called them unto him and said: 'Ye know that petty princes exercise dominion over the Gentiles and certain great ones exercise dominion over the petty princes, and all men do their bidding.

'But it shall not be so among you. Whosoever shall be great among you, let him be your servant; and whosoever shall be chief, let him minister unto you.'

* * * * *

(*d*) This was true in a limited sense only; Jesus here distinguishes the Jewish theory of monarchy from that of Greece, Parthia, and Rome. Many Hebrew rulers, beginning with Moses, had exercised dominion and 'showed a mighty hand and great terror in the sight of all Israel' (*Deuteronomy* xxxiv. 12); yet the author of *Numbers* xii. 3 could write of Moses: 'Now, the man Moses was very meek above all the men which were on the face of the earth.' The judge, or law-giver, though acting as God's mouthpiece, remained in theory a servant of the people on whose behalf he interceded with God; and humiliated himself before God in their presence as being no greater than the least of them. A king who 'gave not God the glory', like Herod Agrippa in *Acts* xii. 23, might expect immediate retribution. Jesus, though exacting strict obedience from his subjects, humbled himself before them on at least one occasion (*see* cvi.*t*).* If he said any words resembling those attributed to him in *Mark* x. 45 and *Matthew* xx. 28, they will have been:

(245) *And he said: 'I am not sent into this world to rule it as mine own, but the Father hath sent me to minister unto all Israel; that I might meekly bring you His command.'*

---

* The Kings of England rule by the same dispensation and formerly were expected to wash the feet of the poor every Maundy Thursday (Holinshed: *Chronicles* iii. *p.* 914).

THE DEMONIAC

Mark v. 1–20

[1]And they came over unto the other side of the sea, into the country of the Gerasenes. [2]And when He was come out of the boat, immediately there met Him out of the tombs a man with an unclean spirit, [3]who had his dwelling among the tombs; and no man could bind him, no, not with chains: [4]because that he had been often bound with fetters and chains, and the chains had been plucked asunder by him, and the fetters broken in pieces: neither could any man tame him. [5]And always, night and day, he was in the mountains, and in the tombs, crying, and ·cutting himself with stones. [6]But when he saw Jesus afar off, he ran and worshipped Him, [7]and cried with a loud voice, and said: 'What have I to do with Thee, Jesus, Son of the most high God? I adjure Thee by God, that Thou torment me not.' [8]For He said unto him: 'Come out of the man, unclean spirit.' [9]And He asked him: 'What is thy name?' And he answered, saying: 'My name is Legion: for we are many.' [10]And he besought Him much that He would not send them away out of the country. [11]Now there was there nigh unto the mountains a great herd of swine feeding. [12]And all the devils besought Him, saying, Send us unto the swine, that we may enter into them. [13]And forthwith Jesus gave them leave. And the unclean spirits went out, and entered unto the swine: and the herd ran violently down a steep place into the sea, (they were about two thousand;) and were choked in the sea. [14]And they that fed the swine fled, and told it in the city, and in the country. And they went out to see what it was that was done. [15]And they come to Jesus, and see him that was possessed with the devil, and had the legion, sitting, and clothed, and in his right mind: and they were afraid. [16]And they that saw it told them how it befell to him that was possessed with the devil, and also concerning the swine. [17]And they began to pray Him to depart out of their coasts. [18]And when He was come into the boat, he that had been possessed with the devil prayed Him that he might be with Him. [19]Howbeit Jesus suffered him not, but saith unto him: 'Go home to thy friends, and tell them how great things the Lord hath done for thee, and hath had compassion on thee.' [20]And he departed, and began to publish in Decapolis how great things Jesus had done for him: and all men did marvel.

Matthew viii. 28–34

[28]And when He was come to the other side into the country of the Gadarenes [or Gergesenes], there met Him two possessed with devils, coming out of the tombs, exceeding fierce, so that no man might pass by that way. [29]And, be-

Matthew viii. 28–34 (contd.)

hold, they cried out, saying: 'What have we to do with Thee, Jesus, Thou Son of God? art Thou come hither to torment us before the time?' [30]And there was a good way off from them an herd of many swine feeding. [31]So the devils besought Him, saying: 'If thou cast us out, suffer us to go away into the herd of swine.' [32]And He said unto them: 'Go.' And when they were come out, they went into the herd of swine: and, behold, the whole herd of swine ran violently down a steep place into the sea, and perished in the waters. [33]And they that kept them fled, and went their ways into the city, and told everything, and what was befallen to the possessed of the devils. [34]And, behold, the whole city came out to meet Jesus: and when they saw Him, they besought Him that He would depart out of their coasts.

Luke viii. 26–39

[26]And they arrived at the country of the Gerasenes, which is over against Galilee. [27]And when He went forth to land, there met Him out of the city a certain man, which had devils long time, and ware no clothes, neither abode in any house, but in the tombs. [28]When he saw Jesus, he cried out, and fell down before Him, and with a loud voice said: 'What have I to do with Thee, Jesus, Son of God most high? I beseech Thee, torment me not.' [29]For He had commanded the unclean spirit to come out of the man. For oftentimes it had caught him: and he was kept bound with chains and in fetters; and he brake the bands, and was driven of the devil into the wilderness. [30]And Jesus asked him, saying: 'What is thy name?' And he said: 'Legion': because many devils were entered into him. [31]And they besought Him that He would not command them to go out into the deep. [32]And there was there an herd of many swine feeding on the mountain: and they besought Him that He would suffer them to enter into them. And He suffered them. [33]Then went the devils out of the man, and entered into the swine: and the herd ran violently down a steep place into the lake, and were choked. [34]When they that fed them saw what was done, they fled, and went and told it in the city and in the country. [35]Then they went out to see what was done; and came to Jesus, and found the man, out of whom the devils were departed, sitting at the feet of Jesus, clothed, and in his right mind: and they were afraid. [36]They also which saw it told them by what means he that was possessed of the devils was healed. [37]Then the whole multitude of the country of the Gerasenes round about besought Him to depart from them; for they were taken with great fear: and He went up into the boat, and returned back again. [38]Now the man out of whom the devils were departed besought Him that he might be with Him: but Jesus sent him away, saying: [39]'Return to thine own house, and shew how great things God hath done unto thee.' And he went his way, and published throughout the whole city how great things Jesus had done unto him.

* * * * *

Matthew xii. 43–45

[43]'When the unclean spirit is gone out of a man, he walketh through dry places, seeking rest, and findeth none. [44]Then he saith, I will return into my house from whence I came out; and when he is come, he findeth it empty,

Matthew xii. 43–45 (*contd.*)

swept, and garnished. [45]Then goeth he, and taketh with himself seven other spirits more wicked than himself, and they enter in and dwell there: and the last state of that man is worse than the first. Even so shall it be also unto this wicked generation.'

Luke xi. 24–26

[24]'When the unclean spirit is gone out of a man, he walketh through dry places, seeking rest; and finding none, he saith, I will return unto my house whence I came out. [25]And when he cometh, he findeth it swept and garnished. [26]Then goeth he, and taketh to him seven other spirits more wicked than himself; and they enter in, and dwell there: and the last state of that man is worse than the first.'

(*a*) The original of *Matthew* xii. 43–45, paralleled in *Luke* xi. 24–26, seems to have been a *midrash* on *Job* i. 7 and *Tobit* viii. 3:

(239) *And Jesus saith unto him again:*

'*Yet watch and pray, lest that evil spirit enter into thee again! For when God asked the Adversary: "Whence comest thou?" he answered Him: "From going to and fro in the earth and from walking up and down in it."*

'*And verily, when he hath been cast out of a man (as Tobias cast out Asmodeus from the body of his bride Sara) he fleeth to the uttermost parts of Egypt and walketh in waterless places, seeking rest and finding none.*

'*Then, presently, unless an angel shall have bound him, he saith: "I will return unto the same house whence I was cast out," and when he is returned thither he findeth it swept and garnished.*

'*And he taketh seven other devils more wicked than himself, and they enter together into the man, and abide in him.*

'*Then is the last state of that man worse than the first.*'

*   *   *   *   *

(*b*) It is likely that Jesus gave this warning to the demoniac of Gerasa, or Gergesa (*Mark* v. 1–20, *Matthew* viii. 28–34 and *Luke* viii. 26–39). The exact name and site of this place has been much disputed ever since the days of Eusebius, who wrote (*Onomastica Sacra* 248. 14):

'Gergesa, where the Lord healed the demoniacs . . . to this day a village of that name is shown on the hills above the Lake of Tiberias into which the swine rushed down.'

He also described Gergesa (*Onomastica Sacra* 242. 68) as:

'. . . a city of Gilead lying on the other side of the Jordan, which the tribe of Manasseh seized. It is said to be Gerasa, a notable town of Arabia. But some say it is Gadara. And the Gospel makes mention of the Gerasenes.'

And again (*Onomastica Sacra* 244. 24):

'. . . Gergasi is in Basanitis, from which the Children of Israel were unable to expel the Geshurites.'

Gospel manuscripts vary in their readings; but by a general consensus of scholars, 'Gadarene' is the correct version in *Matthew;* and 'Gerasene' in *Mark* and *Luke;* and the second *g* which, in some texts of *Matthew* viii. 28, disguises 'Gerasa'—a village lying halfway up the eastern coast of the Lake of Tiberias—is a scribal error probably suggested by 'Girgatha', a place mentioned in *Deuteronomy* vii. 1.

(*c*) The story of the two thousand possessed swine is the oddest in the Gospels, and no plausible guess at its provenience has yet been made. We venture to suggest, however, that shortly after the destruction of the Temple, an editor of *Mark* wrote in the margin of his Gospel the following gloss on Josephus's *Wars* iv. 7. 5:

> 'Gerasa is nigh unto the land of the Gadarenes. It seems that the evil spirits when Jesus forbade them to enter into those that herded swine, did not depart thence to flee into the midst of the wilderness. For not long since a horde of evil spirits entered into the men of Gadara when they suddenly and rashly assaulted a legion on the hills nigh unto the city, where these swine were herded in the time of Jesus, but afterwards flying away, were driven down to the waterside where a prodigious number were drowned, beside two thousand taken prisoners, so that both the Lake and the river were filled with dead bodies.'

This gloss was misread and incorporated into the text of *Mark;* and 'Gerasa' was omitted when the incident was introduced into *Matthew* viii. 28–34. *Luke,* however, copied *Mark's* version almost verbatim.

(*d*) In *Matthew* viii. 28–34, two demoniacs are cured, but only one in *Mark* v. 1–20 and in *Luke* viii. 26–39. The same amendment has apparently been made here as in the cases of the two blind men cured at Jericho and the two cured at Bethsaida in *Matthew* ix. 27 and xx. 30, whereas *Mark* and *Luke* record one cure only in each place (*see* XL.*c*). It seems, then, that *Mark* v. 1–20, the account of the Demoniac of Gerasa, was read by an editor of *Matthew* who did not realize that the sequel to it already appeared in *Matthew* xii. 43–45. Thinking that *Mark's* story referred to a separate miracle, he noted in the margin of his Gospel: 'There were two such demoniacs, not one.' Later, his gloss was misunderstood, like the gloss about the blind men; so that the Gerasa passage, when borrowed from *Mark* and inserted in *Matthew* viii. 28–34, had two demoniacs emerging from their haunts in the tombs.

(*e*) The background of Jesus's expulsion of evil spirits is found in the Talmud (*Pesahim* 112*b*), an account of the conflict between a second-century rabbi and 'the Female' on whom Jesus declared war (*see* XXI.*o*):

> 'The sages have taught us: "Do not walk alone at night either on the Wednesday or on the Sabbath, because *Aggrath Bat Machlat* and her one hundred and eighty thousand devils [*malache habaleh,* 'destructive angels'] are abroad, and each hath licence to wreak destruction severally."

'Once they met with Rabbi Chanina ben Dosa. And Aggrath Bat Machlat said to him: "Had there not come a command from Heaven to spare thee, I should have put thee now in danger."

'Rabbi Chanina answered her: "If it be that I am so well esteemed in Heaven, then I order thee nevermore to appear in inhabited places." '

'My name is Legion, for we are many', has a genuine ring, since Christian editors would never have associated Roman legions with devils that made an Israelite doubly defile himself by touching tombs and eating swine. They accepted Roman rule without question and had no ritual objection either to pork or graveyards. For Jesus, however, the Romans were 'swine' as the Syro-Phoenicians were 'dogs' (*see* xviii.*b,* xxxvi.*h and* xlvii.*d*), and the demoniac's fate was horrible beyond words.

If the devil was indeed *Aggrath Bat Machlat,* she must have been purposely under-estimating the number of her followers, since these amounted to thirty legions at full strength. She walked on Wednesday and Saturday nights because her ally Naku the Cosmocrator claimed to own Wednesday, and because Sabbath repose degenerated into idleness, and idleness into mischief.

(*f*) The swineherds cannot have wished to send Jesus away from the hill; he was doing them no harm. Their objection must have been to the demoniac, who had harassed them by tearing the swine into pieces and eating their flesh in his unclean frenzy.

Jesus's reason for declining to accept the man as a follower, when healed, will have been that he was not completely purified even by washing in the Lake—which counted as 'running water' because the Jordan flowed through it; there was still need for a sin-offering. His refusal to accept any credit for the miracle is emphasized in *Mark* v. 19.

In *Mark* v. 7, the demon addresses Jesus in the same words as the other demon in *Mark* i. 24; the text is therefore suspect (*see* xlii.*b*). Though he may have asked Jesus's permission to enter into a swineherd (*see* xxxi.*b*), this will have been refused.

(238) *Now, this was the region of the Gerasenes, and there was an Israelite with an unclean spirit, which ware no clothes and had his dwelling among the tombs and no man could tame him.*

And those that fed great herds of swine nigh unto the hill where he dwelt, held him in terror, for he rushed violently upon them and tare the swine in sunder with his hands and ate their flesh.

But though these swineherds besought the rulers of the city to drive the man thence, they could not.

For if ever he were bound with chains and fetters, he brake them in pieces and escaped out of the hands of them that guarded him.

And night and day his voice was heard crying from the tombs, as he cut himself with stones.

This man therefore saw Jesus afar off with the disciples, and ran to him and cried:

'Master, I pray thee, let this evil spirit torment me no longer!'

And immediately the evil spirit spake through his mouth, cursing and blaspheming.

Then said Jesus unto the evil spirit: 'What is thy name?'

And the evil spirit dissembled and answered: 'My name is Legion, for we are many.'

Jesus said: 'If my Father hearken to my prayer, He will send thee out of this man. Begone therefore, in God's name, Aggrath Bat Machlat, and take thine one hundred and eighty thousand devils with thee!'

Then the evil spirit besought Jesus through the mouth of the same man, saying: 'Suffer me to enter into one of them that keep the swine.'

But Jesus answered: 'Nay, for they are also sons of Adam and made in God's image.'

At that the evil spirit departed, and Jesus bade the man wash in the Lake, and gave unto him clothing to hide his nakedness.

And he was healed and besought Jesus that he might follow after him.

But Jesus suffered him not, and said: 'Go rather to thy father's house and tell thy kindred how great things the Lord God hath done unto thee, and how He hath had compassion upon thee.

'Ask them also for the price of a sin-offering, and take it unto Jerusalem, and when thy debt is paid, then, if thou wilt, come thou with me.'

* * * * *

[Here follows: 'Yet watch and pray . . .' (*see* (*a*) *above*).]

(240) *And when his kindred saw the man returning, clothed and in his right mind, they were astonished and began to publish the name of Jesus throughout Decapolis.*

* * * * *

LXIV

ON IMPORTUNITY

Luke xi. 5–8

[5]And He said unto them: 'Which of you shall have a friend, and shall go unto him at midnight, and say unto him, Friend, lend me three loaves; [6]for a friend of mine in his journey is come to me, and I have nothing to set before him? [7]And he from within shall answer and say, Trouble me not: the door is now shut, and my children are with me in bed; I cannot rise and give thee. [8]I say unto you, though he will not rise and give him, because he is his friend, yet because of his importunity he will rise and give him as many as he needeth.'

Luke xviii. 1–8

[1]And He spake a parable unto them to this end, that men ought always to pray, and not to faint; [2]saying: 'There was in a city a judge, which feared not God, neither regarded man: [3]and there was a widow in that city; and she came unto him, saying, Avenge me of mine adversary. [4]And he would not for a while: but afterward he said within himself, Though I fear not God, nor regard man; [5]yet because this widow troubleth me, I will avenge her, lest by her continual coming she weary me. [6]And the Lord said: Hear what the unjust judge saith. [7]And shall not God avenge His own elect, which cry day and night unto Him, though He bear long with them? [8]I tell you that He will avenge them speedily. Nevertheless when the Son of Man cometh, shall He find faith on the earth?'

(*a*) Jesus's two parables on Importunity occur in *Luke* only. The first (*Luke* xi. 5–8), is told apparently to mitigate the harshness of another parable in *Luke* xiii. 25 (*see* LXIX.*b*), where the guests invited to a feast arrive late and are refused admittance. It must have been introduced by a question from one of the disciples: 'But if the guests came late through no fault of their own?' and Jesus will have supported it by a quotation from *Isaiah* xxvi. 2.

The last verse of the second, and similar, parable (*Luke* xviii. 1–8), seems to have been mistranslated.

> (128) *His disciples ask Jesus: 'Master, what if they return late through no fault of their own? Shall the door not be opened unto them?'*
> *He answered: 'It shall assuredly be opened. As Isaiah prophesied, saying: "Open ye the gates, that the righteous nation which keepeth the truth may come in."*

'For if one of you goeth at midnight and knocketh at his neighbour's door, and saith: "Neighbour, lend me three loaves, for a friend of mine hath even now turned in unto me and I have no meat to set before him,"

'He from within shall answer: "Trouble me not, the door is shut and my children are with me in bed. I cannot rise and provide for thee."

'Yet I say unto you: though he would not arise for friendship, yet if thou stand and knock long, then at the last, because of thine importunity he will rise and give thee as many loaves as thou needest.

'And if this be the way of a churlish householder, how much sooner will thy Heavenly Father not open unto thee?'

* * * * *

(129) And he spake another parable, saying: 'The judge of a certain city neither feared God nor regarded man.

'And in that city was a widow which came continually to him, pleading: "O judge, give me satisfaction against my adversary!"

'He for a while would not, but at the last he said within himself: "I am wearied by the importunity of this widow. I will avenge her wrongs that she may trouble me no more."

'And if this be the mercy of an unjust judge, how much more mercifully will God not grant the pleas of the faithful which cry unto Him day and night against the Adversary of man?

'Verily, I say unto you: when the Son of Man shall appear, he will avenge them speedily, though he find no justice in the courts of this world.'

* * * * *

TAKE NO THOUGHT

Matthew vi. 25–34

²⁵Therefore I say unto you, take no thought for your life, what ye shall eat, or what ye shall drink; nor yet for your body, what ye shall put on. Is not the life more than meat, and the body than raiment?

²⁶Behold the fowls of the air:
For they sow not, neither do they reap, nor gather into barns;
Yet your heavenly Father feedeth them.
Are ye not much better than they?
²⁷Which of you by taking thought can add one cubit unto his stature?
²⁸And why take ye thought for raiment?
Consider the lilies of the field, how they grow;
They toil not, neither do they spin:
²⁹And yet I say unto you,
That even Solomon in all his glory
Was not arrayed like one of these.
³⁰Wherefore, if God so clothe the grass of the field,
Which to day is, and to morrow is cast into the oven,
Shall He not much more clothe you,
O ye of little faith?

³¹Therefore take no thought, saying, What shall we eat? or, What shall we drink? or, Wherewithal shall we be clothed? ³²(for after all these things do the Gentiles seek) for your heavenly Father knoweth that ye have need of all these things. ³³But seek ye first the kingdom of God, and His righteousness; and all these things shall be added unto you. ³⁴Take therefore no thought for the morrow: for the morrow shall take thought for the things of itself. Sufficient unto the day is the evil thereof.

Luke xii. 22–31

²²And He said unto His disciples: 'Therefore I say unto you, take no thought for your life, what ye shall eat; neither for the body, what ye shall put on. ²³The life is more than meat, and the body is more than raiment.

²⁴Consider the ravens:
For they neither sow nor reap; which neither have storehouse nor barn;
And God feedeth them: how much more are ye better than the fowls?

Luke xii. 22–31 (*contd.*)

²⁵And which of you with taking thought can add to his stature one cubit? ²⁶If ye then be not able to do that thing which is least, why take you thought for the rest?

²⁷Consider the lilies how they grow:
They toil not, they spin not;
And yet I say unto you, that Solomon in all his glory was not arrayed like one of these.

²⁸If then God so clothe the grass, which is to day in the field, and to morrow is cast into the oven; how much more will He clothe you, O ye of little faith? ²⁹And seek not yet what ye shall eat, or what ye shall drink, neither be ye of doubtful mind. ³⁰For all these things do the nations of the world seek after: and your Father knoweth that ye have need of these things. ³¹But rather seek ye the kingdom of God; and all these things shall be added unto you.'

Oxyrhynchus Papyrus 654. ii

. . . saith (who are they that) draw us . . . the kingdom that is in heaven. The fowls of the air . . . whatsoever is beneath the earth . . . the fishes of the sea. (These are they that draw) you . . . And the kingdom (of heaven) is within you: (and whosoever) knoweth . . . shall find it . . . know yourselves . . . ye are . . . of the Father . . . ye shall know yourselves to be in . . . And ye are the city [?] (of God) . . .

(*a*) Jesus's counsel of improvidence in *Matthew* vi. 25–34 is a *midrash* on *Psalms* xxxvii. 3–5 and cxlvii. 9. *Matthew* vi. 27, which does not fit the argument, was probably found next to it in a collection of Oracles under the subject-heading 'Take no Thought'; it belongs to the *midrash* on 1 *Samuel* xvi. 7: 'Take no thought for the height of his stature,' and refers incidentally to Saul's great height (1 *Samuel* ix. 2—*see* LXVIII.*f*). Jesus may have had in mind his own stunted person (*see* VI.*c*).

(278) *'And though a man's stature be a cubit above the stature of other men, hath he taken thought to make it so?'*

* * * * *

(*b*) The lilies of the field are the eight-petalled field-anemones, called 'the blood of Tammuz' in Syria. A distinction is made here between birds that perform none of the work done by men, and flowers that perform none of the work done by women. Thus Jesus will have referred to Solomon's Shunemite bride—compared to a lily in *Canticles* ii. 1–2—rather than to Solomon himself.

This seems to be the context of a fragment found in the *Oxyrhynchus Papyrus* 654. It may be restored as follows:

[Judas] saith: '[What things are they that] draw us [unto God, since] His Kingdom is in Heaven?'
[Jesus answered]: 'The fowls of the air [the beasts, and] whatsoever is be-

neath the earth [that sprouteth, and] the fishes of the sea, [these are the things that] draw you [unto God].

'And the Kingdom [of God] is within you [and whosoever] knoweth [the Law] shall find it.

'[For if ye know the Law ye shall] know yourselves [how that] ye are [sons] of the Father [which is in Heaven. Likewise] ye shall know yourselves [to be in His image].

'Ye are the city [of God over which the Son of Man shall reign].'

* * * * *

Somewhat different restorations have been made by Evelyn White and Lagrange. 'The Kingdom of God is within you', quoted in *Luke* xvii. 21, means: 'You have the power to make yourselves citizens of the Kingdom', not 'it is a figurative Kingdom only', as the editor of *Luke* understood (*see* CI.*b*).

The 'grass cast into the oven' (*Matthew* vi. 30), was the withered scrub harvested as fuel in the late Spring; after it had been set ablaze in a bread oven, the ashes were raked out and the dough was then slapped on the hot stones.

(*c*) The text of *Matthew* vi. 25 and *Luke* xii. 23, 'the life is more than meat and the body than raiment,' has been telescoped.

'Are you not better than they?' in *Matthew* vi. 26, which is not logically parallel with *Matthew* vi. 30, is borrowed from another question concerning birds: 'Are not two sparrows sold for one farthing?' (*Matthew* x. 29–31— *see* L.*a*).

Matthew vi. 32, which has fortunately survived, proves that the Gentiles were outside the immediate scope of Jesus's mission.

Matthew vi. 34 seems to be a separate saying, found under the same subject-heading as the other two; it is a *midrash* on *Proverbs* xxvii. 1.

(166) *And afterwards he preached to them that came up for the Feast, saying:*

'Take no thought for this your life, what ye shall eat or what ye shall drink, nor yet for your body, wherewithal ye shall be clothed.

'For after these things do the Gentiles seek, which know not God.

'Is not the word of the Lord more than meat, and his mercy more than raiment? and is not the life eternal more than this life, and the soul more than the body?'

Judas of Kerioth asketh: 'What things are they that draw us unto God, which ruleth heaven?'

Jesus answered: 'The fowls of the air, the fishes of the sea, the beasts, and whatsoever springeth from the earth, these are the things that draw you unto God.

'Consider the ravens, how they sow not, neither do they reap, nor gather into barns, as men do.

'Yet David spake of them, saying: "The Lord feedeth the young ravens which cry into Him."

'*How much more shall He not feed you, O ye of little faith? For David also saith: "Trust in the Lord and do righteousness, and verily thou shalt be fed."*

'*Consider the lilies of the field, how they grow. They toil not, neither do they spin, as women do.*

'*Yet unto these did Solomon liken his beloved in all her glory. For he said: "As the lily among her thorns, so is my love among other women."*

'*If God so clothe the grass of the field which today is, and tomorrow is cast into the oven, how much more shall He not clothe you, O ye of little faith?*

'*And David saith: "Delight thyself in the Lord, and He shall give thee thy heart's desire."*

'*In righteousness therefore seek ye the Kingdom of God; trust in the Lord and He shall bring it to pass.*

'*The Kingdom of God is within you, and whosoever knoweth the Law shall find it. For if ye know the Law, ye shall know yourselves, how that ye are sons of the Father which is in heaven.*

'*Likewise ye shall know yourselves to be created in His image. Ye are the city of God over which the Son of Man shall reign.*

'*Solomon counselled us: "Boast not thyself of tomorrow, for thou knowest not what a day may bring forth."*

'*Therefore take no thought for the morrow, whether it shall be good or whether evil. Sufficient unto the day are the cares thereof. And let the Law sustain you.*'

* * * * *

(*d*) The saying attributed to Rabbi Eliezer the Great, in *Sotah* 48*b*: 'He that hath yet a morsel of food in his basket and saith: "What shall I eat tomorrow?" is of little faith,' may have been a quotation from Jesus. 'In his basket' suggests that the author was an itinerant ascetic; and Rabbi Eliezer had gleaned from James the Just at least one other saying of Jesus's, though subsequently forced to break all connexion with the Nazarenes (*see* LIII.*b*).

(168) '*He that hath yet a morsel of food in his basket and asketh: "What shall I eat tomorrow?", the same is of little faith.*'

* * * * *

(*e*) A comment made by Rabbi Eliezer, on the 'homer of manna' which was to be preserved for posterity (*Exodus* xvi. 32–34), may have formed the main part of the missing *midrash* concluded by the above passage (*see* XXVII.*c*):

'Rabbi Eliezer said: "The homer of manna was to be preserved against the coming of Jeremiah. For when he asked the Israelites: 'Why do ye not busy yourselves with the Law?', they answered: 'If we busy ourselves with the Law, how will we find food?'

' "Then Jeremiah brought forth the pot in which the manna was, and said unto them: 'O generation, see ye this thing which is of the Lord? [*Jeremiah* ii. 31]. See how your forefathers . . . were sustained! If ye busy yourselves with the words of the Law, God will provide such food for you also.'"'

(*Mekilta* Vol. II, 126; ed. Lauterbach)

(167) *When certain men of the land which heard these things excused themselves, and told Jesus that their labours were many and that they lacked time sufficient to study the Law, he spake this parable unto them:*

'Jeremiah asked our forefathers, saying: "Why busy ye not yourselves with the words of the Law?"

'But they answered him according to their folly, for they said: "How will we then find time to labour for our sustenance?"

'Then brought he forth unto them the pot wherein the manna was kept, according to the word of Moses. And he said unto them: "O faithless generation, see ye this thing which is of the Lord! With this manna were your forefathers sustained in the wilderness.

' "Though ye busy yourselves all day long with the Law, yet will He make provision for you on the morrow." '

* * * * *

THE SOWER

Mark iv. 1–9

^{1}And He began to teach by the sea side: and there was gathered unto Him a great multitude, so that He entered into a boat, and sat in the sea: and the whole multitude was by the sea on the land. ^{2}And He taught them many things by parables, and said unto them in His teaching: ^{3}'Hearken; Behold there went out a sower to sow; ^{4}and it came to pass, as he sowed, some fell by the way side, and the fowls of the air came and devoured it up. ^{5}And some fell on stony ground, where it had not much earth; and immediately it sprang up, because it had no depth of earth; ^{6}but when the sun was up, it was scorched; and because it had no root, it withered away. ^{7}And some fell among thorns, and the thorns grew up, and choked it, and it yielded no fruit. ^{8}And other fell on good ground, and did yield fruit that sprang up and increased; and brought forth, some thirty, and some sixty, and some an hundred.' ^{9}And He said unto them: 'He that hath ears to hear, let him hear.'

Mark iv. 13–20

^{13}And He said unto them: 'Know ye not this parable? and how then will ye know all parables? ^{14}The sower soweth the word. ^{15}And these are they by the way side, where the word is sown; but when they have heard, Satan cometh immediately, and taketh away the word that was sown in their hearts. ^{16}And these are they likewise which are sown on stony ground; who, when they have heard the word, immediately receive it with gladness; ^{17}and have no root in themselves, and so endure but for a time: afterward, when affliction or persecution ariseth for the word's sake, immediately they are offended. ^{18}And these are they which are sown among thorns; such as hear the word, ^{19}and the cares of this world, and the deceitfulness of riches, and the lusts of other things entering in, choke the word, and it becometh unfruitful. ^{20}And these are they which are sown on good ground; such as hear the word, and receive it, and bring forth fruit, some thirtyfold, some sixty, and some an hundred.'

Mark iv. 26–29

^{26}And He said: 'So is the kingdom of God, as if a man should cast seed into the ground; ^{27}and should sleep, and rise night and day, and the seed should spring and grow up, he knoweth not how. ^{28}For the earth bringeth forth

Mark iv. 26–29 (*contd.*)

fruit of herself; first the blade, then the ear, after that the full corn in the ear. [29]But when the fruit is brought forth, immediately he putteth in the sickle, because the harvest is come.'

Matthew xiii. 1–30

[1]The same day went Jesus out of the house, and sat by the sea side. [2]And great multitudes were gathered together unto Him, so that He went into a boat, and sat; and the whole multitude stood on the shore. [3]And He spake many things unto them in parables, saying: 'Behold, a sower went forth to sow; [4]and when he sowed, some seeds fell by the way side, and the fowls came and devoured them up: [5]some fell upon stony places, where they had not much earth: and forthwith they sprang up, because they had no deepness of earth: [6]and when the sun was up, they were scorched; and because they had no root, they withered away. [7]And some fell among thorns; and the thorns sprang up, and choked them. [8]But other fell into good ground, and brought forth fruit, some an hundredfold, some sixtyfold, some thirtyfold. [9]Who hath ears to hear, let him hear.'

[10]And the disciples came, and said unto Him: 'Why speakest Thou unto them in parables?' [11]He answered and said unto them: 'Because it is given unto you to know the mysteries of the Kingdom of Heaven, but to them it is not given. [12]For whosoever hath, to him shall be given, and he shall have more abundance: but whosoever hath not, from him shall be taken away even that he hath. [13]Therefore speak I to them in parables: because they seeing see not; and hearing they hear not, neither do they understand. [14]And in them is fulfilled the prophecy of Isaiah, which saith,

> By hearing ye shall hear, and shall not understand;
> And seeing ye shall see, and shall not perceive:
> [15]For this people's heart is waxed gross,
> And their ears are dull of hearing,
> And their eyes they have closed;
> Lest at any time they should see with their eyes,
> And hear with their ears,
> And should understand with their heart,
> And should be converted, and I should heal them.

[16]But blessed are your eyes, for they see: and your ears, for they hear. [17]For verily I say unto you, That many prophets and righteous men have desired to see those things which ye see, and have not seen them; and to hear those things which ye hear, and have not heard them.

[18]'Hear ye therefore the parable of the sower. [19]When any one heareth the word of the kingdom, and understandeth it not, then cometh the wicked one, and catcheth away that which was sown in his heart. This is he which received seed by the way side. [20]But he that received the seed into stony places, the same is he that heareth the word, and anon with joy receiveth it; [21]yet hath he not root in himself, but dureth for a while: for when tribulation or persecution ariseth because of the word, by and by he is offended. [22]He also that received seed among the thorns is he that heareth the word; and the care

Matthew xiii. 1–30 (*contd.*)

of this world, and the deceitfulness of riches, choke the word, and he be-cometh unfruitful. ²³But he that received seed into the good ground is he that heareth the word, and understandeth it; which also beareth fruit, and bringeth forth, some an hundredfold, some sixty, some thirty.'

²⁴Another parable put He forth unto them, saying: 'The Kingdom of Heaven is likened unto a man which sowed good seed in his field. ²⁵But while men slept, his enemy came and sowed tares among the wheat, and went his way. ²⁷But when the blade was sprung up, and brought forth fruit, then appeared the tares also. So the servants of the householder came and said unto him, Sir, didst not thou sow good seed in thy field? from whence then hath it tares? ²⁸He said unto them, An enemy hath done this. The servants said unto him, Wilt thou then that we go and gather them up? ²⁹But he said, Nay; lest while ye gather up the tares, ye root up also the wheat with them. ³⁰Let both grow together until the harvest: and in the time of harvest I will say to the reapers, gather ye together first the tares, and bind them in bundles to burn them: but gather the wheat into my barn.'

Matthew xiii. 36–43

³⁶Then Jesus sent the multitude away, and went into the house: and His disciples come unto Him, saying: 'Declare unto us the parable of the tares of the field.' ³⁷He answered and said unto them: 'He that soweth the good seed is the Son of Man: ³⁸the field is the world; the good seed are the children of the kingdom; but the tares are the children of the wicked one; ³⁹the enemy that soweth them is the devil; the harvest is the end of the world; and the reapers are the angels. ⁴⁰As therefore the tares are gathered and burned in the fire; so shall it be in the end of this world. ⁴¹The Son of Man shall send forth His angels, and they shall gather out of His kingdom all things that offend, and them which do iniquity: ⁴²and shall cast them into a furnace of fire: there shall be wailing and gnashing of teeth. ⁴³Then shall the righteous shine forth as the sun in the kingdom of their Father. Who hath ears to hear, let them hear.'

Luke viii. 1–8

¹And it came to pass afterward, that He went throughout every city and village, preaching and shewing the glad tidings of the kingdom of God: and the Twelve were with Him, ²and certain women, which had been healed of evil spirits and infirmities, Mary called Magdalene, out of whom went seven devils, ³and Joanna the wife of Chuza, Herod's steward, and Susanna, and many others, which ministered unto Him of their substance.

⁴And when much people were gathered together, and were come to Him out of every city, He spake by a parable: ⁵A sower went out to sow his seed: and as he sowed, some fell by the way side; and it was trodden down, and the fowls of the air devoured it. ⁶And some fell upon the rock; and as soon as it was sprung up, it withered away, because it lacked moisture. ⁷And some fell among thorns; and the thorns sprang up with it, and choked it. ⁸And other fell on good ground, and sprang up, and bare fruit an hundredfold.'

Luke viii. 11–15

[11]Now the parable is this: The Seed is the Word of God. [12]Those by the way side are they that hear; then cometh the devil, and taketh away the Word out of their hearts, lest they should believe and be saved. [13]They on the rock are they which, when they hear, receive the Word with joy; and these have no root, which for a while believe, and in time of temptation fall away. [14]And that which fell among thorns are they, which, when they have heard, go forth, and are choked with cares and riches and pleasures of this life, and bring no fruit to perfection. [15]But that on the good ground are they, which in an honest and good heart, having heard the Word, keep it, and bring forth fruit with patience.

(a) Whenever Gospel editors take it upon themselves to explain Jesus's words, as at the close of The Sower (Mark iv. 13–20, Matthew xiii. 36–43 and Luke viii. 11–15), they must be suspected of either not understanding them, or not wanting to understand.

Here they have been content merely to manipulate Jesus's own brief explanation, instead of inventing a new one as in John xxi. 19 (see cxvii.m), or John ii. 21 (see xc.i). But they have managed to suppress the simple and obvious meaning of the parable, namely the fate of Isaac's seed—the descendants of Jacob and Esau, re-united since Hasmonean days in obedience to the Law—which did not interest them because, having rejected circumcision, they themselves were not even honorary Sons of Abraham. As a result of these manipulations the parable has ceased to be logical: for instance, the 'stony places' cannot symbolize 'him that receiveth the word of God with joy but hath no root in himself'—it is the seed that puts out a root, not the stony places; neither is a stony place an emblem of joy.

(b) Some of this seed 'perished by the way' (Joshua v. 4), and as prophesied in Deuteronomy xxviii. 26, fell a prey to 'the fowls of the air' for disobeying God's word; it was 'seed sown in vain' (Leviticus xxvi. 16). The seed that 'had not much earth' is a reference to Isaiah xl. 24; that which 'fell among thorns', to Jeremiah iv. 3; that which 'fell on good soil', to Hosea x. 12 and Zechariah viii. 12. It is thus seen that the parable progresses chronologically from the Pentateuch to the later prophets, recording the fate of Isaac's seed from its first planting until the Last Days.

(c) For Matthew xiii. 10–17, the verses that intervene between the parable and its explanation, see xxv.b and e.

(52) And Jesus said: 'It is written that the Lord, when He spared our Father Isaac, called out of heaven unto Abraham, saying: "In thy seed shall all the nations of the earth be blessed, because thou hast obeyed My voice."

'Yet not all the seed of Isaac fell on good ground. Hearken therefore to this parable:

'A sower went forth to sow, and as he sowed, some seed fell by the wayside. As it is written in the Book of Joshua: "All the men of war perished in the wilderness, by the way."

'For they obeyed not the word that the Lord spake unto Moses: "If it shall come to pass that thou wilt not hearken to the voice of thy God, thy carcase shall be meat unto all the fowls of the air." And again: "Ye shall sow your seed in vain, for your enemies shall eat it."

'And some fell upon stony places which had not much earth, and when the sun was up, they were scorched, and because they had no root they withered away. As Isaiah prophesied: "Their stock shall not take root in the earth. The Lord shall also blow upon them and they shall wither, and the whirlwind shall take them away."

'And some fell among thorns, and the thorns sprang up and choked them. As Jeremiah prophesied: "Thus saith the Lord to the men of Judah and of Jerusalem: 'Break up your fallow ground and sow not among thorns.'"

'But others fell upon good ground and brought forth fruit: some thirty, some sixty, some an hundredfold. As Hosea spake in the name of the Lord: "Sow in righteousness, reap in mercy." And as Zechariah likewise spake: "For the seed shall be prosperous and the ground shall give her increase, and I will cause the remnant of this people to possess all these things."

'Hear ye therefore the word of God and keep it, fall not by the wayside, spread your roots in the faith, be not choked by the cares of this world, and at the last ye shall enjoy great increase.

'For thus it is written of our forefather Isaac: "He sowed in that land and received in the same year an hundredfold, and the Lord blessed him."'

*   *   *   *   *

(d) This parable appears in an early chapter of *Mark*; but in *Luke* viii. 1–3 it is introduced by an account of Jesus's financial backing which belongs to a later stage of his ministry. It may be placed tentatively between the Return of the Twelve and Jesus's subsequent visit to Samaria.

Since Jesus kept the Twelve journeying up and down the country, it will have been seldom that they could ply their trades or undertake more than casual labour. Galilee being so heavily taxed, a large sum was needed to support their dependants. Even with a 'penny' for a minimum daily wage (*see* LVIII.*b*), Jesus would have had to find nearly five thousand pence a year (in modern money, something like £1,000 or $3,000); but the social condition of the disciples, four of whom were fishermen and one an ex-publican, appears to have been higher than that of casual labourers and they will therefore have expected a larger subsistence allowance for their families. Jesus's support by Joanna, wife of Chuza, Herod's finance-minister, is likely to have prejudiced many of the Pharisees against him; yet he seems to have been scrupulous in accepting no money from her husband's purse, which is why '*their* substance' is specified. Unless Chuza had divorced Joanna, *Luke* must be mistaken when he records that she followed Jesus on his travels.

(e) For Mary Magdelene, *see* VII.*i*; she has here been confused with Mary, daughter of Simeon the Chaste (*see* XI.*d*), and is unjustly accused of being a harlot.

(221) *Afterward it came to pass that he went throughout the cites and vil-*
lages of Judaea which lie towards the sea preaching and expounding the glad
tidings of the Kingdom of God.

And the Twelve were with him, and certain women which had forsaken
this evil world; and Mary the Braider, his mother according to the spirit.

Now, Joanna the wife of Chuza, Herod's steward, and Susanna and other
rich women secretly ministered unto him of their substance, that the house-
holds of the Twelve should suffer no want.

* * * * *

(*f*) The parable of the Tares occurs only in *Matthew* iii. 24–30. Like the
Mustard-seed (*see* XLV.*d*), which breaks its continuity, and the Sower, it was
probably found in a collection of Oracles under the subject-heading 'Sown
Seed'. It is a *midrash* on *Proverbs* xi. 18. These tares, though identified with
corn-cockles by the medieval Church, were darnel, a weed peculiarly liable
to ergot. Darnel is the Devil's plant because its seed is not readily distinguished from wheat and because, if wheat and darnel are sown and harvested together, the ergot, which is poisonous and causes abortions in animals
and women, may smutch the grain. Hence the necessity of first binding the
tares and burning them (*Matthew* xiii. 30). The gathering of the wheat into
the barn is apparently a quotation from *Haggai* ii. 19.

(*g*) In *Matthew* xiii. 37, the sowing of seed is wrongly attributed to the Son
of Man. The Son of Man would appear only in harvest time; the seed was
sown by Isaac, as in the Sower. Jesus will have quoted *Joel* iii. 13–14 and
Psalms xxi. 8–10 and lxxxix. 29 in support of his parable.

(*h*) *Matthew* xiii. 43 is a quotation from *Daniel* xii. 3, and belongs to the
Labourers in the Vineyard (*see* LVII.*h*).

(*i*) *Mark* iv. 26–29 has so little point that it may well be a fragmentary version of the Tares. If so, verse 27, 'And should sleep' would refer to Isaac who
'slept with his forefathers' after having sown the seed, and never revisited
Canaan to observe its subsequent fate. (A 'not' has fallen out in the same
verse before 'rise night and day'.) *Mark's* fragment, if inserted into the fuller
version of *Matthew* xiii. 24–30, makes perfect sense. 'While he slept' then
explains 'while men slept' (*Matthew* xiii. 25), as an evasion of the difficulty
raised by the editor who confused the sower with the Son of Man; in the
Christian doctrine, the Son of Man was God, who 'slumbereth not nor sleepeth'.

The nature note about the gradual growth of wheat is superfluous in *Mark*
iv. 28, its present context; but if placed into the Lord of the Harvest's mouth
after *Matthew* xiii. 29, aptly explains the need for waiting until it ripens.

For the rooting out of plants not sown by God, *see* xx.*j*.

(218) *And because they wondered that God did not instantly destroy the*
guilty as He destroyed Korah, Dathan and Abiram, he taught them, saying:
'Solomon spake a proverb: "The wicked worketh a deceitful work, but to
him that soweth righteousness shall be a sure reward."

'And Joel prophesied also: "Put in the sickle, for the harvest is ripe. Multitudes, multitudes in the valley of decision; for the day of the Lord is near in the valley of decision!"

'Hearken therefore to a parable: the Kingdom of Heaven is like unto a man which sowed good seed in his master's field. And he slept and went not to view the field again either by night or day, and how the seed should spring and grow up he wist not.

'Then, while he slept, his adversary came and sowed tares among the wheat and went his way. When therefore the blade was sprung up, then appeared the tares also.

'The servants of the master said unto him: "Master, did not the sower sow good seed in thy field? From whence then hath it tares?"

'He answered them, saying: "An enemy hath done this."

'The servants said unto him: "Wilt thou then that we go and root them up?"

'But he said: "Nay; lest while ye root up the tares, ye root up also the wheat with them. For the earth bringeth forth fruit of herself, first the blade, then the ear, after that the full corn in the ear. And when the fruit is ripe, immediately the sickle is put in, for it is harvest.

' "Therefore let the wheat and tares both grow together until the harvest, and in that time I will say to the reapers: 'Gather ye together first the tares, and bind them in bundles to burn them; and then gather ye the wheat into my barn.' "

'For David prophesied of the seed of Belial: "Thine hand, O Lord, shall find out all Thine enemies and the fire of Thy wrath shall devour them; their fruit shalt Thou destroy from the earth and their seed from among the children of men. But the chosen seed of David will I make to endure for ever."

'And Haggai spake in the name of the Lord: "Is the seed yet in the barn? Yea, as yet the vine and the fig tree and the pomegranate and the olive tree have not brought forth. From this day will I bless them." '

* * * * *

(195) 'And know that Daniel prophesied of the Last Days: "They that teach the word of God shall shine as the brightness of the firmament, and they that turn many to righteousness shall be as the stars that endure for ever." '

(j) The prophecy about the vine, fig, pomegranate, and olive was referring, Messianically, to the great abundance that would be enjoyed by the elect in the Kingdom of Heaven (see LV.a).

For the quotation from *Isaiah* vi. 9–16 in *Matthew* xiii. 14, *see* xxv.*b* and cv.*e*.

* * * * *

LXVII

THE RICH FOOL

Luke xii. 15–21

[15]And He said unto them: 'Take heed, and beware of covetousness: for a man's life consisteth not in the abundance of the things which he possesseth.'

[16]And He spake a parable unto them, saying: 'The ground of a certain rich man brought forth plentifully: [17]and he thought within himself, saying, What shall I do, because I have no room where to bestow my fruits? [18]And he said, This will I do: I will pull down my barns, and build greater; and there will I bestow all my fruits and my goods. [19]And I will say to my soul, Soul thou hast much goods laid up for many years; take thine ease, eat, drink, and be merry. [20]But God said unto him, Thou Fool, this night thy soul shall be required of thee: then whose shall those things be, which thou hast provided? [21]So is he that layeth up treasure for himself, and is not rich toward God.'

Oecumenius: On James v. 16

'And that happens to us whereof the blessed Peter saith: "One building, another pulling down. They gain nought but their labour." '

(*a*) *Luke* xii. 15–21 is a *midrash* on *Ecclesiasticus* xi. 18–19, itself a variation on the theme of *Psalm* xlix. 6–20; Jesus quotes here also from *Psalm* xxxix. 6 and *Job* xxvii. 8. 'Covetousness' in the first verse stands for 'miserliness', the rich man's failure to relieve the poor; but an ascetic editor of *Luke* held that nothing whatever could save a rich man's soul, not even the giving of alms, and shortened the parable accordingly. The quotation by Oecumenius from the *Teaching of Peter* (*see* cxvii.*l*) apparently refers to the man who pulled down his barns to build greater ones and originally comes from *Ecclesiasticus* xxxiv. 23.

(57) '*And David prophesied, saying: "They that boast themselves in the multitude of their riches, though they see that wise men die, likewise the fool and the brutish person, and leave their wealth to others,*

'*"Nevertheless, their inward thought is that their dwelling places shall continue for ever, and they call their lands after their own names.*

'*"Therefore, like sheep they are laid in the grave and shall never see the light; for a man that is honoured in this world but hath no understanding is like the beasts that perish."*

'And again: "Surely, every man walketh in a vain show, that heapeth up riches and knoweth not who shall enjoy them."

'Therefore take ye heed and beware of covetousness, for a man's life consisteth not in the abundance of the things which he possesseth.

'The Preacher, the Son of Sirach, saith: "This is the reward of him that waxeth rich from covetousness. What time he saith: 'I have found rest, and now will I enjoy my substance,' he knoweth not what is his lot. His lot is that he shall die and leave his goods to be enjoyed of others."

'And it is written in the Book of Job: "For what is the hope of him that maketh a vain show, though he hath gained much, when God taketh away his soul?"'

* * * * *

(58) 'Hearken therefore to this parable: The ground of a certain rich man brought forth plentifully.

'But he was covetous, and gave nought unto his kinsfolk or unto his poor neighbours.

'And he thought within himself: "What shall I do, because I have no room where to bestow my fruits?"

'Therefore he said: "This will I do, I will pull down my barns and build greater, and there will I bestow all my fruits and my goods.

'"And I will assure my soul: 'Soul, thou hast much goods laid up for many years. Take thine ease now, eat, drink and be merry.'"

'But God said unto him: "Settest thou one man a-building, and another pulling down, by which they gain nought but their labour [as the Son of Sirach saith], while thou livest at thy ease? Thou fool, this night thy soul shall be required of thee! Then whose shall those goods be which thou hast provided?"'

* * * * *

(b) [Here follows the substance of Mark viii. 36–37 (see CI.k).]

LXVIII

MAMMON

Matthew vi. 19–21

[19]Lay not up for yourselves treasures upon earth, where moth and rust doth corrupt, and where thieves break through and steal: [20]but lay up for yourselves treasures in heaven, where neither moth nor rust doth corrupt, and where thieves do not break through nor steal: [21]for where your treasure is, there will your heart be also.'

Matthew vi. 24

[24]No man can serve two masters: for either he will hate the one, and love the other; or else he will hold to the one, and despise the other. Ye cannot serve God and mammon.

Luke xii. 32–34

[32]Fear not, little flock; for it is your Father's good pleasure to give you the kingdom.

[33]Sell that ye have and give alms;
Provide yourselves bags which wax not old,
A treasure in the heavens that faileth not,
Where no thief approacheth, neither moth corrupteth.
[34]For where your treasure is,
There will your heart be also.

Luke xvi. 1–15

[1]And he said also unto His disciples: 'There was a certain rich man, which had a steward; and the same was accused unto him that he had wasted his goods. [2]And he called him, and said unto him, How is it that I hear this of thee? give an account of thy stewardship; for thou mayest be no longer steward. [3]Then the steward said within himself, What shall I do? for my lord taketh away from me the stewardship: I cannot dig; to beg I am ashamed. [4]I am resolved what to do, that, when I am put out of the stewardship, they may receive me into their houses. [5]So he called every one of his lord's debtors unto him, and said unto the first, How much owest thou onto my lord? [6]And he said, An hundred measures of oil. And he said unto him, Take thy bill, and sit down quickly, and write fifty. [7]Then said he to an-

Luke xvi. 1–15 (*contd.*)

other, And how much owest thou? And he said, An hundred measures of wheat. And he said unto him, Take thy bill, and write fourscore. [8]And the lord commended the unjust steward, because he had done wisely: for the children of this world are in their generation wiser than the children of light. [9]And I say unto you, make to yourselves friends of the mammon of unrighteousness; that, when ye fail, they may receive you into everlasting habitations. [10]He that is faithful in that which is least is faithful also in much: and he that is unjust in the least is unjust also in much. [11]If therefore ye have not been faithful in the unrighteous mammon, who will commit to your trust the true riches? [12]And if ye have not been faithful in that which is another man's, who shall give you that which is your own? [13]No servant can serve two masters: for either he will hate the one, and love the other; or else he will hold to the one, and despise the other. Ye cannot serve God and mammon.'

[14]And the Pharisees also, who were covetous, heard all these things: and they derided Him. [15]And He said unto them: 'Ye are they which justify yourselves before men; but God knoweth your hearts: for that which is highly esteemed among men is abomination in the sight of God.'

(*a*) Jesus never recommended the complete abandonment of money as a social convenience; this is proved by his punctilious payment of the Sanctuary tax (*see* XLVIII.*a*) and the appointment of Judas as treasurer to his company (*see* CV.*e*). Since money had been used both for the selling of Joseph (*Genesis* xxxvii. 28) and the purchase of the Temple site (2 *Samuel* xxiv. 24), the Pharisees regarded it as neither good nor evil in itself. The *Targum* to *Proverbs* iii. 9 reads: 'Honour thy God with thy mammon.' Thus in the ironically-intended saying of *Luke* xvi. 9, Jesus distinguished between the unrighteous use of wealth and its righteous use. His words in *Matthew* vi. 24 have been misreported as an antithesis between God and riches, rather than between God and the Devil. He will have said: 'No man can serve both God and the Devil with his riches', and quoted 1 *Kings* xviii. 21 in support. It is, in fact, a *midrash* on the First Commandment.

(*b*) *Matthew* vi. 19 appears to be a *midrash* on four passages in *Proverbs,* namely xiii. 7, xxii. 4, xxiii. 4–5 and xxviii. 20, and on the *Testament of Levi* xiii. 5. These same words were used by King Monobazus of Adiabene, who embraced Judaism in 36 A.D., when reproached for spending his treasure on famine relief in Jerusalem (*Jer. Pe'ah* i. 1; *Baba Bathra* 11a and *Tosephta Pe'ah* iv. 18):

'His kinsfolk said: "Thy father gathered treasures, which thou hast squandered."

'He replied: "My father laid up treasures upon earth, but I lay them up in heaven. My father gathered them into a place over which the hand of man had power, but I have laid them in a place over which the hand of man hath no power. My fathers gathered mammon, but I gather souls."'

Matthew vi. 21 should follow verse 24.

> (54) *And he said: 'Lay not up for yourselves riches upon earth that vanish and fly away; for here moth and rust corrupt and thieves break through and steal.*
>
> *'But do ye according to the* Testament of Levi: *"By righteousness lay up riches in the heavenly palace, in bags that wax not old, where neither moth nor rust do corrupt, and where thieves do not break through nor steal."*
>
> *'For there shall ye also find honour and eternal life.'*

* * * * *

> (55) *'It is written: "Thou shalt have none other Gods but Me," and ye have read how Elijah spake to the people on Carmel, saying: "How long halt ye between two opinions? If the Lord be God, follow Him, but if Baal, follow him."*
>
> *'No man that serveth two masters can serve both faithfully with his heart. Either he will hate the one and love the other; or else he will hold to the one and despise the other.*
>
> *'Ye cannot both serve God and God's Adversary with your riches; for wheresoever ye have laid up your treasure, there shall your heart be also.'*

* * * * *

> (56) *'Solomon verily taught us that we should despise earthly riches, for he said:*
>
> *'"He that keepeth faith with God shall abound with blessings, but he that maketh haste to be rich shall not go unpunished."*
>
> *'And he said again: "Labour not to be rich, for riches vanish, they make themselves wings and fly away like an eagle."*
>
> *'And he said again: "Humility and the fear of the Lord are true riches and honour and life."*
>
> *'And he said again: "There is one that maketh himself rich despite his penury; and another that maketh himself poor despite his riches."'*

* * * * *

(c) [Here follows the parable of the Rich Fool (*see* LXVII.*a*).]

* * * * *

(d) The parable of the Unjust Steward is aimed at the Sadducee priesthood who lived on their perquisites and were accused of never doing an honest day's work. In Jesus's view, they had betrayed their trust as God's stewards and spokesmen and, in 79 B.C., were rightly superseded as teachers by hardworking Pharisee laymen. He held that they still demanded far less from the people than these owed to God; it was a prophetic commonplace that He required love, mercy, and humility, as well as sacrifices and tithes. The sting of the parable lay in the ironical reference to *everlasting* habitations—since the Sadducees did not believe in the resurrection.

Luke vi. 8 may refer to *The War Between the Sons of Light and the Sons of Darkness*, a newly recovered apocalyptic book of the second century B.C.

(*see* IV.*e*). The Sons of Darkness, after losing the first three battles out of seven, rallied under the leadership of 'Beliar' and succeeded by superior craft in winning the next three.

(*e*) In *Luke* xvi. 14–15, 'Sadducees' has been substituted for 'Pharisees'; the passage also conceals a *midrash* on 1 *Samuel* xvi. 7.

(276) *Jesus spake this parable against such priests as were covetous:*

'*A certain rich man had a steward and the same was accused unto him that he had wasted his goods.*

'*And he called him and said: "How is it that I hear this of thee? Give an account of thy stewardship. For if these things be true, thou canst no longer be steward."*

'*Then the steward said within himself: "What shall I do? For my lord taketh away from me the stewardship. I cannot dig; to beg I am ashamed.*

'*"I am resolved what to do: that when I am put out of the stewardship I may find men to receive me into their habitations."*

'*So he called every one of his lord's debtors, and said unto the first: "How much owest thou my lord?"*

'*And he answered: "An hundred measures of oil." The steward said unto him: "Take thy bill and sit down quickly, and write fifty!"*

'*Then said he to another: "And how much owest thou?" He answered: "An hundred measures of wheat." And the steward said unto him: "Take thy bill and write fourscore!"*

'*What think ye? Did the lord commend the unjust steward because he had done wisely, when he came to call in those debts?*

'*Ye Sadducees, children of darkness, which are in your generation wiser than the children of light, would ye hear my counsel?*

'*Then go ye with your unrighteous wealth and buy the friendship of God's Adversary, that when your strength faileth, his messengers may receive you into everlasting habitations.*'

* * * * *

(277) *And the priests were wroth when they heard this parable, and asked: 'Are we not priests, sons of Aaron, which Moses anointed? Who art thou to revile us, little one?'*

Jesus answered: 'When Samuel looked on Eliab, the eldest of David's brethren, he said: "Surely, the Lord's anointed is before Him."

'*But the Lord said unto Samuel: "Take no thought for the height of his stature: for the Lord seeth not as a man seeth. Man looketh on the outward appearance, but the Lord looketh on the heart."*

'*Verily, I say unto you: that which is highly esteemed among men is abominable unto God!*'

* * * * *

(*f*) [For the sequel, *see* LXV.*a*.]

* * * * *

LXIX

MASTER, MASTER!

Matthew vii. 21–23

[21]Not every one that saith unto Me, Lord, Lord, shall enter into the Kingdom of heaven; but he that doeth the will of My Father which is in heaven. [22]Many will say to Me in that day, Lord, Lord, have we not prophesied in Thy name? and in Thy name have cast out devils? and in Thy name done many wonderful works? [23]And then will I profess unto them, I never knew you: depart from Me, ye that work iniquity.

Luke xiii. 25–30

[25]When once the master of the house is risen up, and hath shut to the door, and ye begin to stand without, and to knock at the door, saying, Lord, Lord, open unto us; and He shall answer and say unto you, I know you not whence ye are: [26]then shall ye begin to say, We have eaten and drunk in Thy presence, and Thou hast taught in our streets. [27]But He shall say, I tell you, I know you not whence ye are; depart from me, all ye workers of iniquity. [28]There shall be weeping and gnashing of teeth, when ye shall see Abraham, and Isaac, and Jacob, and all the prophets, in the kingdom of God, and you yourselves thrust out. [29]And they shall come from the east, and from the west, and from the north, and from the south, and shall sit down in the kingdom of God. [30]And, behold, there are last which shall be first, and there are first which shall be last.

(*a*) Both *Matthew* vii. 21–23, and the parallel passage in *Luke* xiii. 25–30, are corrupt. Two unrelated sayings, evidently found in a collection of Oracles under the subject-heading 'Master, Master!', have been run together. *Matthew's* first verse clearly distinguishes Jesus from God and probably owes its survival to an editor's misconception that Jesus was foretelling Judas's betrayal. The remaining verses must be rejected, since the disciples were authorized to prophesy and heal in God's name alone; they seem to be a late interpolation aimed at pagan miracle-mongers who borrowed the Gentile Christian formula of healing in the name of Jesus.

(*b*) *Luke's* account of the knocking at the door is confused. The servants cannot be the bridemen of *Luke* xii. 36, because they are outside the house, not inside. And the parable, which is absurdly prefaced by: 'Strive to enter in at the narrow gate' (*Luke* xiii. 24), was originally, perhaps, a continuation of *Luke* xi. 10: 'To him that knocketh it shall be opened' (*see* xxvii.*i*), and ran: 'When once the master of the house shall have risen up from supper and gone to rest . . .' If so, the editor of *Luke,* taking Jesus, not God, to be the master, ingeniously shortened this to 'hath risen up', in reference to the Ascension; thus converting it into a pronouncement that the Jews, who rejected Jesus in his lifetime, are already damned and have no prospect of admission to the Kingdom. Verses 26–27 are an interpolation similar to that in *Matthew* vii. 22–23 (*see* (*a*) *above*).

> (127) *'See therefore that none of you, being yet unbaptized, delay from sloth. For when once the householder shall have risen from supper, and shut to the door and gone to rest, if certain of his household that went elsewhere to make merry shall gather outside and knock at the door, crying: "Master, master, open unto us!" he will answer: "The door is shut, and I know not who ye may be. Depart from me; it is too late."'*

* * * * *

(*c*) Yet in another parable (*Luke* xi. 5–8—*see* LXIV.*a*), Jesus shows that God will listen to the importunate knock of the late guest if he offers a reasonable excuse.

The following is perhaps part of the dialogue between Jesus and his disciples when they try to dissuade him from preaching beyond the Jordan (*see* LXXXIV.*f*).

> (293) *'Not by calling me "Master, master!" will ye enter the Kingdom of Heaven; but only by doing His will.'*

* * * * *

(*d*) *Luke* xiii. 27–30 seems to be addressed to the Sadducaic Chief Rulers who reject the dogma of resurrection (*see* XXI.*l*), but will find too late that they are mistaken (*see* XCIV.*d*). The Sadducees did not accept the prophets but stood on the Law alone; to which the Pharisees retorted (*Sanhedrin* 90*b*): 'Those who deny that the resurrection is taught in the Law, the same will have no part in the world to come.'

This is the correct setting for *Luke* xiii. 30, the wandering saying also found in *Matthew* xix. 30 and *Mark* x. 31 (*see* LXXXII.*d*), and in *Matthew* xx. 16 (*see* LVIII.*a*). Jesus here quotes *Isaiah* xlix 5, 6 and 12.

> (344) *'There shall be weeping and gnashing of teeth when ye shall see Abraham, and Isaac, and Jacob, and all the prophets in the Kingdom of God, and yourselves thrust out.*
>
> *'For Isaiah prophesied in the name of the Lord: "Fear not, Israel, I am with thee! I will bring thy seed from the east, (yea, even from the land of Sinim) and gather thee from the far west.*
>
> *'"I will say to the north: 'Give up!', and to the south: 'Keep not back: bring my sons from far and my daughters from the end of the earth!'"*

'Then shall the scattered seed of Israel come from the east, the west, the north and the south, and shall sit down in the Kingdom of God.

'And behold, there are last which shall be first, and first which shall be last.'

* * * * *

(e) By Jesus's time, Jewish colonies had been founded in Spain, the Sudan, Babylonia, Ceylon, Germany, and most of the intervening countries; which seems to have been the meaning of 'In my Father's house are many mansions' (*John* xiv. 2—*see* cvi.*u* and cxvii.*h*). 'Sinim' is China; the Chinese Jews keep their religious identity to this day.

* * * * *

LXX

JESUS IN SAMARIA

Matthew x. 5–6

⁵These twelve Jesus sent forth and commanded them saying: 'Go not into the way of the Gentiles, and into any city of the Samaritans enter ye not. ⁶But go rather to the lost sheep of the House of Israel.'

Luke ix. 51–56

⁵¹And it came to pass, when the time was come that He should be received up, He steadfastly set His face to go to Jerusalem, ⁵²and sent messengers before His face: and they went, and entered into a village of the Samaritans, to make ready for Him. ⁵³And they did not receive Him, because His face was as though He would go to Jerusalem. ⁵⁴And when His disciples James and John saw this, they said: 'Lord, wilt Thou that we command fire to come down from heaven, and consume them, even as Elijah did?' ⁵⁵But He turned, and rebuked them, and said: 'Ye know not what manner of spirit ye are of. ⁵⁶For the Son of Man is not come to destroy men's lives, but to save them.' And they went to another village.

Luke xvii. 11–12

¹¹And it came to pass as he went to Jerusalem that he passed through the midst of Samaria and Galilee.

¹²And as he entered into a certain village there met him ten men that were lepers . . .

John iii. 22

²²After these things came Jesus and His disciples into the land of Judaea; and there He tarried with them, and baptized.

John iv. 1–42

¹When therefore the Lord knew how the Pharisees had heard that Jesus made and baptized more disciples than John, ²(though Jesus himself baptized not, but His disciples) ³He left Judaea, and departed again into Galilee. ⁴And He must needs go through Samaria. ⁵Then cometh He to a city of Samaria, which is called Sychar, near to the parcel of ground that Jacob gave to his son Joseph. ⁶Now Jacob's well was there. Jesus therefore, being wearied with His journey, sat thus on the well: and it was about the sixth hour. ⁷There cometh a woman of Samaria to draw water: Jesus saith unto

John iv. 1–42 (*contd.*)

her: 'Give me to drink.' ⁸(For His disciples were gone away unto the city to buy meat.) ⁹Then saith the woman of Samaria unto Him: 'How is it that Thou, being a Jew, askest drink of me, which am a woman of Samaria? for the Jews have no dealings with the Samaritans.' ¹⁰Jesus answered and said unto her: 'If thou knewest the gift of God, and Who it is that saith to thee, give me to drink; thou wouldest have asked of Him, and He would have given thee living water.'

¹¹The woman saith unto Him: 'Sir, Thou hast nothing to draw with, and the well is deep: from whence then hast Thou that living water? ¹²Art Thou greater than our father Jacob, which gave us the well, and drank thereof himself, and his children, and his cattle?' ¹³Jesus answered and said unto her: 'Whosoever drinketh of this water shall thirst again; ¹⁴but whosoever drinketh of the water that I shall give him shall never thirst; but the water that I shall give him shall be in him a well of water springing up into everlasting life.'

¹⁵The woman saith unto Him: 'Sir, give me this water, that I thirst not, neither come hither to draw.' ¹⁶Jesus saith unto her: 'Go, call thy husband, and come hither.'

¹⁷The woman answered and said: 'I have no husband.' Jesus said unto her: 'Thou hast well said, I have no husband, ¹⁸for thou hast had five husbands; and he whom thou now hast is not thy husband: in that saidst thou truly.'

¹⁹The woman saith unto Him: 'Sir, I perceive that thou art a prophet. ²⁰Our fathers worshipped in this mountain; and ye say, that in Jerusalem is the place where men ought to worship.' ²¹Jesus saith unto her: 'Woman, believe Me, the hour cometh, when ye shall neither in this mountain, nor yet at Jerusalem, worship the Father. ²²Ye worship ye know not what: we know what we worship: for salvation is of the Jews. ²³But the hour cometh, and now is, when the true worshippers shall worship the Father in spirit and in truth: for the Father seeketh such to worship Him. ²⁴God is a spirit: and they that worship Him must worship Him in spirit and in truth.'

²⁵The woman saith unto Him: 'I know that Messiah cometh, Who is called Christ: when He is come, He will tell us all things.' ²⁶Jesus saith unto her: 'I that speak unto thee am He.'

²⁷And upon this came His disciples and marvelled that He talked with the woman: yet no man said, what seekest Thou? or, why talkest Thou with her? ²⁸The woman then left her waterpot, and went her way into the city, and saith to the men: ²⁹Come, see a Man that told me all things that ever I did: is not this the Christ?' ³⁰Then they went out of the city and came unto Him.

³¹In the mean while His disciples prayed Him, saying, Master, eat. ³²But He said unto them: 'I have meat to eat that ye know not of.'

³³Therefore said the disciples one to another: 'Hath any man brought Him aught to eat?' ³⁴Jesus saith unto them: 'My meat is to do the will of Him that sent Me, and to finish His work. ³⁵Say not ye, There are yet four months and then cometh harvest? behold, I say unto you, Lift up your eyes, and look on the fields; for they are white already to harvest. ³⁶And he that reapeth

John iv. 1–42 (*contd.*)

receiveth wages, and gathereth fruit unto life eternal: that both he that soweth and he that reapeth may rejoice together. [37]And herein is that saying true, One soweth, and another reapeth. [38]I sent you to reap that whereon ye bestowed no labour: other men laboured, and ye are entered into their labours.'

[39]And many of the Samaritans of that city believed on Him for the saying of the woman, which testified, He told me all that ever I did. [40]So when the Samaritans were come unto Him, they besought Him that He would tarry with them: and He abode there two days. [41]And many more believed because of His own word; [42]and said unto the woman: 'Now we believe, not because of thy saying: for we have heard Him ourselves, and know that this is indeed the Christ, the Saviour of the world.'

John viii. 3–11

[3]And the scribes and Pharisees brought unto Him a woman taken in adultery; and when they had set her in the midst, [4]they say unto Him: 'Master, this woman was taken in adultery, in the very act. [5]Now Moses in the law commanded us, that such should be stoned: but what sayest Thou?' [6]This they said, tempting Him, that they might have to accuse Him. But Jesus stooped down, and with His finger wrote on the ground, as though He heard them not. [7]So when they continued asking Him, He lifted up Himself, and said unto them: 'He that is without sin among you, let him first cast a stone at her.' [8]And again He stooped down, and wrote on the ground. [9]And they which heard it, being convicted by their own conscience, went out one by one, beginning at the eldest, even unto the last: and Jesus was left alone, and the woman standing in the midst. [10]When Jesus had lifted up Himself, and saw none but the woman, He said unto her: 'Woman, where are those thine accusers? hath no man condemned thee?' She said: 'No man, Lord.' And Jesus said unto her: 'Neither do I condemn thee: go, and sin no more.'

John viii. 48

[48]Then answered the Jews and said unto him: 'Say we not well that thou art a Samaritan and hast a devil?'

Eusebius: Ecclesiastical History 3. xxix. 17

Papias hath also set forth another story about a woman accused of many sins before the Lord, which the *Gospel according to the Hebrews* also containeth.

(*a*) Jesus's command to the Twelve: 'Go not into the way of the Gentiles and into any city of the Samaritans enter ye not!' (*Matthew* x. 5—*see* LVII.*a*), and his rebuff to the Syro-Phoenician woman (*Mark* vii. 27—*see* XXXVI.*g*): 'Let the children first be filled!' prove that he felt no obligation towards the Samaritans as such. For a discussion of the Samaritan forgeries in the Gospels, *see Introduction* II.*f and* III.*n–t*. His immediate mission was to the lost sheep of the House of Israel, the 'Men of the Land', whose ignorance of the Law was delaying the Kingdom of God (*see* XII.*m–p*).

(*b*) Neither *Mark* nor *Matthew* records that Jesus had any dealings at all with the Samaritans, or even that he passed through their country on his way to Jerusalem. According to *Luke,* however, where the editorial touch of Simon Magus is strongly felt, he remains there during the eight chapters (*Luke* ix. 51–xviii. 34) which contain, among other things, the 'Good Samaritan' (*see* LXXXII.*m–n*) and the cure of the Samaritan leper (*see* XXXII.*c–d*). This misarrangement has resulted in several absurdities: for instance the odd appearance in Samaria of the Scribes and Pharisees (*Luke* xv. 2), and the suggestion (*Luke* xiii. 31) that Herod Antipas's writ ran in Samaria as well as Galilee.

Jesus's tenderness towards the Samaritan village in *Luke* ix. 55–56 stands in contrast not only with the animosity of his Jewish disciples who wanted it to be destroyed by fire from heaven, but with his alleged orders in *Matthew* x. 14–15, that any Galilean village which did not receive them should suffer a worse fate than even Sodom and Gomorrah. The editor of *Luke* ix. 52–53 is at pains to make the Samaritan villagers reject not Jesus himself, but his messengers, and excuses them by suggesting that they mistook the missionaries for pilgrims to Jerusalem.

According to *John* iv. 3–4, Jesus was going in the opposite direction: from Jerusalem to Galilee.

(*c*) It should be noted that, though the woman at the well is described as a Samaritan in *John* iv. 9, she claims Israelite descent three verses later. If she had not done so, Jesus would never have risked defilement by asking to drink from her pitcher. She was, in fact, a descendant of the Ephraimite peasantry who stayed behind in Samaria when their nobility and priesthood were carried off to Assyria and replaced by Cypriots and Cushites; the Galileans, equally, were peasant relics of Isaachar, Zebulon, Dan, and the rest (*see* XLII.*c*). Jesus's message of repentance was meant for her Israelite kinsfolk also; and it is possible that some of these accepted it, though incredible that they acclaimed him as the Messiah (*John* iv. 41–42). Her question in *John* iv. 20 rings true: according to *Joshua* viii. 33, the Ark was brought to Mount Ebal, where Joshua built an altar to God and recited the Law, at a time when Jerusalem was still in the hands of the Canaanites. Jesus, when he tells the woman that 'Salvation is of the Jews', is insisting on the right of the Pharisaic Sanhedrin to legislate for all Israelites, including the descendants of the ten Northern tribes.

(*d*) *John* iv. 22: 'Ye know not what ye worship', is the orthodox Jewish view; the Samaritans were held to be foolish rather than wicked. 'From this day shall Shechem be called the City of Fools' (*Testament of Levi* c. 7). 'With two nations is My soul vexed and also with a third that is no nation: namely with the dwellers on the mountain of Seir* [Edom], and with those of Philistia, and with the foolish race that sojourneth in Shechem' (*Ecclesiasticus* l. 25–26). The Talmud (*Maseketh Kuthim* 28) replies to the question: 'When

---

* The Authorised Version reads 'Samaria'.

shall we accept them [the Samaritans] again?' with: 'When they renounce
Mount Gerizim, acknowledge Jerusalem, and believe in the resurrection of
the dead.' And in the same tractate it is stated: 'We do not give them wives,
nor do we take wives from them, but we allow them the gleanings and the
forgotten sheaf' (*Leviticus* xix. 9—because the Samaritans also observed the
law of gleaning). The ties between Samaria and Jerusalem were never quite
broken, even when, after Bar Cochba's rising, the Romans rewarded their
Samaritan allies by permitting them to re-build the temple on Mount Gerizim. Thus in *Kiddushin* 76a, Rabbi Gamaliel III (about 165 A.D.) acknowledged: 'Every command of the Law that the Samaritans keep [though they
fail to keep many], they keep it more scrupulously than the Israelites themselves', and the view is expressed in *Niddah* vii. 5 that, in certain respects, a
Samaritan is the equal of an Israelite.

(*e*) Jerome in his *Epistle* 86, identifies Sychar with Shechem, but since the
disciples were forbidden to enter a Samaritan city (*see* (*a*) *above*), because
the town-dwellers were predominantly Cyprio-Cushites, they could not have
entered Shechem to buy bread, as stated in *John* iv. 8. They were not, however, forbidden to enter a hamlet; and Lightfoot and Conder, among other
Biblical critics, identify Sychar with a hamlet now called 'Askar, about half a
mile from Jacob's Well, nearly two miles east-north-east from Shechem and
on the slope of Mount Ebal.

For the quotation from *Proverbs* xviii. 4, on which *John* iv. 14 is a *midrash,*
see XLIX.*c.*

The Pharisees generously decided that, since the Samaritans kept the Law,
apart from being served by a non-Aaronic priesthood, 'the Land of the
Cuthim [i.e. the Samaritans] is clean, and so are the gatherings of their
waters, their dwellings and their roads' (*Jer. Abodah Zarah* v. 4: *and see
Tosephta Mikwaoth* vi. 1). Subject to certain precautions, Samaritan meat
was considered 'clean' (*Hullin* 3b and *Maseketh Kuthim* 17) as was also their
wine, until the mid-second century A.D.

(*f*) The 'five husbands' of *John* iv. 18—if this passage is to be regarded as a
Grecian interpolation—are the five senses, which Philo called the seducers of
the soul (*On Genesis* iii. 6 and *Allegories of the Law* i. 131). For Jesus, however, the five senses were not evil in themselves, any more than money was,
but could be put to either righteous or unrighteous use. If, therefore, the passage is authentic, the husbands will be the evil planetary Powers of the five
worldly days of the week, whose sins were listed in the second half of the
Decalogue: namely Witchcraft for Monday, Murder for Tuesday, Theft for
Wednesday, False Oaths for Thursday, and Adultery for Friday. The Essenes
kept holy the first, as well as the seventh, day; and the subsequent fame of
Sunday in the early Church as 'The Lord's Day' suggests that Jesus did the
same. The pretended husband, then, is God's Adversary, the Cosmocrator
and leader of these five evil Powers—whose particular day was Wednesday
(*see* CI.*j*).

It was the Pharisaic view, based on *Ezekiel* xxiii. 1–21, that the worshipping of many gods was like polyandry, and that the soul should acknowledge God as her only husband. Philo's use of this metaphor in his *Allegories of the Law* i. 563 and i. 609 does not prove that Jesus did not use it independently. Philonian influence has also been suspected in *John* iv. 6, where Jesus 'sat thus at the well at about the sixth hour', a time which Philo (*On Genesis* xviii. 1) describes as the fittest for a divine revelation. In *Allegories of the Law* i. 131 he writes that 'Moses sat at the well like an athlete recovering his breath'. But in Palestine and Syria the sixth hour, namely noon, is siesta time—Abraham was also taking a siesta in *Genesis* xviii. 1—and there is no more reason to suspect Philonian allegory here than in *Acts* x. 6 and xxii. 6 (*see* cxviii.*k*). Mention of the sixth hour explains why Jesus rested at the well-head apart from his disciples and how the woman hoped to seduce him unnoticed by her sleeping husband and kinsfolk. Only a loose woman would have engaged in conversation with a stranger met alone at an hour of such erotic notoriety. From the sharpness of Jesus's reproof, indeed, it seems likely that she opened it with the classical *double-entendre* about wells; but that, because of later libels on Jesus's chastity—in one Talmudic passage he is accused of having admired the eyes of an innkeeper's wife—this provocation was suppressed.

(*g*) The proper place for this story is after the healing of the lunatic child (*see* LXXII.*b*). A late editor of *John* seems to have borrowed it from the *Gospel according to the Hebrews*: it does not occur in all manuscripts, but is inserted in a few manuscripts of *Luke*.

(263) *Then cometh he to a village of Samaria which is called Sychar, nigh to the parcel of ground that Jacob gave unto his son Joseph.*

Now, Jacob's well was there. And Jesus, being wearied with his journey sat thus on the well, and it was about the sixth hour.

And the disciples went away to the village to buy food from the men of the land.

Then cometh a woman to the well, and with an impudent face she saith to him: 'Friend, the well is at thy command. Let me draw water and give thee to drink.'

Now, she was an Ephraimite woman, of the daughters of the land, and Jesus perceived that she was an harlot.

He said unto her: 'Woman, suffer me rather to give thee living water, that thou mayest never thirst again.'

She said unto him: 'Art thou greater than our father Jacob, which gave us this well and himself drank thereof, and his children, and his cattle? For though this water be good, yet must I come every day hither to draw more.'

He answered: 'Go, call thy husband, and I will give you both to drink.'

She saith unto him: 'I have no husband', thinking to entice him to lie with her, for unto that purpose was she come out to the well at noon while her husband slept.

He answered again: 'Thou has rightly said: "I have no husband." For thou hast had five husbands: which are Enchantment, Murder, Theft, False Oaths, and Adultery, and he whom thou hast now, God's Adversary, he is not thy husband.'

* * * * *

[Here follows Jesus's explanation of this metaphor (*see* ci.*j*).]

(265) *'Yet I say unto thee, bring hither him which is truly thy husband, that I may teach him the fear of the Lord, which is the beginning of wisdom.*

'For Solomon, when he reigned over your forefathers, said: "The words of a wise man's mouth are as deep waters, and the well-spring of wisdom is as a flowing brook."

'Therefore, that which I will give him to drink from the words of the sages, the same shall be in him as a well of water springing up to everlasting life!'

Then was she abashed, and said: 'Sir, I perceive that thou art a prophet of God.'

And he declared unto the woman her errors, and she repented of them and wept, and he prayed God to forgive her.

Afterward, she asked him: 'Why say ye that in Jerusalem is the place where men should worship, seeing that our fathers worshipped in this mountain according to the blessing that Moses put upon it?'

Jesus answered and said: 'The priests of Samaria worship they know not what; for though they have received the Law, they know not that God will be worshipped in righteousness and truth.

'But we of Jerusalem know Him whom we worship, and salvation is of the Jews.

'Do ye of Samaria therefore beware, lest the time come when ye shall worship the Lord neither here nor there.'

Then came his disciples, marvelling that he conversed with the woman, yet they durst say nought.

And she, perceiving what was in their hearts, said: 'Sirs, he told me all that ever I did, and he hath turned me away from my sins.'

Then left she her waterpot, and went in haste to Sychar to call her husband, which presently came unto Jesus and constrained him to tarry in the house with them.

This man also gathered his neighbours together, such as were Israelites, and Jesus tarried there two days and preached repentance unto them, and many accepted his words.

* * * * *

(*h*) In the account of the woman taken in adultery—which belongs here (*see Introduction* ii.*b–d*) rather than in *John* viii. 3–11, where it serves as a libel on the Pharisees—no mention is made of the paramour who should have been stoned with her. It is likely, therefore, that she had cast a heathen spell on her husband to further her adulterous schemes—magic and adultery are associated in 2 *Kings* ix. 22, *Nahum* iii. 4, and *Malachi* iii. 5—thus breaking four Commandments at once: the First, the Sixth, the Seventh, and the

Tenth. This would agree with Papias's account of her 'many sins'. She would then have been subject to the law of *Deuteronomy* xvii. 2–7; which gives point to Jesus's otherwise idle remark about precedence in casting the stones. He was here opposing the humane Pharisaic view of the Law to the savage literalness of the Samaritans (*see Introduction* 11.*d*), and will have had in mind *Hosea* iv. 14: 'I will not punish your daughters when they commit whoredom, nor your spouses when they commit adultery: for ye yourselves are gone off with whores and do sacrifice with harlots.' Yet it was futile to quote the prophets at Samaritans, and dangerous to exacerbate them by Pharisaic argument; they respected the written Law only. Jesus, therefore, with admirable presence of mind wrote the text of *Deuteronomy* xvii. 2–7 in the dust, and suggested an order of precedence for the eye-witness who, according to this passage, must throw the first stones. But all showed reluctance to claim that they were sinless—it was a commonplace that God alone is perfect (*Proverbs* xx. 9)—and slipped away; then, deprived of their witnesses, the crowd was powerless to carry out the execution and so dispersed.

(*i*) Jesus's intervention to save the life of a city-Samaritan is in keeping with his parable of the Samaritan who fell among thieves (*see* LXXXII.*m–n*). In *John* viii. 11, which Christian commentators relate to *Luke* vi. 37: 'Condemn not, and ye shall not be condemned', there seems to be, as elsewhere (*see* LIV.*b*), a substitution of 'I' for 'God'. As it stands, the pronouncement makes no sense, since Jesus could not have condemned the woman in the absence of all witnesses even if he had been a duly appointed Samaritan judge.

(266) *And he departed thence and as he went, he saw how certain Samaritans brought a woman by force without the gates of the city of Shekem, and the people that were gathered together took up stones in their hands.*

And Jesus asked: 'Why take ye up stones against this woman?'

They answered and said: 'She hath committed an abomination unto the furtherance of her adulteries, and was taken in the very act. Art thou a Jew and knowest not that Moses commanded us to stone her?'

Jesus answered: 'Nevertheless, ye will do well to heed every statute of the Law.'

And he stooped, and began to write on the dust with his finger: how that until the two witnesses, or three witnesses, should have cast their stones, the people must refrain.

And they asked saying: 'What writest thou?'

He answered: 'Read; and he that is without sin among the witnesses, let him cast the first stone!'

And the witnesses, being just men, went away softly one by one, beginning with the eldest. For they remembered the words of Solomon: 'Who can say: "I have made my heart clean, I am pure from my sin"?'

Then Jesus lifted himself up and saw that none of them remained. And he asked the people: 'Where are the witnesses against this woman?'

And the woman which was accused, answered: 'They are gone away, and have not set their hands against me.'

Jesus said unto her: 'Repent and sin no more! For if thou so doest, neither will God's hand be set against thee.'

* * * * *

(*j*) John iv. 31–38 consists of two unrelated sayings. The first belongs probably to the preceding incident of the Lunatic Child, where Jesus discusses fasting with the disciples (*see* LXXIX. *d–e*). The second, which recalls the Labourers in the Vineyard (*see* LVIII.*b*), should be supplemented by a quotation from the *Book of Ahikar* about those who refuse to work (*see* XXI.*g*); Jesus's mention of four months suggests that it was spoken in the January before the Crucifixion, when he was preaching at Beth-Nimrah (*see* LXXXIV.*f* *and* LXXXVII.*d*).

(255) *And they importuned him, saying: 'Master, eat now! Break thy fast. Wait not until the sabbath.'*

But Jesus said unto them: 'I have meat to eat of which ye know not, whereby I am sustained to do the will of Him which sent me, and to finish His work speedily.'

* * * * *

(295) *And when the disciples said unto Jesus: 'Master, there is no haste. Rest awhile, and take thy ease,' he answered:*

'Say not: "There are yet four months remaining before we shall have need to put in the sickle,"

'But lift up your eyes and look on the fields, for they are white already to harvest.

'The reward of him that reapeth now shall be that he gathereth fruit to everlasting life.

'Herein is that saying true: "One soweth and another reapeth." For Moses and the prophets laboured to sow, and we are entered late into their labours.

'Howbeit, in the Kingdom of God the sower and the reaper shall rejoice together.'

* * * * *

(*k*) *Luke* ix. 56: 'I have not come to destroy men's lives', is out of context here (*see* LXXVIII.*g*) and contradicts Jesus's announcement that he has come to bring down fire from heaven (*Luke* xii. 49—*see* CI.*f*). The disciples' demand for a repetition of Elijah's fiery miracle suggests that they had been opposed by soldiers—as happened to Elijah in 2 *Kings* i. 9–13—rather than by villagers; a principal duty of the Roman garrison in Samaria was the prevention of clashes between the Samaritans and Galilean pilgrims passing through their country (*Wars* ii. 12. 3–5). Jesus will have refused the disciples' demand by quoting *Jeremiah* li. 33—the 'daughter of Babylon' being now a Pharisaic term for 'Rome'. However, it was the policy of the Gentile Church to suppress all evidence of friction between Jesus and the Romans, and a new end to this story had to be composed.

(262) *And he steadfastly set his face to go toward Jerusalem. But he first must needs pass through Samaria. And he sent James and John before him to make ready.*

And they entered into a village and preached repentance, and many came together to hear them or to dispute with them.

But the soldiers of the Wicked Kingdom, which were in that place, beat them with rods and cast them out.

Therefore returned they unto Jesus and asked him, saying: 'Lord, wilt thou command fire to come down from heaven and consume these soldiers, even as Elijah did unto the soldiers of Ahaziah which came against him?'

Jesus answered and said: 'Jeremiah prophesied: "The daughter of Babylon is like unto a threshing floor. Yet a little while, and the time of the harvest is come."

'Go ye to another village!' And they went, and were received.

* * * * *

(*l*) The contradiction between *John* iii. 22 and *John* iv. 2 is due to doctrinal confusion. In *John* iii. 5 (*see* LXXXIII.*h*), Jesus is made to insist on the necessity of Christian baptism; in *John* iii. 22, he is said to have himself performed the rite of baptism; and in *John* iv. 2—which really belongs to a later stage of events (*see* LXXXIV. *a–b*)—he is said to have baptized more repentant sinners even than John. But *John* iv. 2 was held by a late editor to detract from the force of *Matthew* iii. 11, where John distinguishes between his own baptism by water and Jesus's baptism by fire (*see* v.*d*); a gloss was therefore added to the text of *John* iv. 2: 'Jesus himself did not baptize, but only his disciples.' This gloss also served as an explanation why, since Jesus baptized such great numbers, the Jews should have utterly rejected him: for if Jesus, now regarded as God, had baptized in person, no subsequent back-sliding would have been possible.

(*m*) *John* viii. 48: 'Say we not well that thou art an Samaritan, and hast a devil?' may be regarded as genuine, if 'Samaritan' is here used as a euphemism for 'fool' (*see* LXX.*d*); to call one's neighbour plain 'fool' was to commit the sin of murder (*see* XXII.*a*). Its proper place will be the Beelzebub context (*see* XXXIV.*f*).

(118) *And he pressed Jesus, saying: 'Art thou not truly a Samaritan, and hast thou not a devil?'*

* * * * *

THE PLUCK-RIGHT

Mark ii. 23–28

²³And it came to pass that He went through the corn fields on the sabbath day; and His disciples began, as they went, to pluck the ears of corn. ²⁴And the Pharisees said unto Him: 'Behold, why do they on the sabbath day that which is not lawful?' ²⁵And He said unto them: 'Have ye never read what David did, when he had need, and was an hungered, he, and they that were with him? ²⁶How he went into the house of God in the days of Abiathar the high priest, and did eat the shewbread, which is not lawful to eat but for the priests, and gave also to them which were with him?' ²⁷And He said unto them: 'The sabbath was made for man, and not man for the sabbath, ²⁸therefore the Son of Man is Lord also of the sabbath.'

Matthew xii. 1–8

¹At that time Jesus went on the sabbath day through the corn; and His disciples were an hungered, and began to pluck the ears of corn, and to eat. ²But when the Pharisees saw it, they said unto Him: 'Behold, Thy disciples do that which is not lawful to do upon the sabbath day.' ³But He said unto them: 'Have ye not read what David did, when he was an hungered, and they that were with him; ⁴how he entered into the house of God, and did eat the shewbread, which was not lawful for him to eat, neither for them which were with him, but only for the priests? ⁵Or have ye not read in the law, how that on the sabbath days the priests in the temple profane the sabbath, and are blameless? ⁶But I say unto you, that in this place is One greater than the temple. ⁷But if ye had known what this meaneth,

I will have mercy, and not sacrifice,

ye would not have condemned the guiltless. ⁸For the Son of Man is Lord even of the sabbath day.'

Luke vi. 1–5

¹And it came to pass on the second sabbath after the first, that He went through the corn fields; and His disciples plucked the ears of corn, and did eat, rubbing them in their hands. ²And certain of the Pharisees said unto them: 'Why do ye that which is not lawful to do on the sabbath days?' ³And Jesus answering them said: 'Have ye not read so much as this, what David did, when himself was an hungered, and they which were with him; ⁴how he went into the house of God, and did take and eat the shrewbread, and gave

Luke vi. 1–5 (*contd.*)

also to them that were with him; which it is not lawful to eat but for the priests alone?' ⁵And He said unto them, that the Son of Man is Lord also of the sabbath.

Oxyrhynchus Papyrus 654, vii.

Jesus saith: 'If ye fast not from the world ye shall not find the Kingdom of God, and if ye keep not the Sabbath for the whole week, ye shall not see the Father.'

Luke vi. 4—*Codex Bezae*

On the same day, seeing one working on the Sabbath, he said to him: 'Man, if indeed thou knowest what thou doest, blessed art thou; but if thou knowest not, thou art accursed and a transgressor against the Law.'

(*a*) The disciples' corn-plucking in *Mark* ii. 23–28, *Matthew* xii. 1–8 and *Luke* vi. 1–5 cannot be reconciled with Sabbath observance of the period. The Sabbath was devoted to joy and loving-kindness and also to complete rest— even the prisoners of Gehenna were released from their torments on that day (*Pirke di Rabbi Eliezer* xix.). *Isaiah* lviii. 13–14 reads:

'If thou turn away thy foot from doing thy pleasure on the Sabbath, My holy day, and call it a delight, the holy of the Lord, honourable; and shalt honour Him, not doing thine own ways, nor finding thine own pleasure, nor speaking thine own words,

'Then shalt thou delight thyself in the Lord and I will cause thee to ride upon the high places of the earth and feed thee with the heritage of Jacob thy father: for the mouth of the Lord hath spoken it.'

The choicest collations were prepared for the Sabbath, and it was forbidden to mourn or fast. Jesus would never have led the Twelve into a field to eat raw corn on the Sabbath, when they could have counted on the hospitality which the town was obliged to provide; nor would there have been any Pharisees present to observe him, if he had.

(*b*) It was laid down in *Exodus* xvi. 29: 'Remain every man where he is, let no man go out of his place on the seventh day!' The Pharisees had lightened this command by permitting a 'Sabbath-day's journey' of about four hundred yards from home. Jesus's party will therefore have arrived at the town where he proposed to spend the Sabbath, not later than the Friday afternoon, thus allowing the local authorities time to arrange for their board and lodging. Moreover, he could not have let the disciples husk corn with their hands; this was reckoned as threshing and strictly forbidden on a Sabbath.

(*c*) Nevertheless, the incident does not read like a wanton invention, and in all the Synoptic it precedes Jesus's healing of the man with a withered hand whom he found in a synagogue—an act which some of those present condemned as a breach of the Sabbath (*see* LXXIV.*a*–*c*). It is possible, therefore, that both disputes were recorded in a collection of Oracles under the subject-heading 'How He Confounded the Rulers of a Certain Synagogue'. If so, it is easy to see how the mistake arose: the two cases were read in sequence as having occurred on the same day, whereas, in fact, the charge of breaking the Second Commandment had been brought in the second only. In the first, which took place on a labouring day, the charge will have been one of breaking the Eighth Commandment, though travellers passing through a field had a statutory right to glean as they went. It was laid down in *Deuteronomy* xxiii. 25: 'When thou comest into the standing corn of thy neighbour, thou mayest pluck the ears with thine hand, but thou shalt not move a sickle against it.'

(*d*) Some essential element is missing from the account of this first dispute. If the alleged offence took place when Jesus and the disciples were returning to Galilee among crowds of Passover pilgrims, hungry after their journey through barren Judaea and inhospitable Samaria, it is likely enough that certain cornfields were placed out of bounds by the legal fiction of *corban* (*see* xx.*c*), lest the pilgrims should strip them clean; and that, when the disciples exercised their pluck-right in defiance of the ban, the owners accused them of sacrilege. This would explain why Jesus quoted 1 *Samuel* xxi. 1–6, where Ahimelech allowed David to set aside a similar prohibition when compelled by hunger. Jesus will certainly not have misquoted, as he is said to have done in *Mark* ii. 26, calling Ahimelech 'Abiathar' and suggesting that David acted without priestly authority.

> (173) *And it came to pass, as he journeyed with his disciples, that they were sore an-hungered, because there was as yet no ripe corn in Judaea, and because the Samaritans gave them not to eat.*

*   *   *   *

[Here follows Judas Iscariot's questions about the abundance of food in the Heavenly Kingdom, and Jesus's answer (*see* LV.*a and b*).]

*   *   *   *

> (177) *At the last, Jesus led them through a field of corn nigh unto the borders of Galilee; and suffered them to pluck the ears as they went, rubbing them in their hands, though the steward would have prevented them, for this corn was sanctified unto the Lord.*
>
> *Therefore did the steward bring them before the rulers of the synagogue, which said unto Jesus: 'Sir, it is written: "Thou shalt not steal!" And have not thy disciples stolen from God Himself?'*
>
> *He answered: 'The Law suffereth us to pluck a neighbour's corn with our hands as we pass through his field, and he may not deny us.'*
>
> *They said: 'Yet are these fruits sanctified unto the Lord; for if every man that cometh from Jerusalem should take an ear, or twain, then would these fields be laid bare and we should lose our labour.'*
>
> *Jesus answered and said: 'Have ye not heard what David did when his men were an-hungered? He went to the House of the Lord which was at*

Nob, and besought Ahimelech the priest to sustain them with the shew bread, which only the priests might eat.

'And Ahimelech, when he learned that they had kept themselves from women three days and that their need was great, gave them freely of what David had asked.

'So likewise were my disciples an-hungered, which have kept themselves from women these many months, and I being a priest, a Son of Aaron, suffered them to eat, but ate not myself.'

At this, the rulers of the synagogue dismissed him, saying: 'Thou hast well said, and hast justified both thyself and thy disciples.'

* * * * *

(e) *Mark* ii. 27: 'The Sabbath is made for man, and not man for the Sabbath', is likely to have figured elsewhere in the Oracles. Jesus here quotes the oral tradition, now preserved in the Talmud (*Yoma* 85b): 'God delivered the Sabbath unto you, not you unto the Sabbath.' This was deduced by the rabbis from *Exodus* xxxi. 14: 'For it is holy unto *you*.' The occasion of Jesus's quotation, since it cannot have been the pluck-right dispute, must be looked for elsewhere and is found precisely here: *Luke* vi. 4, in the *Codex Bezae* ('D' of the Gospels, at Cambridge), though expunged from all other manuscripts. Evidently the man was performing one of those humane actions which, in the *Tosephta Shabbath* xv. 11 are listed as being no true desecration of the Sabbath, and even laudable: 'He who acts promptly deserves praise'. Jesus will have quoted this passage, but added that if the man were a habitual Sabbath-breaker, who would as soon have threshed his own corn as run to quench the fire in a neighbour's barn, he was accursed.

(f) Jesus's claim for a personal exemption does not ring true: it is a deduction made by the Gospel editors from the final verse of the pluck-right dispute. 'Son of man' (*Mark* ii. 28, *Matthew* xii. 8 and *Luke* vi. 5) should read 'sons of men'—who might decide how best to serve God on the Sabbath.

(105) *Jesus, seeing a man do a work of mercy on the sabbath, said unto him: 'Man, if thou knowest indeed what thou doest, blessed art thou! For the Sages have taught us: "God delivered the sabbath unto you, not you unto the sabbath."*

'But if thou knowest not, and wouldst break the sabbath for no good cause, then art thou accursed as a transgressor against the Law.'

And when they that stood by questioned him further, he answered and said: 'Under God which ordained the sabbath, the sons of men are made masters of the sabbath.'

* * * * *

(g) *Matthew* xii. 5–8 is plainly corrupt, since Jesus would never have boasted that he was of greater importance than the Temple. Yet the passage proves that the pluck-right dispute has here been confused with the one about the Sabbath-day healing. Jesus refers his critics to *Numbers* xxviii. 9–10, where a sacrifice of two lambs is prescribed for every Sabbath. He argues that if a work of sacrifice is permitted, a work of mercy should be even more accept-able to God, and supports his argument by quoting *Hosea* vi. 6: 'For I de-sired mercy and not sacrifice, and the knowledge of God more than burnt offerings.' But to eat corn was not, like healing, a work of mercy nor, like the sacrifice of lambs, a work of piety, but a mere gratification of appetite.

(*h*) The concluding phrases of the two sayings quoted in the *Oxyrhynchus Papyrus* 654 seem to have become interchanged. The first may be a *midrash* on the Fourth Commandment.

> (106) *He said also: 'It is written: "Six days shalt thou labour and do all thou hast to do, but the seventh is the sabbath of the Lord thy God."*
>
> *'Verily, I say unto you: if ye keep not the sabbath in joy and holiness every day of the week, casting aside the cares of this world, ye shall not enter into the Kingdom of Heaven.'*

* * * * *

The second saying is an apt sequel to *Matthew* vi. 18 (*see* xxvii.*g*).

* * * * *

LXXII

BREAD FROM HEAVEN

Mark vi. 31–44

[31]And He said unto them: 'Come ye yourselves apart into a desert place, and rest a while,' for there were many coming and going, and they had no leisure so much as to eat. [32]And they departed into a desert place by boat privately. [33]And the people saw them departing, and many knew Him, and ran afoot thither out of all cities, and outwent them, and came together unto Him. [34]And Jesus, when He came out, saw much people, and was moved with compassion toward them, because they were as sheep not having a shepherd: and He began to teach them many things. [35]And when the day was now far spent, His disciples came unto Him, and said: 'This is a desert place, and now the time is far passed. [36]Send them away, that they may go into the country round about, and into the villages, and buy themselves bread: for they have nothing to eat.' [37]He answered and said unto them: 'Give ye them to eat.'

And they say unto Him: 'Shall we go and buy two hundred pennyworth of bread, and give them to eat?' [38]He saith unto them: 'How many loaves have ye? go and see.' And when they knew, they say: 'Five, and two fishes.' [39]And He commanded them to make all sit down by companies upon the green grass. [40]And they sat down in ranks, by hundreds, and by fifties. [41]And when He had taken the five loaves and the two fishes, He looked up to heaven, and blessed, and brake the loaves, and gave them to His disciples to set before them; and the two fishes divided He among them all. [42]And they did all eat, and were filled. [43]And they took up twelve baskets full of the fragments, and of the fishes. [44]And they that did eat of the loaves were about five thousand men.

Mark viii. 1–21

[1]In those days the multitude being very great, and having nothing to eat, Jesus called His disciples, and saith unto them: [2]'I have compassion on the multitude, because they have now been with Me three days, and have nothing to eat: [3]and if I send them away fasting to their own houses, they will faint by the way.' For divers of them came from far. [4]And His disciples answered Him: 'From whence can a man satisfy these men with bread here in the wilderness?' [5]And He asked them: 'How many loaves have ye?' And they said seven. [6]And He commanded the people to sit down on the ground: and He took the seven loaves, and gave thanks, and brake, and gave to His

Mark viii. 1–21 (*contd.*)

disciples to set before them; and they did set them before the people. [7]And they had a few small fishes: and He blessed, and commanded to set them also before them. [8]So they did eat, and were filled: and they took up of the broken meat that was left seven baskets. [9]And they that had eaten were about four thousand: and He sent them away. [10]And straightway He entered into a boat with His disciples, and came into the parts of Dalmanutha.

[11]And the Pharisees came forth, and began to question with Him, seeking of Him a sign from heaven, tempting Him. [12]And He sighed deeply in His spirit, and saith: 'Why doth this generation seek after a sign? verily I say unto you, There shall no sign be given unto this generation.' [13]And He left them, and entering into the boat again departed to the other side.

[14]Now the disciples had forgotten to take bread, neither had they in the boat with them more than one loaf. [15]And He charged them, saying: 'Take heed, beware of the leaven of the Pharisees, and of the leaven of Herod.' [16]And they reasoned among themselves, saying, it is because we have no bread. [17]And when Jesus knew it, He saith unto them: 'Why reason ye, because ye have no bread? perceive ye not, neither understand? have ye your heart yet hardened? [18]Having eyes, see ye not? and having ears, hear ye not? and do ye not remember? [19]When I brake the five loaves among five thousand, how many baskets full of fragments took ye up?' They say unto Him, twelve. [20]'And when the seven among four thousand, how many baskets full of fragments took ye up?' And they said, seven. [21]And He said unto them: 'How is it that ye do not understand?'

Matthew xiv. 15–21

[15]And when it was evening, His disciples came to Him, saying: 'This is a desert place, and the time is now past; send the multitude away, that they may go into the villages, and buy themselves victuals.' [16]But Jesus said unto them: 'They need not depart; give ye them to eat.' [17]And they say unto Him: 'We have here but five loaves, and two fishes.' [18]He said: 'Bring them hither to Me.' [19]And He commanded the multitude to sit down on the grass, and took the five loaves, and the two fishes, and looking up to heaven, He blessed, and brake, and gave the loaves to His disciples, and the disciples to the multitude. [20]And they did all eat, and were filled: and they took up of the fragments that remained twelve baskets full. [21]And they that had eaten were about five thousand men, beside women and children.

Matthew xv. 29–39

[29]And Jesus departed from thence, and came nigh unto the sea of Galilee; and went up into a mountain, and sat down there. [30]And great multitudes came unto Him, having with them those that were lame, blind, dumb, maimed, and many others, and cast them down at Jesus's feet; and He healed them: [31]insomuch that the multitude wondered, when they saw the dumb to speak, the maimed to be whole, the lame to walk, and the blind to see: and they glorified the God of Israel. [32]Then Jesus called His disciples unto Him,

Matthew xv. 29–39 (*contd.*)

and said: 'I have compassion on the multitude, because they continue with
Me now three days, and have nothing to eat: and I will not send them away
fasting, lest they faint in the way.' [33]And His disciples say unto Him:
'Whence should we have so much bread in the wilderness, as to fill so great a
multitude?' [34]And Jesus saith unto them: 'How many loaves have ye?' And
they said: 'Seven, and a few little fishes.' [35]And He commanded the multitude to sit down on the ground. [36]And He took the seven loaves and the
fishes, and gave thanks, and brake them, and gave to His disciples, and the
disciples to the multitude. [37]And they did all eat, and were filled: and they
took up of the broken meat that was left seven baskets full. [38]And they that
did eat were four thousand men, beside women and children. [39]And He sent
away the multitude, and took boat, and came into the coasts of Magdala.

Matthew xvi. 5–12

[5]And when His disciples were come to the other side, they had forgotten to
take bread. [6]Then Jesus said unto them: 'Take heed and beware of the leaven
of the Pharisees and of the Sadducees.' [7]And they reasoned among themselves, saying: 'It is because we have taken no bread.' [8]Which when Jesus
perceived, He said unto them: 'O ye of little faith, why reason ye among
yourselves, because ye have brought no bread? [9]Do ye not yet understand,
neither remember the five loaves of the five thousand, and how many baskets
ye took up? [10]Neither the seven loaves of the four thousand, and how many
baskets ye took up? [11]How is it that ye do not understand that I spake it not
to you concerning bread, that ye should beware of the leaven of the Pharisees
and of the Sadducees?' [12]Then understood they how that He bade them not
beware of the leaven of bread, but of the doctrine of the Pharisees and of the
Sadducees.

Luke ix. 10–17

[10]And the Apostles, when they were returned, told Him all that they had
done. And He took them, and went aside privately into a desert place belonging to the city called Bethsaida. [11]And the people, when they knew it, followed Him, and He received them, and spake unto them of the kingdom of
God, and healed them that had need of healing. [12]And when the day began
to wear away, then came the Twelve, and said unto Him: 'Send the multitude away, that they may go into the towns and country round about, and
lodge, and get victuals: for we are here in a desert place.' [13]But He said unto
them: 'Give ye them to eat.' And they said: 'We have no more but five
loaves and two fishes; except we should go and buy meat for all this people.'
[14]For they were about five thousand men. And He said to His disciples:
'Make them sit down by fifties in a company.' [15]And they did so, and made
them all sit down. [16]Then He took the five loaves and the two fishes, and
looking up to heaven, He blessed them, and brake, and gave to the disciples
to set before the multitude. [17]And they did eat, and were all filled: and there
was taken up of fragments that remained to them twelve baskets.

John vi. 1–14

[1]After these things Jesus went over the sea of Galilee, which is the sea of Tiberias. [2]And a great multitude followed Him, because they saw His miracles which He did on them that were diseased. [3]And Jesus went up into a mountain, and there He sat with His disciples. [4]And the passover, a feast of the Jews, was nigh. [5]When Jesus then lifted up His eyes, and saw a great company unto Him, He saith unto Philip: 'Whence shall we buy bread that these may eat?' [6]And this He said to prove him: for He Himself knew what He would do. [7]Philip answered Him: 'Two hundred pennyworth of bread is not sufficient for them, that every one of them may take a little.' [8]One of His disciples, Andrew, Simon Peter's brother, saith unto Him: [9]'There is a lad here, which hath five barley loaves, and two small fishes: but what are they among so many?' [10]And Jesus said: 'Make the men sit down.' Now there was much grass in the place. So the men sat down, in number about five thousand. [11]And Jesus took the loaves; and when He had given thanks, He distributed to the disciples, and the disciples to them that were set down; and likewise of the fishes as much as they would. [12]When they were filled, He said unto His disciples: 'Gather up the fragments that remain, that nothing be lost.' [13]Therefore they gathered them together, and filled twelve baskets with the fragments of the five barley loaves, which remained over and above them that had eaten.

[14]Then those men, when they had seen the miracle that Jesus did, said: 'This is of a truth that prophet that should come into the world.'

John vi. 27–55

Jesus said: [27]'Labour not for the meat which perisheth, but for that meat which endureth unto everlasting life, which the Son of Man shall give unto you: for Him hath God the Father sealed.' [28]Then said they unto Him: 'What shall we do that we might work the works of God?' [29]Jesus answered and said unto them: This is the work of God, that ye believe on Him whom He hath sent.' [30]They said therefore unto Him: 'What sign shewest Thou then, that we may see, and believe Thee? what dost Thou work? [31]Our fathers did eat manna in the desert; as it is written:

He gave them bread from heaven to eat.'

[32]Then Jesus said unto them: 'Verily, verily, I say unto you, Moses gave you not that bread from heaven; but My Father giveth you the true bread from heaven. [33]For the bread of God is He which cometh down from heaven, and giveth life unto the world.' [34]Then said they unto Him: 'Lord, evermore give us this bread.' [35]And Jesus said unto them: 'I am the bread of life: he that cometh to Me shall never hunger; and he that believeth on Me shall never thirst. [36]But I said unto you, that ye also have seen Me, and believe not. [37]All that the Father giveth Me shall come to Me; and him that cometh to Me I will in no wise cast out. [38]For I came down from heaven, not to do Mine own will, but the will of Him that sent Me. [39]And this is the Father's will Who hath sent Me, that of all which He hath given Me I should lose nothing, but should raise it up again at the last day. [40]And this is the will of Him that sent

John vi. 27–55 (*contd.*)

Me, that every one which seeth the Son, and believeth on Him, may have everlasting life: and I will raise him up at the last day.'

[41]The Jews then murmured at Him, because He said, I am the bread which came down from heaven. [42]And they said: 'Is not this Jesus, the son of Joseph, whose father and mother we know? how is it then that He saith, I came down from heaven?' [43]Jesus therefore answered and said unto them: 'Murmur not among yourselves. [44]No man can come to Me, except the Father Who hath sent Me draw him: and I will raise him up at the last day. [45]It is written in the prophets,

> *And they shall be all taught of God.*

Every man therefore that hath heard, and hath learned of the Father, cometh unto Me. [46]Not that any man hath seen the Father, save He Who is of God, He hath seen the Father. [47]Verily, verily, I say unto you, he that believeth on Me hath everlasting life. [48]I am the bread of life. [49]Your fathers did eat manna in the wilderness, and are dead. [50]This is the bread which cometh down from heaven, that a man may eat thereof, and not die. [51]I am the living bread which came down from heaven: if any man eat of this bread, he shall live for ever: and the bread that I will give is My flesh, which I will give for the life of the world.'

[52]The Jews therefore strove among themselves, saying, how can this man give us His flesh to eat? [53]Then Jesus said unto them: 'Verily, verily, I say unto you, except ye eat the flesh of the Son of Man, and drink His blood, ye have no life in you. [54]Whoso eateth My flesh, and drinketh My blood, hath eternal life; and I will raise him up at the last day. [55]For My flesh is meat indeed, and My blood is drink indeed.'

(*a*) The Feeding of the Five Thousand is reported in all four Gospels, and the Feeding of the Four Thousand in both *Mark* and *Matthew*. This suggests that the first event certainly (and the second probably) has its origin in the authentic Nazarene tradition. Yet the Nazarenes would have scouted any suggestion that Jesus conjured baker's ware from the sky, or from the stones of the desert, since he would thus have been either trying to prove himself greater than God, who had sustained the Israelites with manna only, or else yielding to the Devil's temptation which he claimed to have rejected, namely: 'Command these stones to be made bread!' (*see* LXXVIII.*f*). It is therefore reasonable to conclude that, though Jesus fed the multitude, he did so spiritually, not physically, and that his symbolic acts were later claimed as miracles by Gentile Christians who wished to prove him no less of a magician than Apollonius of Tyana (*see Introduction* IV.*m–p*).

(*b*) When afterwards, according to *Mark* viii. 19, paralleled in *Matthew* xvi. 9, Jesus questioned his disciples about these symbolic acts, he did not ask: 'Lack ye then faith that I can call down bread from heaven, though ye forget to bring sufficient for our needs?', but wanted to know how many baskets of broken bread were collected on each occasion. And on receiving their reply, he asked again, impatiently (*Mark* viii. 21): 'How is it that ye do not understand?' In other words, they should have deduced the meaning of his acts from the detail of the baskets.

(c) This meaning can be recovered only if it is first decided how many diners made up a 'company'. Here *Mark* vi. 39-40, the earliest account, is unintentionally misleading: 'He commanded them to sit down by companies on the green grass, by hundreds and by fifties' shortened in *Luke* ix. 14 to: 'make them sit down by fifties in a company', which is by no means the same thing. The canonical number for a company of guests at a feast (*Judges* xiv. 11 and 1 *Samuel* ix. 22), or a company of soldiers (2 *Samuel* xxiii. 13, 1 *Chronicles* xi. 42 and *Jeremiah* xxxviii. 10) was thirty. What the author of *Mark* probably meant was: 'in companies of thirty, making two or three hundred diners'.

(d) The story now begins to make sense. According to a well-known Egyptian calendar myth, the God Thoth, dicing with the Goddess Isis who ruled the year, won from her a seventy-second part of each day and combined the broken fragments into the five complete days which remained outside the 360 of the calendar; these were the birthdays, kept as public holidays, of the five gods Osiris, Horus, Set, Isis, and Nephthys. Thereafter, the Pharaonic month contained thirty days, each month divided into three ten-day weeks, or *asors*, a measure of time to which several indirect references are found in the Pentateuch, and a direct one in *Genesis* xxiv. 55. The Messiah expected by the apocalyptics was destined to perform many feats, including that of amending the Sadducaic calendar, and Jesus seems to have been giving an esoteric demonstration of how this should be done. If so, the five thousand and the four thousand will have signified so many years (*see* LXXXVIII.*u–x*), and he will have given both displays on the same occasion. The *Book of Enoch* and the *Book of Jubilees* contain other attempts by apocalyptics to reform the calendar.

At the same time Jesus may have been repairing an omission from his coronation ritual: the distribution of bread to his subjects (*see* VIII.*y*).

For *John* ix. 4, *see* XL.*d*: Jesus here insists that he must continue his missionary task until daylight fails (*see* XCIV.*d*) in order to save as many souls as possible before the Day of Judgement dawns.

(e) What happened is discussed at some length in *King Jesus* (pp. 247–251).

(f) The complete account, however, will not have been preserved in the Nazarene Oracles. Since any attempt at reforming the national calendar would have been regarded as revolutionary, the meaning of Jesus's symbolic displays must have been a secret explained to the catechumens by the Nazarene elder who acted as mystagogue. The following is probably as much as would have appeared:

(222) *And Jesus said unto the Twelve: 'Come ye apart into a desert place and rest awhile.' For there were many coming and going and they had no leisure so much as to eat.*

Therefore they departed into a desert place by boat privately. And the people saw them departing and some five thousand of them ran afoot by the lakeside, waiting for him to land.

But the boat drave onward, and all save one thousand of the people returned unto the city whence they came, for they were faint with hunger.

Then Jesus had compassion on them that remained, and came out of the boat and preached unto them.

But the disciples gathered themselves unto him, and asked: 'Is this not a desert place, and is not the day far spent?'

He answered and said: 'I must do the work which I have been sent to do while there is yet light. For behold, the night cometh when no man can work.'

Jesus, in the course of his demonstration, is likely to have quoted a prophecy of Elisha from 2 *Kings* iv. 41–44; and various incidents in the story of Joseph and the corn-famine (*Genesis* xli–xlvii).

(223) *Then Peter said unto him: 'Nay, but send away these people that they may buy bread in the villages, for they have nought to eat.'*

He answered: 'Ye shall yourselves give them to eat.'

They asked again: 'What? Shall we then buy bread for two hundred pence? For though four thousand men and women are departed, as many as one thousand remain, besides children.'

He saith unto them: 'How many loaves have they?'

And when they knew, they answered: 'There is a lad here which hath five barley loaves and a few fishes.'

He said: 'It is enough for fifties and for hundreds.'

Then he commanded that those which were nearest to him, having washed, should sit down by companies of thirty, in a circuit cast about him. And when they were set, he himself went into a room which remained on the northern side.

Then he commanded the Twelve to take baskets and stand, each beside a several company, for there were twelve companies.

And he saith unto the people: 'Elisha prophesied in the name of the Lord: "They shall all eat bread and have bread left over." For this was bread sanctified unto God's use. Therefore bring me your five loaves for sanctification.'

And Jesus sanctified the loaves and brake them into fragments, and put the fragments into the baskets which they brought.

Then went he from company to company about the circle, receiving a basket from the hand of each disciple in turn.

To every man he gave a fragment of bread, and each made as if to eat, yet refrained. For Jesus said: 'This is bread sanctified unto God. Feed on it in your hearts!'

And when he came to the gap that remained on the southern side, he said to the Twelve: 'Gather up the fragments that remain.'

And the fragments were the same five loaves, for nought had been eaten.

Then said he unto them: 'Lo, here is more bread! Call five more men, that they may sit here and be fed.' And this was done.

Likewise he divided the fishes among them all, saying: 'Eat, for He will save!'

And when this was accomplished, he stood and cried: 'Four thousand are gone, one thousand remain! He that hath ears, let him hear!'

* * * * *

(224) *Afterward, he commanded every man which sat in the circle to yield his place to one which had not yet eaten; and stood again in the room which remained on the northern side.*

And he preached unto them, saying : 'Behold, it is written that Joseph, when he foresaw a famine of seven years, built seven granaries in Egypt, filling one in every year of plenty as a surety against a year of famine.'

Then he meted the fragments of bread into seven heaps, and with each heap he filled a basket.

And he said: 'Behold, Joseph's father and his eleven brethren came down to Egypt to be fed, and Joseph appointed his brethren and his own two sons to mete out bread unto the people.

'Each should perform this service for seven days in succession, and draw in turn from each of the seven granaries.'

Then Jesus named the Twelve after the names of the fathers of tribes, and he also called to one that sat apart on the southern side (being the lad which brought the loaves and fishes), and named him Benjamin.

And at his bidding each of the thirteen in turn meted out bread unto seven men, to every man from a different basket; and all made as if to eat, yet ate not.

And when the thirteen had done, each had meted out his bread four times.

Then said Jesus unto the lad: 'Return thou to thy seat!'; and when the fragments of bread were gathered once more, he returned them all unto him, saying: 'It is written: "But Benjamin's mess was five times as much as theirs." '

And he cried: 'Four thousand are gone, one thousand remain! He that hath eyes to see, let him attend!'

* * * * *

Jesus's demonstration was meant to show that the four millennia, elapsed since Adam's day, were ruled by the Pharaonic solar year of 360 days, divided into twelve thirty-day months, or five seasons of seventy-two days, with five residual days, celebrated as public holidays (*see (d) above*); this is likely to have been the calendar observed by the Essenes, whose mysticism was of a purely solar character. But each year of the fifth millennium—which was due to begin with the Pangs of the Messiah—would consist of thirteen four-week months, with one residual day only. Solar time would thus be reconciled with lunar time more accurately than in the contemporary Sadducaic calendar (*see (h) below*). The fish are not so readily explained as the bread. There may be a Zodiacal mystery here connected with the passage of the Sun through Pisces. Or Jesus may have recalled the text of *Numbers* xi. 15: 'We remember the fish we did eat in Egypt'. Or perhaps, as we suggest above, he was referring to Joshua's patronymic, 'Son of Nun'—*Nun* means 'fish', as *Joshua* means 'He will save'—and undertaking to lead them, like his namesake, to the Promised Land. 'The Fish' was a mystical name for Jesus in the Early Church.

(g) This passage is followed by *Mark* iv. 10–11, *Matthew* xiii. 10–11 and *Luke* viii. 9–10: the saying about Jesus's habitual use of parables (*see* xxv.*d*).

John vi. 10: 'There was much grass in that place', is not idle detail, but a reference to *Ezekiel* xxxiv. 14 and 23.

> (225) *Now, there was much grass in that place where Jesus fed them with bread of the spirit, even as Ezekiel prophesied:*
>
> *'I will feed them in a good pasture, there shall they lie in a good fold and in a fat pasture.*
>
> *'And I shall set up one shepherd over them and he shall feed them, even as My servant David.'*

* * * * *

The proper context of *John* vi. 14 is the disciples' realization at Caesarea Philippi of Jesus's identity (*see* LXXVII.*b*).

(h) When Jesus presented his new calendar, he may have had in mind the *Book of Jubilees,* where the year, a sidereal one, consisted of 364 days divided into fifty-two weeks and regulated by the Sun; whereas the contemporary Sadducaic calendar (*see* (*e*) *above*), was ruled by lunations of alternately twenty-nine and thirty days, with an intercalary month, 'Second Adar', inserted about three times every eight years. The author of the *Celestial Physics,* which is included in the *Book of Enoch,* likewise regarded the year, sidereally, as consisting of 364 days; and he, too, rejected the lunation-month, proposing instead twelve solar months of thirty days, which contained four separate intercalary days each (*Enoch* lxxiv.–lxxv.). (There is no reason to believe that these chapters formed part of *Enoch* as Jesus knew it; they are known to be written later than the apocalyptic ones.) Jesus will have intended that the New Moon feasts should be determined by simple sequences of twenty-eight days (sidereal, as opposed to terrestrial, months), and the intercalary 'Second Adar' given a permanent place after Adar, roughly the equivalent of March. His choice of the week as the main unit of time was consistent with Pharisaic mysticism. The Pharisees regarded the Kingdom of Heaven as one unbroken Sabbath; and his reckoning of the years may have been influenced by that of the *Book of Jubilees*—the new Covenanters of Damascus are known to have studied it (*see* VIII.*m*)—where years were to be grouped in sevens as weeks of years, and where a week of year-weeks would constitute a Jubilee period. In neither *Enoch* nor *Jubilees* is any mention to be found of the supernumerary terrestrial day which, if disregarded, would have confused their calendars within a very few years; the manner of its yearly disposal must have been kept secret.

The main object of re-instituting the 364-day year was to let the principal feasts always fall on the same day of the week; but, as the Passover was bound to fall about the beginning of harvest and Tabernacles in the vintage season, Jesus's remedy for the displacement of the Feasts by the use of this year may have been prolongation of a single Sabbath-day from twenty-four to forty-eight hours. This would take place every year except the fourth, when the Sabbath might be prolonged to seventy-two hours and so provide for the 'leap of the moon'—as Julius Caesar had done, but as the Pharaonic Egyptians had failed to do.

(228) *Afterward, as they sailed across the Lake, the Twelve were ashamed and asked Jesus to expound his riddles.*

He answered and said: 'Having eyes, see ye not? Having ears, hear ye not? And do ye not remember?

'When first I brake the bread, how many fragments took ye up in the twelve baskets?'

They answered: 'As many as would feed five men.'

He asked again: 'And how many the second time?'

They answered: 'In the seven baskets we took up a five-fold portion for the lad.'

He said: 'How is it that ye understand not even yet?'

* * * * *

(*i*) The Christological discourse attached to the miracle in *John* vi. 27–55 may have its origin in verses 31, 49, and 51, which concern manna from heaven, and in verse 35, which concerns the bread of life. Its proper context seems to be *Mark* viii. 14, 15, 17, and it will have been found in a collection of Oracles under the subject-heading 'Bread from Heaven'. What remains of this discourse is a late invention, except for verse 30 (*see* xci.*a*), verse 42 (*see* xxxvii.*b*) and verse 54, originally a quotation from *Ecclesiasticus* xxiv. 21–23 but influenced by Paul's theory of the Eucharist (*see* cvi.*p*).

(226) *And when these things were accomplished Jesus sent the multitude away, and desired to cross over unto the coast of Gennesaret.*

Now, the Twelve had themselves forgotten to take bread, neither had they with them in the boat so much as one loaf.

And when they murmured among themselves, Jesus said: 'It is written: "God gave our fathers bread from heaven to eat," namely the manna which He rained upon them in the wilderness when they murmured for hunger. They ate and were filled, but now are dead, for it was food that endured not.

'Yet gave He unto them other bread also, namely the Law, which is the everlasting bread of life. Whosoever feedeth upon it in his heart, the same shall not die but live for ever.

'As the Preacher saith, the Son of Sirach: "They that eat me, namely Wisdom, shall yet hunger after me, and they that drink me shall yet thirst after me.

'"He that obeyeth me shall never be confounded, and they that work by me shall not do amiss.

'"All these things are the book of the covenant of the Most High God,

*even the Law which Moses commanded for an heritage unto the congrega-
tion of Jacob."* '

* * * * *

[For the sequel, *see* LXXIII.*e–f.*]

* * * * *

(*j*) The order of events in *Mark* viii. 1–21 and *Matthew* xv. 29–xvi. 12 is confused, and Biblical critics have long disputed the meaning of 'Dalmanutha'
in *Mark* viii. 10, an otherwise unknown place-name; the corresponding text
in *Matthew* xv. 39 is 'Magdala' or, in some manuscripts, 'Magadan'. Herz
(*Expository Times* viii. 563) has come closest to the solution, though he fails
to account for the 'D' in Dalmanutha. This, however, will have stood for *de,*
the Aramaic for 'of'; therefore 'he came to the coasts of *Magadan de-
demnitha'* (Magadan of the Haven) would mean that Jesus reached the fishing port of Magadan, which should not be confused with an inland village of
the same name. Eusebius identifies 'Magadan' with a town near Gerasa (*see*
LXIII.*b*), called 'Magedane' in his time.

In the original tradition, Jesus's arrival at Magadan will have concluded
the Stilling of the Storm (*see* LXXV.*c*).

The following discreet gloss may be added to the Nazarene account of the
'Feeding of the Five Thousand and of the Four Thousand':

(229) *For these were parables of the year and its months: how it had been
divided in the days of Moses, and how it should be divided in the Kingdom
of Heaven:*

*Namely a year of twelve months, each of thirty days, with five days re-
maining over; and a year of thirteen months, each of four weeks, with one
day remaining over.*

* * * * *

LXXIII

WALKING ON WATER

Mark vi. 45–56

⁴⁵And straightway He contrained His disciples to get into the boat, and to go to the other side before unto Bethsaida, while He sent away the people. ⁴⁶And when He had sent them away, He departed into a mountain to pray. ⁴⁷And when even was come, the boat was in the midst of the sea, and He alone on the land. ⁴⁸And He saw them toiling and rowing; for the wind was contrary unto them: and about the fourth watch of the night He cometh unto them, walking upon the sea, and would have passed by them. ⁴⁹But when they saw Him walking upon the sea, they supposed it had been a spirit, and cried out: ⁵⁰for they all saw Him, and were troubled. And immediately He talked with them, and saith unto them: 'Be of good cheer: it is I: be not afraid.' ⁵¹And He went up unto them into the boat; and the wind ceased: and they were sore amazed in themselves beyond measure, and wondered. ⁵²For they considered not the miracle of the loaves: for their heart was hardened.

⁵³And when they had passed over, they came into the land of Gennesaret, and drew to the shore. ⁵⁴And when they were come out of the boat, straightway they knew Him, ⁵⁵and ran through that whole region round about, and began to carry about in beds those that were sick, where they heard He was. ⁵⁶And whithersoever He entered, into villages, or cities, or country, they laid the sick in the streets, and besought Him that they might touch if it were but the border of His garment: and as many as touched Him were made whole.

Matthew xiv. 22–36

²²And straightway Jesus constrained His disciples to get into a boat and to go before Him unto the other side, while He sent the multitudes away. ²³And when He had sent the multitudes away, He went up into a mountain apart to pray: and when the evening was come, He was there alone. ²⁴But the boat was now in the midst of the sea, tossed with waves: for the wind was contrary. ²⁵And in the fourth watch of the night Jesus went unto them, walking on the sea.

²⁶And when the disciples saw Him walking on the sea, they were troubled, saying it is a spirit; and they cried out for fear. ²⁷But straightway Jesus spake unto them, saying: 'Be of good cheer; it is I; be not afraid.' ²⁸And Peter answered Him and said: 'Lord, if it be Thou, bid me come unto Thee on the water.' ²⁹And He said 'Come.' And when Peter was come down out of the boat, he walked on the water, to go to Jesus. ³⁰But when he saw the wind

Matthew xiv. 22–36 (contd.)

boisterous, he was afraid; and beginning to sink, he cried, saying: 'Lord, save me.' [31]And immediately Jesus stretched forth His hand, and caught him, and said unto him: 'O thou of little faith, wherefore didst thou doubt?' [32]And when they were come into the boat, the wind ceased. [33]Then they that were in the boat came and worshipped Him, saying: 'Of a truth Thou art the Son of God.'

[34]And when they were gone over, they came into the land Gennesaret. [35]And when the men of that place had knowledge of Him, they sent out into all that country round about, and brought unto Him all that were diseased; [36]and besought Him that they might only touch the hem of His garment: and as many as touched were made perfectly whole.

John vi. 15–26

[15]When Jesus therefore perceived that they would come and take Him by force to make Him a king, He departed again into a mountain Himself alone.

[16]And when even was now come, His disciples went down unto the sea, [17]and entered into a boat and went over the sea toward Capernaum. And it was now dark and Jesus was not come to them. [18]And the sea arose by reason of a great wind that blew. [19]So when they had rowed about five and twenty or thirty furlongs, they see Jesus walking on the sea and drawing nigh unto the ship: and they were afraid. [20]But He saith unto them: 'It is I; be not afraid.' [21]Then they willingly received Him into the ship: and immediately the ship was at the land whither they went.

[22]The day following, when the people which stood on the other side of the sea saw that there was none other boat there, save that one whereinto His disciples were entered, and that Jesus went not with His disciples into the boat, but that His disciples were gone away alone; [23](howbeit there came other boats from Tiberias nigh unto the place where they did eat bread, after that the Lord had given thanks) [24]when the people therefore saw that Jesus was not there, neither His disciples, they also took boats, and came to Capernaum, seeking for Jesus. [25]And when they had found Him on the other side of the sea, they said unto Him: 'Rabbi, when camest Thou hither?' [26]Jesus answered them and said: 'Verily, verily, I say unto you, ye seek Me, not because ye saw the miracles, but because ye did eat of the loaves, and were filled.'

John i. 44

[44]Now Philip was of Bethsaida, the city of Andrew and Peter.

(a) In *Mark* vi. 45–56, *Matthew* xiv. 22–36, and *John* vi. 22–26 the Walking on Water follows the Feeding of the Five Thousand; it is missing from *Luke*. The scene of the alleged miracle is not clearly defined, but a place on the eastern lakeshore, some miles south of Bethsaida, would fit what seem to have been the facts. The Land of Gennesaret, which included Capernaum, lay on the north-western shore.

(*b*) Peter's partial success in walking on water is recorded in *Matthew* xiv. 29–30 only, but appears to have some bearing on *John* xxi. 7, where he plunges into the Lake and swims towards Jesus, who stands on the shore beside the loaves and fishes (*see* XVII.*c*).

(*c*) *John's* account contains yet another miracle: no sooner has Jesus entered the boat than the disciples find themselves at their destination (*John* vi. 21). This suggests competition with the biographers of Apollonius of Tyana (*see Introduction* IV.*m*). In an attempt to improve on the story, an editor of *John* has the people take to boats and follow Jesus to Capernaum; forgetting that, according to verse 22, 'there was none other boat there'. Verse 23 is a subsequent attempt to retrieve his error. The statement, in verse 15, that Jesus escaped from the crowd because they tried to make him king has been introduced here to satisfy the Roman authorities that he was no revolutionary; for its correct meaning and context, *see* LXXVIII.*c*.

(*d*) The origin of the story must be looked for in Jesus's *midrash* on *Job* ix. 5–8 (*see* XLV.*b*), where it is mentioned that 'God treadeth upon the waves of the sea'. In proof of his divinity, Jesus is here made to do so himself, whereas Peter fails because he is no more than human.

(*e*) Nevertheless, the incident may have a simple historical basis: a temporary breach between Jesus and the Twelve. Jesus, intending to continue his missionary work, decided to make for Gennesaret; but they were weak from hunger, having forgotten to bring more than a single loaf of bread, if as much (*Mark* viii. 14 and *Matthew* xvi. 5–8—*see* XLIV.*f*), and wanted to go to Bethsaida, which was nearer. This visit would also have given Peter, Andrew, and Philip, who were natives of the place (*John* i. 44—*see* LVI.*h*), an opportunity of visiting their families. Jesus refused to come—probably because Bethsaida had rejected his call to repentance (*see* LIX.*c*)—dismissed them and went off alone to pray on a hill. A strong head wind sprang up, and when the fishermen disciples thought that they had rowed nearly thirty furlongs towards Bethsaida, and were at a safe distance from the shore—though the boat had, in fact, long ceased to make any progress, because exhaustion had obliged them to share the oars with their unskilled companions—they cast anchor, lighted a lantern, and drowsily waited for the dawn. They were, in fact, quite close to their starting point. In the 'fourth watch', which lasted from three o'clock in the morning until six, Jesus descended, saw their lantern and, the wind having abated, waded out into the shallows towards them— walking, of course, *in* the water, not *on* the water. He was wearing his customary white garments, and the disciples, who still believed that they were 'in the midst of the Lake', mistook him for a ghost. When Jesus reassured them: 'It is I', they were confused and ashamed and made no reply, until Peter at last begged for forgiveness. 'Disobedience carries its own punishment', is the moral of this story, which should be placed between the Feeding of the Five Thousand (*see* LXXII.*i*) and the disciples' questions about its hidden meaning (*see* LXXII.*h*).

(*f*) Peter's 'Depart from me, for I am a sinful man, O Lord!' (*Luke* v. 8), seems also to belong to this context, since the miraculous draught of fishes, with which *Luke* connects it, is patently a fiction (*see* XVII.*b*). The story concludes with *Mark* iv. 41, *Matthew* viii. 27 and *Luke* viii. 25, a passage wrongly inserted in the Stilling of the Storm: 'What manner of man is he . . . ?' (*see* LXXV.*d*).

Matthew xiv. 33, which suggests that Jesus permitted the Twelve to worship him as the Son of God, must be rejected (*see* XXXII.*b*).

(227) *Then Philip said unto Jesus: 'Nevertheless, let us go unto Bethsaida, that we may buy bread that endureth not, lest we faint for hunger.'*

And others of the Twelve said likewise.

But Jesus purposed to sail unto the Land of Gennesaret. Wherefore he rebuked them that their minds were set on earthly things,

For Philip was of Bethsaida, the city also of Peter and Andrew, which had rejected the word of repentance.

And when Jesus perceived that they hardened their hearts, he bade them go whither they listed; but he himself went up into a mountain to pray.

Then set they a course for Bethsaida. But their boat was tossed with waves, for the wind was contrary; and already it was night.

And when they had rowed as it seemed five-and-twenty or thirty furlongs, they cast anchor and lighted a lanthorn and slept.

And in the fourth watch, while it was yet dark, they saw a man dressed in white raiment walking toward them through the water.

Then were they greatly troubled, and cried: 'It is a spirit!' For they trusted to be still in the midst of the sea.

And Jesus called unto them, and said: 'It is I, be not afraid!' And straightway they knew him.

Now, because of the violence of the wind, their boat had driven back nigh unto the place whence they came, but they knew it not; therefore went Jesus through the shallow water to meet them, thinking that they were come back to ask forgiveness.

And when they perceived how the matter was, they were confused in their hearts, and made Jesus no answer.

Wherefore he turned again to pass on his way.

But Peter, being ashamed of his frowardness, whereby he had toiled to no purpose, cried out, saying:

'Master, depart from me, if it seemeth good unto thee, for I am a sinful man. Yet if haply thou wilt shew forgiveness unto thy servant, suffer him to come to thee, that he may lift thee into this boat. For now we would go with thee unto the Land of Gennesaret!'

Jesus said: 'Come!'

And Peter cast himself into the waters and came unto the place where Jesus was, and lifted him into the boat. And Jesus forgave them when they had confessed their folly.

Yet were they amazed beyond measure, for so soon as they received him, the wind which was contrary turned about and blew from the east.

And they said to each other in fear: 'What manner of man is this, that even the winds obey him?'

* * * * *

(g) *Mark* vi. 56, the wholesale healing in Gennesaret, differs from the more modest account in *Mark* i. 32–34, where he healed 'many', not all that were brought.

For the touching of Jesus's praying garment, *see* xxxvi.*e.*

(231) *Then came they to Capernaum in the Land of Gennesaret, and drew nigh unto the shore.*

And when the men of that place had knowledge of him, whithersoever he entered, into villages or cities or country, they laid the sick in the streets. They also besought him that they might touch the fringes of his garment and be kept thereby from evil dreams and inclinations.

* * * * *

LXXIV

SABBATH HEALING

Mark iii. 1–6

[1]And He entered again into the synagogue; and there was a man there which had a withered hand. [2]And they watched Him, whether He would heal him on the sabbath day; that they might accuse Him. [3]And He saith unto the man which had the withered hand: 'Stand forth.' [4]And He saith unto them: 'Is it lawful to do good on the sabbath days, or to do evil? to save life, or to kill?' But they held their peace. [5]And when He had looked round about on them with anger, being grieved for the hardness of their hearts, He saith unto the man: 'Stretch forth thine hand.' And he stretched it out: and his hand was restored whole as the other. [6]And the Pharisees went forth, and straightway took counsel with the Herodians against Him, how they might destroy Him.

Matthew xii. 9–14

[9]And when He was departed thence, He went into their synagogue. [10]And, behold, there was a man which had his hand withered. And they asked Him, saying: 'Is it lawful to heal on the sabbath days?' that they might accuse Him. [11]And He said unto them: 'What man shall there be among you, that shall have one sheep, and if it fall into a pit on the sabbath day, will he not lay hold on it, and lift it out? [12]How much then is a man better than a sheep? Wherefore it is lawful to do well on the sabbath days.' [13]Then saith He to the man: 'Stretch forth thine hand.' And he stretched it forth; and it was restored whole, like as the other. [14]Then the Pharisees went out, and held a council against Him, how they might destroy Him.

Luke vi. 6–12

[6]And it came to pass also on another sabbath, that He entered into the synagogue and taught: and there was a man whose right hand was withered. [7]And the scribes and Pharisees watched Him, whether He would heal on the sabbath day; that they might find an accusation against Him. [8]But He knew their thoughts, and said to the man which had the withered hand: 'Rise up, and stand forth in the midst.' And he arose and stood forth. [9]Then said Jesus unto them: 'I will ask you one thing; Is it lawful on the sabbath days to do good, or to do evil? to save life, or to destroy it?' [10]And looking round about upon them all, He said unto the man: 'Stretch forth thy hand.' And he did so: and his hand was restored whole as the other. [11]And they were filled with madness; and communed one with another what they might do to Jesus.

Luke vi. 6–12 *(contd.)*

¹²And it came to pass in those days, that He went out into a mountain to pray, and continued all night in prayer to God.

Jerome: On Matthew xii. 13

In the Gospel which the Nazarenes and Ebionites use, which I have lately translated into Greek from the Hebrew and which is called by many 'the original of Matthew' this man who had the withered hand is described as a mason who prays for help in such words as these: 'I was a mason seeking a livelihood with my hands; I pray thee, Jesu, to restore me mine health that I may not beg meanly for my food.'

John v. 17–18

¹⁷But Jesus answered them: 'My Father worketh hitherto, and I work.' ¹⁸Therefore the Jews sought the more to kill Him, because He not only had broken the sabbath, but said also that God was His Father, making Himself equal with God.

Matthew xii. 5–7

⁵Or have ye not read in the law, how that on the sabbath days the priests in the temple profane the sabbath, and are blameless? ⁶But I say unto you, that in this place is One greater than the temple. ⁷But if ye had known what this meaneth,

I will have mercy, and not sacrifice,

ye would not have condemned the guiltless.

John vii. 21–23

²¹Jesus answered and said unto them: 'I have done one work, and ye all marvel. ²²Moses therefore gave unto you circumcision; (not because it is of Moses, but of the fathers) and ye on the sabbath day circumcise a man. ²³If a man on the sabbath day receive circumcision, that the law of Moses should not be broken; are ye angry at Me, because I have made a man every whit whole on the sabbath day?'

Luke xiii. 10–17

¹⁰And He was teaching in one of the synagogues on the sabbath. ¹¹And behold, there was a woman which had a spirit of infirmity eighteen years, and was bowed together, and could in no wise lift up herself. ¹²And when Jesus saw her, He called her to Him, and said unto her: 'Woman, thou art loosed from thine infirmity.' ¹³And He laid His hands on her: and immediately she was made straight, and glorified God. ¹⁴And the ruler of the synagogue answered with indignation, because that Jesus had healed on the sabbath day, and said unto the people: 'There are six days in which men ought to work: in them therefore come and be healed, and not on the sabbath day.' ¹⁵The Lord then answered him, and said: 'Thou hypocrite, doth not each one of you on the sabbath loose his ox or his ass from the stall, and lead him away to watering? ¹⁶And ought not this woman, being a daughter of

Luke xiii. 10–17 (*contd.*)

Abraham, whom Satan hath bound, lo, these eighteen years, be loosed from this bond on the sabbath day?' [17]And when He had said these things all His adversaries were ashamed: and all the people rejoiced for all the glorious things that were done by Him.

Luke xiv. 1–6

[1]And it came to pass, as He went into the house of one of the chief Pharisees to eat bread on the sabbath day, that they watched Him. [2]And, behold, there was a certain man before Him which had the dropsy. [3]And Jesus answering spake unto the lawyers and Pharisees, saying, Is it lawful to heal on the sabbath day? [4]And they held their peace. And he took him, and healed him, and let him go; [5]and answered them, saying, Which of you shall have an ass or an ox fallen into a pit, and will not straightway pull him out on the sabbath day?

[6]And they could not answer him again to these things.

(*a*) *Mark* iii. 1–5, *Matthew* xii. 9–13, and *Luke* vi. 6–11, all display ignorance of the oral Law. No Pharisee, for instance, could have asked, as in *Matthew* xii. 10: 'Is it lawful to heal on the Sabbath?'; he would have known the answer (*Yoma* 83*a* and *Deuteronomy Rabbah* x. 1): 'The Sages have taught thus: Where there is the least question of danger to life the Sabbath laws are suspended.' This condition could apply to almost every illness, since it might conceivably be fatal to neglect even a slight swelling or rash, and the *Mishna* (*Yoma* viii. 6) specifically permits the treatment of a sort throat on the Sabbath. Moreover, it is not recorded that Jesus prepared a plaster or tied a bandage, which might be reckoned as work; his command: 'Stretch forth thy hand!' was no breach of the Law.

This particular case will have been one of nervous paralysis—like the many thousands caused by modern warfare—when the patient is cured if he can be surprised into the realization that his limbs will indeed obey him.

(*b*) Though it is not credible that the Pharisees in the synagogue expected Jesus to perform a miracle (*Mark* iii. 2 and *Luke* vi. 7), or that he performed one in interruption of divine service, the report of their criticism does not appear to have been wholly invented. If the treatment did, after all, involve mud-plasters or massage, as is suggested by 'Stand forth!' (*see* xxxi.*b* and xl.*a*), a scrupulous elder will have objected that these were unlawful, and that Jesus should have waited until sun-down when both he and his patient would still be in Capernaum (*see* lxxi.*b*). To Jesus's contention that the Law permitted the rescue of a sheep from the pit into which it had fallen on the Sabbath, and that a man was surely of greater value than a sheep, the elder will have replied: 'True, but the sheep's life might be endangered by its fall; whereas this man was in no similar danger.'

(*c*) Jesus might then have rejoined that the healing of the man's hand would henceforth enable him to perform his Sabbath duties in a manner more pleasing to God: 'A man may break one Sabbath so that another may keep many' (*Yoma* 85*b*). But he appears to have preferred the argument found in *John* v. 18, a corrupt passage combining the cure of the withered hand, which happened on a Sabbath, with that of the paralytic (*Mark* ii. 1–12, *Matthew* ix. 1–8 and *Luke* v. 17–26—*see* xxxv.*a–b*), which happened on a week day, and with an otherwise unrecorded cure of a cripple (*see* xl.*f and h*). Here Jesus is made to say: 'My Father worketh hitherto [i.e. on the Sabbath] and I work also.' In other words: 'God Himself, though He keeps the Sabbath (*Exodus Rabbah* xxx. 9), performs cures on the Sabbath'—injuries sustained on a Friday are often healed by the Sunday, even where there has been no reason to fear that life is endangered—'and His cure of this man is in itself a condonation of my technical breach of the Law.'

Another argument on the same topic, with a quotation from *Hosea* vi. 6, has been mistakenly incorporated in *Matthew* xii. 5 and 7 (*see* lxxi.*g*). Jesus insists that where two Commandments conflict, the ethically higher one must be given precedence, and that the Fourth Commandment ranks below *Leviticus* xix. 18, the law of love. His view is supported in *Yoma* 85*b,* on the legalistic ground that the wording of *Exodus* xxxi. 13: *'Only ye* shall keep My Sabbaths!' hints at exceptions.

(*d*) The Pharisees may well have been crestfallen at the outcome of this dispute, but it is incredible that they should thereupon have conspired against Jesus's life with the Herodians, especially as they are elsewhere reported to have warned him of Herod Antipas's murderous intentions (*Luke* xiii. 31— *see* xcvii.*h*).

(130) *And again on a certain sabbath, when Jesus went into the synagogue, a man which had a withered hand stood without.*

The same besought him, and cried: 'Master, I was a mason earning my bread with this hand. I pray thee, restore it to health that I need no longer beg for alms!'

Jesus was moved by compassion, and said unto him: 'Stand forth!' And when the man stood forth from the crowd, he led him to a place apart.

There, after that he had spitted upon his own hands, he rubbed the man's withered hand between them, and prayed to God, saying: 'Lord, let the evil depart from this man.'

Then saith he unto him: 'Stretch forth thy hand!', and he stretcheth it forth and, behold, it was restored whole as the other.

Then some of them that stood by glorified God, but others reproached Jesus, saying: 'Is it lawful to do such a work on the sabbath?'

Jesus looked round upon them with anger, and answered: 'Which of you, having a sheep that hath fallen into a pit, doth not lay hold on it and lift it out on a sabbath, as the Sages permit? And is not this man better than a sheep?'

They answered: 'Thou hast well said. For the Sages have taught us: "Where there is danger to life, the sabbath may be broken." Yet here was no danger. Why hast thou therefore not waited till the morrow?'

He answered and said: 'I obey the Law of righteousness and love. Though our Father rest on the sabbath, yet He performeth works of healing on that day also. Hath He not even now hearkened unto my prayer, and healed this man?'

But they murmured and asked him: 'Though God should work on the sabbath, where is it written that a man may work on the sabbath?'

Jesus answered: 'Have ye not read in the Law, how that on the sabbath day the priests in the Temple shall sacrific two lambs, and yet their work be blameless?'

* * * * *

[Here follows Jesus's argument about circumcision (*see* (*e*) *below*).]

* * * * *

(132) *'And if ye had remembered the words of the prophet Hosea, which he spake in God's name: "I desired mercy and not sacrifice," then would ye not have condemned that I did, when I rubbed this man's hand between mine own.'*

* * * * *

(*e*) The sequel, in *John* vii. 21–23, to the lame man of Bethsaida's cure (*John* v. 1–16—*see* XL.*h*) probably belongs to the argument in *Matthew* xii. 5–7. Jesus was pointing out that not only did Levite butchers break the Sabbath by their sacrifices, and remain blameless, but:

(131) *'Ye yourselves likewise on the eighth day circumcise a male child according to the Law, though that day be a sabbath, and remain blameless.*

'For God commanded our father Abraham to circumcise on the eighth day, before ever He delivered the Law of the sabbath unto Moses.'

* * * * *

Jesus's quotation here is from *Leviticus* xii. 3. (The antithesis implied in *John* vii. 23 between circumcision—which the Gentiles regarded as mutilation—and healing, is gratuitous.) *John* vii. 22: 'Not because it is of Moses, but of the patriarchs', means that the order to circumcise on the eighth day anteceded the Decalogue, having been given to Abraham before the birth of Isaac (*Genesis* xvii. 12). This temporal precedence may equally account for the Talmudic ruling (*Shabbath* 151*a*): 'On behalf of an infant ye may break the Sabbath, but on behalf of none other, not even King David!'

(*f*) Two further Sabbath cures are reported in *Luke* xiii. 10–17 and xiv. 1–6, though not elsewhere. The first reads as if an editor, finding that only men had been cured of major disorders, invented the case of a woman bent double with lumbago—*Luke* mentions Jesus's regard for women more frequently than any other Gospel—and modelled it on the account of the man with the withered hand, and of the paralytic in *John* v. From *Matthew* xii. 11: 'What man shall there be among you, that shall have one sheep . . . ?' he developed: 'Doth not each of you on the Sabbath loose his ox or his ass from the stall and lead him away to watering?'—forgetting that a pious Jew would not do so, but fill a water trough for his beasts on the Friday afternoon. Since, however, wanton inventions are rare in the Synoptics, it is safe to assume the existence of an original:

(114) *And in these days Jesus healed a woman which was bowed together for eighteen years, and could in no wise lift herself up.*

* * * * *

In the second, and similar account, the patient is a dropsical man (*see* XLVI.*d*); Jesus's questions about the sheep in the pit, and the ox or ass led out to water have here been combined. The original may have been simply:

(115) *And he healed a man which had the dropsy.*

* * * * *

LXXV

THE STORM STILLED

Mark iv. 35–41

[35]And the same day, when the even was come, He saith unto them: 'Let us pass over unto the other side.' [36]And when they had sent away the multitude, they took Him even as He was in the boat. And there were also with Him other little boats. [37]And there arose a great storm of wind, and the waves beat into the boat, so that it was now full. [38]And He was in the hinder part of the boat, asleep on a pillow: and they awake Him, and say unto Him: 'Master, carest Thou not that we perish?' [39]And He arose, and rebuked the wind, and said unto the sea: 'Peace, be still.'

And the wind ceased, and there was a great calm. [40]And He said unto them: 'Why are ye so fearful? how is it that ye have no faith?' [41]And they feared exceedingly, and said one to another: 'What manner of man is this, that even the wind and sea obey Him?'

Matthew viii. 18

[18]Now when Jesus saw great multitudes about Him, He gave commandment to depart unto the other side.

Matthew viii. 23–27

[23]And when He was entered into a boat, His disciples followed Him. [24]And, behold, there arose a great tempest in the sea, insomuch that the boat was covered with the waves: but He was asleep. [25]And His disciples came to Him, and awoke Him, saying: 'Lord, save us: we perish.' [26]And He saith unto them: 'Why are ye fearful, O ye of little faith?' Then He arose, and rebuked the winds and the sea; and there was a great calm. [27]But the men marvelled, saying: 'What manner of man is this, that even the winds and the sea obey Him!'

Luke viii. 22–25

[22]Now it came to pass on a certain day, that He went into a boat with His disciples: and He said unto them: 'Let us go over unto the other side of the lake.' And they launched forth. [23]But as they sailed He fell asleep: and there came down a storm of wind on the lake; and they were filled with water, and were in jeopardy. [24]And they came to Him, and awoke Him, saying: 'Master, Master, we perish.' Then He arose, and rebuked the wind and the raging of the water: and they ceased, and there was a calm. [25]And He said unto

Luke viii. 22–25 (contd.)

them: 'Where is your faith?' And they being afraid wondered, saying one to another, 'What manner of man is this! for He commandeth even the winds and water, and they obey Him.'

(a) The details of the Storm incident—which in *Mark* v. 35–41 happens on the day when Jesus preached from the boat; but in *Matthew* viii. 23–27 some time later, when he healed Peter's mother-in-law and the centurion's servant; and in *Luke* viii. 22–25 on an unspecified day—are identical in all three accounts, except that *Mark* has 'other little boats' also crossing the Lake.

The original here is more likely to have been embroidered upon than invented: it seems that a storm sprang up, the other boats ran for port, but Jesus kept on his course. The landsmen among the disciples then grew afraid, but Jesus, quoting *Psalm* cvii. 23–28, ordered them to trust in God who could still the waves which He had Himself raised; and they reached Magadan, a fishing-port near Gerasa, in safety (*Matthew* xv. 39—*see* LXXII.*j*).

(b) It remains an open question whether Jesus slept during the storm. In *Mark* iv. 37–38, *Matthew* viii. 25 and *Luke* viii. 23, the scene has been over-dramatized: he is presented as soundly asleep when the gunwales are already flush with the water. *Mark's* version is the oldest, and a clue to this part of the story is found in the obtrusive pictorial detail of the pillow (*Mark* iv. 38), and in the close literary correspondence between the Greek of *Mark* iv. 35–41 and the Septuagint translation of *Jonah* i. 4–15. On the strength of *Matthew* xii. 40 (*see* XCI.*c*), the early Christians connected the three days spent by Jonah in the whale's belly with the three days which elapsed between the Crucifixion and the Resurrection; Jonah and the Whale therefore became a favourite subject of Catacomb art. To account for the luxurious pillow, a diptych must be assumed, well known to the author of *Mark,* which illustrated Jonah's story. One panel will have shown him roused from sleep by the ship-master (*Jonah* i. 6): 'What meanest thou, O sleeper? Arise, call upon thy God . . . that we perish not!' The other will have shown him being swallowed by the whale (*Jonah* i. 17). The author of *Mark* recognized the principal figure in this second panel as Jonah and, because of Jonah's figurative association with Jesus, mistook the first panel for an illustration of Jesus's courage during the storm.

(c) Eventually, when the Gentile Christians identified Jesus with God, he was said to have himself claimed the power of calming storms. The rebuke to the waves cannot be accepted: according to *Psalm* cvii. 25, it was God, not the Devil, who had raised them. If anyone or anything was rebuked, it will have been the frightened disciples.

(d) *Mark* iv. 41, *Matthew* viii. 27, and *Luke* viii. 25: 'What manner of man is this, that even the winds and the sea obey him?' belongs to the Walking on Water context (*see* LXXIII.*f*). We place this incident after Jesus's mourning for John.

(236) *And when he had broken his fast and the even was come, Jesus entered into a boat with the Twelve, and said unto them: 'Let us pass over unto the other side.' And they launched forth.*

Now, as they sailed, there came down a great storm of wind on the Lake. Yet Jesus would not turn back to seek an haven, as did the masters of other little boats that sailed with him, but held to his course.

And it came to pass that the storm increased in violence, and the waves beat into the boat, whereat certain of the disciples were afraid.

And they cry unto him, saying: 'Master, we perish!'

Jesus rebuked them, and said: 'Peace, be still! Why are ye so fearful, O ye of little faith?

'As David saith in a psalm: "God raiseth a stormy wind which lifteth up the waves so that the shipmen are tossed to and fro, and all their wisdom is swallowed up.

'"Yet they cry unto Him in their trouble, and He bringeth them out of their distress.

'"He maketh the storm a calm, so that the waves thereof are still, and He bringeth them to their desired haven."'

Then prayed they all to God with one voice, and He heard them. And, behold, while they were yet praying, the wind ceased and it was as Jesus had declared.

For when they had cast out the water from the boat, they came safely over the Lake unto Magadan of the Haven.

* * * * *

(e) Here follows Peter's remark in *Luke* ix. 33 (*see* LXXIX.g), which introduces the incident of the demoniac (*see* LXIII.b):

(237) *Then Peter said unto Jesus: 'Master, it is good for us to be here. Let us build a tabernacle and kindle a fire and dry our garments thereat.'*

* * * * *

LXXVI

JOHN IS BEHEADED

Mark vi. 21–30

21And when a convenient day was come, that Herod on his birthday made a supper to his lords, high captains, and chief estates of Galilee; 22and when the daughter of the said Herodias came in, and danced, and pleased Herod and them that sat with him, the king said unto the damsel: 'Ask of me whatsoever thou wilt, and I will give it thee.' 23And he sware unto her: 'Whatsoever thou shalt ask of me, I will give it thee, unto the half of my kingdom.' 24And she went forth, and said unto her mother: 'What shall I ask?' And she said: 'The head of John the Baptist.' 25And she came in straightway with haste unto the king, and asked, saying: 'I will that thou give me by and by in a charger the head of John the Baptist.' 26And the king was exceeding sorry; yet for his oath's sake, and for their sakes which sat with him, he would not reject her. 27And immediately the king sent an executioner, and commanded his head to be brought: and he went and beheaded him in the prison, 28and brought his head in a charger, and gave it to the damsel: and the damsel gave it to her mother. 29And when his disciples heard of it they came and took up his corpse, and laid it in a tomb. 30And the Apostles gathered themselves together unto Jesus, and told Him all things, both what they had done, and what they had taught.

Matthew xiv. 6–14

6But when Herod's birthday was kept, the daughter of Herodias danced before them, and pleased Herod. 7Whereupon he promised with an oath to give her whatsoever she would ask. 8And she, being before instructed of her mother, said: 'Give me here John Baptist's head in a charger.' 9And the king was sorry: nevertheless for the oath's sake, and them which sat with him at meat, he commanded it to be given her. 10And he sent, and beheaded John in the prison. 11And his head was brought in a charger, and given to the damsel: and she brought it to her mother. 12And his disciples came, and took up the body, and buried it, and went and told Jesus.

13When Jesus heard of it, He departed thence by boat into a desert place apart: and when the people had heard thereof, they followed Him on foot out of the cities. 14And Jesus went forth, and saw a great multitude, and was moved with compassion toward them, and He healed their sick.

Luke ix. 9

9And Herod said: 'John have I beheaded: but who is this, of whom I hear such things?' And he desired to see Him.

Luke xiii. 31

[31]The same day there came certain of the Pharisees, saying unto Him: 'Get Thee out, and depart hence: for Herod will kill Thee.'

(*a*) Josephus records (*Antiquities* xviii. 5.2) that Herod Antipas executed John at Machaerus, as a disturber of the people (*see* XLI.*a*), and that the Jews regarded his subsequent defeat by King Aretas as God's punishment for this crime. But though mentioning Antipas's unlawful marriage in the same chapter, he fails to connect it with the execution. However, as Elijah had condemned Ahab and Jezebel for their murder of Naboth (1 *Kings* xxi. 1–24), so John could not have refrained from condemning Antipas and Herodias for this marriage—which, incidentally, threatened to involve the country in a war with King Aretas (*see* LXXXVI.*b*)—neither could Antipas have refrained from taking offence; and according to the Slavonic version of the *Jewish Wars,* this is what did happen (*see* XLI.*b*). Josephus published the *Wars* about 75 A.D., and may have omitted this passage from the *Antiquities* —completed some eighteen years later—because Salome, by a second marriage to her cousin Aristobulus (*Antiquities* xviii. 5. 4), had become an aunt of Agrippa II, now Josephus's close friend.

(*b*) The editor of *Mark* vi. 21–30 disagrees with Josephus: he blames Herodias for John's execution which, he alleges, Antipas regretted deeply. *Matthew* xiv. 6–14 is a compromise between these two versions; in *Luke* ix. 9 no motive appears for the execution; and although the Baptist figures prominently in the early chapters of *John,* his end is nowhere mentioned there.

All this reflects the disingenuous pro-Roman policy of the Gospel editors. Antipas was a Roman magistrate and the fact that he, and none other, eventually condemned Jesus himself to death (*see* CX.*i*) is suppressed or disguised in every Gospel account of his trial, the responsibility being instead absurdly laid upon the Jewish nation.

In *Luke* ix. 9, Antipas 'desired to see Jesus'; in *Luke* xxiii. 8, 'he desired to see him because he had heard many things of him and hoped to have seen a miracle done by him' (*see* CX.*n*). But *Luke* xiii. 31–32 (*see* XCVII.*h*), which betrays the truth, has somehow escaped excision: it is there admitted that Antipas wanted to kill him.

(*c*) Salome's plea for John's execution is credible; but Antipas's extravagant offer of half his kingdom is at variance with what we know of his niggardliness (*Antiquities* xviii. 6. 2), as is his public display of John's head with what we know of his caution (*Antiquities* xviii. 7. 2). Moreover, though a group of noble youths might perform a sword dance in honour of the Emperor (Suetonius: *Tiberius* 6 and *Nero* 12), a *pas seul* by a princess would have been considered disgraceful. Such performances were given only by courtesans or slave-girls.

(*d*) Perhaps this *Arabian Nights* story arose from an iconotropic misunderstanding. The author of *Mark* vi. 21–30 may have seen a synagogue fresco of Judith, decked in all her finery (*Judith* x. 4), being offered a heaped charger of food by Holofernes's servants (*Judith* xii. 1), and then handing the severed head to her maid (*Judith* xiii. 9)—who might easily be mistaken for Herodias. He may also have seen a companion fresco showing Esther, similarly garbed, being granted her request by Ahasuerus,* over the legend: 'Unto half my kingdom' (*Esther* v. 3); and this diptych may have been the source of his picturesque invention.

(*e*) *Mark* vi. 30: 'They told Jesus all things', refers to the return of the Twelve from their mission (*see* LVII.*h*). The corresponding phrase in *Matthew* xiv. 12 refers to John's disciples, not to Jesus's: a slip which proves that an editor of *Matthew* borrowed the anecdote from *Mark*.

Jesus will have mourned John in the desert; if not for the traditional seven days (*Sanhedrin* 108*b*), then perhaps for three weeks, as Daniel mourned before his vision of the Latter Days (*Daniel* x. 2). It was held that the soul of a righteous man clung to its body for thirty days before entering Paradise (*Zohar, Vayakhel*), and national mourning for Aaron and for Moses lasted the whole thirty days (*Numbers* xx. 29 and *Deuteronomy* xxxix. 8)—though this was exceptional.

(232) *Now it came to pass, when Herod's birthday was kept with wine and flute players and dancing women, that Herod was merry with his lords and high captains and the chief estates of Galilee.*

Which, when his wife Herodias perceived, she led in Salome, her daughter, to wish Herod good health.

And when he smiled upon the damsel, and asked her: 'Daughter, what gift shall I give thee for the desire of thy heart?'

She, being instructed by her mother, answered, and said: 'I will that thou slay John the Baptist, for he hath dishonoured both my mother and thy servant.'

Then Herod would not be shamed before them that sat at meat, and sware to do even as she desired.

And he sent and beheaded John in the castle of Machaerus.

And John's disciples went thither sorrowfully, and took up the body and buried it.

* * * * *

(*f*) [Here follows the Pharisees' warning to Jesus, and his reply (*see* XCVII.*h*).]

* * * * *

(235) *And Jesus departed thence by boat unto a desert place apart. There he mourned for John, and fasted for him three full weeks, saving only the sabbaths, even as Daniel mourned before his vision of the Latter Days.*

* * * * *

---

* This is one of the frescoes surviving in the Doura-Europos synagogue. (Comte du Mesnil du Buisson: *Les Peintures de la Synagogue de Doura-Europos, Planche* LII.)

(*g*) Salome, who will have been eighteen years old at the time of John's death, linked Antipas with the High Priestly family at Jerusalem: she was the daughter of Herodias by Herod Philip, whose maternal grandfather, Simon, son of Boethus, had been one of Herod the Great's High Priests. Both Annas and Caiaphas were of the House of Boethus (*see* CIX.*a*), and Antipas seems to have profited by this family connection.

* * * * *

LXXVII

THE REVELATION

Mark vi. 14–16

¹⁴And king Herod heard of Him (for His name was spread abroad): and he said, that John the Baptist was risen from the dead, and therefore mighty works do shew forth themselves in him. ¹⁵Others said, that it is Elijah. And others said, that it is a prophet, or as one of the prophets. ¹⁶But when Herod heard thereof, he said: 'It is John, whom I beheaded: he is risen from the dead.'

Mark viii. 27–29

²⁷And Jesus went out, and His disciples, into the towns of Caesarea Philippi: and by the way He asked His disciples, saying unto them: 'Whom do men say that I am?' ²⁸And they answered: 'John the Baptist: but some say Elijah; and others, one of the prophets.' ²⁹And He saith unto them: 'But whom say ye that I am?' And Peter answereth and saith unto Him, 'Thou art the Christ.'

Matthew xiv. 1–2

¹At that time Herod the tetrarch heard of the fame of Jesus, ²and said unto his servants: 'This is John the Baptist; he is risen from the dead; and therefore mighty works do shew forth themselves in him.'

Matthew xvi. 13–19

¹³When Jesus came into the coasts of Caesarea Philippi, He asked His disciples, saying: 'Whom do men say that I the Son of Man am?' ¹⁴And they said: 'Some say that Thou art John the Baptist: some, Elijah; and others, Jeremiah, or one of the prophets.' ¹⁵He saith unto them: 'But whom say ye that I am?' ¹⁶And Simon Peter answered and said: 'Thou art the Christ, the Son of the living God.' ¹⁷And Jesus answered and said unto him: 'Blessed art thou, Simon Bar-jona: for flesh and blood hath not revealed it unto thee, but My Father which is in heaven. ¹⁸And I say also unto thee, that thou art Peter, and upon this rock I will build My Church; and the gates of hell shall not prevail against it. ¹⁹And I will give unto thee the keys of the Kingdom of Heaven: and whatsoever thou shalt bind on earth shall be bound in heaven: and whatsoever thou shalt loose on earth shall be loosed in heaven.'

Matthew xviii. 18

¹⁸'Verily I say unto you, Whatsoever ye shall bind on earth shall be bound in heaven: and whatsoever ye shall loose on earth shall be loosed in heaven.'

Luke ix. 7–9

[7]Now Herod the tetrarch heard of all that was done by Him: and he was perplexed, because that it was said of some, that John was risen from the dead; [8]and of some, that Elijah had appeared; and of others, that one of the old prophets was risen again. [9]And Herod said: 'John have I beheaded: but who is this, of whom I hear such things?' And he desired to see Him.

Luke ix. 18–20

[18]And it came to pass, as He was alone praying, His disciples were with Him: and He asked them, saying: 'Whom say the people that I am?' [19]They answering said: 'John the Baptist; but some say Elijah; and others say, that one of the old prophets is risen again.' [20]He said unto them: 'But whom say ye that I am?' Peter answering said: 'The Christ of God.'

John vi. 56–71

[56]He that eateth My flesh, and drinketh My blood, dwelleth in Me, and I in him. [57]As the living Father hath sent Me, and I live by the Father: so he that eateth Me, even he shall live by Me. [58]This is that bread which came down from heaven: not as your fathers did eat manna, and are dead; he that eateth of this bread shall live for ever. [59]These things said He in the synagogue, as He taught in Capernaum.

[60]Many therefore of His disciples, when they had heard this, said: 'This is an hard saying; who can hear it?' [61]When Jesus knew in Himself that His disciples murmured at it, He said unto them: 'Doth this offend you? [62]What and if ye shall see the Son of Man ascend up where He was before? [63]It is the spirit that quickeneth; the flesh profiteth nothing: the words that I speak unto you, they are spirit, and they are life. [64]But there are some of you that believe not.' For Jesus knew from the beginning who they were that believed not, and who should betray Him. [65]And He said: 'Therefore said I unto you, that no man can come unto Me, except it were given unto him of My Father.'

[66]From that time many of His disciples went back, and walked no more with Him. [67]Then said Jesus unto the Twelve: 'Will ye also go away? [68]Then Simon Peter answered Him: 'Lord, to Whom shall we go? Thou hast the words of eternal life. [69]And we believe and are sure that Thou art that Christ, the Son of the living God.' [70]Jesus answered them: 'Have not I chosen you Twelve, and one of you is a devil?' [71]He spake of Judas Iscariot the son of Simon: for he it was that should betray Him, being one of the Twelve.

John vi. 14

[14]Then those men, when they had seen the miracle that Jesus did, said: 'This is of a truth that prophet that should come into the world.'

Origen: On Jeremiah, Homilies iii. 3 (*Latin*)

'I have read somewhere that the Saviour said—though I am not sure whether someone put these words in the Saviour's mouth, or whether he truly remembered them—at any rate, I read that he said: "He that is near me is near the fire. He that is far from me is far from the Kingdom." '

Origen: **On Jeremiah, Homilies iii. 3** (*contd.*)

(Didymus on *Psalm* lxxxviii. 8 quotes the same saying in Greek and with greater assurance.)

(*a*) Philip the tetrarch built Caesarea Philippi in 2–3 B.C. on the site of the ancient city of Dan: a high cliff beneath the southern buttress of Mount Hermon. There his father, Herod the Great, had dedicated a temple to the God Augustus. Near the base of the cliff was the grotto of Baal Gad, the goatish God of Good Fortune, formerly worshipped by the tribe of Gad, whom the Syrian Greeks now knew as Pan and whom they associated with the river nymphs (*see* xxxii.*d*) because the main source of the Jordan breaks out from this grotto. The city's official name and title ran: 'Caesarea of Augustus, sacred, with the right of sanctuary under the protection of Pan'; but it became known as 'Caesarea of Philip', to distinguish it from the port of Caesarea Palestinae which Herod the Great had founded.

Jesus avoided the city itself as dedicated to a heathen god, but went to the neighbouring villages in search of 'lost sheep of the House of Israel'. Dan had been the northernmost city of the ancient Israelite Kingdom, outside which Jesus seems never yet to have stepped; while making the statutory circuit of his realm (see viii.*e and y*), he will also have visited Beersheba, its southern-most city (*see* lxxxiv.*a*).

(*b*) The disciples' report of the various guesses made about Jesus's identity appears to be incorrectly recorded in all the Gospels. It is incredible that either Herod Antipas, or his servants, could have mistaken him for John the Baptist risen from the dead; nor does any Jewish tradition survive that Jeremiah was expected to return (*Matthew* xvi. 14). Unless, therefore, Jesus was thought to be Enoch, who, like Elijah, had been spared death, the only possible conjectures will have been the two which, according to *John* i. 21, were made about John the Baptist: namely 'Elijah, or that prophet'—the prophet spoken of in *Deuteronomy* xviii. 18 (*see* xv.*g and* xciv.*c*). An editor of *John* evidently misread a passage in the Oracles where Jesus, not the Baptist, was the subject of these conjectures; his mistake has however, been corrected in *John* vi. 14: 'This is of a truth that prophet which should come into the world.' The Synoptics, using the same collection of Oracles, rightly made the conjectures apply to Jesus; but they misunderstood the meaning of 'that prophet' and therefore altered it to 'a prophet, or as one of the prophets' (*Mark* vi. 15); 'Jeremiah or one of the prophets' (*Matthew* xvi. 14); and 'one of the old prophets' (*Luke* ix. 19).

Matthew xvi. 13: 'Whom do men say that I, the Son of Man, am?', proves that Jesus's modest 'this son of man', meaning 'myself', was misread as a transcendental title. If he did say: 'I, the Son of Man', Peter deserves little credit for deducing from this that he was the Messiah.

(*c*) It cannot be accepted either that Jesus invested the Twelve with authority (*Matthew* viii. 18) to decide the fates of their fellow-Israelites in the afterworld, or that he limited such authority to Peter (*Matthew* vi. 19); God alone could judge a man's soul.

Matthew vi. 18 is also suspect: 'Thou art Peter, and upon this rock I will build my church'; if only because Jesus had expressed unqualified loyalty to the Pharisaic synagogue, and had no thought of abolishing it in favour of a new church organization (*Matthew* xxiii. 2–3—*see* XIII.*a*). His reported gift to Peter of the Heavenly keys (*Matthew* xvi. 19) is not included in Tatian's second-century *Diatessaron,* a combination of the four Gospels into a single narrative, and was evidently invented by a late editor of *Matthew* who wished to exalt the Petrine Church above the Pauline, the Nazarene, the Johannine, the Gnostic, and all others.

Eisler is right in suggesting (*The Messiah and John the Baptist, p.* 147) that Peter's supposed patronymic 'Bar Jonah' (*Matthew* xvi. 17 and *John* xxi. 15) means 'one of the Baryonim', or 'wild men'—in other words, a Zealot (*Gittin* 56a). Jesus will have used it as a rebuke both in this context (*see* LXXVIII.*c*) and in the later one (*see* CXVII.*m*).

(241) *Jesus passed thence, and came unto Caesarea Philippi, where once was the city of Dan; and he preached in the villages thereabout, but into Caesarea, which was of the heathen, entered he not.*

And he asked the sons of Zebedee: 'Whom do men say that I am?'

They answered: 'Some say that thou art Elijah come again, and some that thou art Enoch, the messenger of God.'

He asked them again: 'And whom say ye that I am?'

They answered: 'Verily, thou art the prophet that should come into the world, as foretold by Moses.'

Then he saith unto Peter: 'And whom sayest thou that I am?'

Peter answered: 'Thou art the Anointed King, the Son of the Living God.'

And Jesus rejoiced and said: 'Blessed art thou, Simon! For no man revealed this unto thee, but the Father Himself revealeth it.'

* * * * *

(*d*) The rhetorical passage in *John* vi. 56–71 shows a bland disregard of historical probability: Jesus would have been arrested at once if he had preached the drinking of human blood in a Galilean synagogue, since the drinking of any blood was expressly forbidden in *Genesis* ix. 4 (*see* CVI.*n*). It is an interpolation devised both to justify the Eucharist and to prove that Jesus knew exactly what his fate in Jerusalem was to be. Verse 63, 'the spirit quickeneth', borrowed from 2 *Corinthians* iii. 6, is there more suitably linked with 'the letter killeth'. Verses 60–61 and 65–69 are the only genuine ones in this otherwise fantastic discourse; they continue and complete the account of the Temptation where Jesus discourages Peter's hopes that a successful war for national freedom is about to begin (*see* LXXVIII.*e*). (*John* xv. 20 belongs to the same context, *see* LIV.*j*.) The 'hard saying' which offended many of the disciples (*John* vi. 60), was probably the one preserved by Origen and Didymus.

(243) *And to the disciples he said: 'Yet must I suffer many things in Jerusalem; and as the Chief Rulers persecute me, so likewise will they persecute you.*

'Therefore said I unto you that no man can follow me whither I go, except it be given him of the Father.

'He that is nigh unto me and hearkeneth to my words, the same is also nigh unto the fire which shall consume the world; but he that hearkeneth not, the same is far from the Kingdom of God.'

His disciples answered and said: 'This is a hard saying. Who can bear it?' And from that time many went back and walked no more with him.

Then Jesus asked the Twelve: 'Doth this offend you? Will ye also go from me?'

Simon Peter answered: 'Lord, to whom shall we go? For thou teachest us the way unto everlasting life.'

* * * * *

(*e*) Jesus had not yet revealed to the Twelve that he expected a violent death in Jerusalem; he made this disclosure after his return to Galilee (*Mark* ix. 30–31 and *Matthew* xvii. 22–23—*see* LXXIX.*f*).

(*f*) The following passage appears to belong to a later time, when Jesus had gone to Beth-Nimrah in Peraea, there to continue the Baptist's work (*see* LXXXIV.*a and* LXXXVII.*d*). *Luke* has suppressed all mention of Herod's hostility towards Jesus (*see* XCVII.*a and h*), thus laying the responsibility for his crucifixion on the whole Jewish nation (*Mark* vi. 20, *Luke* ix. 9 and xxiii. 8 —*see* LXXVI.*b*).

(298) *And presently it came to pass that Herod Antipas, the tetrarch of Galilee, himself heard of Jesus, for his fame was spread abroad.*

And he said to those of his household: 'John have I beheaded. But who is this Jesus whereof I hear such things? He seemeth to be his fellow in sedition.'

Therefore he now sought to apprehend Jesus.

* * * * *

LXXVIII

THE TEMPTATION

Mark i. 12–13

[12]And immediately the Spirit driveth Him into the wilderness. [13]And He was there in the wilderness forty days, tempted of Satan; and was with the wild beasts; and the angels ministered unto Him.

Matthew iv. 1–11

[1]Then was Jesus led up of the Spirit into the wilderness to be tempted of the devil. [2]And when He had fasted forty days and forty nights, He was afterward an hungered. [3]And when the tempter came to Him, he said: 'If Thou be the Son of God, command that these stones be made bread.' [4]But He answered and said: 'It is written

Man shall not live by bread alone,
But by every word that proceedeth out of the mouth of God.'

[5]Then the devil taketh Him up into the holy city, and setteth Him on a pinnacle of the temple, [6]and saith unto Him: 'If Thou be the Son of God, cast Thyself down: for it is written

He shall give His angels charge concerning Thee:
And in their hands they shall bear Thee up,
Lest at any time Thou dash Thy foot against a stone.'

[7]Jesus said unto him: 'It is written again

Thou shalt not tempt the Lord thy God.'

[8]Again, the devil taketh Him up into an exceeding high mountain, and sheweth Him all the kingdoms of the world, and the glory of them; [9]and saith unto Him: 'All these things will I give Thee, if Thou wilt fall down and worship me.' [10]Then saith Jesus unto him:

'Get thee hence, Satan: for it is written

Thou shalt worship the Lord thy God,
And Him only shalt thou serve.'

[11]Then the devil leaveth Him, and, behold, angels came and ministered unto Him.

Luke iv. 1–13

[1]And Jesus being full of the Holy Ghost returned from Jordan, and was led by the Spirit into the wilderness, [2]being forty days tempted of the devil. And in those days He did eat nothing: and when they were ended, He afterward

Luke iv. 1–13 (*contd.*)

hungered. ³And the devil said unto Him: 'If Thou be the Son of God, command this stone that it be made bread.' ⁴And Jesus answered him, saying: 'It is written that:

Man shall not live by bread alone, but by every word of God.'

⁵And the devil, taking Him up into an high mountain, shewed unto Him all the kingdoms of the world in a moment of time. ⁶And the devil said unto Him: 'All this power will I give Thee, and the glory of them: for that is delivered unto me; and to whomsoever I will I give it. ⁷If Thou therefore wilt worship me, all shall be Thine.' ⁸And Jesus answered and said unto him: 'Get thee behind Me, Satan: for it is written:

Thou shalt worship the Lord thy God,
And Him only shalt thou serve.'

⁹And he brought Him to Jerusalem, and set Him on a pinnacle of the temple, and said unto Him: 'If Thou be the Son of God, cast Thyself down from hence: ¹⁰for it is written:

He shall give His Angels charge over Thee, to keep Thee:
¹¹*And in their hands they shall bear Thee up,*
Lest at any time Thou dash Thy foot against a stone.'

¹²And Jesus answering said unto him: 'It is said:

Thou shalt not tempt the Lord thy God.'

¹³And when the devil had ended all the temptation, he departed from Him for a season.

Origen: On John ii. 12

And if any accept the *Gospel according to the Hebrews* where the Saviour himself saith: 'Even now did my mother the Holy Spirit take me by one of mine hairs and carried me away unto the great mountain Tabor,' he will be perplexed. . . .

Origen: On Jeremiah, Homilies xv. 4

'And if anyone receive that saying: "Even now my Mother the Holy Spirit took me and carried me up into the great mountain Tabor. . . ." '

Mark viii. 30–33

³⁰And He charged them that they should tell no man of Him.

³¹And He began to teach them, that the Son of Man must suffer many things, and be rejected of the elders, and of the chief priests, and scribes, and be killed, and after three days rise again. ³²And He spake that saying openly. And Peter took Him, and began to rebuke Him. ³³But when He had turned about and looked on His disciples, He rebuked Peter, saying: 'Get thee behind Me, Satan: for thou savourest not the things that be of God, but the things that be of men.'

Mark x. 32–34

³²And they were in the way going up to Jerusalem; and Jesus went before them: and they were amazed; and as they followed, they were afraid. And

Mark x. 32–34 (*contd.*)

He took again the Twelve, and began to tell them what things should happen unto Him: [33]'Behold, we go up to Jerusalem; and the Son of Man shall be delivered unto the chief priests, and unto the scribes; and they shall condemn Him to death, and shall deliver Him to the Gentiles: [34]and they shall mock Him, and shall scourge Him, and shall spit upon Him, and shall kill Him: and the third day He shall rise again.'

Matthew xvi. 20–23

[20]Then charged He His disciples that they should tell no man that He was Jesus the Christ.

[21]From that time forth began Jesus to shew unto His disciples, how that He must go unto Jerusalem, and suffer many things of the elders and chief priests and scribes, and be killed, and be raised again the third day. [22]Then Peter took Him, and began to rebuke Him, saying: 'Be it far from Thee, Lord: this shall not be unto Thee.' [23]But He turned, and said unto Peter: 'Get thee behind Me, Satan: thou art an offence unto Me: for thou savourest not the things that be of God, but those that be of men.'

Matthew xx. 17–19

[17]And Jesus going up to Jerusalem took the twelve disciples apart in the way, and said unto them: [18]'Behold, we go up to Jerusalem; and the Son of Man shall be betrayed unto the chief priests and unto the scribes, and they shall condemn Him to death, [19]and shall deliver Him to the Gentiles to mock, and to scourge, and to crucify Him: and the third day He shall rise again.'

Luke ix. 21–22

[21]And He straitly charged them, and commanded them to tell no man that thing; [22]saying: 'The Son of Man must suffer many things, and be rejected of the elders and chief priests and scribes, and be slain, and be raised the third day.'

Luke xviii. 31–34

[31]Then He took unto Him the Twelve, and said unto them: 'Behold, we go up to Jerusalem, and all things that are written by the prophets concerning the Son of Man shall be accomplished. [32]For He shall be delivered unto the Gentiles, and shall be mocked, and spitefully entreated, and spitted on: [33]and they shall scourge Him, and put Him to death: and the third day He shall rise again.'

[34]And they understood none of these things: and this saying was hid from them, neither knew they the things which were spoken.

John xiv. 22–24

[22]Judas saith unto Him, not Iscariot: 'Lord, how is it that Thou wilt manifest Thyself unto us, and not unto the world?' [23]Jesus answered and said unto him: 'If a man love Me he will keep My words: and My Father will love him, and we will come unto him, and make our abode with him. [24]He that

John xiv. 22–24 (*contd.*)

> loveth Me not keepeth not My sayings: and the word which ye hear is not
> Mine, but the Father's Who sent Me.'

(*a*) The brief account of the Temptation in *Mark* i. 12–13 is given immediately after Jesus's baptism, and may have been associated in the editor's mind
with the mock-combat which formed part of the ancient coronation ritual
(*see* VIII.*d*). A royal contest with the four symbolic beasts that ruled the
cardinal points of the compass was a familiar conception in Syria and Egypt.
These beasts appeared in Ezekiel's vision (*Ezekiel* i. 5) and, in mythically
degenerate form, are shown subjugated around the Throne of the Lamb in
Revelation iv. 6. Professor E. G. Brown in his *A Year Among the Persians*
(1893, *p.* 148), cites a forty-day struggle between a Persian initiate seated in a
circle—apparently divided into four parts by a cross—and four genies in
beast-disguise, who entered and challenged him at set intervals. Solomon
who, according to *Antiquities* viii. 2. 5, subjugated genies, may well have
used the same method.

(*b*) The source of *Mark* i. 12–13 seems to have been a synagogue fresco of
the four beasts—the lion, the bear, the leopard, and the many-horned creature with 'a mouth speaking terrible things'—which raged around the
throne of God (*Daniel* vii. 1–9). This picture will have shown angels in
their thousands ministering to God, and the crowned Son of Man standing
before His throne (*Daniel* vii. 10–13), above the legend: 'Dominion and
glory and a kingdom that all people, nations, and languages should serve
him' (*Daniel* vii. 14). The many-horned creature has been mistaken for the
Devil tempting Jesus in the words of this text, as he does in *Matthew* iv.
8–9 and *Luke* iv. 5–6. The forty days in *Mark* i. 13 are probably derived from
this passage in *Matthew*.

(*c*) But *Matthew* iv. 8–9 is intelligible only in the light of *Matthew* xvi.
20–23, where Jesus is made to address Peter with: 'Get thee behind me,
Satan!'; and this again is intelligible only in the light of *John* vi. 15 (*see*
LXXIII.*b*), a passage which follows Jesus's parable of the Bread from Heaven:

> 'When Jesus therefore perceived that they would take him by force to make
> him king, he departed again into a mountain himself alone.'

Peter, in fact, must have realized that Jesus had been anointed King of
Israel (*Matthew* xvi. 16—*see* LXXVII.*b and d*), and at once acclaimed him as
the Conquering Messiah who would rule an ideally organized kingdom in
justice and peace, as prophesied in *Daniel* vii. 13–14—a theme also enlarged
upon in the Talmud (*Shabbath* 63*a*). Jesus then disillusioned the disciples,
explaining that he was no warrior; and rebuked Peter as a 'wild man', or
Zealot (*see* LXXVII.*c*). But they still had hopes that he would finally reign by
force of arms; which seems to be the meaning of 'they would take him by
force to make him king'.

(*d*) Jesus here identifies himself with the pacific Messiah, the Son of David, as opposed to the warrior Messiah, the Son of Joseph. The rabbis deduced the existence of these two latter-day Messiahs from both the Law and the prophets. According to the *Midrash* (*Genesis Rabbah* lxxv. 6): 'And he sent Judah before him unto Joseph', Joseph should receive the Kingdom before Judah, and the Son of Joseph must therefore reign before the Son of David, who was of the tribe of Judah. In support of this, the rabbis quoted *Isaiah* xxxii. 20: 'Blessed are ye that send forth the feet of the ox and the ass.' The ox was a symbol of the Messiah anointed for battle, namely the Son of Joseph, because in *Deuteronomy* xxxiii. 17, Moses pronounced this blessing on Joseph: 'His glory is like the firstling of his bullock, his horns like the horns of the wild ox; with them shall he push the people together to the ends of the earth.' The ass was a symbol of the pacific Son of David, who would appear 'lowly and riding upon an ass' (*Zechariah* ix. 9—*see* LXXXIX.*a*). A question in *Genesis Rabbah* xxix. 2–3: 'By whose hand will the Kingdom of Edom [i.e. Rome] fall?' is answered: 'By the hand of him, anointed for war, who shall spring from Joseph.' The reign of the Son of Joseph was to be brief; that of the Son of David everlasting (*ibid.*). Nazarene identification of Jesus with the Son of David finds support in the famous Palatine *graffito,* dating from Claudius's reign, of a crucified figure with an ass's head; which scholars insist on mistaking for a caricature of Christ. To this Pharisaic view of the two Messiahs, Jesus contributed the doctrine—first conceived, it may be, by John the Baptist—that the Son of David must die before exercising effective sovereignty in this world, must be avenged by the Son of Joseph, and then rise again to reign in the Kingdom of Heaven for a thousand years. It is not clear whom Jesus envisaged as the Son of Joseph; perhaps one of the two Beni Rehem (*see* LVI.*e*).

(*e*) Peter was disappointed at Jesus's refusal to take up arms; he had intended, it seems, to reveal his identity to the Zealots, who would thereupon rally against Rome under the Davidic standard. According to *John* xiv. 22, Judas—'Judas of James', *alias* 'Jude the Obscure'—also protested. It appears from *Mark* viii. 33 that Jesus, after binding the Twelve to silence and quoting 2 *Samuel* xix. 22, told Peter a dramatic parable: how, just before his coronation, he went into the wilderness to fast and commune with God (*see* VI.*d* and VIII.*f*). He described the subsequent temptations in terms of a conflict between himself and God's Adversary or, perhaps more modestly, between his evil counsellor, *yetzer ha'ra,* and his good counsellor, *yetzer tov*—taking for his model the crucial passage in *Zechariah* iii. 1–10 where Joshua, when about to be crowned Priest-king, hears Satan rebuked by the Angel of the Lord, his adversary. In *Matthew* iv. 8–9 and *Luke* iv. 5–6 this parable has been removed from its context and inserted as literal fact at the close of the coronation.

(*f*) The parable is apparently based on a legend brought back by the Jews from their Persian captivity: how the wicked Angra Mainyu unsuccessfully tempted Zarathustra, with promises of universal conquest, to desert the good law of Mazda, God of Light. It has been carelessly transcribed, and in *Luke* iv. 1–13 the events are in a different order from those in *Matthew* iv. 1–11. In both versions the bread-into-stones temptation is correctly countered with a text from *Deuteronomy* viii. 3. The quotation from *Deuteronomy* vi. 16: 'Thou shalt not tempt the Lord thy God' has, however, been misrepresented as a final reproof to the Devil, implying that Jesus himself claimed to be God. This reproof must originally have countered another temptation: namely, to do as Moses did at Massah and strike the rock for water (*Exodus* xvii. 6). Jesus was thirsty as well as hungry.

(*g*) Three temptations are the rule in legends of this sort, and 'Cast thyself down!' is a challenge rather than a fourth temptation. Evidently it belongs to a subsequent dispute in which Jesus, not the Devil, quotes Scripture—from *Psalm* xvi. 11; but part of the dialogue is to be found elsewhere. 'My Kingdom is not of this world' has been introduced into Jesus's interview with Pilate (*John* xviii. 36—*see* cx.*d*); and 'I am not come to destroy men's lives' into the incident of the Samaritan village which rejected the apostles (*Luke* ix. 56—*see* lxx.*k*). Origen has preserved fragments of the original tradition, altered by *Mark* and *Luke,* and reveals that the mountain was Tabor, whence a wide view could be had of the Israelite kingdom ruled by Solomon the Conqueror. Tabor was the abode of Beelzebub (*see* xxxiv.*b*), who reminds Jesus of this kingdom's modest extent—it could be 'viewed in a moment of time' (*Luke* iv. 5)—and tempts him with its enlargement by conquest.

'My mother the Holy Spirit' is a reference to the Trinitarian mystery (*see Introduction* iii.*q–r and* lxxxiv.*e–f*).

(*h*) Jesus's prophecy of his own death is doubled in the Synoptics (*Mark* viii. 31–32 and x. 32–34; *Matthew* xvi. 21 and xx. 17–19; *Luke* ix. 22 and xviii. 31–34). In the first version, he foretells a clash with the Chief Rulers, and his death and subsequent resurrection 'on the third day', that is, after the end of the world (*see* xcii.*g*). Gentile Christian doctrine, however, insisted that Jesus not only was a willing victim but had exact foreknowledge of his fate. The second version was therefore added. But Jesus could never have preached that the Messiah would be delivered to the Gentiles for scourging and crucifixion; this formed no part of accepted eschatological doctrine. There can be no doubt that he expected to be assassinated by the swords of his own people (*see* ci.*b*); for the proper context of this disclosure, *see* lxxix.*f*. The manner of his death is specified in *Matthew* xx. 19, where the word 'crucify' occurs, but not in *Mark* x. 33–34 and *Luke* xviii. 32–33, the corresponding passages.

The literal Greek of Peter's 'Be it far from thee' (*Matthew* xvi. 22), is 'Pity thyself' and may preserve the original Aramaic phrase. The Syriac reads *Hass lah mari* ('be silent, master!'); but since the letters *heth* and *he* are often mistaken for each other, the Syriac copyist from an Aramaic text may have mistaken *Hass* for *Ḥass,* which again means 'pity thyself'.

(244) *And Jesus straitly charged them to tell no man that he was the King of Israel.*

* * * * *

[Here follows Jesus's statement that he has not come to rule the world as his own (*see* LXII.*d*).]

* * * * *

(246) *Judas asked him (not he of Kerioth): 'Lord, how is it that thou revealest thyself unto us, and not unto the world?'*

And Peter saith: 'Lord, suffer me to proclaim thy kingdom from the housetops, that all Israel may rise and take arms with thee against the Wicked Kingdom.'

But Jesus rebuked them, saying: 'My Kingdom is not of this world. I come not to destroy men's lives, but to save them.'

And Peter asked: 'What if thy people greatly desire thee to do battle?'

But Jesus again rebuked him, saying: 'Thou wild man, knowest thou not what David said unto the sons of Zeruiah, when they pleaded with him that he should do violence?

'He said: "What have I to do with you, ye sons of Zeruiah, that ye should this day be adversaries unto me? For know ye not that I am this day King over Israel?"

'So likewise say I unto thee: stand not against me as mine adversary, but get thee behind me and follow whither I lead.

'For thou savourest not the things that be of God, but those that be of men.'

* * * * *

(247) *And he spake this parable unto the Twelve: 'In the days that I was chosen King, I went apart into the wilderness to commune with God, and I thirsted and was an-hungered.*

'And the Adversary, meeting me in the form of my evil counsellor, said unto me: "If thou be the very Son of God which is prophesied, lift thy rod and strike this rock that water may flow forth for us."

'And my good counsellor, the angel of the Lord, made answer: "It is written: 'Ye shall not tempt the Lord thy God, as ye tempted Him at Massah.'"

'The Adversary said again: "If thou be the very Son of God which is prophesied, pray to thy Father that these stones be made bread for us."

'And my good counsellor, the angel of the Lord, again made answer: "It is written: 'I humbled thee and suffered thee to hunger, that He might make thee know that man liveth not by bread alone, but by every word that proceedeth out of the mouth of the Lord.'"

'Then my mother the Holy Spirit taketh me by the hair of my head and beareth me unto the great mountain Tabor.

'And the Adversary, which sojourneth there, came before me again, and shewed unto me all the lands over which Solomon ruled.

'And he said: "Over this kingdom shalt thou rule. Is it not a little one, and viewed in a moment of time?

'"Yet mayest thou enlarge thy dominion to the ends of the earth, if thou

wilt but fall down and worship me. For the glory of conquest is delivered unto me, and I give it to whomsoever I will."

'*But my good counsellor made answer, rebuking him: "Get thee hence, thou Adversary of God! For it is written: 'Thou shalt worship the Lord thy God and Him only shalt thou serve.'"*

'*Then the Adversary leaveth me, but lo! he is returned and speaketh unto me with the voice of my familiar friends.'*

* * * * *

(248) *And Peter saith again: 'But if thou wilt not lead us into battle, how then shall we overcome?'*

Jesus answered and said: 'I will go up to Jerusalem, and whatsoever the Lord shall put into my mouth, that will I preach against the Chief Rulers and against their scribes, which serve the Wicked Kingdom.

'*For it is there that all things which are prophesied concerning this son of man shall be accomplished.'*

* * * * *

(*i*) [Here follows Jesus's quotation from *Ezekiel* iii. 7 (*see* LIV.*j*), enjoining the Twelve to set their faces sternly against the Chief Rulers.]

* * * * *

(250) *And Peter saith unto Jesus: 'Pity thyself, for then will they cast thee from the highest pinnacle of the Temple.'*

Jesus answered, and said: 'David prophesied in a psalm: "He shall give His angels charge of thee. They shall bear thee up in their hands lest thou dash thy foot against a stone."'

But when Jesus perceived that they would yet have him take arms and reign by conquest and a mighty hand, he departed thence into a mountain apart, and there he fasted.

* * * * *

(*j*) 'Forty days' (*Mark* i. 13, *Matthew* iv. 2 and *Luke* iv. 2) is inacceptable, though it need not be doubted that Jesus possessed both the power and the will to fast for forty days, had he been called upon to do so. No absolute fast by any European has been authoritatively recorded as lasting even thirty-two days; and in only two such cases has death not supervened. Yet in India members of the ascetic Jain sect, whose customs and beliefs recall those of the Essenes, fast without harm to themselves twice, and even three times, as long; they sit in ecstatic contemplation, their bodies in a state of retarded metabolism not unlike that of hibernating bears.

In Hebrew and Aramaic, 'forty days' or 'forty years' means simply 'many days' or 'many years'; and if the preparatory interval between Jesus's acclamation and his coronation lasted for the traditional week (*see* VI.*d*), he will have fasted for six days only. He seems later to have fasted on the so-called Mountain of the Transfiguration (*see* LXXIX.*d*); this will have been his fast in mourning for John (*see* LXXVI.*f*).

The longest fast permitted by the Oral Law was six days, to prevent a breach of the Sabbath (*see* LXXI.*a*), but fasting on week days might be continued indefinitely if this served a legitimate purpose. Zadok, a contemporary of Jesus, who was a priest as well as a Pharisee sage, is said to have kept every labouring day as a fast for 'forty years', in the hope that he would thus stave off the threatened destruction of the Temple (*Gittin* 56*b* and *Lamentations Rabbati* 1.5.31).

* * * * *

LXXIX

THE TRANSFIGURATION

Mark ix. 2–32

²And after six days Jesus taketh with Him Peter, and James, and John, and leadeth them up into an high mountain apart by themselves: and He was transfigured before them. ³And His raiment became shining, exceeding white as snow; so as no fuller on earth can white them. ⁴And there appeared unto them Elijah with Moses: and they were talking with Jesus. ⁵And Peter answered and said to Jesus: 'Master, it is good for us to be here: and let us make three tabernacles; one for Thee, and one for Moses, and one for Elijah.' ⁶For he wist not what to say; for they were sore afraid. ⁷And there was a cloud that overshadowed them: and a voice came out of the cloud, saying:

This is My beloved Son: hear Him.

⁸And suddenly, when they had looked round about, they saw no man any more, save Jesus only with themselves. ⁹And as they came down from the mountain, He charged them that they should tell no man what things they had seen, till the Son of Man were risen from the dead. ¹⁰And they kept that saying with themselves, questioning one with another what the rising from the dead should mean. ¹¹And they asked Him, saying: 'Why say the scribes that Elijah must first come?' ¹²And He answered and told them: 'Elijah verily cometh first, and restoreth all things; and how it is written of the Son of Man, that He must suffer many things, and be set at nought. ¹³But I say unto you, that Elijah is indeed come, and they have done unto him whatsoever they listed, as it is written of him.'

¹⁴And when He came to His disciples, He saw a great multitude about them, and the scribes questioning with them. ¹⁵And straightway all the people, when they beheld Him, were greatly amazed, and running to Him saluted Him. ¹⁶And He asked the scribes: 'What question ye with them?'

¹⁷And one of the multitude answered and said: 'Master, I have brought unto Thee my son, which hath a dumb spirit; ¹⁸and wheresoever he taketh him, he teareth him: and he foameth, and gnasheth with his teeth, and pineth away: and I spake to Thy disciples that they should cast him out; and they could not.' ¹⁹He answereth him, and saith: 'O faithless generation, how long shall I be with you? how long shall I suffer you? bring him unto Me.' ²⁰And they brought him unto Him: and when he saw Him, straightway the spirit tare him; and he fell on the ground, and wallowed foaming. ²¹And He asked his father: 'How long is it ago since this came unto him?' And he said:—'Of a child, ²²and ofttimes it hath cast him into the fire, and into the

Mark ix. 2–32 (*contd.*)

waters, to destroy him: but if Thou canst do any thing, have compassion on us, and help us.' ²³Jesus said unto him: 'If thou canst believe, all things are possible to him that believeth.' ²⁴And straightway the father of the child cried out, and said with tears: 'Lord, I believe; help Thou mine unbelief.' ²⁵When Jesus saw that the people came running together, He rebuked the foul spirit, saying unto him: 'Thou dumb and deaf spirit, I charge thee, come out of him, and enter no more into him.' ²⁶And the spirit cried, and rent him sore, and came out of him: and he was as one dead; insomuch that many said, He is dead. ²⁷But Jesus took him by the hand, and lifted him up; and he arose. ²⁸And when He was come into the house, His disciples asked Him privately: 'Why could not we cast him out?' ²⁹And He said unto them: 'This kind can come forth by nothing, but by prayer and fasting.'

³⁰And they departed thence, and passed through Galilee; and He would not that any man should know it. ³¹For He taught His disciples, and said unto them: 'The Son of Man is delivered into the hands of men, and they shall kill Him; and after that He is killed, He shall rise the third day.' ³²But they understood not that saying, and were afraid to ask Him.

Matthew xvii. 1–23

¹And after six days Jesus taketh Peter, James, and John his brother, and bringeth them up into an high mountain apart, ²and was transfigured before them: and His face did shine as the sun, and His raiment was white as the light. ³And, behold, there appeared unto them Moses and Elijah talking with Him. ⁴Then answered Peter, and said unto Jesus: 'Lord, it is good for us to be here; if Thou wilt, let us make here three tabernacles; one for Thee, and one for Moses, and one for Elijah.' ⁵While he yet spake, behold, a bright cloud overshadowed them: and behold a voice out of the cloud, which said:

This is My beloved Son, in Whom I am well pleased; hear ye him.

⁶And when the disciples heard it, they fell on their face, and were sore afraid. ⁷And Jesus came and touched them, and said: 'Arise, and be not afraid.' ⁸And when they had lifted up their eyes, they saw no man, save Jesus only. ⁹And as they came down from the mountain, Jesus charged them saying: 'Tell the vision to no man, until the Son of Man be risen again from the dead.' ¹⁰And His disciples asked Him, saying: 'Why then say the scribes that Elijah must first come?' ¹¹And Jesus answered and said unto them: 'Elijah truly shall first come, and restore all things. ¹²But I say unto you, that Elijah is come already, and they knew him not, but have done unto him whatsoever they listed. Likewise shall also the Son of Man suffer of them.' ¹³Then the disciples understood that He spake unto them of John the Baptist.

¹⁴And when they were come to the multitude, there came to Him a certain man, kneeling down to Him, and saying: ¹⁵'Lord, have mercy on my son: for he is lunatic, and sore vexed: for ofttimes he falleth into the fire, and oft into the water. ¹⁶And I brought him to Thy disciples, and they could not cure him.' ¹⁷Then Jesus answered and said: 'O faithless and perverse generation, how long shall I be with you? how long shall I suffer you? bring him hither to Me.' ¹⁸And Jesus rebuked the devil; and he departed out of him: and the

Matthew xvii. 1–23 (*contd.*)

child was cured from that very hour. ¹⁹Then came the disciples to Jesus apart, and said: 'Why could not we cast him out?'

²⁰'Because of your unbelief: for verily I say unto you, if ye have faith as a grain of mustard seed, ye shall say unto this mountain, remove hence to yonder place; and it shall remove; and nothing shall be impossible unto you. ²¹Howbeit this kind goeth not out but by prayer and fasting.'

²²And while they abode in Galilee, Jesus said unto them: 'The Son of Man shall be betrayed into the hands of men: ²³and they shall kill Him, and the third day He shall be raised again.' And they were exceeding sorry.

Luke ix. 28–48

²⁸And it came to pass about an eight days after these sayings, He took Peter and John and James, and went up into a mountain to pray. ²⁹And as He prayed, the fashion of His countenance was altered, and His raiment was white and glistering. ³⁰And behold, there talked with Him two men, which were Moses and Elijah: ³¹who appeared in glory, and spake of His decease which He should accomplish at Jerusalem. ³²But Peter and they that were with Him were heavy with sleep: and when they were awake, they saw His glory, and the two men that stood with Him. ³³And it came to pass, as they departed from Him, Peter said unto Jesus: 'Master, it is good for us to be here: and let us make three tabernacles; one for Thee, and one for Moses, and one for Elijah': not knowing what he said. ³⁴While he thus spake, there came a cloud, and overshadowed them: and they feared as they entered into the cloud. ³⁵And there came a voice out of the cloud, saying:

This is My beloved Son: hear Him.

³⁶And when the voice was past, Jesus was found alone. And they kept it close, and told no man in those days any of those things which they had seen.

³⁷And it came to pass, that on the next day, when they were come down from the hill, much people met Him. ³⁸And, behold, a man of the company cried out, saying: 'Master, I beseech Thee, look upon my son: for he is mine only child. ³⁹And, lo, a spirit taketh him, and he suddenly crieth out; and it teareth him that he foameth again, and bruising him hardly departeth from him. ⁴⁰And I besought Thy disciples to cast him out; and they could not.' ⁴¹And Jesus answering said: 'O faithless and perverse generation, how long shall I be with you, and suffer you? Bring thy son hither.' ⁴²And as he was yet a coming, the devil threw him down, and tare him. And Jesus rebuked the unclean spirit, and healed the child, and delivered him again to his father. ⁴³And they were all amazed at the mighty power of God.

But while they wondered every one at all things which Jesus did, He said unto His disciples: ⁴⁴'Let these sayings sink down into your ears: for the Son of Man shall be delivered into the hands of men.' ⁴⁵But they understood not this saying, and it was hid from them, that they perceived it not: and they feared to ask Him of that saying.

⁴⁶Then there arose a reasoning among them, which of them should be greatest. ⁴⁷And Jesus, perceiving the thought of their heart, took a child, and set him by Him, ⁴⁸and said unto them: 'Whosoever shall receive this child in

Luke ix. 28–48 (*contd.*)

My name receiveth Me: and whosoever shall receive Me receiveth Him that sent Me: for he that is least among you all, the same shall be great.'

John xii. 44–45

[44]Jesus cried and said: 'He that believeth on Me, believeth not on Me, but on Him that sent Me. [45]And he that seeth Me seeth Him that sent Me.'

(*a*) The Synoptic account of the Transfiguration (*Mark* ix. 2–9, *Matthew* xvii. 1–9 and *Luke* ix. 28–36) is closely connected with that of the Lunatic Child which, in all three versions, breaks the thread of Jesus's important disclosure about the manner of his death. The reason for this interruption seems to have been the need to separate the Lunatic Child from the ensuing incident of the Little Child, which had been found under the same subject-heading in a collection of Jesus's Oracles. Despite this precaution, however, an editor of *Luke* has run the two incidents together by omitting the parallel passage in *Mark* ix. 30 and 33: 'They departed thence and passed through Galilee and . . . came to Capernaum.' *Luke* ix. 47: 'He set a child by him', must have read once: 'He set *the* child [i.e. the lunatic] by him'—an error subsequently corrected by a more intelligent editor.

Nevertheless, it is likely that the Disclosure, the Lunatic Child, and the Transfiguration originally formed part of a single coherent narrative.

(*b*) The foul spirit is deaf and dumb in *Mark,* though not in either *Matthew* or *Luke:* a detail apparently deduced from Jesus's reference, now suppressed, to the deaf adder that resists the voice of the charmer in *Psalm* lviii. 3–5. This addition to the original account of how Jesus cured an epileptic, makes good the popular comment in *Mark* vii. 37: 'He maketh both the deaf to hear and the dumb to speak'. The deaf man cured in *Mark* vii. 31–37 had merely stuttered (*see* xxxi.*a*).

Mark ix. 14–29 is a more complete account than either *Matthew* xvii. 14–21 or *Luke* ix. 37–42, whose editors have omitted a part of the original Triple Tradition which they found unedifying.

No mention is made in *Matthew* that the boy threw another fit in Jesus's presence; a pious editor may have thought that the foul spirit should have shown greater awe in the presence of its God. The pronouncement in *Mark* and *Matthew* on the need for prayer and fasting has been omitted in *Luke*. Though in both *Luke* and *Matthew* the child's father kneels before Jesus, he fails to do so in *Mark*.

(*c*) *Matthew* xvii. 20 is an interpolation (*see* xlv.*b and d*).

(*d*) An essential passage explaining the people's amazement at Jesus's appearance must have dropped out before *Mark* ix. 15; this will have been an account of the days spent by Jesus in prayer and fasting (verse 29) on a mountain (verse 2—*see* lxxviii.*i and j*) apart from his disciples (verse 14). The Transfiguration itself (verses 2–10) seems to be iconotropically derived (*see Foreword k*) from an illustration to one of Jesus's sayings, in which he quotes *Exodus* xxxiv. 28–35 and 1 *Kings* xix. 8 to prove that human strength need not be overtaxed by fasting 'forty days'.

The scribes' enquiries (*Mark* ix. 14) appear at first sight to form part of the original Lunatic Child incident, because in a Gentile interpolation they would have spoken harshly or deceitfully to Jesus on his arrival; moreover, in verse 16 he is made to ask them a question to which he would, in the view of later editors, have known the answer. It is more likely, however, that two unconnected passages found in a collection of Oracles under the subject-heading 'Questions Concerning Elijah' have been run together: in the first (*Mark* ix. 11–13 and *Matthew* xvii. 10–12) the disciples will have questioned Jesus about Elijah's second coming, and quoted the scribes' opinion, while in the second Jesus questioned the disciples about the effect of a forty-day fast on Elijah.

(*e*) John contributes nothing, unless the sayings in *John* xii. 44 and *John* iv. 31–33 belong to this story rather than (respectively) to Jesus's address to the Grecians (*see* LXXXI.*b*) and his converse with the woman of Samaria (*see* LXX.*j*).

(251) *And on the last day of his fast, Jesus came again unto the disciples, and beheld how a great multitude made mock of them.*

And he asked: 'What meaneth this confusion?'

Then one of the multitude answered, and said: 'Master, my son hath a foul spirit. And whithersoever it taketh him, it teareth him, and he foameth and gnasheth with his teeth, and pineth away.

'Therefore spake I to thy disciples that they should cast out this evil spirit, but they could not.'

And the disciples confessed: 'He speaketh the truth.'

*   *   *   *   *

(252) *And Jesus rebuked them, crying: 'O faithless generation, how long must I bear with you? Bring the boy hither!'*

And he was brought, and when he beheld Jesus, straightway he was torn by the foul spirit, and fell on the ground and wallowed foaming.

And Jesus asked the father: 'How long is it ago since this came unto him?'

He answered and said: 'Of a little child. And ofttimes it hath cast him into the fire and into the water to destroy him. But if thou canst do aught, have compassion on us and help us.'

Jesus said unto him: 'Our father David testified in a psalm: "The wicked are estranged from the womb, they go astray as soon as they be born, speaking lies.

' "They are like the deaf adder that stoppeth her ear and will not listen to the wise voice of the charmer."

'Yet if thou canst believe in God's power to heal, all things are possible.'

And straightway the father of the boy cried out: 'Master, help thou mine unbelief! Yet verily I believe that thou canst do more than these.'

And Jesus cried aloud, saying: 'He that believeth on me, the same believeth not on me, but on Him that sent me!'

* * * * *

(253) *And when he saw that the people came running together, he rebuked them also, and sent them away.*

But unto the foul spirit he said: 'Thou deaf and lying devil, I charge thee in the name of God to come out and enter no more into this child!'

And the foul spirit cried and rent him sore, but came forth, leaving him as one dead; insomuch that many who watched from afar, said: 'He is dead.'

But Jesus took him by the hand and he arose and was healed.

And when he delivered him unto his father, the people glorified the mighty power of God.

* * * * *

(254) *Now, the disciples were amazed to see Jesus of so shining a countenance, for he had fasted three weeks at tidings of John's death, and now again one week.*

* * * * *

(*f*) [Here follows *John* iv. 31–34 (*see* LXX.*j*), where the Twelve urge Jesus to break his fast.]

(256) *And after that he was come with the Twelve into the house where they abode, they asked him privily: 'Why could we not cast out the foul spirit even in the name of God, yet thou couldst cast it out?'*

He answered and said: 'This kind cometh not forth, save after prayer and fasting.'

Then said they unto Jesus: 'Surely, thou fastest beyond reason. Thou wilt do thyself hurt.'

* * * * *

(257) *He answered and said: 'It is written that Moses fasted forty days on Sinai, and afterward his face shone, so that he veiled it because of its brightness; likewise did Elijah fast forty days on Horeb. Yet each came thence to do great works.*

'Think ye then that either of these twain suffered any hurt?

'Or think ye that I shall die because that I fast from a sabbbath even unto a sabbath?

'Verily, I say unto you: my death shall be on a different wise, for I shall be pierced by the sword at Jerusalem! Yet I trust that God will raise me up on the Third Day.'

But they understood not this saying, and it troubled them exceedingly.

* * * * *

(259) *Then departed he thence and passed through the borders of Galilee, going toward Jerusalem.*

* * * * *

Though Elijah was held not to have died, the Psalmist had said explicitly that no man born could escape death in the end (*Psalms* xlix. 7–10 and lxxxix. 8). John's execution therefore, while not disproving his identity with Elijah, made the end of the world seem to Jesus more imminent than ever.

(*g*) The source of the Transfiguration seems to have been an early Christian triptych. In the central panel Jesus stands crowned and surrounded by a nimbus, above the legend: 'Before that I was anointed King, I went out into the wilderness apart to commune with God, and there I thirsted and was an-hungered' (*see* LXXVIII.*e*). In the other panels Moses and Elijah are shown, each saying: 'I fasted forty days upon a mountain and came down to do great things.' From a cloud above Jesus's head, God proclaims: 'This is My beloved Son!' and clouds of witnesses wave branches or lie prostrate in adoration.

Peter's saying: 'Master, it is good for us to be here. Let us build tabernacles . . .' reads authentically, but has strayed into *Mark* ix. 5 and *Luke* ix. 33 from the Stilling of the Storm (*see* LXXV.*e*). The tabernacles which he so ineptly offers to build, 'not knowing what he said', may be a deduction from the same triptych—each of the three fasters being framed in an interlace of palm and olive branches, which the witnesses appear to have constructed themselves.

Jesus's order that the Twelve should keep the Transfiguration a close secret (*Mark* ix. 9 *and Matthew* xvii. 9)—they do so on their own initiative in *Luke* ix. 36—may have been inserted to explain the omission of the story from earlier Gospel texts. Its proper context will have been the Disclosure (*see* (*f*) *above*).

> (258) *And Jesus straitly charged them to tell no man that which he had revealed unto them concerning the manner of his death.*

*   *   *   *   *

(*h*) *Luke* omits all mention of the disciples' question about Elijah (*Mark* ix. 11 and *Matthew* xvii. 10), though the passage is in the main genuine. Jesus answers by quoting *Malachi* iv. 5.

The character in *Mark* ix. 12 who must be 'set at naught and suffer' was the 'Worthless Shepherd' of *Zechariah* xi–xiv (*see* CII.*a–e*).

The word 'betrayed' in *Matthew* xvii. 22 has been borrowed from the Passion narrative (*Matthew* xxvi. 16, 21, and 46—*see* cv.*d*).

> (234) *And the disciples ask Jesus:'Why say the scribes that Elijah must come again before the Kingdom of God can be established?'*
> *He answered and said: 'Malachi prophesied in the name of the Lord: "Behold, I will send you Elijah the prophet before the coming of the great and dreadful day of the Lord."*
> *'And Zechariah likewise prophesied of one which must suffer many things in that day and be set at naught.*

'Verily, I say unto you: Elijah is indeed come again, and hath been put to death, though we would have willingly laid down our lives for him.

'As David saith in a psalm: "None can redeem his brother that he should live for ever." Therefore let them now do unto that other whatsoever they list.'

And the disciples understood that Elijah had come again in the person of John the Baptist. But they wist not that Jesus spake of himself when he told them: 'Another must suffer many things in that day and be set at naught.'

* * * * *

(i) For *Luke* ix. 47–48, see LX.c.

* * * * *

LXXX

A DAUGHTER'S INHERITANCE

Talmud: Shabbath 116a and b

Imma Shalom, the wife of Rabbi Eliezer and a sister of Rabban Gamaliel, lived near to a philosopher who was reputed never to accept bribes.

They sought to expose him. Imma Shalom therefore sent him a golden lamp and said: 'It is my desire that a share in the inheritance of my [father's] house be given me.'

He answered: 'Ye may share.'

Then Gamaliel said: 'The Law lays down that where there is a son, a daughter does not inherit.'

The philosopher answered: 'From the day in which ye were exiled from your land, the Law of Moses has been annulled and the Law of the Gospel has been given; and in the Gospel it is written: "A son and a daughter shall inherit together."'

The next day, Rabban Gamaliel sent to the philosopher a Libyan ass.

[And when they came before him again] the philosopher said: 'I have consulted further in the Gospel and in it I find: "I have not come to take aught away from the Law of Moses, nor am I come to add aught thereto"; and it is written in the Law: "Where there is a son, a daughter does not inherit."'

Imma Shalom said to him: 'Let your light verily shine as a lamp.'

But Rabban Gamaliel said: 'The ass is come and hath overturned the lamp.'

(*a*) The point of this satiric anecdote is Imma Shalom's demonstration for the benefit of her husband—the famous Rabbi Eliezer (*see* LIII.*b*)—that the 'philosophers' (i.e. the Christians) vacillated in their attitude towards the Law, and that even the most upright of them would argue for or against its validity according to pragmatic need. The date will have been about 73 A.D., when the ritual Law could no longer be kept in its entirety because the Temple had been destroyed and the priesthood scattered, and when even the Pharisees were momentarily confused and disorientated.

'The ass is come and hath overturned the lamp', means that the bribe of the Libyan ass—'Libyan' because the Church had gained a peculiarly strong foothold in Libya (*Mark* xv. 21, *Acts* ii. 10, vi. 9 and xi. 20)—outweighed that of the golden lamp; but it also refers to Jesus as the reputed Messiah Son of David, whose symbol was the ass (*see* LXXVIII.*d*). In late Talmudic contexts Jesus is sometimes called 'Balaam', meaning that he too was a false prophet and rode an ass (*see* LXXXIX.*a*).

(*b*) The hard core of the anecdote appears to be a recommendation by Jesus, elsewhere unrecorded, that sons and daughters should inherit equally, and its apparent contradiction by another saying of his: that he came neither to augment nor to diminish the Mosaic Law—according to which daughters should inherit only in the absence of a son (*Numbers* xxvii. 8). Both these sayings seem to have been authentic quotations from a collection of Oracles.*
They cease, however, to contradict each other once the original context of the first is restored and careful consideration is given to the passage in *Numbers*.

(*c*) The Pharisees, who interpreted *Numbers* xxvii. 8 as meaning that daughters should inherit only in the absence of a son, nevertheless made generous provision for the support of unmarried women (*Kethuboth* 52*b* and 108*b*): 'If an inheritance suffice not to maintain both son and daughter, let the son go begging.' They further stipulated (*Kethuboth* 52*b*, *Baba Bathra* 112*b*, and *Bekoroth* 52*a*) that the dowry set aside from the family estate should be no smaller for a younger than for an elder daughter. A married woman was protected by the *Kethubah,* or marriage contract (still read aloud at Jewish weddings), which bound the husband to honour, support, and maintain her; and the family was then quit of any further obligation unless she were divorced, when the dowry would be returned.

(*d*) The daily tasks required of a wife depended on the size of her dowry. If she brought none at all, she must grind corn, bake, cook, wash, suckle her child, make the bed, spin, and sew. If the dowry included a single slave-woman, or the price of one, she was theoretically excused the baking and washing; if two, the cooking and suckling; if three, the bed-making and sewing; if four, she might 'sit at ease in her chair'. Moreover, if she bore twins, her husband must find a wet-nurse for one, while she suckled the other (*Kethuboth* 59*a*).

It was laid down in the Talmud (*Kethuboth* 61*a*): 'She shall ascend with him, but shall not descend.' In other words: 'a wife shares in the advantages of her husband's higher station, but cannot be compelled to forfeit any that she has previously enjoyed.' Yet, however rich a wife might be in her own right, she must herself perform certain small services for her husband, such as anointing his head (*see* xi.*d*) or washing his hands and face. After the destruction of the Temple, Rabbi Eliezer held that though a woman's dowry consisted of a hundred slaves, the husband might still set her to spin and sew, lest idleness should breed mischief (*Kethuboth* v. 5). But no married woman, however poor, could be forced to work in the fields. Since dowries were always as generous as possible, daughters usually derived greater benefit from the family estate than sons; and, by a ruling (*Kethuboth* xiii. 3)

---

* Imma Shalom is capping the philosopher's quotation from a text now incorporated in *Matthew* v. 17 (*see* xiii.*a*), with another now incorporated in *Matthew* v. 16 (*see* xxi.*i*). This suggests that in the Oracles these two sayings were connected by a comparison of the Law with a lamp, lighted in the hearts of the faithful.

promulgated in Jesus's lifetime, the latter were bound to support their un-married sisters, even though they themselves had inherited nothing.

(*e*) Jesus's amendment of the Oral Law did not contradict the written Law, which laid down that a daughter should inherit in the absence of a son, not that the existence of one debarred her from inheritance. Moreover, a prec-edent for the equal division of a patrimony might be found in *Job* xlii. 15, and was probably cited by the Sadducees, who are known to have opposed the Pharisaic view. The Pharisees, at any rate, did not venture to join issue with them on this point; and the only legal arguments recorded in the Talmud concern border-line cases (*Baba Bathra* 115*b; Tosephta Yadaim* ii. 9; *Megalith Ta'anith ch.* 5; *etc.*).* Where Levite families were concerned —and Jesus was a Levite by adoption (*see* 1.*e* and XLVIII.*d*)—the Sanhedrin may have tacitly permitted an equal division on the ground that Joshua had settled no inheritance on the tribe of Levi (*Joshua* xiii. 14 and 33). This would tend to break up the over-large fortunes of the Chief Rulers (*see* LXXXIII.*b*), to the benefit of the community as a whole.

(*f*) Jesus will have accepted the justice of the Pharisaic ruling as suitable for ordinary times, but insisted that these were extraordinary ones: the Day of Judgement loomed, and nobody in his senses would now marry or give in marriage (*Matthew* xxiv. 38—*see* XCVIII.*j*). Young women should be dedi-cated to housework, prayer and sexless companionship (*see* x.*b*); and the division of a patrimony among the entire family without regard for age or sex would distract their thoughts from the *Kethubah* (the scroll of paper con-taining the marriage contract), always a bone of domestic contention.

> (85) *Now, a certain Levite asked Jesus, saying: 'Master, what of a daughter's inheritance? How readest thou the Law?'*
>
> *Jesus answered, and said: 'It is written: "If a man die and have no son, then ye shall cause his inheritance to pass unto his daughter," yet it is no-where forbidden that a daughter should inherit where there is a son.*
>
> *'Did not Job divide his substance equally among sons and daughters? Do thou even as Job did!'*
>
> *His disciples say unto Jesus: 'Yet the sages have taught that where there is a son, a daughter shall not inherit, but a marriage portion shall be given unto her from the substance of her father's house.'*
>
> *He answered: 'Ye say well; but now the times require this other thing, which shall be for a memorial unto the daughters of Israel.*
>
> *'Verily, I say unto you: the season for marrying and for giving in marriage is over past. Let them that hope for the Kingdom remain virgins undefiled,*
>
> *'And let them not ensnare men into lust, neither seek husbands, neither contend with their kinsmen for a marriage portion. But let them labour with-out cease for the Kingdom of Heaven.'*

*　*　*　*　*

* For instance, whether sons and daughters should inherit equally if the estate were left by a widow; or whether if an only son predeceased his father, leaving a daughter, she should inherit her grandfather's estate at the expense of aunts.

(g) Geiger suggests (*Ozar Nehmad* iii) that it was for political reasons that the Pharisees deliberately overlooked the precedent in *Job* and forbade the daughter to inherit if there were sons. Herod the Great, he says, based his title to the throne of Israel on his marriage to the Hasmonean princess Mariamne which took place in the lifetime of her brother Aristobulus (*Antiquities* xv. 3. 1–3); the Pharisees loathed Herod and therefore made the ruling 'because the times required it'. Geiger's view finds support in a tradition quoted by Rabbi Huna (*Baba Bathra* 115*b*):

> 'No one must hearken even to a prince in Israel, if he declares that a daughter must inherit together with the daughter of a son; for this is the view of the Sadducees alone.'

* * * * *

THE GRECIANS

John xii. 20–43

²⁰And there were certain Greeks among them that came up to worship at the feast: ²¹the same came therefore to Philip, which was of Bethsaida of Galilee, and desired him, saying: 'Sir, we would see Jesus.' ²²Philip cometh and telleth Andrew: and again Andrew and Philip tell Jesus. ²³And Jesus answered them, saying: 'The hour is come, that the Son of Man should be glorified. ²⁴Verily, verily, I say unto you, except a corn of wheat fall into the ground and die, it abideth alone: but if it die, it bringeth forth much fruit. ²⁵He that loveth his life shall lose it; and he that hateth his life in this world shall keep it unto life eternal. ²⁶If any man serve Me, let him follow Me; and where I am, there shall also My servant be: if any man serve Me, him will My Father honour. ²⁷Now is my soul troubled; and what shall I say? Father, save Me from this hour: but for this cause came I unto this hour. ²⁸Father, glorify Thy name.' Then came there a voice from heaven:

'I have both glorified it, and will glorify it again.'

²⁹The people therefore, that stood by, and heard it, said that it thundered: others said: 'An angel spake to Him.' ³⁰Jesus answered and said: 'This voice came not because of Me, but for your sakes. ³¹Now is the judgment of this world: now shall the prince of this world be cast out. ³²And I, if I be lifted up from the earth, will draw all men unto Me.' ³³This He said, signifying what death He should die. ³⁴The people answered Him: 'We have heard out of the law that Christ abideth for ever: and how sayest Thou, the Son of Man must be lifted up? Who is this Son of Man?' ³⁵Then Jesus said unto them: 'Yet a little while is the light with you. Walk while ye have the light, lest darkness come upon you; for he that walketh in darkness knoweth not whither he goeth. ³⁶While ye have light, believe in the light, that ye may be the children of light.'

These things spake Jesus, and departed, and did hide Himself from them. ³⁷But though He had done so many miracles before them, yet they believed not on Him. ³⁸That the saying of Isaiah the prophet might be fulfilled, which he spake:

Lord, who hath believed our report?
And to whom hath the arm of the Lord been revealed?

³⁹Therefore they could not believe, because that Isaiah said again:

John xii. 20–43 (*contd.*)

> [40]*He hath blinded their eyes,*
> *And hardened their heart;*
> *That they should not see with their eyes, nor understand with their*
> *heart, and be converted,*
> *And I should heal them.*

[41]These things said Isaiah when he saw His glory, and spake of Him. [42]Nevertheless among the chief rulers also many believed on Him; but because of the Pharisees they did not confess Him, lest they should be put out of the synagogue: [43]for they loved the praise of men more than the praise of God.

Mark ii. 21–22

[21]'No man also seweth a piece of new cloth on an old garment: else the new piece that filled it up taketh away from the old, and the rent is made worse. [22]And no man putteth new wine into old wine-skins: else the new wine doth burst the wine-skins, and the wine is spilled, and the wine-skins will be marred: but new wine must be put into new wine-skins.'

Matthew ix. 16–17

[16]'No man putteth a piece of new cloth unto an old garment, for that which is put in to fill it up taketh from the garment, and the rent is made worse. [17]Neither do men put new wine into old wine-skins: else the skins break, and the wine runneth out, and the skins perish: but they put new wine into new wine-skins, and both are preserved.'

Luke v. 36–39

[36]And He spake also a parable unto them: 'No man putteth a piece of a new garment upon an old; if otherwise, then both the new maketh a rent, and the piece that was taken out of the new agreeth not with the old. [37]And no man putteth new wine into old wine-skins; else the new wine will burst the wine-skins, and be spilled, and the wine-skins shall perish. [38]But new wine must be put into new wine-skins; and both are preserved. [39]No man also having drunk old wine straightway desireth new: for he saith, The old is better.'

John x. 1–20

[1]'Verily, verily, I say unto you, he that entereth not by the door into the sheep-fold, but climbeth up some other way, the same is a thief and a robber. [2]But he that entereth in by the door is the Shepherd of the sheep. [3]To Him the porter openeth; and the sheep hear His voice: and He calleth His own sheep by name, and leadeth them out. [4]And when He putteth forth His own sheep, He goeth before them, and the sheep follow Him: for they know His voice. [5]And a stranger will they not follow, but will flee from him: for they know not the voice of strangers.' [6]This parable spake Jesus unto them, but they understood not what things they were which He spake unto them.

[7]Then said Jesus unto them again: 'Verily, verily, I say unto you, I am the door of the sheep. [8]All that ever came before Me are thieves and robbers: but

John x. 1–20 (*contd.*)

the sheep did not hear them. ⁹I am the door: by Me, if any man enter in, he shall be saved, and shall go in and out, and find pasture. ¹⁰The thief cometh not, but for to steal, and to kill, and to destroy: I am come that they might have life, and that they might have it more abundantly. ¹¹I am the Good Shepherd: the Good Shepherd giveth His life for the sheep. ¹²But he that is an hireling, and not the shepherd, whose own the sheep are not, seeth the wolf coming, and leaveth the sheep, and fleeth: and the wolf catcheth them, and scattereth the sheep. ¹³The hireling fleeth, because he is an hireling, and careth not for the sheep. ¹⁴I am the Good Shepherd, and know My sheep, and am known of Mine. ¹⁵As the Father knoweth Me, even so know I the Father: and I lay down My life for the sheep. ¹⁶And other sheep I have, which are not of this fold: them also I must bring, and they shall hear My voice; and there shall be one flock, and one Shepherd. ¹⁷Therefore doth My Father love Me, because I lay down My life, that I might take it again. ¹⁸No man taketh it from Me, but I lay it down of Myself. I have power to lay it down, and I have power to take it again. This commandment have I received of My Father.'

¹⁹There was division therefore again among the Jews for these sayings. ²⁰And many of them said: 'He hath a devil and is mad; why hear ye Him?'

Luke xii. 32

Fear not, little flock; for it is your Father's good pleasure to give you the kingdom.

(*a*) Though the 'Grecians' of *John* xii. 20 were, in fact, Greek-speaking Jews of the Dispersal—called 'Grecians' in *Acts* ix. 29—they are here represented as Gentile Greeks, like Paul's converts of *Acts* xvii. 4. The editor of *John* does not doubt that Jesus felt great satisfaction when the Gentiles first showed interest in his message; he even improves on the occasion by reporting thunderous approbation from Heaven, not mentioned in the Synoptics. Yet his account of the interview and of its outcome is extremely confused: no Greeks show up for conversion; in verse 34, attention has shifted to 'the people'; in verse 35, Jesus hides himself; and verse 42 is an irrelevant denunciation of the Pharisees. An essential passage seems to have been suppressed, probably Jesus's rebuff to the Grecians. Only the first three verses read authentically. The editor of *John* x. 22 has suppressed Philip's reason for consulting Andrew, the only other Apostle with a Greek name: namely to propose that they should act as interpreters for Jesus who knew only Aramaic and Hebrew. Philip's fluency in Greek is suggested by his conversion of the Ethiopian eunuch, who will almost certainly have been reading *Isaiah* in the Septuagint translation (*Acts* viii. 36-40).

(285) *Now, certain Grecians, coming up from Egypt to keep the Feast of Dedication, saluted Philip, which understood their speech, and said unto him: 'Sir, we would converse with thy master Jesus.'*

Wherefore Philip sought out Andrew, and together they told Jesus of the matter, and undertook to interpret unto him whatever words the Grecians might speak.

*   *   *   *   *

(*b*) A collage of miscellaneous borrowings has replaced the missing passage. The sense of *John* xii. 24 is found in 1 *Corinthians* xv. 36, the phrasing in Simon Magus's *Great Announcement* (*see Introduction* III.*v*); verse 25 appears in several different contexts (*Mark* viii. 35, *Matthew* x. 39 and xvi. 25, *Luke* ix. 24 and xvii. 33—*see* CI.*b and i*); verse 26 anticipates *John* xiv. 3 (*see* CVI.*w*) and *John* xvi. 24 (*see* XXVII.*j*); verse 27 is borrowed from the Passion narrative as reported in *Matthew* xxvi. 38–39 (*see* CVII.*d*) and verses 28 and 29 from the Transfiguration (*Mark* ix. 7 and *Matthew* xvii. 5—*see* LXXIX.*e*), or from the Coronation (*Mark* i. 11 and *Matthew* iii. 17—*see* VIII.*a*); verse 30 repeats *John* xi. 42 (*see* LXXXVII.*c*); verse 31 is paralleled in *John* xvi. 11 (*see* CXVII.*k*)—its proper context is the Passion narrative (*see* CVII.*l*); verse 32 repeats *John* iii. 14 (*see* LXXXIII.*j*); verse 33 anticipates *John* xviii. 32 (*see* CX.*d*); verses 35 and 36*a* add nothing to *John* viii. 12, ix. 5 and xi. 10 (*see* XXIV.*c and* LXXII.*d*); in verse 36*b*, Jesus again hides himself, as in *John* viii. 59 (*see* XCV.*g*) or *Luke* iv. 30 (*see* XXXVII.*f*); verses 37 to 41 are borrowed from the very different context of *Matthew* xiii. 14 (*see* XXV.*b*). For verse 42, *see* XL.*e and* CXVII.*p*.

(*c*) The gist of the Grecians' original interview with Jesus can, however, be recovered from unexplained passages found elsewhere in the Gospels. The first is his parable of the New Patch and the New Wine (*Mark* ii. 21–22, *Matthew* ix. 16–17 and *Luke* v. 36–39). In the Synoptics, these follow Jesus's reply when asked why his disciples do not fast like John the Baptist's: namely, that bridemen are excused fasting at a wedding feast (*see* VIII.*o*). They will have been found in a collection of Oracles under the subject-heading 'On the Drinking of Wine'.

If the 'Grecians' were Alexandrian Jews who tried to interest Jesus in Philo's attempt to reconcile the Mosaic Law with Platonic philosophy, he may well have spoken these parables in disapproval.

> (286) *And Jesus spake to the twain, saying: 'Let them come before me.'*
>
> *And when the Grecians had saluted him, they said unto Jesus: 'Master, we are disciples of that Philo which, for the greater glory of God, seeketh to reconcile unto the Law the wisdom of the learned Greek Plato.'*
>
> *Jesus answered and said: 'No good can proceed therefrom.'*
>
> *They ask him: 'Art thou then more learned than our master Philo?'*
>
> *And Jesus spake a parable unto them, saying: 'No wise man putteth a piece of new cloth upon an old garment; lest the new agree not with the old, but take away from it and make a rent.*
>
> *'Moreover, a good garment lasteth all the years of a man's life.*
>
> *'Likewise no wise man putteth new wine into old wine-skins, lest it burst them, and be spilled, and the wine-skins shall perish.*
>
> *'But old wine abideth in old wine-skins, and groweth better with age.*

'For which of you that hath drunk old wine straightway desireth new? Will he not say: "The old is better"?'

* * * * *

(d) *Luke's* version is the most trustworthy: it retains the preference for old wine (*Luke* v. 39) and does not suggest, as do *Matthew* and *Mark,* that the garment was torn before being patched. These changes in *Matthew* and *Mark* seem to have been made by a Pauline editor who understood the new wine as the new spirit which was to descend upon the Twelve at the Feast of Pentecost—'These men are full of new wine' (*Acts* ii. 13); and the new patch as the doctrine of 'Christ crucified', which did not agree with Judaism. The preference for old wine will have been paralleled by a preference for old clothes—worn by the Essenes until they fell to pieces (*see* LVII.*i*)—which has been suppressed under Pauline influence (2 *Corinthians* viii. 20–21—*see* (g) *below*).

(e) If the Grecians then asked Jesus whether God might not bestow wisdom on the heathen also, citing the case of King Hiram (*Antiquities* viii. 2. 6–8 and *Against Apion* i. 18–19), he may well have replied with a text now buried in the rhetoric of *John* x. 1–20.

> (287) *And the Grecians asked Jesus again: 'But shall God never bestow wisdom on a man that is an heathen such as Plato was? Is it not written that Hiram King of Tyre conversed on high things with Solomon the Wise, and equalled him in understanding?'*

* * * * *

John x. 1–5 reads authentically, but in verse 7 Jesus could never have boasted that he was the Door of Salvation; Jerusalem was so described in *Micah* i. 9, because it was God's seat and the repository of His Law. The pronouncement is a *midrash* on *Psalm* xxiv. 7, since Jesus will have held, with the Pharisees, that every letter of the Law came from God (*Baba Bathra* 15a); that God Himself read it (*Abodah Zarah* 3b); that it had existed in His mind 947 generations before the Creation; that He wept over those who neglected to study it when they might (*Hagigah* 5b); and that a single day so devoted outweighed a thousand sacrifices (*Shabbath* 30a). According to *Midrash Tehilim* 118–119 on *Psalm* c. 4 and cxviii. 19, 'the gate of the Lord into which the righteous shall enter' was the gate to the Kingdom of God, namely the New Jerusalem; and only the Law gave access to the Kingdom. This was the true Law, its every letter numbered by the scribes, which was jealously preserved at Jerusalem in the original Hebrew and correctly expounded by the Pharisees; not the Law as translated into Greek by the Seventy-two Scholars of Pharos—an event deplored among pious Israelites: 'The day when the Law was translated has proved as ill a day for us as that whereon the golden calf was fashioned' (*Sopherim* i. 8–9, ed. Higger)—and put to evil use by Greek philosophers and magicians.

(*f*) In *John* x. 8, a Pauline editor makes Jesus recklessly dismiss the Hebrew prophets and law-givers as 'thieves and robbers', and in verse 9 announce that none can be saved except through faith in himself (*see Introduction* II.*u*). Though in *Matthew* xix. 17 he denies that he is good (*see* LXXXII.*c*), he twice calls himself the 'Good Shepherd' in *John* x. 10—an interpolation designed to obscure his self-identification with the Worthless Shepherd of *Zechariah* xi. and xiii. (*see* CII.*j*). At this point in the original, Jesus will have quoted *Ezekiel* xxxiv. 31–32, held to be a Messianic prophecy, and also *Psalm* xxiii. 1–3.

(*g*) *John* x. 11–13 is acceptable only if a context can be found in which Jesus met with a 'hireling shepherd', that is to say, a preacher who thought more of gain than of his message. But even Judas was unmercenary in his betrayal (*see* CV.*c and f, and* CXII.*a*), and Jesus cannot have been attacking the Sadducees—who were endowed priests, as distinct from the Pharisaic lay-preachers. Though regarding them as lost souls, he admitted their right to collect the Sanctuary tax (*Matthew* xvii. 27—*see* XLVIII.*d*). This passage may have been borrowed from an early Christian polemic against Paul, on the lines of *Acts* viii. 9–24 (*see Introduction* III.*q–t*) and xiii. 8–11 (*see* XL.*g footnote*). Paul, whose establishment of a weekly Church collection (1 *Corinthians* xvi. 2) proves his business acumen, was a hireling when he defrayed his travelling expenses from these funds, using them for the support of a respectable appearance (2 *Corinthians* viii. 20–21)—and even, it may have been, for the purchase of his Roman citizenship (*see Introduction* II.*y*). The hireling's flight (*John* x. 12) will have referred to his cowardly appeal to Caesar (*Acts* xxv. 11—*see Introduction* II.*y and* CXIX.*f*). For verses 14–18, see LXXXIV.*d and f.*

Luke xii. 32 forms part of Jesus's argument.

(288) *Jesus answered, and said: 'Jerusalem is the gate to salvation, whereby the Anointed Son of David shall lead in the chosen ones.*

'As David saith in a psalm: "Lift up your heads, O ye gates, and be ye lift up, ye everlasting doors, for the King of Glory shall come in!"

'And Micah likewise prophesied, saying: "He is come unto the gate of My people, even unto Jerusalem."

'Verily, I say unto you: he that seeketh to enter into this Kingdom not by the gate of the sheepfold, but climbing up some other way, the same is as a thief and a robber!'

And they asked Jesus: 'Wherefore sayest thou this?'

He answered: 'Ezekiel prophesied in the name of the Lord, saying: "I shall set up one shepherd, even My servant David, over My flock, even the House of Israel; and he shall feed them, and they shall be no more a prey to the heathen."

'How then shall David feed the flock, except it be with the Law of God, which is published in Jerusalem? Shall he feed them with the vanities of Egypt?

'Go to! For the shepherd of the sheep entereth in by the gate, and the

porter openeth unto him. He calleth his sheep by name and they know his voice, and he leadeth them out to water and to pasture.

'But a stranger will they not follow, for they know not his voice.'

They said: 'With our master Philo we have drunk deep waters.'

Jesus answered: 'Well said Ezekiel the prophet: "Doth it seem a small thing to you to have drunk deep waters, but ye must foul the residue with your feet?" '

*   *   *   *   *

In *John* x. 19–20, part of the sequel has been confused with the accusation, made in Galilee, that Jesus cast out devils by the power of Beelzebub (*see* xxxiv.*c*).

(289) *And there was a division among the Grecians because of these words. Some said: 'He hath reasoned well,' but the disciples of Philo: 'He is mad.'*

And Jesus arose, and left them, and he said unto the Twelve: 'Fear not, little flock; if ye hearken unto the voice of the Shepherd of shepherds, it will please Him to lead you unto His Kingdom.

'For David testified in a psalm: "The Lord is my shepherd, I shall not want. He maketh me to lie down in green pastures, he leadeth me beside the still waters. He restoreth my soul." '

*   *   *   *   *

(*h*) The Nazarenes, like the Pharisees, rejected neo-Platonic philosophy, which began to influence Gentile Christian doctrine at Rome, and in the Churches of Greece and Asia Minor, only after Bar Cochba's defeat in 132 A.D., when *John* was grudgingly admitted into the Canon. Papias (120–130 A.D.), Basilides (117–138 A.D.), Hermas (114–156 A.D.), and even Justin Martyr (145–149 A.D.), did not accept *John* as authoritative scripture.

*   *   *   *   *

LXXXII

THE RICH YOUTH

Mark x. 17–31

17And when He was gone forth into the way, there came one running, and kneeled to Him, and asked Him: 'Good Master, what shall I do that I may inherit eternal life?'

18And Jesus said unto him: 'Why callest thou Me good? there is none good but one, that is, God. 19Thou knowest the commandments,

Do not commit adultery,
Do not kill,
Do not steal,
Do not bear false witness,
Defraud not,
Honour thy father and mother.'

20And he answered and said unto Him: 'Master, all these have I observed from my youth.'

21Then Jesus beholding him, loved him, and said unto him: 'One thing thou lackest: go thy way, sell whatsoever thou hast, and give to the poor, and thou shalt have treasure in heaven: and come, take up the cross, and follow Me.' 22And he was sad at that saying, and went away grieved: for he had great possessions. 23And Jesus looked round about, and saith unto His disciples: 'How hardly shall they that have riches enter into the kingdom of God!'

24And the disciples were astonished at His words. But Jesus answereth again, and saith unto them: 'Children, how hard is it for them that trust in riches to enter into the kingdom of God! 25It is easier for a camel to go through the eye of a needle, than for a rich man to enter into the kingdom of God.' 26And they were astonished out of measure, saying among themselves, Who then can be saved? 27And Jesus looking upon them saith: 'With men it is impossible, but not with God: for with God all things are possible.'

28Then Peter began to say unto Him: 'Lo, we have left all, and have followed Thee.' 29And Jesus answered and said: 'Verily I say unto you, there is no man that hath left house, or brethren, or sisters, or father, or mother, or wife, or children, or lands, for My sake, and the Gospel's, 30but he shall receive an hundredfold now in this time, houses, and brethren, and sisters, and mothers, and children, and lands, with persecutions; and in the world to come eternal life. 31But many that are first shall be last; and the last first.'

Mark xii. 28–34

²⁸And one of the scribes came, and having heard them reasoning together, and perceiving that He had answered them well, asked Him: 'Which is the first commandment of all?' ²⁹Jesus answered him: 'The first of all the commandments is,

> Hear, O Israel; The Lord our God is one Lord:
> ³⁰Thou shalt love the Lord thy God with all thy heart,
> And with all thy soul, and with all thy mind, and with all thy strength:

This is the first commandment. ³¹And the second is like, namely this,

> Thou shalt love thy neighbour as thyself.

There is none other commandment greater than these.' ³²And the scribe said unto Him: 'Well, Master, Thou hast said the truth: for there is one God; and there is none other but He: ³³and to love Him with all the heart, and with all the understanding, and with all the soul, and with all the strength, and to love his neighbour as himself, is more than all whole burnt offerings and sacrifices.' ³⁴And when Jesus saw that he answered discreetly, He said unto him: 'Thou art not far from the kingdom of God.' And no man after that durst ask Him any question.

Matthew xix. 16–30

¹⁶And, behold, one came and said unto Him: 'Good Master, what good thing shall I do, that I may have eternal life?' ¹⁷And He said unto him: 'Why askest thou me to tell thee what is good? there is none good but One: but if thou wilt enter into life, keep the commandments.' ¹⁸He saith unto Him, Which? Jesus said:

> Thou shalt do no murder,
> Thou shalt not commit adultery,
> Thou shalt not steal,
> Thou shalt not bear false witness,
> ¹⁹Honour thy father and thy mother;
> And, Thou shalt love thy neighbour as thyself.

²⁰The young man saith unto Him: 'All these things have I kept from my youth up: what lack I yet?' ²¹Jesus said unto him: 'If thou wilt be perfect, go and sell that thou hast, and give to the poor, and thou shalt have treasure in heaven: and come and follow Me.' ²²But when the young man heard that saying, he went away sorrowful: for he had great possessions.

²³Then said Jesus unto His disciples: 'Verily I say unto you, that a rich man shall hardly enter into the Kingdom of Heaven. ²⁴And again I say unto you, it is easier for a camel to go through the eye of a needle, than for a rich man to enter into the kingdom of God.' ²⁵When His disciples heard it, they were exceedingly amazed, saying, 'Who then can be saved?' ²⁶But Jesus beheld them, and said unto them: 'With men this is impossible; but with God all things are possible.'

²⁷Then answered Peter and said unto Him: 'Behold, we have forsaken all, and followed Thee; what shall we have therefore?' ²⁸And Jesus said unto them: 'Verily I say unto you, that ye which have followed Me, in the regen-

Matthew xix. 16–30 (contd.)

eration when the Son of Man shall sit in the throne of His glory, ye also shall sit upon twelve thrones, judging the twelve tribes of Israel. ²⁹And every one that hath forsaken houses, or brethren, or sisters, or father, or mother, or wife, or children, or lands, for My name's sake, shall receive an hundredfold, and shall inherit everlasting life. ³⁰But many that are first shall be last; and the last shall be first.'

Luke xviii. 18–30

¹⁸And a certain ruler asked Him, saying: 'Good Master, what shall I do to inherit eternal life?' ¹⁹And Jesus said unto him: 'Why callest thou Me good? none is good, save One, that is God. ²⁰Thou knowest the commandments,

> *Do not commit adultery,*
> *Do not kill,*
> *Do not steal,*
> *Do not bear false witness,*
> *Honour thy father and thy mother.'*

²¹And he said: 'All these have I kept from my youth up.' ²²Now when Jesus heard these things, He said unto him: 'Yet lackest thou one thing: sell all that thou hast and distribute unto the poor, and thou shalt have treasure in heaven, and come, follow Me.' ²³And when he heard this, he was very sorrowful: for he was very rich. ²⁴And when Jesus saw that he was very sorrowful, He said: 'How hardly shall they that have riches enter into the kingdom of God. ²⁵For it is easier for a camel to go through a needle's eye, than for a rich man to enter into the kingdom of God.' ²⁶And they that heard it said: 'Who then can be saved?' ²⁷And He said: 'The things which are impossible with men are possible with God.'

²⁸Then Peter said: 'Lo, we have left all, and followed Thee.' ²⁹And He said unto them: 'Verily I say unto you, there is no man that hath left house, or parents, or brethren, or wife, or children, for the kingdom of God's sake, ³⁰who shall not receive manifold more in this present time, and in the world to come life everlasting.'

Luke xvi. 19–31

¹⁹'There was a certain rich man, which was clothed in purple and fine linen, and fared sumptuously every day: ²⁰and there was a certain beggar named Lazarus, which was laid at his gate, full of sores, ²¹and desiring to be fed with the crumbs which fell from the rich man's table: moreover the dogs came and licked his sores. ²²And it came to pass, that the beggar died, and was carried by the angels into Abraham's bosom: the rich man also died, and was buried: ²³and in hell he lifted up his eyes, being in torments, and seeth Abraham afar off, and Lazarus in his bosom. ²⁴And he cried and said, Father Abraham, have mercy on me, and send Lazarus that he may dip the tip of his finger in water, and cool my tongue; for I am tormented in this flame. ²⁵But Abraham said, Son, remember that thou in thy lifetime receivedst thy good things, and likewise Lazarus evil things: but now he is comforted, and

Luke xvi. 19–31 (*contd.*)

thou art tormented. [26]And beside all this, between us and you there is a great gulf fixed: so that they which would pass from hence to you cannot: neither can they pass to us, that would come from thence. [27]Then he said, I pray thee therefore, father, that thou wouldest send him to my father's house: [28]for I have five brethren; that he may testify unto them, lest they also come into this place of torment. [29]Abraham saith unto him, They have Moses and the prophets: let them hear them. [30]And he said, Nay, father Abraham: but if one went unto them from the dead, they will repent. [31]And he said unto him, If they hear not Moses and the prophets, neither will they be persuaded, though one rose from the dead.'

Matthew xxii. 34–40

[34]But when the Pharisees had heard that He had put the Sadducees to silence, they were gathered together. [35]Then one of them, who was a lawyer, asked Him a question, tempting Him, and saying: [36]'Master, which is the great commandment in the law?' [37]Jesus said unto him:

'Thou shalt love the Lord thy God with all thy heart, and with all thy soul, and with all thy mind.

[38]This is the first and great commandment. [39]And the second is like unto it,

Thou shalt love thy neighbour as thyself.

[40]On these two commandments hang all the law and the prophets.'

Luke x. 25–37

[25]And, behold, a certain lawyer stood up, and tempted Him, saying: 'Master, what shall I do to inherit eternal life?' [26]He said unto him: 'What is written in the law? how readest thou?' [27]And he answering said:

'Thou shalt love the Lord thy God with all thy heart, and with all thy soul, and with all thy strength, and with all thy mind;
And thy neighbour as thyself.'

[28]And He said unto him: 'Thou hast answered right: this do, and thou shalt live.' [29]But he, willing to justify himself, said unto Jesus: 'And who is my neighbour?' [30]And Jesus answering said: 'A certain man went down from Jerusalem to Jericho, and fell among thieves, which stripped him of his raiment, and wounded him, and departed, leaving him half-dead. [31]And by chance there came down a certain priest that way: and when he saw him, he passed by on the other side. [32]And likewise a Levite, when he was at the place, came and looked on him, and passed by on the other side. [33]But a certain Samaritan, as he journeyed, came where he was: and when he saw him, he had compassion on him, [34]and went to him, and bound up his wounds, pouring in oil and wine, and set him on his own beast, and brought him to an inn, and took care of him. [35]And on the morrow when he departed, he took out two pence, and gave them to the host, and said unto him, Take care of him; and whatsoever thou spendest more, when I come again,

Luke x. 25–37 (*contd.*)

> I will repay thee. [36]Which now of these three, thinkest thou, was neighbour unto him that fell among the thieves?' [37]And he said: 'He that shewed mercy on him.' Then said Jesus unto him: 'Go, and do thou likewise.'

Acts xx. 35

> [35]I have shewed you all things, how that so labouring ye ought to support the weak, and to remember the words of the Lord Jesus, how He said, 'It is more blessed to give than to receive.'

(*a*) The Synoptics all report the story of the Rich Young Man in much the same words (*Mark* x. 17–31, *Matthew* xii. 28–34 and *Luke* xviii. 18–30), though *Luke* xviii. 18 makes him a 'ruler', that is to say, a member of a patrician family, and *Mark* x. 21 tells how Jesus felt a sudden love for him.

Hugh Schonfield, in the first chapter of his *Saints Against Caesar,* suggests that the parable of Dives ('the rich man') and Lazarus was spoken to the same person. Citing the *Gospel according to the Hebrews* (*see* LXXXIII.*h*), he identifies him with 'the disciple whom Jesus loved' who was known to the High Priest and entered his house freely (*John* xviii. 15—*see* CVIII.*a and i*), and to whose care—but this is an error—Jesus is said to have commended his mother from the Cross (*John* xix. 26–27—*see* VIII.*i*). Schonfield argues plausibly that this disciple was John (Johanan), a son of the High Priest Annas (*Acts* iv. 6). Like Dives, he had five brothers, all of them in turn High Priests and, according to Eusebius (*Ecc. Hist.* iii. 31. 2–3), became a Christian martyr:

> 'Moreover, John, he who rested on the bosom of the Lord and had been a priest wearing the sacred breastplate' [*the golden frontlet worn only by the High Priest—Schonfield understands from this that John had deputized for the High Priest on some occasion*] 'both a martyr and teacher, has died at Ephesus.'[*]

(*b*) He may be further identified with Papias's 'the elder John'—'elder' being used by Papias not as an honorific, but to distinguish John son of Annas from his junior, John son of Zebedee. Eusebius quotes Papias's exact words in *Ecc. Hist.* iii. 39. 4:

> 'I [Papias, when a young man, at the close of the first century A.D.] enquired into the words of the elders: what Andrew, Peter, Philip, Thomas, John, or Matthew or any other of the Lord's [no longer living] disciples had said; and what Aristion and the elder John, the Lord's [surviving] disciples were saying.'

But two rich men, not one, are particularized in the *Gospel according to the Hebrews.* For the second, *see* LXXXIII.*a–k.*

(*c*) In most manuscripts of *Matthew* xix. 17, the editor has tried to divert at-

---

* Eisler in *The Enigma of the Fourth Gospel,* x–xi, also identifies the beloved disciple with John son of Annas, but holds that John was another name for Annas's son Theophilus.

tention from Jesus's crucial saying: 'Why callest thou me good? None is good but God', preserved in *Mark* x. 18 and *Luke* xviii. 19. He realizes that this cuts at the roots of the Gentile Christian conception of Jesus as God.

Mark x. 21: 'Take up thy cross and follow me!'—though interpreted by the Church as a prophecy of John son of Zebedee's eventual martyrdom—will have referred to the pre-Christian *tau* marked on the brow of the elect (*see* XIII.*d and* CI.*a*) and meant: 'Dedicate yourself to God!'

Luke xviii. 24: 'They that have riches', has been softened in *Mark* x. 24 to: 'Them that trust in riches'.

'For my sake' in *Mark* x. 29 should read 'for God's sake'; and the 'persecutions' in verse 30 are a late addition.

(*d*) Jesus had no power to promise the disciples that they should sit on twelve thrones and judge the tribes of Israel (*Matthew* xix. 28). This must be an interpolation (*see* LXII.*b*); besides, the editor appears to have forgotten that Judas was still one of the Twelve.

For *Matthew* xix. 30, paralleled in *Mark* x. 31, *Luke* xiii. 30 and *Matthew* xx. 16, *see* LVIII.*a* and LXIX.*d*.

According to *Mark* x. 30 and *Luke* xviii. 30, the disciples are told to expect good things in this world too; but according to *Matthew* xix. 28–29, Jesus reserves his promises for the next.

(*e*) The metaphor of the needle's eye was used facetiously in the third century during a Rabbinic dispute (*Baba Mezi'a* 38*b*) : whether the nearest male relative of a man held captive in foreign parts might legally enter and administer his estate. Rabbi Shesheth of the Babylonian Academy decided that he could not. Then Rabbi Amram of Pumpeditha Academy asked: 'If he may not administer the estate, may he sell it?' To which Shesheth retorted: 'Are you not from Pumpeditha, where they draw elephants though a needle's eye?' Whether Jesus's metaphor had, by this time, gained proverbial force, or whether it was of still earlier coinage and quoted by Jesus himself, cannot be determined. It has been plausibly suggested that he had in mind a narrow gate at Jerusalem, called 'The Needle's Eye'—through which a camel could squeeze only after its panniers were removed—and was not speaking in hyperbole (*see* LXXXIII.*g*).

The difficulty of being rich as well as righteous had been appreciated several generations before Jesus's time. 'Happy is the rich man that is found blameless and that hath not gone astray after riches' (*Ecclesiasticus* xxxi. 8). But 'the needle's eye' had a secondary meaning: the chink of repentance which God could enlarge to a broad highway (*see* XLIII.*a*).

(*f*) The disciples' question: 'Who then can be saved?', and Jesus's answer: 'With God all things are possible!' *Mark* x. 26–27, *Matthew* xix. 25–26 and *Luke* xviii. 26–27), cannot belong to this context. If poverty had been the chief qualification for entering Heaven, they would not have wondered how God would find a sufficiency of saints; Jerusalem contained thousands of poor, and the disciples themselves were dedicated to poverty (*see* LVII.*c*). But their question, like Jesus's reply, which suggests a *midrash* on *Zechariah* viii. 6, reads authentically; though both seem to have been fitted into this context to restrain Gentile Christians from taking Jesus's advice too literally and giving away all their possessions without regard for their families' needs. This was a real danger, as is proved by an enactment of the second-century Pharisaic Synod of Usha—aimed at Essenes, Ebionites, and the like—according to which no one might give away more than a fifth of his possessions, lest he became a burden on the community (*Kethuboth* 50a).

Mark x. 24: 'Who trust in their riches', has been interpolated as a reassurance to wealthy Christians that prayer, faith, and good works *may* enable a rich man to enter the Kingdom.

The original dialogue probably referred to the difficulty of survival when God's fire fell from Heaven; and interrupted the so-called 'Little Apocalypse' in *Matthew* xxiv, where Jesus dwells on the horrors of the Last Days (*see* xcviii.*k and l*).

The proper context of the needle's eye metaphor (*Luke* xviii. 25), like Peter's boast 'Lord we have forsaken all!' (*Luke* xviii. 28), seems to be the story of 'Nicodemus' (*see* LXXXIII.*g and l*).

> (372) *And Peter, when he heard these things, asked Jesus: 'Who then can be saved, seeing that we be all sinners?'*
>
> *Jesus answered and said: 'Zechariah prophesied in the name of the Lord: "There shall yet dwell old women and old men in Jerusalem, and the streets shall be full of boys and girls playing.*
>
> *' "Thus saith the Lord of Hosts: 'Though it be a difficult thing in the eyes of the remnant of this people in these days, should it also be difficult in Mine eyes?' "*
>
> *'For with God all things are possible!'*

* * * * *

(g) In *Mark* x. 30 and *Matthew* xix. 29, the editors have clumsily sandwiched 'brethren, sisters, father, mother, wife, and children' between 'houses' and 'lands'. The houses, lands, and the hundredfold reward may belong either to this context or, more probably, to the similar one of Nicodemus's visit; but the mention of the various relatives, and of eternal life, makes sense only in the 'Suffer me first to bury my father' context (*see* LXXXV.*c*). The saying, as it stands, promises a man a hundred celestial bed-fellows in recompense for the earthly one he abandons.

Mark x. 19, *Matthew* xix. 18, and *Luke* xviii. 20 omit the earlier commandments of the Decalogue in an attempt to obscure Jesus's insistence on the Fourth, by which the Gentile Christians no longer felt bound.

> (152) *A rich young man, which was a priest, came hastily to Jesus, and said unto him: 'Good master, what shall I do to inherit everlasting life?'*
>
> *Jesus answered and said: 'Why callest thou me good? None is good save One, that is God!*

'And wherefore askest thou me how thou mayest be saved?

'Knowest thou not the Commandments: "Thou shalt have no God but God, and keep His sabbath, and honour thy parents, and swear no false oath, neither commit adultery or murder or theft, neither bear false witness, neither covet, but love thy neighbour as thyself"?'

He answered: 'All these have I observed from my youth, even as the Sages have expounded them.'

And Jesus, beholding him, loved him, and said: 'Then if thou wilt verily inherit everlasting life, sell all thou hast, give unto the needy, accept the cross of baptism, and joyfully take upon thyself the yoke of the Law.'

But the young man was grieved by these words; for he durst not obey, being of the High Priest's kindred.

* * * * *

(*h*) Here follows Paul's quotation from Jesus in *Acts* xx. 35:

(153) *And Jesus asked him, saying: 'Art thou then grieved? Is it not more blessed to give than to receive?'*

* * * * *

(*i*) *Luke* xvi. 22, 'in Abraham's bosom', suggests that Lazarus, after his death, was guest of honour at a banquet given by Abraham (*cf. John* xiii. 23—*see* cv.*a*). At the close of this parable, evidently addressed to a Sadducee, Jesus insists that obedience to the prophets, as well as the Law, is necessary for salvation. An interpolation would doubtless have been inserted here, stressing the need for belief in Jesus himself, had the editors not misunderstood Abraham's remark in *Luke* xvi. 31. But 'neither will they be persuaded, though one rose from the dead', merely discourages the hope that Lazarus would be able to convert Dives's family by appearing among them as a ghost and warning them of their errors; it is not a prophecy that the Jews as a whole will reject Jesus's message even after the Resurrection. Nor was *Luke* xvi. 29: 'They have Moses and the prophets', spoken in scorn, as is usually supposed.

(*j*) The story of Dives and Lazarus is paralleled in the Talmud. According to a *midrash* on *Ruth* i. 17—'The Lord do so to me and more also, if aught but death part thee and me'—a sinner, finding himself in Hell, complains to the gaolers that one of his former associates is in Paradise (*Ruth Rabbah* iii. 3):

'"We both committed robbery and murder; yet he is among the righteous, while I am here among the wicked."

'The gaolers answered: "Thy companion . . . repented of his evil ways; thou too hadst time to repent, yet didst not."

'He said: "Then suffer me now to go hence and repent."

'They answered: "Fool, knowest thou not that this world is like unto the Sabbath, and that the world from which thou hast come is like unto the day before the Sabbath? If a man prepareth not on the sixth day, what shall he eat on the seventh?"'

(154) *And Jesus spake a parable of the same rich young man:*

'There was a certain rich man, clothed in purple and fine linen, which fared sumptuously every day.

'And there was a certain beggar named Lazarus laid at his gate, full of sores and desiring to be fed with the crumbs which fell from the rich man's table. Moreover, the dogs came and licked his sores.

'And it came to pass that the beggar died, and was carried by the angels into Abraham's bosom.

'The rich man also died, and was buried. And in hell he lifted up his eyes, being in torments, and seeth Abraham afar off, and Lazarus in his bosom.

'And he cried and said: "Father Abraham, have mercy on me, and send Lazarus that he may dip the tip of his finger in water, and cool my tongue; for I am tormented in this flame."

'But Abraham said: "Son, remember that thou in thy lifetime didst receive thy good things, and likewise Lazarus evil things: but now he is comforted, and thou art tormented.

' "And beside all this, between us and you, there is a great gulf fixed. So that they which would pass from hence to you, cannot. Neither can they pass to us, that would come from thence."

'Then he said: "I pray thee therefore, father, that thou wouldest send him to my father's house. For I have five brethren; that he may testify unto them lest they also come into this place of torment."

'Abraham saith unto him: "They have Moses and the prophets. Let them hear them!"

'And he said: "Nay, father Abraham, but if one went unto them from the dead, they would repent."

'But Abraham said again: "If they hear not Moses and the prophets, neither will they be persuaded, though one rose from the dead." '

* * * * *

(*k*) The setting of the lawyer's question in *Luke* x. 25–37, and the question itself, are given differently in *Mark* xii. 28 and *Matthew* xxii. 34–40. According to these, Jesus is preaching in the Temple at Jerusalem; according to *Luke*, he is still in Galilee, and the lawyer's question is the one asked by the rich young man of *Matthew* xix. 16. Yet *Mark* xii. 28 and *Matthew* xxii. 36: 'Which is the great Commandment in the Law?' would have been too ingenuous a question for a lawyer to ask, especially if he wished to 'try' Jesus. (*l*) Jesus is here quoting the well-known story of Shammai, Hillel, and the rich young Gentile (*Shabbath* 31*a*), which makes it easy to restore the first part of the conversation. *Luke's* reason for equating the rich young Sadducee with the lawyer will have been that both incidents were found in a collection of Oracles under the subject-heading 'The Rich Young Man'. Hillel, however, did not quote *Deuteronomy* vi. 5 (a text contained in the *Shemā—see* xxvii.*a*) as well as *Leviticus* xix. 18; and neither will Jesus have done so. *Deuteronomy* vi. 5 must have been the lawyer's contribution.

(267) *Now, when a certain lawyer heard that Jesus preached unto the men of the land which were in Samaria, he said unto him:*

'Master, to expound the Law to an ignorant and unclean multitude is to labour in vain. Canst thou hope to teach them in one hour what the pious may hardly learn in a lifetime?'

Jesus answered and said: 'A certain rich young man, a scoffer from the Wicked Kingdom, desiring to try the sage Shammai, went unto him, and said: "I have no leisure to study the Law. Teach it me, I pray, while I stand upon one foot."

'And Shammai drove him thence with blows.

'But when he went unto the sage Hillel—blessed be his memory!—and asked the same thing of him, Hillel answered and said:

' "Do not to thy neighbour what is hateful unto thee! This is all the Law and the Prophets."

'For, verily, he that loveth his neighbour, the same likewise loveth his God.'

The lawyer, when he heard this, wishing to justify himself, said unto Jesus: 'Master, thou speakest the truth, which is known unto all: that there is one God, and none other than He.

'And it is written: "Thou shalt love the Lord thy God with all thine heart and with all thy soul and with all thy strength!"

'But who is my neighbour, and how shall I know him?'

* * * * *

(m) Here follows the parable of the Samaritan, tampered with by Simon Magus or one of his compatriots (*see Introduction* III.n *and* p). Jesus tells a Pharisaic parable, beginning: 'Once a Priest, a Levite, and a Son of Israel. . . .' The trio occur frequently in the Talmud: for instance, in *Sifra Ahre* xviii. 5 where, quoting 2 *Samuel* vii. 19 and *Isaiah* xxvi. 2, the commentator writes:

> ' . . . And we read in the Scripture: "This is the Law of man, O Lord God," not: "This is the Law of the Priest, the Levite, and the Son of Israel."
>
> 'And again we read: "Open ye the gates that the righteous nation which keepeth the truth may enter in!" not: "Open ye the gates that the Priest, the Levite, and the Son of Israel may enter in!" '

This type of parable seems to have been formalized, as in the familiar anecdotal pattern: 'An Englishman, an Irishman, and a Scot'—the Priest and the Levite, being Sadducees, invariably obey the letter of the Law, and thus offend against its spirit, whereas the Son of Israel (that is to say, the God-loving Pharisee), behaves with charitableness and moral integrity. 'A Priest, a Levite, and . . . a Samaritan', would have been as eccentric a beginning in Jesus's time, as: 'An Englishman, an Irishman, and . . . an Eskimo', would be in ours.

(n) Obviously, the Samaritan was the victim, not the deliverer. The Priest and the Levite refused to help him because of a long-standing feud between Jews and Samaritans, justifying themselves on the ground that he was ritually

unclean, since the Samaritan priesthood was non-Aaronic. But the Son of
Israel, the God-loving Pharisee, came to his aid. Though even more scrupulous not to defile himself, his conscience told him that 'Charity outweighs all
commandments' (*Tosephta Pe'ah* iv. 19), and that 'The poor of the Samaritans are like unto the poor of Israel', that is, entitled to the same consideration
(*Tosephta Pe'ah* iv. 1). The Samaritan, however deficient in religious education, obeyed the Law of Moses and was therefore a co-religionist and, if a
peasant, might well be of Israelite descent (*see* LXX.c–e).* The true Son of
Israel could even forgive the Samaritans their desecration of the Temple at
Passover, some twenty years previously, when they had thrown dead men's
bones in at the gates; though all Samaritans had been forbidden entry ever
since (*Antiquities* xviii. 2. 2).

Once this amendment is made, the rich young man's question: 'Who is my
neighbour whom I am commanded to love?' is logically answered with:
'Even a Samaritan, if he is in distress!' In *Luke* x. 36, however, Jesus is made
to withhold the answer by using 'neighbour' in the novel sense of 'benefactor'.
(*o*) It is ironical that, had the Samaritan been dead, both Priest and Levite
could have touched him without scruple. No Jew, not even the High Priest
(*Baba Kamma* 80b), was exempt from the law which obliged the first passer-
by to take up for burial a dead man found on the highway (*Nazir* 43b).
Josephus (*Against Apion* ii. 29) credits Moses with this law, thus showing
that it was a very early oral tradition. In *Nazir* vii. 1, a moral case is argued
which recalls Jesus's parable: if a High Priest (who must be protected from
defilement by every possible means) travelled with a Nazirite (whose vows
prevented him from touching any corpse, even that of his own father or
mother—*Numbers* vi. 7) and they simultaneously saw a corpse on the road,
which of them should lift it up on his beast—assuming that only one person
was needed for the task?

> (268) *Jesus answered and said: 'A certain Samaritan journeyed to Jericho,
> and on his way he fell among thieves, which stripped him and departed,
> leaving him half dead.*
>
> *'And he cried for help in God's name unto them that passed by.*
>
> *'And by chance there came down that way a priest from Jerusalem, and
> heard his cries but, when he knew him for a Samaritan, passed by on the
> other side, fearing defilement.*
>
> *'Likewise a Levite came where he lay, and stood looking at him, but when
> he knew him for a Samaritan, and perceived that there was yet life in him,
> he too went his way, fearing defilement.*
>
> *'But a righteous Son of Israel, when he heard the man, how he cried out
> for help in God's name, took compassion on him, and feared not to be defiled.*
>
> *'Nay, but he dressed the man's wounds with oil and wine, and bound them
> up, and set him on his own beast and brought him to an inn, and took care
> of him.*

* Rabbi Meir derived the word *Samaria* from *Shimron*, the fourth son of Issachar (*Genesis*
xlvi. 13), thus allowing the Samaritans Israelite descent (*Genesis Rabbah* xciv. 7).

'And on the morrow, when he departed, he gave two pence unto the host, and said: "Take care of him that fell among thieves, and whatsoever thou spendest more, when I come again I will repay thee.

'"For the same is my neighbour, because that when he was in trouble, he cried unto the One God which I also worship."'

* * * * *

(269) *And Jesus saith unto the lawyer: 'Now, which of these three thinkest thou did right? The twain that feared defilement, or the other?'*

The lawyer answered: 'Assuredly he did right that shewed mercy unto his neighbour.'

Then said Jesus unto him: 'Go, and do thou likewise!'

* * * * *

(*p*) Jesus is inviting the lawyer to join him in his missionary work among the Samaritan peasantry: the lost sheep of the House of Israel who, in a spiritual sense, have been stripped, robbed, and left nearly dead by their alien overlords (*see* LXX.*c*).

Mark xii. 34: 'And no man after that durst ask him any questions', is not made good; several others are, in fact, asked him. Its proper context is perhaps the dispute about the Superscription (*see* CXI.*e*).

* * * * *

LXXXIII

NICODEMUS

John ii. 23–25

[23]Now when He was in Jerusalem at the passover, in the feast day, many believed in His name, when they saw the miracles which He did. [24]But Jesus did not commit Himself unto them, because He knew all men, [25]and needed not that any should testify of man: for He knew what was in man.

John iii. 1–15

[1]There was a man of the Pharisees, named Nicodemus, a ruler of the Jews: [2]the same came to Jesus by night, and said unto Him: 'Rabbi, we know that Thou art a teacher come from God: for no man can do these miracles that Thou doest, except God be with him.' [3]Jesus answered and said unto him: 'Verily, verily, I say unto thee, except a man be born again, he cannot see the kingdom of God.' [4]Nicodemus saith unto Him: 'How can a man be born when he is old? can he enter the second time into his mother's womb, and be born?' [5]Jesus answered: 'Verily, verily, I say unto thee, except a man be born of water and of the Spirit he cannot enter into the kingdom of God. [6]That which is born of the flesh is flesh: and that which is born of the Spirit is spirit. [7]Marvel not that I said unto thee, ye must be born again. [8]The wind bloweth where it listeth, and thou hearest the sound thereof, but canst not tell whence it cometh, and whither it goeth: so is every one that is born of the Spirit.' [9]Nicodemus answered and said unto Him: 'How can these things be?' [10]Jesus answered and said unto him: 'Art thou a master of Israel, and knowest not these things? [11]Verily, verily, I say unto thee, We speak that We do know, and testify that We have seen; and ye receive not our witness. [12]If I have told you earthly things, and ye believe not, how shall ye believe, if I tell you of heavenly things? [13]And no man hath ascended up to heaven, but He that came down from heaven, even the Son of Man Which is in heaven. [14]And as Moses lifted up the serpent in the wilderness, even so must the Son of Man be lifted up: [15] that whosoever believeth in Him should not perish, but have eternal life.'

Origen: On Matthew xix. 16–22

It is written in a certain Gospel which is called *According to the Hebrews* ... that the second of the rich men said unto Jesus: 'Master, what good thing can I do and live?' He answered: 'O man, fulfil the Law and the prophets.'

He answered: 'I have kept them.' Jesus said: 'Go sell all that thou ownest and distribute it to the poor and come, follow me.'

But the rich man began to scratch his head and it pleased him not.

Origen: **On Matthew xix. 16–22** (*contd.*)

·　　And the Lord said to him: 'How sayest thou "I have kept the Law and the prophets"? For it is written in the Law "Thou shalt love thy neighbour as thyself" and lo, many of the brethren, sons of Abraham, are clad in dung and perish for hunger, and thine house is full of many good things, and nothing at all goeth out of it to them.'

And he turned and said to Simon his disciple who sat by him: 'Simon son of Jonah, it is easier for a camel to enter in by a needle's eye than for a rich man to enter the kingdom of heaven.'

John of Damascus: **Sacred Parallels A.12 (from** *The Teaching of Peter*)

'Rich is he that hath mercy on many, and he that, imitating God, giveth of that he hath. For God hath given all things unto all, of his own creatures. Understand then, ye rich, that ye ought to minister, for ye have received more than ye yourselves need. Learn that others lack the things that ye possess in superfluity. Be ashamed to keep things that belong to others. Imitate the fairness of God, and none will be poor.'

(*a*) Nicodemus's visit to Jesus is reported only in *John* iii. 1–15, where it has been mischievously edited. He can be identified with Nicodemon, or Nakdimon ben Gorion—one of the wealthiest men in Jerusalem—several times mentioned in the Talmud, and once by Josephus who, however, reverses his name to 'Gorion son of Nicodemon' (*Wars* ii. 17. 10). Nicodemon must have been a young man at the time, since he was actively trying to stave off the Jewish revolt against Rome nearly forty years later. The Talmud praises his generosity, his love of peace, and his services to the nation—for though born into the class of the Chief Rulers, he had embraced Pharisaism—and it appears that he had inherited not only the monopoly of fetching lustral water for Temple use, but also most of the reservoirs in Jerusalem. During the main festivals he provided water for pilgrims by the hundred thousand.

(*b*) One of the chief subjects of dispute between Pharisees and Sadducees were these Temple monopolies, which remained in the hands of a few priestly families even after the Sadducees lost control of the Great Sanhedrin (*see* cviii.*c–d*). In all, there were fifteen chief overseers of Temple services and supplies (*Shekalim* v. 1), including the director of the choir (*al'ha'shir*) and the director of the orchestra (*al'hatziltzul*). Three of the monopolists are reproved in the *Mishnah* (*Yoma* iii. 11):

'These are [remembered] with dishonour: the House of Garmu who would not teach [others] how to make shew bread; the House of Abtines who would not teach [others] how to prepare incense; and Hygros ben Levi [Director of the Choir] who had the art of singing from his fathers and likewise would teach it to none other.'

Only once did the Pharisees try to break the monopoly of the House of Garmu by bringing in bakers from Egypt, but their shew bread was inferior;

and the Garmus, when asked to return, went on strike until their wages had been doubled (*Tosephta Yoma* ii. 5).

(*c*) The following is recorded of Nicodemon in *Ta'anith* 19*b*–20*a*:

'There were three men for whom the sun shone [miraculously], namely Moses, Joshua [*these two should really be Joshua (Joshua* x. 13) *and Hezekiah (Isaiah* xxxviii. 8), *but it seemed wrong to omit Moses*], and Nakdimon ben Gorion.

'The Rabbis have taught us: "It happened during a drought that the Israelites went up to Jerusalem for the feast and there was not enough water. Nakdimon ben Gorion betook himself to a General who still had water [*probably reserves for the Roman garrison*] and said unto him: 'Lend me twelve of thy wells, and presently I will repay thee in kind or give thee twelve talents of silver [*some £6,000 or $18,000 in modern currency*].' To this the General agreed and fixed the day of payment.

' "When that day came and the drought continued, the General sent word to Nakdimon that he should either repay the water or pay the money. Nakdimon replied: 'The day is not yet done.' And at noon the General sent to him again, saying: 'Either give me the water or the money!' Nakdimon answered: 'There is yet time, for the sun is not yet darkened.' In the afternoon the General made the same demand, and was told again: 'The sun is not yet darkened.' Then said he to Nakdimon: 'There hath fallen no rain for one whole year and dost thou expect it to fall before even?' and departed for the baths in a cheerful spirit. But while he was on his way thither, Nakdimon went to the Temple, wrapped himself [in his praying garment] and prayed to God: 'Master of the world! It is well known to Thee that I made this covenant not for my own glory, nor for that of my father's house, but for Thy glory, that the pilgrims might have water.' At once the skies became clouded and rain began to fall, so that all wells overflowed with water.

' "The General returned from the baths and, meeting Nakdimon as he came from the Temple, said to him: 'I know full well that it is for thee alone that thy God hath disturbed His world. Yet will I maintain my claim against thee for the twelve talents. For the sun is already darkened, and therefore this rain hath fallen in the time that was mine.' Nakdimon again went to the Temple, wrapped himself, and stood in prayer, saying: 'Master of the world! As Thou hast performed one miracle for Thy servant, now perform another, I pray Thee!' At once the wind blew, the darkness was dispersed and the sun shone out.

' "Then said the General unto Nakdimon: 'Were it not that the sun shineth again, I should have pressed my claim against thee.' " '

(*d*) After thus explaining that Nakdimon (from the verb root NKD, to shine) was his nickname 'because there shone out for him the sun', the Talmud reveals that his true name was Bunni. This name had been borne by two Levites in early post-Exilic times, one of them an overseer of the Temple (*Nehemiah* ix. 4 and xi. 15); and, according to *Sanhedrin* 43*a*, Bunni was also the name of one of Jesus's five disciples (*see* LVI.g). It is probable, however, that his real nickname was *Nakemidam,* 'Innocent of Blood', a reference to his action at Jesus's trial (*see* CIX.*s*), and that this became transliterated to the Greek *Nicodemon,* 'Conquering Spirit', but was, centuries later, changed to *Nakdimon* by Talmudists who had forgotten the occasion on which he acquired it. An improving anecdote, probably based on an unmiraculous original, was then invented to justify the change.

(*e*) Josephus records (*see* (*a*) *above*) that at the outbreak of the Jewish War, Nicodemon offered a safe-conduct to a party of Roman soldiers if they would surrender. The soldiers assented but, unluckily for Nicodemon, were murdered by Zealots when his back was turned.

Originally, Josephus's Greek text may have run: 'Bunni, Gorion's son (Nicodemon).' If the 'Bunni' dropped out because it was mistaken for 'Ben', the Hebrew equivalent of 'Son of'—a mistake occurring in some Greek translations of *Nehemiah,* where the earlier Bunni is mentioned—the text will then have been amended to 'Gorion, son of Nicodemon'.

(*f*) *Gittin* 56*a* mentions Nicodemon—whom we shall hereafter call 'Bunni'—in connection with the subsequent siege of Jerusalem:

> 'There were three counsellors in Jerusalem: Ben Zizith Hakeseth, Nakdimon ben Gorion, and Ben Kalba-Shebua, each of whom had the means of supplying the city with food for ten years. But Ben Battiah [*leader of the Zealot party*] arose and burned down their store houses [*to induce his men to break out from the beleaguered city and fight; the ample supply of provisions having caused placidity*].
>
> 'When Rabbi Johanan [*Ben Battiah's aged uncle, who had been one of Hillel's favourite disciples and was now leader of the Pharisees*] heard of this outrage, he exclaimed: "Woe!" Ben Battiah had him brought before him, and asked: "Why did you exclaim 'Woe!'?" He answered: "I did not say 'Woe!' [*which would have been a curse*] but 'Wah!'" [*an exclamation denoting merely disapproval*].
>
> 'The difference between "woe" and "wah" saved Rabbi Johanan ben Zakkai's life.'

Rabbi Johanan had officiated at the wedding of Bunni's daughter, whose marriage portion consisted of one million gold pieces, as well as a large present by her father-in-law. Bunni was killed during the siege by the Zealots (*Antiquities* iv. 6. 1):

> 'They slew [the son of] Gorion, a person eminent in dignity, and on the account of his family also. He was for democracy, a man as bold and free in spirit as any Jew living, and it was this outspokenness as much as his other advantages [of rank and riches] that proved his ruin.'

His daughter was left destitute and lived for awhile on grain picked from the dung of Roman horses until forced to appeal for public assistance (*Kethuboth* 66*b*).

(*g*) The rabbis later held that the reason for this disaster was Bunni's failure to achieve perfect charity (*Kethuboth* 67*a*): 'The burden of the camel should accord with his strength.' And if Bunni quoted this proverb in reference to his own case, claiming that he undertook his fair share of the burden of alms-giving, Jesus's proverb about the needle's eye (*see* LXXXII.*e*) will have made an apt rejoinder.

(*h*) When, impressed by Jesus's teaching, Bunni visited him—by night to escape the attention of his fellow-patricians—he will have been advised to undergo baptism in token of a complete breach with his past; and to distrib-ute his wealth among the poor of Jerusalem. The *Gospel according to the Hebrews* (*see* LXXXII.*b*) supplies the missing part of this interview.

(*i*) According to *John* iii. 15, Bunni enquired about eternal life, but he can-not have been so literal-minded and stupid as the Church now teaches: he was merely disinclined to believe in the complete re-generation of a man whose habits were already formed (*John* iii.4). The first part of verse 11 must have been spoken by Bunni, not Jesus; Jesus's answer is found in verses 7–8, a vestigial *midrash* on *Ecclesiasticus* xi. 5. In verse 13, an editor of *John*, who was completely out of touch with Jewish religious belief, makes Jesus deny that any man had ever ascended to Heaven, though both Enoch and Elijah were believed to have done so.

(*j*) *John* iii. 14, Jesus's reference to himself as the 'serpent in the wilderness' (*Numbers* xxi. 9), has also been altered. It will have referred to the Son of Man prophesied for the Last Days in *Daniel* vii. 13 (*see* LXXVIII.*c*); God would set him as a standard in the sky for the elect to fix their eyes upon, since no man could gaze at God directly.

Jesus, who is made to foretell his crucifixion in both *John* viii. 28 and xii. 32 —though he expected death by the sword (*see* CI.*b and* CII.*e–f*)—will have rebuked Bunni for his caution, and warned him that the Last Days were at hand when everyone would have to make public repentance, like the Israel-ites in the wilderness when Moses raised the brazen serpent.

(*k*) Since Bunni arranged for one of his water-carriers to conduct Jesus's disciples to the upper room (*see* CVI.*b*), the meeting here recorded is likely to have taken place during some earlier visit of Jesus's to Jerusalem than when he drove out the money-changers (*John* ii. 13–17—*see* XC.*a and e*).

(279) *Bunni son of Gorion, a chief ruler (which was afterward called Nakemidam), came unto Jesus by night.*

And he said unto him: 'Master, I know that thou art a teacher sent from God, for no man doeth as thou hast done, except God be with him. What then shall I do to be saved?'

Jesus answered, and said: 'Except a man be born again, he cannot see the Kingdom of God. Go therefore and be baptized of water and of the Spirit, and thou shalt live.'

He asked: 'How can these things be? We speak that we do know, and bear witness to that which we have seen, but how shall we believe this?

'Shall a grown man as it were enter a second time into his mother's womb and, proceeding thence, be altogether changed?'

Jesus answered: 'As the Preacher saith: "He that observeth the wind shall not sow, and he that regardeth the clouds shall not reap."

'For the wind bloweth when it listeth, and thou hearest the sound thereof, but canst not tell whence it cometh nor whither it goeth.

'And as the Preacher saith also: "Thou understandest neither the way of the Spirit, nor how the bones are formed in the womb of a woman. Even so thou understandest not the word of God which made all."

'That which is born of the flesh is flesh, that which is born of the spirit is spirit.

'Tell thou me of earthly things and I will believe thee; but when I tell thee of heavenly things, then believe thou me!'

Bunni asked: 'And if I suffer myself to be baptized, what lack I further?'

And Jesus, perceiving that he answered discreetly, said unto him: 'Thou shalt not be far from the Kingdom of Heaven while thou obeyest the Law.'

Bunni answered: 'I have obeyed it from my youth up.'

And Jesus said again: 'How sayest thou: "I have obeyed the Law," when it biddeth thee to love thy neighbour as thyself?

'For lo, many sons of Abraham, thy brethren, are clad in dung and perish for want at thy gates; but thine house is full of good things.'

* * * * *

(*l*) [Here follows the advice about lending to God (*see* xxvi.g).]

* * * * *

The following saying is quoted by John of Damascus from the *Teaching of Peter*, a collection of Oracles.

(281) *'And knowest thou not that, having won a superfluity of riches, thou oughtest to give freely of it unto them that lack?*

'Forasmuch as God freely gave of all that He had created unto our fore-father Adam and to his seed for ever, fearest thou not to hold back that which belongeth also unto thy brethren?

'Consider the wide mercy of God, and do thou even as He did; then shalt thou be truly rich.'

* * * * *

(282) *These words pleased Bunni but little, and he answered: 'It is said: "The burden of a camel should be according to his strength"; behold, the more alms I give, the more do the beggars importune me.'*

Jesus said: 'If this burden be too heavy for thy back, shed thou the greater burden of thy riches and be free.

'Go thy way, sell all thou hast, and give unto the poor!'

Bunni answered and said: 'This I cannot do, being a chief ruler and the master of a great household.'

* * * * *

(283) *And Jesus said unto Bunni: 'Thou comest unto me secretly by night. Yet the day of the Lord's vengeance is nigh when thou must declare thy repentance openly, like as the Children of Israel repented before Moses, be-cause of the fiery serpents.*

'And as Moses raised up the brazen serpent for a standard, that whosoever looked upon it should not die, so shall God set the Son of Man in the sky, that whosoever hath sinned and believeth in God, the same shall look upon him, and not perish, but have everlasting life.'

And Bunni departed thence, being very sorrowful.

But Jesus turned unto Simon, and said to him: 'Verily, it is easier for a laden camel to go through the gate that is called the Eye of the Needle, than for a rich man to enter into the Kingdom of Heaven by the needle's eye of repentance!

'For the camel will more gladly cast the load from off his back.'

*   *   *   *   *

(284) *And Peter saith: 'Lo, we have forsaken all and followed thee.'*

Jesus answered and said: 'He that hath forsaken houses and lands for God's sake, the same shall be repaid an hundredfold in the Kingdom of Heaven!'

*   *   *   *   *

LXXXIV

THE DEDICATION

John x. 14–18

14I am the Good Shepherd, and know My sheep, and am known of Mine.
15As the Father knoweth Me, even so know I the Father: and I lay down
My life for the sheep. 16And other sheep I have, which are not of this fold:
them also I must bring, and they shall hear My voice; and there shall be one
flock, and one Shepherd. 17Therefore doth My Father love Me, because I lay
down My life, that I might take it again. 18No man taketh it from Me, but
I lay it down of Myself. I have power to lay it down, and I have power
to take it again. This commandment have I received of My Father.

John x. 39–42

39Therefore they sought again to take Him: but He escaped out of their
hand.

40And He went away again beyond Jordan into the place where John
at first baptized; and there He abode. 41And many resorted unto Him, and
said: 'John did no miracle: but all things that John spake of this man were
true.' 42And many believed on Him there.

John iv. 1–3

1When therefore the Lord knew how the Pharisees had heard that Jesus
made and baptized more disciples than John, 2(Though Jesus himself
baptized not, but his disciples,) 3He left Judaea, and departed again into
Galilee.

John xi. 53–54

53Then from that day forth they took council together for to put Him
to death.

54Jesus therefore walked no more openly among the Jews; but went thence
unto a country near to the wilderness, into a city called Ephraim, and there
continued with His disciples.

John x. 22–38

22And it was at Jerusalem the feast of the Dedication, and it was winter.
23And Jesus walked in the temple in Solomon's porch. 24Then came the
Jews round about Him, and said unto Him: 'How long dost Thou make
us to doubt? If Thou be the Christ, tell us plainly.' 25Jesus answered them:
'I told you, and ye believed not: the works that I do in My Father's name,

John x. 22–38 (*contd.*)

they bear witness of Me. ²⁶But ye believe not, because ye are not My sheep, as I said unto you. ²⁷My sheep hear My voice, and I know them, and they follow Me: ²⁸and I give unto them eternal life; and they shall never perish, neither shall any man pluck them out of My hand. ²⁹My Father, Who gave them Me, is greater than all: and no man is able to pluck them out of My Father's hand. ³⁰I and My Father are one.' ³¹Then the Jews took up stones again to stone Him. ³²Jesus answered them: 'Many good works have I shewed you from My Father; for which of those works do ye stone Me?' ³³The Jews answered Him, saying: 'For a good work we stone Thee not; but for blasphemy, and because that Thou, being a man, makest Thyself God.' ³⁴Jesus answered them: 'Is it not written in your law,

I said, Ye are gods?

³⁵If He called them gods, unto whom the word of God came, and the scripture cannot be broken; ³⁶say ye of Him, Whom the Father hath sanctified, and sent into the world, Thou blasphemest; because I said, I am the Son of God? ³⁷If I do not the works of My Father, believe Me not. ³⁸But if I do, though ye believe not Me, believe the works: that ye may know, and believe, that the Father is in Me, and I in Him.'

Luke xxi. 19

¹⁹In your patience possess ye your souls.

John xi. 26–27

²⁶'And whosoever liveth and believeth in Me shall never die. Believest thou this?' ²⁷She saith unto Him: 'Yea, Lord: I believe that Thou art the Christ, the Son of God, Who should come into the world.'

John xi. 7–8

⁷Then after that saith He to His disciples: 'Let us go into Judaea again.' ⁸His disciples say unto Him: 'Master, the Jews of late sought to stone Thee; and goest Thou thither again?'

John xi. 16

¹⁶Then said Thomas, which is called Didymus, unto his fellow-disciples: 'Let us also go, that we may die with him.'

Epiphanius: Heresies lxii. 2

The whole deceit and error of the Sabellians, and the strength of it, they draw from some apocryphal books, especially from the so-called Egyptian Gospel. For in it many similar things are recorded as from the person of our Saviour, but said in a corner, purporting that he shewed his disciples that the same person was Father, Son, and Holy Spirit.

Clement of Alexandria: Stromateis v. 10. 63

'For the prophet saith: "Who shall understand a parable of the Lord save he that is wise and knowledgeable and loveth his Lord? For it is given

Clement of Alexandria: **Stromateis v. 10. 63** (*contd.*)

> to few to contain all things: for it is not as grudging (saith he) that the Lord commanded in a certain Gospel: 'my secret for me and the sons of my house.'" '

Clementine Homilies xix. 20

> 'For we remember our Lord and Teacher, how he charged us, saying: "Ye shall keep my secrets for me and for the sons of my house." '

Hippolytus: **Against Heresies v. 7**

> The Naassenes say that the soul is very hard to find and to perceive; for it does not continue in the same fashion or shape or in one passion, so that one can neither describe it nor comprehend it in one essence.
>
> And they have these various changes of the soul set forth in the *Gospel according to the Egyptians.*

(*a*) The sequence in *John* x. and xi. is confused. For instance, *John* xi. 48, where the Chief Rulers fear that the Romans will make Jesus's popularity a pretext for stamping out Judaism, anticipates events by several months. In verse 53, they decide to kill Jesus. It is more likely that the Herodians took this decision, and because he was preaching at Beth-Nimrah, in Herod Antipas's tetrarchy, where John the Baptist had already been arrested for sedition (*see* v.*j and* xli.*a*). This is the proper context for *John* iv. 1–3, though 'Pharisees' has there been substituted for 'Herodians', and 'Galilee' for 'Judaea' (*see* lxx.*l*). Jesus will have moved to safer quarters in Judaea, where Herod's writ did not run; and 'near to the wilderness' must mean in the south of that country.

(*b*) 'Ephraim' in *John* xi. 54 has long puzzled critics—*John's* geographical nomenclature is usually corrupt—and though Jerome identifies it with the village of Efrem, five Roman miles east of Bethel (*Onomastica Sacra* xciv. 7), Bethel does not lie 'near to the wilderness'. The correct reading is probably 'Hebron'. Hebron, David's first capital, was originally named after Ephron the Hittite who sold the neighbouring Cave of Machpelah to Abraham (*Genesis* xxiii. 8–16) and, since the ending *ain* or *aim* is interchangeable with *on, Ephraim* may well have been a local name either for Hebron itself or for Mamre (*Genesis* xiii. 18 and xviii. 1) which lay about a mile to the north, and was also called 'The Field of Ephron' (*Genesis* xxiii. 17). Mamre formed the trade centre of the wild Negeb region (*see* Sozomen: *Ecclestiastical History* ii. 4), and will have attracted Jesus because of its associations with Abraham and its tombs of the patriarchs. Moreover, water for baptismal use was abundant there. When Jesus made the ritual circuit of his realm, he may well have visited Beersheba too, which lay a few miles to the south (*see* lxxvii.*a*).

(220) *And Jesus went again beyond Jordan, unto Beth-Nimrah in the dominion of Herod, where John at first baptized.*

There he abode for awhile with his disciples, and many resorted unto him from the coasts of Edom and from all the country round about.

But the Herodians, when they heard that Jesus baptized and made more disciples even than John, took counsel how they might put him to death.

Wherefore he departed thence into Judaea, to the village of Ephron, which is nigh unto the wilderness of the south, and continued there for a time with the Twelve, preaching and baptizing.

* * * * *

(c) The Feast of Dedication (*John* x. 22) was the eight-day midwinter festival—still kept by the Jews—which required the lighting of an eight-branched candelabrum. Originally, this was a Canaanite charm to make the sun recover his strength and burn eight times as warmly; in Jesus's time, however, it was held to commemorate the anniversary of the Temple's re-dedication by Judas Maccabeus in 164 B.C. (1 *Maccabees* iv. 36–56).

(d) It is unfortunate that the identity of Jesus's questioners in *John* x. 24 has been lost and that his answer is so ineptly reported. He was not empowered to promise everlasting life to his sheep (*John* x. 28); he could only point the way to its attainment. *John* x. 30: 'I and my Father are One', is Johannine doctrine and even if Jesus had said this—which he could never have done— no attempt would have been made to stone him; instead, he would have been examined by the local Sanhedrin. It is likely, however, that he taught a secret Essene doctrine of God as a Trinity-in-unity, hinted at in *Matthew* vii. 7 (*see* xxvii.*i*) and eventually incorporated in the medieval *Zohar* (*see Introduction* III.*q–s*).

Part of his answer can be recovered from *John* x. 14–18 (*see* LXXXI.*g*) and from *Luke* xxi. 19 (*see* XCVIII.*a*), which has been inserted in the 'Little Apocalypse'.

John x. 24: 'How long dost thou make us to doubt?' meaning, 'hold us in suspense', suggests that his questioners were Jesus's Levite kinsmen—whom the Baptist had admitted into the closely-guarded secret of the Coronation— and that they were urging Jesus to reveal himself. This is the proper context for the substance of *John* xii. 2 (*see* XI.*f*) and of *John* xi. 26–27, a dialogue antecedent to the 'Raising of Lazarus' (*John* xi. 40—*see* LXXXVII.*d*).

(e) *John* x. 34: 'Is it not written in your Law: "I said 'ye are gods' "?' cannot be accepted as it stands. To say '*your* Law' would have made Jesus an apostate; and the quotation is not from the Law, but from *Psalm* lxxxii. 6; and 'gods' means no more than 'judges'. The original question belongs to a different context altogether (*see* xxvi.*a*).

John x. 35–38 may be disregarded as a clumsy invention in support of the Trinitarian dogma.

(f) *John* x. 16: 'The other sheep', were certainly not the Gentiles, as is usually supposed, but Jews who were still waiting to hear Jesus's message. It seems to have been on his conscience that he had not completed his mission beyond

Jordan (*see (a) above*). In John xi. 7–8, the apostles are afraid to accompany him until Thomas, in verse 16, encourages them with bold words.

(270) *It was at Jerusalem the Feast of the Dedication.*

* * * * *

(271) *And Jesus went up to the Temple, and as he walked in Solomon's Porch his kinsmen came unto him from Bethany, saying:*

'*Art thou not our King? Why standest thou idle, and how long wilt thou hold us in suspense?*

'*When wilt thou reveal unto all which are in Jerusalem that thou art the Son of David?*'

Jesus answered and said: '*The works which I do in my Father's name bear witness whether or not I be a shepherd even as David was.*

'*Behold, I have sheep that know my voice and will follow me into the fold, neither shall any man pluck them out of my hand.*

'*For I am willing to die if thereby I may guide their feet into the way of everlasting life.*

'*But other sheep I have which are not yet of this fold: them also must I seek out.*

'*Therefore, if I do not the works of the Father, trust me not; but if I do them, possess ye your souls in patience!*'

* * * * *

(272) '*Verily, I say unto you: if ye believe, in a little while ye shall see the Son of Man come in glory.*

'*And whosoever turneth unto him, the same shall not die.*'

And among his kinsmen was Eliezer, whose father was Simeon, the ruler of the Watchers which were in Bethany.

And Eliezer said: '*Of a truth, I believe. For art thou not the Anointed One, which is prophesied for the Last Days?*'

* * * * *

[Here follow Jesus's preaching against the priests, the visit of 'Nicodemus', his interview with the Grecians, and two feats of healing.]

* * * * *

(292) *Now, it came to pass when the Feast was ended, that Jesus said unto his disciples:* '*Let us depart hence and go across Jordan.*'

They ask him: '*Master, goest thou thither again where of late the Herodians sought to take thee?*'

He said: '*This commandment received I of the Father.*'

They said again: '*Master, they will kill both thee and us.*'

* * * * *

[Here follows: 'Not by calling me "Master, master!" will ye enter into the Kingdom of Heaven' (*see* LXIX.*c*).]

* * * * *

(294) *Then said Thomas, which was called the Twin, unto his fellows:*
'Brethren, let us go, that we may die with him.'

* * * * *

[Here follows the account of Jesus's return beyond Jordan (*see* xxi.*a*).]
The next sayings may have been spoken on another occasion.

* * * * *

(204) *And Jesus disclosed to the Twelve the three-fold mystery of the mercy*
and wisdom of God.
    For he said unto them: 'If knowledge be as the Father, then shall the
knower be as the Mother, and the twain engender the thing known, namely
the Word.
    'These three abide together: God the Father which hath created us of
His mercy, and the Holy Spirit of God which shineth upon us in wisdom,
and the Word of God which sheddeth peace.'

* * * * *

(205) *Afterward, he put upon them the blessing which the sons of Aaron*
alone might utter, saying: 'Thus I put upon you the Name of the Lord.
    '"*The Lord bless you and keep you!*
    '"*The Lord make His face to shine upon you and be gracious unto you.*
    '"*The Lord lift up the light of His countenance upon you, and give you*
peace."
    'For the Father is Mercy, and the light of His countenance is Wisdom,
and the Son is Peace.'

* * * * *

[Here follow *Matthew* vii. 7: 'Ask, and ye shall receive [peace]; seek, and
ye shall find [wisdom]; knock, and it [the gate of mercy] shall be opened
unto you' (*see* xxvii.*i*), and the *midrash* on *Psalm* lxxviii. 2 (*see* xliv.*c*).]

* * * * *

(g) We know from Josephus (*Wars* ii. 8. 7), that the Essenes kept certain
mysteries from the world. The saying attributed to Jesus in the *Stromateis*
and *Clementine Homilies* may refer to a similar one (*see* xxv.*d* and lxxii.*f*).
But if Clement's quotation from 'the prophet' refers to *Psalm* xxv. 14 (paralleled in *Proverbs* iii. 32) : 'The secret of the Lord is with them that fear Him',
then this secret might be revealed to all Israelites worthy of receiving it.
However, it was soon to be profaned by non-Israelites, including Simon
Magus (*see Introduction* iii.*g*), and the Gentile Gnostics, who identified
Jesus himself with the Word and his mother with the Divine Wisdom. The
'sons of my house' are the Israelites, since Jesus is here speaking as their King.

(209) *'Yet do ye keep this secret for those of my house which are worthy*
to receive it.

'For David said in a psalm: "The secret of the Lord is with them that fear Him."

'And Solomon said likewise: "His secret is with the righteous." '

* * * * *

(*h*) Jesus's doctrine of the 'changes of the soul', mentioned by Hippolytus, may have been another mystery. Josephus (*Wars* ii. 8. 11) reports that the soul was regarded by the Essenes as having been born in the rarefied parts of Heaven, and subsequently imprisoned in the body until death, when it returned home. Jesus is likely to have shared their view. The intermediate changes may, or may not, have been Zodiacal in character. In Pharisaic doctrine the souls of every generation had been created at the beginning of the world and were kept in store waiting for the bodies to be born (*Leviticus Rabbah* xv. 1). No suggestion of Pythagorean metempsychosis is to be found in the whole of Talmudic literature, though it was adopted by Jewish mystics of the eighth century A.D., and popularized by the *Kabbala*.

(210) *And Jesus also revealed unto them the changes of man's soul, how it abideth not in one form, neither in one passion,*

But as from heaven it proceedeth, so unto heaven shall it return, having suffered many things, and be freed at last from the prison of its flesh.

* * * * *

LXXXV

FOLLOW ME!

Matthew viii. 19–22

[19]And a certain scribe came, and said unto Him: 'Master, I will follow Thee whithersoever Thou goest.' [20]And Jesus saith unto him: 'The foxes have holes, and the birds of the air have nests; but the Son of Man hath not where to lay His head.' [21]And another of His disciples said unto Him: 'Lord, suffer me first to go and bury my father.' [22]But Jesus said unto him: 'Follow Me; and let the dead bury their dead.'

Luke ix. 57–62

[57]And it came to pass, that, as they went in the way, a certain man said unto Him: 'Lord, I will follow Thee whithersoever Thou goest.' [58]And Jesus said unto him: 'Foxes have holes, and birds of the air have nests; but the Son of Man hath not where to lay His head.' [59]And He said unto another: 'Follow Me.' But he said: 'Lord, suffer me first to go and bury my father.' [60]Jesus said unto him: 'Let the dead bury their dead: but go thou and preach the kingdom of God.' [61]And another also said: 'Lord, I will follow Thee; but let me first go bid them farewell, which are at home at my house.' [62]And Jesus said unto him: 'No man, having put his hand to the plough, and looking back, is fit for the kingdom of God.'

(*a*) Jesus used the formula 'Follow me!' to summon Peter, Andrew, James, John (*see* xvii.*f*), Matthew (*see* xix.*g*), and the rich young man (*see* lxxxii.*c*). Here he uses it again to summon 'another' (*Matthew* viii. 22 and *Luke* ix. 59).

(*b*) *Luke* ix. 60: 'Let the dead bury their dead', is a Greek mistranslation of an Aramaic original. As F. Perles has pointed out in the *Zeitschrift der Neutestamentarischen Wissenschaft* xix. 96, the word *LMKBR* (which is unvocalized) has been taken for *lemikbar,* the infinitive of *peal,* which means 'to bury', rather than for *limkaber,* which means 'to the burier' and is a participle of *pael.* The sentence, in its correct form, should read literally: 'Leave the dead to their burier of the dead'—*shevok lemataya limkaber metaya lehon.*

(*c*) This is also the proper context of 'Call no man father' (*Matthew* xxiii. 9 —*see* xiii.*l*), and 'He who hath forsaken father, mother, and brethren for God's sake shall inherit eternal life' (*Mark* x. 30—*see* lxxxii.*g*). However, if Jesus was to avoid a breach of the Fifth Commandment, these pronouncements must have been applied to an unusual case. Under the Law, a father derived his authority from God and might chastize his children if they disobeyed him; only if he repudiated God were they free from all obligations towards him. Such a case might occur if he took an oath of allegiance to the Emperor Tiberius, offered sacrifices to the God Augustus, and tried to make them do the same.

The following will have been spoken after Jesus, for fear of arrest, had abandoned his headquarters at Capernaum, and begun to move rapidly from district to district (*see* xcvii.*h*).

(299) *And a certain scribe said unto Jesus: 'Master, I will follow thee whithersoever thou goest.'*

Jesus answered and said unto him: 'Foxes have holes, and birds of the air have nests, but this son of man hath not where to lay his head.'

* * * * *

(301) *And another said unto Jesus: 'Suffer me first to bury my father, for he serveth the Wicked Kingdom and desireth not that I go with thee.'*

Jesus answered: 'Leave the dead to the burier of the dead, and call thou no man father that hath denied Him which is in Heaven; for He alone is thy Father.

'Verily, he that hath forsaken an evil household for God's sake, the same shall inherit everlasting life.'

* * * * *

(*d*) The mention of a plough in *Luke* ix. 62 points to a *midrash* on 1 *Kings* xix. 20–21. This will have been spoken between the grape harvest and the winter rains, when there was a lull in agriculture.

(302) *And yet another, which was an husbandman, said unto Jesus in the time of gleaning: 'I will bid farewell unto them that are in my house, and then will I follow thee until the time of ploughing be come again.'*

Jesus answered and said: 'It is written of Elisha that when he was called to be a prophet of God, he said unto Elijah: "Suffer me first, I pray thee, to kiss my father and mother." Nor did Elijah deny him.

'But afterward he burned both his plough and his goad, and upon them he sacrificed a yoke of oxen unto the Lord; then ran he and followed after Elijah, and turned not back again.

'Verily, I say unto you: no man which hath put an hand to his plough to burn it, and turneth again to till the field, is fit for the Kingdom of Heaven!'

* * * * *

COUNTING THE COST

Luke xiv. 28–33

²⁸For which of you, intending to build a tower, sitteth not down first, and counteth the cost, whether he have sufficient to finish it? ²⁹Lest haply, after he hath laid the foundation, and is not able to finish it, all that behold it begin to mock him, ³⁰saying, This man began to build, and was not able to finish. ³¹Or what king, going to make war against another king, sitteth not down first, and consulteth whether he be able with ten thousand to meet him that cometh against him with twenty thousand? ³²Or else, while the other is yet a great way off, he sendeth an ambassage, and desireth conditions of peace. ³³So likewise, whosoever he be of you that forsaketh not all that he hath, he cannot be My disciple.

(*a*) *Luke* xiv. 28–33 is a continuation of *Luke* ix. 57–62 (*see* LXXXV. *c–d*). The 'tower' (great building) to which Jesus refers was probably Herod's Temple, which had been begun sixteen years before Jesus's birth (*John* ii. 20—*see* XC.*j*), but remained uncompleted, partly for lack of funds (partly because only priests were allowed to decorate the more sacred courts and chambers) until Albinus became Governor-General of Judaea, more than thirty years after the Crucifixion; and four years later was destroyed by Titus. This identification is suggested by *Proverbs* xxiv. 27, on which *Luke* xiv. 28 is a *midrash,* and which itself refers to 1 *Kings* v. 17. 'Which of you' must be an error; Jesus's lowly hearers were not in a position to build towers.

(*b*) The king mentioned in *Luke* xiv. 31 will have been Herod Antipas—a king by courtesy, though titularly no more than a tetrarch—who had quarrelled over boundaries with his neighbour King Aretas of Nabataea, and had also angered him by divorcing his daughter in favour of Herodias (*Antiquities* xviii. 5. 1 and xvii. 1. 2—*see* XLI.*a*). This divorce was technically unnecessary because, according to the *Mishna,* a king was permitted eighteen wives (*Sanhedrin* ii. 4); but Herodias must have refused to tolerate a rival in the palace and insisted that the rule did not apply to mere tetrarchs. Jesus probably knew from his secret supporters at court (*see* LII.*d*) that Herodias had urged Antipas to accept Aretas's warlike challenge, and that he was prudently pleading lack of troops. The war did not, in fact, break out until some six years later, when Aretas took the initiative and decisively defeated Antipas, whose Transjordanian soldiers ran away (*Antiquities* xviii. 5. 2—*see* LXXVI.*a*).

Luke xiv. 33 is not quite logical; the editor has omitted Jesus's advice to sit down first and consider the cost of following him.

(300) *'A prudent man intending to build a great house sitteth down first and counteth the cost, whether he have sufficient to finish it throughout.*

'As Solomon saith: "Prepare thy work without in a field, and gather together all things fit for building, and then build thine house."

'And it is written that Solomon did even as he counselled. For he raised a levy out of Israel, thirty thousand men to prepare great stones and timber, and to lay them ready; and when all the timber was shaped and all the stones hewn, Solomon built the House of the Lord, and after seven years it was finished throughout.

'But Herod the Wicked counted not the cost, and that which he began six and forty years ago remaineth unfinished unto this day.

'Likewise will a prudent king not rashly make war on his neighbour. He sitteth down first, and counteth whether he be able with his ten thousand men to meet him that cometh against him with twenty thousand.

'And if he be not able, then while the other is yet a great way off, he sendeth an ambassage and desireth conditions of peace.

'Likewise, I say unto you: if a man seek to follow me, let him consider first whether he can endure to the end: for he must forsake all that he hath, and not turn back!'

* * * * *

LAZARUS

Mark iii. 20

²⁰And the multitude cometh together again, so that they could not so much as eat bread.

John xi. 1–6

¹Now a certain man was sick, named Lazarus, of Bethany, the town of Mary and her sister Martha. ²It was that Mary which anointed the Lord with ointment, and wiped His feet with her hair, whose brother Lazarus was sick. ³Therefore his sisters sent unto Him saying: 'Lord, behold, he whom Thou lovest is sick.' ⁴When Jesus heard that, He said: 'This sickness is not unto death, but for the glory of God, that the Son of God might be glorified thereby.' ⁵Now Jesus loved Martha, and her sister, and Lazarus. ⁶When He had heard therefore that he was sick, He abode two days still in the same place where He was.

Mark v. 35

³⁵While He yet spake, there came from the ruler of the synagogue's house certain which said: 'Thy daughter is dead; why troublest thou the Master any further?'

John xi. 11–46

¹¹These things said He: and after that He saith unto them: 'Our friend Lazarus sleepeth, but I go, that I may awake him out of sleep.' ¹²Then said His disciples: 'Lord, if he sleep, he shall do well.' ¹³Howbeit Jesus spake of his death: but they thought that He had spoken of taking of rest in sleep. ¹⁴Then said Jesus unto them plainly: 'Lazarus is dead. ¹⁵And I am glad for your sakes that I was not there, to the intent ye may believe; nevertheless let us go unto him.' ¹⁶Then said Thomas, which is called Didymus, unto his fellow-disciples: 'Let us also go, that we may die with Him.'

¹⁷Then when Jesus came, He found that he had lain in the grave four days already. ¹⁸Now Bethany was nigh unto Jerusalem, about fifteen furlongs off: ¹⁹and many of the Jews came to Martha and Mary, to comfort them concerning their brother. ²⁰Then Martha, as soon as she heard that Jesus was coming, went and met Him: but Mary sat in the house. ²¹Then said Martha unto Jesus: 'Lord, if Thou hadst been here, my brother had not died. ²²But I know, that even now, whatsoever Thou wilt ask of God, God will give it Thee.' ²³Jesus saith unto her: 'Thy brother shall rise again.' ²⁴Martha saith unto Him: 'I know that he shall rise again in the resurrection at the last day.'

John xi. 11–46 (*contd.*)

[25]Jesus said unto her: 'I am the resurrection, and the life: he that believeth in Me, though he were dead, yet shall he live: [26]and whosoever liveth and believeth in Me shall never die. Believest thou this?' [27]She saith unto Him: 'Yea, Lord: I believe that Thou art the Christ, the Son of God, Who should come into the world.'

[28]And when she had so said, she went her way, and called Mary her sister secretly, saying: 'The Master is come, and calleth for thee.' [29]As soon as she heard that, she arose quickly, and came unto Him. [30]Now Jesus was not yet come into the town, but was in that place where Martha met Him. [31]The Jews then which were with her in the house, and comforted her, when they saw Mary, that she rose up hastily and went out, followed her, saying, 'She goeth unto the grave to weep there.' [32]Then when Mary was come where Jesus was, and saw Him, she fell down at His feet, saying unto Him: 'Lord, if Thou hadst been here, my brother had not died.' [33]When Jesus therefore saw her weeping, and the Jews also weeping which came with her, He groaned in the spirit, and was troubled, [34]and said: 'Where have ye laid him?' They said unto Him: 'Lord, come and see.' [35]Jesus wept. [36]Then said the Jews: 'Behold how He loved him!' [37]And some of them said: 'Could not this Man, which opened the eyes of the blind, have caused that even this man should not have died?' [38]Jesus therefore again groaning in Himself cometh to the grave. It was a cave, and a stone laid upon it. [39]Jesus said: 'Take ye away the stone.' Martha, the sister of him that was dead, saith unto Him: 'Lord, by this time he stinketh: for he hath been dead four days.' [40]Jesus saith unto her: 'Said I not unto thee, that, if thou wouldest believe, thou shouldest see the glory of God?' [41]Then they took away the stone from the place where the dead was laid. And Jesus lifted up His eyes, and said: 'Father, I thank Thee that Thou hast heard Me. [42]And I knew that Thou hearest Me always: but because of the people which stand by I said it, that they may believe that Thou hast sent Me.' [43]And when He thus had spoken, He cried with a loud voice: 'Lazarus, come forth.' [44]And he that was dead came forth, bound hand and foot with graveclothes: and his face was bound about with a napkin. Jesus saith unto them: 'Loose him, and let him go.'

[45]Then many of the Jews which came to Mary, and had seen the things which Jesus did, believed on Him. [46]But some of them went their ways to the Pharisees, and told them what things Jesus had done.

John vii. 5

[5]For neither did His brethren believe in Him.

John xii. 10–11

[10]But the chief priests consulted that they might put Lazarus also to death; [11]because that by reason of him many of the Jews went away, and believed on Jesus.

(*a*) 'Lazarus', or Eliezer, seems to have been the only brother of Mary and Martha, daughters of Simeon the Chaste (*see* VIII.*q–v*, XI.*a–c and* CXVI.*b*). His resurrection, described with great circumstantial detail in *John* xi, is neither mentioned nor hinted at in any other early source. Even if it be assumed that Lazarus was not dead but lay in a coma, his successful summons from the tomb would have been too dramatic an incident for the other evangelists to omit; for they had included among Jesus's miracles particular cures of fever (*Matthew* viii. 14-15—*see* XLII.*b*), lumbago (*Luke* xiii. 10-17—*see* LXXIV.*f*) and menstrual irregularity (*Mark* v. 25-34—*see* XXXVI.*d*), and were always anxious to multiply his feats on the least excuse (*see* XXXII.*c and* XL.*a*). But since the compiler of *John* is unlikely to have invented the story, he will have found it among the Oracles—but in an early version which the Synoptics had rejected because of its unmiraculous ending. Recognizing its capabilities, he saved it and converted it into a miracle.

(*b*) It remains then, to isolate the main features and moral of the original narrative. The case of blind Bartimaeus (*see* XL.*c*), who was the first stranger to acclaim Jesus as the Messiah, will be a helpful parallel; it has been assumed that Jesus could not have failed to restore sight to the one, life to the other. Since, by the end of the first century, his identity with God had been established at least in Alexandria, it was supposed that a false and discreditable ending to the story of Lazarus must have been supplied by jealous Nazarenes (*see Foreword–h.*5.), and that Jesus proved himself no less of a wonder-worker than Elijah or Elisha. Various fragments of the original narrative have become embodied in *Mark* v. 35 (*see* XXVI.*f*), and *Mark* iii. 20 (*see* CIV.*d*) as well as in *John* vii. 5 (*see* XLIX.*b*) and *John* iv. 31-38 (*see* LXX.*j*); which suggests that its suppression by the Synoptics was deliberate.

(*c*) *John* xi. 7-8, 16 and 26-27 (*see* LXXXIV.*d and f*), 9-10 (*see* XXIV.*c*) and 44 (*see* CXV.*h*) are borrowed from other contexts, and verse 42 is a late interpolation.

The words most heavily stressed in the narrative are: 'Lord, if thou hadst been here, my brother had not died', with which first Martha (*John* xi. 21) and then Mary (verse 32) greet Jesus; and though in *Luke* xix. 41 he weeps for Jerusalem in general, 'Jesus wept' (verse 35) is the only instance recorded in the four Gospels of his grieving at a personal loss. Both these details carry emotional conviction. The sisters appear to have reproached Jesus for having gone back across Jordan to win more converts (*see* LXXXIV.*f*), and to have said that, had he stayed in Jerusalem and initiated the Last Days by revealing his identity, Lazarus would have entered alive into the Kingdom of Heaven.

(*d*) Jesus wept because, as may be deduced from *John* xi. 40 (*see* LXXXIV.*d*), he had promised that Lazarus, if he showed faith, would live to see the coming of the Son of Man; evidently Lazarus had lost faith and died. Jesus, who loved him, had not thought this possible, and thus refused to take seriously the first news of his sickness. Beth-Nimrah lay, at most, two days' journey from Bethany, and if he had hurried back in answer to the first summons he might have arrived in time. Verses 11 and 14 suggest that a further urgent message was sent: 'Lazarus lieth as if lifeless!' and that only then did Jesus show signs of concern, though still assuming that his friend was peacefully asleep. Indeed, he loved and trusted Lazarus so completely that, even after receiving the news of his death (*see* xxxvi.*a*), he had hopes of reviving him. (*e*) When Jesus arrived at Bethany, having sent a messenger ahead to announce his coming, he found that Lazarus had been four days buried; yet still he refused to abandon hope. He insisted that the grave be opened (probably it was Mary, not Martha, who objected) and summoned him to arise; but without result. Jesus had counted on a private visit to the tomb, accompanied by the sisters only; but friends and kinsfolk gathered, which publicized his failure. Martha, it appears, was bitterly disappointed and Mary undisguisedly ashamed of Jesus; and the kinsmen, loth to blame Lazarus himself for dying—because, as Josephus relates (*Antiquities* xiii. 5. 9), the Essenes regarded fate as governing all things, whereas the Pharisees held that faith limited the power of fate—took Jesus for a fanatic and ceased for awhile to believe in him. This attitude explains not only their attempt to silence him soon afterwards (*see* civ.*a*), but their astonishment and change of heart when, on the road from Emmaus, he convinced two of them that he himself, through faith, had cheated the grave (*see* cxvi.*f*).

The circumstantial details of the original narrative were meant to free Jesus from all suspicion of having deceived Lazarus or the kinsmen; but since he had failed to raise his dead friend, the Pauline evangelists of the first century rejected it altogether.

If the account of Lazarus's dramatic appearance in verse 44 reads authentically, this is because an ingenious editor of *John* has borrowed it from that of Jesus's own Resurrection. *John* xi. 44, the curt: 'Loose him, and let him go!' strikes a false note. One would have expected Jesus to say: 'Loose him, and take him again to your bosoms!' But it could well have been spoken by the centurion at the Holy Sepulchre (*see* cxv.*h*).

(*f*) The sequence begins with an account of Jesus's decision to return across Jordan (*see* lxxxiv.*f*) and his assiduous preaching and baptizing in Antipas's dominions (*Mark* iii. 20).

> (295) *Jesus therefore went again beyond Jordan, and laboured much. And the multitude came together unto him, so that he could not so much as eat bread.*

* * * * *

[Here follows *John* iv. 31–38, the disciples' attempt to dissuade Jesus from overworking (*see* lxx.*j*). Next come Antipas's decision to arrest him (*see* lxxvii.*f*) and three applications for discipleship (*see* lxxxv.*c* and *d*).]

> (304) *And it came to pass, while Jesus was preaching and baptizing beyond Jordan, that Eliezer fell sick, the son of Simeon the Chaste which was the ruler of the Watchers at Bethany.*
>
> *Now, Bethany is nigh unto Jerusalem, about fifteen furlongs.*
>
> *And Mary and Martha, his sisters, sent unto Jesus, saying: 'Lord, behold, he whom thou lovest is sick. Come thou and lay thy hands upon him.'*
>
> *But Jesus supposed that they feared for his life, because of the Herodians,*

and that they made this excuse, as wishing to draw him back from beyond Jordan.

He therefore sent unto them, saying: 'This sickness is not unto death. Let the saints of his household lay their hands upon him, that by their faith he may be made whole.'

And he abode still two days in the same place where he was.

Then sent they again unto him, saying: 'Come in haste; he whom thou lovest lieth as if dead!'

* * * * *

(305) *Then saith Jesus unto his disciples: 'Our brother Eliezer sleepeth, yet will I go, if haply I may awake him.'*

They answered and said: 'Master, if he sleep, he shall do well.'

And even as they spake came yet another from the house of the ruler, which said unto his fellow: 'Trouble thou not the Master; for Eliezer is dead.'

And the disciples mourned together with the messengers. But Jesus said: 'Why mourn ye and why make ye such ado? Surely he is not dead but sleepeth?'

Therefore the messengers laughed him to scorn.

* * * * *

(306) *Then said Jesus unto the Twelve: 'I rejoice that we tarried not in Bethany (as ye would have me do) lest they, by their unbelief, should have made you also stumble. Nevertheless, let us go hither unto him.'*

And he sent the two messengers before his face, saying: 'He cometh.'

But when he drew nigh unto Bethany, Eliezer had lain in the grave four days.

* * * * *

(307) *Now, Martha and Mary were in the house, where many came to comfort them concerning their brother.*

And they which came reproached Jesus, saying: 'Why hastened he not when he was first called? Could not he, which opened the eyes of the blind man of Bethesda, have caused that thy brother should not have died?'

Wherefore, when the two messengers returned, saying: 'He cometh,' Martha went out to meet Jesus; but Mary sat still in the house.

And Martha said unto him: 'Lord, if thou hadst been here, my brother had not died.'

Jesus answered her: 'Said I not unto him that if he would but believe he should see the Glory of God?'

And Martha said: 'Yea, lord, and I trust that even now whatsoever thou askest of God, He will give it thee.'

Jesus saith: 'The Lord giveth resurrection and life. He that believeth in Him, the same shall live, though he were already dead. Believest thou this?'

She answered him: 'Yea, Lord.'

And Jesus saith: 'Send now privily for thy sister Mary, and come ye both to shew me where ye have laid him.'

And Martha sent for her.

* * * * *

(308) *Then they that were with Mary in the house, when they saw how she rose up hastily and went out, followed her, saying: 'She goeth unto the grave to weep there.'*

* * * * *

(309) *And Mary, coming where Jesus was, saw him and fell at his feet.*

She said likewise: 'Lord, if thou hadst but been here, my brother had not died.'

When Jesus therefore saw her weeping, and them also weeping which came with her, he groaned within himself and was troubled, and he asked: 'Where have ye laid him?'

They answered: 'Lord, come and see!'

Jesus wept.

Then said they: 'Behold, how he loved him! Why therefore came he not in haste when we sent for him?'

Jesus, yet weeping, cometh unto the grave, which was a cave, and a stone laid upon it.

And he said: 'Take ye away the stone!'

But Mary said unto him: 'Lord, by this time he stinketh, for now is the fourth day. Why camest thou not before this?'

* * * * *

(310) *Then rolled they away the stone from the place where the dead was laid. And Jesus lifted up his eyes unto heaven, and prayed: 'Lord, if it be possible, restore Thou my brother Eliezer! And praised be Thy name, that Thou hast sent them which stand by, that by their faith he may be raised!'*

And when he had thus spoken, he cried with a loud voice: 'Eliezer, come forth in the name of the Living God!'

Yet Eliezer stirred not.

Then said Jesus plainly unto them: 'He is dead. Yet shall he rise again in the resurrection of the dead.'

Mary answered and said unto him: 'I know that he will rise again on the Last Day. But why didst thou deceive both him and us, declaring that he should never taste of death?'

Jesus saith: 'Said I not unto all of you that if ye would but believe, ye should behold the Glory of God?

'But the faith of our brother Eliezer failed him, neither could any of you restore it, nor heal him while he yet lived.'

Then was Mary wroth and would believe no more on Jesus; neither did her brethren believe on him.

* * * * *

(g) John xii. 10–11, the Chief Priests' alleged decision that Lazarus must be put to death, will have originally been their decision to re-arrest Jesus when they heard from Saul that he had survived the Cross (*see* cxviii.*u*).

(477) *Now, it came to pass, that when the Chief Priests heard these tidings, they consulted together how they might deliver Jesus again unto death.*

For by reason of his resurrection many of those in Jerusalem were now become Nazarenes.

* * * * *

THE LAST DAYS

(*a*) The prophetic books are not arranged in chronological order, and because most of them contain additions or emendations, far later in date than the original text, here is a brief historical summary of Hebrew notions about the 'Day of Judgement', or the 'Great Day of the Lord', held in Jesus's time.

The Great Day of the Lord had been an Israelite obsession since at least the early eighth century B.C., when it was popularly regarded as one of national victory over all Gentiles who defied God (*Amos* v. 18). Amos warned the Israelites that it would be a dark day for them also (*see* cxvii.*l*), unless they were scrupulous in His worship (*Amos* iii. 2, iv. 5 and v. 5, 21–27); but neither he nor his contemporaries associated this event with the end of the world, which was still regarded as eternal.

Isaiah, in the late eighth century B.C., confirmed these gloomy prophecies. Since the Israelites had disregarded Amos's warning, they were to be destroyed on the Great Day of the Lord, or all but a small remnant, as a punishment for their sins. In *Isaiah* i. 24–26 this remnant is envisaged as the nucleus of a more faithful and prosperous kingdom. Before the close of the collection of early Isaianic prophecies—some uttered by Isaiah himself, some by his immediate disciples—the Northern Kingdom had been conquered and its princes carried into captivity (721 B.C), never to return. The warning is then addressed to the Southern Kingdom of Israel—for the book contains numerous later prophecies by several hands and was not given its final recension, according to some critics, until about 220 B.C.

(*b*) Zephaniah (last third of seventh century B.C.) presents the Great Day of the Lord as one of judgement against all nations (*Zephaniah* iii. 8), including Israel, while agreeing with Isaiah that a remnant of Israel will be saved. But the Southern prophets succeeded in pressing partial religious reforms on King Hezekiah (720–693 B.C.), and by the time of Nahum and Habakkuk (end of seventh century B.C.), when the Chaldeans were expanding their empire, it was felt that the remaining Israelites were, at any rate, more righteous than their over-weening Gentile neighbours (*Habakkuk* i). This conception prevailed thereafter and was expressed, for instance, in *Psalms* ix. 5, 16; lxviii. 1–2 and cxxv. 3, most of the psalms being exilic or post-exilic.

(*c*) Next Jeremiah (late seventh and early sixth centuries B.C.) prophesied against the Southern Kingdom, in the style of Isaiah, for forty years. Jerusalem was to be destroyed, but after a change of heart the Jews would repossess their land under a rightful successor to David (*Jeremiah* xxiii. 5–8). In 586 B.C., the first part at least of this prophecy was fulfilled: Jerusalem fell to Nebuchadnezzar, who carried off the leading citizens to Babylon.

Ezekiel, a younger contemporary of Jeremiah's, prophesied in a similar style until he was himself exiled to Babylon; where he declared that, if Israel repented, both the Northern and the Southern Kingdom would be restored by a chosen remnant under a single Davidic king (*Ezekiel* xvii. 22–24, xxxiv. 23–31, *etc.*). The Gentiles would then assemble their armies and march against Jerusalem, to be utterly destroyed there (*Ezekiel* xxxviii. and xxxix.). (*d*) Later prophets laid greater emphasis on God's mercy and repentance, especially the 'Deutero-Isaiah' who wrote during the second half of the Exile. Israel, he said, had already been well punished for her sins. Babylon would be overthrown by Cyrus, the exiles restored, Jerusalem re-built, and her inhabitants would listen to a divine teacher; never again should the Holy City be conquered (*Isaiah* xl.–xlviii.). In the 'Songs of the Servant', also exilic and included among the prophecies of the Deutero-Isaiah, Israel is presented as the humble Servant of God through whom all nations would come to know the truth.

In 538 B.C., the exiles returned to Jerusalem, full of hope, and in 520 B.C., a prophecy of the first Zechariah encouraged them to re-build the Temple. This was accomplished five years later by Zerubbabel, a descendant of David (*see* II.*c*). The same Zechariah also prophesied that Jehovah-worship would be so greatly esteemed among the Gentiles that ten men of different nationalities would seize a single foreign-born Jew by the skirt, begging him to lead them to Jerusalem for prayer (*Zechariah* viii. 21–23). And Malachi wrote, not long after (*Malachi* i. 11):

'From the rising of the sun to its setting My name is great among the Gentiles, and in every place incense is offered unto My name, and a pure offering.'

Similarly, in *Micah* iv. 1–3, a post-exilic passage, all nations are to be converted and partake of God's Kingdom, apparently on equal terms with Israelites.

But presently the tone of the prophecies changed: according to fifth-century passages in *Isaiah,* the Gentiles would be subjected to the Israelites (*Isaiah* xl. 12–14), becoming their bondmen and handmaidens (lxi. 5 and xiv. 1–3)—that is, such few of them as had escaped destruction in the universal judgement (xxxiv. 1–3), since only those who feared the Lord would be spared (lix. 18 and lxvi. 16–24).

(*e*) According to the more precise views of Joel (fourth century B.C.), all nations were to gather for annihilation in the Valley of Decision near Jerusalem—which, in Jesus's day, was identified with the Valley of the Kidron (*see* LXXXIX.*a*). However, according to a mid-second-century proph-

ecy attributed to Zechariah (*Zechariah* xiv. 12), only the hostile Gentiles
would be destroyed; those who remained would be converted, to make good
Malachi's prophecy, and come up yearly for the Feast of Tabernacles under
pain of God's displeasure.

(*f*) Later apocalyptics, brooding over Israel's national misfortunes, came
to believe that the Great Day of the Lord implied the destruction of the
world as it had been, and the initiation of an altogether new one. This
revolutionary view appears first in the apocalypse of *Daniel* vii.–xii., written
after the Seleucid King Antiochus Epiphanes had attempted to Hellenize
the Temple cult, but before the successful Jewish revolt in 167 B.C.: an
emanation of God, known as the Ancient of Days, would come to judge the
world and, after overthrowing the Gentiles, would depute everlasting sovereignty to the Son of Man and his elect (*Daniel* vii. 9–27).

The same view is found in a contemporaneous addition to *Isaiah,* namely,
chapters lxv. and lxvi.: lxvi. 6–18 foretells the re-birth of Israel and the
destruction of God's enemies; lxv. 17 announces a new heaven and earth.
The Messianic kingdom will be a golden age in which the lion eats straw
and lies down with the lamb, and all men live at peace with their neighbours.
Those of the Gentiles who escape God's judgement in the battle of Jerusalem are to preach His glory to distant nations (lxvi. 19), who will then con-
verge on Jerusalem, honourably escorting all descendants of Israelite exiles.

(*g*) Since, however, Israel was a small nation, her righteous dead would
arise and swell her numbers by taking their places in the Kingdom. This
view had already been expressed, though perhaps only figuratively, by the
end of the fourth century. Thus *Isaiah* xxvi. 19 reads: 'Thy dead shall
arise, awake and shout for joy, because Thy dew is a dew of lights and the
earth shall bring the shades to life,' a passage which was associated with
Ezekiel's vision of the valley of dry bones restored to life (*Ezekiel* xxxvii.—
see Foreword-k). According to *Daniel* xii. 2, all the dead were destined to
arise for judgement: whereupon the righteous would obtain their reward of
bliss; but the wicked, everlasting shame and contempt.

(*h*) This closes the prophetic canon of the Old Testament; but Jesus and
his contemporaries accepted many later prophecies as only a little less
authoritative than Scripture, especially the *Book of Enoch* (late second and
early first centuries B.C.), and the *Testaments of the Twelve Patriarchs*
(late second century, but containing additions made in the middle of the
first century B.C., which must be distinguished from Christian interpolations). The theory developed in these apocalyptic books was that seventy
rebel angels—into whose care God had consented to commit Israel for
awhile as a means of testing the faith and virtue of her children (*Enoch*
lxxxix. 59)—were the cause of her backslidings. At the Day of Judgement,
these would be cast into an abyss of fire (*Enoch* xc. 20–25). God Himself
would then establish a new Jerusalem and recall the exiles; the converted
Gentiles would devote themselves to the service of Israel; and the Messiah

(called 'The Son of Man', as in *Daniel*) would appear in his glory (*Enoch* xc. 28–37). The whole world would be ruled by a Messiah of Aaronic descent (*Testament of Levi* xviii.). Next would follow the resurrection of the patriarchs and famous men of old; then all the remaining dead would be roused for judgement (*Testament of Benjamin* x.). The Ancient of Days would restore Jerusalem and make it his dwelling place, and the Son of Man, after judging the nations in God's name (*Testament of Levi* viii) and condemning the wicked to Gehenna (*Enoch* xc. 26), would open the gates of Paradise to the elect and give them to eat of the Tree of Life (*Testament of Levi* xviii. and *Enoch* xxv. 4–6). In this new golden age there would be one nation and one tongue only (*Testament of Judah* xxv.); and the elect would live for ever (*Enoch* xc. 33). The Temple would still stand in its accustomed place, but it would be a Third Temple, newly brought down from Heaven (*Enoch* xc. 28–29), larger and far more beautiful than the old, battered, often desecrated Second Temple of Zerubbabel (*see* xc.g–h).

The dream visions of *Enoch* end with the appearance of the Lamb of God, an enormous creature wearing anomalous black horns on his head (*Enoch* xc. 38)—the horns of power, such as Moses wore, or Zeus Ammon, or Alexander—and with the tears of joy shed by Enoch at this sight (*see* vi.*b*). A preliminary judgement by the Son of Man in the earthly Kingdom of Heaven is foretold (*Enoch* xci. 12); at the final judgement heaven and earth will pass away and all spirits become one with God (*Enoch* xci. 16–17).

(*i*) The *Psalms of Solomon* (70–40 B.C.) trace the Messiah's descent from David, not Aaron. He was to be sinless and, after slaying the ungodly Gentiles with the word of his mouth, was to gather the scattered tribes together and re-sanctify Jerusalem. None of the hostile Gentiles would be allowed to reside in Jerusalem; but all would remain under the Messiah's rule, and bring him gifts from the ends of the earth (*Psalm of Solomon* xii. 25–26, ed. Charles).

The later apocalyptics held that the souls of all dead men went first to Sheol, a purgatory of four divisions—one for the righteous, one for unredeemable sinners, the other two respectively for the not so good and the not so bad—there to await the preliminary judgement. The righteous would then enter the earthly Kingdom of God, while the remainder were detained in Sheol until the final Judgement; and when this had been delivered, Sheol would become Gehenna, a pit of fire.

(*j*) Originally, Gehenna ('the valley of Hinnon'), was not a figure of speech but the gorge of the Valley of the Kidron, dividing the Mount of Olives from Mount Zion, where human sacrifices were offered to the God Moloch (2 *Chronicles* xxviii. 3 and xxxiii. 6). King Josiah, in the course of his reforms, 'defiled' Moloch's altar (2 *Kings* xxiii. 10); and it appears that by Jesus's time Moloch's part of the valley, otherwise known as Topheth (*Jeremiah* vii. 31), had become the municipal rubbish dump of Jerusalem—whatever would burn was raked into heaps and set alight. The figurative

Gehenna is described in *Enoch* xlviii. 9, liv. 1–6 and lxii. 12; it lies 'in the midst of the earth', but this means 'in a central position', not 'in the heart of the earth' (*see Ezekiel* xxxvii. 28). Paradise, mentioned in the *Apocalypse of Baruch* lix. 8, is described both in *Enoch* xxxii. 3–4 and the *Secrets of Enoch* viii. 5.

(*k*) The *Secrets of Enoch,* an apocalyptic book composed by a Grecian follower of Philo during Jesus's lifetime, but based on a lost Hebrew original, is not Messianic in tendency. Paradise there is modelled on the Garden of Eden, but its four rivers flow with milk, honey, oil, and wine, and it contains the 'Tree of Life' on which God rests when He enters the Garden. This book influenced the Grecian Churches while the doctrine of the Second Coming was being formulated (*see* cxvii.*q*). Occasional similarities between Jesus's sayings and the *Secrets* have been detected (*see* xxiii.*c*), but it is most unlikely that he had read it, except perhaps in its Hebrew original. He probably held the Essene view of Paradise, quoted by Josephus, which recalls the Arthurian legend of Avalon and, as Josephus himself notes (*Wars* ii. 8. 11), Homer's account of the Elysian Fields.* The Elysian Fields were originally held to lie in the far North-West—'habitations beyond the ocean in a region oppressed neither with rain nor snow, nor with intense heat, but refreshed by the gentle blowing of a west wind from the ocean' (*ibid.*). In this North-Western region Enoch places the Tree of Life (*Enoch* xxiii.–xxv.)—but describes the Scriptural Garden of Eden, where the Tree of Wisdom grew, as lying far to the east (*Enoch* xxxii. 3 and 6). The Tree of Life, which conferred immortality (*Genesis* iii. 22), bore unwithering leaves, beautiful blossom, and fruit sweet as dates. It was, in fact, a celestial apple-tree: in Hebrew poetry, apples—that is to say quinces—symbolized love (*Canticles* ii. 3–4).

(*l*) Another Grecian work was the *Sibylline Oracles,* a collection of prophecies written in unprosodic hexameters—crudely imitating those venerated by the Graeco-Romans as Cumaean or Delphic. *Book* iii, the oldest and most famous, prophesies the regeneration of Israel in the reign of Ptolemy VII (170–164 B.C., and again, after a temporary abdication, 145–117 B.C.). All Gentiles are invited by the Sibyl to worship the God of Israel lest the Messiah punish them at his coming. *Book* iii. 236–247 describes the Jews as a race who:

'. . . take thought for uprightness and goodness; they keep just measure in town and country, they go not a-stealing from one another by night, nor drive

---

* *Paradise* literally means 'a fruit orchard'; *Avalon* is derived from the Brythonic word for apple; and *Avernus* (despite the classical view that it meant *a-ornis,* 'birdless') probably from a similar Italic word; and *Elysium* from a Ligurian word meaning 'sorb-apple', which yields the French word *alisier.*

The apple, or quince, in Celtic and Mediterranean mythology symbolized immortality through love of the Great Goddess; this seems also to have been the pagan origin of the Garden of Eden story in *Genesis,* where the 'Mother of All Living' (*Genesis* iii. 20) offers the apple to Adam as a life-in-death gift. Adam, the eponymous ancestor of the Edomites, was the oracular hero of the ancient shrine of Hebron (*see* cxiii.*t*), which explains the talking serpent of *Genesis,* his embodied ghost. Hebron was the original Garden of Eden (*see* Graves: *The White Goddess, London,* 1952, p. 154), which after the Exile was placed in the delta of the Euphrates.

off herds of oxen, sheep or goats, nor does neighbour remove neighbour's landmark, nor does a wealthy man oppress a poorer, or deal harshly with the widow, but rather helps her with supplies of corn and wine and oil.

'Always does he who has abundance among the people give a portion of his harvest to them that have nothing and are in poverty, fulfilling the command of the great God, the oracle of the Law; for the Lord of Heaven made the earth to be possessed by all in common.'

These Oracles anticipate Pauline doctrine in so far as no attempt is made in them to preach the observance of the Jewish ceremonial laws; the Gentiles are merely invited to fear God, show brotherly love towards one another, and await their part in the Heavenly Kingdom.

(*m*) Many of the 'God-fearers' converted by the *Sibylline Oracles* later found that Christianity suited them better than Judaism, and not for political reasons only. In *Book* iii. 1–62, a passage written before 30 B.C., occurs the famous Messianic prophecy, echoed in Virgil's *Fourth Eclogue*, of a King who should wield his sceptre over all countries and reign for ever; the Grecian God-fearers were willing to believe that this referred to the spiritual sovereignty of Jesus.* But Jesus himself discouraged the advances of the Grecians (*see* LXXXI.*a and c*), and made no attempt to convert the Gentiles; on the contrary, he placed their cities out of bounds to his apostles (*Matthew* x. 5—*see* LVII.*a*), taking his stand on the purely Hebrew prophecies and on the Gentiles' need for strict observance of the Law as interpreted by the Pharisees.

(*n*) It is difficult to say how many of the apocalyptic books written in the first century A.D. came to Jesus's notice. Two of the four visions in 4 *Esdras* —the *Ezra Apocalypse* and the *Vision of the Son of Man,* which agree with the main concepts of earlier apocalypses—may have been written during his lifetime. The *Ezra Apocalypse* mentions the resurrection of the Elect and their enjoyment of the Messianic Kingdom (vii. 31), which would last for ten generations (400 years), as opposed to the seventy of *Enoch* x. 12—elsewhere called 'a week' (*Enoch* xc. 12). According to the *Vision of the Son of Man,* the Son of Man would appear in the clouds, the nations would assemble to destroy him, but be vanquished by a flaming breath from his mouth, namely 'the Law which is like fire', (as in the *Psalms of Solomon—see* (*i*) *above*); he would then set up the New Jerusalem and restore the ten tribes (xiii. 5–47). Jesus may have known this book which is, however, so orthodox that practically all its elements are found elsewhere.

(*o*) The *Book of Jubilees* (a haggadic commentary on *Genesis,* and apocalyptic only in part), was composed by a Palestinian Jew while the Temple was still standing, and may be as early as 30 B.C. According to *Jubilees,* the Messiah would be physically descended from David, not Aaron (xxxi. 18). After a Gentile invasion of Palestine, Israel would devote herself to the

---

* In Majorcan churches a choir boy, dressed as the Sibyl, still enters the pulpit every Christmas Eve, sword in hand, and chants her prophecy.

Law and repent; then, as the nation became more devout, human life would lengthen by degrees until it reached a span of a thousand years (xxiii. 23–28). This period was called 'The Great Day of Peace' (xxv. 10). After the Great Judgement, the spirits of the righteous would at last enter a blessed immortality (xxiii. 11). Jesus knew this book (see LXXII.*h*).

(*p*) The *Assumption of Moses,* an anti-Sadducaic document dating from 7–29 A.D., places the inauguration of the Kingdom 1750 years after the death of Moses which, according to contemporary reckoning, had occurred in 1485 B.C. If the book was written in 15 A.D., this would allow seven full generations, of forty years apiece, to pass before the Great Day dawned. There is no mention of a Messiah: God Himself would exalt Israel to Heaven after destroying her enemies and having them cast into Gehenna. Jesus does not appear to have been influenced by this book.

(*q*) The Pharisees of the first century B.C. had avoided speculation on the Last Days, as distracting them from the immediate obligations of the Law; they held that if they obeyed these, God would preserve their souls when the End came. However, by the time of Jesus, they had accepted the apocalyptic creed with the single proviso that God should not be hurried —He would choose the date in His own good time, and Israel must patiently contain herself. Some of them believed that *Isaiah* lx. 22: 'I the Lord will hasten it in his time', meant that none knew when the day of Zion's comfort would arrive (*Genesis Rabbah* lxiii. 12); they recorded that, when Jacob on his deathbed wished to reveal the End, God made him tremble and deprived him of his senses (*Genesis Rabbah* xcix. 5). It was useless, they said, to 'force the hour' of the Great Day, which is compared in *Canticles Rabbah* (*end*) to child-bed: if birth is prematurely induced, the child dies. And *Sanhedrin* 97*b* records: 'Cursed be the bones of them that have calculated the End; for when the expected hour arrives but not the Messiah, it will be said: "Now will he never come!"'

(*r*) Thus, although Jesus expected the Great Day to dawn within his own lifetime and that of his disciples (see xci.*f*), he insisted nevertheless that God alone knew precisely when this would be; as Daniel had prophesied (*Daniel* xii. 9): 'The words are closed up and sealed until the end of time.' He held, however, that the signs of the times could be read by any person of common sense (see xcviii.*g and* ci.*c*). In a passage of the *Apocalypse of Baruch** (2 *Baruch* xxvii. 2–13), which was probably written during his lifetime, the twelve signs of the 'Pangs of the Messiah' are recorded as follows:

(1) The beginning of commotion.
(2) The slaying of the great ones.
(3) The sudden death of many.
(4) The sending of the sword.

* Later this book was greatly expanded, and li. 5 even contains a quotation from *Matthew* xvi. 26.

(5) Drought and famine.
(6) Earthquakes and terror.
(7) [Missing—a flood?]
(8) Swarms of spectres and attacks by evil spirits.
(9) A rain of fire.
(10) Oppression and rapine.
(11) Breaches of the Commandments.
(12) Confusion from the mingling together of all the above.

These signs may have been in Jesus's mind. The doctrine that the existing world would be destroyed by fire was deduced by the apocalyptics from God's promise to Noah that He would never again destroy it by flood (*Genesis* ix. 15). This was still, however, to be the fate of Jerusalem (*Daniel* ix. 26).

(*s*) All hitherto unfulfilled prophecies were expected to find their fulfilment in God's good time, and an over-zealous editor had confused Daniel's plain statement that God alone knew, or could know, when the world would end, with a precise prophecy of the death of King Antiochus Epihanes (*Daniel* xii. 11–12):

> 'And from the time that the daily sacrifice shall be taken away and the abomination that maketh desolate set up, shall be 1290 days. Blessed is he that waiteth and cometh to the 1335 days.'

This prophecy—though almost certainly composed after the event (*see* (*f*) *above*)—was now canonical Scripture, and its meaning had been forgotten. So, since all prophecies in the canon were held to refer to the Last Days, it cried out for comment; as did also the date of the Great Day previously announced in *Jeremiah* xxv. 11–33. Jeremiah's seventy years from the destruction of the First Temple (586 B.C.) had long passed, and though the Temple had indeed been rebuilt in 515 B.C., this was not considered to have been the event prophesied by him.

(*t*) Ezekiel also had made an ambiguous prophecy, in terms of 390 years (*Ezekiel* iv. 9). But 390 years from the destruction of the Temple—if that was what Ezekiel had in mind—were fulfilled by 195 B.C.; therefore, this cannot have been what he meant. The author of *Daniel,* in order to justify Jeremiah's more definite prophecy, interpreted his 'seventy years' as seventy weeks of years (*Daniel* ix. 24–27—*see* xcvii.*b*), i.e. 490 years. He reckoned that sixty nine and a half had already passed, leaving only another three and a half; but he had made an error in chronology—no more than fifty nine and a half weeks of years had passed, and when the remaining three and a half went by, again nothing spectacular happened—nor even in 95 B.C., when the full seventy weeks of years ended.

(*u*) The mediaeval *Metsudath David* comments on the 1290 and 1335 days of *Daniel* xii. 11–12: 'We do not know whether this means days or years, or what will happen when they are accomplished.' Yet the Jews continued their speculations on the prophecies of Jeremiah, Ezekiel, Daniel, and Enoch —thus encouraging the appearance of several Messiahs, each of them disparaged by his successors.

(*v*) Jesus may have been influenced in his expectations by the view later expressed in *Tanna debe Eliyahu,* chapter ii.—a *midrash,* containing ancient *baraitas,* compiled in the third century:

> 'This world will exist for six thousand years; the first two thousand are to be void [*without the Law*], the second two thousand are to be the time of the Law, and the third two thousand the days of the Messiah. But because of our many sins, a number of years that should have belonged to the days of our Messiah have passed and we are still subjected [*i.e. the Messiah has not come yet*].'*

But, according to the same calculation, Jesus lived precisely at the close of the fourth millennium, reckoned from the Creation, when the Messiah's two thousand years were due to begin. This period was expected to be an interregnum—distinct from the subsequent 'world to come', or the 'Great Messiah', which was to last one thousand years. These seven thousand years were deduced from the six days of Creation and the seventh Day of Rest, as well as from *Psalm* xc. 4: 'For a thousand years in Thy sight are but as yesterday'; and, according to Lagarde (*Mitteilungen* iv. 135) this interpretation had been held, in about 280 B.C., by the translators of the Pentateuch. Jesus's views on *Daniel* xii. 11-12 are not known; but he may have dated the beginning of the End in the year 5 A.D., by counting the days as 'weeks of days' (*see* xcviii.*b*).

(*w*) The conflict between early and later speculations on the duration of the Messianic Kingdom (as opposed to the 'world to come') is revealed in the Talmud (*Sanhedrin* 99a):

> 'Rabbi Hillel II [*fourth century*] said: "There shall be no Messiah for Israel, because they have already enjoyed him [*lit.: 'they have already eaten him'*] in the days of Hezekiah." [*This view had been held by Alexandrian Jews in Jesus's time.*]
>
> 'Rabbi Eliezer held that the days of the Messiah "will last forty years".
>
> 'Rabbi Doza held: "four hundred years". [*This he took from the Apocalypse of Ezra.*]
>
> 'Rabbi Judah (the patriarch) said: "365 years, even as the days of the solar year."
>
> 'Abimi, the son of Rabbi Abahu [*third century*], taught: "The days of Israel's Messiah shall be seven thousand years, as it is written (*Isaiah* lxii. 5): 'And as the bridegroom rejoiceth over the bride, so shall thy God rejoice over thee.'"' [*The bridegroom's period of rejoicing was seven days—and with God one day was as a thousand years.*]

* In this connexion the Talmud (*Abodah Zarah* 9a) asks:

'From what date are the two thousand years of the Law to be reckoned? Should we date them from the delivery of the Law at Sinai? In that case, not quite two thousand years are passed. . . . Therefore the period is to be reckoned from the time when Abraham and Sarah "had gotten souls in Haran" (*Genesis* xii. 5).'

(*x*) Other conjectures were two thousand eight hundred years (the 'seventy generations' of the *Book of Enoch* x. 12), and one thousand years (*Revelation* xx. 2–5). For a time, under the influence of the Grecian *Secrets of Enoch,* the 'millennium' became orthodox Christian doctrine (Justin: *Dialogue* 80); this was not even scotched by the great disappointment of the year 1000 A.D.—when numbers of pious Christians gave away all their possessions, neglected their fields, and waited on their knees for the fiery storm to break. The relevant passage in the *Secrets of Enoch* is xxxii. 2–xxxiii. 2:

> 'And I appointed the eighth day also, that the eighth day should be the first one created after My work, and that *the first seven* should revolve in the form of the seventh thousand, and that at the beginning of the eighth thousand there should be a time of not-counting, endless, with neither years nor months, nor weeks, nor days, nor hours.'

(*y*) *Sanhedrin* 97*b* records a typical late-first-century argument between Rabbi Eliezer ben Horkynas and Rabbi Joshua ben Hananiah, both disciples of Johanan ben Zakkai, as to when and under what conditions the Kingdom would come. Eliezer, who was influenced by Shammai's teaching, insisted that the Messiah would come only if Israel repented; Joshua, a follower of Hillel, that he would come, whether she repented or not. He triumphantly quoted *Isaiah* lii. 3: 'Ye have sold yourselves for naught: and ye shall be redeemed without money', and commented: 'This means: ye have sold yourselves for the purpose of idolatry, and ye shall be redeemed without repentance or reform.'

(*z*) Speculations about the Messianic Kingdom vary in the Talmud, from ecstatic visions of a new heaven and a new earth, to the dry statement by Mar Samuels (second century) in *Pesahim* 68*a*:

> 'This world differs from the coming Messianic age only in respect of servitude to government [*i.e. delivery from oppression*].'

As for the world to come, Rabbi Johanan aptly quoted *Isaiah* lxiv. 4:

> 'For since the beginning of the world men have not heard, nor perceived by the ear, neither hath the eye seen (O God, beside Thee) what He hath prepared for him that waiteth for Him!'

* * * * *

THE ENTRY

Mark xi. 1–11

[1]And when they came nigh to Jerusalem, unto Bethphage and Bethany, at the mount of Olives, He sendeth forth two of His disciples, [2]and saith unto them: 'Go your way into the village over against you: and as soon as ye be entered into it, ye shall find a colt tied, whereon never man sat; loose him, and bring him. [3]And if any man say unto you, Why do ye this? say ye that the Lord hath need of him; and straightway he will send him hither.' [4]And they went their way, and found the colt tied by the door without in a place where two ways met; and they loose him. [5]And certain of them that stood there said unto them, What do ye, loosing the colt? [6]And they said unto them even as Jesus had commanded: and they let them go. [7]And they brought the colt to Jesus, and cast their garments on him; and He sat upon him. [8]And many spread their garments in the way: and others cut down branches off the trees, and strawed them in the way. [9]And they that went before, and they that followed, cried, saying:

> Hosanna:
> *Blessed is He that cometh in the name of the Lord:*
> [10]*Blessed be the kingdom of our father David,*
> *That cometh in the name of the Lord:*
> Hosanna in the highest.

[11]And Jesus entered into Jerusalem, and into the temple: and when He had looked round about upon all things, and now the eventide was come, He went out unto Bethany with the Twelve.

Matthew xxi. 1–11

[1]And when they drew nigh unto Jerusalem, and were come to Bethphage, unto the mount of Olives, then sent Jesus two disciples, [2]saying unto them: 'Go into the village over against you, and straightway ye shall find an ass tied, and a colt with her: loose them, and bring them unto Me. [3]And if any man say ought unto you, ye shall say, The Lord hath need of them; and straightway he will send them.' [4]All this was done, that it might be fulfilled which was spoken by the prophet, saying:

> [5]*Tell ye the daughter of Sion, Behold, thy King cometh unto thee,*
> *Meek and sitting upon an ass,*
> *And a colt the foal of an ass.*

Matthew xxi. 1–11 (*contd.*)

⁶And the disciples went, and did as Jesus commanded them, ⁷and brought the ass, and the colt, and put on them their clothes, and they set Him thereon. ⁸And a very great multitude spread their garments in the way; others cut down branches from the trees, and strawed them in the way. ⁹And the multitudes that went before, and that followed, cried, saying:

> *Hosanna to the Son of David:*
> *Blessed is He that cometh in the name of the Lord:*
> *Hosanna in the highest.*

¹⁰And when He was come into Jerusalem, all the city was moved, saying, Who is this? ¹¹And the multitude said, This is Jesus the prophet of Nazareth of Galilee.

Matthew xxi. 15–17

¹⁵And when the chief priests and scribes saw the wonderful things that He did, and the children crying in the temple, and saying, Hosanna to the Son of David; they were sore displeased, ¹⁶and said unto Him: 'Hearest Thou what these say?' And Jesus saith unto them: 'Yea; have ye never read—

> *Out of the mouth of babes and sucklings*
> *Thou hast perfected praise'?*

¹⁷And He left them, and went out of the city into Bethany; and He lodged there.

Luke xix. 28–40

²⁸And when He had thus spoken, He went before, ascending up to Jerusalem.

²⁹And it came to pass, when He was come nigh to Bethphage and Bethany, at the mount called the mount of Olives, He sent two of His disciples, ³⁰saying: 'Go ye into the village over against you; in the which at your entering ye shall find a colt tied, whereon yet never man sat: loose him, and bring him hither. ³¹And if any man ask you, Why do ye loose him? thus shall ye say unto him, Because the Lord hath need of him.'

³²And they that were sent went their way, and found even as He had said unto them. ³³And as they were loosing the colt, the owners thereof said unto them, Why loose ye the colt? ³⁴And they said, The Lord hath need of him. ³⁵And they brought him to Jesus: and they cast their garments upon the colt, and they set Jesus thereon. ³⁶And as He went, they spread their clothes in the way. ³⁷And when He was come nigh, even now at the descent of the mount of Olives, the whole multitude of the disciples began to rejoice and praise God with a loud voice for all the mighty works that they had seen; ³⁸saying:

> *Blessed be the King*
> *That cometh in the name of the Lord:*
> *Peace in heaven,*
> *And glory in the highest.*

³⁹And some of the Pharisees from among the multitude said unto Him, Master, rebuke Thy disciples. ⁴⁰And He answered and said unto them: 'I tell you that, if these should hold their peace, the stones would immediately cry out.'

John xi. 55–56

⁵⁵And the Jews' passover was nigh at hand: and many went out of the country up to Jerusalem before the passover, to purify themselves. ⁵⁶Then sought they for Jesus, and spake among themselves, as they stood in the temple: 'What think ye, that He will not come to the feast?'

John xii. 12–19

¹²On the next day much people that were come to the feast, when they heard that Jesus was coming to Jerusalem, ¹³took branches of palm trees, and went forth to meet Him, and cried:

> Hosanna:
> Blessed is the King of Israel,
> That cometh in the name of the Lord.

¹⁴And Jesus, when He had found a young ass, sat thereon; as it is written:

> ¹⁵Fear not, daughter of Zion:
> Behold, thy King cometh,
> Sitting on an ass's colt.

¹⁶These things understood not His disciples at the first: but when Jesus was glorified, then remembered they that these things were written of Him, and that they had done these things unto Him. ¹⁷The people therefore that was with Him when He called Lazarus out of his grave, and raised him from the dead, bare record. ¹⁸For this cause the people also met Him, for that they heard that He had done this miracle. ¹⁹The Pharisees therefore said among themselves: 'Perceive ye how ye prevail nothing? behold, the world is gone after Him.'

Justin Martyr: 1 Apology xxxii.

The prophecy which concerned the binding of his foal to the vine and the washing of his robe in the blood of the grape was a sign of what things Christ should both suffer and do. For the foal of an ass stood bound to a vine at the entering-in of a village and he bade his companions bring it unto him; which when it was brought, he set himself upon it and rode into Jerusalem.

(*a*) It was the Tuesday before Passover and Jesus, to complete the Coronation ritual (*see* VIII.g), now rode in triumph through the streets of Jerusalem (*Mark* xi. 1–11, *Matthew* xxi. 1–11, *Luke* xix. 28–40, and *John* xxi. 12–19). His hour had come at last. Following an ancient tradition, some of the disciples laid their garments on the ass's back, others spread theirs on the ground as a carpet: Jehu's troops had done the same when he seized the throne from King Jehoram (2 *Kings* ix. 13).

After spending the night in Bethany, Jesus with an ecstatic escort of pilgrims rode up the 'Valley of Decision' and entered the city from the east (*Joel* iii. 14—*see* LXXXVIII.*e*); thereby intending to set his torch to the dry tinder of the old world.

Bethpage, 'the house of young figs', lay close to Bethany, at the eastern limit of a Sabbath Day's journey from the city (*Menahoth* xi. 2 and 78*b*).

(*b*) The editor of *Matthew* xxi. 2–5 displays characteristic obtuseness (*see* xLV.*e*) in his account of the ass. Zechariah, using the common Hebrew device of repetition for the sake of emphasis, had written (*Zechariah* ix. 9):

> 'Rejoice greatly, O daughter of Zion; shout, O daughter of Jerusalem! Behold, thy King cometh unto thee! He is just and bringeth salvation, lowly and riding upon an ass, and upon a colt, the foal of an ass.'

This the editor has understood to mean that Jesus would ride two beasts at once, namely the ass and her colt and, in verse 7, actually makes him do so.

Jesus knew that Zechariah had been referring to the Messianic prophecy of *Genesis* xlix. 11; the ass must therefore have been tied to a vine, and he will have stained his white garments with the 'blood of the grape', thus also fulfilling the prophecy of *Isaiah* lxiii. 1–6.

(*c*) The editors of *Mark* and *Matthew* are at pains to suppress all mention of Jesus's acclamation as king, which would have been offensive to the Romans. 'King' has been altered to 'prophet' in *Matthew* xxi. 11, and to 'kingdom' in *Mark* xi. 10. 'King', although retained in *Luke* xix. 38, is used there only in a spiritual sense. *John* alone preserves the original tradition (*John* xii. 13): 'Blessed is the King of Israel!'; but *John* was edited in Alexandria, where the need for caution was less than in Rome or Asia Minor. In *John* xii. 15, which is a quotation from *Zechariah* ix. 9, the word 'meek'— retained by the editor of *Matthew* xxi. 5—has been omitted as derogatory to Jesus.

'Hosanna!', 'Save now!' (*see* xLIX.*e*) was the shout prescribed in *Jeremiah* ii. 27 and xvii. 14–17 for the 'Day of Trouble', or the 'Great Day of the Lord'. 'Hosanna in the highest!' (*Mark* xi. 10 and *Matthew* xxi. 9) makes no sense; neither does 'Hosanna to the Son of David!' (*Matthew* xxi. 9), or 'Blessed be the Kingdom of our father David that cometh in the name of the Lord!' (*Mark* xi. 10). The editors have here run together four separate shouts, three of them from *Psalm* cxviii. 25–26: 'Praise to the Son of David, the King of Israel!', 'Save now, I beseech Thee!', 'Blessed be he that cometh in the name of the Lord!' and the other from *Psalm* cxlviii. 1: 'Glory to God in the highest!'

Because the shout of 'Hosanna!' was also raised at the Feast of Tabernacles, some critics suggest that an editor of *John* has confused the Passover with Tabernacles and thus made the people wave thyrsi of palm, willow, and myrtle in welcome to Jesus (*see* xLIX.*e*). It is likely, however, that some pilgrims carried palm-branches—dried winter-loppings brought up from the Jericho date orchards as fuel for the Passover ovens.

(*d*) Since Jesus quotes *Habakkuk* ii. 10–11, the 'Pharisees' who commanded him to rebuke his followers (*Luke* xix. 39) but admitted their powerlessness to check his progress (*John* xii. 19) must have been Sadducees, members of the High Priest's party. Addressed to anyone else, this prophecy would have been irrelevant. The correct version survives in *Matthew* xxi. 15, where the 'chief priests and scribes' ask Jesus to silence his followers and he answers with a quotation from *Psalm* viii. 2—which has, however, been altered by an editor to disguise its bellicosity. The word 'children' in *Matthew* xxi. 15 appears to have been used contemptuously, in the sense of 'ignorant peasants'. (*e*) Such dense crowds thronged the Temple—it has been estimated that two hundred thousand came up every year for the Passover from distant synagogues of the Dispersal as well as from Judaea, Galilee, and Edom— that Jesus and his small band did not long remain the focus of popular attention, and few later arrivals will have been aware that anything unusual had happened.

The Royal Entry was a failure: Jesus had expected to be acclaimed by all Israel, except perhaps the Chief Rulers, after which he would first cleanse the Temple courts in accordance with *Zechariah* iii. 7 (*see* xc.*a*), then assert his High Priesthood by a visit to the Sanctuary, and his royalty by the customary sacrifice to God (*Antiquities* xvii. 8. 4). He achieved a limited success in cleansing the courts, and won at least a moral victory when he routed the Chief Rulers in Scriptural argument. But since his acclamation was not unanimous, and since he was debarred by Law from using force in the Temple, he could only 'look around upon all things' (*Mark* xi. 11); wait patiently for a sign; and finally retire at nightfall after public prayers, his task still unfulfilled.

(*f*) The 'Jews', in *John* xi. 55–56, who discussed the possibility of Jesus's arrival in Jerusalem, will have been the Herodians; as collaborators with Rome, who constantly broke the ritual law, they needed to come up early and purify themselves by sin-offerings.

(311) *And the Passover was nigh at hand, and many Herodians of the country went up to Jerusalem before the Feast, to purify themselves.*

Then sought they for Jesus, and spake among themselves as they stood in the Temple: 'What think ye, that he will not come to the Feast?'

* * * * *

(*g*) [Here follows the account of Jesus's journey from Jericho to Bethany, and the incident of Blind Bartimaeus (*see* xl.*a–h*); next, that of his reconciliation with Mary (*see* xi.*f–h*).]

* * * * *

(315) *And on the morrow, coming out of Bethany, they drew nigh unto Bethphage, which standeth upon the Mount of Olives, a sabbath day's journey from Jerusalem.*

And Jesus sendeth forth two of his disciples, and saith unto them:

'Go into the village over against you, and when ye be entered into it, ye shall find tied unto a vine an ass's colt, whereon never man sat: loose him, and bring him unto me.

'And if any man say unto you: "Why do ye this?", say ye that your master hath need of him, and straightway he will send him hither.'

Wherefore they went their way, and found the colt tied unto a vine at a place nigh unto Bethphage where two ways met.

And they loosed him, and answered the man which stood by even as Jesus had commanded.

As our forefather Jacob testified: 'The sceptre shall not depart from Judah, nor a law-giver from between his feet until Shiloh come, and unto him shall the gathering of the people be.

'Binding his foal unto the vine and his ass's colt unto the choice vine, he washed his garments in wine and his clothes in the blood of the grape.'

* * * * *

(316) *Therefore, when they brought the colt unto Jesus, he washed his garments in wine.*

* * * * *

(*h*) [Here follows a stray text from *Matthew* x. 27 (*see* XLIV.*d*).]

* * * * *

(318) *And with one accord they heaped their garments upon the colt and he sat upon them, and they shouted and cried: 'Hail, Jesus, King of Israel!'*

And others spread their garments before him, and cut down branches of trees and strawed them in his path, crying: 'Praise be to the Anointed One, the Son of David; King of Israel.

'As Zechariah prophesied: "Rejoice greatly, O daughter of Zion, shout, O daughter of Jerusalem! Behold, thy King cometh unto thee. He is just and bringeth salvation, lowly and riding upon an ass and upon a colt, the foal of an ass."

'And as Isaiah saith: "Speak ye to the daughter of Zion: 'Behold, thy salvation cometh; behold, his reward is with him, and his recompense before him!' "

'And: "Wherefore art thou red in thine apparel, and thy garments like unto him that treadeth in the wine vat?

' "Behold, I have trodden the wine-press alone! For the day of vengeance is in my heart, and the year of my redeemed is come.

' "I looked, and there was none to help me, I wondered that there was none to uphold. Therefore mine own arm brought salvation unto me, and my fury upheld me.

' "I will tread down the people in my anger!" '

And they that went before, and they that followed, cried: 'Hosha-na!' (which is, Save now!) and: 'Blessed be he that cometh in the name of the Lord!' and: 'Glory be to God in the highest!'

And after that they had entered into the city, they continued to cry: 'Hosha-na!'

For so Jeremiah prophesied: 'In the time of their trouble they will say: "Arise, and save us!" And also: "Save me, and I shall be saved. Thou art my hope in the Day of Trouble!" "

* * * * *

(319) *Wherefore, when he was come into Jerusalem, all the city was moved, asking: 'Who is this?'*

And the multitude answered: 'This is Jesus, the prophet of Galilee which is King over Israel. He hath come to overthrow his enemies and trample upon them in his anger!'

And the High Priest sent an officer which said unto Jesus: 'Sir, rebuke thy disciples!'

He answered him: 'How can I rebuke them? Did not Habakkuk prophesy against thy master's house?

'For he said: "Thou hast consulted shame to thy house by cutting off many people, and hast sinned against thy soul. Yea, the stone shall cry out of the wall against thee, and the beam from the socket shall cry in answer!"'

* * * * *

(320) *Now, the High Priest was sore displeased when he heard how they that followed Jesus continued to cry: 'Praise to the Son of David!', and sent again unto him, saying: 'Hearest thou not what these say, being ignorant children?'*

Jesus answered: 'Yea, and have ye not read what David saith in a psalm: "Out of the mouths of babes and sucklings hast Thou ordained strength, that Thou mightest put to silence the enemy and the vengeful man"?'

* * * * *

(*i*) The following is the conclusion of Jesus's subsequent dispute with the Chief Rulers:

(335) *And the Chief Rulers departed thence, but Jesus might not come nigh unto the Sanctuary, for the Levite watchmen prevented him, and he bade them which followed him to use no violence.*

Therefore he looked around upon all things, and waited in patience.

* * * * *

Here follows *Luke* xi. 53–54 (*see* XIII.*w*):

(336) *But the scribes of the Sadducees and the Herodians began to urge him vehemently, and to provoke him to speak of many things, laying wait for him and seeking to catch something out of his mouth, that they might accuse him.*

* * * * *

(337) *Now, the eventide was come, and Jesus prayed with all that were there. Afterward he went out unto Bethany with his disciples.*

* * * * *

THE MONEY-CHANGERS

Mark xi. 15–19

[15]And they come to Jerusalem: and Jesus went into the temple, and began to cast out them that sold and bought in the temple, and overthrew the tables of the moneychangers, and the seats of them that sold doves; [16]and would not suffer that any man should carry any vessel through the temple. [17]And He taught, saying unto them:

> *Is it not written,*
> *My house shall be called of all nations*
> *The house of prayer?*
> *But ye have made it a den of thieves.*

[18]And the scribes and the chief priests heard it, and sought how they might destroy Him: for they feared Him, because all the people were astonished at His teaching. [19]And when even was come, He went out of the city.

Matthew xxi. 12–13

[12]And Jesus went into the temple of God, and cast out all them that sold and bought in the temple, and overthrew the tables of the moneychangers, and the seats of them that sold doves, [13]and said unto them: 'It is written:

> *My house shall be called the house of prayer;*

but ye have made it a den of thieves.'

Luke xix. 45–48

[45]And He went into the temple, and began to cast out them that sold therein, and them that bought; [46]saying unto them: 'It is written,

> *My house is the house of prayer: but ye have made it a den of thieves.'*

[47]And He taught daily in the temple. But the chief priests and the scribes and the chief of the people sought to destroy Him, [48]and could not find what they might do: for all the people were very attentive to hear Him.

John ii. 12–25

[12]After this He went down to Capernaum, He, and His mother, and His brethren, and His disciples: and they continued there not many days.

[13]And the Jews' passover was at hand, and Jesus went up to Jerusalem, [14]and found in the temple those that sold oxen and sheep and doves, and the changers of money sitting: [15]and when He had made a small scourge of small

John ii. 12–25 *(contd.)*

cords, He drove them all out of the temple, and the sheep, and the oxen; and poured out the changers' money, and overthrew the tables: [16]and said unto them that sold doves: 'Take these things hence; make not My Father's house an house of merchandise.' [17]And His disciples remembered that it was written:

> *The zeal of Thine house hath eaten Me up.*

[18]Then answered the Jews and said unto Him: 'What sign shewest Thou unto us, seeing that Thou doest these things?' [19]Jesus answered and said unto them: 'Destroy this temple, and in three days I will raise it up.' [20]Then said the Jews: 'Forty and six years was this temple in building, and wilt Thou rear it up in three days?' [21]But He spake of the temple of His body. [22]When therefore He was risen from the dead, His disciples remembered that He had said this unto them; and they believed the scripture, and the word which Jesus had said.

[23]Now when he was in Jerusalem at the passover, in the feast day, many believed in His name, when they saw the miracles which He did. [24]But Jesus did not commit Himself unto them, because He knew all men, [25]and needed not that any should testify of man: for He knew what was in man.

Thirteenth-century marginal note to *The Aurora* (*Fitzwilliam MSS*) quoting *The Gospel according to the Hebrews*

At the cleansing of the Temple: 'In the books which the Nazarenes use it is read that rays issued from his eyes whereby they were terrified and put to flight.'

Jerome: On Matthew xxi. 12

'They did not resist him, for a certain fiery and starry light shone from his eyes, and the majesty of Godhead gleamed from his face.'

(*a*) At first sight, it seems impossible that Jesus cleansed the Temple courts of the money-changers and vendors of sacrificial birds as described in *Mark* xi. 15–19, *Matthew* xxi. 12–13, *Luke* xix. 45–48, and *John* ii. 12–15; they were stationed there by order of the High Priest and with the Pharisaic leaders' consent. This, however, was Jesus's first action after openly proclaiming himself Israel's Priest-king. He seems to have held that it was now his duty (*Zechariah* iii. 7—*see* VIII.*e–f*) to keep holy all the courts of the Temple, not merely the two inner ones (*Psalms* ii. 6, iii. 4, xv. 1, xl. 3, and xcix. 9).

(*b*) The Booths of Hino, a public poultry market, were on the Mount of Olives; but the Chief Rulers, to spare the pilgrims an arduous climb, bought sacrificial birds wholesale and had them delivered at an outer Temple court, where they were sold at a fixed price—in the same way as drink-offerings—by salaried Levite Temple-servants. The *Mishnah* (*Shekalim* v. 4) explains the procedure:

'The devout would approach Johanan, the overseer of the tokens, and pay money in exchange for a token. Johanan would then approach Ahijah, the overseer of drink-offerings, hand him the token and receive the drink-offering. In the evening, when these two consulted together, Johanan would pay Ahijah the value of his tokens.'

(*c*) The money-changers of the Temple were also salaried Levites. Yearly, on the 15th of *Adar,* their tables were set up in the provinces (*Shekalim* i. 3), and ten days later in the Temple. It was their task to provide clean change—that is, coins without blasphemous emblems or inscriptions—for the payment of the Sanctuary tax. A surcharge of a *half-ma'ah* was levied on every transaction and went to the Temple Funds, as the tax itself did. The money-changers therefore made no personal profit, though they drew a subsistence allowance while away from Jerusalem. Some of them seem to have been permanently stationed at the approaches to the Temple, where they provided clean coin for free-will offerings or the purchase of tokens.

The token system, as well as the ban on private trading, had been introduced by the Pharisees, who also forbade pilgrims to enter the Temple precincts carrying sticks, bags, or coins tied in kerchiefs, or with dusty feet—*Exodus* iii. 5 forbade the wearing of shoes upon the Temple Mount (*Peshahim* vii. 11 and 35*b*).

(*d*) Josephus's statement (*Against Apion* ii. 8), that the Temple grounds might not be used as a thoroughfare, is confirmed by the *Mishnah* (*Berakoth* ix. 5 and *Tosephta* vii. 19): 'They shall not use it to shorten a journey!' This regulation, which must have been strictly enforced, seems to contradict *Mark* xi. 16, where Jesus prevents men from carrying vessels through the Temple. But 'through the Temple' does not necessarily mean 'in at one door and out at the other'; and since Zechariah's prophecies were uppermost in Jesus's mind, he may have been protesting against the shape of the Temple vessels carried. Some two centuries before, these had roused the anger of Zechariah (*Zechariah* xi. 13 and xiv. 20-21), who regarded them as 'unclean'. Apparently they were decorated with an ancient motif which now seemed idolatrous, whereas he wanted them modelled on the plain brass lavers placed before the altar. The Canaanite potters against whom he declaimed (*see* cii.*c*) had worked in the Temple ever since the treaty concluded by their ancestors* with Joshua (*Joshua* ix. 15-21); originally, their vessels will have been made in honour of the Moon-goddess Anatha, a form of Athene, after whom Bethany was named, and relics of whose worship survived in the Day of Willows ceremony (*see* xlix.*d*).

These vessels, in fact, were ordinary Temple vessels used for drink-offerings, lustral water, or for the seething of sacrifices (*Zechariah* xiv. 20-21). No Pharisaic objection to their shape is recorded, though some may have

---

* Their city was Gibeon, *Agabon* in one text of the Septuagint; apparently a worn-down form of *Astu Achaivōn,* 'the city of the Achaeans'; and their suppliant dress when they approached Joshua suggests that they were Achaeans—probably descendants of the *Akaiwasha* who had fought Rameses II at Kadesh in 1335 B.C.

been of the widely-distributed owl-eyed type recalling the demoness Lilith ('the Scritch Owl') who, in Hebrew folklore, had become Adam's succuba but was really Anatha-Athene herself. The rabbis drew a Jahvistic moral from even the most erotic accessories of her former cult—such, for instance, as the two cherubim, interlocked in a sexual embrace, which had been carved above the Mercy-seat of the Ark (*Yoma* 54*a*)—and will have found no difficulty in accounting for these. But since the Temple pots—with the brass moon-amulets worn by horses and mules in the streets of Jerusalem— had been the chief object of Zechariah's preaching against idolatry, Jesus will have wished to emulate his zeal. Thus, in *Mark* xi. 16, the word 'unclean'— deleted by a Pauline editor as un-Christian—should be restored to its place before 'vessels'; the Paulines even ate meat that had previously been offered to idols, except when this might offend weaker brethren (1 *Corinthians* viii. 1–12), since Paul was 'persuaded by Christ Jesus that there is nothing unclean of itself'.

(*e*) Jesus was angry not with the authorized vendors of birds, but with the wholesalers who enriched themselves by retaining a large part of their profits. Although the Pharisees tried to preserve the decencies of the Temple, they could not adequately control the Chief Rulers' business dealings—as is proved by the immense fortunes of Bunni ben Gorion and other monopolists (*see* LXXXIII.*g*). Indeed, by their ban on competitive trading, they unwittingly encouraged extortion. Shortly before the Destruction, the controlled price of doves had risen absurdly high, and Rabbi Simeon ben Gamaliel, discovering that pilgrims were now charged a gold denarius the pair, ruled that in future only one bird need be sacrificed for every five demanded by tradition. At once the price fell to a quarter of a denarius (*Kerithoth* i. 7). The Chief Rulers pretended to blame the dove-breeders for these high prices, but there is little doubt that they themselves connived in the fraud on the people.

Jesus, though angered that the poor were unable to afford sacrifices enjoined by the Law, cannot have resorted to violence against the money-changers and dove-vendors (*see* LXXXIX.*e*). He will have been content to fold up their stools and trestle tables as a sign that business was over, ordering them to leave the court in words that frightened them; and since neither the birds nor the money were their own property, they will have been ready enough to obey. At this point, the Levite Temple-guards should have intervened and arrested Jesus for a breach of the peace; but his action seems to have been so popular with the crowd that they stood aside and left the matter for settlement by the Chief Rulers. They realized that Jesus was fulfilling *Zechariah* xiv. 21, 'In that day there shall be no more the Canaanite in the House of the Lord', for in another sense 'Canaanite' had come to mean 'huckster'—the agricultural and pastoral Israelites despised the Canaanite merchant princes whom they had conquered—and was so used in *Hosea* xii. 8 and *Isaiah* xxiii. 8.

(*f*) It is wrongly assumed in *John* that Jesus cleansed the Temple during an earlier visit (*see Introduction* IV.*i*). This account contains several absurdities—why, for instance, sacrificial oxen (*John* ii. 14) should be on sale in the Temple during Passover week, no Christian apologist has been able to explain; even the bull-calves for the burnt-offerings were public, not private, sacrifices (*Numbers* xxviii. 19–24). Nevertheless, *John* alone retains the important detail of the plaited scourge, which seems also to have been the 'sign' mentioned in *John* ii. 18. Jesus first answered the Chief Rulers' protests with a quotation from *Psalm* lxix. 7–9 and then, when they demanded a sign, threatened them with the scourge foretold in *Isaiah* xxviii. 14–16, and further cited *Isaiah* lvi. 7 and *Jeremiah* vii. 11–14.

(*g*) The quotation from *Jeremiah* led to a discussion of what would happen after the destruction of the Temple, which Jesus had just foretold. But in *John* ii. 19: 'Destroy this Temple, and in three days I will raise it up' (*see* CIX.*b*), 'God' must be substituted for the Johannine 'I'. The saying then makes sense: 'Destroy' here is a conditional imperative as, for instance, in 'Marry in haste, repent at leisure!' Jesus had no wish to see the Temple destroyed; indeed, he subsequently wept over its fate (*see* XCVII. *a–b*), and held with *Enoch* that God, who would Himself kindle the blaze (*Lamentations* iv. 11), must afterwards make restitution in accordance with *Exodus* xxii. 6. The Temple would be replaced on the Third Day—the day of universal resurrection foretold in *Hosea* vi. 2 (*see* LXXVIII.*h*)—with a far more glorious one, not made by human hands (*Enoch* xc. 28–29).

(*h*) The Pharisees had always expected the destruction of this Temple. On a famous occasion mentioned in *Wars* vi. 5. 3 when, one morning, the eastern gate of the inner court was found inexplicably open, though bolted on the previous night, the president of the Great Sanhedrin, Johanan ben Zakkai, is said to have exclaimed (*Yoma* 39a): 'Temple, why troublest thou us? We know that thou wilt be destroyed, for Zechariah son of Iddo hath already prophesied concerning thee: "Open thy doors, O Lebanon, that the fire may devour thy cedars." ' And *Genesis Rabbah* lxix. 7 comments on *Genesis* xxviii. 17:

> 'It means that the Holy One, blessed be He, shewed Jacob the Temple built, destroyed, and re-built. "This is the house of God and this is the Gate of Heaven," refers to the Temple when re-built and firmly established in the Messianic Age.'

Furthermore, the author of *Exodus Rabbah* lii. 4 on *Exodus* xxxix. 33 proves to his own satisfaction that both Moses's Tabernacle and Solomon's Temple rose miraculously after the masons and carpenters had prepared the materials. Would not the building of this Celestial Temple be even more miraculous?

(*i*) The Sadducees, however, pretended not to understand Jesus's reference to the Third Day; and the Church, on the strength of *John* ii. 21, has done the same.

(321) *And Jesus lighted from his ass, and took off his shoes at the outer gate of the Temple.*

And it came to pass, when he entered into the porch over against the Treasury, that he saw the money-changers sitting at their tables, and them that sold doves.

And he rebuked them, saying: 'This is the Holy Hill of Zion, whereof David spake: "O send out Thy light and Thy truth. Let them bring me unto Thy Holy Hill!"

'Therefore, take these things hence! Make not my Father's house an house of merchandise! As Zechariah saith: "In that day shall be no more the huckster in the House of the Lord."'

And when at first they would not obey him, he began to fold up the tables of the money-changers, so that the money was spilt; and the seats of them that sold doves he folded up also, and compelled them to depart.

For a fiery light shone from his eyes, and majesty from his countenance, whereby they were overcome with awe.

Neither would he suffer the porters of the Temple to bear unclean vessels through the courts thereof.

These he rebuked likewise, saying: 'Zechariah prophesied: "The vessels in the Lord's house shall be like unto the lavers before His altar. Yea, every pot in Jerusalem and in Judah shall be holiness unto the Lord!"

'See ye not that the pots which ye bear are in shape like unto the abomination of the heathen?'

Yet the Levite watchmen laid not hold on Jesus, for the multitude were attentive to hear his words.

And when they asked him: 'Hast thou no shame, that thou comest with shouts and bringest confusion into this holy place, forbidding these men to minister unto the needs of the people?'

He answered and said: 'David spake unto the Lord: "For Thy sake have I borne reproach; shame hath covered my face. For the zeal of Thine house hath eaten me up."'

* * * *

(j) [Here follow the Widow's Mites (*see* xcii.*a*); the Chief Rulers' decision to investigate the disturbance (*see* xciii.*d*); the Tribute Penny (*see* xciii.*d and e*); the Chief Rulers' request for a sign (*see* xci.*f*); Jesus's further rebuke to them (*see* xci.*e*); and the discussion about Jonah and the Queen of Sheba (*see* xv.*e and* xci.*g*).]

* * * *

(332) *Howbeit, Jesus plaited a scourge of small cords, and said unto the Chief Rulers: 'Ye have asked for a sign, therefore it shall be given unto you.*

'For this scourge is the sign whereof the prophet Isaiah spake, saying:

'"Wherefore hear the word of the Lord, ye scornful men that rule this people which is in Jerusalem!

'"Ye have said: 'We have made a covenant with death, and agreed with hell: when the overflowing scourge shall pass through, it shall not come nigh

*unto us; for we have made lies our refuge, and under falsehood have we hid
ourselves.'*

' *"But the hail shall sweep away your refuge of lies, and the waters shall
overflow your hiding places."*

'*And Isaiah prophesied also in the name of the Lord: "Mine house shall be
called an house of prayer for all people."*

'*But ye pollute it with your extortions.*

'*Jeremiah verily warned your fathers: "Trust ye not in lying words, saying:
'The Temple of the Lord, the Temple of the Lord, the Temple of the Lord.'
Ye trust in lying words that cannot profit. Is this house, which is called by
My name, become a den of thieves in your eyes?*

' *"Go ye unto My house which was in Shiloh, where I set My name at the
first, and see what I did unto it for the wickedness of My people Israel.*

' *"And now, because ye have done these evil works, therefore will I do unto
this house even as I have done unto Shiloh!"* '

* * * * *

For *John* ii. 20, 'forty and six years', *see* LXXXVI.*a*:

(333) *The Chief Rulers said unto Jesus: 'God forbid! For if it please Him to
destroy this Temple, how then shall Israel keep the Law?'*

*Jesus answered: 'Destroy this Temple, and on the Third Day He will raise
it up again in a twinkling of an eye, a glorious work, not built with hands.'*

*But they laughed him to scorn, saying: 'Forty and six years hath this
Temple been a-building, and sayest thou that it will be raised again in three
days?'*

For they were Sadducees, which believe not in the resurrection.

* * * * *

(*k*) [Here follows the Parable of the King's Heir (*see* XCVI.*c*).]

* * * * *

SIGNS FROM HEAVEN

Mark viii. 10-13

[10]And straightway He entered into a boat with His disciples, and came into the parts of Dalmanutha.

[11]And the Pharisees came forth, and began to question with Him, seeking of Him a sign from heaven, tempting Him. [12]And He sighed deeply in His spirit, and saith: 'Why doth this generation seek after a sign? verily I say unto you, There shall no sign be given unto this generation.' [13]And He left them, and entering into the boat again departed to the other side.

Matthew xii. 38-42

[38]Then certain of the scribes and of the Pharisees answered, saying: 'Master, we would see a sign from Thee.' [39]But He answered and said unto them: 'An evil and adulterous generation seeketh after a sign; and there shall no sign be given to it, but the sign of the prophet Jonah: [40]for as Jonah was three days and three nights in the whale's belly; so shall the Son of Man be three days and three nights in the heart of the earth. [41]The men of Nineveh shall rise in judgment with this generation, and shall condemn it: because they repented at the preaching of Jonah; and, behold, a greater than Jonah is here. [42]The queen of the south shall rise up in the judgment with this generation, and shall condemn it: for she came from the uttermost parts of the earth to hear the wisdom of Solomon; and, behold, a greater than Solomon is here.'

Matthew xvi. 1-4

[1]The Pharisees also with the Sadducees came, and tempting desired Him that He would shew them a sign from heaven. [2]He answered and said unto them: 'When it is evening, ye say, It will be fair weather: for the sky is red. [3]And in the morning, It will be foul weather to day: for the sky is red and lowring. O ye hypocrites, ye can discern the face of the sky; but can ye not discern the signs of the time? [4]A wicked and adulterous generation seeketh after a sign; and there shall no sign be given unto it, but the sign of the prophet Jonah.' And He left them, and departed.

Luke xi. 16

[16]And others, tempting him, sought of him a sign from heaven.

Luke xi. 29-32

[29]And when the people were gathered thick together he began to say, This is an evil generation: they seek a sign; and there shall no sign be given it, but the sign of Jonas the prophet. [30]For as Jonas was a sign unto the Ninevites, so shall also the Son of man be to this generation. [31]The queen of the south shall rise up in the judgment with the men of this generation and condemn them: for she came from the utmost parts of the earth to hear the wisdom of Solomon; and, behold, a greater than Solomon is here. [32]The men of Nineve shall rise up in the judgment with this generation, and shall condemn it: for they repented at the preaching of Jonas; and, behold, a greater than Jonas is here.

John vi. 30

[30]They said therefore unto Him: 'What sign shewest Thou then, that we may see, and believe Thee? what dost Thou work?'

Luke xii. 54-57

[54]And He said also to the people: 'When ye see a cloud rise out of the west, straightway ye say, There cometh a shower; and so it is. [55]And when ye see the south wind blow, ye say, There will be heat; and it cometh to pass. [56]Ye hypocrites, ye can discern the face of the sky and of the earth; and how is it that ye do not discern this time? [57]Yea, and why even of yourselves judge ye not what is right?'

(a) In *Mark* viii. 10-13 and *John* vi. 30, the incident of the Signs from Heaven follows the Feeding of the Four Thousand, but in *Matthew* xii. 38-42 precedes it, and in *Luke* xi. 16 and 29-32 takes place some time afterwards. It will therefore have been recorded in the Oracles without any hint as to time and place.

Mark's account, though commendably brief, is inacceptable in so far as it makes the 'Pharisees' tempt Jesus by demanding a sign from heaven which, they knew, God alone could give. It also omits the sayings about Jonah and the Queen of Sheba found in *Matthew* and *Luke,* which are authentic at least in origin.

(b) The editor of *Luke* does not particularize the tempters: he calls them 'others' (*Luke* xi. 16). In *Matthew* xii. 38 they are said to be Scribes and Pharisees; and in *Matthew* xvi. 1, 'Pharisees and Sadducees'. This second and earlier version, taken from the source used in *Mark,* contains a saying about forecasting the weather which recalls *Mark* xiii. 28-29, *Matthew* xxiv. 32-36, and *Luke* xxi. 29-30, where the leafing of fig-trees is mentioned as a sign that summer is near (*see* ci.*c*). It seems, then, that the editor of *Matthew* xii. 38-42 has borrowed and run together two passages from *Luke* (xi. 29-32 and xii. 54-57), in the first of which Jesus makes Jonah's adventure prophetic of his own death and resurrection—though Jonah spent three nights in the whale's belly, and Jesus only two nights in the tomb. For the general allegorical meaning of Jonah's ordeal (*Matthew* xii. 40), see xcvii.*d*.

(c) The demand for a sign was made, it seems, during Jesus's dispute with the Chief Rulers. They will not, however, have tempted him to perform a miracle, but merely asked for signal proof that his message was authoritative (*see* xc.*f*). In reply, he cannot have claimed to be wiser than Solomon; but will have compared the Chief Rulers unfavourably with the Queen of Sheba (1 *Kings* x. 1) who came from Africa to hear the wisdom that they themselves refused to accept, though it was cried aloud in their streets. So far they could follow Jesus's argument; but *Jonah* was a late prophetic book and the Sadducees rejected even the major prophets.

(*d*) In *Luke* xi. 29–32 a reference to *Proverbs* i. 20–23 has dropped out, and two distinct sayings have been run together—both of them presumably found in a collection of Oracles under the subject-heading 'Signs from Heaven'.

(*e*) *Luke* xii. 54–56 appears, at first sight, to be an idle variant of *Matthew* xvi. 1–4; it may, however, conceal a *midrash* on *Job* xxxvii. 16–24. Paul writes in a chapter of *Romans* which contains numerous brief quotations from Jesus's sayings (*Romans* xii. 16) : 'Be not wise in your own conceits.' This is a quotation from *Proverbs* iii. 7, which refers specifically to the passage from *Job,* and may be the key to Jesus's argument, since Paul (*Romans* xi. 25) repeats it in the context of 'blindness in part'.

> (327) *Then he asked them saying: 'Know ye not that a great day is come unto Israel? Wherefore seek ye to condemn it?*
>
> *'As Solomon saith: "Dost thou know the balancings of the clouds, the wondrous works of Him which is perfect in knowledge: how it is that thy garments grow hot when He quieteth the earth by the south wind?*
>
> *' "Men see not the Glory of God which is in the clouds, when the wind passeth and cleanseth them of their rain. But God careth not for any that are wise in their own conceits."*
>
> *'How is it that, when the sky is red at even, ye say: "It will be fair weather," and when the sky is red and lowering in the morning, ye say: "It will be foul"?*
>
> *'Are ye blind in part, that ye read the face of the sky, but not the signs of the times?*
>
> *'Repent then speedily, for by the signs it is clearly discerned that the Day of the Lord is at hand, whose Glory shineth in the clouds!'*

* * * * *

(*f*) Here follows the heart-searching of the Pharisees (*see* xciv.*j*) and the Chief Rulers' request for a sign:

> (329) *But the Chief Rulers, seeing that the people were gathered thick together about Jesus, said unto him: 'What sign shewest thou then, that we may see and believe that God is with thee?'*
>
> *Jesus sighed deeply in his spirit, and said: 'Why doth this generation seek after a sign? What sign shall be given them but a call to repentance, as when the prophet Jonah was sent unto the men of Nineveh?*
>
> *'Yet at the Day of Judgment the men of Nineveh shall rise up in witness*

against this wicked and adulterous generation, for they hearkened to a call, but ye stop your ears.

'*Likewise at the Day of Judgement the Queen of the South shall rise up in witness against you, for she came here from afar to learn wisdom of Solomon, but ye stop your ears to wisdom when she crieth aloud in your streets.*

'*As Solomon himself prophesied, saying: "I, Wisdom, called and ye refused; I stretched out mine hand and no man regarded.*

'*"Ye have set at nought all my counsel, and would have none of my reproof."* '

* * * * *

(g) [Here follows *John* v. 39: Jesus's recommendation to search the Scriptures (*see* xv.*e*).]

* * * * *

(331) *Then said they:* '*The Queen of Sheba we know, but of Jonah we know nought.*'

Jesus answered and said: '*If ye will not read the prophets, how then can ye learn?*

'*For Jonah lay three nights and three days in the whale's belly for a token that the righteous shall rise again on the third day after the destruction of the world.*'

* * * * *

(h) *Luke* xii. 57 belongs to another context; it is probably part of Jesus's answer to the question about tribute to Caesar (*Luke* xx. 19–26—see xciii.*e*).

(325) *And he said unto them all:* '*Do not your own hearts inform you of what is right?*'

* * * * *

THE WIDOW'S MITES

Mark xii. 41–44

⁴¹And Jesus sat over against the treasury, and beheld how the people cast money into the treasury: and many that were rich cast in much. ⁴²And there came a certain poor widow, and she threw in two mites, which make a farthing. ⁴³And He called unto Him His disciples, and saith unto them: 'Verily I say unto you, that this poor widow hath cast more in, than all they which have cast into the treasury: ⁴⁴for all they did cast in of their abundance; but she of her want did cast in all that she had, even all her living.'

Luke xxi. 1–4

¹And He looked up, and saw the rich men casting their gifts into the treasury. ²And He saw also a certain poor widow, casting in thither two mites. ³And He said: 'Of a truth I say unto you, that this poor widow hath cast in more than they all: ⁴for all these have of their abundance cast in unto the offerings of God: but she of her penury hath cast in all the living that she had.'

(*a*) *Deuteronomy* xvi. 16–17 orders that at the feast of the Passover, Weeks and Tabernacles no man shall appear empty-handed before the Lord, but all must give according to their ability. The order had now been extended: at each of these three principal Feasts every Jew, male or female, must make a free-will offering on entering the Temple. The offerings were devoted to the Temple Repair Fund: a custom supposedly initiated in the time of Elisha by Jehoiada, King Jehoash's High Priest, who bored a hole in the lid of the chest and made it an offertory box (2 *Kings* xii. 9).

> (322) *Jesus sat over against the Treasury and beheld how the people cast money into the chest, and how many that were rich gave much.*
>
> *And there came a certain poor widow which cast in two mites.*
>
> *And he said unto his disciples: 'Verily, I say unto you, this poor widow hath done more than all they which have cast into the treasury!*
>
> *'For it is written: "Every man shall give according to his ability," yet none but she hath obeyed the Law.*
>
> *'Behold, they cast in of their abundance, but she of her want hath cast in all that she had, even her own life.'*

*　*　*　*　*

(*b*) A Talmudic parallel is found in *Leviticus Rabbah* iii. 1:

'Once a poor woman brought a handful of flour for an offering, and the priest despised her, saying: "Look, what an offering thou hast brought! How much is here to eat, and how much to offer upon the altar?"

'But in a dream it was revealed unto this priest: "Despise her not. It is as though she had offered her own life in sacrifice." '

* * * * *

THE TRIBUTE PENNY

Mark xii. 13–17

[13]And they send unto Him certain of the Pharisees and of the Herodians, to catch Him in His words. [14]And when they were come, they say unto Him: 'Master, we know that Thou art true, and carest for no man: for Thou regardest not the person of men, but teachest the way of God in truth: Is it lawful to give tribute to Caesar, or not? [15]Shall we give, or shall we not give?' But He, knowing their hypocrisy, said unto them: 'Why tempt ye Me? bring Me a penny, that I may see it.' [16]And they brought it. And He saith unto them: 'Whose is this image and superscription?' And they said unto Him: 'Caesar's.' [17]And Jesus answering said unto them: 'Render to Caesar the things that are Caesar's, and to God the things that are God's.' And they marvelled at Him.

Matthew xxii. 15–22

[15]Then went the Pharisees, and took counsel how they might entangle Him in His talk. [16]And they sent out unto Him their disciples with the Herodians, saying: 'Master, we know that Thou art true, and teachest the way of God in truth, neither carest Thou for any man: for Thou regardest not the person of men. [17]Tell us therefore, What thinkest thou? Is it lawful to give tribute unto Caesar, or not?' [18]But Jesus perceived their wickedness, and said: 'Why tempt ye Me, ye hypocrites? [19]Shew Me the tribute money.' And they brought unto Him a penny. [20]And He saith unto them: 'Whose is this image and superscription?' [21]They say unto Him, 'Caesar's.' Then saith He unto them: 'Render therefore unto Caesar the things which are Caesar's; and unto God the things that are God's.' [22]When they had heard these words, they marvelled, and left Him, and went their way.

Luke xx. 19–26

[19]And the chief priests and the scribes the same hour sought to lay hands on Him; and they feared the people: for they perceived that He had spoken this parable against them. [20]And they watched Him, and sent forth spies, which should feign themselves just men, that they might take hold of His words, that so they might deliver Him unto the power and authority of the governor. [21]And they asked Him, saying: 'Master, we know that Thou sayest and teachest rightly, neither acceptest Thou the person of any, but teachest the way of God truly. [22]Is it lawful for us to give tribute unto Caesar, or no?'

Luke xx. 19–26 (contd.)

²³But he perceived their craftiness, and said unto them: 'Why tempt ye Me? ²⁴Shew Me a penny. Whose image and superscription hath it?' They answered and said: 'Caesar's.' ²⁵And He said unto them: 'Render therefore unto Caesar the things which be Caesar's, and unto God the things which be God's.' ²⁶And they could not take hold of His words before the people: and they marvelled at His answer, and held their peace.

John viii. 20

²⁰These words spake Jesus in the treasury, as He taught in the temple: and no man laid hands on Him; for His hour was not yet come.

Luke xi. 53–54

⁵³And as He said these things unto them, the scribes and the Pharisees began to urge Him vehemently, and to provoke Him to speak of many things: ⁵⁴laying wait for Him, and seeking to catch something out of His mouth, that they might accuse Him.

(a) *Mark* xii. 17, *Matthew* xxii. 21, and *Luke* xx. 25: 'Render unto Caesar the things that are Caesar's . . .', though one of the most famous of the sayings attributed to Jesus, must for historic reasons be rejected, at least in its traditional form.

Israel had spent most of her national existence under the protection of one or other of the great foreign powers—Philistia, Egypt, Assyria, Persia, or Syria—and Jesus will have regarded her present subjection as a just punishment for sin, not to be remedied by force of arms. Nevertheless, among the provisions of the Law were a ban on numbering the tribe of Levi (*Numbers* i. 49)—originally, none of the tribes were to be numbered (*Exodus* xxx. 12 and 1 *Chronicles* xxi. 1–17)—and another on worshipping any graven image (*Exodus* xx. 4–5). The first of these had been broken in Jesus's childhood when Quirinius, before imposing a poll-tax, conducted a general census of Palestine (*see* 1.t) and the High Priest permitted him to include the Levites. The other had been broken more recently, when his successor made no protest against the introduction into Judaea of the new Imperial silver coins—which showed Tiberius's head on the obverse, with the legend: 'High Pontiff and son of the Holy God Augustus', and on the reverse his mother Livia as priestess of her deified husband. This was a graven image* well within the meaning of the Second Commandment, and Jews who paid tribute in this coinage were technically worshipping the God Augustus.

(b) It was easy, of course, to pay in earlier Roman money, still current, which bore no offensive legend—several hundred types of denarius ('penny') were in circulation—or in money acquired outside the Empire, or from allied states. Thus Jesus could have answered, had he wished, that it was lawful

---

* Herod the Great had never dared to place his own head on the copper coinage which the Romans allowed him to strike; but his grandson Agrippa II, King of the Jews, did so, and this will have been one of the reasons suggested for his horrible death (*Acts* xii. 23).

to pay tribute to Caesar, so long as this involved no breach of *Numbers* i.
49 or *Exodus* xx. 4–5. Indeed, the Chief Rulers, whose emissaries asked the
test question, were offering him an opportunity to say so and thereby prove
that he was not a militant fanatic; the revolt led by Judas of Galilee (*Antiquities* xvii. 10. 4) at the time of the first census was still remembered (*Acts*
v. 37—*see* cxviii.*c*). But Jesus, boldly forcing the issue, called for an example
of the new denarius.

(*c*) That it was produced proves that the Pharisees were not, as *Mark* xii.
13 and *Matthew* xxii. 15 suggest, implicated in the plot against him; they
would not have handled the coin anywhere, least of all in the Temple (*see*
xc.*c*). In both these accounts the Pharisees are impossibly allied with their
enemies, the Herodians. But in *Luke* xx. 19 the plot is attributed to the
Sadducees and the scribes; it is likely, therefore, that the original alliance
was between the Sadducees and the Herodians. Jesus's demand that the
offending coin be displayed—he would never have touched it himself—
proves that he did not say the words ascribed to him. 'Render unto Caesar
that which is Caesar's' would have been an invitation to break the Second
Commandment, whereas his object was to call attention to the coin's offensive
design and legend. He will have said: '*Render not to Caesar that which is
God's*'—namely, the sole right to be worshipped by the Israelites—'*nor unto
God that which is Caesar's*'—namely, a coin which was disqualified by its
design and legend from being paid into the Treasury.

(*d*) Jesus's saying has been altered by Gentile editors in accordance with
Paul's instructions to his converts (*Romans* xiii. 7), whom he freed from all
obligations to the Law: 'Render therefore to all their dues: tribute to whom
tribute is due, custom to whom custom, fear to whom fear, honour to whom
honour.' This is a complete repudiation of Jesus's religious convictions as
expressed elsewhere (*see* xix.*a*, xlvii.*d and* li.*b*).

'Why tempt ye me?' means: 'Why trouble to put me to the test, since
you know well what views I hold?'

> (323) *And the Chief Rulers and their scribes, together with the Herodians,
> when they knew that the people which followed Jesus and hailed him King
> were unarmed, sought to know whether it were in his mind to make insur-
> rection by violence.*
>
> *If he plotted aught, then would they seek to lay hands upon him and de-
> liver him unto the power of Pontius Pilate, which was Governor of Judaea;
> but secretly, for they feared the people.*
>
> *Therefore sent they forth certain of their number, feigning themselves to
> be seekers after knowledge, that they might lead Jesus to disclose the inner-
> most thoughts of his heart.*

* * * * *

> (324) *These men asked him, saying: 'Master, we know that thou teachest the
> way of God in all truth, and as God Himself is no respecter of persons, so thou*

also fearest none but God, neither carest for any man unless he be set over thee by the will of God.

'Tell us therefore: is it lawful to give tribute unto the Romans in token of their lordship over us?'

Jesus answered and said: 'If ye know that I teach the way of God in truth, why try ye me? Shew me the penny of him that exacteth this tribute.'

Then one of the Herodians drew forth a penny from his bosom and shewed it unto Jesus, but he touched it not.

And Jesus asked: 'Whose is this graven image and what meaneth the super-scription?'

The Herodian answered: 'It is the image of Caesar, and the superscription nameth him High Priest and son of the most holy God Augustus.'

Jesus asketh: 'Bringest thou such money into the Temple of the One God? And wouldst thou indeed pay it into His treasury? And askest thou me whether it be right to bow down unto him whose graven image thou shewest me?'

* * * * *

(e) [Here follows: 'Do not your own hearts inform you of what is right?', a stray text from *Luke* xii. 57 (*see* xci.*h*).]

* * * * *

(326) *'Render not unto Caesar that which is God's, nor unto God that which is Caesar's!'*

These words spake Jesus as he watched over against the Treasury, and no man durst lay hands upon him.

* * * * *

BY WHAT AUTHORITY?

John viii. 1–2

[1]Jesus went unto the Mount of Olives. [2]And early in the morning He came again into the temple, and all the people came unto Him; and He sat down, and taught them.

John vii. 14

[14]Now about the midst of the feast Jesus went up into the temple, and taught.

John v. 24

[24]Verily, verily, I say unto you, he that heareth My word, and believeth on Him that sent Me, hath everlasting life, and shall not come into condemnation; but is passed from death unto life.

John vii. 40–41a

[40]Many of the people therefore, when they heard this saying, said: 'Of a truth this is the Prophet.' [41]Others said: 'This is the Christ. . . .'

John vii. 32

[32]The Pharisees heard that the people murmured such things concerning Him; and the Pharisees and the chief priests sent officers to take Him.

John vii. 30

[30]Then they sought to take Him: but no man laid hands on Him, because His hour was not yet come.

John vii. 15

[15]And the Jews marvelled, saying, 'How knoweth this man letters, having never learned?'

John vii. 24

[24]'Judge not according to the appearance, but judge righteous judgement.'

Mark xi. 27–33

[27]And they come again to Jerusalem: and as He was walking in the temple, there come to Him the chief priests, and the scribes, and the elders, [28]and say unto Him: 'By what authority doest Thou these things? and who gave Thee

Mark xi. 27–33 (*contd.*)

this authority to do these things?' [29]And Jesus answered and said unto them: 'I will ask of you one question, and answer Me, and I will tell you by what authority I do these things. [30]The baptism of John, was it from heaven, or of men? answer Me.' [31]And they reasoned with themselves, saying, If we shall say from heaven; He will say, Why then did ye not believe him? [32]But if we shall say, of men; they feared the people: for all men counted John, that he was a prophet indeed. [33]And they answered and said unto Jesus: 'We cannot tell.' And Jesus answering saith unto them: 'Neither do I tell you by what authority I do these things.'

Matthew xxi. 23–27

[23]And when He was come into the temple, the chief priests and the elders of the people came unto Him as He was teaching, and said: 'By what authority doest Thou these things? and who gave Thee this authority?' [24]And Jesus answered and said unto them: 'I also will ask you one thing, which if ye tell Me, I in like wise will tell you by what authority I do these things. [25]The baptism of John, whence was it? from heaven, or of men?' And they reasoned with themselves, saying, If we shall say, from heaven; He will say unto us, Why did ye not then believe him? [26]But if we shall say, of men; we fear the people; for all hold John as a prophet. [27]And they answered Jesus, and said: 'We cannot tell.' And He said unto them: 'Neither tell I you by what authority I do these things.'

Luke xx. 1–8

[1]And it came to pass, that on one of those days, as He taught the people in the temple, and preached the Gospel, the chief priests and the scribes came upon Him with the elders, [2]and spake unto Him, saying: 'Tell us, by what authority doest Thou these things? or Who is he that gave Thee this authority?' [3]And He answered and said unto them: 'I will also ask you one thing; and answer Me: [4]The baptism of John, was it from heaven, or of men?' [5]And they reasoned with themselves, saying, If we shall say, From heaven; He will say, Why then believed ye him not? [6]But and if we say, Of men; all the people will stone us: for they be persuaded that John was a prophet. [7]And they answered, that they could not tell whence it was. [8]And Jesus said unto them: 'Neither tell I you by what authority I do these things.'

Luke xxi. 37–38

[37]And in the day time He was teaching in the temple; and at night He went out, and abode in the mount that is called the mount of Olives. [38]And all the people came early in the morning to Him in the temple, for to hear Him.

John vii. 28–29

[28]Then cried Jesus in the temple as He taught, saying: 'Ye both know Me, and ye know whence I am: and I am not come of Myself, but He that sent Me is true, Whom ye know not. [29]But I know Him: for I am from Him, and He hath sent Me.'

John vii. 16–20

[16]Jesus answered them, and said: 'My doctrine is not Mine, but His that sent Me. [17]If any man will do His will, he shall know of the doctrine, whether it be of God, or whether I speak of Myself. [18]He that speaketh of himself seeketh his own glory: but he that seeketh His glory that sent him, the same is true, and no unrighteousness is in him. [19]Did not Moses give you the law, and yet none of you keepeth the law? Why go ye about to kill Me?' [20]The people answered and said: 'Thou hast a devil: who goeth about to kill Thee?'

John vii. 33–34

[33]Then said Jesus unto them: 'Yet a little while am I with you, and then I go unto Him that sent Me. [34]Ye shall seek Me, and shall not find Me: and where I am, thither ye cannot come.'

John vii. 35–36

[35]Then said the Jews among themselves: 'Whither will He go, that we shall not find Him? will He go unto the dispersed among the Gentiles, and teach the Gentiles? [36]What manner of saying is this that He said, ye shall seek Me, and shall not find Me; and where I am, thither ye cannot come?'

John vii. 44–53

[44]And some of them would have taken Him; but no man laid hands on Him.

[45]Then came the officers to the chief priests and Pharisees; and they said unto them: 'Why have ye not brought Him?' [46]The officers answered: 'Never man spake like this Man.' [47]Then answered them the Pharisees: 'Are ye also deceived? [48]Have any of the rulers or of the Pharisees believed on Him? [49]But this people who knoweth not the law are cursed.' [50]Nicodemus saith unto them, (he that came to Jesus by night, being one of them): [51]'Doth our law judge any man, before it hear him, and know what he doeth?' [52]They answered and said unto him: 'Art thou also of Galilee? Search, and look: for out of Galilee ariseth no prophet.'

[53]And every man went unto his own house.

John vii. 25–27

[25]Then said some of them of Jerusalem: 'Is not this He, Whom they seek to kill? [26]But lo, He speaketh boldly, and they say nothing unto Him. Do the rulers know indeed that this is the very Christ? [27]Howbeit we know this man whence He is; but when Christ cometh, no man knoweth whence He is.'

John vii. 41b–43

[41]But some said: 'Shall Christ come out of Galilee? [42]Hath not the scripture said, that Christ cometh of the seed of David, and out of the town of Bethlehem, where David was?' [43]So there was a division among the people because of Him.

John vii. 31

[31]And many of the people believed on Him, and said: 'When Christ cometh, will He do more miracles than these which this Man hath done?'

John vii. 12–13

^{12}And there was much murmuring among the people concerning Him; for some said: 'He is a good man'; others said: 'Nay, but he deceiveth the people.' ^{13}Howbeit no man spake openly of Him for fear of the Jews.

John xii. 48

^{48}He that rejecteth Me, and receiveth not My words, hath One that judgeth him: the word that I have spoken, the same shall judge him in the last day.

John xvi. 16–23

^{16}'A little while, and ye shall not see Me: and again, a little while, and ye shall see Me, because I go to the Father.'

^{17}Then said some of His disciples among themselves: 'What is this that He saith unto us, A little while, and ye shall not see Me: and again, a little while, and ye shall see Me: and, Because I go to the Father?' ^{18}They said therefore: 'What is this that he saith, A little while? we cannot tell what He saith.' ^{19}Now Jesus knew that they were desirous to ask Him, and said unto them: 'Do ye inquire among yourselves of that I said, A little while, and ye shall not see Me: and again, a little while, and ye shall see Me? ^{20}Verily, verily, I say unto you, that ye shall weep and lament, but the world shall rejoice: and ye shall be sorrowful, but your sorrow shall be turned into joy. ^{21}A woman when she is in travail hath sorrow, because her hour is come: but as soon as she is delivered of the child, she remembereth no more the anguish, for joy that a man is born into the world. ^{22}And ye now therefore have sorrow: but I will see you again, and your heart shall rejoice, and your joy no man taketh from you. ^{23}And in that day ye shall ask Me nothing. Verily, verily, I say unto you, whatsoever ye shall ask the Father in My Name, He will give it you.'

Justin: Dialogue with Tryphon the Jew. ii.

'The Messiah, if he be already born and dwell in any place, the same is unknown both of others and also of himself, and lacketh power until Elias shall come to anoint him and manifest him unto all.'

(*a*) *John* vii. is perhaps the most confused chapter of the New Testament. Verses 1–11 and 37–39 are concerned with an earlier visit of Jesus to Jerusalem, probably for the previous Feast of Tabernacles (*see* XLIX. *a–f*); verses 21–23 with his healing of the blind man at Bethesda (*see* LXXIV.*c*); the remainder with his visit to the Temple on the day which intervened between the Royal Entry and the Arrest. These last are given in haphazard order; and the sequence should be introduced by *John* viii. 1–2. An important omission is the question (*Mark* xi. 27–33; *Matthew xxi.* 23–27, and *Luke* xx. 1–8): 'By what authority doest thou these things?'—which Jesus answers with a reference to his lustration by John the Baptist (*see* VIII.*a–b*). He will have held that his installation as Priest-king freed him to do as he pleased under the Law, regardless of the existing High Priest, who was a Roman nominee and therefore a usurper.

(*b*) In John vii. 15, the Jews are said to marvel at Jesus's preaching and declare that he is self-taught—as they marvel at his 'authority' in *Mark* i. 22 and *Matthew* vii. 28–29 (*see* XLII.*f*). The interpolated 'having never learned' wrongly suggests that Jesus's doctrine was original and divinely inspired, not based on the oral or the written Law; from which Christians are expected to deduce that, since belief in Jesus is sufficient for salvation, they may disregard both of these. Yet Jesus had not only studied the written and oral Law, the historical books, the prophets, and the uncanonical apocalypses under a competent teeacher, but was word-perfect in all of them.

John vii. 16–20 appears to be genuine, and must refer to his conflict with the Chief Rulers' emissaries mentioned in verse 32; this passage contains his final reply to the question: 'By what authority doest thou these things?', and should follow verses 28 and 29, which are part of the same incident.

Jesus's chief questioner will have been the Commander of the Levite Guard, called 'The Captain of the Temple' (*Ish har ha'baith*). It appears that the Chief Rulers had, so far, not taken Jesus's claims seriously; on the previous day he had failed to excite any great enthusiasm among the pilgrim crowd and gone away quietly when evening came. They can hardly have expected that he would make a second attempt to assert his sovereignty and, unless he did so, there would be no need to report the matter to the Romans. Religious demonstrations were punishable only if they caused a breach of the peace. Now, however, they realized that his following was greater than they had supposed, and that he had been neither overawed nor deflected from his purpose.

(*c*) *John* vii. 21–23, a passage about healing on the Sabbath (*see* (*a*) *above*), seems to have superseded a contemptuous speech by the Captain, which the editors found offensive; but its substance has been preserved in verse 15. Jesus's reply in verse 24—a quotation from *Deuteronomy* i. 16–17—has been modified because it was too humbly phrased.

John vii. 25–27 should be joined to verses 41*b*–44 and 12–13. 'A good man' in verse 12, should read 'The Righteous One', that is to say, the Messiah. 'Jews' in verse 13, should read 'Romans'. Verses 27 and 42 are corrupt—but easily amended. Verse 32 is absurd in so far as it makes the Pharisees conspire with the Chief Rulers, though these may well have sent officers to arrest Jesus. It should precede *Mark* xi. 27–33, which is paralleled in *Matthew* xxi. 23–27 and *Luke* xx. 1–8. The view expressed in verse 35 should be the disciples'; here it is wrongly attributed to Jesus's audience and the Jews in general. Verse 40 refers to 'that prophet' (*Deuteronomy* xviii. 15— *see* LXVII.*b*), and will have been spoken in the Temple.

(*d*) The substance of *John* viii. 33–34, repeated in *John* xiii. 33 and xvi. 16, seems authentic, though abbreviated, and should follow *John* vii. 20. Jesus is addressing the officers who have orders to arrest him, and announces that he will soon be slain, though not by them; that, when they finally come for him, they will grope in the darkness prophesied for the Last Days—which will be inaugurated by his death (*see* LXXXVIII.*e and* CII.*d*). If God accepts his sacrifice, the Day of Judgement will soon dawn and, unless they repent speedily, they will find themselves separated from him by a great gulf (*see* (*e*) *below;* LXIX.*d and* LXXXII.*j*). *John* vii. 45–49 is a sequel to Jesus's clash with these officers.

(338) *Jesus went up into the Mount of Olives, and tarried there all night; but early in the morning he came again into the Temple and the people thronged unto him.*

And he sat down and taught them, and they marvelled at his teaching.

Then said some of them that heard him: 'Of a truth, this is that prophet of which Moses spake!'

And others said: 'This is the Anointed King which shall redeem Israel!'

Wherefore the Chief Rulers when they heard how the people murmured such things, bade the Captain of the Temple lead forth officers to take him.

* * * * *

(339) *And Jesus said unto the multitude: 'He that heareth my word and believeth in Him that sent me and straightway repenteth, the same shall not be condemned, but be passed from death into life.'*

* * * * *

[Here follow 'The hour is at hand when the dead shall hear the voice of the Son of Man' (*see* XXVI.*d*); and 'Some that stand here shall not taste of death' (*see* CI.*k*).]

* * * * *

(342) *And as he spake these words, the Captain of the Temple, coming unto Jesus with his officers, saw that the people hearkened unto him with awe.*

Therefore they durst not take him, but asked: 'Why boastest thou thyself somewhat, being a poor man of Galilee, neither a priest nor a lawyer?'

Jesus answered and said: 'It is written: "Ye shall not respect persons in judgment; but ye shall hearken unto the small as well as the great." '

* * * * *

(*e*) [Here follow the argument about Abraham (*see* XCV.*c*); the substance of *Luke* xiii. 27–30 (*see* LXIX.*d*); and Jesus's refusal to bear witness to his own righteousness (*see* XCV.*e*).]

* * * * *

(346) *Then said the Captain of the Temple: 'By what authority sayest and doest thou these things? And who gave thee leave?'*

Jesus answered and said unto him, and unto them that were with him: 'I will also ask one question of you and when ye have answered it, then will I tell you by what authority I say and do these things.'

They said: 'Say on!'

Jesus asked: 'The baptism with which John baptized me, and my anointing at his hands, were they of heaven, or were they of men?'

And they reasoned within themselves, saying: 'If we say "of heaven," he will answer: "Why, then, do ye not acknowledge me King?" But if we say "of men," the people will be moved to anger, for they account John a prophet indeed.'

Wherefore they answered him, saying: 'We cannot tell thee.'

Jesus asked again: 'If, then, ye will not answer me, why should I answer you?'

They said: 'Because that we ask thee these things in the name of the Chief Rulers!'

Whether John was Elijah (*see* xiii.*a*), and thus capable of anointing the Messiah, is still hotly debated in Justin's mid-second-century Dialogue with Tryphon.

* * * * *

(347) *Then cried Jesus, saying: 'Ye know both who I am and whence I come! But I do nought of my own authority, nor seek I mine own glory; but am sent of God, and seek God's glory.*

'Whosoever obeyeth God's will, the same shall know within his heart whether these things which I say and do proceed from God or from mine own vain imaginings.'

* * * * *

(*f*) [Here follows *John* v. 46, which refers to *Deuteronomy* xviii. 18–19 (*see* xv.*f*). Jesus proves that no one can logically obey the Law while rejecting the prophets authorized by it.]

* * * * *

Here follows *John* xii. 48:

(349) *'Beware therefore: he that rejecteth me and receiveth not my words, the same shall be judged of Him that sent me; and the words that I speak shall testify against him in the Last Day!'*

* * * * *

(350) *'Ye sons of Levi, why go ye about to kill me? Did not Moses give you the Law, and appoint you priests of God to serve Him according to the Law? Are ye wroth, then, that I preach the observance of the Law?'*

They answered: 'Thou art beside thyself. Who goeth about to kill thee?'

Jesus said unto them: 'Yet a little while am I with you, and then I go hence unto my Father.

'And ye shall seek to lay hands on me, but shall not find me.

'And again in a little while ye shall see me, but haply ye shall not be able to come thither where I go.'

They that heard him, questioned among themselves: 'What manner of saying is this?'

* * * * *

(*g*) [Here follows a missing part of Jesus's discourse, to be recovered from *John* viii. 13–14, 19, 25, and 28 (*see* xcv.*a* and *f*).]

* * * * *

(353) *But they durst not yet lay hands on him, and departed thence.*

* * * * *

(*h*) [Here follows the account of his safe escape from the Temple (*see* xcv.*g*).]

* * * * *

(357) *The Captain of the Temple and his officers went unto the Chief Rulers, which asked them: 'Why have ye not brought him that ye were commanded to bring?'*

They answered, and said: 'We feared the people. Never spake a man like unto this man, neither gave he us any occasion against him.'

And the Chief Rulers asked: 'Are ye then also deceived? Hath any man of our number believed that he is the Anointed One? Or hath any ruler of the Pharisees?

'Behold, this Galilean stirreth up the ignorant people; may God's curse fall upon him and upon them!'

* * * * *

(*i*) John vii. 50–52 belongs to a later context (*see* cix.*q*); at this stage 'Nicodemus' will still have been referred to as 'Bunni son of Gorion':

(416) *Bunni son of Gorion, being one of their number, saith: 'Doth the Law suffer us to condemn any man without hearing?'*

They asked him: 'Art thou also a Galilean?'

* * * * *

(*j*) John vii. 52 has been misreported: several prophets had come from Galilee, including Hosea of Belemoth (St Ephraim the Syrian: *Commentaries* ii. 234) and Jonah of Gath-Hepher (2 *Kings* xiv. 25).

John vii. 53: 'And every man returned to his own house' apparently refers to the Council held early in the morning of the Crucifixion (*see* cix.*s*).

(328) *Then said certain of the Pharisees and other devout people of Jerusalem: 'Is not this he whom the Herodians seek to kill? But lo, he speaketh boldly, and they do nought against him.*

'Know the Chief Rulers then that he is verily the Anointed One, and therefore hold their hands?'

But others said: 'Why think ye that this man is the Anointed One? He is indeed of the seed of David, but we know whence he cometh: he cometh of Bethlehem Nazara.

'Shall not the Anointed come of Bethlehem Ephratah, whence David was?'

Then said the first: 'He hath wrought great wonders both in Galilee and in Judaea.'

But the others answered: 'When the Anointed One cometh, will he not work greater?'

Then was there a division among the Pharisees and other devout people of Jerusalem because of him.

Some said: 'This is verily the King, the Righteous One,' and others: 'Nay, but he deceiveth the people.'

But none durst openly acknowledge him to be King, for all waited for a sure proof that God had appointed him to redeem Israel.

* * * * *

(*k*) This passage is supplemented in *John* xvi. 16–23—which refers to the Pangs of the Messiah—by Jesus's quotations from *Micah* iv. 9–10 and v. 3, and from *Isaiah* lxvi. 9. The original may have read:

(355) *And afterward Jesus made plain the words which he spake: 'Yet a little while am I with you, and then I go hence.'*

For some of the disciples thought that he purposed to go unto the dispersed among the Gentiles.

Therefore he said: 'This I spake because I must suffer death according to the word of my Father which sent me. And when I am gone, they that seek me shall grope in the darkness whereof Daniel prophesied.

'For then shall ensue the pangs of her that bringeth forth, whereof Micah and Isaiah prophesied, saying: "Be in pain and labour to bring forth, O daughter of Zion!"

'Verily, ye shall weep and lament, but presently your sorrow shall be turned to joy.

'A woman in her travail weepeth and lamenteth that her hour is come; but when she is delivered of her child, straightway she remembereth no more her anguish for joy that a man is born into the world.'

* * * * *

(*l*) Here follows the saying concealed in *John* v. 25–29 (*see* xxvi.*d*):

(356) *'So likewise the Kingdom of God shall come, and if it please Him to number me among the elect, they that now seek my life will behold me, but not come thither where I am.*

'For a great gulf is fixed between them that are condemned and them that are saved.

'And in that day ye shall have no more need to question me; for all things shall be revealed unto every man!'

* * * * *

(*m*) Jesus's condemnation of the Sadducees accorded with *Zechariah* vii. 9–10, where God commands Zechariah to tell the people and priests:

'Execute true judgement, shew mercy and compassion every man to his brother.

'And oppress not the widow, nor the fatherless, nor the stranger, nor the poor, and let none of you imagine evil in his heart against his brother.'

The passage continues (*Zechariah* vii. 11–14):

'But they refused to hearken and pulled away the shoulder and stopped their ears that they should not hear.

'Yea, they made their hearts as an adamant stone, lest they should hear the Law, and the words which the Lord of Hosts hath sent in His spirit by the former prophets: therefore came a great wrath from the Lord of Hosts.

' "Therefore also it is come to pass that, as He cried and they would not hear, so they cried and I would not hear," saith the Lord of Hosts.

' "But I scattered them with an whirlwind among all the nations which they knew not. Thus the land was desolate after them, that no man passed through or returned: for they laid the pleasant land desolate." '

* * * * *

SONS OF ABRAHAM

John viii. 13–14

[13]The Pharisees therefore said unto Him: 'Thou bearest record of Thyself: Thy record is not true.' [14]Jesus answered and said unto them: 'Though I bear record of Myself, yet My record is true: for I know whence I came, and whither I go; but ye cannot tell whence I come, and whither I go.'

John viii. 19–59

[19]Then said they unto Him, 'Where is Thy Father?' Jesus answered: 'Ye neither know Me, nor My Father: if ye had known Me, ye should have known My Father also.' [20]These words spake Jesus in the treasury, as He taught in the temple: and no man laid hands on Him; for His hour was not yet come.

[21]Then said Jesus again unto them: 'I go My way, and ye shall seek Me, and shall die in your sins: whither I go, ye cannot come.' [22]Then said the Jews: 'Will He kill Himself? because He saith, Whither I go, ye cannot come.' [23]And He said unto them: 'Ye are from beneath; I am from above: ye are of this world; I am not of this world. [24]I said therefore unto you, that ye shall die in your sins: for if ye believe not that I am He, ye shall die in your sins.' [25]Then said they unto Him: 'Who art Thou?' And Jesus saith unto them: 'Even the same that I said unto you from the beginning. [26]I have many things to say to judge of you: but He that sent Me is true; and I speak to the world those things which I have heard of Him.' [27]They understood not that He spake to them of the Father. [28]Then said Jesus unto them: 'When ye have lifted up the Son of Man, then shall ye know that I am He, and that I do nothing of Myself; but as My Father hath taught Me, I speak these things. [29]And He that sent Me is with Me: the Father hath not left Me alone; for I do always those things that please Him.' [30]As He spake these words, many believed on Him.

[31]Then said Jesus to those Jews which believed on Him: 'If ye continue in My word, then are ye My disciples indeed; [32]and ye shall know the truth, and the truth shall make you free.' [33]They answered Him: 'We be Abraham's seed, and were never in bondage to any man: how sayest Thou, ye shall be made free?' [34]Jesus answered them: 'Verily, verily, I say unto you, whosoever committeth sin is the servant of sin. [35]And the servant abideth not in the house for ever: but the Son abideth ever. [36]If the Son therefore shall make you free, ye shall be free indeed. [37]I know that ye are Abraham's seed; but ye seek to kill Me, because My word hath no place in you. [38]I speak that

John viii. 19–59 (*contd.*)

which I have seen with My Father: and ye do that which ye have seen with your father.' [39]They answered and said unto Him: 'Abraham is our father.' Jesus saith unto them: 'If ye were Abraham's children, ye would do the works of Abraham. [40]But now ye seek to kill Me, a man that hath told you the truth, which I have heard of God: this did not Abraham. [41]Ye do the deeds of your father.' Then said they to Him: 'We be not born of fornication; we have one Father, even God.' [42]Jesus said unto them: 'If God were your Father, ye would love Me: for I proceeded forth and came from God; neither came I of Myself, but He sent Me. [43]Why do ye not understand My speech? even because ye cannot hear My word. [44]Ye are of your father the devil, and the lusts of your father ye will do. He was a murderer from the beginning, and abode not in the truth, because there is no truth in him. When he speaketh a lie, he speaketh of his own: for he is a liar, and the father of it. [45]And because I tell you the truth, ye believe Me not. [46]Which of you convinceth Me of sin? And if I say the truth, why do ye not believe Me? [47]He that is of God heareth God's words: ye therefore hear them not, because ye are not of God.' [48]Then answered the Jews, and said unto Him: 'Say we not well that Thou art a Samaritan, and hast a devil?' [49]Jesus answered: 'I have not a devil; but I honour My Father, and ye do dishonour Me. [50]And I seek not Mine own glory: there is One that seeketh and judgeth. [51]Verily, verily, I say unto you, if a man keep My saying, he shall never see death.' [52]Then said the Jews unto Him: 'Now we know that Thou hast a devil. Abraham is dead, and the prophets: and Thou sayest, If a man keep My saying, he shall never taste of death. [53]Art Thou greater than our father Abraham, which is dead? and the prophets which are dead: whom makest Thou Thyself?' [54]Jesus answered: 'If I honour Myself, My honour is nothing: it is My Father that honoureth Me; of Whom ye say, that He is your God. [55]Yet ye have not known Him: but I know Him: and if I should say, I know Him not, I shall be a liar like unto you: but I know Him, and keep His saying. [56]Your father Abraham rejoiced to see My day: and he saw it, and was glad.' [57]Then said the Jews unto Him: 'Thou art not yet fifty years old, and hast Thou seen Abraham?' [58]Jesus said unto them: 'Verily, verily, I say unto you, before Abraham was, I am.' [59]Then took they up stones to cast at Him: but Jesus hid Himself, and went out of the temple, going through the midst of them, and so passed by.

(*a*) *John* viii. is another confused chapter. Verses 1–2 introduce 'By what authority?' (*see* XCIV.*a*). Verses 13–14, 19, 25, and the last clause of 28, seem authentic parts of the dispute which follows (*see* XCIV.*e–g*); verses 21–30 are its Christological expansion.

(351) *But the Captain of the Temple said: 'Thou foretellest what shall become of thee, but no man knoweth certainly what shall become of him; therefore is thy record not true.'*

Jesus answered and said: 'I speak as my Father hath taught me; for he hath instructed me whither I shall go.'

Then the Captain asked: 'Who art thou, then, and where is thy father?'

He answered: 'If ye know not my Father which sent me, and which is from the Beginning, how then shall ye know me?'

* * * * *

(*b*) *John* viii. 3–11 refers to events in Samaria (*see* LXX.*h*); verse 12 is the Christological version of a saying about the Glory of God (*see* XXIV.*c*). Verses 15–18 are part of Jesus's discourse of judgement (*see* XXVI.*c*), and verse 20 of the Tribute Penny incident (*see* XCIII.*e*).

(*c*) *John* viii. 31–59 is a Christological sermon based, probably, on Matthew iii. 9: 'We have Abraham for our father' (*see* v.*g*), and on certain passages from the *Epistle to the Romans* (vi. 14–22, viii. 2 and ix. 7). It concludes, impossibly, with Jesus's claim to be God. Verse 41: 'We be not born of fornication' reflects the second-century Jewish libel that Jesus was himself so born (*see* I.*a*, VII.*g* and XL.*e*). For verse 48, *see* LXX.*m*. A nucleus of authentic tradition seems to be embedded in verses 39, 44, 51–52 and 24, another fragment of the previous day's dispute, which should follow *Mark* ix. 1: 'Some that stand here will not taste of death' (*see* XCI.*f and* CI.*k*). Part of Jesus's answer has dropped out, but can be deduced from the Pharisaic doctrine that the righteous dead were still living, to which *Mark* xii. 27 refers (*see* XXI.*l*). Jesus could not have called the Sadducees 'liars' and Devil's bastards, or accused them of being murderers; this would have made him a murderer himself, in the eyes of the Law (*see* XXII.*b*).

> (343) *The Captain saith unto him: 'How prophesiest thou to these men, that they shall not see death if they hearken unto thee?*
>
> *'Art thou then greater than our father Abraham which is dead, and the prophets which are dead?'*
>
> *Jesus answered and said: 'They died, but live yet. Beware, that ye Sadducees die not in your sins, and perish everlastingly!*
>
> *'If ye be true sons of Abraham, then do the works of Abraham, and not the works of the father of lies, which was a murderer from the beginning.'*

* * * * *

(*d*) [Here follows *Luke* xiii. 25–28, a warning that there will be weeping and gnashing of teeth when the Sadducees see Abraham, Isaac and Jacob and all the prophets in the Kingdom of God, but find themselves thrust out (*see* LXIX.*d*).]

* * * * *

(*e*) *John* viii. 54: 'If I honour myself, my honour is nothing', recalls *John* v. 31: 'If I bear witness of myself, my witness is not true' (*see* XV.*b and* XXVI.*f*). This, also, seems to be part of the previous day's dispute, and will have provoked the question: 'By what authority sayest and doest thou these things?' (*see* XCIV.*e*).

> (345) *Then said the Captain: 'Art thou indeed an honourable person, filled with righteousness?'*

He answered: 'If I honour myself, my honour is nothing; if I bear witness to my own righteousness, my witness is not true.'

* * * * *

(*f*) *John* viii. 58 may be part of Jesus's answer to the question (*see* (*a*) *above*): 'Where is thy father?' For 'I am' as God's name, *see* LIV.*b*; 'I' has again been substituted for 'God'. Jesus here quotes *Exodus* iii. 13–14:

> (352) *'For it is written that when Moses enquired of God, and asked Him by what name He should be known, God answered:*
> *'"Say: I AM THAT I AM, the Lord God of your Fathers, the God of Abraham and Isaac and Jacob hath sent thee!"*
> *'Yet in the ages before Abraham, God was!'*

* * * * *

(*g*) *John* viii. 59 must be rejected, since no Sadducee would have dared to stone a blasphemer either in the Temple or out of it and, in any case, Jesus had not blasphemed. The incident ends with:

> (355) *And they laid wait for him outside the Temple, but he went forth in the midst of a great throng, and they could do nothing.*

* * * * *

(*h*) At this point, it will have been the Captain's duty to inform Pilate of Jesus's persistent claims to the throne of Israel. He will have submitted that no violence had so far been used, but that Jesus had the support of numerous Galilean fanatics; his presence in the Temple area during the coming Feast Days might cause a serious breach of the peace.

* * * * *

THE KING'S SON

Mark xii. 1–9

[1]And He began to speak unto them by parables. 'A man planted a vineyard, and set an hedge about it, and digged the winefat, and built a tower, and let it out to husbandmen, and went into a far country. [2]And at the season he sent to the husbandmen a servant, that he might receive from the husbandmen of the fruit of the vineyard. [3]And they caught him, and beat him, and sent him away empty. [4]And again he sent unto them another servant; and at him they cast stones, and wounded him in the head, and sent him away shamefully handled. [5]And again he sent another; and him they killed, and many others; beating some, and killing some. [6]Having yet therefore one son, his well-beloved, he sent him also last unto them, saying, They will reverence my son. [7]But those husbandmen said among themselves, This is the heir; come, let us kill him, and the inheritance shall be ours. [8]And they took him, and killed him, and cast him out of the vineyard. [9]What shall therefore the lord of the vineyard do? he will come and destroy the husbandmen, and will give the vineyard unto others.'

Matthew xxi. 33–41

[33]'Hear another parable: There was a certain householder, which planted a vineyard, and hedged it round about, and digged a winepress in it, and built a tower, and let it out to husbandmen, and went into a far country: [34]and when the time of the fruit drew near, he sent his servants to the husbandmen, that they might receive the fruits of it. [35]And the husbandmen took his servants, and beat one, and killed another, and stoned another. [36]Again, he sent other servants more than the first: and they did unto them likewise. [37]But last of all he sent unto them his son, saying, They will reverence my son. [38]But when the husbandmen saw the son, they said among themselves, This is the heir; come, let us kill him, and let us seize on his inheritance. [39]And they caught him, and cast him out of the vineyard, and slew him. [40]When the lord therefore of the vineyard cometh, what will he do unto those husbandmen?' [41]They say unto Him, 'He will miserably destroy those wicked men, and will let out his vineyard unto other husbandmen, which shall render him the fruits in their seasons.'

Luke xx. 9–16

[9]Then began He to speak to the people this parable: 'A certain man planted a vineyard, and let it forth to husbandmen, and went into a far country for a

Luke xx. 9–16 (*contd.*)

long time. [10]And at the season he sent a servant to the husbandmen, that they should give him of the fruit of the vineyard: but the husbandmen beat him, and sent him away empty. [11]And again he sent another servant: and they beat him also, and entreated him shamefully, and sent him away empty. [12]And again he sent a third: and they wounded him also, and cast him out. [13]Then said the lord of the vineyard, What shall I do? I will send my beloved son: it may be they will reverence him when they see him. [14]But when the husbandmen saw him, they reasoned among themselves, saying, This is the heir: come, let us kill him, that the inheritance may be ours. [15]So they cast him out of the vineyard, and killed him. What therefore shall the lord of the vineyard do unto them? [16]He shall come and destroy these husbandmen, and shall give the vineyard to others.'

(*a*) Jesus spoke the parable of the King's Son (*Mark* xii. 1–9, *Matthew* xxi. 33–41 and *Luke xx.* 9–16) against the Sadducee priesthood of Jerusalem, who had, he thought, failed in their spiritual duty. Since they did not now recognize his claim to the throne it followed that, when opportunity offered, they would arrest him as a rebel against Rome; which indeed he was. He may also have been warned by John, son of Annas the High Priest, his secret disciple (*see* LXXII.*a*), of what was being plotted against him.

The vineyard of the parable was Israel (*Isaiah* v. 7—*see* LVIII.*b*), and Jesus will have pointed to the great gold vine, adorning the gate of the Sanctuary (*see* LIV.*c*), which was the priests' reminder that they were Israel's husbandmen—answerable for their conduct not to the Romans, but to God. Only the Sadducee priesthood and their Herodian allies rejected the prophets, as the husbandmen in the parable did; the Pharisees and the Jewish nation as a whole accepted them without reserve.

(*b*) *Luke* xx. 9–16 is more credible than either *Mark* xii. 1–9 or *Matthew* xxi. 31–41, because more restrained. Since pre-Exilic days, the priests had killed no authorized prophets (*see* XIII.*t*) and, in the time of Nehemiah, had made a public confession of ancestral guilt and promised to mend their ways (*Nehemiah* ix. 26). The letter of this promise had since been kept, except for a single lapse, two centuries before Jesus's ministry, when Jason, the Hellenizing High Priest, taking orders from the Seleucid Governor of Jerusalem, had crucified a few devout Jews who opposed his reforms (*Antiquities* xii. 5. 4—*see* CXIII.*f, footnote*). It even seems from Josephus's account (*Antiquities* xvii. 6. 3), that when forty young Pharisees, disciples of Judas son of Zippori and Matthias son of Margalot, cut down an idolatrous golden eagle which Herod the Great had fixed above the East Gate of the Temple, and professed themselves ready to burn for their faith, the High Priest Matthias tried, though unsuccessfully, to save them from Herod's vengeance. For this presumption he was deposed and replaced by his brother-in-law, Joasar of the House of Boethus, a collaborationist. The Boethians had since, however, condoned the murder of John the Baptist by their kinsman

Herod Antipas, and not forbidden him entry into the Temple. Their use of club-law against malcontents (*see* xii.*l, footnote and* xx.*c*) and the common people in general, is recalled in a popular song composed by Abba Shaul ben Bothnith (*Pesahim* 57a):

> *Woe is me because of the House of Boethus;*
> *Woe is me because of their staves!*
> *Woe is me because of the House of Hanin* [Annas];
> *Woe is me because of their whisperings!*
> *Woe is me because of the House of Kathros* [Cantheras];
> *Woe is me because of their pens!*
> *Woe is me because of the House of Ishmael the son of Phabi*
>   [Phabi himself was held to be righteous];
> *Woe is me because of their fists!*
> *For they are the High Priests,*
> *And their sons are* [Temple] *treasurers,*
> *And their sons-in-law are overseers,*
> *And their servants beat the people with staves.*

The 'whisperings' were their secret conclaves on Roman business; the 'pens' stood for their oppressive decrees and dishonest accountancy.

(*c*) The parable is introduced by the first two verses of Isaiah's song about the vineyard that brought forth wild grapes (*Isaiah* v. 1–7), and a quotation from *Canticles* viii. 11–12. Jesus combines the two texts and this time directs God's anger against the husbandmen of the *Canticles,* not against the vineyard of *Isaiah.* In the original parable, it is unlikely that the heir to the vineyard was murdered; its point lay in the treacherous whisperings of the House of Annas, not in the successful execution of their designs.

> (334) *And Jesus said unto the Chief Rulers: 'Isaiah made a song concerning this vineyard:*
> '"*My beloved hath a vineyard in a very fruitful hill (which is the House of Israel). And he fenced it, and gathered out the stones thereof, and planted it with the choicest vines, and built a tower in the midst of it.*"
> '*As it is written in the* Song of Songs: "*Solomon had a vineyard at Baal-hamon. He let out the vineyard unto husbandmen. Every one for the fruit thereof was to bring a thousand pieces of silver.*
> '"*My vineyard, which is mine, is before me. Thou, O Solomon, must have a thousand, and the husbandmen must have two hundred for themselves.*"
> '*Hearken now unto a new parable concerning this same vineyard, which was let out to husbandmen.*
> '*Behold, when the season of the fruit drew nigh, the Lord of the vineyard sent a servant unto the husbandmen, and required from each of them the thousand pieces of silver.*
> '*But the husbandmen took the servant, and beat him with clubs, and sent him away emptyhanded.*
> '*Then the Lord sent another servant, more honourable than the first, to require from them the sum which had been agreed.*

'*At him they cast stones and wounded him in the head, and sent him away shamefully handled.*

'*But having yet one son, his well-beloved, he sent him also last unto them, saying: "They will reverence my son."*

'*But the wicked husbandmen whispered among themselves: "Here cometh the heir! What say ye? Let us kill him, and the heritage shall fall unto us."*

'*Now, therefore, if the Lord of the vineyard, which overheareth all, take heed to their whisperings, what will He do unto those wicked husbandmen?*

'*Hath He not power to destroy them with the breath of His mouth, and let out His vineyard unto others?*'

* * * *

O JERUSALEM, JERUSALEM!

Mark xiii. 1–2

[1]And as He went out of the temple, one of His disciples saith unto Him: 'Master, see what manner of stones and what buildings are here!' [2]And Jesus answering said unto him: 'Seest thou these great buildings? there shall not be left one stone upon another, that shall not be thrown down.'

Matthew xxiii. 37–39

[37]'O Jerusalem, Jerusalem, thou that killest the prophets, and stonest them which are sent unto thee, how often would I have gathered thy children together, even as a hen gathereth her chickens under her wings, and ye would not! [38]Behold, your house is left unto you desolate. [39]For I say unto you, Ye shall not see Me henceforth, till ye shall say,

Blessed is He that cometh in the name of the Lord.'

Matthew xxiv. 1–2

[1]And Jesus went out, and departed from the temple: and His disciples came to Him for to shew Him the buildings of the temple. [2]And Jesus said unto them: 'See ye not all these things? verily I say unto you, There shall not be left here one stone upon another, that shall not be thrown down.'

Luke xiii. 31–35

[31]The same day there came certain of the Pharisees, saying unto Him: 'Get Thee out, and depart hence: for Herod will kill Thee.' [32]And He said unto them: 'Go ye, and tell that fox, Behold, I cast out devils, and I do cures to day and to morrow, and the third day I shall be perfected. [33]Nevertheless I must walk to day and to morrow, and the day following: for it cannot be that a prophet perish out of Jerusalem. [34]O Jerusalem, Jerusalem, which killest the prophets, and stonest them that are sent unto thee; how often would I have gathered thy children together, as a hen doth gather her brood under her wings, and ye would not! [35]Behold your house is left unto you desolate: and verily I say unto you, ye shall not see Me, until the time come when ye shall say,

Blessed is He that cometh in the name of the Lord.'

Luke xix. 41–44

[41]And when He was come near, He beheld the city, and wept over it, [42]saying: 'If thou hadst known, even thou, at least in this thy day, the things

Luke xix. 41–44 (*contd.*)

which belong unto thy peace! but now they are hid from thine eyes. [43]For the days shall come upon thee, that thine enemies shall cast a trench about thee, and compass thee round, and keep thee in on every side. [44]And shall lay thee even with the ground, and thy children within thee; and they shall not leave in thee one stone upon another; because thou knewest not the time of thy visitation.'

Luke xxi. 5–6

[5]And as some spake of the temple, how it was adorned with goodly stones and gifts, He said: [6]'As for these things which ye behold, the days will come, in the which there shall not be left one stone upon another, that shall not be thrown down.'

)

(*a*) Jesus's lament for Jerusalem does not appear in *Mark*. In *Matthew* xxiii. 37 it follows his alleged outburst in the Temple against the Pharisees (*see* XIII.*t–z*), whom he accuses of killing the prophets. In *Luke* xiii. 34 it follows on the Pharisees' friendly warning that Herod Antipas will kill him if he remains in Galilee.

The similarity of the two distinct sayings about Jerusalem, found in this verse and the preceding one, explains why they were run together. In *Luke* xix. 41–44, Jesus again mourns for Jerusalem during his triumphal entry, but here the accusations against the Pharisees have been omitted.

(*b*) The proper context for the lament seems to be Jesus's apocalyptic prophecy (*Mark* xiii. 3–33, *Matthew* xxiv. 3–41, *Luke* xvii. 22–27 and xxi. 7–28—*see* XCVIII.*a–k*) made to his disciples when he left the Temple after disputing with the Captain (*see* xcv.*g*). A suggestion in Mark xiii. 1 and *Matthew* xxiv. 1 that the disciples pointed out its beauties to him, as though he had never before seen these, is an ingenuous addition by an editor who wants to prove that Jesus, because of his hostility towards Judaism, had not visited the Temple since infancy. *Matthew* xxiii. 37 and *Luke* xiii. 34, the saying about the hen and her brood, is a *midrash* on *Psalm* xci. 4; but it should be God, not Jesus, who cares for the brood. *Luke* xiii. 35: 'Your house is left desolate', provides the clue to the origin of 'thou that killest the prophets'; it is a concealed *midrash* on *Jeremiah* xxvi.

(*c*) In *Luke* xix. 41–44, Jesus refers to the destruction of Jerusalem prophesied in *Isaiah* xxix. 3–4, lxvi. 1–16 and *Micah* iii. 11–12. A missing part of this speech seems to have been preserved in *Acts* vii. 49, where it is attributed to Stephen.

Since there is no mention in the Scriptures of a trench to be dug about Jerusalem (*Luke* xix. 43), it is likely that this detail was added, after the siege of Jerusalem, from a memory of *Micah* iii. 12: 'Zion shall be ploughed as a field.' Josephus describes the work of the Roman sappers in many chapters of *Wars* v.

'The time of thy visitation' in *Luke* xix. 44 means the conclusion of the seventy weeks prophesied in *Daniel* ix. 24 (*see* LXXXVIII.*t*).

(*d*) *Luke* xiii. 32, Jesus's prophecy of his 'perfection' on the third day, is a Pauline interpolation modelled on *Hebrews* ii. 10: 'For it became Him . . . to make the captain of their salvation perfect through sufferings.' It need not, however, be doubted that Jesus foretold his resurrection on the Third Day (*Mark* viii. 31–33 and x. 32–34; *Matthew* xvi. 21 and xx. 17–19; *Luke* ix. 22 and xviii. 33–34—*see* LXXVIII.*h*). But he was referring to his belief, shared with Pharisees and all Jews other than the Sadducees, that on the third day after the end of this false Creation a general resurrection of the dead would take place. The belief was based on *Hosea* vi. 1–2:

> 'Come and let us return unto the Lord, for He hath torn and He will heal us, He hath smitten and He will bind us up. After two days will He revive us and in the third day He will raise us up and we shall live in His sight.'

It was on the third day that the Temple 'not built with hands' would descend from Heaven (*Enoch* xc. 28—*see* xc.*g*).

(*e*) In *Genesis Rabbah* xci. 7 it is explained:

> 'God never leaves the righteous in distress for more days than three. This we learn from Joseph ("And he put his brethren all together into ward three days," *Genesis* xlii. 17); from Jonah ("Jonah was in the belly of the fish three days and three nights," *Jonah* i. 17) and from David ("that there be three days' pestilence in the land," 2 *Samuel* xxiv. 13).'

Jesus's reference to Jonah in *Matthew* xii. 40 (*see* XCI.*c*) suggests that this *midrash* was current in his day. Similarly, a comment in *Genesis Rabbah* lvi. 1, on *Genesis* xxii. 4—Abraham's release on the third day from the command to sacrifice Isaac—emphasizes the importance of the third day as one of relief from distress; not only Joseph and Jonah are quoted here, but also *Ezra* viii. 32 (the felicitous end of Ezra's three-day stay in Jerusalem), *Esther* v. 1 (Esther's favourable reception by King Ahasuerus after three days) and *Exodus* xix. 16 (the Revelation on Sinai after Israel's three days of sanctification). And it is explained:

> 'The Rabbis asked: "For whose sake were these things done?" and answered: "For the sake of the third day, when Revelation took place." But Rabbi Levi maintained: "Because of what Abraham did on the third day." '

It is likely, therefore, that Jesus's message to Antipas concluded with: 'For on the third day cometh relief.'

(*f*) The sequence may be restored as follows:

> (358) *When Jesus went forth from the Temple, and saw how it was adorned with goodly stones and gifts, he wept, and said unto his disciples:*
> *'See ye not these great buildings? O Jerusalem, Jerusalem, when the nations are gathered together to destroy thee, there shall scarce be left one stone upon another that shall not be thrown down!*

O JERUSALEM, JERUSALEM! [XCVII] 585

'*For thou hast not known the time of thy visitation, neither hearkened to the voice that cried unto thee to repent.*

'*If thou couldst but know, in this thy last day, the things which belong to thy peace! But even now are they hid from thine eyes.*

'*As Isaiah prophesied in the name of the Lord: "I will camp against thee round about and will lay siege against thee, and raise forts against thee, and thou shalt be brought low."*

'*And again: "The heaven is My throne and the earth is My footstool. Where is the house that ye build unto Me, and where is the place of My rest?*

'*"For he that offereth an oblation there, it is as if he offered swine's blood;* he that burneth incense, as if he blessed an idol. Yea, they have chosen their own ways, and their soul delighteth in abomination.*

'*"Behold, the Lord will come with fire and with His chariots like a whirl- wind, to rebuke with flames of fire."*

'*And Micah likewise prophesied: "Zion shall be plowed as a field, for the sake of the princes of Israel that abhor judgement, and Jerusalem shall be- come heaps."*

'*Now is it again as in the days when the Lord spake unto Jeremiah, saying: "Stand in the court of the Temple, and say unto all men that come up to worship:*

'*"If ye will not walk in the Law which I have set before you, to hearken unto the words of My servants the prophets, which I sent you, to which ye have not hearkened, then will I make this house like unto that of Shiloh, and this city shall be desolate without an inhabitant!"*

'*Then would the priests have stoned Jeremiah until he died, yet they could not. But in his stead they slew the prophet Urijah; whose innocent blood was on their heads until the prophecy of Jeremiah was fulfilled.*

'*Verily, I say unto you: so it shall be again!*'

* * * * *

[Here follow Jesus's quotation of Malachi's prophecy against the priests (*see* XXXIII.*c*), and the passage about the blood of Zechariah (*see* XIII.*z*).]

* * * * *

(361) '*Yet shall the Lord raise up the righteous man and the prophet, before three days are fulfilled; as Hosea prophesied: "In the third day He will raise us up and we shall live in His sight."*

'*In the third day also He shall restore the Temple which He Himself hath destroyed. As Enoch prophesied, saying: "I saw till the Lord of the sheep brought a new house, greater and loftier than the first, and set it up in the place of the first."*'

* * * * *

(g) [Here follows Jesus's woe intended for Jerusalem, but mistakenly made to fall upon Capernaum (*Matthew* vi. 23—*see* LIX.*c*).]

* * * * *

* As the Hellenizing High Priest Jason did, according to *Antiquities* xii. 5. 4.

(363) *'Yet fear ye not, little ones, for David spake in a psalm, saying: "The Lord shall cover the earth with His feathers, and under His wings shalt thou trust.*

'"A thousand shall fall at thy side, and ten thousand at thy right hand; but it shall not come nigh thee!"'

* * * * *

(*h*) The following belongs to the account of the Baptist's execution (*see* LXXVI.*f*):

(233) *On the same day come certain of the Pharisees unto Jesus, saying: 'John the Baptist is slain. Get thee out and depart hence, lest Herod kill thee also, as he hath killed John!'*

And Jesus rent his clothes, and lamented sore, and unto them that warned him he said: 'Go ye, and tell that fox that I must walk in Galilee today and tomorrow and the day following, and he shall have no power to slay me as he slew John.

'For it cannot be that this prophet shall perish out of Jerusalem.

'But on the third day cometh relief, and the Kingdom of God is now at hand.'

As a prophet by virtue of his coraration, Jesus was referring, in *Luke* xiii. 33, to his destined death as the Worthless Shepherd (*see* CII.*a*).

* * * * *

(*i*) Matthew xxiii. 39, paralleled in *Luke* xiii. 35, records Jesus's farewell on the Mount of Olives to the remainder of his disciples, when he took Peter, James, and John aside immediately before the Arrest (*see* CVII.*l*). It is a *midrash* on *Psalm* cxviii. 17–26.

(402) *'Ye shall not see me again until we meet together in the Resurrection, if so it be that God shall make good in us the prophecy which David spake: "I shall not die but live. The Lord hath chastened me sore, but hath not given me over unto death."*

'Then shall we lift our eyes to heaven, and cry with the voice of David: "Blessed be he that cometh in the name of the Lord!"'

* * * * *

THE LITTLE APOCALYPSE

Mark xiii. 3–8

³And as He sat upon the mount of Olives over against the temple, Peter and James and John and Andrew asked Him privately: ⁴'Tell us, when shall these things be? and what shall be the sign when all these things shall be fulfilled?' ⁵And Jesus answering them began to say: 'Take heed lest any man deceive you: ⁶for many shall come in My name, saying, I am the Christ; and shall deceive many. ⁷And when ye shall hear of wars and rumours of wars, be ye not troubled: for such things must needs be: but the end shall not be yet. ⁸For nation shall rise against nation, and kingdom against kingdom: and there shall be earthquakes in divers places and there shall be famines and troubles: these are the beginnings of sorrows.'

Mark xiii. 12–27

¹²'Now the brother shall betray the brother to death, and the father the son; and children shall rise up against their parents, and shall cause them to be put to death. ¹³And ye shall be hated of all men for My name's sake: but he that shall endure unto the end, the same shall be saved.

¹⁴'But when ye shall see the abomination of desolation, spoken of by Daniel the prophet, standing where it ought not, (let him that readeth understand,) then let them that be in Judaea flee to the mountains: ¹⁵and let him that is on the housetop not go down into the house, neither enter therein, to take any thing out of his house: ¹⁶and let him that is in the field not turn back again for to take up his garment. ¹⁷But woe to them that are with child, and to them that give suck in those days! ¹⁸And pray ye that your flight be not in the winter. ¹⁹For in those days shall be affliction, such as was not from the beginning of the creation which God created unto this time, neither shall be. ²⁰And except that the Lord had shortened those days, no flesh should be saved: but for the elect's sake, whom He hath chosen, He hath shortened the days. ²¹And if any man shall say to you, Lo, here is the Christ; or, lo, He is there; believe him not: ²²for false Christs and false prophets shall rise, and shall shew signs and wonders, to seduce, if it were possible, even the elect. ²³But take ye heed: behold I have foretold you all things.

²⁴'But in those days, after that tribulation, the sun shall be darkened, and the moon shall not give her light, ²⁵and the stars of heaven shall fall, and the powers that are in heaven shall be shaken. ²⁶And then shall they see the Son of man coming in the clouds with great power and glory. ²⁷And then shall He send His angels, and shall gather together His elect from the four winds, from the uttermost part of the earth to the uttermost part of heaven.'

Mark xiii. 32–33

[32]But of that day and hour knoweth no man, no, not the angels which are in heaven, neither the Son, but the Father. [33]Take ye heed, watch and pray: for ye know not when the time is.

Matthew x. 21–23

[21]And the brother shall deliver up the brother to death, and the father the child: and the children shall rise up against their parents, and cause them to be put to death. [22]And ye shall be hated of all men for My name's sake: but he that endureth to the end shall be saved. [23]But when they persecute you in this city, flee ye into another: for verily I say unto you, ye shall not have gone over the cities of Israel, till the Son of man be come.

Matthew xxiv. 3–31

[3]And as He sat upon the mount of Olives, the disciples came unto Him privately, saying: 'Tell us, when shall these things be? and what shall be the sign of Thy coming, and of the end of the world?' [4]And Jesus answered and said unto them: 'Take heed that no man deceive you. [5]For many shall come in My name, saying I am Christ; and shall deceive many. [6]And ye shall hear of wars and rumours of wars: see that ye be not troubled: for all these things must come to pass, but the end is not yet. [7]For nation shall rise against nation, and kingdom against kingdom: and there shall be famines, and pestilences, and earthquakes, in divers places. [8]All these are the beginning of sorrows. [9]Then shall they deliver you up to be afflicted, and shall kill you: and ye shall be hated of all nations for My name's sake. [10]And then shall many be offended, and shall betray one another, and shall hate one another. [11]And many false prophets shall rise, and deceive many. [12]And because iniquity shall abound, the love of many shall wax cold. [13]But he that shall endure unto the end, the same shall be saved. [14]And this Gospel of the Kingdom shall be preached in all the world for a witness unto all nations; and then shall the end come. [15]When ye therefore shall see the abomination of desolation, spoken of by Daniel the prophet, stand in the holy place (whoso readeth, let him understand), [16]then let them which be in Judaea flee into the mountains: [17]let him which is on the housetop not come down to take any thing out of his house: [18]neither let him which is in the field return back to take his clothes. [19]And woe unto them that are with child, and to them that give suck in those days! [20]But pray ye that your flight be not in the winter, neither on the sabbath day: [21]for then shall be great tribulation, such as was not since the beginning of the world to this time, no, nor ever shall be. [22]And except those days should be shortened, there should no flesh be saved: but for the elect's sake those days shall be shortened. [23]Then if any man shall say unto you, Lo, here is the Christ, or there; believe it not. [24]For there shall arise false Christs, and false prophets, and shall shew great signs and wonders; insomuch that, if it were possible, they shall deceive the very elect. [25]Behold, I have told you before. [26]Wherefore if they shall say unto you, "Behold, He is in the desert"; go not forth: "Behold, He is in the secret chambers"; believe it not. [27]For as the lightning cometh out of the east, and shineth even unto the west; so shall

Matthew xxiv. 3–31 *(contd.)*

also the coming of the Son of man be. ²⁸For wheresoever the carcase is, there will the eagles be gathered together. ²⁹Immediately after the tribulation of those days

> *The sun shall be darkened, and the moon shall not give her light,*
> *And the stars shall fall from the heaven,*
> *And the powers of the heavens shall be shaken.*

³⁰And then shall appear the sign of the Son of man in heaven: and then shall all the tribes of the earth mourn, and they shall see the Son of man coming in the clouds of heaven with power and great glory. ³¹And He shall send His angels with a great sound of a trumpet, and they shall gather together His elect from the four winds, from one end of heaven to the other.'

Matthew xxiv. 37–41

³⁷But as the days of Noah were, so shall also the coming of the Son of man be. ³⁸For as in the days that were before the flood they were eating and drinking, marrying and giving in marriage, until the day that Noah entered into the ark, ³⁹and knew not until the flood came, and took them all away; so shall also the coming of the Son of man be. ⁴⁰Then shall two be in the field; the one shall be taken, and the other left. ⁴¹Two women shall be grinding at the mill; the one shall be taken, and the other left.

Matthew xxv. 31–34

³¹'When the Son of man shall come in His glory, and all the holy angels with Him, then shall He sit upon the throne of His glory: ³²and before Him shall be gathered all nations: and He shall separate them one from another, as a shepherd divideth his sheep from the goats: ³³and He shall set the sheep on His right hand, but the goats on the left. ³⁴Then shall the King say unto them on His right hand, Come, ye blessed of My Father, inherit the kingdom prepared for you from the foundation of the world.'

Luke xvii. 22–32

²²And He said unto the disciples: 'The days will come, when ye shall desire to see one of the days of the Son of man, and ye shall not see it. ²³And they shall say to you, See here; or, see there: go not after them, nor follow them. ²⁴For as the lightning, that lighteneth out of the one part under heaven, shineth unto the other part under heaven; so shall also the Son of man be in His day. ²⁵But first must He suffer many things, and be rejected of this generation. ²⁶And as it was in the days of Noah, so shall it be also in the days of the Son of man. ²⁷They did eat, they drank, they married wives, they were given in marriage, until the day that Noah entered into the ark, and the flood came, and destroyed them all. ²⁸Likewise also as it was in the days of Lot; they did eat, they drank, they bought, they sold, they planted, they builded; ²⁹but the same day that Lot went out of Sodom it rained fire and brimstone from heaven, and destroyed them all. ³⁰Even thus shall it be in the day when the Son of man is revealed. ³¹In that day, he which shall be upon the housetop, and his stuff in the house, let him not come down to take it

Luke xvii. 22–32 (contd.)

away: and he that is in the field, let him likewise not return back. [32]Remember Lot's wife.'

Luke xvii. 34–37

[34]'I tell you, in that night there shall be two men in one bed; the one shall be taken, and the other shall be left. [35]Two women shall be grinding together; the one shall be taken, and the other left. [36]Two men shall be in the field; the one shall be taken, and the other left.' [37]And they answered and said unto Him: 'Where, Lord?' And He said unto them: 'Wheresoever the body is, thither will the eagles be gathered together.'

Luke xxi. 7–13

[7]And they asked Him, saying: 'Master, but when shall these things be? and what sign will there be when these things shall come to pass?' [8]And He said: 'Take heed that ye be not deceived: for many shall come in My name, saying, I am Christ: and the time draweth near: go ye not therefore after them. [9]But when ye shall hear of wars and commotions, be not terrified: for these things must first come to pass; but the end is not straightway.' [10]Then said He unto them: 'Nation shall rise against nation, and kingdom against kingdom: [11]and great earthquakes shall be in divers places, and famines, and pestilences; and fearful sights and great signs shall there be from heaven. [12]But before all these, they shall lay their hands on you, and persecute you, delivering you up to the synagogues, and into prisons, being brought before kings and rulers for My name's sake. [13]And it shall turn to you for a testimony.'

Luke xxi. 16–17

[16]And ye shall be betrayed both by parents, and brethren, and kinsfolk, and friends; and some of you shall they cause to be put to death. [17]And ye shall be hated of all men for My name's sake.

Luke xxi. 20–28

[20]'And when ye shall see Jerusalem compassed with armies, then know that the desolation thereof is nigh. [21]Then let them which are in Judaea flee to the mountains; and let them which are in the midst of it depart out; and let not them that are in the countries enter thereinto. [22]For these be the days of vengeance, that all things which are written may be fulfilled. [23]But woe unto them that are with child, and to them that give suck, in those days! for there shall be great distress in the land, and wrath upon this people. [24]And they shall fall by the edge of the sword, and shall be led away captive into all nations: and Jerusalem shall be trodden down of the Gentiles, until the times of the Gentiles be fulfilled. [25]And there shall be signs of the sun, and in the moon, and in the stars; and upon the earth distress of nations, with perplexity; the sea and the waves roaring; [26]men's hearts failing them for fear, and for looking after those things which are coming on the earth: for the powers of heaven shall be shaken. [27]And then shall they see the Son of man coming in a cloud with power and great glory. [28]And when these things begin to

Luke xxi. 20–28 (*contd.*)

come to pass, then look up, and lift up your heads; for your redemption draweth nigh.'

Luke xxiii. 29–30

²⁹'For, behold, the days are coming, in the which they shall say, Blessed are the barren, and the wombs that never bare, and the paps which never gave suck. ³⁰Then shall they begin to say to the mountains, Fall on us; and to the hills, Cover us.'

(*a*) *Mark* xiii. 3–33, *Matthew* xxiv. 3–41, *Luke* xvii. 22–37, and xxi. 7–28, commonly known as the 'Little Apocalypse', cannot be understood without reference to the Apocalypse of Daniel (*Daniel* vii.–xii.), which foretold that the 'Great Day of the Lord' would follow the struggle of the Hasmoneans against the Seleucid Kings. Since this prophecy had not been fulfilled, Jesus expected its culmination in his own times.

Afterwards, when he proved to have been mistaken—for 30 A.D., the year of the Crucifixion, happened to be one of more than usual peace and prosperity, and another generation was to elapse before the Destruction of the Temple—the Gentile Christians understood his words as a prophecy of future troubles, and manipulated them accordingly.

(*b*) Jesus may have foreseen, as a consequence of Roman policy in Judaea, the reappearance of the 'Abomination of Desolation' (*shikuz shomen*); this was a Hebrew cacophemism (*see* xxxiv.*b*) used by the author of *Daniel* to describe the statue of Zeus, the 'Lord of Heaven' (*baal-shamaim*), with which Antiochus Epiphanes had desecrated the Sanctuary in 186 B.C. If so, his expectations were nearly fulfilled a few years later when the Emperor Caligula ordered his own statue to be set up in the Temple (*Antiquities* xviii. 8. 2). However, King Herod Agrippa persuaded Caligula to change his mind (*Antiquities* xviii. 8. 8), and the evil day was postponed until after Bar Cochba's abortive revolt in 132 A.D.; then the Emperor Hadrian re-built the ruined Temple in honour of the same Zeus, and it is to this desecration that most of the Gentile Christian additions to the 'Little Apocalypse' refer. *Mark* xiii. 14: 'Let him that readeth understand', is a cautious second-century gloss which has crept into the text. Jesus would have said, rather: 'Let him that *heareth* understand.'

But it is more likely that Jesus regarded the Abomination as having already been set up: interpreting *Daniel* xii. 12 as a prophecy that the 'Pangs of the Messiah' would begin 1335 *weeks,* not days, after Judaea had passed directly into the power of the Roman Emperor—namely in 30 A.D.

(*c*) No false Messiah is known to have appeared in Israel during Jesus's ministry: but in *Mark* xiii. 6, he may have referred in retrospect to the three or four rebellions which Josephus records (*Wars* ii. 4. 1–3) at the beginning of the 1335-week period. After 132 A.D., this saying was twisted into a prophecy, because the majority of the Jews, and even Rabbi Akiba the Pharisee leader, regarded Bar Cochba as the Messiah, and many 'deceived' Nazarenes rallied to his standard—which also explains *Mark* xiii. 22: 'False Christs and false prophets shall rise and shall show signs and wonders* to seduce, if it were possible, even the elect.' Another false Messiah was Apollonius of Tyana, whose feats tempted the second-century Gospel editors to turn Jesus's symbolic acts into miracles (*see Introduction* IV.*m–p*).

(*d*) *Mark* xiii. 12 and *Matthew* x. 21, the prophecy about the brother 'delivering' (the Greek word carries no sense of 'betraying') his brother to death, and the father his son, has been confused with Jesus's *midrash* on *Micah* vii. 6 (*see* CI.*d*) which concerns dissensions in a household. As a result, it has been expanded with: 'and children shall rise up against their parents and cause them to be put to death.' The same saying in *Matthew* xxiv. 10 and *Luke* xxi. 16, has strayed still farther from its original meaning. Its proper context is *Mark* iii. 31–35 (*see* CIV.*e*).

(381) *'For in the last days the brother shall deliver his brother unto death for God's sake, and the father his son.'*

* * * * *

(*e*) *Mark* xiii. 14–27, paralleled in *Matthew* xxiv. 15–31 and *Luke* xvii. 22–37, is a *midrash* on *Daniel* ix. 24–26 and vii. 13–14, with quotations from *Amos* v. 2, *Joel* iii. 15–16, *Isaiah* lx. 22, *Enoch* xc. 33, *Apocalypse of Baruch* xxvii. 2–13, and *Zechariah* ix. 14–16, xii. 9–14 and xiv. 1–5; it continues Jesus's prophecy about the destruction of the Temple. In *Daniel* ix. 24–26 seventy weeks are given as the period of Israel's last opportunity for reconciliation with God; the first seven being devoted to 'the building of the street and the wall'. It is likely that Jesus read the street and the wall as metaphorical of the call to repentance and resistance; and that he planned his ministry to last seventy weeks—from the New Year of 29 A.D. to the Passover of 30 A.D.

(365) *'Behold, these are the days whereof Daniel prophesied, saying: "Seventy weeks are determined upon Thy people and upon Thy holy city to finish the transgression, and to make an end of sins, and to make reconciliation for iniquity, and to bring in everlasting righteousness.*

' *"Know therefore that from the going forth of the commandment to restore and build Jerusalem unto the Anointed One shall be seven weeks, and three score and two weeks: the street shall be built again, and the wall as in troublous times.*

' *"And after three score and two weeks shall the Anointed One be cut off and have nothing, and the people of the prince that shall come shall destroy both the city and the Sanctuary. And the end thereof shall be with a flood."'*

* * * * *

---

* Bar Cochba's rising may be said to have been heralded by signs and wonders. At his first assault on the Roman forces under the procurator of Judaea, nearly fifty strongholds and close on a thousand towns and villages surrendered to him. Publius Marcellus, the Commander-in-Chief of Syria, who brought reinforcements down from Antioch, was defeated in his turn, and Roman military recovery began only when Hadrian recalled Julius Severus from his British campaign to take command in Judaea.

(*f*) Here follows *Luke* xvii. 37, Jesus's saying about the eagles—a *midrash* on *Job* xxxix. 29-30—which refers to the Roman legions:

(366) *The disciples ask Jesus: 'Lord, which shall this prince be?'*

He answered: 'It is written in the Book of Job: "The eyes of the eagle behold afar off. Her young ones also suck up blood and where the slain lie, there shall she be also."

'Verily, I say unto you: wheresoever the carcase is, there shall the eagles be gathered together!'

* * * * *

(*g*) *Mark* xiii. 7 and *Matthew* xxiv. 6, 'rumours of war', will have referred to the expected clash between Herod Antipas and King Aretas of Nabataea (*see* LXXXVI.*b*). For the 'signs' of *Baruch* xxvii. 2–13, *see* LXXXVIII.*r*.

(367) *'Therefore, when ye shall hear of wars and rumours of wars, see that ye be not troubled. All these things must be, before the end cometh.*

'For it was revealed unto Baruch how that nation shall rise against nation and kingdom against kingdom, and that famines and pestilences and earth-quakes shall be known in divers places.

'And there shall be signs in the heavens, and upon the earth distress and perplexity; the sea and the waves roaring;

'Men's hearts failing them for fear, and for looking after those things which are coming on the earth. And because of iniquity the love of many shall wax cold.

These are the beginnings of sorrows, but when they come to pass, lift up your heads: for your redemption draweth nigh.'

* * * * *

(*h*) [Here follows the prophecy about a brother delivering his erring brother to death (*see* (*d*) above). Jesus was not denouncing fratricide: so long as a sinner was given every opportunity to repent (*see* XIX.*d*) and then was tried by an authorized court, such executions were, in his view, necessary.]

* * * * *

(*i*) Part of the 'Little Apocalypse' has been transferred to *Luke* xxiii. 29-30, which concerns the journey to Golgotha and in which a quotation from *Hosea* x. 8 is preserved (*see* CXIII.*s*).

(369) *And Jesus spake further of the Last Days, saying: 'Zechariah prophe-sied: "Behold, the Day of the Lord cometh, and I will gather all nations against Jerusalem to battle.*

' "And the city shall be taken, and the houses plundered, and the women ravished, and half of the city shall go into captivity."

'Blessed in those days shall be the barren, and the wombs which never bare, and the paps which never gave suck!

'But woe unto them that are with child, and unto them that give suck in those days!

'*For there shall be great distress on the land, and wrath upon this people, and some shall fall by the sword and some be led away into captivity.*

'*As Hosea prophesied: "They shall say unto the mountains: 'Cover us!' and unto the hills: 'Fall on us!'"*

'*Verily, I say unto you: in that night two men shall be in one bed; the one shall be taken, and the other shall be left.*

'*And two women shall be grinding together; the one shall be taken, and the other shall be left.*

'*And Jerusalem shall be trodden down of the nations until their time be fulfilled.*

'*But Zechariah prophesied also: "Then shall the Lord go forth and fight against those nations.*

'*"And His feet shall stand in that day upon the Mount of Olives, and the Mount of Olives shall cleave in the midst thereof.*

'*"Then ye shall flee like as ye fled from the earthquake in the days of King Uzziah."*

'*And again: "In the day that I go about to destroy all the nations that come against Jerusalem, I will pour upon the House of David, and upon the inhabitants of Jerusalem, the spirit of grace and supplication, and the land shall mourn for the Anointed One, every family apart."*'

* * * * *

(*j*) It is fortunate that *Luke* xvii. 32 'Remember Lot's wife!' has been preserved; this saying points to Jesus's careful antithesis between the deluge prophesied, in *Daniel* ix. 26, for the destruction of the Gentiles who have assaulted Jerusalem, and the rain of fire, prophesied in *Enoch* and elsewhere, for the Israelite apostates. The evangelists, by concealing this antithesis—in order to distract attention from the purely local incidence of the deluge which was to destroy the Temple—make Jesus's pronouncement illogical. It would be natural to seek refuge in the hills from a rain of fire, as Lot had been advised to do, or to take refuge on the roof top from a sudden deluge of water. But anyone caught on the roof, when the rain of fire descended, was left no choice: he would get burned whether he fled or stayed. And since the deluge of water was to fall only on the high ground about Jerusalem, the man in the field would be ill-advised to 'flee to the hills' when it came.

(*k*) From Noah's flood (*Genesis* vi.–vii.), and from the destruction of Sodom (*Genesis* xix. 1–28), only God's elect were saved. Since neither buying nor selling is mentioned in the account of Sodom's fall, this part of the saying is probably an interpolation by some ascetic editor. Jesus's quotations are always accurate; thus he would have spoken, rather, of the fornication and sodomy which made the Cities of the Plain notorious. Certain marriages, hateful to God, were one of the main causes of the Flood (*Genesis* vi. 4); and the pair of dogs saved in the Ark imitated the obscene marital customs of their drowned masters (*see* xxxvi.*h*). But Jesus regarded all physically consummated marriage as being now hateful to God (*see* x.*b*, xxi.*k* and *n*, and lxxx.*f*).

(370) *'Daniel likewise prophesied concerning the destruction of Jerusalem: "And the end thereof shall be with a flood, and it shall be cut off with desolations."*

'Therefore shall it be again as in the days of Noah. They did eat, they drank, they raged, they were corrupt, they married and were given in marriage: until the day that Noah entered into the ark with his elect, and the flood came and destroyed the wicked.

'Therefore, when this flood cometh upon Jerusalem, let him that is on the house top not go down into his house, nor enter therein to take up his stuff, lest the waters ensnare him!

'And afterward it shall be again as in the days of Lot. They did eat, they drank, they committed fornication and all manner of uncleanness: until the day that Lot with his elect went forth from Sodom and fled unto the mountains and God rained fire and brimstone from heaven and destroyed the city.

'Therefore, ere that this rain of fire fall upon the cities of Judaea, let them that be there likewise flee unto the barren mountains! And let him that is in the field remember Lot's wife, and return not back to take up his garment.

'Verily, I say unto you: the Gentiles shall be swept away by the flood, but they that rebel against the Law, the same shall be destroyed by the rain of fire!'

* * * * *

(371) *'And pray ye that your flight be not in the winter, neither on the sabbath day.*

'For Daniel prophesied, saying: "And there shall be a time of trouble such as never hath been since the beginning of creation.

' "Yet at that time Thy people shall be delivered, every one that shall be found enrolled in the book."

'For Joel wrote of those days of tribulation, how that the sun and the moon should be darkened, and the stars should withdraw their shining, and the heavens and earth should be shaken.

'And Amos likewise prophesied: "Shall not the day of the Lord be darkness and not light? Even very dark and no brightness in it?"'

* * * * *

(*l*) [Here follows Peter's question: 'Who, then, can be saved?' and Jesus's reassurance (*see* LXXXII.*f* and c.*b*).]

* * * * *

(374) *'But except those days should be shortened, no flesh should be saved; only for them which God hath chosen and enrolled in the book shall He shorten those days.*

'And Isaiah prophesied of their deliverance: "The sun shall no more go down, neither the moon withdraw herself, for the Lord shall be thine everlasting light. I, the Lord, will hasten it in his time."

'For in the midst of this darkness shall the elect perceive the Son of Man coming in the clouds with great power and glory, like unto the lightning that lighteneth out of the east and shineth unto the west.

'As Daniel saw in a vision: "Behold, one like the Son of Man came with the clouds of heaven and came to the Ancient of Days, and they brought him nearer before Him.

' "And there was given him dominion and glory and a kingdom that all people, nations and languages should serve him." '

* * * * *

(m) *Matthew* xxv. 32 is a *midrash* on *Ezekiel* xx. 38 and xxxiv. 17. The shepherd of Ezekiel's parable separates the sheep from the goats. Goats, being notorious for barking fruit-trees, would be unwelcome in an orchard Paradise; and the he-goat, which symbolized lechery, was commonly chosen as a sin-offering (*Leviticus* x. 16, *Numbers* vii. 16, *Ezra* viii. 35 and *Ezekiel* xliii. 25).

(375) 'And the Son of Man will judge them that are brought before him in God's name.

'As Ezekiel prophesied: "I will purge out from among you the rebels and them that trespass against Me."

'And again: "I judge between small cattle of lambs and kids, between the rams also and the great he-goats."

'So shall He separate one from another, as a shepherd divideth his sheep from the goats, and shall set the sheep on his right hand, but the goats on his left.

'And He shall send forth His angels with a sound of trumpet to gather His elect from the four winds, and from the uttermost part of the earth to the uttermost part of heaven, and they shall be united in the Kingdom.

'For Zechariah saith: "The Lord God shall blow the trumpet and save His flock on that day."

'And Enoch saw in a vision how all the sheep that had been destroyed and dispersed gathered together in one house, and the shepherd of the flock rejoiced with great joy because they were righteous and had returned.'

* * * * *

(376) Afterward, Jesus sat upon the Mount of Olives over against the Temple. And Peter and James and John and Andrew asked him privately: 'Tell us, Master, when shall these things be? And by what sign shall we know whether the cup of evil be full?'

Jesus answered them saying: 'Daniel asked this same thing of the angel, which bade him go his way, for the secret of the hour was closed up and sealed.

'Nevertheless, he revealed unto Daniel how, when one thousand and three hundred, five and thirty days should have passed, from that day in which the abomination that maketh desolate was set up, there would then be a beginning of the Last Days.

'Now, by a day Daniel signifieth a week; for when these days began and Israel fell subject unto the Wicked Kingdom, immediately false deliverers arose, deceiving many, and there were wars in the land, and great distress.'

* * * * *

(*n*) In *Mark* xiii. 28–33, *Matthew* x. 34–36 and xxiv. 32–36, and *Luke* xii. 49–53 and xxi. 29–33, Jesus insists that the signs of the times can be read, though the exact date of the End is a secret known to the Father only (*see* ci.*b–i*). This seems to have been an earlier message; he was now confident that the End would come within a day or two.

(*o*) The first part of *Mark* xiii. 13 is Christological, dating perhaps from the second century; the second part appears to be a *midrash* on *Psalm* cxix. 112–117 and, to judge by the reference to the 'abomination of desolation' in the next verse, on *Daniel* xii. 12.

> (377) '*David said in a psalm: "I have inclined mine heart to perform Thy statutes always unto the end: hold Thou me up and I shall be safe."*
>
> '*So also spake the angel unto Daniel: "Blessed is the heart that endureth and cometh to the thousand and three hundred, five and thirty days!*
>
> '*"But go thou thy way until the end be. For thou shalt rest and stand in thy lot at the end of days."*
>
> '*Verily, I say unto you: he that endureth faithfully unto the end, the same shall be saved!*
>
> '*But first must the Anointed One be cut off and brought to naught.*'

* * * * *

TWO OR THREE GRAPES

Matthew xviii. 19–20

[19]'Again I say unto you, that if two of you shall agree on earth as touching any thing that they shall ask, it shall be done for them of My Father which is in heaven. [20]For where two or three are gathered together in My name, there am I in the midst of them.'

Oxyrhynchus Papyrus I

Wheresoever there are two, they are not without God; and where there is one alone, I say: I am with him. Raise the stone and thou shalt find me; cleave the wood and I am there.

(*a*) *Matthew* xviii. 19–20 is Christological in form and probably influenced by the *First Epistle of John* v. 14–15:

'And this is the confidence that we have in the Son of God that if we ask anything according to his will he heareth us, and that if he hear us we have the petitions granted that we desired of him.'

In *Mark* xi. 24 Jesus had insisted that prayers should be offered to God alone (*see* xxvii.*j*).

(*b*) The saying is the remains of a *midrash* on *Isaiah* xvii. 4–7; the conclusion of which has been preserved in the first part of the first saying in *Oxyrhynchus Papyrus* I. Jesus may also have quoted *Genesis* iii. 8 and I *Kings* xix. 10 to support his statement that God stands at the side of even two devotees, or only one.

It is possible that 'two or three' carries the secondary meaning of 'men and women' (*see* x.*b*).

(364) *'Isaiah prophesied of these days, saying: "Then shall the glory of Jacob be made thin, and his flesh shall wax lean, and it shall be as when the harvestman gathereth the corn and leaveth the gleanings.*

'*"Yet, gleaning grapes shall be left on his vine, two or three berries at the top of the uppermost bough.*

'*"In that day shall a man look to his Maker, and his eyes shall have respect for the Holy One of Israel."*

'*Verily, I say unto you: where even two or three are gathered in God's name, He is in the midst of them and will hearken unto their prayer!*

'*Yea, and wheresoever there are but two, they are not without God. For Adam and Eve heard His voice as He walked in the Garden in the cool of the day.*

'*And where there is but one alone, yet is God also with him. When Elijah made complaint unto Him, saying: "The children of Israel have forsaken Thy covenant, and thrown down Thine altars, and slain Thy prophets with the sword, and I, even I only, am left, and they seek to take my life also," God comforted him.*

'*For He said: "I have left me seven thousand in Israel, knees which have not bowed unto Baal."* '

*   *   *   *   *

(*c*) The second part of *Oxyrhynchus Papyrus* i. x has puzzled commentators since its discovery in 1903. It is a *midrash* on *Genesis* xxii. 1–14, the trial of Abraham's faith; but 'me' has once more been substituted for 'God'.

(368) '*It is written that Abraham hearkened unto God's voice and clave the wood for the burnt offering of his son Isaac, and raised the stone for an altar to bind Isaac thereto;*

'*Yet even as he stretched forth his hand for the knife, a voice called unto him from heaven, and bade him spare Isaac his son. And lo, a ram was provided in his stead.*

'*Do ye therefore as Abraham did: cleave the wood and ye shall find God; raise the stone and He shall be with you!*'

*   *   *   *   *

THE REJECTED STONE

Mark xii. 10–12

[10]'And have ye not read this scripture;

"The stone which the builders rejected
Is become the head of the corner:
[11]*This was the Lord's doing,*
And it is marvellous in our eyes"?'

[12]And they sought to lay hold on Him, but feared the people: for they knew that He had spoken the parable against them: and they left Him, and went their way.

Matthew xxi. 42–44

[42]Jesus·saith unto them: 'Did ye never read in the scriptures,

The stone which the builders rejected,
The same is become the head of the corner:
This is the Lord's doing,
And it is marvellous in our eyes?

[43]Therefore say I unto you, the kingdom of God shall be taken from you, and given to a nation bringing forth the fruits thereof. [44]And whosoever shall fall on this stone shall be broken: but on whomsoever it shall fall, it will grind him to powder.'

Luke xx. 17–18

[17]And He beheld them, and said: 'What is this then that is written:

The stone which the builders rejected,
The same is become the head of the corner?

[18]Whosoever shall fall upon that stone shall be broken; but on whomsoever it shall fall, it will grind him to powder.'

(*a*) The saying in *Mark* xii. 10-12, *Matthew* xxi. 42-44, and *Luke* xx. 17-18 is placed after the parable of the King's Son, apparently because the evangelists believed, with the author of *Acts* iv. 11, that Jesus was the 'stone which the builders rejected'. But Jesus is quoting from *Psalms* cxviii. 2-22, where the metaphor is applied to the people of Israel:

'Let Israel now confess that His mercy endureth for ever . . . The stone which the builders refused is become the head stone of the corner.'

This quotation he amplified with two others. The first came from *Zecha-riah* xii. 3, where the stone stands for Jerusalem against which the waves of Gentile oppressors shall break in vain:

> 'And I shall make Jerusalem a burdensome stone for all people: they that burden themselves with it shall be cut in pieces, though all the peoples of the earth shall be gathered together against it.'

The second came from *Daniel* ii. 34–45, the explanation of Daniel's dream about the golden-headed image:

> 'Thou sawest that a stone was cut out without hands [*a reference to the unhewn altar stone of the Temple*] which smote the image upon his feet of iron and clay [*the Ptolemies, Seleucids, and other successors of Alexander*] and brake them to pieces. . . . In the days of these Kings shall the God of Heaven set up a kingdom which shall never be destroyed [*the Hasmonean kingdom of Israel*] but shall break in pieces and consume all these kingdoms, and shall stand for ever.'

(*b*) Though in *Genesis* xxvii. 40 God promised Esau his revenge on Jacob (i.e. Edom would revolt against Israel), that promise had already been ful-filled in King Joram's reign (2 *Kings* viii. 20); and the Edomites, since their forcible conversion by the Hasmoneans a century before, were now regarded as full members of the Israelite congregation. *Matthew* xxi. 43 is therefore likely to be an interpolation (*see Introduction* iii.*n, p, w*) by a Samaritan editor who wished to suggest that his own nation would inherit the Kingdom of God expected by the Jews.

The parable of the Stone will have been told to reassure Peter, when he asked: 'Who, then, shall be saved?' (*see* LXXXII.*f*).

> (373) '*David spake concerning Israel in a psalm: "The stone which the builder rejected is become the headstone of the corner. This is the Lord's doing and is marvellous in our eyes."*
>
> '*Behold, it is the same stone, not cut with hands, of which Zechariah prophesied: how that in the last days all the nations of the earth should be broken against it.*
>
> '*And Daniel likewise prophesied that it should grind them all to powder; for Israel shall inherit the Kingdom of Heaven and stand for ever.*'

* * * * *

(*c*) The corner stone of *Isaiah* xxviii. 16 was not the head-stone on which the roof rested, but a foundation stone.

* * * * *

THE IMMINENT END

Mark viii. 34–38

³⁴And when He had called the people unto Him with His disciples also, He said unto them: 'Whosoever will come after Me, let him deny himself, and take up his cross, and follow Me. ³⁵For whosoever will save his life shall lose it; but whosoever shall lose his life for My sake and the Gospel's, the same shall save it. ³⁶For what shall it profit a man, if he shall gain the whole world, and lose his own soul? ³⁷Or what shall a man give in exchange for his soul? ³⁸Whosoever therefore shall be ashamed of Me and My words in this adulterous and sinful generation; of him also shall the Son of Man be ashamed, when He cometh in the glory of His Father with the holy angels.'

Mark ix. 1

¹And he said unto them: 'Verily I say unto you, That there be some of them that stand here which shall not taste of death, till they have seen the kingdom of God come with power.'

Mark xiii. 28–33

²⁸Now learn a parable of the fig tree: 'When her branch is yet tender, and putteth forth leaves, ye know that summer is near: ²⁹so ye in like manner, when ye shall see these things come to pass, know that it is nigh, even at the doors. ³⁰Verily I say unto you, that this generation shall not pass, till all these things be done. ³¹Heaven and earth shall pass away: but My words shall not pass away. ³²But of that day and hour knoweth no man, no, not the angels which are in heaven, neither the Son, but the Father. ³³Take ye heed, watch and pray: for ye know not when the time is.'

* * * * *

Matthew x. 32–39

³²Whosoever therefore shall confess Me before men, him will I confess also before My Father which is in heaven. ³³But whosoever shall deny Me before men, him will I also deny before My Father which is in heaven.

³⁴"Think not that I am come to send peace on earth: I came not to send peace, but a sword. ³⁵For I am come to set a man at variance against his father, and the daughter against her mother, and the daughter in law against her mother in law. ³⁶And a man's foes shall be they of his own household.

Matthew x. 32–39 (contd.)

³⁷He that loveth father or mother more than Me is not worthy of Me: and he that loveth son or daughter more than Me is not worthy of Me. ³⁸And he that taketh not his cross, and followeth after Me, is not worthy of Me. ³⁹He that findeth his life shall lose it: and he that loseth his life for My sake shall find it.'

Matthew xvi. 24–28

²⁴Then said Jesus unto His disciples: 'If any man will come after Me, let him deny himself, and take up his cross, and follow Me. ²⁵For whosoever will save his life shall lose it: and whosoever will lose his life for My sake shall find it. ²⁶For what is a man profited, if he shall gain the whole world, and lose his own soul? or what shall a man give in exchange for his soul? ²⁷For the Son of Man shall come in the glory of His Father with His angels; and then He shall reward every man according to his works. ²⁸Verily I say unto you, there be some standing here, which shall not taste of death, till they see the Son of Man coming in His kingdom.'

Matthew xxiv. 32–36

³²'Now learn a parable of the fig tree; When its branch is yet tender, and putteth forth leaves, ye know that summer is nigh: ³³So likewise ye, when ye shall see all these things, know that it is near, even at the doors. ³⁴Verily I say unto you, this generation shall not pass till all these things be fulfilled. ³⁵Heaven and earth shall pass away, but My words shall not pass away. ³⁶But of that day and hour knoweth no man, no, not the angels of heaven, but My Father only.'

Old Syriac Version of Matthew xxiv. 32–33
(Hebr. MSS. 132 Bibliothèque Nationale, Paris.)

'Learn ye this parable from the fig tree; when its branch is tender and it putteth out leaves, ye know that the summer fruit [Qa'itz] is nigh; so likewise ye, when ye shall see all these things, know that it [the end, "Qetz"] is nigh, even at the doors.'

* * * * *

Luke ix. 23–27

²³And He said to them all: 'If any man will come after Me, let him deny himself, and take up his cross daily, and follow Me. ²⁴For whosoever will save his life shall lose it; but whosoever will lose his life for My sake, the same shall save it. ²⁵For what is a man advantaged, if he gain the whole world, and lose himself, or be cast away? ²⁶For whosoever shall be ashamed of Me and of My words, of him shall the Son of Man be ashamed, when He shall come in His own glory, and in His Father's, and of the holy angels. ²⁷But I tell you of a truth, there be some standing here, which shall not taste of death, till they see the kingdom of God.'

Luke xii. 49–53

⁴⁹'I am come to send fire on the earth; and what will I, if it be already kindled? ⁵⁰But I have a baptism to be baptized with; and how am I straitened till it be accomplished! ⁵¹Suppose ye that I am come to give peace on earth? I tell you, nay; but rather division: ⁵²for from henceforth there shall be five in one house divided, three against two, and two against three. ⁵³The father shall be divided against the son, and the son against the father; the mother against the daughter, and the daughter against the mother; the mother in law against her daughter in law, and the daughter in law against her mother in law.'

Luke xvii. 20–21

²⁰And when He was demanded of the Pharisees, when the kingdom of God should come, He answered them and said: 'The kingdom of God cometh not with observation: ²¹neither shall they say, Lo here! or, lo there! for behold, the kingdom of God is within you.'

Luke xvii. 33

³³Whosoever shall seek to save his life shall lose it; and whosoever shall lose his life shall preserve it.

Luke xix. 11

¹¹And as they heard these things, he added and spake a parable, because he was nigh to Jerusalem, and because they thought that the kingdom of God should immediately appear.

Luke xiv. 27

²⁷And whosoever doth not bear his cross, and come after Me, cannot be My disciple.

Luke xxi. 29–33

²⁹And He spake to them a parable: 'Behold the fig tree, and all the trees: ³⁰when they now shoot forth, ye see and know of your own selves that summer is now nigh at hand. ³¹So likewise, ye, when ye see these things come to pass, know ye that the kingdom of God is nigh at hand. ³²Verily I say unto you, this generation shall not pass away, till all be fulfilled. ³³Heaven and earth shall pass away: but My words shall not pass away.'

John xii. 25

²⁵He that loveth his life shall lose it; and he that hateth his life in this world shall keep it unto life eternal.

Clement of Rome: First Epistle to the Corinthians xxiii.

Let this scripture be far from us where he saith: 'Wretched are the double-minded which doubt in their soul, and say: "These things did we hear in the days of our fathers also, and behold, we are grown old and none of these things hath befallen us." Ye fools, liken yourselves unto a tree; take a vine, that first sheddeth its leaves, then putteth forth a shoot, and afterwards a leaf, and a flower, and a sour fruit, but at last the ripe grape.'

(*a*) Jesus cannot have expected to be crucified, because that was not the Messiah's destined fate. Thus in *Mark* viii. 34, *Matthew* x. 38, xvi. 24 and *Luke* ix. 23, xiv. 27 (*see* xiii.*d*), where he is credited with: 'Take up your cross!', the original will have run: 'Accept the cross of baptism and take up your burden!' According to *Ezekiel* ix. 4–6 (*see* cxiii.*e*), the Elect were marked on their brows with a cross; and Paul writes in *Galatians* vi. 2–5: 'Bear ye one another's burdens and so fulfil the Law of Christ. But . . . every man shall [also] bear his own burden.' And in the *Epistle to the Philippians* iii. 18, 'enemies to the cross of Christ' plainly refers to the baptismal symbol.

(*b*) Jesus awaited death by the sword, in accordance with *Zechariah* xiii. 3; which explains *Mark* viii. 35, *Matthew* x. 39 and xvi. 25, *Luke* ix. 24 and xvii. 33, and *John* xii. 25: 'Whosoever shall lose his life shall keep it unto life eternal.' This was the sword to which he alluded in *Matthew* x. 34; it is omitted from the parallel passage in *Luke* xii. 50–51, though implied there too. He expected the end of the world—the false world created by God's adversary (*see* lxx.*f*)—to follow immediately on his own death, in accordance with the same prophecy; as is proved by *Mark* ix. 1, *Matthew* xvi. 28 and *Luke* ix. 27, where he declares that some of those who stand by will escape the cataclysm, enter the Kingdom alive and not taste of death until the whole earth shall have passed away.

This premature statement is now generally taken as a prophecy of his Resurrection which, according to Catholic doctrine, has initiated a new religious epoch; but that it was read literally when the Gospels were compiled is shown by its modification in *Matthew* xxiv. 34, *Mark* xiii. 30, and *Luke* xxi. 32: 'This generation shall not pass till all these things be fulfilled'—which allowed for an extension of about a hundred years. By the middle of the second century A.D., however, when everyone had died who could claim contemporaneity with Jesus, an editor of *Luke* concluded that the Kingdom of God on earth had been a figure of speech (*see Introduction* iii.*l and* iv.*k*), and used an authentic saying, spoken by Jesus in a different context, to prove his point: 'For behold, the Kingdom of God is within you!' (Luke xvii. 21—*see* lxv.*b*). In *Luke* xix. 11 the same editor explains the parable of the Talents as meaning that the Kingdom of God would not come immediately (*see* lii.*i*).

In *Mark* xi. 31, *Matthew* xxiv. 35 and *Luke* xxi. 33, 'my words' have been substituted for 'the Law'. The original version survives in *Matthew* v. 18 and *Luke* xvi. 17 (*see* xxi.*i*).

(*c*) The fig-tree, a symbol of Israel—'all the trees' is an interpolation by a Lucan editor—leafs in Palestine just before the Passover, which was when Jesus set out for Jerusalem. The saying in *Mark* xiii. 28–29, *Matthew* xxiv. 32–36, and *Luke* xxi. 29–31 conceals a play on words which has survived in the Hebrew text of *Matthew* xxiv. 32–33 (*Heb. MSS.* 132. *Bibliothèque Nationale, Paris*); this points to a lost *midrash* on *Amos* viii. 2: i.e. *qa'itz* is 'ripe fruit', and *qetz* is 'the end'. Jesus decides that he must die and is impatient to

see the preliminaries completed. In *Luke* xii. 49 he wishes that the fire of
universal destruction were already kindled, and in the following verse—if
the baptism is one of blood, not water, as 'the sword' in *Matthew* x. 34 suggests—that he were already thrust through the eye and arm. Though named
'The Prince of Peace' in *Isaiah* ix. 6, he believed himself fated to let loose
apocalyptic disaster.

(*d*) *Luke* xii. 52: 'Five shall be in one house divided', is originally unrelated
to the saying about the son, the father, the daughter, the mother, the daughter-in-law, and the mother-in-law. The latter is a *midrash* on *Micah* vii. 6,
where the family disputes are a sign that the times are ripe for God's intervention. The editor of *Luke*, over-ingeniously, tries to explain 'two against
three' by setting the younger generation, son and (presumably widowed)
daughter against the elder generation of father, mother, and mother-in-law.

(*e*) The original will have run: '*In one house shall five be divided against
two*'—namely the evil planetary powers which ruled the five central days of
the week, against those of the Sabbath and the Sunday. These five were: *Sin,*
the Moon; *Nergal,* Mars; *Nabu,* Mercury or Thoth, the Cosmocrator; *Mar-
duk,* Jupiter; and *Ishtar,* Venus. They symbolized, respectively, witchcraft,
murder, theft, false oaths, and adultery—the five 'shalt not's' in the second
half of the Decalogue, which are introduced by a sixth forbidding their worship. *Ninib* (Saturn), the planet of the Sabbath, was a symbol of Peace; and
Samas, the Sun, of Light. Jesus's reference to the five husbands of the Samaritan woman at Sychar carried the same meaning (*see* LXX.*f*).*

(*f*) However, Jesus was not content to borrow this antithetical word-play
from *Amos.* He himself made two similar ones, which recall the bitter complaint of *Isaiah* v. 7 (*see* XLVII.*b*):

> '*Va'yekav le*' *mishpat*, vehine *mispah; lizedakah,* vehine *zeakah.*' 'He
> looked for *judgement* and behold, a *scab:* for *righteousness* and behold, a
> *cry.*'

His original words may be restored as follows:

> '*Lo tisbrun d'atit ana le'maite shalvitah be'arah; ana lo atit le'maite* shal-
> vitah *ela* shalhovitah; *ana lo atit le-maite* pluga *ela* plugta.'

> 'Think not that I have come to bring peace on earth. I am come not to
> bring peace on earth (*shalvitah*), but a flaming fire (*shalhovitah*); I am come
> not to bring division (*pluga*), but dissension (*plugta*).'

---

* Jehovah appointed seven archangels to guard the days of the week: Raphael for Sunday,
Gabriel for Monday, Sammael for Tuesday, Michael for Wednesday, and so forth (*see* Weber:
Altsynag. Pal. Theol. p. 164). The command of the heavenly host against the Cosmocrator,
leader of the five evil powers, was given to Michael (*Daniel* xii. 1 and *Revelation* xii. 7) be-
cause he had been God's instrument for the creation of the First Adam (*Midrash Konen in
Beth Ha'Midrash ed. Jellinek* ii. 27). Michael disputed the possession of Wednesday with his
adversary (*see* LXIII.*e*). (The Germanic days of the week correspond with the Babylonian,
Greek, and Latin; Wotan was the Cosmocrator.)

This struggle, which must continue until the Day of Judgment, began when Michael ordered
all angels to pay homage to God, and Satan refused. In punishment he will be hurled into the
abyss (*see* LVII.*f*), and his place in Heaven given to the Second Adam (*Slavonic Book of
Enoch* xxxi. 3–6, *Chronicle of Jerahmeel* xxii. and *Pirke di Rabbi Eliezer* xiii).

The word *shalvitah* occurs in *Targum on Psalm* lxxiii. 12, and *Targum Jona-than on Genesis* xxxvii. 1; and *shalhovitah* in *Targum Onḳelos on Exodus* iii. 2. *Pluga* is 'division' in a joyful sense—a division of booty, or of an inherit-ance. In this case 'booty' will have been meant: Jesus denies that he has come to lead the armed Zealots against the Wicked Kingdom.

(*g*) Jesus's two antitheses were, however, separated by his interjection about the baptism of blood which he must undergo; and since only the second referred to his *midrash* on *Micah* vii. 6, the evangelists grew confused. The author of *Luke,* who seems to have used a Greek translation without con-sulting the Aramaic original, has preserved three of the four elements in Jesus's play on words, but their order is wrong; he also fails to establish the first antithesis and, by mistaking *division* for *dissension,* telescopes the second. Thus:

> 'I am come to bring fire.
> I am not come to bring peace.
> I am come to bring [*dissension*
> *I am not come to bring*] division.'

The author of *Matthew* has preserved two elements only:

> 'I am not come to bring peace.
> [*I am come to bring fire.*
> *I am not come to bring division.*]
> I am come to bring dissension.'

and makes *sword,* borrowed from Jesus's saying about the baptism of blood, the antithesis of *peace.* (No verbal approximations in Aramaic can be found to connect *peace* with either *sword* or *division.*)

(*h*) *Mark* viii. 38, *Matthew* x. 32–33, and *Luke* xii. 8–9, passages about deny-ing or being ashamed of Jesus, are Christological; in the original, the disciples must have been enjoined not to be ashamed either of their vow of poverty or of their mission. In *Matthew* this saying is irrelevantly linked with the quotation from *Micah,* and also with Jesus's declaration that he had no rela-tives except those who love God (*Matthew* xii. 48–49—*see* CIV.*d*).

Matthew xvi. 26 is a separate and distinct *midrash* on *Job* xxxvi. 18.

(*i*) *Mark* xiii. 32, paralleled in *Matthew* xxiv. 36, is a *midrash* on *Isaiah* lxiii. 4. According to the Talmud (*Hagigah* 16*a,* and some other passages), the angels' knowledge of God's plans was limited to hints caught while they lis-tened '*Me'ahure ha'pargud',* i.e. 'from behind the curtain'. It was deduced from *Genesis* i. 26 and xi. 7 that God at times consulted His angels; but the precise day and hour of the Son of Man's coming would remain a close secret from them. The mention of the Son of God in *Mark* xiii. 32 is probably au-thentic, though misplaced. This verse should read: 'But of that day and hour knoweth no man, no, *neither the Son of God, neither the angels which are in heaven,* but the Father only.' Later, when Jesus was believed to be one with the Father, 'the son' was omitted from *Matthew* xxiv. 32.

(273) 'Let not Israel think that I am come to bring peace on earth. I am come not to bring shalvitah (*which is peace*) on earth, but I am come to bring shalhovitah (*which is a flaming fire*), and would that it were already kindled!

'For I have a baptism of blood wherewith I must be baptized, and how straitened am I till it come upon me with the sword!

'Verily, I say unto you: he that would save his life shall lose it; and he that loseth his life for God's sake, the same shall save it!'

* * * * *

(274) 'Neither let Israel think that I am come to divide the spoils of the Wicked Kingdom among her children.

'I come not to bring pluga (*which is a division of spoil*), but I am come to bring plugta (*which is dissension*)!

'Behold, this is the evil day whereof Micah prophesied, saying: "The good man is perished out of the earth. Therefore the day of thy visitation cometh.

'"For the son dishonoureth the father, the daughter riseth against her mother, the daughter-in-law against her mother-in-law; a man's foes shall be those of his own household. Now will I wait for the God of my salvation."'

* * * * *

(139) 'Learn a parable of the fig tree:

'When her branch is tender and putteth forth leaves, ye know that the summer fruit is nigh.

'For the Lord shewed unto Amos a basket of summer fruit, and said: "What seest thou?" And he answered: "A basket of summer fruit."

'Then said the Lord: "Nay, not qa'itz (*which is summer fruit*), but qetz (*which is the end*)! I will not again pass by them. And the songs of the Temple shall be howlings in that day!"

'So in like manner, when ye see those things prophesied by Micah come to pass, ye shall know that the end is nigh, even at the doors.

'Yet of that day and hour knoweth no man, nay, not the Son of God, neither the angels of heaven which listen from behind the veil, but the Father only.

'As Isaiah prophesied in the name of God: "For the day of vengeance is in My heart."

'Take heed, therefore, watch and pray: for ye know not when the time is!'

* * * * *

(*j*) The following (*see* (*a*) *above*) may be Jesus's answer to the three applicants for discipleship (*see* LXXXV.*c and d*).

(303) 'But whosoever will follow with me now in the preaching of the Kingdom, let him accept the cross upon his brow and deny himself, and take up his burden, and the burdens of his brethren.

'And let him be ashamed neither of poverty nor of much preaching.

'For whosoever shall be ashamed in this adulterous and sinful generation, of him also shall the Son of Man be ashamed, when he cometh in the glory of the Father.'

* * * * *

The following (*see (e) above*) is an explanation of the Samaritan woman's five husbands (*see* LXX.*g*).

(264) *'For in the house of the heavenly bodies, five are divided against two.*
'The evil powers that seek to gain dominion over the five middle days of the week are ranged against the holy powers of the first day and of the sabbath; and God's Adversary is their prince.'

* * * * *

(*k*) The following (*see (h) above*) belongs to the parable of the Rich Fool (*see* LXVII.*b*).

(59) *'For it is written in the Book of Job: "Beware lest the Lord take thee away with His stroke; then a great ransom shall not deliver thee."*
'And what shall it profit a man if he gain the whole world and lose his soul, which is beyond all price?'

* * * * *

The following (*see (b) above*) seems to have been spoken in the Temple (*see* XCIV.*e*).

(341) *'Verily, I say unto you, that there be some which stand here that shall not taste of death, till they have seen the Kingdom of Heaven come with power!'*

* * * * *

(*l*) The quotation from 'Scripture' in Clement of Rome's *First Epistle to the Corinthians* xxiii., written about 95 A.D., is paralleled in the much later *Second Epistle,* of which St Clement cannot have been the author. In each case the context suggests that these are Jesus's own words, and not, as has been suggested, those of some apocryphal prophet, perhaps the author of *Eldad and Medad.*

(140) *'Woe unto them that are of divided heart, which doubt and say: "These same things did we hear in the days of our fathers also, and behold, we are grown old, and none of them is befallen us."*
'Ye slow of heart, liken yourselves unto a tree, yea, unto a vine that first sheddeth her leaves, then putteth forth a shoot, from which springeth a leaf and a flower, and a green berry, and at the last a ripe grape.
'For behold, the time of vintage is at hand!'

* * * * *

THE WORTHLESS SHEPHERD

(*a*) Jesus's subsequent actions are intelligible only in the light of the long prophetic vision which closes the *Book of Zechariah* (xi.–xiv.). A main difficulty is the accidental displacement of several verses in the canonical text, and the subsequent editorial changes intended to repair this. The sequence may be restored as follows:

(xi. 3) A voice of the howling of the shepherds, for their glory is spoiled. A voice of the roaring of young lions, for the pride of Jordan is spoiled. (xi. 8) Three shepherds also I cut off in one month; my soul loathed them and their soul also abhorred me. (xi. 4) [And the Lord spake unto me, saying]: 'Thus saith the Lord my God: "Feed the flock of the slaughter, (xi. 5) whose possessors slay them and hold themselves not guilty, or sell them and say: 'Blessed be the Lord, now I am rich,' and whose own shepherds pity them not." ' (xi. 7a and 7c) And I said 'I will feed the flock of the slaughter, even you, the poor of the flock.' And I fed the flock.

(xi. 12) Then said I [unto the shpherds]: 'If ye think good, give me my price, and if not, forbear.' So they weighed for my price thirty pieces of silver. (xi. 13) And the Lord said unto me: 'Cast it unto the potter: a goodly price that I was prized at of them!' And I took the thirty pieces of silver and cast them unto the potter in the House of the Lord.

(xi. 15) And the Lord said unto me: 'Take now unto thee the instruments of a foolish shepherd. (xi. 16) For lo, I will raise up a shepherd in the land, which shall not visit them that be cut off, neither shall seek the young one, nor heal that which is broken, nor feed that which standeth still: but he shall eat the flesh of the fat and tear their claws in pieces.' (xi. 7b) And I got me two staves, the one I named *Noam,* which is Grace, and the other I named *Hoblim,* which is Corrupters.

(xi. 10) And I took my staff, even Grace, and cut it asunder, saying: 'Thus I break my covenant which I have made with all the people. (xi. 14) I have cut asunder my staff that I may break the fellowship that is between Judah and Israel.' (xi. 11) And it was broken in that day, and the poor of the flock that waited upon me certainly knew that this was the word of the Lord.

* * * * *

(*b*) [An omission here may be made good from *Zechariah* xi. 4 and xiii. 3: 'And the Lord said unto this man: "Take now thine other staff and preach lies in My name!" ']

* * * * *

(xi. 9) 'Tell them: "I will not feed you. That which dieth, let it die, and that which is cut off, let it be cut off, and let the rest eat every one the flesh of another. (xi. 6) For I will no more pity the inhabitants of the land, but lo, I will deliver the men every one into his neighbour's hand, and into the hand of his king; and they shall smite the land and out of their hand I will not deliver them."'

(xiii. 3) 'And it shall come to pass, while this man shall yet prophesy, that his father and his mother that begat him shall say unto him: "Thou shalt not live. For thou speakest lies in the name of the Lord! (xi. 17) Woe unto the worthless shepherd that leaveth the flock! The sword shall be upon his arm and upon his right eye. His arm shall be clean dried up and his right eye shall be utterly darkened." (xii. 3b) And his father and his mother that begat him shall thrust him through when he prophesieth.'

(xiii. 7) 'Awake therefore, O sword, against My shepherd, though he is My fellow,' saith the Lord of Hosts. 'Smite the shepherd and the sheep shall be scattered, but I will turn My hands upon the little ones. (xii. 10) For I will pour upon the House of David and upon the inhabitants of Jerusalem the spirit of grace and supplication; and they shall look upon him whom they have pierced, and they shall mourn for him, as one that mourneth for his only son, and shall be in bitterness for him as one that is in bitterness for his firstborn.'

(xii. 11) In that day shall there be great mourning in Jerusalem as the mourning of women that weep for Rimmon* in the valley of Megiddo. (xii. 12) And the land shall mourn every family apart; the family of those of David apart, the family of the House of Nathan apart, and their wives apart; (xii. 13) the family of the House of Levi apart, and their wives apart; the family of Shimei apart, and their wives apart. (xii. 14) All the families that remain, every family apart, and their wives apart.

(xiii. 1) In that day shall there be a fountain opened to the House of David and to the inhabitants of Jerusalem for sin and for uncleanness. (xiii. 2) 'And it shall come to pass in that day,' saith the Lord of Hosts, 'that I will cut off the names of the idols out of the land and they shall be no more remembered: and also I will cause the [false] prophets and the unclean spirit to pass out of the land. (xiii. 4) And it shall come to pass in that day that the false prophets shall be ashamed every one of his vision, when he hath prophesied, neither shall they wear a hairy garment to deceive. (xiii. 5) But [the false prophet] shall say: 'I am no prophet, I am an husbandman, for I was taught to keep cattle from my youth.' (xiii. 6) And when one shall say unto him: 'What are these wounds in thine hands?' he shall answer: 'Those with which I was wounded in the house of my friends.'

* * * * *

(c) The meaning of this vision is as follows. The Deutero-Zechariah, who lived in the age of the Seleucids when the Hellenizing priesthood tried to undo Ezra's religious reforms, preached true doctrine to the people of Jeru-

* Tammuz of the Pomegranates.

salem. But when he went to dedicate himself officially for his task, the High Priests did not value him at the full price of fifty shekels (*Leviticus* xxvii. 3), but at a lesser one (*Leviticus* xxvii. 8). They added to the insult by offering him thirty shekels, the price of a mere woman devotee (*Leviticus* xxvii. 4) or of a Canaanite slave (*Exodus* xxi. 32); thus also insulting God, who inspired Zechariah to refuse their money and cast it into the trough in which the Gibeonite potter was kneading clay for Temple vessels (*see* xc.*d*).

In his vision, he then breaks his staff of 'Grace' before the people, and chooses another called 'Corrupters'—the 'instruments of a worthless shepherd'. Supported by this new staff, he preaches falsehoods and denies the continuance of God's Grace, until he provokes his father and mother to kill him as a liar.

His death breaks the spell of evil. The people are moved to sudden repentance, and God proves merciful. A fountain of Grace gushes forth in Jerusalem for the removal of sin and uncleanness. All idols are thrown down, and the false prophets who have taken part in the worship of the Queen of Heaven, of Tammuz, Dionysus, and Zeus, are hounded from the city. Zechariah sees them taking refuge in the suburban villages, and there pretending to be simple cattlemen; they explain the wounds which they have dealt themselves in their Orgies as inflicted in a brawl at the house of friends. Meanwhile, the people of Jerusalem gaze upon the corpse of the dead prophet and understand at last: he was really 'God's fellow' and his provocative falsehoods have saved them from destruction. They mourn him as bitterly as if he were an only son.

Thereupon the Great Day of the Lord dawns. All the nations of the world march against Jerusalem, the city is taken and sacked, the women ravished, and half the population carried off into captivity. But suddenly the Son of Man manifests himself; and his feet bestride the Mount of Olives, which splits in two. The elect, preserved from slaughter, take refuge in his shadow. That day the sky is darkened to a twilight, but at nightfall it clears again and living waters—a metaphor interpreted by the Pharisees as meaning 'the Law of God'—flow out from the city eastward to the Dead Sea and westward to the Mediterranean. Two-thirds of the nation have perished; but the remnant is refined, as gold and silver are refined by fire. God says: 'It is My people', and they: 'It is our God'.

God then strikes the Gentile oppressors with a plague. They fight one another furiously and myriads perish, but at last strife ceases for very exhaustion, and the plague is stayed. Their survivors are converted and go up every year to Jerusalem for the Feast of Tabernacles. Plague has also stricken those horses and mules that wore brass moon-amulets in honour of the Queen of Heaven, and every one has succumbed. All is now clean and holy throughout the city: Canaanite potters are no longer found in the Temple, and the horses and mules display Jehovah's name on the bells that jingle from their harness —bells as holy as those sewn on the High Priest's robes.

Thus the vision ends; but Zechariah never dared to translate it into action, and it had therefore become one more prophecy awaiting fulfilment.

(e) Jesus, rebuffed by the Chief Rulers and insufficiently supported by the populace, decided as a desperate measure to impersonate the Worthless Shepherd and rouse Jerusalem to a sense of shame by preaching false doctrine. He expected that the people would assassinate him but that general repentance would follow when they looked on his pierced body, and induce the Pangs of the Messiah. As Israel's Priest-king, he could combine Zechariah's prophecy with that of the Suffering Servant in *Isaiah* liii. 1–12: the marred man of sorrows, who would die willingly for the sins of his people and be 'numbered among the sinners'. To be thus numbered was to sin deliberately; and the very consciousness of his sins, though they were committed in God's name, would make him a man of sorrows.

The Passion narrative is based upon the Worthless Shepherd prophecy: 'Lowly and riding upon an ass's colt' (*Zechariah* ix. 9 and *Matthew* xxi. 5); 'Thirty pieces of silver' (*Zechariah* xi. 12 and *Matthew* xxvii. 9); 'Smite the shepherd and the sheep shall be scattered' (*Zechariah* xiii. 7 and *Matthew* xxvi. 31); 'They shall look on me whom they pierced' (*Zechariah* xii. 10 and *John* xix. 37); 'The tribes of the world shall mourn' (*Zechariah* xii. 12 and *Matthew* xxiv. 30).

(f) Jesus, having released his disciples from their prophetic discipline by plying them with wine (*Amos* ii. 11–12 and *Micah* ii. 11—see cvi.*k*), assumes the role of the Worthless Shepherd and orders them no longer to count on God's bounty (*Luke* xxii. 35–36), but to buy swords: thus destroying the fence planted by the Pharisees around the Sixth Commandment. Then he warns them that he is about to offend them still further (*Matthew* xxvi. 31); quotes the relevant texts (*Luke* xxii. 37 and *Matthew* xxvi. 31) and satisfies himself that they have bought the two swords needed for taking revenge on him (*Luke* xxii. 38); next appoints, or accepts, Judas as the chief executioner (*John* xiii. 26–27) in the absence of his 'father and mother'—having said that he has no mother, brother, nor sister except those that do God's will (*Luke* viii. 21)—and awaits his own assassination. This he expects to take place on the Mount of Olives (*Mark* xiv. 26–27), the refuge for the elect few who are to be saved when the Son of Man alights there (*see* cvi.*t and* cvii.*b*).

(g) The glory of dying in ransom for Israel's iniquity had been celebrated in the *Fourth Book of Maccabees*, a 'Grecian' homily composed a few years before the Crucifixion. *Chapter* xvii. 20–22 is an apocryphal legend of the aged priest Eleazar and his seven sons who were cruelly tortured by the enemies of God—the same Hellenizing priesthood against whom the Deutero-Zechariah contended—but did not flinch:

> 'And these men, therefore, having sanctified themselves for God's sake, not only have received this honour [of dying for the nation], but also [the honour] that through them the enemy had no more power over our people, and the tyrant suffered punishment, and our country was purified, they hav-

ing as it were become a ransom for our nation's sin; and through the blood of
these righteous men and the propitiation of their death, the divine Providence
delivered Israel that before was evilly entreated.'

It is unlikely that Jesus had read this horrific book, unless in an Aramaic
translation. Its existence, however, proves that his purpose was in keeping
with contemporary religious thought. All sacrifice was 'ransom', an averting
of divine vengeance, and a king must be ready, if called upon, to suffer for
his nation. In 2 *Samuel* xxiv. 17, David voiced an ancient tradition: 'Let
Thine hand, I pray Thee, O God, be upon me and upon my father's house,
and not on Thy people that they should be plagued!'

(*h*) Jesus, in his heroic attempt to make the Great Day dawn quickly, laid
himself open to the charge of 'forcing the hour'. *Midrash Canticles Rabbah*
viii. 14. 1 runs:

> 'The salvation of Israel shall be likened unto four things:
>
> 'To the harvest: since when a field is harvested untimely, even the straw is
> poor, but when in due season, all is good. As it is written in the *Book of Joel*
> (iv. 13): "Put ye in the sickle, for the harvest is ripe!"
>
> 'To the vintage: since when the grapes are gathered untimely, even the
> vinegar is poor, but when in due season, all is good. As it is written in *Isaiah*
> (xxvii. 2–9): "Sing ye unto her, a vineyard of red wine"—for the grapes are
> cut when red.
>
> 'To spices: for the savour of spices gathered untimely is not so sweet as
> when they are gathered in due season. As it is written in the *Canticles* (iv.
> 16): "Blow upon my garden that the spices thereof may flow out."
>
> 'To a woman in travail: since when a child is born untimely, it dies, but
> when in due season, it lives. As it is written in *Micah* (v. 3): "Therefore will
> he give them up, until the time when she that travaileth shall bring forth;
> for then the remnant of his brethren shall return unto the Children of
> Israel." '

But *Sanhedrin* 98a contains a comment on Isaiah lx. 22, a text which was held
to refer to the Great Day:

> ' "I will hasten it in his time," signifies: "If they are worthy I will hasten
> it; if not [the Messiah will come] in due time." '

In Pharisaic tradition, the Messiah would come in a generation that was
either wholly righteous or wholly evil (*ibid.*). Jesus hoped that he would
precipitate the end by self-sacrifice: forcing his generation to repent and become wholly righteous.

(*i*) Afterwards, the Nazarenes understood and approved Jesus's desire to ransom Israel, though he misjudged the hour; this is proved by the record of
events which underlies the canonical Gospels. The Gentile Christians, however, deliberately misunderstood. They have, in fact, used the false doctrine
preached by him when he impersonated the Worthless Shepherd, as a dispen-

sation to reject the strict discipline of poverty and pacifism which he had hitherto enjoined on his followers.

(*j*) *John* x. 14, Jesus's alleged boast 'I am the *good* shepherd' (*see* LXXXI.*f*), which contradicts *Luke* xviii. 19—is apparently meant to distract attention from his grim histrionics.

(*k*) The Talmudic verdict that Jesus was a 'deceiver' (*Sanhedrin* 43*a*), is based on *Deuteronomy* xviii. 22, where it is laid down that if a prophet fore-tells events that do not come to pass, he is no prophet, but a presumptuous deceiver: Jesus had undoubtedly prophesied the coming of the Kingdom in the lifetime of many, and it had not come. This verdict is justified, moreover, if one considers the result, as opposed to the intention, of his actions. In his name the Jews have been forced into ghettos, and subjected to hatred, slanders, pogroms, persecutions, and forcible conversions to Catholicism, rather than led into the earthly paradise which he promised to them. Yet he acted in perfect good faith: he wholeheartedly believed himself to be 'God's fellow' when he adopted the part of *Zechariah's* Worthless Shepherd and, despite all libels from the time of Simon Magus to that of Renan and his successors, preserved his integrity to the end.

* * * * *

THE BARKED FIG-TREE

Mark xi. 12–14

¹²And on the morrow, when they were come from Bethany, He was hungry; ¹³and seeing a fig tree afar off having leaves, He came, if haply He might find any thing thereon: and when He came to it, He found nothing but leaves; for the time of figs was not yet. ¹⁴And Jesus answered and said unto it: 'No man eat fruit of thee hereafter for ever.' And His disciples heard it.

Mark xi. 20–23

²⁰And in the morning, as they passed by, they saw the fig tree dried up from the roots. ²¹And Peter calling to remembrance saith unto Him: 'Master, behold the fig tree which thou cursedst is withered away.' ²²And Jesus answering saith unto them: 'Have faith in God. ²³For verily I say unto you, that whosoever shall say unto this mountain, Be thou removed, and be thou cast into the sea; and shall not doubt in his heart, but shall believe that those things which he saith shall come to pass; he shall have whatsoever he saith.'

Matthew xxi. 17–22

¹⁷And He left them, and went out of the city into Bethany; and He lodged there.

¹⁸Now in the morning as He returned into the city, He hungered. ¹⁹And when He saw a fig tree in the way, He came to it, and found nothing thereon, but leaves only, and said unto it: 'Let no fruit grow on thee henceforward for ever.' And presently the fig tree withered away. ²⁰And when the disciples saw it, they marvelled, saying, How soon is the fig tree withered away! ²¹Jesus answered and said unto them: 'Verily I say unto you, if ye have faith, and doubt not, ye shall not only do this which is done to the fig tree, but also if ye shall say unto this mountain, be thou removed, and be thou cast into the sea; it shall be done. ²²And all things, whatsoever ye shall ask in prayer, believing, ye shall receive.'

Luke xvii. 5–6

⁵And the Apostles said unto the Lord: 'Increase our faith.' ⁶And the Lord said: 'If ye had faith as a grain of mustard seed, ye might say unto this sycamine tree, Be thou plucked up by the root, and be thou planted in the sea; and it should obey you.'

(*a*) This incident, reported in *Mark* xi. 12–14, 20–23, *Matthew* xxi. 17–22, and *Luke* xvii. 5–6, has troubled devout Christians more than any other passage in the Gospels. Not only is it at variance with Jesus's parable of the Barren Fig-Tree, which was to have one last opportunity for repentance (*see* XVI.*a*) but, as the author of *Mark* frankly points out, April is not the season for figs in Palestine. Moreover, Jesus curses the harmless tree for purely selfish reasons, though the cursing of any but a deliberate sinner, and then only by the inspiration of God, would have revolted the moral conscience of every devout first-century Jew. Cursing and lying are linked in *Psalm* lix. 12; and *Psalm* cix. 17 reads: 'As he loved cursing, so let it come unto him.'

(*b*) Nevertheless, this spectacular action, performed on the day before the Crucifixion, must be accepted as, in the main, historical. It marks the beginning of Jesus's impersonation of the Worthless Shepherd, and will have been preceded by his symbolic breaking of the staff named 'Grace' (*Zechariah* xi. 10—*see* CII.*a*). In *Mark* xi. 20, the curse takes effect after twenty-four hours have passed; in *Matthew* xxi. 20, the tree withers away before the disciples' eyes. Both Matthew and Mark interpret the incident as demonstrating the power of faith. So, it seems, did *Luke,* until an editor, noticing the discrepancy between the parable of the Barren Fig Tree and this act of cursing, altered 'fig' to 'sycomore' (or fig-mulberry). A later editor omitted the cursing and substituted: 'The apostles said unto the Lord: "Increase our faith!"'', though retaining the moral which Jesus was alleged to have drawn from his action, and misreading 'sycomore' for 'sycamine'—mulberry (*see* XLV.*e*).

(*c*) It may be asked: 'Was Jesus hungry after praying all night?' But in *John* iv. 31–34 he had assured the disciples that he could sustain himself on spiritual food (*see* LXX.*j* and LXXIX.*d*). Unless his hunger was feigned, 'he was hungry' must be an interpolation. Part of the dialogue is omitted from *Mark* xi. 13, where Jesus is made to answer without having first been questioned.

(*d*) The clue to the withering of the tree is found in *Joel* i. 12: 'The fig-tree languisheth'. Jesus will have implemented his curse by symbolically 'barking' or girdling this emblem of Israel, as prophesied in *Joel* i. 7–15, and the young leaves will soon have wilted.

(*e*) If the tree belonged to Annas, the head of the High-priestly House of Boethus—whose palace lay beside the road from Bethany to Jerusalem— Jesus's action would be in keeping with Joel's prophecy, which continues:

> 'Gird yourselves to lament, ye priests, howl, ye ministers of the altar! Alas, for the day! The day of the Lord is at hand and as a destruction from the Almighty shall it come!'

Jeremiah viii. 7–13, the prophecy about the fig-tree, was similarly aimed at the Chief Priests who 'worked abomination', and at the Temple scribes; all were promised destruction because of their failure to observe the signs of the times.

(378) *On the morrow, which was the day of preparation for the Passover, Jesus and his disciples were come from Bethany nigh unto the palace of Annas, which had been High Priest.*

And there Jesus took his staff and cut it asunder, even as Zechariah prophesied, saying: 'Thus doth God break the covenant which He hath made with His people!'

And looking up, he perceived a fig tree having branches that overhung the highway.

And he said unto the disciples: 'Go ye, and look if haply ye may find any fruit thereon!'

The disciples went, and found nothing but leaves. And they tell Jesus: 'We find nothing.'

Then said Jesus unto the tree: 'No man eat fruit of thee hereafter for ever! As Joel prophesied: "He hath barked my fig tree; the fig tree languisheth."

And as Jeremiah likewise saith: "There shall be no more figs on the fig tree, and the leaf shall wither."'

And Jesus barked the tree with a sharp stone, so that when certain of the disciples passed on the morrow, the leaves were already withered.

And the disciples marvelled greatly, because of the parable which he had spoken before, how that the Lord would spare the barren fig tree until the next season.

Neither was it yet the time of figs.

* * * * *

(*f*) By fulfilling these two prophecies Jesus was, in fact, 'forcing the hour'. The tree did not belong to him and, however just his case against the priesthood, he had no right to deprive the owner of a possession which symbolized his personal freedom (2 *Kings* xviii. 31); but he had already 'taken unto himself the instruments of the foolish shepherd' (*Zechariah* xi. 15—see CII.*a*), and turned his back on ethical principles.

At this point a lacuna occurs in the story. Jesus could not have visited the Temple again, since this was the Day of Preparation for the Passover, when its gates were shut. Instead, he seems to have gone into the streets of Jerusalem—probably the Ophel quarter where the Galileans congregated—there to fulfil the prophecy of *Zechariah* xi. 9 by deliberately preaching false doctrine. It will have been on this occasion that his kinsfolk thought him mentally deranged (*see* CIV.*c*).

(379) *And Jesus went into the streets and lanes of Jerusalem and there preached false doctrine,*

Declaring that God should no longer shew mercy unto Israel, because that the fig tree was now barked: wherefore let every man go his own way, and take a weapon in his hand and do what seemed good in his own eyes, neither be obedient to authority.

For God had put in his heart to fulfil the prophecy concerning the worthless shepherd, which preached lies in His name, that he might provoke the men of Jerusalem to indignation against him.

As Zechariah prophesied: 'God hath said: "I will not feed you. That which dieth, let it die; and that which is to be cut off, let it be cut off, let the rest eat every one the flesh of another."'

* * * * *

THE KINSMEN

Mark iii. 20–21

And they went into an house, [20]and the multitude cometh together again, so that they could not so much as eat bread. [21]And when His friends heard of it, they went out to lay hold on Him: for they said, He is beside Himself.

Mark iii. 31–35

[31]There came then His brethren and His mother, and standing without, sent unto Him, calling Him. [32]And the multitude sat about Him, and they said unto Him: 'Behold Thy mother and Thy brethren without seek for Thee.' [33]And He answered them saying: 'Who is My mother, or My brethren?' [34]And He looked round about on them which sat about Him, and said: 'Behold My mother and My brethren! [35]For whosoever shall do the will of God, the same is My brother, and My sister, and mother.'

Matthew xii. 46–50

[46]While He yet talked to the people, behold, His mother and His brethren stood without, desiring to speak with Him. [47]Then one said unto Him: 'Behold, Thy mother and Thy brethren stand without, desiring to speak with Thee.' [48]But He answered and said unto him that told Him: 'Who is My mother? and who are My brethren?' [49]And He stretched forth His hand toward His disciples, and said: 'Behold My mother and My brethren! [50]For whosoever shall do the will of My Father which is in heaven, the same is My brother, and sister, and mother.'

Luke viii. 19–21

[19]Then came to Him His mother and His brethren and could not come at Him for the press. [20]And it was told Him by certain which said: 'Thy mother and Thy brethren stand without, desiring to see Thee.' [21]And He answered and said unto them: 'My mother and My brethren are these which hear the word of God, and do it.'

Luke xi. 27–28

[27]And it came to pass, as He spake these things, a certain woman of the company lifted up her voice, and said unto Him: 'Blessed is the womb that bare

Luke xi. 27–28 (contd.)

Thee, and the paps which Thou hast sucked.' [28]But He said: 'Yea, rather, blessed are they that hear the word of God, and keep it.'

Luke xiv. 25–26

[25]And there went great multitudes with Him: and He turned, and said unto them: [26]'If any man come to Me, and hate not his father, and mother, and wife, and children, and brethren, and sisters, yea, and his own life also, he cannot be My disciple. And whosoever doth not bear his cross, and come after Me, cannot be My disciple.'

(a) Exactly what Jesus's kinsmen—the Greek phrase in *Mark* iii. 21 means 'those of his own'—heard about him that made them think he was mentally deranged, is not explained. They could hardly have thought so during his Galilean ministry, as the passage suggests. If his Davidic 'brethren according to the flesh' are meant, these were converts of John the Baptist (*see* vi. *a–g*) and could not have objected either to his healing of the sick, his preaching, or his choosing of disciples. Neither could they have feared that he would embarrass them by leading an armed rebellion against Rome; so far he had shown no signs of abandoning his Pharisaic quietism. It may be assumed, therefore, that the protest came from Jesus's 'brethren according to the spirit', his Levite kinsmen of Bethany, and that it was raised not at Capernaum, but in Jerusalem on the day before the Crucifixion, when in accordance with *Zechariah* xiii. 3 he began to impersonate the Worthless Shepherd and 'speak lies in the name of the Lord' (*see* cii.*e* and ciii.*b*).

'Who is my mother, or my brethren?' in *Mark* iii. 33 and *Matthew* xii. 48, is a repudiation of the Third Commandment, which he could never have uttered; and the order in *Luke* xiv. 26 to hate one's father and mother for Jesus's sake, is one of the grossest forgeries in the Gospels.

(b) The sister mentioned in *Matthew* xii. 50 is a clue to Jesus's real answer. If he was told: 'Thy sister and brethren stand without', he will have been justified in countering this with: 'Who is my sister, who are my brethren?', and in quoting *Deuteronomy* xxxiii. 9, Moses's praise of the tribe of Levi for the murder of their rebellious sons and brothers (*Exodus* xxxii. 27); and, perhaps also, *Numbers* xii. 1–15 where Moses's sister Miriam is punished with leprosy for doubting his prophetic pretensions. However, the Levites had taken good care to observe *Deuteronomy* xiii. 6, which excepted a father and mother from vengeance; and in *Numbers* xii. 14 the father's right to spit in his children's faces is asserted by God in person. If, therefore, it was Jesus's mother who sent for him, his quotation would have been inept.

(c) *Mark* alone has retained the kinsmen's charge that Jesus was out of his senses; *Matthew* ii. 46–50 and *Luke* vii. 19–21 might be read as though they had come merely to wish him well.

Jesus will have been aware of their hostile intentions before he rebuked them; they had already ceased to believe in him, if *John* vii. 5 (*see* xlix.*b*) is, as we suggest, the misplaced conclusion of the Lazarus incident (*see* LXXXVII.*e*), and no record survives that his parable of the Two Debtors (*Luke* vii. 41–42—*see* XI.*f*) re-converted them to belief in himself.

The situation was charged with irony: his kinsmen were right to protest against the false doctrine and he was secretly approving their attitude when he praised those who remained faithful to God. It is reasonable to conclude that, after quoting *Deuteronomy* xiii. 6, he said: 'The same is my mother and my father'; but that 'and my father' was subsequently omitted—though hinted at in *Luke* xiv. 26—partly because he was held not to have had an earthly father, and partly because it was an embarrassingly clear reference to Zechariah's prophecy of the vengeance taken on the Worthless Shepherd by both his parents (*see* CII.*b and f*).

There is some doubt whether 'James the brother of our Lord' was among the protesting kinsmen. It is likely that he remained loyal to Jesus until the barking of the fig-tree and the preaching of false doctrine (*see* CIII.*d–f*); but then hurried back to Bethany, where he reported with horror what was now a-foot. Jesus's 'sister' will have been Martha, his sister-in-law, who was nursing her resentment since his failure to raise Lazarus. Though a close relative, she is not mentioned as having either attended the Crucifixion (*see* CXIII.*v*) or gone to anoint Jesus's dead body (*see* VII.*f*).

(*d*) *Mark* iii. 20: 'And the multitude cometh together again, so that Jesus and his disciples could not so much as eat bread'—paralleled in *Mark* vi. 31 (*see* LXXII.*f*)—seems to have introduced the Lazarus incident (*see* LXXXVII.*f*).

(380) *And Martha, daughter of Simeon the Chaste, hearing from James, her brother, what things Jesus did and preached, went with certain of her kinsmen to lay hold on him, saying: 'He is beside himself.'*

But when they were nigh unto the place where he was, they could not come at him because of the press.

Then a certain man said unto Jesus: 'Behold, thy sister and thy brethren stand without, desiring to speak with thee.'

And he asked: 'What would they of me?'

He that told him, answered: 'That thou wouldst hold thy peace and preach no more in Jerusalem.'

Jesus answered and said: 'Who is my sister, and who are my brethren?

'Verily, I say unto you: Moses praised the Sons of Levi because they regarded not their brethren which trespassed against the Lord, but took sword and slew them.

'Neither was Miriam spared, which was the sister of Moses, when she spake evil against him at Hazeroth.'

And he stretched forth his hands towards his disciples and the women which ministered unto him, and said: 'Behold my sisters and my brethren!

'Yea, whosoever doeth the will of our Father which is in heaven and slayeth the deceiver, the same is my brother or my sister—yea, and my father or my mother!'

* * * * *

(e) [Here follows *Mark* xiii. 12, paralleled in *Matthew* x. 21: 'For in the last days the brother shall deliver his brother unto death, for God's sake, and the father his son' (*see* xcviii.*d*).]

* * * * *

(f) *Luke* xi. 27–28, a saying which has been abbreviated to the point of illogic, may belong to this context. It does not imply that Jesus's mother according to the flesh had disobeyed God's word; he brusquely waives the personal compliment—irrelevant now that he has been re-born from a virgin—and limits his blessing to those mothers whose sons obey God. He will have quoted *Proverbs* x. 1 in support of his saying.

> (382) *Then one cried, saying: 'Yet blessed is the womb that bare thee, blessed are the paps which thou didst suck!'*
>
> *And Jesus answered: 'Say, rather, that blessed is she whose children hearken unto the word of God and delight to keep it.*
>
> *'For Solomon saith: "An unwise son is the heaviness of his mother."'*

* * * * *

THE SOP

Mark xiv. 1–2

[1]After two days was the feast of the Passover, and of unleavened bread: and the chief priests and the scribes sought how they might take Him by craft, and put Him to death. [2]But they said, Not on the feast day, lest there be an uproar of the people.

Mark xiv. 10–11

[10]And Judas Iscariot, one of the Twelve, went unto the chief priests, to betray Him unto them. [11]And when they heard it, they were glad, and promised to give him money. And he sought how he might conveniently betray Him.

Mark xiv. 18–21

[18]And as they sat and did eat, Jesus said: 'Verily I say unto you, one of you which eateth with Me shall betray Me.' [19]And they began to be sorrowful, and to say unto Him one by one: 'Is it I?' and another said, 'Is it I?' [20]And He answered and said unto them: 'It is one of the Twelve, that dippeth with Me in the dish. [21]The Son of Man indeed goeth, as it is written of Him: but woe to that man by whom the Son of Man is betrayed! good were it for that man if he had never been born.'

Matthew xxvi. 1–2

[1]And it came to pass, when Jesus had finished all these sayings, He said unto His disciples: [2]'Ye know that after two days is the feast of the passover, and the Son of Man is betrayed to be crucified.'

Matthew xxvi. 14–16

[14]Then one of the Twelve, called Judas Iscariot, went unto the chief priests, [15]and said unto them, What will ye give me, and I will deliver Him unto you? And they covenanted with him for thirty pieces of silver. [16]And from that time he sought opportunity to betray Him.

Matthew xxvi. 21–25

[21]And as they did eat, He said: 'Verily I say unto you, that one of you shall betray Me.' [22]And they were exceeding sorrowful, and began every one of them to say unto him, Lord, is it I? [23]And He answered and said: 'He that dippeth his hand with Me in the dish, the same shall betray Me. [24]The Son

Matthew xxvi. 21–25 (*contd.*)

of Man goeth as it is written of Him: but woe unto that man by whom the Son of Man is betrayed! it had been good for that man if he had not been born.' 25Then Judas, which betrayed Him, answered and said: 'Master, is it I?' He said unto him: 'Thou hast said.'

John xii. 38–41

38That the saying of Isaiah the prophet might be fulfilled, which he spake:

Lord, who hath believed our report?
And to whom hath the arm of the Lord been revealed?

39Therefore they could not believe, because that Isaiah said again:

40*He hath blinded their eyes,*
And hardened their heart;
That they should not see with their eyes, nor understand
with their heart, and be converted,
And I should heal them.

41These things said Isaiah when he saw His glory, and spake of Him.

John xi. 57

57Now both the chief priests and the Pharisees had given a commandment, that, if any man knew where He were, he should shew it, that they might take Him.

Luke xxii. 1–6

1Now the feast of unleavened bread drew nigh, which is called the Passover. 2And the chief priests and scribes sought how they might kill Him; for they feared the people.

3Then entered Satan into Judas surnamed Iscariot, being of the number of the Twelve. 4And he went his way, and communed with the chief priests and captains, how he might betray Him unto them. 5And they were glad, and covenanted to give him money. 6And he promised, and sought opportunity to betray Him unto them in the absence of the multitude.

Luke xxii. 21–23

21'But, behold, the hand of him that betrayeth Me is with Me on the table. 22And truly the Son of Man goeth, as it was determined: but woe unto that man by whom He is betrayed!' 23And they began to inquire among themselves, which of them it was that should do this thing.

John xiii. 1–2

1Now before the feast of the passover, when Jesus knew that His hour was come that He should depart out of this world unto the Father, having loved His own which were in the world, He loved them unto the end. 2And supper being ended, the devil having now put into the heart of Judas Iscariot, Simon's son, to betray Him.

John xiii. 18–32

[18]'I speak not of you all: I know whom I have chosen: but that the scripture may be fulfilled,

He that eateth bread with Me
Hath lifted up his heel against Me.

[19]Now I tell you before it come, that, when it is come to pass, ye may believe that I am He. [20]Verily, verily, I say unto you, he that receiveth whomsoever I send receiveth Me; and he that receiveth Me receiveth Him that sent Me.'

[21]When Jesus had thus said, He was troubled in spirit, and testified, and said: 'Verily, verily, I say unto you, that one of you shall betray me.' [22]Then the disciples looked one on another, doubting of whom He spake. [23]Now there was leaning on Jesus' bosom one of His disciples, whom Jesus loved. [24]Simon Peter therefore beckoned to him, that he should ask who it should be of whom He spake. [25]He then lying on Jesus' breast saith unto Him: 'Lord, who is it?' [26]Jesus answered: 'He it is, to whom I shall give a sop, when I have dipped it.' And when he had dipped the sop, He gave it to Judas Iscariot, the son of Simon. [27]And after the sop Satan entered into him. Then said Jesus unto him: 'That thou doest, do quickly.' [28]Now no man at the table knew for what intent He spake this unto him. [29]For some of them thought, because Judas had the bag, that Jesus had said unto him, Buy those things that we have need of against the feast; or, that he should give something to the poor. [30]He then having received the sop went immediately out: and it was night.

[31]Therefore, when he was gone out, Jesus said: 'Now is the Son of Man glorified, and God is glorified in Him. [32]If God be glorified in Him, God shall also glorify Him in Himself, and shall straightway glorify Him.'

(a) The Synoptics state (*Mark* xiv. 1–10, *Matthew* xxvi. 1–14, and *Luke* xxii. 1–16) that Satan entered into Judas two days before the Passover; and that, having then sold his master to the Chief Priests, he waited until the Last Supper was over before stealing away to act as their guide. But these three accounts do not agree in all respects.

According to *Mark* xiv. 18 Jesus said, just before instituting the Sacrament: 'One of you will betray me!' and when asked who this would be, replied: 'One of the Twelve!'—which excluded from the number of suspects only John son of Annas, 'the disciple whom Jesus loved'. But according to *Luke* xxii. 21–23 everyone present was suspect, including the beloved disciple; and Jesus foretold his betrayal after the Sacrament, of which Judas had presumably partaken. Again, according to *Matthew* xxvi. 2 and 14–16, this announcement, which included a reference to the Crucifixion, had been made shortly before Judas decided to approach the Chief Priests; and his villainy was either broadly hinted at during the supper (*Matthew* xxvi. 25), if 'thou hast said' is a translation of the idiomatic Aramaic phrase *'atta amarta'*, 'You say so, not I!'; or else clearly exposed, if it has the force of the Greek 'That is so!' (*see* cix.k).

A very different story is told in *John* xiii. 26–27: Jesus, by giving Judas a sop, singles him out as the criminal and tells him to do quickly what he has to do. After this Satan enters into Judas, for the first time, and he runs out to bargain with the Chief Priests. The Sacrament is not mentioned in *John's* account of the scene, which contains two obvious inconsistencies. According to *John* xiii. 2 the supper has ended, and grace must therefore have been said, yet Jesus hands Judas a sop from the dish; and in *John* xiii. 26 the beloved disciple is privately informed who will betray Jesus, yet fails to realize (verse 28) what is meant when Jesus urges Judas to hasten the betrayal.

(*b*) *John* xiii. 21 does not explain why Jesus should suddenly have been troubled in spirit, though already aware (verse 18) that his familiar friend would 'lift up his heel' against him. It must, rather, have been Judas who was troubled, when Jesus succeeded in offending him.

For the proper context of the quotation from *Psalm* xli. 9 in *John* xiii. 18, see CIX.*p*.

(*c*) The evangelists wished to emphasize that Jesus, being God, had always been aware of Judas's intentions, and was now urging him to act. This has left theologians with a difficult problem: if Jesus was God, how could Judas be blamed for obeying his instructions? And if Judas's actions were predestined, should he not be praised as the man who sent Christ to the Cross and thus brought about universal salvation? But if his actions were not predestined and therefore evil, why did Christ urge him on?

The *Zechariah* references prove that Jesus, though expecting death at the hand of a ritual slayer, never foresaw that Judas would fail in the part for which he had been cast. Judas was not a traitor in the vulgar sense but, when called upon to act, thought that he knew better than his master. Two details in the account of his 'betrayal' exculpate him of the desire to have Jesus crucified or in any way punished: first the kiss, which was an assurance that his actions were in Jesus's best interests; next the peculiar sum which he demanded as blood-money. Had he bargained for three hundred pence, or even three thousand, these would have been forthcoming, since the knowledge that Jesus was still at large gravely embarrassed the Chief Priests. The thirty pence mentioned in *Matthew* xxvi. 15 was too paltry a sum to have satisfied a man who, as *John* suggests, took so great an interest in money (*see* XI.*h*); if he was indeed a villain he could have gained far more by remaining treasurer of the Twelve, fleecing such rich women supporters as Joanna and Susanna, and blackmailing the secret disciples, Bunni ben Gorion and John son of Annas. His choice of thirty pence proves, on the contrary, that he understood Jesus's message and agreed that the Chief Priests—in *John* xi. 57 'Pharisees' has been substituted for 'Herodians', the Chief Priests' allies—misprized and undervalued him as grossly as their forebears had misprized the Worthless Shepherd (*see* CII.*c*). He was asking for the exact sum mentioned in *Zechariah* xi. 12–13, neither more nor less, and intended to return it later to the Treasury (*see* CXII.*a*).

(*d*) Jesus must have said: 'One of you is destined to kill me!', not: 'One of you shall betray me!'; and when he realized that Judas was the only person present who had taken offence at his false doctrine, rewarded him with a sop, or titbit—such as is still selected by a Bedouin sheikh from the common dish of mutton and pressed on his favoured guest. He was, in fact, honouring him as the most faithful and perceptive of his disciples; and when Judas asked: 'Is it I?', did not definitely appoint him executioner—which would have been inconsistent with the spirit of *Zechariah's* prophecy—but used the non-committal phrase 'So thou sayest!', thus placing the burden of choice on Judas himself.

(*e*) At this, Judas started to his feet in indignation, and Jesus, believing that he had accepted the task, told him: 'Use what money is necessary!', namely for buying the swords. Meanwhile, the remaining disciples did not understand what had happened. Some thought that since all shops would close at noon on the following day, he had ordered Judas, as treasurer of the Twelve, to lay in a two-days' store of provisions before supplies were exhausted. (*John* xiii. 29: 'That he should give something to the poor', was another guess.)

The thoughtless acceptance of false doctrine by everyone present but Judas made Jesus quote first *Isaiah* liii. 1, the prophecy about the Suffering Servant; and next *Isaiah* vi. 9–10, the passage about the blind eyes and hard hearts, which is misplaced and misquoted in *John* xii. 40 (*see* LXXXI.*b*), in *Matthew* xiii. 14 (*see* LXVI.*j*), in *Mark* iv. 12 and in *Luke* viii. 10 (*see* XXV.*b*).

(*f*) Judas must have deeply disapproved of Jesus's attempt to 'force the hour' by fulfilling *Zechariah's* prophecies. God alone knew when the hour would come and, if Jesus were wrong in thinking it close at hand, those who were to take ritual vengeance on the Worthless Shepherd would be common murderers. Judas shrank from the task assigned to him: how could he raise a sword against a virtuous man who was merely impersonating a sinner? He decided that the only way to save Jesus from taking a false step was to make a pretence of betraying him for the described sum, and thus place him in protective custody. The Great Sanhedrin, when it tried Jesus after the Feast, would either acclaim him King of Israel, and thus rally the nation in his support; or else sentence him to death in unwitting fulfilment of *Zechariah's* prophecy. It never occurred to Judas that Jesus might be handed over to the Romans instead, as is proved by his horror when he heard of the coming crucifixion (*see* CXII.*a*).

(*g*) *Mark* xiv. 21, paralleled in *Matthew* xxvi. 24 and *Luke* xxii. 22, has been misplaced: its proper context is Jesus's arrest in the Garden (*see* CVII.*n*). *Isaiah* liii. 7, here quoted by Jesus, later prevented him from pleading his case, for the passage continues: 'and as a sheep before his shearers is dumb, so opened he not his mouth' (*see* CIX.*j* and CX.*i*).

(406) *'Behold, this son of man goeth now as Isaiah prophesied: "He is brought as a lamb unto the slaughter."*

'But woe unto him that hath betrayed me! It were better for that man that he had never been born!'

* * * *

John xiii. 19 may be disregarded; verse 20 is paralleled both in *Luke* x. 16 (*see* LIX.*a*) and in *Matthew* x. 40 (*see* LVII.*e*), which seems to be its correct context. Verse 32 may also be disregarded.

(*h*) *Matthew* xxvi. 17: 'the first day of the feast of unleavened bread', contradicts the Nazarene tradition that Jesus was sacrificed at the same time as the Passover Lamb (*see* CXIII.*q*). The *Seder,* or Passover Supper, was eaten at sundown of the fourteenth of *Nisan,* when the fifteenth day began and, with it, the Feast of Unleavened Bread. And though, in 30 A.D., this happened to fall on a Sabbath, yet the Jews ate the *Seder* at the usual hour: because Hillel, when President of the Great Sanhedrin, had ruled that the Passover, being a public sacrifice, took precedence over the Sabbath (*Tosephta Pesahim* iv. 1–2), and that the preparations for the *Seder,* which could not be completed by dusk and involved considerable work, were no breach of the Fourth Commandment.*

If, therefore, the main Gospel tradition that Jesus was crucified on the Friday (*Mark* xv. 42 and *Luke* xxiii. 54—*see* CXIV.*e*) is accepted—and this also finds support in the Talmud (*Sanhedrin* 43*a*): 'On the Eve of Passover they hanged Yeshu of Nazareth'—the Last Supper cannot have been the *Seder*. It will have been a *seudath mizwah,* or friendly club-feast, as common an institution among the Jews as it was among the Greeks and Romans. The *Seder* required a Passover lamb sacrificed by the Temple Levites, which could not have been available on the Thursday; neither does any Gospel mention such a lamb. In *John* xiii. 1–2 it is, in fact, stated that the Last Supper was eaten before the Passover.

(*i*) *Mark* xiv. 1 and *Matthew* xxvi. 2: 'After two days was (or 'is') the Passover,' should be read in conjunction with the corresponding text in *Luke* xxii. 1: 'Now the feast of unleavened bread drew nigh which is called the Passover.' The decision to arrest Jesus was reached by the Chief Rulers between Wednesday and Thursday night.

(383) *Now, the Feast of Unleavened Bread drew nigh, and in that year the Passover fell on a sabbath.*

And the Chief Priests and scribes sought how they might yet take Jesus by craft, and deliver him unto the Romans.

For they feared that there might be a rebellion of the people if they took

---

* Chwolson's contention (*Das Letzte Passamahl Christie und der Tag Seines Todes,* 1892, *p.* 31) that the Passover lamb in Jesus's day was regarded as a private sacrifice which did not suspend the Sabbath laws, and that in 30 A.D. it was therefore offered on the Thursday evening, cannot be accepted. The Sadducees disagreed with Hillel on this point (*Tosephta Pesahim* iv. 1–2), but though, as agents of Rome, they were politically dominant, the President of the Great Sanhedrin took the final decision in all questions of religious procedure. There is no evidence that this particular ruling had been altered or annulled since Hillel had made it some forty years previously.

him not before the feast began; yet the multitude thronged him, and they dared do nothing against him openly.

* * * * *

(*j*) [Here follows the Last Supper and Jesus's further preaching of false doctrine (*see* cvi.*u–v*).]

* * * * *

(390) *And when Jesus had thus said, he cried in a loud voice: 'Verily, verily, I say unto you: the hand of him that shall slay me is on this table and dippeth into the dish!'*

Then the disciples looked on one another, doubting whereof he spake.

Which when Jesus perceived, he said: 'Isaiah prophesied: "Who hath believed our report? And to whom is the arm of the Lord revealed?"

'And again: "Hear ye indeed, but understand not; and see ye indeed, and perceive not?

' "Make the heart of this people fat and make their ears heavy and shut their eyes; lest they see with their eyes and hear with their ears and understand with their heart, and be converted and be healed." '

Now, there was leaning on Jesus's bosom the disciple which he loved; and Peter beckoned unto him that he should ask who it was that should slay him.

He then, lying on Jesus's bosom, asketh of him: 'Lord, who is it?'

And Jesus, when he perceived that Judas of Kerioth, the son of Simon, alone of them that sat at meat, was offended in him, gave him a sop, after that he had dipped it in the dish.

And Judas saith unto him privately: 'Is it I?'

Jesus answered: 'So thou sayest!'

And Judas was wroth thereat, and rose to depart.

Then saith Jesus unto him: 'Spend what money is needful, and that thou doest, do it quickly!'

But no man at the table understood to what intent he spake this unto Judas.

Some thought that Jesus had said unto him: 'Give alms to the poor.'

Others thought that he had said: 'Buy the food that we have need of against the sabbath.'

But Judas knew that he said: 'Buy the swords that are needed against the fulfilment of that prophecy which Zechariah spake: of him that feigned himself to be a false prophet, yet was God's fellow.'

* * * * *

(391) *Judas, when he had received the sop, went forth immediately; and it was night. And Satan entered into his soul, for he loathed the task that was laid upon him.*

And Satan spake within his heart, saying: 'Doth not thy master force the hour and bring it to birth untimely? Beware, lest he make thee a murderer!'

Then Judas, greatly longing to deliver Jesus from error, considered how to put him in ward.

Wherefore he went hastily unto the Captain of the Temple, and said unto him: 'Sir, I am a disciple of Jesus the Galilean, which is called the King of Israel; but that he doeth now, my soul abhorreth.

'Suffer me therefore to lead thee tonight unto the place where he lieth, that he may be put in ward, and cause no man to sin.

'But after the feast, let him be judged by the Council, whether he be truly the King of Israel, or whether a deceiver of the people.'

* * * * *

(392) *The Captain of the Temple therefore leadeth Judas unto the two Catholics which were set over the Treasury, being kinsmen of the High Priest.*

And the Catholics say unto him: 'Wilt thou indeed shew us the place where thy master lieth? Then will we pay thee well.'

Judas answered in the words of Zechariah: 'If ye think good, give me my price, and if not, forbear!'

Then the Catholics ask him: 'Man, what is thy price?'

He answered: 'It is written: "So they weighed for my price thirty pieces of silver, a goodly price that I was prized at by them." '

But they knew not whereof Judas spake, being Sadducees which regard not the prophets.

* * * * *

THE LAST SUPPER

Mark xiv. 12–17

¹²And the first day of unleavened bread, when they killed the passover, His disciples said unto Him: 'Where wilt Thou that we go and prepare that Thou mayest eat the passover?' ¹³And he sendeth forth two of His disciples, and saith unto them: 'Go ye into the city, and there shall meet you a man bearing a pitcher of water: follow him. ¹⁴And wheresoever he shall go in, say ye to the goodman of the house, the Master saith, where is the guestchamber, where I shall eat the passover with My disciples? ¹⁵And he will shew you a large upper room furnished and prepared: there make ready for us.' ¹⁶And His disciples went forth, and came into the city, and found as He had said unto them: and they made ready the passover.

¹⁷And in the evening He cometh with the Twelve.

Mark xiv. 22–25

²²And as they did eat, Jesus took bread, and blessed, and brake it, and gave to them, and said:

'Take, eat: this is My body.'

²³And He took the cup, and when He had given thanks, He gave it to them: and they all drank of it. ²⁴And He said unto them:

'This is My blood of the new testament, which is shed for many.

²⁵Verily I say unto you, I will drink no more of the fruit of the vine, until that day that I drink it new in the kingdom of God.'

Mark xiv. 27–31

²⁷And Jesus saith unto them: 'All ye shall be offended because of Me this night: for it is written,

I will smite the shepherd,
And the sheep shall be scattered.

²⁸But after that I am risen, I will go before you into Galilee.'

²⁹But Peter said unto Him: 'Although all shall be offended, yet will not I.' ³⁰And Jesus saith unto him: 'Verily I say unto thee, that this day, even in this night, before the cock crow twice, thou shalt deny Me thrice.' ³¹But he spake the more vehemently: 'If I should die with Thee, I will not deny Thee in any wise.' Likewise also said they all.

Matthew xxvi. 17–20

[17]Now the first day of the feast of unleavened bread the disciples came to Jesus, saying unto Him: 'Where wilt Thou that we prepare for Thee to eat the passover?' [18]And He said: 'Go into the city to such a man, and say unto him, The Master saith, My time is at hand; I will keep the passover at thy house with My disciples.' [19]And the disciples did as Jesus had appointed them; and they made ready the passover.

[20]Now when the even was come, He sat down with the Twelve.

Matthew xxvi. 26–29

[26]And as they were eating, Jesus took bread, and blessed it, and brake it, and gave it to the disciples, and said:

'Take, eat; this is My body.'

[27]And He took the cup, and gave thanks, and gave it to them, saying:

'Drink ye all of it;

[28]for this is My blood of the new testament, which is shed for many for the remission of sins. [29]But I say unto you, I will not drink henceforth of this fruit of the vine, until that day when I drink it new with you in My Father's kingdom.'

Matthew xxvi. 31–35

[31]Then saith Jesus unto them: 'All ye shall be offended because of Me this night: for it is written,

I will smite the shepherd,
And the sheep of the flock shall be scattered abroad.

[32]But after I am risen again, I will go before you into Galilee.' [33]Peter answered and said unto Him: 'Though all men shall be offended because of Thee, yet will I never be offended.' [34]Jesus said unto him: 'Verily I say unto thee, that this night, before the cock crow, thou shalt deny Me thrice.' [35]Peter said unto Him: 'Though I should die with Thee, yet will I not deny Thee.' Likewise also said all the disciples.

Luke xxii. 7–20

[7]Then came the day of unleavened bread, when the passover must be killed. [8]And He sent Peter and John, saying: 'Go and prepare us the passover, that we may eat.' [9]And they said unto Him: 'Where wilt Thou that we prepare?' [10]And He said unto them: 'Behold, when ye are entered into the city, there shall a man meet you, bearing a pitcher of water; follow him into the house where he entereth in. [11]And ye shall say unto the goodman of the house, The Master saith unto thee, Where is the guestchamber, where I shall eat the passover with My disciples? [12]And he shall shew you a large upper room furnished: there make ready.' [13]And they went, and found as He had said unto them: and they made ready the passover.

[14]And when the hour was come, He sat down, and the twelve Apostles with Him. [15]And He said unto them: 'With desire I have desired to eat this passover with you before I suffer. [16]For I say unto you, I will not any more

Luke xxii. 7–20 (*contd.*)

eat thereof, until it be fulfilled in the kingdom of God.' [17]And He took the cup, and gave thanks, and said: 'Take this, and divide it among yourselves: [18]for I say unto you, I will not drink of the fruit of the vine, until the kingdom of God shall come.' [19]And He took bread, and gave thanks, and brake it, and gave unto them, saying:

'This is My body which is given for you: this do in remembrance of Me.' [20]Likewise also the cup after supper, saying:

'This cup is the new testament in My blood, which is shed for you.'

Luke xxii. 33–34

[33]And he said unto Him: 'Lord, I am ready to go with Thee, both into prison, and to death.' [34]And He said: 'I tell thee, Peter, the cock shall not crow this day, before that thou shalt thrice deny that thou knowest Me.'

Luke xxii. 35–38

[35]And He said unto them: 'When I sent you without purse, and scrip, and shoes, lacked ye any thing?' And they said: 'Nothing.' [36]Then said He unto them: 'But now, he that hath a purse, let him take it, and likewise his scrip: and he that hath no sword, let him sell his garment, and buy one. [37]For I say unto you, that this that is written must yet be accomplished in Me,

And He was reckoned among the transgressors:

for the things concerning Me have an end.' [38]And they said: 'Lord, behold, here are two swords.' And He said unto them: 'It is enough.'

Luke xxii. 49

[49]When they which were about Him saw what would follow, they said unto Him: 'Lord, shall we smite with the sword?'

John xiii. 3–17

[3]Jesus knowing that the Father had given all things into His hands, and that He was come from God, and went to God; [4]He riseth from supper, and laid aside His garments; and took a towel, and girded Himself. [5]After that He poureth water into a bason, and began to wash the disciples' feet, and to wipe them with the towel wherewith He was girded. [6]Then cometh He to Simon Peter: and Peter saith unto Him: 'Lord, dost Thou wash my feet?' [7]Jesus answered and said unto him: 'What I do thou knowest not now; but thou shalt know hereafter.' [8]Peter saith unto Him: 'Thou shalt never wash my feet.' Jesus answered him: 'If I wash thee not, thou hast no part with Me.' [9]Simon Peter saith unto Him: 'Lord, not my feet only, but also my hands and my head.' [10]Jesus saith to him: 'He that is washed needeth not save to wash his feet, but is clean every whit: and ye are clean, but not all.' [11]For He knew who should betray Him; therefore said He, 'Ye are not all clean.' [12]So after He had washed their feet, and had taken His garments, and was set down again, He said unto them: 'Know ye what I have done to you? [13]Ye call me Master and Lord: and ye say well; for so I am. [14]If I then, your Lord and

John xiii. 3–17 (*contd.*)

Master, have washed your feet; ye also ought to wash one another's feet. [15]For I have given you an example, that ye should do as I have done to you. [16]Verily, verily, I say unto you, the servant is not greater than his lord; neither he that is sent greater than he that sent him. [17]If ye know these things, happy are ye if ye do them.'

John xiii. 33–38

[33]'Little children, yet a little while I am with you. Ye shall seek me: and as I said unto the Jews, whither I go, ye cannot come; so now I say to you. [34]A new commandment I give unto you, that ye love one another; as I have loved you, that ye also love one another. [35]By this shall all men know that ye are My disciples, if ye have love one to another.'

[36]Simon Peter said unto Him: 'Lord, whither goest Thou?' Jesus answered him: 'Whither I go, thou canst not follow Me now; but thou shalt follow Me afterwards.' [37]Peter said unto Him: 'Lord, why cannot I follow Thee now? I will lay down my life for Thy sake.' [38]Jesus answered him: 'Wilt thou lay down thy life for My sake? Verily, verily, I say unto thee, the cock shall not crow, till thou hast denied Me thrice.'

John xiv. 1–6

[1]'Let not your heart be troubled: ye believe in God, believe also in Me. [2]In My Father's house are many mansions: if it were not so, I would have told you. [3]I go to prepare a place for you, and if I go and prepare a place for you, I will come again, and receive you unto Myself: that where I am, there ye may be also. [4]And whither I go ye know, and the way ye know.'

[5]Thomas saith unto Him: 'Lord, we know not whither Thou goest; and how can we know the way?' [6]Jesus saith unto him: 'I am the way, the truth, and the life: no man cometh unto the Father, but by Me.'

John xiv. 15

[15]'If ye love Me, keep My commandments.'

John xiv. 31b

[31b]And as the Father gave Me commandment, even so I do. Arise, let us go hence.

John xvi. 25–33

[25]'These things have I spoken unto you in proverbs: but the time cometh, when I shall no more speak unto you in proverbs, but I shall show you plainly of the Father. [26]At that day ye shall ask in My Name: and I say not unto you, that I will pray the Father for you: [27]for the Father Himself loveth you, because ye have loved Me, and have believed that I came out from God. [28]I came forth from the Father, and am come into the world: again, I leave the world, and go to the Father.' [29]His disciples said unto Him: 'Lo, now speakest Thou plainly, and speakest no proverb. [30]Now are we sure that Thou knowest all things, and needest not that any man should ask Thee: by this

John xvi. 25–33 (contd.)

we believe that Thou camest forth from God.' [31]Jesus answered them: 'Do ye now believe? [32]Behold, the hour cometh, yea, is now come, that ye shall be scattered, every man to his own, and shall leave Me alone: and yet I am not alone, because the Father is with Me. [33]These things I have spoken unto you, that in Me ye might have peace. In the world ye shall have tribulation: but be of good cheer; I have overcome the world.'

I Corinthians xi. 23–26

[23]For I have received of the Lord that which also I delivered unto you, That the Lord Jesus the same night in which He was betrayed took bread: [24]and when He had given thanks, He brake it, and said,

> Take, eat:
> This is My body, which is broken for you:
> This do in remembrance of Me.

[25]After the same manner also He took the cup, when He had supped, saying,

> This cup is the new testament in My blood:
> This do ye, as oft as ye drink, in remembrance of Me.

[26]For as often as ye eat this bread, and drink this cup, ye do shew the Lord's death till He come.

The Gospel of the Ebionites quoted by Epiphanius: Heresies xxx.

The Ebionites have changed the saying . . . and made the Disciples say: 'Have I heartily desired this flesh of the Passover with you?'

John xii. 49–50

[49]'For I have not spoken of Myself; but the Father Who sent Me, He gave Me a commandment, what I should say, and what I should speak. [50]And I know that His commandment is life everlasting: whatsoever I speak therefore, even as the Father said unto Me, so I speak.'

Fayoum Gospel Fragment
(Third Century)

'. . . all ye in this night shall be offended according to the Scripture: "I will smite the shepherd and the sheep shall be scattered." And when Peter said: 'Even if all, not I,' the Lord said: 'The cock shall twice crow and thou first shalt thrice deny me.'

(a) Mark xiv. 13 and Luke xxii. 10 preserve the detail of the guide who carried a water-pitcher; in Matthew xxvi. 18 he is merely called 'such a man'. The disciples' meeting with him must not be regarded as an instance of Jesus's prophetic foresight; it will have been pre-arranged, and Jesus must have known where to find the room, since Peter and John went ahead of him. But he feared that an attempt might be made to arrest him and secrecy had therefore to be observed; moreover, as the sequel shows, he wished for privacy. Most commentators are content to point out that a man with a water-pitcher would have been an unusual sight in Jerusalem, since the carrying of water was women's work. This explanation is illogical. Less spectacular means of recognition could easily have been found, such as a basket of spring flowers, or an ox-goad; if women alone carried pitchers, a ribald and inquisitive crowd would soon have gathered around the guide. Since, on the contrary, he must have been chosen to divert rather than attract public attention, and since Jesus was now regarded as a Galilean revolutionary, it is reasonable to assume that the guide was a Temple Levite employed in carrying lustral water up from Siloam—in fact a servant of Bunni ben Gorion's (*see* LXXXIII.*b and* ḳ), who will have lent Jesus the upper room (*Mark* xiv. 15) for use during the Feast.

(*b*) The identity of the 'goodman of the house' remains a mystery. He cannot have been 'the disciple whom Jesus loved'—as some deduce from his reclining in the place of honour—nor Bunni himself since, according to *Mark* xiv. 14, Peter and John were not expected to know him.

(*c*) Jesus was crucified on the Friday morning, the 'Day of Preparation for the Passover'. Therefore, despite *Mark* xiv. 12 and *Matthew* xxvi. 17, the Last Supper will have been a *seudath mizwah,* which might be eaten on almost any occasion, not the *Seder* (*see* cv.*h*). It has been argued that according to *Mark* xiv. 16, *Matthew* xxvi. 19, and *Luke* xxii. 13, Jesus intended to eat the *Seder* and that, between them, the four Gospels describe the correct observance of its laws and ordinances, namely:

(1) The thanksgiving for the first cup of wine (*Matthew* xxvi. 27 and *Luke* xxii. 17).
(2) The breaking and blessing of the 'bread of affliction' (*Luke* xxii. 19).
(3) The dipping in the common dish (*Matthew* xxvi. 23).
(4) The second cup (*Luke* xxii. 20).
(5) The singing of a psalm (*Mark* xiv. 26).

However, these arguments are inconclusive (*see* cv.*i and* (*h–i*) *below*).

It has further been argued that if the Last Supper had been a *seudath mizwah,* the disciples would not have been allowed to recline in the presence of their master (*John* xiii. 23); since this was a custom reserved for the *Seder* —an annual reminder of a common servitude from which the Israelites were now freed. But, when Jesus had sent the apostles on their mission, he made them prophets in their own right, releasing them from all bonds of subservience (*see* LVII.*n*) and making them his equals. They were thus free to recline in his presence, at least on an intimate occasion like this.

(*d*) The *Seder,* which had to be 'eaten in haste', consisted of unleavened bread, minute pieces of roast lamb, and bitter herbs—symbolizing the bitterness of Egyptian bondage—which were dipped into the *haroseth,* a sauce of chopped almonds mixed with fruit and wine, a reminder of the Israelites' brick-making in Egypt. The common dish was passed around and everyone took his share of all the ingredients, which were kept in separate compartments; it was then returned to the head of the table. Next, *Psalms* cxiii. and cxiv. were sung, followed by a prayer giving thanks for liberation from bondage. Then the second cup of wine was drunk. All present had to drain four cups, symbolizing the four different expressions used by God when He related His feats of deliverance. At the fourth cup the *hallel* (*Psalms* cxv.-cxviii.) was sung, and this ended the proceedings, except for the singing of the *Canticles* which, though customary, was not obligatory. The *Seder* began at dusk on the fourteenth of *Nisan* (*see* cv.*h*) and ended shortly before midnight, the hour of the Exodus from Egypt; then everyone rose hastily from table and, staff in hand, left the house as if setting out on a journey.

(*e*) In *Mark* xiv. 12 and *Matthew* xxvi. 17 the events are placed one day ahead of their occurrence; since the Passover lamb was slaughtered on the Friday afternoon, and the 'first day of unleavened bread', namely the fifteenth of *Nisan,* began at dusk, when it was already too late to ask: 'Where wilt thou that we go to prepare the Passover?'

(*f*) It is unlikely that Jesus would have eaten the full *Seder* even if he had escaped arrest. Here he seems to have differed from the Pharisees on a point of doctrine and, like the Essenes, John the Baptist, and the apocalyptics in general, taken Amos's view (*Amos* vi. 6—*see* LXXI.*g*) that God desired mercy, not sacrifice. If so, he will have abstained from eating sacrificial meat on any occasion, regarding the Passover lamb as a particular dispensation made 'because of the troublesomeness of the flight from Egypt' (*see* XLI.*b*). Moreover, though the draining of four cups of wine was an integral part of the *Seder* (*Pesahim* x. 1),* wine was forbidden to prophets, lest they 'prophesied foolishness' (*see* x.*d*). Jesus not only regarded himself as a prophet, but had imposed his prophetic discipline on the Twelve when he sent them on their mission (*see* LVII.*a*). Moreover, *Luke* xxii. 15: 'I have heartily desired to eat this Passover with you' was, Epiphanius says, contradicted by the Nazarene Ebionites who recorded it as: '*Have I* heartily desired to eat the flesh of this Passover with you?'—meaning: 'Surely I have not?' Indeed, the only dietary law of the Passover which Jesus is likely to have observed will have been the eating of unleavened bread and bitter herbs, and the keeping of the day as a Sabbath.

(*g*) The Pharisees insisted that the *Seder* was a solemn rite rather than an occasion for gluttonous feasting. They ruled that each lamb should be distributed among as many mouths as possible and that a share no bigger than an olive would suffice. This gave rise to the proverb (*Pesahim* 85*b*): 'Though the Passover be but as an olive, let the *hallel* split the roof.' In part, this extreme economy was due to practical considerations: though the Levite butchers had rationalized the processes of killing, bleeding, and jointing the victims, they had to cater for many thousands of pilgrims between midday and nightfall. If every ten pilgrims expected to share one lamb, the work

---

* The poor were given their full share and the cost met from the Temple funds (*ibid.*).

could not possibly be done in the time available. Each victim, therefore, was divided among more than a hundred people, and the custom was for households to expand by inviting relatives or neighbours who filled the houses and overflowed into the courtyards and even on to the flat roofs; such an arrangement was called a *haburah,* or fellowship. According to *Pesahim* 89a,* those wishing to 'eat the flesh of the Passover' had to register with the head of their fellowship a day or two before the Feast; one might change to another only while the victim was still alive.

(*h*) No member of a fellowship was permitted to absent himself during the *Seder* (*Pesahim* vii. 13); thus, had this been Passover night, Jesus could not have sent Judas on the errand described in *John* xiii. 27–30 (*see* cv.*e*). The 'hymn' mentioned in *Mark* xiv. 26, may have been either the *birkath ha'mazon,* 'grace after meat', which concluded with *Psalms* xxxvii. 24, cvi. 1, and xxix. 11, or the song of praise mentioned in *Psalm* xl. 3 (*see t below*). But the bread broken cannot have been the unleavened 'bread of affliction'; the 'first day of unleavened bread' would not begin until dusk on Friday.

(*i*) According to *Mark* xiv. 13–14, *Matthew* xxvi. 18, and *Luke* xxii. 8–10, Jesus sent Peter and John to 'prepare for the Passover'. These instructions will have been given on the Thursday afternoon. To 'prepare for the Passover' did not, however, imply as the Synoptics have understood, the laying of the table for the *Seder,* but merely the acquisition of a room where the 'Day of Preparation' could be spent in the Galilean manner—'the Galileans took their ease all that day' (*Pesahim* iv. 5)—and, incidentally, the cooking of a supper for the Thursday night while work was still permitted.

(*j*) The tradition of the sop dipped in the dish (*see* cv.*d*) cannot be disregarded: it suggests that the Last Supper consisted of something better than mere bread. And since the only valid explanation of what happened during it is that Jesus continued to impersonate the 'Worthless Shepherd', he is likely to have ordered a dish of fat mutton in accordance with *Zechariah* xi. 16: 'He shall eat the flesh of the fat and tear their claws (joints) in pieces.'

(*k*) The young man's fleeing away naked at Gethsemane (*see* cvii.*j*) calls

---

* Heads of fellowships, carrying the live victims, were received in three 'shifts' by the Levite butchers. Rabbi Isaac (*Pesahim* 64b) estimated that at least thirty fellowships were represented at each shift. When the first entered the Temple court its gates were closed behind them; the second and third shifts waited outside for their turn. The third was called the 'lazy shift', because it came late; and was so small that their lambs had usually been sacrificed before the Levite choir—which sang while the butchers worked—had time to complete the *hallel* (*Pesahim* v. 7).

This suggests that far fewer pilgrims came up to Jerusalem for the Passover than appears from Josephus (*Wars* vi. 9. 3), even if an obtuse editor has confused the number of people with the number of lambs, which are put at 256,500—an impossible task for the butchers; this editor further reveals his ignorance when he allows an average of only eleven people to each fellowship. Rabbi Isaac, on the other hand, must have greatly underestimated the number of fellowships. His account allows for the sacrifice of only seventy-five lambs between noon and dusk, which would have fed, at the most, twenty thousand people. The original tradition probably was that each fellowship, not each shift, consisted of at least thirty people; and that some three thousand lambs were sacrificed, which would have sufficed for 256,500 people. (*Wars* vi. 9. 3 puts them at 2,700,200!)

attention to *Amos* ii. 11–16, the prophecy which it was afterwards held to have fulfilled. This begins:

> 'I raised up your sons for prophets, and of your young men for Nazirites.
> 'But ye gave the Nazirites wine to drink and commanded the prophets to cease.
> 'Behold, I am pressed under you as a cart is pressed under a full weight of sheaves.'

And ends:

> 'And he that is courageous among the mighty shall flee away naked on that day,' saith the Lord.

The balanced clauses of verses 11 and 12 are in poetic apposition, as in *Zechariah's* prophecy of the ass's colt (*see* LXXXIX.*b*), and mean: 'I raised up your young sons for prophets who should be as Nazirites and drink no wine; but ye gave them wine and commanded them to cease from prophesy.' Jesus was seducing the disciples from their prophetic duty when he offered them the wine-cup. But it is nowhere stated that he drink the wine himself.

(*l*) According to *Mark* xiv. 22–25, *Matthew* xxvi. 26–29, *Luke* xxii. 17–20, and 1 *Corinthians* xi. 23–26, Jesus followed this act of seduction with another so terrible, from the Jewish point of view, that Klausner (*Jesus of Nazareth p.* 329) rightly refuses to accept it as historical. He is said to have performed a heathen mystery-rite: identifying himself with the God Dionysus (Tammuz)—whose body, as Corn-king, was ritually eaten in the form of bread by his Greek and Syrian devotees, and whose blood, as Vine-king, was ritually drunk in the form of wine*—and imitating the sacramental oath taken by the 'soldiers of Mithras' at a mystery feast eaten in honour of the Persian Tammuz, whose sacrificial victim was a bull.

(*m*) Paul, if he is in fact the author of 2 *Timothy* ii. 3–4, refers to 'good soldiers chosen by Christ' and twice, elsewhere, uses a similar metaphor: *Hebrews* xi. 34 and 1 *Corinthians* ix. 26. Jesus never regarded his disciples as soldiers who had taken the *sacramentum,* or oath of allegiance, to himself. But Paul, who paid scant attention to any other action or saying of Jesus's, used the so-called 'Sacrament of the Holy Communion' as a means of detaching converts from Judaism; his account of its institution is, of course, the earliest extant.

1 *Corinthians* xi. 25: 'Do this as often as ye drink in memory of me', must be spurious, since Jesus expected the end of the world on the following Sabbath. This happened to be the most felicitous date in many years: not only

---

* Jesus can hardly have known that the *Seder* itself, despite the detailed traditional account of its institution in *Exodus* xii., was originally eaten by the Jews in honour of the Corn-king. But he must have known that the heathen celebrated their harvest-mysteries at the same time, that the Hebrew word for Passover, *pesach,* means 'hobbling', and was applied to the priests of Baal (Tammuz) when they danced in a frenzy on Mount Carmel and cut themselves with knives (1 *Kings* xviii. 26); and that the sacrificial lamb was still being spitted on pomegranate-wood, the tree of Tammuz. He will, however, have regarded the Tammuz cult as a travesty of Jehovah worship, not as its antecedent.

was the world created on a Sunday and therefore likely to end on a Saturday, but it was at the Passover that the Angel of Death had smitten the Egyptians while sparing the Israelite elect, as he was now expected to do again.

(*n*) Paul's mischievous account of the Last Supper has displaced a genuine one. Though Jesus plied the disciples with wine, and thus relaxed their prophetic discipline, he cannot have ordered them to drink his own blood. Such an order, even if it was intended figuratively, would have contravened *Genesis* ix. 4—one of God's earliest commandments: 'The blood, which is the life, shall ye not eat!' Educated Nazarenes would at once have recalled David's scruples about drinking the water fetched by his bold captains from a well held by the Philistines (2 *Samuel* xxiii. 17):

'He would not drink thereof but poured it out unto the Lord.

'And he said: "Be it far from me, O Lord, that I should drink this, which is the blood of the men that went in jeopardy of their lives."'

David here referred to *Leviticus* xvii. 10: 'I will even set My face against that soul that eateth blood and will cut him off from among his people.' Moreover, the *new* testament of blood in 1 *Corinthians* xi. 25 and *Mark* xiv. 24 would annul the old testament of blood in *Exodus* xxiv. 6–8, and thus be idolatrous. The Jews compared red wine to blood because of its colour (*Sanhedrin* 70*a*), but the blood of the vine differed from the blood of a creature that drew 'the breath of life'.

Hegesippus's statement, quoted by Eusebius (*Ecc. Hist.* 2. xxiii. 5), that James the Just never touched wine suggests, since he was head of the Church, that the original disciples did not thereafter drink Jesus's blood in memory of him. Nevertheless, the drinking of 'blood' must have been a topic discussed at the Last Supper, and Jesus may have quoted *Zechariah* ix. 7: 'And I will take away his blood out of his mouth and his abominations from between his teeth, but he that remaineth, even he shall be for our God [i.e. judge] and he shall be as a governor in Judah.'

(*o*) Jesus will also have meant to fulfil *Zechariah* xii. 2: 'Behold, I will make Jerusalem a cup of trembling for all the people round about', which in *Yalkut Shimeoni* 11. 578 is associated with a similar prophecy in *Isaiah* li. 17–22:

' "Behold, I will make Jerusalem a reeling cup." This signifies that God will force the nations to drink blood. For this cup certainly contains blood, as it is written (*Exodus* xii. 22): "Ye shall take hyssop and dip it in the blood which lieth in the cup." It is the same reeling cup of which Isaiah prophesied.'

Isaiah's prophecy runs:

'Awake, awake, stand up, Jerusalem, which hast drunken at the hand of the Lord the cup of His fury; thou hast drunken the dregs of the reeling cup and wrung them out.

'There is none to guide her among all her sons whom she hath brought forth, neither is there any that taketh her by the hand of all the sons she hath brought up.

'These two things are come upon thee; who shall be sorry for thee? Desolation and destruction and the famine and the sword: by whom shall I comfort thee?

'Thy sons have fainted, they lie at the head of all the streets, as a wild bull in the net: they are full of the fury of the Lord, the rebuke of thy God.

'Therefore hear now this, thou afflicted and drunken, though not with wine:

'Thus saith thy Lord the Lord, and thy God that pleadeth the cause of His people: "Behold, I have taken out of thine hand the reeling cup, even the dregs of the cup of My fury; thou shalt no more drink it again!" '

(*p*) It should be noted that God's final injunction reads: '*Thou* shalt no more drink it again!' not '*I* shall no more drink it again.' If this, then, is one of the texts on which Paul based his theory of the Holy Sacrament, the sequence of events is obvious enough: Jesus blesses the wine-cup with the customary thanks to the Creator of the Vine, which proves that he is about to honour Jehovah, and no other god. He hands it to the disciples and, when all have drunk, quotes *Isaiah,* and declares that this is a reeling cup, in effect, a cup of blood; closing with Isaiah's final injunction: 'Thou shalt no more drink it again!' Paul has altered this text to: 'Thou *shalt* drink it again!', and the evangelists have confused it with: 'I will drink no more of the fruit of the vine until I drink it new in the Kingdom of Heaven', which belongs to the Coronation context (*see* x.*d*). The author of *Luke* makes Jesus say much the same thing about the bread, but *Mark, Matthew,* and Paul differ, and *Luke* xxii. 19–20*a* is generally regarded as an interpolation.

Jesus's reference to the cup of blood was topical; on the next day, the Preparation, all Jewish door-posts and lintels would be marked with blood to commemorate the passing-over of the Angel of Death. Judas may well have cried out in horror at having been made to drink blood, even figuratively, and if so, Jesus will have quoted *Zechariah* ix. 7 in reassurance.

Nevertheless, it is unlikely that Paul invented 'This is my blood' (*Mark* xiv. 24 and *Matthew* xxvi. 28). Jesus will have said, quoting *Zechariah* xi. 16, that his flock should be torn in pieces as he tore the bread, and their blood poured out as he poured the wine—and that his own blood must also be so spilt. Later, this may have been confused by the evangelists with his *midrash* on *Ecclesiasticus* xxiv. 21–23: 'They that eat me (namely Wisdom) shall yet hunger after me, and they that drink me shall yet thirst after me' (*see* LXXII.*i*).

(*q*) The disciples, though puzzled by Jesus's new mood, evidently enjoyed the long forgone exhilaration of the wine-cup; their eyes were blinded and their hearts hardened (*see* cv.*e*). Judas alone realized that Jesus was deliberately leading them astray—unless perhaps Jesus had taken John son of Annas into his confidence; as is suggested by Peter's asking John to pass on a question which he dared not put himself (*John* xiii. 23–25—*see* cv.*a*).

(*r*) It was with relief that Jesus accepted Judas as the ritual slayer and encouraged him to make haste. Soon, however, after saying his preliminary farewells, he grew anxious at Judas's failure to return with the swords and his anxiety spread to the company. If Judas had been arrested or had betrayed his trust, a substitute must be found. But how could the substitute buy swords, now that Judas had taken the money-bag with him, and how could Jesus, at this stage, provoke the happy, slow-witted disciples to take offence at his false doctrine?

Time pressed. He must dare to speak even plainer falsehoods which they could not possibly accept as truth. Thus he ordered them no longer to trust in God's bounty, but to invoke the power of the sword—'He that hath no sword, let him sell his cloak and buy one!' (*Luke* xxii. 36). The disciples were quietists and hitherto the sword had been an abomination to them; to own one was to consider the possibility of using it, and to use it was murder— Jesus had taught them that they should not use even their bare hands in self-defence (*see* xxviii.*c*). Yet they accepted this false doctrine too; regarding it, perhaps, as a temporary shift of policy 'because the times required it'. Peter, at least, had already urged an armed revolt against the Wicked Kingdom (*see* lxxviii.*c*), and 'Simon the Canaanite' was a Zealot (*see* lvi.*b*) before he became a disciple. Both will now have thought that the Chief Rulers' enmity had induced Jesus to change his mind, and that he would soon place himself at the head of the Zealots. Jesus, however, envisaged no such thing*; he expected Michael and his angels to do all the necessary fighting, and the wicked to be destroyed by fire from the Son of Man's mouth (*see* lxxxviii.*i and n*).

(*s*) The order to buy swords seems to have been taken literally by Peter and the sons of Zebedee only. Apparently they were supping in the Ophel quarter, the poorest and most rebellious of Jerusalem, where it was not difficult either to sell a cloak or to buy a weapon. The swords favoured by the Zealots were short enough to hide up a sleeve, or in a victual-bag. Jesus was pleased when Peter returned from his errand, quoted the relevant texts from *Zechariah* xi. 17 and xiii. 7, and accepted him as the slayer in place of Judas; but the succeeding dialogue ran at cross-purposes. Peter, who had declared that he would never be offended at anything that Jesus might say or do (*Matthew* xxvi. 33) remained blindly loyal. The editor of *Luke* xxii. 33 has replaced his: 'I will not be offended' with: 'I will go with thee to prison or to death', which belongs to a later context (*see* cxvii.*m*). Peter misunderstood 'the shepherd who leaveth the flock', and thought that he was meant to kill Judas. Yet Jesus gathered from Peter's question, misplaced in *Luke* xxii. 49— 'Shall we smite with the sword?'—that he understood well enough who the

---

* This misconception, perpetuated by the Gentile Church, has been responsible for the Church Militant, the Crusades, Chivalry, the consecration of Regimental Colours, Service Chaplains, and all the bloody religious wars of the last sixteen hundred years.

The Quakers have been among the few Christian sects to follow Jesus's real intentions, and even they have not always been consistent. In the American War of Independence, for instance, there were 'wet' and 'dry' Quakers; among the 'wet' was Nathanael Greene, probably the best of Washington's generals.

victim was to be. Peter's triple denial was intended by Jesus to be a solemn repudiation of his discipleship—as the Mohammedan says to an erring wife: 'I divorce thee, I divorce thee, I divorce thee!'—but still Peter missed the point.

Mark xiv. 28 and *Matthew* xxvi. 32: 'When I am risen I will go before you into Galilee', is an interpolation; it does not, at least, occur in the early *Fayoum Gospel Fragment.*

In *John* xiii. 36–38 the sequence is further confused by the insertion of the cock-crow saying in a dialogue which took place after the Crucifixion, and most of which is recorded in *John* xxi. 15–35 (*see* cxvii.*m*). This dialogue, which was concerned with Jesus's departure from Palestine and his wandering over the face of the earth, bears a misleading resemblance to the dialogue in *John* xiv. 1–6 where, at the Last Supper, he discusses his departure from this world to the next. *John* xiv. 2 apparently belongs to the former.

In *John* xiv. 6, Jesus is made to declare himself the Way, the Truth, and the Life; but 'I' has been characteristically substituted for 'the Law' (*see* LIV.*b*). This passage must be completed from *Luke* xxiii. 43, a saying which has there been wrongly attributed to the Repentant Thief (*see* cxiii.*k*).

(*t*) *John* xiii. 3–17, the symbolic washing of the disciples' feet, was more than an act of humility; it was performed in preparation for the journey to the Mount of Olives, soon to be sanctified by the feet of the transcendental Son of Man. The lustral water brought by Bunni's waterman will have been used for this purpose. *John* xiii. 10–11: 'Ye are clean but not all of you', probably stands for 'not every part of you—namely not your feet.' It conceals a reference to the mire into which Jesus's falsehoods had led the disciples; he washed it symbolically from their feet and may have quoted *Psalm* xl. 2–3, which fits the context aptly, and *Zechariah* ix. 11, which has influenced Paul's account of the new covenant of blood. The disciples themselves had not sinned so far, but had been led astray. According to *Mark,* they had drunk the cup *before* Jesus pronounced its contents to be blood. Even their drinking of wine (*see* xx.*e*) was no sin; Jesus, who had imposed this ban when they wished to follow him, had now himself withdrawn it.

Peter's request in *John* xiii. 9: 'My hands and my head also,' seems to have been misreported; he must have said 'my body and head', since he would have washed his own hands when he finished eating. It was surprise at seeing Jesus wash the disciples' feet after the meal, when these had already been washed before it, that made him protest; but *John* xiii. 8 reads as though he protested against Jesus's self-abasement. Some verses belonging to the sequence can be recovered from *John* xvi. 25–33, a Christological discourse, which is there placed in Jesus's mouth at the Last Supper: namely *John* xvi. 29 and 31–32.

(*u*) This cleansing rite brought Jesus's impersonation of the Worthless Shepherd to a close. The stage was now set for the disciples' expected vengeance (*see* cii.*c and e*).

John xiii. 34 carries no conviction. 'Love one another' was not a 'new commandment' but a quotation from the *Testament of Gad* (*see* xxviii.*f*).

John xiii. 37 (*see* cxvii.*m*) and *John* xiv. 2 (*see* cxvii.*h*) are misplaced.

(384) *The next day was the preparation for the Passover, wherefore Peter and John say unto him:* 'Master, where wilt thou that we go and prepare, that thou mayest eat this Passover?'

He asketh them: 'Have I indeed desired to eat it?

'Behold, my time is at hand. After this night I will eat no more with you until, if God so grant, we sit down together in His Kingdom.

'But go ye twain before me now, and at such a place there ye shall find a Levite bearing a pitcher of water. Beckon unto him and follow him.

'And wheresoever he shall enter in to deliver the water, enter ye in also, and say unto the goodman of the house: "Our master asketh: 'Where is the guest chamber, that I may eat there with my disciples?' "

'Then will he shew unto you a large upper room furnished. There prepare both flesh and wine.'

Peter and John did as Jesus appointed them; and, when even was come, he entered in with others of the Twelve, and the disciple which he loved likewise joined himself unto him.

* * * * *

(385) *And Jesus saith unto them:* 'Because of me ye shall all be offended this night!

'For this that is prophesied by Isaiah must yet be accomplished in me: "And he was numbered among the transgressors, and bare the sin of many, and made intercession for the transgressors." '

Peter saith: 'Master, though all others shall be offended because of thee, yet will I never be offended!'

* * * * *

(*v*) Here Jesus orders the Twelve to recline with him (*see* lvii.*n*).

(386) *And he bade them lie down, and take their ease.*

And when they marvelled at the wine which before was forbidden unto them, Jesus saith: 'Ye shall all drink wine tonight and cease for awhile from prophecy.'

This he spake that the word of Amos might be accomplished, which said:

'I raised up of your sons for prophets, and of your young men for Nazarites.

'But ye gave the Nazarites wine to drink, and commanded the prophets to cease.

'Behold, I am pressed under you as a cart is pressed under a full weight of sheaves.'

* * * * *

(387) *And when they marvelled at the flesh which before was forbidden unto them, Jesus saith:* 'It is written: "I shall raise up a shepherd which shall eat the flesh of the fat and tear their joints in pieces." '

And he brake bread and sanctified it, and he took the wine pot and poured out into cups and sanctified them.

Then he said: 'Yea, even as I tear this bread, so shall the sheep be torn; and even as I pour this wine, so shall their blood be poured out.

'And so likewise shall mine be spilt!'

Yet understood they not that Jesus spake of the worthless shepherd which should perish by the sword, though he was God's fellow.

* * * * *

(388) *And Jesus, perceiving that they murmured not against him, neither were offended, again poured wine into the cups, and sanctified them, and they drank.*

And afterwards he said unto them: 'Verily, that which ye drank was the reeling cup whereof Zechariah prophesied, saying: "Behold, I will make Jerusalem a reeling cup."

'This was also the cup whereof Isaiah prophesied, saying: "Awake, awake, stand up, Jerusalem, which hast drunk the cup of God's fury at His hands; thou hast drunken the dregs of the reeling cup and wrung them out.

' "There is none to guide her among all her sons whom she hath brought forth, neither is there any that taketh her by the hand of all her sons that she hath brought up.

' "These things are come upon thee; who shall be sorry for thee? Desolation and destruction and the famine and the sword: by whom shall I comfort thee?

' "Thy sons have fainted, they lie at the head of all the streets, as a wild bull in the net: they are full of the fury of the Lord, the rebuke of thy God.

' "Therefore hear now this, thou afflicted and drunken, though not for wine:

' "Thus saith the Lord thy God, and thy God that pleadeth the cause of His people: 'Behold, I have taken out of thine hand the reeling cup of My fury; thou shalt no more drink of it again!' " '

* * * * *

(389) *They ask him: 'Master, what is this reeling cup, if they that drain it are not drunken with wine?'*

He answereth: 'It is the cup of blood with which the door posts and the lintels shall be marked tomorrow in preparation for the Lord's Passover.'

Then was Judas of Kerioth troubled in spirit, and asketh him: 'How sayest thou, Master? Is it not written: "Ye shall not eat of the blood, which is the life"?'

Jesus answered and said: 'Zechariah prophesied in the name of the Lord: "And I will take away his blood out of his mouth, and his abomination from between his teeth; but he that remaineth, even he shall be for your judge and he shall be as a governor in Judah." '

* * * * *

(w) [Here follows Jesus's order: 'One of you shall kill me!' (*see* cv.d), and Judas's errand (*see* cv.j).]

* * * * *

(393) *And Jesus said unto the disciples: 'Little children, I am with you but a little while yet.'*

Simon Peter asked him: 'Lord, whither goest thou?'

And Jesus answered and said: 'Whither I go thou canst not follow me now, but afterward shall ye follow me. Let not your hearts be troubled; ye believe in God, believe then also that He will uphold and guide me.'

Thomas saith unto him: 'Master, we know not whither thou goest, and how shall we know the way?'

Jesus answered and said: 'Nay, but whither I go ye know, and the way ye know. For the Law is the way, and the truth, and the life.

'Verily, I say unto you: no man cometh unto the Father but by the Law!

'I go now to prepare a place for you. If I come again, then will I receive you unto myself, that where I am, there may ye be also.'

* * * * *

(394) *Presently, Jesus saith unto the disciples: 'Cometh Judas not again? Hath he haply fled away, as a traitor fleeth?'*

And again he sought to offend them, saying: 'When I sent you to preach without purse or scrip or shoes, lacked ye ought?'

They answer: 'Nothing.'

Then said he unto them: 'Yet trust ye no more in God's mercy, for in these days it is withheld from you!

'Wherefore let him that hath a purse and a scrip buy a sword, and hide it in the scrip against need.

'And let him that hath neither purse nor scrip sell his cloak and buy him a sword and a scrip, and do likewise!'

And Peter and the sons of Zebedee, being full of flesh and wine, when they heard this saying, went out and sold their cloaks and bought them scrips and swords.

For Peter said unto the other twain: 'Now shall he lead us in arms against the Wicked Kingdom!'

And they come again unto Jesus, and say: 'Master, here are two swords.'

He saith: 'It is enough.'

* * * * *

(*x*) This is the proper context for *Luke* xxiii. 43, which has been altered by the editor and ascribed to Jesus on the Cross: 'Today shalt thou be with me in Paradise' (*see* cxiii.*k*).

In *Sifre* (*Haazinu*) it is recorded:

> 'A certain philosopher [i.e. *heretic*] who was restored to the faith because of the great devotion shewn by Hanina ben Teradion and his wife [*in the time of Hadrian, when they were burned alive for refusing to disobey the Law*] and who, in the end, died as they did, exclaimed [*when sentence was passed upon him*]: "Thou hast told me good tidings: tomorrow my portion shall be with them in the World to Come." '

According to *Abodah Zarah* 18a, Hanina's words on hearing his sentence pronounced had been a quotation from *Deuteronomy* xxxii. 4: 'He is the

Rock, His way is perfect, for all His ways are judgement!' It is not impossible that the unknown 'heretic' has here been credited with Jesus's saying as preserved in the Nazarene tradition.

'Tomorrow' was evidently altered to 'today' by a Gentile editor of *Luke* who wished Jesus to reward the Repentant Thief with immediate Salvation.

(395) *'Ye have told me good tidings, for now the things concerning me have an end.*

'Tomorrow, if God will, my portion will be with them that dwell in Paradise, and ye shall be there with me also!'

* * * * *

(396) *And Peter saith: 'Master, I will lay down my life for thy sake.'*

Jesus answered: 'Wilt thou verily lay down thy life for my sake? Then before the second cock crow shalt thou thrice deny that ever thou knewest a certain worthless shepherd, and shalt take vengeance upon him for what he hath done.

'For Zechariah prophesied, saying: "Woe unto the worthless shepherd which leaveth the flock!

' "The sword shall strike his right arm and his right eye; his arm shall be made powerless and his eye utterly darkened!"

'For so shall vengeance be taken upon him.'

And Peter saith: 'What, shall we then smite with these swords?'

He answereth: 'Yea.'

Then said Peter: 'Now thou speakest plainly and no riddles.'

And Jesus saith: 'This commandment that I give you truly proceedeth from the Father.

'Behold, I speak not of myself; but of my Father which sent me, for He commanded me what I should do and what I should speak.

'Verily, I say unto you: if ye truly love God, keep His commandments which are life everlasting! Therefore, whatsoever the Father biddeth me to do, that do I.'

Nevertheless, Simon Peter understood not even yet, but supposed that he should slay Judas, as a shepherd which had left the flock.

And Jesus saith: 'Do ye now believe? Behold, then, the hour cometh, yea is now at hand, that ye shall be scattered every man to his own, and I shall abide by myself.'

* * * * *

(397) *And when the supper was ended, and they had washed their hands, Jesus arose and laid aside his garments, and took a towel and girded himself.*

Then he poureth water into a basin, and saith: 'Ye are clean, but not all.'

And he began to wash the feet of the disciples, and to wipe them with the towel.

And he saith unto them: 'Zechariah prophesied unto Jerusalem: "As for thee also, whose covenant is by blood," which is the covenant that our fathers sware unto Moses, "I have sent forth thy prisoners out of the pit where is no water."

'And David prophesied: "The Lord delivered me also out of an horrible pit, out of the miry clay, and set my feet upon a rock and established my goings."

'And He hath put a new song in my mouth, even praise unto our God.'

* * * * *

(398) *Then cometh he to Simon Peter, and Peter saith unto him: 'Master, dost thou wash my feet? Did not I myself wash them before I came in hither?'*

Jesus answered and said: 'What I do, thou knowest not now, but soon thou shalt know.'

Peter saith: 'Master, thou shalt never wash my feet!'

He answered: 'If I wash thee not, then shalt thou have no part in the Kingdom.'

Peter saith: 'Master, not my feet only, but my body and my head.'

Jesus saith: 'He that hath washed his hands tonight and is clean of heart, the same needeth not save to wash his feet of the miry clay, for they shall stand on that rock whereon the feet of the Son of Man shall also stand.

'Come, now, let us sing the new psalm of praise whereof David spake!'

* * * * *

THE ARREST

Mark xiv. 26

[26]And when they had sung an hymn, they went out into the mount of Olives.

Mark xiv. 32–52

[32]And they came to a place which was named Gethsemane: and He saith to His disciples: 'Sit ye here, while I shall pray.' [33]And He taketh with Him Peter and James and John, and began to be sore amazed, and to be very heavy; [34]and saith unto them: 'My soul is exceeding sorrowful unto death: tarry ye here, and watch.' [35]And He went forward a little, and fell on the ground, and prayed that, if it were possible, the hour might pass from Him. [36]And He said: 'Abba, Father, all things are possible unto Thee; take away this cup from Me: nevertheless not what I will, but what Thou wilt.' [37]And He cometh, and findeth them sleeping, and saith unto Peter: 'Simon, sleepest thou? couldest not thou watch one hour? [38]Watch ye and pray, lest ye enter into temptation. The spirit truly is ready, but the flesh is weak.' [39]And again He went away, and prayed, and spake the same words. [40]And when He returned, He found them asleep again, (for their eyes were heavy,) neither wist they what to answer Him. [41]And He cometh the third time, and saith unto them: 'Sleep on now, and take your rest: it is enough, the hour is come; behold, the Son of Man is betrayed into the hands of sinners. [42]Rise up, let us go: lo, he that betrayeth Me is at hand.'

[43]And immediately, while He yet spake, cometh Judas, one of the Twelve, and with him a great multitude with swords and staves, from the chief priests and the scribes and the elders. [44]And he that betrayed Him had given them a token, saying, Whomsoever I shall kiss, that same is He; take Him, and lead Him away safely. [45]And as soon as he was come, he goeth straightway to Him, and saith, Master, Master, and kissed Him. [46]And they laid their hands on Him, and took Him. [47]And one of them that stood by drew a sword, and smote a servant of the high priest, and cut off his ear. [48]And Jesus answered and said unto them: 'Are ye come out, as against a thief, with swords and with staves to take Me? [49]I was daily with you in the temple teaching, and ye took Me not: but the scriptures must be fulfilled.' [50]And they all forsook Him, and fled. [51]And there followed Him a certain young man, having a linen cloth cast about his naked body; and the young men laid hold on him: [52]and he left the linen cloth and fled from them naked.

Matthew xxvi. 30

[30]And when they had sung an hymn, they went out into the mount of Olives.

Matthew xxvi. 36–56

[36]Then cometh Jesus with them unto a place called Gethsemane, and saith unto the disciples: 'Sit ye here, while I go and pray yonder.' [37]And He took with Him Peter and the two sons of Zebedee, and began to be sorrowful and very heavy. [38]Then saith He unto them: 'My soul is exceeding sorrowful, even unto death: tarry ye here, and watch with Me.' [39]And He went a little farther, and fell on His face, and prayed, saying: 'O My Father, if it be possible, let this cup pass from Me: nevertheless not as I will, but as Thou wilt.' [40]And He cometh unto the disciples, and findeth them asleep, and saith unto Peter: 'What, could ye not watch with Me one hour? [41]Watch and pray, that ye enter not into temptation: the spirit indeed is willing, but the flesh is weak.' [42]He went away again the second time, and prayed, saying: 'O My Father, if this cup may not pass away from Me, except I drink it, Thy Will be done.' [43]And He came and found them asleep again: for their eyes were heavy. [44]And He left them, and went away again, and prayed the third time, saying the same words. [45]Then cometh He to His disciples, and saith unto them: 'Sleep on now, and take your rest: behold, the hour is at hand, and the Son of Man is betrayed into the hands of sinners. [46]Rise, let us be going: behold, he is at hand that doth betray Me.'

[47]And while He yet spake, lo, Judas, one of the Twelve, came, and with him a great multitude with swords and staves, from the chief priests and elders of the people. [48]Now he that betrayed Him gave them a sign, saying, Whomsoever I shall kiss, that same is He: hold Him fast. [49]And forthwith he came to Jesus, and said, Hail, Master; and kissed Him. [50]And Jesus said unto him: 'Friend, wherefore art thou come?' Then came they, and laid hands on Jesus, and took Him. [51]And, behold, one of them which were with Jesus stretched out his hand, and drew his sword, and struck a servant of the high priest's, and smote off his ear. [52]Then said Jesus unto him: 'Put up again thy sword into its place: for all they that take the sword shall perish with the sword. [53]Thinkest thou that I cannot now pray to My Father, and He shall presently give Me more than twelve legions of angels? [54]But how then shall the scriptures be fulfilled, that thus it must be?' [55]In that same hour said Jesus to the multitudes: 'Are ye come out as against a thief with swords and staves for to take Me? I sat daily with you teaching in the temple, and ye laid no hold on Me. [56]But all this was done, that the scriptures of the prophets might be fulfilled.' Then all the disciples forsook Him, and fled.

Luke xxii. 31–32

[31]'Simon, Simon, behold, Satan hath desired to have you, that he may sift you as wheat: [32]but I have prayed for thee, that thy faith fail not: and when thou art converted, strengthen thy brethren.'

Luke xxii. 37

37'For I say unto you, that this that is written must yet be accomplished in Me,

And He was reckoned among the transgressors:

for the things concerning Me have an end.'

Luke xxii. 39–53

39And He came out, and went, as He was wont, to the mount of Olives; and His disciples also followed Him. 40And when He was at the place, He said unto them: 'Pray that ye enter not into temptation.' 41And He was withdrawn from them about a stone's cast, and kneeled down, and prayed, 42saying: 'Father, if Thou be willing, remove this cup from Me: nevertheless not My will, but Thine, be done.' 43And there appeared an angel unto Him from heaven, strengthening Him. 44And being in an agony He prayed more earnestly: and His sweat was as it were great drops of blood falling down to the ground. 45And when He rose up from prayer, and was come to His disciples, He found them sleeping for sorrow. 46And said unto them: 'Why sleep ye? rise and pray, lest ye enter into temptation.'

47And while He yet spake, behold a multitude, and he that was called Judas, one of the Twelve, went before them, and drew near unto Jesus to kiss Him. 48But Jesus said unto him: 'Judas, betrayest thou the Son of Man with a kiss?' 49When they which were about Him saw what would follow, they said unto Him: 'Lord, shall we smite with the sword?' 50And one of them smote the servant of the high priest, and cut off his right ear. 51And Jesus answered and said: 'Suffer ye thus far.' And He touched his ear, and healed him. 52Then Jesus said unto the chief priests, and captains of the temple, and the elders, which were come to Him: 'Be ye come out, as against a thief, with swords and staves? 53When I was daily with you in the temple, ye stretched forth no hands against Me: but this is your hour, and the power of darkness.'

John xii. 27

27'Now is my soul troubled; and what shall I say? Father, save me from this hour: but for this cause came I unto this hour.'

John xviii. 1–11

1When Jesus had spoken these words, He went forth with His disciples over the brook Cedron, where was a garden, into the which He entered, and His disciples. 2And Judas also, which betrayed Him, knew the place: for Jesus ofttimes resorted thither with His disciples. 3Judas then, having received a band of men and officers from the chief priests and Pharisees, cometh thither with lanterns and torches and weapons. 4Jesus, therefore, knowing all things that should come upon Him, went forth, and said unto them: 'Whom seek ye?' 5They answered Him: 'Jesus of Nazareth.' Jesus saith unto them: 'I am He.' And Judas also, which betrayed Him, stood with them. 6As soon then as He had said unto them, I am He, they went back-

John xviii. 1–11 *(contd.)*

ward, and fell to the ground. [7]Then asked He them again: 'Whom seek ye?' And they said, 'Jesus of Nazareth.' [8]Jesus answered: 'I have told you that I am He: if therefore ye seek Me, let these go their way:' [9]that the saying might be fulfilled, which He spake:

> *Of them which Thou gavest Me have I lost none.*

[10]Then Simon Peter having a sword drew it, and smote the high priest's servant, and cut off his right ear. The servant's name was Malchus. [11]Then said Jesus unto Peter: 'Put up thy sword into the sheath: the cup which My Father hath given Me, shall I not drink it?'

John xvii. 1–26

[1]These words spake Jesus, and lifted up His eyes to heaven, and said: 'Father, the hour is come; glorify Thy Son, that Thy Son also may glorify Thee: [2]as Thou hast given Him power over all flesh, that He should give eternal life to as many as Thou hast given Him. [3]And This is life eternal, that they might know Thee the only true God, and Jesus Christ, Whom Thou hast sent. [4]I have glorified Thee on the earth: I have finished the work which Thou gavest Me to do. [5]And now, O Father, glorify Thou Me with Thine own self with the glory which I had with Thee before the world was.

[6]'I have manifested Thy name unto the men which Thou gavest Me out of the world: Thine they were, and Thou gavest them Me; and they have kept Thy word. [7]Now they have known that all things whatsoever Thou hast given Me are of Thee. [8]For I have given unto them the words which Thou gavest Me; and they have received them, and have known surely that I came out from Thee, and they have believed that Thou didst send Me. [9]I pray for them: I pray not for the world, but for them which Thou hast given Me; for they are Thine. [10]And all Mine are Thine, and Thine are Mine; and I am glorified in them. [11]And now I am no more in the world, but these are in the world, and I come to Thee. Holy Father, keep through Thine own name those whom Thou hast given Me, that they may be one, as We are. [12]While I was with them in the world, I kept them in Thy Name: those that Thou gavest me I have kept, and none of them is lost, but the son of perdition; that the scripture might be fulfilled. [13]And now come I to Thee; and these things I speak in the world, that they might have My joy fulfilled in themselves. [14]I have given them Thy word; and the world hath hated them, because they are not of the world, even as I am not of the world. [15]I pray not that Thou shouldest take them out of the world, but that Thou shouldest keep them from the evil. [16]They are not of the world, even as I am not of the world. [17]Sanctify them through Thy truth: Thy word is truth. [18]As Thou hast sent Me into the world, even so have I also sent them into the world. [19]And for their sakes I sanctify Myself, that they also might be sanctified through the truth.

[20]'Neither pray I for these alone, but for them also which shall believe on Me through their word: [21]that they all may be one; as Thou, Father, art in Me, and I in Thee, that they also may be one in Us: that the world may believe that Thou hast sent Me. [22]And the glory which Thou gavest Me I

John xvii. 1–26 (*contd.*)

have given them; that they may be one, even as We are one: [23]I in them, and Thou in Me, that they may be made perfect in one; and that the world may know that Thou hast sent Me, and hast loved them, as Thou hast loved Me. [24]Father, I will that they also, whom Thou hast given Me, be with Me where I am; that they may behold My glory, which Thou hast given Me: for Thou lovedst Me before the foundation of the world. [25]O righteous Father, the world hath not known Thee: but I have known Thee, and these have known that Thou hast sent Me. [26]And I have declared unto them Thy name, and will declare it: that the love wherewith Thou hast loved Me may be in them, and I in them.'

The Strasbourg Coptic Papyrus (fourth century)

Now when he had ended all the . . . . he turned himself to us and said: 'The hour is come when I shall be taken from you. The spirit is willing but the flesh is weak: . . . and watch with me.'

But we the apostles wept, saying . . . .

(*a*) Jesus had signally failed to rouse his disciples to action. They had all drunk more than one cup of wine each (*see* cvi.*p and v*) which, since they had tasted none for many months, went to their heads, leaving them sleepy and dull-witted; and had understood neither his quotation from *Isaiah* liii. 12, which was an admission of deliberate sin, nor his quotation from *Zechariah* xiii. 7, which was a challenge to their vengeance.

(*b*) The final scene was to be staged on the Mount of Olives, the refuge of the elect when the Messiah came (*Jeremiah* iii. 17 and *Zechariah* xiv. 4) and the Last Trump sounded (*Joel* ii. 2).

(*c*) *Mark* xiv. 26–52, *Matthew* xxvi. 30–56, and *Luke* xxii. 31–53, probably based on Peter's eye-witness report, provide the fullest account of Jesus's arrest. But it has been over-dramatized: even if all the disciples were not asleep, how could they see the drops falling from Jesus's brow as he prayed a stone's cast away? The detail of the sweat that looked like blood is important. Some twelve hours later a sand-storm from the Elamite desert blotted out the sun—a common enough phenomenon at that season (*see* cxiii.*n*)—and if the east wind had already risen, the Passover moon, now all but full, would turn red and the sweat would reflect its colour. One of the signs of the Last Days was the moon's turning into blood (*Joel* ii. 31), which Peter subsequently mentioned (*Acts* ii. 20) as though he had witnessed it.

(*d*) Jesus's heart was heavy and his prayers agonized (*Mark* xiv. 33–35, *Matthew* xxvi. 38–39, and *Luke* xxii. 44), not because he feared death, but because the disciples had still shown no sign of righteous anger. He feared that he might need to provoke them further—by an incitement to armed rebellion, perhaps—and doubted whether he could summon up the necessary courage. His words about going before them into Galilee have been misquoted; it seems that he begged them to watch lest he succumbed to temptation, leaving his task unfinished and fleeing back to Galilee. This is supported by the *Strasbourg Coptic Papyrus,* where *Mark* xiv. 38 and *Matthew* xxvi. 41: 'The spirit is willing but the flesh is weak' is spoken by Jesus himself, not Peter.

(*e*) Although altered and embroidered upon in *John* xvii. 1 and xiii. 31–32, 'Father, glorify Thy son, that Thy son also may glorify Thee' seems to be based on an authentic tradition.

(*f*) Jesus had decided 'to drink the cup' just before second cock-crow—*Mark* xiv. 30 is the better version, because at first cock-crow it was still night, and he will have wished the assassination to take place in the light of the sun. His most trusted disciples were at hand, armed with swords, and the cup seemed to be already at his lips when Judas's sudden arrival dashed it away; yet despite this disappointment, he still hoped to drink the bitter draught.

(*g*) The composition of the armed force which followed behind Judas differs in all four accounts. The original version will have mentioned a small band of men sent by the High Priest under the command of the Captain of the Temple: Levite guards, detached from Temple duty, whom the Romans permitted to carry swords and clubs. This tradition is preserved in *John* xviii. 3; though 'and Pharisees' has there been interpolated by an editor who wished to suggest that Jesus was about to be tried by the Great Sanhedrin, and not by a special Sadducaic court of 'the Chief Priests and elders' (*see* cix.*g*–*h*). But the Pharisees, even if they had controlled the Levite guard, could not have arrested him, because the Sanhedrin were on holiday and, by a Pharisaic ruling, suspected criminals could not be placed under restraint two days before their trial. The editors of *Mark* xiv. 43 and *Matthew* xxvi. 47, trying to lay the blame for Jesus's crucifixion on the whole Jewish nation, have turned the Levite guards into a wild lynching party, illegally armed and let loose by the Chief Priests and elders. According to *Luke* xxii. 52, the Chief Priests, 'captains of the Temple' and elders straggled along in the wake of the mob.

(*h*) Jesus's complaint that the Levites came against him as though he were a bandit proves that the disciples' two swords were intended for ritual use only. He was innocently oblivious of the Roman ban on the bearing of arms by private persons. The Captain seems to have pointed out Jesus's double breach of the peace: he had both proclaimed himself King and permitted his servants to carry arms. Part of Jesus's reply to these charges (*John* xviii. 36) has been transferred to the account of his trial before Pilate (*see* cx.*d*).

(*i*) Judas's kiss was, in fact, a loving one. He wanted to convince Jesus that he acted in his best interests by placing him in preventive custody before murder would be committed. Indeed, one might suppose at first sight that the order for Peter to put up his sword came from Judas, not Jesus, since it was supported by a condemnation of murder quoted from *Genesis* ix. 6; but Jesus did not regard his own assassination as murder, and felt outraged when Malchus was attacked. In this tragedy of errors, Peter had misunderstood Jesus's reference to the Worthless Shepherd 'which leaveth the flock' (*see* cvi.*s*) and tried to kill Judas, but instead wounded Malchus when he intervened.

(*j*) *John* alone mentions Peter by name. But the unnamed young man with the linen cloth in *Mark* xiv. 51 can only have been Peter: the one disciple who showed fight and therefore the man whom the guards were most anxious to arrest. The detail of his nakedness is introduced to show that the Messianic prophecy of *Amos* ii. 16 was now fulfilled (*see* cvi.*k*). Peter slept without his cloak because he had just sold it to buy a sword.

It may well have been Judas who requested that the other disciples should go free: he did not want his companions flogged for their part in acclaiming Jesus as King.

(*k*) Like all similar visitations, the angel's strengthening of Jesus as he prayed will have been deduced from a sacred picture (*see* i.*s*, lxxix.*g and* cxv.*m*). That the guards (*John* xviii. 6) 'went back and fell to the ground' is probable, but this cannot have been caused by awe at hearing his divine name. Judaean olive orchards are stony and uneven, and Peter's surprise attack in the moonlight, launched after Jesus had announced the pacific intentions of his party, will have sent the Levites sprawling on their backs. Even Judas was unaware that any of the disciples were armed.

(*l*) The legions of angels (*Matthew* xxvi. 53) were those who, according to the *Testament of Levi* iii. 3, live in the second of the seven heavens 'and are ordained for the Day of Judgement to wreak vengeance on the spirit of deceit and of Beliar.' Jesus cannot have boasted of his power to summon them by prayer, but may have spoken of their part in the coming battle of Armageddon.

Since the restoration of Malchus's ear is mentioned in *Luke* xxii. 51 only, it may be dismissed as a pious addition, like the cure of Blind Bartimaeus (*see* xl.*b*) or the raising of Lazarus (*see* lxxxvii. *a–e*). The editor will have felt that Jesus, of his infinite mercy and power, would not have left Malchus maimed for life.

(399) *And after that they had sung David's psalm of praise, they went forth and passed over the brook Kidron.*

And going up into the Mount of Olives, they came unto a garden called Gethsemane and entered in.

Now, Judas also knew the place for Jesus ofttimes resorted thither with the disciples.

* * * * *

(400) *Then said Jesus unto Peter: 'Simon, Simon, behold Satan hath desired to have you all, that he may sift you as wheat.*

'But I have prayed for thee, that thy faith in God fail not; and that when thou art persuaded of that which must be accomplished, thou wilt also strengthen thy brethren!'

These words spake Jesus, and lifted up his eyes unto heaven. And, seeing that the face of the moon grew red, he prayed: 'Father, the hour is come!

'*Strengthen Thou Thy son which hath glorified Thee, O Lord, that he may perfect the work which Thou gavest him to do, whereby as many as Thou ordainest shall taste of everlasting life.*

'*For their sakes have I sanctified myself, that they also may be sanctified through truth.*

'*As it is written: "O Lord, Thou art God and Thy words are true, and Thou hast promised this goodness unto Thy servant."*'

Then Jesus went with Peter and James and John, having the two swords, and they withdrew themselves about a stone's cast.

And unto them which were left he said: '*Abide ye here, and pray that ye enter not into temptation!*'

*   *   *   *   *

(*m*) [Here follow *John* xii. 31 (*see* cxvii.*k*); *Matthew* xxiii. 39, and *Luke* xiii. 35: Jesus's farewell to the disciples (*see* xcvii.*i*).]

*   *   *   *   *

(403) *And unto the three which came with him, he said:* '*My soul is exceeding sorrowful even unto death, because of that which must be accomplished in me.*

'*Shall I pray: "Father, save me from this hour"? But was it not for the Father's sake that I came unto this hour?*

'*Tarry ye therefore with me, and watch that I rise not and flee from you into Galilee. Behold, the spirit is willing but the flesh is weak.*'

And he went away a little farther, and fell to the ground, and prayed aloud in an agony: '*Father, if it be possible, let this cup pass from me! Nevertheless, let it not be as I will, but as Thou wilt.*'

Then cometh he back unto the three, and in the light of the moon the sweat broke from his brow as it were drops of blood.

And he findeth the sons of Zebedee awake, but Peter sleeping, and he saith unto him: '*Simon, sleepest thou? Couldst not thou watch one hour? Watch, therefore and pray!*'

And Jesus went forward again but, as he prayed, Peter slept and they which watched likewise grew drowsy, for all their sorrow.

Then cometh he unto them a second time, and rebuketh them, neither wist they what to answer him, but roused themselves from slumber.

And he went forward the third time, but what he did they knew not, for presently they slept.

Again he roused them, saying: '*Do ye slumber yet and take your rest?*

'*Behold, the hour is now come when ye shall verily know that ye have been led astray.*

'*Arise, let us stand upon our feet! For he that should slay me is at hand.*'

And as they arose and followed him, on a sudden he cried out: '*Awake, sword! Smite the shepherd and the sheep shall be scattered!*'

For even as he spake, Judas was at hand, and with him a company of Levites, servants of the High Priest, armed with swords and staves.

And Judas saith: '*Hail, Master!*'

Jesus's heart was glad, and he saith unto Judas: '*Friend, wherefore art thou come?', thinking that he verily came in the way of vengeance according to the prophecy.*

And Judas kissed Jesus, but unto the Captain he said: 'This is he!'

Jesus saith: 'Betrayest thou the Son of God with a kiss?'

* * * * *

(404) *Then Jesus asked the Captain of the Temple, saying: 'Whom seekest thou?'*

He answered: 'I seek Jesus of Nazara.'

Jesus saith: 'I am he, but why comest thou against me with swords and staves as against a robber? For two days I sat in the Temple teaching, yet ye laid no hold on me.'

The Captain answered: 'Thou settest up thyself for a King, which is against the law of Caesar.'

Jesus saith unto him: 'If my Kingdom were of this world, then might I order my disciples to take arms against Caesar and the Wicked Kingdom.

'Yet have I no need of these, for presently the Father shall send twelve legions of angels to destroy His enemies.'

And Judas, turning unto the Captain, said: 'Yea, I pray thee, let these other men go their ways.'

* * * * *

(405) *Then Judas would have led Jesus from the garden, but Peter perceiving it, cried out in wrath.*

And Jesus saith unto Peter: 'Simon, suffer thus far. The cup that is given unto me to drink, shall I not drink it?'

* * * * *

(n) [Here follows *Mark* xiv. 21, paralleled in *Matthew* xxvi. 24 and *Luke* xxii. 22: 'Behold, this son of man goeth as Isaiah prophesied' (*see* cv.g).]

* * * * *

(407) *But Peter drew his sword and, running against Judas, thought to slay him.*

Then went the Levites a pace backward for fear of him, and some fell to the ground, and Peter smote a servant of the High Priest, by name Malchus, which sought to deliver Judas, and cut off his right ear.

Which, when the other disciples saw, they fled.

And Jesus rebuked Peter saying: 'Simon, put up thy sword into its place! For it is written: "Whosoever sheddeth a man's blood, by man shall his blood be shed." '

* * * * *

(408) *Then sought the High Priest's servants to take Peter, and they caught hold of the linen garment in which he was clothed, having sold his cloak.*

But he left the garment in their hands, and fled away naked.

As Amos prophesied in the name of the Lord: ' "He that is courageous among the mighty shall flee away naked in that day," saith the Lord.'

* * * * *

BARABBAS

Mark xiv. 54

[54]And Peter followed Him afar off, even into the palace of the high priest: and he sat with the servants, and warmed himself at the fire.

Mark xiv. 66–72

[66]And as Peter was beneath in the palace, there cometh one of the maids of the high priest: [67]and when she saw Peter warming himself, she looked upon him, and said: 'And thou also wast with Jesus of Nazareth.' [68]But he denied, saying: 'I know not, neither understand I what thou sayest.' And he went out into the porch; and the cock crew. [69]And a maid saw him again, and began to say to them that stood by: 'This is one of them.' [70]And he denied it again. And a little after, they that stood by said again to Peter: 'Surely thou art one of them: for thou art a Galilaean, and thy speech agreeth thereto.' [71]But he began to curse and to swear, saying: 'I know not this man of whom ye speak.' [72]And the second time the cock crew. And Peter called to mind the word that Jesus said unto him, Before the cock crow twice, thou shalt deny Me thrice. And when he thought thereon, he wept.

Mark xv. 7

[7]And there was one named Barabbas, which lay bound with them that had made insurrection with him, who had committed murder in the insurrection.

Matthew xxvi. 69–75

[69]Now Peter sat without in the palace: and a damsel came unto him, saying: 'Thou also wast with Jesus of Galilee.' [70]But he denied before them all, saying: 'I know not what thou sayest.' [71]And when he was gone out into the porch, another maid saw him, and said unto them that were there: 'This fellow was also with Jesus of Nazareth.' [72]And again he denied with an oath: 'I do not know the man.' [73]And after a while came unto him they that stood by, and said to Peter: 'Surely thou also art one of them; for thy speech bewrayeth thee.' [74]Then began he to curse and to swear, saying: 'I know not the man.' And immediately the cock crew. [75]And Peter remembered the word of Jesus, which said unto him, 'Before the cock crow, thou shalt deny Me thrice.' And he went out, and wept bitterly.

Matthew xxvii. 16

[16]And they had then a notable prisoner, called Barabbas.

Acts xxiii. 1–5

[1]And Paul, earnestly beholding the council, said: 'Men and brethren, I have lived in all good conscience before God until this day.' [2]And the high priest Ananias commanded them that stood by him to smite him on the mouth. [3]Then said Paul unto him: 'God shall smite thee, thou whited wall: for sittest thou to judge me after the law, and commandest me to be smitten contrary to the law?' [4]And they that stood by said: 'Revilest thou God's high priest?' [5]Then said Paul: 'I wist not, brethren, that he was the high priest: for it is written:

Thou shalt not speak evil of the ruler of thy people.'

Luke xxii. 54–62

[54]And Peter followed afar off. [55]And when they had kindled a fire in the midst of the hall, and were set down together, Peter sat down among them. [56]But a certain maid beheld him as he sat by the fire, and earnestly looked upon him, and said: 'This man was also with Him.' [57]And he denied Him, saying: 'Woman, I know Him not.' [58]And after a little while another saw him, and said: 'Thou art also of them.' And Peter said: 'Man, I am not.' [59]And about the space of one hour after another confidently affirmed, saying: 'Of a truth this fellow also was with Him: for he is a Galilaean.' [60]And Peter said: 'Man, I know not what thou sayest.' And immediately, while he yet spake, the cock crew. [61]And the Lord turned, and looked upon Peter. And Peter remembered the word of the Lord, how He had said unto him, Before the cock crow, thou shalt deny Me thrice. [62]And Peter went out, and wept bitterly.

Luke xxiii. 18–19

[18]And they cried out all at once, saying: 'Away with this man, and release unto us Barabbas:' [19](who for a certain sedition made in the city, and for murder, was cast into prison).

John xviii. 15–18

[15]And Simon Peter followed Jesus, and so did another disciple: that disciple was known unto the high priest, and went in with Jesus into the palace of the high priest. [16]But Peter stood at the door without. Then went out that other disciple, which was known unto the high priest, and spake unto her that kept the door, and brought in Peter. [17]Then saith the damsel that kept the door unto Peter: 'Art not thou also one of this man's disciples?' He saith: 'I am not.' [18]And the servants and officers stood there, who had made a fire of coals; for it was cold: and they warmed themselves: and Peter stood with them, and warmed himself.

John xviii. 25–27

[25]And Simon Peter stood and warmed himself. They said therefore unto him: 'Art not thou also one of His disciples?' He denied it, and said: 'I am not.' [26]One of the servants of the high priest, being his kinsman whose ear Peter cut off, saith: 'Did not I see thee in the garden with Him?' [27]Peter then denied again: and immediately the cock crew.

John xviii. 40

⁴⁰ . . . Now Barabbas was a robber.

(*a*) Peter, in fulfilment of his vow not to desert Jesus (*see* cvi.*s*), waited outside Annas's 'palace' where Jesus had been led by the Levite guards; he wanted to 'see the end' (*Matthew* xxvi. 58) and expected this to be introduced by a miracle. Since, however, none occurred, the editor of *Luke* xxiii. 8 has absurdly transferred Peter's expectations to Herod Antipas.

Presently, another disciple—not one of the Twelve, all of whom had fled except Peter—arranged for him to be let in. This man was 'known to the High Priest' and may be identified with 'the beloved disciple' (*see* lxxxii.*a*). He must first have provided Peter with clothes.

(*b*) Peter was recognized by one, or (according to *Matthew* xxvi. 71) by two palace maids, including the janitrix (*John* xviii. 17) as a companion of Jesus —which suggests that both Jesus and he had visited the palace on a previous occasion—and later, according to *John* xviii. 26, by a kinsman of Malchus's, whose ear he had just cut off. Peter's Galilean accent betrayed him (*Mark* xiv. 70), and though he denied his identity on oath (*Mark* xiv. 71), he cannot have avoided being held for an official examination. *John* xix. 9: 'Whence are thou?', was probably addressed to him by one of Annas's officers, not to Jesus by Pilate (*see* cx.*d*).

(*c*) It seems that in order to shield John son of Annas, and perhaps also his brother Andrew whose patronymic and birthplace were the same as his own, Peter refused to give his name. 'Barabbas' merely means 'my father's son'.* *John* xviii. 40: 'Now Barabbas was a robber' is a mistranslation. In Roman Law, Peter's crime was 'banditry', i.e. the illegal possession and use of arms†; and in Jewish Law his attack on Malchus, though not in effect fatal, ranked as murder.

(*d*) *Luke* xxiii. 19: 'A certain sedition', is equally misleading; the original Greek word means 'rising'. The identity of the two 'bandits' crucified with Jesus is not known; they cannot have been members of the Twelve—all of whom, except Judas, were alive a few weeks later (*Acts i.* 15–26)—and must have been condemned by Pilate. No record survives of any other disturbance in Jerusalem at the time; and that at least one of the bandits knew about Jesus's royal entry into the city, and bitterly reviled him, suggests that he had been only a few hours in Roman hands, and that he held Jesus responsible for his present plight (*see* cxiii.*t*).

(410) *But Peter followed Jesus afar off to the Palace, and stood at the door without.*

---

* Jerome, *On Matthew* xxvii. 11, quotes the *Gospel according to the Hebrews* where 'Barabbas' is explained as '*Filius magistri eorum*'—'the son of one of their prominent men'; but the author of this Gospel did not necessarily know who 'Barabbas' was.

† The Greek word *lestai*, 'bandits', became *listim* in Hebrew. The Jewish nationalists used this in an honourable sense; and when the Talmud was eventually committed to writing, its original meaning had been forgotten.

And presently cometh the disciple which Jesus loved, being of the family of Annas, and Peter crieth out to him.

Then goeth the disciple in to fetch garments wherewith to cover Peter's nakedness.

And speaketh unto the maid at the door and, coming out again, bringeth in Peter also.

Then said the maid unto Peter: 'Art thou not a disciple of Jesus?'

He answered: 'I am not.'

Now, the servants and officers sat there, which had kindled a fire of coals, for it was cold.

And Peter sat down with them, and warmed himself, and waited for the end, hoping to have seen some miracle done by Jesus.

But another maid beheld him as he sat by the fire, and looking earnestly upon him, she said: 'This man was also with him.'

And he denied again, saying: 'Woman, I was not!'

But they that stood by, said: 'Surely he is a Galilean, for his speech bewrayeth him.'

About the space of an hour after, there came a kinsman of Malchus whose ear Peter cut off, and said: 'Of a truth, this fellow was with him!'

And he asked Peter: 'Did I not see thee in the garden with him?'

But Peter denied a third time with oaths. And immediately the cock crew.

Then wept Peter bitterly, and went out into the porch, and sought to escape, but the servants prevented him.

And an officer said unto Peter: 'Who are thou?'

He answered: 'I am Barabbas,' which is to say: 'The son of my father.'

Then they led Peter away and accused him before Annas.

* * * * *

(*e*) Peter's trial has been omitted from the Gospels. Because of the hour at which it was held, it will not have been a trial by a regular court, but a hurried examination only—by a small junta of leading collaborationists, called to decide whether there was *prima facie* evidence for detaining him, and whether he had been acting under Jesus's orders.

(*f*) *Acts* xxii. 29–30 and xxiii. 1–9, the report of Paul's trial by the Great Sanhedrin on a charge of polluting the Temple, contains a great deal of unhistorical and extraneous material. The High Priest, whose name was 'Ananias son of Nedabiah' (*Antiquities* xx. 5. 2), was not qualified to preside over the Great Sanhedrin before which the case must have come; neither would he have dared to order the smiting of a Roman citizen; neither was Paul's remark in *Acts* xxiii. 1 sufficient provocation for a blow, even if he had not been a Roman. Nor is it credible that a brawl took place in open court; or that Paul was ignorant of Ananias's office. But if the first five verses of *Acts* xxiii. are removed, and also part of xxii. 30: 'The chief captain commanded the chief priests and all their council to appear'—because the Great Sanhedrin, being in continuous session except for feast days, could not be 'summoned'—what remains is historically plausible:

(*Acts* xxii. 29) The chief captain also was afraid after he knew that Paul was a Roman, because he had bound him.

(30) On the morrow, because he would have known the certainty wherefore he was accused of the Jews, he loosed him from his bonds and brought him down and set him before the Council.

(xxiii. 6) But when Paul perceived that the one part were Sadducees and the other Pharisees, he cried out in the Council: 'Men and brethren, I am a Pharisee, the son of a Pharisee: of the hope and resurrection of the dead I am called in question, etc. . . .'

It seems, however, that the need to suppress all mention of Peter's condemnation as a 'bandit', and the desire both to present Paul as less pusillanimous than he really was* (*see* cxviii.*m*), and to denigrate the predomi-

---

* It is difficult to believe Paul when, in 2 *Corinthians* xi. 23–33, he boasts that he has suffered more for the faith than any other of the brethren, and then lists his dismal adventures.

According to the *Acts*, he was shipwrecked once, not thrice as he here claims; flogged once, not thrice, by the Romans; and never flogged by the Jews, though he alleges that this happened five times. The climax of his boasts is the danger that he ran when lowered in a basket from the walls of Damascus; he does not mention that, on this occasion, he was being saved from the consequences of his bloody persecutions of the Grecians. Yet one might give him the benefit of the doubt if his story in *Acts* xvi. were more credible: how, at Philippi, he meekly allowed Silas and himself to be flogged on a charge of curing a young woman of demonic possession, and how that night God miraculously unshackled every prisoner in the jail and opened all doors so that the terrified prison governor first tried to commit suicide and was then converted with all his household; after which Paul revealed his Roman citizenship and made the magistrates come on bended knees to release him.

It may, of course, have been Silas who invented this story; but 1 *Corinthians* xv. 32 shows that Paul could fall back on pure fantasy when he wished to repair his tattered reputation for courage. He hints (in a modest parenthesis) that he fought wild beasts in the amphitheatre at Ephesus, whereas all that seems to have happened during his only recorded stay there (*Acts* xix. 23–41) was that the silversmiths' guild held an indignation meeting against him in the local theatre—not the amphitheatre—which Paul was 'dissuaded' from attending and which was eventually quieted by the town-clerk. Yet he was in a state of abject terror: 'We were weighed down exceedingly, beyond our power, insomuch that we despaired of our life' (2 *Corinthians* i. 8); and when the uproar died down he made a hurried departure for Macedonia (*Acts* xx. 1).

A year later, on his return eastward along the coast of Asia Minor, he did not venture into Ephesus, but (*Acts* xx. 16) 'determined to sail by it, because he would not spend time in Asia, for he hasted if it were possible for him to be at Jerusalem the day of Pentecost.' The excuse was lamentably thin. If he considered the Law annulled by Jesus, he had no need to keep Pentecost at Jerusalem; and on his arrival at Miletus farther along the coast, he sent a message back to Ephesus, desiring the elders of the Church to join him there and be confirmed in the faith. It is clear from *Acts* that Paul could have spent a fortnight or more at Ephesus if he had chosen—instead of tarrying seven days at Tyre (*Acts* xxi. 4), and many days at Caesarea (*Acts* xxi. 10)—and still reached Jerusalem in good time for Pentecost (*Acts* xxi. 26).

Nero's insane persecutions of the Church had not yet begun, and if Paul was indeed condemned at Ephesus to fight wild beasts, he must have been charged with parricide, incest, cannibalism, or some other atrocity, as were Sanctus, Blandina, and the other martyrs of Lyons who suffered under Marcus Aurelius in the late second century (*Ecc. Hist.* 5. i. 14–38). But even at Lyons such of the condemned criminals as proved to be Romans were spared the indignity of the wild beast show and beheaded instead (*Ecc. Hist.* 5. i. 47). Moreover, Paul's being free to leave Ephesus proves that no sentence had yet been passed upon him. It may be that 2 *Corinthians* i. 9, the account of how he went about like one already condemned to death, hourly awaiting execution of his sentence, is a lie; or it may be that he had, in fact, committed some serious crime that weighed on his conscience and prevented him from returning to Ephesus. He does not say on what occasion Priscilla and Aquila (*Romans* xvi. 4) had 'laid down their own necks' for his life, but preaching the Gentile Gospel of Christ was not even a minor felony at the time. Perhaps the Grecians had tried to avenge Stephen's murder; which would explain why he told the Ephesian elders at Miletus (*Acts* xx. 26) that he had never in his life been implicated in a murder.

nantly Pharisaic Sanhedrin, have combined here in transferring Peter's preliminary and irregular examination in 30 A.D. by Annas (Ananias, or Hananiah) son of Boethus, to the account of Paul's trial in 58 A.D. by a court of Priestly Elders (*see* CIX.*h–i*) presided over by the High Priest Ananias son of Nedabiah.

(*g*) If 'Peter' is substituted for 'Paul', *Acts* xiii. 1–5 becomes credible, and 'until this day' is explained by Peter's admitted use of the sword. But he must have said more to earn the blow, and his words may be deduced from verse 5, where he quotes *Exodus* xxii. 28: 'Thou shalt not curse the ruler of thy people!'—who, in *Ecclesiastes* x. 20, is clearly defined as the King, not the High Priest. Peter here upholds his right to draw a sword in defence of his King, and will have quoted 2 *Samuel* xviii. 5 and 14 in support. The blow was dealt him (*Acts* xxiii. 2) in violation of legal procedure (*see* (*h*) *below*); but this was not a properly constituted court and old Annas will have been vexed at being kept from his bed by Peter's stubbornness.

> (411) *And Peter, earnestly beholding the Council, said:* 'Men and brethren, I have lived in all good conscience before God until this day.
>
> 'And now have I done no evil, save to defend my King from them which sought to take him.'
>
> *Annas therefore charged him straitly, saying:* 'Tell me whether this man Jesus commanded thee to draw thy sword against my servant?'
>
> *Peter answered and said:* 'Nay, but I sought vengeance on him which hath betrayed my master. I struck thy servant in error, and my master rebuked me therefor.
>
> 'Yet though David commanded his captains to do nothing against the youth Absalom which had made rebellion, was it accounted a sin in Joab son of Zeruiah that he thrust him through the heart?
>
> 'For that which Joab did was done lest Israel should be shamed. As he said unto David, his King and master: "In that thou lovest thine enemies and hatest thy friends."'
>
> *Then said Annas:* 'Callest thou this deceiver thy King?'
>
> *And Peter answered:* 'He is no deceiver, but thy King and mine.'
>
> *Wherefore Annas commanded them that stood by to smite him on the mouth.*
>
> *Then said Peter unto him:* 'God shall smite thee also, thou whited sepulchre! Sittest thou to judge me according to the Law, and commandest me to be smitten contrary to the Law?'
>
> *And they that stood by, asked him:* 'Revilest thou the High Priest of God?'
>
> *Then said Peter:* 'I wist not that he was the High Priest.'
>
> *And he spake unto Annas, saying:* 'Art thou then a High Priest, and hast not read the Scripture: "Thou shalt not speak evil of thy King"?'
>
> *And Annas, being exceeding wroth thereat, commanded Peter to be bound, and put in ward.*

* * * * *

(*h*) Annas was, in point of fact, an ex-High Priest, his son-in-law Joseph Caiaphas being the present holder of office, which explains the otherwise unaccountable 'I wist not'. Caiaphas will have been asleep at the time; he had a long and arduous day ahead of him and Annas therefore took his place as president of the examining court, which must have consisted mainly of his own sons.

'Thou whited wall!' is a typical Galilean outburst against the white-robed priesthood—Peter here improves on Jesus's 'unwhited sepulchre', and his remark has caused an editor of *Matthew* to misreport the original (*Matthew* xxiii. 27—*see* XIII.s). 'Contrary to the Law' refers to a Pharisaic regulation deduced from *Leviticus* xix. 35 and *Deuteronomy* xxv. 2, protecting the person of the accused until he had been found guilty by a judge. The Mishnah (*Aboth* i. 8) lays down that a judge must not show prejudice before a case opened, or bear resentment after it was closed:

> Judah ben Tabbai [*2nd. century* B.C.] said: '[In the judge's office] act not the counsel's part: when the parties to a suit are standing before thee, regard them both as alike guilty; but when they are departed from thy presence, regard them both as innocent, since they accepted thy judgement.'

(*i*) If the other disciple was Annas's son John, as seems likely, respect for his father would have effectively prevented him from offering the least word of protest; he appears, however, to have attended the Council of Priestly Elders early in the morning and kept a record of its proceedings.

* * * * *

BEFORE CAIAPHAS

Mark xiv. 53–65

[53]And they led Jesus away to the high priest: and with him were assembled all the chief priests and the elders and the scribes. [54]And Peter followed Him afar off, even into the palace of the high priest: and he sat with the servants, and warmed himself at the fire. [55]And the chief priests and all the council sought for witnesses against Jesus to put Him to death; and found none. [56]For many bare false witness against Him, but their witness agreed not together. [57]And there arose certain, and bare false witness against Him, saying: [58]'We heard Him say, I will destroy this temple that is made with hands, and within three days I will build another made without hands.' [59]But neither so did their witness agree together. [60]And the high priest stood up in the midst, and asked Jesus, saying: 'Answerest Thou nothing? what is it which these witness against Thee?' [61]But He held His peace, and answered nothing. Again the high priest asked Him, and said unto Him: 'Art Thou the Christ, the Son of the Blessed?' [62]And Jesus said: 'I am: and ye shall see the Son of Man sitting on the right hand of power, and coming in the clouds of heaven.' [63]Then the high priest rent his clothes, and saith: 'What need we any further witnesses? [64]Ye have heard the blasphemy: what think ye?' And they all condemned Him to be guilty of death. [65]And some began to spit on Him, and to cover His face, and to buffet Him, and to say unto Him, Prophesy: and the servants did strike Him with the palms of their hands.

Matthew xxvi. 57–68

[57]And they that had laid hold on Jesus led Him away to Caiaphas the high priest, where the scribes and the elders were assembled. [58]But Peter followed Him afar off unto the high priest's palace, and went in, and sat with the servants, to see the end. [59]Now the chief priests, and elders, and all the council, sought false witness against Jesus, to put Him to death; [60]but found none: yea, though many false witnesses came, yet found they none. At the last came two false witnesses, [61]and said: 'This fellow said, I am able to destroy the temple of God, and to build it in three days.' [62]And the high priest arose, and said unto Him: 'Answerest Thou nothing? what is it which these witness against Thee?' [63]But Jesus held His peace. And the high priest answered and said unto Him: 'I adjure Thee by the living God, that Thou tell us whether Thou be the Christ, the Son of God.' [64]Jesus saith unto him:

Matthew xxvi. 57–68 (*contd.*)

'Thou has said: nevertheless I say unto you,
Hereafter shall ye see the Son of Man sitting on the right hand of power,
And coming in the clouds of heaven.'

[65]Then the high priest rent his clothes, saying: 'He hath spoken blasphemy; what further need have we of witnesses? behold, now ye have heard His blasphemy. [66]What think ye?' They answered and said, He is guilty of death. [67]Then did they spit in His face, and buffeted Him; and others smote Him with the palms of their hands, [68]saying, Prophesy unto us, Thou Christ, Who is he that smote Thee?

Matthew xxvii. 1–2

[1]When the morning was come, all the chief priests and elders of the people took counsel against Jesus to put Him to death: [2]and when they had bound Him, they led Him away, and delivered Him to Pontius Pilate the governor.

Luke xxii. 54

[54]Then took they Him, and led Him, and brought Him into the high priest's house. And Peter followed afar off.

Luke xxii. 63–71

[63]And the men that held Jesus mocked Him, and smote Him. [64]And when they had blindfolded Him, they struck Him on the face, and asked Him, saying: 'Prophesy, who is it that smote Thee?' [65]And many other things blasphemously spake they against Him.

[66]And as soon as it was day, the elders of the people and the chief priests and the scribes came together, and led Him into their council, saying: [67]'Art Thou the Christ? tell us.' And He said unto them: 'If I tell you, ye will not believe: [68]and if I also ask you, ye will not answer Me, nor let Me go. [69]Hereafter shall the Son of Man sit on the right hand of the power of God.' [70]Then said they all: 'Art Thou then the Son of God?' And He said unto them: 'Ye say that I am.' [71]And they said: 'What need we any further witness? for we ourselves have heard of His own mouth.'

John xi. 47–52

[47]Then gathered the chief priests and the Pharisees a council, and said: 'What do we? for this Man doeth many miracles. [48]If we let Him thus alone, all men will believe on Him: and the Romans shall come and take away both our place and nation.' [49]And one of them, named Caiaphas, being the high priest that same year, said unto them: 'Ye know nothing at all, [50]nor consider that it is expedient for us, that one man should die for the people, and that the whole nation perish not.' [51]And this spake he not of himself: but being high priest that year, he prophesied that Jesus should die for that nation; [52]and not for that nation only, but that also He should gather together in one the children of God that were scattered abroad.

John xviii. 12–14

¹²Then the band and the captain and officers of the Jews took Jesus and bound Him, ¹³and led Him away to Annas first; for he was father in law to Caiaphas, which was the high priest that same year. ¹⁴Now Caiaphas was he, which gave counsel to the Jews, that it was expedient that one man should die for the people.

John xviii. 19–24

¹⁹The high priest then asked Jesus of His disciples, and of His doctrine. ²⁰Jesus answered him: 'I spake openly to the world: I ever taught in the synagogue, and in the temple, whither the Jews always resort: and in secret have I said nothing. ²¹Why askest thou Me? ask them which heard Me, what I have said unto them; behold, they know what I said.' ²²And when He had thus spoken, one of the officers which stood by struck Jesus with the palm of his hand, saying: 'Answerest Thou the high priest so?' ²³Jesus answered him: 'If I have spoken evil, bear witness of the evil: but if well, why smitest thou Me?' ²⁴Now Annas had sent Him bound unto Caiaphas the high priest.

John vii. 53

⁵³And every man went unto his own house.

(*a*) The High Priest Joseph—nicknamed Caiaphas ('the Prophet') even before the incident recorded in *John* xi. 49–52—had been nominated by the Romans and collaborated with them throughout his term of office from 18–36 A.D. He was married to a daughter of his predecessor Annas (Hananiah)—five, and perhaps six, of whose sons were also destined to wear the High Priestly frontlet (*see* LXXXII.*a*), and who had originally been appointed by Quirinius, the Governor of Syria, to help him enforce the poll-tax (*Luke* ii. 2—*see* I.*t*). Annas's family, the 'Grecian' House of Boethus, were much hated by the populace (*see* XCVI.*d*) but remained in power until shortly before the siege of Jerusalem, when the Zealots burned down their palace on the Mount of Olives.

(*b*) *Matthew's* account of the proceedings at this palace differs in important particulars from *Mark's* version which, like *Luke's*, does not mention Caiaphas by name. According to *Matthew* xxvi. 59, the Great Sanhedrin—the Jewish Supreme Court alleged to have tried Jesus—attempted to secure *false* evidence, but they could at first find none sufficiently false for their purpose. According to *Mark* xiv. 55–59, they attempted merely to secure evidence, but could find none sufficiently conclusive. According to *Matthew* xxvi. 50, two men came forward at last and testified: 'This fellow declared: "I can destroy the Temple of God and build it up in three days" '—whereupon Caiaphas began to interrogate Jesus. According to *Mark* xiv. 57–58, the witnesses declared: 'We heard him say: "I will destroy this Temple made by hands, and in three days I will build another Temple, not made by hands," ' but this evidence was disqualified.

Both *Matthew* and *Mark* suggest that the Sanhedrin sat all night and, at daybreak, unanimously condemned Jesus to death for blasphemy, spat on him, buffeted him, and then handed him over to Pilate. According to *Luke* xxii. 66, the session was held early in the morning; after the High Priest's servants had spat on Jesus and buffeted him; and other members of the court, not Caiaphas alone, interrogated him. 'They said to him: "If thou art the Christ, tell us"' (*Luke* xxii. 67). *John* does not mention any session of the Sanhedrin; but according to *John* xviii. 13, Jesus was brought before Annas, who questioned him briefly and then sent him on to Caiaphas (*John* xviii. 24). The proceedings before Caiaphas are, however, omitted; all that remains is: 'they led Jesus from Caiaphas into the Praetorium' (*John* xviii. 28).

In none of the Gospels does any witness mention Jesus's regal entry into Jerusalem, his brush with the money-changers, or Peter's attack on Malchus. The principal charge is always blasphemy.

The four Gospel accounts of Pilate's examination are even less credible and more contradictory, since they incorporate much of the proceedings at the palace, but with the speaking parts redistributed.

(*c*) The Great Sanhedrin, consisting of seventy-one members, was predominantly Pharisaic, and though, according to *Mark* xiv. 54, Jesus came before it in 'the Palace of the High Priest', its regular venue was the *Beth Din,* 'the House of Hewn Stone', a part of the Temple (*Sanhedrin* xi. 2). In theory, this Court was competent to try every crime committed in Israel against God or man—blasphemy, idolatry, perjury, theft, adultery, murder, and the like; but ever since the accession of Herod the Great, to whom the Pharisaic judges refused their allegiance, it had been forbidden to try political cases. That Jesus's case was a political rather than a religious one is proved by the charges subsequently brought against him when he appeared before Pilate (*Luke* xxiii. 2–5): 'We have found this fellow perverting our nation, forbidding tribute to be paid to Caesar and saying that he is the Anointed King. He stirs up the people by teaching throughout Judaea; he began in Galilee and now he is here.'

(*d*) Moreover, though the Great Sanhedrin sat almost continuously, no sessions might take place on Sabbaths, Feasts, or the days preceding these*; neither might its members be convened on such days even in an emergency; nor did they ever meet at night. But Jesus was tried on the night before the Passover which, that year, fell on a Sabbath (*see* cv.*h*). Thus he could not have come before the Great Sanhedrin, or any Lower Court responsible to it and governed by the same rules—there were several such Lower Sanhedrins in Israel, of twenty-three members each (*Tosephta Hagigah* ii. 9)—nor could he have come before a court consisting of the Great Sanhedrin's Sadducaic minority, since such a court could be called only to try cases wholly concerned

---

* Augustus himself issued an edict that no Jew should be compelled to stand trial in a Roman court on a Sabbath, or on a day of preparation for a Sabbath after the ninth hour (*Antiquities* xvi. 6. 2).

with the priesthood, and Jesus's priestly claims were not recognized at the Palace. He was arrested as a Galilean, not as a Judaean of Ramathaim-Zophim. Moreover, according to Josephus (*Antiquities* xviii. 1. 4), even these Sadducaic judges were obliged to follow Pharisaic procedure:

'They [*the Sadducees*] are able to do almost nothing of themselves; for when they become magistrates, unwillingly and by force sometimes, they addict themselves to the notions of the Pharisees, because the multitude would not otherwise listen to them.'

(*e*) The following judicial rules governing the Great Sanhedrin and its subsidiary courts are pertinent to Jesus's trial.

Non-capital cases might be begun, after the reading of the indictment, by either the defence or the prosecution; capital cases must be begun by the defence. A verdict of acquittal might be carried by a majority of one; a verdict of conviction must be carried by a majority of at least two. A verdict might be reversed from conviction to acquittal, but not from acquittal to conviction. Anyone arguing in favour of conviction might change his mind and argue for acquittal, but not contrariwise. All trials must be held in daytime, and the verdict must be delivered while it was still light; a verdict of acquittal might be reached on the first day of a trial but, to allow due time for deliberation and for the production of fresh evidence by the defence, a verdict of conviction must always be delivered on the following day*—it was for this reason that trials could not be held on the eve of a Sabbath or of a Feast.

(*f*) Witnesses were warned, before interrogation, of the dire consequences if their testimony should prove to be mere hearsay or gossip. In capital cases they were addressed as follows (*Sanhedrin* iv. 1–5):

'Perhaps you know not that we shall test you by examination and enquiry? Understand that capital cases differ from non-capital ones. In non-capital cases a man may atone by a payment of money, but in capital cases the witness is responsible for the blood of a man wrongfully condemned and for the blood of the posterity [*that should have been born to him*] until the end of the world . . .

'One man [*Adam*] was created first to teach that, if any man causes a single soul to perish, the Law will treat him as though he caused an entire world to perish; and that if any man saves the life of a single soul, the Law will treat him as though he had saved the life of an entire world.'

The witnesses must then confirm that the accused had been forewarned as to the criminality and consequences of his alleged actions (*ibid*. v. 1).

Several of these judicial rules were disregarded in Caiaphas's examination of Jesus.

(*g*) Because of *John* xviii. 31, it has been much debated whether in Jesus's

---

* This regulation changed Jewish history. When Herod the Great as a young man was tried for murder by the Great Sanhedrin, and attempted to awe them by his royal purple, it is clear even from Josephus's garbled account (*Antiquities* xiv. 9. 4–5) that Shemaiah the President adjourned the trial not from cowardice, but because he held that Herod deserved the death penalty; and Herod was thus able to make his escape.

time the Great Sanhedrin, or its subsidiaries, were empowered to condemn an accused man to death. It is true that a *baraita* in the Jerusalem Talmud (*Sanhedrin* 41*a*) states that 'forty years before the destruction' of the Temple the right to exercise capital punishment was taken away by the Romans; but if this *baraita,* which has no parallel in the Babylonian Talmud, is indeed historical, it must refer to a range of quasi-political offences which the Romans now claimed the sole right to judge. The Romans did not, however, interfere with the administration of Jewish religious laws; and 'forty years before the destruction'—namely 30 A.D.—may refer to an edict published after the Crucifixion. Moreover, the Talmud (*Sanhedrin* 37*b*) discusses the four Jewish forms of capital punishment abolished after the Temple was destroyed; which means that they were in force during Jesus's lifetime. This tallies with Josephus's statement (*Wars* vi. 2. 4) that Titus, when calling on the Jews to surrender, reminded them of their religious freedom: they were even, he said, permitted to execute Romans found guilty of entering a part of the Temple reserved for Jews alone (*see* cxix.*e–j*). In other words: the Romans recognized the Jewish right to pass sentence of death on offenders against the Mosaic Law and to execute them. Thus the Great Sanhedrin could have condemned Jesus to death, without referring the case to Pilate, if his offence had been a religious one. But political offences lay outside its jurisdiction.

(*h*) At the outset of the Herodian régime, a compromise had been reached which was maintained under the Roman protectorate: the Great Sanhedrin would try religious cases—offences committed against God or one's neighbour—and leave disputes between the King and his subjects, or between the Emperor and his subjects, to be tried by special courts. Herod, for instance, could not ask the Great Sanhedrin to try Hyrcanus the Hasmonean on a charge of lese-majesty, or his sister-in-law on a charge of alienating her husband's loyalty; because these were not considered crimes in Jewish Law, he had to try them before a court of his own choosing. Similarly, Pontius Pilate used special Courts of Inquiry, consisting of the collaborationist Chief Rulers, to investigate political disorders or disputes not provided for by the Mosaic Law, and to recommend, though not award, a fitting punishment. The Chief Rulers, headed by the High Priest, stood in such dread of a Roman ban on Temple worship—the Romans had them by the throat, and even kept the High Priestly regalia in military custody—that these courts could be counted upon to do Pilate's work most efficiently; indeed, the Chief Rulers seem to have arrested Jesus on their own initiative. But, except by courtesy of the Procurator, these special courts had no standing, and when about the year 62 A.D. the High Priest Annas II convened one in the temporary absence of the Procurator and sentenced James the Just to be stoned as a political offender, King Agrippa II at once deposed him for his presumption (*Antiquities* xx. 9. 1).

(*i*) In the normal course of events, Jesus would have been tried by the Great Sanhedrin after the Passover, on a charge of interfering with the Temple administration, the maximum penalty being thirty-nine stripes; he would doubtless have recognized the authority of the court, quoted *Isaiah* lvi. 7 (*see* xc.*f*), and been released with a caution. But the Chief Priests' special court was not one that he could recognize as competent to judge him, though it was larger and more formal than the skeleton court which examined Peter. It will have consisted of fifteen members: the High Priest; the Deputy High Priest (*segan*), a permanent official; the two Treasurers, called 'Catholics' (*Jer. Shekalim* v. 2); the seven 'Wardens of the Gates'; the Captain of the Temple; and three Chief Rulers whose monopolies entitled them to a part in the Temple administration—among them Bunni ('Nicodemus') son of Gorion. The court's official name was the 'Council of Priestly Elders' (*zikne kehunah*).

(*j*) According to *Mark* xiv. 60-61 and *Matthew* xxvi. 62-63, Jesus refused to answer his interrogators, and paid no attention to the evidence of the witnesses for the prosecution. He knew that this Council did not abide by the judicial rules of the Pharisees, nor were its members individually qualified to judge capital cases. Every member of the Great Sanhedrin had to be perfect in both the oral and the written Law, and was generally promoted to a seat only after service in a lower Sanhedrin of twenty-three.

(*k*) An apparent exception to Jesus's withholding of evidence when brought before this Council, is his reply to the question: 'Art thou the Anointed King, the son of the Blessed One?' (*Mark* xiv. 62); which *Mark*, however, has misunderstood. The original phrase, again used by Jesus when brought before Pilate, is preserved in *Luke* xxii. 70, namely: 'Thou sayest (or "Ye say") that I am' (*see* cx.*i*). Here the editor is literally translating an Aramaic or Hebrew idiom, *amarta* or *atta amarta* (*see* cv.*d*), which carries a negative sense: 'So *you* say, but I reserve my opinion'; whereas the corresponding words in Greek and Latin carry a positive sense: 'What you say is true.'

In the *Tosephta Kelim* (*Baba Kamma*) i. 6, it is related that, some twenty-five years after the Crucifixion, Simeon the Chaste—who seems to have been Simon the son of Cleophas, the successor of James the Just as head of the Nazarene Church* and father of Mary, Martha, and Lazarus (*see* VIII.*s and* XI.*b*)—told Rabbi Eliezer ben Horkinas:

> ' "I entered between the *ulam* (vestibule) and the altar and I did not wash my hands or my feet." [*Such washing was prescribed for all priests. Simeon meant by this that the regulations were not binding on a man who lived a clean and retiring life.*]
>
> 'Then said Rabbi Eliezer unto him: "Which is the more honourable, thou or the High Priest?"
>
> 'Simeon remained silent.

---

* According to Hegesippus, quoted by Eusebius (*Ecc. Hist.* 2. xxiii. 5), James the Just never anointed himself, nor went to the baths, nor ate sacrificial meat, and lived as a Nazarite. And, according to an Ebionite work, *The Ascent of James,* quoted by Epiphanius (*Heresies* xxvi. 6), he condemned certain parts of the Temple ritual, particularly burnt sacrifices. For this he had the support of *Psalms* xl. 6 and li. 16, and *Hosea* vi. 6 which was quoted by Jesus (*see* LXXI.*g*). Simeon seems to have held the same views.

'Then Rabbi Eliezer said: "Thou art ashamed to admit that even the High Priest's dog is more honourable than thou art."

'Simeon replied: "Rabbi, so thou sayest!" '

Simeon did not of course accept Rabbi Eliezer's hot-tempered suggestion, but seems to have spoken in humble disagreement. Rabbi Elijah of Vilna interprets his words as meaning: 'I am grieved that thou shouldst say this.' However, Jesus had used the phrase defiantly: and it was his defiance, not his alleged blasphemy, which provoked a blow on the mouth from the Court officer. This will, however, have been the only blow struck; the other buffets belong to a different context altogether (*see* viii.*k*).

(*l*) It seems, then, that Jesus was arrested on the Mount of Olives, taken to the near-by Palace of the Boethians, and briefly cross-examined by Annas, who, though he had ceased to be High Priest fifteen years previously, remained the power behind the scenes (*Acts* iv. 6). There he was confined for the rest of the night, and at dawn brought before a specially convened Council of Priestly Elders, presided over by Caiaphas. It is also likely that Peter was tried first and found guilty of armed rebellion; that he would not incriminate Jesus and escaped with an exemplary scourging; that Jesus was first privately interviewed by Caiaphas; and that, after a violent disagreement in Court, where Bunni tried to secure an acquittal, Caiaphas on his own responsibility handed Jesus over to Pilate.

It must be said in Caiaphas's favour that, while acting as the trusted agent of the invader, he regarded himself as serving his country's best interests; further, it is clear from *John* xi. 49: 'Ye know nothing at all, nor consider that it is expedient for us that one man should die for the people,' that Pilate had already heard of Jesus's activities from the Captain of the Temple and privately threatened to take stern measures if Caiaphas did not surrender him at once to Roman justice.

(*m*) According to *Mark* xiv. 62 and *Matthew* xxvi. 64, Jesus uttered no blasphemy. Blasphemy consisted in taking the name of God in vain (*Exodus* xx. 7 and *Leviticus* xxiv. 10–16), but the Pharisees held that it was not punishable by Law unless God had been cursed in His own name (*Sanhedrin* vii. 5), which implied the pronunciation of the Tetragrammaton: 'The blasphemer is not guilty unless he pronounces the Name itself.' Jesus had used the phrase 'the right hand of *Power*', and thus did not blaspheme even if he could be accused of wrongful invocation, for which God Himself would strike him dead if it were necessary to do so. The High Priest came far closer to blasphemy when he said: 'I adjure thee by the Living God!' uttered in a nonjudicial capacity. Moreover, until the Passover had ended, not even the Great Sanhedrin could have tried a blasphemy charge, and the Council of Priestly Elders were not competent to take so much as a summary of evidence in such a case.

The correct procedure for blasphemy trials is laid down in the *Mishna* (*Sanhedrin* vii. 5):

'When sentence was to be pronounced, they cleared the court and told the first witness: "Repeat precisely what you heard." He repeated it; and (if it was adjudged blasphemy) the judges rose to their feet and rent their garments . . . and the second witness testified: "I also heard the like," and then the third likewise.'

(n) 'Blasphemy' therefore should read 'treason', namely rebellion against Rome. This agrees with *Luke* xxii. 70, where the charge of blasphemy is not mentioned, but where the Court satisfy themselves that Jesus has claimed to be 'Son of God', that is to say, King; and with *John* xi. 48, where the charge is one of endangering the national security.

Yet the utterance of treason against Rome could not have induced Caiaphas to rend his clothes. If anyone present did so, it will have been Bunni: in anticipatory mourning for Jesus, whose life he found himself unable to save. Clothes were rent on three occasions only: on hearing the Unspeakable Name blasphemed, at news of death or misfortune befallen a relative or close friend (*Job* i. 20 and ii. 12), or when the entire nation had sinned (*Ezra* ix. 3).

(409) *And they led Jesus away to the Palace of Annas which had been the High Priest; for he was father-in-law to Joseph, called Caiaphas, which was now the High Priest.*

* * * * *

(o) [Here follows Peter's arrest and examination by Annas (*see* cviii.*d–h*).]

* * * * *

(412) *And when he had heard the testimony which the Captain of the Temple brought against Jesus, he kept him also in ward until the morrow.*

* * * * *

(413) *Now, as soon as it was day, Peter was brought bound before Caiaphas. And the Chief Priests and elders were assembled in Council, and the scribes sat by.*

Then Caiaphas, when he heard from Annas of the wounding of Malchus, asked Peter, which called himself Barabbas: 'Did thy master bid thee draw thy sword against my servants?

'For if so, thou art somewhat the less guilty.'

He answered and said: 'Nay, but I drew it of mine own will, and he rebuked me therefor.'

Then Caiaphas judged Peter to be guilty of sedition, and said: 'Thou art worthy of death!'

And they led him away.

* * * * *

(414) *Then came out Caiaphas to the place where Jesus was, and asked him privately of his disciples and of his doctrine, whether he had provoked any man to violence.*

Jesus answered: 'I spake to all the world and taught in the synagogues and in the Temple; neither have I kept anything secret.

'*Why askest thou me? Ask them which hearkened unto me!*'

Wherefore Caiaphas went in again, and Jesus was led before him and the Council of the Chief Priests and elders.

And Caiaphas sent for witnesses, which testified that Jesus had provoked his disciples to violence. But their testimony did not agree.

Then sent he for others, which said: 'This fellow called himself the King of Israel. Yesterday he provoked the multitude to burn the Temple, saying: "Destroy ye this Temple, which is a den of robbers, for God will raise up a better Temple in three days!"'

Jesus held his peace and answered nothing.

Caiaphas arose, and said unto him: 'Answerest thou nothing? What is it that these men witness against thee?'

But Jesus held his peace.

Caiaphas said unto him: 'I adjure thee by the Living God, that thou tell us whether thou be the Anointed King, the Son of God!'

Jesus answered: 'So thou sayest. Yet if I ask thee by what authority thou hast brought me to judgement, thou wilt not answer me, neither let me go.

'Wherefore I do not answer thee, whether I be King or no King.'

And when he had thus spoken, one of the officers which stood by struck Jesus with the palm of his hand, saying: 'Answerest thou the High Priest so?'

Jesus said: 'If I am at fault, testify to the fault; but if I speak the truth, why smitest thou me?'

* * * *

(*p*) The substance of the following passage, in the course of which Jesus quotes *Psalm* xli. 9 (*see* cv.*b*), has been transferred by the evangelists to Pilate's trial of Jesus (*see* cx.*d*) with certain necessary omissions and modifications. 'He that delivered me', is Judas, not Caiaphas, as in *John* xix. 11.

(415) *Caiaphas saith again unto Jesus: 'Knowest thou not that I have power to deliver thee unto the Romans to be crucified, and power likewise to release thee?'*

Jesus answered: 'Thou canst have no power over me, except it were given thee from above. Therefore thou sinnest in judging me.

'For this is not the Council by which Israelites are judged. Nevertheless, he that delivered me unto thee hath the greater sin.

'As David prophesied: "Mine own familiar friend in whom I trusted, which did eat of my bread, hath lifted up his heel against me."

'But hath not Caesar, which boweth down unto false gods, appointed thee to judge Israelites according to his laws? Why then askest thou me these things in the name of the Living God?

'Beware, lest thou sin against Him in judging for His enemies!'

And the High Priest cried aloud, and said: 'Is this not treason? For we ourselves have heard of his own mouth that he speaketh against Caesar.

'What further need have we of witnesses? What think ye? Is he not deserving of death?

'If we let him go free, all men will follow him, and Caesar will destroy both our dwelling place and our nation.'

* * * * *

(*q*) [Here follows *John* vii. 50–52 (*see* xciv.*i*), Bunni's protest, part of which has been transferred to an earlier meeting held by the Chief Priests. Another part: 'Why, what evil hath he done?' has been attributed to Pilate in *Luke* xxiii. 22 (*see* cx.*e*), and still another to 'the Chief Priests and Pharisees' in *John* xi. 47. *John* xi. 48–50 contains Caiaphas's reply.]

* * * * *

(417) *Then said Bunni: 'Why, what evil hath he done? He hath not offended against the Law, neither hath he risen in arms against Caesar.*

'Ye know well that we may not deliver an innocent man unto death. What do we? This man worketh many miracles of healing by the finger of God.'

And others said likewise.

Then said the High Priest: 'Ye know nothing at all, nor consider that it is expedient that one man should die for the people and that the whole people perish not.'

* * * * *

(418) *And Jesus saith unto the Council of Chief Priests and Elders: 'Take heed what ye do with me, being no judges!*

'Verily, I say unto you: if ye deliver me unto death, and thereby seek favour with the Wicked Kingdom, it shall go hard with you when ye see the Son of Man coming on the clouds of heaven, to sit on the right hand of Power!

'For he shall judge them that pervert justice, and that make friends of the enemies of God.'

* * * * *

(*r*) Here follows a passage which has been broken up, modified, and woven into Pilate's trial of Jesus (*see* cx.*j*). Bunni seems to have quoted *Proverbs* iii. 3, *Deuteronomy* xxi. 7–8, 2 *Samuel* i. 16 and *Susannah* v. 46.

(419) *Wherefore, when Bunni heard these words, he was sore afraid and sought the more to release Jesus, and answered the High Priest, saying: 'Should this man also die because his disciple drew a sword? For he rebuked the fault.*

'Moreover, it is the Law that one man only may be delivered unto death on the one day, lest they that judge become as murderers.

'Beware, therefore, of the people; for tomorrow is the Passover when they drink much wine and make merry in the streets of the city!'

And again others said likewise.

Then Caiaphas asked them, saying: 'Whether of the twain will ye that I release unto you?

'Would ye have me release him that maketh himself King and condemn his servant?

'Nay, I will not release this man, but Barabbas, after that I have chastised him well.'

And Bunni answered: 'It is written: "Let not mercy and truth forsake thee."'

Caiaphas asked: 'What is truth?'

Bunni answered and said: 'Behold, every Israelite that is of the truth heareth God's voice; to this end was he born, and for this cause came he into the world that he should bear witness to the truth.'

Caiaphas said: 'If thou wouldst let this man go, then art thou not Caesar's friend.'

And the Chief Priests and scribes were instant with loud voices, requiring that Jesus might be delivered unto Pilate for crucifixion.

Bunni saith: 'Shall he then be crucified?'

They answer: 'What is that to us? Let him that spake against Caesar stand at Caesar's judgement-seat.'

Bunni saith: 'I find no fault in the man. As Daniel, which was the advocate of Susannah, declared: "I am clear from his blood." And when he shewed how the testimony of the two accusers agreed not together, the innocent soul was released.'

But the Chief Priests and the scribes cried out again, saying: 'Let him be delivered unto Pilate!'

* * * * *

(s) *Matthew* xxvii. 22: 'Let him be crucified!' is a better reading than 'Crucify him!' The High Priest had no power to crucify. But the council will have been content with: 'Let him be delivered to Pilate!'

(420) *And Bunni, perceiving that he could in no wise prevail, but that rather a tumult was made, took water and washed his hands before them all, and said: 'My hands have not shed this blood, neither have mine eyes seen it.'*

And he prayed: 'Be merciful, O God, unto Thy people Israel, whom thou hast redeemed, and lay not innocent blood unto Thy people's charge!'

And he rent his garments.

They that consented with him, prayed likewise, and said unto Caiaphas: 'As it is written: "Thy blood be upon thy head!" See thou to it.'

But the Chief Priests and the scribes cried out the more exceedingly: 'Let him be delievered unto Pilate!'

And Caiaphas gave sentence that it should be as they required.

And he scourged Peter, which had been found guilty of rebellion and murder, and afterward released him.

But Bunni was called Nakemidam of all the people, which is 'Innocent of Blood'.

* * * * *

Here follows the substance of *John* vii. 53:

(421) *Then was an end made to the Council, and every man returned to his own house.*

* * * * *

(*t*) The scourging would account for Peter's failure to appear at the Crucifixion; he clearly lacked neither courage nor loyalty.

Several years later, a Boethian High Priest disclaimed responsibility, on behalf of his family, for Jesus's death (*Acts* v. 28); and technically, at least, he was justified. Though they had handed Jesus over to Pilate for breaking the Roman peace by entering Jerusalem in regal style, Pilate had not tried him on this charge, but had transferred the case to Antipas's jurisdiction. And Antipas had condemned him for a quite different misdemeanour: that of preaching sedition against his régime in the border province of Peraea (*see* cx.*n and* cxi.*c*).

* * * * *

(*u*) Since even the editors of *John* refrain from suggesting that Judas was among the hostile witnesses, though the council can hardly have neglected to call him, it may have been he who corrected the report that Jesus had incited the mob to burn the Temple.

* * * * *

BEFORE PILATE

Mark xv. 1–20

[1]And straightway in the morning the chief priests held a consultation with the elders and scribes and the whole council, and bound Jesus, and carried Him away, and delivered Him to Pilate. [2]And Pilate asked Him: 'Art Thou the King of the Jews?' And He answering said unto him: 'Thou sayest it.' [3]And the chief priests accused Him of many things: but He answered nothing. [4]And Pilate asked Him again, saying: 'Answerest Thou nothing? behold how many things they witness against Thee.' [5]But Jesus yet answered nothing; so that Pilate marvelled. [6]Now at that feast he released unto them one prisoner, whomsoever they desired. [7]And there was one named Barabbas, which lay bound with them that had made insurrection with him, who had committed murder in the insurrection. [8]And the multitude crying aloud began to desire him to do as he had ever done unto them. [9]But Pilate answered them, saying: 'Will ye that I release unto you the King of the Jews?' [10]For he knew that the chief priests had delivered Him for envy. [11]But the chief priests moved the people, that he should rather release Barabbas unto them. [12]And Pilate answered and said again unto them: 'What will ye then that I shall do unto Him Whom ye call the King of the Jews?' [13]And they cried out again: 'Crucify Him.' [14]Then Pilate said unto them: 'Why, what evil hath He done?' And they cried out the more exceedingly: 'Crucify Him.' [15]And so Pilate, willing to content the people, released Barabbas unto them, and delivered Jesus, when he had scourged Him, to be crucified.

[16]And the soldiers led Him away into the hall, called Praetorium; and they call together the whole band. [17]And they clothed Him with purple, and platted a crown of thorns, and put it about His head, [18]and began to salute Him: 'Hail, King of the Jews!' [19]And they smote Him on the head with a reed, and did spit upon Him, and bowing their knees worshipped Him. [20]And when they had mocked Him, they took off the purple from Him, and put His own clothes on Him.

Matthew xxvii. 11–31

[11]And Jesus stood before the governor: and the governor asked Him, saying: 'Art Thou the King of the Jews?' And Jesus said unto him: 'Thou sayest.' [12]And when He was accused of the chief priests and elders, He answered nothing. [13]Then said Pilate unto Him: 'Hearest Thou not how many things they witness against Thee?' [14]And He answered him to never a word;

Matthew xxvii. 11–31 (*contd.*)

insomuch that the governor marvelled greatly. [15]Now at that feast the governor was wont to release unto the people a prisoner, whom they would. [16]And they had then a notable prisoner, called Barabbas. [17]Therefore when they were gathered together, Pilate said unto them: 'Whom will ye that I release unto you? Barabbas, or Jesus which is called Christ?' [18]For he knew that for envy they had delivered Him. [19]When he was set down on the judgment seat, his wife sent unto him, saying: 'Have thou nothing to do with that just man: for I have suffered many things this day in a dream because of Him.' [20]But the chief priests and elders persuaded the multitude that they should ask Barabbas, and destroy Jesus. [21]The governor answered and said unto them: 'Whether of the twain will ye that I release unto you?' They said, Barabbas. [22]Pilate saith unto them: 'What shall I do then with Jesus which is called Christ?' They all say unto him: 'Let Him be crucified.' [23]And the governor said: 'Why, what evil hath He done?' But they cried out the more, saying: 'Let Him be crucified.' [24]When Pilate saw that he could prevail nothing, but that rather a tumult was made, he took water, and washed his hands before the multitude, saying: 'I am innocent of the blood of this just person: see ye to it.' [25]Then answered all the people, and said: 'His blood be on us, and on our children.' [26]Then released he Barabbas unto them: and when he had scourged Jesus, he delivered Him to be crucified.

[27]Then the soldiers of the governor took Jesus into the common hall, and gathered unto Him the whole band of soldiers. [28]And they stripped Him, and put on Him a scarlet robe. [29]And when they had platted a crown of thorns, they put it upon His head, and a reed in His right hand: and they bowed the knee before Him and mocked Him, saying: 'Hail, King of the Jews!' [30]And they spit upon Him, and took the reed, and smote Him on the head. [31]And after that they had mocked Him, they took the robe off from Him, and put His own raiment on Him, and led Him away to crucify Him.

Luke xxiii. 1–25

[1]And the whole multitude of them arose, and led Him unto Pilate. [2]And they began to accuse Him, saying: 'We found this fellow perverting the nation, and forbidding to give tribute to Caesar, saying that He Himself is Christ a King.' [3]And Pilate asked Him, saying: 'Art Thou the King of the Jews?' And He answered him and said: 'Thou sayest it.' [4]Then said Pilate to the chief priests and to the people: 'I find no fault in this Man.' [5]And they were the more fierce, saying: 'He stirreth up the people, teaching throughout all Jewry, beginning from Galilee to this place.' [6]When Pilate heard of Galilee, he asked whether the man were a Galilaean. [7]And as soon as he knew that He belonged to Herod's jurisdiction, he sent Him to Herod, who himself was also at Jerusalem at that time. [8]And when Herod saw Jesus, he was exceeding glad: for he was desirous to see Him of a long season, because he had heard many things of Him; and he hoped to have seen some miracle done by Him. [9]Then he questioned with Him in many words; but He answered him nothing. [10]And the chief priests and scribes

Luke xxiii. 1–25 (contd.)

stood and vehemently accused Him. [11]And Herod with his men of war set Him at nought, and mocked Him, and arrayed Him in a gorgeous robe, and sent Him again to Pilate. [12]And the same day Pilate and Herod were made friends together: for before they were at enmity between themselves.

[13]And Pilate, when he had called together the chief priests and the rulers of the people, [14]said unto them: 'Ye have brought this Man unto me, as one that perverteth the people: and, behold, I, having examined Him before you, have found no fault in this Man touching those things whereof ye accuse Him: [15]no, nor yet Herod: for I sent you to him: and, lo, nothing worthy of death is done unto Him. [16]I will therefore chastise Him, and release Him.' [17]For of necessity he must release one unto them at the feast. [18]And they cried out all at once, saying: 'Away with this man, and release unto us Barabbas:' [19](who for a certain sedition made in the city, and for murder, was cast into prison.) [20]Pilate, therefore, willing to release Jesus, spake again to them. [21]But they cried, saying: 'Crucify Him, crucify Him.' [22]And he said unto them the third time: 'Why, what evil hath He done? I have found no cause of death in Him: I will therefore chastise Him, and let Him go.' [23]And they were instant with loud voices, requiring that He might be crucified. And the voices of them and of the chief priests prevailed. [24]And Pilate gave sentence that it should be as they required. [25]And he released unto them him that for sedition and murder was cast into prison, whom they had desired; but he delivered Jesus to their will.

John xviii. 28–40

[28]Then led they Jesus from Caiaphas unto the hall of judgment: and it was early; and they themselves went not into the judgment hall, lest they should be defiled; but that they might eat the passover. [29]Pilate then went out unto them, and said: 'What accusation bring ye against this man?' [30]They answered and said unto him: 'If He were not a malefactor, we would not have delivered Him up unto thee.' [31]Then said Pilate unto them: 'Take ye Him, and judge Him according to your law.' The Jews therefore said unto him: 'It is not lawful for us to put any man to death,' [32]that the saying of Jesus might be fulfilled, which He spake, signifying what death He should die.

[33]Then Pilate entered into the judgment hall again, and called Jesus, and said unto Him: 'Art Thou the King of the Jews?' [34]Jesus answered him: 'Sayest thou this thing of thyself, or did others tell it thee of Me?' [35]Pilate answered: 'Am I a Jew? Thine own nation and the chief priests have delivered Thee unto me; what hast Thou done?' [36]Jesus answered: 'My kingdom is not of this world: if My kingdom were of this world, then would My servants fight, that I should not be delivered to the Jews: but now is My kingdom not from hence.' [37]Pilate therefore said unto Him: 'Art Thou a king then?' Jesus answered: 'Thou sayest that I am a king. To this end was I born, and for this cause came I into the world, that I should bear witness unto the truth. Every one that is of the truth heareth My voice.'

[38]Pilate saith unto Him: 'What is truth?' And when he had said this, he went out again unto the Jews, and saith unto them: 'I find in Him no fault

John xviii. 28–40 (contd.)

at all. [39]But ye have a custom, that I should release unto you one at the passover: will ye therefore that I release unto you the King of the Jews?' [40]Then cried they all again, saying: 'Not this man, but Barabbas.' Now Barabbas was a robber.

John xix. 1–16

[1]Then Pilate therefore took Jesus, and scourged Him. [2]And the soldiers platted a crown of thorns, and put it on His head, and they put on Him a purple robe, [3]and said: 'Hail, King of the Jews!' and they smote Him with their hands. [4]Pilate therefore went forth again, and saith unto them: 'Behold, I bring Him forth to you, that ye may know that I find no fault in Him.' [5]Then came Jesus forth, wearing the crown of thorns, and the purple robe. And Pilate saith unto them: 'Behold the man!' [6]When the chief priests therefore and officers saw Him, they cried out, saying: 'Crucify Him, crucify Him.' Pilate saith unto them: 'Take ye Him, and crucify Him: for I find no fault in Him.' [7]The Jews answered him: 'We have a law, and by our law He ought to die, because He made Himself the Son of God.' [8]When Pilate therefore heard that saying, he was the more afraid; [9]and went again into the judgment hall, and saith unto Jesus: 'Whence art Thou?' But Jesus gave him no answer. [10]Then saith Pilate unto Him: 'Speakest Thou not unto me? knowest Thou not that I have power to crucify Thee, and have power to release Thee?' [11]Jesus answered: 'Thou couldest have no power at all against Me, except it were given thee from above: therefore he that delivereth Me unto thee hath the greater sin.' [12]And from thenceforth Pilate sought to release Him: but the Jews cried out, saying: 'If thou let this man go, thou art not Caesar's friend: whosoever maketh himself a king speaketh against Caesar.'

[13]When Pilate therefore heard that saying, he brought Jesus forth, and sat down in the judgment seat in a place that is called the Pavement, but in the Hebrew, Gabbatha. [14]And it was the preparation of the passover, and about the sixth hour: and he saith unto the Jews: 'Behold your King!' [15]But they cried out: 'Away with Him, away with Him, crucify Him.' Pilate saith unto them: 'Shall I crucify your King?' The chief priests answered: 'We have no king but Caesar.' [16]Then delivered he Him therefore unto them to be crucified. And they took Jesus, and led Him away.

(a) The early Gentile Christians found the Nazarene account of Jesus's death and resurrection embarrassing. They realized that their faith could make little progress in the Roman Empire if responsibility for the Saviour's Crucifixion were laid upon Pontius Pilate. Pilate, the sixth Procurator of Judaea, though a nominee of Sejanus's—the Commander of the Praetorian Guard who tried to usurp the Empire during Tiberius's stay on Capri—and though subsequently recalled on a charge of oppression (see (c) below) had, after all, been the accredited representative of Roman justice.

(b) The evangelists decided on so drastic a revision of the narrative that Pilate would not only find Jesus innocent but even try to save his life; thus they made him yield reluctantly to the pressure of a fanatical Jewish mob who howled for Jesus's blood as a blasphemer.* Indeed, their rehabilitation of Pilate was so successful that the Ethiopian Church (of 'Grecian' origin) finally canonized him as a martyr—on the strength of the *Paradosis of Pilate*, an appendix to the apocryphal *Gospel of Nicodemus*. They deduced the charge of blasphemy, allegedly brought against Jesus, from a subsequent Jewish condemnation of themselves for breaking the First Commandment (*see* cix.*m*).

(*c*) King Agrippa I, in a letter to the Emperor Caligula, described Pilate as 'inflexible, merciless, and obstinate'. Philo (*Legatio ad Gaium* 38) charged him with 'corruption, violence, robbery, ill-usage, oppression, illegal executions, and never-ending most grievous cruelty,' and recorded his provocative hanging up of votive shields, inscribed with the Emperor's name, in what had been Herod's palace. Josephus mentions (*Antiquities* viii. 6. 5) that Tiberius retained him in office for ten years (26–36 A.D.) on the principle that it was better to leave the gorged flies on a sore than to drive them off and replace them with fresh. But, shortly before his own death, he recalled Pilate to answer a Samaritan complaint forwarded from the Governor of Syria: a religious gathering had been held on Mount Gerizim (*Antiquities* xviii. 4. 2) and though it was Imperial policy to recruit Samaritan cavalry as a means of keeping the Jews in check (*Antiquities* xx. 8. 7), Pilate had been stupid enough to make this the occasion for a massacre.† His obstinacy in the case of the Roman military standards and the Emperor's statue which he brought into Jerusalem is described in *Antiquities* xviii. 3. 1 and *Wars* ii. 9. 2–3.

(*d*) Thus Pilate's administrative career cannot be reconciled with the trial narrative. The obstinate, headstrong, cruel Pilate—his standing garrison at the citadel reinforced for the Passover—is presented in *John* as bustling to and fro, terrified of the unarmed Jews, pleading and cajoling, trying to pacify them, finding no fault in Jesus who had claimed to be King in defiance of Caesar, finally offering to release whichever prisoner they chose. This fantastic sequence (*John* xviii. 28–xix. 22) runs as follows:

> (1) Jesus is brought before Pilate who, without enquiring what the charges are, refuses to try him, and orders the Jews to do so themselves.
>
> (2) The Jews reply that they cannot legally put Jesus to death.
>
> (3) Pilate asks Jesus whether he is, in fact, the King of the Jews.
>
> (4) Jesus and Pilate enjoy an amicable chat in private. Jesus charges Caiaphas with having betrayed him, and states that his kingdom is not of this world, and that if it were, his servants would take arms against the Jews —presumably on the Roman side.

---

* Loisy in his *Origins of the New Testament* (*p.* 103) rightly concludes:

'The crucifixion of Jesus is explicable on one ground only: he was sentenced to death and executed by the Roman Authority as a sower of sedition against itself, and simply so. The efforts of the traditional legend have been concentrated on transferring responsibility for his death to the Jews, and on doing this in such a way as to make it appear that the death sentence was extorted from Pilate, or imposed upon him, while he, for his part, acknowledged the perfect innocence of the accused.'

† For a previous massacre of unarmed Jewish pilgrims, *see* li.*a*.

(5) Pilate proclaims Jesus innocent and offers to release him.

(6) The Chief Priests demand the release of Barabbas, instead; and Pilate scourges Jesus.

(7) When the Roman soldiers have playfully dressed Jesus in royal robes and buffeted him, Pilate leads him out and proudly displays him to the Jews in his regal finery.

(8) Nevertheless, he instructs the Jews to crucify Jesus, as though he were guilty and as though this were a Jewish form of punishment.

(9) The Jews now admit that, after all, they have a law by which he must die for having proclaimed himself the Son of God.

(10) Pilate therefore returns to Jesus and asks him: 'Whence art thou?'— which should have been the first question put to him. (It was probably addressed to Peter—*see* cviii.*b*.)

(11) Jesus refuses to answer; and when threatened with crucifixion, utters a defiance of Roman law.

(12) Pilate then grows alarmed, tries to release him, and again presents him to the Jews as their King.

(13) The Jews remind Pilate that Caesar does not permit anyone to proclaim himself King without special permission—a constitutional point which has apparently slipped Pilate's memory.

(14) Pilate gives way at last and the Jews illegally crucify Jesus in Roman style.

(15) Yet Pilate insists on supplying a *titulus,* by way of a minority verdict, which publicly proclaims Jesus the King of the Jews.

(*e*) *Luke* xxiii. 1–25 is a little more plausible, though Pilate there attempts three times to save Jesus but is overborne by popular clamour; and Herod Antipas, after welcoming Jesus—not because he wants to kill him (*see* lxxvi.*b*), but because he is eager to witness a miracle—finds no fault in him either. Even in *Mark* xv. 1–20 and *Matthew* xxvii. 11–31, which are the most restrained accounts, Pilate asks: 'Why, what evil hath he done?'—of a prisoner charged with claiming the throne of Israel—and is fully prepared to release him.

(*f*) That the accusers remained outside the Roman Praetorium (*John* xviii. 28) is likely enough. They would not have been 'defiled' if they had entered, but perhaps they wished to avoid the popular accusation of having given sworn evidence in the name of the God Augustus. It was beneath Pilate's dignity to act as go-between, as he is made to do, or even to 'come out'; it must have been Caiaphas who, earlier that morning, 'came out' to examine Jesus (*see* cix.*l*). By this hour, however, Caiaphas's duty lay in the Temple, where he had to supervise the preparations for the Passover, and he cannot therefore have been present.

(*g*) If *Matthew* xxvii. 24, the strange account of how Pilate washed his hands, excites no suspicion nowadays, even among reputable historians, this is only because the phrase has become proverbially familiar. Washing one's hands of a crime was not a Roman custom, but in *Deuteronomy* xxi. 1–9 the elders of a city within the boundaries of which a man is found murdered by persons unknown, are ordered to sacrifice a heifer (in placation of the 'avenger of blood') and to wash their hands over it with the words: 'Our hands have not shed this blood, etc.' Since Pilate did not interest himself in the Pentateuch, as is proved by his 'Am I a Jew?', the proper context of this action must be the proceedings at the Palace of Annas; and it will have been performed by a dissident member of the Priestly Council of Elders, almost certainly Bunni ben Gorion (*see* CIX.*q*).

(*h*) *Matthew* xxvii. 19, the story of Pilate's wife, is not necessarily an invention; Bunni may well have bribed her to secure Jesus's release. On the whole, however, the account reads suspiciously like a sop for second-century Roman matrons whose husbands happened to be magistrates. Pilate's wife 'Procla', or 'Claudia', was afterwards wishfully believed to have embraced Christianity; she has been identified with the Claudia of 2 *Timothy* iv. 21.

(*i*) When all extraneous matter is removed from the narrative of the trial, including the soldiers' mockery of Jesus (*see* VIII.*j*), little remains. It is evident from *Mark* xv. 3–5, *Matthew* xxvii. 14, *Luke* xxiii. 3, and *John* xix. 9, that Jesus refused to recognize the jurisdiction of the Roman Court and answered Pilate's question: 'Art thou then King?' as he had previously answered Caiaphas, with: 'So thou sayest!' (*see* CIX.*k*); and that the subsequent proceedings were short. Pilate, finding on enquiry that Jesus commanded a powerful popular backing and was a subject of Herod Antipas, decided not to exasperate the Galilean pilgrims by crucifying him for lese-majesty; if they rioted and thus compelled him to call out the garrison, the Grecian Jews might lodge a complaint against him with their friends in the Imperial Secretariat at Rome. It amused him to fasten the burden of unpopularity on the shoulders of Antipas.

When in Jerusalem for the Passover, Antipas occupied one wing of Herod's Palace, the remainder of which was Pilate's residence; thus the transfer and return of a prisoner need not have taken long. Antipas, who had been on bad terms with Pilate since the affair of the votive shields, regarded this extradition as an act of courtesy rather than of ill-will. He condemned Jesus to death without hesitation but, since he could not carry out a capital sentence except in his own tetrarchy, asked Pilate to supply the crucifixion party. Josephus's record (*Antiquities* xviii. 3. 3) that Jesus was condemned by Pilate 'at the suggestion of the principal men of our nation', is thus seen to be accurate: the three principal men, from the Roman point of view, were Caiaphas, Annas, his father-in-law, and Herod Antipas. The President of the Great Sanhedrin would not have been included (*see* I.*k*).

(*j*) The proper context for *John* xviii. 38: 'What is truth?' and 'I find no fault in him at all' is the Council of Priestly Elders at the Palace of Annas (*see* CIX.*q*).

John xviii. 39: 'Ye have a custom that I should release unto you one prisoner at the Passover', is unhistorical and seems to reflect another saying from the earlier proceedings: namely, that 'a council cannot condemn two persons to death on the same day' (according to *Sanhedrin* vi. 4)—'wherefore it is expedient to release one of them' (*see* cix.*r*). Indeed, the Pharisees were so chary of taking human life that it is recorded in *Makkoth* i. 10: 'A court which condemned to death one man in seven years was called "murderous".'

It must have been on this occasion, too, that Caiaphas said: 'Not this man but Barabbas' (*John* xviii. 40), to which Bunni ben Gorion, aware that Jesus had been anointed King, replied: 'Thy blood be upon thy head' (*Matthew* xxvii. 25)—a reference to 2 *Samuel* i. 16, where David rebukes the murderer of the Lord's anointed.

Pilate's characteristic 'Am I a Jew?' (*John* xviii. 35) must have been addressed not to Jesus, but to Annas's emissaries when these pressed a point of Jewish law which he thought irrelevant to the matter in hand. 'Thine own nation hath delivered thee unto me' (*ibid.*) cannot be accepted; Pilate will have known that Jesus had not appeared before the Great Sanhedrin, the only national tribunal. He may, however, have said: 'The Chief Priests of thine own nation . . .'

(*k*) It is impossible that the people of Jerusalem either howled for Jesus's blood or proclaimed themselves friends of Caesar's; that an angry mob was permitted to assemble outside the Praetorium; or that the Chief Priests were actively concerned with the Crucifixion. The *Annals* of Tacitus (xv. 44), which have escaped Christian interpolation, contain this brief record:

> 'Christus, the founder of the sect, was put to death by Pontius Pilate, the procurator of Judaea, in the reign of Tiberius.'

In so far as Pilate approved the sentence and carried it out, this statement is correct; but it must have been Herod Antipas who condemned Jesus.

(*l*) When the four accounts of the trial are compared, it is remarkable how little of the original tradition seems to be missing; the evangelists have been content merely to re-arrange and modify, not to invent. This explains why their fantastic narratives carry as much conviction as they do (*see Introduction* iii.*z*).

> (422) *But Jesus was led to judgement unto the place called Gabbatha, and it was yet early.*
>
> *And certain of the family of Annas came to accuse him before Pilate.*
>
> *Wherefore, when Pilate drew nigh, they delivered Jesus unto him but went not in, lest the people should say of them: 'They entered into Caesar's judgement hall and sware an oath by false gods.'*
>
> *And unto Pilate they said: 'Lest we defile ourselves for the Feast.'*
>
> *Then Pilate asked: 'What accusation bring ye against this man?'*
>
> *And they began to accuse Jesus, saying: 'We found this fellow perverting the nation and saying that he is the Son of God; he hath also ridden into the city upon an ass.'*
>
> *Pilate answered and said: 'Am I a Jew? If he hath transgressed against your religion, let him be judged according to your Law.'*

They say: 'Lord, if he were not a malefactor, we would not have delivered him unto thee.

'But he that calleth himself the Son of God, the same proclaimeth himself the King and Deliverer of Israel which must ride into Jerusalem upon an ass,

'And whosoever maketh himself King, the same speaketh against Caesar.

'Likewise hath he preached in the Temple, forbidding the people to pay tribute unto Caesar.'

* * * * *

They could not, however, report either that Jesus had interfered with the Temple administration—because that was a religious offence; or that his disciple Peter had been arrested for bearing arms—because the Priestly Council had let him off with a flogging.

(423) *And Pilate spake scornfully: 'What would ye then that I should do unto your King?'*

They answered and said: 'Lord, we have no King but Caesar. Take thou him and do what seemeth good unto thee. For the whole city is witness to his offences.'

Thus did they deliver Jesus unto Pilate to be judged.

* * * * *

(*m*) Here follows a fragment of *John* xviii. 28:

(424) *Then they departed every man, that they might make ready to eat the Passover.*

* * * * *

(*n*) After their departure, Pilate had to rely on evidence supplied by the Captain of the Temple or by Jesus's Levite escort. Jesus's single question to Pilate shows that he could not yet bring himself to believe that the Priestly Council, which included Bunni and his supporters, had dared to transfer the case, with a summary of evidence, to a Roman court.

(425) *And Pilate went in, and sat on the judgement seat, and when Jesus was brought before him, he asked: 'Art thou the King of the Jews?'*

Jesus answered: 'Sayest thou this of thine own knowledge or did others tell it thee?'

Pilate saith: 'The Chief Priests of thine own nation have delivered thee unto me. Tell me therefore: art thou the King of the Jews?'

Jesus answered: 'So thou sayest.'

And Pilate marvelled at his stubbornness.

Then the Captain of the Temple, which stood by, bare witness and said: 'This mad fellow stirreth up the people, teaching through all Jewry, beginning from Galilee unto this place.'

Pilate, when he heard of Galilee, asked whether the man were a Galilean,

And when he knew that Jesus belonged to Herod's jurisdiction, he sent him to Herod to be judged by him.

For he would provoke the people to complain against Herod rather than against himself.

Now, Herod was at Jerusalem in this time, dwelling in a mansion of the palace where Pilate also was.

* * * * *

(426) *Wherefore, when Herod saw Jesus brought before him, he was exceeding glad, being desirous of a long season to put him to death.*

And he questioned Jesus with many words, but Jesus made no answer, though men stood and vehemently accused him.

Now, Herod lacked authority to condemn a Galilean for any crime which he had committed in Judaea.

Nevertheless, he found Jesus guilty of death, as having followed in the way of John the Baptist and stirred up the people at Beth-Nimrah.

And he sent him unto Pilate again, saying: 'I pray thee, have him crucified.'

Pilate therefore, when he had commanded Jesus to be scourged in the common hall, delivered him to be crucified. And it was the preparation of the Passover, about the sixth hour.

* * * * *

(*o*) [Here follows *John* xix. 19–22, the dispute about the wording of the *titulus* (*see* cxi.*c–d*).]

* * * * *

(429) *And it came to pass that on this day Pilate and Herod were made friends together.*

These twain had long been at enmity between themselves, because of the image of Caesar which the soldiers of Pilate had brought into Jerusalem.

For Herod had joined himself with them that raised their voices against this desecration of the City of God.

* * * * *

THE SUPERSCRIPTION

Mark xv. 26

[26]And the superscription of His accusation was written over, THE KING OF THE JEWS.

Matthew xxvii. 37

[37]And set up over His head His accusation written, THIS IS JESUS THE KING OF THE JEWS.

Luke xxiii. 38

[38]And a superscription was also written over Him in letters of Greek, and Latin, and Hebrew,

THIS IS THE KING OF THE JEWS.

John xix. 19–22

[19]And Pilate wrote a title, and put it on the cross. And the writing was:

JESUS OF NAZARETH THE KING OF THE JEWS.

[20]This title then read many of the Jews: for the place where Jesus was crucified was nigh to the city: and it was written in Hebrew, Greek, and Latin. [21]Then said the chief priests of the Jews to Pilate: 'Write not, The King of the Jews; but that He said, I am King of the Jews.' [22]Pilate answered: 'What I have written I have written.'

(a) *John* xix. 22: 'What I have written I have written', is one of the few remarks ascribed to Pilate that correspond with King Agrippa's account of his 'obstinate and inflexible' character (*see* cx.c). Yet it is inconceivable that he composed the *titulus,* or 'superscription', in so odd a way. This was a statement of the crime for which a felon had been condemned, and Roman law required that it should be hung around his neck and subsequently affixed to the cross. If Pilate meant his statement to be taken seriously, he was himself committing treason; but if he meant it as a contemptuous joke, why had he pronounced Jesus innocent?

It is equally inconceivable that Jews who were hurrying to keep the Passover at Jerusalem—there can have been no outward-bound traffic—and happened to pass by Golgotha, would have called at Pilate's headquarters to complain that the superscription, far from being an accusation, was an assertion of Jesus's innocence.

(*b*) If, therefore, John's account is not wholly fictitious, the words for which Pilate was requested to substitute: 'He claimed to be King of the Jews', must have been altogether different from: 'This is the King of the Jews', and the request will have been made before the crucifixion party set off. The evangelists' version is a clumsy attempt to show that the Jews, not the Romans, were responsible for Jesus's crucifixion and that Pilate persisted in his minority verdict to the end.

(*c*) Pilate had transferred the case to Herod Antipas, who thereupon condemned Jesus to death. *Luke* xxiii. 15, Pilate's alleged statement that Antipas had found Jesus innocent, must be rejected; if only because it is absent from the other accounts. However, since Antipas was competent to try crimes committed only in his tetrarchy, he could not charge Jesus with lese-majesty—an offence for which Pilate himself should have indicted him on the evidence of the Captain of the Temple—but merely with having preached against the Herodian régime in Peraea and Galilee; and it must have been for this crime that he was sent to the Cross. It was now Pilate's duty to confirm the sentence and provide the superscription, namely: 'SEDITION: to wit, fomenting disaffection against Prince Herod Antipas, Caesar's ally'. But Antipas will have begged him to substitute the graver charge of: 'LESE-MAJESTY: to wit, proclaiming himself King of the Jews without Caesar's consent.'

(*d*) Pilate proved obdurate, since his main object in waiving the charge of lese-majesty had been to lay the odium of Jesus's condemnation on Antipas. He must also have known that it is prudent to lessen the force of popular indignation by trying a rebel on a minor, rather than a major, charge.

> (427) *And Pilate wrote an accusation in Latin, which should be hanged about the neck of Jesus and should afterward be set upon the cross.*
>
> *And the writing was:* 'Sedition: this is Jesus the Galilean which by his preaching hath offended against Herod Antipas his lord, Caesar's friend.'
>
> *Then said Herod:* 'I pray thee, write rather: "Treason: this is Jesus the Galilean which hath offended against Caesar, saying: 'I am the King of the Jews.'"'
>
> *Pilate answered:* 'What I have written I have written.'

*   *   *   *   *

(*e*) Antipas's reaction is perhaps concealed in *Mark* xii. 34 (*see* LXXXII.*p*):

> (428) *And Herod durst ask him nothing more.*

*   *   *   *   *

(*f*) Thus, though it has long pleased Christians to believe that Jesus was condemned to death by the Jews for proclaiming himself God, and though recent scholars have assumed that the Romans condemned him for treasonably proclaiming himself King, the truth seems to be that he was the chance victim of a woman's political ambitions and condemned to death because he had publicly insulted her.

Herodias, wife of Herod the Great's exiled son Herod Philip, had agreed to marry Herod Antipas, her brother-in-law, in defiance of the Mosaic Law; but apparently stipulated that he must first divorce his present queen—though Antipas was legally entitled to several wives. This queen was a daughter of King Aretas IV of Nabataea, whose kingdom marched with Antipas's province of Peraea; and Aretas, grossly offended, threatened war. When John the Baptist denounced the marriage to the crowds which came to be baptized at Beth-Nimrah in Peraea, Herodias not only felt personally affronted but feared that John's preaching would cause disaffection and expose the province to Aretas's inroads. He was arrested and beheaded at her insistence (*see* xli.*a–b and* lxxvi.*a–b*). This tradition has been preserved only in the apocryphal *Gospel of Peter* (about 140 A.D.), which makes Herod the King—and inevitably the Jewish people—responsible for his death.

(*g*) Jesus had then preached and baptized in the same place and in the same style—he also held strict views on divorce (*see* xxi.*c*)—until Antipas asked: 'Is this John returned from the dead?' (*see* lxxvii.*f*), and decided to silence him too (*see* lxxxiv.*a and* xcvii.*h*). But Jesus had been warned in time by the Pharisees and managed to evade arrest. As events proved, Antipas and Herodias had not underestimated the political effect of this preaching: Josephus relates that when King Aretas finally struck, Antipas's Transjordanian troops fled and he suffered a decisive defeat (*see* lxxxvi.*b*).

* * * * *

THE DEATH OF JUDAS

Matthew xxvii. 3–10

³Then Judas, which had betrayed Him, when he saw that He was condemned, repented himself, and brought again the thirty pieces of silver to the chief priests and elders, ⁴saying: 'I have sinned in that I have betrayed the innocent blood.' And they said: 'What is that to us? see thou to that.' ⁵And he cast down the pieces of silver in the temple, and departed, and went and hanged himself. ⁶And the chief priests took the silver pieces, and said, 'It is not lawful for to put them into the treasury, because it is the price of blood.' ⁷And they took counsel, and bought with them the potter's field, to bury strangers in. ⁸Wherefore that field was called, 'The field of blood,' unto this day. ⁹Then was fulfilled that which was spoken by Jeremiah the prophet, saying,

> *And they took the thirty pieces of silver (the price of Him that was valued; Whom they of the children of Israel did value)* ¹⁰*and gave them for the potter's field, as the Lord appointed me.*

Acts i. 15–26

¹⁵And in those days Peter stood up in the midst of the disciples, and said, (the number of names together were about an hundred and twenty): ¹⁶'Men and brethren, this scripture must needs have been fulfilled, which the Holy Ghost by the mouth of David spake before concerning Judas, which was guide to them that took Jesus. ¹⁷For he was numbered with us, and had obtained part of this ministry. ¹⁸Now this man purchased a field with the reward of iniquity; and falling headlong, he burst asunder in the midst, and all his bowels gushed out. ¹⁹And it was known unto all the dwellers at Jerusalem; insomuch as that field is called in their proper tongue, *Aceldama,* that is to say, The field of blood. ²⁰For it is written in the book of Psalms:

> *Let his habitation be desolate,*
> *And let no man dwell therein:*

And

> *His bishopric let another take.*

²¹Wherefore of these men which have companied with us all the time that the Lord Jesus went in and out among us, ²²beginning from the baptism of John, unto that same day that He was taken up from us, must one be ordained to be a witness with us of His resurrection.' ²³And they appointed two, Joseph called Barsabas, who was surnamed Justus, and Matthias. ²⁴And they prayed,

Acts i. 15–26 (contd.)

and said: 'Thou Lord, Who knowest the hearts of all men, shew whether of these two Thou hast chosen, ²⁵that he may take part of this ministry and apostleship, from which Judas by transgression fell, that he might go to his own place.' ²⁶And they gave forth their lots; and the lot fell upon Matthias; and he was numbered with the eleven Apostles.

(a) The account of Judas's death in *Acts* i. 15–25 differs greatly from that in *Matthew* xxvii. 3–10. According to *Matthew,* Judas realized his mistake as soon as Jesus had been handed over to the Romans, and unsuccessfully tried to undo it. He offered to return the thirty pieces of silver, and when they were refused by the 'Catholics' (*see* cix.*i*), 'cast them to the potter' in fulfilment of *Zechariah's* prophecy (*see* cii.*c*), went away and hanged himself. The Catholics then decided that the money, being the price of a man's blood, might neither go to the Treasury nor be laid out on any Israelite charity; they therefore used it to buy a field in which to bury Gentiles.

This account, though attributing the *Zechariah* prophecy to *Jeremiah,* and also misquoting it, is historically acceptable. It had never been Judas's intention to hand Jesus over to the Romans; he merely wanted him placed in protective custody (*see* cv.*f*). The decision to buy the field was probably forced upon the Catholics by Bunni and his supporters. What might be accepted by the Treasury, and what might not, was a vexed subject: the Pharisees frequently protested against Sadducaic laxity (*see* liii.*c*).

(b) According to *Acts* i. 15–25, Judas himself unrepentantly used the blood-money to buy a field, but was struck down by God when he visited it and burst into pieces. The source of this fabulous misadventure is the *Book of Ahikar* (*see* xviii.*b*), the Arabic version of which describes Nadan's well-deserved death (*Ahikar* viii. 38) as follows:

'And when Nadan heard that speech . . . he swelled up immediately and became like unto a blown-out bladder. And his limbs swelled up and his legs and his feet and his side, and he was torn and his belly burst asunder and his entrails were scattered, and he perished and died.'

(c) It may be argued against *Matthew's* account that no devout Jew of that period would have hanged himself, since suicide in any form was strictly forbidden by the Law, and hanging carried with it a special Deuteronomic curse (*see Introduction* ii.*u*). But Judas had read the Scriptures and evidently decided to punish himself in a manner befitting his crime; he will have remembered 2 *Samuel* xvii. 23, the closest Biblical parallel, where Achitophel hangs himself after he has betrayed the Lord's Anointed and the elders of Israel have rejected him.

Aceldama is translated in *Acts* i. 19 as 'the field of blood', and substantiated by the story of the burst stomach. But *hakel demākh,* the nearest verbal equivalent in Aramaic, does not mean 'the field of blood'; it means either 'the field of *thy* blood' or (as Klostermann argues in his *Probleme in den*

Aposteltexten 1–8) 'the field of sleep', i.e. 'the cemetery', which substantiates *Matthew's* account of how the Chief Priests used the money. Fourth-century tradition places the site of 'Aceldama' on the plateau above the Valley of the Hinnon ('Gehenna'), near the north-eastern slope of the Hill of Evil Counsel. This tradition seems based on *Jeremiah* xviii.–xix., where the potter's house is mentioned as being in that neighbourhood. Christian pilgrims were buried in the cemetery from at least the sixth century onwards.

The attribution of *Zechariah's* prophecy to *Jeremiah* is probably due to the telescoping of two texts, namely *Zechariah* xi. 13 and *Jeremiah* xviii. 1–4; the latter will have been quoted by Peter, after Judas's death, as authority for bringing the company of Twelve, one apostle for each tribe (*see* LVI.*f*), up to strength again. His quotations from *Psalms* lxix. 35 and cix. 8 are directed against living enemies, presumably the Priestly Council.

(*d*) 'Joseph Barsabas' in *Acts* i. 23, is probably 'Joseph bar Sabbath', 'the son of the Sabbath', i.e. he lived as holy a life on week-days as on the Sabbath; and 'surnamed the Just' shows that he was a Watcher. He may have been James the Just's brother 'Joses', Mary of Cleophas's son (*see* LVI.*f*).

(430) *Now Judas, when he saw that Jesus was delivered to be crucified, was exceeding troubled; for he had not thought to betray him to death, but contrariwise, to save him.*

Wherefore he brought the thirty pieces of silver again unto the two Catholics, which were set up over the Treasury, saying: 'I have sinned in that I betrayed innocent blood.'

They answered: 'What is that to us? See thou to that.'

And they would not take the money.

Then Judas said unto them: 'It is written: "And the Lord said unto me: 'Cast it unto the potter, a goodly price that I was prized at of them.'

'"And I took the thirty pieces of silver and cast them to the potter in the house of the Lord."'

Wherefore Judas went and cast the money unto the potter which made vessels for the Temple, and departed from the city.

For he remembered how Achitophel had made rebellion against his anointed King, and had sought to take him by night when he was weary and weakhanded; and how the rulers of Israel afterward treated Achitophel with despite.

As it is written: 'And when Achitophel saw that his counsel was not followed, he saddled his ass and arose and gat him home to his house to his own city, and put his household in order, and hanged himself and died, and was buried in the sepulchre of his fathers.'

Judas therefore did likewise, returning to his own city of Kerioth, and there he hanged himself and died.

But the potter brought the thirty pieces of silver unto the Catholics again, which durst not put them into the Treasury to spend them upon any work whereby Israelites might be profited.

For Nakemidam and the Pharisees said: 'It is the price of innocent blood.'

Therefore, they took counsel and bought a field, which was called The

Potter's Field, nigh unto the Valley of the Sons of Hinnon, to bury Gentiles in that had no kindred.

That field is now called Hakeldemach, which is The Field of Sleep.

* * * * *

(*e*) The following (*see* (*c*) *above*) occurred after the resurrection and departure of Jesus:

(466) *And it came to pass afterward, that Peter, when he heard what the Chief Priests had done with the money which Judas received of them, stood up in the midst of the disciples (the number of names together were about an hundred and twenty) and said:*

'That field which they have bought with the thirty pieces whereof Zechariah prophesied, behold, the same is the very field wherein Jeremiah stood and prophesied of the Last Days.

'As it is written: "Then went I down to the potter's house and, behold, he wrought a work on his wheels; and the vessel that he made of clay was marred in his hand, so he made it again, another vessel as seemed good to the potter to make it."

'Wherefore, seeing that our Master chose us out to be Twelve, one for each of the tribes of Israel, let us now renew our number and make another vessel in the place of that which was marred.

'Yet not us but the Lord, for He alone is the potter!

'And as touching the Chief Priests, let it be unto them even as David prayeth in his Psalms:

' "Seeing that they compassed me about with words of hatred and fought against me without a cause.

' "Set thou, O Lord, a wicked man over them, let each man's days be but few, and let another take his office;

' "Pour out Thy wrath upon them, that their habitation be desolate!" '

And when it seemed good unto them what Peter said, they appointed two: Joseph called the Son of the Sabbath, the Watcher; and Matthias.

And they prayed: 'Thou O Lord, which knowest the hearts of all, shew whether of these twain Thou hast chosen, that he may take part of this ministry and apostleship from which Judas by transgression fell, and that he may go into the place that is left open!'

And they gave forth their lots, and the lot fell upon Matthias; and he was numbered among the Twelve.

* * * *

THE CRUCIFIXION

Mark xv. 20b–41

20bAnd they led Him out to crucify Him. 21And they compel one Simon a Cyrenian, who passed by, coming out of the country, the father of Alexander and Rufus, to bear His cross. 22And they bring Him unto the place Golgotha, which is, being interpreted, The place of a skull. 23And they gave Him to drink wine mingled with myrrh: but He received it not. 24And when they had crucified Him, they parted His garments, casting lots upon them, what every man should take. 25And it was the third hour, and they crucified Him. 26And the superscription of His accusation was written over, THE KING OF THE JEWS. 27And with Him they crucify two thieves; the one on His right hand, and the other on His left. 28And the scripture was fulfilled, which saith:

And he was numbered with the transgressors.

29And they that passed by railed on Him, wagging their heads, and saying: 'Ah, Thou that destroyest the temple, and buildest it in three days, 30save Thyself, and come down from the cross.' 31Likewise also the chief priests mocking said among themselves with the scribes: 'He saved others; Himself He cannot save. 32Let Christ the King of Israel descend now from the cross, that we may see and believe.' And they that were crucified with Him reviled Him.

33And when the sixth hour was come, there was darkness over the whole land until the ninth hour. 34And at the ninth hour Jesus cried with a loud voice, saying:

Eloi, Eloi, lama sabachthani?

which is, being interpreted, My God, My God, why hast Thou forsaken Me? 35And some of them that stood by, when they heard it, said: 'Behold, He calleth Elijah.' 36And one ran and filled a spunge full of vinegar, and put it on a reed, and gave Him to drink, saying: 'Let alone; let us see whether Elijah will come to take Him down.' 37And Jesus cried with a loud voice, and gave up the ghost. 38And the veil of the temple was rent in twain from the top to the bottom. 39And when the centurion, which stood over against Him, saw that He so cried out, and gave up the ghost, he said: 'Truly this man was the Son of God.' 40There were also women looking on afar off: among whom was Mary Magdalene, and Mary the mother of James the less and of Joses, and Salome; 41(who also when He was in Galilee, followed Him, and ministered unto Him;) and many other women which came up with Him unto Jerusalem.

Matthew xxvii. 32–56

³²And as they came out, they found a man of Cyrene, Simon by name: him they compelled to bear His cross. ³³And when they were come unto a place called Golgotha, that is to say, 'a place of a skull', ³⁴they gave Him vinegar to drink mingled with gall: and when He had tasted thereof, He would not drink. ³⁵And they crucified Him, and parted His garments, casting lots: that it might be fulfilled which was spoken by the prophet:

> They parted My garments among them,
> And upon My vesture did they cast lots.

³⁶And sitting down they watched Him there; ³⁷and set up over His head His accusation written, THIS IS JESUS THE KING OF THE JEWS. ³⁸Then were there two thieves crucified with Him, one on the right hand, and another on the left. ³⁹And they that passed by reviled Him, wagging their heads, ⁴⁰and saying: 'Thou that destroyeth the temple, and buildest it in three days, save Thyself. If Thou be the Son of God, come down from the cross.' ⁴¹Likewise also the chief priests mocking Him, with the scribes and elders, said: ⁴²'He saved others; Himself He cannot save. If He be the King of Israel, let Him now come down from the cross, and we will believe Him. ⁴³He trusted in God; let Him deliver Him now, if He will have Him: for He said, I am the Son of God.' ⁴⁴The thieves also, which were crucified with Him, cast the same in His teeth.

⁴⁵Now from the sixth hour there was darkness over all the land unto the ninth hour. ⁴⁶And about the ninth hour Jesus cried with a loud voice, saying,

> ELI, ELI, LAMA SABACHTHANI?

that is to say,

> My God, My God, why hast Thou forsaken Me?

⁴⁷Some of them that stood there, when they heard that, said: 'This man calleth for Elijah.' ⁴⁸And straightway one of them ran, and took a spunge, and filled it with vinegar, and put it on a reed, and gave Him to drink. ⁴⁹The rest said: 'Let be, let us see whether Elijah will come to save Him.' ⁵⁰Jesus, when He had cried again with a loud voice, yielded up the ghost. ⁵¹And, behold, the veil of the temple was rent in twain from the top to the bottom; and the earth did quake, and the rocks rent; ⁵²and the graves were opened; and many bodies of the saints which slept arose, ⁵³and came out of the graves after His resurrection, and went into the holy city, and appeared unto many. ⁵⁴Now when the centurion, and they that were with him, watching Jesus, saw the earthquake, and those things that were done, they feared greatly, saying: 'Truly this was the Son of God.' ⁵⁵And many women were there beholding afar off, which followed Jesus from Galilee, ministering unto Him: ⁵⁶among which was Mary Magdalene, and Mary the mother of James and Joses, and the mother of Zebedee's children.

Luke xxiii. 26–49

²⁶And as they led Him away, they laid hold upon one Simon, a Cyrenian, coming out of the country, and on him they laid the cross, that he might bear it after Jesus. ²⁷And there followed Him a great company of people, and of

Luke xxiii. 26–49 (*contd.*)

women, which also bewailed and lamented Him. [28]But Jesus turning unto them said: 'Daughters of Jerusalem, weep not for Me, but weep for yourselves, and for your children. [29]For, behold, the days are coming, in the which they shall say, Blessed are the barren, and the wombs that never bare, and the paps which never gave suck. [30]Then shall they begin to say to the mountains, Fall on us; and to the hills, Cover us. [31]For if they do these things in a green tree, what shall be done in the dry?' [32]And there were also two other, malefactors, led with Him to be put to death.

[33]And when they were come to the place, which is called Calvary, there they crucified Him, and the malefactors, one on the right hand, and the other on the left. [34]Then said Jesus: 'Father, forgive them; for they know not what they do.' And they parted His raiment, and cast lots. [35]And the people stood beholding. And the rulers also with them derided Him, saying: 'He saved others; let Him save Himself, if He be Christ, the chosen of God.' [36]And the soldiers also mocked Him, coming to Him, and offering Him vinegar, [37]and saying: 'If Thou be the king of the Jews, save Thyself.' [38]And a superscription was also written over Him in letters of Greek, and Latin, and Hebrew,

THIS IS THE KING OF THE JEWS.

[39]And one of the malefactors which were hanged railed on Him, saying: 'If Thou be Christ, save Thyself and us.' [40]But the other answering rebuked him, saying: 'Dost not thou fear God, seeing thou art in the same condemnation? [41]And we indeed justly; for we receive the due reward of our deeds: but this man hath done nothing amiss.' [42]And he said unto Jesus: 'Lord, remember me when Thou comest into Thy kingdom.' [43]And Jesus said unto him: 'Verily I say unto thee, today shalt thou be with Me in paradise.' [44]And it was about the sixth hour, and there was a darkness over all the earth until the ninth hour. [45]And the sun was darkened, and the veil of the temple was rent in the midst. [46]And when Jesus had cried with a loud voice, He said: 'Father, into Thy hands I commend My spirit.' And having said thus, He gave up the ghost. [47]Now when the centurion saw what was done, he glorified God, saying: 'Certainly this was a righteous man.' [48]And all the people that came together to that sight, beholding the things which were done, smote their breasts, and returned. [49]And all His acquaintance, and the women that followed Him from Galilee, stood afar off, beholding these things.

John xix. 17–37

[17]And He bearing His cross went forth into a place called the place of a skull, which is called in the Hebrew Golgotha; [18]where they crucified Him, and two other with Him, on either side one, and Jesus in the midst. [19]And Pilate wrote a title, and put it on the cross. And the writing was:

JESUS OF NAZARETH THE KING OF THE JEWS.

[20]This title then read many of the Jews: for the place where Jesus was crucified was nigh to the city: and it was written in Hebrew, Greek, and Latin. [21]Then said the chief priests of the Jews to Pilate: 'Write not, The King of the Jews; but that He said, I am King of the Jews.' [22]Pilate answered: 'What I have written I have written.'

John xix. 17–37 (*contd.*)

[23]Then the soldiers, when they had crucified Jesus, took His garments, and made four parts, to every soldier a part; and also His coat: now the coat was without seam, woven from the top throughout. [24]They said therefore among themselves: 'Let us not rend it, but cast lots for it, whose it shall be:' that the scripture might be fulfilled, which saith:

> They parted My raiment among them,
> And for My vesture they did cast lots.

These things therefore the soldiers did. [25]Now there stood by the cross of Jesus His mother, and His mother's sister, Mary the wife of Cleophas, and Mary Magdalene. [26]When Jesus therefore saw His mother, and the disciple standing by, whom He loved, He saith unto His mother: 'Woman, behold thy son!' [27]Then saith He to the disciple: 'Behold thy mother!' And from that hour that disciple took her unto his own home.

[28]After this, Jesus knowing that all things were now accomplished, that the scripture might be fulfilled, saith: 'I thirst.' [29]Now there was set a vessel full of vinegar: and they filled a spunge with vinegar, and put it upon hyssop, and put it to His mouth. [30]When Jesus therefore had received the vinegar, He said: 'It is finished.' And He bowed His head, and gave up the ghost.

[31]The Jews therefore, because it was the preparation, that the bodies should not remain upon the cross on the sabbath day, (for that sabbath day was an high day,) besought Pilate that their legs might be broken, and that they might be taken away. [32]Then came the soldiers, and brake the legs of the first, and of the other which was crucified with Him. [33]But when they came to Jesus, and saw that He was dead already, they brake not his legs: [34]but one of the soldiers with a spear pierced His side, and forthwith came there out blood and water. [35]And he that saw it bare record, and his record is true: and he knoweth that he saith true, that ye might believe. [36]For these things were done, that the scripture should be fulfilled:

> A bone of Him shall not be broken.

[37]And again another scripture saith:

> They shall look on Him Whom they pierced.

Hebrews xiii. 12

[12]Wherefore Jesus also, that He might sanctify the people with His own blood, suffered without the gate.

Jerome: On Matthew xxvii. 51

In the *Gospel* [*according to the Hebrews*] I so often mention, we read that a lintel of the Temple of immense size was broken and divided.

Jerome: Letter to Hedibia (epistle 120) 8

But in the Gospel that is written in Hebrew letters we read, not that the veil of the Temple was rent but that a lintel of the Temple, of wondrous size, fell.

(*a*) Since there is no reason to suppose that the technique of crucifixion was modified in Jesus's case, the Gospel accounts can be checked against Classical references to other crucifixions. Because of *Deuteronomy* xxi. 23: 'He that is hanged is accursed of God', the Romans favoured it as a deterrent to Galilean Zealotry. In 1 *Corinthians* i. 23, Paul describes this Deuteronomic curse as 'a stumbling-block to the Jews', and in *Galatians* iii. 13 quotes it to prove that Jesus released the world from the curse of the Mosaic Law by being hanged and yet achieving salvation. Paul must have been aware, however, that this curse was relevant only if the victim were justly condemned, as Jesus was not.

(*b*) The Deuteronomic curse had been inserted in the Law, either shortly before or during the Exile, to discourage Israelites from offering tree-sacrifices to 'the Lord' Tammuz. 2 *Samuel* xxi. 6 records such a sacrifice of seven royal youths, offered with David's consent at Gibeah, where their father Saul had 'tarried under a pomegranate tree' sacred to Tammuz (1 *Samuel* xiv. 2). *Deuteronomy* contains a number of similar prohibitions against Canaanite religious practices: for instance, ritual prostitution and ritual sodomy, the sacramental eating of a kid seethed in its mother's milk, and tonsures worn by priests in honour of Tammuz.

(*c*) Crucifixion began as a religious rite and was imported as such from Palestine to Carthage in the eighth century B.C. Originally the victim had been the Sacred King himself, the divine incarnation of Tammuz, god of the sacred grove (*see The Golden Bough, passim*), whose blood was symbolized by the red juice of the pomegranate. Later, the King provided substitute victims, first from the royal family, next from royal enemies captured in battle (*Joshua* viii. 29 and x. 26), and finally from rebels and felons. By the time of the Punic Wars, when the Romans borrowed the practice from the 'Canaanites', as the Carthaginians preferred to be known, it had ceased to be a rite and was now a degrading form of execution; they reserved it for the most obdurate criminals and, until some centuries later, inflicted it on no Roman citizen, however heinous his offence (Cicero: *In Verrem* i. 5 and v. 61–64).

(*d*) The cross of Christian baptism, identical with that marked on the brow of an anointed Hebrew prophet, is historically connected with the Cross on which Jesus suffered. In ancient Palestine, royal personages seem to have had a T branded on their foreheads as a sign of their eligibility for crucifixion; and the mark of Cain in *Genesis* iv. 15—the subject of an improving anecdote to discredit ritual murder—is this very mark. 'Cain' was the eponymous ancestor of the Kenites, or Canaanites, his name in Phoenician legend being 'Chnas' and in Greek, 'Agenor'. 'Abel', the name of Cain's victim, was derived by the Massoretic editors of the Pentateuch from 'Hebel' ('vanity'), evidently a cacophemism for 'Tammuz', the lamenting of whose annual death was the greatest religious event of the Canaanite year; but etymologists now derive it from *ablu* ('son'), an abridgement of one of Tammuz's titles. The Canaanite (i.e. Phoenician) character *tav,* or 'T', used in the archaic Hebrew alphabet, had the same shape as the Christian cross, and represented the *crux ansata* of Osiris, the looped cross which was the Egyptian symbol of immortality. Osiris worship had been brought in pre-Dynastic times from Phoenicia—where Osiris was a tree-Tammuz—to Egypt where he became a god of corn. The *tav,* then, was the initial of Tammuz, and the traditional 'mourning for Tammuz' forbidden by the prophets (*Ezeziel* viii. 14) continued, under thin disguise, in the annual four-day lamentation for Jephthah's daughter (*Judges* xi. 40).

(*e*) These mythological origins would be irrelevant here, were it not for *Ezekiel* ix. 4–6, where the letter *tav* is branded on the foreheads of the elect in Jerusalem to *spare* them from slaughter; because Adonai ('Lord'), which is a form of 'Tammuz' (Greek: *Adonis*), was one of Jehovah's titles. A reminiscence of this branding occurs in *Revelation* vii. 3–8: 144,000 servants of God, twelve thousand from each tribe of Israel, are 'sealed' upon their brows. Thus in *Mark* viii. 34 and *Matthew* x. 38, where Jesus orders the disciples to take up their cross, two texts seem to have been run together: an injunction to take up the burden of saintliness, and an unjunction to be marked with the *tav* sign and so be spared in the Last Days as God's elect (*see* cɪ.*a*). Since *Leviticus* xxi. 5 prohibited 'cuttings in the flesh', that is to say tattoo marks, the Pharisees used phylacteries, tied to their foreheads, which displayed the name *Adonai* (*Matthew* xxiii. 5—*see* xɪɪɪ.*k*); but Jesus, like John the Baptist, seems to have held that a *tav* marked with water, though invisible to man, would be discerned by God.

(*f*) Thus, though Jesus had expected to die by the sword, the uncanny aptness of his punishment on the Cross, in atonement for the sins of Israel, was seized upon by the Nazarenes as justifying his Messianic claims. Moreover, among Paul's Syrian-Greek converts the connexion between the cross and the letter *tav*—*tau* in Greek—was well known: Lucian mentions it in his *Trial in the Court of Vowels.*

> 'Men weep and bewail their lot and curse Cadmus with many curses for introducing *tau* into the family of letters; they say it was his body that tyrants took for a model, his shape they imitated when they set up the erections on which men are crucified. *Stauros* the vile engine is called and it derives its vile name from him.'

Psalm xxii, which Jesus quoted from the Cross, refers in verses 12–18 to a Jew crucified by hostile 'dogs' (i.e. 'sodomites'—*see* xxxvɪ.*h*). Evidently the crucifixion ritual had not changed for many hundreds of years, and Roman practice was almost identical with that current in Canaan itself long before the arrival of Pompey; which made the psalm seem wonderfully prophetic.*

(*g*) The Roman cross in use during Tiberius's reign consisted of an upright stake, permanently fastened to a tree or planted in a socket, and a cross-piece—a baulk of timber about nine feet long but of no great weight—which

---

* *Psalm* xxii, though ascribed by the Pharisees to David himself, is a poetic record of the persecutions which provoked the Maccabean revolt: Jason the High Priest crucified devout Jews who refused to Hellenize (*see* xcvɪ.*b* and cɪɪ.*g*).

the victim himself carried to the place of execution. A notch near the top of the stake allowed the cross-piece to engage in it and be securely fixed (Horace: *Carmina* i. 35 and Cicero: *In Verrem* v. 21). A peg was then inserted in the stake, about four feet from the ground, to support the victim's crotch; thus his weight would not wholly fall on the arms and feet (Irenaeus: *Heresies* ii. 24; Justin: *Dialogue* xci. and Tertullian: *Against Marcion* iii. 18). (*h*) The condemned was first scourged with a *flagrum*, a multiple chain-whip with a stud at the end of each lash (Valerius Maximus: *Book* i. 16 and Livy: *History* xxxiii. 36); this was a relic of the ritual flagellation intended to fructify the soil with the blood and sperm of Tammuz's representative. He was then led, bearing his cross-piece (Plutarch: *De Sera Numinis Vindicata* ix. and Artemidorus: *Book* ii. 56) along a public highway to an eminence beyond the city gates (Cicero: *In Verrem* 66 and Plautus: *Miles Gloriosus* 2. iv. 6). Ahead went a herald carrying the *titulus,* unless the condemned wore it around his neck (Suetonius: *Caligula* 32 and *Domitianus* 10; Dio Cassius: *History* liv. 3). At the place of execution, where the stake was already fixed (Cicero: *In Verrem* v. 66 and Polybius: *Book* i. lxxxvi. 6), he was stripped naked and laid supine, his neck against the cross-piece, the peg against his crotch. His arms were then fastened to the cross-piece with cords (Pliny: *Natural History* 28. iv. 11), and a nail was driven through each palm, fixing his hands to the wood (Lucan: *Pharsalia* vi. 543); this could be done without either piercing an artery or damaging bones or tendons. The cross-piece was then hoisted up the stake by means of a pulley (Pliny: *Natural History* 29. iv. 57), until it engaged in the notch. Two more nails, driven through the victim's feet just behind the Achilles tendon, secured them to the sides of the stake (Plautus: *Mostellaria* 2. i. 13). These nails, again, would not injure a bone or tendon and, unless a projecting foot-stool were used, could be hammered in far more easily than through the instep.

(*i*) The cross was guarded by soldiers until the victim died; his body then remained hanging, if no relatives claimed it, until it decayed (Lucan: *Pharsalia* vi. 543 and Quinctilian: *Declamationes* vi. 9). Death was normally caused by exhaustion and pain (Eusebius: *Ecc. Hist.* 8. viii. 1 and Seneca: *Epistles* 101). Since the stronger victims lingered for three, or even five, days, their guards sometimes hastened the end with a *coup de grâce* (Origen: *On Matthew* xxvii. 54). The Canaanites, to judge from *Psalm* xxii. 20, despatched the victim with a sword when at his last gasp. *Scelocopia,* the breaking of legs, was no part of the crucifixion ritual, but a distinct form of punishment (Seneca: *De Ira* iii. 32); Augustus inflicted it on one of his freedmen who had divulged official secrets (Suetonius: *Augustus* 67).

(*j*) The only departure from normal practice in this case was that a passing Jew had to be forced to carry Jesus's cross-piece, because he could not do so himself (*Mark* xv. 20, *Matthew* xxvii. 32, and *Luke* xxiii. 26). This does not suggest that he was too weak to fulfil the requirements of Roman Law; if he had protested his inability, he would have been scourged again until he either carried the cross-piece or fainted. It suggests, rather, that being lame, as Talmudic tradition has it, he lost his balance as soon as he tried to walk with a weight on his shoulder (*see* xxxvii.*d*). That a stranger was called in, points to the absence of any male disciples capable of volunteering for the service. The author of *John,* feeling perhaps that Jesus should have carried his own cross, does not mention Simon of Cyrene (*John* xix. 17).

(*k*) Accounts of Jesus's last words differ greatly. According to *Mark* xv. 34 and *Matthew* xxvii. 46, he merely quoted *Psalm* xxii. and disregarded the two malefactors who reviled him. According to *Luke* xxiii. 34, he said: 'Father, forgive them, they know not what they do', and when the 'repentant thief' begged to be remembered in the Kingdom, assured him: 'Today shalt thou be with me in Paradise' (*Luke* xxiii. 43). Since God alone could decide a sinner's fate, this answer cannot be accepted: it is evidently an adaptation of words spoken by Jesus during the Last Supper (*see* cvi.*x*). In *Luke* xxiii. 46, he is credited with: 'Father, into Thy hands I commend my spirit', at a point where, in *Mark* xv. 37 and *Matthew* xxvii. 50, he merely utters a loud cry. According to *John* xix. 26–27, he committed the beloved disciple to the care of his mother—this incident, however, belongs to an altogether different context (*see* viii.*i*); and also said 'I thirst', but since he was forbidden to utter the least complaint in his torments (*Isaiah* liii. 7) this may have been said when he emerged from his tomb on the third day (*see* cxv.*g*). According to *John* xix. 30, his last words, after drinking the sour wine, were: 'It is finished'. But since in *Matthew* xxvii. 34 he refused to drink, this remark also seems to be out of context; it will have been spoken by the women when they saw him bow his head in physical collapse.

(*l*) It is probable that both malefactors reviled Jesus. One said mockingly: 'Remember me when thou comest into thy Kingdom'; and the other: 'If thou art the Saviour, give proof thereof by saving thyself and us.' Jesus made no answer, but prayed aloud that God might spare their souls the Deuteronomic curse, on the ground that they had not known what they did, and were condemned by an alien court; '*they* know not what they do' or 'knew not what they did' implies that he took the responsibility for their crimes upon himself. *Luke* xxiii. 33–34 makes it clear enough that his prayer was offered for these two; it certainly cannot have been for the Roman soldiers, who were ignorant of the Law and merely obeying orders.

The Synoptics' suggestion that the Chief Priests and Rulers attended the Crucifixion and mocked Jesus, is inacceptable. Those of the Priests who were not on Temple duty will have gone home to prepare the Passover. Perhaps, however, representatives of Herod Antipas were present, since the execution took place at his request. Being only nominal Jews, they will not have recognized '*Eloi, eloi, lama sabachthani?*' as the opening verse of *Psalm* xxii. in Aramaic, and may even have mocked him, as suggested by *Mark* xv. 29–32.

(*m*) It is possible also that they misheard Jesus's words as an appeal to Elijah. Elijah was already a character in Jewish folklore, though not yet credited—as after the destruction of the Temple—with such fanciful feats as, for instance, hurling a hostile witness four hundred leagues to save Eleazar ben Prata from his Roman judges (*Abodah Zarah* 17*b*). Since Elijah had never suffered death, he was liable to appear at any door, at any moment, usually in a time of crisis and often disguised as a peasant. At the *Seder,* an extra glass of wine was placed for him, and an extra chair at circumcision ceremonies (*Zohar, Lek Leka*); again, in the Great Sanhedrin of seventy-one members, difficult cases were sometimes adjourned 'until Elijah comes' (*Malachi* iv. 5-6)—Elijah would then bring the membership of the court up to the perfect seventy-two, the number of letters in God's longest name. According to *Pesikta Rabbati* 161*a* (ed. Friedmann):

> 'Three days before the coming of the Messiah, Elijah, standing upon the mountains of Israel, shall weep and wail, saying: "Alas for the land of Israel! How long will she stand barren and desolate . . . ?" '

(*n*) Jesus must have thought, at first, that the sponge, resting on a bunch of hyssop—wild caper—tied to the end of a rod, contained water; but when he found that it was sour wine, forbidden him as a king and prophet (*see* x.*d*), he refused it. The soldiers' offer of the sponge (*Luke* xxiii. 36) was kindly intended; a guild of pious women used to provide frankincense—not myrrh —as an anaesthetic for criminals on their way to the place of execution (*Sanhedrin* 43*a*). They seem also to have provided the wine, in accordance with *Proverbs* xxxi. 6: 'Give strong drink unto him that is ready to perish, and wine unto those that be of heavy hearts.'

If Jesus opened his mouth to cry, it will have been in exultation: he thought that the end of the world had come, because a cloud of red dust— still a common natural phenomenon in Palestine at this season—blown by a hot wind from the east or south-east, was blotting out the midday sun. Simultaneously, a mild earthquake shock may have been felt; both being recognized signs of the approaching End (*Joel* iii. 15-16—*see* LXXXVIII.*r and* XCVIII.*e, g, and k*).

Luke xxiii. 46: 'Father, into Thy hands I commend my spirit!' is an attempt to improve on *Matthew* xxvii. 46: 'My God, my God, why hast thou forsaken me?' which seemed too unfilial for quotation; and on *Matthew* xxvii. 50: 'He cried aloud and gave up the ghost', which seemed too bald. The words are found in the hymn *Adon Olam,* based on *Psalm* xxxi. 5, with which all Jewish prayers conclude and which, in an earlier form perhaps, was used in the first century. These would be the last words repeated by a pious man before falling asleep. The original tradition may have been that Jesus bowed his head *as though* saying his good-night prayer.

(*o*) The earthquake, mentioned in *Matthew* xxvii. 51 only, is there stated to have opened numerous tombs—by rolling back the circular sliding stones from their entrances. But if it had been of such strength, many buildings in Jerusalem would have collapsed, and no chronicler reports such a catastrophe.

The author of *Matthew* xxvii. 52–53, by stating that ghosts were subsequently seen in the streets of Jerusalem, suggests that this was the prophesied Resurrection of the Just (*see* LXXXVIII.*g–h*); but the proper context for the earthquake is the Pentecost narrative (*see* CXVIII.*a*). The report that the shock tore the Sanctuary curtain in half (*Mark* xv. 38 and *Matthew* xxvii. 51) as Jesus yielded up the ghost, is due to an editorial confusion. This curtain was of remarkable thickness (*see* VII.*a*) and could not have been 'torn' by even the most violent earthquake, unless the Sanctuary walls had collapsed outwards and ripped it in half. Also, Jerome states in his *Letter to Hedibia* 8, that, according to the *Hebrew Gospel,* only a large lintel fell down. This appears to be the original account, subsequently combined and confused with a verse referring to an event of three hours later: 'the dark curtain of cloud was rent by a wind, and the sun shone again.' The falling of the lintel will have been held to fulfil *Isaiah* vi. 4.

Although Palestine is subject to earth tremors, none of major importance had been recorded since the days of King Uzziah (*Zechariah* xiv. 5), and if it was not a major earthquake which, according to *Matthew* xxviii. 2 (*see* cxv.*f*), rolled back the stone from Jesus's own tomb—then what was it? The other evangelists offer no explanation. If we reject the earthquake theory, we shall have to admit that, since Jesus could not have released himself from the tomb, the stone must have been rolled back either by the soldiers if they were still on duty, or if not, by a gang of grave-robbers (*see ibid.*). It was a task for two or three strong men; and the disciples arrived at the tomb after the women.

(*p*) *Mark* xv. 39, *Matthew* xxvii. 54 and *Luke* xxiii. 47, the Centurion's glorifying of God, is a pro-Roman manipulation. An editor of *Luke,* alive to the absurdity of making a Roman soldier call Jesus 'the son of God', has contented himself with 'a righteous man'. This saying makes historical sense only if attributed to Bunni (*see* cxv.*l*).

(*q*) The Nazarene tradition calls attention to several prophecies which were thought to have been fulfilled on this occasion. These are *Psalm* xxii. 18, 'they parted my garments among them and for my vesture did they cast lots'; *Psalm* lxix. 21, 'In my thirst they gave me vinegar to drink'—*Luke* improves on this by gratuitously adding 'gall,' which is mentioned in the first part of the same verse, to Jesus's potion; *Exodus* xii. 46, 'A bone of him shall not be broken'—the Levite butchers began their slaughter of the Passover lambs to which this refers, at the sixth hour (midday),* the time when Jesus 'bowed his head'; and *Zechariah* xii. 10, 'They shall look on him whom they pierced'—as though the Worthless Shepherd prophecy had after all been fulfilled by the piercing of his side. A reference to the same prophecy is concealed in *Luke* xxiii. 44–45: 'And it was about the sixth hour, and there was darkness over all the earth until the ninth hour. And the sun was darkened.'

---

* The Jewish twelve-hour day began at sunrise and ended at sunset. Thus the hour varied in length, according to the season, from forty-nine to seventy-one minutes.

This the Nazarenes held to prove beyond possibility of error that the Crucifixion day was 'the Day of the Lord'; since *Zechariah* xiv. 6–7 runs:

> 'And it shall come to pass in that day that the light shall not be clear, nor
> dark. It shall be one day known to the Lord which is neither day nor night;
> but it shall come to pass that at evening time it shall be light.'

(*r*) *John* xix. 34 contains a reference to the next four verses: 'forthwith came
there out blood and water'. Since according to *Genesis* ix. 4 'the blood is the
life', *Zechariah* xiv. 8, the prophecy that 'living waters shall go out from
Jerusalem'—itself a reference to *Proverbs* x. 11 and concerned with the
preaching of any righteous prophet—was taken to be fulfilled in this re-
deeming flow from Jesus's side. If no blood had been shed, his sacrifice would
not have been a perfect one. The tradition that Jesus, the Lamb of God
(*see* vi.*b*), became the Paschal lamb is recorded in 1 *Corinthians* v. 7.

The unhistorical taunts of the Chief Priests, elders, scribes and passers-by
in *Matthew* xxvii. 39–43 conceal a reference to *Psalm* xxii. 7–8:

> 'All they that see me, laugh me to scorn, they shoot out the lip, they shake
> the head, saying: "He trusted on the Lord that He would deliver him. Let
> Him deliver him seeing he delighted in Him!"'

(*s*) *Luke's* main contribution to the Crucifixion narrative is his account of
Jesus's address to the woman who mourned for his approaching death (*Luke*
xxiii. 27–31); but the address as it stands is too long to shout over the
shoulder when marching under military escort. Part of it is a quotation from
Jeremiah xxii. 10, which Jesus relates to *Zechariah* xiv. 2 where the women
of Jerusalem are threatened with rape and captivity. Most of the remainder
is borrowed from *Luke* xxi. 23–24, and belongs to an earlier context (*see*
xcviii.*i*).

Luke xxiii. 31: 'If they do these things in a green tree, what shall be done
in a dry?' is a proverb. Certain trees were sacred in Palestine, as they still
are in Arabia, and no one dared take their branches for fire-wood (Doughty:
Arabia Deserta i. 448); these were the 'green trees', some of them immensely
old and luxuriant. They had originally been the scene of Canaanite fertility
rites, but were now associated with legends of ancient Israelite kings, judges,
or prophets. The dry trees were the common ones, smaller and much lopped.
Jesus means: 'If the King of Israel, the Son of God, is delivered to crucifixion
by the Romans, what fate can the common people expect?' He may have been
recalling *Ezekiel* xx. 47:

> 'Behold, I will kindle a fire in thee, and I shall devour every green tree in
> thee, and every dry tree; the flaming flame shall not be quenched and all
> faces from the south to the north shall be burned therein.'

(*t*) According to the apocryphal *Acts of Pilate* and the *Story of Joseph of
Arimathea*, the names of the two malefactors were Dysmas and Gestas; but

the fanciful accounts there given of their history are not worth quoting. Whether they had listened to Jesus when he preached false doctrine in the streets and lanes of Jerusalem (*see* cIII.*f*), and taken it literally, or whether they had rioted at news of his arrest and fallen foul of a Roman patrol, cannot be determined; but the animosity they displayed towards him, even under the shadow of death, proves that they held him responsible for their fate.

Priests were privileged to wear a seamless tunic, like that for which the soldiers cast lots in *John* xix. 23; this garment was woven on a special loom (*see* vIII.*k*).

Golgotha, 'the place of the skull'—translated *Cranion* in the Greek and *Calvarium* ('Calvary') in the Vulgate Latin—lay 'without the gate' according to *Hebrews* xiii. 12. According to Jerome (*Commentary on Ephesians* v. 14 and *Epistle* 46), Adam's skull lay buried there. Anciently, the skull of a royal hero was often buried near a highway outside a city to protect it from invasion: thus the skull of Eurystheus, Hercules's overlord, buried at Macaria (Marathon), had been said to protect Athens (Strabo: *Geography* viii. 6. 19 and Euripides: *Heraclidae* 1026–55). Adam, the eponymous ancestor of the Edomites, was the oracular hero of Hebron, and when David moved his capital from Hebron to Jerusalem, a stronger fortress, he may have brought the skull with him; Adam's body was believed to be still at Hebron (*Baba Bathra* 58a and *Genesis Rabbah* lviii.), where it was worshipped by the Melchizedekians. Whatever the historical truth of the legend connecting Adam's skull with Golgotha, it was evidently current among the Nazarenes, who regarded Jesus as the 'Second Adam' come to redeem the First Adam by his sacrificial death (1 *Corinthians* xv. 22–45).

(*u*) Biblical scholars dispute the precise whereabouts of Golgotha. The Church of the Holy Sepulchre stands on a site—accepted by the Emperor Constantine on doubtful evidence (Eusebius: *Constantine* iii. 45)—three hundred yards north-east of Herod's Palace, where Pilate and Antipas were at the time occupying different wings (*see* cx.*i*). A more likely site, on a skull-shaped hillock dominating a main road and close to the Grotto of Jeremiah, was pointed out by Thenius in 1849; this hillock lies a thousand yards north-east from Herod's Palace, but only half that distance, nearly due north, from the Temple Hill. In either case, Jesus will have been led out of the city by the Western, or Joppa, Gate and then sun-wise around the walls to Golgotha. Few people were still out on the roads at that hour. All the pilgrims from Judaea, Galilee, and the far north had already arrived for the Feast. However, a late arrival from Cyrene in North Africa was now hastily entering Jerusalem, apparently on his way from Joppa, where he had disembarked. Jesus's escort seized on him and forced him to carry the cross-piece.

(*v*) Since the women stood afar off—the guards will have ordered the crowd to remain on the highway—they could not have heard Jesus's words from the Cross. A crucified man, after a severe scourging and on a hot day, could hardly speak above a hoarse whisper. Probably the only Jewish eyewitness on Golgotha itself, apart from the Herodians, was Simon of Cyrene, 'the father of Rufus and Alexander', who overheard Jesus's last words before hurrying back to Jerusalem to enroll himself in a *haburah* (*see* cvi.*g*). It seems likely that Rufus and Alexander were later converted and that this was their contribution to the original Nazarene Gospel.

Luke does not name any of the women. In *Mark* xv. 40, they are described as Mary Magdalene, Mary the mother of James the Less, and Salome; in *Matthew* xxvii. 56 as, among others, Mary Magdalene, Mary the mother of James and Joses, and the mother of Zebedee's children; in *John* xix. 25, as 'his mother and his mother's sister Mary of Cleophas, and Mary Magdalene'. The witness to the wound in his side must have been Joseph of Arimathea, who had meanwhile obtained permission to bury the body (*see* cxiv.*e*).

(*w*) Despite *John* xix. 31, 'the Jews' cannot have asked Pilate to break the criminals' legs; they knew that this act would not greatly hasten the end but only cause additional pain. It was doubtless a supererogatory punishment ordered by Pilate, to offset his leniency in despatching the three criminals with cold steel after a mere six hours of torture; but the evangelists have decided to shift all blame from Pilate to the Jews. The author of *John* xix. 31 is unaware that, Sabbath or no Sabbath, no Jew might be left hanging on the cross after nightfall (*Deuteronomy* xxi. 23), and that the Romans deferred to Jewish sentiment except in time of war. The soldiers broke the legs of the two malefactors and then ran them through but, when they came to Jesus and thought that he was already dead, did not trouble to break his legs; one of them, however, pierced his side perfunctorily with a spear (or according to the Copts, with a sword), and out flowed water mixed with blood.

Since corpses do not bleed, the trace of blood in the water proves that Jesus's heart was still feebly beating. The origin of the aqueous fluid is debatable. Either—as Dr. George Simon, the London physician and radiologist has suggested to us—the short upward thrust tapped a secretion of water in the pleural cavity, caused by the scourging; or else—as Mr. W. B. Primrose, the Scottish surgeon and anaesthetist, believes*—it tapped a similar secretion in the abdominal cavity. Mr. Primrose points out that a state of low vitality combined with a minimal circulation cannot be easily distinguished from death, and believes that in Jesus's case this condition was due to the delayed shock of the scourging.† Jesus collapsed at the ninth hour

---

* *A Surgeon Looks at the Crucifixion* (*Hibbert Journal*, July 1949).

† I apologize for intruding autobiography into this argument, but I had an experience medically analogous to Jesus's, when I 'died of wounds' during the Battle of the Somme on July 21st, 1916, and was officially resurrected on August 4th.

During the 19th Infantry Brigade's assault on High Wood an eight-inch shell burst within a few feet of me and a splinter penetrated my right lung; other fragments caused superficial injuries and I lost consciousness. An experienced Scottish medical officer, Dr. J. C. Dunn, D.C.M., D.S.O., of Glasgow, came up under fire to attend me and had me carried back to the advanced dressing station, an open shelter.

He mistook a complete anaesthesia for death: because a deep, undressed wound in my finger had ceased to bleed. So I was left in a corner, unburied, for some twenty-four hours,

(three o'clock) when the aqueous secretion, also caused by the scourging—a phenomenon resembling the familiar 'water on the knee'—will have been at its most copious.

(*x*) It did not occur to those present that Jesus might still be alive, since he remained in complete anaesthesia both when he was wounded in the side, and when the nails were drawn out. His quoting from *Psalm* xxii. proves, however, that he expected to survive his ordeal. This psalm, though beginning with 'My God, my God, why hast Thou forsaken me?', and describing a man's torments on the cross, ends on a more hopeful note. Verses 19–23 run:

> 'But be Thou not far from me, O Lord. O my strength, haste to help me.
> 'Deliver my soul from the sword, mine only begotten from the power of the dog.
> 'Save me from the lion's mouth, for Thou has heard me and saved me from between the horns of the wild oxen.
> 'Ye that fear the Lord, praise Him . . . for He hath not despised nor abhorred the afflicted, neither hath He hid His face . . .'

Verse 20: 'Mine only begotten', may be a misreading of 'thine only begotten' by an editor of the *Psalms* who recalled *Wisdom of Solomon* vii. 22: 'In her [Wisdom] is the spirit of understanding, holy, only-begotten . . .' If 'thine only begotten' is the correct version, it refers to Israel, here symbolized by a crucified man.

(*y*) The question whether the thrust in Jesus's side was dealt by a spear (*John* xix. 34) or a sword, is more important than appears at first sight. Coptic pictorial tradition shows a Roman stabbing-sword; and this would have been a far handier weapon for the purpose than a spear. If it was a spear, then Simeon's prophecy (*see* viii.*w*): 'The sword shall pierce thy heart also', remained unfulfilled, and so did the entire *Zechariah* prophecy; it may be that 'sword' was changed to 'spear' to divert attention from the Worthless Shepherd.

(431) *And they led Jesus out to crucify him. And with him they also led out two malefactors which were condemned of Pilate that day to be crucified.*

For they had hearkened unto the false doctrine that Jesus taught in the

---

while the battle went on and Dr. Dunn was kept continuously at work. Then I began to show signs of life, though remaining unconscious.

I attribute my recovery to a superstitious conviction that I was fated to survive the battle; to the shock caused by the shell-burst which slowed down my circulation and prevented my lungs from filling with blood; and to my extreme exhaustion at the time.

Mr. Primrose argues that Jesus could not have retained sufficient vital heat in a rock sepulchre, clad only in a linen shroud, for more than an hour or so. But the sepulchre had been open to the hot air, and Jesus was wrapped in linen clothes thickly smeared with ointment, which would have kept him warm.

I managed to conserve my vital heat for little less than the thirty hours which Jesus spent in the tomb, while lying with only a stretcher between myself and the bare earth; and the physical resistance of Oriental saints is notoriously greater than that of European sinners (*see* LXXVIII.*j*). R. G.

streets and lanes of Jerusalem, how that every man should fend for himself in despite of his neighbour; and had shed blood.

And as they went forth from the city by the western gate, behold, a man of Cyrene, Simon by name, which was the father of Alexander and Rufus, came up late from Joppa for the Feast.

But Jesus, being lame, could not bear his cross-piece, as the other twain did; wherefore the soldiers compelled Simon to bear it for him.

* * * * *

(432) Now, a company of women followed behind, which bewailed and lamented him.

And Jesus, turning unto them, said: 'Daughters of Jerusalem, it is written: "Weep ye not for the dead, neither bemoan him. But weep sore for him that goeth away, for he shall return no more, neither see his native country."

'Wherefore weep for yourselves, who shall be ravished and carried away into bondage!'

And he said likewise: 'Behold, if these things are done to a green tree, what shall be done unto a dry?'

* * * * *

(433) And they came unto the mount which is called Golgotha, where the skull of Adam lieth buried, nigh unto the highway that leadeth to the north.

There the soldiers crucified Jesus with the other twain,

And the women stood afar off, beholding what was done, among whom were Mary the Braider, his mother; and Mary, the mother of James and Joses, which was the wife of Joseph of Ramathaim; and Salome the midwife; and the mother of Zebedee's children.

But Simon of Cyrene remained for awhile with the soldiers, and hearkened unto the words which Jesus spake, after that his hands and feet were made fast to the wood with sharp nails and he was raised upon the cross.

Then the superscription which Pilate had ordained was set above his head; and it was written in Latin and Greek and Hebrew.

* * * * *

(434) Now, when the other twain were crucified with Jesus, the superscriptions shewed that they were guilty of bloodshed.

And he which hanged on the left hand of Jesus, reviled him, saying: 'If thou be the Son of God, come down from the Cross! Save thyself and us that we may believe on thee.

'For because of thy lies we are crucified.'

And he which hanged on the right hand of Jesus, cast the like in his teeth, mocking him and saying: 'Lord, remember me when thou comest into thy Kingdom!'

But Jesus prayed aloud: 'Father, forgive them! They wist not what they did.'

Then saith Simon unto the malefactors: 'Why revile ye this man, seeing that he is of the same condemnation as yourselves, and did no violence such as ye did? Fear ye not God?'

But certain of the Herodians which stood by, likewise mocked Jesus, saying: 'He saved others; himself he cannot save!'

* * * * *

(435) *And the soldiers took the clothes of Jesus, and of his garment of prayer they made four parts, and took every man a part.*

But his tunic was without seam, woven from the top throughout, being a priestly garment.

Therefore they said: 'Let us not rend it, but cast lots for it.'

And when Jesus saw this, he said: 'Eloi, eloi, lama sabachthani?', which is: 'My God, my God, why hast Thou forsaken me?'

For he remembered the psalm in which David prophesied of him, saying: 'My God, my God, why hast Thou forsaken me? Why art Thou so far from helping me, and from the words of my roaring?

'Our fathers trusted in Thee, they trusted and Thou didst deliver them.

'But I am a worm, and no man, a reproach of the people.

'All they that see me laugh me to scorn, they shoot out the lip and shake the head, saying: "He trusted on the Lord, that He would deliver him. Let Him deliver him, seeing He delighted in him."

'But Thou art He that took me out of the womb, Thou didst make me hope when I was upon my mother's breasts.

'Be not far from me, for trouble is near and there is none to help.

'Many bulls have encompassed me about, strong bulls of Bashan.

'They gaped on me like a ravening and a roaring lion.

'I am poured out like water, all my bones are racked by my hanging.

'My heart is melted within me like wax; I am dried up like a potsherd, and my tongue is swollen and cleaveth to my jaws. Thou hast brought me to the dust of death.

'For the dogs have beset me, the assembly of the wicked have closed me in. They have pierced my hands and feet.

'I am naked and an-hungered so that I shew all my bones; they look and stare upon me.

'They have parted my garments among them and cast lots for my vesture.

'But be not Thou far from me, O Lord! O my Strength, hasten to help me!

'Deliver my soul from the sword, thine only begotten from the power of the dog.

'Save me from the lion's mouth, hear me from between the horns of the wild oxen.

'Ye that fear the Lord, praise ye the Lord, for He hath not despised nor abhorred the affliction of him that is afflicted!

'Neither hath He turned His face from him. When he called upon Him, He heard.'

But the Herodians, when they heard Jesus cry 'Eloi, Eloi!', said: 'Now he calleth upon Elijah to save him!'

* * * * *

(436) *And it came to pass that certain pious women, which were in Jerusalem, had provided frankincense that it might be mixed with vinegar and*

given unto them which were crucified, that their torments might be eased.

One of the soldiers took a spunge and filled it with the vinegar, and set it upon a branch of hyssop which was fastened to a reed, and gave it unto the malefactors, and they drank thereof and held their peace.

But Jesus, when he perceived by the smell that it was vinegar, would not taste thereof, because he might not drink of the fruit of the vine.

* * * * *

(437) Now, Jesus was raised upon the cross at about the third hour; and at the sixth hour, which was the hour of the sacrifice in the Temple, behold, a great cloud came up from the east and the sun was darkened, and the earth began to shake.

As Joel prophesied: 'The day of the Lord is near in the valley of decision.

'The sun and the moon shall be darkened, and the heavens and the earth shall shake.'

Which when Jesus saw, he opened his mouth to cry out.

And the earth quaked again, and a lintel of wondrous size fell from a doorway of the Temple.

As Isaiah prophesied: 'The posts of the door moved at the voice of him that cried.'

And because of the trembling of the earth a great shout of fear arose; but Jesus bowed his head upon his breast, as one which, praying before he falleth on sleep, saith: 'Father, into Thy hands I commend my spirit.

'Thou hast redeemed me, O Lord, God of Truth. For Thy salvation have I waited, O Lord!'

And Jesus hanged there as dead, and the women that watched wept to see him, and cried: 'It is finished!'

* * * * *

(438) And there was darkness over all the land until the ninth hour, yet at evening it grew light, for a wind rent in twain the curtain of darkness.

As Zechariah prophesied: 'And it shall come to pass in that day that the light shall not be clear, nor dark.

'It shall be one day known to the Lord which is neither day nor night, yet it shall come to pass that at evening time it shall be light.'

* * * * *

(439) Then Mary, the wife of Joseph of Ramathaim, goeth hastily unto him at Bethany, and saith: 'Husband, the Anointed One is dead.'

* * * * *

(z) [Here follows Joseph of Arimathea's request to Pilate for the dead body, and Bunni's journey with him to Golgotha (*see* cxiv.e).]

* * * * *

(441) Now, the Chief Priests had aforetime made known unto Pilate that they which were condemned might not hang on the cross when night fell, lest the Law be set at naught.

Wherefore he had sent word to the centurion, saying: 'At evening, let their legs be broken and let their bodies be thrust through and taken down for burial.'

* * * * *

(442) *And when even was come, the centurion commanded the soldiers that they should break the legs of them which were crucified, and that their bodies should be thrust through with swords.*

And they brake the legs of the one and the other of the malefactors, and afterward they slew them both.

But finding Jesus dead, they brake not his legs.

As it is written of the lamb which is slain for the Passover: 'A bone of him shall not be broken.'

Howbeit, a soldier with a sword pierced his side but a little, and forthwith came there out water mixed with blood.

As Zechariah prophesied: 'Living waters shall go out from Jerusalem.'

And also: 'They shall look on him which they pierced.'

* * * * *

(444) *And the soldiers took down the body of Jesus with care, as Nakemidam bade them, and anointed the clothes with ointment and wrapped him therewith, and tied a napkin about his head.*

* * * * *

THE BURIAL

Mark xv. 42–47

[42]And now when the even was come, because it was the Preparation, that is, the day before the sabbath, [43]Joseph of Arimathaea, an honourable counsellor, which also waited for the kingdom of God, came, and went in boldly unto Pilate, and craved the body of Jesus. [44]And Pilate marvelled if He were already dead: and calling unto him the centurion, he asked him whether He had been any while dead. [45]And when he knew it of the centurion, he gave the body to Joseph. [46]And he bought fine linen, and took Him down, and wrapped Him in the linen, and laid Him in a sepulchre which was hewn out of a rock, and rolled a stone unto the door of the sepulchre. [47]And Mary Magdalene and Mary the mother of Joses beheld where He was laid.

Matthew xxvii. 57–61

[57]When the even was come, there came a rich man of Arimathaea, named Joseph, who also himself was Jesus' disciple: [58]he went to Pilate, and begged the body of Jesus. Then Pilate commanded the body to be delivered. [59]And when Joseph had taken the body, he wrapped it in a clean linen cloth, [60]and laid it in his own new tomb, which he had hewn out in the rock: and he rolled a great stone to the door of the sepulchre, and departed. [61]And there was Mary Magdalene, and the other Mary, sitting over against the sepulchre.

Luke xxiii. 50–56

[50]And, behold, there was a man named Joseph, a counsellor; and he was a good man, and a just: [51](the same had not consented to the counsel and deed of them,) he was of Arimathaea, a city of the Jews: who also himself waited for the kingdom of God. [52]This man went unto Pilate, and begged the body of Jesus. [53]And he took it down, and wrapped it in linen, and laid it in a sepulchre that was hewn in stone, wherein never man before was laid. [54]And that day was the preparation, and the sabbath drew on. [55]And the women also, which came with Him from Galilee, followed after, and beheld the sepulchre, and how His body was laid. [56]And they returned, and prepared spices and ointments.

And they rested the sabbath day according to the commandment.

John xix. 38–42

[38]And after this Joseph of Arimathaea, being a disciple of Jesus, but secretly for fear of the Jews, besought Pilate that he might take away the body of

John xix. 38–42 (contd.)

Jesus: and Pilate gave him leave. He came therefore, and took the body of Jesus. [39]And there came also Nicodemus, which at the first came to Jesus by night, and brought a mixture of myrrh and aloes, about an hundred pound weight. [40]Then took they the body of Jesus, and wound it in linen clothes with the spices, as the manner of the Jews is to bury. [41]Now in the place where He was crucified there was a garden; and in the garden a new sepulchre, wherein was never man yet laid. [42]There laid they Jesus therefore because of the Jews' preparation day; for the sepulchre was nigh at hand.

(a) Under Roman law the body of a crucified felon was the property of his next-of-kin, but since Jesus had ceased to be a member of Joseph the Carpenter's family, his Galilean brothers did not come forward to assert their claim. This was done by the head of the Levite family into which he had been adopted (see VIII.r–s and u); namely, Joseph, brother of Mary the Braider and of Cleophas, and father of 'James the brother of our Lord'. Joseph is here distinguished from other Josephs as being 'of Arimathea', probably Ramathaim-Zophim, near Lydda (1 Samuel i. 1 and 1 Maccabees xi. 34). The use of 'just' in Luke xxiii. 50—as well as his description in the next verse: 'who also himself waited for the Kingdom of God'—suggests that he was an Essene apocalyptic. He would have been simply called 'The Essene' (Alpheios), if his son and namesake had not also belonged to this sect.

(b) Luke xxiii. 51: 'Who also himself waited (or "watched") for the Kingdom of God'—paralleled in Mark xv. 43 and in Luke ii. 25 (see VIII.q and v) —points to an association with the name 'Ramathaim-Zophim', since the Targum of Jonathan on 1 Samuel i. takes zophim to mean 'a place of watching', and renders the word ramathaim as 'of the disciples of the prophets'. It was one of several Levite villages in the Emmaus district, and distinguished as the birthplace of the prophet Samuel. There may have been two allied establishments of Levite Essenes, one at 'Arimathea', another at Bethany. References to the Zophim,* or 'Watchers', as a distinct society or sect are found in Genesis Rabbah i. 15 and Megillah 2b, where they are said to have anciently shaped the five final letters of the Hebrew alphabet.

(c) According to Luke xxiii. 50, Joseph was a counsellor, and according to Mark xv. 42 an honourable counsellor; but this does not necessarily imply membership of the Great Sanhedrin—he may have sat in a lower court or, more likely, in the council which governed his Essene organization. The awkward parenthetical statement in Luke (ibid.): 'the same had not consented to the counsel and deed of them', must have originally referred to some other person. An important passage has been suppressed here, since 'them' is left without an antecedent; 'the same' probably refers to Bunni

---

*Zophim (plural of zopheh) is one of ten Biblical words meaning 'prophets' (Aboth di Rabbi Nathan 34). It is used in Isaiah iii. 8, xvi. 10; Jeremiah vi. 17; Ezekiel iii. 17 and xxxiii. 2, 6–7.

('Nicodemus'). Thus *John* xix. 39, 'Nicodemus which at first came to Jesus by night', should be completed with the misplaced phrases in the previous verse: 'secretly, for fear of the Jews [i.e. the Chief Rulers],' and with: 'but afterward withstood them, and had not consented to the counsel and deed of them.' *John's* 'secretly' contradicts the 'boldly' of *Mark* xv. 43.

(*d*) If *John's* account alone had survived it might be assumed that Bunni provided the tomb; and since Joseph of Arimathea, an Essene, could hardly have made such lavish provision for his own burial as a rock-hewn sepulchre in a private garden, it seems likely that the Synoptics have suppressed all reference to Bunni. Because *Deuteronomy* xxi. 22-23 forbade the burial of a crucified man *if he had committed a sin worthy of death,* Bunni seems to have pointedly undertaken the funeral arrangements as a sign that he dissociated himself from the verdict of the Council of Priestly Elders.

According to *John* xix. 39, 'Nicodemus' provided a hundred pounds' weight of myrrh and aloes—which, to judge from the value of Mary's boxful (*see* xi.*j*), would be worth at least 30,000 pence. According to *Matthew* xxvii. 57-61, it was Joseph's tomb; but this account is suspect as the only one in which Joseph is stated to have been rich—the Essenes were a communistic society. 'Rich' has here evidently been borrowed from the suppressed account of Bunni's generosity, in which *Isaiah* liii. 9, where the Suffering Servant is promised a 'grave with the wicked and with the rich' will have been quoted. This editor of *Matthew* has overreached himself, since Isaiah meant 'with the wicked rich', and Joseph and his family were not wicked, neither was Jesus buried with the two malefactors. The sepulchre, in fact, was Bunni's, not Joseph's; and *Isaiah's* prophecy seemed fulfilled because Bunni's unregenerate relatives had been buried in the same private cemetery. Bunni's name has been suppressed by the Synoptics, because he was a Pharisee and they were therefore loth to give him credit either for his firm stand in Caiaphas's court or for his subsequent piety in arranging the funeral.

(*e*) The sequence of events seems to have been as follows. When Joseph was informed of Jesus's death, he visited Pilate, who, though surprised that the end had come as early as three o'clock, granted him the body after an enquiry into his *bona fides.* Then Joseph, at a loss because the combined Passover and Sabbath ruled out an immediate funeral, consulted Bunni, who promised to arrange everything for him. They went at once to Golgotha, where Bunni supervised the careful removal of the body from the cross; and since there was now no time even to lay it out, he had it wrapped in the linen shroud and temporarily laid in his own tomb. He also engaged soldiers to guard it until the Sunday morning. The centurion must have been well paid for removing the body to the tomb and leaving a maniple to watch over it for the next thirty-six hours. Despite the evangelists, neither Joseph nor Bunni would have touched a corpse now that the Sabbath had begun, since to do so would have prevented them from eating the *Seder* with their families; nor would Bunni have allowed his servants to become defiled. And

Joseph, being of Rechabite family (*see* VIII.*v*), was prohibited from any contact with corpses.

(*f*) Jesus's body was not guarded 'lest his disciples steal him away'—*Matthew* xxvii. 62–64 is a clumsy forgery—but lest grave-robbers should despoil the corpse of its extremities. Lucan and Apuleius both mention that parts of crucified men were used in black magic, for which the province of Syria was notorious;* Germanicus had recently been done to death at Antioch by a witch who had employed such relics (Tacitus: *Annals* ii. 69). Thus Mary the Braider and Mary, Joseph of Ramathaim's wife, seem to have temporarily watched at the tomb while the soldiers went back to barracks in search of food and bedding for the night.

(*g*) It is most unlikely that, as stated in *Mark* xv. 44, Pilate recalled the centurion from Golgotha to confirm Jesus's death; and impossible that the women prepared the spices before the Saturday night—the Sabbath had begun and any kind of work was forbidden. Bunni seems to have brought one load of spices to Golgotha for immediate use, and promised the women another when they came at dawn on the Sunday to lay the corpse out properly.

(440) *Now, Joseph of Ramathaim, which was a just man and waited for the Kingdom, when he heard that Jesus was dead, went unto Pilate and begged him for the body.*

For this duty fell unto him, being brother of Mary the Braider and reckoned a father unto Jesus.

And Pilate, marvelling if Jesus were already dead, called unto him an officer, that he might learn whether aught were known of Joseph.

And when he learned that Joseph was of good repute and an honourable counsellor, he gave him leave to take the body.

But Joseph wist not what to do therewith, because this was the preparation for the sabbath and for the Passover; he was also of the Rechabites, which handle not the dead.

Wherefore he sought out Bunni, called Nakemidam, the same which at the first came unto Jesus by night for fear of the Chief Rulers, but afterward boldly withstood them, consenting neither to their counsel nor to their deed.

And Nakemidam saith unto him: 'I will gladly see to the matter.'

Then took Nakemidam pieces of fine linen and much ointment of myrrh, and straightway went forth with Joseph unto Golgotha.

---

* Apuleius: *Golden Ass* iii. 17:

'Pamphile made ready the members of dead men brought from their tombs. Here she set out their nostrils and fingers; there the nails, with lumps of flesh adhering, of such as had been crucified.'

Lucan: *Civil Wars* vi. 540–8:

'When the dead are confined in stone, then the witch eagerly vents her savagery on all the limbs, scooping out the stiffened eye-balls, gnawing the yellow nails on the withered hand; or . . . mangling the carcase as it dangles from the cross, tears away the rain-beaten flesh and the sun-calcined bones, purloins the nails that pierced the hands, the clotted filth and the oozing black humour of corruption . . .'

*There they watched until what time the soldiers took down the body of
Jesus from the cross.*

* * * * *

[Here follows the breaking of the malefactors' legs and the piercing of
Jesus's side (*see* CXIII.*z*).]

* * * * *

(443) *Afterward, Nakemidam said unto the centurion: 'Sir, this is the preparation for the sabbath and for the Passover, and all my servants keep the
Feast with me.*

*'Now, therefore, I pray thee, lest we be defiled, let thy soldiers anoint these
linen clothes with the ointment of myrrh and wrap the dead body of Jesus
therewith and lay him in the tomb which I have provided.*

'Behold, if thou seest to all this, I will pay thee well.'

And the centurion answered:'As thou sayest, so shall it be done.'

*Then said Nakemidam again: 'Wilt thou then also provide a watch lest
witches come by night and despoil the body?*

*'For when the sabbath is ended, this man, which is a counsellor, will send
women early in the morning, to wash and anoint the body and bury it. And
then shall I likewise set a guard of my own servants over the tomb.'*

*The centurion answered and said: 'Truly ye shall have a watch. Go your
ways in peace!'*

* * * * *

[Here follows the removal of the body from the Cross (*see* CXIII.*z*).]

(445) *Then Nakemidam shewed them where the body should be laid.*

*And it was a new sepulchre which had been hewn out of a rock in the
midst of a garden, against Nakemidam himself fell on sleep.*

*But there were also in that place the graves of Nakemidam's kinsmen,
Chief Rulers, wicked men and exceeding rich.*

*Thus was the prophecy of Isaiah fulfilled, which saith: 'He was cut off out
of the land of the living, for the transgression of My people was he stricken.*

'And he made his grave with the wicked, and with the rich in his death.'

* * * * *

(446) *And forthwith they laid him in the new sepulchre, and rolled a stone
across the mouth thereof, and set a seal upon the stone, and departed to fetch
all things needful for their watch.*

*And Mary the Braider and the other Mary sat over against the sepulchre
and watched awhile.*

*But, when the soldiers were come again, the women hastened to Jerusalem
to eat the Passover there.*

*And on the morrow Nakemidam shewed them an hundred pound weight
of myrrh mixed with aloes, with which they should anoint the body of Jesus
when the sabbath was ended, and when they had rested according to the commandment.*

* * * * *

THE RESURRECTION

Mark xvi. 1–11

[1]And when the sabbath was past, Mary Magdalene, and Mary the mother of James, and Salome, had bought sweet spices, that they might come and anoint Him. [2]And very early in the morning the first day of the week, they came unto the sepulchre at the rising of the sun. [3]And they said among themselves, Who shall roll us away the stone from the door of the sepulchre? [4]And when they looked, they saw that the stone was rolled away: for it was very great. [5]And entering into the sepulchre, they saw a young man sitting on the right side, clothed in a long white garment; and they were affrighted. [6]And he saith unto them: 'Be not affrighted: Ye seek Jesus of Nazareth, which was crucified: He is risen; He is not here: behold the place where they laid Him. [7]But go your way, tell His disciples and Peter that He goeth before you into Galilee: there shall ye see Him, as He said unto you.' [8]And they went out quickly, and fled from the sepulchre; for they trembled and were amazed: neither said they any thing to any man; for they were afraid.

[9]Now when Jesus was risen early the first day of the week, He appeared first to Mary Magdalene, out of whom He had cast seven devils. [10]She went and told them that had been with Him, as they mourned and wept. [11]And they, when they had heard that He was alive, and had been seen of her, believed not.

Matthew xxviii. 1–15

[1]In the end of the sabbath, as it began to dawn toward the first day of the week, came Mary Magdalene and the other Mary to see the sepulchre. [2]And, behold, there was a great earthquake: for the angel of the Lord descended from heaven, and came and rolled back the stone from the door, and sat upon it. [3]His countenance was like lightning, and his raiment white as snow: [4]and for fear of him the keepers did shake, and became as dead men. [5]And the angel answered and said unto the women: 'Fear not ye: for I know that ye seek Jesus, Who was crucified. [6]He is not here: for He is risen, as He said. Come, see the place where the Lord lay. [7]And go quickly, and tell His disciples that He is risen from the dead; and, behold, He goeth before you into Galilee; there shall ye see Him: lo, I have told you.' [8]And they departed quickly from the sepulchre with fear and great joy; and did run to bring His disciples word. [9]And as they went to tell His disciples, behold, Jesus met them, saying: 'All hail.' And they came and held Him by the feet, and wor-

Matthew xxvii. 1–15 (*contd.*)

shipped Him. [10]Then said Jesus unto them: 'Be not afraid: go tell My brethren that they go into Galilee, and there shall they see Me.'

[11]Now when they were going, behold, some of the watch came into the city, and shewed unto the chief priests all the things that were done. [12]And when they were assembled with the elders, and had taken counsel, they gave large money unto the soldiers, [13]saying: 'Say ye, His disciples came by night, and stole Him away while we slept. [14]And if this come to the governor's ears, we will persuade him, and secure you.' [15]So they took the money, and did as they were taught: and this saying is commonly reported among the Jews until this day.

Luke xxiv. 1–12

[1]Now upon the first day of the week, very early in the morning, they came unto the sepulchre, bringing the spices which they had prepared, and certain others with them. [2]And they found the stone rolled away from the sepulchre. [3]And they entered in, and found not the body of the Lord Jesus. [4]And it came to pass, as they were much perplexed thereabout, behold, two men stood by them in shining garments: [5]and as they were afraid, and bowed down their faces to the earth, they said unto them: 'Why seek ye the living among the dead? [6]He is not here, but is risen: remember how He spake unto you when He was yet in Galilee, [7]saying, The Son of Man must be delivered into the hands of sinful men, and be crucified, and the third day rise again.' [8]And they remembered His words, [9]and returned from the sepulchre, and told all these things unto the Eleven and to all the rest. [10]It was Mary Magdalene, and Joanna, and Mary the mother of James, and other women that were with them, which told these things unto the Apostles. [11]And their words seemed to them as idle tales, and they believed them not.

[12]Then arose Peter, and ran unto the sepulchre; and stooping down, he beheld the linen clothes laid by themselves, and departed, wondering in himself at that which was come to pass.

John xi. 44

[44]And he that was dead came forth, bound hand and foot with graveclothes: and his face was bound about with a napkin. Jesus saith unto them: 'Loose him, and let him go.'

John xx. 1–18

'The first day of the week cometh Mary Magdalene early, when it was yet dark, unto the sepulchre, and seeth the stone taken away from the sepulchre. [2]Then she runneth, and cometh to Simon Peter, and to the other disciple, whom Jesus loved, and saith unto them: 'They have taken away the Lord out of the sepulchre, and we know not where they have laid Him.'

[3]Peter therefore went forth, and that other disciple, and came to the sepulchre. [4]So they ran both together: and the other disciple did outrun Peter, and came first to the sepulchre. [5]And he stooping down, and looking in, saw the linen clothes lying; yet went he not in. [6]Then cometh Simon Peter following

John xx. 1–18 (*contd.*)

him, and went into the sepulchre, and seeth the linen clothes lie, [7]and the napkin, that was about His head, not lying with the linen clothes, but wrapped together in a place by itself. [8]Then went in also that other disciple, which came first to the sepulchre, and he saw, and believed. [9]For as yet they knew not the scripture, that He must rise again from the dead. [10]Then the disciples went away again unto their own home.

[11]But Mary stood without at the sepulchre weeping: and as she wept, she stooped down, and looked into the sepulchre, [12]and seeth two angels in white sitting, one at the head, and the other at the feet, where the body of Jesus had lain. [13]And they say unto her: 'Woman, why weepest thou?' She saith unto them: 'Because they have taken away my Lord, and I know not where they have laid Him.' [14]And when she had thus said, she turned herself back, and saw Jesus standing, and knew not that it was Jesus. [15]Jesus saith unto her: 'Woman, why weepest thou? Whom seekest thou?' She, supposing Him to be the gardener, saith unto Him: 'Sir, if Thou hast borne Him hence, tell me where Thou hast laid Him, and I will take Him away.' [16]Jesus saith unto her: 'Mary.' She turned herself, and saith unto Him: 'Rabboni'; which is to say, Master. [17]Jesus saith unto her: 'Touch Me not; for I am not yet ascended to My Father: but go to My brethren, and say unto them, I ascend unto My Father, and your Father; and to My God, and your God.' [18]Mary Magdalene came and told the disciples that she had seen the Lord, and that He had spoken these things unto her.

(*a*) The evangelists' accounts of the Resurrection are strewn with 'stumbling blocks'—the Church's term for 'irreconcileable contradictions'; and only by a supreme effort of faith are intelligent Christians able to believe that Jesus indeed rose from the dead. It is, of course, a criminological common-place that, when a group of accomplices have not agreed on the details of a collusive story, the truth which they are trying to hide will eventually be betrayed by discrepancies in their evidence; yet, surprisingly enough, after all impossibilities and contradictions in these four accounts have been examined, and the true sequence of events pieced together, the central fact of the Resurrection still resists all critical attempts to disprove it.

(*b*) No mention is made in *Mark, Luke* or *John* of the watch at the tomb, or of an earthquake. According to *Matthew* xxviii. 4, the watchmen were terrified to see an angel seated on the stone which he had just rolled back by means of an earthquake; and there had been an earlier shock which rent the veil of the Temple and opened many other tombs (*see* cxiii.*o*). They returned to Jerusalem, where the Chief Priests bribed them to give out that the body had been stolen by the disciples. Meanwhile Mary Magdalene ('the Braider') and 'the other Mary', who arrived at first dawn, did not enter the tomb, because the same angel told them that Jesus was no longer inside, but had gone ahead to Galilee, where the disciples were to meet him; so back they went to inform Peter and the others. Jesus met them on the road, confirmed the angel's message, and permitted both to clasp his feet; and the disciples, when they had received the glad tidings, hastened to keep the appointment.

(c) According to *Mark* xvi. 1-11, the two Marys, accompanied by Salome —whom the other evangelists do not mention—entered the tomb at sunrise and found a young man dressed in white, not an angel, sitting within. His message was similar to that of *Matthew's* angel, but the frightened women did not pass it on to the disciples. The editor of *Mark* offers no explanation for the removal of the stone; and at this point the earliest manuscripts break off. According to the addition supplied by a late editor from the other Gospels, Jesus then appeared to Mary Magdalene alone, but the disciples refused to believe her when she told them of her experience; he next appeared to two disciples on a country walk, and finally to most of the apostles in Jerusalem.

(d) According to *Luke* xxiv. 1-12, the Marys, arriving very early in the morning, found two men inside the tomb, clad in shining garments, who asked them to advise the disciples of Jesus's resurrection—no mention is made here of an appointment in Galilee—but the disciples would not believe this story. Peter, going to the tomb which was empty, found the linen clothes laid apart and went away in perplexity. Jesus then revealed himself to two disciples on the road to Emmaus, broke bread with them, but vanished suddenly. They later visited the Eleven in Jerusalem, where Jesus appeared to them all soon afterwards and was mistaken for a ghost. *Luke's* omission of Jesus's appearance to the Marys is apparently due to his mistrust of women's testimony (*see* cxvii.*d*).

(e) According to *John* xx. 1-18, Mary Magdalene went alone to Golgotha, while it was still dark, and found the stone rolled back. She saw no angel, nor even a man in white raiment, neither did she enter the tomb, but hurried to tell Peter and 'the beloved disciple' (John son of Annas), that the body seemed to have been stolen. John arrived first, looked into the tomb and saw only the linen clothes and the napkin. Next Peter arrived, went in, and John, encouraged to do the same, also 'saw and believed'—namely that the body had disappeared. They departed together and Mary Magdalene, venturing now to look into the tomb, noticed two angels clad in white who asked her why she wept. She explained that someone had removed the body which she had come to wash and anoint. Then she turned and, seeing a man whom she took to be the cemetery keeper, told him that, if he had moved the body, she would be grateful to have it restored to her. Suddenly she recognized Jesus. He would not let her touch him, but asked her to tell the disciples that he would soon be ascending to Heaven. This she did, and the disciples' reaction is not given. Afterwards he appeared to them in Jerusalem.

(f) The stone, like many grave-stoppers of the period, seems to have resembled a small mill-stone running in a groove. Jesus, in his exhausted condition, could not have moved it from the inside of the tomb, even if unencumbered by his cere-clothes. Had an earthquake rolled the stone away and left the entrance of the tomb uncovered, as the Marys found it, the shock must have been exceptionally severe (*see* cxiii.*o*); because, according to *Mark* xvi. 3, their combined powers were insufficient to move it. Yet, since Jesus's body had disappeared, it must have been rolled back by some person or force; and all four Gospels agree that this happened without the knowledge or connivance of his followers.

If the problem is examined as an incident in profane, rather than sacred, history, an obvious solution suggests itself. According to *Matthew* xxviii. 11, soldiers watched over the body—a fact which is unlikely to have been invented. The other evangelists make no mention of the watch, aware perhaps that, in the original tradition, the soldiers themselves rolled away the stone; that, in fact, 'while it was yet dark', and their officer lay asleep, they were inspired to break into the tomb. They came in search of loot: probably the precious ointment, which could have been sold at a very high price in the brothels of Caesarea or Tyre. A few minutes' work was worth several years' pay; and even the best Roman troops would have found it hard to resist the temptation of quietly enriching themselves at the expense of a dead Jewish criminal.

(*g*) They rolled away the stone and, as they stood listening, to make certain that their officer had not been aroused by the rumbling noise, a rustle and a groan from inside the tomb scattered them in terror. Jesus, recovering from his trance, slowly emerged from the low entrance, clad in pall and head-cloth, and sat on the stone in the moonlight. *Luke* xxiv. 37: 'They mistook him for a ghost', fits this context better than that of his appearance to the disciples in Jerusalem. The officer, awakened by shouts of alarm, realized that the seated figure was Jesus, and asked his men how the stone came to be rolled back. They answered that the earth had quaked while he slept— and perhaps this was the truth, though not the whole truth. *John* xix. 28: 'I thirst!', omitted by the Synoptics, seems to have been spoken on this occasion (*see* cxiii.*k*).

(*h*) The author of *John* has ingeniously inserted at the close of the Raising of Lazarus the suppressed account of Jesus's emergence from the tomb (*see* lxxxviii.*e*). That is to say: the officer will have given his men the curt order 'Loose him and let him go!' (*John* xi. 44) and, as soon as the women approached in the distance, will have marched them off and reported the affair to Bunni. Bunni, it seems—not the Chief Priests—paid them all well to keep the secret of Jesus's survival, lest it came to the ear of Pilate; and advised them, if questioned, to say no more than that the disciples had come, as expected, and taken away the body. (Eventually, the Chief Priests learned the truth and decided to re-arrest Jesus because it was now popularly rumoured that he was immortal—*see* lxxxvii.*g*.)

(*i*) The two Marys, coming at first dawn and carrying a heavy load of spices to anoint the body, must have seen the soldiers come off duty. They found the tomb open. When Mary the Braider peered into the dark interior she saw what appeared to be two men in white raiment, but what must have been Jesus, who had taken refuge in the tomb again to hide his nakedness, and the discarded cere-clothes which the officer of the guard had ordered his men to fold and replace on the slab. Both Marys then hurried in terror back to the city and, meeting Peter and John son of Annas, told them that two men were in the tomb and that the body must have been stolen. The 'they' in *John* xx. 2: '*They* have taken away the Lord out of the sepulchre', has lost its antecedent, which is likely to have been 'the soldiers'. It seems that Bunni had told John son of Annas, under a pledge of secrecy, of Jesus's re-appearance. John and Peter hastened to the tomb, the Marys following behind; but John outran Peter—stiff from his scourging (*see* cix.*t*)—found Jesus shivering inside, took off his own cloak, wrapped it around him, and led him out again. Then Jesus, wishing to avoid Peter, who had narrowly escaped crucifixion for his sake, and hastily agreeing to meet John in Jerusalem that night, concealed himself elsewhere in the cemetery.

Thus, when Peter and the Marys arrived, they found John sitting in the tomb wearing his white priestly garment. He advised them not to seek the living with the dead and reminded Peter that Jesus had foretold his Resurrection on the Third Day; but made no mention of having met him. Peter noticed the linen cloth and the napkin lying apart, and concluded that these were the two men in white of whom Mary the Braider had told him.* He was, however, unable to understand what had happened to the body, knowing that the soldiers had been on guard until the Marys came in sight. It appeared to have been stolen, but he was struck by the detail of the carefully folded napkin and the linen pall, still heavy with precious ointment. Why had these not been removed with the body? Since there was no one to enlighten him, he presently went away with John and Mary the Braider, carrying the unused spices back to Bunni.

The other Mary remained weeping outside the tomb. Suddenly a man's voice behind her asked why she wept; she half turned, and failed at first to recognize Jesus, because he was not dressed in his customary white robe and praying-garment. (It seems to have been on a later occasion that he was mistaken for the cemetery keeper—*see* cxvi.*d*.) Then she heard her name called, faced about and knew him at once. She tried to clasp his feet, but he would not permit this. *John* xx. 17: 'Touch me not, for I am not yet ascended to my Father' cannot be accepted. He will have said: 'Touch me not, for I have been raised (i.e. on a cross) and am not yet purified.' Jesus feared to defile her, being himself defiled through contact with a cross on which previous victims had died. He asked her to give Peter and the other Galilean disciples a message: they were to re-assemble in the place from which they had come— namely the upper room in which the Last Supper had been eaten, but Mary

---

* Samuel Butler makes this suggestion in *The Fair Haven*.

thought that he meant 'Galilee'—where he would presently join them. When she returned to Jerusalem, Peter did not believe her.

(*k*) The Mary to whom Jesus revealed himself was his Queen, not Mary the Braider, as is suggested by her calling him 'my lord', and then trying to clasp his feet. Had she been his adoptive mother, she would neither have abased herself nor would he have addressed her familiarly as 'Mary'.

(*l*) The Synoptics suppress all mention of John son of Annas; probably because Jesus held him in higher regard than Peter, who was afterwards venerated in the West as the true head of the Church. They have even recorded a special appearance to Peter which was, in fact, granted to Simeon son of Cleophas (*see* cxvi.*c*).

Mark xv. 39, the Centurion's alleged testimony that Jesus was the Son of God (*see* cxiii.*p*), will have been Bunni's when told of the Resurrection. A Roman officer would never have glorified God because His Son was crucified; or even because a 'righteous man' was crucified. However, the officer of the guard who witnessed the Resurrection may well have cried: 'Surely, this was a righteous man!' and been so deeply impressed by Jesus's survival that he forbore to hinder his escape; taking the characteristic Graeco-Roman view, 'Since fortune has preserved this man, is he not proved innocent of any crime?', and expressing this without special regard either for the God of Israel or for Jesus's claims to royalty.

(*m*) As for the miraculous appearance of the angels in *Matthew* xxviii. 2: if the editor knew the original tradition—namely that the soldiers were inspired 'by an angel' to roll back the stone, and that they told their officer: 'There has been an earthquake'—he would naturally simplify the narrative by crediting the angel with both the earthquake and the removal of the stone. His version may have found confirmation in synagogue murals which showed the Angel Gabriel opening the tombs of the Just on the Third Day, to the amazement of spectators.

> (447) *When the sabbath was ended and it was yet dark, an angel of the Lord put it into the hearts of certain of the watchmen to come privily to the tomb, and roll back the stone.*
>
> *And even as they did so, lo! a noise, and he that was dead came forth, bound hand and foot with grave-clothes, and his face bound about with a napkin, and sat upon the stone in the moonlight.*
>
> *His countenance was pale and his raiment shone; and for fear of him the watchmen did tremble and cry out, and their cries awakened the officer of the watch.*
>
> *The same beheld how they bowed their faces to the earth, supposing that they had seen a spirit, and became as dead men.*
>
> *But Jesus said: 'I thirst.'*
>
> *Then the officer, knowing that it was Jesus and no spirit, straitly enquired of the watchmen: 'How came the stone to be rolled back?'*
>
> *They answered, for fear of him: 'Sir, while thou layest sleeping the earth trembled, and behold the tomb was opened.'*

Then said he: 'This cometh surely of the gods, not of men. Loose this man therefore, and let him go!'

*   *   *   *   *

(448) *And when they had loosed Jesus, they gave him to drink, and straightway the officer went unto Jerusalem with the watchmen, and sought out Nakemidam, and told him all that had passed.*

Then Nakemidam glorified God, and said: 'Truly, this man is the Son of God and no deceiver!'

And he gave large money unto the soldiers, and said unto them: 'Ye did well to loose him, but beware!

'For if this come to Pilate's ear, he will cast you into prison because that ye freed him which was condemned to die on the cross.

'Therefore, if any man ask aught of you, answer ye that his disciples came at dawn and wrapped him in the linen clothes with the spices, and carried him away for burial.'

And they gladly took the money, and spake as they were taught, and their saying is commonly reported among unbelievers unto this day.

Then Nakemidam sent hastily for John the son of Annas, and saith unto him: 'Hearken unto a marvellous thing: Jesus is not dead but risen. Go thou to him, but tell no man that the soldiers have freed him!'

Wherefore John goeth forth from the city and overtaketh Peter, which also went sorrowing to the sepulchre.

*   *   *   *   *

(449) *Now, it came to pass, even as the watchmen departed from the sepulchre, while it began to dawn toward the first day of the week, that Mary the Braider and the other Mary also, the sister-wife of Jesus, came bearing spices which they had prepared to anoint the body withal, after that they had washed it.*

They, coming unto the sepulchre, found the stone rolled away, and stood perplexed.

Howbeit, Mary the Braider went and stooped down and looked into the sepulchre; and it was dark within.

She thinketh that she seeth two men in white garments seated one at the head and the other at the foot of the place where Jesus had lain.

And she runneth and cometh unto the other Mary, and saith unto her: 'I saw two men in white garments!'

And they fled from the sepulchre, for they were sore amazed, and meeting Peter and John coming forth from Jerusalem, the other Mary cried unto them:

'Brethren, the watchmen have taken away my lord out of the sepulchre, and we know not where they have laid him!'

Then said Mary the Braider: 'Yea, and even now I saw two men in white raiment sitting within, as it might be angels.'

*   *   *   *   *

(450) *And John and Peter hastened forward together, but John did outrun Peter, which halted because of the scourging, and came first unto the sepul-*

chre; and stooping down, he saw Jesus sitting naked within, and the linen clothes lying apart.

And he believed that which Nakemidam had told him and was exceeding glad, and beckoned unto Jesus to come forth.

Then John put his cloak upon Jesus to cover his nakedness, and led him unto a place apart, and they covenanted together to meet that night in Jerusalem, in the upper room where they had supped.

* * * *

(451) And John returneth straightway unto the sepulchre, and there cometh Simon Peter following, with Mary the Braider and the other Mary, and went in after him; but as yet only John had seen Jesus, and these others had not.

John therefore saith unto them: 'Why seek ye the living with the dead? He is not here. Hath he not been restored to life?

'As he himself said unto us: "I trust that God will raise me up on the third day," and behold, is this not the third day since he died?'

And Peter, when he heard this, wondered. And seeing the linen clothes lie and the napkin, that had been about the head of Jesus, wrapped together in a place apart, he saith unto Mary the Braider: 'Here verily are the two angels whereof thou spakest!'

And John departed thence, neither said he aught unto any man, for the sake of Nakemidam which had charged him to reveal unto none that Jesus was yet alive.

Peter also went with him unto Jerusalem, and Mary the Braider, bearing the spices.

* * * *

(452) But the other Mary stood without the sepulchre, weeping, and as she wept, she heard a voice behind her, which said: 'Woman, why weepest thou?'

She answered, saying: 'Because they have taken away my lord, and I know not where they have laid him.'

And when she had thus said, she turned about and saw Jesus standing, but wist not that it was he, because of her tears.

Jesus saith unto her: 'Mary!'

She answereth: 'My lord!', and would have clasped his feet, but he forbade her, saying: 'Touch me not, for I was raised and hanged upon a cross whereon men had died.

'Wherefore must I first be purified, and then shalt thou touch me.

'But go now unto Peter and the other brethren which are with him. Tell them to go before me thither whence we came; there shall they see me when it is night.'

And Mary sought out Peter, and told him, saying: 'I have seen Jesus and held converse with him, and he commandeth that ye go before him into Galilee.'

(For she understood not that they should go unto the upper room wherein they had supped.)

Yet her words seemed to Peter but as an idle tale, like unto that told by Mary the Braider concerning the two men clad in white raiment.

* * * *

(*n*) That Judas offered himself as a surrogate for Jesus, and that Jesus did not die on the cross but on some later occasion, is also the Moslem view, however Mohammed may have arrived at it. The Koran (*Sura* iv. 158) is perhaps a recollection of the apocryphal *Travels of the Apostles,* quoted by Photius (*Bibl. Cod.* cxiv.) : 'Christ was not crucified, but another in his stead.'

> 'And for their saying: "Verily we have slain the Messiah Jesus the son of Mary, an apostle of God"—yet they slew him not, and crucified him not, but one who was made to appear in his likeness. And they were in doubt about him, no sure knowledge had they of him, but followed only an opinion; and did not indeed slay him, but God took him to Himself, which is mighty and wise.'

The late mediaeval *Gospel of Barnabas,* written by an Italian convert to Islam, makes this other man Judas. Mohammed seems to have believed that Jesus went to Heaven [for three hours?] while his substitute hung on the Cross (*Sura* xlvii. 48) :

> 'Remember how that God said: O Jesus, verily I will cause thee to die.'

and that he subsequently met with a natural death; though exactly when or where this took place is not suggested. Jesus is made to say (*Sura* xix. 34) :

> 'And the peace of God was on me in the day of my birth and will be on me in the day of my death and likewise in the day of my resurrection.'

According to Sir Richard Burton's *Pilgrimage* (vol. ii), the Moslems also share the Nazarene view that Jesus will reappear on earth in the Last Days, slay the Antichrist, die and be raised to Heaven again. A vacant place is reserved for his body in the Prophet's tomb at Medina.

* * * * *

THE RETURN FROM EMMAUS

Mark xvi. 12–13

¹²After that He appeared in another form unto two of them, as they walked, ¹³and went into the country. And they went and told it unto the residue: neither believed they them.

Luke xxiv. 13–36

¹³And, behold, two of them went that same day to a village called Emmaus, which was from Jerusalem about threescore furlongs. ¹⁴And they talked together of all these things which had happened. ¹⁵And it came to pass, that, while they communed together and reasoned, Jesus Himself drew near, and went with them. ¹⁶But their eyes were holden that they should not know Him. ¹⁷And He said unto them: 'What manner of communications are these that ye have one to another, as ye walk, and are sad?' ¹⁸And the one of them, whose name was Cleopas, answering said unto Him: 'Art Thou only a stranger in Jerusalem, and hast not known the things which are come to pass there in these days?' ¹⁹And He said unto them: 'What things?' And they said unto Him: 'Concerning Jesus of Nazareth, which was a prophet mighty in deed and word before God and all the people: ²⁰and how the chief priests and our rulers delivered Him to be condemned to death, and have crucified Him. ²¹But we trusted that it had been He which should have redeemed Israel: and beside all this, to day is the third day since these things were done. ²²Yea, and certain women also of our company made us astonished, which were early at the sepulchre; ²³and when they found not His body, they came, saying, that they had also seen a vision of angels, which said that He was alive. ²⁴And certain of them which were with us went to the sepulchre, and found it even so as the women had said: but Him they saw not.' ²⁵Then He said unto them: 'O fools, and slow of heart to believe all that the prophets have spoken: ²⁶ought not Christ to have suffered these things, and to enter into His glory?' ²⁷And beginning at Moses and all the prophets, He expounded unto them in all the scriptures the things concerning Himself. ²⁸And they drew nigh unto the village, whither they went: and He made as though He would have gone further. ²⁹But they constrained Him, saying: 'Abide with us: for it is toward evening, and the day is far spent.' And He went in to tarry with them. ³⁰And it came to pass, as He sat at meat with them, He took bread, and blessed it, and brake, and gave to them. ³¹And their eyes were opened, and they knew Him; and He vanished out of their sight. ³²And they said one to another: 'Did not our heart burn within us,

Luke xxiv. 13–36 (*contd.*)

while He talked with us by the way, and while He opened to us the scriptures?'

[33]And they rose up the same hour, and returned to Jerusalem, and found the Eleven gathered together, and them that were with them, [34]saying: 'The Lord is risen indeed, and hath appeared to Simon.' [35]And they told what things were done in the way, and how He was known of them in breaking of bread.

[36]And as they thus spake, Jesus Himself stood in the midst of them, and saith unto them: 'Peace be unto you.'

Luke xxiv. 40–43

[40]And when He had thus spoken, He sheweth them His hands and His feet. [41]And while they yet believed not for joy, and wondered, He said unto them: 'Have ye here any meat?' [42]And they gave Him a piece of broiled fish, and of an honeycomb. [43]And He took it, and did eat before them.

Luke ii. 28–32

[28]Then took he him up in his arms, and blessed God, and said:
[29]'Lord, now lettest thou thy servant depart in peace, according to thy word:
[30]'For mine eyes have seen thy salvation,
[31]'Which thou preparest before the face of all people;
[32]'A light to lighten the Gentiles and the glory of thy people Israel.'

Jerome: Of Illustrious Men, 2. (On James the Brother of Our Lord.)

Also the Gospel called 'according to the Hebrews' tells, after the resurrection of the Saviour:

Now the Lord, when he had given the linen cloth unto the servant of the priest, went and appeared to James (for James had sworn that he would not eat bread from that hour wherein he had drunk the Lord's cup until he should see him risen again from among them that sleep) and again, after a little, 'Bring ye,' saith the Lord, 'a table and bread.' And, immediately after, it is added: 'He took bread and blessed and brake and gave it unto James the Just and said: "My brother, eat thy bread, for the Son of Man is risen from among them that sleep."'

(*a*) Jesus's meeting with two disciples on the road to Emmaus is fully related only in *Luke* xxiv. 13–36, where it has been given a miraculous twist. Though he talks to them at great length in the course of a seven-mile walk, they do not recognize him until he breaks bread at Emmaus. There he vanishes, to re-appear presently in their midst at Jerusalem. *Luke's* account has strong literary affinities with the first chapter of Apuleius's *Golden Ass,* where a traveller overtakes two countrymen earnestly discussing a local miracle, becomes engrossed in their talk, and continues with them until they reach their goal. Later, one of the countrymen says: 'You must surely be very much of a stranger here, if you are ignorant . . .' of a further wonder. The disciples' failure to recognize Jesus during their long journey also recalls several episodes in the Clementine *Recognitions,* a devotional novel on which Voltaire mischievously modelled his *Candide.*

(*b*) Since Emmaus, which lay 'about sixty furlongs' (seven miles) northwest of Jerusalem on the highway to Lydda, was a town, not a 'village', it may have been used merely as a point of reference for the 'village' to which they went— probably Ramathaim-Zophim, or 'Arimathea' (*see* cxiv.*a*). Another Emmaus is mentioned by Josephus (*Wars* vii. 6. 6) as lying only four Roman miles from Jerusalem in the same direction. But Jesus, after all his sufferings, culminating in nearly three days of starvation, will hardly have been able to walk even eight miles, let alone fifteen.

Luke's account may, however, be accepted as basically true, and a simple combination of verses 18 and 34 reveals the identity of one disciple at least. He was Simeon son of Cleophas, or *Garosh* ('the Chaste'), father of Mary, Martha and Lazarus, brother of Mary of Cleophas, and destined later to succeed his cousin James the Just as head of the Nazarene Church (*see* viii.*q–v*). Luke xxiv. 32, 'did not our hearts burn?' makes it clear that they had both been among the disbelieving kinsmen (*see* lxxxvii.*e*) who held that he was out of his senses (*see* civ.*a–c*).

(*c*) *Luke* xxiv. 33–34 is curiously worded:

> 'They rose up the same hour and found the Eleven gathered together and them that were with them, saying: "The Lord is risen indeed and hath appeared unto Simon." '

Simon is the Greek form of 'Simeon'—thus Simon Peter (*Acts* xv. 14) is also called 'Simeon'—and 'saying' is in the accusative case, in apposition to 'them that were with them'; so that the Greek reads as though two travellers were greeted with news of a special and otherwise unrecorded appearance to Simon Peter. However, by the change of a single letter, *legontes* for *legontas,* the sense is restored: these two disciples are excitedly recounting their own meeting with Jesus. Since it was Simeon's companion who spoke, he must have been of greater authority among the Eleven even than Simeon, and it is therefore likely that he was James the Just (or 'James the brother of Our Lord'). His name will have been suppressed because he later quarrelled with Paul and reproved Peter for eating with Gentiles: the editor of *Luke* likes to believe that, after Simeon's daughter Mary, Peter was granted the first vision of the Risen Lord.

(*d*) James and Simeon had probably walked out to 'Arimathea', escorting James's father Joseph back to his home after the *Seder*; their route lay from the east of Jerusalem to the north-west, skirting the walls. It seems that on their return, towards evening, accompanied by a servant, they passed near Bunni's private cemetery, not far from Golgotha and therefore to the north of the city, where they paused to discuss the stealing of Jesus's body, about which they had been informed early that morning. Their earnest talk was interrupted by the appearance of Jesus, whom they mistook for the cemetery-keeper, and who will have been waiting to enter Jerusalem under cover of dusk. When he enquired what they were discussing so sorrowfully, they told him of the great disappointment which their dead master's last actions had caused them, of the mysterious disappearance of his body, and of the rumour that he was still alive. Jesus then revealed himself and asked them for food—*Luke* xxiv. 40–43 has been misplaced—which their servant found for him.

(*e*) If the main details of the account quoted by Jerome from the *Gospel according to the Hebrews** are to be accepted, Jesus showed them one of the sweet-smelling linen cloths—perhaps the napkin—in evidence of his identity, and gave it to their Levite servant. The parenthetical gloss giving the reasons for James's fasting must be rejected; James, being a Rechabite (*see* viii.*v*), would not have 'drunken the Lord's cup' even if he had attended the Last Supper; nor would Jesus, who was still defiled, have offered him bread. Both James and Simeon were fasting for Jesus, and he will have told them that this was now no longer necessary. (The table mentioned in Jerome's quotation is a reminiscence of Jesus's visit to Bethany in *Luke* xxiv. 28.) When he had satisfied his hunger with unleavened bread and broiled fish—the best manuscripts omit the honeycomb—supplied by the servant, who was under no obligation to fast, he accompanied James and Simeon and explained why he had preached the false doctrine. He may have called them 'slow of heart', but he certainly did not call them 'fools', which would have been a sin (*see* xxii.*b*).

(*f*) James and Simeon now understood all and repentantly begged him to spend the night at Bethany: but he left them, to meet John son of Annas, and disappeared into the dusk. At this point Simeon seems to have uttered the *Nunc Dimittis* of *Luke* ii. 29–32 (*see* iii.*a*); it consists largely of quotations from *Genesis* xlvi. 30 and from *Isaiah* lii. 10, and xlix. 3 and 6. He was inwardly at peace again, though feeling bitterly ashamed. He remembered his recent scornful denial that his son Lazarus could have escaped from the tomb by a supreme effort of faith; but Jesus had now justified his own contention by doing so himself.

After dining at Bethany, James and Simeon set out for Jerusalem, where they visited John son of Annas in the upper room. They found most of the other disciples closeted with him, discussing Mary's report, which they at once confirmed. When Peter still doubted, they assured him that they had not seen a phantom: Jesus had eaten and drunk, had blessed the bread with his own particular prayer, and showed them the nail marks in his hands and feet. John son of Annas kept silent. Jesus himself was still on his way, and it is indeed remarkable that, in his condition, he managed the steep ascent to Ophel through the narrow, crowded streets.

---

*This is an important passage, because it identifies 'James the Just' with James the Apostle, the brother of our Lord, *alias* 'James the Less' or 'James the son of Alphaeus'.

(g) *John* xx. 24, where it is stated that Thomas was absent, contradicts *Luke* xxiv. 34, where 'all the Eleven' were present; thus the latter cannot be quoted to prove that Simeon's companion was not also of the Eleven. Origen's quotation from this verse (*Against Celsus* i. 31), lends further support to our interpretation of *legontas*. He writes: 'When Simon and Cleophas were talking of what happened to them . . .' This dichotomy of 'Simon Cleopas' into 'Simon' and 'Cleopas' is understandable if James's name had already been suppressed by Celsus's time.

(453) *And on the same day it came to pass that James the brother of Jesus went forth from Bethany with his father Joseph.*

And they journeyed to Ramathaim, a village nigh unto the town of Emmaus, where Joseph dwelt; and his cousin Simeon the Chaste, son of Cleophas went with them.

And before it was night, James and Simeon returned unto Bethany, which was a journey of about sixty furlongs.

Now, as they passed by the garden where the body of Jesus had been laid, they stood without, and communed together and reasoned.

Jesus himself drew nigh, and said unto them: 'What manner of communications are these that ye have one to another, being so sad?'

But they, supposing him to be the gardener, knew him not.

And Simeon said: 'We speak concerning Jesus the Galilean, our kinsman, which was a prophet mighty in deed and word before God, and before all the people.

'And we trusted that it had been he which should have redeemed Israel. But an evil spirit entered into him and he deceived the people, bidding them trust every man in the strength of his own right hand and in the sword.

'Therefore was he taken and delivered by the Chief Priests unto the Romans, which have crucified him.

'But now this is the third day, and certain women of our household which were early in this garden to anoint the body, found it not, but said that they had seen a vision of angels, yea, also that they had found him yet alive.

'And afterward two of his disciples came hither, but found him not. Knowest thou truly naught of the matter?'

* * * *

(454) *Then said Jesus unto the twain: 'O slow of heart to believe all that the prophets have spoken!'*

When he had thus said, he shewed unto them his hands and his feet, and the linen napkin, smelling of spices.

And while they yet believed not for joy, and marvelled, he said unto them: 'Have ye any meat?'

They answer: 'Nay, for we fast in mourning for him that is dead.'

Howbeit, their servant which came with them set bread and a piece of broiled fish before him; and to him Jesus gave the linen napkin.

And when Jesus had washed his hands, he sanctified the bread and brake it, and did eat before them.

*Then saith he unto James and Simeon: 'My brethren, break your fast like-
wise, for this son of man is risen from among them that sleep.'*   .

And at last they believed.

* * * *

(455) *Then Jesus arose and departed with the twain, and as they walked, he
asked them: 'Ought not the Anointed One to have done even as he did?'*

*And he expounded unto them all the prophecies that were fulfilled in him,
beginning with Moses even unto Zechariah.*

*And their eyes were opened, and they understood wherefore he had
preached false doctrine.*

*Now, as they drew nigh unto Bethany, he made as if to turn toward Jeru-
salem, and they sought to constrain him, saying: 'Abide with us, the day is far
spent and darkness falleth.'*

But he would not, and said: 'Go your way. Peace be unto you.'

*And Simeon took Jesus in his arms, though he was as yet in his unclean-
ness, and said: 'Lord, I shall indeed depart in peace according to Thy word.*

*'As Jacob, our forefather, said unto his son Joseph: "Now let me die, for I
have seen thy face and thou art yet alive." '*

*And Simeon blessed God, saying: 'Today is come to pass the prophecy
which Isaiah spake: "All the nations of the world shall see the salvation of
our God.*

' "Thou art My servant, O Israel, in whom I will be glorified.

*' "I will also give thee for a light unto the Gentiles, that thou mayest be My
salvation to the ends of the earth." '*

Then Jesus went from them and vanished out of their sight.

* * * *

(456) *Afterward, as they sat at meat in Bethany, they said to one another:
'Did not our heart burn within us, when he spake to us by the way?'*

*For it repented them that they had withstood him as touching the death of
Eliezer, seeing that he himself now by faith was enlarged from the sepulchre.*

*And they rose up in the same hour and went unto Jerusalem to seek out
John the son of Annas, and found him and Peter and certain of the disciples
gathered together in the upper room.*

*Then said James: 'The master hath risen indeed, as Mary told you, and
hath appeared unto Simeon and myself.'*

*And he set forth what things were said and done by the way, that it might
be certified that they had seen no spirit, but Jesus himself, and no other man.*

*For he was known unto them by the words wherewith he blessed the bread
when he brake it, and by the wounds in his hands and feet.*

* * * *

THE GOODBYE

Mark xvi. 14–20

[14]Afterward He appeared unto the Eleven as they sat at meat, and upbraided them with their unbelief and hardness of heart, because they believed not them which had seen Him after He was risen. [15]And He said unto them: 'Go ye into all the world, and preach the Gospel to every creature. [16]He that believeth and is baptized shall be saved; but he that believeth not shall be condemned. [17]And these signs shall follow them that believe: In My name shall they cast out devils; they shall speak with new tongues; [18]they shall take up serpents; and if they drink any deadly thing, it shall not hurt them; they shall lay hands on the sick, and they shall recover.'

[19]So then after the Lord had spoken unto them, He was received up into heaven, and sat on the right hand of God. [20]And they went forth, and preached every where, the Lord working with them, and confirming the word with signs following.

Amen.

Matthew xxviii. 16–20

[16]Then the eleven disciples went away into Galilee, into a mountain where Jesus had appointed them. [17]And when they saw Him, they worshipped Him: but some doubted. [18]And Jesus came and spake unto them, saying: 'All power is given unto Me in heaven and in earth. [19]Go ye therefore, and teach all nations, baptizing them in the name of the Father, and of the Son, and of the Holy Ghost, [20]teaching them to observe all things whatsoever I have commanded you: and, lo, I am with you alway, even unto the end of the world.'

Amen.

Luke xxiv. 36–53

[36]And as they thus spake, Jesus Himself stood in the midst of them, and saith unto them: 'Peace be unto you.' [37]But they were terrified and affrighted, and supposed that they had seen a spirit. [38]And He said unto them: 'Why are ye troubled? and why do thoughts arise in your hearts? [39]Behold My hands and My feet, that it is I Myself: handle Me, and see; for a spirit hath not flesh and bones, as ye see Me have.' [40]And when He had thus spoken, He shewed them His hands and His feet. [41]And while they yet believed not for joy, and wondered, He said unto them: 'Have ye here any meat?' [42]And they gave

Luke xxiv. 36–53 *(contd.)*

Him a piece of broiled fish, and of an honeycomb. ⁴³And He took it, and did eat before them.

⁴⁴And He said unto them: 'These are the words which I spake unto you, while I was yet with you, that all things must be fulfilled, which were written in the law of Moses, and in the prophets, and in the psalms, concerning Me.' ⁴⁵Then opened He their understanding, that they might understand the scriptures, ⁴⁶and said unto them: 'Thus it is written, and thus it behoved Christ to suffer, and to rise from the dead the third day: ⁴⁷and that repentance and remission of sins should be preached in His name among all nations, beginning at Jerusalem. ⁴⁸And ye are witnesses of these things. ⁴⁹And, behold, I send the promise of My Father upon you: but tarry ye in the city of Jerusalem, until ye be endued with power from on high.'

⁵⁰And He led them out as far as to Bethany, and He lifted up His hands, and blessed them. ⁵¹And it came to pass, while He blessed them, He was parted from them, and carried up into heaven. ⁵²And they worshipped Him, and returned to Jerusalem with great joy: ⁵³and were continually in the temple, praising and blessing God.

Amen.

Acts i. 1–14

THE ACTS OF THE APOSTLES

¹The former treatise have I made, O Theophilus, of all that Jesus began both to do and teach, ²until the day in which He was taken up, after that He through the Holy Ghost had given commandments unto the Apostles whom He had chosen, ³to whom also He shewed Himself alive after His passion by many infallible proofs, being seen of them forty days, and speaking of the things pertaining to the kingdom of God: ⁴and, being assembled together with them, commanded them that they should not depart from Jerusalem, but wait for the promise of the Father, which, saith He, ye have heard of Me. ⁵For John truly baptized with water: but ye shall be baptized with the Holy Ghost not many days hence. ⁶When they therefore were come together, they asked of Him, saying: 'Lord, wilt Thou at this time restore again the kingdom to Israel?'

⁷And He said unto them: 'It is not for you to know the times or the seasons, which the Father hath put in His own power. ⁸But ye shall receive power, after that the Holy Ghost is come upon you: and ye shall be witnesses unto Me both in Jerusalem, and in all Judaea, and in Samaria, and unto the uttermost part of the earth.' ⁹And when He had spoken these things, while they beheld, He was taken up; and a cloud received Him out of their sight. ¹⁰And while they looked stedfastly toward heaven as He went up, behold, two men stood by them in white apparel; ¹¹which also said: 'Ye men of Galilee, why stand ye gazing up into heaven? this same Jesus, which is taken up from you into heaven, shall so come in like manner as ye have seen Him go into heaven.' ¹²Then returned they unto Jerusalem from the mount called Olivet, which is from Jerusalem a sabbath day's journey.

¹³And when they were come in, they went up into an upper room, where

Acts i. 1–14 (*contd.*)

abode both Peter, and James, and John, and Andrew, Philip, and Thomas, Bartholomew, and Matthew, James the son of Alphaeus, and Simon Zelotes, and Judas the brother of James. [14]These all continued with one accord in prayer and supplication, with the women, and Mary the mother of Jesus, and with His brethren.

John xx. 19–31

[19]Then the same day at evening, being the first day of the week, when the doors were shut where the disciples were assembled for fear of the Jews, came Jesus and stood in the midst, and saith unto them: 'Peace be unto you.' [20]And when He had so said, He shewed unto them His hands and His side. Then were the disciples glad when they saw the Lord. [21]Then said Jesus to them again: 'Peace be unto you: as My Father hath sent Me, even so send I you.' [22]And when He had said this, He breathed on them, and saith unto them: 'Receive ye the Holy Ghost: [23]whose soever sins ye remit, they are remitted unto them; and whose soever sins ye retain, they are retained.'

[24]But Thomas, one of the Twelve, called Didymus, was not with them when Jesus came. [25]The other disciples therefore said unto him: 'We have seen the Lord.' But he said unto them: 'Except I shall see in His hands the print of the nails, and put my finger into the print of the nails, and thrust my hand into His side, I will not believe.'

[26]And after eight days again His disciples were within, and Thomas with them: then came Jesus, the doors being shut, and stood in the midst, and said: 'Peace be unto you.' [27]Then saith He to Thomas: 'Reach hither thy finger, and behold My hands; and reach hither thy hand, and thrust it into My side: and be not faithless, but believing.' [28]And Thomas answered and said unto Him: 'My Lord and my God.' [29]Jesus saith unto him: 'Thomas, because thou hast seen Me, thou hast believed: blessed are they that have not seen, and yet have believed.'

[30]And many other signs truly did Jesus in the presence of His disciples, which are not written in this book: [31]but these are written, that ye might believe that Jesus is the Christ, the Son of God; and that believing ye might have life through His name.

John xxi. 15–25

[15]So when they had dined, Jesus saith to Simon Peter: 'Simon, son of Jonas, lovest thou Me more than these?' He saith unto Him: 'Yea, Lord; Thou knowest that I love Thee.' He saith unto him: 'Feed My lambs.' [16]He saith to him again the second time: 'Simon, son of Jonas, lovest thou Me?' He saith unto Him: 'Yea, Lord; Thou knowest that I love Thee.' He said unto him: 'Feed My sheep.' [17]He saith unto him the third time: 'Simon, son of Jonas, lovest thou Me?' Peter was grieved because He said unto him the third time, Lovest thou Me? And he said unto Him: 'Lord, Thou knowest all things; Thou knowest that I love Thee.' Jesus saith unto him: 'Feed My sheep. [18]Verily, verily, I say unto thee, when thou wast young, thou girdest thyself, and walkedst whither thou wouldest: but when thou shalt be old,

John xxi. 15–25 *(contd.)*

thou shalt stretch forth thy hands, and another shall gird thee, and carry thee whither thou wouldest not.' [19]This spake He, signifying by what death he should glorify God. And when He had spoken this, He saith unto him: 'Follow Me.'

[20]Then Peter, turning about, seeth the disciple whom Jesus loved following; which also leaned on His breast at supper, and said, Lord, which is he that betrayeth Thee? [21]Peter seeing him saith to Jesus: 'Lord, and what shall this man do?' [22]Jesus saith unto him: 'If I will that he tarry till I come, what is that to thee? follow thou Me.' [23]Then went this saying abroad among the brethren, that that disciple should not die: yet Jesus said not unto him: 'He shall not die;' but 'If I will that he tarry till I come, what is that to thee?'

[24]This is the disciple which testifieth of these things: and wrote these things: and we know that his testimony is true.

[25]And there are also many other things which Jesus did, the which, if they should be written every one, I suppose that even the world itself could not contain the books that should be written.

Amen.

John xiv. 2

[2]In my Father's house are many mansions: if it were not so, I would have told you. I go to prepare a place for you.

John xiv. 16–21

[16]'And I will pray the Father, and He shall give you another Comforter, that He may abide with you for ever; [17]even the Spirit of truth; Whom the world cannot receive, because it seeth Him not, neither knoweth Him: but ye know Him; for He dwelleth with you, and shall be in you. [18]I will not leave you comfortless: I will come to you. [19]Yet a little while, and the world seeth Me no more: but ye see Me: because I live, ye shall live also. [20]At that day ye shall know that I am in My Father, and ye in Me, and I in you. [21]He that hath My commandments, and keepeth them, he it is that loveth Me: and he that loveth Me shall be loved of My Father, and I will love him, and will manifest Myself to him.'

John xvi. 25–31

[25]'These things have I spoken unto you, being yet present with you. [26]But the Comforter, Who is the Holy Ghost, Whom the Father will send in My name, He shall teach you all things, and bring all things to your remembrance, whatsoever I have said unto you. [27]Peace I leave with you, My peace I give unto you: not as the world giveth, give I unto you. Let not your heart be troubled, neither let it be afraid. [28]Ye have heard how I said unto you, I go away, and come again unto you. If ye loved Me, ye would rejoice, because I said, I go unto the Father: for My Father is greater than I. [29]And now I have told you before it come to pass, that, when it is come to pass, ye might believe. [30]Hereafter I will not talk much with you: for the prince of this world cometh, and hath nothing in Me. [31]But that the world may know that

John xvi. 25–31 (*contd.*)

I love the Father; and as the Father gave Me commandment, even so I do. Arise, let us go hence.'

John xvi. 1–15

[1]'These things have I spoken unto you, that ye should not be offended. [2]They shall put you out of the synagogues: yea, the time cometh, that whosoever killeth you will think that he doeth God service. [3]And these things will they do unto you, because they have not known the Father, nor Me. [4]But these things have I told you, that when the time shall come, ye may remember that I told you of them. And these things I said not unto you at the beginning, because I was with you. [5]But now I go My way to Him that sent Me; and none of you asketh Me, whither goest Thou? [6]But because I have said these things unto you, sorrow hath filled your heart. [7]Nevertheless I tell you the truth; it is expedient for you that I go away: for if I go not away, the Comforter will not come unto you; but if I depart, I will send Him unto you. [8]And when He is come, He will reprove the world of sin, and of righteousness, and of judgment: [9]of sin, because they believe not on Me; [10]of righteousness, because I go to My Father, and ye see Me no more; [11]of judgment, because the prince of this world is judged. [12]I have yet many things to say unto you, but ye cannot bear them now. [13]Howbeit when He, the Spirit of truth, is come, He will guide you into all truth: for He shall not speak of Himself; but whatsoever He shall hear, that shall He speak: and He will shew you things to come. [14]He shall glorify Me: for He shall receive of Mine, and shall shew it unto you. [15]All things that the Father hath are Mine: therefore said I, that He shall take of Mine, and shall shew it unto you.'

John xiii. 37

[37]Peter said unto Him: 'Lord, why cannot I follow Thee now? I will lay down my life for Thy sake.'

1 Corinthians xv. 3–7

[3]For I delivered unto you first of all that which I also received, how that Christ died for our sins according to the scriptures: [4]and that He was buried, and that He rose again the third day according to the scriptures, [5]and that He was seen of Cephas, then of the twelve: [6]after that, He was seen of above five hundred brethren at once; of whom the greater part remain unto this present, but some are fallen asleep. [7]After that, He was seen of James; then of all the Apostles.

John xxi. 14

[14]This is now the third time that Jesus shewed Himself to His disciples, after that He was risen from the dead.

The Gospel according to the Hebrews.
(*Jerome:* On Isaiah, preface to Book xviii.)

'For when the Apostles took him for a spirit, or in the words of the Gospel which is of the Hebrews, "a bodiless demon".'

Ignatius (2nd Bishop of Antioch—about 70–105 A.D.)
Letter to the Smyrnaeans (*Eusebius: Ecc. Hist.* 34. xi.)

> 'That he is in the flesh ever since his resurrection I both know and believe.
> 'And when he came to them that were with Peter he said to them: "Take, handle me and see that I am not a demon without a body!"
> 'And immediately they touched and believed.'

John of Damascus: **Sacred Parallels A.12**
(From the *Teaching of Peter*)

> 'Wretched that I am, I remembered not that God seeth the mind and observeth the voice of the soul. Allying myself with sin, I said unto myself: "God is merciful and will bear with thee." And because I was not immediately smitten, I ceased not but rather despised pardon, and wore out the long-suffering of God.'

The Freer Logion

(This fifth-century Greek manuscript of *Mark* has the following passage, attested by St Jerome (*Dialogue against Pelagius* ii. 15), inserted at *Mark* xvi. 14; it may have formed part of the original ending of *Mark* before Aristion rewrote it.)

> . . . and they made excuse, saying: 'This age of wickedness and unbelief is under Satan, who by means of unclean spirits permitteth not to apprehend the power of God, therefore do thou now reveal thy righteousness.' They spoke thus unto Christ. And Christ answered: 'The limit of the years of the power of Satan is fulfilled, but other fearful things draw nigh even upon them for whom, because they had sinned, I was delivered unto death, that they may return to truth and sin no more; that they may inherit the spirit and incorruptible glory of righteousness which is in heaven.'

(*a*) Records of Jesus's last appearances differ more widely even than those of the Resurrection. The original ending of *Mark* is no longer extant; a mid-second-century editor has substituted for it accounts of the appearance to the Eleven at Jerusalem, and of the subsequent Ascension, which would agree more closely with the orthodox dogma of his day. According to *Matthew* xxviii. 16–20, Jesus did not meet the disciples in Jerusalem but was last seen on a mountain in Galilee, where they had met him by appointment. According to *Luke* xxiv. 50–51, he met them in Jerusalem, and then ascended to Heaven from Bethany. This version is repeated in *Acts*—the authorship of which is also ascribed to *Luke*—with the additional detail (*Acts* i. 3) that, before the Ascension, he had stayed forty days in Jerusalem. According to *John* xx. 19–29, Jesus appeared there twice within eight days, and a third time to eight disciples beside the Lake of Galilee (*John* xxi. 1–14); but the Ascension is not mentioned.

(*b*) In 1 *Corinthians* xv. 3–7 Paul records the Resurrection and six subsequent appearances. These were: to Peter; to the rest of the 'Twelve'; to 'above five hundred brethren at once'; to James (though he does not specify which James); to 'all the apostles'; finally to himself (*see* cxviii.*j*). But if he did indeed appear to five hundred brethren at once, why is this grand manifestation not mentioned in the Gospels or *Acts?* Moreover, according to *Acts* i. 15, only one hundred and twenty persons believed in Jesus at the time of his departure; and the smaller the number, the more credible.

(*c*) 1 *Corinthians* xv. 3–7 is the earliest written account of the Resurrection. The original text can be freed of its corruptions only if it is borne in mind that Paul wrote in Greek, not Aramaic, about the year 54 A.D., and that Jesus appeared first to John son of Annas (who kept this a close secret for years, perhaps until the death of Bunni); next to Mary, daughter of Simeon Cleophas; then to her father and her cousin James the Just; finally to Peter and the rest of the Eleven. The five hundred disciples mentioned in verse 6 are, like St Ursula's Eleven Thousand Virgins,* created by a simple misreading of an abbreviation. Paul seems to have written:

(4) . . . and that he rose again the third day according to the Scriptures:

(5) And that he was seen of Mary, the daughter of Simeon Cleophas, and that then he was seen again of Simeon Cleophas and of James, brethren, at the same time; and then of all the apostles.

(6) And last of all he was seen of me also, as of one born out of due time.

(*d*) It seems that at the close of the first century the appearance to Mary, daughter of Simeon Cleophas, was quietly deleted from verse 5 because the evangelists had described her as Mary Magdalene, a very different character; and also because the testimony of women was, in any case, considered of little value. Next, 'Simeon Cleophas' was changed to 'Simon Cephas' (Simon Peter), either by mistake or design, to substantiate Peter's precedence over James. Finally an editor—forgetting that Judas had hanged himself—added 'and then of the Twelve', after 'Cephas', to make the account correspond with the already falsified text of *Luke* xxiv. 34 (*see* cxvi.*g*). He also took the words 'and of James' from their original place in the sentence and inserted them after 'at the same time'. The text will then have read:

(4) . . . and that he rose again the third day according to the Scriptures:

(5) And that he was seen; and then was seen again of Simon *Cephas;* and *then* of *the twelve* brethren at the same time; and of James; then of all the apostles.

(6) And last of all, etc.

(*e*) At this point an editor questioned verse 5, which read in Greek:

Epeita ōphthē, epeita authis ōphthē . . .

('then he was seen and then was seen again . . .')

---

* A ninth-century German martyrology, under the date 21st October, contained the following entry: '*Dasius Zoticus cum XII millibus.*' This was combined with a quotation from another martyrology: '*XI VV: Ursula, Sensia, Gregoria, Pinosa, Martha, Saula, Britula, Satnina, Rabacia, Saturia, Paladia.*' In later martyrologies *Dasius Zoticus* dropped out, and *millibus,* an abbreviation for *militibus,* 'soldiers', was mistranslated as *millibus,* 'thousands'. Then the resultant '*XII millibus et XI VV: Ursala, Sensia, etc.*' ('twelve thousand and eleven virgins: Ursala, Sensia, etc.') was further simplified to: 'Eleven thousand virgins, led by Ursula.'

and, in a marginal gloss, marked the second of these phrases for deletion, as being unnecessary. He also commented on 'the twelve brethren at the same time' by adding: 'of whom the greater part remain unto this present, but some are fallen asleep.' Finally he omitted *Simon* as unnecessary too, remembering that Paul elsewhere (1 *Corinthians* i. 12, iii. 22, ix. 5 and *Galatians* ii. 9) calls him merely 'Cephas'. The text will then have read:

(4) . . . and that he rose again the third day according to the Scriptures:

(5) And that he was seen of *Cephas, and then of the twelve* brethren at the same time, *of whom the greater part remain unto this present, but some are fallen asleep,* and of James; then of all the apostles.

(*f*) An ingenious editor then asked himself: 'What difference is there between "twelve brethren at the same time" and "all the apostles"?' He found the answer in his predecessor's gloss, the second part of which was set down in abbreviated form to show that these were the words intended for deletion:

aph: epeita ōphthē ep. au. ōph.

He mistook the *u* in *authis* for an *n* (which happens as easily in Greek as in English script); read *aph.* not as 'delete'; but as 'there has been deleted'; compressed *ep. an. ō.* into a single word, *epanō,* meaning 'above'; and read *ph* as the Greek numeral expressing 500. Thus:

aph: epeita ōphthē epanō ph.

(' "And after that he was seen of above five hundred," has been deleted.')

Then, in all good faith, he inserted this apocryphal appearance after the word *twelve*:

(4) And that he was buried, and that he rose again the third day according to the Scriptures:

(5) And that he was seen of *Cephas, then of the twelve:*

(6) *After that, he was seen of above five hundred* brethren at once; *of whom the greater part remain unto this present, but some are fallen asleep.*

(7) *After that, he was seen* of James; then of all the apostles.

(8) And last of all he was seen of me also, as of one born out of due time.

And so the verses are printed today.

(*g*) Paul does not mention the Ascension, and makes no visual distinction between Jesus's appearance to Simeon Cleophas and James, to all the apostles, and to himself. By 54 A.D., in fact, the theory of the Ascension was not yet fully developed, and Paul regarded Jesus as having still been physically alive in the year 35, when they met each other near Damascus (*see* CXVIII.*j–n*). In the absence of contrary evidence, Paul's testimony may be accepted, since he wrote at a time when the original disciples could have been called upon to disprove any gross factual mis-statements made by him.

It has been shown that *John* xxi. 1–14, Jesus's appearance to the disciples beside the Lake of Galilee, is a late intrusion into the text (*see* XVII.*c and d*);

thus the meal which follows it must have been the one which they were eating in Jerusalem before this interruption of the narrative. Therefore, in *John's* original account, Jesus will have bade his disciples farewell in, or near, Jerusalem and never gone to Galilee. In *Matthew* he is made to go there because of Mary's message to Peter and the other Galilean disciples (*see* cxv.*j*), namely to return thither whence they came (i.e. to the upper room) and await his arrival; she thought that 'thither whence they came' referred to 'Galilee', and the editor of *Matthew* thought so too, and felt certain that Jesus would have kept his appointment.

(*h*) The sequence of events may now be restored as follows. Peter and several other apostles forgathered in the upper room. There Jesus met them and explained that God had delivered him from death, and that most of the prophecies concerning the Imminent End were now fulfilled: the Son of Man was due to appear at any moment. He then retired into hiding, under the protection of Bunni and John son of Annas, until his wounds had healed. But it was slowly borne in upon him that, despite his reconciliation with the kinsmen and Peter's forgiveness, he had acted prematurely. All Israel had not repented, neither had the world come to an end; therefore Zechariah's prophecy was still unfulfilled and he had misread the signs of the times. He also realized with anguish that, as a direct result of his error, Judas had hanged himself, two fellow-Galileans had been crucified, and Peter had nearly suffered the same fate. What was he to do? Discredited as a prophet, he could not boldly resume his missionary work. Neither could he remain much longer in hiding, and thus expose his friends to the charge of harbouring a criminal. The scars of crucifixion would betray his identity.* Suicide, too, was forbidden him. He read *Genesis* iv. 1-6 as the only Scriptural precedent to his case: God refused to accept the sacrifice which he offered, his own life, as He had formerly refused Cain's. And like Cain he was branded a murderer with the scars left by the sword and by the four nails. He, too, would have to become 'a fugitive and vagabond', and seek refuge 'in the Land of Nod to the east of Eden'—namely, in the trans-Euphratean province of Susiana—doomed to 'bear the sins of many' until the end of the world, which he still expected to come within his lifetime. Meanwhile, he could preach repentance to his coreligionists in the far East; and this seems to be the meaning of *John* xiv. 2: 'In my Father's house are many mansions' (*see* cvi.*u*).

(*i*) A letter written by Ignatius to the Smyrnaeans proves that Jesus was still regarded as alive and in the flesh towards the end of the first century; because Ignatius writes in the present, not the past tense. He had, in fact, become the Wandering Jew, popularly associated with Judas's thirty pieces of silver. This legend—though not recorded until the 13th century, and

---

* No other contemporary case is known of a felon's having cheated the cross; though Josephus records (*Life*, 75) another which took place forty years later. The survivor was one of Josephus's three friends crucified at Thecoa after the fall of Jerusalem. Josephus persuaded the Emperor Titus to have them taken down after some hours, while still alive; but two died under the hands of the physician.

then confused by the theory that he was Joseph of Arimathea—may be ultimately based on a Nazarene tradition that Jesus doomed himself to a fugitive
life until he had redeemed his sin of leading Judas into error: only when the
Last Days dawned would the prophecy of the thirty pieces be truly fulfilled.
In Germany, the Wandering Jew of the legend is called Ahasuerus, an impossible name for an Israelite but, according to *Esther* i. 1, borne by the
Babylonian king who saved Mordecai from hanging and hanged Haman instead.

(*j*) It is known from *Acts* and the Early Fathers that James the Just, Simeon
Cleophas, Mary the Braider, Peter and the rest of the disciples remained in
Palestine; but there is no further mention of Mary the daughter of Simeon
Cleophas. She will have accompanied Jesus into exile; and since it was
dangerous to remain anywhere in the Roman Empire while still under sentence of crucifixion, they will have been heading for safety in Parthia, which
contained many large Jewish colonies, each with its synagogue.

(*k*) Of the Canonical Gospels, *John* alone preserves any convincing details
of the first meeting in the upper room, and even these are confused and
half-buried under a mound of Christological accretions. *John* xvi. 25–31,
John xiv. 25–28 (a development of *John* xiv. 16–17) and *John* xx. 21–23, are
very late insertions meant to prove that the apostles were pardoned for their
flight at Gethsemane and awarded a peculiar gift of the Holy Ghost em-
powering them to forgive sins or not, as they chose.

Two verses of the *Freer Logion,* a missing passage from *Mark* xiv., refer
to this first meeting.

John xii. 31 is explained by *John* xvi. 11. It refers to the Cosmocrator and
is part of an authentic but misplaced saying (*see* cvii.*l*).

> (401) '*Now is the judgement of this world; now shall the prince of Evil be
> cast out.*'

* * * * *

(*l*) Jesus, before making his second appearance—which Thomas also witnessed—will have had time to purify himself and decide whether or not he
should try to expiate his sin of ignorance, and thus free himself from God's
curse, by offering the required Levitical sacrifice. Since he ranked as a ruler,
a he-goat, not a she-goat, was demanded (*Leviticus* iv. 22–26); and he must,
moreover, take an active part in its slaughter. It is probable that he decided
against this unusual sacrifice—which even John son of Annas and his Levite
kinsmen could hardly have arranged without attracting the Chief Priests'
attention—and that he quoted *Amos* v. 18–27 to prove that one who had
longed for the Day of the Lord, yet none the less preached false doctrine,
could not propitiate God by a mere burnt offering, but must face the ordained punishment: 'captivity beyond Damascus'.

John of Damascus's quotation from *The Teaching of Peter*—a lost Gospel
which Origen regarded as genuine in parts (Origen: *On John* xiii. 17), and

which must be distinguished from the Gnostic *Preaching of Peter*—supplies Jesus's missing acknowledgement of sin. Theodoret in his *On Heretical Fables* ii. 2, seems to be referring to this Gospel, when he writes: 'The Nazarenes are Jews who know Christ as a just man [i.e. as an Essene saint, not as God] and use the Gospel called *According to Peter.*' All the surviving quotations (*see* XIX.*k*, LXVII.*a and* LXXXIII.*l*) are consonant with the authentic Nazarene tradition; but it is most unlikely that the Nazarenes themselves reduced this Gospel to writing, since to do so would have been a breach of Pharisaic custom. That Peter was still honoured by the Nazarenes in Theodoret's day shows that though he permitted the preaching of the Gospel to uncircumcized God-fearers (*Acts* xi. 1–48) he never again broke the Mosaic ritual laws, which he considered necessary for salvation (*see* Introduction ii.*t–v* and cxix.*d*) after his reproof by James (*Galations* ii. 12) for eating with the uncircumcized. His alleged speech about the unbearable burden of the Law (*Acts* xv. 6–11) is certainly a Pauline forgery (*see* xv.*a–d*).

(*m*) *John* xxi. 12–22 evidently belongs to the account of Jesus's second appearance, or all but the latter half of verse 12. 'After eight days' shows that this was a Sunday, when the Essenes and the early Christians celebrated their love-feast. On the previous Sunday they will have fasted in mourning for Jesus; now they could keep the feast with him (*John* xxi. 13), and he could also permit Thomas to touch him—though Thomas would not, of course, have addressed him as 'My God'. Jesus had now appeared three times to the disciples; and since his meeting with James and Simeon has been suppressed in *John,* this is the proper context for *John* xxi. 14 (*see* XVII.*c*).

Peter, one of the eight disciples present, seems to have asked: 'What of the Kingdom?' To which Jesus replied that he was no longer expecting it immediately or, indeed, at any particular time: in spite of what he had previously taught (*see* CI.*l*), Peter might well die of old age before its advent. (These words—*John* xxi. 19—were later glossed as a prophecy of Peter's crucifixion.) He then required all the apostles to follow him to Bethany; but John son of Annas remained, apparently with instructions where to meet him on the following day.

Jesus told Peter, who wanted to know more about this arrangement and felt jealous of John, to mind his own business and not to think of coming into exile with him. (*John* xiii. 37 has been misplaced.) In ordering him to stay in Israel and feed the now shepherdless sheep, Jesus recalled his own quotation from *Zechariah* xi. 9: 'I will not feed you!' (*see* CII.*b* and CIII.*f*). He may also have had in mind *Jeremiah* xxiii. 1–4:

> 'Woe be to the shepherds that destroy and scatter the sheep of My pasture,' saith the Lord.
>
> Therefore thus saith the Lord God of Israel against the shepherds that feed this people: 'Ye have scattered My flock and driven them away and have not visited them: behold, I will visit upon you the evil of your doings.
>
> 'And I will gather the remnant of My flock out of all countries whither I

have driven them and will bring them again to their folds and they shall be fruitful and increase.

'And I will set up shepherds over them which shall feed them, and they shall fear no more, neither be dismayed; nor shall they be lacking,' saith the Lord.

He told Peter, who still clung to his Zealotry and had to be once more reproachfully addressed as Bar Jonah, 'wild man' (*see* LXXVIII.*c*), that he could best show his love by continuing his missionary work at home. Part of this sequence has been incorporated in *John* xiii. and xiv., the Last Supper narrative (*see* CV.*s*).

John xx. 21–23, where Jesus is represented as breathing the Holy Spirit upon the disciples, is a typical Gnostic interpolation. The Holy Spirit could not be magically conveyed by human lungs.

(*n*) Jesus then seems to have visited his kinsmen at Bethany—neither James nor Simeon Cleophas are mentioned as having been present at this Sunday gathering—to bid them farewell and take Mary away with him. John son of Annas followed independently to avoid recognition, and will afterwards have escorted Jesus through Peraea into King Aretas's territory. The men in white raiment who sent the disciples back to Jerusalem (*Acts* i. 10–12) must have been members of Simeon's household. Their message was that the royal power which descended upon Jesus at the Coronation had now departed: the Crown remained once more in demise until the Son of David should come to claim it. The disciples last saw Jesus disappearing into low-lying cloud as he ascended the Mount of Olives on his way to Bethany.

The miraculous account in *Acts* i. 9 of Jesus the Saviour's ascension into Heaven from the Mount of Olives has evidently been influenced by that of Hercules the Saviour from Mount Oeta in Euboea. According to the Augustan writers, Apollodorus (ii. 7. 7) and Ovid (*Metamorphoses* i. 270–271), a cloud 'coming underneath' Hercules by the Almighty Father's order, received him out of the sight of Iolaus, Poeas, Philoctetes, Hyllus and his other followers, and wafted him to Heaven, where he attained immortality.

(457) *And as they spake, Jesus himself came and stood in their midst, and saith unto them: 'Peace be unto you!'*

Then were the disciples glad when they saw him, and none durst ask him: 'Who art thou?'; knowing that he was their master.

And Jesus said unto them again: 'Peace be unto you! Why are ye troubled? And why do doubts arise in your hearts? Behold my hands and my feet, that it is I myself.'

And when he had thus spoken, he shewed them his hands and his feet.

But they made excuse, saying: 'Master, thou knowest well that this age of wickedness and unbelief is under Satan which, by means of rebellious angels, permitteth man to doubt the power of God.

'But do thou now make all things plain unto us.'

Then said Jesus: 'Behold, the limit of Satan's power is fulfilled, and other fearful things shall draw nigh.

'For to this end was I delivered unto death: that all Israel might return to truth and sin no more, and inherit the glory of righteousness which is in heaven.

'Howbeit, it is expedient for you that I go away. I am with you but a little while yet.

'And I will pray the Father that He shall send you another to comfort you when I am gone, and abide with you for ever:

'Even the spirit of truth, which they of this world cannot receive, because they know it not. But ye do know it now, and it shall dwell within you.'

And unto James and Simeon son of Cleophas he said: 'Rehearse now the words which I spake unto you while I was with you on the way, how all things must be fulfilled which were written in the Law, and in the Prophets, and in the Psalms, concerning this son of man.'

Then opened James their eyes, that they likewise might understand.

And he said unto them: 'Thus and thus is it written, and it behoved the Anointed One to suffer and to rise from the dead on the third day.

'That repentance and remission of sins should be preached in his name to all Israel, beginning at Jerusalem and going forth even unto the Jews of the Dispersal.'

Afterwards, Jesus went forth into the night, for he was not yet purified of his uncleanness; and James and Simeon went with him.

* * * * *

(458) Now Thomas, called The Twin, one of the Eleven, was not with them when Jesus came.

And to him, coming late, they say: 'We have seen the master, and we knew him by the prints in his feet and his hands, and by the wound in his side.'

Thomas answered: 'Did ye handle him?'

They say: 'Nay, he suffered us not, because that he was yet in his uncleanness.'

Then saith Thomas: 'Surely, ye have seen a vision. Except I shall touch with my finger the nail-prints which are in his hands and the wound which is in his side, I will not believe!'

* * * * *

(459) And again after eight days, certain of the disciples sat in the same room and were about to break bread, for it was the first day of the week, the doors being shut.

And there were together Simon Peter, and Thomas called The Twin, and Nathanael which had been a Zealot, and John the son of Annas, and Judas (not he of Kerioth), and the sons of Zebedee.

Then came Jesus again, and stood in their midst, saying: 'Peace be unto you!'

This was the third time that Jesus shewed himself unto his disciples, after that he was risen from the dead.

And being now purified of his uncleanness, he saith unto the disciples: 'Come, let us dine!'

And he waiteth upon them, and breaketh the bread, and sanctifieth it, and giveth it unto them, and fish also.

And when they had dined, he saith unto Thomas: 'Reach hither thy finger and touch my hands and my side, to learn whether or no I be a bodiless spirit. And be not faithless, but believe in the power of God.'

Thomas answered: 'Nay, master, but I have seen; may the Lord forgive me my unbelief!'

Jesus saith: 'So be it. But more blessed are they that have not seen and yet have believed!'

* * * * *

(460) *Then Simon Peter asketh Jesus, saying: 'Master, will God at this time restore thee thy Kingdom of Israel?'*

And he answered: 'It is not for me to know the times or the seasons, which the Father keepeth in His power.'

Peter saith again: 'Didst thou not foretell that many of us which are now here shall never taste of death, but enter alive into the Kingdom of Heaven? I would gladly go in thither.'

Jesus answered: 'Now that thou art yet young, thou girdest thyself and walkest whither it pleaseth thee. But who may comprehend the purposes of God?

'Thou canst not enter His Kingdom unless it be first opened unto thee.

'What if thou shouldest live to be old and stretch out thine hand before thee, because thy sight faileth?

'Then shall another gird thee and carry thee whither thou wouldest not.'

And he said unto them all: 'Ye heard how I told you: "I go away and am with you but a little while." Yet none of you hath asked me: "Master, whither goest thou?"'

And Simon Peter saith: 'Master, whither goest thou?'

Jesus answered and said: 'In my Father's house are many mansions. I go whither He sendeth me.

'For because of the Scripture which I sought to fulfil, behold, thy brother Judas hath taken his life; yet I live, and his thirty pieces of silver shall witness against me until the day of judgement.

'Better that I had died in his stead, as Haman was hanged by Ahasuerus in the stead of Mordecai!'

* * * * *

(461) *'Wretched that I am: I remembered not how that God readeth the heart of man and observeth his soul.*

'I made alliance with sin, saying unto myself: "The Lord is merciful and will bear with me. Am I not his fellow?"

'And because He did not straightway smite me, I ceased not then but provoked the long-suffering of God.

'Behold, I put in the sickle before the harvest was ripe, greatly desiring the day of the Lord, and thereby I caused my neighbour to sin.

'For thou, Simon, hearkening unto the words of my mouth, didst draw a sword to do murder, and other twain that hearkened likewise shed blood, and were crucified and suffered death.

'As Amos saith: "Woe unto you that desire the day of the Lord! To what end is it for you? The day of the Lord is darkness and not light.

' "*As if a man did flee from a lion and a bear met him, or went into the house and leaned his hand on the wall and a serpent bit him.*

' "*Though ye offer Me burnt offerings and your meat offerings, yet I will not accept them, but I will cause you to go into captivity beyond Damascus.*"

'*Yea, even the sacrifice of my life by the sword, this my Father refused, because that I sinned from presumption.*

'*As it is written: "Unto Cain and his offering had the Lord no respect.*

' "*And the Lord said unto Cain: 'If thou doest well, shalt thou not be respected? But if thou doest not well, sin lieth at thy door.'*

' "*And it came to pass that Cain slew his brother, which was a shepherd, and the Lord said unto him: 'The voice of thy brother's blood crieth unto Me from the ground, and now thou art cursed from the earth, which hath opened her mouth to receive thy brother's blood from thy hand.*

' " '*A fugitive and a vagabond shalt thou be in the earth.'*

' "*And the Lord set a mark upon Cain. And he went out from the presence of the Lord, and dwelt in the Land of Nod, on the east of Eden.*"

'*Behold, that is the land where the city of Susa now standeth. Thither will I go, for His marks are upon my hands and feet, and in my side, whereby every man shall know me.*

'*But do ye tarry in Jerusalem until ye be blessed with wisdom and power from on high to do the will of the Father.*

'*And lo, my heart shall be with you alway, even unto the end of the world.*

'*Arise, let us go hence!*'

* * * * *

(462) *And when he had thus spoken, he said: 'I go tonight unto the house of my kinsmen, and by the way will I bid you farewell.'*

But unto John son of Annas he said: 'Tarry thou here, and afterward come unto Bethany, and we will privily depart from this land together.'

Simon Peter, turning about, saith unto Jesus: 'Master, what shall this man do that I may not do? Why cannot I follow with thee? I will lay down my life for thy sake.'

Jesus saith unto him: 'Simon, if I will that he tarry here, and that he should come unto me after that ye have all departed, what is that to thee?'

(Therefore hath the saying now gone abroad, that Jesus spake in parables and said: 'John shall tarry on earth and enjoy the Kingdom with me after that ye are all dead.')

* * * * *

(463) *But Peter desired yet that Jesus should lead Israel in arms against the Wicked Kingdom.*

Then saith Jesus unto him: 'Simon, thou wild man, lovest thou me?' For they had eaten the Feast of the First Day, which is called the feast of love.

Simon answered and said: 'Yea, master.'

Jesus saith: 'Feed my lambs!'

He saith unto him again: 'Simon, thou wild man, lovest thou me truly?'

Simon answered and said: 'Yea, master, I love thee with all my heart.'

Jesus saith: 'Feed my sheep!'

He said unto him yet again: 'Simon, thou wild man, art thou sure that thou lovest me?'

Then was Simon Peter grieved because that Jesus seemed to doubt, and he answered: 'Master, thou readest all my thoughts. Thou knowest that I love thee.'

Jesus saith: 'He that hath God's commandments and keepeth them, the same also loveth me, for I likewise love the Father.

'Rememberest thou how I spake and said before thee: "I will not feed my sheep"?

'Behold, now I may not feed them though I would. But do thou feed them, for the love of the Father.

'This same thing I speak unto you all, that ye be no more offended in me.

'Even as Jeremiah prophesied in the name of the Lord: "Woe be unto the shepherds that destroy and scatter the sheep. But I will set up shepherds which shall feed the flock and they shall fear no more, neither be dismayed."'

* * * * *

(464) And he led them forth as far towards Bethany as is a sabbath day's journey, and there he lifted up his hands, and blessed them, saying: 'Peace remain with you!'

Then they saw him no more, for a cloud received him out of their sight as he went up into the mountain of Olives unto the house of Simeon son of Cleophas.

And they stood watching from afar, and presently come two of the kinsmen of Jesus, clad in white linen, and say unto them: 'Ye men of Galilee, why stand ye gazing upwards?

'For as the power of God descended upon Jesus at his anointing, so hath it departed again, and he is now no more our King.'

Then returned the disciples unto Jerusalem, with Mary the mother of Jesus, and with his kinsmen, and with Mary of Cleophas, and Martha, and Salome, and they went again together unto the upper room, and all continued with one accord in prayer and supplication.

* * * * *

(465) But Jesus gat him from the land of Israel, he and Mary his sister-wife, and John the son of Annas went with him a part of the way.

And he came unto the Land of Nod, where are many Israelites which dwell under the rule of the Parthians.

Then was he as a fugitive and a vagabond in the earth, and returned not again unto his own people.

But the disciples which he taught know and believe him to be still in the flesh, watching for the deliverance of Israel.

And his heart is with them alway, even unto the end of the world.

* * * * *

(o) Here the Nazarene Gospel ends, except for a short summary of the events leading to Saul of Tarsus's experience on the road to Damascus (*see* cxviii.*j–n*)—which proves that Jesus was alive at least five years later—and a homiletic epilogue supplied by James the Just (*see* cxviii.*z*).

(*p*) *John* xvi. 2: 'They shall put you out of the synagogue'—paralleled in *John* ix. 22, 34 and xii. 42, where this punishment is threatened for individual cases (*see* xl.*e and* lxxxi.*b*)—has been put into Jesus's mouth as a prophecy of the Pharisees' eventual decision to shut the synagogues against all Jews who accepted Paulinism. The Great Sanhedrin had ruled that there was no room in the Kingdom of Heaven for the following (*Tosephta Sanhedrin* xiii. 5):

> 'Heretics; apostates; informers; Epicureans; those that deny the Revelation [*i.e. the Mosaic Law*]; those that separate themselves from the ways of the congregation; those that deny the resurrection of the dead; those that by their sin cause the people to sin, like unto Jeroboam and Ahab; those that cause terror in the land of the living [*Ezekiel* xxxii. 23]; and those that raise their hands against the Temple. On these will Gehenna be locked fast and they will suffer punishment therein for all generations to come . . .'

Pauline Christians could be justly charged by the Nazarenes with five or six of these shortcomings. The second part of *John* xvi. 2 and *John* xvi. 3, Jesus's alleged prophecy:

> 'Whosoever killeth you will think he doeth God service. These things they will do because they have not known the Father nor me; but these things have I told you, so that when the time shall come ye may remember.'

probably commemorates the violence done by the turbulent followers of Bar Cochba, more than a century later, to certain Pauline Jews who set their allegiance to Rome (*Romans* xiii. 1) above the cause of Israel's freedom.

(*q*) The Gentile Christians' theory of the Second Coming, implied in *John* xxi. 23, derives from their identification of Jesus with God, whose Second Coming was expected. In the *Secrets of Enoch* xxxii. 1–2, God expels Adam from the Garden of Eden, saying:

> 'Dust thou art and to the dust whence I took thee shalt thou return. Yet I will not utterly destroy thee but will send thee thither whence I took thee; then can I again take thee at My second coming.'

* * * * *

(*r*) The last verse of *John* xxi. may well have formed part of the original Aramaic tradition. Rabbi Johanan ben Zakkai is recorded to have said (*Tractate Soforim* xvi. 8, ed. Müller):

> 'If all the heavens were parchment, and all the trees pens, and all the seas ink, it would not be possible to write down all the wisdom that I learned from my master [Hillel].'

Much the same praise of Rabbi Johanan himself was given by Rabbi Eliezer ben Horkinas (*Canticles* i. 20):

'If all the seas were ink, and all the reeds pens, and the heaven and earth scrolls, and all mankind scribes, they would not suffice to record all the instruction in the Law which I had from him.'

And Joshua ben Hananiah, his fellow-pupil, used almost the same words. It is unlikely that Jesus's deeds, as opposed to his teachings, were the subject of the Apostles' praise; or that they greatly varied the hyperbolic convention, which was still being used in the third century (*Shabbath* 1*a*).

(PROEM)

(iii) *Behold, if all the earth were parchment, and all the seas were ink, and every reed a pen, the wisdom which he taught us concerning the Law and the prophets could not easily be written down.*

* * * * *

THE ROAD TO DAMASCUS

Acts ii. 1–5

¹And when the day of Pentecost was fully come, they were all with one accord in one place. ²And suddenly there came a sound from heaven as of a rushing mighty wind, and it filled all the house where they were sitting. ³And there appeared unto them cloven tongues like as of fire, and it sat upon each of them. ⁴And they were all filled with the Holy Ghost, and began to speak with other tongues, as the Spirit gave them utterance.

⁵And there were dwelling at Jerusalem Jews, devout men, out of every nation under heaven.

Matthew xxvii. 51–53

⁵¹And, behold, the veil of the temple was rent in twain from the top to the bottom; and the earth did quake, and the rocks rent; ⁵²and the graves were opened; and many bodies of the saints which slept arose, ⁵³and came out of the graves after His resurrection, and went into the holy city, and appeared unto many.

Acts ii. 12–21

¹²And they were all amazed, and were in doubt, saying one to another: 'What meaneth this?' ¹³Others mocking said: 'These men are full of new wine.'

¹⁴But Peter, standing up with the Eleven, lifted up his voice, and said unto them: 'Ye men of Judaea, and all ye that dwell at Jerusalem, be this known unto you, and hearken to my words; ¹⁵for these are not drunken, as ye suppose, seeing it is but the third hour of the day. ¹⁶But this is that which was spoken by the prophet Joel:

> ¹⁷*And it shall come to pass in the last days, saith God,*
> *I will pour out of My Spirit upon all flesh:*
> *And your sons and your daughters shall prophesy,*
> *And your young men shall see visions,*
> *And your old men shall dream dreams:*
> ¹⁸*And on My servants and on My handmaidens I will*
> *pour out in those days of My Spirit;*
> *And they shall prophesy:*
> ¹⁹*And I will shew wonders in heaven above,*
> *And signs in the earth beneath:*
> *Blood, and fire, and vapour of smoke:*

Acts ii. 12–21 (*contd.*)

> ²⁰*The sun shall be turned into darkness,*
> *And the moon into blood,*
> *Before that great and notable day of the Lord come:*
> ²¹*And it shall come to pass that whosoever shall call*
> *on the name of the Lord shall be saved.*

Acts ii. 37–47

³⁷Now when they heard this, they were pricked in their heart, and said unto Peter and to the rest of the apostles: 'Men and brethren, what shall we do?' ³⁸Then Peter said unto them: 'Repent, and be baptized every one of you in the name of Jesus Christ for the remission of sins, and ye shall receive the gift of the Holy Ghost. ³⁹For the promise is unto you, and to your children, and to all that are afar off, even as many as the Lord our God shall call.' ⁴⁰And with many other words did he testify and exhort, saying, Save yourselves from this untoward generation. ⁴¹Then they that gladly received his word were baptized: and the same day there were added unto them about three thousand souls. ⁴²And they continued stedfastly in the apostles' doctrine and fellowship, and in breaking of bread, and in prayers.

⁴³And fear came upon every soul: and many wonders and signs were done by the apostles. ⁴⁴And all that believed were together, and had all things common, ⁴⁵and sold their possessions and goods, and parted them to all men, as every man had need. ⁴⁶And they, continuing daily with one accord in the temple, and breaking bread from house to house, did eat their meat with gladness and singleness of heart, ⁴⁷praising God, and having favour with all the people. And the Lord added to the church daily such as should be saved.

Acts v. 1–5

¹But a certain man named Ananias, with Sapphira his wife, sold a possession, ²and kept back part of the price, his wife also being privy to it, and brought a certain part, and laid it at the Apostles' feet. ³But Peter said: 'Ananias, why hath Satan filled thine heart to lie to the Holy Ghost, and to keep back part of the price of the land? ⁴Whilst it remained, was it not thine own? and after it was sold, was it not in thine own power? why hast thou conceived this thing in thine heart? thou hast not lied unto men, but unto God.' ⁵And Ananias hearing these words fell down, and gave up the ghost: and great fear came on all them that heard these things.

Acts v. 12

¹²And by the hands of the Apostles were many signs and wonders wrought among the people. And they were all with one accord in Solomon's porch.

Acts v. 14

¹⁴And believers were the more added to the Lord, multitudes both of men and women.

Acts iv. 1–3

¹And as they spake unto the people, the priests, and the captain of the temple, and the Sadducees, came upon them, ²being grieved that they taught the people, and preached through Jesus the resurrection from the dead. ³And they laid hands on them, and put them in hold unto the next day: for it was now eventide.

Acts iv. 5–7

⁵And it came to pass on the morrow, that their rulers, and elders, and scribes, ⁶and Annas the high priest, and Caiaphas, and John, and Alexander, and as many as were of the kindred of the high priest, were gathered together at Jerusalem. ⁷And when they had set them in the midst, they asked: 'By what power, or by what name, have ye done this?'

Acts iv. 18–21

¹⁸And they called them, and commanded them not to speak at all nor teach in the name of Jesus. ¹⁹But Peter and John answered and said unto them: 'Whether it be right in the sight of God to hearken unto you more than unto God, judge ye. ²⁰For we cannot but speak the things which we have seen and heard.' ²¹So when they had further threatened them, they let them go, finding nothing how they might punish them, because of the people: for all men glorified God for that which was done.

Acts v. 16–21a

¹⁶There came also a multitude out of the cities round about unto Jerusalem, bringing sick folks, and them which were vexed with unclean spirits: and they were healed every one.

¹⁷Then the high priest rose up, and all they that were with him, (which is the sect of the Sadducees,) and were filled with indignation, ¹⁸and laid hands on the Apostles, and put them in the common prison. ¹⁹But the angel of the Lord by night opened the prison doors, and brought them forth, ²⁰and said: 'Go, stand and speak in the temple to the people all the words of this life.' ²¹ᵃAnd when they heard that, they entered into the temple early in the morning, and taught.

Acts v. 24–33

²⁴Now when the high priest and the captain of the temple and the chief priests heard these things, they doubted of them whereunto this would grow. ²⁵Then came one and told them, saying: 'Behold, the men whom ye put in prison are standing in the temple, and teaching the people.' ²⁶Then went the captain with the officers, and brought them without violence: for they feared the people, lest they should have been stoned. ²⁷And when they had brought them, they set them before the council: and the high priest asked them, ²⁸saying: 'Did not we straitly command you that ye should not teach in this name? and, behold, ye have filled Jerusalem with your doctrine, and intend to bring this man's blood upon us.' ²⁹Then Peter and the other Apostles answered and

Acts v. 24–33 (*contd.*)

said: 'We ought to obey God rather than men. [30]The God of our fathers raised up Jesus, Whom ye slew and hanged on a tree. [31]Him hath God exalted with His right hand to be a Prince and a Saviour, for to give repentance to Israel, and forgiveness of sins. [32]And we are His witnesses of these things; and so is also the Holy Ghost, Whom God hath given to them that obey Him.' [33]When they heard that, they were cut to the heart, and took counsel to slay them.

Acts v. 34–40

[34]Then stood there up one in the council, a Pharisee, named Gamaliel, a doctor of the law, had in reputation among all the people, and commanded to put the Apostles forth a little space; [35]and said unto them: 'Ye men of Israel, take heed to yourselves what ye intend to do as touching these men. [36]For before these days rose up Theudas, boasting himself to be somebody; to whom a number of men, about four hundred, joined themselves: who was slain; and all, as many as obeyed him, were scattered, and brought to nought. [37]After this man rose up Judas of Galilee in the days of the taxing, and drew away much people after him: he also perished; and all, even as many as obeyed him, were dispersed. [38]And now I say unto you, Refrain from these men, and let them alone: for if this counsel or this work be of men, it will come to nought: [39]but if it be of God, ye cannot overthrow it; lest haply ye be found even to fight against God.' [40]And to him they agreed: and when they had called the Apostles, and beaten them, they commanded that they should not speak in the name of Jesus, and let them go.

Acts vi. 1–15

[1]And in those days, when the number of the disciples was multiplied, there arose a murmuring of the Grecians against the Hebrews, because their widows were neglected in the daily ministration. [2]Then the Twelve called the multitude of the disciples unto them, and said: 'It is not reason that we should leave the word of God, and serve tables. [3]Wherefore, brethren, look ye out among you seven men of honest report, full of the Holy Ghost and wisdom, whom we may appoint over this business. [4]But we will give ourselves continually to prayer, and to the ministry of the word.' [5]And the saying pleased the whole multitude: and they chose Stephen, a man full of faith and of the Holy Ghost, and Philip, and Prochorus, and Nicanor, and Timon, and Parmenas, and Nicolas a proselyte of Antioch: [6]whom they set before the Apostles: and when they had prayed, they laid their hands on them.

[7]And the word of God increased; and the number of the disciples multiplied in Jerusalem greatly; and a great company of the priests were obedient to the faith.

[8]And Stephen, full of faith and power, did great wonders and miracles among the people. [9]Then there arose certain of the synagogue, which is called the synagogue of the Libertines, and Cyrenians, and Alexandrians, and of them of Cilicia and of Asia, disputing with Stephen. [10]And they were not able to resist the wisdom and the spirit by which he spake. [11]Then they

Acts vi. 1–15 (*contd.*)

suborned men, which said: 'We have heard him speak blasphemous words against Moses, and against God.' [12]And they stirred up the people, and the elders, and the scribes, and came upon him, and caught him, and brought him to the council, [13]and set up false witnesses, which said: 'This man ceaseth not to speak blasphemous words against this holy place, and the law: [14]for we have heard him say, that this Jesus of Nazareth shall destroy this place, and shall change the customs which Moses delivered us.' [15]And all that sat in the council, looking stedfastly on him, saw his face as it had been the face of an angel.

Acts vii. 44–50

[44]Our fathers had the tabernacle of witness in the wilderness, as He had appointed, speaking unto Moses, that he should make it according to the fashion that he had seen. [45]Which also our fathers that came after brought in with Joshua into the possession of the Gentiles, whom God drave out before the face of our fathers, unto the days of David; [46]who found favour before God, and desired to find a tabernacle for the God of Jacob. [47]But Solomon built Him an house. [48]Howbeit the most High dwelleth not in temples made with hands; as saith the prophet:

> [49]*Heaven is My throne*
> *And the earth is My footstool:*
> *What house will ye build Me? saith the Lord:*
> *Or what is the place of My rest?*
> [50]*Hath not My hand made all these things?*

Acts vii. 54–58

[54]When they heard these things, they were cut to the heart, and they gnashed on him with their teeth. [55]But he, being full of the Holy Ghost, looked up stedfastly into heaven, and saw the glory of God, and Jesus standing on the right hand of God, [56]and said: 'Behold, I see the heavens opened, and the Son of Man standing on the right hand of God.' [57]Then they cried out with a loud voice, and stopped their ears, and ran upon him with one accord, [58]and cast him out of the city, and stoned him: and the witnesses laid down their clothes at a young man's feet, whose name was Saul.

Acts viii. 1–4

[1]And Saul was consenting unto his death.

And at that time there was a great persecution against the Church which was at Jerusalem; and they were all scattered abroad throughout the regions of Judaea and Samaria, except the Apostles. [2]And devout men carried Stephen to his burial, and made great lamentation over him. [3]As for Saul, he made havoc of the church, entering into every house, and haling men and women committed them to prison.

[4]Therefore they that were scattered abroad went every where preaching the word.

Acts ix. 1–31

[1]And Saul, yet breathing out threatenings and slaughter against the disciples of the Lord, went unto the high priest, [2]and desired of him letters to Damascus to the synagogues, that if he found any of this 'Way,' whether they were men or women, he might bring them bound unto Jerusalem.

[3]And as he journeyed, he came near Damascus: and suddenly there shined round about him a light from heaven: [4]and he fell to the earth, and heard a voice saying unto him: 'Saul, Saul, why persecutest thou Me?' [5]And he said: 'Who art Thou, Lord?' And the Lord said: 'I am Jesus Whom thou persecutest: it is hard for thee to kick against the goad.' [6]And he trembling and astonished said: 'Lord, what wilt Thou have me to do?' And the Lord said unto him: 'Arise, and go into the city, and it shall be told thee what thou must do.' [7]And the men which journeyed with him stood speechless, hearing a voice, but seeing no man. [8]And Saul arose from the earth; and when his eyes were opened, he saw no man: but they led him by the hand, and brought him into Damascus. [9]And he was three days without sight, and neither did eat nor drink.

[10]And there was a certain disciple at Damascus, named Ananias; and to him said the Lord in a vision: 'Ananias.' And he said: 'Behold, I am here, Lord.' [11]And the Lord said unto him: 'Arise, and go into the street which is called Straight, and inquire in the house of Judas for one called Saul of Tarsus: for, behold, he prayeth, [12]and hath seen in a vision a man named Ananias coming in, and putting his hand on him, that he might receive his sight.' [13]Then Ananias answered: 'Lord, I have heard by many of this man, how much evil he hath done to Thy saints at Jerusalem: [14]and here he hath authority from the chief priests to bind all that call on Thy name.' [15]But the Lord said unto him: 'Go thy way: for he is a chosen vessel unto Me, to bear My name before the Gentiles, and kings, and the children of Israel: [16]for I will shew him how great things he must suffer for My name's sake.' [17]And Ananias went his way, and entered into the house; and putting his hands on him said: 'Brother Saul, the Lord, even Jesus, that appeared unto thee in the way as thou camest, hath sent me, that thou mightest receive thy sight, and be filled with the Holy Ghost.' [18]And immediately there fell from his eyes as it had been scales: and he received sight forthwith, and arose, and was baptized. [19]And when he had received meat, he was strengthened.

Then was Saul certain days with the disciples which were at Damascus. [20]And straightway he preached Christ in the synagogues, that He is the Son of God. [21]But all that heard him were amazed, and said: Is not this he that destroyed them which called on this name in Jerusalem, and came hither for that intent, that he might bring them bound unto the chief priests? [22]But Saul increased the more in strength, and confounded the Jews which dwelt at Damascus, that this is very Christ.

[23]And after that many days were fulfilled, the Jews took counsel to kill him: [24]but their laying await was known of Saul. And they watched the gates day and night to kill him. [25]Then the disciples took him by night, and let him down by the wall in a basket.

[26]And when Saul was come to Jerusalem, he assayed to join himself to the

Acts ix. 1–31 *(contd.)*

disciples: but they were all afraid of him, and believed not that he was a disciple. [27]But Barnabas took him, and brought him to the Apostles, and declared unto them how he had seen the Lord in the way, and that He had spoken to him, and how he had preached boldly at Damascus in the name of Jesus. [28]And he was with them coming in and going out at Jerusalem. [29]And he spake boldly in the name of the Lord Jesus, and disputed against the Grecians: but they went about to slay him. [30]Which when the brethren knew, they brought him down to Caesarea, and sent him forth to Tarsus.

[31]Then had the churches rest throughout all Judaea and Galilee and Samaria, and were edified: and walking in the fear of the Lord, and in the comfort of the Holy Ghost, were multiplied.

Acts xxii. 3–21

[3]'I am verily a man which am a Jew, born in Tarsus, in Cilicia, yet brought up in this city at the feet of Gamaliel, and taught according to the perfect manner of the law of the fathers, and was zealous toward God, as ye all are this day. [4]And I persecuted this Way unto the death, binding and delivering into prisons both men and women. [5]As also the high priest doth bear me witness, and all the estate of the elders: from whom also I received letters unto the brethren, and went to Damascus, to bring them which were there bound unto Jerusalem, to be punished. [6]And it came to pass, that, as I made my journey, and was come nigh unto Damascus about noon, suddenly there shone from heaven a great light round about me. [7]And I fell unto the ground, and heard a voice saying unto me: "Saul, Saul, why persecutest thou Me?" [8]And I answered: "Who art Thou, Lord?" And He said unto me: "I am Jesus of Nazareth, Whom thou persecutest." [9]And they that were with me saw indeed the light, and were afraid; but they heard not the voice of Him that spake to me. [10]And I said: "What shall I do, Lord?" And the Lord said unto me: "Arise, and go into Damascus, and there it shall be told thee of all things which are appointed for thee to do." [11]And when I could not see for the glory of that light, being led by the hand of them that were with me, I came into Damascus. [12]And one Ananias, a devout man according to the law, having a good report of all the Jews which dwell there, [13]came unto me, and stood, and said unto me: "Brother Saul, receive thy sight." And the same hour I looked up upon him. [14]And he said: "The God of our fathers hath chosen thee, that thou shouldest know His will, and see that Just One, and shouldest hear the voice of His mouth. [15]For thou shalt be His witness unto all men of what thou hast seen and heard. [16]And now why tarriest thou? arise, and be baptized, and wash away thy sins, calling on the name of the Lord." [17]And it came to pass, that, when I was come again to Jerusalem, even while I prayed in the temple, I was in a trance; [18]and saw Him saying unto me: "Make haste, and get thee quickly out of Jerusalem: for they will not receive thy testimony concerning Me." [19]And I said: "Lord, they know that I imprisoned and beat in every synagogue them that believed on Thee: [20]and when the blood of Thy martyr Stephen was shed, I also was standing by, and consenting unto his death, and kept the raiment of them that slew him." [21]And He said unto me: "Depart: for I will send thee far hence unto the Gentiles." '

1 Corinthians xv. 8–10

[8]And last of all He was seen of me also, as of one born out of due time. [9]For I am the least of the Apostles, that am not meet to be called an Apostle, because I persecuted the Church of God. [10]But by the grace of God I am what I am: and His grace which was bestowed upon me was not in vain; but I laboured more abundantly than they all: yet not I, but the grace of God which was with me.

Galatians i. 13–20

[13]For ye have heard of my conversation in time past in the Jews' religion, how that beyond measure I persecuted the Church of God, and wasted it: [14]and profited in the Jews' religion above many my equals in mine own nation, being more exceedingly zealous of the traditions of my fathers. [15]But when it pleased God, Who separated me from my mother's womb, and called me by His grace, [16]to reveal His Son in me, that I might preach Him among the heathen: immediately I conferred not with flesh and blood: [17]neither went I up to Jerusalem to them which were Apostles before me: but I went into Arabia, and returned again unto Damascus. [18]Then after three years I went up to Jerusalem to see Peter, and abode with him fifteen days. [19]But other of the Apostles saw I none, save James the Lord's brother. [20]Now the things which I write unto you, behold, before God I lie not.

Acts xxvi. 1–23

[1]Then Agrippa said unto Paul, 'Thou art permitted to speak for thyself.' Then Paul stretched forth the hand, and answered for himself:

[2]'I think myself happy, king Agrippa, because I shall answer for myself this day before thee touching all the things whereof I am accused of the Jews: [3]especially because I know thee to be expert in all customs and questions which are among the Jews: wherefore I beseech thee to hear me patiently. [4]My manner of life from my youth, which was at the first among mine own nation at Jerusalem, know all the Jews, [5]which knew me from the beginning, if they would testify, that after the most straitest sect of our religion I lived a Pharisee. [6]And now I stand and am judged for the hope of the promise made of God unto our fathers: [7]unto which promise our twelve tribes, instantly serving God day and night, hope to come. For which hope's sake, king Agrippa, I am accused of the Jews. [8]Why should it be thought a thing incredible with you, that God should raise the dead? [9]I verily thought with myself, that I ought to do many things contrary to the name of Jesus of Nazareth. [10]Which thing I also did in Jerusalem: and many of the saints did I shut up in prison, having received authority from the chief priests; and when they were put to death, I gave my voice against them. [11]And I punished them oft in every synagogue, and compelled them to blaspheme; and being exceedingly mad against them, I persecuted them even unto strange cities. [12]Whereupon as I went to Damascus with authority and commission from the chief priests, [13]at midday, O king, I saw in the way a light from heaven, above the brightness of the sun, shining round about me and them which journeyed with me. [14]And when we were all fallen to the earth, I heard a

Acts xxvi. 1–23 (*contd.*)

voice speaking unto me, and saying in the Hebrew tongue, "Saul, Saul, why persecutest thou Me? it is hard for thee to kick against the goad." [15]And I said, "Who art Thou, Lord?" And He said: "I am Jesus, whom thou persecutest. [16]But rise, and stand upon thy feet: for I have appeared unto thee for this purpose, to make thee a minister and a witness both of these things which thou hast seen, and of those things in the which I will appear unto thee: [17]delivering thee from the people, and from the Gentiles, unto whom now I send thee, [18]To open their eyes, and to turn them from darkness to light, and from the power of Satan unto God, that they may receive forgiveness of sins, and inheritance among them which are sanctified by faith that is in Me." [19]Whereupon, O king Agrippa, I was not disobedient unto the heavenly vision: [20]but shewed first unto them of Damascus, and at Jerusalem, and throughout all the coasts of Judaea, and then to the Gentiles, that they should repent and turn to God, and do works meet for repentance. [21]For these causes the Jews caught me in the temple, and went about to kill me. [22]Having therefore obtained help of God, I continue unto this day, witnessing both to small and great, saying none other things than those which the prophets and Moses did say should come: [23]that Christ should suffer, and that He should be the first that should rise from the dead, and should shew light unto the people, and to the Gentiles.'

2 Corinthians xi. 32–33

[32]In Damascus the governor under Aretas the king kept the city of the Damascenes with a garrison, desirous to apprehend me: [33]and through a window in a basket was I let down by the wall, and escaped his hands.

2 Peter ii. 9–22

[9]The Lord knoweth how to deliver the godly out of temptations, and to reserve the unjust unto the day of judgment to be punished: [10]but chiefly them that walk after the flesh in the lust of uncleanness, and despise government. Presumptuous are they, self-willed, they are not afraid to speak evil of dignities. [11]Whereas angels, which are greater in power and might, bring not railing accusation against them before the Lord. [12]But these, as natural brute beasts, made to be taken and destroyed, speak evil of the things that they understand not; and shall utterly perish in their own corruption: [13]and shall receive the reward of unrighteousness, as they that count it pleasure to riot in the day time. Spots they are and blemishes, sporting themselves with their own deceivings while they feast with you; [14]having eyes full of adultery, and that cannot cease from sin; beguiling unstable souls: an heart they have exercised with covetous practices; cursed children, [15]which have forsaken the right way, and are gone astray, following the way of Balaam the son of Bosor, who loved the wages of unrighteousness; [16]but was rebuked for his iniquity: the dumb ass speaking with man's voice forbade the madness of the prophet. [17]These are wells without water, clouds that are carried with a tempest; to whom the mist of darkness is reserved for ever. [18]For when they speak great swelling words of vanity, they allure through the lusts of the flesh, through

2 Peter ii. 9–22 (*contd.*)

much wantonness, those that were clean escaped from them who live in error. [19]While they promise them liberty, they themselves are the servants of corruption: for of whom a man is overcome, of the same is he brought in bondage. [20]For if after they have escaped the pollutions of the world through the knowledge of the Lord and Saviour Jesus Christ, they are again entangled therein, and overcome, the latter end is worse with them than the beginning. [21]For it had been better for them not to have known the way of righteousness, than, after they have known it, to turn from the holy commandment delivered unto them. [22]But it is happened unto them according to the true proverb: The dog is turned to his own vomit again; and the sow that was washed to her wallowing in the mire.

Epistle of James ii. 1–10

[1]My brethren, have not the faith of our Lord Jesus Christ, the Lord of glory, with respect of persons. [2]For if there come unto your assembly a man with a gold ring, in goodly apparel, and there come in also a poor man in vile raiment; [3]and ye have respect to him that weareth the gay clothing, and say unto him, Sit thou here in a good place; and say to the poor, Stand thou there, or sit here under my footstool: [4]are ye not then partial in yourselves, and are become judges of evil thoughts? [5]Hearken, my beloved brethren, Hath not God chosen the poor of this world rich in faith, and heirs of the kingdom which He hath promised to them that love Him? [6]But ye have despised the poor. Do not rich men oppress you, and draw you before the judgment seats? [7]Do not they blaspheme that worthy name by the which ye are called? [8]If ye fulfil the royal law according to the scripture,

> *Thou shalt love thy neighbour as thyself,*

ye do well: [9]but if ye have respect to persons, ye commit sin, and are convinced of the law as transgressors. [10]For whosoever shall keep the whole law, and yet offend in one point, he is guilty of all.

Epistle of James v. 1–10

[1]Go to now, ye rich men, weep and howl for your miseries that shall come upon you. [2]Your riches are corrupted, and your garments are moth-eaten. [3]Your gold and silver is cankered; and the rust of them shall be a witness against you, and shall eat your flesh as it were fire. Ye have heaped treasure together for the last days. [4]Behold, the hire of the labourers who have reaped down your fields, which is of you kept back by fraud, crieth: and the cries of them which have reaped are entered into the ears of the Lord of sabaoth. [5]Ye have lived in pleasure on the earth, and been wanton; ye have nourished your hearts as in a day of slaughter. [6]Ye have condemned and killed the just; and he doth not resist you.

[7]Be patient therefore, brethren, unto the coming of the Lord. Behold, the husbandman waiteth for the precious fruit of the earth, and hath long patience for it, until he receive the early and latter rain. [8]Be ye also patient; stablish your hearts: for the coming of the Lord draweth nigh. [9]Grudge not one against another, brethren, lest ye be condemned: behold, the Judge

Epistle of James v. 1–10 (*contd.*)

standeth before the door. [10]Take, my brethren, the prophets, who have spoken in the name of the Lord, for an example of suffering affliction, and of patience.

Epistle of James v. 16–18

[16]Confess your faults one to another, and pray one for another, that ye may be healed. The effectual fervent prayer of a righteous man availeth much. [17]Elijah was a man subject to like passions as we are, and he prayed earnestly that it might not rain: and it rained not on the earth by the space of three years and six months. [18]And he prayed again, and the heaven gave rain, and the earth brought forth her fruit.

(*a*) The early chapters of the *Acts* have been severely edited for various political and doctrinal reasons. Thus Peter is given greater prominence than he enjoyed, James the Just has been relegated to the background, and no hint is allowed to appear that Stephen's Christological doctrine was a scandalous Grecian heresy. Nevertheless, much of the genuine Nazarene tradition remains.

Acts ii. 42–47 and v. 1–15 show that, after Jesus's departure, his disciples still organized their lives on communistic Free Essene lines and hourly expected the end of the world. Nazarene converts sold all their property, ceased to ply trades, spent as much time as they could praying in the Temple, enjoyed only spiritual relations with their wives, and lived in a continuous state of religious ecstasy. According to *Acts* ii. 46 and v. 12, they met regularly in 'Solomon's Porch' and took meals at one another's lodgings.

The account of their miraculous use of foreign tongues in *Acts* ii. 1–21 travesties a religious experience which they seem to have enjoyed in common. It closely resembled Elijah's on Mount Horeb (1 *Kings* xix. 11–12) and consisted, like his, of four distinct manifestations: a rushing wind, an earthquake that rent rocks, a fire, and a still small voice. Only one of these is missing from the Pentecost narrative: the earthquake, said to have opened the graves and initiated the Resurrection of the saints, which has been clumsily transferred to the account of the Crucifixion (*Matthew* xxvii. 51–53—*see* cxiii.*o*). A late editor who realized that 'the saints' should not have risen before the third day, when Jesus himself arose, has added 'after the Resurrection' in *Matthew* xxvii. 53—thus absurdly keeping the saints, who 'arose' on the Friday, waiting until the Sunday morning before their emergence from the tomb.

This account of the graves' miraculous opening may shed light on the Emperor Claudius's remarkable edict against tomb-robbing, carved on the marble tablet found at Nazareth, and first published by Fr. Cumont in the *Rèvue Historique* clxiii. (1930), which Professor Momigliano and others regard as an anti-Christian measure. It is suggested that Claudius, having heard of Jesus's resurrection, decided to prevent any further troubles of the same sort by making the desecration of tombs a capital offence. But Jesus's tomb had not been desecrated: his crucified body was temporarily laid in Bunni's own vault, and then, according to the soldiers' report, taken elsewhere for burial by his kinsmen. Nor would Claudius's foreign secretary have drafted such an inept edict for his master to sign. The Resurrection had taken place two reigns before, and its most unusual circumstances could never be repeated. Probably, therefore, what prompted the edict was a report from Jerusalem that many tombs had been secretly opened, and the dead bodies removed, by unscrupulous fanatics who wished to strengthen the belief that the Last Days were at hand and the Resurrection of the Just had already begun.

(b) The disciples, freed from Jesus's restraining hand, worked themselves into a sufficiently hysterical state to believe any wild tale of ghostly visitations. They seem to have justified their excitement by quoting *Joel* ii. 29–32, calling loudly on the Name of God and exhorting the devout to repentance. An editor of *Acts* ii. 15, trying to disguise their total abstention from wine—and therefore from the Eucharist—makes Peter aver that they could not possibly be drunk at nine o'clock in the morning. Their reason for expecting an important event will have been the apocalyptic tradition preserved in *Numbers Rabbah* xi. 2 where, by a deduction from *Daniel* xii. 11–12, it is prophesied:

'As it was with Moses, the first redeemer which appeared to the Israelites and then vanished, so it shall be with the last redeemer . . . The last redeemer shall also appear unto them and vanish for forty-five days.'

Pentecost was supposed to mark the anniversary of God's gift of the Law at Sinai. It also coincided with the end of the seven weeks' Harvest festivities, which began with the offering of the barley-sheaf on the second day of the Passover. This was the day of Jesus's Resurrection, and he had lived in hiding ever since; thus the disciples may have been hourly awaiting news of his return, now four days overdue. The *Midrash* continues with an exhortation to follow this redeemer into the wilderness, there to eat the roots of wild-broom and salt-wort. A variant text is found in the *Canticles Rabbah* ii. 9:

'Whosoever believeth in this redeemer and followeth him and waiteth for him, the same shall live, but whosoever doth not believe in him and joineth himself unto the Gentiles, the same shall in the end be slain by them.'

When the forty-five days had elapsed and Jesus did not appear, he was thought to have sent the Spirit of Truth to comfort the disciples according to his promise (*see* cxvii.*n*). They will then have argued resignedly: 'Forty-five days must mean forty-five weeks of days, or perhaps even years. Watch and pray!'

(c) Afterwards, the apostles preached repentance in Jesus's name, styling him 'the Son of God'—which meant 'King of Israel'—and insisting on the imminence of the Kingdom, now that all the relevant prophecies had been fulfilled. The Chief Rulers warned them to hold their tongues (*Acts* iv. 18), but found no excuse for judicial action against them until they converted Solomon's Porch into a lazar-house, thus causing an obstruction in the Temple, and were duly arrested (*Acts* v. 18). However, 'an angel of the Lord' opened the prison doors (*Acts* v. 19): in other words, a protest against their unlawful detention was made in the Great Sanhedrin, and they were released pending trial. The charge which then confronted them (*Acts* v. 27) was 'resisting the High Priest's religious authority by continuing, when warned, to act in a manner likely to cause a breach of the peace'; but Gamaliel I, the Pharisaic President, acquitted them when they pleaded that God commanded them to preach as they did (*Acts* v. 34–40). He ruled that the effects of their message would prove whether it were true or false, and mentioned the cases of Judas (*Antiquities* xvii. 10. 4) and perhaps Theudas (*Antiquities* xx. 5. 1).* At this point, an important passage is likely to have been omitted: how Gamaliel nevertheless upheld the Captain of the Temple's protest against the apostles' misuse of Solomon's Porch. No more, at any rate, is heard of cures performed there. Gamaliel's attitude to the Law was faithfully modelled on that of his grandfather Hillel.

(*d*) Next, a number of Grecians were converted, probably by Philip (*John* xii. 21–22 and *Acts* viii. 5–40) and, after a dispute about the distribution of a benevolent fund for 'widows'—apparently the unregenerate wives of men who had taken vows of chastity and poverty—certain Grecian deacons were appointed to administer it. One of these, Stephen, was soon brutally stoned to death; but this can certainly not have been by order of the Great Sanhedrin, as stated in *Acts* vii. 54–58. The account of his trial is unhistorical, the procedure is illegal, and his address to the judge carries no conviction. Stephen, it seems, had been preaching some form of Philonism (*see* LXXXI.*c*) and identifying Jesus with the Son of Man who sat on the right hand of God and partook of His nature—a doctrine which other Grecians resented as blasphemous. He had also 'blasphemed Moses'—a capital crime among the Essenes (*Wars* ii. 8–9)—and had urged his associates not to worship in the Temple, because Jehovah was a Universal Deity and did not dwell in houses made by hands: a heretical deduction from 1 *Kings* viii. 27 and *Isaiah* lxvi. 1–6 (*see* XCVII.*c*). A young Grecian named Saul, a citizen of Tarsus, pretending indignant horror, led a lynching party which pursued Stephen beyond the city-walls and there stoned him; he himself, however, cast no stone, but guarded the garments which his men had removed to prevent their being spattered with blood.

(*e*) Saul's claim that he was born and bred a Jerusalem Pharisee and had sat at the feet of Gamaliel (*Acts* xxii. 3 and xxvi. 5), does not stand up to

---

* Whether Josephus or the editor of the *Acts* has misdated Theudas's uprising is a matter of opinion; according to Josephus, it took place some fourteen years later, in 44 A.D.

scrutiny. Gamaliel's pupils were young law-students so thoroughly grounded in the Pentateuch, the Prophets, and the Oral Tradition, that they could benefit by his post-graduate instruction. Tarsus, Saul's native city (*Acts* ix. 11, xxi. 39 and xxii. 3), was predominantly Greek and a centre of Stoic philosophy. His *Epistles* reveal a smattering of synagogue education, but this must have been Grecian, since all his quotations from the Old Testament are based on the Septuagint, even where its text wrongly diverges from the Hebrew original. He had a grounding in Greek philosophy, but nowhere quotes either Zeno or Cleanthes, as might be expected from an educated Tarsian; and though his language and style betray the native Greek, his syntax is faulty. In 1 *Corinthians* ix. 20–22 (*see* cxix.*l*), he says that he *became* a Jew when among Jews, not that he *remained* one; and the Ebionite account quoted by Epiphanius (*Heresies* xxx. 16)—that he was the son of a Greek mother and father, that after spending some time in Jerusalem he adopted circumcision because he wished to marry into the High Priest's family, and that, when disappointed in his ambition, he turned apostate and attacked the Mosaic Law—should be amended rather than summarily rejected.

(*f*) In view of his many conspicuous failures to tell the truth (*see* cxix.*d, f, and j–k*), no credence need be paid to his declaration that he was a Hebrew of the Hebrews, a member of the tribe of Benjamin (*Romans* xi. 1–2, *Corinthians* xi. 22 and *Philippians* iii. 5); he may have chosen Benjamin as being the smallest of the tribes ('Paul'='small') and having, moreover, bred his namesake King Saul. The probability is that he was a 'free-born' but undistinguished citizen of Tarsus whose father had become a 'God-fearer', that his real name was Solon, which he changed to Saul when he came to Jerusalem and acted as *agent provocateur* for the Boethians; and that when at home he sacrificed to the *Tyche* (or presiding Goddess) of his city, who appears on local coins with the river Cydnus flowing at her feet.

If it is true that Saul was a tent-maker by trade (*Acts* xviii. 3), the story of his proposed marriage into a patrician Sadducaic family makes no sense, unless his achievements as a gang-leader in the Boethian service allowed him to hope for so great distinction. The Ebionites, at any rate, are unlikely to have invented these details, and it is therefore probable that he was promised a Boethian bride if he brought off a delicate secret mission on foreign soil—the precise nature of which Epiphanius, rather than the Ebionites whom he quotes, did not dare to dwell upon—and that his failure was ignominious enough to make him turn his coat again, temporarily at least, to that of a Nazarene. Epiphanius has telescoped the Ebionite account: Saul, as a genuine or pretended convert to Pharisaism must have adopted circumcision before entering the secret service of the Boethians, and his failure to carry out his side of the marriage bargain will have turned him into a Nazarene, a scrupulous observer of the Law, after indoctrination by the Saints of the New Covenant at Damascus. The apostasy recorded by the Ebionites took place later: when he had quarrelled with Peter, James and the other Nazarene leaders.

(g) Stephen's 'martyrdom', as it was subsequently called by the Grecians, provides an important link in the chain of reasoning by which Jesus became posthumously identified with God. This depended on a misunderstanding of the true meaning of certain Scriptual texts, and afterwards found support in a Gnostic argument probably drawn from the Essene doctrine of God as a Trinity of Wisdom (*see Introduction* iii.*q–r*).

(1) God figuratively seated His Son, the King of Israel, on His right hand while making foot-stools of His enemies (*Psalm* ii. 7 and cx. 1).

(2) Jesus was such a King and was formally acclaimed the Son of God at his Coronation (*Matthew* iii. 17).

(3) Before the Crucifixion, Jesus spoke of his return to the Father [*that is to say, his death*] (*John* xvi. 16).

(4) He constantly referred to himself as 'the son of man' [*by which he meant: 'this man, myself'*] (*Matthew* viii. 20, *Luke* xxii. 48, *etc.*).

(5) He spoke of the transcendental Son of Man who was to appear in the Last Days (*Matthew* xxv. 31) and was an emanation of the Messiah, the Son of David.

(6) Stephen, in a vision, recognized Jesus as this Son of Man (*Acts* vii. 56).

(7) The Son of Man would come near to God and rule the world in His name (*Daniel* vii. 13–14).

(8) The Son of Man was the Messiah, and according to Pharisaic mystical tradition (*Pesikta Rabbati* xxxiii.): 'At the beginning of Creation was born the Messiah, who mounted into God's thoughts before the world was made.'

(9) Eventually, as 'Mine Elect', the Son of Man would occupy God's throne of glory and judge the works of man (*Enoch* xlv. 3).

(10) The Son of Man, namely Jesus, must therefore be an aspect of God, not merely an idea of God's, since God alone shall judge every man (*Ecclesiastes* xii. 14 and Psalm lxxv. 7).

(h) The apostles will have disowned these conclusions with horror, because Jesus was not only a man, and therefore a sinner, but so far as they knew, still alive; nevertheless, Stephen's murder shocked their quietistic consciences. Saul then showed his hand by obtaining a commission from the High Priest —necessarily countersigned by the Roman authorities—to warn all Christians in Judaea and neighbouring parts of the Roman Empire that they must cease preaching in Jesus's name, and to bring them to trial if they persisted. It will have been alleged, in justification, that Stephen, a Nazarene official, had caused a breach of the peace by inveighing against the Law, and that his associates had murdered him in an access of sectarian rage. The truth was, however, that since Jesus had been executed for sedition, any revival of his teaching was politically dangerous, the more so when it ceased to be a purely Palestinian doctrine and was exploited by the Grecians of Alexandria.

Stephen's murderers were, in fact, Boethian gangsters led by Saul himself; otherwise they would have been brought to justice.

Moreover, the apostles were full-time evangelists and thus regarded as endangering trade, industry, and family life. The Pharisees disapproved of their attempt to divorce themselves completely from the everyday life of the nation. Even members of the Great Sanhedrin plied trades between sessions, holding that the 'six days shalt thou labour' of the Fourth Commandment was a positive injunction which must be literally interpreted: an Israelite should not content himself with spiritual exercises only, but should be prepared, if need be, even to turn knacker for his livelihood—'Let none say: "I am a priest", or "I am a great one", or "such work is beneath my dignity,"' (*Pesahim* 113a). Every member of the congregation must actively contribute towards the fulfilment of God's sentence on Adam (*Genesis* iii. 19): 'In the sweat of thy face shalt thou eat bread, till thou return unto the ground!' Besides, the Nazarenes' complete abstention from women infringed *Genesis* i. 28: 'Be fruitful, and multiply!' Yet since the Great Sanhedrin had acquitted the apostles themselves of the charge of irreligion, and they had neither licensed nor approved Stephen's preaching of Alexandrian doctrine (*see* LXXXI.*c*), Saul was powerless against them.

(*i*) The Chief Rulers' attitude towards the Nazarene movement is clearly defined by Josephus. In *Wars* ii. 13. 3–4, after writing about the *Sicarii,* or Zealots, who a generation later began to murder the leading Sadducee collaborationists, including the High Priest Jonathan, and plundered their palaces, he records:

> 'There was also another body of wicked men not so impure in their actions, but more wicked in their intentions, who laid waste the happy state of the city no less than these murderers. These were such men as deceived and deluded the people under pretence of divine inspiration, but were for procuring innovations and changes of government; and these prevailed with the multitude to act like madmen, and went before them into the wilderness, as pretending that God would shew them the signals of liberty.'

These Apocalyptics, who included the Nazarenes, were anti-Roman and anti-collaborationist, yet not militant: they expected God's angels to fight their battles for them. Thus, though the apostles themselves were spared, many of those who kept to the same way of life, and even had no dealings with the Grecians, underwent persecution.

According to *Acts* viii. 5, Philip left Jerusalem for Samaria when the persecutions were at their height; and, according to *Galatians* i. 18–19, Saul found only James and Peter living there three years later. Saul seems to have kept within Judaean and Galilean territory, except on one occasion when, in 35 A.D., he visited Damascus—a Roman city which had recently been ceded to King Aretas of Nabataea (2 *Corinthians* xi. 32–33). Aretas had defeated the Herodian armies (*see* LXXXVI.*b*) and, though Tiberius declared war on him just before his own death, was awarded Damascus as a peace-offering when the Emperor Caligula succeeded to the throne.*

(*j*) The question whether Saul did, in fact, meet Jesus on the road to Damascus is obscured by discrepancies between the five accounts in the *Acts,* four of which disagree with his own apparently authentic statement, in 1 *Corinthians* xv. 8–10, that he saw Jesus in the same direct visual way as Peter, James and the other apostles. According to the three main accounts in the *Acts,* he saw only a blinding light and then heard a voice; and these accounts contradict one another in describing the effect on his companions. If *Acts* ix. 7 is to be accepted, they heard a voice and stood speechless, but saw no one; if *Acts* xxii. 9, they saw the light and were afraid, but heard no voice; if *Acts* xxvi. 1–23, they saw the light and fell to the ground, but had no share in the 'vision'. In *Acts* ix. 27, however, Barnabas assures the apostles that Saul had *seen* Jesus, not merely heard him.

(*k*) Sudden blindness is a common enough phenomenon and not necessarily due to any physical shock, such as a shell-burst or severe concussion; in the case of Saul—as in that of Adolph Hitler when serving as a stretcher-bearer in the La Bassée sector during the First World War—it was clearly caused by hysterical fright.

The story may be reconstructed as follows. About noon, while Saul's party were enjoying their after-dinner siesta by the roadside not far from Damascus, he heard himself suddenly addressed by name and threatened. Jesus is reported to have said: 'Why persecutest thou me?' It may be argued that his original words were: 'Why persecutest thou *my brethren*?', and that 'me' was substituted later. But it is far more likely that Saul's illegal raid into 'strange' territory (*Acts* xxvi. 11) was made with the sole object of arresting Jesus, news of whose re-appearance in Damascus had reached Jerusalem. If he had succeeded in handing back his prisoner to Pilate for a second crucifixion, the Nazarene movement, which was founded on the knowledge of Jesus's continued existence in the flesh and on the hope of his eventual triumphant return, would have collapsed in ridicule. According to Hegesippus (Eusebius: *Ecc. Hist.* 2. xxiii. 9), James the Just was eventually martyred because he had testified to Jesus's bodily resurrection.

(*l*) There can be little doubt that Saul went to Damascus with official credentials, but in all three accounts of his mission (*Acts* ix. 2, xxii. 5 and xxvi. 12) these are carefully distinguished from the real object of his journey. Indeed, the High Priest could not have signed an order to the Damascene synagogue authorities requiring them to fetter and send him by Saul's hands all Christians found in their city. They owed him no political allegiance; to obey him would have been defiance to King Aretas's sovereignty; and he must have known in advance that religious scruples would prevent them from surrendering fellow-Jews to his vengeance, especially when the Romans had not endorsed any such order.

---

* Damascene coins of the period are evidence of this change in sovereignty.

Saul would, in fact, have been obliged to act on his own responsibility, and since the only letter with which the High Priest could frank him on a journey to Damascus was one ordaining him an 'apostle of the Catholics'— a tax collector sent out by the Temple Treasurers, six weeks before the Passover (*see* XLVIII.*a*)—this is what Saul must have been given. His position as tax-collector carried two advantages: it would enable him both to identify Jesus when he came to pay his half-shekel, and to take a party of armed Levites with him—ostensibly as an escort for the tax-money when he returned—whose task would be to follow and waylay Jesus after he had paid the tax, bind him, and carry him off.

(*m*) However, this plan miscarried because Jesus had boldly taken the initiative. Saul roused himself when he heard his name called and, though dazzled by the glare of the midday sun on Jesus's white robes, peered at the stigmata in his outstretched hands and recognized him. In terror that Jesus had come with an armed following to take his life, he closed his eyes, bowed low, trembled, and begged for mercy—Saul made no secret of his cowardice (2 *Corinthians* x. 1): 'I am cringing when among you, but bold when I am away.' The situation strangely resembled that of 1 *Samuel* xxiv. 1–20, which Jesus can hardly have refrained from quoting: another fugitive, David, had caught another murderous Saul at a disadvantage, but left the task of vengeance to God. When Saul asked what he had to do, he was directed to the house of one Judas where he should await orders.

Presently Saul, opening his eyes, realized that he was blind. His shouts of alarm roused the Levites from sleep; and they led him to Judas's house where, feeling himself under God's curse, he remained without food or drink for three days (*see* 2 *Samuel* xii. 16–17) until a certain Brother Ananias was sent to relieve his misery. Since Saul's blindness was of hysterical origin, Ananias cured it without difficulty; but as King Saul had purchased his life by an acknowledgement of David's sovereignty (1 *Samuel* xxiv. 20), so his namesake must now become a Nazarene convert. However, being a tax-collector, he was expected to preach in the local synagogues on the importance of paying the half-shekels in token of national unity under the Law; and this he seems to have done for some days (*Acts* ix. 20) until the secret object of his mission, divulged by the Levite guards, came to the ears of the Ethnarch. He would then have either been publicly executed for attempted kidnapping or privately lynched by the Grecians, had not 'the brethren' smuggled him out of the city in a basket (*Acts* ix. 25 and 2 *Corinthians* xi. 33).

(*n*) The pseudo-Clementine *Recognitions* i. 70*ff.* suggests how Jesus came to know of Saul's intentions. 'A certain hostile man' raises a tumult in the Temple, snatches a firebrand from the altar, and hurls James the Just down the fifteen steps of the Nicanor Gate (leading from the Court of Women to the Court of Israel) so that he lies as one dead. Three days later, the brethren who have fled to Jericho learn that Caiaphas has given Saul—apparently the same 'hostile man'—a general commission to persecute them, and that he is on his way to Damascus, having heard that Peter is there. Caution prevents the author of the *Recognitions* from revealing the identity of Saul's intended victim, and he contents himself with mentioning Peter's presence in the city. But, according to *Acts* viii. 1, Peter had no need to leave Jerusalem for his own safety, since the Great Sanhedrin had already acquitted him of a charge of heresy (*Acts* v. 38–39); however, if he had heard of Saul's appointment as tax-collector for Damascus, he might well have hurried there to see Jesus again and warn him what to expect. Saul's fear for his life is understandable if Peter—who had once engaged an armed party of Levites single-handed in Jesus's defence, and later defied the High Priest (*see* cvii.*i and* cviii.*g*)— now accompanied Jesus as his bodyguard.

(*o*) Three years passed (*Galatians* i. 17–18). Then, after a return to Damascus for further indoctrination by the brethren who had baptized, or re-baptized, him (*Acts* xxii. 16), Saul insinuated himself into the Nazarene Church at Jerusalem; and tried to prove his loyalty by denouncing Grecian heresies (*Acts* ix. 26–29). He even, it seems, went so far as to tattoo himself with certain marks which dedicated him to Jesus's service (*Galatians* vi. 17), in the manner of the 'slaves of the God Hercules' (Herodotus: *History* ii. 113). Yet the apostles decided that they liked him no better than before—tattooing was against the Law (*see* cxiii.*e*)—and, a fortnight later, sent him back to Tarsus (*Acts* ix. 30), having heard that the Sadducees meant to kill him. Not only did the apostles feel compromised by Saul's presence, but he seems to have been incapable of telling the truth. He could not even make up his mind whether it was Jesus himself on the road to Damascus, or Brother Ananias in the Street called Straight, who had nominated him as an apostle to the Gentiles (*Acts* ix. 15, xxii. 15 and xxvi. 16).

(*p*) Schechter's *Fragments of a Zadokite Work* (*Documents of Jewish Sectaries* i.) throw further light on Jesus's presence in Damascus. These refer to an apocalyptic group known as 'The Saints of the New Covenant' (or 'The Covenant of Repentance'—*see* viii.*l*), an other-worldly ascetic sect of Levites self-exiled from Jerusalem, who placed the authority of the prophets and hagiographers almost on an equal footing with the Law. They believed in spirits, angels, the coming of the Messiah, and a blessed life after death; blamed the Pharisees for 'removing a neighbour's landmark' (*Deuteronomy* xix. 14) by setting fences about the Law; and forbade divorce. Canon Charles (*The Apocrypha and Pseudepigrapha of the Old Testament,* 1913, ii. 791) holds that they may have been among the 'great company of priests' (*Acts* vi. 71), who became converts to the Nazarene faith.

It is not known whether the New Covenanters had ever lived at Ramathaim or in its neighbourhood, but they seem to have had close doctrinal relations with the 'Watchers'. Jesus will have been on a visit to the New Covenanters at Damascus, the home of a large Jewish colony and seemingly a safe retreat now that it was no longer a Roman city and ruled over by

Herod Antipas's mortal enemy. Brother Ananias, whose name is a Zadokite one, will have been a New Covenanter.

(*q*) No historical evidence survives for determining Jesus's subsequent movements and eventual decease or apotheosis, unless Suetonius's statement in his *Twelve Caesars* (*Claudius* 25)—reading 'Chrestos' as 'Christos'—refers to him:

> '[*Claudius*] *Judaeos impulsore Chresto assidue tumultantes Roma expulit.*'
> 'Claudius expelled from Rome the Jews who were in a state of continuous tumult under the instigation of Christ.'

Suetonius was a careful, if uncritical, transcriber of Julio-Claudian memoirs and official annals, and must have had good reason to think that 'Chrestos' was a living person. Unless, therefore, another self-styled Messiah of whom nothing is known appeared in Rome between the years 41 and 54 A.D., invested with sufficient authority to throw the prosperous Jews there into a fever of millennary excitement, it is at least possible that Jesus himself ventured into the lion's den. Suetonius does not say what happened to 'Chrestos', nor does he connect him with the Neronian persecutions of the Pauline Church (*Nero* 16); but this Messiah cannot have been Simon Magus,* since no devout Jew would have accepted a Samaritan Messiah.

(*r*) Fourteen years later, in 52 A.D., Saul quarrelled with James the Just on a question of ritual cleanliness, again turned his coat and became Paul, toyed with Philonism even more heretically than Stephen and, after a temporary return to Pharisaic discipline in 55 A.D. (*Acts* xxi. 26—*see* cxix.*a–f*), eventually tore the Church apart (*see Introduction* ii.*s–y*). Yet he persisted in believing that, at the Second Coming, which he expected in his own lifetime, Jesus would approve of all that he had done and catch him up alive to Heaven with the other saints (1 *Thessalonians* iv. 16–17).

(*s*) A credible description of Paul in middle age appears in the *Acts of Paul,* written in his honour about 160 A.D., by an Asian presbyter. According to Tertullian, this presbyter was degraded from office for the lies contained in his book; but Professor W. M. Ramsay shows that he must have worked from earlier authentic material:

> 'And he [Onesiphorus] went by the king's highway that leads to Lystra and stood expecting him, and watching the passers-by, having in mind the description which Titus had given. And he saw Paul coming: a short man, almost bald, with crooked legs, in good bodily health, with eyebrows that met and a somewhat hooked nose, of great charm; for though sometimes he seemed an ordinary man, at others he had the face of an angel.' (*Acts of Paul* iii.)

Early apprenticeship to the trade of tent-making would account for his 'crooked legs'; the 'somewhat hooked nose' suggests that, though speaking like a Greek, he looked Jewish; the 'eyebrows that met', combined with his

---

* As Eisler suggests (*The Messiah Jesus and John the Baptist*, p. 581).

baldness, must have given him a sinister look at variance with his rapt evangelical smile—because the superstition that such eyebrows bespeak the trickster or murderer is ancient and widespread. This portrait is corroborated by a hostile writer's description of Paul as 'bald in front, with a pretty big nose, who had taken an aerial journey into the third heaven' (pseudo-Lucian: *Philopatris* 12).

The tradition that Paul suffered martyrdom at, or about, the same time as Peter is both late and suspect; it occurs in a passage—quoted by Eusebius (*Ecc. Hist.* 2. xxv. 5) from Dionysius of Corinth, a late second-century writer —where Peter and Paul are unhistorically said to have 'taught in Italy just as they also planted and taught in Corinth.' Though it is not difficult to believe in Peter's martyrdom, Paul is far more likely to have died peacefully in bed. No historical evidence of his end survives, except a vague statement by Clement of Rome (*Epistle C.* v) who wrote, a generation later, that:

> 'Paul having taught the whole world righteousness and reached the goal of the West [*Rome? Spain?*] and having borne witness before the rulers [*which?*] so was released from the world [*by execution? by natural death?*] and went to the Holy Place, having become the greatest example of patience.'

In the *Second Epistle of Peter,* most of which dates from the late second century, occurs a passage (ii. 9–22) apparently borrowed from a Nazarene diatribe against Paul, of which Peter himself may have been the author (*see Introduction* III.*i*). It describes a foreign proselyte to the Nazarene faith who has contumaciously resisted the authority of the Church leaders, and drawn away other converts by a false promise of liberty from the Law. The dog and sow in the last verse are Jewish symbols for the Syrians and Romans respectively (*see* XLVII.*d*).

(*t*) The following sequence is introduced by Matthias's election to fill the gap left by Judas's death (*see* CXII.*d*).

(467) *Now, when the day was come for the joy of the harvest to be fulfilled, the disciples were all with one accord in the same place.*

And suddenly they heard as it were a rushing tempest of wind that filled the house wherein they prayed.

And after the tempest, behold the earth quaked and rocks were rent and the graves were opened, and many bodies of the saints arose,

And came forth from their graves, and went into Jerusalem and were seen of much people.

And after the earthquake, behold a fire like unto cloven flames, that sat upon them.

And after the fire, a still small voice, that spake first in one and then in the other.

Now, this same thing happened aforetime unto Elijah, when he watched upon Mount Horeb.

And the spirit of God came upon them, and they arose hastily and ran into the streets, crying aloud unto the men of Jerusalem: 'Repent! Repent!'

But these were sore amazed and in doubt, saying one to another: 'What meaneth this? Are these men full of new wine?'

* * * * *

(468) *Then Peter stood up with the Eleven, and testified, saying: 'Ye men of Jerusalem, and all ye that have come up hither for the feast, be it known unto you that we are not drunken.*

'For we are of them that drink no wine.

'But hearken unto the prophecy which Joel spake: "It shall come to pass afterwards that I will pour out My spirit upon all flesh, and your sons and daughters shall prophesy, your old men shall dream dreams, and your young men shall see visions.

' "The sun shall be turned into darkness, and the moon into blood before the great and the terrible day of the Lord come.

' "And it shall come to pass that whosoever shall call on the name of the Lord shall be delivered; for in Mount Zion and in Jerusalem shall be deliverance."

'Repent therefore, and be baptized unto the remission of your sins in the name of Jesus, the son of David, which died upon the Cross, and rose again, and in which all these Scriptures are fulfilled.

'Save yourselves from this untoward generation, for the promise is unto you and your children, and unto all Israelites even as many as the Lord shall call.'

* * * * *

(469) *And many of the multitude were pricked to the heart and repented, and were baptized.*

The same continued steadfastly in the fellowship of the Twelve, and in breaking of bread and in prayers.

And James the Just and Peter, and the sons of Zebedee were their leaders.

Then they that believed sold their rich possessions and gave alms unto the poor, and afterwards dwelt together, and had all things common.

Howbeit, a Levite named Ananias sold a possession and kept back part of the price, Sapphira his wife being privy to it; but brought the residue, and laid it at the feet of the Twelve.

Then said James: 'Brother Ananias, why hath Satan filled thine heart to keep back part of the price of thy land? Behold, thou hast lied not unto man but unto God.'

And Ananias hearing these words, fell down and gave up the ghost.

Then came great fear upon all that believed.

But they, continuing daily with one accord in Solomon's Porch, and breaking bread from house to house, did eat their meat with gladness and singleness of heart, praising God and having favour with all devout people.

And the Lord added to the Church daily such as should be saved.

* * * * *

(470) *And it came to pass on a certain day, when the Twelve spake unto the people there, that the Chief Priests and the Captain of the Temple with other Sadducees came upon them.*

Being vexed that they taught the people and preached the resurrection of the just, through Jesus the Anointed One which was delivered unto death by Pilate the Governor of Judaea.

And laid hands upon them and put them in ward until the next day, for it was now eventide.

Therefore, on the morrow, Annas and Caiaphas and John and Alexander and as many as were of the kindred of the High Priest, gathered together in Jerusalem.

And when Caiaphas had set the Twelve in their midst, he commanded them neither to preach nor to speak at all in the name of Jesus.

* * * *

(471) *Then would James not open his mouth in their presence.*

But Peter and John the son of Zebedee answered, and said: 'Whether it be right in the sight of God to hearken unto you more than unto God, judge ye.

'For we cannot but speak the things which we have seen and heard.'

Wherefore, when they had further threatened the Twelve, they let them go, finding nothing how they might punish them; and fearing the people.

But a multitude came forth from the cities round about, bringing sick folk and them that were troubled with unclean spirits unto Solomon's Porch, that they might be healed by the Twelve.

Then were the High Priest and all that came with him filled with wrath, and laid hands upon the Twelve to put them in the common prison-house.

Howbeit, the Pharisees, when they heard this, made protest, and said: 'Wherefore do ye these things?

'If these men have sinned, let them come before the Council which alone may judge them.'

Thus the Lord opened the prison doors unto the Twelve, and they came forth and taught again in Solomon's Porch, until what time they were summoned by the Captain of the Temple and led without violence before the Council.

There Caiaphas the High Priest accused them, saying: 'Did I not straitly command you that ye should not teach in his name?

'But, behold, ye have filled Jerusalem with your doctrine, and seek to bring this man's blood upon us.'

And James made answer unto Caiaphas: 'It behoves us to obey God rather than them which ally themselves with the enemies of God.

'For He exalted our master Jesus to be a King and a Deliverer which preached repentance unto Israel and the remission of sins.

'But thou and thy kindred delivered him unto Pilate, by whose command he was hanged upon a tree.

'Now hath God raised him from the dead, whereof we are witnesses.'

And Caiaphas, when he heard these things, was cut to the heart and would have slain James, but he could not.

Then Gamaliel stood up, the leader of the Pharisees, which was in reputation among all the people, and commanded to put the Twelve forth a little space.

And he said unto the Council: 'Ye men of Israel, take heed to yourselves what ye intend to do as touching these men.

'Before these days rose up Theudas, which boasted himself to be King, and about four hundred men believed and joined themselves to him; but he was slain and they were scattered.

'And after Theudas rose up Judas of Galilee in the days of the taxing, and drew away much people after him. He likewise perished and as many as believed in him were brought to naught.

'Now, therefore say I unto you: Ye dwellers in Jerusalem, refrain from these men and let them alone, for if this counsel or this work be of men, it will come to naught.

'But if the same be of God, ye cannot overthrow it, lest haply ye be found even to fight against God.'

And the Chief Priests hearkened unto Gamaliel, and let the Twelve go, but forbad them to suffer the sick and lunatic to be brought unto them in the Porch.

Yet daily in the Temple and in the houses of devout persons they ceased not to preach the words which Jesus had put into their mouths to preach.

* * * * *

(472) And it came to pass that, when the number of the disciples was multiplied, and many of the Grecians also joined themselves unto the Twelve, there arose a murmuring of the Grecians against the Hebrews, because that their widows were neglected in the daily ministration.

Then the Twelve called an assembly of the Grecian brethren, and said unto them: 'It is not reason that we should leave the word of God and serve tables.

'Wherefore do ye seek out from among you seven men of honest report, which we may appoint over this business.

'And let other seven be sought out for the ministration unto the Hebrews.

'But we will give ourselves continually to prayer and to preaching.'

These words pleased the Grecians, and they chose Stephen, Philip, Prochorus, Nicanor, Timon, Parmenas, and Nicolas, which was a proselyte of Antioch.

* * * * *

(473) Howbeit, Stephen preached false doctrine, how that Jesus had despised the Law of Moses, and had commanded his disciples not to worship in the Temple.

And he perverted the Scriptures, preaching also that David had said: 'The Lord shall not dwell in temples made with hands,' and Isaiah likewise: 'I will not dwell in the house that ye built unto Me.'

And when certain other Grecians arose, of the Libyan, the Cyrenean, the Alexandrian, the Cilician and the Asian synagogues, which would have brought Stephen before the Council, he spake terrible things, saying:

'Behold, I saw the heavens opened and Jesus, being the Son of Man, sat at the right hand of God, and he it is which shall judge the world.'

And the Chief Rulers, when they heard of it, feared that the Council would not condemn Stephen, as they had not condemned the Twelve, but set him free.

Therefore they suborned certain sons of Belial to come unto Stephen, and lay hold on him as he went forth from the city, and there stone him.

* * * * *

(474) *Now, a young man named Saul was leader of them that laid hold on Stephen and stoned him that he gave up the ghost.*

(Yet Saul forbore to cast a single stone, but watched over the garments which the sons of Belial laid at his feet while they went about to do murder.)

And the followers of Stephen carried him to his burial and made great lamentation over him, and called woe upon all the Grecians which lamented not with them.

Then, because that blood had been shed, albeit by their own provocation, the Chief Rulers, with the consent of Pilate, made great persecution both against them which had been led astray by Stephen, and against them which followed true doctrine.

Yet they refrained from doing aught against the Twelve, for the Council that judged them had found no fault in them.

* * * * *

(475) *This Saul was a Greek of Tarsus in Cilicia, and a tent-maker.*

The same had been converted and was circumsised and feigned himself to be a Pharisee, but for gain served Caiaphas the High Priest, and strove to root out the faith of the Nazarenes.

And he was given authority of Caiaphas to enter into houses and hale forth men and women that believed, and commit them for trial.

Nor forbore he to raise a tumult in the very Temple, casting James the brother of Jesus headlong down the fifteen steps of the Inner Court, so that he lay as one dead.

Then the elect of Jerusalem were scattered abroad for fear of him, and preached the word in Samaria and in Galilee and beyond Jordan.

* * * * *

(476) *And Saul, yet breathing out threatenings and slaughter against the disciples of Jesus, went unto the Chief Priests, saying:*

'Behold, I have true tidings that the man Jesus, which was the cause of this mischief, liveth yet and hath come from the province of Susiana, whither he first went.

'The same now sojourneth at Damascus, among the Levites which are of the New Covenant of Repentance,

'And the marks of the nails are yet in his hands and his feet.

'What will ye give me therefore, if I draw him back thence and bring him unto you, that Pilate may crucify him afresh?

'For if this be accomplished, the people will believe no longer that he hath conquered death, and ye shall have peace.'

* * * * *

(*u*) [Here follows Caiaphas's consultation with his kinsmen (*John* xii. 10–11 —*see* LXXXVII.g).]

* * * * *

(478) *Then they called Saul again, and Caiaphas asked him, saying: 'Man, what is thy price?'*

Saul answered: 'That I be given a wife of the daughters of thine own household.'

And the High Priest was vexed thereat, and asked: 'Is this a small thing that thou desirest, being but a proselyte and a tent-maker of Cilicia?'

Saul answered and said: 'Nay, but that which I would do is likewise no small thing, and my life will be in jeopardy.

'For the city of Damascus, being now given unto King Aretas by Caesar, is a strange land, and I must go thither in stealth.

'And though thou hadst five daughters, yet wouldst thou give them all to proselytes if thereby thou mightest rid thyself of this plague.'

Then the High Priest considered and said: 'So be it. Thou shalt marry a daughter of our house on the day that this Jesus is crucified afresh.'

Saul said again: 'I pray thee give me letters unto the leaders of the synagogues which are in Damascus, testifying that I am an apostle of the Catholics, come to take up the yearly tax, and they shall entreat me well.

'Then will Jesus come unto my table to pay the half-shekel that is due of him, and I shall know him by the marks in his hands.

'But when he hath departed, then my armed servants, which thou shalt give me to guard the tax-money, will lie in wait and bind him.

'And I will straightway return hither and deliver him unto Pilate, as one which hath already suffered condemnation.'

And Caiaphas did as Saul desired, and provided armed servants to go with him, and letters testifying that he was an apostle of the Catholics.

* * * * *

(479) *And it came to pass that Saul, as he journeyed, came nigh unto the city of Damascus, and it was about noon; and he and his fellows, when they had dined, slumbered in the shade by the roadside.*

And on a sudden, he heard a voice saying in the Hebrew language: 'Saul, Saul, why persecutest thou me?'

And he opened his eyes, and saw a man standing, and the sun shone fiercely upon his white raiment, and the eyes of Saul were dazzled.

Then said Saul: 'Sir, who art thou?'

He that had come, answered: 'I am Jesus, whose life thou seekest. It is ill for thee to kick against the goad, like unto an ox that hath no understanding.'

For Jesus had warning of Simon Peter that Saul sought to take him, and came forth boldly, and Peter with him.

And Saul seeth the nail prints in his hands, and likewise the angry countenance of Peter, which stood by.

Wherefore, trembling and astonished, he falleth all along on the earth, and there was no strength in him.

And he closeth his eyes, and crieth: 'Have mercy upon me, thou son of David! Art thou come to destroy us?'

For he doubted not that Peter bore a sword.

Jesus answered: 'Thus said David, when he surprised Saul in the cave: "I have not sinned against thee, yet thou huntest my life to take it.

' "*The Lord judge between me and thee, and the Lord avenge me of thee,
but mine hand shall not be upon thee." '

And in a moment Saul's eyes were blinded, yet he knew it not.

And he asked Jesus, saying: 'Lord, what wilt thou have me do?'

*Jesus answered: 'Arise, and go into Damascus to the street called Straight,
and enquire in the house of Judas for one called Ananias.*

'The same will tell thee what thou shalt do.'

*And when he had said these things, he departed, and Simon Peter with
him.*

* * * * *

(480) *Then Saul rose up, but when he opened his eyes there was no sight in
them, and he cried out aloud and his fellows roused themselves from slumber.*

*(These men saw not Jesus, for they were drowsy with sleep, yet they heard
his voice.)*

*And they took Saul by the hand and led him into Damascus, where he
abode in the house of Judas, three days without sight, neither eating nor
drinking, until Ananias came unto him, being sent by Jesus.*

As it is written: 'On the third day cometh relief.'

*And in like manner as Saul the king sware unto David, saying: 'Inasmuch
as when the Lord had delivered me into thine hand thou killedst me not,
behold, now I know well that the Kingdom of Israel shall be established in
thine hand,'*

*So likewise Saul the tent-maker sware unto Ananias that by Jesus the son
of David should the Kingdom of God be established.*

*Then did Ananias lay his hands upon him, and there fell from his eyes as
it had been a sheet of white stone, such as is set in a lanthorn, and he did see
again.*

*And he was baptized, and took meat and, being strengthened, straight-
way preached in the synagogues, how that all Israelites should pay the tax as
Moses commanded.*

*Now, it became known unto the Grecians that Saul had been sent of the
Chief Priests to seize Jesus without leave of King Aretas.*

*And they laid in wait to apprehend him, and bring him before the ethnarch
which ruled the city for the King, and to accuse him of the murders which
he had done in Judaea.*

*But Ananias and the brethren, forasmuch as Saul had made a full repent-
ance and desired also to preach the Gospel to the Gentiles, took him by night,
and through a window let him down by the wall in a basket.*

* * * *

(481) *Afterwards, when Saul had dwelt three years in the land of Arabia, he
journeyed again from Damascus unto Jerusalem, and would have joined himself to the disciples, but all feared him and believed not that he walked in the
way of righteousness.*

Then Barnabas, a Levite of Cyprus, brought Saul unto Peter and unto

James the brother of Jesus, and declared that he had repented him of his evil and had boldly preached at Damascus in Jesus's name.

Therefore they rejected not Saul, for in those days he walked discreetly.

* * * * *

(482) And Saul abode with Peter and James fifteen days, coming in and going out of the Temple, speaking in the name of Jesus, and preaching against the false doctrine of the Grecians.

But the servants of the High Priest went about to seize him; which when the Twelve knew, they brought him down to Caesarea and thence sped him unto Tarsus, whereof he was a free-born citizen.

And the Church had rest awhile throughout Judaea and Galilee and Samaria, for the brethren obeyed the Twelve and followed not after the Grecian heresies which Stephen had preached.

* * * * *

(483) But afterwards Saul turned him back again unto the Wicked Kingdom, and spake terrible things in the name of Jesus.

And drew after him many that were weak in the faith, so that because of them we are now fallen into suspicion and hatred.

* * * * *

(484) Yet the Lord knoweth how to deliver the godly from temptation, and to reserve the unjust unto the day of judgement to be punished: but chiefly them that walk after the flesh in the lust of uncleanness, and despise government.

Presumptuous are they, self-willed, unafraid to speak evil of their rulers, though even angels, which are of greater power, bring not railing accusation against these before the Lord.*

But, as natural brute beasts, born to be destroyed, they contemn that they understand not; and shall utterly perish, as they that count it pleasure to riot in the daytime.†

Spots they are and blemishes, sporting themselves with their own deceits; having eyes full of adultery, and unstable souls and an heart which they have exercised with covetous practices.

Cursed children, which have forsaken the Law and are gone astray, following the way of Balaam the son of Beor who, loving the wages of unrighteousness, was rebuked and brought to shame.

The dumb ass speaking with a man's voice forbad the madness of the prophet.

* * * * *

(485) Wells without water are they, clouds that are carried with a tempest; to whom the mist of darkness is reserved for ever.

For when they speak great swelling words of vanity, they allure through the lusts of the flesh them that thought themselves clean escaped from terror.

While they promise liberty, they serve corruption: for of whom a man is overcome, of the same is he brought into bondage.

* These are the guardian angels of kings (*see* LX.*c footnote*).
† (*See* footnote to XXI.*l*).

> *Yea, it were better for them never to have known the way of righteousness, which is the Law, than, after that they have known it, to turn aside and be entangled in error.*
>
> *But it is happened unto them according to the proverb which Solomon spake:*
>
> *'The dog is turned to his own vomit again; and the sow that was washed to her wallowing in the mire.'*

*   *   *   *

(*v*) The remainder of the New Testament is largely an account of Paul and Paulinism. Scandals, riots, libels, and counter-libels, provoked by the complete breach between the Pharisees and the Gentile Christians (*see Introduction* 1.*o*, II.*y* and III.*k–l*), made certain pious Jews—the most famous of whom was Hillel II, who lived in the third century—denounce the feverish apocalyptic expectation of the Messiah as damaging to true religion. He taught that the Messiah had come centuries before Jesus (*Sanhedrin* 99*a*):

> 'There shall be no Messiah for Israel, for they have already consumed him [*that is, "enjoyed his presence"*] in the days of King Hezekiah.'

But Hillel was refuted by Rabbi Joseph with a quotation from *Zechariah* ix., which proved to the general satisfaction that the Messiah was still to come. In days of national crisis, therefore, Messiahs continued to appear in Jewry until modern times.*

(*w*) Shortly before the destruction of the Temple the Nazarenes, 'commanded by a divine revelation', left Jerusalem and settled at Pella in Decapolis (Eusebius: *Ecc. Hist.* 3. v. 3); later, their leaders John the Elder—that is to say, John the son of Annas—and Philip, accompanied by his virgin daughters, fled from Pella to Ephesus in Asia Minor (Irenaeus: *Heresies* iii. 1. 1 and Eusebius: *Ecc. Hist.* 3. xxxi. 2). John seems to have been still alive in the second century, having survived Andrew, Peter, John the son of Zebedee, Philip, Thomas, and James the Just (Eusebius: *Ecc. Hist.* 3. xxxix. 5) but, probably because he had kept silence at the Council of Priestly Elders which handed Jesus over to Pilate, was never raised to Apostolic rank. According to Hegesippus (Eusebius: *Ecc. Hist.* 3. xxxii. 3), Simeon Cleophas was martyred under Trajan in the year 106 A.D., being then one hundred and twenty years old. A passage in the *Toldoth Yeshu* (Huldreich's text)—which is for once so temperate that it may be historical—records that Mary the mother of Jesus (presumably 'Mary the Braider') died about the year 65 A.D., and was buried by her kinsmen near Golgotha. Her headstone is said to have borne the following inscription:

> 'Lo, this is a ladder set upon earth, whose head reaches unto heaven, and the angels of God ascend and descend upon it, and the mother rejoices here in her children—HALLELUJAH!'

---

* The last important pseudo-Messiah was Jacob Frank (1726–91), who claimed, by metempsychosis, to possess the soul that had dwelt successively in David, Elijah, Jesus, and Mohammed.

(*x*) The respectful, but by no means uncritical, attitude towards Jesus of
the original Nazarene leaders is preserved in the *Epistle of James,* a genuine
letter written by James the Just to the Jews of the Dispersal, 'the twelve
tribes which are scattered abroad'. Although grudgingly accepted into the
Canon after a slight process of Paulinization (*James* i. 21, 25; ii. 12 and v. 14),
its standing was still disputed in the time of Eusebius (*Ecc. Hist.* 2. xxiii. 25);
Jerome records that it had been 'published by another in the name of James.'
Since, however, all educated Jews of the first century were bilingual, it need
not be doubted that a Temple priest could have written a simple letter in
Greek, and Jerome's statement may mean no more than that James's letter
was known to have been re-written by later hands. In *James* ii. 1–3, the following remarkable criticism occurs:

> 'My brethren, in your acceptance of persons do not have the trust in repu-
> tation which our master, Jesus the Anointed One, had.'
> [*'Mē en prosōpolēmsiais echete tēn pistin tou kuriou hēmōn Iēsou Christou
> tēs doxēs.'*]
> 'For if a man cometh into your synagogue with a golden ring on his finger
> and with bright raiment, and also a poor man in vile raiment and ye cast
> your eye upon the man in bright raiment, and say: "Sit thou there at thy
> ease," and to the poor man: "Stand thou there, or sit thou against my foot-
> stool," are ye not partial in yourselves and evil-minded judges?'

Then follows a vigorous diatribe against the rich. The first verse has escaped
revision only through being mistranslated in the *Vulgate:*

> '*Fratres mei, ne cum acceptione personarum habete fidem Domini nostri
> Jesu Christi gloriosi.*'
> 'My brethren, do not combine the faith of our Lord Jesus Christ, the Glori-
> ous One, with a respect for persons.'

But the central meaning of *doxē* is 'opinion', 'estimation', 'credit', 'repute';
and though Paul speaks of Jesus as 'the Lord of Glory', the phrase *Iēsou
Christou tēs doxēs,* 'Jesus Christ of Glory', is not even New Testament Greek.
Nor do *doxē,* in the sense of 'glory', or the verb 'glorify' formed from it, appear elsewhere in this epistle, which is far better Greek than most of the New
Testament. Frequent use of *pistis* in the Gospels and Pauline Epistles, where
it always stands for 'religious faith', has blinded translators to its meaning
here, which is simply 'confidence'. The word is thus used by Demosthenes
(Reiske's paging: 300. 11): '*sōphrosunēs echein pistin*', 'to have confidence in
[someone's] probity'.
(*y*) *James* v. begins:

> 'Go to now, ye rich men, weep and howl for your miseries that shall come
> upon you. Your riches are corrupted, your garments are moth-eaten, your
> gold and silver is cankered and the rest of them shall eat your flesh as it were
> fire . . . Ye have lived in pleasure on the earth and been wanton, ye have

nourished your hearts as in a day of slaughter. Ye have condemned and killed The Righteous One.'

James's diatribe seems to be aimed at such fellow-travellers as John son of Annas and even Bunni ben Gorion who, despite his devotion to Jesus, kept one foot in the collaborationist camp. He is saying that the rich and influential friends whom Jesus trusted—but who dared not cast off their burden as the Apostles did—had failed to save him from the Cross; and that he should not, for instance, have given John the seat of honour at the Last Supper. It is, of course, taken for granted that Jesus, being the Righteous One, was an 'evil-minded judge' only in so far as he fixed his affections upon John son of Annas, who was unworthy of them; the brethren are told to take warning from Jesus's fate and never judge a man by his social position. Respect for such might lead to contempt of the poor, or (*James* ii. 5 and iv. 13) abandonment of ideal communism and indulgence in competitive trade. (*z*) Even pious interpolations and a frequent use of 'the Lord' to mean God and Jesus indiscriminately—which is the hall-mark of Pauline editing—fail to obscure James's argument. He closes with the traditional exhortation: to watch for the Second Coming of God (*see* cxvii.*q*), to be as patient as the prophet Job, to support suffering with prayer, and to regard the end (or 'fate', or 'consummation') of the prophet Jesus as a crowning example of God's merciful forgiveness.

> (486) 'Yet be patient, brethren, unto the second coming of God.
>
> 'Behold, the husbandman waiteth for the precious fruit of the earth, and hath long patience for it until he receive the early and the latter rain.
>
> 'Be ye likewise patient and stablish your hearts, for the coming of the Lord draweth nigh.
>
> 'Consider, my brethren, the prophets which testified in the name of God and gave an ensample of affliction suffered in patience.
>
> 'Behold, we count them happy which endured.
>
> 'Ye have heard of the patience of Job, and ye have seen what the end was of Jesus, our master; how God is very pitiful and of tender mercy.
>
> 'Is any among you afflicted? Let him then pray! The prayer of a righteous man availeth much.
>
> 'Elijah was subject to like passions as we are, and he prayed earnestly that it might not rain; and it rained not on the earth for the space of three years and six months.
>
> 'And he prayed again, and the heaven gave rain, and the earth brought forth her fruit.'

* * * * *

James's meaning is: 'Even an anointed prophet hath something of sin in him, as our master Jesus frankly confessed (*see* xix.*d*). Jesus himself was subject to error; and even Elijah, whom God received alive into Heaven, was of like passions with ourselves. God alone is good, and the consummation of Jesus's life, though he was The Righteous One of the prophecies, proves God's mercy rather than man's perfectability.'

The Nazarene Gospel closes with this homily, the missing last verse of which may be supplied from the *Apocalypse of Baruch* (*see* LV.*a*):

(487) *'Pray ye therefore with all your heart that the Kingdom may come speedily, wherein the earth shall yield fruit ten thousandfold both of grapes and wheat.*

'And the Righteous One the Son of David shall rule it in peace and righteousness for a thousand years.

'Amen.'

* * * * *

ALL THINGS TO ALL MEN

1 Corinthians ix. 20–22

20And unto the Jews I became as a Jew, that I might gain the Jews; to them that are under the law, as under the law, that I might gain them that are under the law: 21to them that are without law, as without law, (being not without law to God, but under the law to Christ,) that I might gain them that are without law. 22To the weak became I as weak, that I might gain the weak: I am made all things to all, that I might by all means save some.

(*a*) A.D. 58 is a far more crucial date in ecclesiastical history than either A.D. 425, when the Council of Nicaea was held, or 1517, when Luther rebelled against the Papacy at Wittenberg.

In the early summer of that year Paul, who had been covertly preaching the annulment of the Mosaic Law to the Jews of the Dispersal, was exposed before his Nazarene superiors at Jerusalem. Charged with heresy by James the Just, he proved ready to recant, and had indeed done so, when suddenly he was confronted with the far more serious accusation of having committed sacrilege. He could escape Jewish justice only by openly allying himself with the Wicked Kingdom, and thus severing all relations with the Nazarenes; whereupon he was repudiated even by his former collaborationist employers, the Boethian Chief Priests who had handed Jesus over to Pilate.

(*b*) The falsifying of Jesus's own doctrine by the publication of tendentious Greek Gospels now began. Mark, a Greek-speaking friend of Peter's (*Acts* xii. 12) who sided with Barnabas against Paul during the quarrel at Antioch (*Acts* xv. 39), had set down and translated Peter's recollections of Jesus, but without troubling to arrange them in chronological sequence (*see Introduction* iv.g). The Paulines, who borrowed this translation and transmogrified it into something like the present form of *Mark,* pretended later that not only Mark, but Luke, was a companion of Paul's; they clumsily inserted into 2 *Timothy* iv. 10–12, where it interrupts a syntactical sequence:

> 'Only Luke is with me. Take Mark and bring him with thee, for he is profitable to me for the ministry.'

But Luke, even if he was a 'fellow-labourer' of Paul's (*Philemon* 24)—though this is contradicted in *Colossians* iv. 10–14—is unlikely to have been the author of *Luke* as we now have it, or of the *Acts,* since his association with these is first recorded towards the end of the second century.

(*c*) Some Biblical scholars, aware that the narrative of Paul's trial and its sequel, which forms the conclusion of *Acts,* is full of inconsistencies, suggest that editors have tampered with it, rather than that Paul himself prevaricated (*see Introduction* ii.*y*). However, except for transferring part of Peter's trial in 30 A.D. to Paul's in 58 A.D. (*see* cviii.*f–g*), and making one or two minor adjustments (*see* (*h*) *and* (*i*) *below*), they seem to have left the narrative much as they found it. Paul's account, written in the first person plural, is merely supported with critical glosses, by a far from hostile hand, on his frequent ingenious changes of front.

(*d*) According to *Acts* xxi. 15–40 Paul, with certain brethren from Caesarea and Cyprus, arrives in Jerusalem by way of Miletus, Tyre, and Caesarea. He brings a large sum of money collected for the Nazarene poor, and is greeted by James the Just who, though rejoicing to hear of his missionary success, asks to be reassured that he has not been preaching against the Mosaic Law, as rumour reports. James rightly concedes that full acceptance of the Law is, of course, not incumbent on uncircumcised God-fearers, but on the Israelites only. Thereupon Paul consents to undergo ritual purification in the Temple with four companions, as a token that there is no truth in the charges made against him, and that he himself, though working among the uncircumcised, is a devout Jew. Yet *Galatians* iii. and v. (*see Introduction* ii.*u*) prove that these charges were true; Paul was already teaching that Jesus had annulled the Law.

However, before the purification ceremony can be completed, certain Jews arrive from Asia Minor and indignantly confirm the rumours; and Paul is further charged with having introduced an uncircumcised Ephesian named Trophimus into the Temple, and thus polluted it. He is dragged out and man-handled by the mob; but soldiers from the Roman garrison in the Tower of Antony rescue him. Paul tells their commander—who has mistaken him for Satda, the Egyptian impostor, wanted by the Romans for rebellion (*see* vii.*h*)—that he is really a Cilician Jew and that the crowd's indignation has been due to another, equally unfortunate, misapprehension. He is therefore allowed to pacify them with an address from the steps of the Tower.

(*e*) In *Acts* xxii. 1–21, Paul explains to the crowd that he is a Jew from Tarsus who first studied under Gamaliel, next persecuted the Nazarenes on behalf of the Sadducees, and was finally converted by Jesus himself, who appointed him an apostle to the Gentiles. The crowd interrupts this harangue and roars: 'Away with him! Such a man [i.e. a liar and a turncoat] is not fit to live!' He is then taken into the Tower, where the Commander, Claudius Lycias, orders that the truth be extracted from him by flogging. Paul, in great fear, discloses his Roman citizenship to the centurion about to execute the order. The surprised centurion reports the matter to Lycias, who wonders how Paul has managed to raise the large fee needed (*see Introduction* II.*y, footnote*), but satisfies himself that the claim is genuine. Paul is then released, and his case transferred to the 'Council', which must have been the same Council of Priestly Elders which had examined both Peter and Jesus (*see* CIX.*i–l*).

(*f*) This untoward disclosure of Paul's Roman citizenship will have immediately severed his remaining ties with the Nazarenes: no one could serve both God and Nero. For better or worse, he was now free of all Apostolic restraint. So far the narrative seems to be substantially true; but in *Acts* xxiii. Paul's trial by Annas II has been deliberately confused with Peter's examination by Annas I (*see* CVIII.*f–g*). Again, verse 7 describes the council as a 'multitude' to make it appear that they were the predominantly Pharisaic Great Sanhedrin; but, since the High Priest presided, this is impossible. It seems, however, that Paul appealed to Bunni ben Gorion and the Pharisaic minority in the Council of Priestly Elders by claiming that a false charge had been brought against him because he had preached Jesus's resurrection: an ingenious lie which opened old wounds among his judges. The High Priest pressed home the charge of sacrilege and Paul would have been remanded for trial by the Great Sanhedrin, had not news reached Lycias that the court was in an uproar and Paul in danger of being 'pulled in pieces'. He at once sent a detachment of troops to bring him back to the Tower.

(*g*) Next, Paul's nephew secretly informs Lycias that forty men, with the High Priest's connivance, have banded together to kill Paul when he appears again before the Council. Lycias swallows this improbable tale and, to avoid a riot, sends him by night under an exceptionally strong escort of infantry and cavalry to Caesarea-upon-Sea. At the same time he writes a letter to Felix, the Governor-General—a freedman of the late Emperor Claudius—to the effect that his prisoner, who is a Roman citizen, has fallen foul of the Jews in some ceremonial matter and is being sent to headquarters for safety; whereupon Felix orders Paul to await his trial.

(*h*) In *Acts* xxiv., the High Priest visits Caesarea, where he complains to Felix that Lycias has forcibly removed Paul from the Council during his preliminary examination on a capital charge of polluting the Temple. He accuses Paul of being a pestilent mover of sedition and a ringleader of the Nazarene sect; but does not disclose that he is a former Roman agent.

Paul boldly challenges the High Priest to produce evidence for the charge of sacrilege—since Trophimus seems to have escaped (*see* 2 *Timothy* iv. 20); and claims that despite his Roman citizenship he is one of the Pharisaic quietists with whom the Sadducees have a long-standing disagreement on eschatological questions; that he was seized in the Temple while ritually purifying himself; and that the commotion which prompted Lycias to rescue him was due to his having told the Council that he believed in the resurrection of the dead. He is careful, however, not to mention Jesus. Felix then adjourns the case until Lycias can come to Caesarea and give evidence, but has no intention of sending for him.

Acts xxiv. 24-26 is a later interpolation: it recounts how Paul very nearly converted Felix, and what frequent conversations they had; though Felix, not being altogether serious, was holding out for a bribe. According to verse 27, Paul remained in custody for two years, until Festus became Governor-General in 60 A.D.

(*i*) In *Acts* xxv., the High Priest requests Festus to re-open Paul's case and have him brought before the Council—that is to say, the Great Sanhedrin—on a charge of sacrilege. The appropriate punishment for such a crime was death, even if the offender were a Roman citizen (*see* CIX.*g*); though, in that case, the sentence would first have to be confirmed by the Governor-General. An editor of the *Acts* here suggests, most improbably, that the Chief Priests planned to waylay and kill Paul on his return to Jerusalem. However, according to verse 4, Festus orders the High Priest to bring Paul's accusers to Caesarea and make out a *prima facie* case for handing him over to the Great Sanhedrin, as they had been engaged in doing when Lycias rudely interrupted their examination two years previously.

His order is obeyed, but Festus, on hearing the charges, asks Paul whether he will be prepared to stand trial in Jerusalem 'before me'—which means no more than that the Great Sanhedrin's verdict would be submitted to him for confirmation. Paul dares not face the trial, though it would have been a scrupulously fair one, knowing that he can no longer count on Boethian support. He requests that his case be transferred to Rome. This is granted, and he feels safe again; being aware that the Great Sanhedrin do not acknowledge the Emperor's right to try Jewish religious offences, and will not therefore send representatives to Rome. If the Churches in Greece and Asia Minor are puzzled by his action, he can justify it by declaring that the order to appeal to Caesar was given him by Jesus in a vision (*Acts* xxiii. 11 and xxii. 17-18).

Next, the puppet-king Agrippa II, inheritor of his grandfather Herod the Great's extensive dominions, happens to visit Caesarea accompanied by his sister Berenice; and Festus, who is the power behind the throne, brings Paul before these two. Festus admits that he does not quite understand the charges, which concern Jewish superstitions and especially one Jesus, whom the Chief Priests believe dead but Paul asserts to be still alive.

(*j*) In *Acts* xxvi., Paul assures Agrippa that he is a strict Pharisee bred at Jerusalem from his earliest youth—no word about Tarsus—and once more recounts his former activities on behalf of the Boethians and his subsequent conversion to the Nazarene faith. He explains that 'the Jews' then seized and tried to kill him because he preached repentance and the Kingdom of Heaven.

Festus interrupts Paul's remarkable lie by saying that he must be out of his wits to talk in this strain—'much study doth make thee mad'—but Paul flatters Agrippa as being no less pious than his father (though well aware that he is almost a heathen and living in incest with Berenice) and convinces him of his innocence. This would not have been difficult even for a man less eloquent than Paul, since Agrippa heard one side of the question only and was ignorant of the niceties of Jewish law. According to *Acts* xxvi. 28, he tells Paul amiably: 'In brief time [mistranslated "almost"] thou persuadest me to be a Christian,' that is to say: 'It will take you a long time to persuade me, I fear.'

He is also reported to have told Festus: 'This man might have been set at liberty, if he had not appealed unto Caesar'; but he is more likely to have said: 'Now that he has appealed unto Caesar, you might as well release him. The Great Sanhedrin will let the matter lie "until Elijah comes"' (*see* cxiii.*m*).

According to *Acts* xxvi. 29, which is an interpolation, Paul then wishes that Festus were altogether as he himself is, 'except for these bonds'. These 'bonds', and those mentioned in *Acts* xxiv. 27 and xxv. 14, contradict xxii. 30 and xxiii. 23 where Paul, as a Roman citizen against whom no charge has been proved, is free from all restraint.

(*k*) In *Acts* xxvii., Paul, on his way to Rome, is shipwrecked at Malta, where he survives the bite of a non-venomous snake (*see* xiii.*y*).

In *Acts* xxviii., he reaches Rome safely, and is there kept under house-arrest while awaiting trial. He then summons the heads of the Jewish colony in Rome and tells them a new lie—this was early in the reign of Nero, who had apparently repealed Claudius's edict banishing the Jews—that he is a strict Pharisee whom the Chief Priests have handed over to the Romans for punishment because of his Messianic beliefs, and whom Festus, though finding no fault in him, has forced to appeal to Caesar because 'the Jews' are after his blood. When the elders express astonishment at his Roman citizenship, he hastens to explain—and this comes oddly from the mouth of a strict Pharisee—that he has no quarrel with the Jews as a nation.

The elders reply that they know nothing to his personal discredit, but have heard ill reports of the Nazarenes. Paul then delivers his Messianic message, makes some converts, but not many, and remains for two years in his own hired house, preaching without hindrance. That is as much as can be learned about Paul's life from the New Testament, unless the later *Epistles* doubtfully ascribed to him are really his, and belong to this period.

(*l*) One of the most striking differences between the Gentile and the Judaic Churches was their attitude towards money. Though at Jerusalem the 'saints' held all in common, and therefore had no incentive to work for personal gain, the Gentile Christians, freed by Paul from the Written Law which forbade lending at interest (*see* lii.*f*), and from the Oral Law which forbade anyone to make preaching a paid profession (*see* xiii.*j and* lvii.*c*), soon found that this liberty led them into temptation. Paul (if he is the author of the *First Epistle to Timothy*) had to insist that bishops should not be money-lovers, nor deacons swindlers (1 *Timothy* iii. 3 and 8); nor did he himself avoid the suspicion of being more interested in making money than in saving souls, and of 'loving the wages of unrighteousness'. The precise nature of his 'thorn in the flesh', from which he thrice vainly besought God to free him (2 *Corinthians* xii. 7–8) and which was 'like a buffet from Satan to humiliate' him, has been much discussed. Though the usual charitable suggestion is that it was a physical disorder, perhaps epilepsy, stuttering, or myopia, this same infirmity seems to be described in *Galatians* iv. 4 as a 'temptation' (*peirasmon,* a word which does not mean 'trial of patience' but 'temptation to sin'). Moreover, the phrase 'thorn in the side' is applied in *Numbers* xxxiii. 55 and *Judges* ii. 3 to the idolatrous inhabitants of Canaan whom the Israelites failed to expel under Joshua—'their gods shall ensnare thee'—and in *Ezekiel* xxviii. 24 to the idolatrous people of Sidon. Paul records that the Galatians on his first visit condoned 'the temptation which was in my flesh', because of the heavenly message that he brought.

Since a physical disorder can hardly be a temptation to sin, his infirmity will have been a moral one. Sexual unchastity, or perversion, had he displayed it, would doubtless have figured in the anti-Pauline polemics; but these concentrate attention mainly on his greed, and his boastful lying (*see* cxviii.*u*). That Paul was conscious of showing too much interest in money is suggested by his frequent repudiations of the charge (e.g. 1 *Corinthians* viii. 31; x. 33 and 2 *Corinthians* xii. 14); by his seemingly penitent remark that 'love of silver', the root of all evil, had caused certain men's departures from the faith and subsequent remorse (1 *Timothy* vi. 10), and by his irresponsible suggestion that the synagogue Jews who tried to suppress his heresies were actuated by a desire for 'filthy lucre' (*Titus* i. 11). It was, after all, the riches of Sidon which made her a thorn in the side of poverty-stricken Judaea, and Paul specifically identifies idolatry with greed in *Colossians* iii. 5 and *Ephesians* v. 5. Thus, although he feels the need, in defiance of Pharisaic Law and Jesus's express command (*see* xxiii.*a*) to support a simple autobiographical statement by an oath before God that he is not lying (*Galatians* i. 20), the thorn in his flesh is more likely to have been dishonesty in money matters than an inability to tell the truth about himself. Boastful exaggeration was a fault which Paul found it difficult to check (2 *Corinthians* x. 16 and 33), but could not afford to confess, since to do so would have been to discredit the authenticity of his new gospel.

Why, however, should Paul dwell so emphatically upon this 'thorn' unless its public disclosure had forced him at some time or other to make a virtue of repentance? When he reminds the Galatians (iv. 13) of his having first preached to them 'because of infirmity'—a remark which nobody has been able to explain—does this mean that he had to leave the populous Southern coast of Asia Minor and pursue his missionary labours far inland, because he had been convicted of fraud? Was this why the chief men of Antioch, urged by the 'devout and honourable women' of the city, expelled him from their frontiers? And had this sort of thing happened so often that Paul was forced to pray to God three times for the thorn's removal?

Again: what did in fact happen at Lystra in Lycaonia, where Paul went with Barnabas when expelled from Antioch (*Acts* xiv.)? Are the readers of *Acts* seriously expected to believe that because Paul healed a cripple, the Lystraeans, headed by their chief magistrate, the priest of Juppiter, were about to sacrifice to them both as gods, calling Barnabas 'Zeus', and Paul 'Hermes because he was the principal speaker'? But that then, suddenly, at the instigation of some new arrivals from Antioch and Iconium, they threw Paul out of the city, where he was stoned and left for dead? Not even the most backward provincial Greeks behaved like that in the first century. Has a Pauline editor re-written an anti-Pauline document, according to which the Priest of Zeus, apprised of Paul's reputation in Antioch and Iconium, arrested him for miracle-mongering; and when Barnabas protested himself a servant of 'Jehovah, the Hebrew Zeus', dismissed him and turning to Paul, said: 'But you, wretch, have no god but Hermes, patron of thieves and swindlers,' and hustled him out of Lystra? That the women of Antioch were 'devout and honourable', a detail out of keeping with the story as it now stands, may have been overlooked in the revision; and the finality of Paul's shaking the dust off his shoes when he leaves Antioch (*Acts* xiii. 51—*see* LIX.*c*) is denied by his joyful return there after the visit to Lycaonia (*Acts* xiv. 28). A similarly radical editing has long been suspected earlier in this sequence: the account of Paul's interview with Sergius Paullus (*Acts* xiii. 4–13).

Paul's followers condoned, and even praised, the serpentine cunning with which he extricated himself from danger (*see* LVII.*f*) and succeeded in being 'all things to all men'. Those were, of course, difficult times, and even the Pharisees permitted a law-abiding Jew to dissemble when hard-pressed by unscrupulous enemies of God (*see* XXIII.*b*); yet to the law-abiding he owed unfailing truth and must choose between serving God with all his heart and serving God's Adversary.

Paul, however, saw that it would one day become impossible to keep the whole Law: sooner or later Jewish nationalism must be suppressed by Rome and Temple worship abolished. He determined to transfer the title deeds of the Heavenly Kingdom from the Children of the House to unclean and Lawless strangers; and cynically did so in the name of Jesus, who had paid the uttermost farthing of his debt to the Law, believed it to be everlastingly valid, and preached salvation only to those who would observe it in every particular. Was this Paul's revenge on Jesus and Peter for having been prevented, by their surprise appearance on the road to Damascus, from marriage into the rich and influential House of Boethus (*see* CXVIII.*f*)?

(*m*) One further problem remains: in Paul's claims to have been personally instructed by Jesus (1 *Corinthians* xi. 23 and *Galatians* i. 11-12), is he identifying him with the Spirit of Divine Wisdom (1 *Corinthians* i. 24), which speaks in the heart? The first passage at least reads as though Jesus had visited him in flesh and blood at Damascus, after his conversion, and confided a personal reminiscence to him.

Part Three

Part Three

SUMMARY OF CRITICAL PRINCIPLES

In *Matthew* xxiii. 1–3, Jesus orders his Nazarene followers to obey the religious authority of the Pharisees. It is, therefore, only reasonable to check the Gospel accounts of his teaching against the two Talmuds and the *Mishnah*, which provide full information about the tenets held by the Pharisees during his lifetime. Like them, he regarded the Mosaic Law as immutable (*Matthew* v. 18) and avoided all contact with ritually unclean Gentiles (*Matthew* x. 5 and xv. 24). Close scrutiny of his sayings proves him to have been well-versed in the oral and written Law, in the prophets and in the later Apocalyptics; thus it is most unlikely that he either misquoted or interpreted these in a heterodox sense. Since Pharisaic teaching was mainly delivered in the form of *midrashim,* or Scriptural commentaries, it may be assumed that so was Jesus's; thus the meaning, context, and original wording of many of his 'hard sayings' can usually be restored by finding the Biblical or apocryphal texts to which they refer.

No Aramaic Gospel survives, or is likely ever to have existed in manuscript; not because the Apostles were unlettered, but because the Pharisees of the first and early second centuries, whose religious discussions were held in Aramaic, refrained from writing down even the more important pronouncements of their sages. There is evidence to show that at least some of Jesus's disciples were men of high education, and that they carefully memorized his sayings, or 'Oracles', though arranging them in Pharisaic style under subject-headings, not in chronological order. A generation later, these 'Oracles' were surreptitiously jotted down and translated by Greek-speaking converts. Several Greek lives of Jesus, published towards the end of the first century for the various Gentile Churches in Egypt, Syria, Asia Minor, and Greece, were based on such collections of Oracles. One (The Gospel According to the Hebrews) was written in Syriac.

According to *Luke* i. 1–4, the handling of this pirated material varied greatly. An unbridgeable gulf now separated the original Church of Jerusalem from the Gentile Churches, which did not even agree among themselves on doctrinal questions; thus the evangelists, having only a scanty knowledge of Jewish institutions, made many mistakes in reporting Jesus's acts and sayings, and frequently contradicted one another. Not before the mid-second century were *Matthew, Mark,* and *Luke* collated, and some clumsy attempts made to reconcile their divergencies.

The Gentile Christians were anxious, for political as well as doctrinal reasons, to dissociate themselves from the Jews; but especially from the Pharisees, who continued to be the spiritual leaders of Jewry after Bar Cochba's revolt had failed in 132 A.D. Thus the evangelists falsely represented Jesus as having himself quarrelled with the Pharisees, annulled the Law of Moses, and kept on friendly terms with the Romans. Though hesitating to suppress any large part of the original Apostolic tradition, they nevertheless disguised its true meaning by ingenious omissions or interpolations, and by wholesale re-arrangement. Wanton fictions, however, are rare; if, therefore, a saying or event does not fit its Canonical context, even after critical restoration of the passage in question, a lacuna can usually be found elsewhere into which it fits exactly.

Before the Nazarene tradition can be restored, it must first be decided whether each Gospel passage under scrutiny tallies with accepted historical fact. If not, the reason must be sought for its misplacement, distortion, or invention; and this is more often found in ecclesiastical politics than in scribal error, and never in original misreporting. After those passages that betray the greatest editorial ineptitude have been closely examined, several techniques of textual manipulation can be detected and isolated, familiarity with which becomes an aid in the detection of more skilful changes. References to Jesus in Jewish or Classical literature, though meagre, are valuable to investigators, once the anti-Christian bias has been discounted; and so, of course, are suppressed Gospel passages surviving in Patristic literature and elsewhere.

Catholic Christianity combines the Aramaic Apostolic tradition with Paul's heretical teaching—a 'free' variety of Judaism—and with extraneous and alien religious theory derived largely from Alexandrian Gnostic philosophy by way of the *Gospel according to St. John*. This Gospel, though embodying valuable material omitted from the Synoptics, is textually the most corrupt in the Canon, and was not accepted as genuine by the Catholics until towards the end of the second century.

Most Catholic views on Jesus's identity and life must be discounted. He was set apart from his contemporaries because John the Baptist had acclaimed him as the Saviour of his nation; was crowned King with all the ancient rites; ceremonially re-born from a Levite virgin, and made an honorary High Priest, though physically descended from the royal House of David. Thereafter, as the King-Messiah, he had to follow a rule of conduct laid down by the Prophets and hagiographers; and since the precise details of this rule are known, the truth of the Gospel narratives can be tested by it.

Jesus expected the present world to end during his lifetime in a series of catastrophes known as the 'Pangs of the Messiah'. The Kingdom of Heaven, which would then be inaugurated and last for a thousand years, with Jerusalem for its capital, was to be a heaven on earth, peopled partly by resurrected saints, partly by a few living saints who would not die until the world ended. True to his Pharisaic principles, Jesus declined to perform miracles in proof of his divine authority (*Mark* viii. 12), and apart from a few faith-cures, the accounts of which have been greatly exaggerated and for which he gave all credit to God, was content to foretell the wonders of the coming Kingdom. Yet certain of his acts that conveyed a moral lesson have been misreported as miracles, to rival those reputedly performed by Apollonius of Tyana. The appearance of angels in the Gospel narrative—except where they are inspired human messengers, or dream visitants—formed no part of the original Apostolic tradition, which will have been as free from supernatural embellishments as the Talmudic accounts of first-century sages.

Jesus never identified himself with God, or even with the transcendental Son of Man. His title 'Son of God' was an ancient religious one, acquired at the Coronation. He preached that only devout Jews, who kept the spirit as well as the letter of the Law, could qualify for the Kingdom of Heaven; Gentiles who had not accepted circumcision and the yoke of the Law were excluded. In his view, the imminence of the Pangs was manifested by many signs of the times, and all who desired salvation must therefore cease to live a normal life, observe strict chastity and avoid every kind of pollution. He made the statutory round of his dominions, and by preaching as he went and sending out chosen missionaries, gave his whole people the chance to repent and be saved: and presently decided that the time had come to offer himself as a royal sacrifice for them. The manner of the sacrifice had been laid down in the last chapters of *Zechariah,* which deal with the 'Worthless Shepherd'. Only by careful examination of these can Jesus's actions during Passion Week be intelligibly reconstructed.

Though our restoration of the Nazarene Gospel may not be correct in every detail, it is at least free from the historical objections to which the Canonical Gospels are exposed. We hold that Jesus, a well-documented personage of the first century, can be understood only in terms of his contemporary background, and are at pains to emphasize what the Church has been at pains to suppress: that he neither preached to the Gentiles, nor encouraged his apostles to do so, nor showed any concern for their fate; and that he hourly expected the literal fulfilment of eschatological prophecies. We hold also that he officially died on the Cross; but afterwards, when he recovered from his death-like coma, and found that the Kingdom of Heaven had not come, it was gradually borne in upon him that his sacrifice had been premature. He therefore tried to expiate his error by self-exile from Palestine, intending to return only when the 'Day of the Lord' finally dawned. The Apostles continued the missionary work in obedience to his parting orders. Later, their expectation that he would triumphantly re-appear became a dogma with the Gentile Churches; but he was then believed to be seated in Heaven on the right hand of God, rather than wandering somewhere in the far East among the Jews of the Dispersal, a penitent and branded fugitive.

* * * * *

THE NAZARENE GOSPEL

PROLEGOMENA

HYMN

IV.f

(i) *Blessed be the Lord God of Israel, which hath visited and redeemed His people,*

To perform the mercy promised to our fathers, and to remember His holy covenant, the oath which He sware to our father Abraham and his seed for ever:

That he would grant us delivery from our enemies and from the hands of all that hate us,

To serve Him with fear, in holiness and righteousness before Him, all the days of our life.

For He hath raised up an horn of salvation for us in the house of His servant David,

To give knowledge of salvation unto His people for the remission of their sins and to guide our feet into the way of peace.

Come, let us exalt the tender mercy of our God, which hath been since the world began and which shall continue on them that fear Him from generation to generation!

For thereby the dayspring from on high hath visited us, with healing in his wings: to give light to them that sit in darkness and in the shadow of death.

As God spake by the mouth of His holy prophets, saying:

'O Israel, all nations shall call you blessed, for ye shall be a delightful land.

'Thy righteousness, O God, is very high, which hast done great things. O who is like unto God?

'For He hath sent redemption unto His people; He hath commanded His covenant for ever; holy and reverend is His name!'

PROEM

V.k

(ii) THE BEGINNING OF THE GOSPEL CONCERNING JESUS, THE ANOINTED SON OF GOD.

* * * * *

CXVII.2

(iii) Behold, if all the earth were parchment, and all the seas were ink, and every reed a pen, the wisdom which He taught us concerning the Law and the prophets could not easily be written down.

* * * * *

CHAPTER I

THE NATIVITY OF JESUS

I.w

(1) Glory to God in the highest; on earth peace; good will towards men!

The birth of Jesus which became our Master, the Anointed One, was on this wise:

There went out a decree of Herod the Wicked, King of the Jews, that all they of the House of David should be gathered together at the city of David, which is called Bethlehem Ephratah, and there prove their lineage.

And one Joseph, son of Eli, which dwelt in that other Bethlehem called Nazara, a just man, took the roll of his lineage and went thither with his wife Mary, being great with child.

But when they entered into the city they found no room at the inn, for a great concourse of the Sons of David lodged there.

Then were the days accomplished that Mary should be delivered. And as they sought a house or a stable where they might find rest until morning, behold the pangs of travail came upon her and she cried out.

Now, there were shepherds abiding in the field, keeping watch over their flocks by night,

Which, when they heard her cries, came running and cared for her.

And she brought forth her first-born son in a cave that was nigh at hand, and wrapped him in swaddling clothes and laid him in a harvest basket which the shepherds gave unto her.

And she called his name Jehoshua (which is Jesus); the same signifieth 'He shall save'.

For behold, an angel of the Lord had appeared unto her husband Joseph in a dream, saying: 'That which is conceived in thy wife Mary is full of the Holy Spirit.

'And she shall bring forth a son, and thou shalt call his name Jesus, for he shall save Israel from their sins.'

Now, certain of the Sons of David, when they heard the tidings of Jesus's birth which were given to them by the shepherds, came to salute Joseph and Mary and found them in the cave, and the babe lying in the basket.

And when they heard of the dream that Joseph had dreamed, they wondered and made known abroad the saying which was told them concerning the child, and returned to their own cities, glorifying and praising God.

I.w

(2) This Jesus was the prophet which should redeem Israel from the hands of Belial. Therefore he tasted no wine, like unto Samson the Nazirite which redeemed Israel from the hands of the Philistines.

Yea, more, he was that Branch whereof Isaiah prophesied: 'A branch shall grow out of the roots of Jesse, and the Spirit of the Lord shall rest upon him, the Spirit of wisdom and understanding, the Spirit of counsel and might, the Spirit of knowledge and of the fear of the Lord.

'And shall make him of quick understanding in the fear of the Lord, and righteousness shall be the girdle of his loins.

'And it shall come to pass in that day that the Lord shall set His hand again the second time to recover the remnant of His people.

'In that day the Branch of the Lord shall be beautiful and glorious and the fruit of the earth excellent for them that are escaped of Israel.

'And he that is left in Zion shall be called holy, even every one that is written among the living of Jerusalem.'

Jeremiah also spake of him, saying: 'I will raise unto David a righteous Branch, and a King shall reign and prosper.'

That day was the prophecy of Micah fulfilled: 'But thou, Bethlehem Ephratah, though thou be little among the thousands of Judah, yet out of thee shall come forth unto Me that is to be ruler in Israel!'

I.w

(3) Then Herod the King, when they of the House of David brought their records unto him, destroyed them; for he was envious. Yet Mary kept the lineage of Jesus in her heart.

And it came to pass that, while Jesus was yet a suckling, this same Herod having slain other children of his own, princes innocent of the charges he laid against them, went further and slew Antipater, his eldest son, which reigned beside him in Edom.

After these things Herod also died himself; nor did the Romans grant the title of King to Archelaus when he came to reign in Judaea in the room of his father Herod, nor unto any other man.

Thus was the prophecy fulfilled which Isaiah spake, saying: 'Behold, a damsel shall conceive and bear a son and shall call his name "Emmanuel", which is "God with us",

'Milk and honey shall he eat, that he may know to refuse the evil and choose the good.

'But before the child shall know to refuse the evil and choose the good, the land which Thou abhorrest shall be forsaken of both her Kings.'

III.c

(4) Now this is the genealogy, according to the flesh, of Jesus which afterwards was called The Branch:

> He was the son of Joseph,
> The son of Eli,
> The son of Matthan,
> The son of Levi,
> The son of Johanan,
> The son of Joseph,

III.c
(contd.)

The son of Mattathias,
The son of Amos,
The son of Nahum,
The son of Esli,
The son of Naggai,
The son of Maaz,
The son of Mattathias,
The son of Shimei,
The son of Joseph,
The son of Judah,
The son of Johanan,
The son of Zerubbabel the Governor,
The son of Salathiel,
The son of Jechoniah the captive,
The son of Melcheiram,
The son of Addi,
The son of Osamoth,
The son of Elmodam,
The son of Er,
The son of Joseph,
The son of Eliezer,
The son of Joram,
The son of Matthan,
The son of Levi,
The son of Simeon,
The son of Judah,
The son of Joseph,
The son of Johanan,
The son of Eliakim,
The son of Malchiah,
The son of Menahem,
The son of Mattathias,
The son of Nathan,
The son of David.

III.b   (5) And when the eight days were accomplished, the child was circumcised, and when forty days were accomplished for the purification of Mary his mother, Joseph brought these twain from Bethlehem to the Temple at Jerusalem.

There he offered the sacrifice ordained by the Law, namely a lamb for a burnt offering, and a turtledove for a sin-offering, and he presented the child Jesus to the Lord.

Now, there was one Hannah a prophetess, the daughter of Phanuel of the tribe of Assher. She was of great age and had lived with an husband seven years from her virginity.

And she was now a widow of about fourscore and four years, which departed not from the women's court of the Temple, but served God with fastings and prayers night and day.

III.b
(contd.) She coming in that instant when the child was presented, gave thanks unto the Lord, and prophesied of him to all the saints of her acquaintance, saying: 'He will be a great one and a present help in the redemption of Israel.'

But when his parents had performed all things according to the Law they returned into Galilee, to their own city Nazara.

And the child grew and waxed strong in spirit, filled with wisdom, and the grace of the Lord was upon him.

III.b (6) When the child Jesus was twelve years old, his parents went to Jerusalem to keep the feast of Passover, as their custom was.

And after that they had fulfilled the days, as they returned, the child tarried behind in Jerusalem.

But his mother and father supposing him to have been in the company of their kinsfolk and acquaintance, went a day's journey.

And when they found him not that night, on the morrow they turned back again to Jerusalem, seeking him. And it came to pass that on the third day they found him in a porch of the Temple, where the doctors expounded the Law, sitting in the midst of their disciples.

Now, the doctors were astonished to find such love of learning in so young a child; for he had asked them many questions as they entered into the porch where they taught.

But Mary said unto him: 'Son, why hast thou thus dealt with us? Behold, thy father and I have sought thee sorrowing.'

And Jesus fell at their feet and desired their forgiveness, but he asked them: 'How is it that ye sought me?'

For one of his kinsfolk, having business to perform in Jerusalem, had undertaken to plead with Joseph and Mary that Jesus might tarry with him there for certain days, and afterwards return to Galilee in his company.

And when they asked further: 'But wherefore didst thou desire to tarry here, not being also a merchant?' he answered: 'Wist ye not that I must be about the Father's business?'

Then he went down with them and came again to Nazara, and was subject unto them until Joseph his father died.

And he increased in wisdom and stature, and in the favour of God and man.

CHAPTER II

THE PREACHING OF JOHN THE BAPTIST

IV.f

(7) There was also in the days of Herod the Wicked, King of the Jews, a certain priest named Zechariah of the course of Abijah, and his wife was of the daughters of Aaron and her name was Elisabeth.

And they were both righteous before God, walking in all the commandments and ordinances of the Lord after the manner of the Pharisees, blameless.

And a son was born unto them which was called John, and he waxed strong in spirit.

Now, John was great in the sight of the Lord and drank neither wine nor strong drink, and was filled with the Holy Spirit even from his mother's womb.

Many were the children of Israel which afterwards he turned to the Lord their God,

For he would not minister in the Temple as his father did,

But was seized by the spirit of prophecy, and driven out into the wilderness.

And there he went before God in the spirit and power of Elijah, to turn the hearts of the fathers unto the children (even as Malachi prophesied) and the disobedient unto the wisdom of the just, to make ready a people prepared for the Lord.

V.k

(8) John baptized in the wilderness of Beth-Nimrah and preached the baptism of repentance, for the remission of sins.

And there went over unto him multitudes from Jerusalem and from all the land of Judaea, and confessed their sins, and were baptized.

V.k

(9) And when there came out unto him certain priests of his kinsfolk, which were Pharisees, to enquire what he did, he answered: 'It is written in the book of the prophet Malachi:

' "Behold, I will send my messenger and he shall prepare the way before me, and the Lord whom ye seek shall suddenly come to His Temple.

' "But who may abide the day of His coming? For He is like a refiner's fire. And I will come near to you in judgement."

'Also it is written in the book of the prophet Isaiah: "The voice of one crying in the wilderness: Prepare ye the way of the Lord, make straight in the desert a highway to our God.

' "For the glory of the Lord shall be revealed and all flesh shall see it together." '

V.k   (10) And John was clothed with a rough garment of camel's hair and with breeches of skin about his loins, and his meat was carobs of repentance.

He ate wild honey also from the rock. For he said: 'Moses testified: "The Lord found Israel in this desert land, in the waste wilderness, and made him to suck honey out of the rock and oil out of the flinty rock.

' "But when Israel went into Canaan and ate butter of kine and milk of sheep and fat of lambs and wheat and drank the pure blood of the grape, then he waxed fat and kicked and forsook God and lightly esteemed the rock of his salvation." Therefore am I returned hither to the desert.'

And John preached: 'Now is the axe laid unto the root of trees in the vineyard; as Isaiah prophesied that every vine bearing wild grapes shall be hewn down and cast into the fire. Bring forth therefore the fruits of repentance.

'For there cometh one mightier than I, whose shoes I am not worthy to bear, nor stooping down to set them upon his feet.

'I indeed have baptized you with water, but he shall baptize you with consuming fire.

'Of him Malachi prophesied: "Behold, the day cometh that all the proud, and they that do wickedly, shall be burned up as stubble; but unto them that fear God shall the Sun of Righteousness arise with healing in his wings."

'And Jeremiah spake in the name of the Lord: "I will fan them with a winnowing fan and bereave them of children."

'Behold, now, God's fan is in His hand, and He will thoroughly cleanse His threshing floor and gather the wheat into the garner, but He will burn the chaff with unquenchable fire.

'For the anointed King is at hand, the Son of God.'

V.k   (11) And when certain men also of the Sadducees came to John to enquire what he did, he cried unto them: 'O ye that are hatched from the eggs of vipers, as the prophet Isaiah testified, who hath warned you to flee from the wrath to come?

'Say not within yourselves: "We are children of Abraham, which is called the Rock." For in like manner as God once made the twelve stones that our forefather Jacob gathered to be his sons, and tribes in Israel, so He is able of these *abanim,* which is stones, to raise up new *banim,* which is children, unto Abraham!'

XXXIX.h   (12) Then all they that were baptized of John, glorified God, saying: 'Is not this Elijah, which is come to fulfill the prophecy spoken of Malachi?'

But the rulers of the Pharisees would not accept John that he was Elijah, for they declared that the signs prophesied of the Last Days were not yet appeared in Israel.

CHAPTER III

HOW JESUS WAS CHOSEN TO BE KING

VI.d (13) Now it came to pass after that Joseph the son of Eli was dead in Nazara, that the brethren of Jesus called him from where he sat under a fig-tree; and his mother said unto him before them all:

'John the Baptist baptizeth beyond Jordan unto the remission of sins. Let us go, thou and I and thy brethren, to be baptized of him.'

Jesus answered and said unto her: 'Have we so greatly offended against God or against our neighbours that thou shouldst say this thing?

'Nevertheless, our father David prayed: "O cleanse Thou me of my secret faults. Keep me from the sin of presumption." Therefore will I go with thee and with my brethren, according to thy word.'

VI.g (14) And forthwith they left their dwellings and went to Beth-Nimrah across Jordan.

John, seeing Jesus coming unto him in the midst of his brethren, stood amid two of his disciples,

And looking upon Jesus as he walked, he said unto them: 'Behold Emmanuel, an Israelite indeed in whom there is no guile! Here cometh the Lamb of God which shall take away the sins of the world.

'For He that sent me to baptize with water, the same said unto me: "In whom thou shalt see the Spirit of the Lord dwelling, the same is he which shall be called the Son of God."'

John therefore baptized the mother of Jesus and his brethren, but when Jesus came to be baptized John forbade him, saying privily: 'Nay, for thou art set aside from all thy brethren, as was my father Levi.'

Jesus saith unto him: 'Whence knowest thou me?'

He answered him, saying: 'Wert thou not called hither from under thy fig-tree?'

Jesus said: 'I perceive that thou art indeed a prophet.'

John spake and said: 'I prophesy greater things than these. Thou shalt become the Son of God, thou shalt become the King of Israel! Hereafter thou shalt see Heaven open and the spirit of God poured in a fountain upon thee! Then shall I have need to be baptized of thee.

'Now behold, as the prophet Samuel spake to Saul, so speak I to thee: "Seven days shalt thou tarry till I come unto thee and shew thee what thou shalt do."'

VI.g
(*contd.*)   Jesus therefore went apart into a mountain to pray, but his mother and his brethren turned back into Galilee.

VII.1   (15) And John, the messenger of the Lord, in likeness of the Angel Gabriel which leadeth in the Last Days, came filled with the Holy Spirit to Jerusalem unto a virgin named Mary, a daughter of Aaron.

The same had been given by her father and mother to the service of the Temple, in accordance with the Law.

She it is that was called Mary Magaddla (which is Mary the Braider) because she was of the women that wove the veil of the Sanctuary and braided the fringes thereof.

VII.1   (16) Now it came to pass, when the virgins which braided the veil were athirst, that Mary took a pitcher and went out to fill it with water.

And John, standing by the well, saluted her, saying: 'Hail, Mary, thou art highly favoured, the Lord is with thee: blessed art thou among women!'

But Mary, when she heard his words, was troubled, and cast in her mind what manner of salutation this should be and she set down the pitcher.

And John said unto her: 'Fear not, Mary, for thou hast found favour with God.

'Behold, not many days shall pass and thou shalt bring forth a son and shalt call his name The Branch.

'He shall be great, and shall be called the Son of the Most High, and the Lord God shall give unto him the throne of his father David,

'And he shall reign over the House of Jacob until this world hath ended.'

Then said Mary unto John: 'How may this be, seeing that I have known no man, to lie with him carnally? Shall I in truth bring forth as every woman bringeth forth?'

John answered and said: 'Not so, Mary, for the Holy Spirit shall come upon thee, and the power of the Highest shall overshadow thee.

'Therefore also that holy one which shall be born of thee shall be called the Son of God; and his name is now Jesus, for he shall save the people from their sins.'

And Mary said: 'Let thine handmaid find grace in thy sight. If that thou sayest is true, be it unto me according to thy word.'

John answered: 'Go to the house of my mother Elisabeth, which is thy kinswoman, and hasten with her to the place that I have appointed.'

And he departed from her, and when she had filled the pitcher she went away trembling and sat down in her seat, saying naught to her companions.

VII.1   (17) Mary arose in those days and went with haste into the hill country and entered into the house of Zechariah and saluted Elisabeth, her kinswoman.

And Elisabeth said: 'Blessed art thou among women! And whence is this that the mother of my Lord should come to me?'

VII.1
(*contd.*)
When therefore Mary knew that the messenger spake no deceit, she said:

'Let me rejoice as our mother Hannah rejoiced in the birth of her son Samuel, saying:

' "My heart rejoiceth in the Lord, mine horn is exalted in Thee, O Lord, because I rejoice in Thy salvation!

' "The Lord maketh poor, and maketh rich; He bringeth low, He lifteth up.

' "He raiseth up the poor from the dust and the beggar from the dung hill to set them among princes and to make them inherit the throne of glory.

' "He will keep the feet of the saints, and the wicked shall be silent in darkness, for by strength shall no man prevail over God.

' "The adversaries of the Lord shall be broken into pieces, out of heaven shall He thunder upon them. The Lord shall judge the ends of the earth, He shall give strength unto His king and exalt the horn of His Messiah." '

And Mary abode with Elisabeth about three days and afterward went with her to Beth-Nimrah across Jordan, even as John had appointed.

CHAPTER IV

HOW HE WAS CROWNED

VIII.y (18) When therefore Mary came with Elisabeth unto Beth-Nimrah, and Jesus which should be made King was also returned thither from the mountain where he fasted,

He, being clad in filthy garments, stood before John the messenger of the Lord, even as Zechariah prophesied.

And John said to the seven priests which stood by: 'Take away these filthy garments!' And unto Jesus he said: 'Behold, I have caused thine iniquity to pass from thee, and I will clothe thee with change of raiment.'

VIII.y (19) Then John protested unto Jesus according to the prophecy of Zechariah, saying:

'Thus saith the Lord of Hosts: "If thou wilt walk in My ways and if thou wilt keep My charge, then shalt thou also judge My house and keep My courts, and I will give thee walks to walk in among them that stand by.

' "Hear now, Jesus, thou and thy fellows that sit before thee, for they are men of a sign; behold, I will bring forth my servant The Branch!" '

Then it came to pass that Jesus went into the water of his cleansing and when he came out a great light shone upon him.

John bare record, saying: 'Behold, I saw the heavens opened, as my father Levi prophesied, and the Spirit of God that descended and lighted upon thee in the form of a dove. And the voice of the Lord uttered glory upon thee.'

And John, casting his eye upon Mary the Braider, said unto her: 'Woman, behold thy son!' and to Jesus he said: 'Son, behold thy mother!'

Then Mary spread her skirt over Jesus to cover his nakedness, and he was born again of her and was received into the tribe of Levi.

And Salome, her kinswoman, who ministered unto her as a midwife, testified saying: 'This child is born of a virgin which hath known no man.'

Thereafter Jesus took Mary unto him as his own mother, and she called his name The Branch.

VIII.y (20) John took a cruse of sacred oil and anointed the brow of Jesus.

VIII.y Then went Jesus into the tiring chamber and there his mother set
(contd.) upon his brow a wreath of thorn which she had plaited for his
espousals.

As it is written: 'Go forth, ye daughters of Zion, and behold the
King with the wreath wherewith his mother crowned him in the day
of his espousals and in the gladness of his heart.'

Then of the seven priests which stood by, the first fastened shoes
upon his feet.

And the second clad him in a tunic of fine linen without seam, and
the third put a purple mantle upon him.

And the fourth set a green reed in his right hand, and the fifth, a
branch of fruitful olive.

And the sixth filled his left hand with frankincense, and the
seventh crowned him with a diadem of gold.

VIII.m (21) For certain wise men had journeyed from Damascus to Jerusalem, being Zadokite priests of the New Covenant,

Which came unto the Watchers of Bethany (the same is nigh to
Jerusalem) and said unto them: 'Where is he that shall be re-born
King of Israel? Behold, the Star, the Coming One, is foretold in the
heavens; and we are journeyed hither to worship him.'

Then the Watchers enquired diligently of them at what time this
birth should come to pass, and they answered 'on such a day'.

These wise men therefore were abiding in Jerusalem until the time
that John chose Jesus to be King.

And when they heard that Jesus was chosen, they rejoiced with
exceeding great joy and went out with the Watchers unto Beth-
Nimrah,

Where seeing Mary and her new-born son, they fell down and
worshipped him.

And when they had opened their treasures, they presented unto him
gifts: a golden diadem and precious ointment and frankincense.

VIII.y (22) When he therefore came forth from the tiring chamber, wearing the diadem and the crown of thorn and the purple mantle, John
saith: 'Behold, the man!'

Then Jesus, seeing the solemn assembly, went up into a mount, as
David his father had prophesied, saying: 'Yet have I set my King
upon my holy hill,

'I will declare the statute: the Lord hath said unto me: "Thou art
My Son, this day art thou born to Me." '

And when Jesus was set, the disciples came unto him and they
began to salute him, saying: 'Hail, King of the Jews!' and bowed the
knee before him and worshipped him.

IX.c (23) And he opened his mouth and uttered ten blessings upon
those that forsook all for the Kingdom's sake, saying:

'Blessed are the poor in spirit; theirs is the Kingdom of Heaven!
For Isaiah prophesied in God's name, saying: "I dwell in the high
and holy place with him also that is of a contrite and humble spirit."

'Blessed are they that mourn; they shall be comforted! For Isaiah

IX.c
(*contd.*)

also prophesied, saying: "The Lord shall be thine everlasting light and the days of thy mourning shall be ended."

'Blessed are the meek; they shall inherit the earth! For David prophesied: "The meek shall inherit the earth, and shall delight themselves in the abundance of peace."

'Blessed are they that hunger and thirst after righteousness and mercy; they shall be filled! For Solomon prophesied: "He that loveth wine and oil shall not be rich, but he that seeketh after righteousness and mercy findeth life and righteousness and honour."

'Blessed are the merciful; they shall receive mercy! For David prophesied: "He that hath mercy upon the poor, the Lord will deliver him in time of trouble."

'Blessed are the pure in heart; they shall see God! For David prophesied: "He that hath clean hands and a pure heart, he shall receive the blessing of the Lord." And David also declared this blessing, what it was, saying: "I will behold Thy face in righteousness, when I awaken."

'Blessed are the peacemakers; they shall be called the Children of God! For David prophesied, saying: "Come, ye children, hearken unto me and I will teach you the fear of the Lord: which is to depart from evil and to do good, to seek peace and to ensue it."

'Blessed are they that are reproached for righteousness's sake; they shall not be confounded! For Isaiah prophesied: "I hid not my face from shame and spitting. But the Lord God will help me; therefore shall I not be confounded and I have set my face like a flint."

'Blessed are they that men hate and forsake; many generations shall love them! For Isaiah prophesied: "Whereas thou hast been forsaken and hated, I will make thee an eternal excellence, a joy of many generations."'

IX.c

(24) And he uttered also ten woes upon those that repented not, saying:

'Woe unto them that take delight in riches and put far off the evil day; they shall perish in the destruction of their palaces. For Amos prophesied of them: "Woe unto them that are at ease in Zion and lie upon beds of ivory and chant to the sound of viols; if there remain ten men in one house, they shall all die."

'Woe unto them that are filled; they shall hunger! For Isaiah prophesied against them in the name of the Lord: "Behold, My servants shall eat, but ye shall be hungry."

'Woe unto them that laugh now; they shall weep! For Isaiah prophesied against them also: "Behold My servants shall sing for joy of heart, but ye shall weep for sorrow of heart and cry for vexation of spirit."

'Woe unto the proud; they shall be left without shelter! For Solomon prophesied: "The Lord will break down the house of the proud."

'Woe unto the deceitful; they shall be destroyed! For David prophesied: "Thou shalt destroy them that speak leasing."

'Woe unto the fools that despise righteousness; they shall receive

IX.c
(*contd.*)
many stripes! For Solomon prophesied: "Judgements are prepared for scorners and stripes for the backs of fools."

'Woe unto the hard-hearted; they shall find no mercy! For Solomon prophesied: "He that hardeneth his heart shall fall into mischief."

'Woe unto them that are greedy of gain; they shall want! For Isaiah prophesied: "Woe unto them that join house to house, that lay field to field! Of a truth many great and fair houses shall be desolate, and the seed of an homer shall yield but an ephah."

'Woe unto the blood-thirsty; they shall be cut off! For David prophesied: "Bloody and deceitful men shall not live out half their days."

'Woe unto them that speak well of false prophets, but despise the messengers of God; they shall perish utterly! As it is written in the Chronicles of the Kings of Judah: "But they mocked the messengers of God and despised His prophets, until the wrath of the Lord arose against His people and He sent him against them which slew their young men with the sword in the house of their sanctuary, and had no compassion upon young man or maiden, or him that stooped for age." '

VIII.w
(25) And John spake from beside the throne, saying in a voice of mighty thunderings: 'Praise our God, all ye His servants, and ye that fear Him, both great and small!'

And they that stood by answered in a voice of many waters: 'Halleluiah! For the Lord God Omnipotent reigneth!'

Then said John: 'Let us be glad and rejoice and give honour to our King. For the marriage of the Lamb is come, and his wife hath made herself ready.

'And to her is granted that she should be arrayed in fine linen, clean and white; for fine linen is the righteousness of saints.

'Blessed are they that are called to the marriage supper of the Lamb.'

CHAPTER V

THE MARRIAGE OF THE LAMB

VIII.v (26) Then John brought unto Jesus the other Mary, daughter of Simeon the Chaste, of Bethany, arrayed in white linen and espoused her unto him.

VIII.w (27) And Simeon the Chaste, a just and devout man, of those Watchers which awaited the consolation of Israel, was filled with the Holy Spirit.

He blessed the bridegroom and the bride and said unto Mary the Braider, the mother of Jesus:

'This thy son is set for the fall and rising again of many in Israel, and for a sign that shall be spoken against, that the thoughts of many hearts may be revealed.

'Yea, a sword shall pierce thy soul also.'

And the mother of Jesus and Joseph of Ramathaim, her brother, marvelled at these things which were spoken of him.

VIII.v (28) Now Jesus, after the manner of the saints, had kept himself from women all the days of his life lest the Day of Judgement might find him defiled. As Moses said on Sinai: 'Be ready against the third day' (which is the Day of Resurrection); 'come not at your wives!'

VIII.v (29) Then he, being a just man, was minded to put her away privily, not wishing to shame her before the guests.

But while he thought on these things, John counselled him saying: 'Fear not, thou son of David, to take unto thee Mary, thy espoused wife,

'For she shall be unto thee as Abishag the Shunemite was, that ministered unto thy father David; though she was very fair, yet David knew her not and he named her his sister, though she was his spouse.'

And Jesus said unto Mary his wife: 'Suffer it to be so, for thus it becometh us to fulfil all righteousness.'

Therefore he took unto him his wife as John bade, but he knew her not. Yet he entered with her into the bride chamber which the disciples had builded for him, and tarried there awhile with her.

VIII.o (30) When presently these twain came out of the bride chamber they found a feast prepared for them.

But Jesus, perceiving that the disciples of John fasted and were of a sorrowful countenance, said unto them:

'Shall the sons of the bride chamber mourn and fast while the bridegroom is with them?' (For the espousals of a king absolve men

VIII.o
(contd.) of their vows of fasting.) 'But when the bridegroom is gone from you, then may ye fast again.'

Therefore did they also eat with him, and were merry.

VIII.p (31) And the disciples of John the Baptist, seeing him of good cheer which before was sorrowful, and full of laughter and blessings which before was full of lamentations and curses, were amazed, because it was as though he were himself the bridegroom.

But he answered and said unto them: 'The friend of the bridegroom which standeth and heareth him, rejoiceth greatly in his voice. This my joy therefore is fulfilled, that the Father loveth His son and hath given all things into his hand.

'He must increase, but I must decrease.'

XI.i (32) As Jesus sat at meat, Mary took an alabaster box of ointment of nard, mixed with myrrh, very precious, and breaking the box, poured it upon his head. And the house was filled with the savour.

And the disciples were offended and one said: 'Why was this waste of ointment made? It might have been sold for three hundred pence and given to the poor?' And they murmured against her.

Jesus said: 'Let her alone, why trouble ye her?

'For it is written: "The poor shall never cease out of the land," and whensoever ye will, ye may open your hand wide unto them. But me ye have not always with you.

'My sister hath wrought a good work: she hath done this as a memorial unto me, anointing my body aforehand for the grave, that my soul may live for ever more.'

XI.k (33) And Jesus sang the psalm of David which saith:

'Behold, how good and pleasant it is for brethren to dwell in unity!

'It is like the precious ointment upon the head that ran down upon the beard, even the beard of Aaron, that went down to the skirts of his garments,

'As the dew that fell upon Hermon and upon the mountains of Zion: for there the Lord commanded the blessing, even life for ever more.'

X.e (34) Then Jesus took a cup of wine that was prepared for him, and blessed it and gave thanks. And unto the sons of the bride chamber he said: 'Take this and drink ye all of it. But I will not drink henceforth of the fruit of the vine until I may drink it new in the Kingdom of my Father.

'That wine shall be pressed from grapes which have been since the world began.'

VIII.y (35) Afterward, according to the word that John had spoken, Jesus kindled a great fire of thorns, and burned incense therein, wherewith the disciples were baptized, and John, and all the company.

VIII.y (36) But certain of the sons of the bride chamber took the reed from Jesus and smote him on the head withal, and did spit on his face.

And others blindfolded him and smote him with the palms of their hands, saying: 'Prophesy unto us, thou Anointed One: which is he that smote thee?'

VIII.y   And they heaped many curses upon him and buffeted him.
(*contd.*)   That it might be fulfilled which was spoken of Isaiah the prophet:
'Behold, my servant shall be exalted and extolled and be very high.
And many were astonished: his visage was so marred more than any
man's, and his form more than the sons of men.'

VIII.y   (37) And when they had done mocking him, they took the purple
off him and put his own raiment on him, and led him away, for his
visage was bruised so that for awhile he had no sight, and his body
was maimed.
          Thus Jesus himself began to be, about thirty years of age.

VIII.p   (38) When therefore all things were accomplished, Jesus returned
into Galilee, and John was baptizing in Karim, nigh unto Jerusalem,
because there was much water there.

VIII.u   (39) Now, this was the generation of Joseph of Ramathaim, which
was called the father of Jesus, seeing that Mary the Braider, his sister
of whom Jesus was born by the spirit, was an unwedded virgin:

> Joseph was the son of Jacob,
> Which was the son of Matthan,
> Which was the son of Eleazar,
> Which was the son of Elihu,
> Which was the son of Jachin,
> Which was the son of Zadok,
> Which was the son of Azur,
> Which was the son of Eliakim,
> Which was the son of Abner,
> Which was the son of Abihu,

Which was of the line of Zadok son of Ahitub, which was of the
line of Eleazar son of Aaron, whom the Lord God (blessed be He!)
chose to be High Priest of Israel.

CHAPTER VI

CONCERNING THE PHARISEES

XIII.w   (40) When therefore Jesus returned in power of the spirit unto Galilee, there went out a fame of him in all the region round about. And he preached in the synagogues, being glorified of all.

XIII.w   (41) Thus he taught the people, saying:

'The scribes and the Pharisees sit in Moses's seat. For Moses received the Law upon Sinai, and delivered it to Joshua, and Joshua to the elders, and the elders to the prophets, and they to the men of the Great Council, the sages of whose line came Hillel—blessed be his memory!

'All therefore that they bid you observe, that observe and do.

'But take heed ye walk not in the way of the feigned Pharisees.

'For the feigned ones are they of whom Isaiah prophesied, saying: "This people draw near Me with their mouth, and with their lips do honour Me, but have removed their heart from Me, and their fear towards Me is taught by the precept of men."

'Behold, they worship not God for His own sake as do the true Pharisees;

'And hark ye how Isaiah beareth witness against their dissembling, saying: "Woe unto them that seek deep to hide their counsel from the Lord, and whose works are in the dark! They say: 'Who seeth us, and who knoweth us?'"

'Woe therefore unto those feigned Pharisees that serve not for love of God, but think only of rewards. For they make broad their phylacteries and enlarge the fringes of their garments of prayer, to be seen of men!'

XXVII.g   (42) 'Being but feigned Pharisees, they give alms as it were with trumpets sounded before them. They have their reward: to be praised of men.

'But thou, when thou givest alms, let not thy left hand know what thy right hand doth, that thine alms may be in secret; then in the world to come shalt thou earn praise from thy Father which watcheth in secret.

'Being but feigned Pharisees, they love also to pray openly in the synagogue or at the street corner. They have their reward: to be praised of men.

'But thou, when thou prayest, enter into thy closet and pray in

XXVII.g
(contd.) secret; then in the world to come shalt thou earn praise from thy
Father which hearkeneth in secret.

'Being but feigned Pharisees, they disarray their hair when they
come from fasting, and make foul their cheeks with ashes and shew
a sorrowful countenance. They have their reward: to be praised of
men.

'But thou, when thou comest from fasting, comb thy hair and wash
thy cheeks and be of a merry countenance. Then, though thou appearest unto men not to have fasted, yet shalt thou earn praise in the
world to come from thy Father which watcheth in secret.'

XIV.b   (43) And Jesus said also:

'Moses spake in God's name: "Unto Me the children of Israel are
bondmen which I brought from Egypt."

'Now, a bondman serveth not for reward, but because he is a bondman.

'Therefore Elihu the Jebusite asked of Job: "If thou be righteous,
what givest thou unto God? Or what receiveth He of thine hand?"

'For which of you, having a bondman ploughing or feeding cattle,
will say unto him, by and by, when he is come from the field: "Go
and sit down to meat"?

'But will not rather say unto him: "Make ready wherewith I may
sup, and gird thyself and serve me, till I have eaten and drunken, and
afterward thou shalt eat and drink"?

'Doth he praise that servant because he doeth the things that were
commanded him? I trow not.

'So likewise ye, when ye shall have done all those things which are
commanded you in the Law, shall say: "We are unprofitable bondmen: we have done no more than was our duty."

'As the Preacher saith: "Fear God and keep His commandments;
for this is the whole duty of man." '

XV.c   (44) But lest they should deceive themselves and suppose that such
bondage was weariness, he said:

'Come unto the Lord, all ye that labour and are heavily laden under
the burdens of this world, and He will give you rest.

'Take upon you the easy yoke of the Law, and learn wisdom of
God.

'As Jeremiah prophesied: "Thus saith the Lord: 'Ask ye for the old
paths, where is the good way, and walk therein, and ye shall find rest
for your souls.' "

'And as the Preacher, the Son of Sirach, exhorted us: "Put your
neck under the yoke of the Law and let your soul receive instruction;
for wisdom is close at hand to find.

' "Behold with your eyes how I have had but little labour and have
gotten unto me much rest."

'And the Preacher saith likewise of Wisdom: "An ornament of gold
is her yoke, and her traces a ribband of purple silk." '

XIII.x   (45) He said also:

'Woe unto those feigned Pharisees that serve only for fear! For they

XIII.x
(contd.)
tithe mint and dill and cummin, as indeed they ought to do, but hope thereby to abate a punishment; and omit the weightier matters of judgement, mercy, and faith.

'Against them Isaiah witnesseth: "They make haste to shed innocent blood; there is no judgement in their goings; they have made them crooked paths, whosoever goeth in them shall not know peace. They hatch vipers' eggs, and weave the spider's web."

'Woe therefore unto those feigned Pharisees! For they strain that which they drink lest they swallow a gnat, but (as men say) swallow a camel.

'Which wash well the outside of their dish, yet eat therefrom the meat of defilement.

'Which triumph in the rich proselyte coming from a land that lieth beyond the sea, yet despise the lost sheep of the House of Israel,

'By their scorn repelling them from the synagogue, and taking away the key of knowledge, whereby the Kingdom of Heaven is shut against them; for they know not that by so doing they shut themselves out also.

'Beware of such, for they are like sepulchres that appear not, being unwhited, against which ye may stumble and be defiled.

'Avoid their crooked paths, lest the vipers that lurk therein bite you and ye die.

'But keep faith with God, shew mercy, use judgement, and ye shall live!

XIII.y
(46) 'For David prophesied in a psalm, saying:
' "If thou makest the Most High God thy refuge and dwelling, no evil shall befall thee: thou shalt trample upon the asp and viper." '

XX.i
(47) And he spake again of the feigned Pharisees, saying:
'It is not only that which goeth into a man that defileth a man, but also that which cometh out of him.

'For though ye eat clean food it entereth into the belly and descendeth into the draught and is presently voided as dung that defileth.

'The Lord gave Ezekiel a scroll of a book to eat, and it was in his mouth as honey for sweetness.

'Yet some there are which, when the scroll of the Law is given them to feed upon in their hearts, void it wickedly in murders, adulteries, thefts, false witness and covetousness.

XX.i
(48) 'Walk not in their company, open thine eyes to their deceit, and be not guided by them: for if the blind lead the blind, shall they not both fall into a ditch?

XX.k
(49) 'To be blind is no sin, but to be blind and say: "We see, let us guide thee," the same is deceit and sin.'

CHAPTER VII

HOW JESUS PREACHED BY THE LAKE

XVII.f (50) Jesus, walking by the Sea of Galilee, preached to the great multitude that followed him, and lest they should throng him he entered into a small boat.

And he preached unto them, saying: 'The Day of Judgement is like to a net that was cast into a sea and gathered of every kind of fish, clean and unclean, which when it was full the fishers drew to shore. Then gathered they the clean into baskets, but cast the unclean away.

'So it shall be in the last days. The angels shall come forth and sever the wicked from the just.

'For Enoch testifieth: "The Most High will deliver those evil ones to His angels for punishment because they have oppressed His children,

' "But the righteous and elect shall be saved on that day and shall never thenceforward see the face of the sinners and unrighteous." '

Now, in a boat near by were Simon, afterwards called Peter, and Andrew his brother; and in another boat were James and John the sons of Zebedee, mending their nets.

Jesus said: 'Who will preach the way of repentance? Come with me, that will, and I will make you fishers of men!'

Simon and Andrew, hearing those words, forsook their nets and, when Jesus departed, they followed him. Then Jesus turned and saw them following, and said unto them: 'What seek ye?'

They asked him: 'Master, where dwellest thou?' He saith unto them: 'Come and see!'

They came and saw where he dwelt, and abode with him that day, for it was about the tenth hour, and became his disciples.

XVI.a (51) And he taught them of the fig-tree which is Israel, how God would yet once more shew mercy unto her and spare her; but if this time also she repented not, nor gave forth the fruits of repentance, she should be hewn down.

For he said: 'A certain man had a fig-tree planted in his vineyard; and he came and sought fruit thereon, but found none.

'Then spake he unto the dresser of the vineyard: "Behold, these three years I come seeking fruit on my fig-tree, and find none; cut it down; why cumbereth it the ground?"

'And he, answering, said unto him: "Lord, let it alone this year also,

XVI.a till I dig about it, and dung it: and if it bear fruit, well: and if not,
(contd.) then after that thou shalt cut it down." '

LXVI.c (52) And Jesus said: 'It is written that the Lord, when He spared
our father Isaac, called out of heaven unto Abraham, saying: "In thy
seed shall all the nations of the earth be blessed, because thou hast
obeyed My voice."

'Yet not all the seed of Isaac fell on good ground. Hearken therefore
to this parable:

'A sower went forth to sow, and as he sowed, some seed fell by the
wayside. As it is written in the Book of Joshua: "All the men of war
perished in the wilderness, by the way."

'For they obeyed not the word that the Lord spake unto Moses: "If
it shall come to pass that thou wilt not hearken to the voice of thy
God, thy carcase shall be meat unto all the fowls of the air." And
again: "Ye shall sow your seed in vain, for your enemies shall eat it."

'And some fell upon stony places where they had not much earth,
and when the sun was up, they were scorched, and because they had
no root they withered away. As Isaiah prophesied: "Their stock shall
not take root in the earth. The Lord shall also blow upon them and
they shall wither, and the whirlwind shall take them away."

'And some fell among thorns, and the thorns sprang up and choked
them. As Jeremiah prophesied: "Thus saith the Lord to the men of
Judah and of Jerusalem: 'Break up your fallow ground and sow not
among thorns.' "

'But others fell upon good ground and brought forth fruit: some
thirty, some sixty, some an hundredfold. As Hosea spake in the name
of the Lord: "Sow in righteousness, reap in mercy." And as Zechariah
likewise spake: "For the seed shall be prosperous and the ground shall
give her increase, and I will cause the remnant of this people to possess all these things."

'Hear ye therefore the word of God and keep it, fall not by the wayside, spread your roots in the faith, be not choked by the cares of this
world, and at the last ye shall enjoy great increase.

'For so it is written of our forefather Isaac: "He sowed in that land
and received in the same year an hundredfold, and the Lord blessed
him." '

XLVII.e (53) He expounded also a proverb of Solomon: 'If thou seekest
Wisdom as silver and searchest for her as for hid treasures, then shalt
thou find the knowledge of God,' saying:

'Hearken therefore unto this parable: the Kingdom of Heaven is
like unto a treasure of silver and gold and precious stones hid in a
field, the which when a wise man hath found he hideth again, and for
joy thereof goeth and selleth all that he hath and buyeth that field.

'Or it is like unto a merchant man, seeking goodly pearls, which
when he hath found one pearl of price goeth and selleth all that he
hath and buyeth it.

'As Job also saith: "Behold the fear of the Lord, that is wisdom; and
to depart from evil, that is understanding.

XLVII.e
(contd.)
' "The gold and the sapphire shall not equal wisdom, nor shall it be exchanged for jewels of fine gold. No mention shall be made of coral or of pearls, for the price of wisdom is above rubies." '

LXVIII.c
(54) And he said: 'Lay not up for yourselves riches upon earth that vanish and fly away; for here moth and rust do corrupt and thieves break through and steal.

'But do ye according to the Testament of Levi: "By righteousness lay up riches in the heavenly palace," in bags that wax not old, where neither moth nor rust do corrupt, and where thieves do not break through and steal.

'For there shall ye also find honour and eternal life.

LXVIII.c
(55) 'It is written: "Thou shalt have none other Gods but Me," and ye have read how Elijah spake to the people on Carmel, saying: "How long halt ye between two opinions? If the Lord be God, follow Him; but if Baal, follow him."

'No man that serveth two masters can serve both faithfully with his heart. Either he will hate the one and love the other; or else he will hold to the one and despise the other.

'Ye cannot serve both God and God's Adversary with your riches; for wheresoever ye have laid up your treasure, there shall your heart be also.

LXVIII.b
(56) 'Solomon verily taught us that we should despise earthly riches, for he said:

' "He that keepeth faith with God shall abound with blessings, but he that maketh haste to be rich shall not go unpunished."

'And he said again: "Labour not to be rich, for riches vanish, they make themselves wings and fly away like an eagle."

'And he said again: "Humility and the fear of the Lord are true riches and honour and life."

'And he said again: "There is one that maketh himself rich despite his penury; and another that maketh himself poor despite his riches."

LXVII.a
(57) 'And David prophesied, saying: "They that boast themselves in the multitude of their riches, though they see that wise men die, likewise the fool and the brutish person, and leave their wealth to others,

' "Nevertheless, their inward thought is that their dwelling places shall continue for ever, and they call their lands after their own names.

' "Therefore, like sheep they are laid in the grave and shall never see the light; for a man that is honoured in this world but hath no understanding is like the beasts that perish."

'And again: "Surely, every man walketh in a vain show, that heapeth up riches and knoweth not who shall enjoy them."

'Therefore take ye heed and beware of covetousness, for a man's life consisteth not in the abundance of the things which he possesseth.

'The Preacher, the Son of Sirach, saith: "This is the reward of him that waxeth rich from covetousness. What time he saith: 'I have found rest, and now will I enjoy my substance,' he knoweth not what is his

LXVII.a   lot. His lot is that he shall die and leave his goods to be enjoyed of
(contd.)   others."

    'And it is written in the Book of Job: "For what is the hope of him
that maketh a vain show, though he hath gained much, when God
taketh away his soul?"

LXVII.a   (58) 'Hearken therefore unto this parable: the ground of a certain
rich man brought forth plentifully.

    'But he was covetous, and gave naught unto his kinsfolk or unto his
poor neighbours.

    'And he thought within himself: "What shall I do, because I have
no room where to bestow my fruits?"

    'Therefore he said: "This will I do, I will pull down my barns and
build greater, and there will I bestow all my fruits and my goods.

    ' "And I will assure my soul: 'Soul, thou hast much goods laid up
for many years. Take thine ease now, eat, drink and be merry.' "

    'But God said unto him: "Settest thou one man a-building, and
another pulling down, by which they gain naught but their labour
[as the Son of Sirach saith], while thou livest at thy ease? Thou fool,
this night thy soul shall be required of thee! Then whose shall those
goods be which thou hast provided?"

CI.k   (59) 'For it is written in the Book of Job: "Beware lest the Lord
take thee away with His stroke; then a great ransom shall not deliver
thee."

    'And what shall it profit a man if he gain the whole world and lose
his soul, which is beyond all price?'

CHAPTER VIII

HOW HE HEALED DIVERS SICK AND
GAVE WATER FOR WINE

XLII.e (60) It was a sabbath, and when Jesus was come out of the synagogue, he entered into the house of Simon Peter and Andrew to eat bread, and James and John were with him.

But Peter's wife's mother kept her bed and would do naught for them, no, not so much as arise to greet Jesus.

For since Peter and Andrew had left their nets and followed after him, she feared lest her daughter might lack and suffer hunger.

They tell Jesus: 'She hath a fever. It were well for thee to dine in the house of another.'

But Jesus went to where she lay on her bed, and took her by the hand and spake a word to her privily: how that those which fear the Lord shall want no manner of thing that is good.

And immediately she arose and ministered unto them.

XLII.e (61) And when the sun had set, the men of Capernaum brought unto Jesus many that were lunatic or possessed of evil spirits, and all the city was gathered together at his door.

Then was it granted unto him to work cures upon them; but he suffered no man to name him King, lest the matter should come to the ears of them that served the Wicked Kingdom.

And rising up a great while before day was come, he went out and departed unto a solitary place and there prayed.

But Peter and they that were with him followed after, and when they find him, they say: 'Master, all men seek for thee.'

He answered: 'Let us go into the next cities, that I may preach there also; for unto this end was I sent: to proclaim the acceptable year of the Lord, and the day of His vengeance.'

LVI.h (62) On the morrow, therefore, Jesus would go forth into Galilee.

And Philip besought him, saying: 'Master, suffer me to be thy disciple.'

Jesus answered and said: 'Follow me!'

Then Philip sought out Nathanael his brother, and said unto him: 'He hath been found, whom Moses and the prophets foretold. The same is Jesus, of Bethlehem Nazara, and he is dedicated unto God.'

But Nathanael asked: 'Is it not written that the Holy One shall proceed from Bethlehem Ephratah? And how can any man that

LVI.h
(contd.)
proceedeth from Bethlehem Nazara be *nazir* (which is dedicated unto God)?'

Philip said: 'Come and see! He is more than a man dedicated, he is *Netzer* (which is The Branch), whereof Isaiah prophesied, saying: "And a branch from his roots shall blossom." '

(Wherefore to this day we are called Nazarenes.)

And Nathanael likewise was chosen to be a disciple.

XLII.e
(63) Jesus preached in the synagogues throughout Galilee, and his fame went forth even to the coasts of Tyre and Sidon. And it passed also through Decapolis and across Jordan and came unto Jerusalem. And great multitudes followed him,

XLII.f
(64) Which marvelled at his teaching, for he spake with authority, though not being of the scribes.

LVI.g
(65) And there pressed upon him, to touch the fringe of his garment, as many as were plagued by evil dreams and evil inclinations.

X.c
(66) There was a marriage in Cana of Galilee. And Jesus was called thither, for the bridegroom was his kinsman according to the flesh.

And coming on the third day with his disciples, he found the guests merry with music and laughter, but Jesus would drink no wine with them.

Then Mary his wife, said unto him: 'Lord, thou hast no wine. Let me command the servants to fill thy cup.'

He answered and said unto her: 'Woman, what have I to do with thee? The time of my drinking is not yet come.'

But his mother, which was of the House of David, said unto him: 'Yet this day looseth all vows.'

He answered her: 'Our forefather Judah commanded us: "My children, be not drunk with wine, which turneth the mind away from the truth, leadeth in lust, and guideth the eyes into error."

'And Isaiah prophesied against the drunken, saying: "The tabret and pipe are in their feasts but they regard not the work of the Lord."

'Therefore will I drink no wine until the Kingdom of God cometh. I pray thee, let me now command the servants as it seemeth good unto me. For behold, that time is at hand when, as Zechariah prophesied, every pot shall be holiness unto the Lord of Hosts.'

His mother commanded the servants, saying: 'Whatsoever he may bid you do, do it!'

And he bade them fill up six stone water-pots being of two or three firkins apiece. They filled them with water to the brim.

And when that the ruler of the feast had tasted of the water that was poured out as wine, he understood, and said unto the bridegroom: 'The better drink is used to be set out first, and then, when men have well drunk, that which is worse. But thou hast kept the better until now.'

Jesus answered and said unto him: 'These six pots shall be as the six days of the week wherein we labour: each shall be holiness unto the Lord, both for the male and for the female, even as the sabbath is holy.'

X.c
(*contd.*)   This was the first notable act which Jesus performed in Galilee after that he turned back thither from his anointing.

XLVI.g   (67) And when Jesus marked how they which were bidden to the wedding chose out the chief seats, he taught them, saying: 'Solomon spake a proverb: "Put not forth thyself in the presence of the king, and stand not in the place of great men:

' "For better it is that it be said unto thee: 'Come up hither,' than that thou shouldest be put lower in the presence of the prince whom thine eyes have seen."

'And Job declareth: "When men are cast down then shalt thou say: 'There is lifting up, and He shall save the humble person.' "

'Verily, I say unto you: as it is in the presence of the prince whom thine eyes have seen, so shall it also be in the presence of Him whom they have not seen.

'For whosoever exalteth himself shall be abased; and he that humbleth himself, the same shall be exalted.

'As David saith: "For Thou wilt save the afflicted people and bring down high lords." '

CHAPTER IX

HOW HE CALLED MATTHEW THE PUBLICAN

XIX.g (68) As Jesus passed by the receipt of custom, he saw Matthew the Levite, which had been a Watcher, sitting there and said unto him:

'Why sittest thou there, Matthew? Art thou not also a son of Aaron? Make haste and come down!'

Matthew, being overcome with shame, asked him: 'Sir, what shall I do to be saved?'

Jesus answered, and said: 'Restore fourfold whatsoever thou hast taken by fraud, as the Law commandeth, and bestow upon thy household the remainder of thy substance, and come, follow me!'

Matthew said: 'Sir, I will do even as thou sayest.'

And he made haste and came down and followed him.

Now, it came to pass that many Hebrew publicans, which saw it, repented likewise and were drawn to follow after Matthew.

And they all entered into the house where Jesus lodged with his disciples, and sat down there.

Then did Jesus rejoice, saying: 'This day is salvation come to this house!' And he preached the word of God unto them, but certain of his disciples were offended that the publicans were come into the house.

XVIII.b (69) Jesus said: 'A certain man had two sons, and he divided unto them his living.

'And not many days after, the younger son gathered all together and took his journey into a far country, and there wasted his substance in riotous living.

'Now, when he had spent all, there arose a mighty famine in that land; and he began to be in want.

'Therefore he went and joined himself to a citizen of that country; and he sent him into his fields to feed swine, where he would fain have filled his belly with the carobs that the swine did eat: and no man gave aught else unto him.

'As the prophet Isaiah saith: "If ye be willing and obedient, the good of the land shall ye eat; but if ye rebel and resist, *hereb* (which is the sword), shall eat you."

'Let the rebellious ones therefore hasten to eat *harub* (which is carobs), for verily this is the food of repentance!

'And when the son came to himself, he said: "How many hired

XVIII.b
(contd.)

servants of my father's have bread enough and to spare, and I perish with hunger!

' "I will arise and go to my father, and will say unto him: 'Father, I have sinned against heaven, and before thee.' "

'For David spake in a psalm: "I acknowledged my sin unto Thee, and mine iniquity have I not hid. I said: 'I will confess my transgressions unto the Lord.' And Thou forgavest the iniquity of my sin."

'And the son arose and came to his father.

'But when he was yet a great way off, his father saw him, and had compassion, and ran, and fell on his neck, and kissed him.

'Then said the son unto him: "Father, I have sinned against heaven and before thee and am no more worthy to be called thy son. Forgive me this my folly and I will be thy bondman and will tend thy asses and feed thy cattle."

'But the father said to his servants: "Bring forth the best robe, and put it on him; and put a ring on his hand, and shoes on his feet: for this my son was dead, and is alive again; he was lost, and is found."

'And they began to be merry.

'Now, his elder son was in the field: and as he came and drew nigh to the house, he heard music and dancing.

'And he called one of the servants, and asked what these things meant. The servant said unto him: "Thy brother is come; and thy father hath killed the fatted calf, because he hath received him safe and sound."

'The elder son was angry thereat, and would not go in; therefore came his father out, and intreated him.

'And he answering said to his father: "Lo, these many years do I serve thee, neither transgressed I at any time thy commandment: and yet thou never gavest me a kid, that I might make merry with my friends:

' "But as soon as this thy son was come, which hath devoured thy living with harlots, thou hast killed for him the fatted calf."

'The father said unto him: "Son, thou art ever with me, and all that I have is thine.

' "It was meet that we should make merry, and be glad: for this thy brother was dead, and is alive again; and was lost, and is found." '

XIX.g

(70) But when certain Pharisees came to converse with Jesus and desired him to preach in their synagogue, they also were offended at that they saw and would not enter into his house.

They said to the disciples privily: 'How is this? Why doth your master preach to publicans and sinners?'

When Jesus heard that the Pharisees were offended, he went out and said unto them: 'They that are whole have no need of the physician, but they that are sick. They that are well filled have no need of bread, but they that are hungry. I am come not to call the righteous, but sinners to repentance.'

XIX.h

(71) And he spake this parable unto them, saying:

'The words of the prophet Zechariah: "Thus saith the Lord my

XIX.h
(contd.)

God, feed the flock of the slaughter. Therefore will I feed the flock of the slaughter, even you, the poor of the flock."

'What man of you having an hundred sheep, if he lose one of them doth not leave the ninety and nine in the fold, and go into the mountains and seek that which is gone astray?

'And if so be that he find it, verily I say unto you, he calleth to his friends and neighbours, saying unto them: "Rejoice with me, for I have found my sheep which was lost."

'Or what woman having ten pieces of silver, if she lose one doth not light a lamp and sweep the house, and seek diligently until she find it?

'And when she hath found it, she calleth her friends and neighbours together, saying unto them: "Rejoice with me, for I have found my piece which was lost."

'Likewise I say unto you, that there is joy in the presence of the angels of God over one sinner that repenteth.

'This son of man is sent to seek and save that which is lost, and today he hath found him.'

XIX.k

(72) And Jesus also spake this parable:

'Two men went up into the Temple to pray, the one a Pharisee which fasted when fasting was required of him and paid tithes of all his produce; the other a publican which had repented of his evil.

'The Pharisee stood and prayed: "O Lord, I thank Thee that Thou hast heard my prayer, and kept me from adultery and theft and blasphemy and from all such greater offences. Were it not for Thy grace I might be even as a publican."

'But the publican, standing far from the Sanctuary, would not lift up so much as his eyes unto heaven but smote upon his breast, saying: "God be merciful unto me, a sinner!"

'I say unto you: that the Lord bestowed His peace first upon this publican, and then upon the Pharisee. For Isaiah prophesied: "Peace, peace to him that is far off, and to him that is nigh."

'Behold, a soul which is in trouble standeth nigh unto God. And joy shall be in heaven over one such sinner that repenteth more than over nine and ninety just persons that need no repentance.'

CHAPTER X

HIS EXHORTATIONS TO CHASTITY

XXI.h   (73) Jesus went across Jordan and a multitude followed him, and as he was wont he taught them.

And a Pharisee asked Jesus: 'Master, holdest thou that a man may put away his wife for any cause, or for fornication only?'

Jesus answered and said: 'Hast thou not read how that He which made man at the beginning made them male and female,

'For which cause shall a man leave his father and mother and shall cleave to his wife, and they twain shall be one flesh?

'What therefore God hath joined, let no man lightly put asunder.'

The Pharisee asked him again: 'Why then did Moses suffer a man to give a bill of divorcement, and to put away his wife?'

Jesus answered: 'Moses, truly, because of the hardness of our fathers' hearts, suffered them to put away their wives, if matter of uncleanness were found in them.

'Yet have ye not read what the prophet Jeremiah spake in the name of the Lord?

'For he said: "It is written: 'If a man put away his wife, and she go from him and become another man's, shall he return unto her again? Shall not that land be greatly polluted?' But thou, Israel, hast played the harlot with many lovers and under every green tree. Yet return again to Me, saith the Lord."

'Therefore, if God thus forgiveth Israel her manifold whoredoms, how much more should not a man forgive a matter of uncleanness in the wife of his bosom?

'And I say unto you that if a man put away his wife for slight cause he guideth her feet in the path of adultery; and if he then take another in her stead, he himself committeth adultery.'

XXI.i   (74) They said unto him: 'But what Moses permitted, is not that the Law?'

He answered and said: 'Think not that I am come to subvert the Law. I am come neither to increase it nor to diminish it but to fulfil the Will of God, which hath interpreted the Law by the mouth of His holy prophets.

'For Moses commanded Israel: "Ye shall not add unto the word which I command you, neither shall ye diminish aught from it, but ye shall keep the commandments of the Lord for ever!"

'Verily, therefore, until heaven and earth pass away, not one jot or

XXI.i
(contd.)

tittle shall in any wise pass from the Law, but all shall be fulfilled!

'And whosoever breaketh the least of the commandments that God committed unto His prophets and excuseth himself, saying: "It is permitted in the Law," the same shall be called the least in the Kingdom of Heaven.'

XXI.l

(75) But a Sadducee said to Jesus: 'If then the twain be one flesh, there can be no resurrection.'

Jesus asked: 'How so?'

He answered and said: 'Moses wrote that if a man die and leave no children, his brother shall take the widow and raise up seed unto him that is dead.

'Now, there were seven brethren, the first of which died without issue.

'The second took the widow unto himself and married her, neither left he any issue.

'The third likewise, and the fourth, until all seven had her.

'Last of all the woman died also.

'If there be a resurrection, how can this woman be one flesh with seven men?'

Jesus answered and said: 'Thou errest. Those that arise from the dead shall neither marry nor be given in marriage, but shall be like the angels in heaven. None thereafter shall either be born or die.

'And ye Sadducees that reject the prophets, how do ye reject the resurrection of the dead, having read the Law and knowing the power of God?

'Did not God speak to Moses out of the bush, saying: "I am the God of Abraham, Isaac and Jacob"?

'He therefore is not the God of the dead, but of the living. They that are called dead according to the flesh live unto Him in the spirit and shall be raised again at the Last Judgement when the Anointed One, the Son of David, cometh to judge the world.

XXI.l

(76) 'And the Kingdom of Heaven to which they are called shall be in this land where we now are. As it is written: "And I also kept My covenant with Abraham, Isaac and Jacob to give them the Land of Canaan."'

XXI.m

(77) Then certain of the scribes answered: 'Master, thou hast well said!'

But the same Sadducee asked again: 'By what authority sayest thou that the Anointed One, the Son of David, will come to judge the world?'

He answered and said: 'Though ye Sadducees reject the prophets, yet sing ye the psalm of David, which saith: "The Lord said unto my Lord: 'Sit thou on My right hand till I make thine enemies thy footstool.'"'

But the Sadducee laughed him to scorn, saying: 'If David calleth him Lord, how is he then his son? And if he is David's son, how shall he be given greater honour than David?'

XXI.m   (78) Jesus answered and said: 'It is written in the same psalm: "The Lord at thy right hand shall strike through kings in the day of His wrath."

'Therefore shall David sit on the left hand, for something of sin was found in him, but his son shall be perfected and shall sit on the right hand.'

XXI.o   (79) Jesus also said:

'It is written: "Thou shalt not commit adultery!"

'Yet whosoever looketh upon a woman to lust after her, the same committeth adultery with her in his heart.

'Therefore, if thine eye offend thee, pluck it out and cast it from thee; or if thy foot offend against thee, cut it off.

'It is better to enter halt or blind into the Kingdom, than that thy whole body should be cast into hell. Save thyself and thy soul!

'For Isaiah the prophet saith: "In the carcases of those that transgress against Thee, O Lord, their worm dieth not and the fire is not quenched." '

His disciples say unto him: 'Not all men can receive this saying.'

Jesus answered: 'I speak not according to the flesh. Some are born eunuchs and earn no praise therefrom, neither condemnation; some are made eunuchs of men and earn condemnation; but some shall make themselves as it were eunuchs for the Kingdom of God, and these shall earn praise from the Father.

'He that can receive this saying, let him receive it!

XXI.r   (80) 'And let him strive with the flesh and chasten it, not yielding unto its lusts, but making his soul to wax strong by faith and wisdom.

'For no man that is not tried can be approved, and no man that is not approved shall enter into the Kingdom.'

XXI.r   (81) The disciples say unto him: 'Master, we receive this saying.'

And Jesus rejoiced, and said: 'Now, behold, I see Satan as lightning falling from heaven.'

XXI.o   (82) Salome (which was midwife when he was born again of Mary the Braider by the Spirit of God, and which testified to her virginity) asked Jesus: 'Lord, how long shall Death prevail?'

He answered: 'So long as ye women bear children.'

She asked again: 'I have done well, then, in bearing none?'

He said unto her: 'It is written: "To the hungry soul, every bitter thing is sweet." Eat of every healthful plant, but of that which is bitter eat not; for the time will come wherein the childless shall account themselves blessed.'

She asked: 'Shall a man then marry a wife and know her not?'

He answered: 'It is written that the Alukah hath two daughters, which are the womb and the grave, and they cry "Give, give!" I am sent to destroy her works.'

She asked him again: 'Lord, when shall these things be accomplished?'

He said unto her: 'When ye women shall have trampled upon the

XXI.o garment of shame: and when the two shall have become one in spirit,
(contd.) the male with the female being neither male nor female.

'Verily, I say unto you all, both men and women: if ye make not
that which was on the left hand to be neither on the right nor yet on
the left; and that which was below to be neither above nor yet below;
and that which was behind to be neither before nor yet behind, ye
shall not know the Kingdom of God!

XXVII.h (83) 'But if ye fast not from the fleshly deceits of this world, ye
shall not see the Father in the world to come.'

XXVII.j (84) Philip saith: 'Teach us to see our Father, and it is enough. For
wisdom dwelleth in thee, and thou revealest unto us new things.'

Jesus answered: 'Have I been so long with thee, Philip, and yet hast
thou not known me?

'The words that I speak, I speak not of myself, but I deliver the
word of God to thee as it is delivered unto me in the scriptures and in
the tradition of the elders.'

LXXX.f (85) Then a certain Levite asked Jesus, saying: 'Master, what of a
daughter's inheritance? How readest thou the Law?'

Jesus answered, and said: 'It is written: "If a man die and have no
son, then ye shall cause his inheritance to pass unto his daughter," yet
it is nowhere forbidden that a daughter should inherit where there is
a son.

'Did not Job divide his substance equally among sons and daughters? Do thou even as Job did!'

His disciples say unto Jesus: 'Yet the sages have taught that where
there is a son, a daughter shall not inherit, but a marriage portion
shall be given unto her from the substance of her father's house.'

He answered: 'Ye say well; but now the times require this other
thing, which shall be for a memorial unto the daughters of Israel.

'Verily, I say unto you: the season for marrying and for giving in
marriage is overpast. Let them that hope for the Kingdom remain
virgins undefiled.

'And let them not ensnare men into lust, neither seek husbands,
neither contend with their kinsmen for a marriage portion. But let
them labour without cease for the Kingdom of Heaven.'

XLVI.f (86) Jesus said also: 'Hearken to the words of the Preacher: "Go
thy way, eat thy bread, drink thy wine with a merry heart, for God
now accepteth thy works. Let thy garment be always white and let thy
head lack no ointment."

'For to obey the Law is to be clothed in purity as in a linen garment; and to hearken unto the prophets is to be anointed with God's
mercy as with ointment. Thus doing shalt thou rejoice as a guest
rejoiceth at a wedding feast.

'Take heed therefore: behold, the Kingdom of Heaven is like unto
a King that went to view the guests at the wedding feast to which he
had called them,

'Among whom was one that had not on a wedding garment.

XLVI.f
(contd.)
'And he said unto him: "Friend, how camest thou in hither not wearing a wedding garment?" And he was speechless.

'Then said the King unto his servants: "Bind him hand foot and take him away! Cast him into outer darkness; there shall he weep and gnash his teeth!" '

CHAPTER XI

HOW HE EXPOUNDED CERTAIN OF THE TEN COMMANDMENTS

XXII.d   (87) Jesus spake of others of the Ten Commandments, saying: 'It is written: "Thou shalt bear no false witness!", and likewise: "If a man heareth the voice of swearing and is a witness to an oath, and afterwards concealeth his knowledge of it, then when he confesseth to his sin he shall bring a trespass offering unto the Lord, according to his substance, and the priest shall sprinkle of its blood upon the altar."

'But if ever thou bringest such a trespass offering unto the Lord, first consider whether by any words lightly spoken thou hast offended thy neighbour, whose oath thou concealedst because he wronged thee.

'And if thou rememberest aught, leave there thine offering before the altar and go thy way. First be reconciled to thy neighbour, and then come again and offer thy gift.

XXII.e   (88) 'Moreover, Solomon counselleth thee: "Go not forth hastily to strive lest thou know not what to do in the end thereof, when thy neighbour hath put thee to shame.

' "Debate thy cause with thy neighbour himself, and discover it not to another, lest he that heareth thee put thee to shame."

'Therefore, agree with thy neighbour whilst thou art with him in this world, lest in a time to come the Adversary deliver thee to the Judge and the Judge to his officer, and the officer cast thee into prison,

'Whence thou shalt not depart until thou hast paid the uttermost farthing of the debt that thou owest unto thy neighbour.

XXIII.b   (89) 'It is written also: "Thou shalt not take the name of the Lord thy God in vain!"

'Therefore do thou set a fence about this commandment, and swear not at all save under compulsion, lest haply thou forswear thyself.

'Let thy yea be yea, and thy nay, nay; for what is more than this proceedeth from evil.

'As who would seek to deceive with an oath sworn by heaven, or by earth, or by Jerusalem, seeming to swear by Him that sitteth enthroned in heaven and that maketh the earth His footstool and that hath chosen Jerusalem as the city whereof He is the Great King.

XX.h   (90) 'It is written also: "Thou shalt honour thy father and thy mother!"

'And know ye not that whosoever hath possessions and will neither

XX.h
(*contd.*)
feed nor clothe his father or mother, the same is before God like unto a murderer?

'Therefore make no rash vow, by which they may haply be deprived of that thou owest unto them!

'But if thou hast made such a vow, yet shalt thou be released from it, as one that spake in ignorance.'

A certain lawyer therefore asked Jesus, saying: 'Master, how may a man be released from his vow because he spake rashly? Was Jephthah released from the vow which he made concerning the burnt offering?

'For he said unto his daughter: "Alas, daughter, I have opened my mouth unto the Lord, and I cannot go back." And she, lest the word of God might be dishonoured, agreed thereto, saying: "Let the thing be done unto me."

'This, therefore, that thou preachest hangeth in the air without support from the Law. Dost thou indeed love God and wouldst thou make His word of none effect?'

Jesus answered and said: 'Love is of God, and hereby we know the spirit of truth and the spirit of error.

'For though men rightly fear to break a rash vow which they have made, yet perfect love casteth out fear; and he that saith "I love God" but doeth his neighbour an injury, or dishonoureth his parents, the same is a liar.

'For he that loveth not his neighbour or his parents which he hath seen, how can he love God which he hath not seen?

XXIV.c   (91) 'It is written also: "Thou shalt not covet thy neighbour's house, nor his wife, nor his servant, nor his maid, nor his ox, nor his ass, nor anything that is his!"

'Therefore take heed that ye cast not looks that do injury.

'For verily, the light of the body is the eye: if thine eye be good and covet not, thine whole body shall be full of light; but if evil, then thy body shall be full of darkness,

'As it is written in the testament of the patriarch Judah: "A blinded soul stumbleth by day as though it were night."

'Take heed then that thine inner eye be good and covet not, that thou mayest see God; for if it be evil, how gross shall thy darkness be!

'Strive to look upon all things even as doth the eye of our Heavenly Father: for the prophet Habakkuk saith: "Thou art of purer eyes, O God, than to behold evil." '

XXIV.c   (92) 'Know ye not the words of Solomon? "The way of the just is as a shining light, that shineth more unto the perfect day; but the way of the wicked is darkness."

'For the Law is a lamp lighted within the heart of them that love the Lord.

'Be ye therefore as a light to the world, shine ye openly! For he that lighteth a lamp hideth it not under a bushel nor under a bed, but setteth it upon a lampstand, whence it giveth light to all the household.

'Let your light so shine before men that they may know whence

XXIV.c your good works proceed and may glorify our Father which is in
(*contd.*) heaven.

XXIV.d   (93) 'Is it not written in the Book of Job: "They rebel against the
light; they know not the ways thereof.

'"The thief worketh by night; the eye also of the adulterer waiteth
for the twilight; and in the dark they dig through the walls of houses.

'"The morning is to them even as the shadow of death"?

'But he that doeth truth, the same feareth not the light, for it is
manifest that his deeds are wrought in the name of God.

XXIV.c   (94) 'And have ye not heard what Isaiah said? "Arise, be enlightened; for thy light cometh and the glory of the Lord is risen upon
thee.

'"For behold, a darkness shall cover the earth, and a gross darkness the people, but the Lord shall rise upon thee and His glory shall
be seen upon thee.

'"And the generations shall come to Thy light, and kings to the
brightness of Thy rising."

'Truly, God is the light of the world: he that obeyeth His Law, the
same shall not walk in darkness but shall have the light of life.

'And know ye not what Isaiah also prophesieth? "And it shall come
to pass in the last days that the mountain of the Lord's house shall be
established on the mountain top and shall be exalted above the hills;
and all nations shall flow unto it. O House of Jacob, come ye and let
us walk in the light of the Lord!"

'Therefore fix ye your hearts upon this heavenly city; which is an
easy thing. For a city that is set on the top of a high mountain and
established of God can neither fall nor be hidden.'

CHAPTER XII

HIS EXHORTATIONS TO MERCY

XXIX.a   (95) Jesus said:

'Hearken unto the words which Ezekiel the prophet spake, saying: "If a man be just and hath not oppressed any, but hath restored the debtor his pledge, he shall live; but he that hath oppressed the poor and needy and hath not restored the pledge, the same shall surely die."

XXIX.a   (96) 'Therefore is the Kingdom of Heaven likened unto a certain king which would take account of his servants.

'And when he had begun to reckon, one was brought unto him, which owed him ten thousand pounds.

'But forasmuch as he had not to pay, his lord commanded him to be sold, and his wife, and his children, and all that he had, and payment to be made.

'The servant therefore fell down, and besought him, saying: "Lord, have patience with me, and I will pay thee all!"

'Then the king was moved with compassion, and loosed him and forgave him his debt.

'But the same servant went out, and found one of his fellow-servants, which owed him an hundred pence: and he laid hands on him, and took him by the throat, saying: "Pay me that thou owest!"

'And his fellow-servant fell down at his feet, and besought him, saying: "Have patience with me, and I will pay thee all!"

'Yet he would not: but went and cast him into prison, till he should pay the debt. So when the other servants saw this thing, they were very sorry, and came and told unto the king all that was done.

'Then the king, after that he had called him, said unto him: "O thou wicked servant, I forgave thee all thy debt, because thou desiredst me: shouldst not thou also have had compassion on thy fellow-servant, even as I had pity on thee?"

'And the king was wroth, and delivered him to the tormentors, till he should pay all that was due unto him.

'So, likewise, shall our Heavenly Father do also unto you, if ye from your hearts forgive not every one his fellows their trespasses.'

XXIX.b   (97) Jesus said also: 'It is written: "Ye shall not afflict any widow or child!"

'Woe, then, unto the lawyers which serve the Chief Rulers! For they love long clothing, and salutations in the market place,

XXIX.b
(*contd.*) 'And the chief seats in council, and the uppermost places at feasts, and for a show make long prayers.

'The same forbear to take a widow's raiment in pledge, yet will take her ox (as Job testifieth), yea, and her house and land, and if she cannot pay her debt, will drive her thence, and her orphans with her,

'And will ask: "Was the woman not my debtor?"

'Therefore Job saith: "They are of those that rebel against the light." '

XXVIII.c (98) Jesus said also: 'It is written: "An eye for an eye and a tooth for a tooth."

'Now, if the eye of him that put out his neighbour's eye be likewise put out, or the tooth of him that broke his neighbour's tooth be likewise broken, is the neighbour's loss restored?

'Therefore, he giveth his neighbour satisfaction in silver or works, according to his loss. For the law of mercy is not to be broken that the law of vengeance may be kept.'

XXVIII.c (99) 'Moreover, Solomon counselled you: "Say not thou: 'I will recompense evil, I will so do to my neighbour as he hath done to me,' but wait on the Lord and He shall save thee."

'And it is written in the Book of Lamentations: "The Lord is good unto him that waiteth for Him, and unto him that giveth his cheek to the smiter."

'Therefore, resist not evil, and if a man will sue thee at the law and take away thy coat, let him have thy cloak also, if so be that thou mayest be at peace with him.

'And if he smite thee on the right cheek, turn thou also the other to him.

'And if he compel thee to go a mile, go with him twain.

XXVI.h (100) 'Know ye not the proverb which Solomon spake? "A false balance is abomination to the Lord, but a just weight is His delight."

'Therefore, according to the measure wherewith ye mete, so shall He measure unto you.

LII.h (101) 'It is written in the Law: "If thou lend money to any of God's people, thou shalt not be to him as an usurer, neither shalt thou lay any usury upon him."

'Now, a certain nobleman before that he went to the Wicked Kingdom to sue for the title of King in his own country, called his ten servants to which he entrusted money, giving unto each of them a talent.

'He said unto them: "Occupy yourselves until I return." Then straightway he took his journey.

'But his fellow-citizens hated the nobleman, for the violence that he did them, and sent an embassy after him to Caesar, saying: "We will not have this man to reign over us."

'And it came to pass that, when he had received the kingdom and returned, he sent for the ten servants that he might know how much each had gained by his trading.

LII.h
(*contd.*)

'Then came the first, saying: "O King, thy talent hath gained ten talents."

'And he said unto him: "Well done, thou good and faithful servant: thou hast been faithful over a few things; I will make thee ruler over much. Have thou authority over ten cities."

'Then came another, saying: "O King, thy talent hath gained five talents."

'He said unto him likewise: "Well done, thou good and faithful servant: have thou authority over five cities."

'Then came the other seven and likewise earned their master's praise.

'For these nine servants had oppressed the poor and needy and used usury and fraudulent wiles, whereby they had increased the money committed unto them.

'Last of all came the tenth servant, which was a just man, and said: "O King, I knew thee for a hard man which reapest from fields where others have sown, and gatherest where others have reaped; and I feared to do as thou wouldst have had me do, lest I might offend against the Law.

' "Wherefore I wrapped my talent in a napkin and digged a hole and hid it in the ground: lo, here thou hast that is thine!"

'The King answered and said unto him: "Thou slothful and unprofitable servant, since thou knewest me for an hard man which reaped from fields where others had sown, why didst thou not at the least entrust my money to the bankers, and then at my coming I should have received mine own again with usury?"

'But the just servant asked him, saying: "Did not Ezekiel prophesy: 'He that hath given his money upon usury and taken increase, and hath oppressed the poor and needy, and hath spoiled by violence, the same shall surely die'?"

'Whereat the King was wroth, and said: "Cast this servant into prison; there shall he be fed upon bread of affliction and water of affliction! And those mine enemies which would not that I should reign over them, bring them hither and slay them!"

'Howbeit, the servants of the King could not prevail against them that made complaint, for all the people hated him.

'Then made they insurrection, running by night with torches to set fire to the King's house, and with swords to slay the King and his nine wicked servants withal.

'But the just servant which had not defiled his hands with offences against the Law, him they set free and entreated him well, as Jeremiah was likewise set free, and appointed him to be their judge.

'He that hath ears to hear, let him hear!'

XXVIII.d   (102) And again Jesus taught them, saying: 'Moses commanded: "Thou shalt open thine hand wide unto thy poor neighbour and lend him sufficient for his need and turn not away from him."

'But to him that asketh thee to lend, give and exact no pledge, whosoever he may be.

XXVIII.d   'For if thou takest a pledge, what love shewest thou? The publicans
(*contd.*)   also lend to their fellows, to receive as much again.

'Be ye therefore merciful, as your Father also is merciful: lend looking for no payment, and without respect for persons, whether they be just or unjust.

'For it is written in the Book of Job: "Upon whom doth not the light of God arise? And how can any man that is born of woman be clean in His sight?"

'Therefore, as He maketh the sun to rise both on the just and the unjust, and sendeth rain (as it is written in the same book) both upon the field that is plowed and upon the desolate waste ground,

'So do ye likewise give freely and judge not of your neighbour whether he be just or no, and your reward shall be great: ye shall be called the Children of the Highest.

'For David saith in a psalm: "He that is ever merciful and lendeth, his seed is blessed."

'And he saith also: "With the merciful Thou wilt shew Thyself merciful, O God, and with the upright man wilt Thou shew Thyself upright."

XXVIII.e   (103) 'Heed not them that counsel thee: "Let it be thy prayer that poverty and sickness may be the lot of thine enemies."

'For Moses commanded: "Thou shalt love thy neighbour as thyself," and Solomon declared: "It is a man's glory to pass over a transgression."

'Therefore, return not evil for evil, but pray for thy neighbour if he be at enmity with thee, and forgive him if he curse thee, and do good to him if he hate thee and use thee despitefully.

'As Aristeas counselleth: "All men hold that we should return good to those that do good unto us; but should we not also open our hand with gifts to those that shew enmity, that thereby we may draw them to righteousness?"

'Likewise the patriarch Joseph commanded in his testament: "And if any man seek to do you evil, do ye well unto him, and pray for him, and the Lord shall redeem you from evil."

'Likewise the patriarch Gad in his testament: "Love ye one another from the heart. If a man sin against thee, speak peaceably unto him, and hold no guile in thy soul. And if he repent and confess, forgive him, lest catching the poison from thee he take to swearing and thou sin doubly."

'Do all these things therefore, and ye shall be called the children of your Father which reigneth in glory.

XXI.j   (104) 'Verily, I say unto you, that except your righteousness shall exceed the righteousness of the Sadducees, which keep all the laws but not that of mercy and lovingkindness, ye shall in no wise enter into the Kingdom of Heaven!'

CHAPTER XIII

HIS DISCOURSES UPON JUDGEMENT

LXXI.f   (105) Jesus, seeing a man doing a work of mercy on the sabbath, said unto him: 'Man, if thou knowest indeed what thou doest, blessed art thou! For the Sages have taught us: "God delivered the sabbath unto you, not you unto the sabbath."

'But if thou knowest not, and wouldst break the sabbath for no good cause, then art thou accursed as a transgressor against the Law.'

And when they that stood by questioned him further, he answered and said: 'Under God which ordained the sabbath, the sons of men are made masters of the sabbath.'

LXXI.h   (106) He said also: 'It is written: "Six days shalt thou labour and do all thou hast to do, but the seventh is the sabbath of the Lord thy God."

'Verily, I say unto you: if ye keep not the sabbath in joy and holiness every day of the week, casting aside the cares of this world, ye shall not enter into the Kingdom of Heaven.'

XXVI.f   (107) On another day a certain man besought Jesus, saying: 'Speak to my brother that he divide the inheritance with me.'

Jesus said unto him: 'Man, who made me a judge or divider over you? I can of mine own self do nothing: I judge only as I hear men speak.

'But were I appointed to be a judge and sit in Moses's seat, then would my judgement be just, because I should seek not mine own will but the will of the Father which appointed me; the same readeth every man's heart.

'It is written that Jehoshaphat the King of Judah said unto the judges: "Take heed what ye do, for ye judge not for men, but for the Lord which is with you in judgement."

'Moses also said: "I charged your judges not to be respecters of persons in judgement, seeing that the judgement is the Lord's."

'And Jehoshaphat the King spake also with the voice of David, saying: "I have called my judges 'gods'; all of you are sons of the Most High God."

'Yet even Moses, before that he was sent of God to judge Israel, by the hand of the angel which appeared to him in the bush, the same suffered a reproach from his fellows as having judged without authority.

XXVI.f
(*contd.*)

'For seeing one of them suffer wrong, he avenged him and smote the Egyptian. And the next day he shewed himself unto two of them as they strove and would have set them at one again, saying: "Ye are brethren, why wrong ye one another?"

'But he that did his neighbour wrong thrust Moses away, saying: "Who made thee a ruler and a judge over us? Wilt thou kill me, as thou didst the Egyptian yesterday?"

'Therefore, let no man of you which is not appointed by authority, set himself up as a judge, lest judgement itself be judged.

'For if thou sayest: "Restore the splinter that is between thy teeth," he that is judged shall answer: "First do thou restore the beam that is in the wall before thy very eyes!"

'Or if thou sayest: "Thy silver is mingled with dross," he shall answer: "The wine which I bought from thee therewith is mingled with water."'

XIX.d

(108) And Jesus taught them, saying: 'Take heed to yourselves. If thy brother trespass against thee, rebuke him gently; and if he repent, forgive him.

'Though he trespass against thee seven times in a day, and seven times in a day turn again to thee saying: "I repent", thou shalt forgive him.'

Peter saith: 'Shall I indeed forgive him seven times?'

Jesus answered: 'Yea, and unto seventy times seven! For even in the prophets, after that they were anointed and the Spirit of the Lord had come upon them, something of sin was yet found.

'Moreover, if thy brother shall have trespassed against thee and repented not, the Law giveth thee redress.

'But first go and tell him his fault between him and thee alone, and if he shall hear thee and acknowledge it, thou hast regained thy brother.

'For the patriarch Gad exhorted his sons in his testament, saying: "My children, love ye one another from the heart! And if a man sin against thee, speak peaceably to him and in thy soul hold not guile; and if he repent and confess, forgive him."

'But if thy brother will not hear thee, then take with thee another witness or, if thou wilt, twain. For Moses said: "One witness shall not rise up against a man for any sin that he sinneth: at the mouth of two witnesses or three shall the matter be established." And if he shall hear them, well.

'But if he shall neglect to hear them, tell it unto the council; and if he shall hear the council, well.

'But if he shall neglect to hear the council, let him be unto thee as a heathen and a publican, and thou hast lost thy brother.

'Nevertheless, forgive him from thy heart. For Gad saith again: "But if he be shameless and persist in his wrongdoing, even so forgive him from the heart, and leave to God the avenging."

LXI.c

(109) 'Yea, have peace with all men, and take no vengeance, for it is written: " 'Vengeance is Mine, I will repay,' saith the Lord."

LXI.c
(*contd.*)
'And Solomon likewise saith: "If thine enemy be hungry, give him bread to eat, and if he be thirsty, give him water to drink. For thou shalt heap coals of fire upon his head, and the Lord shall reward thee."

'Wherefore, be not overcome of evil, but overcome evil with good.

XXI.q
(110) 'Moreover, if the neighbour of a man that accounteth himself righteous should sin, then hath he also something of sin in him.

'For if he had kept the Law according to the spirit of righteousness, then his neighbour would have repented him of his own ways and not sinned.'

XXII.b
(111) Again he taught them, saying: 'It is written: "Thou shalt do no murder!", and he that doth murder shall be in danger of judgement.

'Also Solomon hath declared that he that slandereth his neighbour is a fool, and deserving of stripes.

'These are the punishments of this world; but verily, in the world to come he that hath been angry with his neighbour without cause, the same shall be in danger of God's judgement; and he that hath slandered his neighbour, or hath shamed him, the same shall be in danger of hell fire!

XXII.c
(112) 'But since from the abundance of the heart the mouth speaketh, good if it be good, evil if it be evil,

'Therefore, if thy heart be evil, hold thy peace; for of every vain word that thou shalt speak, thou shalt be called to account in the Day of Judgement.

'By thy words as much as by thy deeds thou shalt be justified, or shalt be condemned.

'As David prophesied in the name of the Lord: "O ye sons of men, how long will ye turn My glory into shame? How long will ye love vanity and seek after leasing?

' "Stand in awe of Me and sin not, commune with your own heart upon your bed and let your tongues be still."

'As it is written in the testament of the patriarch Dan: "Unless ye keep yourselves from the spirit of lying and anger ye shall perish. For anger is blindness and suffereth not a man to see the face of his neighbour with truth."

'Therefore, let your mouths never speak so freely as doth your heart, save when ye behold your neighbour with joy and love.'

XXXI.c
(113) Jesus preached in the seaward parts of Galilee, even unto the coasts of Tyre and Sidon.

And departing thence he came again unto the Lake of Galilee by way of Philip's tetrarchy.

Now, men bring unto him one that was deaf and had an impediment in his speech, and they beseech him to lay his hand upon him.

And Jesus took him aside, and spat upon his own fingers and put them into the man's ears, and also touched the man's tongue withal.

Then, looking up to heaven, he sighed and prayed to God in his heart, and said: 'May they be opened; may it be loosed!'

XXXI.c
(*contd.*)
And straightway his ears were opened and he heard; and the string of his tongue was loosed, and he spake plain.

Then Jesus charged them that stood by to tell no man; yet the more he charged them, so much the more they published it,

For they were beyond measure astonished, and said: 'He hath performed his twofold task well.

'By his intercession he that was dumb and deaf both speaketh and heareth.'

LXXIV.f (114) And in those days he healed a woman which was bowed together for eighteen years, and could in no wise lift herself up.

LXXIV.f (115) And he healed a man which had the dropsy.

XXXVI.d (116) Jesus also laid his hands upon a woman which for many years had a bloody issue.

For thus he suffered himself to be made unclean until the evening, if haply she might be delivered of her plague for the remainder of her life.

And it pleased God to hearken unto his prayers, and straightway the fountain of her blood was dried up, though she had spent all her living on physicians and none had been able to heal her.

CHAPTER XIV

HOW HE HEALED OTHER SICK AND ANSWERED JOHN'S DISCIPLES

XXXIV.f (117) In those days Jesus cast out a dumb devil from a man, and the man spake, so that the people wondered, saying: 'The like was never seen in Israel!'

But one of them said: 'He casteth out devils through Beelzebub, the prince of the devils.'

LXX.m (118) And he pressed Jesus, saying: 'Art thou not truly a Samaritan, and hast thou not a devil?'

XXXIV.f (119) Jesus answered: 'Believest thou in truth that I cast out devils through him they call the Lord of the House? What sayest thou then? If the kingdom and household of the Lord of the House are divided against him, how shall they stand?

'And if by the finger of God I am granted to cast out devils, will not God's kingdom be brought so much the nearer to you all?'

XXXIV.f (120) And he said also: 'When a strong man guardeth his house, with arms in his hand, his goods are secure. But if an enemy find the strong man sleeping, then will he bind him and spoil his goods.

'Watch, therefore, that the Lord of the House become not also the lord of thine house, to carry thy soul with him to the abode of darkness.

XXXIV.f (121) 'Verily, I say unto you: all sins shall be forgiven the sons of men if they repent, yea, even the taking in vain of God's name.

'But if any of you shall mutter magical spells in God's name, like as He were Beelzebub, the same standeth in danger of eternal damnation.'

XXXIII.c (122) Now, when Jesus entered into Capernaum, a centurion sent a messenger which should bring him unto the camp.

Jesus went thither, but would not enter in, lest he defile himself.

Then came the centurion out to him, and said: 'My servant which is a Jew lieth within, grievously tormented with the palsy and desireth to be healed.

'Know now, that I am a man of authority. I say to this man "Go!" and he goeth; and to another "Come!" and he cometh; and to another "Do this!" and he doeth it.

'Therefore say I unto thee: Come in, and heal my servant! For I have heard that thy God worketh wonders for thee.'

XXXIII.c   Jesus turned to them that stood by him, and said as one that mock-
(contd.) eth: 'I have not seen such faith, no, not in Israel!'

    The centurion asked Jesus: 'Why delayest thou? Thinkest thou thyself unworthy to enter?'

    Jesus answered: 'I may not come in, lest I defile myself. Yet will I pray to God, and peradventure thy servant shall be healed.'

    And he prayed to God, and the sick man that lay within heard the voice of Jesus which called him to repentance; and was made whole, and consorted no more with the Wicked Kingdom.

XXXVIII.c (123) And Jesus departed thence and came to the village of Nain.

    But the rumour of his healing of the centurion's servant ran ahead of him; and men said: 'A great prophet is arisen among us, like unto Elisha!'

    (For Nain lieth not far from the city of Shunem where he restored the rich woman's son to life.)

    And there came to meet Jesus at Nain certain disciples of John the Baptist.

XXXIX.g   (124) Now, John the Baptist expected to hear great things of Jesus which he had anointed; but Jesus had not revealed himself to the people as King.

    Therefore John sent two disciples to say unto him: 'What doest thou of the things that are prophesied? Wherefore liftest thou not up thy voice, that all may know thee who thou art? Art thou verily he that should come, or shall I seek another to anoint him?'

    Jesus answered them, and said: 'Isaiah prophesied in the name of the Lord: "Behold My servant whom I uphold, Mine elect in whom My soul delighteth. I have put My spirit upon him: he shall bring forth judgement to the Gentiles.

    ' "He shall not cry, nor lift up, nor cause his voice to be heard in the streets.

    ' "A bruised reed shall he not break and smoking flax shall he not quench, yet he shall bring forth judgement unto truth.

    ' "He shall not fail nor be discouraged till he have set judgement in the earth: I the Lord have called thee in righteousness, and will hold thine hand and will keep thee and give thee for a covenant of the people, for a light to the Gentiles,

    ' "To open the blind eyes, to bring out the prisoners from confinement, and them that sit in darkness of the prison house."

    'Go now, and shew John those things that ye have heard and seen!'

    And they returned to John and delivered unto him the words of Jesus, and said:

    'The blind indeed see, and the prisoners are freed, for he preacheth the Kingdom to the Men of the Land that hitherto dwelt in darkness.

    'Moreover, the sick are healed, the dumb speak, the crooked are made straight, and they that were dead in the spirit are quickened.'

XL.i   (125) And they said also: 'Was it not of him that Job spake, saying: "I was eyes to the blind, and feet to the lame; I was a father to the

XL.i
(contd.) poor. The blessing of him that was ready to perish came upon me, and I caused the widow's heart to sing with joy"?'

XXXIX.g (126) And when the disciples of John had departed, Jesus began to preach unto the multitude concerning John.

He said: 'What went ye out into the wilderness for to see? A murmuring reed shaken by the wind? Nay, but such a thing speaketh foolishness.

'But what went ye out to see? A prophet? Yea, I say unto you, and more than a prophet! He is a burning and a shining light, and happy are ye to have rejoiced in his light for a season.

'Verily, among them that are born of woman, there hath not risen a greater than John!

'He that hath ears to hear, let him hear: this is Elijah come again!

'As Malachi saith: "Behold, I will send you Elijah the prophet before the coming of the great and terrible Day of the Lord.

' "And he shall turn the hearts of the fathers to their children and the hearts of the children to their fathers, lest I come and smite the earth with a curse."

'Lo, with his coming all prophecy hasteneth to fulfilment; for he hath preached repentance, and all men press into the Kingdom of Heaven.

LXIX.b (127) 'See therefore that none of you, being yet unbaptized, delay from sloth. For when once the householder shall have risen from supper, and shut to the door and gone to rest, if certain of his household that went elsewhere to make merry shall gather outside and knock at the door, crying: "Master, master, open unto us!" he will answer: "The door is shut, and I know not who ye may be. Depart from me; it is too late." '

LXIV.a (128) His disciples ask Jesus: 'Master, what if they return late through no fault of their own? Shall the door not be opened unto them?'

He answered: 'It shall assuredly be opened. Isaiah prophesied, saying: "Open ye the gates, that the righteous nation which keepeth the truth may come in."

'For if one of you goeth at midnight and knocketh at his neighbour's door, and saith: "Neighbour, lend me three loaves, for a friend of mine hath even now turned in unto me and I have no meat to set before him,"

'He from within shall answer: "Trouble me not, the door is shut and my children are with me in bed. I cannot rise and provide for thee."

'Yet I say unto you: though he would not arise from friendship, nevertheless if thou stand and knock long, then at the last, because of thine importunity he will rise and give thee as many loaves as thou needest.

'And if this be the way of a churlish householder, how much sooner will thy Heavenly Father not open unto thee?'

LXIV.a　　　(129) And he spake another parable, saying:

'The judge of a certain city neither feared God nor regarded man.

'And in that city was a widow which came continually to him, pleading: "O judge, give me satisfaction against my adversary!"

'He for awhile would not, but at the last he said within himself: "I am wearied by the importunity of this widow. I will avenge her wrongs that she may trouble me no more."

'And if this be the mercy of an unjust judge, how much more mercifully will God not grant the pleas of the faithful which cry unto Him day and night against the Adversary of man?

'Verily, I say unto you: when the Son of Man shall appear, he will avenge them speedily, though he find no justice in the courts of this world!'

CHAPTER XV

HOW HE PERFORMED A CURE ON THE SABBATH AND REPROACHED THE MEN OF NAZARA

LXXIV.d (130) And again on a certain sabbath, when Jesus went into the synagogue, a man which had a withered hand stood without.

The same besought him, and cried: 'Master, I was a mason earning my bread with this hand. I pray thee, restore it to health that I need no longer beg for alms!'

Jesus was moved by compassion, and said unto him: 'Stand forth!' And when the man stood forth from the crowd, he led him to a place apart.

There, after that he had spat upon his hands, he rubbed the man's withered hand between them, and prayed to God, saying: 'Lord, let the evil depart from this man.'

Then saith he unto him: 'Stretch forth thy hand!', and he stretched it forth and, behold, it was restored whole as the other.

Then some of them that stood by glorified God, but others reproached Jesus, saying: 'Is it lawful to do such work on the sabbath?'

Jesus looked round upon them with anger, and answered: 'Which of you, having a sheep that hath fallen into a pit, doth not lay hold on it and lift it out on a sabbath, as the Sages permit? And is not this man better than a sheep?'

They answered: 'Thou hast well said. For the Sages have taught us: "Where there is danger to life, the sabbath may be broken." Yet here was no danger. Why hast thou therefore not waited till the morrow?'

He answered and said: 'I obey the Law of righteousness and love. Though our Father rest on the sabbath, yet He performeth works of healing on that day also. Hath He not even now hearkened unto my prayer, and healed this man?'

But they murmured and asked him: 'Though God should work on the sabbath, where is it written that a man may work on the sabbath?'

Jesus answered: 'Have ye not read in the Law, how that on the sabbath day the priests in the Temple shall sacrifice two lambs, and yet their work be blameless?

LXXIV.e (131) 'Ye yourselves likewise on the eighth day circumcise a male child according to the Law, though that day be a sabbath, and remain blameless.

'For God commanded our father Abraham to circumcise on the eighth day, before ever He delivered the Law of the sabbath unto Moses.

LXXIV.d (132) 'And if ye had remembered the words of the prophet Hosea, which he spake in God's name: "I desired mercy and not sacrifice," then would ye not have condemned that I did, when I rubbed this man's hand between mine own.'

XXXVII.g (133) And he came to Bethlehem Nazara, where he had been brought up, and his fame had gone thither before him.

But it was not granted unto him to do any mighty works among the people there, because of their unbelief.

And when the sabbath was come he went into the synagogue and, after the Law had been expounded, the roll of the prophet Isaiah was delivered unto him.

And standing up, he read:

'The spirit of the Lord God is upon me, because the Lord hath appointed me to preach good tidings unto the meek; He hath sent me to bind up the brokenhearted, to proclaim liberty to the captives and the opening of the prison to them that are bound.

'To proclaim the acceptable year of the Lord, and the day of vengeance of our God, to comfort all that mourn.'

Then said he: 'This scripture is fulfilled today.' And he preached the Kingdom to them, as had been desired of him.

And they all hearkened unto the gracious words that proceeded out of his mouth.

But many were offended when he likewise preached the vengeance of God and called them unto repentance; and they said one to another:

'Is not this the carpenter, the son of Joseph and Mary, the brother of James and Joses and Judah and Simon? And are not his sisters here with us? Who hath given him authority to speak thus threateningly unto us?'

And Jesus answered and said: 'A prophet is not acceptable in his own country, nor doth a physician do cures upon them that know him.

'It is written that, when Israel hearkened not to the warning of God's vengeance which Elijah the Tishbite preached, he departed into Sidon.

'There he was well received by a widow of Zarephath; and by the Lord's grace he replenished her cruse of oil and her barrel of meal and also healed her son, though many sons of Israel perished in the famine which God sent upon them.

'For they lacked faith in the Lord, as ye likewise now lack faith.'

XXXVII.g Then one that sat near by, beholding that Jesus now halted upon
(*contd.*) his thigh (even as our father Israel halted), mocked him, and said:
'Physician, heal thyself!'

Jesus answered: 'Because of his baldness the prophet Elisha was
mocked by certain little children of Israel, and forty-two of them were
destroyed by two she-bears.'

And he said also: 'When Naaman the Syrian came to Elisha from
afar to be healed of his leprosy, he was made whole by the finger of
God, though there were many lepers of Israel in that day.

'For they lacked faith to be made whole, as ye likewise now lack
faith.'

And they in the synagogue, when they heard these things, were
filled with wrath.

But Jesus delivered the roll again into the hands of the minister
and, passing through the midst of them, he went his way.

And he came to the brow of the hill whereon the city was built, and
there prayed for forgiveness, because that he had not answered the
man with mildness. As it is written: 'A soft answer turneth away
wrath.'

And he humbled himself before God, saying in the words of his
father David:

' "As for me, I was almost gone, my steps had well nigh slipped.

' "Verily, I have cleansed my heart in vain and washed my hands
in innocency.

' "So foolish was I and ignorant, like as a beast before Thee.

' "Nevertheless, I am continually with Thee, Thou hast holden me
by the right hand." '

XLI.b (134) At this time Herod Antipas sent forth and laid hold on John
and bound him in the Castle of Machaerus for Herodias's sake, the
widow of his brother Herod Philip, which he had married.

For John had stirred up the people against Herod, testifying of the
many evil things that he did, and saying: 'He hath uncovered the
nakedness of his brother's wife, and this was done for carnal lust, not
that he might raise up seed unto his brother, as the Law requireth.

'Already she hath issue of Philip, namely four children.

'Shall this man continue to rule over us?'

And he spake these things to Herod himself and would not be
silent, though many stripes were laid upon him.

Therefore Herod would have put him to death, but that he feared
the multitude because they accounted him a prophet.

CHAPTER XVI

HOW HE PREACHED REPENTANCE

XLII.d   (135) Now, after that John was cast into prison, Jesus came into Galilee, preaching and proclaiming: 'The time is now fulfilled and the Kingdom of God is at hand.

'Accept ye this gospel: that if ye repent, ye shall be saved by God's mercy.'

LIV.d   (136) 'David said in a psalm: "Thou didst bring a vine out of Egypt," and Jeremiah prophesied in the name of the Lord: "Yet I had planted you a noble vine of right good stock."

'For Israel is the vine, our Father is the vine-dresser; without Him we are as nothing.

'The branches that bear no grapes, those He cutteth off and casteth away; they wither and are gathered up for burning.

'But the fruitful branches He pruneth that they may bear yet more abundantly.

LIV.e   (137) 'Delight therefore in the pruner's hook; thus shall God be glorified with much fruit in a latter season.

'For David said also: "Blessed is he whom Thou chastenest, O Lord, and teachest of Thy Law! For the Lord will not cast off His people, neither will He forsake His inheritance." '

XLVII.b   (138) And he expounded the prophecy of Isaiah, which saith: ' "My well-beloved hath a vineyard in a very fruitful place, and he gathered out the stones thereof, and planted it with the choicest vines, and built a tower in the midst of it. And he looked that it should bring forth grapes and it brought forth wild grapes.

' "I will therefore lay it waste, it shall not be pruned nor digged and there shall come up briers and thorns. For the Lord looked for judgement, but behold a scab; for righteousness, but behold a cry." '

He told them: 'Now, Israel is the vine which is judged by her fruit, whether it be good or whether it be cankered.

'As Joel prophesied, saying: "He hath laid My vine waste and barked My fig-tree, the branches thereof are made white."

'And ye have heard how John the Baptist testified: "The axe is now laid to the root of the trees, and everyone that bringeth not forth good fruit is hewn down and cast into the fire."

'Beware, therefore, that ye bring forth the fruit of repentance! For if this vineyard be laid waste, shall men gather grapes of the thorns that spring up thereafter, or figs of the briers?

CI.i   (139) 'Learn a parable of the fig tree:

'When her branch is tender and putteth forth leaves, ye know that the summer fruit is nigh.

'For the Lord sheweth unto Amos a basket of summer fruit, and said: "What seest thou?" And he answered: "A basket of summer fruit."

'Then said the Lord: "Nay, not *qa'itz* (which is summer fruit), but *qetz* (which is the end)! I will not again pass by them. And the songs of the Temple shall be howlings in that day!"

'So in like manner, when ye see those things prophesied by Micah come to pass, ye shall know that the end is nigh, even at the doors.

'Yet of that day and hour knoweth no man, nay, not the Son of God, neither the angels of heaven which listen from behind the veil, but the Father only.

'As Isaiah prophesied in the name of God: "For the day of vengeance is in My heart."

'Take heed therefore, watch and pray: for ye know not when the time is!

CI.l   (140) 'Woe unto them that are divided of heart, which doubt and say: "These same things did we hear in the days of our fathers also, and behold, we are grown old, and none of them is befallen us."

'Ye slow of heart, liken yourselves unto a tree, yea, unto a vine that first sheddeth her leaves, then putteth forth a shoot, from which springeth a leaf and a flower, and a green berry, and at the last a ripe grape.

'For behold, the time of vintage is at hand!'

XLVII.c   (141) And he expounded unto them of the words of David: 'God is the rock of my heart and my portion for ever,' saying:

'Whosoever heareth the word of God and keepeth it, the same is like unto a wise man which builded his house on a rock.

'For the rain descended and the floods came and the winds blew and beat upon the house, but it fell not.

'But whosoever heareth not the word of God, but trusteth in his own conceits, the same is like unto a foolish man which builded his house upon the sands of the seashore.

'For the winds arose and the waves of the sea beat vehemently against the house, and great was the fall thereof.

'As Ezekiel prophesied: "Its place shall be for the spreading of nets." '

XLII.d   (142) And Jesus came with his disciples to Capernaum, where presently he entered into the synagogue and preached repentance.

But as he taught, a certain man that was possessed with an unclean spirit, cried out: 'Let us alone, Jesus of Nazara! What have we to do with thee?'

And when Jesus rebuked him, speaking as one with authority, the unclean spirit tore the man, and cried: 'Art thou come to destroy us? I know thee who thou art. Thou art the son of the Most High God.'

Jesus therefore spake to the evil spirit, saying: 'If the Father shew me favour, let Him suffer me to cast thee out of this man. Hold thy peace and begone!'

XLII.d   And the devil cried again with a loud voice and came forth.

   (contd.)   Then were the people all amazed, and asked: 'What was this name by which the unclean spirit called him? And by what authority was he cast forth?'

XXXVI.h   (143) Jesus departed thence and went across the Lake to Decapolis, and entered into the house of a Galilean and would have no man know it.

But he could not be hid, and when he came out at eventide, behold, a Canaanite woman cried unto him: 'Have mercy on me, Jesus of Nazara! My daughter is grievously vexed with a devil.'

He answered her not and turned again to go into the house. But though his disciples would have prevented her, she fell at his feet and took hold on the fringe of his garment, crying: 'Master, help me!'

He answered and said: 'Woman, I am not sent but unto the lost sheep of the House of Israel. Let the children first be filled. It is not meet to take their bread and cast it to the dogs.'

Then said she: 'Yea, but the little dogs that are taught to walk discreetly, the same eat of the crumbs that fall from their master's table.

'Behold, I would be baptized into the congregation of Israel, and my daughter also.'

Jesus answered: 'Woman, great is thy faith. Be it unto thee as thou wilt. Bring thy daughter hither, but tell no man.'

And he commanded the devil to go out of the damsel, and she was healed, and both the woman and her daughter believed and were baptized.

XXXVI.f   (144) And when Jesus was passed over again by boat unto the other side of the Lake, much people gathered unto him; and he was nigh to the water.

And behold, there cometh one of the rulers of the synagogue, Jairus by name, who fell at Jesus's feet and besought him greatly, saying: 'My little daughter lieth at the point of death: come, lay thy hands upon her and pray that she may be healed.'

And Jesus went with him and much people followed him, and he cometh to the ruler's house and heareth the dirges which the minstrels played.

And the kinsfolk and servants of the ruler wept and wailed greatly about the bed whereon the damsel lay, and she was about twelve years of age.

And Jesus asked: 'Why wail ye, as if for one already dead? Pray ye rather that the damsel may be restored to health!'

When therefore Jesus had caused them all to be put out, he entereth into the room with Jairus and the damsel's mother, and with his disciples Peter and James and John.

And having prayed to God, he saith to the damsel: *'Talyetha cumi!'*

And straightway she arose and walked, and they were greatly astonished and wist not what to do.

But Jesus commanded that something should be given her to eat.

CHAPTER XVII

HOW HE WENT TO KEEP THE PASSOVER

XLVIII.f (145) Jesus and Peter returned together unto Capernaum, and the other disciples followed behind.

And an apostle of the High Priest, which gathered tribute for the Sanctuary, came to Peter and asked him: 'Doth not thy master pay tribute?'

He answered: 'Yea, but both he and I have a vow of poverty.'

The apostle said: 'Yet go ye and earn an half-shekel apiece. For every son of Israel must pay according to the Law, both rich and poor alike.'

When Peter was returned to the house where they lodged, Jesus said unto him:

'Thinkest thou, Simon, that I should pay that which is required of me? For this tribute is ordained of God as a ransom for every man's soul when the Children of Israel are numbered, lest a plague fall upon them. Every man shall bring an half-shekel to the Sanctuary.

'But to the intent that the number of the congregation shall not be known by a computation of the shekels gathered, and the sin thereby multiplied, God hath set a fence about the offering.

'For He commanded Moses: "Thou shalt not number the tribe of Levi!"

'How, therefore, should they that are not numbered offer a ransom for their numbering? And that the Levites paid naught unto Moses, the word of tribute proveth.

'For of whom do the rulers of this world take tribute? Of their own children or of strangers?'

Peter answered: 'Of strangers.'

Jesus said: 'Then are the children of the Temple free, and I with them, who am enrolled in the House of Levi.

'Notwithstanding: lest we offend the Council which hath ruled otherwise, go thou to the Lake and cast an hook, if peradventure God may grant thee to catch aught.'

Peter therefore went to the Lake and did even as Jesus bade him, and with an hook he caught a great musc-fish and sold it in the market for four pence, which make one shekel.

And he told it unto Jesus, which said: 'Go thou and give both for thyself and for me also, as though I were a stranger.'

XLVIII.f   Peter took the money unto the apostle, which asked him: 'Whence,
(contd.)   son of idleness, came this shekel? Hast thou begged it in alms?'

He answered: 'With this coin did a great musc-fish stop her mouth
against her enemies; let it likewise stop thy mouth against my master!'

XLVIII.g   (146) Then the money changer proved the piece and found it good.
LX.e   (147) And the other disciples also came to Capernaum, and when
they were together in the house, Jesus asked them: 'What was it that
ye disputed among yourselves by the way?'

They answered: 'We disputed who should be counted most honourable in the Kingdom of God, whether our father Abraham which died
and was buried, or whether his forefather the prophet Enoch, which
was spared death as being a man without sin.'

Jesus said: 'Neither the one nor the other. For Isaiah hath testified:
"A little child shall lead them all."

LX.e   (148) 'Know ye not what David spake in a psalm? He said: "Lord,
my heart is not haughty, neither do I exercise myself in great matters
or things too high for me.

'"Surely, I have behaved and quieted my soul as a weaned child."

'Now, the things that are too high signify the Works of the Chariot,
namely the vision of the Glory of God which Ezekiel saw, whereof
we are warned by the Sages: "Enquire not what is above, nor what is
below, nor what is ahead, nor what is behind."

'Be ye therefore as the little children. For it is written in the Book
of Lamentations: "Her children are gone into captivity, from Zion
her glory is departed."

'And the Sages have taught us: "See how beloved the little children
are before God. When the Council went into captivity, the Glory of
God went not with them; nor went it with the priests; but when the
little children went into captivity, then went the Glory of God with
them."

'If therefore ye be not humble in heart and become as little children,
ye shall neither see the Glory nor enter into the Kingdom.'

XLVIII.g   (149) Afterwards, when Jesus saw the money changers, how they
rejected unclean money brought unto them, and also money that was
of light weight, he exhorted his disciples, saying:

'Be ye like unto approved money changers, working for God, not
for private gain! Mark all things with care and weigh them in a just
balance; reject that which is evil, hold fast that which is good.'

XXXII.f   (150) Now, the Passover drew nigh, and Jesus went to Jerusalem
by way of Galilee and the eastern coasts of Samaria, and came to a
certain village that lay nigh unto the Jordan.

And when he had passed through to the other side, he saw ten
lepers standing afar off, which lifted up their voices, and cried:
'Master, have mercy on us. If thou wilt, thou canst save us!'

Jesus said: 'Go, wash seven times in Jordan. For so Elisha commanded Naaman the Syrian.'

Then went they off hastily and did as he commanded. And one of

XXXII.f them, when he saw that he was healed, returned to Jesus glorifying
(contd.) God.

Jesus asked him: 'Were there not ten lepers? But where are the
nine? Arise now and go thy way, shew thyself to the priest and offer
the sacrifice of purification that Moses commanded, namely two sparrows.

'For thy faith hath made thee whole, but thy fellows doubted,
though power was present from the Lord to heal them also.'

And he charged him that had been a leper to tell no man by whose
orders he had washed in Jordan.

But so much the more went there a fame abroad of him, and great
multitudes came together to hear and to be healed. And he withdrew
himself into the wilderness and prayed.

XLIII.a (151) And he went through the cities and villages teaching and
journeying toward Jerusalem.

And one of the disciples asked of him: 'Master, are there few that
shall be saved?'

He answered and said: 'Knowest thou not the Song of Solomon,
how that he cried to his beloved, saying: "Open unto me, my sister,
my spouse," whereat she put her hand to the hole of the door and
opened it?

'Now, Solomon spake a parable of the Virgin of Israel which should
open the door unto God.

'For God crieth: "Behold, I stand at the door and knock. Open unto
Me, make Me an opening for repentance, and though it be as strait as
the needle's eye, yet will I open the door widely, that wagons and
chariots may enter."

'Yea, wide is the highway of repentance, of which the prophet
Jeremiah spake, saying: "Set thine heart towards the highway, turn
again, thou Virgin of Israel!" '

LXXXII.g (152) A rich young man, which was a priest, came hastily to Jesus,
and said unto him: 'Good master, what shall I do to inherit everlasting life?'

Jesus answered and said: 'Why callest thou me good? None is good
save One, that is God!

'Knowest thou not the Commandments: "Thou shalt have no God
but God, and keep His sabbath, and honour thy parents, and swear no
false oath, neither commit adultery or murder or theft, neither bear
false witness, neither covet, but love thy neighbour as thyself"?'

He answered: 'All these have I observed from my youth.'

And Jesus, beholding him, loved him, and said: 'Then if thou wilt
verily inherit everlasting life, sell all thou hast, give unto the needy,
accept the cross of baptism, and joyfully take upon thyself the yoke of
the Law, even as the Sages have expounded them.'

But the young man was grieved by these words; for he durst not
obey, being of the High Priest's kindred.

LXXXII.h (153) And Jesus asked him, saying: 'Art thou then grieved? Is it
not more blessed to give than to receive?'

LXXXII.j (154) And Jesus spake a parable of the same rich young man: 'There was a certain rich man, clothed in purple and fine linen, which fared sumptuously every day.

'And there was a certain beggar named Lazarus laid at his gate, full of sores and desiring to be fed with the crumbs which fell from the rich man's table. Moreover, the dogs came and licked his sores.

'And it came to pass that the beggar died and was carried by the angels into Abraham's bosom.

'The rich man also died, and was buried. And in hell he lifted up his eyes, being in torments, and seeth Abraham afar off, and Lazarus in his bosom.

'And he cried and said: "Father Abraham, have mercy on me, and send Lazarus that he may dip the tip of his finger in water, and cool my tongue: for I am tormented in this flame."

'But Abraham said: "Son, remember that thou in thy lifetime didst receive thy good things, and likewise Lazarus evil things: but now he is comforted, and thou art tormented.

'"And beside all this, between us and you, there is a great gulf fixed. So that they which would pass from hence to you, cannot. Neither can they pass to us, that would come from thence."

'Then he said: "I pray thee therefore, father, that thou wouldst send him to my father's house. For I have five brethren; that he may testify unto them lest they also come into this place of torment."

'Abraham saith unto him: "They have Moses and the prophets. Let them hear them!"

'And he said: "Nay, father Abraham, but if one went unto them from the dead, they would repent."

'But Abraham said again: "If they hear not Moses and the prophets, neither will they be persuaded, though one rose from the dead."'

CHAPTER XVIII

HOW HE BADE THE PEOPLE WATCH

XXV.a (155) Jesus preached in the streets and lanes of Jerusalem, saying: 'Solomon spake this proverb of them that hearkened to the Law:

' "My son incline thine ear unto wisdom. If thou seekest after her as silver, then shalt thou understand the fear of the Lord, and understanding shall deliver thee from the ways of darkness."

'And Ezekiel spake of them that hearkened not. For he said:

' "Man, thou dwellest in the midst of a rebellious house which have eyes to see, and see not, and ears to hear, but hear not."

'And Isaiah likewise prophesied in God's name:

' "Inasmuch as this people have removed their heart from Me, the wisdom of their learned men shall perish."

'Therefore, he that hath ears to hear, let him hearken; for unto him that hearkeneth shall be given wisdom. And from him that hearkeneth not shall be taken even that wisdom which he seemeth to have.

XXV.e (156) 'Blessed be your eyes if they see, and your hearts if they hear, that by wisdom ye may live and not die!

'For verily, I say unto you that many prophets and kings and righteous men of old have desired to see and hear such things as shall soon be seen and heard among you, but have neither seen nor heard them.'

XXX.e (157) And he spake this parable unto them:

'The Kingdom of Heaven is as when a man, taking a far journey, leaveth his house, and giveth authority to his steward, and allotteth to each man his work, and commandeth the porter to watch.

'Watch ye therefore, for ye know not when the master of the house shall come from travelling—at even, or at midnight, or at cock-crow, or in the morning—lest coming suddenly, he find you sleeping or having neglected your tasks.

'As Solomon saith to the sluggard: "Desirest thou a little sleep, a little slumber, a little folding of the hands?

' "So shall thy poverty come upon thee as a man that travelleth."

'Blessed is that servant which the Lord shall find ready to receive Him, for he shall be rewarded.

'And Solomon saith likewise: "The soul of the sluggard desireth, and hath nothing; but the soul of the diligent shall be made fat.

' "Therefore give not sleep to thine eyes, my son, nor slumber to thine eyelids." '

XXX.e   (158) Peter asked him: 'And what of the servant which shall be found unready?'

Jesus answered and said: 'If a servant, knowing his lord's will, neglect it, then when the lord cometh in a day and an hour of which he is unaware, that servant shall be beaten with many stripes.

'And if a servant, not well knowing his lord's will, neglect it, that servant shall be beaten with few stripes.

'But if a servant hearken to the wiles of an adulteress, like her of which Solomon testifieth that she said: "Come, I have perfumed my bed. Let us take our fill of love until the morning. For the goodman is not at home, he is gone a long journey. He hath taken a bag of money with him and will come home at the day appointed";

'And if he, likewise, go in unto her as a bird goeth to a snare, and be drunken with the kisses of her mouth;

'And if the lord when he returneth find them in a bed together, he shall strike him in the liver with a dart.

'Verily I say unto you that he shall afterwards cut the adulterous servant in sunder and bury him with unbelievers.

'Therefore take heed to yourselves lest at any time your hearts be overcharged with surfeiting, and drunkenness, and wantonness, so that the day come upon you unawares.

'For as a snare shall the Last Day come on all them that dwell on the face of the whole earth.

'Watch therefore, and pray always, that ye may be accounted worthy to escape the slaughter of that day, and stand on the Mount of Olives with the Son of Man.

'That which I say unto you, I say unto all: Watch!

'For Isaiah testifieth against the foolish: "His watchmen are blind and ignorant, dumb dogs that cannot bark, sleeping, lying down, loving to slumber, looking everyone to his own gain,

' "Which say: 'Come, I will fetch wine, we will fill ourselves with strong drink, and tomorrow shall be as this day, but much more abundant.' " '

XXX.e   (159) Then said Jesus:

'The Kingdom of Heaven is like unto ten bridesmaids which lighted their lamps and went forth to meet the bridegroom by the way.

'And five of them were wise, but five foolish.

'The wise took oil in their oil vessels, besides that which was in their lamps, but the foolish took none.

'While the bridegroom tarried, the wise bridesmaids beholding how their lamps burned low, presently replenished and trimmed them.

'The foolish said to the wise: "Give us of your oil, for our lamps also burn low."

'The wise answered: "There is not enough both for us and for you. Go quickly to them that sell oil, and buy more while there is yet time."

XXX.e
(contd.)
'But they answered: "We go anon"; and they slumbered and slept, while the others kept watch.

'And at midnight a cry was made: "Behold, the bridegroom cometh: go ye out to meet him!"

'Then all the bridesmaids arose together and those that were ready went forth to meet the bridegroom.

'And those that were not ready ran to buy oil for their lamps, but coming to the house of the seller of oil found the door shut.

'Thus of the ten bridesmaids, only five went in to the wedding; and these were well received.

'As it is written in the psalm of David: "The virgins, the companions that follow the bride shall be brought unto Thee: with gladness and rejoicing they shall enter the King's palace."

'Watch, therefore, and be prepared, for ye know neither the day nor the hour wherein the Son of Man cometh!'

XXX.e
(160) He said also:

'The Kingdom of Heaven shall come like a thief in the night.

'As Jeremiah saith: "If thieves come by night they will destroy till they have enough of destruction."

'Let not the porter therefore excuse himself to his master, saying: "Lord, had I known in what watch the thief would come, I should not have slept."

'The porter's office is to watch from nightfall even unto cock-crow.'

XXX.e
(161) And he said:

'While ye wait for the Kingdom of God, be like them that keep the Passover, with their loins girded and with shoes on their feet and with staffs in their hands, as for a journey undertaken in haste; for so Moses commanded our fathers as an ordinance for ever.'

XVII.g
(162) All these things spake Jesus in parables, and without a parable spake he not unto them.

But some said among themselves: 'What are these new things he telleth? Sufficeth it not to deliver the Law plainly unto us as it is written in the roll thereof?'

Jesus answered and said: 'The prophet Ezekiel cried unto God: "Ah, Lord, they say of me: 'Doth he not speak parables?'"

'Yet he that is instructed in the imminent coming of the Kingdom of Heaven and expoundeth the Scriptures, the same shall be like an householder that bringeth forth from his store-room meat which is old, and also meat which is new.

'As Moses commanded: "Ye shall eat old store and bring forth the old because of the new. And I will set My tabernacle among you, and abhor you not. I will walk among you and will be your God, and ye shall be My people."'

CHAPTER XIX

HOW HE BADE THEM TAKE NO THOUGHT
FOR THE MORROW

XLVI.f   (163) On a sabbath day, when Jesus dined with a rich man of Jerusalem, the same asked him: 'Friend, why preachest thou in the streets and lanes of this city?'

Jesus answered and said: 'Solomon prophesied that the poor of Jerusalem shall inherit everlasting life if they do but hearken to the voice of Wisdom.

'For she crieth in these streets, saying: "Wisdom hath killed her fatlings, she hath mingled her wine and also furnished her table.

' "She hath sent forth her maidens, she crieth upon the highest places of the city: 'Whoso is simple, let him turn in hither!'

' "And to him that is poor of understanding, she saith: 'Come, eat of my bread and drink of the wine which I have mingled. Forsake the foolish and live, and go in the way of understanding.' "

'For the foolish are the rich that hearken not unto her voice, but are busied with the cares of this world.

'Therefore, the Kingdom of Heaven is like unto one that prepared a great supper and invited many, and sent a servant at supper time to say: "Come, for all is now ready!"

'But they began with one consent to make excuses. The first said:

' "A piece of ground is offered for sale and I must view it forthwith, lest I lose the occasion of purchase. I pray thee, have me excused."

'Another said: "I have bought five yoke of oxen on a pledge that, if they serve not my purpose, their price shall be restored to me tomorrow; therefore I must go to prove them. I pray thee, have me excused."

'A third said: "I have lately married a wife and am wearied with feasting. Moreover, the Law biddeth me to stay at home and cheer up my wife which I have taken. I pray thee, have me excused."

'When the servant came and told his master these words, the master, being angry, said unto him: "Go out quickly into the streets and lanes of the city, and bring hither whatsover poor and hungry thou mayest find, until all the places be filled!" '

XLVI.f   (164) Jesus said again: 'In the day when Ezra the scribe first read the Law to our fathers after that they returned unto Jerusalem from captivity, Nehemiah and Ezra beheld how the people wept.

XLVI.f
(contd.)
'Then said they: "This day is holy to the Lord, therefore weep not, but go your way, eat the fat and drink the sweet. Yet send portions of your feast unto him for which nothing is prepared."

'Wherefore, when thou preparest a supper, call not thy brethren, nor thy kinsmen, nor thy rich neighbours, hoping that they will bid thee in return,

'But rather call the poor unto thy table, and thou shalt be blessed; for though they cannot recompense thee, thou shalt be recompensed at the resurrection of the just.'

XLVI.f
(165) The rich man which heard these things sighed and said unto Jesus: 'Blessed is he that shall eat bread in the Kingdom of Heaven.'

Jesus answered: 'Many are called, but few are chosen.'

LXV.c
(166) And afterward he preached to them that had come up for the Feast, saying: 'Take no thought for this your life, what ye shall eat or what ye shall drink, nor yet for your body, wherewithal ye shall be clothed.

'For after these things do the Gentiles seek, which know not God.

'Is not the word of the Lord more than meat, and His mercy more than raiment? And is not the life eternal more than this life, and the soul more than the body?'

Judas of Kerioth asketh: 'What things are they that draw us unto God, which ruleth in heaven?'

Jesus answered: 'The fowls of the air, the fishes of the sea, the beasts, and whatsoever sprouteth from the earth, these are the things that draw you unto God.

'Consider the ravens, how they sow not, neither do they reap, nor gather into barns, as men do.

'Yet David spake of them, saying: "The Lord feedeth the young ravens which cry unto Him."

'How much more shall He not feed you, O ye of little faith? For David also saith: "Trust in the Lord and do righteousness, and verily thou shalt be fed."

'Consider the lilies of the field, how they grow. They toil not, neither do they spin as women do.

'Yet unto these did Solomon liken his beloved in all her glory. For he said: "As the lily among thorns, so is my love among other women."

'If God so clothe the grass of the field which today is, and tomorrow is cast into the oven, how much more shall He not clothe you, O ye of little faith?

'And David saith: "Delight thyself in the Lord, and He shall give thee thy heart's desire."

'In righteousness therefore seek ye the Kingdom of God; trust in the Lord and He shall bring it to pass.

'The Kingdom of God is within you, and whosoever knoweth the Law shall find it. For if ye know the Law, ye shall know yourselves, how that ye are sons of the Father which is in heaven.

LXV.c   'Likewise ye shall know yourselves to be created in His image. Ye
(*contd.*)   are the city of God over which the Son of Man shall reign.

'Solomon counselled us: "Boast not thyself of tomorrow, for thou
knowest not what a day may bring forth."

'Therefore take no thought for the morrow, whether it shall be good
or whether evil. Sufficient unto the day are the cares thereof. And let
the Law sustain you.'

LXV.e   (167) When certain men of the land which heard these words
excused themselves, and told Jesus that their labours were many and
that they lacked time sufficient to study the Law, he spake this parable
unto them:

'Jeremiah asked our forefathers, saying: "Why busy ye not yourselves with the words of the Law?"

'But they answered him according to their folly, for they asked:
"How will we then find time to labour for our sustenance?"

'Then brought he forth unto them the pot wherein the manna was
kept, according to the word of Moses. And he said unto them: "O
faithless generation, see ye this thing which is of the Lord! With this
manna were your forefathers sustained in the wilderness.

' "Though ye busy yourselves all day long with the Law, yet will He
make provision for you on the morrow."

LXV.d   (168) 'He that hath yet a morsel of meat in his basket and saith:
"what shall I eat tomorrow?", the same is of little faith.'

XLIV.b   (169) And because that these were the days of unleavened bread,
he taught them saying: 'Beware of the leaven of the Sadducees and
Herodians, which watch not for the Kingdom of God but adulterously ally themselves with the Wicked Kingdom, and sleep and are in
danger of Gehenna.

'For the prophet Amos saith: "Come to Bethel and transgress; at
Gilgal multiply your transgression, and offer a burnt sacrifice of
thanksgiving with leaven."

'And likewise the prophet Hosea saith: "They are all adulterers, as
the oven is heated by the baker, which kneadeth the dough until he
hath leavened it and thereafter sleepeth all night, and in the morning
it burneth like a flaming fire."

'Know ye not that a little leaven leaveneth the whole lump? Therefore feed in your hearts upon the unleavened bread of righteousness.'

LXI.a   (170) In these same days, when the disciples murmured, saying
that the salt which they bought had no savour, Jesus said: 'The Chief
Rulers, the sons of Aaron, love the princes of the Wicked Kingdom;
wherefore the salt is corrupted.

'For the Lord said unto Aaron: "With all thy sacrifices shalt thou
offer salt and it shall be a covenant of salt for ever before the Lord
unto thee and thy seed for ever."

'But these sons of Aaron have forsaken His covenant. And this salt,
that hath lost its savour, wherewith shall it be salted?

'It is fit neither for the land, nor yet for the dung hill, but only to be
cast upon the highway and trodden underfoot.

LXI.a
(*contd.*)　'Is it not written: "Every sacrifice that is burned upon the altar shall be seasoned with pure salt"?

'Therefore keep ye faith, though they fail. Be ye as the salt which Elijah cast into the corrupt springs of Jericho, crying in the name of the Lord: "I have healed these waters. There shall not be from thence any more death or barren land." '

XXXIX.g　(171) And a report came unto Jesus how that certain men reproached him, saying: 'He preacheth that a man shall take no heed what he shall eat or what he shall drink, yet he dineth every day with rich men of this city.'

Jesus answered: 'Whereunto shall I liken the men of this generation?

'They are like unto little children sitting in the market place that reproach their fellows, crying: "We have piped as for a wedding, but ye have not danced; and we have wept as for a burial, but ye have not lamented."

'Wherefore should I heed their reproaches?

'When they saw that John's meat was carobs and his drink water they said: "He hath a devil that driveth him into the wilderness and mortifieth his flesh."

'And when they see that I dine with honourable men and that bread is my meat and milk my drink, they say: "Behold a glutton and a belly-server!"

'But wisdom is proved in her fruits.'

CHAPTER XX

HOW HE TAUGHT HIS DISCIPLES TO PRAY

XXXVII.g   (172) And when the Feast was accomplished, Jesus returned to Galilee in the power of the Spirit.

LXXI.d   (173) And it came to pass, as he journeyed with his disciples, that they were sore an-hungered, because there was as yet no ripe corn in Judaea, and because the Samaritans gave them not to eat.

LV.a   (174) Then Judas of Kerioth asked Jesus: 'Shall the earth verily bring forth fruit of herself in the Kingdom of Heaven?'

Jesus answered and said: 'Baruch foretold these things: "Behold, the earth will yield fruit ten thousandfold, and one vine shall bear a thousand branches, and each branch a thousand clusters, and each cluster a thousand grapes, and from each grape shall be pressed a cor of wine."

'And I say unto you that when any of the elect shall take hold on a cluster of such a vine, another will (as it were) cry out to him: "I am better, take thou me and through me bless the Lord!"

'Likewise shall it be with the wheat. One grain shall bring forth ten thousand ears, and each ear ten thousand grains, and from every grain shall be ground five double pounds of clean white flour.

'And so shall it be with all other fruits and grains and herbs according to the same measure.

LV.b   (175) 'But every plant which our heavenly Father hath not planted shall be rooted out.

LV.b   (176) 'Moreover, the beasts that eat of these fruits and grains and herbs shall be at peace one with another and subject unto men in all obedience.

'For Isaiah likewise prophesied of those days: "The wolf shall dwell with the lamb and the leopard shall lie down with the kid, the calf and the young lion and the fatling together, and a little child shall lead them.

' "The lion shall eat straw like an ox; they shall not hurt nor destroy in all My holy mountain, saith the Lord; for the earth shall be full of the knowledge of the Lord." '

And Judas asked: 'But how shall all these things be accomplished?'

Jesus answered and said: 'They shall see that are worthy to come thereto.'

LXXI.d   (177) At the last, Jesus led them through a field of corn nigh unto the borders of Galilee; and suffered them to pluck the ears as they

LXXI.d
(contd.)

went, rubbing them in their hands, though the steward would have prevented them, for this corn was sanctified unto the Lord.

Therefore did the steward bring them before the rulers of the synagogue, which said unto Jesus: 'Sir, it is written: "Thou shalt not steal!" And have not thy disciples stolen from God Himself?'

He answered: 'The Law suffereth us to pluck a neighbour's corn with our hands as we pass through his field, and he may not deny us.'

They said: 'Yet are these fruits sanctified unto the Lord; for if every man that cometh from Jerusalem should take an ear, or twain, then would these fields be laid bare and we should lose our labour.'

Jesus answered and said: 'Have ye not heard what David did when his men were an-hungered? He went to the House of the Lord which was at Nob, and besought Ahimelech the priest to sustain them with the shew bread, which only the priests might eat.

'And Ahimelech, when he learned that they had kept themselves from women three days and that their need was great, gave them freely of what David had asked.

'So likewise were my disciples an-hungered, which have kept themselves from women these many months, and I being a priest, a Son of Aaron, suffered them to eat, but ate not myself.'

At this, the rulers of the synagogues dismissed him, saying: 'Thou hast well said and hast justified both thyself and thy disciples.'

XXXV.c

(178) And he entered into Capernaum, and it was noised abroad that he was in the house where he dwelt at this time.

And straightway many were gathered together, insomuch as there was no room to receive them, no, not so much as about the door: and he preached the word unto them.

And there come four men to the house, bearing between them on a litter one that lay sick of the palsy.

And when they could not come nigh unto him, for the press, they went upon the roof of the house, and took off a part of the tiling and let the bed down by cords into the midst before Jesus, and themselves leaped down after.

And when Jesus saw their faith he prayed aloud, saying: 'O God, in Thy mercy forgive this man his sins!'

But they that brought the sick man murmured within themselves.

Jesus, perceiving their downcast countenances, said unto them: 'Why murmur ye within yourselves because I prayed that God might forgive him his sins, rather than that He should suffer him to rise and walk?

'For the Lord spake to Solomon by night, saying: "If I send sickness among My people, and if they humble themselves and turn from their wicked ways, then will I hear their prayers from heaven. I will forgive their sins and heal them."'

And even as he said these things, the man stirred and stood upon his feet, and gave thanks to God.

And Jesus said unto him: 'Son, take this bed hence that others may have the more room.'

XXXV.c
(contd.) And when he took up the bed and went forth before them all, they were amazed.

And certain of the scribes that sat by, said: 'We never saw it on this fashion.'

LX.e (179) And when little children were brought unto Jesus that he should teach them the Law, his disciples drave them away, and rebuked those that brought them.

But, Jesus, being much displeased, took a little child in his arms and stood in their midst, and said: 'Suffer little children to come unto me and drive them not hence.

'For David saith: "Touch not Mine anointed nor do My prophets any harm," and the Sages have taught us that the anointed signify the little children which learn the Law.

'Therefore care ye well for the children of the Men of the Land; from them the Law shall proceed.

'Verily, I say unto you: whosoever shall offend against one of these little ones, it were better for him that a millstone were hanged about his neck and that he were drowned in the depth of the sea.

'For Enoch, which is God's messenger unto such children as learn the Law, he ever beholds the face of our Father which is in heaven.'

XXVII.h (180) Jesus therefore taught them, saying: 'Little children, when ye stand in prayer, forgive them that have wronged you; for if ye forgive not, neither will the Father forgive you the wrongs that ye have done Him.

'Ask ye for the greater things, and the lesser shall be added unto you; ask for the heavenly things and the earthly shall be added unto you.

'And pray only for a sufficiency, saying: "Feed me with the bread of my allowance." For your Father will know before ye ask Him what your needs may be.

'But when ye pray to Him for aught, add thereto: "Yet not as I will, but as Thou wilt."

'And make not long prayers, thinking to be better heard by much speaking.'

XXVII.h (181) Then said the disciples: 'Master, teach us to pray, as John also taught his disciples.'

He answered and said: 'Thus pray ye:

'"Our Father which art in heaven!

'"Hallowed be Thy exalted name.

'"Thy Kingdom come speedily and be acknowledged by all the world.

'"Thy will be done in heaven,

'"And on earth be peace of heart to them that fear Thee.

'"Feed us with the bread of our allowance, which is grace, favour and mercy in Thy sight.

'"Forgive us our trespasses, Father,

'"And forgive them that trespass against us, as we also forgive them.

XXVII.h
(contd.)
‘ “And lead us not into the power of sin,

‘ “Nor into temptation that is too great for us to bear.

‘ “Yet in all things do what seemeth good unto Thee.

‘ “For Thine is the Kingdom and ever more wilt Thou reign in glory!” ’

CHAPTER XXI

HOW HE SENT FORTH THE TWELVE

LVI.g   (182) And Jesus took apart into a mountain twelve men of his disciples, which he chose that they might abide with him until he should send them forth to preach: to heal all them that were sick in spirit and to destroy the works of the devil.

First he chose Simon, and called him Cephas (which is The Stone), for he said: 'On this stone will I raise my pillar to the Lord.'

And he chose also James and John the sons of Zebedee, and called them Beni Rehem (which is The Sons of the Wild Ox); and Andrew, Simon's brother;

And Philip, and Nathanael his brother, sons of Tholomaeus, and Matthew the Levite, and Thomas called The Twin;

And his own brother James, and Judas, called Of the Bosom; and that Simon which had been a Zealot; and lastly Judas of Kerioth.

And he said unto them: 'Behold, I will you to be twelve apostles for a testimony unto Israel, one man for every tribe.'

And they went together into his house at Capernaum, and abode there.

LXII.c   (183) And it came to pass one day that Jesus departed from the house where he abode and went to pray upon a mountain alone. And he committed the ten disciples unto the charge of James his brother, and of Simon Peter.

Then were the ten filled with wrath and murmured, saying: 'Are these then greater than we?'

Therefore Jesus called them unto him and said: 'Ye know that petty princes exercise dominion over the Gentiles and certain great ones exercise dominion over the petty princes, and all men do their bidding.

'But it shall not be so among you. Whosoever shall be great among you, let him be your servant; and whosoever shall be chief, let him minister unto you.'

LVII.f   (184) And when certain days had passed, Jesus called unto him the Twelve and began to send them forth two by two, and commanded them that they should take naught for their journey save a staff only.

No scrip, no bread, no money in the fold of their garments; neither two pairs of shoes, nor two tunics, nor two shifts; nor salute any man by the way.

And if any of them would eat, let him undertake any labour that fell to him to do.

LIV.f

(185) And he said: 'I send you out two by two, for Amos saith: "Can two walk together except they be agreed?"; and ye know that God commandeth you so to love one another as He hath loved you.

LVII.g

(186) 'But go not into any region of the Gentiles, nor into any city of the Samaritans.

XLVII.d

(187) 'For ye shall not give what is holy unto the dogs, neither shall ye cast your pearls before swine, lest they trample them under their feet and turn again to rend you.

LVII.g

(188) 'Go only to the strayed sheep of the House of Israel.

'And as ye go, preach, saying: "The Kingdom of Heaven is at hand!"

'Into whatsoever city or village ye shall enter, enquire which house in it is worthy to receive you.

'And when ye come to that house, salute it, and if it be worthy, let your peace come thereupon. But if not, let your peace return unto you.

'And when ye have found a house that is worthy, enter in and abide until ye go thence.

'And know that whosoever receiveth a prophet, the same shall be rewarded by God in the prophet's name; as was the widow of Zarephath which received Elijah, and the great woman of Shunem which received Elisha.

'And whosoever receiveth a righteous man, the same shall be rewarded by God in that righteous man's name, as when Jacob blessed Pharaoh which received him into Egypt for Joseph's sake.

LX.e

(189) 'And whosoever receiveth any of you little ones, and give him so much as a cup of cold water in God's name, the same shall receive his reward in the Day of Judgement.

'For Solomon prophesied: "He that hath pity upon the poor lendeth unto the Lord, and the Lord will repay him."

'In that day the King of Glory shall say unto certain righteous men that come before him: "Come, ye blessed of my Father, inherit the Kingdom of Heaven prepared for you from the foundation of the world.

' "For I was an-hungered and ye gave me meat; I was a-thirst and ye gave me drink; I was a stranger and ye took me in."

'Then shall the righteous ask: "Lord, when did we so?"

'And the King of Glory shall answer and say unto them: "Insomuch as ye have done it unto the least of my children, ye have done it unto me."

'And it is written in the same book: "He that useth the poor ill, the same reproacheth his Maker."

'Therefore, in that day the King of Glory shall say unto certain others: "I was an-hungered and ye gave me no meat; I was a-thirst and ye gave me no drink, but ye reproached me and sent me away empty-handed."

'Then shall these unrighteous ones ask: "Lord, when did we so?"

'And the King of Glory shall answer and say unto them: "Inso-

LX.e
(contd.)

much as ye have done unto the least of my children, ye have done unto me to my reproach.

'"Depart from me, -cursed ones, into the everlasting fire prepared for Belial and his angels!"

LVII.g

(190) 'And if there be any sick brought unto you, or any tormented by evil spirits, anoint them with oil and pray God to heal them.

'And as He spake by the mouth of the prophet Hosea, saying: "I will love you freely," so, having freely received, do ye freely give.

'Fall not into the sin of Gehazi, which sought to exact payment for the healing that Elisha had wrought by the finger of God.

'Neither boast ye if evil spirits obey your voice and come forth; for the glory is God's. But pray to Him that your names be inscribed among the stars of heaven.

'Even as Enoch testified, saying: "God called the stars by their names and they hearkened unto Him; and these are the names of the holy which dwell on earth and believe in the name of the Lord of Spirits for ever and ever."

XXVII.e

(191) 'When ye pray that God will heal a sick person, peep not, neither mutter as the heathen do, but before the laying on of hands say openly: "Believe in God: He shall save!"

LVII.g

(192) 'And if there be found no house in that city or village that is worthy, go your ways out from the streets of the same, and say:

'"The dust of your city which cleaveth to our shoes, we shake off as a testimony against you."

'And if they do not hearken to these words, and so repent, I say unto you it shall be less tolerable in the Day of Judgement for that city than it was for Sodom and Gomorrah, when God rained fire and brimstone upon them.

'For he that heareth you, heareth Him that sent you; and he that despiseth you, despiseth Him that sent you. Depart thence and go to another.

'Verily, when ye have visited all the cities of the land, the time shall be at hand that the Son of Man is revealed.

'Even as Daniel spake in the name of the Lord: "Go thou thy way until the end be; for thou shalt find rest and stand in thy allotted place at the end of the days."

XXXIV.g

(193) 'In that day he that is not with God shall be against Him; and he that is not against Him shall be with Him.

'He that gathereth not shall be as one which scattereth; he that scattereth not shall be as one which gathereth.

LVII.g

(194) 'Behold, I send you forth as harmless sheep into the midst of ravening wolves, and as guileless doves into the midst of subtle serpents.

'And if ye are taken before the rulers of synagogues, or before magistrates, or before the servants of Herod, take no thought beforehand what ye shall speak.

'But whatsoever shall be given you in that same hour, that speak ye; the Holy Spirit shall teach you what words ye may use.

LVII.g
(contd.)
 'For David saith in a psalm: "I will speak of Thy testimonies even before kings, and will not be ashamed."

LXVI.i
 (195) 'And know that Daniel prophesied of the Last Days: "They that teach the word of God shall shine as the brightness of the firmament, and they that turn many to righteousness shall be as the stars that endure for ever." '

XLV.b
 (196) And he strengthened their spirits, saying: 'Ezekiel prophesied of the tender twig that the Lord shall plant: "In the mountain of the height of Israel will I plant it, and it shall bring forth boughs and bear fruit and it shall be a goodly cedar tree, and under it shall be gathered all birds of every wing."

'And though the work that ye are sent to do be as a grain of mustard seed, which is among the least of seeds that the earth yields,

'Yet when the grain is sown, it sprouteth and runneth up and becometh greater than all other herbs; it throweth forth branches like unto a tree, and to them likewise shall the birds of the air be gathered.

'Have faith therefore in God, whose Kingdom ye preach. Of Him Job prophesieth, saying: "He removeth the mountains, He casteth the earth out of her place, He treadeth upon the waves of the sea."

'And He shall also hearken unto your prayers.

LIV.i
 (197) 'But if this world hate you without a cause, rejoice; for it loveth but its own.'

XXXIV.g
 (198) And, seeing that they were sent forth to the House of Israel alone, the disciples said unto him: 'Master, at the Great Day shall all men, save only the elect of Israel, truly be cast into the everlasting fire?'

He answered: 'Not so; for God shall spare them that set not their face against Him.

'The prophet Zechariah hath testified that even such as are left alive of the Gentiles shall come up yearly to Jerusalem and worship the Lord of Hosts.'

CHAPTER XXII

HOW HE DISCLOSED CERTAIN MYSTERIES

LVII.h (199) And the Twelve went forth as Jesus bade them and preached that men should repent.

They also anointed with oil those that were sick or possessed of devils, and healed many.

LVII.h (200) And they gathered themselves together unto Jesus again, and told him all things, both that they had done and that they had taught.

LIV.f (201) And Jesus received them joyfully, saying: 'I chose and ordained you to go and gather fruit, and ye were my servants, for ye obeyed me.

'But henceforth I call you not my servants, for the servant knoweth not that which his master doeth. I call you my friends; for the work of love which God hath granted me to perform, that ye likewise now perform.

LVII.n (202) 'Yet think not that the disciple is above his master or the servant above his lord; it is enough for the disciple that he be as his master, and the servant as his lord.'

LIX.c (203) And when Jesus heard that they had shaken the dust off their feet as a testimony against Chorazin and against Bethsaida, he said:

'Woe unto thee, Chorazin! Woe unto thee, Bethsaida! For if the mighty words spoken in your streets had been spoken in Sodom and Gomorrah, they would have repented in sack-cloth and ashes, and have remained standing until this day.'

LXXXIV.f (204) And Jesus disclosed to the Twelve the threefold mystery of the mercy and wisdom of God.

For he said unto them: 'If knowledge be as the Father, then shall the knower be as the Mother, and the twain engender the thing known, namely the Word.

'These three abide together: God the Father which hath created us of His mercy, and the Holy Spirit of God which shineth upon us in wisdom, and the Word of God which sheddeth peace.'

LXXXIV.f (205) Afterward, he put upon them the blessing which the sons of Aaron alone might utter, saying: 'Thus I put upon you the Name of the Lord:

' "The Lord bless you and keep you!

' "The Lord make His face to shine upon you and be gracious unto you.

LXXXIV.f ' "The Lord lift up the light of His countenance upon you, and give
(*contd.*) you peace."

'For the Father is Mercy, and the light of His countenance is
Wisdom, and the Son is Peace.'

XXVII.i (206) And he taught them, saying: 'David spake in the name of the
Lord: "Ask of Me and I will give unto thee the heathen for thine
inheritance and the uttermost parts of the earth for thy possession."

'And Solomon saith likewise of Wisdom: "They that seek Me
diligently shall find Me; with Me are riches and honour."

'And it is written in the Book of Esther: "Let nothing fail of all that
thou hast spoken for him that sitteth at the King's gate."

'Therefore ask for peace, (which is the humbling of the heathen),
and it shall be given you; seek wisdom (which is the Holy Spirit),
and ye shall find it; knock at the Gate of Mercy, and it shall be opened
to you, as it was opened to Mordecai the son of Kish.

'If a son ask his father for bread, will he give him a stone? Or a
serpent, if he ask for a fish? Or a scorpion, if he ask for an egg?

'Since therefore men that are sinners give good things to their
children, how much more shall our heavenly Father give good things
to them that pray to Him?

XXVII.i (207) 'For David saith: "Like as a father pitieth his children, so
the Lord pitieth them that fear him."

XLIV.c (208) 'David saith also: "Give ear, O my people, to my Law, incline
your ears to the words of my mouth.

' "I will open my mouth in a parable, I will utter dark sayings of
old which our fathers have told us.

' "We will not hide them from our children, but shew to the
generation to come the praises of the Lord and His strength and His
wonderful works."

'For now there is nothing covered that shall not be revealed, neither
hid that shall not be known.

LXXXIV.g (209) 'Yet do ye keep this secret for those of my house which are
worthy to receive it.

'For David said in a psalm: "The secret of the Lord is with them
that fear Him."

'And Solomon said likewise: "His secret is with the righteous." '

LXXXIV.h (210) And Jesus also revealed unto them the changes of a man's
soul, how it abideth not in one form, neither in one passion,

But as from heaven it proceedeth, so unto heaven shall it return,
having suffered many things, and be freed at last from the prison of
its flesh.

LVIII.b (211) Now, certain jealous men, feigning themselves to be Pharisees, heard that Jesus made much of the Twelve, and were offended,
saying: 'Shall these verily be received with as much honour as they
that have studied the Law and kept it from their youth up?

'For some of these were sinners but yesterday, and today they
continue in ignorance of the Law.'

Therefore Jesus spake a parable unto them, saying:

LVIII.b
(*contd.*)

'The Kingdom of Heaven is like unto an householder, which went out early in the morning to hire labourers unto his vineyard.

'And when he had agreed with certain tried labourers of his acquaintance for a penny a day, he sent them into his vineyard.

'About the third hour he went out again and saw men standing idle in the market place as sheep having no shepherd, and said unto them: "Go ye also into the vineyard and whatsoever is right I will give you. For the harvest truly is plenteous and the labourers are few." And they went their way.

'Now, it chanced as he passed through the market place at about the eleventh hour, that he saw a poor man, which had been waiting there since the third hour, and saith unto him: "Why standest thou here all the day idle?"

'He answered and said: "Because no man hath hired me; wherefore tomorrow we must go hungry, I and my children."

'Then he was filled with compassion and said unto the man: "Go thou also into the vineyard and whatsoever is right, that thou shalt receive."

'When even was come, the householder saith unto his steward: "Call the labourers and give them their hire."

'And when the first came, they received every man a penny, but when they saw that those which were hired at the third hour likewise received a penny, they murmured among themselves and waited to see how much the last man should receive.

'But the householder said unto his steward: "Let this man likewise receive a penny."

'Then were those which were first hired filled with wrath, and said unto the householder: "This last hath laboured one hour only, and thou hast made him equal unto us which have borne the burden and heat of the day."

'But he answered one of them, and said: "Friend, I do thee no wrong. Didst thou not agree with me for a penny? Take that thine is and go thy way. Wherefore shall I not give unto this last even as unto thee? Is it not lawful for me to do what I will with mine own?

' "Let not thine eye be evil because I do good unto this man which laboureth for me." '

And Jesus said unto them: 'Pray ye rather the Lord of the Vineyard, that He will send forth many more labourers into His harvest. For the harvest is great, but the labourers are few.'

LVIII.d

(212) They said again: 'Every sabbath day the Law is expounded in the synagogue, whither all they that are faithful come to be taught.'

But since they had rejected John's counsel which bade them preach to the men of the land, Jesus answered:

'It is not enough to teach the righteous only.'

He said unto them also: 'A certain householder had two sons. And he came to the first, and said: "Son, go work to-day in my vineyard!"

'He answered and said: "I will not," but afterwards he repented, and went.

LVIII.d
(*contd.*)

'And the householder came to the second, and said likewise.

'And this son answered him dutifully, and said: "I go, sir," but went not.

'Did not the first of the twain honour his father rather than the second?

'Verily, I say unto you: these men which aforetime served the Wicked Kingdom and partook of her harlotries, but repented and were baptized of John, shall they be less honoured in the Kingdom of Heaven than ye?

'For John came and shewed unto you the way of righteousness, but ye which are skilled in the Law heeded him not, and went not forth to preach as he counselled you in God's name.

'But these, which are less skilled, hearkened to him and now they go forth to preach in your stead.'

CHAPTER XXIII

HOW HE KEPT THE FEAST OF
TABERNACLES

XLIX.e (213) Now, the Feast of Tabernacles was at hand, and James the brother of Jesus according to the spirit, said unto him: 'Comest thou not with us to the feast? Let those of Judaea likewise see such works as thou doest in Galilee. Shew thyself to the world, for no man which seeketh to be known openly worketh alway in secret.'

Jesus answered and said: 'Go thither now with thy brethren, and I follow. But that I do must not be openly done, for mine hour is not yet come.'

And when they had gone up, then went he up also.

LI.d (214) And the disciples met Jesus and told him concerning the Galileans whose blood Pilate had mingled with the offerings which they brought to the Temple.

(For they made a great outcry against him because that he had built a conduit and paid the labourers with money consecrated to God.)

Jesus answered and said: 'Those were just men which fell as an acceptable sacrifice to God, for they stood up unarmed to make protest against the despoilers of His House, and would not be silenced.

L.c (215) 'Serve not the Wicked Kingdom, neither make to yourselves friends of the Herodians.

'As Isaiah prophesied: "Say ye not: 'Let us make a confederacy,' and fear not the fear of such as say so, neither be afraid. But fear the Lord Himself, in holiness, and He shall be for a sanctuary."

'Fear not them that kill the body, and are not able to kill the soul; fear, rather, Him which, after He hath killed, is able to cast both soul and body into the flames of hell.

'Are not two sparrows sold for one farthing to the leper that cometh for purification? Yet I say unto you: that sparrow of the twain which falleth a sacrifice to God shall not be forgotten of Him.

'Therefore, fear not lest ye likewise fall a sacrifice. Ye are of more value than many sparrows.

'As the people spake unto Saul, saying: "Shall he die which hath wrought this great salvation in Israel?", and Saul answered: "God forbid that an hair of his head shall fall to the ground,"

'So it shall likewise be with you. At the resurrection ye shall be

L.c
(*contd.*)
LIV.g

LI.e

LXVI.i

raised up whole. For even the very hairs of your head are all numbered, and not one of them shall perish.

(216) 'And what though ye perish in your labours, which ye perform that others may repent and be saved?

'Greater love hath no man than this, that he lay down his life for his
friends.'

(217) Again, they asked Jesus, saying: 'Of those eighteen whereon
the tower of the conduit fell and slew them, thinkest thou that they
were sinners above all men in Jerusalem?'

He answered: 'Nay, for the Chief Priests consented to the work.
Yet it pleased the Lord to take these lives before the Last Days; and
presently, if their rulers repent not, He will not only slay them, but
condemn their souls to hell also.'

(218) And because they wondered that God did not instantly
destroy the guilty as He destroyed Korah, Dathan, and Abiram, he
taught them, saying:

'Solomon spake a proverb: "The wicked worketh a deceitful work,
but to him that soweth righteousness shall be a sure reward."

'And Joel prophesied also: "Put in the sickle, for the harvest is ripe.
Multitudes, multitudes in the valley of decision; for the day of the
Lord is near in the valley of decision!"

'Hearken therefore to a parable: the Kingdom of Heaven is like
unto a man which sowed good seed in his master's field. And he slept
and went not to view the field again either by night or day, and how
the seed should spring and grow up he wist not.

'Then, while he slept, his adversary came and sowed tares among
the wheat and went his way. When therefore the blade was sprung
up, then appeared the tares also.

'The servants of the master said unto him: "Master, did not the
sower sow good seed in thy field? From whence then hath it tares?"

'He answered them, saying: "An enemy hath done this."

'The servants said unto him: "Wilt thou then that we go and root
them up?"

'But he said: "Nay; lest while ye root up the tares, ye root up also
the wheat with them. For the earth bringeth forth fruit of herself,
first the blade, then the ear, after that the full corn in the ear. And
when the fruit is ripe, immediately the sickle is put in, for it is harvest.

' "Therefore let the wheat and tares both grow together until the
harvest, and in that time I will say to the reapers: 'Gather ye together
first the tares, and bind them in bundles to burn them; and then
gather ye the wheat into my barn.' "

'For David prophesied of the seed of Belial: "Thine hand, O Lord,
shall find out all Thine enemies and the fire of Thy wrath shall
devour them; their fruit shalt Thou destroy from the earth and their
seed from among the children of men. But the chosen seed of David
will I make to endure for ever."

'And Haggai spake in the name of the Lord: "Is the seed yet in the
barn? Yea, as yet the vine and the fig tree and the pomegranate and

LXVI.i   the olive tree have not brought forth. From this day will I bless
(contd.)   them." '

XLIX.f   (219) And on the seventh day of the Feast, when the priest stooped
to fill his pitcher at the Pool of Siloam, Jesus lifted up his voice, and
cried in the words of the prophet Isaiah:

' "Ho, everyone that thirsteth, come ye to the waters, and he that
hath no money; come ye, buy and eat; yea, come, buy wine and milk
without money and without price!

' "Wherefore spend ye money on that which is not bread, and your
labour on that which satisfieth not? Hearken diligently unto Me, and
eat ye that which is good, and let your soul delight in fatness!" '

And many that stood by, knowing the Scriptures, continued to cry
out the words of Isaiah, saying:

' "Incline your ear and come unto Me and your soul shall live, and
I will make an everlasting covenant with you, even the sure mercies
of David.

' "Behold, I have given him for a witness to the people, a leader and
a commander to the people!" '

Then were the Chief Rulers wroth, and asked: 'Who is this man
that breaketh the holy silence?'

And they sought him out, but found him not; for the multitude
was great.

LXXXIV.b   (220) And Jesus went again beyond Jordan, unto Beth-Nimrah in
the dominion of Herod, where John at first baptized.

There he abode for awhile with his disciples, and many resorted
unto him from the coasts of Edom and from all the country round
about.

But the Herodians, when they heard that Jesus baptized and made
more disciples even than John, took counsel how they might put him
to death.

Wherefore he departed thence into Judaea, to the village of Ephron,
which is nigh unto the wilderness of the south, and continued there
for a time with the Twelve, preaching and baptizing.

LXVI.e   (221) Afterward it came to pass that he went throughout the cities
and villages of Judaea which lie towards the sea, preaching and expounding the glad tidings of the Kingdom of God.

And the Twelve were with him, and certain women which had forsaken this evil world; and Mary the Braider, his mother according to
the spirit.

Now, Joanna the wife of Chuza, Herod's steward, and Susanna and
other rich women secretly ministered unto him of their substance, that
the households of the Twelve should suffer no want.

CHAPTER XXIV

HOW HE ORDERED THE YEAR

LXXII.f (222) And Jesus said unto the Twelve: 'Come ye apart into a desert place and rest awhile.' For there were many coming and going and they had not leisure so much as to eat.

Therefore they departed into a desert place by boat privately. And the people saw them departing and some five thousand of them ran afoot by the lakeside, waiting for him to land.

But the boat drave onward, and all save one thousand of the people returned unto the city whence they came, for they were faint with hunger.

Then Jesus had compassion on them that remained, and came out of the boat and preached unto them.

But the disciples gathered themselves unto him, and asked: 'Is this not a desert place, and is not the day far spent?'

He answered and said: 'I must do the work which I have been sent to do while there is yet light. For behold, the night cometh when no man can work.'

LXXII.f (223) Then Peter said unto him: 'Nay, but send away these people that they may buy bread in the villages, for they have naught to eat.'

He answered: 'Ye shall yourselves give them to eat.'

They asked again: 'What? Shall we then buy bread for two hundred pence? For though four thousand men and women are departed, as many as one thousand remain, besides children.'

He saith unto them: 'How many loaves have they?'

And when they knew, they answered: 'There is a lad here which hath five barley loaves and a few fishes.'

He said: 'It is enough for fifties and for hundreds.'

Then he commanded that those which were nearest to him, having washed, should sit down by companies of thirty in a circuit cast about him. And when they were set, he himself went into a room which remained on the northern side.

Then he commanded the Twelve to take baskets and stand, each beside a several company, for there were twelve companies.

And he saith unto the people: 'Elisha prophesied in the name of the Lord: "They shall all eat bread and have bread left over." For this was bread sanctified unto God's use. Therefore bring me your five loaves for sanctification.'

LXXII.f
(contd.)   And Jesus sanctified the loaves and brake them into fragments, and put the fragments into the baskets which they brought.

They went he from company to company about the circle, receiving a basket from the hand of each disciple in turn.

To every man he gave a fragment of bread, and each made as if to eat, yet refrained. For Jesus said: 'This is bread sanctified unto God. Feed on it in your hearts!'

And when he came to the room that remained on the southern side, he said to the Twelve: 'Gather up the fragments that remain.'

And the fragments were the same five loaves, for naught had been eaten.

Then said he unto them: 'Lo, here is more bread! Call five more men, that they may sit here and be fed.' And this was done.

Likewise he divided the fishes among them all, saying: 'Eat, for He will save!'

And when this was accomplished, he stood and cried: 'Four thousand are gone, one thousand remain! He that hath ears, let him hear!'

LXXII.f   (224) Afterward, he commanded every man which sat in the circle to yield his place to one which had not yet eaten; and stood again in the room which remained on the northern side.

And he preached unto them, saying: 'Behold, it is written that Joseph, when he foresaw a famine of seven years, built seven granaries in Egypt, filling one in every year of plenty as a surety against a year of famine.'

Then he meted the fragments of bread into seven heaps, and with each heap he filled a basket.

And he said: 'Behold, Joseph's father and his eleven brethren came down to Egypt to be fed, and Joseph appointed his brethren and his own two sons to mete out bread unto the people.

'Each should perform this service for seven days in succession, and draw in turn from each of the seven granaries.'

Then Jesus named the Twelve after the names of the fathers of tribes, and he also called to one that sat apart on the southern side (being the lad which brought the loaves and fishes), and named him Benjamin.

And at his bidding each of the thirteen in turn meted out bread unto seven men, to every man from a different basket; and all made as if to eat, yet ate not.

And when the thirteen had done, each had meted out his bread four times.

Then said Jesus unto the lad: 'Return thou to thy seat!'; and when the fragments of bread were gathered once more, he returned them all unto him, saying: 'It is written: "But Benjamin's mess was five times as much as theirs." '

And he cried: 'Four thousand are gone, one thousand remain! He that hath eyes to see, let him attend!'

LXXII.g   (225) Now, there was much grass in that place where Jesus fed them with bread of the spirit, even as Ezekiel prophesied:

LXXII.g
(*contd.*)
'I will feed them in a good pasture, there shall they lie in a good fold and in a fat pasture.

'And I shall set up one shepherd over them and he shall feed them, even as My servant David.'

LXXII.i
(226) And when these things were accomplished, Jesus sent the multitude away, and desired to cross over unto the coast of Gennesaret.

Now, the Twelve had themselves forgotten to take bread, neither had they with them in the boat so much as one loaf.

And when they murmured among themselves, Jesus said: 'It is written: "God gave our fathers bread from heaven to eat," namely the manna which He rained upon them in the wilderness when they murmured for hunger. They ate and were filled, but now are dead, for it was food that endured not.

'Yet gave He unto them other bread also, namely the Law, which is the everlasting bread of life. Whosoever feedeth upon it in his heart, the same shall not die but live for ever.

'As the Preacher saith, the Son of Sirach: "They that eat me, namely Wisdom, shall yet hunger after me, and they that drink me shall yet thirst after me.

'"He that obeyeth me shall never be confounded, and they that work by me shall not do amiss.

'"All these things are the book of the covenant of the Most High God, even the Law which Moses commanded for an heritage unto the congregation of Jacob."'

LXXIII.f
(227) Then Philip saith unto Jesus: 'Nevertheless, let us go unto Bethsaida, that we may buy bread that endureth not, lest we faint for hunger.'

And others of the Twelve said likewise.

But Jesus purposed to sail unto the land of Gennesaret. Wherefore he rebuked them that their minds were set on earthly things,

For Philip was of Bethsaida, the city also of Peter and Andrew, which had rejected the word of repentance.

And when Jesus perceived that they hardened their hearts, he bade them go whither they listed; but he himself went up into a mountain to pray.

Then set they a course for Bethsaida. But their boat was tossed with waves, for the wind was contrary; and already it was night.

And when they had rowed as it seemed five-and-twenty or thirty furlongs, they cast anchor and lighted a lanthorn and slept.

And in the fourth watch, while it was yet dark, they saw a man dressed in white raiment walking toward them through the water.

Then were they greatly troubled, and cried: 'It is a spirit!' For they trusted to be still in the midst of the sea.

And Jesus called unto them, and said: 'It is I, be not afraid!' And straightway they knew him.

Now, because of the violence of the wind their boat had driven back nigh unto the place whence they came, but they knew it not;

LXXIII.f
(contd.)
therefore went Jesus through the shallow water to meet them, think-ing that they were come back to ask forgiveness.

And when they perceived how the matter was, they were confused in their hearts, and made Jesus no answer.

Wherefore he turned again to pass on his way.

But Peter, being ashamed of his frowardness, whereby he had toiled to no purpose, cried out, saying:

'Master, depart from me, if it seemeth good unto thee, for I am a sinful man. Yet if haply thou wilt shew forgiveness unto thy servant, suffer him to come to thee, that he may lift thee into this boat. For now we would go with thee unto the land of Gennesaret!'

Jesus said: 'Come!'

And Peter cast himself into the waters and came unto the place where Jesus was, and lifted him into the boat. And Jesus forgave them when they had confessed their folly.

Yet were they amazed beyond measure, for so soon as they received him, the wind which was contrary turned about and blew from the east.

And they said to each other in fear: 'What manner of man is this, that even the winds obey him?'

LXXII.h
(228) Afterward, as they sailed across the Lake, the Twelve were ashamed and asked Jesus to expound his riddles.

He answered and said: 'Having eyes, see ye not? Having ears, hear ye not? And do ye not remember?

'When first I brake the bread, how many fragments took ye up in the twelve baskets?'

They answered: 'As many as would feed five men.'

He asked again: 'And how many the second time?'

They answered: 'In the seven baskets we took up a fivefold portion for the lad.'

He said: 'How is it that ye understand not even yet?'

LXXII.k
(229) For these were parables of the year and its months: how it had been divided in the days of Moses, and how it should be divided in the Kingdom of Heaven:

Namely a year of twelve months, each of thirty days, with five days remaining over; and a year of thirteen months, each of four weeks, with one day remaining over.

XXV.d
(230) The disciples asked him: 'Why speakest thou in parables?'

He answered them, saying: 'Unto you it is given to understand the mysteries of the Kingdom of Heaven, but to others it is not yet given.'

LXXIII.g
(231) Then came they to Capernaum in the land of Gennesaret, and drew nigh unto the shore.

And when the men of that place had knowledge of him, whitherso-ever he entered, into villages or cities or country, they laid the sick in the streets. They also besought him that they might touch the fringes of his garment and be kept thereby from evil dreams and inclinations.

CHAPTER XXV

HOW HE MOURNED FOR JOHN AND
HEALED A DEMONIAC

LXXVI.e (232) Now it came to pass, when Herod's birthday was kept with wine and flute players and dancing women, that Herod was merry with his lords and high captains and the chief estates of Galilee.

Which, when his wife Herodias perceived, she led in Salome, her daughter, to wish Herod good health.

And when he smiled upon the damsel, and asked her: 'Daughter, what gift shall I give thee for the desire of thy heart?'

She, being instructed by her mother, answered and said: 'I will that thou slay John the Baptist, for he hath dishonoured both my mother and thy servant.'

Then Herod would not be shamed before them that sat at meat, and sware to do even as she desired.

And he sent and beheaded John in the castle of Machaerus.

And John's disciples went thither sorrowfully, and took up the body and buried it.

XCVII.h (233) On the same day come certain of the Pharisees unto Jesus, saying: 'John the Baptist is slain. Get thee out and depart hence, lest Herod kill thee also, as he hath killed John!'

And Jesus rent his clothes, and lamented sore, and unto them that warned him he said: 'Go ye, and tell that fox that I must walk in Galilee today and tomorrow and the day following, and he shall have no power to slay me as he slew John.

'For it cannot be that this prophet shall perish out of Jerusalem.

'But on the third day cometh relief, and the Kingdom of God is now at hand.'

LXXIX.h (234) And the disciples ask Jesus: 'Why say the scribes that Elijah must come again before the Kingdom of God can be established?'

He answered and said: 'Malachi prophesied in the name of the Lord: "Behold, I will send you Elijah the prophet before the coming of the great and dreadful day of the Lord."

'And Zechariah likewise prophesied of one which must suffer many things in that day and be set at naught.

'Verily, I say unto you: Elijah is indeed come again, and hath been put to death though we would have willingly laid down our lives for him.

LXXIX.h
(contd.) 'As David saith in a psalm: "None can redeem his brother that he should live for ever."

'Therefore let them now do unto that other whatsoever they list.'

And the disciples understood that Elijah had come again in the person of John the Baptist. But they wist not that Jesus spake of himself when he told them: 'Another must suffer many things in that day and be set at naught.'

LXXVI.f (235) And Jesus departed thence by boat unto a desert place apart. There he mourned for John, and fasted for him three full weeks, saving only the sabbaths, even as Daniel mourned before his vision of the Latter Days.

LXXV.d (236) And when he had broken his fast, and even was come, Jesus entered into a boat with the Twelve, and said unto them: 'Let us pass over unto the other side.' And they launched forth.

Now, as they sailed, there came down a great storm of wind on the Lake. Yet Jesus would not turn back to seek an haven, as did the masters of other little boats that sailed with him, but held to his course.

And it came to pass that the storm increased in violence, and the waves beat into the boat, whereat certain of the disciples were afraid.

And they cry unto him, saying 'Master, we perish!'

Jesus rebuked them, and said: 'Peace, be still! Why are ye so fearful, O ye of little faith?

'As David saith in a psalm: "God raiseth a stormy wind which lifteth up the waves so that the shipmen are tossed to and fro, and all their wisdom is swallowed up.

' "Yet they cry unto Him in their trouble, and He bringeth them out of their distress.

' "He maketh the storm a calm, so that the waves thereof are still, and He bringeth them to their desired haven." '

Then prayed they all to God with one voice, and He heard them. And, behold, while they were yet praying, the wind ceased and it was as Jesus had declared.

For when they had cast out the water from the boat, they came safely over the Lake unto Magadan of the Haven.

LXXV.e (237) Then Peter said unto Jesus: 'Master, it is good for us to be here. Let us build a tabernacle and kindle a fire and dry our garments thereat.'

LXIII.f (238) Now, this was the region of the Gerasenes, and there was an Israelite with an unclean spirit, which ware no clothes and had his dwelling among the tombs and no man could tame him.

And those that fed great herds of swine nigh unto the hill where he dwelt, held him in terror, for he rushed violently upon them and tare the swine in sunder with his hands and ate their flesh.

But though these swineherds besought the rulers of the city to drive the man thence, they could not.

For if ever he were bound with chains and fetters, he brake them in pieces and escaped out of the hands of them that guarded him.

LXIII.f
(contd.)
And night and day his voice was heard crying from the tombs, as he cut himself with stones.

This man therefore saw Jesus afar off with the disciples, and ran to him and cried:

'Master, I pray thee, let this evil spirit torment me no longer!'

And immediately the evil spirit spake through his mouth, cursing and blaspheming.

Then said Jesus unto the evil spirit: 'What is thy name?'

And the evil spirit dissembled and answered: 'My name is Legion, for we are many.'

Jesus said: 'If my Father hearken to my prayer, He will send thee out of this man. Begone therefore, in God's name, Aggrath Bat Machlat, and take thine one hundred and eighty thousand devils with thee!'

Then the evil spirit besought Jesus through the mouth of the same man, saying: 'Suffer me to enter into one of them that keep the swine.'

But Jesus answered: 'Nay, for they are also sons of Adam and made in God's image.'

At that the evil spirit departed, and Jesus bade the man wash in the Lake, and gave unto him clothing to hide his nakedness.

And he was healed and besought Jesus that he might follow after him.

But Jesus suffered him not, and said: 'Go rather to thy father's house and tell thy kindred how great things the Lord God hath done unto thee, and how He hath had compassion upon thee.

'Ask them also for the price of a sin-offering, and take it unto Jerusalem, and when thy debt is paid, then, if thou wilt, come thou with me.'

LXIII.a
(239) And Jesus saith unto him again: 'Yet watch and pray, lest that evil spirit enter into thee again! For when God asked the Adversary: "Whence comest thou?" he answered Him: "From going to and fro in the earth and from walking up and down in it."

'And verily, when he hath been cast out of a man (as Tobias cast out Asmodeus from the body of his bride Sara) he fleeth to the uttermost parts of Egypt and walketh in waterless places, seeking rest and finding none.

'Then, presently, unless an angel shall have bound him, he saith: "I will return unto the same house whence I was cast out," and when he is returned thither he findeth it swept and garnished.

'And he taketh seven other devils more wicked than himself, and they enter together into the man, and abide in him.

'Then is the last state of that man worse than the first.'

LXIII.f
(240) And when his kindred saw the man returning, clothed and in his right mind, they were astonished and began to publish the name of Jesus throughout Decapolis.

CHAPTER XXVI

HOW HE REVEALED HIMSELF TO THE TWELVE

LXXVII.c   (241) Jesus passed thence, and came unto Caesarea Philippi, where once was the city of Dan; and he preached in the villages thereabout, but into Caesarea, which was of the heathen, entered he not.

And he asked the sons of Zebedee: 'Whom do men say that I am?'

They answered: 'Some say that thou art Elijah come again, and some that thou art Enoch, the messenger of God.'

He asked them again: 'And whom say ye that I am?'

They answer: 'Verily, thou art the prophet that should come into the world, as foretold by Moses.'

Then he saith unto Peter: 'And whom sayest thou that I am?'

Peter answered: 'Thou art the Anointed King, the Son of the Living God.'

And Jesus rejoiced, and said: 'Blessed art thou, Simon! For no man revealed this unto thee, but the Father Himself revealeth it.'

LIX.d   (242) And he lifted his eyes to heaven, and gave thanks to God, saying: 'I rejoice, Father, that Thou hast not hid from simple men things that before were revealed to the wise and prudent alone.'

LXXVII.d   (243) And to the disciples he said: 'Yet must I suffer many things in Jerusalem; and as the Chief Rulers persecute me, so likewise will they persecute you.

'Therefore said I unto you that no man can follow me whither I go, except it be given him of the Father.

'He that is nigh unto me and hearkeneth to my words, the same is also nigh unto the fire which shall consume the world; but he that hearkeneth not, the same is far from the Kingdom of God.'

His disciples answered and said: 'This is a hard saying. Who can bear it?' And from that time many went back and walked no more with him.

Then Jesus asked the Twelve: 'Doth this offend you? Will ye also go from me?'

Simon Peter answered: 'Lord, to whom shall we go? For thou teachest us the way unto everlasting life.'

LXXVIII.h   (244) And Jesus straitly charged them to tell no man that he was the King of Israel.

LXII.d   (245) And he said: 'I am not sent into this world to rule it as mine own, but the Father hath sent me to minister unto all Israel; that I might meekly bring you His command.'

LXXVIII.h (246) Judas asked him (not he of Kerioth): 'Lord, how is it that thou revealest thyself unto us, and not unto the world?'

And Peter saith: 'Lord, suffer me to proclaim thy kingdom from the housetops, that all Israel may rise and take arms with thee against the Wicked Kingdom.'

But Jesus rebuked them, saying: 'My kingdom is not of this world. I come not to destroy men's lives, but to save them.'

And Peter asked: 'What if thy people greatly desire thee to do battle?'

But Jesus again rebuked him, saying: 'Thou wild man, knowest thou not what David said unto the sons of Zeruiah, when they pleaded with him that he should do violence?

'He said: "What have I to do with you, ye sons of Zeruiah, that ye should this day be adversaries unto me? For know I not that I am this day King over Israel?"

'So likewise say I unto thee: stand not against me as mine adversary, but get thee behind me and follow whither I lead.

'For thou savourest not the things that be of God, but those that be of men.'

LXXVIII.h (247) And he spake this parable unto the Twelve: 'In the days that I was chosen King, I went apart into the wilderness to commune with God, and I thirsted and was an-hungered.

'And the Adversary, meeting me in the form of my evil counsellor, said unto me: "If thou be the very Son of God which is prophesied, lift thy rod and strike this rock that water may flow forth for us."

'And my good counsellor, the angel of the Lord, made answer: "It is written: 'Ye shall not tempt the Lord thy God, as ye tempted Him at Massah.'"

'The Adversary said again: "If thou be the very Son of God which is prophesied, pray to thy Father that these stones be made bread for us."

'And my good counsellor, the angel of the Lord, again made answer: "It is written: 'I humbled thee and suffered thee to hunger, that He might make thee know that man liveth not by bread alone, but by every word that proceedeth out of the mouth of the Lord.'"

'Then my mother the Holy Spirit taketh me by the hair of my head and beareth me unto the great mountain Tabor.

'And the Adversary, which sojourneth there, came before me again, and shewed unto me all the lands over which Solomon ruled.

'And he said: "Over this kingdom shalt thou rule. Is it not a little one, and viewed in a moment of time?

'"Yet mayest thou enlarge thy dominion to the ends of the earth, if thou wilt but fall down and worship me. For the glory of conquest is delivered unto me, and I give it to whomsoever I will."

LXXVIII.h 'But my good counsellor made answer, rebuking him: "Get thee
(*contd.*) hence, thou Adversary of God! For it is written: 'Thou shalt worship
the Lord thy God and Him only shalt thou serve.'"

'Then the Adversary leaveth me, but lo! he is returned and speaketh
unto me with the voice of my familiar friends.'

LXXVIII.h (248) And Peter saith again: 'But if thou wilt not lead us into
battle, how then shall we overcome?'

Jesus answered and said: 'I will go up to Jerusalem, and whatsoever
the Lord shall put into my mouth, that will I preach against the Chief
Rulers and against their scribes, which serve the Wicked Kingdom.

'For it is there that all things which are prophesied concerning this
son of man shall be accomplished.

LIV.j (249) 'The Lord said unto Ezekiel the prophet: "The House of
Israel will not hearken unto thee, for they will not hearken unto Me.

'"Behold, I have made thy face strong against their faces, and thy
forehead strong against their foreheads. Fear them not, neither be dismayed."'

LXXVIII.i (250) And Peter saith unto Jesus: 'Pity thyself, for then will they
cast thee from the highest pinnacle of the Temple.'

Jesus answered and said: 'David prophesied in a psalm: "He shall
give His angels charge of thee. They shall bear thee up in their hands
lest thou dash thy foot against a stone."'

But when Jesus perceived that they would yet have him take arms
and reign by conquest and a mighty hand, he departed thence into a
mountain apart, and there he fasted.

CHAPTER XXVII

HOW HE FORETOLD HIS DEATH

LXXIX.e (251) And on the last day of his fast, Jesus came again unto the disciples, and beheld how a great multitude made mock of them.

And he asked: 'What meaneth this confusion?'

Then one of the multitude answered and said: 'Master, my son hath a foul spirit. And whithersoever it taketh him, it teareth him, and he foameth and gnasheth with his teeth, and pineth away.

'Therefore spake I to thy disciples that they should cast out this evil spirit, but they could not.'

And the disciples confessed: 'He speaketh the truth.'

LXXIX.e (252) And Jesus rebuked them, crying: 'O faithless generation, how long must I bear with you? Bring the boy hither!'

And he was brought, and when he beheld Jesus, straightway he was torn by the foul spirit, and fell on the ground and wallowed foaming.

And Jesus asked the father: 'How long is it ago since this came unto him?'

He answered and said: 'Of a little child. And ofttimes it hath cast him into the fire and into the water to destroy him. But if thou canst do aught, have compassion on us and help us.'

Jesus said unto him: 'Our father David testified in a psalm: "The wicked are estranged from the womb, they go astray as soon as they be born, speaking lies.

' "They are like the deaf adder that stoppeth her ear and will not listen to the wise voice of the charmer."

'Yet if thou canst believe in God's power to heal, all things are possible.'

And straightway the father of the boy cried out: 'Master, help thou mine unbelief! Yet verily I believe that thou canst do more than these.'

And Jesus cried aloud, saying: 'He that believeth on me, the same believeth not on me but on Him that sent me!'

LXXIX.e (253) And when he saw that the people came running together, he rebuked them also and sent them away.

But unto the foul spirit he said: 'Thou deaf and lying devil, I charge thee in the name of God to come out and enter no more into this child!'

And the foul spirit cried and rent him sore, but came forth, leaving him as one dead; insomuch that many who watched from afar, said: 'He is dead.'

LXXIX.e   But Jesus took him by the hand and he arose and was healed.
(*contd.*)   And when he delivered him unto his father, the people glorified the mighty power of God.

LXXIX.e   (254) Now, the disciples were amazed to see Jesus of so shining a countenance, for he had fasted three weeks at tidings of John's death, and now again one week.

LXX.j   (255) And they importuned him, saying: 'Master, eat now! Break thy fast. Wait not until the sabbath.'

But Jesus said unto them: 'I have meat to eat of which ye know not, whereby I am sustained to do the will of Him which sent me, and to finish His work speedily.'

LXXIX.e   (256) And after that he was come with the Twelve into the house where they abode, they asked him privily: 'Why could we not cast out the foul spirit even in the name of God, yet thou couldst cast it out?'

He answered and said: 'This kind cometh not forth, save after prayer and fasting.'

Then said they unto Jesus: 'Surely, thou fastest beyond reason. Thou wilt do thyself hurt.'

LXXIX.f   (257) He answered and said: 'It is written that Moses fasted forty days on Sinai, and afterward his face shone, so that he veiled it because of its brightness; likewise did Elijah fast forty days on Horeb. Yet each came thence to do great works.

'Think ye then that either of these twain suffered any hurt?

'Or think ye that I shall die because that I fast from a sabbath even unto a sabbath?

'Verily, I say unto you: my death shall be on a different wise, for I shall be pierced by the sword at Jerusalem! Yet I trust that God will raise me up on the Third Day.'

But they understood not this saying, and it troubled them exceedingly.

LXXIX.g   (258) And Jesus straitly charged them to tell no man that which he had revealed unto them concerning the manner of his death.

LXXIX.f   (259) Then departed he thence and passed through the borders of Galilee, going toward Jerusalem.

LXII.c   (260) And as they went Jesus taught his disciples, saying:

'Isaiah prophesied unto Jerusalem in the name of the Lord: "I will restore thy judges as at the first and thou shalt be called the City of Righteousness."

'And David also prophesied, saying: "Jerusalem is built as a city that is at unity with itself; and thither the tribes go up to give thanks unto the name of the Lord. For there are set thrones of judgement, the thrones of the household of David."

'Verily, I say unto you: in the Heavenly Jerusalem they that have continued faithful under temptation, the same shall be chosen to be judges and shall sit on thrones beside the Son of David to judge the tribes and to judge the Gentiles that come up thither to worship.'

LXII.c   (261) Then came the mother of James and John unto Jesus, desiring a boon of him.

And he asked her, saying: 'What wilt thou?'

She saith unto him: 'Grant that these my sons may sit, the one on thy right hand and the other on thy left in the Kingdom, when thou deliverest judgement.'

Jesus was moved with indignation, and said: 'Thou knowest not what thou askest!'

And in the presence of James and John he said unto her: 'To drink of the bitter cup that I must drink of, and to be baptized with the fiery baptism that I must be baptized with, that can I give thy sons, if they are able to receive it.

'But to sit on the right hand and on the left of the Son of David, is not mine to give. For the Father shall give it unto them for whom it is prepared.'

LXX.k   (262) And he steadfastly set his face to go toward Jerusalem. But he first must needs pass through Samaria. And he sent James and John before him to make ready.

And they entered into a village and preached repentance, and many came together to hear them or to dispute with them.

But the soldiers of the Wicked Kingdom, which were in that place, beat them with rods and cast them out.

Therefore returned they unto Jesus and asked him, saying: 'Lord, wilt thou command fire to come down from heaven and consume these soldiers, even as Elijah did unto the soldiers of Ahaziah which came against him?'

Jesus answered and said: 'Jeremiah prophesied: "The daughter of Babylon is like unto a threshing floor. Yet a little while, and the time of the harvest is come."

'Go ye to another village!'

And they went, and were received.

CHAPTER XXVIII

HOW HE PREACHED IN SAMARIA

LXX.g (263) Then cometh he to a village of Samaria which is called Sychar, nigh to the parcel of ground that Jacob gave unto his son Joseph.

Now, Jacob's well was there. And Jesus, being wearied with his journey sat thus on the well, and it was about the sixth hour.

And the disciples went away to the village to buy food from the men of the land.

Then cometh a woman to the well, and with an impudent face she saith to him: 'Friend, the well is at thy command. Let me draw water and give thee to drink.'

Now, she was an Ephraimite woman, of the daughters of the land, and Jesus perceived that she was an harlot.

He said unto her: 'Woman, suffer me rather to give thee living water, that thou mayest never thirst again.'

She said unto him: 'Art thou greater than our father Jacob, which gave us this well and himself drank thereof, and his children, and his cattle? For though this water be good, yet must I come every day hither to draw more.'

He answered: 'Go, call thy husband, and I will give you both to drink.'

She saith unto him: 'I have no husband,' thinking to entice him to lie with her, for unto that purpose was she come out to the well at noon while her husband slept.

He answered again: 'Thou hast rightly said: "I have no husband." For thou hast had five husbands: which are Enchantment, Murder, Theft, False Oaths, and Adultery, and he whom thou hast now, God's Adversary, he is not thy husband.'

CI.j (264) 'For in the house of the heavenly bodies, five are divided against two.

'The evil powers that seek to gain dominion over the five middle days of the week are ranged against the holy powers of the first day and of the sabbath; and God's Adversary is their prince.

LXX.g (265) 'Yet I say unto thee, bring hither him which is truly thy husband, that I may teach him the fear of the Lord, which is the beginning of wisdom.

'For Solomon, when he reigned over your forefathers, said: "The

LXX.g
(*contd.*)

words of a wise man's mouth are as deep waters, and the wellspring of wisdom is as a flowing brook."

'Therefore, that which I give him to drink from the words of the sages, the same shall be in him as a well of water springing up to everlasting life!'

Then was she abashed, and said: 'Sir, I perceive that thou art a prophet of God.'

And he declared unto the woman her errors, and she repented of them and wept, and he prayed God to forgive her.

Afterward, she asked him: 'Why say ye that in Jerusalem is the place where men should worship, seeing that our fathers worshipped in this mountain according to the blessing that Moses put upon it?'

Jesus answered and said: 'The priests of Samaria worship they know not what; for though they have received the Law, they know not that God will be worshipped in righteousness and truth.

'But we of Jerusalem know him whom we worship, and salvation is of the Jews.

'Do ye of Samaria therefore beware, lest the time come when ye shall worship the Lord neither here nor there.'

Then came his disciples, marvelling that he conversed with the woman, yet they durst say naught.

And she, perceiving what was in their hearts, said: 'Sirs, he told me all that ever I did, and he hath turned me away from my sins.'

Then left she her waterpot, and went in haste unto Sychar to call her husband, which presently came unto Jesus and constrained him to tarry in the house with them.

This man also gathered his neighbours together, such as were Israelites, and Jesus tarried there two days and preached repentance unto them, and many accepted his words.

LXX.i

(266) And he departed thence and as he went, he saw how certain Samaritans brought a woman by force without the gates of the city of Shechem, and the people that were gathered together took up stones in their hands.

And Jesus asked: 'Why take ye up stones against this woman?'

They answered and said: 'She hath committed an abomination unto the furtherance of her adulteries and was taken in the very act. Art thou a Jew and knowest not that Moses commanded us to stone her?'

Jesus answered: 'Nevertheless, ye will do well to shew respect unto every statute of the Law.'

And he stooped, and began to write on the dust with his finger: how that until the two witnesses, or three witnesses, should have cast their stones, the people must abstain.

And they asked saying: 'What writest thou?'

He answered: 'Read; and he that is without sin among the witnesses, let him cast the first stone!'

And the witnesses, being just men, went away softly one by one, beginning with the eldest. For they remembered the words of Solo-

LXX.i
(contd.) mon: 'Who can say: "I have made my heart clean, I am pure from my sin"?'

Then Jesus lifted himself up, and saw that none of them remained. And he asked the people: 'Where are the witnesses against this woman?'

And the woman which was accused, answered: 'They are gone away, and have not set their hands against me.'

Jesus said unto her: 'Repent and sin no more! For if thou so doest, neither will God's hand be set against thee.'

LXXXII.1 (267) Now, when a certain lawyer heard that Jesus preached unto the men of the land which were in Samaria, he said unto him:

'Master, to expound the Law to an ignorant and unclean multitude is to labour in vain. Or canst thou hope to teach them in one hour what the pious may hardly learn in a lifetime?'

Jesus answered and said: 'A certain rich young man, a scoffer from the Wicked Kingdom, desiring to try the sage Shammai, went unto him, and said: "I have no leisure to study the Law. Teach it me, I pray, while I stand upon one foot."

'And Shammai drove him thence with blows.

'But when he went unto the sage Hillel—blessed be his memory!— and asked the same thing of him, Hillel answered, and said:

' "Do not to thy neighbour what is hateful unto thee! This is all the Law, and the Prophets."

'For, verily, he that loveth his neighbour, the same likewise loveth his God.'

The lawyer, when he heard this, wishing to justify himself, said unto Jesus: 'Master, thou speakest the truth, which is known unto all: that there is One God, and none other than He.

'And it is written: "Thou shalt love the Lord thy God with all thine heart and with all thy soul and with all thy strength."

'But who is my neighbour, and how shall I know him?'

LXXXII.o (268) Jesus answered and said: 'A certain Samaritan journeyed to Jericho, and on his way he fell among thieves, which stripped him and departed, leaving him half dead.

'And he cried for help in God's name unto them that passed by.

'Now it chanced that there came down that way a priest from Jerusalem, and heard his cries but, when he knew him for a Samaritan, passed by on the other side, fearing defilement.

'Likewise a Levite came where he lay, and stood looking at him, but when he knew him for a Samaritan, and perceived that there was yet life in him, he too went his way, fearing defilement.

'But a righteous Son of Israel, when he heard the man, how he cried out for help in God's name, took compassion on him, and feared not to be defiled.

'Nay, but he dressed the man's wounds with oil and wine, and bound them up, and set him on his own beast and brought him to an inn, and took care of him.

'And on the morrow, when he departed, he gave two pence unto the

LXXXII.o host, and said: "Take care of him that fell among thieves, and what-
(*contd.*) soever thou spendest more, when I come again I will repay thee.

'"For the same is my neighbour, because that, when he was in trouble, he cried unto the One God which I also worship."'

LXXXII.o (269) And Jesus saith unto the lawyer: 'Now, which of these three thinkest thou did right? The twain that feared defilement, or the other?'

The lawyer answered: 'Assuredly he did right that shewed mercy unto his neighbour.'

Then said Jesus unto him: 'Go, and do thou likewise!'

CHAPTER XXIX

HOW HE KEPT THE FEAST OF THE DEDICATION

LXXXIV.f (270) It was at Jerusalem the Feast of the Dedication.

LXXXIV.f (271) Jesus went up to the Temple, and as he walked in Solomon's Porch his kinsmen came unto him from Bethany, saying:

'Art thou not our King? Why standest thou idle, and how long wilt thou hold us in suspense?

'When wilt thou reveal unto all which are in Jerusalem that thou art the Son of David?'

Jesus answered and said: 'The works which I do in my Father's name bear witness whether or not I be a shepherd even as David was.

'Behold, I have sheep that know my voice and will follow me into the fold, neither shall any man pluck them out of my hand,

'For I am willing to die if thereby I may guide their feet into the way of everlasting life.

'But other sheep I have which are not yet of this fold: them also must I seek out.

'Therefore, if I do not the works of the Father, trust me not; but if I do them, possess ye your souls in patience!

LXXXIV.f (272) 'Verily, I say unto you: if ye believe, in a little while ye shall see the Son of Man come in glory.

'And whosoever turneth unto him, the same shall not die.'

And among his kinsmen was Eliezer, whose father was Simeon, the ruler of the Watchers which were in Bethany.

And Eliezer said: 'Of a truth, I believe. For art thou not the Anointed One, the Prince of Peace, which is prophesied for the Last Days?'

CI.i (273) Jesus answered and said: 'Let not Israel think that I am come to bring peace on earth. I am come not to bring *shalvitah* (which is peace) on earth, but I am come to bring *shalhovitah* (which is a flaming fire), and would that it were already kindled!

'For I have a baptism of blood wherewith I must be baptized, and how straitened am I till it come upon me with the sword!

'Verily, I say unto you: he that would save his life shall lose it; and he that loseth his life for God's sake, the same shall save it!

CI.i (274) 'Neither let Israel think that I am come to divide the spoils of the Wicked Kingdom among her children.

CI.i
(contd.)

'I come not to bring *pluga* (which is a division of spoil), but I am come to bring *plugta* (which is dissension)!

'Behold, this is the evil day whereof Micah prophesied, saying: "The good man is perished out of the earth. Therefore the day of thy visitation cometh.

' "For the son dishonoureth the father, the daughter riseth against her mother, the daughter-in-law against her mother-in-law; a man's foes shall be those of his own household. Now will I wait for the God of my salvation." '

LIII.c

(275) It was told unto him by James, his brother according to the spirit:

'There was brought unto the Treasury the hire of an harlot and with it the Chief Rulers have builded a chamber of easement for the High Priest, against the Day of Atonement when he abideth in the Temple.'

Wherefore James asked him: 'Master, what sayest thou? Is it not written: "Thou shalt not bring the hire of an harlot into the House of the Lord"?'

Jesus answered and said: 'Yea, and shall a High Priest which fasteth on the Day of Atonement have need of a chamber of easement? Verily, that which was gained in filth, is spent upon a work of filth.

'Therefore did Micah preach against the Temple which was in Samaria, saying of the golden adornment that hanged there, the hire of harlots: "She gathered it from the hire of harlots, and unto such it will return again."

'And he prophesied, saying: "This evil is incurable; it is also come unto Judah." '

LXVIII.e

(276) Jesus spake this parable against such priests as were covetous:

'A certain rich man had a steward and the same was accused unto him that he had wasted his goods.

'And he called him and said: "How is it that I hear this of thee? Give an account of thy stewardship. For if these things be true, thou canst no longer be steward."

'Then the steward said within himself: "What shall I do? For my lord taketh away from me the stewardship. I cannot dig; to beg I am ashamed.

' "I am resolved what to do: that when I am put out of the stewardship I may find men to receive me into their habitations."

'So he called every one of his lord's debtors, and said unto the first: "How much owest thou my lord?"

'And he answered: "An hundred measures of oil." The steward said unto him: "Take thy bill and sit down quickly, and write fifty!"

'Then said he to another: "And how much owest thou?" He answered: "An hundred measures of wheat." And the steward said unto him: "Take thy bill and write fourscore!"

'What think ye? Did the lord commend the unjust steward because he had done wisely, when he came to call in those debts?

LXVIII.e   'Ye Sadducees, children of darkness, which are in your generation
(*contd.*)   wiser than the children of light, would ye hear my counsel?

'Then go ye with your unrighteous wealth and buy the friendship
of God's Adversary, that when your strength faileth, his angels may
receive you into everlasting habitations.'

LXVIII.f   (277) And the priests were wroth when they heard this parable,
and asked: 'Are we not priests, sons of Aaron, which Moses anointed?
Who art thou to revile us, little one?'

Jesus answered: 'When Samuel looked on Eliab, the eldest of
David's brethren, he said: "Surely, the Lord's anointed is before
Him."

'But the Lord said unto Samuel: "Take no thought for the height
of his stature: for the Lord seeth not as a man seeth. Man looketh on
the outward appearance, but the Lord looketh on the heart."

'Verily, I say unto you: that which is highly esteemed among men
is abominable unto God!'

LXV.a   (278) 'And though a man's stature be a cubit above the stature of
other men, hath he taken thought to make it so?'

CHAPTER XXX

HOW HE ADMONISHED BUNNI SON OF GORION

LXXXIII.k (279) Bunni son of Gorion, a chief ruler (which was afterward called Nakemidam), came unto Jesus by night.

And he said unto him: 'Master, I know that thou art a teacher sent from God, for no man doeth as thou hast done, except God be with him. What then shall I do to be saved?'

Jesus answered and said: 'Except a man be born again, he cannot see the Kingdom of God. Go therefore and be baptized of water and of the Spirit, and thou shalt live.'

He asked: 'How can these things be? We speak that we do know, and bear witness to that which we have seen, but how shall we believe this?

'Shall a grown man as it were enter a second time into his mother's womb and, proceeding thence, be altogether changed?'

Jesus answered: 'As the Preacher saith: "He that observeth the wind shall not sow, and he that regardeth the clouds shall not reap."

'For the wind bloweth when it listeth, and thou hearest the sound thereof, but canst not tell whence it cometh nor whither it goeth.

'And as the Preacher saith also: "Thou understandest neither the way of the Spirit, nor how the bones are formed in the womb of a woman. Even so thou understandest not the work of God which made all."

'That which is born of the flesh is flesh, that which is born of the spirit is spirit.

'Tell thou me of earthly things and I will believe thee; but when I tell thee of heavenly things, then believe thou me!'

Bunni asked: 'And if I suffer myself to be baptized, what lack I further?'

And Jesus, perceiving that he answered discreetly, said unto him: 'Thou shalt not be far from the Kingdom of Heaven while thou obeyest the Law.'

Bunni answered: 'I have obeyed it from my youth up.'

And Jesus said again: 'How sayest thou: "I have obeyed the Law," when it biddeth thee to love thy neighbour as thyself?

'For lo, many sons of Abraham, thy brethren, are clad in dung and perish for want at thy gates; but thine house is full of good things.

XXVI.g   (280) 'Solomon spake a proverb: "He that hath pity upon the poor lendeth unto the Lord, and that which he hath given shall the Lord pay him again."

'David also saith in a psalm: "He that reproacheth his neighbour shall have the reproach repaid by the Lord sevenfold into his bosom." Then shall not God of His mercy likewise repay a kindness?

'Verily, sevenfold shall He repay it: good measure, pressed down, shaken together and running over shall He give into thy bosom!

LXXXIII.1   (281) 'And knowest thou not that, having won a superfluity of riches, thou oughtest to give freely of it unto them that lack?

'Forasmuch as God freely gave of all that He created unto our forefather Adam and to his seed for ever, fearest thou not to hold back that which belongeth also unto thy brethren?

'Consider the wide mercy of God, and do thou even as He did; then shalt thou be truly rich.'

LXXXIII.1   (282) These words pleased Bunni but little, and he answered: 'It is said: "The burden of a camel should be according to his strength"; behold, the more alms I give, the more do the beggars importune me.'

Jesus said: 'If this burden be too heavy for thy back, shed thou the greater burden of thy riches and be free.

'Go thy way, sell all thou hast, and give unto the poor!'

Bunni answered and said: 'This I cannot do, being a chief ruler and the master of a great household.'

LXXXIII.1   (283) And Jesus said unto Bunni: 'Thou comest unto me secretly by night. Yet the day of the Lord's vengeance is nigh when thou must declare thy repentance openly, like as the Children of Israel repented before Moses, because of the fiery serpents.

'And as Moses raised up the brazen serpent for a standard, that whosoever looked upon it should not die, so shall God set the Son of Man in the sky, that whosoever hath sinned and believeth in God, the same shall look upon him, and not perish, but have everlasting life.'

And Bunni departed thence, being very sorrowful.

But Jesus turned unto Simon, and said to him: 'Verily, it is easier for a laden camel to go through the gate that is called the Eye of the Needle, than for a rich man to enter into the Kingdom of Heaven by the needle's eye of repentance!

'For the camel will more gladly cast the load from off his back.'

LXXXIII.1   (284) And Peter saith: 'Lo, we have forsaken all and followed thee.'

Jesus answered and said: 'He that hath forsaken houses and lands for God's sake, the same shall be repaid an hundredfold in the Kingdom of Heaven!'

CHAPTER XXXI

HOW HE REJECTED THE GRECIANS

LXXXI.a (285) Now, certain Grecians coming up from Egypt to keep the Feast of Dedication, saluted Philip, which understood their speech, and said unto him: 'Sir, we would converse with thy master Jesus.'

Wherefore Philip sought out Andrew, and together they told Jesus of the matter, and undertook to interpret unto him whatsoever the Grecians might speak.

LXXXI.c (286) And Jesus spake to the twain, saying: 'Let them come before me.'

And when the Grecians had saluted him, they said unto Jesus: 'Master, we are disciples of Philo which, for the greater glory of God, seeketh to reconcile unto the Law the wisdom of the learned Greek Plato.'

Jesus answered and said: 'No good can proceed therefrom.'

They ask him: 'Art thou then more learned than our master Philo?'

And Jesus spake a parable unto them, saying: 'No wise man putteth a piece of new cloth upon an old garment; lest the new agree not with the old, but take away from it and make a rent.

'Moreover, a good garment lasteth all the years of a man's life.

'Likewise no wise man putteth new wine into old wine skins, lest it burst them, and be spilled, and the wine skins shall perish.

'But old wine abideth in old wine skins, and groweth better with age.

'For which of you that hath drunk old wine straightway desireth new? Will he not say: "The old is better"?'

LXXXI.e (287) And the Grecians asked Jesus again: 'But shall God never bestow wisdom on a man that is an heathen, such as Plato was? Is it not written that Hiram King of Tyre conversed on high things with Solomon the Wise, and equalled him in understanding?'

LXXXI.g (288) Jesus answered and said: 'Jerusalem is the gate to salvation, whereby the Appointed Son of David shall lead in the chosen ones.

'As David saith in a psalm: "Lift up your heads, O ye gates, and be ye lift up, ye everlasting doors, for the King of Glory shall come in!"

'And Micah likewise prophesied, saying: "He is come unto the gate of My people, even unto Jerusalem."

'Verily, I say unto you: he that seeketh to enter into this Kingdom not by the gate of the sheepfold, but climbing up some other way, the same is a thief and a robber!'

LXXXI.g   And they asked Jesus: 'Wherefore sayest thou this?'
(contd.)   He answered: 'Ezekiel prophesied in the name of the Lord, saying:
"I shall set up one shepherd, even My servant David, over My flock,
even the House of Israel; and he shall feed them, and they shall be no
more a prey to the heathen."

'How then shall David feed the flock, except it be with the Law of
God, which is published in Jerusalem? Shall he feed them with the
vanities of Egypt?

'Go to! For the shepherd of the sheep entereth in by the gate, and
the porter openeth unto him. He calleth his sheep by name and they
know his voice, and he leadeth them out to water and to pasture.

'But a stranger will they not follow, for they know not his voice.'
They said: 'With our master Philo we have drunk deep waters.'

Jesus answered: 'Well said Ezekiel the prophet: "Doth it seem a
small thing to you to have drunk deep waters, but ye must foul the
residue with your feet?"'

LXXXI.g   (289) And there was a division among the Grecians because of
these words. Some said: 'He hath reasoned well,' but the disciples of
Philo: 'He is mad.'

And Jesus arose, and left them, and he said unto the Twelve: 'Fear
not, little flock; if ye hearken unto the voice of the Shepherd of shepherds, it will please Him to lead you unto His Kingdom.

'For David testified in a psalm: "The Lord is my shepherd, I shall
not want. He maketh me to lie down in green pastures, He leadeth me
beside the still waters. He restoreth my soul."'

XL.h   (290) There is at Jerusalem by the sheep-market a pool called
Bethesda (which is the Pool of Mercy), having five porches.

(For this is a parable of God's mercy towards the sheep of His
hand; it lieth as a pool of healing amid the five books of the Law.)

In this place were gathered together a great multitude of impotent
folk, the blind, the lame, and the withered, awaiting a troubling of the
water.

For at a certain season an angel went down into the pool and
troubled it; then whosoever first entered the water trusted to be healed
of his infirmity.

And Jesus finding there a man which was crippled of both his legs,
asked: 'How long hast thou lain here?'

He answered: 'For a great while, Master. Behold, I have no fellow
to put me into the pool when it is troubled, and while I drag myself
thither, another forestalleth me.'

Jesus said: 'It is written that Israel came to the waters of Zered, but
was not suffered to wet her feet therein until all that was evil in her
had perished.

'Therefore our fathers waited patiently for eight-and-thirty years,
until at the last they were freed of their former evil and passed
through and entered into the kingdom of their desire.'

The man answered: 'So be it with me!'

And Jesus, when he heard these words, prayed to God and laid his

XL.h
(contd.)

hands upon the man, and healed him, so that he stood upon his feet and walked.

And Jesus said: 'Go now, and make a thank-offering in the Temple.'

But meeting him there after a little while, he said: 'Behold, thou art made whole; sin no more lest a worse thing come upon thee!'

XL.h

(291) Also among them that waited in Bethesda was a blind man. And his fellows, which brought him there, came unto Jesus and besought him urgently, saying: 'Lord, pray that our fellow may be healed!'

He answered: 'According to your faith be it unto him.'

And they call the blind man, saying: 'Be of good comfort, rise; he calleth thee!'

Then the blind man cast away the garment in which he was wrapped, and arose and came unto Jesus.

And Jesus said: 'What wilt thou of me?'

He answered: 'That through thee I may receive my sight of God.'

Then Jesus took the blind man by the hand and led him out from the city, to a place apart where he spat upon the ground and made clay of the spittle.

And, having anointed the blind man's eyes therewith, he prayed to God in silence and afterwards asked him whether he saw aught.

And he looked up, and said: 'I see men as trees walking.'

Then Jesus said: 'Go, wash in the Pool of Siloam and say no word to any man as thou goest, but return to me again.'

He went his way therefore, and washed, and returned seeing clearly. And he praised Jesus for what he had done.

But Jesus said: 'Give God the praise, not me which am a sinner. If any man worship God and do His will, to him will He hearken.'

CHAPTER XXXII

HOW HE PREACHED BEYOND JORDAN

LXXXIV.f (292) Now, it came to pass, when the Feast was ended, that Jesus said unto his disciples: 'Let us depart hence and go across Jordan.'

They ask him: 'Master, goest thou thither again where of late the Herodians sought to take thee?'

He said: 'This commandment received I of the Father.'

They said again: 'Nay, Master, they will kill both thee and us.'

LXIX.c (293) Jesus answered: 'Not by calling me "Master, master!" will ye enter the Kingdom of Heaven; but only by doing His will.'

LXXXIV.f (294) Then said Thomas, which was called The Twin, unto his fellows: 'Brethren, let us go, that we may die with him.'

LXXXVII.f (295) Jesus therefore went again beyond Jordan, and laboured much. And the multitude came together unto him, so that he could not so much as eat bread.

LXX.j (296) And when the disciples said unto Jesus: 'Master, there is no haste. Rest awhile, and take thy ease,' he answered:

'Say not: "There are yet four months remaining before we shall have need to put in the sickle,"

'But lift up your eyes and look on the fields, for they are white already to harvest.

'The reward of him that reapeth now shall be that he gathereth fruit to everlasting life.

'Herein is that saying true: "One soweth and another reapeth." For Moses and the prophets laboured to sow, and we are entered late into their labours.

'Howbeit, in the Kingdom of God the sower and the reaper shall rejoice together.'

XXI.g (297) 'And see that ye labour abundantly. For it is written in the Book of Ahikar: "The hand that laboureth not shall be cut off at the shoulder, and the eye in which there is no vision, the raven shall pluck it out." '

LXXVII.f (298) And presently it came to pass that Herod Antipas, the tetrarch of Galilee, himself heard of Jesus, for his fame was spread abroad.

And he said to those of his household: 'John I have beheaded. But who is this Jesus whereof I hear such things? He seemeth to be his fellow in sedition.'

Therefore he now sought to apprehend Jesus.

LXXXV.c   (299) And a certain scribe said unto Jesus: 'Master, I will follow thee whithersoever thou goest.'

Jesus answered and said unto him: 'Foxes have holes, and birds of the air have nests, but this son of man hath not where to lay his head.'

LXXXVI.b   (300) And Jesus spake a parable: 'A prudent man intending to build a great house sitteth down first and counteth the cost, whether he have sufficient to finish it throughout.

'As Solomon saith: "Prepare thy work without in a field, and gather together all things fit for building, and then build thine house."

'And it is written that Solomon did even as he counselled. For he raised a levy out of Israel, thirty thousand men to prepare great stones and timber, and to lay them ready; and when all the timber was shaped and all the stones hewn, Solomon built the House of the Lord, and after seven years it was finished throughout.

'But Herod the Wicked counted not the cost, and that which he began six and forty years ago remaineth unfinished unto this day.

'Likewise will a prudent king not rashly make war on his neighbour. He sitteth down first, and counteth whether he be able with his ten thousand men to meet him that cometh against him with twenty thousand.

'And if he be not able, then while the other is yet a great way off, he sendeth an ambassage and desireth conditions of peace.

'Likewise, I say unto you: if a man seek to follow me, let him consider first whether he can endure to the end: for he must forsake all that he hath, and not turn back!'

LXXXV.c   (301) And another said unto Jesus: 'Suffer me first to bury my father, for he serveth the Wicked Kingdom and desireth not that I go with thee.'

Jesus answered: 'Leave the dead to the burier of the dead, and call thou no man father that hath denied Him which is in Heaven; for He alone is thy Father.

'Verily, he that hath forsaken an evil household for God's sake, the same shall inherit everlasting life.'

LXXXV.d   (302) And yet another, which was an husbandman, said unto Jesus in the time of gleaning: 'I will bid farewell unto them that are in my house and then will I follow thee until the time of ploughing be come again.'

Jesus answered and said: 'It is written of Elisha that when he was called to be a prophet of God, he said unto Elijah: "Suffer me first, I pray thee, to kiss my father and mother." Nor did Elijah deny him.

'But afterward he burned both his plough and his goad, and upon them he sacrificed a yoke of oxen unto the Lord; then ran he and followed after Elijah, and turned not back again.

'Verily, I say unto you: no man which hath put an hand to his plough to burn it, and turneth again to till the field, is fit for the Kingdom of Heaven!

CI.j   (303) 'But whosoever will follow with me now in the preaching of

CI.j
(contd.) the Kingdom, let him accept the cross upon his brow and deny himself, and take up his burden, and the burdens of his brethren.

'And let him be ashamed neither of poverty nor of much preaching.

'For whosoever shall be ashamed in this adulterous and sinful generation, of him also shall the Son of Man be ashamed, when he cometh in the glory of the Father.'

CHAPTER XXXIII

HOW HE COULD NOT RAISE ELIEZER

LXXXVII.f (304) And it came to pass, while Jesus was preaching and baptizing beyond Jordan, that Eliezer fell sick, the son of Simeon the Chaste which was ruler of the Watchers at Bethany.

Now, Bethany is nigh unto Jerusalem, about fifteen furlongs.

And Mary and Martha, his sisters, sent unto Jesus, saying: 'Lord, behold, he whom thou lovest is sick. Come thou, and lay thy hands upon him.'

But Jesus supposed that they feared for his life, because of the Herodians, and that they made this excuse, as wishing to draw him back from beyond Jordan.

He therefore sent unto them, saying: 'This sickness is not unto death. Let the saints of his household lay their hands upon him, that by their faith he may be made whole.'

And he abode still two days in the same place where he was.

Then sent they again unto him, saying: 'Come in haste; he whom thou lovest lieth as if dead!'

LXXXVII.f (305) Then saith Jesus unto his disciples: 'Our brother Eliezer sleepeth, yet will I go, if haply I may awake him.'

They answered and said: 'Master, if he sleep, he shall do well.'

And even as they spake came yet another from the house of the ruler, which said unto his fellow: 'Trouble thou not the Master; for Eliezer is dead.'

And the disciples mourned together with the messengers. But Jesus said: 'Why mourn ye and why make ye such ado? Surely he is not dead but sleepeth?'

Therefore the messengers laughed him to scorn.

LXXXVII.f (306) Then said Jesus unto the Twelve: 'I rejoice that we tarried not in Bethany (as ye would have had me do) lest they, by their unbelief, should have made you also stumble. Nevertheless, let us go thither unto him.'

And he sent the two messengers before his face, saying: 'He cometh.'

And when he drew nigh unto Bethany, Eliezer had lain in the grave four days.

LXXXVII.f (307) Now, Martha and Mary were in the house, where many came to comfort them concerning their brother.

LXXXVII.f And they which came reproached Jesus, saying: 'Why hastened he
(*contd.*)   not when he was first called? Could not he, which opened the eyes of
the blind man of Bethesda, have caused that thy brother should not
have died?'

Wherefore, when the two messengers returned, saying: 'He cometh,'
Martha went out to meet Jesus; but Mary sat still in the house.

And Martha said unto him: 'Lord, if thou hadst but been here, my
brother had not died.'

Jesus answered her: 'Said I not unto him that if he would but
believe he should see the Glory of God?'

And Martha said: 'Yea, lord, and I trust that even now whatsoever
thou askest of God, He will give it thee.'

Jesus saith: 'The Lord giveth resurrection and life. He that believeth in Him, the same shall live, though he were already dead.
Believest thou this?'

She answered him: 'Yea, lord.'

And Jesus saith: 'Send now privily for thy sister Mary, and come ye
both to shew me where ye have laid him.'

And Martha sent for her.

LXXXVII.f (308) Then they that were with Mary in the house, when they saw
how she rose up hastily and went out, followed her, saying: 'She goeth
unto the grave to weep there.'

LXXXVII.f (309) And Mary, coming where Jesus was, saw him and fell at his
feet.

She said likewise: 'Lord, if thou hadst but been here, my brother
had not died.'

When Jesus therefore saw her weeping, and them also weeping
which came with her, he groaned within himself and was troubled,
and he asked: 'Where have ye laid him?'

They answered: 'Lord, come and see!'

Jesus wept.

Then said they: 'Behold, how he loved him! Why therefore came he
not in haste when we sent for him?'

Jesus, yet weeping, cometh unto the grave, which was a cave, and a
stone laid upon it.

And he said: 'Take ye away the stone!'

But Mary said unto him: 'Lord, by this time he stinketh, for now is
the fourth day. Why camest thou not before this?'

LXXXVII.f (310) Then rolled they away the stone from the place where the
dead was laid. And Jesus lifted up his eyes unto heaven, and prayed:
'Lord, if it be possible, restore Thou my brother Eliezer! And praised
be Thy name, that Thou hast sent them which stand by, that by their
faith he may be raised!'

And when he had thus spoken, he cried with a loud voice: 'Eliezer,
come forth in the name of the Living God!'

Yet Eliezer stirred not.

Then said Jesus plainly unto them: 'He is dead. Yet shall he rise
again in the resurrection of the dead.'

LXXXVII.f Mary answered, and said unto him: 'I know that he will rise again
(*contd.*) on the Last Day. But why didst thou deceive both him and us, declaring that he should never taste of death?'

Jesus saith: 'Said I not unto all of you that if ye would but believe, ye should behold the Glory of God?

'But the faith of our brother Eliezer failed him, neither could any of you restore it, nor heal him while he yet lived.'

Then was Mary wroth and would believe no more on Jesus; neither did her brethren believe on him.

CHAPTER XXXIV

HOW HE RODE INTO JERUSALEM

LXXXIX.f (311) And the Passover was nigh at hand, and many Herodians of the country went up to Jerusalem before the Feast, to purify themselves.

Then sought they for Jesus, and spake among themselves as they stood in the Temple: 'What think ye, that he will not come to the Feast?'

XL.h (312) As Jesus went out from Jericho with his disciples, being in the midst of a great throng that went toward Jerusalem, one Bartimaeus (which is the Son of Uncleanness) sat begging by the highway, and he was blind from birth.

The same, when he heard that Jesus of Nazara was passing by, began to cry out for alms, saying: 'Have mercy upon me, Jesus! Have mercy upon me, thou anointed Son of David!'

And Jesus, giving him alms, charged him to hold his peace. But he cried the more: 'Thou anointed Son of David, blessed be thou!'

The disciples ask Jesus of the same Bartimaeus: 'Master, which hath sinned, this man or his parents, that he should be blind?'

Jesus answered: 'Neither he nor his parents, but this is done that the works of God might be manifested in him.

'For God of His compassion hath given him inward sight.'

XI.g (313) And he came unto Bethany and entered into the home of Simeon the Chaste. He said: 'Peace be to this house!' and offered no reproaches either unto his kinsmen or unto Mary his wife.

As he sat at meat with Simeon and his other kinsmen, Mary stood behind him and ministered unto him, weeping.

On a sudden she cried out and came and fell at his feet, and began to wet them with tears and wipe them with the hairs of her head, and kissed them.

And Simeon spake within himself, saying: 'If this man were indeed a prophet he would know how greatly she hath trespassed against him.'

Then Jesus said unto Simeon: 'I have somewhat to say unto thee.' And Simeon answered: 'Say on!'

He said again: 'There was a certain creditor which had two debtors: the one owing five hundred pence and the other fifty.

'And when they had nothing to pay, he frankly forgave them both. Tell me therefore which of them will love him the most?'

XI.g
(contd.) Simeon answered and said: 'I suppose, he to whom he forgave most.'

And Jesus said: 'Thou hast rightly judged. Thou gavedst me no kiss when I entered, nor weepedst upon my neck; but Mary hath both kissed my feet and washed them with her tears since the time I came in.

'Wherefore I say: her trespasses against me which are many, are forgiven, for she loved me much. Thy trespasses, which are few, are likewise forgiven, but I see that thou lovest me less.'

XI.h (314) Now, Martha the sister of Mary also ministered unto the company.

And when she saw that Mary sat at Jesus's feet and heard his words and did naught, she came unto him, saying:

'Behold, I am cumbered with much serving. Dost thou not care, Master, that my sister hath left me to serve alone? Bid her therefore that she help me.'

Jesus answered and said: 'Martha, Martha, thou art careful and troubled about many things. But one thing is needful, which is repentance.

'Mary hath chosen that good part which shall not be taken away from her. For seven devils entered into her, but now are they come forth.'

LXXXIX.g (315) And on the morrow, coming out of Bethany, they drew nigh unto Bethphage, which standeth upon the Mount of Olives, a Sabbath day's journey from Jerusalem.

And Jesus sendeth forth two of his disciples, and saith unto them:

'Go into the village over against you, and when ye be entered into it, ye shall find tied unto a vine an ass's colt, whereon never man sat: loose him, and bring him unto me.

'And if any man say unto you: "Why do ye this?", say ye that your master hath need of him, and straightway he will send him hither.'

Wherefore they went their way, and found the colt tied unto a vine at a place nigh unto Bethphage where two ways met.

And they loosed him, and answered the man which stood by even as Jesus had commanded.

As our forefather Jacob testified: 'The sceptre shall not depart from Judah, nor a law-giver from between his feet until Shiloh come, and unto him shall the gathering of the people be.

'Binding his foal unto the vine and his ass's colt unto the choice vine, he washed his garments in wine and his clothes in the blood of the grape.'

LXXXIX.g (316) Therefore, when they brought the colt unto Jesus, he washed his garments in wine.

XLIV.d (317) Then he called the Twelve unto him and said: 'Behold, what I have told you in darkness, that speak ye now in light; what ye whispered in the ear, that shout ye now from the housetops!'

LXXXIX.h (318) And with one accord they heaped their garments upon the colt and he sat upon them, and they shouted and cried: 'Hail, Jesus, King of Israel!'

And others spread their garments before him, and cut down branches of trees and strawed them in his path, crying: 'Praise be to the Anointed One, the Son of David; King of Israel!

'As Zechariah prophesied: "Rejoice greatly, O daughter of Zion, shout, O daughter of Jerusalem! Behold, thy King cometh unto thee. He is just and bringeth salvation, lowly and riding upon an ass and upon a colt, the foal of an ass.

'And as Isaiah saith: "Speak ye to the daughter of Zion: 'Behold, thy salvation cometh; behold, his reward is with him, and his recompense before him!' "

'And: "Wherefore art thou red in thine apparel, and thy garments like unto him that treadeth in the wine vat?

' "Behold, I have trodden the wine-press alone! For the day of vengeance is in my heart and the year of my redeemed is come.

' "I looked, and there was none to help me, I wondered that there was none to uphold. Therefore mine own arm brought salvation unto me, and my fury upheld me.

' "I will tread down the people in my anger!" '

And they that went before, and they that followed, cried: 'Hosha-na!' (which is, Save now!) and: 'Blessed be he that cometh in the name of the Lord!' and: 'Glory be to God in the highest!'

And after that they had entered into the city, they continued to cry: 'Hosha-na!'

For so Jeremiah prophesied: 'In the time of their trouble they will say: "Arise, and save us!" And also: "Save me, and I shall be saved. Thou art my hope in the Day of Trouble!" '

LXXXIX.h (319) Wherefore, when he was come into Jerusalem, all the city was moved, asking: 'Who is this?'

And the multitude answered: 'This is Jesus, the prophet of Galilee which is King over Israel. He hath come to overthrow his enemies and trample upon them in his anger!'

And the High Priest sent an officer which said unto Jesus: 'Sir, rebuke thy disciples!'

He answered him: 'How can I rebuke them? Did not Habakkuk prophesy against thy master's house?

'For he said: "Thou hast consulted shame to thy house by cutting off many people, and hast sinned against thy soul. Yea, the stone shall cry out of the wall against thee, and the beam from the socket shall cry in answer!" '

CHAPTER XXXV

HOW HE PURGED THE TEMPLE

LXXXIX.h (320) Now, the High Priest was sore displeased when he heard how they that followed Jesus continued to cry: 'Praise to the Son of David!', and sent again unto him, saying:

'Hearest thou not what these say, being ignorant children?'

Jesus answered: 'Yea, and have ye not read what David saith in a psalm: "Out of the mouths of babes and sucklings hast Thou ordained strength, that Thou mightest put to silence the enemy and the vengeful man"?'

XC.i (321) And Jesus lighted from his ass, and took off his shoes at the outer gate of the Temple.

And it came to pass, when he entered into the porch over against the Treasury, that he saw the money changers sitting at their tables, and them that sold doves.

And he rebuked them, saying: 'This is the Holy Hill of Zion, whereof David spake: "O send out Thy light and Thy truth. Let them bring me unto Thy Holy Hill!"

'Wherefore, take these things hence! Make not my Father's house an house of merchandise! As Zechariah saith: "In that day shall be no more the huckster in the house of the Lord."'

And when at first they would not obey him, he began to fold up the tables of the money changers, so that the money was spilt; and the seats of them that sold doves he folded up also, and compelled them to depart.

For a fiery light shone from his eyes, and majesty from his countenance, whereby they were overcome with awe.

Neither would he suffer the porters of the Temple to bear unclean vessels through the courts thereof.

These he rebuked likewise, saying: 'Zechariah prophesied: "The vessels in the Lord's House shall be like unto the lavers before His altar. Yea, every pot in Jerusalem and in Judah shall be holiness unto the Lord!"

'See ye not that the pots which ye bear are in shape like unto the abomination of the heathen?'

Yet the Levite watchmen laid not hold on Jesus, for the multitude were attentive to hear his words.

And when they asked him: 'Hast thou no shame, that thou comest

XC.i with shouts and bringest confusion into this holy place, forbidding
(contd.) these men to minister unto the needs of the people?',

He answered and said: 'David spake unto the Lord: "For Thy sake
have I borne reproach; shame hath covered my face. For the zeal of
Thine house hath eaten me up." '

XCII.a (322) Jesus sat over against the Treasury and beheld how the
people cast money into the chest, and how many that were rich gave
much.

And there came a certain poor widow which cast in two mites.

And he said unto his disciples: 'Verily, I say unto you, this poor
widow hath done more than all they which have cast into the treasury!

'For it is written: "Every man shall give according to his ability,"
yet none but she hath obeyed the Law.

'Behold, they cast in of their abundance, but she of her want hath
cast in all that she had, even her own life.'

XCIII.d (323) And the Chief Rulers and their scribes, together with the
Herodians, when they knew that the people which followed Jesus and
hailed him King were unarmed, sought to know whether it were in
his mind to make insurrection by force.

If he plotted aught, then would they seek to lay hands upon him
and deliver him unto the power of Pontius Pilate which was Governor
of Judaea; but secretly, for they feared the people.

Therefore sent they forth certain of their number, feigning themselves to be seekers after knowledge, that they might lead Jesus to
disclose the innermost thoughts of his heart.

XCIII.d (324) These men asked him, saying: 'Master, we know that thou
teachest the way of God in all truth, and as God Himself is no re-
specter of persons, so thou also fearest none but God, neither carest for
any man unless he be set over thee by the will of God.

'Tell us therefore: is it lawful to give tribute unto the Romans in
token of their lordship over us?'

Jesus answered and said: 'If ye know that I teach the way of God in
truth, why try ye me? Shew me a penny of him that exacteth this
tribute.'

Then one of the Herodians drew a penny from his bosom and
shewed it unto Jesus, but he touched it not.

And Jesus asked: 'Whose is this graven image and what meaneth
the superscription?'

The Herodian answered: 'It is the image of Caesar, and the superscription nameth him High Priest aand son of the most holy God
Augustus.'

Jesus asketh: 'Bringest thou such money into the Temple of the
One God? And wouldst thou indeed pay it into His treasury? And
askest thou me whether it be right to bow down unto him whose
graven image thou shewest me?'

XCI.h (325) And he said unto them all: 'Do not your own hearts inform
you of what is right?

XCIII.e   (326) 'Render not unto Caesar that which is God's, nor unto God that which is Caesar's!'

These words spake Jesus as he watched over against the Treasury, and no man durst lay hands upon him.

XCI.e   (327) Then he asked them, saying: 'Know ye not that a great day is come unto Israel? Wherefore seek ye to contemn it?

'As Solomon saith: "Dost thou know the balancings of the clouds, the wondrous works of Him which is perfect in knowledge: how it is that thy garments grow hot when He quieteth the earth by the south wind?

' "Men see not the Glory of God which is in the clouds, when the wind passeth and cleanseth them of their rain. But God careth not for any that are wise in their own conceits."

'How is it that, when the sky is red at even, ye say: "It will be fair weather," and when the sky is red and lowering in the morning, ye say: "It will be foul"?

'Are ye blind in part, that ye read the face of the sky, but not the signs of the times?

'Repent then speedily, for by many signs it is clearly discerned that the Day of the Lord is at hand, whose Glory shineth in the clouds!'

XCIV.j   (328) Then said certain of the Pharisees and other devout people of Jerusalem: 'Is not this he whom the Herodians seek to kill? But lo, he speaketh boldly, and they do naught against him.

'Know the Chief Rulers then that he is verily the Anointed One, and therefore hold their hands?'

But others said: 'Why think ye that this man is the Anointed One? He is indeed of the seed of David, but we know whence he cometh: he cometh of Bethlehem Nazara.

'Shall not the Anointed come of Bethlehem Ephratah, whence David was?'

Then said the first: 'He hath wrought great wonders both in Galilee and in Judaea.'

But the others answered: 'When the Anointed One cometh, will he not work greater?'

Then was there a division among the Pharisees and other devout people of Jerusalem because of him.

Some said: 'This is verily the King, the Righteous One,' and others: 'Nay, but he deceiveth the people.'

But none durst openly acknowledge him to be King, for all waited for a sure proof that God had appointed him to redeem Israel.

CHAPTER XXXVI

HOW HE DISPUTED WITH THE CHIEF PRIESTS

XCI.f (329) But the Chief Rulers, seeing that the people were gathered thick together about Jesus, said unto him: 'What sign shewest thou, then, that we may see and believe that God is with thee?'

Jesus sighed deeply in his spirit, and said: 'Why doth this generation seek after a sign? What sign shall be given them but a call to repentance, as when the prophet Jonah was sent unto the men of Nineveh?

'Yet at the Day of Judgement the men of Nineveh shall rise up in witness against this wicked and adulterous generation, for they hearkened to a call, but ye stop your ears.

'Likewise at the Day of Judgement the Queen of the South shall rise up in witness against you, for she came here from afar to learn wisdom of Solomon, but ye stop your ears to Wisdom when she crieth aloud in your streets.

'As Solomon himself prophesied, saying: "I, Wisdom, called and ye refused; I stretched out mine hand and no man regarded.

' "Ye have set at naught all my counsel, and would have none of my reproof."

XV.e (330) 'Search the Scriptures therefore, for in them ye shall find the way of everlasting life.'

XCI.g (331) Then said they: 'The Queen of Sheba we know, but of Jonah we know naught.'

Jesus answered and said: 'If ye will not read the prophets, how then can ye learn?

'For Jonah lay three nights and three days in the whale's belly for a token that the righteous shall rise again on the third day after the destruction of the world.'

XC.j (332) Howbeit, Jesus plaited a scourge of small cords, and said unto the Chief Rulers: 'Ye have asked for a sign, therefore it shall be given unto you.

'For this scourge is the sign whereof the prophet Isaiah spake, saying:

' "Wherefore hear the word of the Lord, ye scornful men that rule the people which is in Jerusalem!

' "Ye have said: 'We have made a covenant with death, and agreed with hell: when the overflowing scourge shall pass through, it shall

XC.j
(*contd.*)

not come nigh unto us; for we have made lies our refuge, and under falsehood have we hid ourselves.'

' "But the hail shall sweep away your refuge of lies, and the waters shall overflow your hiding places."

'And Isaiah prophesied also in the name of the Lord: "Mine house shall be called an house of prayer for all people. But ye pollute it with your extortions."

'Jeremiah verily warned your fathers: "Trust ye not in lying words, saying: 'The Temple of the Lord, the Temple of the Lord, the Temple of the Lord.' Ye trust in lying words that cannot profit. Is this house, which is called by My name, become a den of thieves in your eyes?

' "Go ye unto My house which was in Shiloh, where I set My name at the first, and see what I did unto it for the wickedness of My people Israel.

' "And now, because ye have done these evil works, therefore will I do unto this house even as I have done unto Shiloh!" '

XC.j

(333) The Chief Rulers said unto Jesus: 'God forbid! For if it please Him to destroy this Temple, how then shall Israel keep the Law?'

Jesus answered: 'Destroy this Temple, and on the Third Day He will raise it up again in a twinkling of an eye, a glorious work, not built with hands.'

But they laughed him to scorn, saying: 'Forty and six years hath this Temple been a-building, and sayest thou that it will be raised again in three days?'

For they were Sadducees, which believe not in the resurrection.

XCVI.c

(334) And Jesus said unto the Chief Rulers: 'Isaiah made a song concerning this vineyard:

' "My beloved hath a vineyard in a very fruitful hill (which is the House of Israel). And he fenced it, and gathered out the stones thereof, and planted it with the choicest vines, and built a tower in the midst of it."

'As it is written in the Song of Songs: "Solomon had a vineyard at Baal-hamon. He let out the vineyard unto husbandmen. Every one for the fruit thereof was to bring a thousand pieces of silver.

' "My vineyard, which is mine, is before me. Thou, O Solomon, must have a thousand, and the husbandmen must have two hundred for themselves."

'Hearken now unto a new parable concerning this same vineyard, which was let out to husbandmen.

'Behold, when the season of the fruit drew nigh, the lord of the vineyard sent a servant unto the husbandmen, and required from each of them the thousand pieces of silver.

'But the husbandmen took the servant, and beat him with clubs and sent him away empty-handed.

'Then the lord sent another servant, more honourable than the first, to require from them the sum which had been agreed.

'At him they cast stones and wounded him in the head, and sent him away shamefully handled.

XCVI.c   'But having yet one son, his well-beloved, he sent him also last unto
(*contd*.)   them, saying: "They will reverence my son."

'But the wicked husbandmen whispered among themselves: "Here
cometh the heir! What say ye? Let us kill him, and the heritage shall
fall unto us."

'Now, therefore, if the Lord of the vineyard, which overheareth all,
take heed to their whisperings, what will He do unto those wicked
husbandmen?

'Hath He not power to destroy them with the breath of His mouth,
and let out His vineyard unto others?'

LXXXIX.i (335) And the Chief Rulers departed thence, but Jesus might not
come nigh unto the Sanctuary, for the Levite watchmen prevented
him, and he bade them which followed him to use no violence.

Therefore he looked around upon all things and waited in patience.

LXXXIX.i (336) But the scribes of the Sadducees and the Herodians began to
urge him vehemently, and to provoke him to speak of many things,
laying wait for him and seeking to catch something out of his mouth,
that they might accuse him.

LXXXIX.i (337) Now the eventide was come, and Jesus prayed with all that
were there. Afterward he went out unto Bethany with his disciples.

CHAPTER XXXVII

HOW HE CONFOUNDED THE CAPTAIN OF THE TEMPLE

XCIV.d (338) Jesus went up into the Mount of Olives, and tarried there all night; but early in the morning he came again into the Temple and the people thronged unto him.

And he sat down and taught them, and they marvelled at his teaching.

Then said some of them that heard him: 'Of a truth, this is that prophet of which Moses spake!'

And others said: 'This is the Anointed King which shall redeem Israel!'

Wherefore the Chief Rulers, when they heard how the people murmured such things, bade the Captain of the Temple lead forth officers to take him.

XCIV.d (339) And Jesus said unto the multitude: 'He that heareth my word and believeth in Him that sent me and straightway repenteth, the same shall not be condemned, but be passed from death into life.

XXVI.d (340) 'Marvel not when I say: The hour is at hand when the dead shall hear the voice of the Son of Man and come forth from their tombs: they that have done righteousness into the Kingdom of Heaven, they that have done evil into the torments of hell.

'For Isaiah prophesied: "Thy dead shall live and arise with their dead bodies.

' "Come, my people, enter into thy chambers and shut the door behind thee, hide thyself until His indignation be overpast.

' "For behold, the Lord cometh out of His place to punish the inhabitants of the earth for their iniquity."

'And He shall give the Son of Man authority to execute judgement in His name, even as Daniel saith.

CI.k (341) 'Verily, I say unto you, that there be some which stand here that shall not taste of death, till they have seen the Kingdom of Heaven come with power!'

XCIV.d (342) And, as he spake these words, the Captain of the Temple, coming unto Jesus with his officers, saw that the people hearkened unto him with awe.

Therefore they durst not take him, but asked: 'Why boastest thou thyself somewhat, being a poor man of Galilee, neither a priest nor a lawyer?'

XCIV.d   Jesus answered and said: 'It is written: "Ye shall not respect persons
(contd.) in judgement; but ye shall hearken unto the small as well as the
great." '

XCV.c   (343) The Captain saith unto him: 'How prophesiest thou to these
men, that they shall not see death if they hearken unto thee?

'Art thou then greater than our Father Abraham which is dead, and
the prophets which are dead?'

Jesus answered and said: 'They died, but live yet. Beware, that ye
Sadducees die not in your sins, and perish everlastingly!

'If ye be true sons of Abraham, then do the works of Abraham, and
not the works of the father of lies, which was a murderer from the
beginning.

LXIX.d   (344) 'There shall be weeping and gnashing of teeth when ye shall
see Abraham, and Isaac, and Jacob, and all the prophets in the Kingdom of God, and yourselves thrust out.

'For Isaiah prophesied in the name of the Lord: "Fear not, Israel, I
am with thee! I will bring thy seed from the east, (yea, even from the
land of Sinim) and gather thee from the far west.

' "I will say to the north: 'Give up,' and to the south: 'Keep not
back: bring my sons from far and my daughters from the end of the
earth!' "

'Then shall the scattered seed of Israel come from the east, the west,
the north, and the south, and shall sit down in the Kingdom of God.

'And behold, there are last which shall be first, and first which shall
be last.'

XCV.e   (345) Then said the Captain: 'Art thou indeed an honourable
person, filled with righteousness?'

He answered: 'If I honour myself, my honour is nothing; if I bear
witness to my own righteousness, my witness is not true.'

XCIV.e   (346) Then said the Captain of the Temple: 'By what authority
sayest and doest thou these things? And who gave thee leave?'

Jesus answered and said unto him, and unto them that were with
him: 'I will also ask one question of you and when ye have answered
it, then will I tell you by what authority I say and do these things.'

They said: 'Say on!'

Jesus asked: 'The baptism with which John baptized me, and my
anointing at his hands, were they of heaven, or were they of men?'

And they reasoned within themselves, saying: 'If we say "of
heaven," he will answer: "Why, then, do ye not acknowledge me
King?" But if we say "of men," the people will be moved to anger,
for they account John a prophet indeed.'

Wherefore they answered him, saying: 'We cannot tell thee.'

Jesus asked again: 'If, then, ye will not answer me, why should I
answer you?'

They said: 'Because that we ask thee these things in the name of
the Chief Rulers!'

XCIV.e (347) Then cried Jesus, saying: 'Ye know both who I am and whence I come! But I do naught of my own authority, nor seek I mine own glory; but am sent of God, and seek God's glory.

'Whosoever obeyeth God's will, the same shall know within his heart whether these things which I say proceed from God or from mine own vain imaginings.

XV.f (348) 'And if ye believe Moses, which ye know and acknowledge, ye are accused by him that ye reject the prophets.

'For Moses spake in the name of the Lord: "I will raise them up a prophet from among their brethren, like unto thee and will put My words in his mouth; and he shall speak unto them all that I shall command him.

' "And it shall come to pass that whosoever will not hearken unto My words which he shall speak in My name, I will require it of him."

XCIV.f (349) 'Beware therefore: he that rejecteth me and receiveth not my words, the same shall be judged of Him that sent me; and the words that I speak shall testify against him in the Last Day!

XCIV.f (350) 'Ye sons of Levi, why go ye about to kill me? Did not Moses give you the Law, and appoint you priests of God to serve Him according to the Law? Are ye wroth, then, that I preach the observance of the Law?'

They answered: 'Thou art beside thyself. Who goeth about to kill thee?'

Jesus said unto them: 'Yet a little while am I with you, and then I go hence unto my Father.

'And ye shall seek to lay hands on me, but shall not find me.

'And again in a little while ye shall see me, but haply ye shall not be able to come thither where I go.'

They that heard him questioned among themselves: 'What manner of saying is this?'

XCV.a (351) But the Captain of the Temple said: 'Thou foretellest what shall become of thee, but no man knoweth certainly what shall become of him; and therefore is thy record not true.'

Jesus answered and said: 'I speak as my Father hath taught me; for He hath instructed me whither I shall go.'

Then the Captain asked: 'Who art thou, then, and where is thy father?'

He answered: 'If ye know not my Father which sent me, and which is from the Beginning, how then shall ye know me?

XCV.f (352) 'For it is written that when Moses enquired of God, and asked Him by what name He should be known, God answered:

' "Say: I AM THAT I AM, the Lord God of your fathers, the God of Abraham and Isaac and Jacob hath sent thee."

'Yet in the ages before Abraham, God was!'

XCIV.g (353) But they durst not yet lay hands on him, and departed thence.
XCV.g (354) And they laid wait for him outside the Temple, but he went forth in the midst of a great throng, and they could do nothing.

XCIV.k   (355) And afterward Jesus made plain the words which he spake: 'Yet a little while am I with you, and then I go hence.'

For some of the disciples thought that he purposed to go for awhile unto the dispersed among the Gentiles.

Therefore he said: 'This I spake because I must suffer death according to the word of my Father which sent me. And when I am gone, they that seek me shall grope in the darkness whereof Daniel prophesied.

'For then shall ensue the pangs of her that bringeth forth, whereof Micah and Isaiah prophesied, saying: "Be in pain and labour to bring forth, O daughter of Zion!"

'Verily, ye shall weep and lament, but presently your sorrow shall be turned to joy.

'A women in her travail weepeth and lamenteth that her hour is come; but when she is delivered of her child, straightway she remembereth no more her anguish for joy that a man is born into the world.

XCIV.l   (356) 'So likewise the Kingdom of God shall come, and if it please Him to number me among the elect, they that now seek my life will behold me, but not come thither where I am.

'For a great gulf is fixed between them that are condemned and them that are saved.

'And in that day ye shall have no more need to question me; for all things shall be revealed unto every man!'

XCIV.h   (357) The Captain of the Temple and his officers went unto the Chief Rulers, which asked them: 'Why have ye not brought him that ye were commanded to bring?'

They answered and said: 'We feared the people. Never spake a man like unto this man, neither gave he us any occasion against him.'

And the Chief Rulers asked: 'Are ye then also deceived? Hath any man of our number believed that he is the Anointed One? Or hath any ruler of the Pharisees?

'Behold, this Galilean stirreth up the ignorant people; may God's curse fall upon him and upon them!'

CHAPTER XXXVIII

HOW HE WEPT FOR JERUSALEM

XCVII.f (358) When Jesus went forth from the Temple, and saw how it was adorned with goodly stones and gifts, he wept, and said unto his disciples:

'See ye not these great buildings? O Jerusalem, Jerusalem, when the nations are gathered together to destroy thee, there shall scarce be left one stone upon another that shall not be thrown down!

'For thou hast not known the time of thy visitation, neither hearkened to the voice that cried unto thee to repent.

'If thou couldst but know, in this thy last day, the things which belong to thy peace! But even now are they hid from thine eyes.

'As Isaiah prophesied in the name of the Lord: "I will camp against thee round about and will lay siege against thee, and raise forts against thee, and thou shalt be brought low."

'And again: "The heaven is My throne and the earth is My footstool. Where is the house that ye build unto Me, and where is the place of My rest?

' "For he that offereth an oblation there, it is as if he offered swine's blood; he that burneth incense, as if he blessed an idol. Yea, they have chosen their own ways, and their soul delighteth in abomination.

' "Behold, the Lord will come with fire and with His chariots like a whirlwind, to rebuke with flames of fire."

'And Micah likewise prophesied: "Zion shall be plowed as a field, for the sake of the princes of Israel that abhor judgement, and Jerusalem shall become heaps."

'Now is it again as in the days when the Lord spake unto Jeremiah, saying: "Stand in the court of the Temple, and say unto all men that come up to worship:

' " 'If ye will not walk in the Law that I have set before you, to hearken unto the words of My servants the prophets, which I sent you, to which ye have not hearkened, then will I make this house like unto that of Shiloh, and this city shall be desolate without an inhabitant!' "

'Then would the priests have stoned Jeremiah until he died, yet they could not. But in his stead they slew the prophet Urijah; whose innocent blood was on their heads until the prophecy of Jeremiah was fulfilled.

'Verily, I say unto you: so it shall be again!'

XXXIII.c   (359) Jesus said also:

'Malachi prophesied against the priests of Israel, saying: "Ye that offer polluted bread upon Mine altar, will I regard your persons?

' "For from the east unto the west shall My name be great among the Gentiles; yet have ye said of the table of the Lord: 'Behold, what a weariness it is,' and ye have sniffed at it."

'Therefore I say unto you, that though strangers come from the east and west and accept the Law with joy, and sit down to eat bread with Abraham, Isaac, and Jacob in the Kingdom of Heaven, yet of these sons of Levi, the children of the Kingdom, many shall be cast into outer darkness where shall be weeping and gnashing of teeth!

XIII.z   (360) 'Woe unto these faithless priests, unbelievers! For on their head shall fall all the righteous blood shed upon the earth; from the blood of righteous Abel until that of which Zacharias the son of Barachias prophesied, which is yet to be shed.

XCVII.f   (361) 'Yet shall the Lord raise up the righteous man and the prophet, before three days are fulfilled; as Hosea prophesied: "In the third day He will raise us up and we shall live in His sight."

'In the third day also He shall restore the Temple which He Himself hath destroyed. As Enoch prophesied, saying: "I saw till the Lord of the sheep brought a new house, greater and loftier than that first, and set it up in the place of the first."

LIX.c   (362) 'Woe unto thee, Zion! As it is prophesied in the Book of Lamentations:

' "How hath the Lord cast down from heaven unto earth the beauty of Israel, and in the day of His anger remembered not His footstool!

' "He hath cast off His altar, He hath abhorred His sanctuary, He hath given up into the hand of the enemy the walls of her palaces."

XCVII.g   (363) 'Yet fear ye not, little ones, for David spake in a psalm, saying: "The Lord shall cover the earth with His feathers, and under His wings shalt thou trust.

' "A thousand shall fall at thy side and ten thousand at thy right hand; but it shall not come nigh thee!"

XCIX.b   (364) 'Isaiah prophesied of these days, saying: "Then shall the glory of Jacob be made thin, and his flesh shall wax lean, and it shall be as when the harvestman gathereth the corn and leaveth the gleanings.

' "Yet, gleaning grapes shall be left on his vine, two or three berries at the top of the uttermost bough.

' "In that day shall a man look to his Maker, and his eyes shall have respect for the Holy One of Israel."

'Verily, I say unto you: where even two or three are gathered in God's name, He is in the midst of them and will hearken unto their prayer!

'Yea, and wheresoever there are but two, they are not without God. For Adam and Eve heard His voice as He walked in the Garden in the cool of the day.

'And where there is but one alone, yet is God also with him. When Elijah made complaint unto Him, saying: "The children of Israel

XCIX.b
(contd.)
have forsaken Thy covenant, and thrown down Thine altars, and slain Thy prophets with the sword, and I, even I only, am left, and they seek to take my life also," God comforted him.

'For He said: "I have left me seven thousand in Israel, knees which have not bowed unto Baal."

XCVIII.e
(365) 'Behold, these are the days whereof Daniel prophesied, saying: "Seventy weeks are determined upon Thy people and upon Thy holy city to finish the transgression, and to make an end of sins, and to make reconciliation for iniquity, and to bring in everlasting righteousness.

' "Know therefore that from the going forth of the commandment to restore and build Jerusalem, unto the Anointed One, shall be seven weeks, and three score and two weeks: the street shall be built again, and the wall as in troublous times.

' "And after three score and two weeks shall the Anointed One be cut off and have nothing, and the people of the prince that shall come shall destroy both the city and the Sanctuary. And the end thereof shall be with a flood." '

XCVIII.f
(366) The disciples ask Jesus: 'Lord, which shall this prince be?'
He answered: 'It is written in the Book of Job: "The eyes of the eagle behold afar off. Her young ones also suck up blood and where the slain lie, there shall she be also."

'Verily, I say unto you: wheresoever the carcase is, there shall the eagles be gathered together!

XCVIII.g
(367) 'Therefore, when ye shall hear of wars and rumours of wars, see that ye be not troubled. All these things must be, before the end cometh.

'For it was also revealed unto Baruch how that nation shall rise against nation and kingdom against kingdom, and that famines and pestilences and earthquakes shall be known in divers places.

'And there shall be signs in the heavens, and upon the earth distress and perplexity; the sea and the waves roaring;

'Men's hearts failing them for fear, and for looking after those things which are coming on the earth. And because of iniquity the love of many shall wax cold.

'These are the beginnings of sorrows, but when they come to pass, lift up your heads: for your redemption draweth nigh.

XCIX.c
(368) 'It is written that Abraham hearkened unto God's voice and clave the wood for the burnt offering of his son Isaac, and raised the stone for an altar to bind Isaac thereto;

'Yet even as he stretched forth his hand for the knife, a voice called unto him from heaven, and bade him spare Isaac his son. And lo, a ram was provided in his stead.

'Do ye therefore as Abraham did: cleave the wood and ye shall find God; raise the stone and He shall be with you!'

CHAPTER XXXIX

HOW HE FORETOLD THE LAST DAYS

XCVIII.i   (369) And Jesus spake further of the Last Days, saying: 'Zechariah prophesied: "Behold, the Day of the Lord cometh, and I will gather all nations against Jerusalem to battle.

' "And the city shall be taken, and the houses plundered, and the women ravished, and half of the city shall go into captivity."

'Blessed in those days shall be the barren, and the wombs which never bare, and the paps which never gave suck!

'But woe unto them that are with child, and unto them that give suck in those days!

'For there shall be great distress on the land, and wrath upon this people, and some shall fall by the sword and some be led away into captivity.

'As Hosea prophesied: "They shall say unto the mountains: 'Cover us!' and unto the hills: 'Fall on us!' "

'Verily, I say unto you: in that night two men shall be in one bed; the one shall be taken, and the other shall be left.

'And two women shall be grinding together; the one shall be taken, and the other shall be left.

'And Jerusalem shall be trodden down of the nations until their time be fulfilled.

'But Zechariah prophesied also: "Then shall the Lord go forth and fight against those nations.

' "And His feet shall stand in that day upon the Mount of Olives, and the Mount of Olives shall cleave in the midst thereof.

' "Then ye shall flee like as ye fled from the earthquake in the days of King Uzziah."

'And again: "In the day that I go about to destroy all the nations that come against Jerusalem, I will pour upon the House of David, and upon the inhabitants of Jerusalem, the spirit of grace and supplication, and the land shall mourn for the Anointed One, every family apart."

XCVIII.k   (370) 'Daniel likewise prophesied concerning the destruction of Jerusalem: "And the end thereof shall be with a flood, and it shall be cut off with desolations."

'Therefore shall it be again as in the days of Noah. They did eat, they drank, they raged, they were corrupt, they married, and were given in marriage: until the day that Noah entered into the ark with his elect, and the flood came and destroyed the wicked.

XCVIII.k   'Therefore, when this flood cometh upon Jerusalem, let him that is
(*contd.*)   on the house top not go down into his house, nor enter therein to take
up his stuff, lest the waters ensnare him!

'And afterward it shall be again as in the days of Lot. They did eat,
they drank, they committed fornication and all manner of uncleanness: until the day that Lot with his elect went forth from Sodom and
fled into the mountains and God rained fire and brimstone from
heaven and destroyed the city.

'Therefore, ere that this rain of fire falleth upon the cities of Judaea,
let them that be there likewise flee unto the barren mountains! And
let him that is in the field remember Lot's wife, and return not back
to take up his garment.

'Verily, I say unto you: the Gentiles shall be swept away by the
flood, but they that rebel against the Law, the same shall be destroyed
by the rain of fire!

XCVIII.k   (371) 'And pray ye that your flight be not in the winter, neither
on the sabbath day.

'For Daniel prophesied, saying: "And there shall be a time of
trouble such as never hath been since the beginning of creation.

' "Yet at that time Thy people shall be delivered, every one that
shall be found enrolled in the book."

'For Joel wrote of those days of tribulation, how that the sun and
the moon should be darkened, and the stars should withdraw their
shining, and the heavens and earth should be shaken.

'And Amos likewise prophesied: "Shall not the Day of the Lord be
darkness and not light? Even very dark and no brightness in it?" '

LXXXII.f   (372) And Peter, when he heard these things, asked Jesus: 'Who
then can be saved, seeing that we be all sinners?'

Jesus answered and said: 'Zechariah prophesied in the name of the
Lord: "There shall yet dwell old women and old men in Jerusalem,
and the streets shall be full of boys and girls playing.

' "Thus saith the Lord of Hosts: 'Though it be a difficult thing in
the eyes of the remnant of this people in these days, should it also be
difficult in Mine eyes?' "

'For with God all things are possible!

C.b   (373) 'David spake concerning Israel in a psalm: "The stone which
the builder rejected is become the headstone of the corner. This is the
Lord's doing and is marvellous in our eyes."

'Behold, it is the same stone, not cut with hands, of which Zechariah prophesied: how that in the last days all the nations of the earth
should be broken against it.

'And Daniel likewise prophesied that it should grind them all to
powder; for Israel shall inherit the Kingdom of Heaven and stand
for ever.

XCVIII.l   (374) 'But except those days should be shortened, no flesh should
be saved; only for them which God hath chosen and enrolled in the
book shall He shorten those days.

'And Isaiah prophesied of their deliverance: "The sun shall no more

XCVIII.1 go down, neither the moon withdraw herself, for the Lord shall be
(contd.) thine everlasting light. I, the Lord, will hasten it in his time."

'For in the midst of this darkness shall the elect perceive the Son of
Man coming in the clouds with great power and glory, like unto the
lightning that lighteneth out of the east and shineth unto the west.

'As Daniel saw in a vision: "Behold, one like the Son of Man came
with the clouds of heaven and came to the Ancient of Days and they
brought him nearer before Him.

' "And there was given him dominion and glory and a kingdom
that all people, nations, and languages should serve him."

XCVIII.m (375) 'And the Son of Man will judge them that are brought before
him in God's name.

'As Ezekiel prophesied: "I will purge out from among you the
rebels and them that trespass against Me."

'And again: "I judge between small cattle of lambs and kids, between the rams also and the great he-goats."

'So shall He separate one from another, as a shepherd divideth his
sheep from the goats, and shall set the sheep on his right hand, but
the goats on his left.

'And He shall send forth His angels with a sound of trumpet to
gather His elect from the four winds, and from the uttermost part of
the earth to the uttermost part of heaven, and they shall be united in
the Kingdom.

'For Zechariah saith: "The Lord God shall blow the trumpet and
save His flock on that day."

'And Enoch saw in a vision how all the sheep that had been destroyed and dispersed were gathered together in one house, and the
shepherd of the flock rejoiced with great joy because they were righteous and had returned.'

XCVIII.m (376) Afterward, Jesus sat upon the Mount of Olives over against
the Temple. And Peter and James and John and Andrew asked him
privily: 'Tell us, Master, when shall these things be? And by what
sign shall we know whether the cup of evil be full?'

Jesus answered them, saying: 'Daniel asked this same thing of the
angel, which bade him go his way, for the secret of the hour was
closed up and sealed.

'Nevertheless, he revealed unto Daniel how, when one thousand
and three hundred, five and thirty days should have passed from that
day in which the abomination that maketh desolate was set up, there
would then be a beginning of the Last Days.

'Now, by a day Daniel signifieth a week; for when these days began
and Israel fell subject unto the Wicked Kingdom, immediately false
deliverers arose, deceiving many, and there were wars in the land, and
great distress.

XCVIII.o (377) 'David said in a psalm: "I have inclined mine heart to perform Thy statutes always unto the end: hold Thou me up and I shall
be safe."

'So also spake the angel unto Daniel: "Blessed is the heart that

XCVIII.o   endureth and cometh to the thousand and three hundred, five and
(*contd.*)   thirty days!

> ' "But go thou thy way until the end be. For thou shalt rest and
> stand in thy lot at the end of days."

> 'Verily, I say unto you: he that endureth faithfully unto the end,
> the same shall be saved!

> 'But first must the Anointed One be cut off and brought to naught.'

CHAPTER XL

HOW HE FULFILLED THE PROPHECY OF
THE SHEPHERD

CIII.e   (378) On the morrow, which was the day of preparation for the Passover, Jesus and his disciples were come from Bethany nigh unto the palace of Annas, which had been High Priest.

And there Jesus took his staff and cut it asunder, even as Zechariah prophesied, saying: 'Thus doth God break the covenant which He hath made with His people!'

And looking up, he perceived a fig tree having branches that overhung the highway.

And he said unto the disciples: 'Go ye, and look if haply ye may find any fruit thereon!'

The disciples went, and found nothing but leaves. And they tell Jesus: 'We find nothing.'

Then said Jesus unto the tree: 'No man eat fruit of thee hereafter for ever! As Joel prophesied: "He hath barked my fig tree; the fig tree languisheth."

'And as Jeremiah likewise saith: "There shall be no more figs on the fig tree, and the leaf shall wither." '

And Jesus barked the tree with a sharp stone, so that when certain of the disciples passed on the morrow, the leaves were already withered.

And the disciples marvelled greatly, because of the parable which he had spoken before, how that the Lord would spare the barren fig tree until the next season.

Neither was it yet the time of figs.

CIII.f   (379) And Jesus went into the streets and lanes of Jerusalem and preached false doctrine,

Declaring that God should no longer shew mercy unto Israel, because that the fig tree was now barked; wherefore let every man go his own way, and take a weapon in his hand and do what seemed good in his own eyes, neither be obedient to authority.

For God had put in his heart to fulfil the prophecy concerning the worthless shepherd, which preached lies in His name, that he might provoke the men of Jerusalem to indignation against him.

As Zechariah prophesied: 'God hath said: "I will not feed you. That which dieth, let it die, and that which is to be cut off, let it be cut off, and let the rest eat every one the flesh of another." '

CIV.d (380) And Martha, daughter of Simeon the Chaste, hearing from James, her brother, what things Jesus did and preached, went with certain of her kinsmen to lay hold on him, saying: 'He is beside himself.'

But when they were nigh unto the place where he was, they could not come at him because of the press.

Then a certain man said unto Jesus: 'Behold, thy sister and thy brethren stand without, desiring to speak with thee.'

And he asked: 'What would they of me?'

He that told him, answered: 'That thou wouldst hold thy peace and preach no more in Jerusalem.'

Jesus answered and said: 'Who is my sister, and who are my brethren?

'Verily, I say unto you: Moses praised the Sons of Levi because they regarded not their brethren which trespassed against the Lord, but took sword and slew them.

'Neither was Miriam spared, which was the sister of Moses, when she spake evil against him at Hazeroth.'

And he stretched forth his hands towards his disciples and the women which ministered unto him, and said: 'Behold my sisters and my brethren!

'Yea, whosoever doeth the will of our Father which is in heaven and slayeth the deceiver, the same is my brother or my sister—yea, and my father or my mother!

XCVIII.d (381) 'For in the last days the brother shall deliver his brother unto death, for God's sake, and the father his son.'

CIV.f (382) Then one cried, saying: 'Yet blessed is the womb that bare thee, blessed are the paps which thou didst suck!'

And Jesus answered: 'Say, rather, blessed is she whose children hearken unto the word of God and delight to keep it.

'For Solomon saith: "An unwise son is the heaviness of his mother." '

CHAPTER XLI

HOW HE WAS BETRAYED BY JUDAS

CV.i   (383) Now the Feast of Unleavened Bread drew nigh, and in that year, the Passover fell on a sabbath.

And the Chief Priests and scribes sought how they might yet take Jesus by craft, and deliver him unto the Romans.

For they feared that there might be a rebellion of the people if they took him not before the feast began; yet the multitude thronged him, and they dared do nothing against him openly.

CVI.u   (384) The next day was the preparation for the Passover, wherefore Peter and John say unto him: 'Master, where wilt thou that we go and prepare, that thou mayest eat this Passover?'

He answereth: 'Have I indeed desired to eat it?

'Behold, my time is at hand. After this night I will eat no more with you until, if God so grant we sit down together in His Kingdom.

'But go ye twain before me now, and at such a place there ye shall find a Levite bearing a pitcher of water. Beckon unto him and follow him.

'And wheresoever he shall enter in to deliver the water, enter ye in also, and say unto the goodman of the house: "Our master asketh: 'Where is the guest chamber, that I may eat there with my disciples?' "

'Then will he shew unto you a large upper room furnished. There prepare both flesh and wine.'

Peter and John did as Jesus appointed them; and, when even was come, he entered in with others of the Twelve, and the disciple which he loved likewise joined himself unto him.

CVI.u   (385) And Jesus saith unto them: 'Because of me ye shall all be offended this night!

'For this that is prophesied by Isaiah must yet be accomplished in me: "And he was numbered among the transgressors, and bare the sin of men, and made intercession for the transgressors." '

Peter saith: 'Master, though all others shall be offended because of thee, yet will I never be offended!'

CVI.v   (386) And he bade them lie down, and take their ease.

And when they marvelled at the wine which before was forbidden unto them, Jesus saith: 'Ye shall all drink wine tonight and cease for awhile from prophecy.'

CVI.v
(contd.)   This he spake that the word of Amos might be accomplished, which said:

'I raised up of your sons for prophets, and of your young men for Nazirites.

'But ye gave the Nazirites wine to drink, and commanded the prophets to cease.

'Behold, I am pressed under you as a cart is pressed under a full weight of sheaves.'

CVI.v   (387) And when they marvelled at the flesh which before was forbidden unto them, Jesus saith: 'It is written: "I shall raise up a shepherd which shall eat the flesh of the fat and tear their joints in pieces." '

And he brake bread and sanctified it, and he took the wine pot and poured out into cups and sanctified them.

Then said he: 'Yea, even as I tear this bread, so shall the sheep be torn; and even as I pour this wine, so shall their blood be poured out.

'And so likewise shall mine be spilt!'

Yet understood they not that Jesus spake of the worthless shepherd which should perish by the sword, though he was God's fellow.

CVI.v   (388) And Jesus, perceiving that they murmured not against him, neither were offended, again poured wine into the cups, and sanctified them, and they drank.

And afterward he said unto them: 'Verily, that which ye drank was the reeling cup whereof Zechariah prophesied, saying: "Behold, I will make Jerusalem a reeling cup."

'This was also the cup whereof Isaiah prophesied, saying: "Awake, awake, stand up, Jerusalem, which hast drunk the cup of God's fury at His hands; thou hast drunken the dregs of the reeling cup and wrung them out.

' "There is none to guide her among all her sons whom she hath brought forth, neither is there any that taketh her by the hand of all her sons that she hath brought up.

' "These things are come upon thee; who shall be sorry for thee? Desolation and destruction and the famine and the sword: by whom shall I comfort thee?

' "Thy sons have fainted, they lie at the head of all the streets, as a wild bull in the net: they are full of the fury of the Lord, the rebuke of thy God.

' "Therefore hear now this, thou afflicted and drunken, though not for wine:

' "Thus saith the Lord thy God, and thy God that pleadeth the cause of His people: 'Behold, I have taken out of thine hand the reeling cup of My fury; thou shalt no more drink of it again!' " '

CVI.v   (389) They ask him: 'Master, what is this reeling cup, if they that drain it are not drunken with wine?'

He answereth: 'It is the cup of blood with which the door posts and the lintels shall be marked tomorrow in preparation for the Lord's Passover.'

CVI.v
(contd.)

Then was Judas of Kerioth troubled in spirit, and asked him: 'How sayest thou, Master? Is it not written: "Ye shall not eat of the blood, which is the life"?'

Jesus answered and said: 'Zechariah prophesied in the name of the Lord: "And I will take away his blood out of his mouth, and his abomination from between his teeth; but he that remaineth, even he shall be for your judge and he shall be as a governor in Judah."'

CV.j

(390) And when Jesus had thus said, he cried in a loud voice: 'Verily, verily, I say unto you: the hand of him that shall slay me is on this table and dippeth into the dish!'

Then the disciples looked on one another, doubting whereof he spake,

Which when Jesus perceived, he said: 'Isaiah prophesied: "Who hath believed our report? And to whom is the arm of the Lord revealed?"

'And again: "Hear ye indeed, but understand not; and see ye indeed, and perceive not?

'"Make the heart of this people fat and make their ears heavy and shut their eyes; lest they see with their eyes and hear with their ears and understand with their heart, and be converted and be healed."'

Now, there was leaning on Jesus's bosom the disciple which he loved; and Peter beckoned unto him that he should ask who it was that should slay him.

He then, lying on Jesus's bosom, asketh of him: 'Lord, who is it?'

And Jesus, when he perceived that Judas of Kerioth, the son of Simon, alone of them that sat at meat, was offended in him, gave him a sop, after that he had dipped it in the dish.

And Judas saith unto him privately: 'Is it I?'

Jesus answered: 'So thou sayest!'

And Judas was wroth thereat, and rose to depart.

Then saith Jesus unto him: 'Spend what money is needful, and that thou doest, do it quickly!'

But no man at the table understood to what intent he spake this unto Judas.

Some thought that Jesus had said unto him: 'Give alms to the poor.'

Others thought that he had said: 'Buy the food that we have need of against the sabbath.'

But Judas knew that he said: 'Buy the swords that are needed against the fulfilment of that prophecy which Zechariah spake: of him that feigned himself to be a false prophet, yet was God's fellow.'

CV.j

(391) Judas, when he had received the sop, went forth immediately; and it was night. And Satan entered into his soul, for he loathed the task that was laid upon him.

And Satan spake within his heart, saying: 'Doth not thy master force the hour and bring it to birth untimely? Beware, lest he make thee a murderer!'

Then Judas, greatly longing to deliver Jesus from error, considered how to put him in ward.

CV.j
(*contd.*)   Wherefore he went hastily unto the Captain of the Temple, and said unto him: 'Sir, I am a disciple of Jesus the Galilean, which is called the King of Israel; but that he doeth now, my soul abhorreth.

'Suffer me therefore to lead thee tonight unto the place where he lieth, that he may be put in ward, and cause no man to sin.

'But after the feast, let him be judged by the Council whether he be truly the King of Israel, or whether a deceiver of the people.'

CV.j   (392) The Captain of the Temple therefore leadeth Judas unto the two Catholics which were set over the Treasury, being kinsmen of the High Priest.

And the Catholics say unto him: 'Wilt thou indeed shew us the place where thy master lieth? Then will we pay thee well.'

Judas answered in the words of Zechariah: 'If ye think good, give me my price, and if not, forbear!'

Then the Catholics ask him: 'Man, what is thy price?'

He answered: 'It is written: "So they weighed for my price thirty pieces of silver, a goodly price that I was prized at by them." '

But they knew not whereof Judas spake, being of the Sadducees which regard not the prophets.

CHAPTER XLII

HOW HE PROVOKED THE OTHER
DISCIPLES

CVI.w (393) And Jesus said unto the disciples: 'Little children, I am with you but a little while yet.'

Simon Peter asked him: 'Lord, whither goest thou?'

And Jesus answered and said: 'Whither I go thou canst not follow me now, but afterward shall ye follow me. Let not your hearts be troubled; ye believe in God, believe then also that He will uphold and guide me.'

Thomas saith unto him: 'Master, we know not whither thou goest, and how shall we know the way?'

Jesus answered and said: 'Nay, but whither I go ye know, and the way ye know. For the Law is the way, and the truth and the life.

'Verily, I say unto you: no man cometh unto the Father but by the Law!

'I go now to prepare a place for you. If I come again, then will I receive you unto myself, that where I am, there may ye be also.'

CVI.w (394) Presently, Jesus saith unto the disciples: 'Cometh Judas not again? Hath he haply fled away, as a traitor fleeth?'

And again he sought to offend them, saying: 'When I sent you to preach without purse or scrip or shoes, lacked ye aught?'

They answer: 'Nothing.'

Then said he unto them: 'Yet trust ye no more in God's mercy, for in these days it is withheld from you!

'Wherefore let him that hath a purse and a scrip buy a sword, and hide it in the scrip against need.

'And let him that hath neither purse nor scrip sell his cloak and buy unto him a sword and a scrip, and do likewise!'

And Peter and the sons of Zebedee, being full of flesh and wine, when they heard this saying, went out and sold their cloaks and bought them scrips and swords.

For Peter said unto the other twain: 'Now shall he lead us in arms against the Wicked Kingdom!'

And they come again unto Jesus, and say: 'Master, here are two swords.'

He saith: 'It is enough.

CVI.x (395) 'Ye have told me good tidings, for now the things concerning me have an end.

CVI.x
(contd.)

'Tomorrow, if God will, my portion will be with them that dwell in Paradise, and ye shall be there with me also!'

CVI.x

(396) And Peter saith: 'Master, I will lay down my life for thy sake.'

Jesus answered: 'Wilt thou verily lay down thy life for my sake? Then before the second cock crow shalt thou thrice deny that ever thou knewest a certain worthless shepherd, and shalt take vengeance upon him for what he hath done.

'For Zechariah prophesied, saying: "Woe unto the worthless shepherd which leaveth the flock!

' "The sword shall strike his right arm and his right eye; his arm shall be made powerless and his eye utterly darkened!"

'For so shall vengeance be taken upon him.'

And Peter saith: 'What, shall we then smite with these swords?'

He answereth: 'Yea.'

Then said Peter: 'Now thou speakest plainly and no riddles.'

And Jesus saith: 'This commandment that I give you truly proceedeth from the Father.

'Behold, I speak not of myself; but of my Father which sent me, for He commanded me what I should do and what I should speak.

'Verily, I say unto you: if ye truly love God, keep His commandments which are life everlasting! Therefore, whatsoever the Father biddeth me to do, that do I.'

Nevertheless, Simon Peter understood not even yet, but supposed that he should slay Judas, as a shepherd which had left the flock.

And Jesus saith: 'Do ye now believe? Behold, then, the hour cometh, yea is now at hand, that ye shall be scattered every man to his own, and I shall abide by myself.'

CVI.x

(397) And when the supper was ended and they had washed their hands, Jesus arose and laid aside his garments, and took a towel and girded himself.

Then he poureth water into a basin, and saith: 'Ye are clean, but not all.'

And he began to wash the feet of the disciples, and to wipe them with the towel.

And he saith unto them: 'Zechariah prophesied unto Jerusalem: "As for thee also, whose covenant is by blood," which is the covenant that our fathers swore unto Moses, "I have sent forth thy prisoners out of the pit where is no water."

'And David prophesied: "The Lord delivered me also out of an horrible pit, out of the miry clay, and set my feet upon a rock and established my goings.

' "And He hath put a new song in my mouth, even praise unto our God." '

CVI.x

(398) Then cometh he to Simon Peter, and Peter saith unto him: 'Master, dost thou wash my feet? Did not I myself wash them before I came in hither?'

CVI.x
(contd.)
Jesus answered and said: 'What I do, thou knowest not now, but soon thou shalt know.'

Peter saith: 'Master, thou shalt never wash my feet!'

He answered: 'If I wash thee not, then shalt thou have no part in the Kingdom.'

Peter saith: 'Master, not my feet only, but my body and my head.'

Jesus saith: 'He that hath washed his hands tonight and is clean of heart, the same needeth not save to wash his feet of the miry clay, for they shall stand on that rock whereon the feet of the Son of Man shall also stand.

'Come now, let us sing the new psalm of praise whereof David spake!'

CHAPTER XLIII

HOW HE WAS TAKEN AT GETHSEMANE

CVII.l (399) And after that they had sung David's psalm of praise, they went forth and passed over the brook Kidron.

And going up into the Mount of Olives, they come unto a garden called Gethsemane and entered in.

Now, Judas also knew the place, for Jesus ofttimes resorted thither with the disciples.

CVII.l (400) Then said Jesus unto Peter: 'Simon, Simon, behold Satan hath desired to have you all, that he may sift you as wheat.

'But I have prayed for thee, that thy faith in God fail not; and that when thou art persuaded of that which must be accomplished, thou wilt also strengthen thy brethren!'

These words spake Jesus, and lifted up his eyes unto heaven. And, seeing that the face of the moon grew red, he prayed: 'Father, the hour is come!

'Strengthen thou Thy son which hath glorified Thee, O Lord, that he may perfect the work which Thou gavest him to do, whereby as many as Thou ordainest shall taste of everlasting life.

'For their sakes have I sanctified myself, that they also may be sanctified through truth.

'As it is written: "O Lord, Thou art God and Thy words are true, and Thou hast promised this goodness unto Thy servant." '

Then Jesus went with Peter and James and John, having the two swords, and they withdrew themselves about a stone's cast.

And unto them which were left he said: 'Abide ye here, and pray that ye enter not into temptation!

CXVII.k (401) 'Now is the judgement of this world; now shall the Prince of Evil be cast out.

XCVII.i (402) 'Ye shall not see me again until we meet together in the Resurrection, if so it be that God shall make good in us the prophecy which David spake: "I shall not die but live. The Lord hath chastened me sore, but hath not given me over unto death."

'Then shall we lift our eyes to heaven, and cry with the voice of David: "Blessed be he that cometh in the name of the Lord!" '

CVII.l (403) And unto the three which came with him, he said: 'My soul is exceeding sorrowful even unto death, because of that which must be accomplished in me.

CVII.1
(contd.)

'Shall I pray: "Father, save me from this hour"? But was it not for the Father's sake that I came unto this hour?

'Tarry ye therefore with me, and watch that I rise not and flee from you into Galilee. Behold, the spirit is willing but the flesh is weak.'

And he went away a little farther, and fell to the ground, and prayed aloud in an agony: 'Father, if it be possible, let this cup pass from me! Nevertheless, let it not be as I will, but as Thou wilt.'

Then cometh he back unto the three, and in the light of the moon the sweat broke from his brow as it were drops of blood.

And he findeth the sons of Zebedee awake, but Peter sleeping, and he saith unto him: 'Simon, sleepest thou? Couldst not thou watch one hour? Watch therefore and pray!'

And Jesus went forward again but, as he prayed, Peter slept and they which watched likewise grew drowsy for all their sorrow.

Then cometh he unto them a second time, and rebuketh them, neither wist they what to answer him, but roused themselves from slumber.

And he went forward the third time, but what he did they knew not, for presently they slept.

Again he roused them, saying: 'Do ye slumber yet and take your rest?

'Behold, the hour is now come when ye shall verily know that ye have been led astray.

'Arise, let us stand upon our feet! For he that should slay me is at hand.'

And as they arose and followed him, on a sudden he cried out: 'Awake, sword! Smite the shepherd and the sheep shall be scattered!'

For even as he spake, Judas was at hand, and with him a company of Levites, servants of the High Priest, armed with swords and staves.

And Judas saith: 'Hail, Master!'

Jesus's heart was glad, and he saith unto Judas: 'Friend, wherefore art thou come?', thinking that he verily came in the way of vengeance according to the prophecy.

And Judas kissed Jesus, but unto the Captain he said: 'This is he!'

Jesus saith: 'Betrayest thou the Son of God with a kiss?'

CVII.1

(404) Then Jesus asked the Captain of the Temple, saying: 'Whom seekest thou?'

He answered: 'I seek Jesus of Nazara.'

Jesus saith: 'I am he, but why comest thou against me with swords and staves as against a robber? For two days I sat in the Temple teaching, yet ye laid no hold on me.'

The Captain answered: 'Thou settest up thyself for a King, which is against the law of Caesar.'

Jesus saith unto him: "If my Kingdom were of this world, then might I command my disciples to take arms against Caesar and the Wicked Kingdom.

'Yet have I no need of these, for presently the Father shall send twelve legions of angels to destroy His enemies.'

CVII.1   And Judas, turning unto the Captain, said: 'Yea, I pray thee, let
(*contd.*)   these other men go their ways.'

CVII.1   (405) Then Judas would have led Jesus from the garden, but Peter
perceiving it, cried out in wrath.

And Jesus saith unto Peter: 'Simon, suffer thus far. The cup that
is given unto me to drink, shall I not drink it?

CV.g   (406) 'Behold, this son of man goeth now as Isaiah prophesied:
"He is brought as a lamb unto the slaughter."

'But woe unto him that hath betrayed me! It were better for that
man that he had never been born!'

CVII.m   (407) But Peter drew his sword and, running against Judas, sought
to slay him.

Then went the Levites a pace backward for fear of him, and some
fell to the ground, and Peter smote a servant of the High Priest, by
name Malchus, which sought to deliver Judas, and cut off his right
ear.

Which, when the other disciples saw, they fled.

And Jesus rebuked Peter, saying: 'Simon, put up thy sword into its
place! For it is written: "Whosoever sheddeth a man's blood, by man
shall his blood be shed." '

CVII.m   (408) Then sought the High Priest's servants to take Peter, and
they caught hold of the linen garment in which he was clothed, having sold his cloak.

But he left the garment in their hands, and fled away naked.

As Amos prophesied in the name of the Lord: ' "He that is courageous among the mighty shall flee away naked in that day," saith the
Lord.'

CHAPTER XLIV

HOW PETER WAS JUDGED OF THE CHIEF PRIESTS

CIX.n (409) And they led Jesus away to the Palace, of Annas which had been the High Priest; for he was father-in-law to Joseph, called Caiaphas, which was now the High Priest.

CVIII.d (410) But Peter followed Jesus afar off to the Palace, and stood at the door without.

And presently cometh the disciple which Jesus loved, being of the family of Annas, and Peter crieth out to him.

Then goeth the disciple in to fetch garments wherewith to cover Peter's nakedness,

And speaketh unto the maid at the door and, coming out again, bringeth in Peter also.

Then said the maid unto Peter: 'Art thou not a disciple of Jesus?'

He answered: 'I am not.'

Now, the servants and officers sat there, which had kindled a fire of coals, for it was cold.

And Peter sat down with them, and warmed himself, and waited for the end, hoping to have seen some miracle done by Jesus.

But another maid beheld him as he sat by the fire, and looking earnestly upon him, she said: 'This man was also with him.'

And he denied again, saying: 'Woman, I was not!'

But they that stood by said: 'Surely he is a Galilean, for his speech bewrayeth him.'

About the space of an hour after, there came a kinsman of Malchus whose ear Peter cut off, and said: 'Of a truth this fellow was with him!'

And he asked Peter: 'Did I not see thee in the garden with him?'

But Peter denied a third time with oaths. And immediately the cock crew.

Then wept Peter bitterly and went out into the porch, and sought to escape, but the servants prevented him.

And an officer said unto Peter: 'Who art thou?'

He answered: 'I am Barabbas,' which is to say: 'The son of my father'.

Then they led Peter away and accused him before Annas.

CVIII.g (411) And Peter, earnestly beholding the Council, said: 'Men and brethren, I have lived in all good conscience before God until this day.

CVIII.g
(*contd.*)

'And now have I done no evil, save to defend my King from them which sought to take him.'

Annas therefore charged him straitly, saying: 'Tell me whether this man Jesus commanded thee to draw thy sword against my servants?'

Peter answered and said: 'Nay, but I sought vengeance on him which hath betrayed my master. I struck thy servant in error, and my master rebuked me therefor.

'Yet though David commanded his captains to do nothing against the youth Absalom which had made rebellion, was it accounted a sin in Joab son of Zeruiah that he thrust him through the heart?

'For that which Joab did was done lest Israel should be shamed. As he said unto David, his King and master: "In that thou lovest thine enemies and hatest thy friends." '

Then said Annas: 'Callest thou this deceiver thy King?'

And Peter answered: 'He is no deceiver, but thy King and mine.'

Wherefore Annas commanded them that stood by to smite him on the mouth.

Then said Peter unto him: 'God shall smite thee also, thou whited sepulchre! Sittest thou to judge me according to the Law, and commandest me to be smitten contrary to the Law?'

And they that stood by, asked him: 'Revilest thou the High Priest of God?'

Then said Peter: 'I wist not that he was the High Priest.'

And he spake unto Annas, saying: 'Art thou then a High Priest, and hast not read the Scripture: "Thou shalt not speak evil of thy King"?'

And Annas, being exceeding wroth thereat, commanded Peter to be bound, and put in ward.

CIX.o

(412) And when he had heard the testimony which the Captain of the Temple brought against Jesus, he kept him also in ward until the morrow.

CIX.o

(413) Now, as soon as it was day, Peter was brought bound before Caiaphas. And the Chief Priests and elders were assembled in Council, and the scribes sat by.

Then Caiaphas, when he heard from Annas of the wounding of Malchus, asked Peter, which called himself Barabbas: 'Did thy master bid thee draw thy sword against my servants?

'For if so, thou art somewhat the less guilty.'

He answered and said: 'Nay, but I drew it of mine own will, and he rebuked me therefor.'

Then Caiaphas judged Peter to be guilty of sedition, and said: 'Thou art worthy of death!'

And they led him away.

CHAPTER XLV

HOW THE CHIEF PRIESTS DELIVERED
JESUS TO PILATE

CIX.o (414) Then came out Caiaphas to the place where Jesus was, and asked him privately of his disciples and of his doctrine, whether he had provoked any man to violence.

Jesus answered: 'I spake to all the world and taught in the synagogues and in the Temple; neither have I kept any thing secret.

'Why askest thou me? Ask them which hearkened unto me!'

Wherefore Caiaphas went in again, and Jesus was led before him and the Council of the Chief Priests and elders.

And Caiaphas sent for witnesses, which testified that Jesus had provoked his disciples to violence. But their testimony did not agree.

Then sent he for others, which said: 'This fellow calleth himself the King of Israel. Yesterday he provoked the multitude to burn the Temple, saying: "Destroy ye this Temple, which is a den of robbers, for God will raise up a better temple in three days!"'

Jesus held his peace and answered nothing.

Caiaphas arose, and said unto him: 'Answerest thou nothing? What is it that these men witness against thee?'

But Jesus held his peace.

Caiaphas said unto him: 'I adjure thee by the Living God, that thou tell us whether thou be the Anointed King, the Son of God!'

Jesus answered: 'So thou sayest. Yet if I ask thee by what authority thou hast brought me to judgement, thou wilt not answer me, neither let me go.

'Wherefore I do not answer thee, whether I be King or no King.'

And when he had thus spoken, one of the officers which stood by struck Jesus with the palm of his hand, saying: 'Answerest thou the High Priest so?'

Jesus said: 'If I am at fault, testify to the fault; but if I speak the truth, why smitest thou me?'

CIX.p (415) Caiaphas saith again unto Jesus: 'Knowest thou not that I have power to deliver thee unto the Romans to be crucified, and power likewise to release thee?'

Jesus answered: 'Thou canst have no power over me, except it were given thee from above. Therefore thou sinnest in judging me.

'For this is not the Council by which Israelites are judged. Nevertheless, he that delivered me unto thee hath the greater sin.

CIX.p
(*contd.*)
'As David prophesied: "Mine own familiar friend in whom I trusted, which did eat of my bread, hath lifted up his heel against me."

'But hath not Caesar, which boweth down unto false gods, appointed thee to judge Israelites according to his laws? Why then askest thou me these things in the name of the Living God?

'Beware, lest thou sin against Him in judging for His enemies!'

And the High Priest cried aloud, and said: 'Is this not treason? For we ourselves have heard of his own mouth that he speaketh against Caesar.

'What further need have we of witnesses? What think ye? Is he not deserving of death?

'If we let him go free, all men will follow him, and Caesar will destroy both our dwelling place and our nation.'

XCIV.i
(416) Bunni son of Gorion, being one of their number, saith: 'Doth the Law suffer us to condemn any man without hearing?'

They asked him: 'Art thou also a Galilean?'

CIX.q
(417) Then said Bunni: 'Why, what evil hath he done? He hath not offended against the Law, neither hath he risen in arms against Caesar.

'Ye know well that we may not deliver an innocent man unto death. What do we? This man worketh many miracles of healing by the finger of God.'

And others said likewise.

Then said the High Priest: 'Ye know nothing at all, nor consider that it is expedient that one man should die for the people and that the whole people perish not.'

CIX.q
(418) And Jesus saith unto the Council of Chief Priests and Elders: 'Take heed what ye do with me, being no judges!

'Verily, I say unto you: if ye deliver me unto death, and thereby seek favour with the Wicked Kingdom, it shall go hard with you when ye see the Son of Man coming on the clouds of heaven, to sit on the right hand of Power!

'For he shall judge them that pervert justice, and that make friends of the enemies of God.'

CIX.r
(419) Wherefore, when Bunni heard these words, he was sore afraid and sought the more to release Jesus, and answered the High Priest, saying: 'Should this man also die because his disciple drew a sword? For he rebuked the fault.

'Moreover, it is the Law that one man only may be delivered unto death on the one day, lest they that judge become as murderers.

'Beware, therefore, of the people; for tomorrow is the Passover when they drink much wine and make merry in the streets of the city!'

And again others said likewise.

Then Caiaphas asked them, saying: 'Whether of the twain will ye that I release unto you?

CIX.r
(*contd.*)

'Would ye have me release him that maketh himself King and condemn his servant?

'Nay, I will not release this man, but Barabbas, after that I have chastised him well.'

And Bunni answered: 'It is written: "Let not mercy and truth forsake thee." '

Caiaphas asked: 'What is truth?'

Bunni answered and said: 'Behold every Israelite that is of the truth heareth God's voice; to this end was he born, and for this cause came he into the world that he should bear witness to the truth.'

Caiaphas said: 'If thou wouldst let this man go, then art thou not Caesar's friend.'

And the Chief Priests and scribes were instant with loud voices, requiring that Jesus might be delivered unto Pilate.

Bunni saith: 'Shall he then be crucified?'

They answer: 'What is that to us? Let him that spake against Caesar stand at Caesar's Judgment seat.'

Bunni saith: 'I find no fault in the man. As Daniel, which was the advocate of Susannah, declared: "I am clear from his blood." And when he shewed how the testimony of the two accusers agreed not together, the innocent soul was released.'

But the Chief Priests and the scribes cried again, saying: 'Let him be delivered unto Pilate!'

CIX.s

(420) And Bunni, perceiving that he could in no wise prevail, but that rather a tumult was made, took water and washed his hands before them all, and said: 'My hands have not shed this blood, neither have mine eyes seen it.'

And he prayed: 'Be merciful, O God, unto Thy people Israel, whom Thou hast redeemed, and lay not innocent blood unto Thy people's charge.'

And he rent his garments.

They that consented with him, prayed likewise, and said unto Caiaphas: 'As it is written: "Thy blood be upon thy head!" See thou to it.'

But the Chief Priests and the scribes cried out the more exceedingly: 'Let him be delivered unto Pilate!'

And Caiaphas gave sentence that it should be as they required.

And he scourged Peter, which had been found guilty of rebellion and murder, and afterwards released him.

But Bunni was called Nakemidam of all the people, which is 'Innocent of Blood'.

CIX.s

(421) Then was an end made to the Council, and every man returned to his own house.

CHAPTER XLVI

HOW HEROD ANTIPAS CONDEMNED HIM TO DEATH

CX.1 (422) But Jesus was led to judgement unto the place called Gabbatha, and it was yet early.

And certain of the family of Annas came to accuse him before Pilate.

Wherefore, when Pilate drew nigh, they delivered Jesus unto him but went not in, lest the people should say of them: 'They entered into Caesar's judgement hall and sware an oath by false gods.'

And unto Pilate they said: 'Lest we defile ourselves for the Feast.'

Then Pilate asked: 'What accusation bring ye against this man?'

And they began to accuse Jesus, saying: 'We found this fellow perverting the nation and saying that he is the Son of God; he hath also ridden into the city upon an ass.'

Pilate answered and said: 'Am I a Jew? If he hath transgressed against your religion, let him be judged according to your Law.'

They say: 'Lord, if he were not a malefactor, we would not have delivered him unto thee.

'But he that calleth himself the Son of God, the same proclaimeth himself the King and Deliverer of Israel which must ride into Jerusalem upon an ass,

'And whosoever maketh himself King, the same speaketh against Caesar.

'Likewise hath he preached in the Temple, forbidding the people to pay tribute unto Caesar.'

CX.1 (423) And Pilate spake scornfully: 'What would ye then that I should do unto your King?'

They answered and said: 'Lord, we have no King but Caesar. Take thou him and do what seemeth good unto thee. For the whole city is witness to his offences.'

Thus did they deliver Jesus unto Pilate to be judged.

CX.m (424) Then they departed every man, that they might make ready to eat the Passover.

CX.n (425) And Pilate went in, and sat on the judgement seat, and when Jesus was brought before him, he asked: 'Art thou the King of the Jews?'

Jesus answered: 'Sayest thou this of thine own knowledge or did others tell it thee?'

CX.n
(contd.) Pilate saith: 'The Chief Priests of thine own nation have delivered thee unto me. Tell me therefore: art thou the King of the Jews?'

Jesus answered: 'So thou sayest.'

And Pilate marvelled at his stubbornness.

Then the Captain of the Temple, which stood by, bare witness and said: 'This mad fellow stirreth up the people, teaching through all Jewry, beginning from Galilee unto this place.'

Pilate, when he heard of Galilee, asked whether the man were a Galilean.

And when he knew that Jesus belonged to Herod's jurisdiction, he sent him to Herod to be judged by him.

For he would provoke the people to complain against Herod rather than against himself.

Now, Herod was at Jerusalem in this time, dwelling in a mansion of the palace where Pilate also was.

CX.n (426) Wherefore, when Herod saw Jesus brought before him he was exceeding glad, being desirous of a long season to put him to death.

And he questioned Jesus with many words, but Jesus made no answer, though men stood and vehemently accused him.

Now, Herod lacked authority to condemn a Galilean for any crime which he had committed in Judaea.

Nevertheless, he found Jesus guilty of death, as having followed in the way of John the Baptist and stirred up the people at Beth-Nimrah.

And he sent him unto Pilate again, saying: 'I pray thee, have him crucified.'

Pilate therefore, when he had commanded Jesus to be scourged in the common hall, delivered him to be crucified. And it was the preparation of the Passover, about the sixth hour.

CXI.d (427) And Pilate wrote an accusation in Latin, which should be hanged about the neck of Jesus and should afterward be set upon the cross.

And the writing was: 'Sedition: this is Jesus the Galilean which by his preaching hath offended against Herod Antipas his lord, Caesar's friend.'

Then said Herod: 'I pray thee, write rather: "Treason: this is Jesus the Galilean which hath offended against Caesar, saying: 'I am the King of the Jews.'"'

Pilate answered: 'What I have written I have written.'

CXI.e (428) And Herod durst ask him nothing more.

CX.o (429) And it came to pass that on this day Pilate and Herod were made friends together.

These twain had long been at enmity between themselves, because of the image of Caesar which the soldiers of Pilate had brought into Jerusalem.

For Herod had joined himself with them that raised their voices against this desecration of the City of God.

CXII.d (430) Now Judas, when he saw that Jesus was delivered to be

CXII.d
(*contd.*)

crucified, was exceeding troubled; for he had not thought to betray him to death, but contrariwise, to save him.

Wherefore he brought the thirty pieces of silver again unto the Catholics which were set over the Treasury, saying: 'I have sinned in that I betrayed innocent blood.'

They answered: 'What is that to us? See thou to that.'

And they would not take the money.

Then Judas said unto them: 'It is written: "And the Lord said unto me: 'Cast it unto the potter, a goodly price that I was prized at of them.'

' "And I took the thirty pieces of silver and cast them to the potter in the house of the Lord." '

Wherefore Judas went and cast the money unto the potter which made vessels for the Temple.

And he remembered how Achitophel had made rebellion against his Anointed King, and sought to take him by night when he was weary and weakhanded; and how the rulers of Israel afterward treated Achitophel with despite.

As it is written: 'And when Achitophel saw that his counsel was not followed, he saddled his ass and arose and gat him home to his house to his own city, and put his household in order, and hanged himself and died, and was buried in the sepulchre of his fathers.'

Judas therefore did likewise, returning to his own city of Kerioth, and there he hanged himself and died.

But the potter brought the thirty pieces of silver unto the Catholics again, which durst not put them into the Treasury to spend them upon any work whereby Israelites might be profited.

For Nakemidam and the Pharisees said: 'It is the price of innocent blood.'

Therefore, they took counsel and bought a field, which was called The Potter's Field, nigh unto the Valley of the Sons of Hinnon, to bury Gentiles in that had no kindred.

That field is now called Hakeldemach, which is The Field of Sleep.

CHAPTER XLVII

HOW JESUS WAS CRUCIFIED

CXIII.y (431) And they led Jesus out to crucify him. And with him they also led out two malefactors which were condemned of Pilate that day to be crucified.

For they had hearkened unto the false doctrine that Jesus taught in the streets and lanes of Jerusalem, how that every man should fend for himself in despite of his neighbour; and had shed blood.

And as they went forth from the city by the western gate, behold, a man of Cyrene, Simon by name, which was the father of Alexander and Rufus, came up late from Joppa for the Feast.

But Jesus, being lame, could not bear his cross-piece, as the other twain did; wherefore the soldiers compelled Simon to bear it for him.

CXIII.y (432) Now, a company of women followed behind, which bewailed and lamented him.

And Jesus, turning unto them, said: 'Daughters of Jerusalem, it is written: "Weep ye not for the dead, neither bemoan him. But weep sore for him that goeth away, for he shall return no more, neither see his native country."

'Wherefore weep for yourselves, who shall be ravished and carried away into bondage!'

And he said likewise: 'Behold, if these things are done to a green tree, what shall be done unto a dry?'

CXIII.y (433) And they came unto the mount which is called Golgotha, where the skull of Adam lieth buried, nigh unto the highway that leadeth to the north.

There the soldiers crucified Jesus with the other twain.

And the women stood afar off, beholding what was done, among whom were Mary the Braider, his mother; and Mary, the mother of James and Joses, which was the wife of Joseph of Ramathaim; and Salome the midwife; and the mother of Zebedee's children.

But Simon of Cyrene remained for awhile with the soldiers, and hearkened unto the words which Jesus spake after that his hands and feet were made fast to the wood with sharp nails and he was raised upon the cross.

Then the superscription which Pilate had ordained was set above his head; and it was written in Latin and Greek and Hebrew.

CXIII.y (434) Now, when the other twain were crucified with Jesus, the superscriptions shewed that they were guilty of bloodshed.

And he which hanged on the left hand of Jesus, reviled him, saying:

CXIII.y
(contd.)

'If thou be the Son of God, come down from the Cross! Save thyself and us that we may believe on thee.

'For because of thy lies we are crucified.'

And he which hanged on the right hand of Jesus, cast the like in his teeth, mocking him and saying: 'Lord, remember me when thou comest into thy Kingdom!'

But Jesus prayed aloud: 'Father, forgive them! They wist not what they did.'

Then saith Simon unto the malefactors: 'Why revile ye this man, seeing that he is of the same condemnation as yourselves, and did no violence such as ye did? Fear ye not God?'

But certain of the Herodians which stood by, likewise mocked Jesus, saying: 'He saved others; himself he cannot save!'

CXIII.y

(435) And the soldiers took the clothes of Jesus, and of his garment of prayer they made four parts, and took every man a part.

But his tunic was without seam, woven from the top throughout, being a priestly garment.

Therefore they said: 'Let us not rend it, but cast lots for it.'

And when Jesus saw this, he said: *'Eloi, eloi, lama sabachthani?'* which is: 'My God, my God, why hast Thou forsaken me?'

For he remembered the psalm in which David prophesied of him, saying: 'My God, my God, why hast Thou forsaken me? Why art Thou so far from helping me, and from the words of my roaring?

'Our fathers trusted in Thee, they trusted and Thou didst deliver them.

'But I am a worm, and no man, a reproach of the people.

'All they that see me laugh me to scorn, they shoot out the lip and shake the head, saying: "He trusted on the Lord, that He would deliver him. Let Him deliver him, seeing that He delighted in him."

'But Thou art He that took me out of the womb, Thou didst make me hope when I was upon my mother's breasts.

'Be not far from me, for trouble is near and there is none to help.

'Many bulls have encompassed me about, strong bulls of Bashan.

'They gaped on me like a ravening and a roaring lion.

'I am poured out like water, all my bones are racked by my hanging.

'My heart is melted within me like wax; I am dried up like a potsherd, and my tongue is swollen and cleaveth to my jaws. Thou hast brought me to the dust of death.

'For the dogs have beset me, the assembly of the wicked have closed me in. They have pierced my hands and feet.

'I am naked and an-hungered so that I shew all my bones; they look and stare upon me.

'They have parted my garments among them and cast lots for my vesture.

'But be not Thou far from me, O Lord! O my Strength, hasten to help me!

'Deliver my soul from the sword, thine only begotten from the power of the dog.

CXIII.y
(contd.) 'Save me from the lion's mouth, hear me from between the horns of the wild oxen.

'Ye that fear the Lord, praise ye the Lord, for He hath not despised nor abhorred the affliction of him that is afflicted!

'Neither hath He turned His face from him. When he called upon Him, He heard.'

But the Herodians, when they heard Jesus cry *'Eloi, Eloi!'*, said: 'Now he calleth upon Elijah to save him!'

CXIII.y (436) And it came to pass that certain pious women, which were in Jerusalem, had provided frankincense that it might be mixed with vinegar and given unto them which were crucified, that their torments might be eased.

One of the soldiers took a spunge and filled it with the vinegar, and set it upon a branch of hyssop which was fastened to a reed, and gave it unto the malefactors, and they drank thereof and held their peace.

But Jesus, when he perceived by the smell that it was vinegar, would not taste thereof, because he might not drink of the fruit of the vine.

CXIII.y (437) Now, Jesus was raised upon the cross at about the third hour; and at the sixth hour, which was the hour of sacrifice in the Temple, behold, a great cloud came up from the east and the sun was darkened, and the earth began to shake.

As Joel prophesied: 'The day of the Lord is near in the valley of decision.

'The sun and the moon shall be darkened, and the heavens and the earth shall shake.'

Which when Jesus saw, he opened his mouth to cry out.

And the earth quaked again, and a lintel of wondrous size fell from a doorway of the Temple.

As Isaiah prophesied: 'The posts of the door moved at the voice of him that cried.'

And because of the trembling of the earth a great shout of fear arose; but Jesus bowed his head upon his breast, as one which, praying he falleth on sleep, saith: 'Father, into Thy hands I commend my spirit.

'Thou hast redeemed me, O Lord, God of Truth. For Thy salvation have I waited, O Lord!'

And Jesus hanged there as dead, and the women that watched wept to see him and cried: 'It is finished!'

CXIII.y (438) And there was darkness over all the land until the ninth hour, yet at evening it grew light, for a wind rent in twain the curtain of darkness.

As Zechariah prophesied: 'And it shall come to pass in that day that the light shall not be clear, nor dark.

'It shall be one day known to the Lord which is neither day nor night, yet it shall come to pass that at evening time it shall be light.'

CXII.y (439) Then Mary, the wife of Joseph of Ramathaim, goeth hastily unto him at Bethany, and saith: 'Husband, the Anointed One is dead.'

CHAPTER XLVIII

HOW HE WAS BURIED

CXIV.g   (440) Now, Joseph of Ramathaim, which was a just man and waited for the Kingdom, when he heard that Jesus was dead, went unto Pilate and begged him for the body.

For this duty fell unto him, being brother of Mary the Braider and reckoned a father unto Jesus.

And Pilate, marvelling if Jesus were already dead, called unto him an officer, that he might learn whether aught were known of Joseph.

And when he learned that Joseph was of good repute and an honourable counsellor, he gave him leave to take the body.

But Joseph wist not what to do therewith, because this was the preparation for the sabbath and for the Passover; he was also of the Rechabites which handle not the dead.

Wherefore he sought out Bunni, called Nakemidam, the same which at the first came unto Jesus by night for fear of the Chief Rulers, but afterward boldly withstood them, consenting neither to their counsel nor to their deed.

And Nakemidam saith unto him: 'I will gladly see to the matter.'

Then took Nakemidam pieces of fine linen and much ointment of myrrh, and straightway went forth with Joseph unto Golgotha.

There they watched until what time the soldiers took down the body of Jesus from the cross.

CXIII.z   (441) Now, the Chief Priests had aforetime made known unto Pilate that they which were condemned might not hang on the cross when night fell, lest the Law be set at naught.

Wherefore he had sent word to the centurion, saying: 'At evening, let their legs be broken and let their bodies be thrust through and taken down for burial.'

CXIII.z   (442) And when even was come, the centurion commanded the soldiers that they should break the legs of them which were crucified, and that their bodies should be thrust through with swords.

And they brake the legs of the one and the other of the malefactors, and afterwards they slew them both.

But finding Jesus dead, they brake not his legs.

As it is written of the lamb which is slain for the Passover: 'A bone of him shall not be broken.'

Howbeit, a soldier with a sword pierced his side but a little, and forthwith came there out water mixed with blood.

CXIII.z
(contd.)   As Zechariah prophesied: 'Living waters shall go out from Jerusalem.'

And also: 'They shall look on him which they pierced.'

CXIV.g   (443) Afterward, Nakemidam said unto the centurion: 'Sir, this is the preparation for the sabbath and for the Passover, and all my servants keep the Feast with me.

'Now, therefore, I pray thee, lest we be defiled, let thy soldiers anoint these linen clothes with the ointment of myrrh and wrap the dead body of Jesus therewith and lay him in the tomb which I have provided.

'Behold, if thou seest to all this, I will pay thee well.'

And the centurion answered: 'As thou sayest, so shall it be done.'

Then said Nakemidam again: 'Wilt thou then also provide a watch lest witches come by night and despoil the body?

'For when the sabbath is ended, this man, which is a counsellor, will send women early in the morning, to wash and anoint the body and bury it. And then shall I likewise set a guard of my own servants over the tomb.'

The centurion answered and said: 'Truly ye shall have a watch. Go your ways in peace!'

CXIII.z   (444) And the soldiers took down the body of Jesus with care, as Nakemidam bade them, and anointed the clothes with ointment and wrapped him therewith, and tied a napkin about his head.

CXIV.g   (445) Then Nakemidam shewed them where the body should be laid.

And it was a new sepulchre which had been hewn out of a rock in the midst of a garden, against Nakemidam himself fell on sleep.

But there were also in that place the graves of Nakemidam's kinsmen, Chief Rulers, wicked men and exceeding rich.

Thus was the prophecy of Isaiah fulfilled, which saith: 'He was cut off out of the land of the living, for the transgression of My people was he stricken.

'And he made his grave with the wicked, and with the rich in his death.'

CXIV.g   (446) And forthwith they laid him in the new sepulchre, and rolled a stone across the mouth thereof, and set a seal upon the stone, and departed to fetch all things needful for their watch.

And Mary the Braider and the other Mary sat over against the sepulchre and watched awhile,

But, when the soldiers were come again, they hastened to Jerusalem to eat the Passover there.

And on the morrow Nakemidam shewed them an hundred pound weight of myrrh mixed with aloes, with which they should anoint the body of Jesus when the sabbath was ended, and when they had rested according to the commandment.

CHAPTER XLIX

HOW HE ROSE AGAIN FROM THE DEAD

CXV.g   (447) When the sabbath was ended and it was yet dark, an angel of the Lord put it into the hearts of certain of the watchmen to come privily to the tomb, and roll back the stone.

And even as they did so, lo! a noise, and he that was dead came forth, bound hand and foot with grave-clothes, and his face bound about with a napkin, and sat upon the stone in the moonlight.

His countenance was pale and his raiment shone; and for fear of him the watchmen did tremble and cry out, and their cries awakened the officer of the watch.

The same beheld how they bowed their faces to the earth, supposing that they had seen a spirit, and became as dead men.

But Jesus said: 'I thirst.'

Then the officer, knowing that it was Jesus and no spirit, straitly enquired of the watchmen: 'How came the stone to be rolled back?'

They answered, for fear of him: 'Sir, while thou layest sleeping the earth trembled, and behold! the tomb was opened.'

Then said he: 'This cometh surely of the gods, not of men. Loose this man therefore, and let him go!'

CXV.m   (448) And when they had loosed Jesus, they gave him to drink, and straightway the officer went unto Jerusalem with the watchmen, and sought out Nakemidam, and told him all that had passed.

Then Nakemidam glorified God, and said: 'Truly, this man is the Son of God and no deceiver!'

And he gave large money unto the soldiers, and said unto them: 'Ye did well to loose him, but beware!

'For if this come to Pilate's ear, he will cast you into prison because that ye freed him which was condemned to die on the cross.

'Therefore, if any man ask aught of you, answer ye that his disciples came at dawn and wrapped him in the linen clothes with the spices, and carried him away for burial.'

And they gladly took the money, and spake as they were taught, and their saying is commonly reported among unbelievers unto this day.

Then Nakemidam sent hastily for John the son of Annas, and saith unto him: 'Hearken unto a marvellous thing: Jesus is not dead but risen! Go thou to him, but tell no man that the soldiers have freed him.'

CXV.m
(*contd.*)

Wherefore John goeth forth from the city and overtaketh Peter which also went sorrowing to the sepulchre.

CXV.m

(449) Now, it came to pass, even as the watchmen departed from the sepulchre, while it began to dawn toward the first day of the week, that Mary the Braider and the other Mary also, the sister-wife of Jesus, came bearing spices which they had prepared to anoint the body withal, after that they had washed it.

They, coming unto the sepulchre, found the stone rolled away, and stood perplexed.

Howbeit, Mary the Braider went and stooped down and looked into the sepulchre; and it was dark within.

She thinketh that she seeth two men in white garments seated one at the head and the other at the foot of the place where Jesus had lain.

And she runneth and cometh unto the other Mary, and saith unto her: 'I saw two men in white garments!'

And they fled from the sepulchre, for they were sore amazed, and meeting Peter and John coming forth from Jerusalem, the other Mary cried unto them:

'Brethren, the watchmen have taken away my lord out of the sepulchre, and we know not where they have laid him!'

Then said Mary the Braider: 'Yea, and even now I saw two men in white raiment sitting within, as it might be angels.'

CXV.m

(450) And John and Peter hastened forward together, but John did outrun Peter, which halted because of the scourging, and came first unto the sepulchre; and stooping down, he saw Jesus sitting naked within, and the linen clothes lying apart.

And he believed that which Nakemidam had told him and was exceeding glad, and beckoned unto Jesus to come forth.

Then John put his cloak upon Jesus to cover his nakedness, and led him unto a place apart, and they covenanted together to meet that night in Jerusalem, in the upper room where they had supped.

CXV.m

(451) And John returneth straightway unto the sepulchre, and there cometh Simon Peter following, with Mary the Braider and the other Mary, and went in after him; but as yet only John had seen Jesus, and these others had not.

John therefore saith unto them: 'Why seek ye the living with the dead? He is not here. Hath he not been restored to life?

'As he himself said unto us: "I trust that God will raise me up on the third day," and behold, is this not the third day since he died?'

And Peter, when he heard this, wondered. And seeing the linen clothes lie and the napkin, that had been about the head of Jesus, wrapped together in a place apart, he saith unto Mary the Braider: 'Here verily are the two angels whereof thou spakest!'

And John departed thence, neither said he more unto any man, for the sake of Nakemidam which had charged him to reveal unto none that Jesus had been freed by the soldiers.

Peter also went with him unto Jerusalem, and Mary the Braider, bearing the spices.

CXV.m   (452) But the other Mary stood without the sepulchre, weeping and, as she wept, she heard a voice behind her, which said: 'Woman, why weepest thou?'

She answered, saying: 'Because they have taken away my lord, and I know not where they have laid him.'

And when she had thus said, she turned about and saw Jesus standing, but wist not that it was he, because of her tears.

Jesus saith unto her: 'Mary!'

She answereth: 'My lord!', and would have clasped his feet, but he forbade her, saying: 'Touch me not, for I was raised and hanged upon a cross whereon men had died.

'Wherefore must I first be purified, and then shalt thou touch me.

'But go now unto Peter and the other brethren which are with him. Tell them to go before me thither whence we came; there shall they see me when it is night.'

And Mary sought out Peter, and told him, saying: 'I have seen Jesus and held converse with him, and he commandeth that ye go before him into Galilee.'

(For she understood not that they should go unto the upper room wherein they had supped.)

Yet her words seemed to Peter but as an idle tale, like unto that told by Mary the Braider concerning the two men clad in white raiment.

CHAPTER L

HOW HE RETURNED UNTO HIS DISCIPLES

CXVI.g   (453) And on the same day it came to pass that James the brother of Jesus went forth from Bethany with his father Joseph.

And they journeyed to Ramathaim, a village nigh unto the town of Emmaus, where Joseph dwelt; and his cousin Simeon the Chaste, the son of Cleophas went with him.

And before it was night, James and Simeon returned together unto Bethany, which was a journey of about sixty furlongs.

Now, as they passed by the garden where the body of Jesus had been laid, they stood without, and communed together and reasoned.

Jesus himself drew nigh, and said unto them: 'What manner of communications are these that ye have one to another, being so sad?'

But they, supposing him to be the gardener, knew him not.

And Simeon said: 'We speak concerning Jesus the Galilean, our kinsman, which was a prophet mighty in deed and word before God, and before all the people.

'And we trusted that it had been he which should have redeemed Israel. But an evil spirit entered into him and he deceived the people, bidding them trust every man in the strength of his own right hand and in the sword.

'Therefore was he taken and delivered by the Chief Priests unto the Romans, which have crucified him.

'But now this is the third day, and certain women of our household which were early in this garden to anoint the body, found it not, but said that they had seen a vision of angels, yea, also that they had found him yet alive.

'And afterward two of his disciples came hither, but found him not. Knowest thou truly naught of the matter?'

CXVI.g   (454) Then said Jesus unto the twain: 'O slow of heart to believe all that the prophets have spoken!'

When he had thus said, he shewed unto them his hands and his feet, and the linen napkin smelling of spices.

And while they yet believed not for joy, and marvelled, he said unto them: 'Have ye any meat?'

They answer: 'Nay, for we fast in mourning for him that is dead.'

Howbeit, their servant which came with them set bread and a piece of broiled fish before him; and to him Jesus gave the linen napkin.

CXVI.g
(contd.)   And when Jesus had washed his hands, he sanctified the bread and brake it, and did eat before them.

Then saith he unto James and Simeon: 'My brethren, break your fast likewise, for this son of man is risen from among them that sleep.'

And at last they believed.

CXVI.g   (455) Then Jesus arose and departed with the twain, and as they walked, he asked them: 'Ought not the Anointed One to have done even as he did?'

And he expounded unto them all the prophecies that were fulfilled in him, beginning with Moses even unto Zechariah.

And their eyes were opened, and they understood wherefore he had preached false doctrine.

Now, as they drew nigh unto Bethany, he made as if to turn toward Jerusalem, and they sought to constrain him, saying: 'Abide with us, the day is far spent and darkness falleth.'

But he would not, and said: 'Go your way. Peace be unto you.'

And Simeon took Jesus in his arms, though he was yet in his uncleanness, and said: 'Lord, I shall indeed depart in peace according to Thy word.

'As Jacob, our forefather, said unto his son Joseph: "Now let me die, for I have seen thy face and thou art yet alive." '

And Simeon blessed God, saying: 'Today is come to pass the prophecy which Isaiah spake: "All the nations of the world shall see the salvation of our God.

' "Thou art My servant, O Israel, in whom I will be glorified.

' "I will also give thee for a light unto the Gentiles, that thou mayest be My salvation to the ends of the earth." '

Then Jesus went from them and vanished out of their sight.

CXVI.g   (456) Afterward, as they sat at meat in Bethany, they said to one another: 'Did not our heart burn within us, when he spake to us by the way?'

For it repented them that they had withstood him as touching the death of Eliezer, seeing that he himself now by faith was enlarged from the sepulchre.

And they rose up in the same hour and went unto Jerusalem to seek out John the son of Annas, and found him and Peter and certain of the disciples gathered together in the upper room.

Then said James: 'The master hath risen indeed, as Mary told you, and hath appeared unto Simeon and myself.'

And he set forth what things were said and done by the way, that it might be certified that they had seen no spirit, but Jesus himself, and no other man.

For he was known unto them by the words wherewith he blessed the bread when he brake it, and by the wounds in his hands and feet.

CXVIII.n   (457) And as they spake, Jesus himself came and stood in their midst, and saith unto them: 'Peace be unto you!'

Then were the disciples glad when they saw him, and none durst ask him: 'Who art thou?'; knowing that he was their master.

CXVIII.n And Jesus said unto them again: 'Peace be unto you! Why are ye
(*contd.*) troubled? And why do doubts arise in your hearts? Behold my hands
and my feet, that it is I myself.'

And when he had thus spoken, he shewed them his hands and his
feet.

But they made excuse, saying: 'Master, thou knowest well that this
age of wickedness and unbelief is under Satan which, by means of
rebellious angels, permitteth man to doubt the power of God.

'But do thou now make all things plain unto us.'

Then said Jesus: 'Behold, the limit of Satan's power is fulfilled, and
other fearful things shall draw nigh.

'For to this end was I delivered unto death: that all Israel might
return to truth and sin no more, and inherit the glory of righteousness
which is in heaven.

'Howbeit, it is expedient for you that I go away. I am with you but
a little while yet.

'And I will pray the Father that He shall send you another to comfort you when I am gone, and abide with you for ever:

'Even the spirit of truth, which they of this world cannot receive,
because they know it not. But ye do know it now, and it shall dwell
within you.'

And unto James and Simeon the Chaste, the son of Cleophas, he
said: 'Rehearse now the words which I spake unto you while I was
with you on the way, how all things must be fulfilled which were
written in the Law, and in the Prophets, and in the Psalms, concerning this son of man.'

Then opened James their eyes, that they likewise might understand.

And he said unto them: 'Thus and thus is it written, and it behoved the Anointed One to suffer and to rise from the dead on the
third day.

'That repentance and remission of sins should be preached in his
name to all Israel, beginning at Jerusalem and going forth even unto
the Jews of the Dispersal.'

Afterwards, Jesus went forth into the night, for he was not yet
purified of his uncleanness, and James and Simeon went with him.

CXVII.n (458) Now Thomas, called The Twin, one of the Eleven, was not
with them when Jesus came.

And to him, coming late, they say: 'We have seen the master, and
we knew him by the prints in his feet and his hands, and by the
wound in his side.'

Thomas answered: 'Did ye handle him?'

They say: 'Nay, he suffered us not, because that he was yet in his
uncleanness.'

Then saith Thomas: 'Surely, ye have seen a vision. Except I shall
touch with my finger the nail-prints which are in his hands and the
wound which is in his side, I will not believe!'

CHAPTER LI

HOW HE DEPARTED UNTO THE LAND OF NOD

CXVII.n (459) And again after eight days, certain of the disciples sat in the same room and were about to break bread, for it was the first day of the week, the doors being shut.

And there were together Simon Peter, and Thomas called The Twin, and Nathanael which had been a Zealot, and John the son of Annas, and Judas (not he of Kerioth), and the sons of Zebedee.

Then came Jesus again, and stood in their midst, saying: 'Peace be unto you!'

This was the third time that Jesus shewed himself unto his disciples, after that he was risen from the dead.

And being now purified of his uncleanness, he saith unto the disciples: 'Come, let us dine!'

And he waiteth upon them, and breaketh the bread, and sanctifieth it and giveth it unto them, and fish also.

And when they had dined, he saith unto Thomas: 'Reach hither thy finger and touch my hands and my side to learn whether or no I be a bodiless spirit. And be not faithless, but believe in the power of God.'

Thomas answered: 'Nay, master, but I have seen; may the Lord God forgive me my unbelief!'

Jesus saith: 'So be it. But more blessed are they that have not seen and yet have believed!'

CXVII.n (460) Then Simon Peter asketh Jesus, saying: 'Master, will God at this time restore thee thy Kingdom of Israel?'

And he answered: 'It is not for me to know the times or the seasons, which the Father keepeth in His power.'

Peter saith again: 'Didst thou not foretell that many of us which are now here shall never taste of death, but enter alive into the Kingdom of Heaven? I would gladly go in thither.'

Jesus answered: 'Now that thou are yet young, thou girdest thyself and walkest whither it pleaseth thee. But who may comprehend the purposes of God?

'Thou canst not enter His Kingdom unless it be first opened unto thee.

'What if thou shouldest live to be old and stretch out thine hand before thee, because thy sight faileth?

CXVII.n
(contd.)
'Then shall another gird thee and carry thee whither thou wouldst not.'

And he said unto them all: 'Ye heard how I told you: "I go away and am with you but a little while." Yet none of you hath asked me: "Master, whither goest thou!" '

And Simon Peter saith: 'Master, whither goest thou?'

Jesus answered and said: 'In my Father's house are many mansions. I go whither He sendeth me.

'For because of the Scripture which I sought to fulfil, behold, thy brother Judas hath taken his life; yet I live, and his thirty pieces of silver shall witness against me until the day of judgement.

'Better that I had died in his stead, as Haman was hanged by Ahasuerus in the stead of Mordecai!'

CXVII.n
(461) 'Wretched that I am: I remembered not how God readeth the heart of man and observeth his soul.

'I made alliance with sin, saying unto myself: "The Lord is merciful and will bear with me. Am I not his fellow?"

'And because He did not straightway smite me I ceased not, but provoked the long-suffering of God.

'Behold, I put in the sickle before the harvest was ripe, greatly desiring the day of the Lord, and thereby I caused my neighbour to sin.

'For thou, Simon, hearkening unto the words of my mouth, didst draw a sword to do murder, and other twain that hearkened likewise shed blood, and were crucified and suffered death.

'As Amos saith: "Woe unto you that desire the day of the Lord! To what end is it for you? The day of the Lord is darkness and not light.

' "As if a man did flee from a lion and a bear met him, or went into the house and leaned his hand on the wall and a serpent bit him.

' "Though ye offer Me burnt offerings and your meat offerings, yet I will not accept them, but I will cause you to go into captivity beyond Damascus."

'Yea, even the sacrifice of my life by the sword, this my Father refused, because that I sinned from presumption.

'As it is written: "Unto Cain and his offering had the Lord no respect.

' "And the Lord said unto Cain: 'If thou doest well, shalt thou not be respected? But if thou doest not well, sin lieth at thy door.'

' "And it came to pass that Cain slew his brother, which was a shepherd, and the Lord said unto him: 'The voice of thy brother's blood crieth unto Me from the ground, and now thou art cursed from the earth, which hath opened her mouth to receive thy brother's blood from thy hand.

' " 'A fugitive and a vagabond shalt thou be in the earth.'

' "And the Lord set a mark upon Cain. And he went out from the presence of the Lord, and dwelt in the Land of Nod, on the east of Eden."

'Behold, that is the land where the city of Susa now standeth.

CXVII.n
(*contd*.)

Thither will I go, for His marks are upon my hands and feet, and in my side, whereby every man shall know me.

'But do ye tarry in Jerusalem until ye be blessed with wisdom and power from on high to do the will of the Father.

'And lo, my heart shall be with you alway, even unto the end of the world.

'Arise, let us go hence!'

CXVII.n

(462) And when he had thus spoken, he said: 'I go tonight unto the house of my kinsmen, and by the way will I bid you farewell.'

But unto John son of Annas he said: 'Tarry thou here, and afterward come unto Bethany, and we will privily depart from this land together.'

Simon Peter, turning about, saith unto Jesus: 'Master, what shall this man do that I may not do? Why cannot I follow with thee? I will lay down my life for thy sake.'

Jesus saith unto him: 'Simon, if I will that he tarry here, and that he should come unto me after that ye have all departed, what is that to thee?'

(Therefore hath the saying now gone abroad that Jesus spake in parables and said: 'John shall tarry on earth and enjoy the Kingdom with me after that ye are all dead.')

CXVII.n

(463) But Peter desired yet that Jesus should lead Israel in arms against the Wicked Kingdom.

Then saith Jesus unto him: 'Simon, thou wild man, lovest thou me?' For they had eaten the Feast of the First Day, which is called the feast of love.

Simon answered and said: 'Yea, master.' Jesus saith: 'Feed my lambs!'

He saith unto him again: 'Simon, thou wild man, lovest thou me truly?'

Simon answered and said: 'Yea, master, I love thee with all my heart.'

Jesus saith: 'Feed my sheep!'

He said unto him yet again: 'Simon, thou wild man, art thou sure that thou lovest me?'

Then was Simon Peter grieved because that Jesus seemed to doubt, and he answered: 'Master, thou readest all my thoughts. Thou knowest that I love thee.'

Jesus saith: 'He that hath God's commandments and keepeth them, the same also loveth me, for I likewise love the Father.

'Rememberest thou how I spake and said before thee: "I will not feed my sheep"?

'Behold, now I may not feed them though I would. But do thou feed them, for the love of the Father.

'This same thing I speak unto you all, that ye be no more offended in me.

'Even as Jeremiah prophesied in the name of the Lord: "Woe be unto the shepherds that destroy and scatter the sheep. But I will set up

CXVII.n
(contd.)
CXVII.n shepherds which shall feed the flock and they shall fear no more, neither be dismayed."'

(464) And he led them forth as far towards Bethany as is a sabbath day's journey, and there he lifted up his hands and blessed them, saying: "Peace remain with you."

Then they saw him no more, for a cloud received him out of their sight as he went up into the mountain of Olives unto the house of Simeon son of Cleophas.

And they stood watching from afar, and presently come two of the kinsmen of Jesus, clad in white linen, and say unto them: 'Ye men of Galilee, why stand ye gazing upwards?

'For as the power of God descended upon Jesus at his anointing, so hath it departed again, and he is now no more our King."

Then returned the disciples unto Jerusalem, with Mary the mother of Jesus, and with his kinsmen, and with Mary of Cleophas, and Martha, and Salome, and they went again together unto the upper room, and all continued with one accord in prayer and supplication.

CXVII.n (465) But Jesus gat him from the Land of Israel, he and Mary his sister-wife, and John the son of Annas went with him a part of the way.

And he came unto the Land of Nod, where are many Israelites which dwell under the rule of the Parthians.

Then was he as a fugitive and a vagabond in the earth, and returned not again unto his own people.

But the disciples which he taught know and believe him to be still in the flesh, watching for the deliverance of Israel.

And his heart is with them alway, even unto the end of the world.

CHAPTER LII

HOW THE DISCIPLES FOLLOWED IN
HIS WAY

CXII.e (466) And it came to pass afterward that Peter, when he heard what the Chief Priests had done with the money which Judas received of them, stood up in the midst of the disciples (the number of names together were about an hundred and twenty) and said:

'That field which they have bought with the thirty pieces whereof Zechariah prophesied, the same is the very field wherein Jeremiah stood and prophesied of the Last Days.

'As it is written: "Then went I down to the potter's house and, behold, he wrought a work on his wheels; and the vessel that he made of clay was marred in his hand, so he made it again, another vessel as seemed good to the potter to make it."

'Wherefore, seeing that our Master chose us out to be Twelve, one for each of the tribes of Israel, let us now renew our number and make another vessel in the place of that which was marred.

'Yet not us but the Lord, for He alone is the potter!'

And when it seemed good unto them what Peter said, they appointed two: Joseph called the Son of the Sabbath, the Essene; and Matthias.

And they prayed: 'Thou, O Lord, which knowest the hearts of all, shew whether of these twain Thou hast chosen, that he may take part of this ministry and apostleship from which Judas by transgression fell, and that he may go into the place that is left open!'

And they gave forth their lots, and the lot fell upon Matthias; and he was numbered among the Twelve.

CXVIII.t (467) Now, when the day was come for the joy of the harvest to be fulfilled, the disciples were all with one accord in the same place.

And suddenly they heard as it were a rushing tempest of wind that filled the house wherein they prayed.

And after the tempest, behold the earth quaked and rocks were rent, and the graves were opened, and many bodies of the saints arose,

And came forth from their graves, and went into Jerusalem and were seen of much people.

And after the earthquake, behold a fire like unto cloven flames, that sat upon them.

And after the fire, a still small voice, that spake first in one and then in the other.

CXVIII.t   Now, this same thing happened aforetime unto Elijah, when he
(contd.)   watched upon Mount Horeb.

And the spirit of God came upon them, and they arose hastily and
ran into the streets, crying aloud unto the men of Jerusalem: 'Repent!
Repent!'

But these were sore amazed and in doubt, saying one to another:
'What meaneth this? Are these men full of new wine?'

CXVIII.t   (468) Then Peter stood up with the Eleven, and testified, saying:
'Ye men of Jerusalem, and all ye that have come up hither for the
feast, be it known unto you that we are not drunken.

'For we are of them that drink no wine.

'But hearken unto the prophecy which Joel spake: "It shall come to
pass afterwards that I will pour out My spirit upon all flesh, and your
sons and daughters shall prophesy, your old men shall dream dreams,
and your young men shall see visions.

' "The sun shall be turned into darkness, and the moon into blood
before the great and terrible day of the Lord come.

' "And it shall come to pass that whosoever shall call on the name
of the Lord shall be delivered; for in Mount Zion and in Jerusalem
shall be deliverance."

'Repent therefore, and be baptized unto the remission of your sins
in the name of Jesus, the son of David, which died upon the cross and
rose again, and in which all these Scriptures are fulfilled.

'Save yourselves from this untoward generation, for the promise is
unto you and your children, and to all Israelites even as many as the
Lord shall call.'

CXVIII.t   (469) And many of the multitude were pricked to the heart and
repented, and were baptized.

The same continued steadfastly in the fellowship of the Twelve,
and in breaking of bread and in prayers.

And James the Just and Peter, and the sons of Zebedee were their
leaders.

Then they that believed sold their rich possessions and gave alms
unto the poor, and afterwards dwelt together, and had all things common.

Howbeit, a Levite named Ananias sold a possession and kept back
part of the price, Sapphira his wife being privy to it; but brought the
residue, and laid it at the feet of the Twelve.

Then said James: 'Brother Ananias, why hath Satan filled thine
heart to keep back part of the price of thy land? Behold, thou hast
lied not unto man but unto God.'

And Ananias hearing those words, fell down and gave up the ghost.

Then great fear came upon all that believed.

But they, continuing daily with one accord in Solomon's Porch, and
breaking bread from house to house, did eat their meat with gladness
and singleness of heart, praising God and having favour with all
devout people.

And the Lord added to the Church daily such as should be saved.

CXVIII.t　　(470) And it came to pass on a certain day, when the Twelve spake unto the people there, that the Chief Priests and the Captain of the Temple with other Sadducees came upon them,

Being vexed that they taught the people and preached the resurrection of the just, through Jesus the Anointed One which was delivered unto death by Pilate the Governor of Judaea.

And laid hands upon them, and put them in ward until the next day, for it was now eventide.

Therefore, on the morrow, Annas and Caiaphas and John and Alexander, and as many as were of the kindred of the High Priest, gathered together in Jerusalem.

And when Caiaphas had set the Twelve in their midst, he commanded them neither to preach nor to speak at all in the name of Jesus.

CXVIII.t　　(471) Then would James not open his mouth in their presence.

But Peter and John the son of Zebedee answered, and said: 'Whether it be right in the sight of God to hearken unto you more than unto God, judge ye.

'For we cannot but speak the things we have seen and heard.'

Wherefore when they had further threatened the Twelve, they let them go, finding nothing how they might punish them; and fearing the people.

But a multitude came forth from the cities round about, bringing sick folk and them that were troubled with unclean spirits, unto Solomon's Porch, that they might be healed by the Twelve.

Then were the High Priest and all that came with him filled with wrath, and laid hands upon the Twelve to put them in the common prison-house.

Howbeit, the Pharisees, when they heard this, made protest and said: 'Wherefore do ye these things?

'If these men have sinned, let them come before the Council which alone may judge them.'

Thus the Lord opened the prison doors unto the Twelve, and they came forth and taught again in Solomon's Porch, until what time they were summoned by the Captain of the Temple and led without violence before the Council.

There Caiaphas the High Priest accused them, saying: 'Did I not straitly command you that ye should not teach in his name?

'But, behold, ye have filled Jerusalem with your doctrine, and seek to bring this man's blood upon us.'

And James made answer unto Caiaphas: 'It behoves us to obey God rather than them which ally themselves with the enemies of God.

'For He exalted our master Jesus to be a King and a Deliverer which preached repentance unto Israel and the remission of sins.

'But thou and thy kindred delivered him unto Pilate, by whose command he was hanged upon a tree.

'Now hath God raised him from the dead, whereof we are witnesses.'

CXVIII.t   And Caiaphas, when he heard these things, was cut to the heart
(contd.)   and would have slain James, but he could not.

Then Gamaliel stood up, the leader of the Pharisees, which was in reputation among all the people, and commanded to put the Twelve forth a little space.

And he said unto the Council: 'Ye men of Israel, take heed to yourselves what ye intend to do as touching these men.

'Before these days rose up Theudas, which boasted himself to be King, and about four hundred men believed and joined themselves to him; but he was slain and they were scattered.

'And after Theudas rose up Judas of Galilee in the days of the taxing, and drew away much people after him. He likewise perished and as many as believed in him were brought to naught.

'Now, therefore, say I unto you: Ye dwellers in Jerusalem, refrain from these men and let them alone, for if this counsel or this work be of men, it will come to naught.

'But if the same be of God, ye cannot overthrow it, lest haply ye be found even to fight against God.'

And the Chief Priests hearkened unto Gamaliel, and let the Twelve go, but forbade them to suffer the sick and lunatic to be brought unto them in the Porch.

Yet daily in the Temple and in the houses of devout persons they ceased not to preach the words which Jesus had put into their mouths to preach.

CHAPTER LIII

HOW HE WAS SEEN AGAIN OF SAUL

CXVIII.t (472) And it came to pass that, when the number of the disciples were multiplied, and many of the Grecians also joined themselves unto the Twelve, there arose a murmuring of the Grecians against the Hebrews, because that their widows were neglected in the daily ministration.

Then the Twelve called an assembly of the Grecian brethren, and said unto them: 'It is not reason that we should leave the word of God and serve tables.

'Wherefore do ye seek out from among you seven men of honest report, which we may appoint over this business.

'And let other seven be sought out for the ministration unto the Hebrews.

'But we will give ourselves continually to prayer and to preaching.'

These words pleased the Grecians, and they chose Stephen, Philip, Prochorus, Nicanor, Timon, Parmenas, and Nicolas, which was a proselyte of Antioch.

CXVIII.t (473) Howbeit, Stephen preached false doctrine, how that Jesus had despised the Law of Moses, and had commanded his disciples not to worship in the Temple.

And he perverted the Scriptures, preaching also that David had said: 'The Lord shall not dwell in temples made with hands,' and Isaiah likewise: 'I will not dwell in the house that ye built unto Me.'

And when certain other Grecians arose, of the Libyan, the Cyrenean, the Alexandrian, the Cilician, and the Asian synagogues, which would have brought Stephen before the Council, he spake terrible things, saying:

'Behold, I saw the heavens opened and Jesus, being the Son of Man, sat at the right hand of God, and he it is which shall judge the world.'

And the Chief Rulers, when they heard of it, feared that the Council would not condemn Stephen, as they had not condemned the Twelve, but set him free.

Therefore they suborned certain sons of Belial to come upon Stephen, and lay hold on him as he went forth from the city, and there stone him.

CXVIII.t (474) Now, a young man named Saul was leader of them that laid hold on Stephen and stoned him that he gave up the ghost.

CXVIII.t   (Yet Saul forbore to cast a single stone, but watched over the gar-
(contd.)   ments which the sons of Belial laid at his feet while they went about
to do murder.)

And the followers of Stephen carried him to his burial and made
great lamentation over him, and called woe upon all the Grecians
which lamented not with them.

Then, because that blood had been shed, albeit by their own provocation, the Chief Rulers, with the consent of Pilate, made great
persecution both against them which had been led astray by Stephen,
and against them which followed true doctrine.

Yet they refrained from doing aught against the Twelve, for the
Council that judged them had found no fault in them.

CXVIII.t   (475) This Saul was a Greek of Tarsus in Cilicia, and a tent-maker.

The same had been converted and was circumcised and feigned
himself to be a Pharisee, but for gain served Caiaphas the High Priest,
and strove to root out the faith of the Nazarenes.

And he was given authority of Caiaphas to enter into houses and
hale forth men and women that believed, and commit them for trial.

Nor forbore he to raise a tumult in the Temple, casting James the
brother of Jesus headlong down the fifteen steps of the Inner Court,
so that he lay as one dead.

Then the elect of Jerusalem were scattered abroad for fear of him,
and preached the word in Samaria and in Galilee and beyond Jordan.

CXVIII.t   (476) And Saul, yet breathing out threatenings and slaughter
against the disciples of Jesus, went unto the Chief Priests, saying:

'Behold, I have true tidings that the man Jesus, which was the
cause of this mischief, liveth yet and hath come from the province of
Susiana, whither he first went.

'The same now sojourneth at Damascus, among the Levites which
are of the New Covenant of Repentance,

'And the marks of the nails are yet in his hands and his feet.

'What will ye give me therefore, if I draw him back thence and
bring him unto you, that Pilate may crucify him afresh?

'For if this be accomplished, the people will believe no longer that
he hath conquered death, and ye shall have peace.'

LXXXVII.g (477) Now, it came to pass, when the Chief Priests heard these
tidings, that they consulted together how they might deliver Jesus
again unto death.

For by reason of his resurrection many of those in Jerusalem were
now become Nazarenes.

CXVIII.u   (478) Then they called Saul again, and Caiaphas asked him, saying: 'Man, what is thy price?'

Saul answered: 'That I be given a wife of the daughters of thine
own household.'

And the High Priest was vexed thereat, and asked: 'Is this a small
thing that thou desirest, being a proselyte and a tent-maker of Cilicia?'

Saul answered and said: 'Nay, but that which I would do is likewise no small thing, and my life will be in jeopardy.

CXVIII.u
(contd.) 'For the city of Damascus, being now given unto King Aretas by Caesar, is a strange land, and I must go thither in stealth.

'And though thou hadst five daughters, yet wouldst thou give them all to proselytes if thereby thou mightest rid thyself of this plague.'

Then the High Priest considered and said: 'So be it. Thou shalt marry a daughter of our house on the day that this Jesus is crucified afresh!'

Saul said again: 'I pray thee give me letters unto the leaders of the synagogues which are in Damascus, testifying that I am an apostle of the Catholics, come to take up the yearly tax, and they shall entreat me well.

'Then will Jesus come unto my table to pay the half-shekel that is due of him, and I shall know him by the marks in his hands.

'But when he hath departed, then my armed servants, which thou shalt give me to guard the tax-money, will lie in wait and bind him.

'And I will straightway return hither and deliver him unto Pilate, as one which hath already suffered condemnation.'

And Caiaphas did as Saul desired, and provided armed servants to go with him, and letters testifying that he was an apostle of the Catholics.

CXVIII.u (479) And it came to pass that Saul, as he journeyed, came nigh unto the city of Damascus, and it was about noon; and he and his fellows, when they had dined, slumbered in the shade by the wayside.

And on a sudden he heard a voice saying in the Hebrew tongue: 'Saul, Saul, why persecutest thou me?'

And he opened his eyes, and saw a man standing, and the sun shone fiercely upon his white raiment, and the eyes of Saul were dazzled.

Then said Saul: 'Sir, who art thou?'

He that had come, answered: 'I am Jesus, whose life thou seekest. It is ill for thee to kick against the goad, like unto an ox that hath no understanding.'

For Jesus had warning of Simon Peter that Saul sought to take him, and came forth boldly, and Peter with him.

And Saul seeth the nail prints in his hands, and likewise the angry countenance of Peter, which stood by.

Wherefore, trembling and astonished, he falleth all along on the earth, and there was no strength in him.

And he closeth his eyes, and crieth: 'Have mercy upon me, thou son of David! Art thou come to destroy us?'

For he doubted not that Peter bore a sword.

Jesus answered: 'Thus said David, when he surprised Saul in the cave: "I have not sinned against thee, yet thou huntest my life to take it.

' "The Lord judge between me and thee, and the Lord avenge me of thee, but mine hand shall not be upon thee." '

And in a moment Saul's eyes were blinded, yet he knew it not.

And he asked Jesus, saying: 'Lord, what wilt thou have me do?'

CXVIII.u   Jesus answered: 'Arise, and go into Damascus to the street called
(*contd.*)   Straight, and enquire in the house of Judas for one called Ananias.
'The same will tell thee what thou shalt do.'

And when he had said these things, he departed, and Simon Peter with him.

CXVIII.u   (480) Then Saul rose up but when he opened his eyes there was no sight in them, and he cried out aloud and his fellows roused themselves from slumber.

(These men saw not Jesus, for they were drowsy with sleep, yet they heard his voice.)

And they took Saul by the hand and led him into Damascus, where he abode in the house of Judas, three days without sight, neither eating nor drinking, until Ananias came unto him, being sent by Jesus.

As it is written: 'On the third day cometh relief.'

And in like manner as Saul the king sware unto David, saying: 'Inasmuch as when the Lord had delivered me into thine hand thou killedst me not, behold, now I know well that the Kingdom of Israel shall be established in thine hand,'

So likewise Saul the tent-maker sware unto Ananias that by Jesus the Son of David should the Kingdom of God be established.

Then did Ananias lay his hands upon him, and there fell from his eyes as it had been a sheet of white stone, such as is set in a lanthorn, and he did see again.

And he was baptized, and took meat and, being strengthened, straightway preached in the synagogues, how that all Israelites should pay the tax as Moses commanded.

Now, it became known unto the Grecians that Saul had been sent of the Chief Priests to seize Jesus without leave of King Aretas.

And they laid in wait to apprehend him, and bring him before the ethnarch which ruled the city for the King, and to accuse him of the murders which he had done in Judaea.

But Ananias and the brethren, forasmuch as Saul had made a full repentance and desired also to preach the Gospel to the Gentiles, took him by night, and through a window let him down by the wall in a basket.

CXVIII.u   (481) Afterwards, when Saul had dwelt three years in the land of Arabia, he journeyed again from Damascus unto Jerusalem, and would have joined himself to the disciples, but all feared him and believed not that he walked in the way of righteousness.

Then Barnabas, a Levite of Cyprus, brought Saul unto Peter and unto James the brother of Jesus, and declared that he had repented him of his evil and had boldly preached at Damascus in Jesus's name.

Therefore they rejected not Saul, for in those days he walked discreetly.

CXVIII.u   (482) And Saul abode with Peter and James fifteen days, coming in and going out of the Temple, speaking in the name of Jesus, and preaching against the false doctrine of the Grecians.

CXVIII.u   But the servants of the High Priest went about to seize him; which
(*contd.*)   when the Twelve knew, they brought him down to Caesarea and
thence sped him unto Tarsus, whereof he was a free-born citizen.

And the Church had rest awhile throughout Judaea and Galilee and
Samaria, for the brethren obeyed the Twelve and followed not after
the Grecian heresies which Stephen had preached.

CXVIII.u   (483) But afterwards Saul turned him again unto the Wicked
Kingdom, and spake terrible things in the name of Jesus.

And drew after him many that were weak in the faith, so that because of them we are now fallen into suspicion and hatred.

EPILEGOMENA BY JAMES THE JUST
UNTO THE FAITHFUL

CXVIII.u   (484) *Yet the Lord knoweth how to deliver the godly from temptation, and to reserve the unjust unto the day of judgement to be punished: but chiefly them that walk after the flesh in the lust of uncleanness, and despise government.*

Presumptuous are they, self-willed, unafraid to speak evil of their rulers, though even angels, which are of greater power, bring not railing accusation against these before the Lord.

But, as natural brute beasts, born to be destroyed, they contemn that they understand not; and shall utterly perish, as they that count it pleasure to riot in the daytime.

Spots they are and blemishes, sporting themselves with their own deceits; having eyes full of adultery, and unstable souls and an heart which they have exercised with covetous practices.

Cursed children, which have forsaken the Law and are gone astray, following the way of Balaam the son of Beor who, loving the wages of unrighteousness, was rebuked and brought to shame.

The dumb ass speaking with a man's voice forbade the madness of the prophet.

CXVIII.u   (485) *Wells without water are they, clouds that are carried with a tempest; to whom the mist of darkness is reserved for ever.*

For when they speak great swelling words of vanity, they allure through the lusts of the flesh them that thought themselves clean escaped from error.

While they promise liberty, they serve corruption: for of whom a man is overcome, of the same is he brought into bondage.

Yea, it were better for them never to have known the way of righteousness, which is the Law, than, after that they have known it, to turn aside and be entangled in error.

But it is happened unto them according to the proverb which Solomon spake:

'The dog is turned to his own vomit again; and the sow that was washed to her wallowing in the mire.'

CXVIII.z   (486) *Yet be patient, brethren, unto the second coming of God.*

Behold, the husbandman waiteth for the precious fruit of the earth, and hath long patience for it until he receive the early and the latter rain.

Be ye likewise patient and stablish your hearts, for the coming of the Lord draweth nigh.

CXVIII.z
(contd.) *Consider, my brethren, the prophets which testified in the name of God and gave an ensample of affliction suffered in patience.*

Behold, we count them happy which endured.

Ye have heard of the patience of Job, and ye have seen what the end was of Jesus, our master: how God is very pitiful and of tender mercy.

Is any among you afflicted? Let him then pray! The prayer of a righteous man availeth much.

Elijah was subject to like passions as we are, and he prayed earnestly that it might not rain; and it rained not on the earth for the space of three years and six months.

And he prayed again, and the heaven gave rain, and the earth brought forth her fruit.

CXVIII.z *(487) Pray ye therefore with all your heart that the Kingdom may come speedily, wherein the earth shall yield fruit ten thousandfold both of grapes and wheat.*

And the Righteous One the Son of David shall rule it in peace and righteousness for a thousand years.

Amen.

THE END

CHAPTER INDEX